DISCARD

INTERNATIONAL BIBLIOGRAPHY
OF THE SOCIAL SCIENCES
BIBLIOGRAPHIE INTERNATIONALE
DES SCIENCES SOCIALES

Publications of the ICSSD / Publications du CIDSS

INTERNATIONAL BIBLIOGRAPHY OF THE SOCIAL SCIENCES / BIBLIOGRAPHIE INTERNATIONALE DES SCIENCES SOCIALES.

[published annually in four parts / paraîssant chaque année en quatre parties. Until 1961 / Jusqu'en 1961 : UNESCO, Paris].

International bibliography of sociology | Bibliography internationale de sociologie [red cover / couverture rouge]. Vol. 1 : 1951 (Publ. 1952).
International bibliography of political science | Bibliographie internationale de science politique [grey cover/couverture grise]. Vol. 1 : 1952 (Publ. 1954).
International bibliography of economics | Bibliographie internationale de science économique [yellow cover/couvertrue jaune]. Vol. 1 : 1952 (Publ. 1955).
International bibliography of social and cultural anthropology|Bibliographie internationale d'anthropologie sociale et culturelle [green cover/couverture verte]. Vol. 1 : 1955 (Publ. 1958).

Other series / Autres collections:

INTERNATIONAL POLITICAL SCIENCE ABSTRACTS / DOCUMENTATION POLITIQUE INTERNATIONALE.

[Bimonthly / Bimestriel. IPSA / AISP, Paris].

CONFLUENCE, Surveys of research in the social sciences / CONFLUENCE, états des recherches en sciences sociales.
[Irregular / irrégulier. Mouton, The Hague-Paris.]

DOCUMENTATION IN THE SOCIAL SCIENCES / DOCUMENTATION DANS LES SCIENCES SOCIALES.

[UNESCO, Paris].

Catalogue des sources de documentation juridique dans le monde|A register of legal documentation in the world (2nd Ed. / 2è édition, 1957).
Liste mondiale des périodiques spécialisés dans les sciences sociales|World list of social science periodicals (4th Ed/4è édition, 1976).
International repertory of social science documentation centres|Répertoire international des centres de documentation de sciences sociales (1952).
International register of current team research in the social sciences|Répertoire international des recherches collectives en cours dans le domaine des sciences sociales (1955).

INTERNATIONAL BIBLIOGRAPHY OF THE SOCIAL SCIENCES

BIBLIOGRAPHIE INTERNATIONALE DES SCIENCES SOCIALES

1977

International Bibliography of
SOCIOLOGY

Bibliographie internationale de
SOCIOLOGIE

VOL. XXVII

Prepared by the
International Committee for Social Science Information and Documentation

Établie par le
Comité international pour l'information et la documentation en sciences sociales

LONDON: TAVISTOCK PUBLICATIONS
CHICAGO: ALDINE PUBLISHING COMPANY

Manuscript prepared under the auspices of the International Sociological Association by the ICSSD with the financial support of Unesco (Subvention — 1977/1978, DG/3.3/41/53)

Manuscrit préparé sous les auspices de l'Association Internationale de Sociologie par le CIDSS avec l'aide financière de l'Unesco (Subvention — 1977/1978, DG/3.3/41/53)

ISBN 0 422 80830 X

ISSN 0085 2066

© ICSSD / CIDSS 1979

Published in 1979 by
Tavistock Publications Limited
11 New Fetter Lane, London EC4P 4EE

Printed in Great Britain by
Richard Clay (The Chaucer Press) Ltd,
Bungay, Suffolk

TABLE OF CONTENTS
TABLE DES MATIÈRES

Preface... vi

Préface.. vii

List of periodicals consulted / Liste des périodiques consultés......... xi

Classification scheme / Plan de classification...................... lv

Bibliography for 1977 / Bibliographie pour 1977...................... 1

Author index / Index des auteurs.................................... 293

Subject index... 347

Index des matières.. 381

PREFACE

The 27th volume of the *International Bibliography of Sociology* is similar in format to the volumes published since 1972, at which time the classification scheme was completely revised and the subject index extensively developed and expanded. Elaborated over twenty years ago, the initial classification scheme no longer corresponded to the conception sociologists have of their discipline today; as for the subject index it was ill-adapted to the needs of retrospective research, not being based upon a sufficiently stable and standardized documentary language.

In order to comply with the requirements of the progressive automation of sociological documentation, we have chosen to adopt the framework established in the *Thesaurus for information processing in sociology*[+], compiled at the request of the Department of Social Sciences of UNESCO, and published by the ICSSD, utilizing the descriptors therein for the subject index. In this format, only the major divisions of the classification scheme have a heading; within each of these divisions, themes have been regrouped in subdivisions which do not have headings, the retrieval of information (processed) being assured by the descriptors in the subject index.

We should be most happy to receive the opinion of our readers regarding this format, which should greatly improve the quality and usefulness of the bibliography.

As is the custom, we take pleasure in thanking, here, the institutions which have rendered special assistance by supplying information on the sociological publications issued throughout a country or even a region. The editorial staff also wish to express their gratitude to the following experts who have closely co-operated with them particularly: Valentina Fernandez Vargas (Madrid), Dr. T. Kitagawa (Tokyo), Mr. Gerhard J. A. Riesthuis (Utrecht), Mrs. María Vágh (Budapest), Professor Vladimir A. Vinogradov (Moscow).

Last, but not least, it seems only fair to mention here those who have this year, once again selected and coded the bibliographical material and prepared the manuscript: Germaine George, Agnès Majoros, Edith Molle and Geneviève Mordini.

[+]VIET, Jean. *Thesaurus for information processing in sociology / Thesaurus pour le traitement de l'information en sociologie*. Paris-La Haye, Mouton, 1971, 336 p.

PRÉFACE

Ce vingt-septième volume de la *Bibliographie internationale de sociologie* est conforme, en sa présentation, à ceux publiés depuis 1972: le plan de classification avait été alors refondu et.l'index des matières développé de façon notable. Élaboré voilà plus de vingt ans, le premier ne correspondait plus guère à la vision que les sociologues prennent aujourd'hui de leur discipline; quant au second, il se prêtait mal à la recherche rétrospective faute de s'appuyer sur un langage documentaire suffisamment stable et normalisé.

Afin de satisfaire autant que possible aux exigences d'une automatisation progressive de la documentation en sociologie, on a choisi de suivre la disposition prescrite par le *Thesaurus pour le traitement de l'information en sociologie*[+], rédigé à la demande du Département des sciences sociales de l'UNESCO et publié par le CIDSS, et d'utiliser, pour l'index des matières, les descripteurs dont il préconise l'emploi. Dans cette disposition seules les grandes divisions du plan de classification comportent un intitulé; à l'intérieur de chacune d'elles, des regroupements par thèmes ont été opérés, sans qu'il ait paru nécessaire de leur donner un titre, le dépistage des matières traitées étant assuré par l'index des sujets.

Comme à l'accoutumée, nous remercions les institutions dont le concours a été particulièrement important, et qui nous ont permis de connaître les publications sociologiques de l'ensemble d'un pays ou même d'une région. La rédaction tient en outre à exprimer sa reconnaissance à plusieurs personnalités qui ont collaboré avec elle de façon particulièrement étroite, à savoir: Mme Valentina Fernandez Vargas (Madrid), le Dr Takayoshi Kitagawa (Tokyo), M. Gerhard J. A. Riesthuis (Utrecht), Mme Maria Vagh (Budapest), le Professeur Vladimir A. Vinogradov (Moscou).

Enfin il est juste de mentionner ici les personnes qui ont, cette année encore, recensé et traité les données bibliographiques et préparé le manuscrit: Germaine George, Agnès Majoros, Edith Molle et Geneviève Mordini.

[+]VIET, Jean. *Thesaurus for information processing in sociology / Thesaurus pour le traitement de l'information en sociologie*. Paris-La Haye, Mouton, 1971, 336 p.

LIST OF PERIODICALS CONSULTED
LISTE DES PÉRIODIQUES CONSULTÉS

Accounting Review	*Accting R.*	Columbus, Ohio
Acta ethnographica Academiae Scientiarum Hungaricae	*Acta ethnogr.*	Budapest
Acta Facultatis politico-iuridicae Universitatis Scientiarum budapestiensis de Lorando Eötvös nominatae	*Acta Fac. polit. iur. Univ. Sci. budapest.*	Budapest
Acta geographica. Bulletin officiel de la Société de Géographie	*Acta geogr.*	Paris
Acta juridica	*Acta jur. (Budapest)*	Budapest
Acta oeconomica	*Acta oecon.*	Budapest
Acta politica	*Acta polit.*	Meppel
Acta sociologica	*Acta sociol.*	København
Acta Universitatis Ÿódziensis	*Acta Univ. Ÿódz.*	Lódz
Actes de la Recherche en Sciences sociales	*Actes Rech. Sci. soc.*	Paris
Actualité économique	*Actual. écon.*	Montréal
Actualité en Chine populaire	*Actual. Chine popul.*	Hong Kong
Actualité juridique	*Actual. jur.*	Paris
Administration	*Administration (Dublin)*	Dublin
Administration	*Administration (Paris)*	Paris
Administration and Society	*Adm. and Soc.*	Durham, N.C.
Administration publique du Canada	*Adm. publ. Canada*	Toronto
Administrative Change	*Adm. Change*	Jaipur
Administrative Science Quarterly	*Adm. Sci. Quart.*	Ithaca, N.Y.
Adult Education in Finland	*Adult Educ. Finland*	London
Affari esteri	*Aff. est.*	Roma
Affari sociali internazionali	*Aff. soc. int.*	Milano
Africa	*Africa (London)*	London
Africa	*Africa (Roma)*	Roma
Africa Development	*Afr. Develop.*	Dakar
Africa Institute Bulletin	*Afr. Inst. B.*	Pretoria
Africa Report	*Afr. Rep.*	Washington, D.C.
Africa today	*Afr. today*	Denver, Col.
African Affairs	*Afr. Aff.*	London
African Perspectives	*Afr. Perspect.*	Leiden
African Review	*Afr. R.*	Dar Es Salaam
African Studies	*Afr. Stud.*	Johannesburg
African Studies Review	*Afr. Stud. R.*	Boston, Mass.
Africana Bulletin	*Africana B.*	Warszawa
Afrika Spectrum	*Afr. Spectrum*	Hamburg
Afrique-Agriculture	*Afr.-Agric.*	Paris
Afrique contemporaine	*Afr. contemp.*	Paris
Afrique et Asie modernes	*Afr. Asie mod.*	Paris
Afrique-Industrie-Infrastructure	*Afr.-Industr.-Infrastruct.*	Paris
Aggiornamenti sociali	*Aggiorn. soc.*	Milano

Agrártörténeti Szemle	*Agrártört. Szle*	Budapest
Agrarwirtschaft	*Agrarwirtschaft*	Braunschweig
Agricultura y Sociedad	*Agric. y Soc.*	
Agricultural Economics Research	*Agric. Econ. Res.*	Washington, D.C.
Aikyodai Kenpô (Kyoiku Kagaku)	*Aikyodai Kenpô (Kyôiku Kagaku)*	[Nihon]
Ajia Keizai	*Ajia Keizai*	Tokyo
Akita Daigaku Kenkyû Kiyô	*Akita Daigaku Kenkyû Kiyô*	Akita
Alkoholipolitiikka	*Alkoholipolitiikka*	[Suomi]
Állam és Igazgatás	*Állam és Igazg.*	Budapest
Állam- és Jogtudomány	*Állam- és Joytud.*	Budapest
Allemagne d'aujourd'hui	*Allem. aujourd.*	Paris
Aménagement et Nature	*Aménag. et Nature*	Paris
América indígena	*Amér. indíg.*	México
America latina	*Amer. lat. (Moscu)*	Moskva
América latina	*Amer. lat. (Rio de Janeiro)*	Rio de Janeiro
American Anthropologist	*Amer. Anthropol.*	Washington, D.C.
American behavioral Scientist	*Amer. behav. Scientist*	Princeton, N.Y.
American economic Review	*Amer. econ. R.*	Menasha, Wisc.
American Economist	*Amer. Economist*	New York
American historical Review	*Amer. hist. R.*	New York
American Jewish Yearbook	*Amer. Jew. Yb.*	Philadelphia, Pa.
American Journal of agricultural Economics	*Amer. J. agric. Econ.*	Menasha, Wisc.
American Journal of Economics and Sociology	*Amer. J. Econ. Sociol.*	New York
American Journal of international Law	*Amer. J. int. Law*	Washington, D.C.
American Journal of political Science	*Amer. J. polit. Sci.*	Detroit, Mich.
American Journal of Sociology	*Amer. J. Sociol.*	Chicago, Ill.
American political Science Review	*Amer. polit. Sci. R.*	Washington, D.C.
American Politics Quarterly	*Amer. Polit. Quart.*	Beverly Hills, Calif.
American Psychologist	*Amer. Psychol.*	Washington, D.C.
American Scholar	*Amer. Scholar*	Washington, D.C.
American sociological Review	*Amer. sociol. R.*	New York
American Sociologist	*Amer. Sociologist*	Washington, D.C.
Amministrare	*Amministrare*	Milano
Amministrazione italiana	*Amm. ital.*	Roma
Ampo	*Ampo*	Tokyo
Anales de la Cátedra Francisco Suarez	*A. Cátedra F. Suarez*	Granada
Análise social	*Anál. soc.*	Lisbôa
Analyse financière	*Anal. financ.*	Paris
Annales (Économies - Sociétés - Civilisations)	*Annales*	Paris
Annales africaines	*A. afr.*	Dakar
Annales d'Économie politique	*A. Écon. polit.*	Paris
Annales d'Études internationales	*A. Ét. int.*	Genève
Annales de Criminologie	*A. Criminol.*	Paris
Annales de Droit	*A. Dr.*	Bruxelles
Annales de Droit international médical	*A. Dr. int. médic.*	Monaco
Annales de Géographie	*A. Géogr.*	Paris
Annales de Sciences économiques appliquées	*A. Sci. écon. appl.*	Louvain

Annales de l'Économie publique, sociale et coopérative	*A. Écon. publ. soc. coop.*	Liège
Annales de l'Université d'Abidjan. Série Droit	*A. Univ. Abidjan Sér. Dr.*	Abidjan
Annales de l'Université des Sciences sociales de Toulouse	*A. Univ. Sci. soc. Toulouse*	Toulouse
Annales de l'Université Jean Moulin	*A. Univ. Jean Moulin*	Lyon
Annales de l'Université Jean Moulin. Faculté de Droit	*A. Univ. Jean Moulin Fac. Dr.*	Lyon
Annales de la Faculté de Droit du Centre universitaire de Toulon et du Var	*A. Fac. Dr. Centre univ. Toulon Var*	Toulon
Annales de la Faculté de Droit et de Science politique (Clermont)	*A. Fac. Dr. Sci. polit. (Clermont)*	Clermont-Ferrand
Annales économiques	*A. écon. (Clermont)*	Clermont
Annales internationales de Criminologie	*A. int. Criminol.*	Paris
Annales Universitatis Scientiarum budapestiensis de Rolando Eötvös nominatae. Sectio iuridica	*A. Univ. Sci. budapest. Sect. iur.*	Budapest
Annali del Mezzogiorno	*A. Mezzogiorno*	Catania
Annali della Facoltà di Agraria	*A. Fac. Agrar. (Bari)*	Bari
Annali della Facoltà di Economia e Commercio	*A. Fac. Econ. Com. (Palermo)*	Palermo
Annali della Facoltà di Economia e Commercio dell' Università di Messina	*A. Fac. Econ. Com. Messina*	Messina
Annali di Sociologia	*A. Sociol. (Milano)*	Milano
Annals of economic and social Measurement	*A. econ. soc. Measurement*	New York
Annals of the American Academy of political and social Science	*A. Amer. Acad. polit. soc. Sci.*	Philadelphia, Pa.
Annals of the Association of American Geographers	*A. Assoc. Amer. Geogr.*	Lawrence, Kan.
Année africaine	*Année afr.*	Paris
Année sociologique	*Année sociol.*	Paris
Annuaire de l'Aménagement du Territoire	*Annu. Aménag. Territ.*	Grenoble
Annuaire des Pays de l'Océan Indien	*Annu. Pays Océan Indien*	Aix-en-Provence
Annuaire européen	*Annu. europ.*	La Haye
Annuaire français de Droit international	*Annu. franç. Dr. int.*	Paris
Annuaire suisse de Science politique	*Annu. suisse Sci. polit.*	Genève
Annual Review of Sociology	*Annu. R. Sociol.*	Palo Alto, Calif.
Annuals of Air and Space Law	*A. Air. Space Law*	
Anthropologie et Sociétés	*Anthropol. et Soc.*	Québec
Antitrust Bulletin	*Antitrust B.*	New York
Anuario del Instituto de Ciencia política	*Anu. Inst. Cienc. polit.*	
Anuario del Instituto de Ciencias penales i criminológicas	*Anu. Inst. Cienc. pen. criminol.*	Caracas
Anuario del Instituto de Estudios políticos	*Anu. Inst. Estud. polit.*	
Anuario indígenista	*Anu. indíg.*	México

Aperçus sur l'Économie tchéco-slovaque	*Aperçus Écon. tchécosl.*	Prague
Applied Economics	*Appl. Econ.*	London
Arbitration Journal	*Arbitr. J.*	New York
Arc	*Arc*	Aix-en-Provence
Arche	*Arche*	Paris
Archipel	*Archipel*	Paris
Archiv des öffentlichen Rechts	*Archiv öff. Rechts*	Tübingen
Archiv des Völkerrechts	*Archiv Völkerrechts*	Tübingen
Archiv für Kommunalwissen-schaften	*Archiv Kommunalwiss.*	Stuttgart
Archiv für Rechts- und Sozial-philosophie	*Archiv Rechts- u. soz.-Philos.*	Berlin-Neuwied-am-Rhein
Archives de Politique crimi-nelle	*Archiv. Polit. crim.*	Paris
Archives de Sciences sociales des Religions	*Archiv. Sci. soc. Re-lig.*	Paris
Archives européennes de Socio-logie / European Journal of Sociology / Europäische Ar-chiv für Soziologie	*Archiv. europ. Sociol.*	Paris
Argument	*Argument*	Karlsruhe
Artha Vijñana	*Artha Vijñana*	Poona
Asia Quarterly	*Asia Quart.*	Bruxelles
Asian Affairs	*Asian Aff. (New York)*	New York
Asian Affairs. Journal of the Royal Central Asian Society	*Asian Aff. (London)*	London
Asian and African Studies	*Asian Afr. Stud.*	Bratislava
Asian and Pacific Quarterly of cultural and social Affairs	*Asian Pacific Quart. cult. soc. Aff.*	Seoul
Asian Economies	*Asian Econ.*	Seoul
Asian Profile	*Asian Profile*	Hong Kong
Asian Studies (University of the Philippines)	*Asian Stud. (Quezon)*	Quezon
Asian Survey	*Asian Surv.*	Berkeley, Calif.
Aspects statistiques de l'Ile de France	*Aspects statist. Ile-de-France*	Paris
Aspects statistiques de la Ré-gion parisienne	*Aspects statist. Région paris.*	Paris
Association des Cadres diri-geants de l'Industrie pour le Progrès social et éco-nomique. Bulletin	*Assoc. Cadres dir. Industr. B.*	Paris
Atarashii Shakaigaku no tame ni	*Atarashii Shakaigaku no tame ni*	[Nihon]
Atlantic	*Atlantic*	Boston, Mass.
Atlantic Community Quarterly	*Atlantic Community Quart.*	Washington, D.C.
Atomic Energy Law Journal	*Atomic Energy Law J.*	Boston
Aussenpolitik	*Aussenpolitik*	Stuttgart
Aussenwirtschaft	*Aussenwirtschaft (St. Gallen)*	St. Gallen
Australian and New Zealand Journal of Sociology	*Austral. New Zealand J. Sociol.*	Melbourne
Australian foreign Affairs Record	*Austral. for. Aff. Rec.*	Canberra
Australian Journal of agricul-tural Economics	*Austral. J. agric. Econ.*	Armindale, N.S.W.
Australian Journal of Politics and History	*Austral. J. Polit. Hist.*	Sydney
Australian Journal of public Administration	*Austral. J. publ. Adm.*	Sydney

Australian Outlook	*Austral. Outlook*	Melbourne
Australian Quarterly	*Austral. Quart.*	Sydney
Austriaca. Cahiers universi- taires d'Information sur l'Autriche	*Austriaca*	Rouen
Autogestion et Socialisme	*Autogestion et Social.*	Paris
Autrement	*Autrement*	Paris
AWR Bulletin	*AWR Bull.*	Paris
Banca nazionale del Lavoro. Quarterly Review	*Banca naz. Lav. quart. R.*	Roma
Bancaria	*Bancaria*	Roma
Bangladesh Development Stu- dies	*Bangladesh Develop. Stud.*	Dacca
Bank of Finland monthly Bulletin	*Bank Finland mthly B.*	Helsinki
Bank of London and South Amer- ica Review	*Bank London South Amer. R.*	London
Bank of New South Wales Re- view	*Bank New South Wales R.*	Sydney
Banker	*Banker*	London
Banque	*Banque*	Paris
Banque française et italienne pour l'Amérique du Sud	*Banque franç. ital. Amér. Sud*	Paris
Baranyai Müvelödés	*Baranyai Müv.*	Pécs
Behavior Science Research	*Behav. Sci. Res.*	New Haven
Behavioral Science	*Behav. Sci.*	Ann Arbor, Mich.
Behavioural Sciences and Com- munity Development	*Behav. Sci. Community Develop.*	Hyderabad
Behaviormetrika	*Behaviormetrika*	[Japan]
Beiträge zur Konfliktforschung	*Beitr. Konfliktforsch.*	Köln
Béke és Szocializmus	*Béke és Szocial.*	Budapest
Beleid en Maatschappij	*Beleid en Mij*	[Nederland]
Bénélux	*Bénélux*	Bruxelles
Berkeley Journal of Sociology	*Berkeley J. Sociol.*	Berkeley, Calif.
Betriebswirtschaftliche For- schung und Praxis	*Betriebswirtsch. Forsch. Praxis*	Göttingen
Bevolking en Gezin	*Bevolking en Gezin*	Bruxelles
Biblioteca della Libertà	*Bibl. Libertà*	Torino
Biuletyn Instytutu Gospodarst- wa Społecznego	*Biul. IGS*	Warszawa
Bulleten' inostrannoj kommer- českoj Informacii Priloženie	*B. inostr. kommerc. Inform. Prilož.*	Moskva
Blätter für deutsche und inter- nationale Politik	*Blätt. dtsche u. int. Polit.*	Köln
Boletín de Documentación del Fondo para la Investigación económica y social	*Bol. Docum. Fondo Invest. econ. soc.*	Madrid
Boletín de Estudios económi- cos	*Bol. Estud. econ.*	Bilbao
Boletín de Estudios latino- americanos y del Caribe	*Bol. Estud. latino- amer.*	Amsterdam
Boletín mensual de Estadística	*Bol. mens. Estadíst.*	Bogotà
Bollettino della DOXA	*Boll. DOXA*	Milano
Bollettino della Società geografica italiana	*Boll. Soc. geogr. ital.*	Roma
Bollettino di Psicologia appli- cata	*Boll. Psicol. appl.*	Firenze
Borsodi Szemle	*Borsodi Szle*	Budapest-Miskolc
British Journal of industrial Relations	*Brit. J. industr. Relat.*	London
British Journal of political Science	*Brit. J. polit. Sci.*	London

British Journal of political Science	*Brit. J. polit. Sci.*	London
British Journal of social and clinical psychology	*Brit. J. soc. clinic. Psychol.*	London
British Journal of Sociology	*Brit. J. Sociol.*	London
British political Sociology Yearbook	*Brit. polit. Sociol. Yb.*	London
British Yearbook of international Law	*Brit. Yb. int. Law*	London
Brookings Papers on economic Activity	*Brookings Pap. econ. Activ.*	Washington, D.C.
Budapesti Müszaki Egyetem Marxizmus-Leninizmus Tanszék-Csoportjának Közleményei	*Bpesti Müsz. Egy. Marx.-Lenin. Közlem.*	Budapest
Bukkyo-daigaku daigakuin kinkyû kiyô	*Bukkyo-daigaku daigakuin kinkyû kiyô*	[Nihon]
Bulletin-Africa Institute	*B. Afr. Inst.*	Pretoria
Bulletin. Agence internationale de l'Énergie atomique	*B. Agence int. Énergie atom.*	Vienne
Bulletin. Association de Cadres dirigeants de l'Industrie pour le Progrès social et économique	*B. Assoc. Cadres dir. Industr. Progrès soc. écon.*	Paris
Bulletin. Société française de Sociologie	*B. Soc. franç. Sociol.*	Paris
Bulletin d'Information du CENADDOM	*B. Inform. CENADDOM*	Paris
Bulletin d'Information du Ministère de l'Agriculture	*B. Inform. Minist. Agric.*	Paris
Bulletin d'Information régionale Champagne-Ardenne	*B. Inform. région. Champagne-Ardenne*	Reims
Bulletin d'Informations économiques	*B. Inform. écon. (New Delhi)*	New Delhi
Bulletin d'Informations économiques	*B. Inform. écon. (Washington)*	Washington. D.C.
Bulletin de Conjoncture régionale. Région de Bretagne	*B. Conjonct. région. Bretagne*	Rennes
Bulletin de Documentation pratique des Impôts directs et des Droits d'Enregistrement	*B. Docum. prat. Impôts dir. Dr. Enregistr.*	Paris
Bulletin de Droit tchécoslovaque	*B. Dr. tchécosl.*	Prague
Bulletin de Liaison et d'Information de l'Administration centrale de l'Économie et des Finances	*B. Liaison Inform. Adm. centr. Écon. Finances*	Paris
Bulletin de Statistique	*B. Statist. (Bruxelles)*	Bruxelles
Bulletin de l'Association des Géographes français	*B. Assoc. Géogr. franç.*	Paris
Bulletin d'Information fondamental d'Afrique noire	*B. Inst. fondam. Afr. noire*	Dakar
Bulletin de la Banque nationale de Belgique	*B. Banque nat. Belgique*	Bruxelles
Bulletin de la Fédération des Entreprises de Belgique	*B. Féd. Entr. Belgique*	Bruxelles
Bulletin de la Société générale de Banque	*B. Soc. gén. Banque*	Bruxelles
Bulletin des Séances de l'Académie royale des Sciences d'Outre-Mer	*B. Séances Acad. roy. Sci. O.-Mer*	Bruxelles
Bulletin des Stupéfiants	*B. Stupéfiants*	New York

Bulletin du Bois pour l'Europe	*B. Bois Europe*	Genève
Bulletin du Centre de Documentation d'Études juridiques économiques et sociales	*B. Centre Docum. Ét. jur. écon. soc.*	Le Caire
Bulletin du Centre européen de la Culture	*B. Centre europ. Cult.*	Genève
Bulletin du Pacifique Sud	*B. Pacifique Sud*	Nouméa
Bulletin économique pour l'Europe	*B. écon. Europe*	Genève
Bulletin for international fiscal Documentation	*B. int. fisc. Docum.*	Amsterdam
Bulletin mensuel Economie et Statistique agricoles	*B. mens. Econ. Statist. agric.*	Rome
Bulletin of concerned Asian Scholars	*B. concerned Asian Scholars*	San Francisco, Calif.
Bulletin of economic Research	*B. econ. Res.*	Hull
Bulletin of Indonesian economic Studies	*B. Indones. econ. Stud.*	Canberra
Bulletin of Peace Proposals	*B. Peace Propos.*	Oslo
Bulletin of the atomic Scientists	*B. atomic Scientists*	Chicago, Ill.
Bulletin trimestriel de l'École nationale de la Santé publique	*B. trim. École nat. Santé publ.*	Rennes
Bungaku Kenkyûka Kiyô	*Bungaku Kenkyûka Kiyô*	[Nihon]
Buraku Mondai Kenkyû	*Buraku Mondai Kenkyû*	Osaka
Bureaucrat	*Bureaucrat*	Washington, D.C.
Business and Society Review	*Busin. Soc. R.*	Boston, Mass.
Business Economics	*Busin. Econ.*	Washington, D.C.
Business Review	*Busin. R.*	Washington, D.C.
Cadernos de Departamento de Ciência politica	*Cad. Dept. Ciênc. polit.*	Belo Horizonte
Cahier et Revue de l'OURS	*Cah. Rev. OURS*	Paris
Cahiers africains d'Administration publique	*C. afr. Adm. publ.*	Tanger
Cahiers Bernard Lazare	*C. Bernard Lazare*	Paris
Cahiers d'Études africaines	*C. Ét. afr.*	La Haye-Paris
Cahiers d'Histoire de l'Institut Maurice Thorez	*C. Hist. Inst. Maurice Thorez*	Paris
Cahiers d'Outre-Mer	*C. O.-Mer*	Bordeaux
Cahiers de Droit européen	*C. Dr. europ.*	Louvain
Cahiers de Sociologie et de Démographie médicales	*C. Sociol. Démogr. médic.*	Paris
Cahiers de Tunisie	*C. Tunisie*	Tunis
Cahiers de l'Actualité religieuse et sociale	*C. Actual. relig. soc.*	Paris
Cahiers de l'ERIS	*Cah. ERIS*	Paris
Cahiers de l'Expansion régionale	*C. Expans. région.*	Paris
Cahiers de l'Institut d'Aménagement et d'Urbanisme de la Région d'Ile-de-France	*C. Inst. Aménag. Urb. Région Ile de France*	Paris
Cahiers de l'Institut d'Aménagement et d'Urbanisme de la Région parisienne	*Cah. IAURP*	Paris
Cahiers de l'Office de la recherche scientifique et technique Outre-Mer. Série Sciences humaines	*Cah. ORSTOM Sér. Sci. hum.*	Paris
Cahiers des Amériques latines	*C. Amér. lat.*	Paris

Cahiers des Ingénieurs agro-nomes	*C. Ingén. agron.*	Paris
Cahiers du CEDAF	*Cah. CEDAF*	Bruxelles
Cahiers du Communisme	*C. Communisme*	Paris
Cahiers du GRECOH	*Cah. GRECOH*	Paris
Cahiers du Monde hispano et luso-brésilien	*C. Monde hisp. luso-brésil.*	Toulouse
Cahiers du Monde russe et soviétique	*C. Monde russe sov.*	Paris
Cahiers économiques de Bre-tagne	*C. écon. Bretagne*	Rennes
Cahiers économiques de Bruxelles	*C. écon. Bruxelles*	Bruxelles
Cahiers européens	*C. europ.*	Bruxelles
Cahiers français	*C. franç.*	Paris
Cahiers internationaux de So-ciologie	*C. int. Sociol.*	Paris
Cahiers mensuels de Statistique agricole de la Région Langue-doc	*C. mens. Statist. agric agric. Région Langue-doc*	Perpignan
Cahiers pédagogiques	*C. pédag.*	Paris
California Management Review	*Calif. Manag. R.*	Los Angeles, Calif.
Cambridge Journal of Economics	*Cambridge J. Econ.*	London
Canadian geographical Journal	*Canad. geogr. J.*	Ottawa
Canadian Journal of African Studies	*Canad. J. Afr. Stud.*	Ottawa
Canadian Journal of agricul-tural Economics	*Canad. J. agric. Econ.*	Toronto
Canadian Journal of Economics/ Revue canadienne d'Économie	*Canad. J. Econ.*	Montréal
Canadian Journal of political and social Theory	*Canad. J. polit. soc. Theory*	[Canada]
Canadian Journal of political Science	*Canad. J. polit. Sci.*	Toronto
Canadian Journal of Sociology	*Canad. J. Sociol.*	Edmonton
Canadian public Administration / Administration publique du Canada	*Canad. publ. Adm.*	Toronto
Canadian Review of Sociology and Anthropology / Revue ca-nadienne de Sociologie et d'Anthropologie	*Canad. R. Sociol. Anthropol.*	Calgary
Canadian Slavonic Papers	*Canad. Slavonic Pap.*	Ottawa
Canadian Yearbook of interna-tional Law	*Canad. Yb. int. Law*	Vancouver
Carnets de l'Enfance	*Carnets Enfance*	Paris
Casa de las Américas	*Casa Amér.*	La Habana
Case Western Reserve Journal of international Law	*Case West. J. int. Law*	Cleveland, Ohio
CEPAL Review	*CEPAL Rev.*	Santiago de Chile
Challenge	*Challenge*	New York
Chambres d'Agriculture	*Ch. Agric.*	Paris
Chiffres pour l'Alsace	*Chiffres Alsace*	Strasbourg
Chiiki Fukushi Kenkyû	*Chiiki Fukushi Kenkyû*	Osaka
Chiiki-kai-hatsu	*Chiiki-kai-hatsu*	[Nihon]
Chile-América	*Chile-América*	Roma
China Quarterly	*China Quart.*	London
China Report	*China Rep.*	New York
Chinese Culture	*Chinese Cult.*	Yang Ming Shan
Chinese economic Studies	*Chinese econ. Stud.*	White Plains, N.Y.
Chronique de l'Organisation Mondiale de la Santé	*Chron. OMS*	Genève

Chronique sociale de France	*Chron. soc. France*	Lyon
Chroniques d'Actualité de la SEDEIS	*Chron. Actual. SEDEIS*	Paris
Chûkyô-shôgaku Ronsô	*Chûkyô-shôgaku Ronsô*	[Nihon]
Chûô Daigaku Bungakubu Kiyô	*Chûô Daigaku Bungakubu Kiyô*	Tokyo
Ciência e Trópico	*Ciênc. e Trop.*	Recife
Ciências econômicas e sociais	*Ciênc. econ. soc.*	São Paulo
Civilisations	*Civilisations*	Bruxelles
Civiltà cattolica	*Civiltà catt.*	Roma
Civitas	*Civitas (Roma)*	Roma
Civitas. Jahrbuch für Sozial-wissenschaften	*Civitas (Mannheim)*	Mannheim
Classe. Quaderni sulla Condizione e sulla Lotta operaia	*Classe*	Milano
Co-existence	*Co-existence*	Ontario-Chicago, Ill.
Collections de Statistique agricole. Étude	*Coll. Statist. agric. Ét.*	Paris
Collections de l'INSÉE	*Coll. INSÉE*	Paris
Columbia Journal of transnational Law	*Columbia J. transnat. Law*	New York
Columbia Journal of World Business	*Columbia J. Wld Busin.*	New York
Columbia Journalism Review	*Columbia J-ism R.*	New York
Columbia Law Review	*Columbia Law R.*	New York
Comercio exterior de México	*Com. ext. México*	México
Commentary	*Commentary*	New York
Commerce extérieur tchéco-slovaque	*Com. ext. tchécosl.*	Prague
Common Market Law Review	*Common Market Law R.*	Leyden
Communauté. Archives internationales de Sociologie de la Coopération et du Développement	*Communauté*	Paris
Communautés et Continents	*Communautés et Continents*	Paris
Communes modernes	*Communes mod.*	Paris
Communication et Languages	*Communic. et Lang.*	Paris
Communications	*Communications (Köln)*	Köln
Communications	*Communications (Paris)*	Paris
Communisme	*Communisme*	Paris
Community Development Journal	*Community Develop. J.*	Manchester
Comparative political Studies	*Comp. polit. Stud.*	Beverly Hills, Calif.
Comparative Politics	*Comp. Polit.*	Chicago, Ill.
Comparative Studies in Society and History	*Comp. Stud. Soc. Hist.*	The Hague-Ann Arbor, Mich.
Comparative urban Research	*Comp. urb. Res.*	New York
Comptes-rendus hebdomadaires des Séances de l'Académie d'Agriculture de France	*CR heb. Séances Acad. Agric. France*	Paris
Comptes-rendus trimestriels des Séances de l'Académie des Sciences d'Outre-Mer	*CR trim. Acad. Sci. O.-Mer*	Paris
Comunicación	*Comunicación*	Caracas
Comunidad	*Comunidad*	México
Comunità	*Comunità*	Milano
Comunità europee	*Comunità europ.*	Roma
Comunità internazionale	*Comunità int.*	Roma
Conflict Studies	*Conflict Stud.*	London

Conjuntura econômica	*Conjunt. econ.*	Rio de Janeiro
Connaissance de la République démocratique allemande	*Connaissance RDA*	Paris
Connexions	*Connexions*	Paris
Conseiller du Commerce extérieur	*Cons. Com. ext.*	Paris
Consommation. Annales du CREDOC	*Consommation*	Paris
Construction, Aménagement	*Construct. Aménag.*	Paris
Contemporary Crises	*Contemp. Crises*	Amsterdam
Contemporary Review	*Contemp. R.*	London
Contradictions	*Contradictions*	Paris
Contrepoint	*Contrepoint*	Paris
Contribution to Indian Sociology. New Series	*Contrib. Ind. Sociol. New Ser.*	Bombay
Convergence	*Convergence*	Toronto
Coopération agricole	*Coop. agric.*	Paris
Cooperation and Conflict	*Coop. and Conflict*	Stockholm
Coopération-Distribution-Consommation	*Coop.-Distrib.-Consom.*	Paris
Correspondance municipale	*Corresp. municip.*	Paris
Courrier de l'Extrême-Orient / Berichten uit het Verre Oosten	*Courr. Extr.-Orient*	Bruxelles
Courrier de la Normalisation	*Courr. Normalis.*	Paris
Courrier des Pays de l'Est	*Courr. Pays-Est*	Paris
Cristianismo y Sociedad	*Crist. y Soc.*	Montevideo
Criterio	*Criterio*	Buenos Aires
Criterio económico	*Crit. econ.*	Bogotà
Critica marxista	*Crit. marx.*	Roma
Critica sociologica	*Crit. sociol. (Roma)*	Roma
Critique	*Critique*	Paris
Critique communiste	*Crit. commun.*	Paris
Critique socialiste	*Crit. social. (Rome)*	Rome
Critiques de l'Économie politique	*Crit. Écon. polit.*	Paris
Cuadernos américanos	*Cuad. amér.*	México
Cuadernos de Economía	*Cuad. Econ. (Barcelona)*	Barcelona
Cuban Studies / Estudios cubanos	*Cuban Stud.*	Pittsburg, Pa.
Culture française	*Cult. franç.*	Paris
Cultures	*Cultures*	Paris
Cultures et Développement	*Cult. et Dévelop.*	Louvain
Current	*Current*	Washington, D.C.
Current Affairs Bulletin	*Curr. Aff. B.*	Sydney
Current Anthropology	*Curr. Anthropol.*	Chicago, Ill.
Current History	*Curr. Hist.*	Philadelphia, Pa.
Current Sociology	*Curr. Sociol.*	Oxford
Czechoslovak economic Papers	*Czechosl. econ. Pap.*	Prague
Dados	*Dados*	Rio de Janeiro
Daedalus. Journal of the American Academy of Arts and Sciences	*Daedalus*	Cambridge, Mass.
Daigaku Ronshû	*Daigaku Ronshû*	[Nihon]
DE...	*DE*	Praha
Debate	*Debate*	Paris
De Economia	*De Economia*	Madrid
Défense de l'Occident	*Déf. Occident*	Paris
Défense nationale	*Déf. nat.*	Paris
De franse Nederlanden / Les Pays-Bas français	*De frans. Nederl. / Pays-Bas franç.*	

Democrazia e Diritto	*Democr. e Dir.*	Roma
Demográfia	*Demográfia*	Budapest
Demografía y Economía	*Demogr. y Econ.*	México
Demografie	*Demografie*	Praha
Demography	*Demography*	Ann Arbor
Demosta	*Demosta*	Praha
Den'gi i Kredit	*Den'gi i Kred.*	Moskva
Department of Employment Gazette	*Dept. Employment Gaz.*	London
Derecho de la Integración	*Der. Integr.*	Buenos-Aires
Desarrollo	*Desarrollo*	Santiago de Chile
Desarrollo económico	*Desarr. econ.*	Buenos Aires
Desarrollo indoamericano	*Desarr. indoamer.*	Bogotá
Deutsche Aussenpolitik	*Dtsche Aussenpolit.*	Berlin
Deutsche Jugend	*Dtsche Jugend*	München
Deutsche Studien. Viertel- jahreshefte für vergleichen- de Gegenwartskunde	*Dtsche Stud.*	Lüneburg
Deutsche Zeitschrift für Phi- losophie	*Dtsche Z. Philos.*	Berlin
Deutschland Archiv	*Deutschland Archiv*	Köln
2000, Revue de l'Aménagement du Territoire	*2000 R. Aménag. Territ.*	Paris
Developing Economies	*Develop. Econ.*	Tokyo
Development and Change	*Develop. and Change*	The Hague
Development Dialogue	*Develop. Dialogue*	Uppsala
Development Policy and Admi- nistration Review	*Develop. Pol. Adm. R.*	Jaipur
Dialectiques	*Dialectiques*	Paris
Dialogue	*Dialogue (Washington)*	Washington, D.C.
Difesa sociale	*Dif. soc.*	Roma
Dimensions économiques de la Bourgogne	*Dim. écon. Bourgogne*	Dijon
Diogène	*Diogène*	Paris
Direction et Gestion des Entre- prises	*Dir. Gestion Entr.*	Paris
Dirigeant	*Dirigeant*	Paris
Dispersion et Unité	*Dispersion et Unité*	Jérusalem
Dissent	*Dissent*	New York
Documentación administrativa	*Docum. adm.*	Madrid
Documentación jurídica	*Docum. jur.*	Madrid
Documentation sur l'Europe centrale	*Docum. Europe centr.*	Louvain
Documentos políticos	*Doc. polít.*	Bogotá
Documents. Revue des Questions allemandes	*Documents (Cologne)*	Cologne
Documents CEPESS. Centre d'É- tudes politiques, économiques et sociales	*Doc. CEPESS*	Bruxelles
Documents d'Information et de Gestion	*Doc. Inform. Gestion*	Paris
Documents du Centre d'Étude des Revenus et des Coûts	*Doc. Centre Ét. Revenus Coûts*	Paris
Documents européens	*Docum. europ.*	Paris
Dokkyô-daigaku kyôyô-shogaku	*Dokkyo-daigaku kyôyô- shogaku*	[Nihon]
Donauraum	*Donauraum*	Salzburg
Données statistiques du Li- mousin	*Données statist. Limou- sin*	Limoges
Doshisha Amerika Kenkyû	*Doshisha Amerika Kenkyû*	Kyoto
Dossiers bis "Jeune Afrique" et "Economia"	*Doss. bis Jeune Afr. Economia*	Paris

Dossiers de l'Économie lorraine	*Doss. Écon. lorraine*	Nancy
Dossiers de la Politique agricole commune	*Doss. Polit. agric. commune*	Paris
Double-Point. Information économique Champagne-Ardennes	*Double-Point*	Reims
Dritte Welt	*Dritte Welt*	Meisenheim
Droit et Pratique du Commerce international	*Dr. Pratique Com. int.*	Paris
Droit et Ville	*Dr. et Ville*	Toulouse
Droit maritime français	*Dr. marit. franç.*	Paris
Droit social	*Dr. soc.*	Paris
East Africa economic Review	*East Afr. econ. R.*	Nairobi
East Asian Review	*East Asian R.*	Seoul
East European Quarterly	*East Europ. Quart.*	Boulder, Col.
Eastern Anthropologist	*East. Anthropol.*	Lucknow
Échanges internationaux et Développement	*Échanges int. Dévelop.*	Toulouse
École et Nation	*École et Nation*	Paris
Ecologist	*Ecologist*	London
Econometrica	*Econometrica*	Chicago, Ill.
Economía	*Economía (Quito)*	Quito
Economia del Lavoro	*Econ. del Lav.*	Roma
Economia internazionale	*Econ. int. (Genova)*	Genova
Economia internazionale delle Fonti di Energia	*Econ. int. Fonti Energia*	Milano
Economía y Administración	*Econ. y Adm.*	Concepción
Economía y Desarrollo	*Econ. y Desarr.*	La Habana
Economic and political Weekly	*Econ. polit. Wkly*	Bombay
Economic and social Review	*Econ. soc. R.*	Dublin
Economic Bulletin	*Econ. B. (Oslo)*	Oslo
Economic Bulletin. National Bank of Egypt	*Econ. B. (Cairo)*	Cairo
Economic Development and cultural Change	*Econ. Develop. cult. Change*	Chicago, Ill.
Economic Geography	*Econ. Geogr. (Worcester)*	Worcester, Mass
Economic Inquiry	*Econ. Inquiry*	Los Angeles, Calif.
Economic Journal	*Econ. J.*	London
Economic Papers	*Econ. Pap.*	Warsaw
Economic Record	*Econ. Rec.*	Melbourne
Economic Review	*Econ. R. (Helsinki)*	Helsinki
Economic Review	*Econ. R. (Jerusalem)*	Jerusalem
Económica	*Económica (La Plata)*	La Plata
Economica	*Economica (London)*	London
Economics and Business	*Econ. and Busin.*	Champaign, Ill.
Economics and Sociology	*Econ. and Sociol.*	
Economie	*Economie (Tilburg)*	Tilburg
Économie appliquée	*Écon. appl.*	Paris
Économie corse	*Écon. corse*	Ajaccio
Économie du Centre-Est	*Écon. Centre-Est*	Dijon
Économie et Finances agricoles	*Écon. Finances agric.*	Paris
Économie et Humanisme	*Écon. et Human.*	Caluire
Économie et Politique	*Écon. et Polit.*	Paris
Économie et Statistique	*Écon. et Statist.*	Paris
Économie - Géographie	*Écon.-Géogr.*	Paris
Économie rurale	*Écon. rur.*	Paris
Économies et Sociétés, Cahiers de l'ISEA	*Écon. et Soc.*	Paris
Economisch en sociaal Tijdschrift / Vie économique et sociale	*Econ. soc. Tijds.*	Antwerpen

Economy and Society	*Econ. and Soc.*	London
Ecumenical Review	*Ecumen. R.*	Geneva
Éducation et Gestion	*Éduc. et Gestion*	Paris
Éducation permanente	*Éduc. perm.*	Nancy
Egészségnevelés	*Egészségnevelés*	Budapest
Einheit	*Einheit*	Berlin
Ekistics	*Ekistics*	Athens
Ekonomi dan keuangan Indonesia	*Ekon. keuangan Indonesia*	Djakarta
Ekonomia	*Ekonomia (Warszawa)*	Warszawa
Ěkonomičeskie Nauki	*Ěkon. Nauki*	Moskva
Ekonomicko-matematický Obzor	*Ekon.-matem. Obzor*	Praha
Ekonomický Časopis	*Ekon. Čas.*	Bratislava
Ěkonomika i matematičeskie Metody	*Ěkon. matem. Metody*	Moskva
Ěkonomika sel'skogo Hozjajstva	*Ěkon. sel'sk. Hoz.*	Moskva
Ěkonomika Sovetskoj Ukrainy	*Ěkon. Sov. Ukr.*	Kiev
Ekonomisk Revy	*Ekon. R. (Stockholm)*	Stockholm
Ekonomska Revija	*Ekon. R. (Ljubljana)*	Ljubljana
Ekonomska Samfundet Tidskrift	*Ekon. Samfund. Ts.*	Helsinki
Ekonomist	*Ekonomist (Zagreb)*	Zagreb
Ekonomista	*Ekonomista*	Warszawa
Élet és Tudomány	*Élet. és Tud.*	Budapest
Elmélet és Politika	*Elmélet és Polit.*	[Magyarország]
Emigrazione	*Emigrazione*	Roma
Employment Gazette	*Empl. Gaz.*	London
Encounter	*Encounter*	London
Energy Policy	*Energy Pol.*	Guildford
Energy Systems and Policy	*Energy Systems Pol.*	New York
Entwicklungspolitik	*Entwicklungspolitik*	Frankfurt-am-Main
Environment and Behaviour	*Environ. and Behav.*	Beverly Hills, Calif.
Épitési Kutatás, Fejlesztés	*Épit. Kut. Fejleszt.*	[Magyarország]
Épithéorisis dimossiou Dikaiou kai Dioikitikou Dikaiou	*Épithéor. dimos. Dikaiou Dioikit. Dikaiou*	Athênaï
Équipement - Logement - Transports	*Équipement*	Paris
Espace géographique	*Espace géogr.*	Paris
Espaces et Sociétés	*Espaces et Soc.*	Paris
Esprit	*Esprit*	Paris
Est	*Est (Milano)*	Milano
Est et Ouest, Bulletin de l'Association d'Études et d'Informations politiques internationales	*Est et Ouest*	Paris
Est européen	*Est europ.*	Paris
Est-Ovest	*Est-Ovest*	Trieste
Estadística	*Estadística (Washington)*	Washington, D.C.
Estrategía	*Estrategía*	Buenos Aires
Estudios andinos	*Estud. andin.*	La Paz
Estudios de Derecho	*Estud. Der. (Antioquia)*	Antioquia
Estudios empresariales	*Estud. empresar.*	San Sebastian
Estudios geográficos	*Estud. geogr.*	Madrid
Estudios internacionales	*Estud. int.*	Santiago de Chile
Estudios políticos	*Estud. polít.*	Mexico
Estudios sociales centroamericanos	*Estud. soc. centroamer.*	San José
Estudos CEBRAP	*Estud. CEBRAP*	São Paulo
Et cetera	*Et cetera*	San Francisco, Calif.
Ethics. An international Journal of social political and legal Philosophy	*Ethics*	Chicago

Ethiopiques	*Ethiopiques*	Dakar
Ethnie française	*Ethnie franç.*	Bruxelles
Ethnographia	*Ethnographia*	Budapest
Ethnographie	*Ethnographie*	Paris
Ethnology	*Ethnology*	Pittsburgh, Pa.
Études	*Études (Paris)*	Paris
Études balkaniques	*Ét. balkan.*	Sofia
Études économiques	*Ét. écon. (Mons)*	Mons
Études et Documents. Conseil d'État	*Ét. Doc. Conseil d'É- tat*	Paris
Études et Documents. Éduca- tion nationale	*Ét. et Doc. (Éduc. nat.)*	Paris
Études et Expansion	*Ét. et Expans.*	Liège
Études internationales	*Ét. int.*	Québec
Études normandes	*Ét. normandes*	Le Havre
Études polémologiques	*Ét. polémol.*	Paris
Études rurales	*Ét. rur.*	Paris
Études sociales	*Ét. soc. (Paris)*	Paris
Études sociales et syndicales	*Ét. soc. synd.*	Paris
Études statistiques de l'Équi- pement	*Ét. statist. Équipement*	Paris
Études vietnamiennes	*Ét. vietnam.*	Hanoï
EURE. Revista latinoamericana de Estudios urbano-regionales	*EURE*	Santiago de Chile
Eurépargne	*Eurépargne*	Luxembourg
Eurocoopération. Études éco- nomiques et européennes	*Eurocoopération*	Paris
Euromoney	*Euromoney*	London
Europa-Archiv	*Europa-Archiv*	Frankfurt-am-Main
Europäische Rundschau	*Europ. Rdsch.*	Wien
Europäische Wehrkunde	*Europ. Wehrkunde*	München
Europarecht	*Europarecht*	München
Europe-Outre-Mer	*Europe-O.-Mer*	Paris
European economic Review	*Europ. econ. R.*	Bruxelles
European Journal of political Research	*Europ. J. polit. Res.*	Amsterdam
European Journal of social Psychology	*Europ. J. soc. Psychol.*	The Hague
European Judaism	*Europ. Judaism*	London
European Law Review	*Europ. Law R.*	Brighton
European Quarterly	*Europ. Quart.*	
European Review of agricul- tural Economics	*Europ. R. agric. Econ.*	The Hague
Expansion	*Expansion*	Paris
Explorations in economic Res- earch	*Explor. econ. Res.*	New York
Family Coordinator	*Family Coordinator*	Eugene, Ore.
Family Process	*Family Process*	Baltimore, Md.
Federal Reserve Bank of New York	*Fed. Reserve Bank New York*	New York
Federal Reserve Bank of St. Louis	*Fed. Reserve Bank St. Louis*	St. Louis, Mo.
Federalista	*Federalista*	Pavia-Milano-Lyon
Felsöoktatasi Szemle	*Felsöokt. Szle*	Budapest
Filosofija naučnyj Kommunizm	*Filos. nauč. Kommunizm*	Minsk
Filosofskie Nauki	*Filos. Nauki*	Alma-Ata
Finance and Trade Review	*Finance Trade R.*	Pretoria-Johannes- burg
Finances et Développement	*Finances et Dévelop.*	Washington, D.C.
Financial Analysts Journal	*Financ. Analysts J.*	New York
Finanse	*Finanse*	Warszawa

Finansy SSSR	*Finansy SSSR*	Moskva
Finanzarchiv	*Finanzarchiv*	Frankfurt-am-Main
Finsk Tidskrift	*Finsk Ts.*	Åbo
Földrajzi Értesitö	*Földr. Ért.*	Budapest
Földrajzi Közlemények	*Földr. Közlem.*	Budapest
Folia historica	*Folia hist.*	Budapest
Folia oeconomica cracoviensia	*Fol. oecon. cracov.*	Kraków
Food Research Institute Studies in agricultural Economics, Trade and Development	*Food Res. Inst. Stud.*	Stanford, Calif.
Foreign Affairs	*For. Aff.*	New York
Foreign Affairs Report	*For. Aff. Rep.*	Delhi
Foreign Policy	*For. Pol. (Ankara)*	Ankara
Foreign Policy	*For. Pol. (New York)*	New York
Foro internacional	*Foro int.*	México
Forrás	*Forrás*	Kecskemét
Fortune	*Fortune*	Chicago, Ill.
France-Forum	*France-Forum*	Paris
Frankfurter Hefte	*Frankfurt. H.*	Frankfurt-am-Main
Futures	*Futures*	Guildford
Futuribles	*Futuribles*	Paris
Futurist	*Futurist*	Washington, D.C.
Futuro presente	*Futuro presente*	Madrid
Gazdálkodás	*Gazdálkodás*	Budapest
Gazdaság	*Gazdaság*	Budapest
Gazdaság és Jogtudomány	*Gazd. és Jogtud.*	Budapest
Gazette	*Gazette (Amsterdam)*	Amsterdam
Gazette du Travail	*Gaz. Trav.*	Ottawa
Gegenwartskunde	*Gegenwartskunde*	Opladen
Gendai no Rôdô	*Gendai no Rôdô*	[Nihon[
Gendai Shakaigaku	*Gendai Shakaigaku*	Tokyo
Gendai Shisô	*Gendai Shisô*	[Nihon]
Gendai to Shisô	*Gendai to Shisô*	Tokyo
General Systems	*Gen. Systems*	New York
Genève-Afrique	*Genève-Afr.*	Genève
Geographical Journal	*Geogr. J.*	London
Geographical Review	*Geogr. R.*	New York
Géographie et Recherche	*Géogr. et Rech.*	Dijon
German economic Review	*German econ. R.*	Tübingen
Gérontologie	*Gérontologie*	Paris
Gewerkschaften und Klassen-kampf	*Gewerksch. u. Klassen-kampf*	Frankfurt-am-Main
Gewerkschaftliche Monats-hefte	*Gewerkschaftl. Mh.*	Köln
Giornale degli Economisti e Annali di Economia	*G. Economisti*	Milano
Gledišta	*Gledišta*	Beograd
Godišnik na ekonomski ot Fakultet (Skopje)	*Godiš. ekon. Fak. (Skopje)*	Skopje
Gospodarka planowa	*Gosp. planowa*	Warszawa
Government and Opposition	*Gvt. and Opposition*	London
GPSA Journal	*GPSA J.*	Atlanta, Ga.
Growth and Change	*Growth and Change*	Lexington, Ky.
Guatemala indígena	*Guatemala indíg.*	Guatemala
H Revue de l'Habitat social	*H Rev. Habitat soc.*	Paris
Habitat et Vie sociale	*Habitat Vie soc.*	Paris
Hallinto	*Hallinto*	[Suomi]
Hamburg in Zahlen	*Hamburg in Zahlen*	Hamburg
Hamburger Jahrbuch für Wirt-schafts- und Gesellschafts-politik	*Hamburg. Jb. Wirtsch.- u. Ges.-Polit.*	Hamburg

Handel wewnętrzny	*Handel wewn.*	Warszawa
Handel zagraniczy	*Handel zagran.*	Warszawa
Hanzai-shakaigaku Kenkyû	*Hanzai-shakaigaku Kenkyû*	[Nihon]
Harper's Magazine	*Harper's Mag.*	New York
Harvard Business Review	*Harvard Busin. R.*	Boston, Mass.
Harvard educational Review	*Harvard educ. R.*	Cambridge, Mass.
Harvard Law Review	*Harvard Law R.*	Cambridge, Mass.
Hérodote	*Hérodote*	Paris
Híd	*Híd*	Budapest
Higher Education	*Higher Educ.*	Amsterdam
Higher Education and Research in the Netherlands	*Higher Educ. Res. Netherlands*	The Hague
Himičeskaja Promyšlennost' za rubežom	*Himič. Promyšl. rubežom*	Moskva
Hiroshima Shôdai Ronshû	*Hiroshima Shôdai Ronshû*	Hiroshima
Hiroshima Shudo-daigaku Ronshu	*Hiroshima Shudo-daigaku Ronshu*	Hiroshima
Historiallinen Aikakauskirja	*Hist. Aikakausk.*	Helsinki
Historiens et Géographes	*Hist. et Géogr.*	Paris
Historiskt Tidskrift för Finland	*Hist. Ts. Finland*	Helsinki
History and Theory	*Hist. and Theory*	Middletown, Conn.
History of political Economy	*Hist. polit. Econ.*	Durham, N.C.
Hitotsubashi Journal of Commerce and Management	*Hitotsubashi J. Com. Manag.*	Tokyo
Hitotsubashi Journal of Economics	*Hitotsubashi J. Econ.*	Tokyo
Hôgaku Kenkyû	*Hôgaku Kenkyû (Tokyo)*	Tokyo
Homme. Revue française d'Anthropologie	*Homme*	Paris
Hommes et Commerce	*Hommes et Com.*	Paris
Hommes et Migrations. Documents	*Hommes et Migr. Doc.*	Paris
Hôpital à Paris	*Hôpital Paris*	Paris
Hôritsu Jihô	*Hôritsu Jihô*	Tokyo
Human Factor	*Hum. Factor*	Santa Monica, Calif.
Human Orgnization	*Hum. Org.*	New York
Human Relations	*Hum. Relat.*	London
Human Rights Journal	*Hum. Rights J.*	Paris
Human Rights Review	*Hum. Rights R.*	London
Humanisme	*Humanisme*	Paris
Humanisme et Entreprise	*Human. et Entr.*	Paris
Humanizacja Pracy	*Human. Pracy*	Warszawa
Hyôron Shakaikagaku	*Hyôron Shakaikagaku*	[Nihon]
Hyôronsha shakai-kagaku	*Hyôronsha shakai-kagaku*	[Nihon]
IDOC-internazionale	*IDOC int.*	Brescia
IDS Bulletin	*IDS Bull.*	Brighton
IDSA Journal	*IDSA J.*	New Delhi
Impact. Science et Société	*Impact*	Paris
Impresa	*Impresa*	Roma
India Quarterly	*India Quart.*	New Delhi
Indian Journal of agricultural Economics	*Ind. J. agric. Econ.*	Bombay
Indian Journal of Economics	*Ind. J. Econ.*	Allahabad
Indian Journal of political Science	*Ind. J. polit. Sci.*	Lucknow
Indian Journal of political Studies	*Ind. J. polit. Stud.*	Jodhpur
Indian Journal of Politics	*Ind. J. Polit.*	Aligarh
Indian Journal of public Administration	*Ind. J. publ. Adm.*	New Delhi

Indian Journal of social Research	*Ind. J. soc. Res.*	Baraut
Indian Journal of social Work	*Ind. J. soc. Wk*	Bombay
Indian Labour Journal	*Ind. Lab. J.*	Simla
Indian political Science Review	*Ind. polit. Sci. R.*	Delhi
Indice	*Indice*	Madrid
Indonesia	*Indonesia*	Ithaca, N. Y.
Indonesian economic Studies	*Indones. econ. Stud.*	
Indonesian Quarterly	*Indones. Quart.*	Diakarta
Industria	*Industria*	Milano
Industria e Produtividade	*Industr. e Produtiv.*	Rio de Janeiro
Industrial and Labor Relations Review	*Industr. Lab. Relat. R.*	Ithaca, N. Y.
Industrial Relations	*Industr. Relat. (Berkeley)*	Berkeley, Calif.
Industrie française du Coton et des Fibres alliées	*Industr. franc. Coton Fibres alliees*	Paris
Industries et Travaux d'Outre-Mer	*Industr. Trav. O.-Mer*	Paris
Industry of free China	*Industry free China*	Taipei
Información comercial española	*Inform. com. esp.*	Madrid
Information. Zukunfts- und Friedensforschung	*Information (Hannover)*	Hannover
Information agricole	*Inform. agric.*	Paris
Information géographique	*Inform. géogr.*	Paris
Informationen zur Raumentwicklung	*Inform. Raumentwicklung*	Bad Godesberg
Informations	*Informations (Bruxelles)*	Bruxelles
Informations constitutionnelles et parlementaires	*Inform. constit. parl.*	Genève
Informations coopératives	*Inform. coop (BIT)*	Genève
Informations et Documents	*Inform. et Doc.*	Paris
Informations sociales	*Inform. soc. (Paris)*	Paris
Ingénieurs des Villes de France	*Ingén. Villes France*	Paris
Inquiry	*Inquiry*	Oslo
Instant Research on Peace and Violence	*Instant Res. Peace Violence*	Tampere
Institut des Belles Lettres Arabes	*IBLA*	Tunis
Institute for Defence Studies and Analyses Journal	*Inst. Def. Stud. Anal. J.*	New Delhi
Insurgent Sociologist	*Insurgent Sociologist*	Eugene, Ore.
Integración latinoamericana	*Integr. latinoamer.*	Buenos Aires
Intégration	*Intégration (Alger)*	Alger
Inter-American economic Affairs	*Inter-Amer. econ. Aff.*	Washington, D.C.
Inter-Nord	*Inter-Nord*	Paris
Interchange	*Interchange*	Ontario
Intereconomics	*Intereconomics*	Hamburg
Interfaces	*Interfaces*	Providence, R.I.
Internasjonal Politikk	*Int. Polit. (Bergen)*	Bergen
International Affairs	*Int. Aff. (London)*	London
International and comparative Law Quarterly	*Int. comp. Law Quart.*	London
International behavioural Scientist	*Int. behav. Scientist*	Meerut
International Currency Review	*Int. Currency R.*	London
International Development Review	*Int. Develop. R.*	Washington, D.C.
International economic Review	*Int. econ. R.*	Philadelphia, Pa.
International Journal	*Int. J.*	Toronto
International Journal of comparative Sociology	*Int. J. comp. Sociol.*	Leiden

International Journal of contemporary Sociology	*Int. J. contemp. Sociol.*	Ghaziabad
International Journal of Group Psychotherapy	*Int. J. Group Psychother.*	New York
International Journal of Group Tensions	*Int. J. Group Tensions*	London
International Journal of Middle East Studies	*Int. J. Mid. East Stud.*	London
International Journal of Politics	*Int. J. Polit.*	New York
International Journal of social Economics	*Int. J. soc. Econ.*	Bradford
International Journal of Sociology	*Int. J. Sociol.*	New York
International Library Review	*Int. Library R.*	New York
International Migration Review	*Int. Migration R.*	New York
International Organization	*Int. Org.*	Boston, Mass.
International Problems	*Int. Probl. (Belgrade)*	Belgrade
International Problems	*Int. Probl. (Tel Aviv)*	Tel-Aviv
International Relations	*Int. Relat. (London)*	London
International Relations	*Int. Relat. (Prague)*	Prague
International Review of Community Development	*Int. R. Community Develop.*	Rome
International Review of social History	*Int. R. soc. Hist.*	Assen
International Review of Sport Sociology	*Int. R. Sport Sociol.*	Warszawa
International Studies	*Int. Stud. (New Delhi)*	New Delhi
International Studies Quarterly	*Int. Stud. Quart.*	Detroit, Mich.
International Yearbook of foreign Policy Analysis	*Int. Yb. for. Pol. Anal.*	London
International Yearbook of foreign Policy Studies	*Int. Yb. for. Pol. Stud.*	
Internationale Spectator	*Int. Spectator*	's_Gravenhage
Internationales Afrika Forum	*Int. Afr. Forum*	München
Internationales Asien Forum	*Int. Asien Forum*	München
Internationales Recht und Diplomatie	*Int. Recht u. Diplom.*	Hamburg
Internationella Studier	*Int. Stud. (Stockholm)*	Stockholm
Interrogations	*Interrogations*	Paris
Intertax	*Intertax*	Paris
Investigación economica	*Invest. econ.*	México
Inwestycje i Budownictwo	*Inwest. i Budown.*	Warszawa
Ipargazdaság	*Ipargazdaság*	Budapest
Ipargazdasági Szemle	*Ipargazd. Szle*	Budapest
IPSA Journal	*IPSA J.*	Paris
IPW Berichte	*IPW Ber.*	Berlin
Iranian Review of international Relations	*Iran. R. int. Relat.*	Tehran
Iranian Studies	*Iran. Stud.*	Tehran
Irish Banking Review	*Irish Banking R.*	Dublin
Iskusstvo	*Iskusstvo*	Moskva
Islam and modern Age	*Islam mod. Age*	New Delhi
Islas	*Islas*	La Habana
Israel Annual of public Administration and public Policy	*Israel Annu. publ. Adm. publ. Pol.*	Jerusalem
Israël et Société	*Israel et Soc.*	
Israel Law Review	*Israel Law R.*	Jerusalem
Issue. Quarterly Journal of Opinion	*Issue*	Waltham, Mass.
Issues and Studies	*Issues and Stud.*	Taîpeh
Istina	*Istina*	Paris

Istorija SSSR	*Ist. SSSR*	Moskva
Italian Yearbook of international Law	*Ital. Yb. int. Law*	
Item	*Item*	Paris
Itinéraires	*Itinéraires*	Paris
Iz Istorii sovetskoj Kul'tury i kul'turno-prosvetitel'noj Raboty	*Iz Ist. sov. Kul't. kul't.-prosvet. Raboty*	Moskva
Izvestija Akademii Nauk Azerbajdžanskoj SSR. Serija Istorii, Filosofii i Prava	*Izv. Akad. Nauk Ažerb. SSR Ser. Ist. Filos. Prava*	Baku
Izvestija Akademii Nauk Kazahskoj SSR. Serija obščestvennaja	*Izv. Akad. Nauk. Kazah. SSR Ser. obšč.*	Alma-Ata
Izvestija Akademii Nauk Kazahskoj SSR. Serija obščestvennyh Nauk	*Izv. Akad. Nauk Kazah. SSR Ser. obšč. Nauk*	Alma-Ata
Izvestija Akademii Nauk Moldavskoj SSR. Serija obščestvennyh Nauk	*Izv. Akad. Nauk Moldav. SSR Ser. obšč. Nauk*	Kišinev
Izvestija Akademii Nauk SSR. Serija ėkonomičeskaja	*Izv. Akad. Nauk SSSR Ser. ėkon.*	Moskva
Izvestija Sibirskogo Otdelenija Akademii Nauk SSSR. Serija obščestvennyh Nauk	*Izv. Sib. Otdel. Akad. Nauk SSSR Ser. obšč. Nauk*	Novosibirsk
Jahrbuch der diplomatischen Akademie Wien	*Jb. diplom. Akad. Wien*	Wien
Jahrbuch des öffentlichen Rechts der Gegenwart	*Jb. öff. Rechts*	Tübingen
Jahrbuch für Geschichte der sozialistischen Länder Europas	*Jb. Gesch. sozial. Länd. Europas*	Berlin
Jahrbuch für Ostrecht	*Jb. Ostrecht*	München
Jahrbuch für Sozialwissenschaften	*Jb. soz.-Wiss.*	Göttingen
Jahrbuch für Wirtschaftsgeschichte	*Jb. Wirtsch.-Gesch.*	Berlin
Jahrbücher für Nationalökonomie und Statistik	*Jb-r nat.-Ökon. Statist.*	Stuttgart
Japan Echo	*Japan Echo*	Tokyo
Japan Interpreter	*Japan Interpreter*	Tokyo
Japan Quarterly	*Japan Quart.*	Tokyo
Japanese Annual of international Law	*Japan. Annu. int. Law*	Tokyo
Japanese Journal of religious Studies	*Japan. J. relig. Stud.*	Tokyo
Javeriana	*Javeriana*	Bogotá
Jerusalem Journal of international Relations	*Jerusalem J. int. Relat.*	Jerusalem
Jerusalem Quarterly	*Jerusalem Quart.*	Jerusalem
Jeunes Travailleurs	*Jeunes Trav.*	Paris
Jewish Journal of Sociology	*Jew. J. Sociol.*	London
Jinbun Kenkyû	*Jinbun Kenkyû (Osaka)*	Osaka
Jinko Mondai Kenkyû	*Jinko Mondai Kenkyû*	Tokyo
Jôchi-daigaku shakaigaku Ronshû	*Jôchi-daigaku shakaigaku Ronshû*	[Nihon]
Jogtudományi Közlöny	*Jogtud. Közl.*	Budapest
Jordbruksekonomiska Meddelanden	*Jord.-ekon. Medd.*	Stockholm
Journal de la Planification du Développement	*J. Planif. Dévelop.*	New York

Journal de la Société de Statistique de Paris	*J. Soc. Statist. Paris*	Paris
Journal des Caisses d'Épargne	*J. Caisses Épargne*	Paris
Journal des Tribunaux	*J. Tribunaux*	Bruxelles
Journal du Droit international	*J. Dr. int.*	Paris
Journal for the Theory of social Behaviour	*J. Theory soc. Behav.*	Oxford
Journal of Administration Overseas	*J. Adm. Overseas*	London
Journal of African History	*J. Afr. Hist.*	London
Journal of African Law	*J. Afr. Law*	London
Journal of African Studies	*J. Afr. Stud.*	Berkeley, Calif.
Journal of agricultural Economics	*J. agric. Econ.*	Manchester
Journal of Alcohol and Drug Education	*J. Alcohol Drug Educ.*	Lansing, Mich.
Journal of American Studies	*J. Amer. Stud.*	Cambridge, Engl.
Journal of applied behavioral Science	*J. appl. behav. Sci.*	New York
Journal of applied social Psychology	*J. appl. soc. Psychol.*	Lafayette, Ind.
Journal of Asian and African Studies	*J. Asian Afr. Stud.*	Toronto
Journal of Asian Studies	*J. Asian Stud.*	Ann Arbor, Mich.
Journal of Bank Research	*J. Bank Res.*	Park Ridge, Ill.
Journal of Black Studies	*J. Black Stud.*	Los Angeles, Calif.
Journal of Broadcasting	*J. Broadcasting*	Philadelphia, Pa.
Journal of Common Market Studies	*J. Common Market Stud.*	Oxford
Journal of Commonwealth and comparative Politics	*J. Commonwealth comp. Polit.*	Leicester
Journal of comparative Family Studies	*J. comp. Family Stud.*	Calgary, Alta
Journal of Conflict Resolution	*J. Conflict Resol.*	Ann Arbor, Mich.
Journal of constitutional and parliamentary Studies	*J. const. parl. Stud.*	New Delhi
Journal of Consumer Affairs	*J. Consumer Aff.*	Columbia, Miss.
Journal of contemporary Asia	*J. contemp. Asia*	Stockholm
Journal of contemporary Business	*J. contemp. Busin.*	Washington, D.C.
Journal of contemporary History	*J. contemp. Hist.*	London
Journal of cross-cultural Psychology	*J. cross-cult. Psychol.*	Bellingham, Wash.
Journal of developing Areas	*J. develop. Areas*	Macomb, Ill.
Journal of Development Studies	*J. Develop. Stud.*	London
Journal of Econometrics	*J. Econometrics*	Madison, Wis.
Journal of economic Education	*J. econ. Educ.*	New York
Journal of economic History	*J. econ. Hist.*	New York
Journal of economic Issues	*J. econ. Issues*	Austin, Texas
Journal of economic Literature	*J. econ. Liter.*	Menasha, Wis.
Journal of economic Theory	*J. econ. Theory*	Philadelphia, Pa.
Journal of ecumenical Studies	*J. ecumen. Stud.*	Pittsburgh, Pa.
Journal of experimental Analysis of Behavior	*J. exper. Anal. Behav.*	Bloomington, Ind.
Journal of experimental social Psychology	*J. exper. soc. Psychol.*	London-New York
Journal of Family Planning Studies	*J. Family Planning Stud.*	Seoul
Journal of Finance	*J. Finance*	Madison, Wis.
Journal of financial and quantitative Analysis	*J. financ. quant. Anal.*	Seattle, Wash.

Journal of general Management	*J. gen. Manag.*	London
Journal of industrial Economics	*J. industr. Econ.*	London
Journal of inter-American Studies and World Affairs	*J. inter-Amer. Stud.*	Coral Gables, Fla.
Journal of international Affairs	*J. int. Aff.*	New York
Journal of international Economics	*J. int. Econ.*	Amsterdam
Journal of international Law	*J. int. Law*	
Journal of Latin American Studies	*J. Latin Amer. Stud.*	Cambridge
Journal of Law and Economics	*J. Law Econ.*	Chicago, Ill.
Journal of Management Studies	*J. Manag. Stud.*	Oxford
Journal of Marketing	*J. Mkting*	Chicago, Ill.
Journal of Marketing Research	*J. Mkting Res.*	Chicago, Ill.
Journal of Marriage and the Family	*J. Marriage Family*	Minneapolis, Minn.
Journal of mathematical Sociology	*J. math. Sociol.*	London
Journal of modern African Studies	*J. mod. Afr. Stud.*	Cambridge-Dar es Salam
Journal of Palestine Studies	*J. Palestine Stud.*	Beyrouth
Journal of Peace Research	*J. Peace Res.*	Oslo
Journal of Peasant Studies	*J. Peasant Stud.*	London
Journal of Personality and social Psychology	*J. Person. soc. Psychol.*	Washington, D.C.
Journal of political and military Sociology	*J. polit. milit. Sociol.*	DeKalb, Ill.
Journal of political Economy	*J. polit. Econ.*	Chicago, Ill.
Journal of Politics	*J. Polit.*	Gainesville, Fla.
Journal of public Economics	*J. publ. Econ.*	Amsterdam
Journal of regional Science	*J. region. Sci.*	Philadelphia, Pa.
Journal of social Issues	*J. soc. Issues*	New York
Journal of social Philosophy	*J. soc. Philos.*	[Japan]
Journal of social Policy	*J. soc. Pol.*	London
Journal of social Psychology	*J. soc. Psychol.*	Provincetown, Mass.
Journal of Southeast Asian Studies	*J. Southeast Asian Stud.*	Singapore
Journal of Southern African Studies	*J. South. Afr. Stud.*	London
Journal of Space Law	*J. Space Law*	University, Miss.
Journal of Transport Economics and Policy	*J. Transport Econ. Pol.*	London
Journal of vocational Behavior	*J. vocat. Behav.*	Ann Arbor, Mich.
Journal of World Trade Law	*J. Wld Trade Law*	London
Journal of the American Institute of Planners	*J. Amer. Inst. Planners*	Washington, D.C.
Journal of the History of Ideas	*J. Hist. Ideas*	New York, N.Y.-Lancaster, Pa.
Journal of the Royal Statistical Society	*J. roy. statist. Soc.*	London
Journalism Quarterly	*J-ism Quart.*	Minneapolis, Minn.
Jugoslovenski Pregled	*Jugosl. Pregl.*	Beograd
Juridičeskie Garantii Primenenija Prava i Režim socialisti-českoj Zakonnosti v SSSR	*Jur. Garantii Primen. Prava Režim social. Zakonnosti SSSR*	Jaroslavl'
Juridičeskie Nauki	*Jur. Nauki*	Alma-Ata
Jurisuto	*Jurisuto*	Tokyo
Jurisuto Gendai no Kazoku	*Jurisuto Gendai no Kazoku*	[Nihon]

Kagaku to Shiso	*Kagaku to Shiso*	[Nihon]
Kagawa-daigaku Kyoikugakubu Kenkyu-hokoku	*Kagawa-daigaku Kyoiku-gakubu Kenkyu-hokoku*	[Nihon]
Kaisei-gakuindaigaku Shakaiga-kubu	*Kaisei-gakuindaigaku Shakaigakubu Kiyo*	[Nihon]
Kanazawa-daigaku Hobungakubu Ronshû Tetsugaku-hen	*Kanazawa-daigaku Hobun-gakubu Ronshû Tetsuga-ku-hen*	[Nihon]
Kanazawa-keizai-daigaku Ronshû	*Kanazawa-keizai-daigaku Ronshû*	[Nihon]
Kankyô to Ningen	*Kankyô to Ningen*	[Nihon]
Kansantaloudellinen Aikakaus-kirja	*Kansantal. Aikakausk.*	Helsinki
Kanseigakuindaigaku Shakaiga-ku-bu Kiyô	*Kanseigakuindaigaku Shakaigaku-bu Kiyô*	[Nihon]
Kapitalistate	*Kapitalistate*	Berlin
Kasvatus	*Kasvatus*	Ivaskyla
Katolikus Szemle	*Katol. Szle*	Roma
Kazokukenkyû-Nenpô	*Kazokukenkyû-Nenpô*	[Nihon]
Keiô-gijuku Daigaku Daigakuin Shakaigaku Kenkyûka Kiyô	*Keiô-gijuku Daigaku Daigakuin Shakaigaku Kenkyûka Kiyô*	Tokyo
Keiri Kenkyu	*Keiri Kenkyu*	[Nihon]
Keizai to Shakai	*Keizai to Shakai*	[Nihon]
Keizagaku Kenkyû	*Keizagaku Kenkyû (Hokkaido)*	Hokkaido
Keizaigaku Kihô	*Keizaigaku Kihô*	Tokyo
Kenkyû Hôkoku	*Kenkyû Hôkoku*	Tokyo
Kenkyûju Nenpô	*Kenkyûju Nenpô*	[Nihon]
Khamsin	*Khamsin*	Paris
Kikan Shakai Hoshô Kenkyû	*Kikan Shakai Hoshô Ken-kyû*	[Nihon]
Kobe-daigaku Bungakubu Kiyo	*Kobe-daigaku Bungakubu Kiyo*	Kobe
Kobe economic and Business Review	*Kobe econ. Busin. R.*	Kobe
Kobe University economic Review	*Kobe Univ. econ. R.*	Kobe
Koeki-jigyô Kenkyû	*Koeki-jigyô Kenkyû*	Tokyo
Kokumin Seikatsu Kenkyû	*Kokumin Seikatsu Kenkyû*	[Nihon]
Kokuritsu Minzokugaku Haku-butsukan Kenkyu-hokoku	*Kokuritsu Minzokugaku Hakubutsukan Kenkyu-hokoku*	[Nihon]
Kokusai-kankeigaku Kenkyû	*Kokusai-kankeigaku Kenkyû*	[Nihon]
Kokusai Shukyo News	*Kokusai Shukyo News*	[Nihon]
Kölner Zeitschrift für So-ziologie und Sozialpsycho-logie	*Kölner Z. Soziol. u. soz.-Psychol.*	Köln-Opladen
Komazawa Shakaigaku Kenkyû	*Komazawa Shakaigaku Kenkyû*	[Nihon]
Kommunist	*Kommunist (Moskva)*	Moskva
Kommunist	*Kommunist (Vil'njus)*	Vil'njus
Kommunist Belorussii	*Kommunist Belorussii*	Minsk
Kommunist Êstonii	*Kommunist Êstonii*	Tallin
Kommunist Sovetskoj Latvii	*Kommunist Sov. Latvii*	Riga
Kommunist Tatarii	*Kommunist Tatarii*	Kazan'
Kommunist vooružennyh Sil	*Kommunist vooruž. Sil*	Moskva
Kommunisti	*Kommunisti*	
Konan-joshi-daigaku Ningen-kagaku Nenpo	*Konan-joshi-daigaku Ningen-kagaku Nenpo*	[Nihon]

Konjunkturpolitik	*Konjunkturpolitik*	Berlin
Korea and World Affairs	*Korea Wld Aff.*	Seoul
Korea Journal	*Korea J.*	Seoul
Korean Journal of international Studies	*Korean J. int. Stud.*	Seoul
Korunk	*Korunk*	Budapest
Közgazdasági Szemle	*Közgazd. Szle*	Budapest
Kritische Justiz	*Krit. Justiz*	Frankfurt-am-Main
Külgazdaság	*Külgazdaság*	Budapest
Kuljetus. Materiaalitaloudellinen Aikakauslehti	*Kuljetus*	Helsinki
Külpolitika	*Külpolitika*	Budapest
Kultura	*Kultura*	Paryż
Kultura és Közösség	*Kult. és Köz.*	Budapest
Kultura i Społeczenstwo. Polska Akademia Nauk. Komitet Badań nad Kulturą wspołczesną	*Kult. i Społecz.*	Warszawa
Kumamoto-tandai Ronshû	*Kumamoto-tandai Ronshû*	Kumamoto
Kyklos	*Kyklos*	Berne
Kyoka to Kyogaku	*Kyoka to Kyogaku*	[Nihon]
Kyôto-daigaku Bungakubu Kenkyûkiyô	*Kyôto-daigaku Bungakubu Kenkyûkiyô*	Kyôto
Kyûdai Shakaigaku Kenkyû Nenpô	*Kyûdai Shakaigaku Kenkyû Nenpô*	[Nihon]
Kyushu Bunkashi Kenkyujo Kiyo	*Kyushu Bunkashi Kenkyujo Kiyo*	[Nihon]
Kyûshû Jinruigaku Kaihô	*Kyûshû Jinruigaku Kaihô*	[Nihon]
Lakimies	*Lakimies*	Helsinki
Lamalif	*Lamalif*	Casablanca
Land Economics	*Land Econ.*	Madison, Wis.
Langages	*Langages*	Paris
Latin American Perspectives	*Latin Amer. Perspect.*	Riverside, Calif.
Latin American Research Review	*Latin Amer. Res. R.*	Austin, Tex.
Latin American urban Research	*Latin Amer. urb. Res.*	Beverly Hills, Calif.
Latina-América	*Latina-Amér.*	México
Latinskaja Amerika	*Latinsk. Amer.*	Moskva
Latohatár	*Latohatár*	Budapest
Law and contemporary Problems	*Law contemp. Probl.*	Durham, N.C.
Law and Society Review	*Law Soc. R.*	New York
Law Quarterly Review	*Law Quart. R.*	London
Legi-social	*Legi-social*	Paris
Legislative Studies Quarterly	*Legisl. Stud. Quart.*	Iowa, Iowa
Lendemains	*Lendemains*	Berlin
Leningrad	*Leningrad*	Leningrad
Létünk	*Létünk*	Subotica
Leviathan	*Leviathan*	Bonn
Liberal	*Liberal (Bonn)*	Bonn
Liberal	*Liberal (Copenhagen)*	Copenhague
Ličnost' i Obščestvo	*Ličnost' i Obščestvo*	Kaliningrad
Liiketaloudellinen Aikakauskirja / Journal of Business Economics	*Liiketal. Aikakausk.*	Helsinki
Lloyds Bank Review	*Lloyds Bank R.*	London
Local Finance	*Loc. Finance*	The Hague
Long Range Planning	*Long Range Planning*	Oxford

Maandschrift Economie	*Maandschr. Econ.*	Tilburg
Maataloushallinon Aikakauskirja	*Maataloushal. Aika-kausk.*	Helsinki
Maghreb-Machrek	*Maghreb*	Paris
Magyar filozófiai Szemle	*Magyar filoz. Szle*	Budapest
Magyar Jog	*Magyar Jog*	Budapest
Magyar Nyelv	*Magyar Nyelv*	Budapest
Magyar Pedagógia	*Magyar Pedag.*	Budapest
Magyar pedagógiai Szemle	*Magyar pedag. Szle*	Budapest
Magyar pszichologiai Szemle	*Magyar pszichol. Szle*	Budapest
Magyar Tudomány	*Magyar Tud.*	Budapest
Malayan economic Review	*Malayan econ. R.*	Singapore
Management-France	*Management-France*	Paris
Management international Review	*Manag. int. R.*	Wiesbaden
Manchester School of economic and social Studies	*Manchester Sch. econ. soc. Stud.*	Manchester
Manpower Journal	*Manpower J.*	New Delhi
Mardom nâmeh	*Mardom nâmeh*	*Berlin*
Marquette Business Review	*Marquette Busin. R.*	Milwaukee, Wisc.
Marxism today	*Marxism today*	London
Massacommunicatie	*Massacommunicatie*	*[Nederland]*
Masses ouvrières	*Masses ouvr.*	Paris
Matekon	*Matekon*	White Plains, N.Y.
Materialen zur politischen Bildung	*Mater. polit. Bildung*	Bonn
Mathématiques et Sciences humaines	*Math. Sci. hum.*	Paris
McKinsey Quarterly	*McKinsey Quart.*	New York
Medicus universalis	*Med. univ.*	*[Magyarország]*
Méditerranée	*Méditerranée*	Aix-en-Provence
Medunarodni Problemi	*Medun. Probl.*	Beograd
Meiji Gakuin Ronsô	*Meiji Gakuin Ronsô*	Tokyo
Mens en Maatschappij	*Mens en Mij*	Amsterdam
Mens en Onderneming	*Mens en Onderneming*	Leiden-Haarlem
Mensaje	*Mensaje*	Santiago de Chile
Mercanzia	*Mercanzia*	Bologna
Metodologičeskie Problemy Nauki	*Metodol. Probl. Nauki*	Novosibirsk
Metroeconomica	*Metroeconomica*	Trieste
Metropolis	*Metropolis*	Paris
Metsä ja puu	*Metsä ja puu*	Helsinki
Meždunarodnaja Žizn'	*Meždun. Žizn'*	Moskva
Meždunarodnyj Ežegodnik. Politika i Ekonomika	*Meždun. Ežeg. Polit. Ekon.*	Moskva
Miasto	*Miasto*	Warszawa
Middle East Journal	*Mid. East J.*	Washington, D.C.
Middle East Review	*Mid. East R.*	New York
Middle Eastern Studies	*Mid. East. Stud.*	London
Midwest Review of public Administration	*Midwest R. publ. Adm.*	Parkville, Mo.
Mie-daigaku Kyôikugakubu Kenkyu Kiyô	*Mie-daigaku Kyôikugakubu Kenkyu Kiyô*	*[Nihon]*
Migrations dans le Monde	*Migr. dans le Monde*	Genève
Migrations internationales	*Migr. int.*	La Haye
Milbank Memorial Fund Quarterly	*Milbank Memor. Fund Quart.*	New York
Militärgeschichte	*Militärgeschichte*	Berlin
Military Review	*Military R.*	Fort Leavenworth, Kan.
Millennium	*Millennium*	Londres
Minerva	*Minerva*	London

Mirovaja Ékonomika i meždu-narodnye Otnošenija	*Mir. Ēkon. meždun. Otnoš.*	Moskva
Mirovoe Rybolovstvo	*Mir. Rybolovstvo*	[SSSR]
Mitteilungen des Direktoriums des Österreichischen Na-tionalbank	*Mitt. Direktor. österr. nat.-Bank*	Wien
Modern Age	*Mod. Age*	Chicago, Ill.
Modern Asian Studies	*Mod. Asian Stud.*	London
Modern Law Review	*Mod. Law R.*	London
Modern Review	*Mod. R. (Calcutta)*	Calcutta
Momoya-gakuin-daigaku Sôgô-kenkyûjohô	*Momoya-gakuin-daigaku Sôgô-kenkyûjohô*	[Nihon]
Monatsberichte der deutschen Bundesbank	*Monatsber. dtschen Bundesbank*	Frankfurt-am-Main
Monatsberichte des Österrei-chischen Instituts für Wirtschaftsforschung	*Monatsber. österr. Inst. Wirtsch.-Forsch.*	Wien
Monde de l'Éducation	*Monde Éduc.*	Paris
Monde juif	*Monde juif*	Paris
Monde moderne	*Monde mod.*	Paris
Mondes asiatiques	*Mondes asiat.*	Paris
Mondes en Développement	*Mondes en Dévelop.*	Paris
Mondo aperto	*Mondo aperto*	Roma
Moneda y Crédito	*Moneda y Créd.*	Madrid
Moneta e Credito	*Moneta e Cred.*	Roma
Montana Journalism Review	*Montana J-ism R.*	Missoula, Mont.
Monthly Labor Review	*Mthly Lab R.*	Washington, D.C.
Monthly public Opinion Sur-veys	*Mthly publ. Opin. Surv.*	New Delhi
Monthly Review	*Mthly R.*	New York
Morioka-tankidaigaku Kenkyu-hokoku	*Morioka-tankidaigaku Kenkyu-hokoku*	[Nihon]
Mozgó Világ	*Mozgó Világ*	[Magyarország]
Mulino	*Mulino*	Bologna
Mundo social	*Mundo soc.*	Madrid
Munkaügyi Szemle	*Munkaügyi Szle*	Budapest
Muslim World	*Muslim Wld*	Hartford, Conn.
Nara-daigaku Kiyô	*Nara-daigaku Kiyô*	[Nihon]
Narody Azii i Afriki	*Narody Azii Afr.*	Moskva
National civic Review	*Nat. civic R.*	New York
National Geographic	*Nat. Geogr.*	Washington, D.C.
National Institute economic Review	*Nat. Inst. econ. R.*	London
National Westminster Bank quarterly Review	*Nat. Westminster Bank quart. R.*	London
Nationaløkonomisk Tidsskrift	*Nat.-økon. Tss.*	København
NATO's fifteen Nations	*NATO's fift. Nations*	Amsterdam
Natural Resources Journal	*Natur. Resources J.*	Albuquerque, N.M.
Naučnye Doklady vysšej Školy. Naučnyj Kommunizma	*Nauč. Dokl. vysš. Ško-ly nauč. Kommunizma*	Moskva
Naučnye Trudy (Central'nyj naučno-issledovatel'skij ékonomičeski Institut)	*Nauč. Trudy (Centr. nauč. issled. ékon. Inst.)*	Moskva
Naučnye Trudy Kurskogo pedago-gičeskogo Instituta	*Nauč. Trudy Kursk. pedag. Inst.*	Kursk
Naučnye Trudy Sverdlovskogo pedagogičeskogo Instituta. Problemy izučenija socia-lističeskogo Obraza Žizni	*Nauč. Trudy Sverdlovsk. pedag. Inst. Probl. izučen. social. Obraza Žizni*	Sverdlovsk

Naučnye Trudy (Taškentskij pedagogičeskij Institut)	*Nauč. Trudy (Taškent. pedag. Inst.)*	Taškent
Naučnye Trudy Taškentskogo Instituta narodnogo obščestva	*Nauč. Trudy Taškent. Inst. nar. obšč.*	Taškent
Naučnye upravlenie Obščestvom	*Nauč. upravl. Obšč.*	Moskva
Naučnyj Kommunizm	*Nauč. Kommunizm*	Moskva
Naval War College Review	*Naval War College R.*	Newport, R.J.
Navigator	*Navigator*	Copenhagen
Nef	*Nef*	Paris
Nenpô Shakai Shinrigaku	*Nenpô Shakai Shinri-gaku*	Tokyo
Netherlands Journal of Sociology	*Netherlands J. Sociol.*	Assen
Neue Gesellschaft	*Neue Gesellsch.*	Bielefeld
Neue Praxis	*Neue Praxis*	Neuwied
New African Development	*New Afr. Develop.*	London
New Europe	*New Europe*	London
New Hungarian Quarterly	*New Hung. Quart.*	Budapest
New Internationalist	*New Internat.*	Oxford
New Left Review	*New Left R.*	London
New Outlook	*New Outlook*	Tel-Aviv
New Universities Quarterly	*New Univ. Quart.*	London
New World Review	*New Wld R.*	New York
New Zealand Journal of public Administration	*New Zealand J. publ. Adm.*	Wellington
N.H.K. Hôsôbunka Kenkyu Nenpo	*N.H.K. Hôsôbunka Kenkyu Nenpo*	Tokyo
Nihon Bunka Kenkyûjo Kinkyû-hôkoku	*Nihon Bunka Kenkyûjo Kinkyû-hôkoku*	[Nihon]
Nihon Rôdô Kyôikai Zasshi	*Nihon Rôdô Kyôkai Zas-shi*	Tokyo
Nihon Shakai-kyoiku gakukai kiyô	*Nihon Shakai-kyoiku gakukai kiyô*	[Nihon]
Nihon Toshi-gakukai Nenpô	*Nihon Toshi-gakukai Nenpô*	[Nihon]
Ningen-kagaku	*Ningen-kagaku*	[Nihon]
Nord e Sud	*Nord e Sud*	Milano-Napoli
Nordisk administrativt Tidsskrift	*Nord. adm. Tss.*	København
Norois	*Norois*	Poitiers
Notas de Población	*Notas Pobl.*	Santiago de Chile
Notes and Documents, United Nations Unit on Apartheid	*Notes Docum. UN Unit Apartheid*	New York
Notes d'Information et Statistiques. Banque centrale des États de l'Afrique de l'Ouest	*Notes Inform. Statist. Banque centr. Afr. Ouest*	Paris
Nouveaux Cahiers	*Nouv. Cah.*	Paris
Nouvelle Revue internationale	*Nouv. R. int.*	Paris
Nouvelle Revue socialiste	*Nouv. R. social.*	Paris
Nouvelles Études hongroises	*Nouv. Ét. hongr.*	Budapest
Novaja i novejšaja Istorija	*Nov. novejš. Ist.*	Moskva
Nowe Drogi	*Nowe Drogi*	Warszawa
Nueva Política	*Nueva Polít.*	México
Nuovi Quaderni del Meridione	*Nuovi Quad. Merid.*	Palermo
Nyelvtudományi Közlemények	*Nyelvtud. Közl.*	Budapest

Obščestvenno-politečeskoe Vos-pitanie učaščihsja	Obšč.-polit. Vospitanie učašč.	Irkutsk
Obščestvennye Nauki	Obšč. Nauki (Moskva)	Moskva
Obščestvennye Nauki v Uzbekis-tane	Obšč. Nauki Uzbek.	Taškent
Ocean Development and interna-tional Law	Ocean Develop. int. Law	Washington, D.C.
Octant. Cahiers statistiques de la Bretagne	Octant	Rennes
ODI Review	ODI Rev.	London
Oeconomica polona	Oecon. polona	Warszawa
Öffentliche Verwaltung	Öff. Verw.	Stuttgart
Ohtemaejoshi-tanki-daigaku Kenkyû-shûroku	Ohtemaejoshi-tanki-daigaku Kenkyû-shûroku	[Nihon]
Oikeus	Oikeus	
Okinawa kokusai-daigaku Bunga-kubu kiyô	Okinawa kokusai-daigaku Bungakubu kiyô	[Nihon]
Økonomi og Politik	Økon. og Polit.	København
Openbare Uitgaven	Openbare Uitgaven	Utrecht
Opština	Opština	Beograd
Optima	Optima	Johannesburg
Options	Options	Paris
Options méditerrannéennes	Options méditerr.	Paris
Orbis	Orbis	Philadelphia, Pa.
Ordo. Jahrbuch für die Ord-nung von Wirtschaft und Gesellschaft	Ordo	Düsseldorf
Orient (Opladen)	Orient (Opladen)	Opladen
Orientamenti sociali	Orientam. soc.	Roma
Orientation scolaire et pro-fessionnelle	Orientat. scol. profes.	Paris
Oriente moderno	Oriente mod.	Roma
Orita	Orita	
Osaka Daigaku Ningenkagakubu Kiyô	Ôsaka Daigaku Ningenka-gakubu Kiyô	Ôsaka
Ôsaka Kyoiku Daigaku Kiyô	Ôsaka Kyoiku Daigaku Kiyô	Ôsaka
Osaka-shiritsu-daigaku Seikat-su-kagakubu kiyô	Ôsaka-shiritsu-daigaku Seikatsu-kagakubu kiyô	[Nihon]
Österreichische Monatshefte	Österr. Mh.	Wien
Österreichische Osthefte	Österr. Osth.	Wien
Österreichische Zeitschrift für Aussenpolitik	Österr. Z. Aussenpolit.	Wien
Österreichische Zeitschrift für öffentliches Recht	Österr. Z. öff. Recht	Wien
Österreichische Zeitschrift für Politikwissenschaft	Österr. Z. Polit.-Wiss.	Wien
Osteuropa	Osteuropa	Stuttgart
Osteuropa Recht	Osteuropa Recht	Stuttgart
Osteuropa Wirtschaft	Osteuropa Wirtsch.	Stuttgart
Ostsee-Jahrbuch	Ostsee-Jb.	
Osuuspankkijärjestön Taloudel-linen Katsaus	Osuuspankkijärjestön Taloudellinen Katsaus	Helsinki
Ôtani Gakuhô	Ôtani Gakuhô	Kyotô
Overzicht internazionale uni-versitaire Samenverking	Overzicht int. univ. Samenwk.	[Nederland]
Oxford Bulletin of Economics and Statistics	Oxford B. Econ. Sta-tist.	Oxford
Oxford economic Papers	Oxford econ. Pap.	Oxford
Oyo-shakaigaku Kenkyû	Oyo-shakaigaku Kenkyû	[Nihon]

Pacific Affairs	*Pacific Aff.*	New York
Pacific Community	*Pacific Community*	Tokyo
Pacific sociological Review	*Pacific sociol. R.*	San Diego, Calif.
Pacific Viewpoint	*Pacific Viewpoint*	Wellington
Pakistan Development Review	*Pakistan Develop. R.*	Karachi-Islamabad
Pakistan Horizon	*Pakistan Horizon*	Karachi
Pályaválasztási Tanácsadás	*Pályavál. Tanács.*	Budapest
Państwo i Prawo	*Pań. i Prawo*	Warszawa
Papers of the regional Science Association	*Pap. region. Sci. Assoc.*	
Paradoxes	*Paradoxes*	
Parliamentarian	*Parliamentarian*	London
Partijnaja Žizn'	*Partijn. Žizn' (Moskva)*	Moskva
Párttörténeti Közlemények	*Párttört. Közlem.*	Budapest
Patterns of Prejudice	*Patterns of Prejudice*	London
Paysans	*Paysans*	Paris
Peace and the Sciences	*Peace and Sci.*	Vienna
Pedagógiai Szemle	*Pedag. Szle*	Budapest
Penant. Revue de Droit des Pays d'Afrique	*Penant*	Paris
Pensamiento político	*Pensamiento polít.*	México
Pensamiento y Acción	*Pensamiento y Acción*	Santiago de Chile
Pensée. Revue du Rationalisme moderne	*Pensée*	Paris
Pensiero politico	*Pensiero polit.*	Firenze
Pénzügyi Szemle	*Pénzügyi Szle*	Budapest
Permanences	*Permanences*	Paris
Personnel	*Personnel (Paris)*	Paris
Personnel Psychology	*Personnel Psychol.*	Baltimore, Md.
Perspectives	*Perspectives (Unesco)*	Paris
Perspectives internationales	*Perspect. int.*	Ottawa
Perspectives polonaises	*Perspect. polon.*	Varsovie
Philippine Journal of public Administration	*Philippine J. publ. Adm.*	Manila
Philosophical Forum	*Philos. Forum*	Boston, Mass.
Philosophy and public Affairs	*Philos. publ. Aff.*	New York
Philosophy of the social Sciences	*Philos. soc. Sci.*	Aberdeen
Phylon	*Phylon*	Atlanta, Ga.
Pitanja	*Pitanja*	Zagreb
Planning and Administration	*Planning and Adm.*	The Hague
Planning and Development in the Netherlands	*Planning Develop. Netherl.*	Assen
Plánované Hospodářství	*Plán. Hospod.*	Praha
Planovoe Hozjajstvo	*Plan. Hoz.*	Moskva
Point économique de l'Auvergne	*Point écon. Auvergne*	Clermont-Ferrand
Points d'Appui pour l'Économie Rhône-Alpes	*Points Appui Écon. Rhône-Alpes*	Paris
Policy	*Policy*	London
Policy and Politics	*Pol. and Polit.*	London
Policy Science	*Pol. Sci.*	Santa Monica, N.Y.
Policy Studies Journal	*Pol. Stud. J.*	Urbana, Ill.
Polish Perspectives	*Polish Perspect.*	Warsaw
Polish Review	*Polish R.*	New York
Polish sociological Bulletin	*Polish sociol. B.*	Warsaw
Politica del Diritto	*Polit. Dir.*	Bologna
Politica ed Economia	*Polit. ed Econ.*	Roma
Politica internazionale	*Polit. int. (Milano)*	Milano
Political Affairs	*Polit. Aff.*	New York
Political Quarterly	*Polit. Quart.*	London
Political Science	*Polit. Sci. (Wellington)*	Wellington

Political Science Annual	*Polit. Sci. Annu.*	New York
Political Science Quarterly	*Polit. Sci. Quart.*	New York
Political Science Review	*Polit. Sci. R.*	Jaipur
Political Science Reviewer	*Polit. Sci. R-er*	Hampden-Sydney, Virginia
Political Studies	*Polit. Stud. (Oxford)*	Oxford
Political Theory	*Polit. Theory*	London
Politíčeskaja Ékonomija	*Polit. Ékon.*	Minsk
Politíčeskoe Samoobrazovanie	*Polit. Samoobr.*	Moskva
Politička Misao	*Polit. Misao*	Beograd
Politico	*Politico*	Pavia
Politics	*Politics (Kensington)*	Kensington, N.S.W.
Politics and Society	*Polit. and Soc.*	Washington, D.C.
Politiek Perspectief	*Polit. Perspect.*	Den Hague
Politiikka	*Politiikka*	Helsinki
Politik und Zeitgeschichte (Aus)	*Polit. u. Zeitgesch.*	Bonn
Politikai Föiskola Közleményei	*Polit. Föisk. Közlem.*	Budapest
Politique aujourd'hui	*Polit. aujourd.*	Paris
Politique étrangère	*Polit. étr.*	Paris
Politische Meinung	*Polit. Meinung*	Köln
Politische Rundschau	*Polit. Rdsch.*	Bern
Politische Studien	*Polit. Stud. (München)*	München
Politische Vierteljahresschrift	*Polit. Vjschr.*	Heidelberg-Köln-Opladen
Polity	*Polity*	Amherst, Mass.
Polityka społeczna	*Polit. społecz.*	Warszawa
Pologne contemporaine	*Pologne contemp.*	Varsovie
Pologne et les Affaires occidentales (La)	*Pologne Aff. occid.*	Poznań
Ponte	*Ponte*	Firenze
Population	*Population*	Paris
Population and Development Review	*Popul. Develop. R.*	Ann Arbor, Mich.
Population et Avenir	*Popul. et Avenir*	Paris
Population et Famille / Bevolking en Gezin	*Popul. et Famille*	Bruxelles
Population et Sociétés	*Popul. et Soc.*	Paris
Population Index	*Popul. Index*	Princeton, N.J.
Population Studies	*Popul. Stud.*	London
Populi	*Populi*	New York, N.Y.
Pouvoirs	*Pouvoirs*	Paris
Praca i Zabezpieczenie społeczne	*Praca Zabezp. społecz.*	Warszawa
Prace naukowe Akademii ekonomicznej we Wrocławiu	*Prace nauk. Akad. ekon. Wrocław.*	Wrocław
Premier Mai	*Premier Mai*	Paris
Présence africaine	*Présence afr.*	Paris
Presse Actualité	*Presse-Actual.*	Paris
Previdenza sociale	*Previd. soc.*	Roma
Problemas del Desarrollo	*Probl. Desarr.*	México
Probleme economice	*Probl. econ. (Bucuresti)*	Bucureşti
Problèmes politiques et sociaux	*Probl. polit. soc.*	Paris
Problemi del Socialismo	*Probl. Social. (Milano)*	Milano
Problemi della Sicurezza sociale	*Probl. Sicur. soc.*	Roma
Problems of Communism	*Probl. Communism*	Washington
Problemy Dal'nego Vostoka	*Probl. Dal'nego Vost.*	Moskva
Problemy Dialektiki	*Probl. Dialektiki*	Leningrad

Problemy ekonomiczne	*Probl. ekon. (Warszawa)*	Warszawa
Problemy Filosofii	*Probl. Filos.*	Kiev
Problemy Mira i Socializma	*Probl. Mira Social.*	Moskva
Problemy naučnogo Upravlenija socialističeskim Obščestvom	*Probl. nauč. Uprav. social. Obšč.*	Riga
Problemy organizacji	*Probl. organ.*	Warszawa
Problemy Pravovedenija	*Probl. Pravovedenija*	Kiev
Problemy Razvitija proizvodi-tel'nyh sil TSSR	*Probl. Razvit. proiz-vod. TSSR*	Ašhabad
Proceedings of the Academy of political Science	*Proc. Acad. polit. Sci.*	New York
Professions et Entreprises	*Professions et Entr.*	Paris
Profisl de l'Économie Nord-Pas-de-Calais	*Profils Écon. Nord-Pas-de-Calais*	Lille
Progrès scientifique	*Progr. scientif.*	Paris
Projet	*Projet*	Paris
Promotions	*Promotions*	Paris
Przegląd komunikacyjny	*Przegl. komunik.*	Warszawa
Przegląd organizacji	*Przegl. organ.*	Warszawa
Przegląd socjologiczny	*Przegl. socjol.*	Łódz
Przegląd statystyczny	*Przegl. statyst.*	Warszawa
Przegląd zachodni	*Przegl. zachod.*	Poznan
Public Administration	*Publ. Adm. (London)*	London
Public Administration	*Publ. Adm. (Sydney)*	Sydney
Public Administration Review	*Publ. Adm. R.*	Chicago, Ill.
Public Choice	*Publ. Choice*	Blacksburg, Va.
Public Finance / Finances publiques	*Publ. Finance*	The Hague
Public Finance Quarterly	*Publ. Finance Quart.*	Gainesville, Fla.
Public Interest	*Publ. Interest*	New York
Public Law	*Publ. Law (London)*	London
Public Opinion Quarterly	*Publ. Opin. Quart.*	Princeton, N.J.
Public Personnel Management	*Publ. Personnel Manag.*	Chicago, Ill.
Public Policy	*Publ. Pol.*	Cambridge, Mass.
Public Welfare	*Publ. Welfare*	London
Publius	*Publius*	Bremen
Publizistik	*Publizistik*	Münster-in-Westfalen
Purpan	*Purpan*	Toulouse
Quaderni di Azione sociale	*Quad. Azione soc.*	Roma
Quaderni di Sociologia	*Quad. Sociol.*	Torino
Quality and Quantity	*Quality and Quantity*	Padova
Quarterly Bulletin. Central Bank of Ireland	*Quart. B. centr. Bank Ireland*	Dublin
Quarterly Journal of Admi-nistration	*Quart. J. Adm.*	Ibadan
Quarterly Journal of Econo-mics	*Quart. J. Econ.*	Cambridge, Mass.
Quarterly Review of agri-cultural Economics	*Quart. R. agric. Econ.*	Canberra
Quarterly Review of Economics and Business	*Quart. R. Econ. Busin.*	Champaign, Ill.
Queen's Quarterly	*Queen's Quart.*	Kingston, Ont.
Questions actuelles du So-cialisme	*Quest. act. Socialisme*	Paris
Rabočij Klass i sovremennyj Mir	*Rabočij Klass sovrem. Mir*	Moskva
Race and Class	*Race and Class*	London
Radical Humanist	*Rad. Humanist*	New Delhi
Rádió és Televizió Szemle	*Rádió és TV Szle*	Budapest
Raison présente	*Raison présente*	Paris

Rakennustekniikka	*Rakennustekniikka*	Helsinki
Rassenga di Statistiche del Lavoro	*Rass. Statist. Lav.*	Roma
Rassegna economica	*Rass. econ. (Napoli)*	Napoli
Rassegna italiana di Sociologia	*Rass. ital. Sociol.*	Firenze
Rassegna sindacale Quaderni	*Rass. sind. Quad.*	Roma
Raumforschung und Raumordnung	*Raumforsch. u. -Ordnung*	Bad-Godesberg
Razón y Fe	*Razón y Fe*	Madrid
Réalités franc-comtoises	*Réalités franc-comtoises*	Besançon
Realtà economica	*Realtà econ.*	Milano
Recherche sociale	*Rech. soc. (Paris)*	Paris
Recherches économiques de Louvain	*Rech. écon. Louvain*	Louvain
Recherches économiques et sociales	*Rech. écon. soc.*	Paris
Recherches et Débats	*Rech. et Débats*	Paris
Recherches sociographiques	*Rech. sociogr.*	Québec
Recherches sociologiques	*Rech. sociol.*	Louvain
Recherches sur les Migrations	*Rech. Migr.*	Paris
Recht in Ost und West	*Recht in Ost West*	Berlin
Reconciliation Quarterly	*Reconciliation Quart.*	New Malden
Reflets de l'Économie franc-comtoise	*Reflets Écon. franc-comtoise*	Paris
Reflets et Perspectives de la Vie économique	*Reflets Perspect. Vie écon.*	Bruxelles
Regards sur l'Actualité	*Regards Actual.*	Paris
Regional Science and urban Economics	*Region. Sci. urb. Econ.*	Amsterdam
Regional Studies	*Region. Sci.*	Oxford
Relaciones internacionales	*Relac. int.*	México
Relais statistiques de l'Économie picarde	*Relais*	Paris
Relations industrielles	*Relat. industr.*	Québec
Relations internationales	*Relat. int. (Genève)*	Genève
Remarques africaines	*Remarques afr.*	Bruxelles
Rencontre. Chrétiens et Juifs	*Rencontre*	Paris
Repères	*Repères*	Paris
Repères-Economic du Languedoc-Roussillon	*Repères-Écon. Languedoc-Roussillon*	Montpellier
Res publica	*Res publ.*	Bruxelles
Research Policy	*Res. Pol.*	Amsterdam
Réseaux	*Réseaux*	Mons
Reserve Bank of India Bulletin	*Reserve Bank India B.*	Bombay
Résultats. Statistiques du Poitou-Charentes	*Résultats*	Limoges
Review. International Commission of Jurists	*R. int. Commiss. Jurists*	Geneva
Review of Income and Wealth	*R. Income Wealth*	New Haven
Review of Indonesian and Malayan Affairs	*R. Indones. Malay. Aff.*	Sydney
Review of Marketing and agricultural Economics	*R. Mkting agric. Econ.*	Sydney
Review of Middle East Studies	*R. Mid. East Stud.*	
Review of Politics	*R. Polit.*	Notre Dame, Ind.
Review of radical political Economics	*R. radic. polit. Econ.*	Ann Arbor. Mich.
Review of the economic Conditions in Italy	*R. econ. Condit. Italy*	Rome

Revista brasileira de Economia	*R. brasil. Econ.*	Rio de Janeiro
Revista brasileira de Estatística	*R. brasil. Estatíst.*	Rio de Janeiro
Revista brasileira de Estudos políticos	*R. brasil. Estud. polít.*	Belo Horizonte
Revista de Administração de Emprêsas	*R. Adm. Emprêsas*	Rio de Janeiro
Revista de Administração municipal	*R. Adm. municip. (Rio de Janeiro)*	Rio de Janeiro
Revista de Administração pública	*R. Adm. públ. (Rio de Janeiro)*	Rio de Janeiro
Revista de Administración pública	*R. Adm. públ. (Madrid)*	Madrid
Revista de Ciências sociais	*R. Ciênc. soc. (Ceara)*	Ceara
Revista de Ciencias sociales	*R. Cienc. soc. (Puerto Rico)*	Puerto Rico
Revista de Derecho	*R. Der. (Quito)*	Quito
Revista de Derecho público	*R. Der. públ. (Santiago de Chile)*	Santiago de Chile
Revista de Derecho y Ciencias políticas. Universidad de San Marcos	*R. Der. Cienc. polít.*	Lima
Revista de Direito administrativo	*R. Dir. adm.*	Rio de Janeiro
Revista de Economía	*R. Econ. (Córdoba)*	Córdoba
Revista de Economía latinoamericana	*R. Econ. latinoamer.*	Caracas
Revista de Economía política	*R. Econ. polít. (Madrid)*	Madrid
Revista de Economía y Estadística	*R. Econ. Estadíst.*	Córdoba (Argentina)
Revista de Educación	*R. Educ. (Madrid)*	Madrid
Revista de Estudios agrosociales	*R. Estud. agro-soc.*	Madrid
Revista de Estudios de la Vida local	*R. Estud. Vida loc.*	Madrid
Revista de Estudios políticos	*R. Estud. polít.*	Madrid
Revista de Estudios sindicales	*R. Estud. sindic.*	Madrid
Revista de Estudios sociales	*R. Estud. soc.*	Madrid
Revista de Fomento social	*R. Fomento soc.*	Madrid
Revista de Planeación y Desarrollo	*R. Plan. Desarr. (Bogotà)*	Bogotà
Revista de Política internacional	*R. Polít. int. (Madrid)*	Madrid
Revista de Política social	*R. Polít. soc.*	Madrid
Revista de la Academía diplomática del Perú	*R. Acad. diplom. Perú*	Lima
Revista de la Facultad de Derecho	*R. Fac. Der. (Caracas)*	Caracas
Revista de la Facultad de Derecho de México	*R. Fac. Der. México*	México
Revista de la Universidad industrial de Santander	*R. Univ. industr. Santander*	Bucaramanga
Revista del Instituto de Ciencias sociales	*R. Inst. Cienc. soc.*	Barcelona
Revista do Centro de Estudos demográficos	*R. Centro Estud. demogr.*	Lisbôa
Revista española de Derecho internacional	*R. esp. Der. int.*	Madrid
Revista española de la Opinión pública	*R. esp. Opin. públ.*	·Madrid

Revista geográfica	*R. geogr. (México)*	México
Revista geográfica	*R. geogr. (Rio de Ja-neiro)*	Rio de Janeiro
Revista iberoamericana de Se-guridad social	*R. iberoamer. Segur. soc.*	Madrid
Revista interamericana de Planificación	*R. iberoamer. Planif.*	Bogotà
Revista internacional de So-ciología	*R. int. Sociol. (Mad-rid)*	Madrid
Revista javeriana	*R. javer.*	Bogotà
Revista latinoamericana de Psicología	*R. latinoamer. Psicol.*	Bogotà
Revista mexicana de Ciencias políticas y sociales	*R. mexic. Cienc. polít.*	México
Revista mexicana de Sociología	*R. mexic. Sociol.*	México
Revista peruana de Derecho internacional	*R. peru. Der. int.*	Lima
Revista sindical de Estadís-tica	*R. sind. Estadíst.*	Madrid
Revista venezolana de Sanidad y Asistencia social	*R. venezol. Sanid. Asist. soc.*	Caracas
Revolutionary World	*Revol. Wld*	Amsterdam
Revue administrative	*R. adm.*	Paris
Revue algérienne des Sciences juridiques, économiques et politiques	*R. algér. Sci. jur. écon. polit.*	Alger
Revue belge de Droit interna-tional	*R. belge Dr. int.*	Bruxelles
Revue belge de Sécurité socia-le	*R. belge Sécur. soc.*	Bruxelles
Revue bimensuelle d'Informa-tion. Banque marocaine de Commerce extérieur	*R. bimens. Inform. Banque maroc. Com. ext.*	Casablanca
Revue canadienne des Études africaines	*R. canad. Ét. afr.*	Ottawa
Revue critique de Droit inter-national privé	*R. crit. Dr. int. privé*	Paris
Revue d'Allemagne	*R. Allem.*	Paris
Revue d'Économie et de Gestion	*R. Écon. Gestion*	Nice
Revue d'Économie politique	*R. Écon. polit. (Paris)*	Paris
Revue d'Études comparatives Est-Ouest	*R. Ét. comp. Est-Ouest*	Paris
Revue d'Histoire moderne et contemporaine	*R. Hist. mod. contemp.*	Paris
Revue d'Intégration européenne	*R. Intégr. europ.*	Montréal
Revue de Droit contemporain	*R. Dr. contemp.*	Bruxelles
Revue de Droit international et de Droit comparé	*R. Dr. int. Dr. comp.*	Bruxelles
Revue de Droit rural	*R. Dr. rur.*	Paris
Revue de Géographie alpine	*R. Géogr. alpine*	Grenoble
Revue de Politique interna-tionale	*R. Polit. int.*	Belgrade
Revue de Science criminelle et de Droit pénal comparé	*R. Sci. crimin. Dr. pénal comp.*	Paris
Revue de Science financière	*R. Sci. financ.*	Paris
Revue de Tourisme	*R. Tourisme*	Berne
Revue de l'Association cana-dienne d'Éducation de Langue française	*R. Assoc. canad. Éduc. Langue franç.*	Québec
Revue de l'Économie du Centre-Est	*R. Écon. Centre-Est*	Dijon

Revue de l'Économie méridionale	R. Écon. mérid.	Montpellier
Revue de l'Énergie	R. Énergie	Paris
Revue de l'Europe	R. Europe	Paris
Revue de l'Institut de Socio-logie	R. Inst. Sociol.	Bruxelles
Revue de la Coopération inter-nationale	R. Coop. int.	Londres
Revue de la Navigation flu-viale européenne	R. Navig. fluv. europ.	Strasbourg
Revue de la Société d'Études et d'Expansion	R. Soc. Ét. Expans.	Liège
Revue des Droits de l'Homme	R. Dr. Homme	Paris
Revue des Études coopératives	R. Ét. coop.	Paris
Revue des Études sud-est européennes	R. Ét. Sud-Est europ.	Bucarest
Revue des Pays de l'Est	R. Pays Est	Bruxelles
Revue des Sciences sociales de la France de l'Est	R. Sci. soc. France Est	Strasbourg
Revue des Travaux de l'Aca-démie des Sciences morales et politiques	R. Trav. Acad. Sci. mor. polit.	Paris
Revue du Droit public et de la Science politique en France et à l'étranger	R. Dr. publ. Sci. polit.	Paris
Revue du Marché commun	R. Marché commun	Paris
Revue du Travail	R. Trav. (Bruxelles)	Bruxelles
Revue économique	R. écon. (Paris)	Paris
Revue économique du Sud-Ouest	R. écon. Sud-Ouest	Bordeaux
Revue économique et sociale	R. écon. soc.	Lausanne
Revue économique française	R. écon. franç.	Paris
Revue égyptienne de Droit international	R. égypt. Dr. int.	Le Caire
Revue européenne des Sciences sociales. Cahiers Vilfredo Pareto	R. europ. Sci. soc.	Genève
Revue française d'Administra-tion publique	R. franç. Adm. publ.	Paris
Revue française d'Études poli-tiques africaines	R. franç. Ét. polit. afr.	Paris
Revue française d'Études po-litiques méditerranéennes	R. franç. Ét. polit. médit.	Paris
Revue française d'Histoire d'Outre-Mer	R. franç. Hist. O.-Mer	Paris
Revue française de Gestion	R. franç. Gestion	Paris
Revue française de Science po-litique	R. franç. Sci. polit.	Paris
Revue française de Sociologie	R. franç. Sociol.	Paris
Revue française des Affaires sociales	R. franç. Aff. soc.	Paris
Revue française du Marketing	R. franç. Mkting	Paris
Revue générale	R. gén.	Bruxelles
Revue générale de Droit inter-national public	R. gén. Dr. int. publ.	Paris
Revue géographique de l'Est	R. géogr. Est	Nancy
Revue géographique des Pyré-nées et du Sud-Ouest	R. geogr. Pyrénées	Toulouse
Revue hospitalière de France	R. hospital. France	Lyon
Revue internationale de Droit comparé	R. int. Dr. comp.	Paris
Revue internationale de Poli-tique criminelle	R. int. Polit. crim.	New York

Revue internationale de Socio-logie / International Review of of Sociology	*R. int. Sociol. (Rome)*	Rome
Revue internationale de la Croix-Rouge	*R. int. Cr.-Rouge*	Genève
Revue internationale des Sciences administratives	*R. int. Sci. adm.*	Bruxelles
Revue internationale des Sciences sociales / Interna-tional social Science Journal	*R. int. Sci. soc.*	Paris
Revue internationale du Tra-vail	*R. int. Trav.*	Genève
Revue iranienne des Relations internationales	*R. iran. Relat. int.*	Téhéran
Revue juridique et politique - Indépendance et Coopération	*R. jur. polit.*	Paris
Revue nouvelle	*R. nouv.*	Tournai
Revue politique et parlemen-taire	*R. polit. parl.*	Paris
Revue roumaine d'Études in-ternationales	*R. roum. Ét. int.*	Bucarest
Revue roumaine des Sciences so-ciales. Série de Psychologie	*R. roum. Sci. soc. Sér. Psychol.*	Bucarest
Revue roumaine des Sciences so-ciales. Série Sciences éco-nomiques	*R. roum. Sci. soc. Sér. Sci. écon.*	Bucarest
Revue roumaine des Sciences so-ciales. Série Sciences juri-diques	*R. roum. Sci. soc. Sér. Sci. jur.*	Bucarest
Revue trimestrielle de Droit européen	*R. trim. Dr. europ.*	Paris
Revue tunisienne de Sciences sociales	*R. tunis. Sci. soc.*	Tunis
Revue zaïroise de Psychologie et de Pédagogie	*R. zaïr. Psychol. Pédag.*	Kisangani
Ricerca sociale	*Ric. soc.*	Bologna
Ricerche economiche	*Ric. econ.*	Venezia
Risshô-daigaku bungakubu Ronsô	*Risshô-daigaku bunga-kubu Ronsô*	[Nihon]
Risshô-daigaku Jinbunkagaku kenkyujo nenpo	*Risshô-daigaku Jinbun-kagaku kenkyujo nenpo*	[Nihon]
Risparmio	*Risparmio*	Roma
Rivista di Diritto agrario	*Riv. Dir. agr.*	Milano
Rivista di Diritto europeo	*Riv. Dir. europ.*	Roma
Rivista di Economia agraria	*Riv. Econ. agr.*	Roma
Rivista di Politica agraria	*Riv. Polit. agr.*	Bologna
Rivista di Politica economica	*Riv. Polit. econ.*	Roma
Rivista di Sociologia	*Riv. Sociol.*	Roma
Rivista di Studi politici in-ternazionali	*Riv. Studi polit. int.*	Firenze
Rivista geografica italiana	*Riv. geogr. ital.*	Firenze
Rivista internazionale di Fi-losofia politica e sociale e di Diritto comparato	*Riv. int. Filos. polit. soc. Dir. comp.*	Bologna
Rivista internazionale di Sci-enze economiche e commerciali	*Riv. int. Sci. econ. com.*	Milano-Padova
Rivista internazionale di Sci-enza sociale	*Riv. int. Sci. soc.*	Milano
Rivista italiana di Scienza politica	*Riv. ital. Sci. polit.*	Bologna
Rivista trimestrale di Diritto pubblico	*Riv. trim. Dir. pubbl.*	Milano

Roczniki Instytutu Handlu wewnętrznego	Roczn. Inst. Handlu wewn.	Warszawa
Round Table	Round Table	London
RS Cuadernos de Realidades sociales	RS Cuad. Realidad. soc.	[España]
Ruch prawniczy, ekonomiczny i socjologiczny	Ruch prawn. ekon. socjol.	Poznań
Rural Sociology	Rur. Sociol.	Lexington, Ky.
Saga-daigaku Kyôyôbu Kenkyû Kiyô	Saga-daigaku Kyôyôbu Kenkyû Kiyô	[Nihon]
Sage electoral Studies Yearbook	Sage elect. Stud. Yb.	Beverly Hills, Calif.
Sage Yearbook in Politics and public Policy	Sage Yb. Polit. publ. Pol.	Beverly Hills, Calif.
Sage Yearbook in Women's Policy Studies	Sage Yb. Women's Pol. Stud.	Beverly Hills, Calif.
Sbornik naučnyh Statej voenno-političeskoj Akademii	Sb. nauč. Statej voenno-polit. Akad.	Moskva
Scandinavian Journal of Economics	Scand. J. Econ.	Stockholm
Scandinavian Journal of Work, Environment and Health	Scand. J. Wk Environ. Health	Gothenburg
Scandinavian political Studies	Scand. polit. Stud.	Helsinki
Schriften des Instituts für Asienkunde	Schr. Inst. Asienkunde	Hamburg
Schweizer Monatshefte	Schweiz. Mh.	Zürich
Schweizerische Zeitschrift für Volkswirtschaft und Statistik / Revue suisse d'Économie politique et de Statistique	Schweizer. Z. Volkswirtsch. u. Statist.	Bern
Science and public Policy	Sci. publ. Pol.	London
Science and Society	Sci. and Soc.	New York
Sciences sociales. Académie des Sciences de l'URSS	Sci. soc. (Moscou)	Moscou
Scientific American	Scient. Amer.	New York
Scottish Journal of political Economy	Scott. J. polit. Econ.	Glasgow
Scuola e Città	Scuola e Città	Firenze
Seikei Ronso	Seikei Ronso	[Nihon]
Seminar	Seminar	New Delhi
Service social	Serv. soc. (Québec)	Québec
Service social dans le Monde	Serv. soc. Monde	Bruxelles
Shakai Fukushigaku	Shakai Fukushigaku	[Nihon]
Shakai Fukushi Hyôron	Shakai Fukushi Hyôron	Osaka
Shakai-fukushi Kenkyû	Shakai-fukushi Kenkyû	[Nihon]
Shakai-jigyôshi Kenkyû	Shakai-jigyôshi Kenkyû	[Nihon]
Shakai-kagaku	Shakai-kagaku	[Nihon]
Shakai-kagaku-Jânaru	Shakai-kagaku-Jânaru	[Nihon]
Shakai Kagaku Tôkyû	Shakai Kagaku Tôkyû	Tokyo
Shakai-rônengaku	Shakai-rônengaku	[Nihon]
Shakaigaku Hyôron	Shakaigaku Hyôron	Tokyo
Shakaigaku Jânaru	Shakaigaku Jânaru	[Nihon]
Shakaigaku Kenkyû	Shakaigaku Kenkyû	[Nihon]
Shakaigaku Kenkyû Nenpô	Shakaigaku Kenkyû Nenpô	[Nihon]
Shakaigaku Ronsô	Shakaigaku Ronsô	Tokyo
Shakaigakunenshi	Shakaigakunenshi	[Nihon]
Shaken shirizu	Shaken shirizu	[Nihon]
Shigakenritsu-tankidaigaku Gakujutsu-zasshi	Shigakenritsu-tankidaigaku Gakujutsu-zasshi	[Nihon]

Shinbun kenkyûjo Nenpô	*Shinbun kenkyûjo Nenpô*	[Nihon]
Shinbungaku Hyôron	*Shinbungaku Hyôron*	[Nihon]
Shirasagi Ronsô	*Shirasagi Ronsô*	[Nihon]
Shisô	*Shisô*	Tokyo
Shogaku Ronsan	*Shogaku Ronsan*	[Nihon]
Shôtokugakuen Gifukyoiku-daigaku Kiyô	*Shôtokugakuen Gifukyoiku-daigaku Kiyô*	[Nihon]
Shôwa-daigaku Kyôyôbu Kiyô	*Shôwa-daigaku Kyôyôbu Kiyô*	[Nihon]
Sicurezza sociale	*Sicur. soc.*	Roma
Siirtolaisuus	*Siirtolaisuus*	[Suomi]
Simulation and Games	*Simul. and Games*	Beverly Hills, Calif.
Síntesis-Asociación latino-americana de libre Comercio	*Síntesis*	Montevideo
Sistema. Revista de Ciencias sociales	*Sistema*	Madrid
Skandinaviska enskilda Banken quarterly Review	*Skand. ensk. Bank. quart. R.*	Stockholm
Slavic Review	*Slavic R.*	New York
Sloan Management Review	*Sloan Manag. R.*	Cambridge
Sociaal Maandblad Arbeid	*Soc. Maandbl. Arb.*	Alphen-aan-den-Rijn-Rotterdam
Social Action	*Soc. Action*	Poona
Social Biology	*Soc. Biology*	New York
Social Compass	*Soc. Compass*	The Hague
Social Forces	*Soc. Forces*	Chapel Hill, N.C.
Social Policy	*Soc. Pol.*	New York
Social Praxis	*Soc. Praxis*	Paris
Social Problems	*Soc. Probl.*	New York-Rochester, Mich.
Social Research	*Soc. Res.*	New York
Social Science	*Soc. Sci. (Winfield)*	Winfield
Social Science and Medicine	*Soc. Sci. Medic.*	Boston, Mass.
Social Science and modern Society	*Soc. Sci. mod. Soc.*	
Social Science Information / Information sur les Sciences sociales	*Soc. Sci. Inform.*	Paris
Social Science Journal	*Soc. Sci. J. (Fort Collins)*	Fort Collins
Social Science Quarterly	*Soc. Sci. Quart.*	Austin, Tex.
Social Science Research	*Soc. Sci. Res.*	Ann Arbor, Mich.
Social Theory and Practice	*Soc. Theory Practice*	Tallahassee, Fla.
Social Trends	*Soc. Trends*	London
Social Work	*Soc. Wk (Albany)*	Albany, N.Y.
Sociale Wetenschappen	*Soc. Wetensch.*	Tilburg
Socialisme	*Socialisme*	Bruxelles
Socialisme en Democratie	*Social. en Democr.*	Amsterdam
Socialist Revolution	*Social. Revol.*	San Francisco, Calif.
Social'no-psihologičeskie Problemy čtenija	*Soc.-psihol. Probl. čtenija*	Moskva
Social'nye Problemy novyh proizvodstvennyh Kollektivov	*Soc. Probl. nov. proizvodstv. Kollektiv.*	Krasnojarsk
Socialt Tidsskrift	*Soc. Tss.*	København
Société royale d'Économie politique de Belgique	*Soc. roy. Écon. polit. Belgique*	Bruxelles
Society	*Society*	St. Louis, Mo.
Society and Leisure	*Soc. and Leisure*	Prague
Socijalizam	*Socijalizam*	Beograd
Socio-economic Planning Sciences	*Soc.-econ. Plan. Sci.*	New York
Sociologia	*Sociologia (Roma)*	Roma

Sociologia internationalis	*Sociol. int. (Berlin)*	Berlin
Sociologia ruralis	*Sociol. rur.*	Assen
Sociological Analysis	*Sociol. Anal. (San Antonio)*	San Antonio, Tex.
Sociological Analysis and Theory	*Sociol. Anal. Theory*	Sheffield
Sociological Bulletin	*Sociol. B. (Bombay)*	Bombay
Sociological Focus	*Sociol. Focus*	Akron, Ohio
Sociological Inquiry	*Sociol. Inquiry*	Toronto
Sociological Methods and Research	*Sociol. Meth. Res.*	Beverly Hills, Calif.
Sociological Quarterly	*Sociol. Quart.*	Carbondale, Ill.
Sociological Review	*Sociol. R.*	Keele
Sociologičeskie Issledovanija	*Sociol. Issled. (Moskva)*	Moskva
Sociologický Časopis	*Sociol. Čas.*	Praha
Sociologie contemporaine	*Sociol. contemp.*	La Haye
Sociologie du Travail	*Sociol. Trav.*	Paris
Sociologie et Sociétés	*Sociol. et Soc.*	Montréal
Sociologija	*Sociologija*	Beograd
Sociologija sela	*Sociol. sela*	Zagreb
Sociologische Gids	*Sociol. Gids*	Meppel
Sociologus. Zeitschrift für empirische Soziologie, sozialpsychologische und ethnologische Forschung	*Sociologus*	Berlin
Sociology	*Sociology (London)*	London
Sociology and social Research	*Sociol. soc. Res.*	Los Angeles, Calif.
Sociology of Education	*Sociol. Educ.*	Washington, D.C.
Sociology of Work and Occupations	*Sociol. Wk Occupat.*	Beverly Hills, Calif.
Sociometry	*Sociometry*	New York
Somogy	*Somogy*	[Magyarország]
Sondages	*Sondages*	Paris
Sorevnovanie i Ličnost' pri Socializme	*Sorevnov. Ličnost' Social.*	Perm'
Sosharu Wâku Kenkyû	*Sosharu Wâku Kenkyû*	[Nihon]
Soshiki Kagaku	*Soshiki Kagaku*	[Nihon]
Soshiki Kodo Kenkyû	*Soshiki Kodo Kenkyû*	[Nihon]
Soshioloji	*Soshioloji*	Kyoto
Soshiorojika	*Soshiorojika*	[Nihon]
Sosiologia	*Sosiologia*	Helsinki
Sotilasaikakauslehti	*Sotilasaikakauslehti*	Helsinki
South Africa international Quarterly	*South Afr. int. Quart.*	Johannesburg
South African Journal of Economics / Suid-Afrikaanse Tydskrif vir Ekonomie	*South Afr. J. Econ.*	Johannesburg
Southeast Asian Affairs	*Southeast Asian Aff.*	Singapore
Southeast Asian Journal of social Science	*Southeast Asian J. soc. Sci.*	Singapore
South East Asian Spectrum	*South East Asian Spectrum*	Bangkok
Southern Exposure	*Southern Exposure*	Chapel Hill, N.C.
Southern Quarterly	*South. Quart.*	Hattiesburg, Miss.
Sovetskaja Pedagogika	*Sov. Pedag.*	Moskva
Sovetskoe Gosudarstvo i Pravo	*Sov. Gos. Pravo*	Moskva
Sovetskoe Slavjanovedenie	*Sov. Slavjanoved.*	Moskva
Soviet and Eastern European foreign Trade	*Sov. East. Europ. for. Trade*	White Plains, N.Y.
Soviet Geography	*Sov. Geogr.*	New York

Soviet Jewish Affairs	*Sov. Jew. Aff.*	London
Soviet Law and Government	*Sov. Law Gvt*	New York
Soviet Sociology	*Sov. Sociol.*	New York
Soviet Studies	*Sov. Stud.*	Glasgow
Soziale Welt	*Soz. Welt*	Dortmund
Sozialistische Politik	*Sozial. Polit.*	Berlin
Sozialwissenschaftliches Jahrbuch für Politik	*Soz.-wiss. Jb. Polit.*	München
Spettatore internazionale	*Spettatore int.*	Roma
Spółdzielczy Kwartalnik naukowy	*Spółdz. Kwartal. nauk.*	Warszawa
Sprawy międzynarodowe	*Spr. międzyn.*	Warszawa
Sri Lanka Labour Gazette	*Sri Lanka Lab. Gaz.*	Sri Lanka
SŠA	*SŠA*	Moskva
Staat (Der)	*Staat*	Berlin
Staat und Recht	*Staat u. Recht*	Potsdam
Staff Papers	*Staff Pap.*	Washington, D.C.
Stanford Journal of international Studies	*Stanford J. int. Stud.*	Stanford, Calif.
Statistika	*Statistika (Praha)*	Praha
Statistiques et Développement. Pays de la Loire	*Statist. et Dévelop. Loire*	Paris
Statistiques du Travail. Supplément au Bulletin mensuel	*Statist. Trav. Suppl. B. mens.*	Paris
Statistiques et Études financières	*Statist. Ét. financ.*	Paris
Statistiques et Études financières. Études économiques. Série orange	*Statist. Ét. financ. Ét. écon. Sér. orange*	Paris
Statistiques et Études financières. Série bleue	*Statist. Ét. financ. Sér. bleue*	Paris
Statistiques et Études financières. Série rouge	*Statist. Ét. financ. Sér. rouge*	Paris
Statistiques pour l'Économie normande	*Statist. Écon. normande*	Rouen
Statisztikai Szemle	*Statiszt. Szle*	Budapest
Statsvetenskaplig Tidskrift	*Statsvet. Ts.*	Lund
Storia e Politica	*Storia e Polit.*	Milano
Strategic Review	*Strategic R.*	Washington, D.C.
Stratégie	*Stratégie*	Paris
Studi di Sociologia	*Studi Sociol.*	Milano
Studi economici	*Stud. econ.*	Napoli
Studi Emigrazione	*Studi Emigr.*	Roma
Studia demograficzne	*Stud. demogr.*	Warszawa
Studia diplomatica	*Stud. diplom.*	Bruxelles
Studia finansowe	*Stud. finans.*	Warszawa
Studia Nauk politycznych	*Stud. Nauk polit.*	Warszawa
Studia prawno-ekonomiczne	*Stud. prawno-ekon.*	Łódź
Studia socjologiczne	*Stud. socjol.*	Warszawa
Studies in comparative Communism	*Stud. comp. Communism*	Los Angeles, Calif.
Studies in Family Planning	*Stud. Family Plan.*	New York
Studies in Soviet Thought	*Stud. Sov. Thought*	Fribourg
Studies on international Relations	*Stud. int. Relat.*	Warsaw
Studii şi Cercetări economice	*Studii Cercet. econ.*	Bucureşti
Sud. Information économique Provence-Côte d'Azur-Corse	*Sud. Inform. écon. Provence-Côte d'Azur-Corse*	Marseille
Suisan-keizai Kenkyû	*Suisan-keizai Kenkyû*	Shimonoseki
Supreme Court Review	*Supreme Court R.*	Chicago, Ill.
Survey. A Journal of Soviet and East European Studies	*Survey*	London

Survey of current Business	*Surv. curr. Busin.*	Washington, D.C.
Surveys of Consumers	*Surv. Consumers*	Ann Arbor, Mich.
Survival	*Survival*	London
Svědectví	*Svědectví*	Paris
Swedish Economy	*Swedish Econ.*	Stockholm
Syrie et Monde arabe	*Syrie et Monde arabe*	Damas
Szakszervezeti Szemle	*Szakszerv. Szle*	Budapest
Századok	*Századok*	Budapest
Szervezés és Vezetés	*Szerv. és Vez.*	[Magyarország]
Szigma	*Szigma*	Budapest
Szociológia	*Szociológia*	Budapest
Tájékoztató	*Tájékoztató*	Budapest
Tamagawa-daigaku Bungakubu Ronsô	*Tamagawa-daigaku Bunga-kubu Ronsô*	[Nihon]
Társadalmi Szemle	*Társad. Szle*	Budapest
Társadalomtudományi Közlemények	*Társad.-tud. Közlem.*	Budapest
Teaching political Science	*Teaching polit. Sci.*	London
Teaching Politics	*Teaching Polit.*	London
Technological Forecasting and social Change	*Technol. Forecasting soc. Change*	New York
Temps modernes	*Temps mod.*	Paris
Teorija in Praksa	*Teorija in Praksa*	Ljubljana
Terra	*Terra*	Helsinki
Területi Statisztika	*Területi Statiszt.*	Budapest
Területrendezés	*Területrendezés*	Budapest
Terzo Mondo	*Terzo Mondo*	Milano
Testimonianze	*Testimonianze*	Firenze
Tetsugaku	*Tetsugaku*	Tokyo
Tetsugaku Nenpô	*Tetsugaku Nenpô*	Fukuoka
Tetsugaku Ronshû	*Tetsugaku Ronshû*	[Nihon]
Textes et Documents	*Textes et Doc. (Bruxelles)*	Bruxelles
Theory and Society	*Theory and Soc.*	Amsterdam
Three Banks Review	*Three Banks R.*	Edinburgh
Tidskrift utgiven av juridiska Föreningen i Finland	*Ts. jur. För. Finland*	Helsinki
Tie ja liikenne	*Tie ja liikenne*	Helsinki
Tiers-Monde	*Tiers-Monde*	Paris
Tilastollisia-kuukausitietoja Helsingistä	*Tilastoll. kuukausit. Helsingistä*	Helsinki
Tohô-daigaku Kyôyô Kiyô	*Toho-daigaku Kyôyô Kiyô*	[Nihon]
Tôhoku Fukushi-daigaku Kiyô	*Tôhoku Fukushi-daigaku Kiyô*	[Nihon]
Tokyo Daigaku-shinbunkenkyûsho-kiyô	*Tokyo Daigaku-shinbun-kenkyûsho-kiyô*	Tokyo
Tôkyô-toritsu-daigaku Jinbun-gakuhô	*Tôkyô-toritsu-daigaku Jinbun-gakuhô*	Tokyo
Tonan Ajia Kenkyû	*Tonan Ajia Kenkyû*	[Nihon]
Történelmi Szemle	*Tört. Szle*	Budapest
Toshi Mondai	*Toshi Mondai*	Tokyo
Toshi Mondai Kenkyû	*Toshi Mondai Kenkyû*	Osaka
Toshiseisaku	*Toshiseisaku*	[Nihon]
Toxicomanies	*Toxicomanies*	Québec
Tôyô-gakujutsu Kenkyû	*Tôyô-gakujutsu Kenkyû*	[Nihon]
Transports	*Transports*	Paris
Travail et Société	*Trav. et Soc.*	Genève
Travaux et Communications. Académie des Sciences morales et juridiques (Montréal)	*Trav. Communicat. Acad. Sci. mor. jur. (Montréal)*	Montréal

Travaux et Communications. Académie des Sciences morales et politiques (Montréal)	*Trav. Communicat. Acad. Sci. mor. polit. (Montréal)*	Montréal
Tricontinental	*Tricontinental*	La Habana
Trimestre económico	*Trim. econ.*	México
Trudy Akademii Nauk Litovskoj SSR. Obščestvennye Nauk	*Trudy Akad. Nauk Litovsk. SSR obšč. Nauk*	Viln'jus
Trudy Gor'kovskoj vysšej Školy MVD SSSR	*Trudy Gor'k. vyšš. Školy MVD SSSR*	Gor'kij
Trudy Kirgizskogo Universiteta. Serija obščestvennyh Nauk	*Trudy Kirgiz. Univ. Ser. obšč. Nauk*	Frunze
Trudy naučno-issledovatel'skogo Instituta Kul'tury	*Trudy nauč.-issled. Inst. Kul't.*	[SSSR]
Trudy Tallinskogo politehničeskogo Instituta	*Trudy Tallinsk. politehn. Inst.*	Tallin
Trudy Tbilisijskogo Universiteta	*Trudy Tbilis. Univ.*	Tbilisi
Trudy Vsesojuznogo juridičeskogo zaočnogo Instituta	*Trudy Vsesojuz. jur. zaoč.*	Moskva
Trybuna spóldzielcza	*Tryb. spóld.*	Warszawa
Tsudajuku-daigaku Kiyô	*Tsudajuku-daigaku Kiyô*	[Nihon]
Tudomány és Mezögazdaság	*Tud. és Mezög.*	[Magyarország]
Turkish public Administration Annual	*Turk. publ. Adm. Annu.*	Ankara
Turkish Yearbook of international Relations	*Turk. Yb. int. Relat.*	Ankara
Turkmenistan SSR Ylmar Akademijasynyh Habarlary	*Turkmen. SSR Ylmar Akad. Habarl.*	Ashabad
Tutzinger Studien	*Tutzing. Stud.*	München
Työväen Taloudellinen Tutkimuslaitos-Katsaus	*Työväen Taloudell. Tutkimus. Katsaus*	[Suomi]
Työvoimakatsaus	*Työvoimakatsaus*	[Suomi]
Učenye Zapiski (Azerbajdžanskij Institut narodnogo Hozjajstva). Serija ěkonomičeskih Nauk	*Učen. Zap. (Azerb. In Inst. nar. Hoz.) Ser. ěkon. Nauk*	Baku
Učenye Zapiski (Azerbajdžanskij Universitet). Serija istoričeskih i filosofskih Nauk	*Učen. Zap. (Azerb. Univ.) Ser. ist. filos. Nauk*	Baku
Učenye Zapiski Kafedry obščestvennyh nauk Vuzov goroda Leningrada. Problemy naučnogo Kommunizma	*Učen. Zap. Kaf. obšč. nauk Vuzov g. Leningr. Probl. nauč. Kommunizma*	Leningrad
Učenye Zapiski (Kazanskij pedagogičeskij Institut)	*Učen. Zap. (Kazan. pedag. Inst.)*	Kazan'
Učenye Zapiski (Vysšej partijnoj Školy pri CK KPSS)	*Učen. Zap. (Vyšš. part. Školy CK KPSS)*	Moskva
Ufahamu	*Ufahamu*	Los Angeles, Calif.
Új Irás	*Új Irás*	Budapest
Ukrainian Quarterly	*Ukrainian Quart.*	New York
Ulkopolitiikka	*Ulkopolitiikka*	Helsinki
Unasylva	*Unasylva*	Roma
Universidad de Antioquia	*Univ. Antioquia*	Medellín
Universitas. Pontificia Universidad católica javeriana	*Universitas (Bogotá)*	Bogotá
Urban Affairs annual Review	*Urb. Aff. ann. R.*	Beverly Hills, Calif.
Urban Affairs Quarterly	*Urb. Aff. Quart.*	Beverly Hills, Calif.
Urban and social Change Review	*Urb. soc. Change R.*	Boston, Mass.
Urban Studies	*Urb. Stud.*	Edinburgh

Urbanisme	*Urbanisme*	Paris
Urbanistica	*Urbanistica*	Torino
Utsunomiya-daigaku Kyôyôbu Kenkyûhôkoku	*Utsunomiya-daigaku Kyôyôbu Kenkyûhôkoku*	Utsunomiya
Üzenet	*Üzenet*	[Magyarország]
Valóság	*Valóság*	Budapest
Városépítés	*Városépítés*	Budapest
Verfassung und Recht in Übersee	*Verfassung u. Recht Übersee*	Hamburg
Verfassung und Verfassungswirklichkeit	*Verfassung u. -Wirklichkeit*	Köln
Verwaltung	*Verwaltung*	Heidelberg
Vesitalous	*Vesitalous*	Helsinki
Vestnik Akademii Nauk SSSR	*Vestn. Akad. Nauk SSSR*	Moskva
Vestnik Leningradskogo Universiteta. Serija Ėkonomiki, Filosofii i Pravo	*Vestn. Leningr. Univ. Ser. Ėkon. Filos. Pravo*	Leningrad
Vestnik Leningradskogo Universiteta. Serija Istorii, Jazyka i Literatury	*Vestn. Leningr. Univ. Ser. Ist. Jaz. Lit.*	Leningrad
Vestnik Moskovskogo Universiteta. Serija Ėkonomika	*Vestn. Moskov. Univ. Ser. Ėkon.*	Moskva
Vestnik Moskovskogo Universiteta. Serija Istorija	*Vestn. Moskov. Univ. Ser. Ist.*	Moskva
Vestnik Moskovskogo Universiteta. Serija Pravo	*Vestn. Moskov. Univ. Ser. Pravo*	Moskva
Vestnik Moskovskogo Universiteta. Serija Žurnalistika	*Vestn. Moskov. Univ. Ser. Žurnal.*	Moskva
Vestnik Moskovskogo Universiteta. Teorija naučnogo Kommunizma	*Vestn. Moskov. Univ. Teorija nauč. Kommunizma*	Moskva
Vestnik obščestvennyh Nauk. Akademija Nauk Armjanskoj SSR	*Vestn. obšč. Nauk Akad. Nauk Arm. SSR*	Ėrevan
Vestnik Statistiki	*Vestn. Statist.*	Moskva
Vezetéstudomány	*Vezetéstud.*	Budapest
Vie économique	*Vie écon. (Berne)*	Berne
Vie et Sciences économiques	*Vie Sci. écon.*	Paris
Vie sociale	*Vie soc.*	Paris
Vierteljahresberichte	*Vierteljahresberichte*	Hannover
Vierteljahreshefte für Zeitgeschichte	*Vjh. Zeitgesch.*	Stuttgart
Vierteljahreshefte zur Wirtschaftsforschung	*Vjh. Wirtsch.-Forsch.*	Berlin
Vigilia	*Vigilia*	Budapest
Viitorul social	*Viitor. soc.*	Bucarest
Világosság	*Világosság*	Budapest
Vita e Pensiero	*Vita e Pensiero*	Milano
Vita italiana	*Vita ital.*	Roma
Vnešnaja Torgovlja	*Vnešn. Torg.*	Moskva
Voprosy Cenoobrazovanija	*Vopr. Cenoobraz.*	Moskva
Voprosy Ėkonomiki	*Vopr. Ėkon.*	Moskva
Voprosy Filosofii	*Vopr. Filos.*	Moskva
Voprosy Istorii	*Vopr. Ist.*	Moskva
Voprosy Istorii KPSS	*Vopr. Ist. KPSS*	Moskva
Voprosy Literatury	*Vopr. Lit.*	Moskva
Voprosy naučnogo Kommunizma	*Vopr. nauč. Kommunizma (Kiev)*	Kiev
Voprosy političeskoj Ėkonomii	*Vopr. polit. Ėkon.*	Kiev
Voprosy Psihologii	*Vopr. Psihol.*	Moskva
Voprosy Teorii i Metodov ideologičeskoj Raboty	*Vopr. Teorii Metod. ideol. Raboty*	Moskva

Vorgänge	*Vorgänge*	Hamburg
Vozes. Revista católica de Cultura	*Vozes*	Petropolis
Vues sur l'Économie d'Aquitaine	*Vues Écon. Aquitaine*	Paris
Vuoriteollisuus	*Vuoriteollisuus*	Helsinki
Wallonie	*Wallonie*	Namur
Waseda-daigaku daigakuin Bungaku Kenkyûka Kiyô	*Waseda-daigaku daigakuin Bungaku Kenkyûka Kiyô*	Tokyo
Waseda political Studies	*Waseda polit. Stud.*	Tokyo
Weltwirtschaft	*Weltwirtschaft*	Kiel
Weltwirtschaftliches Archiv	*Weltwirtsch. Archiv*	Kiel
West African Journal of Sociology and political Science	*West Afr. J. Sociol. polit. Sci.*	Exeter
Western political Quarterly	*West. polit. Quart.*	Salt Lake City, Utah
Wiadomości statystyczne	*Wiadom. statyst.*	Warszawa
Więź	*Więź*	Warszawa
Wijsgerig Perspectief op Maatschappij en Wetenschap	*Wijsig Perspect.*	Amsterdam
Wirtschaft und Gesellschaft	*Wirtsch. u. Ges.*	Wien
Wissenschaftliche Zeitschrift der Hochschule für Ökonomie Berlin	*Wiss. Z. Hochschule Ökon. Berlin*	Berlin
Wissenschaftlicher Dienst Südosteuropa	*Wiss. Dienst Südosteuropa*	München
WIST. Wirtschaftswissenschaftliches Studium	*WIST*	München
Wirtschaftsberichte. Credit Anstalt-Bauverein Wien	*Wirtschaftsberichte*	Wien
Wirtschaftsdienst	*Wirtsch.-Dienst*	Hamburg
Wirtschaftswissenschaft	*Wirtsch.-Wiss.*	Berlin
Work and People	*Work and People*	Melburn
World Affairs	*Wld Aff.*	Washington, D.C.
World Politics	*Wld Polit.*	Princeton, N.J.
World today	*Wld today*	London
WSI Mitteilungen. Wirtschafts- und sozialwissenschaftliche Institut der DGB	*WSI Mitt.*	Köln
Yale Law Journal	*Yale Law J.*	New Haven, Conn.
Yale Review	*Yale R.*	New Haven, Conn.
Yamagachi-daigaku Bungaku-kaichi	*Yamagachi-daigaku Bungaku-kaichi*	[Nihon]
Yamanashi Daigaku Kyôikugakubu Kenkyûhokoku	*Yamanashi Daigaku Kyôikugakubu Kenkyûhokoku*	Kôfu
Yearbook of World Affairs	*Yb. Wld Aff.*	London
Yokohama Shiritsu Daigaku Ronsô	*Yokohama Shiritsu Daigaku Ronsô*	Yokohama
Youth and Society	*Youth and Soc.*	Los Angeles, Calif.
Yugoslav Law	*Yugosl. Law*	Belgrade
Yugoslav Survey	*Yugosl. Surv.*	Belgrade
Zagadnienia Ekonomiki rolnej	*Zagadn. Ekon. roln.*	Warszawa
Zaïre-Afrique	*Zaïre-Afr.*	Kinshasa
Zambezia	*Zambezia*	Salisbury
Zeitschrift für ausländisches öffentliches Recht und Völkerrecht	*Z. ausländ. öff. Recht Völkerrecht*	Stuttgart
Zeitschrift für Betriebswirtschaft	*Z. Betriebswirtsch.*	Wiesbaden

Zeitschrift für Geschichts-wissenschaft	*Z. Gesch.-Wiss.*	Berlin
Zeitschrift für Nationalökono-mie / Journal of Economics	*Z. nat.-Ökon.*	Wien-New York
Zeitschrift für Parlaments-fragen	*Z. Parlamentsfragen*	Opladen
Zeitschrift für Politik	*Z. Polit.*	Berlin
Zeitschrift für Rechtspolitik	*Z. Rechtspolit.*	München
Zeitschrift für Sozialpsycho-logie	*Z. soz.-Psychol.*	Frankfurt-am-Main
Zeitschrift für Soziologie	*Z. Soziol.*	Stuttgart
Zeitschrift für Wirtschafts-und Sozialwissenschaften	*Z. Wirtsch.- u. soz.-Wiss.*	Berlin
Zeitschrift für den Erdkunde-unterricht	*Z. Erdkundeunterricht*	Berlin
Zeitschrift für die gesamte Staatswissenschaft	*Z. ges. Staatswiss.*	Tübingen
Zeszyty naukowe Akademii Ekonomicznej w Katowicach	*Zesz. nauk. Akad. Ekon. Katowic.*	Katowice
Zeszyty naukowe Akademii Ekonomicznej w Krakówie	*Zesz. nauk. Akad. Ekon. Kraków.*	Krakówie
Zeszyty naukowe Akademii Ekonomicznej w Poznaniu	*Zesz. nauk. Akad. Ekon. Poznan.*	Poznań
Zeszyty naukowe Uniwersytetu Łódzkiego. Nauki humanistycz-no-społeczne	*Zesz. nauk. Uniw. Łódz. Nauki humanist.-spo-łecz.*	Łódz
Zukunft	*Zukunft*	Wien
Żurnalist - Pressa - Auditorija	*Żurnal. Pressa Audit.*	Leningrad
Żurnalistika	*Żurnalistika*	Alma-Ata

CLASSIFICATION SCHEME
PLAN DE CLASSIFICATION

10.	Social sciences. Research. Documentation Sciences sociales. Recherche. Documentation	
10100.	Social sciences. Sociology/ Sciences sociales. So- ciologie.	1-46
10200.	Research worker. Sociologist / Chercheur. Sociologue	47-63
10300.	Organization of research. Research policy / Organi- sation de la recherche. Politique de la recherche	
10310.	Current research / Recherche en cours	64-98
10320.	Applied research. Interdisciplinary research / Recher- che appliquée. Recherche interdisciplinaire	99-102
10330.	Research centre / Centre de recherche	103-107
10340.	Organization of research. Research policy / Organisa- tion de la recherche. Politique de la recherche . . .	108-119
10350.	Research equipment / Équipement de recherche.	120-126
10360.	Sociological association / Association de sociologie.	127-129
10400.	Congress. Meeting / Congrès. Réunion.	130
10500.	Document. Information processing / Document. Traite- ment de l'information . . .	
10510.	Documentation	131-136
10520.	Document analysis. Reference book / Analyse documen- taire. Ouvrage de référence	137-144
10530.	Documentation centre / Centre de documentation. . . .	145-149
10540.	Documentalist / Documentaliste	
10550.	Terminology / Terminologie.	150-158
10560.	Biography / Biographie	159-180
10570.	Article. Periodical / Article. Périodique	181-185
10580.	Proceedings. Report / Actes. Rapport	
10590.	Textbook. Thesis / Manuel. Thèse.	186-197
11.	Methodology. Theory Méthodologie. Théorie	
11100.	Epistemology. Research method. Theory / Epistémologie. Méthode de recherche. Théorie	
11110.	Philosophy. Theory / Philosophie. Théorie	198-332
11120.	Epistemology. Explanation. Understanding / Epistémolo- gie. Explication. Compréhension	333-388
11130.	Research method. Sociological analysis / Méthode de recherche. Analyse sociologique	389-436
11200.	Data collection. Experiment / Rassemblement des don- nées. Expérience	
11210.	Experimentation. Observation / Expérimentation. Ob- servation	437-450
11220.	Sampling. Survey / Échantillonnage. Enquête	451-464
11230.	Interview. Questionnaire / Entretien. Questionnaire .	465-483

11240.   Personality measurement. Test / Mesure de la person-.
          nalité. Test.   484-490
11250.   Sociodrama / Sociodrame   491-492

11300.   Mathematical analysis. Statistical analysis / Analyse
          mathématique. Analyse statistique
11310.   Algebra. Calculus. Logic / Algèbre. Calcul. Logique .   493-500
11320.   Statistical analysis / Analyse statistique.   501-542
11330.   Cybernetics. Information theory / Cybernétique. Théo-
          rie de l'information.   543-546
11340.   Graph theory / Théorie des graphes.   547-548
11350.   Stochastic processes. Statistical decision. Game theo-
          ry / Processus stochastiques. Décision statistique.
          Théorie des jeux.   549-558
11360.   Attitude scale / Echelle d'attitude   559-572

12.   Individual. Group. Organization
          Individu. Groupe. Organisation

12100.   Psychology. Social psychology. Sociometry / Psycholo-
          gie. Psychologie sociale. Sociométrie
12110.   Psychoanalysis. Social psychology / Psychanalyse. Psy-
          chologie sociale.   573-606
12120.   Psychological factor / Facteur psychologique

12200.   Individual. Personality / Individu. Personnalité
12210.   Ego. Identity / Ego. Identité   607-623
12220.   Egocentrism. Self concept / Égocentrisme. Conception
          de soi.   624-654
12230.   Personality / Personnalité.   655-683
12240.   Cognition. Emotion. Motivation / Cognition. Émotion.
          Motivation.   684-770

12300.   Interpersonal relations / Relations interpersonnelles
12310.   Human relations. Sociability / Relations humaines.
          Sociabilité   771-788
12320.   Social perception / Perception sociale.   789-795
12330.   Interpersonal attraction / Attraction interpersonnelle   796-832
12340.   Interpersonal influence / Influence interpersonnelle.   833-839
12350.   Interpersonal conflict / Conflit interpersonnel . . .   840-858
12360.   Intergroup relations / Relations intergroupes   859-890

12400.   Group / Groupe
12410.   Group dynamics / Dynamique de groupe.   891-919
12420.   Primary group. Training group / Groupe primaire. Grou-
          pe de formation   920-934
12430.   Group size / Dimension du groupe.   935-943
12440.   Group integration / Intégration du groupe   944-956
12450.   Group membership / Appartenance au groupe   957-969
12460.   Group performance / Performance du groupe   970-972

12500.   Bureaucracy. Organization / Bureaucratie. Organisa-
          tion
12510.   Sociology of organization / Sociologie des organisa-
          tions   973-995
12520.   Complex organization / Organisation complexe.   996-1004
12530.   Bureaucracy / Bureaucratie.   1005-1069

12600.   Leadership. Role / Commandement. Rôle
12610.   Authority / Autorité.   1070-1077
12620.   Leadership / Commandement   1078-1091
12630.   Role / Rôle   1092-1108

12700.   Attitude. Opinion
12710.   Behaviour / Comportement.   1109-1141

12720. Cognitive dissonance. Prejudice / Dissonance cognitive. Préjugé. 1142-1165
12730. Dogmatism. F scale / Dogmatisme. Échelle F 1166-1170
12740. Opinion. 1171-1188
12750. Ideology / Idéologie 1189-1210
12760. Collective behaviour / Comportement collectif. . . . 1211-1223

13. Culture. Socialization. Social life
     Culture. Socialisation. Vie sociale

13100. Culture. Social environment. Value / Culture. Milieu
social. Valeur
13110. Social and cultural anthropology / Ethnologie. . . . 1224-1238
13120. Civilization. Culture. Society / Civilisation. Société 1239-1314
13130. Cultural dynamics. Cultural relations / Dynamique culturelle. Relations culturelles 1315-1378
13140. Norm. Social control. Value / Norme. Régulation sociale. Valeur 1379-1403
13150. Alienation. Socialization. Social conformity / Aliénation. Socialisation. Conformité sociale. 1404-1510

13200. Custom. Tradition/ Coutume. Tradition. 1511-1515

13300. Ethics. Morals / Éthique. Morale 1516-1539

13400. Law. Regulation / Loi. Règlementation. 1540-1583

13500. Magic. Mythology. Religion / Magie. Mythologie. Religion
13510. Religion. Sociology of religion / Religion. Sociologie religieuse 1584-1607
13520. Magic. Primitive religion / Magie. Religion primitive 1608-1618
13530. Buddhism. Christianiy / Bouddhisme. Christianisme. . 1619-1640
13540. Church. Religious community. Sect / Église. Communauté religieuse. Secte 1641-1669
13550. Clergy. Religious authority / Clergé. Autorité religieuse 1670-1678
13560. Cult. Rite / Culte. Rite 1679-1695
13570. Myth. Religious doctrine / Mythe. Doctrine religieuse 1696-1717
13580. Religious behaviour / Comportement religieux 1718-1737
13590. Church and State. Religious practice / Église et État.
Pratique religieuse. 1738-1784

13600. Science. Sociology of knowledge / Science. Sociologie
de la connaissance 1785-1837

13700. Communication. Language / Communication. Langage
13710. Linguistics. Semiotics / Linguistique. Sémiotique. . 1838-1866
13720. Communication. Sign / Communication. Signe 1867-1903
13730. Language / Langage 1904-1938
13740. Audience 1939-1941
13750. Advertising. Propaganda / Publicité. Propagande. . . 1942-1956
13760. Mass communication / Communication de masse. 1957-2039

13800. Art
13810. Aesthetics. Artist. Museum / Esthétique. Artiste. Musée. 2040-2061
13820. Literature / Littérature 2062-2079
13830. Fine arts / Beaux-arts 2080-2084
13840. Music / Musique. 2085-2095
13850. Dramatic art / Art dramatique. 2096-2102
13860. Folk art / Art populaire 2103-2107

13900. Education
13910. Educational sociology / Sociologie de l'éducation. . 2108-2147

13920. Educational system. Educational policy / Système d'enseignement. Politique de l'enseignement 2148-2241
13930. Primary education. Secondary education / Enseignement primaire. Enseignement secondaire. 2242-2276
13940. School environment / Milieu scolaire. 2277-2294
13950. Higher education / Enseignement supérieur 2295-2361
13960. Adult education / Éducation des adultes 2362-2398
13970. Civic education. Technical education / Instruction civique. Enseignement technique 2399-2404
13980. Academic achievement. School failure / Réussite des études. Échec scolaire. 2405-2414
13990. Pedagogy. Teaching. Teacher / Pédagogie. Enseignement. Enseignant. 2415-2453

14. Social structure
Structure sociale

14100. Social system / Système social. 2454-2488

14200. Social stratification / Stratification sociale
14210. Social differentiation / Différenciation sociale. . . 2489-2528
14220. Caste. Slavery / Caste. Esclavage 2529-2546
14230. Social class / Classe sociale 2547-2656
14240. Status. 2657-2677
14250. Elite. Intellectual / Élite. Intellectuel 2678-2705
14260. Social mobility / Mobilité sociale. 2706-2728

14300. Social change / Changement social
14310. History / Histoire. 2729-2734
14320. Future / Futur. 2735-2737
14330. Social change / Changement social 2738-2789
14340. Changing society / Société en transformation. . . . 2790-2837

15. Population. Family. Ethnic group
Population. Famille. Groupe ethnique

15100. Demography. Genetics / Démographie. Génétique
15110. Population research / Recherche démographique 2838-2864
15120. Household. Man. Woman / Ménage. Homme. Femme. 2865-2895
15130. Eugenism. Heredity / Eugénisme. Hérédité. 2896-2906

15200. Age group./ Groupe d'âge
15210. Age. Cohort. Generation / Âge. Cohorte. Génération. . 2907-2910
15220. Childhood / Enfance 2911-2943
15230. Youth / Jeunesse. 2944-2977
15240. Adult / Adulte. 2978-2981
15250. Old age / Vieillesse. 2982-3007

15300. Population evolution. Population policy / Évolution de la population. Politique démographique
15310. Population growth / Accroissement de la population. . 3008-3069
15320. Morbidity / Morbidité 3070-3094
15330. Mortality / Mortalité 3095-3131
15340. Fertility. Natality / Fécondité. Natalité 3132-3185
15350. Family planning / Planification de la famille . . . 3186-3232

15400. Marriage. Family / Mariage. Famille
15410. Sexual behaviour / Comportement sexuel. 3233-3264
15420. Marriage. Nuptiality / Mariage. Nuptialité. 3265-3320
15430. Family / Famille. 3321-3463
15440. Woman's status / Condition de la femme. 3464-3533

15500.   Ethnic group / Groupe ethnique
15510.   Ethnicity. Tribe / Ethnicité. Tribu   3534-3612
15520.   Interethnic relations. Racism / Relations interethni-
         ques. Racisme   3613-3653

15600.   Migration
15610.   Migrant. Migration policy / Migrant. Politique migra-
         toire   3654-3666
15620.   External migration / Migration externe.   3667-3743
15630.   Internal migration / Migration interne.   3744-3798

16.   Environment. Community. Rural. Urban
         Environnement. Communauté. Rural. Urbain

16100.   Ecology. Geography. Population settlement / Écologie.
         Géographie. Habitat
16110.   Human geography / Géographie humaine.   3799-3816
16120.   Nature. Soil. Water / Nature. Sol. Eau.   3817-3820
16130.   Citizen. Inhabitant / Citoyen. Habitant   3821-3833

16200.   Community / Communauté.   3834-3847

16300.   Rural. Urban / Rural. Urbain
16310.   Rural sociology / Sociologie rurale   3848-3878
16320.   Urban sociology / Sociologie urbaine.   3879-4234

17.   Economics
         Science économique

17100.   Economic sociology / Sociologie économique.   4235-4238

17200.   Economic system / Système économique
17210.   Economic doctrine / Doctrine économique   4239-4240
17220.   Capitalism. Collectivism / Capitalisme. Collectivisme   4241-4271

17300.   Economic situation. Standard of living / Situation
         économique. Niveau de vie
17310.   Economy. Economic development./ Économie. Développe-
         ment économique   4272-4284
17320.   Income. Living conditions / Revenu. Conditions de vie   4285-4315

17400.   Enterprise. Production / Entreprise. Production
17410.   Business economics. Management/ Économie de l'entre-
         prise. Gestion.   4316-4344
17420.   Productivity. Technology / Productivité. Technologie.   4345-4385
17430.   Agriculture. Commerce. Industry / Agriculture. Com-
         merce. Industrie.   4386-4427

17500.   Consumption. Market. Price / Consommation. Marché.
         Prix
17510.   Consumer behaviour / Comportement du consommateur . .   4428-4448
17520.   Demand. Supply / Demande. Offre   4449-4452

17600.   Credit. Financing. Money / Crédit. Financement. Mon-
         naie.   4453-4460

17700.   Economic policy. Planning / Politique économique. Pla-
         nification.   4461-4465

18.   Labour
         Travail

18100.   Industrial sociology. Sociology of work / Sociologie
         industrielle. Sociologie du travail   4466-4468

18200. Employment. Labour market / Emploi. Marché du travail
18210. Labour. Manpower / Travail. Main-d'oeuvre   4469-4484
18220. Employment. Unemployment / Emploi. Chômage.   4485-4493
18230. Employment service. Job evaluation / Service d'emploi.
        Évaluation d'emploi   4494-4495
18240. Woman worker. Young worker / Travailleur féminin.
        Jeune travailleur   4496-4535

18300. Personnel management. Working conditions / Administra-
        tion du personnel. Conditions de travail
18310. Labour standard. Work study / Norme de travail. Étude
        du travail.   4536-4553
18320. Working conditions / Conditions de travail.   4554-4599
18330. Labour turnover / Renouvellement de la main-d'oeuvre.   4600-4606

18400. Occupation. Vocational training / Profession. Forma-
        tion professionnelle
18410. Occupational sociology / Sociologie de la profession.   4607-4616
18420. Occupational life. Vocational guidance / Vie profes-
        sionnelle. Orientation professionnelle.   4617-4666

18500. Employee. Technician. Worker / Employé. Technicien.
        Travailleur
18510. Worker / Travailleur.   4667-4687
18520. Employee / Employé.   4688-4692
18530. Manager. Technician / Cadre. Technicien   4693-4705
18540. Liberal profession / Profession libérale.   4706-4709

18600. Labour management relations / Relations du travail   4710-4724
18610. Labour law / Droit du travail   4725-4733
18620. Employers' organization / Organisation patronale. . .   4734-4736
18630. Trade union / Syndicat.   4737-4779
18640. Labour conflict / Conflit du travail.   4780-4798
18650. Arbitration. Mediation / Arbitrage. Médiation   4799-4806
18660. Collective agreement. Joint management / Convention
        collective. Cogestion   4807-4821

18700. Leisure / Loisir.   4822-4847
18710. Leisure time / Temps de loisir.   4848-4851
18720. Leisure utilization / Utilisation des loisirs   4852-4899

19.   Politics. State. International relations
        Politique. État. Relations internationales

19100. Political science. Political sociology / Science po-
        litique. Sociologie politique   4900-4907

19200. Political doctrine. Political thought / Doctrine po-
        litique. Pensée politique . . . .
19210. Political philosophy / Philosophie politique.   4908-4910
19220. Power / Pouvoir   4911-4921
19230. Communism. Nationalism / Communisme. Nationalisme . .   4922-4956
19240. Democracy. Dictatorship / Démocratie. Dictature . . .   4957-4966

19300. Constitution. State / Constitution. État
19310. Political system / Système politique.   4967-4994
19320. Human rights / Droits de l'homme.   4995-5003
19330. Political representation / Représentation politique
19340. Government / Gouvernement   5004-5019
19350. Parliament / Parlement.   5020-5021
19360. Judiciary power / Pouvoir judiciaire.   5023-5030

19400. Public administration / Administration publique
19410. Civil service. Technocracy / Fonction publique. Techno-
        cratie.   5031-5049

19420.	Central government. Local government / Administration centrale. Administration locale	5050-5060
19500.	Political party. Pressure group / Parti politique. Groupe de pression	
19510.	Party system. Political party / Système de parti. Par ti politique.	5061-5083
19520.	Pressure group. Protest movement / Groupe de pression. Mouvement contestatiare	5084-5098
19530.	Political majority. Political opposition / Majorité politique. Opposition politique	5099-5100
19600.	Political behaviour. Elections. Politics / Comportement politique. Élections. Politique	
19610.	Political leader. Political society / Leader politique. Société politique.	5102-5111
19620.	Political attitude. Political participation / Attitude politique. Participation politique	5112-5165
19630.	Elections	5166-5192
19640.	Politics / Politique.	5193-5204
19700.	Army. Military sociology / Armée. Sociologie militaire	5205-5233
19800.	International relations / Relations internationales	
19810.	International law. International organization / Droit international. Organisation internationale.	5234-5240
19820.	Foreign policy. Sovereignty / Politique étrangère. Souveraineté	5241-5245
19830.	International cooperation. War / Coopération internationale. Guerre	5246-5255
19840.	Disarmament. Weapon / Désarmement. Arme	5256-5259
20.	Social problem. Social service. social work Problème social. Service social. Travail social	
20100.	Social problem / Problème social	
20110.	Applied sociology / Sociologie appliquée.	5260-5269
20120.	Social pathology / Pathologie sociale	5270-5282
20130.	Disaster / Catastrophe.	5283-5287
20140.	Poverty / Pauvreté.	5288-5303
20150.	Alcoholism. Drug / Alcoolisme. Stupéfiants.	5304-5351
20160.	Crime. Delinquency / Délit. Délinquance	5352-5472
20200.	Social policy / Politique sociale	
20210.	Social action. Social planning / Action sociale. Planification sociale.	5473-5524
20220.	Social security / Sécurité sociale.	5525-5535
20300.	Social work / Travail social.	5536-5556
20400.	Social service / Service social	
20410.	Medical sociology. Medicine / Sociologie médicale. Médecine.	5557-5575
20420.	Public health / Santé publique.	5576-5621
20430.	Hospital / Hôpital.	5622-5639
20440.	Social worker / Travailleur social.	5640-5681

10100. SOCIAL SCIENCES. SOCIOLOGY
        SCIENCES SOCIALES. SOCIOLOGIE

1   ÁGH, A. "A társadalomtudományok közvetlen termelöerövé válása" (The
     transformation of the social sciences into immediate means of pro-
     duction), *Szociológia* 6(1), 1977 : 11-27.
2   BARKER, Paul. (ed.). *The social sciences today*. Totowa, N.J., Little-
     field, Adams, 77, viii-118 p.
3   Bibl.XXVI-2. BENN, S. I.; MORTIMORE, G. W. (eds.). *Rationality in
     the social sciences: contributions to the philosophy and methodo-
     logy of the social sciences.* CR: Eileen O'KEEFE, *Brit. J. Sociol.*
     28(4), dec 77 : 512; J. David LEWIS, *Contemp. Sociol. (Washington)*
     6(2), mar ·77 : 254
4   BENTON, Ted. *Philosophical foundations of the three sociologies.* Lon-
     don, Routledge and Kegan Paul, 77, x-225 p.
5   BOGUE, Allan G.; CLUBB, Jerome M. "History and the social sciences:
     progress and prospects", *Amer. behav. Scientist* 21(1), nov 77 :
     165-312.
6   BORONEV, A. O.; BOVKALOV, A. F. "Konkretno-istoričeskij podhod v so-
     cial'nom issledovanii" (A concrete historical approach towards so-
     cial studies), in: *Rol' naučnyh principov i ponjatij v social'nom
     issledovanii.* Leningrad, 1976 : 11-20.
7   CLOWERS, Myles L.; MORI, Steven H. *Understanding sociology through
     fiction.* New York, McGraw-Hill Book Co., 77, x-223 p.
8   COSER, Lewis A.; LARSEN, Otto N. (eds.). *The uses of controversy in
     sociology.* New York, Free Press, 76, xvi-398 p.
9   CRAWFORD, Elisabeth; ROKKAN, Stein (eds.). *Sociological praxis. Cur-
     rent roles and settings.* London, Sage, 76, 175 p.
10   EISENSTADT, Shmuel Noah. "La tradizione sociologica: origini, confini,
     modelli di innovazione e crisi" (Sociological tradition: origins,
     borders, innovation models and crisis), *Rass. ital. Sociol.* 17(4),
     oct-dec 76 : 499-539.
11   EISENSTADT, Shmuel Noah; CURELARU, M. *The form of sociology: paradigms
     and crises.* New York, Wiley, 76, xvii-386 p.
12   ELLIS, Lee *et al.* "The decline and fall of sociology, 1975-2000",
     Amer. Sociologist 12(2), mai 77 : 56-80.
13   FRANKEL, Charles (ed.). *Controversies and decisions: the social scien-
     ces and public policy.* New York, Russell Sage Foundation, 76, x-
     299 p.
14   FREIDHEIM, Elizabeth A. *Sociological theory in research and practice.*
     Cambridge, Mass., Schenkman Publishing Co., 76, xii-325 p.
15   FRISS, Istvan. "A társadalomtudományok növekvö jelentöségéröl" (The
     growing importance of social sciences), *Társad. Szle* (2), 1977 :
     50-63.
16   FUJINO, Ryûichi; SENGOKU, Yoshiro; MARUYAMA, Sadami (eds.). *Gendai
     seikatsu to shakaigakuteki shiten* (The modern life and sociological
     perspective). Fukuoka, Ashi shobô, 77, 284 p.
17   HANSEN, Donald A. *An invitation to critical sociology. Involvement,
     criticism, exploration.* New York, Free Press, 76, xiv-258 p.

18   HAWTHORN, Geoffrey. *Enlightenment and despair: a history of sociolo-gy*. Cambridge, Eng.-New York, Cambridge University Press, 76, 295 p. CR: Mark MITCHELL, *Brit. J. Sociol.* 28(2), jun 77 : 253-254.

19   HOSOYA, Takashi; YAGI, Tadashi (eds.). *Gendai eno shakaigaku-teki sekken* (Sociological approaches to modern times). Kyoto, Akademia Shuppankai, 77, 240 p.

20   IKEDA, Giyû. "Shakaigaku no genten" (The original problem of modern sociology), *Tetsugaku Ronshû* 23, 1977 : 54-59.

21   INOSHITA, Osamu. "Kôdô sho-kagaku ni okeru ecological perspective ni tsuiteno ichikosatsu" (On the meaning of socio-ecological perspec-rives in the behavioral sciences), *Keiô-gijuku-daigaku daigakuin Shakaigaku Kenkyuka Kiyo*. 17, 1977 : 75-83.

22   Bibl.XXVI-9. LEPSIUS, M. Rainer. *Zwischenbilanz der Soziologie* (In-termediary balancesheet of sociology). CR: Heine von ALEMANN, *Kölner Z. Soziol. u. soz.-Psychol.* 29(3), sep 77 : 583-584.

23   LOURAU, René. *Le gai savoir des sociologues*. Paris, Union générale d'éditions, 77, 312 p.

24   MacRAE, Duncan Jr. *The social function of social science*. New Haven, Yale University Press, 76, xv-352 p.

25   MERTON, Robert King. *Sociological ambivalence and other essays*. New York, Free Press, 76, xii-287 p.

26   MITCHELL, G. Duncan. "The popularization of sociology and the received tradition", *Brit. J. Sociol.* 28(3), sep 77 : 394-400.

27   MOREL, Julius. *Enthüllung der Ordnung: Grundbegriffe und Funktionen der Soziologie* (Revelation of the order: basic concepts and func-tions of sociology). Innsbruck-Wien-München, Tyrolia Verlag, 77, 168 p.

28   NIANG, Mamdou. "Le rôle des sciences sociales dans le développement", *B. Inst. fondam. Afr. noire* 38(2), apr 76 : 339-350.

29   NISBET, Robert. *Sociology as an art form*. London, Heinemann, 76, 145 p. CR: Frederick R. LYNCH, *Contemp. Sociol. (Washington)* 6(3), mai 77 : 354-356.

30   PACH, Zsigmond Pál. "A társadalomtudományok gyakorlati funkciójáról" (Practical function of the social sciences), *Magyar Tud.* (3), 1977 : 161-163.

31   ROSE, Peter Isaac; GLAZER, Myron; GLAZER, Penina Migdal. *Sociology: inquiring into society*. San Francisco, Canfield Press, 77, 605-22 22 p.

32   RYBICKI, Pawel. "The role of social sciences in interpreting social reality", *Polish sociol. B.* 37(1), 1977 : 5-17.

33   SAITO, Shôji. *Shakaigaku-shi kôgi* (Lectures on history of sociology). Tokyo, Shin-Hyôron, 77, 338 p.

34   SICARD, Gerald L.; WEINBERGER, Philip. *Sociology of our times*. Glen-view, Ill., Scott, Foresman, 77, xii-329 p.

35   SZCZEPAŃSKI, Jan. "The social sciences and solutions to practical problems", *Polish sociol. B.* 1976 : 9-21.

36   "Szociológia helyzetéről és feladatáról (A)" (On the situation and tasks of sociology), *Szociológia* 6(1), 1977 : 1-10.

37   SZTOMPKA, Piotr. "On the peculiarities of social sciences once again", *Polish sociol. B.* 1976 : 33-56.

38   THERBORN, Göran. *Science, class and society: on the formation of so-ciology and historical materialism*. London, New Left Books, 76, 461 p. CR: Arto NORO, *Acta sociol.* 20(1), 1977 : 97-105; M. S. HICKOX, *Brit. J. Sociol.* 18(3), sep 77 : 404-405.

39   THURLINGS, J. M. G. *De wetenschap der samenleving. Een drieluik van de sociologie* (The science of society. A triptych of sociology). Alphen aan de Rijn, Samsom, 77, 256 p.

40   TOIVIAINEN, Seppo. "Sosiologian historian käsittämisestä" (On under-standing the history of sociology), *Sosiologia* 14(5-6), 1976 : 191-200.

41   VARMA, Baidya Nath (ed.). *The new social sciences*. Westport, Conn., Greenwood Press, 76, xi-276 p.

42   WARREN,Carol A. B. *Sociology, change and continuity*. Homewood, Ill.,
      Dorsey Press, 77, xiii-427 p.
43   WEINSTEIN, Deena; WEINSTEIN, Michael A. *Choosing sociology: an intro-
      duction to critical inquiry*. New York, McKay, 76, viii-182 p.
44   WILLMOTT, Peter. "L'intégrité dans les sciences sociales: les retom-
      bées d'un scandale", *R. int. Sci. soc.* 29(2), 1977 : 359-362.
45   WRONG, Dennis Hume. *Skeptical sociology*. New York, Columbia Univer-
      sity Press, 76; viii-322 p.
46   ZULKE, Frank (ed.). *Through the eyes of social science*. Dubuque,
      Iowa, Kendall/Hunt Publishing Co., 76, x-261 p.

10200. RESEARCH WORKER. SOCIOLOGIST
CHERCHEUR. SOCIOLOGUE

[See also / Voir aussi: 1535, 4342, 5269]

47   BILLETER, Jean-François. "Contribution à une sociologie historique
      du mandarinat", *Actes Rech. Sci. soc.* 15, jun 77 : 3-30.
48   BOGDANOVIĆ, Marija. "Sociolog u praksi; naučnik ili podanik ?" (The
      sociologist in practice: a scientist or a technician ?), *Sociolo-
      gija* 19(4), 1977 : 641-655.
49   Bibl.XXV-21. BRYANT, Christopher G. A. *Sociology in action: a criti-
      que of selected conceptions of the social role of the sociologist*.
      CR: Stephen MENNELL, *Brit. J. Sociol.* 28(1), mar 77 : 103-104.
50   BÜCKER-GÄRTNER, Heinz *et al. Sozialwissenschaftler in der offentli-
      chen Verwaltung: eine Beitrag Berufsfeldanalyse von Soziologen* (So-
      cial scientists in government: a contribution to the analysis of
      sociologists' working field). Frankfurt-am-Main-New York, Campus-
      Verlag, 77, 200 p.
51   DMITRIEV, A. V. "Dejatel'nost' sociologa na predprijatii" (The socio-
      logist's activity in an enterprise), in: *Aktual'nye problemy soci-
      al'nogo planirovanija*. Irkutsk, 1975 : 252-257.
52   FISCH, Rudolf. "Aspekte sozialer Orientierung bei Wissenschaftlern.
      Untersucht am Beispiel des Fachs Psychologie" (Aspects of scien-
      tists' social orientation. Studies by the example of the subject's
      psychology), *Kölner Z. Soziol. u. soz.-Psychol.* 29(1), mar 77 :
      137-156.
53   GIESEN, Bernard. "Die Soziologen vor der Praxis: ratlos ? Ein kriti-
      sches Nachwordt. zum 18. Deutschen Soziologentag in Bielefeld" (So-
      ciologists in front of practice: helpless ? A critical epilogue to
      the 18th German sociologists' day in Bielefeld), *Soz. Welt* 27(4),
      1976 : 504-516.
54   LOURAU, René. *Sociologue à plein temps: analyse institutionnelle et
      pédagogie: Aire-sur-l'Adour, Nanterre, Poitiers*. Paris, Épi, 76,
      284 p.
55   MARTINDALE, Don. "Sociology's student and teachers", *Int. J. contemp.
      Sociol.* 13(3-4), jul-oct 76 : 183-208.
56   MILLER, J. S. "New directions for the sociologist of education: theory,
      policymaking and professionalization", *R. int. Sociol. (Madrid)*
      34(18-19-20), apr-dec 76 : 91-107.
57   MORRISSEY, Joseph P.; STEADMAN, Henry J. "'Practice and perish ?':
      some overlooked career contingencies for sociologists in nonacadem-
      ic settings", *Amer. Sociologist* 12(4), nov 77 : 154-162.
58   RONAYNE, J. "Anti-science and the politicisation of scientists",
      Austral. New Zealand J. Sociol. 12(3), oct 76 : 219-227.
59   SIMONEN, Leila; SUHONEN, Pertti. "Mitä sosiologit tekevät ?" (What
      sociologists do ?), *Sosiologia* 14(5-6), 1976 : 200-207.
60   "Szociológia-oktatás és szociologusképzés helyzetéről és tovabbfej-
      lesztésének feladatairól (A)" (On the contemporary situation and
      further development of training sociologist and teaching sociology),
      Szociológia 6(2), 1977 : 234-239.
61   VARGA, K. "Tudományos pályafutás, tudományos hatékonyság" (Scientist's

career, scientific efficiency), *Gazdaság és Jogtud.* 10(1-2),
1976 : 215-230.

62 VERHAEGEN, B. "L'engagement du chercheur en sciences sociales", *R. zaïr. Psychol. Pédag.* 4(1), 1975 : 21-32.

63 WOLFELSPERGER, Alain. "De la contestation de l'orthodoxie à la tentation du sociologisme chez les économistes", *R. franç. Sociol.* 18(3), jul-sep 77 : 397-434. Suivi d'une discussion par Xavier GREFFE et l'auteur: 435-438.

10300. ORGANIZATION OF RESEARCH. RESEARCH POLICY ORGANISATION DE LA RECHERCHE. POLITIQUE DE LA RE-CHERCHE

10310. Current research.
Recherche en cours
[See also / Voir aussi: 317, 1230, 1584, 3323, 3328, 3332, 3340, 3359, 3538, 3549, 3656, 3851, 3984, 3992]

64 ATAL, Yogesh. *Social sciences: the Indian scene.* New Delhi, Abhinav Publications, 76, xiv-281 p.

65 BON ESPASANDIN, Mario. "La sociología uruguaya a la muerte del Dr. Isaac Ganón" (Uruguayan sociology at the Dr. Isaac Ganon's death), *R. int. Sociol. (Madrid)* 36(21), 1977 : 159-170.

66 BONJEAN, Charles M.; SCHNEIDER, Louis; LINEBERRY, Robert L. (eds.). *Social science in America: the first two hundred years.* Austin-London, University of Texas Press, 76, 22 p.

67 BUSLOV, K. P. "Obščestvennye nauki v Belorussii" (Social sciences in Belorussia), *Vestn. Akad. Nauk SSSR* 48(4), apr 77 : 54-63.

68 CACCAMO DE LUCA, Rita. "Tematiche e prospettive dell'analisi sociale in Polonia" (Topics and prospects of the social analysis in Poland), *Crit. sociol. (Roma)* 38, 1976 : 185-207.

69 CIECHOCIŃSKA, Maria. "Socjologia regionalna w Polsce na tle świato-wym. Przegląd problematyki" (Regional sociology in Poland as viewed from the international standpoint. A review of problems), *Stud. socjol.* 63(4), 1976 : 197-226.

70 DEUTSCH, Steven. "Sociological currents in contemporary Yugoslavia", *Amer. Sociologist* 12(3), aug 77 : 141-147.

71 FENNER VARGAS, R. "Balance crítico de la sociología latinoamericana" (Critical balance-sheet of Latin-American sociology), *Estud. polít.* 2(6), apr-jun 76 : 39-53.

72 FERNANDES, Florestan. *A sociologia numa era de revolução social* (Sociology in a social revolution period). 2nd rev. ed. Rio de Janeiro, Zahar Editores, 76, 377 p. *[Brazil.]*

73 FUKUTAKE, Tadashi (ed.). *Sengo Nihon no nôson chosa* (Rural social surveys in Japan). Tokyo, Tokyo-daigaku Shuppankai, 77, xii-540 p.

74 HANÁK, Tibor. *Die marxistische Philosophie und Soziologie in Ungarn* (The Marxist philosophy and sociology in Hungary), Stuttgart, Enke, 76, vii-231 p.

75 HAYASE, Toshio. "Senzen no nihon shakaigaku" (Japanese sociology before the war), *Shakaigaku Hyôron* 110, 1977 : 2-28.

76 HOGEWEG-DE-HAART, H. "Social science research and policy", *Higher Educ. Res. Netherlands* 20(3), 1976 : 38-44. *[Netherlands.]*

77 HONG, Sung Chick. "A profile on social science research in Korea", *Korea Wld Aff.* 1(1), 1977 : 87-100.

78 KOCH, Ursula. "Soziologie in der DDR zwischen 1971 und 1976" (Sociology in the GDR between 1971 and 1976), *Soz. Welt* 28(1-2), 1977 : 239-254.

79 KOYANO, S. "Sociological studies in Japan: prewar, postwar and contemporary states", *Sociol. contemp.* 24(1), 1976 : 1-208.

80 KULCSÁR, Kálmán. "Marxistická sociologie v maďarské společnosti sedm-desátých let" (Marxist sociology in the Hungarian society of the seventies), *Sociol. Čas.* 13(4), 1977 : 372-382.

81   LEIMU, Heikki. "Sociology in Finland – notes on main traditions in
      sociology and on some of their exponent with an emphasis on the
      period since 1945", *Z. Soziol.* 6(2), apr 77 : 222-249.
82   LIPSET, S. M. "Orientations de la sociologie américaine", *Dialogue
      (Washington)* 7(2), 1976 : 3-18.
83   MORRISSEY, M. "Imperial designs: a sociology of knowledge; study of
      British and American dominance in the development of Caribbean
      social science", *Latin Amer. Perspect.* 3(4), 1976 : 97-116.
84   NÚÑEZ ENCABO, Manuel. *Manuel Sales y Ferré: los orígenes de la so-
      ciología en España* (Manuel Sales y Ferré: origins of sociology in
      Spain). Madrid, Editorial Cuadernos para el Diálogo, 76, 397 p.
85   OTEIZA, Enrique. "Interregional co-operation in the social sciences:
      the Latin-American experience", *IDS Bull.* 8(3), mar 77 : 13-18.
86   PODGÓRECKI, Adam. "Perspektywy rozwoju socjologii polskiej" (Pers-
      pectives of development of Polish sociology), *Stud. socjol.* 60(1),
      1976 : 287-306.
87   RABIER, Jean-Claude *et al.* "La sociologie en Finlande", *R. franç.
      Sociol.* 18(1), jan-mar 77 : 109-131.
88   ROUX, Yvonne (éd.). *Questions à la sociologie française.* Paris,
      Presses universitaires de France, 76, 280 p.
89   SANO, Makoto (ed.). *Shakaigaku kenkyû bunken yoran, 1965-1974* (Bib-
      liography of sociological research in Japan: 1965-1974). Tokyo,
      Nichigai Asoshietsu, 77, 406 p.
90   "Scandinavian sociology", *Sociol. contemp.* 25(1), 1977 : 165 p.
91   SHALIN, Dmitri N. "On current trends in Soviet sociology", *Crit.
      sociol. (Roma)* 38, 1976 : 173-184.
92   "Social science in America. The first two hundred years", *Soc. Sci.
      Quart.* 57(1), jun 76 : 1-207.
93   STERNBERG, David Joel. *Radical sociology: an introduction to American
      behavioral science.* Hicksville, N.Y., Exposition Press, 77, xiii-
      338 p.
94   TORRANCE, John. "The emergence of sociology in Austria, 1885-1935",
      Archiv. europ. Sociol. 17(2), 1976 : 185-219.
95   WISAN, Gail; MUREN, Gary. "Gouldner's *Coming crisis of Western so-
      ciology:* description or symptom of the crisis ?", *Int. J. contemp.
      Sociol.* 13(1-2), jan-apr 76 : 59-72.
96   YAMAMOTO, Shizuo. "Sengo Nishi-Doitsu shakaigaku no kenkyû dôkô"
      (Trends of West German sociology), *Shakaigaku Hyôron* 27(3), 1977 :
      70-81.
97   YOUNG, T. R. "Research in the land of Oz: the yellow brick road to
      success in American sociology", *Sociol. Inquiry* 47(1), 1977 : 65-
      71.
98   ZASLAVSKY, V. "Sociology in the contemporary Soviet Union", *Soc. Res.*
      44(2), 1977 : 330-353.

10320. Applied research. Interdisciplinary research
       Recherche appliquée. Recherche interdisciplinaire

[See also / Voir aussi: 587]

99   CLARK, Alfred W. (ed.). *Experimenting with organizational life: the
      action research approach.* New York, Plenum Press, 76, x-259 p. CR:
      Andrew H. VAN DE VEN, *Amer. J. Sociol.* 82(6), mai 77 : 1410-1412.
100   CUNNINGHAM, Bart. "Action research", *Hum. Relat.* 29(3), mai 76 :
      215-238.
101   "Facettes de l'interdisciplinarité", *R. int. Sci. soc.* 29(4), 1977 :
      617-724. [Propos d'ensemble sur la recherche interdisciplinaire
      en sciences sociales, et champs d'étude: recherches sur la paix,
      religions, développement, culture.]
102   SHERWOOD, F. P. "Action research: some perspectives for learning or-
      ganizations", *Adm. and Soc.* 8(2), aug 76 : 175-192.

10330. Research centre
Centre de recherche

[See also / Voir aussi: 1589]

103   BOOLSEN, Merete Watt; SØRENSEN, Ole Aagaard. *Samfundsvidenskabelige
institutioner og publikationer i Danmark: undersøgelse foretaget
for Statens samfundsvidenskabelige forskningsråd* (Social science
institutions and publications in Denmark: study made for the
State Council of Social Science Research). København, Forsknings-
sekretariatet, 76, 105-135 p.

104   DOBROVOL'SKAJA, N. P. *et al. Sociologičeskie centry SSSR (1976g.)*
(USSR sociological centres, 1976). Moskva, 76, 209 p.

105   GESER, Hans. "Forschungsinfrastruktur und Organisationsform von
Universitätsinstituten" (Infrastructure of research and the organization of university institutes), *Z. Soziol.* 6(2), apr 77 :
150-173.

106   NEGROTTI, Massimo; PADOVANI, Giuseppe. "La diffusione degli istitu-
ti di ricerca sociale: un'indagine sul *World Index* dell'UNESCO"
(The distribution of social research centres: a study on the
UNESCO's *World Index*), *Rass. ital. Sociol.* 18(3), jul-sep 77 :
415-429.

107   "Osnovnye napravlenija dejatel'nosti Instituta sociologičeskih issledovanij" (Essential directions of the activity of the Institute
for sociological research), *Vestn. Akad. Nauk SSSR* 47(11), nov
76 : 12-19.

10340. Organization of research. Research policy
Organisation de la recherche. Politique de la recherche

108   Bibl.XXVI-80. BERNSTEIN, Ilene N.; FREEMAN, Howard E. *Academic and
entrepreneurial research: the consequences of diversity in federal evaluation studies.* CR: Thomas D. COOK, *Amer. J. Sociol.* 82(6),
mai 77 : 1375-1377.

109   BLAZKO, N. I. "Central'nyj organ upravlenija-ob'ekt sociologičeskogo issledovanija" (Central organ of management is an object of
sociological research), in: *Voprosy teorii i metodov sociologičeskih issledovanij. II.* Moskva, 1976 : 109-116.

110   CRAWFORD, Elisabeth. "Setting priorities for research in the social
sciences: the role of national social science councils and similar bodies", *Soc. Sci. Inform.* 16(3-4), 1977 : 431-450.

111   EVERSLEY, David Edward Charles; MOODY, Mary; BARRITT, Adrian. *The
growth of planning research since the early 1960s.* London, Social Science Research Council, 76, 87 p. *[Social sciences research in the United Kingdom.]*

112   FEDOSEEV, P. N. "XXV s'ezd KPSS i zadaci naučnyh issledovanij u
oblasti obščestvennyh nauk" (The XXVth Congress of PCUS and objectives of scientifical research in the field of social sciences), *Nov. novejš. Ist.* 20(1), jan-feb 77 : 3-24.

113   GAIN, Nicole. "Le CNRS face à la nouvelle politique de la recherche:
stratégie gouvernementale et résistance des structures", *R. Dr.
publ. Sci. polit.* 93(3), mai-jun 77 : 587-654.

114   HOVEDKOMITEEN FOR NORSK FORSKNING. *Forskningsbehov og forskningspo-
litik* (Research needs and research politics). Oslo, Komiteen, 76,
115 p. *[Norway.]*

115   JOHNSTON, Ron. "Finalization: a new start for science policy ?",
Soc. Sci. Inform. 15(2-3), 1976 : 331-336.

116   KULCSÁR, K. "Unesco and the social sciences", *New Hungar. Quart.*
18(67), 1977 : 132-139.

117   LEVINE, Herbert M.; OWEN, Dolores B. *An American guide to British
social science resources.* Metuchen, N.J., Scarecrow Press, 76,
xii-281 p.

118   RIST, R. C. "Federal funding and social science research: the emer-
        gent transformation", *Hum. Org.* 35(3), 1976 : 263-268.
119   SYMES, John M. D. "Policy and maturity in science", *Soc. Sci. In-
        form.* 15(2-3), 1976 : 337-347.

        10350. Research equipment
               Équipement de recherche

120   ADAMS, J. Mack; HADEN, Douglas H. *Social effects of computer use
        and misuse.* New York, Wiley, 76, x-326 p.
121   ANDERSON, Ronald; COOVER, Edwin R. "Academic social research organ-
        izations and computerization", *Soc. Sci. Inform.* 15(4-5), 1976 :
        741-754.
122   GIRARD, Thierry; TYSTRAM, Jean-Paul. *Informatique pour les sciences
        sociales.* Paris, Presses universitaires de France, 76, 181 p.
123   HY, Ronn J. *Using the computer in the social sciences: a nontech-
        nical approach.* New York, Elsevier, 77, xiii-155 p.
124   SILVA DE MEJÍA, Luz María. *Realidades y fantasías de las computa-
        doras: un punto de vista sociológico* (Realities and fictions of
        computers: a sociological point of view). México, Universidad
        Nacional Autónoma de México, 76, 144 p.
125   "Using computers in the social sciences", *Amer. behav. Scientist*
        20(3), jan-feb 77 : 293-427.
126   WEIZENBAUM, Joseph. *Computer power and human reason:from judgment
        to calculation.* San Francisco, W. H. Freeman, 76, 300 p. CR: John
        F. CROWTHER, *Contemp. Sociol. (Washington)* 6(1), jan 77 : 125-
        126.

        10360. Sociological association
               Association de sociologie

127   DAVIS, Ann E. "North Central Sociological Association: members pers-
        pectives - past and present", *Sociol. Focus* 10(3), aug 77 : 275-
        285.
128   PEASE, John; HETRICK, Barbara. "Association for whom ? The regionals
        and the American Sociological Association", *Amer. Sociologist*
        12(1), feb 77 : 42-47.
129   YONEZAWA, Kazuhiko. "Doitsu shakaigaku seiritsushiron josetsu -
        Gakkai setsuritsu to Max Weber" (A study of the German Associa-
        tion for sociology - its foundation and Max Weber), *Tetsugaku
        Nenpô* 36, 1977 : 101-128.

        10400. CONGRESS. MEETING
               CONGRÈS. RÉUNION

        [See also / Voir aussi: 6, 427, 1613, 1708, 2846, 2867, 3820]

130   "18. Deutsche Soziologentag. Bielefeld, 29 sept-1 okt. 1976 (Der)"
        (The 18th German sociologists' day. Bielefeld, 29th Sept.-1st
        Oct. 1976), *Kölner Z. Soziol. u. soz.-Psychol.* 29(1), mar 77 :
        160-194.

        10500. DOCUMENT. INFORMATION PROCESSING
               DOCUMENT. TRAITEMENT DE L'INFORMATION

        10510. Documentation

131   BATSCHA, Robert. *The effectiveness of dissemination methods for
        social and economic development research.* Washington, OECD Pub-
        lications Center, 76, 201 p.
132   HURTUBISE, Rolland. *Informatique et information: la conception des
        systèmes d'information, les banques de données.* Paris, Éditions
        d'organisation, 76, xx-357 p.
133,   McHALE, John. *The changing information environment.* Boulder, Colo.,
        Westview Press; London, Elek, 75, 117 p.

134   PFEFFER, Jeffrey; LEBLEBICI, Huseyin. "Information technology and
       organizational structure", *Pacific sociol. R.* 20(2), apr 77 :
       241-261.

135   RUSSO, F. "Les fichiers", *Études (Paris)* jan 77 : 45-58.

136   WESSEL, Andrew E. *The social use of information - ownership and
       access.* New York, Wiley, 76, xviii-244 p.

10520. Document analysis. Reference book
Analyse documentaire. Ouvrage de référence

*[See also / Voir aussi: 89, 90, 271, 739, 991, 1612, 1637, 1705,
2112, 2128, 2193, 2206, 3344, 3456, 3467, 3470, 3727, 3935, 4002,
4012, 4160, 4170, 4806, 5082, 5087, 5135, 5357, 5530]*

137   ALLEN, Patricia R. B.; RUTLEDGE, Albert J. "An annotated bibliogra-
       phy of mostly obscure articles on human territorial behavior",
       Soc. Sci. Inform. 15(2-3), 1976 : 403-413.

138   "Analyses bibliographiques et notes critiques", *Année sociol.* 26,
       1975 : 203-580. *[Bibliographie d'ouvrages classée par domaines:
       sociologie générale et sociologie politique, sociologie de la
       connaissance, sociologie et psychologie, morphologie sociale,
       systèmes sociaux et civilisations, sociologie religieuse, socio-
       logie juridique et morale, sociologie du travail.]*

139   ARMAND, Monique; AYMARD, Marguerite. "Travaux et publications parus
       en français en 1974 sur la Russie et l'URSS. Domaine des sciences
       sociales", *C. Monde russe sov.* 17(2-3), apr-sep 76 : 335-400.

140   COCO, Nicola; SCARAMUCCI, Fabio. *Bibliografia criminologica italia-
       na, 1970-1975* (Bibliography concerning the Italian criminology,
       1970-1975). Roma, Nuove Dimensioni, 76, 104 p.

141   McCLELLAND, Robyn. *Bibliography - social networks, social planning,
       and community needs.* Monticello, Ill., Council of Planning Libra-
       rians, 76, 52 p.

142   "Raboty po sociologii, opublikovannye v 1975-1976 gg." (Works in
       sociology published in the 1975-1976 years), *Sociol. Issled.
       (Moskva)* (3), 1976 : 234-235. *[USSR.]*

143   ROTH, Guenther. "Max Weber: a bibliographical essay", *Z. Soziol.*
       6(1), jan 77 : 91-118.

144   SUŁEK, Antoni. "Bibliography of sociological works written by Po-
       lish authors and published in languages other than Polish", *Po-
       lish sociol. B.* 1976 : 139-202.

10530. Documentation centre
Centre de documentation

145   LEBEL, M. "Considérations sur le rôle des bibliothèques dans le
       développement culturel du Québec", *Trav. Communicat. Acad. Sci.
       mor. jur. (Montréal)* (2), 1974 : 174-186.

146   PEREZ ALVAREZ-OSORIO, J. R. "El sistema de centros de documenta-
       ción en España" (The system of documentation centres in Spain),
       Bol. Docum. Fondo Invest. econ. soc. 8(4), oct-dec 76 : 708-716.

147   PREIBISHA. "Polish libraries: their structure, organization and
       aims", *Int. Library R.* 9(2), apr 77 : 161-174.

148   TERWINDT, Jan Gaston Frederik. *De openbare bibliotheken in Noord-
       Brabant in sociografisch perspectief* (Public libraries in North-
       Brabant within a sociographical perspective). Tilburg, Katho-
       lieke Hogeschool, 76, viii-117 p.

149   WILSON, Pauline. *A community elite and the public library; the uses
       of information in leadership.* Westport, Conn., Greenwood Press,
       77, xiv-172 p.

10550. Terminology
Terminologie

150 DEMARCHI, Franco; ELLENA, Aldo. *Dizionario di soziologia* (Dictionary of sociology). Cinisello Balsamo, Edizioni paoline, 76,
1436 p.

151 DUMONT, Louis. "Terminology and prestations revisited", *Contrib.
Ind. Sociol.* 9(2), jul-dec 75 : 197-215.

152 HAMASHIMA, Akira; TAKEUCHI, Ikurô; ICHIKAWA, Akihiro (eds.).
Shakaigâku shojiten (Small dictionary of sociology). Tokyo,
Yûhikaku, 77, 543 p.

153 HARTFIEL, Günter. *Wörterbuch der Soziologie* (Dictionary of sociology). Stuttgart, Kröner, 76, vi-715 p.

154 KURIAN, George Thomas. *Historical and cultural dictionary of India.*
Metuchen, N.J., Scarecrow Press, 76, xxii-307 p.

155 LABOVITZ, Sanford. *An introduction into sociological concepts.* New
York, Wiley, 77, xii-244 p.

156 POVIÑA, Alfredo. *Diccionario de sociología a través de los sociólo-
gos* (Dictionary of sociology through sociologists). Buenos Aires,
Editorial Astrea de A y R. Depalma, 76, 1283 p.

157 READING, Hugo F. *A dictionary of the social sciences.* London, Sociologia, 76, 231 p.

158 VALK, J. M. M. DE *et al.* *Encyclopedie van de sociologie* (Encyclopedia of sociology). Amsterdam, Elsevier, 77, 301 p.

10560. Biography
Biographie

[See also / Voir aussi: 420]

159 ABE, Minoru. "Charles Booth no 'hinkon chosa' ni tsuite" (Charles
booth and the First Survey of London), *Kumamoto-tandai Ronshû*
56, 1977 : 1-36.

160 AYALA, Francisco J.; PROUT, Timothy. "In memoriam Theodosius Dobzhansky, 1900-1975", *Soc. Biology* 23(2), 1976 : 103-107.

161 BOGDANOVIĆ, Marija. "Paul Lazarsfeld", *Sociologija* 18(3-4), 1976 :
433-436.

162 DULCZEWSKI, Zygmut. "Eileen Markley Znaniecka, 1886-1976", *Przegl.
socjol.* 29, 1977 : 405-407.

163 ELLEMERS, J. E. "In memoriam Prof. A. N. J. den Hollander, 1906-
1976", *Sociol. Gids* 23(4), jul-aug 76 : 198-200.

164 "George Davy, 1883-1976", *Année sociol.* 26, 1975 : 5.

165 "Georges Friedmann, 1902-1977", *R. franç. Sociol.* 18(3), jul-sep
77 : 367.

166 HULA,Erich. "Arnold Brecht, 1884-1977", *Soc. Res.* 44(4), 1977 : 601.

167 "In memoriam: Herman D. Bloch, 1914-1976", *Amer. J. Econ. Sociol.*
36(3), jul 77 : 334-336.

168 "In memoriam Jean-Charles Bonenfant". *Rech. sociogr.* 18(1), jan-apr
77 : 7.

169 "In memoriam Vojislavu Đuricu", *Sociol. sela* 14(3-4), 1976 : 5-11.

170 LISSNER, Will. "In memoriam Geoffrey W. Esty", *Amer. J. Econ. Sociol.* 36(4), oct 77 : 400.

171 LISSNER, Will. "In memoriam: Meredith B. Givens", *Amer. J. Econ.
Sociol.* 36(1), jan 77 : 64.

172 LISSNER, Will. "On the passing of Paul F. Lazarsfeld", *Amer. J.
Econ. Sociol.* 36(2), apr 77 : 169-170.

173 LÓPEZ TEJEIRO, L. "In memoriam Mariano González Rothvoss", *R. int.
Sociol. (Madrid)* 34(18-19-20), apr-dec 76 : 129-134.

174 MARCHELLO, Giuseppe. "Ricordo di Felice Battaglia" (In memoriam
Felice Battaglia), *Sociologia (Roma)* 11(1), jan-apr 77 : 3-8.

175 MARKIEWICZ-LAGNEAU, Janina. "L'autobiographie en Pologne ou de
l'usage social d'une technique sociologique", *R. franç. Sociol.*
17(4), oct-dec 76 : 591-613.

176   NAKANO, Takashi. *Kôjutsu no seikatsushi* (A narrative life history). Tokyo, Ochanomizu shobô, 77, 289 p.

177   SAAL, C. D. "In memoriam Prof. Dr. P. J. Bouman, 1902-1977", *Sociol. Gids* 23(3), mai-jun 77 : 162-166.

178   SZALAI, Sándor. "Paul Lazarsfeld, 1901-1976", *Szociológia* 6(2), 1977 : 190-192.

179   VAN HOUTEN, B. C. "In memoriam P. J. Bouman", *Mens en Mij* 52(2), 1977 : 121-126.

180   WATSON, Roy E. L. "Donald W. Ball, 1934-1976", *Canad. J. Sociol.* 2(1), 1977 : v-vii.

10570. Article. Periodical
Article. Périodique

181   COMITÉ INTERNATIONAL POUR L'INFORMATION ET LA DOCUMENTATION EN SCIENCES SOCIALES. *Liste mondiale des périodiques specialisés dans les sciences sociales / World list of social science periodicals.* 4e éd. rev. augm. Paris, Unesco, 76, 382 p.

182   MACKIE, Marlene. "Professional women's collegial relations and productivity: female sociologists' journal publications, 1967 and 1973", *Sociol. soc. Res.* 61(3), apr 77 : 277-293.

183   MAISON DES SCIENCES DE L'HOMME. Service d'Échange d'Informations Scientifiques. "Additifs à la *Liste mondiale des périodiques spécialisés dans les sciences sociales*", *R. int. Sci. soc.* 29(1), 1977 : 201-211; 29(3), 1977 : 541-552.

184   McGEE, Reece; HEDLEY, R. Alain; TAVEGGIA, Thomas C. "The college market in commercial publishing: the case of the convertible ?", *Amer. Sociologist* 12(3), aug 77 : 102-129.

185   ORLIK, Jacek. "Polish sociological periodicals", *Polish sociol. B.* 35(3), 1976 : 65-68; 37(1), 1977 : 81-84.

10590. Textbook. Thesis
Manuel. Thèse

[See also / Voir aussi: 2206]

186   BENSMAN, Joseph; ROSENBERG, Bernard. *An introduction to sociology: mass, class, and bureaucracy.* New York, Praeger, 76, x-534 p.

187   CERRONI, Umberto. *Introduzione alla scienza sociale* (Introduction to the social sciences). Roma, Editori riuniti, 76, 271 p.

188   CONGALTON, Athol Alexander; DANIEL, Ann E. *The individual in the making: an introduction to sociology.* Sydney-New York, J. Wiley, 76, x-285 p.

189   CURRAN, Joseph Jr. *Introductory sociology; a basic self-instructional guide.* New York, McGraw-Hill, 77, vi-218 p.

190   GIESEN, Bernard; SCHMID, Michael. *Basale Soziologie. Wissenschaftstheorie.* München, Goldmann, 76, 272 p.

191   GOODE, William Josiah. *Principles of sociology.* New York, McGraw-Hill, 77, xv-543 p.

192   GUIDICINI, Paolo. *Manuale di sociologia urbana e rurale* (Textbook of urban and rural sociology). Milano, F. Angeli, 77, 269 p.

193   KISS, Gábor; WITJES, Claus Winfried. *Steckbrief der Soziologie* (Handbook of sociology). Heidelberg, Quelle und Meyer, 76, 242 p.

194   McGEE, Reece *et al.* (eds.). *Sociology; an introduction.* Hinsdale, Ill., Dryden Press, 77, xii-647 p.

195   OSIPOV, G. V. (ed.). *Rabočij kniga sociologa* (The working book of the sociologist). Moskva, Nauka, 76, 511 p.

196   SAITÔ, Shôji. *Gendai Shakaigaku* (Contemporary sociology). Tokyo, Fukumura Shuppan, 77, 278 p.

197   SAITÔ, Shôji. *Gendai Shakaigaku kôgi* (Lectures on contemporary sociology). Tokyo, Shin-Hyôron, 77, 272 p.

II. METHODOLOGY. THEORY
MÉTHODOLOGIE. THÉORIE

11100. EPISTEMOLOGY. RESEARCH METHOD. THEORY
ÉPISTEMOLOGIE. MÉTHODE DE RECHERCHE. THÉORIE

11110. Philosophy. Theory
Philosophie. Théorie

[See also / Voir aussi: 80, 143, 339, 361, 608, 756, 766, 1034, 1221, 1280, 1713, 1796, 1802, 2326, 2636, 3361, 4237, 4244, 4786, 4900, 5084]

198   ADRAANSENS, H. P. M. *Talcott Parsons en het conceptuele dilemma* (Talcott Parsons and the conceptual dilemma). Deventer, Van Loghum Slaterus, 76, 272 p.

199   ATOJI, Yoshio. "Fututsu no Weber-zô-Jaspers to Rickert" (Two images on Max Weber - K. Jaspers and H. Rickert), *Gendai Shisô* 5(4), 1977 : 220-235.

200   AVVAKUMOV, Ju. G. "Razvitie leninskogo učenija o protivorečijah v uslovijah socializma" (Development of Leninist teaching on contradictions under conditions of socialism), in: *Social'no-političeskie problemy razvitogo socialističeskogo obščestva*. Barnaul, 1976 : 39-55.

201   AXELROD, C. D. "Toward an appreciation of Simmel's fragmentary style", *Sociol. Quart.* 18(2), 1977 : 185-196.

202   Bibl.XXVI-207. BADCOCK, C. R. *Lévi-Strauss: structuralism and sociological theory*. CR: C. E. ASHWORTH, *Brit. J. Sociol.* 28(1), mar 77 : 110-111.

203   BADER, Veit-Michael *et al. Einführung in die Gesellschaftstheorie: Gesellschaft, Wirtschaft und Staat bei Marx und Weber* (Introduction to the sociological theory: society, economy and State in Marx and Weber). Frankfurt-am-Main-New York, Campus-Verlag, 76.

204   BERG, Lars-Erik. *Människans födelse: en socialpsykologisk diskussion kring G. H. Mead och J. Piaget* (The birth of man: a socio-psychological discussion about G. H. Mead and J. Piaget). Göteborg, Korpen, 76, 182 p.

205   BERGNER, Dieter; MOCEK, Reinhard. *Bürgerliche Gesellschaftstheorien: Studien zu den weltanschaulichen Grundlagen und ideologischen Funktionen bürgerlicher Gesellschaftsauffassungen* (Bourgeois sociological theories: studies on the ideological bases and functions of the bourgeois conceptions of society). Berlin, Deutscher Verlag der Wissenschaften, 76, 295 p.

206   BERNSTEIN, Richard J. *The restructuring of social and political theory*. New York, Harcourt Brace Jovanovich, 76, xxiv-286 p.

207   BEZERRA, Felte. *Problemas de antropologia: do estruturalismo de Lévi-Strauss* (Problems of anthropology: Lévi-Strauss' structuralism). Rio de Janeiro, Gráfica Ouvidor, 76, 239 p.

208   BOGART, Robert W. "A critique of existential sociology", *Soc. Res.* 44(3), 1977 : 502-528.

209   BOGART, Robert W. "An assessment of Max Weber's contribution to the debate over positivism", *Sociol. Anal. Theory* 7(1), feb 77 : 1-19.

210   Bibl.XXVI-214. BOTTOMORE, Tom. *Marxist sociology*. CR: Michael BURAWOY, *Contemp. Sociol. (Washington)* 6(1), jan 77 : 9-17.

211   BOURRICAUD, François. *L'individualisme institutionnel: essai sur la sociologie de Talcott Parsons*. Paris, Presses universitaires de France, 77, 350 p.

212   BOUVERESSE, Jacques. "L'animal cérémoniel: Wittgenstein et l'anthropologie", *Actes Rech. Sci. soc.* 16, sep 77 : 43-54.

213   BUCHIGNANI, Norman I. "The Weberian thesis in India", *Archiv. Sci. soc. Relig.* 42(2), jul-dec 76 : 17-33.

214   BUCK, Günther. "La structure de l'expérience herméneutique et le problème de la tradition", *Soc. Sci. Inform.* 15(2-3), 1976 : 239-268.

215   Bibl.XXVI-219. BURGER, Thomas. *Max Weber's theory of concept formation. History, laws, and ideal types*. CR: Guenther ROTH, *Amer. J. Sociol.* 82(6), mai 77 : 1350-1355; Johannes WEISS, *Kölner Z. Soziol. u. soz.-Psychol.* 29(2), jun·77 : 381-387.

216   BURGER, Thomas. "Talcott Parsons, the problem of order in society and the program of an analytical sociology", *Amer. J. Sociol.* 83(2), sep 77 : 320-334. With a comment by Talcott PARSONS: 335-339.

217   BUTTS, Stewart. "Parsons' interpretation of Weber: a methodological analysis", *Sociol. Anal. Theory* 7(3), oct 77 : 227-240.

218   CAHNMAN, Werner J. "Tönnies, Durkheim and Weber", *Soc. Sci. Inform.* 15(6), 1976 : 839-853.

219   CALLINICOS, Alex. *Althusser's marxism*. London, Pluto Press; New York, E. P. Dutton, 76, 133 p.

220   CARACCIOLO, Alberto; SCALIA, Gianni. *La citta futura: saggi figura e il pensiero di Antonio Gramsci* (The city in the future: essays on Antonio Gramsci's personality and thought). Milano, Feltrinelli, 76, 203 p.

221   CARVETH, Donald L. "The disembodied dialectic: a psychoanalytic critique of sociological relativism", *Theory and Soc.* 4(1), 1977 : 73-102.

222   CAVAZUTTI, Tommaso. "A epistemologia de Louis Althusser",(Louis Althusser's epistemology), *Vozes* 71(5), jun-jul 77 : 48-53.

223   CAVAZUTTI, Tommaso. "O pensamento científico de Marx" (Marx's scientific thought), *Vozes* 71(6), aug 77 : 41-52.

224   CONSTANTINESCU, Virgil. *Sistemul sociologic al lui Dumitru Drăghicescu* (Dimitrie Drăgicescu's sociological system). București, Editura Academiei Republicii Socialiste România, 76, 305 p.

225   COPPENS, Peter Roche DE. *Ideal man in classical sociology. The views of Comte, Durkheim, Pareto and Weber*. University Park, Pa., Penssylvania State University Press, 76, viii-174 p.

226   CRAIB, Ian. *Existentialism and sociology: a study of Jean-Paul Sartre*. New York, Cambridge University Press, 76, ix-242 p. CR: Mark POSTER, *Amer. J. Sociol.* 83(3), nov 77 : 775-777; Dean MacCANNELL, *Contemp. Sociol. (Washington)* 6(4), jul 77 : 493-494.

227   DANIELJAN, M. S. "Ob opredelnii ponjatija v obščesociologičeskoj teorii" (On the determination of a concept in general sociological theory), in: *Metodologičeskie problemy analiza jazyka*. Erevan, 1976 : 155-174.

228   DESANTI, Jean-Toussaint. *Introduction à la phénoménologie*. Paris, Gallimard, 76, 157 p.

229   DODGE, Peter. "Ideological preconceptions and sociology: reflections on the contemporary significance of Hendrik de Man", *Sociol. int. (Berlin)* 12(1-2), 1974 : 5-23.

230   DUBIEL, Helmut. "Soziologisches Lesen theoretischer Texte" (Sociological reading of theoretical texts), *Kölner Z. Soziol. u. soz.-Psychol.* 29(2), jun 77 : 201-232.

231   ELIAESON, Sven. "Some recent interpretations of Max Weber's methodology", *Sociol. Anal. Theory* 7(1), feb 77 : 21-71.

232   "Erdei Ferenc publikálatlan írásai, levelei" (Ferenc Erdei's unpublished works and letters", *Forrás* 9(2), 1977 : 3-33.

233   FACTOR, Regis A.; TURNER, Stephen P. "The critique of positivist
       social science in Leo Strauss and Jürgen Habermas", *Sociol.
       Anal. Theory* 7(3), oct 77 : 185-206.
234   FINLEY, M. I. "The ancient city: from Fustel de Coulanges to Max
       Weber and beyond", *Comp. Stud. Soc. Hist.* 19(3), jul 77 : 305-
       327.
235   FORMÁNEK, Miloslav. "Jednota marxismu leninismu a odpovědnost so-
       ciologie" (Unity of marxism-leninism and responsibility of so-
       ciology), *Sociol. Čas.* 13(4), 1977 : 337-351.
236   FURTER, Pierre. "Ernst Bloch et ses interprètes", *Archiv. Sci. soc.
       Relig.* 44(1), jul-sep 77 : 8-23.
237   GINER, Salvador; SALCEDO, Juan. "The ideological practice of Nicos
       Poulantzas", *Archiv. europ. Sociol.* 17(2), 1976 : 344-365.
238   GLASER, Barney G.; STRAUSS, Anselm L. *De ontwikkeling van gefundeer-
       de theorie* (The development of fundamental theories). Alphen aan
       de Rijn, Samson, 76, 268 p.
239   GONOS, George. "'Situation' versus 'frame': the 'interactionist'
       and the 'structuralist' analyses of everyday life", *Amer. sociol.
       R.* 42(6), dec 77 : 854-867.
240   GORMAN, Robert A. *The dual vision, Alfred Schutz and the myth of
       phenomenological social science*. London, Routledge and Kegan
       Paul, 77, 234 p.
241   GREISMAN, H. C. "'Disenchantment of the world': romanticism, aes-
       thetics and sociological theory", *Brit. J. Sociol.* 27(4), dec
       76 : 496-507.
242   GULIAN, C. I. *Marxism şi structuralism* (Marxism and structuralism).
       Bucureşti, Editura Politică, 76, 259 p.
243   HABERMAS, Jürgen. *Zur Rekonstruktion des historischen Materialis-
       mus* (The reconstruction of the historical materialism). Frankfurt-
       am-Main, Suhrkamp, 76, 346 p.
244   HAFERKAMP, Hans. "Handlungstheorie und abweichendes Verhalten. Ein
       Beitrag zum Theorievergleich in der Soziologie" (Theory of action
       and deviant behaviour. A contribution to the theory comparison in
       sociology), *Soz. Welt* 28(3), 1977 : 257-270.
245   HALL, J. A. "Sincerity and politics: 'existentialists' vs. Goffman
       and Proust", *Sociol. R.* 25(3), aug 77 : 535-550.
246   HAMASHIMA, Hikaru. "Genshôgaku-teki shakaigaku no shiza kozo" (The
       perspective of phenomenological sociology), *Bungaku Kenkyûka
       Kiyô* (3), 1977 : 35-51.
247   "Hannah Arendt", *Soc. Res.* 44(1), 1977 : 3-190.
248   HARDING, Neil. "Lenin and his critics: some problems of interpre-
       tation", *Archiv. europ. Sociol.* 17(2), 1976 : 366-383.
249   HIBBERD, Dominico. "A sociological cure for shellshock: Dr. Brock
       and Wilfred Owen", *Sociol. R.* 25(2), mai 77 : 377-386.
250   HINDESS, Barry. *Philosophy and methodology in the social sciences*.
       Hassocks, Sussex, Harvester Press, 77, viii-258 p.
251   Bibl.XXVI-319. HIRST, Paul Q. *Durkheim, Bernard and epistemology*.
       CR: Terry JOHNSON, *Brit. J. Sociol.* 28(4), dec 77 : 509-510.
252   HOEBEN-KRUISINGA, Renée. "Sociologische theorievorming door middel
       van historisch onderzoek; een voorbeeld" (Sociological theory
       formation through historical research: an example), *Mens en Mij*
       52(3), 1977 : 342-351.
253   HOUGHTON, John. "Ideology: a Marxian-Paretean critique of the We-
       berian orientation", *J. polit. milit. Sociol.* 5(2), 1977 : 155-
       168.
254   HUGHES, John A. "Wittgenstein and social science: some matters of
       interpretation", *Sociol. R.* 25(4), nov 77 : 721-741.
255   "In honour of Talcott Parsons", *Ind. J. soc. Res.* 16(3), dec 75 :
       395-479; 17(1), apr 76 : 1-70.
256   JANIČIJEVIČ, M. "Karl Marx i Max Weber danas" (Karl Marx and Max
       Weber today), *Sociologija* 18(3-4), 1976 : 359-369.

257   JENKS, Craig. "T. H. Green, the Oxford philosophy of duty and the
       English middle class", *Brit. J. Sociol.* 28(4), dec 77 : 481-497.
258   JONES, Robert Alun. "On understanding a sociological classic",
       Amer. J. Sociol. 83(2), sep 77 : 279-319.
259   JORAVSKY, David. "The mechanical spirit: the Stalinist marriage of
       Pavlov to Marx", *Theory and Soc.* 4(4), 1977 : 457-477.
260   KAHL, Joachim. *Positivismus als Konservatismus. Eine philosophische
       Studie zu Struktur und Funktion der positivistischen Denkweise
       am Beispiel Ernst Topitsch* (Positivism as conservatism. A philos-
       ophical study of structure and function of the positivist thought
       on the example of Ernst Topitsch). Köln, Pahl-Rugenstein, 76, iv-
       301 p.
261   Bibl.XXVI-243. KARADY, Victor. *Durkheim: textes.* CR: Edward A.
       TIRYAKIAN, *Contemp. Sociol. (Washington)* 6(1), jan 77 : 17-19.
262   KATZ, Fred. E. *Structuralism in sociology: an approach to know-
       ledge.* Albany, State University of New York Press, 76, 218 p.
       CR: Ino ROSSI, *Contemp. Sociol. (Washington)* 6(2), mar 77 : 255-
       256.
263   KEANE, John. "On turning theory against itself: review article on
       Habermas", *Theory and Soc.* 4(4), 1977 : 561-572.
264   KHOZINE, Grigori. "Illusions et réalité: études futurologiques
       d'Alvin Toffler", *Sci. soc. (Moscou)* (4), 1977 : 174-184.
265   KINLOCH, Graham Charles. *Sociological theory: its development and
       major paradigms.* New York, McGraw-Hill, 77, x-319 p.
266   KIRN, M. "Behavioralism, post-behavioralism, and the philosophy of
       science: two houses, one plague", *R. Polit.* 39(1), jan 77 : 82-
       102. *[USA.]*
267   KŌTŌ, Yōsuke. *Weber shakairiron no kenkyu* (Max Weber's social
       theory). Tokyo, Tokyo-daigaku Shuppankai, 77, vi-234 p.
268   KUBIK, Włodzimierz. "Socjologia Herberta Spencera" (The sociology
       of Herbert Spencer), *Przegl. socjol.* 29, 1977 : 339-348.
269   KURZWEIL, Edith. "Michel Foucault: end in the era of man", *Theory
       and Soc.* 4(3), 1977 : 395-420.
270   LACROIX, Bernard. "Dynamique sociale et subordination relative du
       politique selon Émile Durkheim", *C. int. Sociol.* 24(62), jan-jun
       77 : 27-44.
271   LAPOINTE, François; LAPOINTE, Claire C. *Claude Lévi-Strauss and
       his critics; an international bibliography of criticism, 1950-
       1976.* New York, Garland Publishers, 77, vi-219 p.
272   LAWRENCE, Peter A. *Georg Simmel: sociologist and European.* London,
       Nelson, 76, xii-275 p.
273   LEVINE, Donald N. "Simmel at a distance: on the history and system-
       atics of the sociology of the stranger", *Sociol. Focus* 10(1),
       jan 77 : 15-29.
274   LOUBSER, Jan C. *et al.* (eds.). *Explorations in general theory in
       social science.* 2 vols. New York, Free Press, 76, xvi-909-xv p.
275   LUHMANN, Niklas *et al. Teorie en praxis in de sociologiese teorie*
       (Theory and practice in the sociological theory). Amsterdam,
       Amsterdams Sociologies Tijdschrift, 76, 110 p.
276   LYNCH, Frederick R. "Social theory and the progressive era",
       Theory and Soc. 4(2), 1977 : 159-210.
277   MADSEN, Allan. *Samfundsvidenskabelig teori som reproduktion eller
       kritik: om de teoretiske arbejde* (Sociological theory as repro-
       duction or criticism: about the theoretical work). København,
       Akademisk Forlag, 76, 124 p.
278   MAGGIONI, Guido. *La sociologia di Malthus: classi e istituzioni
       alle origini della società industriale* (Malthus' sociology:
       classes and institutions in the origins of the industrial so-
       ciety). Milano, A. Giuffrè, 76, xv-375 p.
279   MAGHAMI, Farhat Ghaem. "Sociological positivism: a critique", *Int.
       J. contemp. Sociol.* 13(1-2), jan-apr 76 : 43-58.

280   MANSILLA, H. C. F. "La controversia metodologica entre positivis-
       mo y dialéctica" (Methodological controversy between positivism
       and dialectics), *R. int. Sociol. (Madrid)* 35(24), 1977 : 485-
       494.

281   MARTÍN SERRANO, Manuel. *Comte, el padre negado: orígenes de la
       deshumanización en las ciencias sociales* (Comte, the denied
       father: origins of dishumanization in the social sciences).
       Madrid, Akal, 76, 101 p.

282   McCLUNG LEE, Alfred. "Ernest Becker's lost science of man: on the
       fate of humanism in social science", *Crit. sociol. (Roma)* 37,
       1976 : 89-93.

283   McINTOSH, Donald. "Habermas on Freud", *Soc. Res.* 44(3), 1977 :
       562-598.

284   McKNIGHT, S. A. "Voegelin on the modern intellectual and political
       crises", *Sociol. Anal. (San Antonio)* 37(3), 1976 : 265-271.

285   MEYER, A. G. "The *Aufhebung* of Marxism", *Soc. Res.* 43(2), 1976 :
       199-219.

286   MOHAN, Raj P. "Sociological career of Carle C. Zimmerman", *Int. J.
       contemp. Sociol.* 13(3-4), jul-oct 76 : 173-182.

287   MOKRZYCKI, Edmund. "The methodological dogma of naturalism", *Po-
       lish sociol. B.* 1976 : 57-73.

288   MRKŠIĆ, Danilo. "Mertonove teorija srednjeg obima" (Merton's
       middle-range theories), *Sociologija* 19(4), 1977 : 657-677.

289   NATSUKARI, Yasuo. "Durkheim shakaigaku-shiso no keisei to tenkai"
       (The formation and development of sociological thought of Emile
       Durkheim), *Shakaigaku Ronso* 18, 1977 : 50-63.

291   NIELSEN, Joyce McCarl; SHELBY, Bo; HAAS, J. Eugene. "Sociological
       carrying capacity and the last settler syndrome", *Pacific so-
       ciol. R.* 20(4), oct 77 : 568-581.

292   NYE, William P. "George Herbert Mead and the paradox of prediction",
       Sociol. Anal. (San Antonio) 38(2), 1977 : 91-105.

293   OVERINGTON, Michael A. "Kenneth Burke and the method of dramatism",
       Theory and Soc. 5(1), 1977 : 131-156.

294   OVERINGTON, Michael A. "Kenneth Burke as social theorist", *Sociol.
       Inquiry* 47(2), 1977 : 133-141.

295   PARYS, Jan. "Metodologiczne znaczenie historyzmu w socjologii"
       (The methodological significance of historicism in sociology),
       Przegl. socjol. 29, 1977 : 295-306.

296   PELLICANI, Luciano. "La sociologia di Ortega y Gasset" (Ortega y
       Gasset's sociology), *Riv. Sociol.* 14(1-3), jan-dec 76 : 61-106.

297   PFAFF, Martin (ed.). *Frontiers in social thought: essays in honor
       of Kenneth E. Boulding.* New York, American Elsevier; Amsterdam-
       Oxford, North-Holland, 76, viii-386 p.

298   PODGÓRECKI, Adam. "Socjologia krytyczna (Szkoła Frankfurcka)" (Cri-
       tical sociology: Frankfurt School), *Przegl. socjol.* 29, 1977 :
       327-337.

299   POLLINI, Gabriele. "Osservazione critiche circa l'attualità della
       teoria sociologica parsonsiana" (Critical observations concern-
       ing the current reality of Parsons' sociological theory), *Studi
       Sociol.* 15(2-3), apr-sep 77 : 173-200.

300   PORTIS, Edward B. "Society and political choice: social science in
       Emile Durkheim's sociology", *Sociol. Anal. Theory* 7(2), jun 77 :
       117-133.

301   POSTER, Mark. *Existential Marxism in postwar France: from Sartre
       to Althusser.* Princeton, Princeton University Press, 76, 415 p.
       CR: Barry SMART, *Brit. J. Sociol.* 28(2), jun 77 : 259-260.

302   RAPAPORT, Elizabeth. "Anarchism and authority in Marx's socialist
       politics", *Archiv. europ. Sociol.* 17(2), 1976 : 333-343.

303   RENZINA, I. M. "K probleme ēdinstva teorii i metoda v sociologi-
       českom issledovanii" (On the problem of the unity of theory and
       method in sociological research), in: *Voprosy teorii i metodov
       sociologičeskih issledovanij. II.* Moskva, 1976 : 3-12.

304   RUBIO CARRACEDO, José. *Lévi-Strauss. Estructuralismo y ciencias humanas* (Lévi-Strauss. Structuralism and sciences of man). Madrid, Ediciones Istmo, 76, 368 p.

305   RUST, Holger. "Dialektik als Gestaltungsprinzip gesellschaftswissenschaftlicher Argumentationen" (Dialectics as a principle of the formation of sociological argumentation), *Kölner Z. Soziol. u. soz.-Psychol.* 29(3), sep 77 : 543-560.

306   "Sciences sociales avant et après Jean Piaget (Les)", *R. europ. Sci. soc. C. Vilfredo Pareto* 14(38-39), 1976 : 525 p.

307   SCIMECCA, Joseph A. *The sociological theory of C. Wright Mills.* Post Washington, N.Y., Kennikat Press, 77, 148 p.

308   SEGATTI, Paolo. "Una critica dialettica alla teoria di Parsons. Appunti sul libro *Economia e stato sociale* di C. Di Leonardis" (A dialectical criticism of the Parsons' theory. Comments on C. di Leonardis' book *Economia e stato sociale*), *Rass. ital. Sociol.* 18(3), jul-sep 77 : 453-464.

309   SEGRE, Landro. "Max Weber, our contemporary", *Int. J. contemp. Sociol.* 13(1-2), jan-apr 76 : 73-78.

310   SEIDMAN, Steven; GRUPER, Michael. "Capitalism and individuation in the sociology of Max Weber", *Brit. J. Sociol.* 28(1), dec 77 : 498-508.

311   SERRAVEZZA, Antonio. *Musica, filosofia e società in Th. W. Adorno* (Music, philosophy and society in Th. W. Adorno's thought). Bari, Dedalo libri, 76, 255 p.

312   SMELSER, Neil J.; WARNER, R. Stephen. *Sociological theory. Historical and formal.* Morristown, General Learning Press, 76, xvi-284 284 p.

313   SPENCER, Martin E. "History and sociology: an analysis of Weber's 'The City'", *Sociology (London)* 11(3), sep 77 : 507-525.

314   SRZEDNICKI, Jan T. J. *Elements of social and political philosophy.* The Hague, Martinus Nijhoff, 76, 189 p.

315   STEINWORTH, Ulrich. "Böhm-Bawerks Marx-Kritik. Eine Kritik ihrer Engelsschen Voraussetzungen" (Böhm-Bawerk's critique of Marx. A critique of its Engelsian presupposition), *Z. Soziol.* 6(3), jul 77 : 302-314.

316   Bibl.XXVI-300. STRASSER, Hermann. *The normative structure of sociology: conservative and emancipatory themes in social thought.* CR: Phil BACON, *Brit. J. Sociol.* 28(2), jun 77 : 255.

317   SZACKI, Jerzy. "Szkoła chicagowska i teorie Roberta E. Parka" (The Chicago School and Ezra Park's theory), *Stud. socjol.* 60(1), 1976 : 5-32.

318   SZTOMPKA, Piotr. "Strategy of theory-construction in sociology", *Polish sociol. B.* 36(4), 1976 : 5-16.

319   TAKAHASHI, Yoshinori. "Weber to sôgo-sayôha - Weber no seijiron o megutte" (Max Weber and symbolic interactionism - an interpretation of Weber's political writings), *Soshioroji* 70, 1977 : 55-77.

320   TAKUBA, Ê. A. "Metodologičeskie funkcii marksistko-leninskoj sociologii" (Methodological functions of the marxist-leninist sociology), *Probl. Filos.* 40, 1977 : 3-8.

321   TANGE, Ryûchi. "Shakaigaku ni okeru kotoba to joshiki - Durkheim 'hohoron' no sai-kentô" (Sociological language and commen sense knowledge - Durkheim's "règles" reconsidered), *Shakaigaku Nenshi* 18, 1977 : 99-119.

322   TROŠKINA, V. P. "Ogjust Kont i sovremennaja buržuaznaja sociologija" (A. Comte and contemporary bourgeois sociology), in: *Voprosy teorii i metodov sociologičeskih issledovanij. II.* Moskva, 1976 : 32-38.

323   TURNER, Bryan S. "The structuralist critique of Weber's sociology", *Brit. J. Sociol.* 28(1), mar 77 : 1-16.

324   TURNER, Jonathan H. "Building social theory: some questions about Homan's strategy", *Pacific sociol. R.* 20(2), apr 77 : 203-220.

325   URDANOZ, T. "Teoría y praxis en el pensamiento filosófico y en las nuevas teologías socio-políticas" (Theory and practice in the philosophical thought and the new socio-political theologies), *R. Estud. polít.* 211, jan-feb 77 : 171-210.

326   VACCARINI, Italo. "Dinamica e crisi della teoria marxista contemporanea" (Dynamics and crisis of the contemporary Marxist theory), *Studi Sociol.* 15(2-3), apr-sep 77 : 137-172.

327   VÁMOS, Vera. "Freudizmus és marxismuz" (Freudism and marxism), *Bpesti Müsz. Egy. Marx.-Lenin. Közlem.* (2), 1976 : 241-251.

328   VERGATI, Stefania. "Louis Wirth e la scuola di sociologia di Chicago" (Louis Wirth and the Chicago School of sociology), *Crit. sociol. (Roma)* 38, 1976 : 164-172.

329   VERICAT, José. *Ciencia, historia y sociedad. Problemas de metodología e ideología de las ciencias sociales a partir de Max Weber* (Science, history and society. Problems of methodology and ideology of the social sciences from Max Weber). Madrid, Editorial Istmo, 76, 285 p.

330   VOGEL, Ulrike. "Das Werk Max Webers im Spiegel aktueller soziologischer Forschung" (Max Weber's work in the mirror of today's sociological research), *Kölner Z. Soziol. u. soz.-Psychol.* 29(2), jun 77 : 343-354.

331   WANDERSMAN, Abraham; POPPEN, Paul J.; RICKS, David F. (eds.). *Humanism and behaviorism: dialogue and growth.* Oxford-New York, Pergamon Press, 76, xx-436 p.

332   ZDRAVOMYSLOV, A. G. "Maks Veber i ego 'preodolenie' marksizma" (Max Weber and its "victory" on marxism), *Sociol. Issled. (Moskva)* (4), 1976 : 158-173.

11120. Epistemology. Explanation. Understanding
Épistémologie. Explication. Compréhension

11121.

[See also / Voir aussi: 222, 1803, 1827, 1869]

333   BRAND, Arie. *Toetsing en kritiek. Over objectiviteit en kennisbelang bij Weber en Habermas* (Testing and criticism. On objectivity and value of knowledge in Weber and Habermas). Meppel, Boom, 76, 353 p.

334   BRAND, Arie. "Truth and Habermas' paradigm of a critical social science", *Sociol. Gids* 23(5), sep-oct 76 : 285-295.

335   CULEA, Haralambie. *Cunoaşterea sociologică: consideratii gnoseologico-epistemologice* (Sociological knowledge: gnoseological and epistemological considerations). Bucureşti, Editura Academiei Republicii Socialiste România, 76, 196 p.

336   JONES, Kenneth. "Some epistemological considerations of paradigm shifts: basic steps towards a formulated model of alteration", *Sociol. R.* 25(2), mai 77 : 253-271.

337   KICIŃSKI, Krzysztof. "The problem of truth and generality of propositions in the social sciences", *Polish sociol. B.* 1976 : 75-88.

338   KRAMM, L. "Der Wahrscheinlichkeitscharakter der Sozialwissenschaften" (The verisimilitude of the social sciences), *Z. Polit.* 23(4), dec 76 : 348-365.

339   MARTIN SERRANO, Manuel. "Epistemología de la dialectica social" (Epistemology of social dialectics), *R. esp. Opin. públ.* 47, 1977 : 57-76.

340   MONOD-HERZEN, Gabriel E. *L'analyse dimensionnelle et l'épistémologie.* Paris, Maloine, 76, 129 p.

341   MOULOUD, Noël. *L'analyse et le sens: essai sur les préalables sémantiques de la logique et de l'épistémologie.* Paris, Payot, 76, 335 p.

342   MULLIGAN, Glenn; LEDERMAN, Bobbie. "Social facts and rules of practice", *Amer. Sociol.* 83(3), nov 77 : 538-550.

343   REYES, Román. "Objetividad en la investigación social" (Objecti-
       vity in social research), *RS Cuad. Realidad soc.* 13, mar 77 :
       107-110.
344   SCIVOLETTO, Angelo. "Da Emile Durkheim ad Alfred Schutz: momenti
       dell'epistemologia sociale" (From Emile Durkheim to Alfred
       Schutz: stages of social epistemology), *Studi Sociol.* 15(4),
       oct-dec 77 : 301-337.
345   THOMSEN, Hand Jørgen. "Epistemology and the problem of materialism",
       Acta sociol. 20(4), 1977 : 349-368.
346   TSUTSUI, Kiyotada."'Shakai-kagaku ni okeru kyakkansei' no gendan-
       kai - Weber to Popper" (Objectivity in the social sciences to-
       day - Max Weber and Karl R. Popper), *Shisô* 641, 1977 : 34-51.

       11122.
       [See also / Voir aussi: 214, 341, 448, 501, 514, 2845]

347   BALL, Richard A. "Equitable evaluation through investigative so-
       ciology", *Sociol. Focus* 10(1), jan 77 : 1-14.
348   BESTUŽEV-LADA, I. B. "Problema optimuma v social'no-ėkologičeskom
       prognozirovanii" (Problems of optimum in socioecological forecast-
       ing), in: *Vzaimosvjaz' nauk pri rešeni ėkologičeskih problem.*
       Moskva, Obninsk, 1976 : 81-85.
349   BESTUŽEV-LADA, I. V. "Prognozirovanie v sociologičeskih issledo-
       vanijah (metodologičeskie problemy)" (Forecast in sociological
       research. Methodological problems), *Sociol. Issled. (Moskva)*
       (1), 1977 : 47-58.
350   BURGER, Thomas. "Max Weber, interpretive sociology, and the sense
       of historical science: a positivistic conception of Verstehen",
       Sociol. Quart. 18(2), 1977 : 165-176.
351   BURGER, Thomas. "Max Weber's interpretive sociology, the under-
       standing of actions and motives, and a Weberian view of man",
       Sociol. Inquiry 47(2), 1977 : 127-132.
352   DALLMAYR, Fred R.; McCARTHY, Thomas A. (eds.). *Understanding and
       social inquiry.* Notre Dame, Ind., University of Notre Dame Press,
       77, vi-365 p.
353   DECOUFLE, André-Clément. *Sociologie de la prévision: l'exemple de
       la prospective sociale en France.* Paris, Presses universitaires
       de France, 76, 144 p.
354   GIDDENS, Anthrony. *New rules of sociological method: a positive
       critique of interpretative sociologies.* New York, Basic Books,
       76, 192 p. CR: Barry HINDESS, *Brit. J. Sociol.* 28(4), dec 77 :
       510-512.
355   JADOV, V. A. "O dialektike sootnošenija istoričeskogo i struktur-
       no-funkcional'nogo podhodov k ob'jasneniju social'nyh javlenij"
       (On dialectics of correlation between historical and structural-
       functional approaches to social events explanation), *Probl.
       Dialektiki* (6), 1976 : 116-121.
356   KOTO, Yôsuke. "Weber to imi no shakaigaku-teki haaku" (On the me-
       thod of understanding of Weber), *Osaka-daigaku Ningen kagakubu
       Kiyo* (3), 1977 : 247-284.
357   NOWAK, Stefan. *Understanding and prediction: essays in the methodo-
       logy of social and behavioral theories.* Dordrecht-Boston, R.
       Reidel Publishing Co., 76, xix-482 p.
358   PAWŁOWSKI, Zbigniew. "Alternative predictions and their properties",
       in: SZANIAWSKI, Klemens (ed.). *Problems of formalization in the
       social sciences.* Wrocław-Warszawa-Kraków-Gdańsk, Zakład Narodowy
       Imienia Ossolińskich Wydawnictwo, 1977 : 113-126.
359   ROGERS, Tommy W. "The generational principle in social explanation",
       R. int. Sociol. (Madrid) 34(17), jan-mar 76 : 187-197.
360   ROSS, Lee *et al.* "Social explanation and social expectation: effects
       of real and hypothetical explanations on subjective likelihood",
       J. Person. soc. Psychol. 35(11), nov 77 : 817-829.

361   RYCHTAŘIK, Karel. "Dialektika faktů a verifikace soudů" (Dialectics of facts and verification of statements), *Sociol. Čas.* 13(2), 1977 : 137-144.

362   SHIMODA, Naoharu. "Shakaigakuteki rikai to setsumei no shiten: 'Setsumei kagaku' toshiteno shakaigaku no tachiba kara" (Sociological understanding and explanation from the standpoint of an "explanatory science"), *Gendai Shakaigaku* 4(1), 1977 : 93-119.

363   SHIMODA, Naoharu. "Shakaigakuteki setsumei no hohoronteki shomondai" (Methodological problems of sociological explanation), *Oyo-shakaigaku Kenkyu* 18, 1977 : 1-17.

364   TURUK, G. P. "Izmerenie suščestvennosti faktorov pri ob'jasnenii konkretnyh social'nyh javlenij" (Measurement of factors for the explanation of concrete social events), in: *Voprosy teorii i metodov sociologičeskih issledovanij. II.* Moskva, 1976 : 116-126.

365   VAN PARYJS, P. "La syntaxe de l'explication dans les sciences sociales", *Rech. sociol.* 8(2), 1977 : 211-243.

366   YOSHIDA, Hiroshi. "Max Weber no rikai shakai-gaku ni okeru nijigenron no mondaiten" (The controversial point of dualism in Max Weber's interpretive sociology), *Kanazawa daigaku Hobungakubu Ronshu Tetsugaku-hen.* 24, 1977 : 45-69.

11123.

[See also / Voir aussi: 215, 405, 2466, 2659, 5256]

367   KERVIN, John B. "An information-combining model for expectation states theory: derivation and tests", *J. math. Sociol.* 5(2), 1977 : 199-214.

368   MIRKIN, Boris G. "On a criterion of classification and analysis of structure", in: SZANIAWSKI, Klemens (ed.). *Problems of formalization in the social sciences.* Wrocław-Warszawa-Kraków-Gdansk, Zaklad Narodowy Imienia Ossolińskich Wydawnictwo, 1977 : 127-138.

369   MISURACA, Pasquale. "Sulla ricostruzione gramsciana dei concetti di struttura e superstruttura" (On Gramsci's reconstruction of the concepts of structure and superstructure), *Rass. ital. Sociol.* 18(3), jul-sep 77 : 439-451.

370   PEAY, Edmund R. "Indices for consistency in qualitative and quantitative structures", *Hum. Relat.* 30(4), 1977 : 343-361.

371   REINHARTH, Leon; WAHBA, Mahmoud A. "A test of alternative models of expectancy theory", *Hum. Relat.* 29(3), mar 76 : 257-272.

372   SAHAY, Arun. "An ideal-type of Luther's and Calvin's system of doctrines and ethics: the norm in Weber's Protestant ethic thesis", *Sociol. Anal. Theory* 7(1), feb 77 : 73-82.

373   WILLAIME, Jean-Paul. "L'opposition des infrastructures et des superstructures: une critique", *C. int. Sociol.* 23(61), jul-dec 76 : 309-327.

11124.

[See also / Voir aussi: 368, 1408]

374   CHERNS, Albert B. "Behavioral science engagements taxonomy and dynamics", *Hum. Relat.* 29(10), oct 76 : 905-910.

375   STYCZEŃ, Marek. "Two methods of taxonomy", in: SZANIAWSKI, Klemens (ed.). *Problems of formalization in the social sciences.* Wroc-ław-Warszawa-Kraków-Gdansk, Zakład Narodowy Imienia Ossolińskich Wydawnictwo, 1977 : 139-162.

11126.

[See also / Voir aussi: 429, 1962, 3255]

376   BALDAMUS, Wilhelm. *Structure of sociological inference*. London, M. Robertson; New York, Barnes and Noble, 76, x-238 p. CR: Barry HINDESS, *Brit. J. Sociol.* 28(4), dec 77 : 510-512.

377   EATON, William W. "An addendum to causal models for the study of prevalence", *Soc. Forces* 56(2), dec 77 : 703-706.

378   HUMMEL, Hans J.; ZIEGLER, Rolf (eds.). *Korrelation und Kausalität* (Correlation and causality). 3 vols. Stuttgart, F. Enke, 76, 137-610 p. CR: Mohamed CHERKAOUI, *R. franç. Sociol.* 18(2), apr-jun 77 : 339-341.

379   MAC DONALD, K. I. "Causal modelling in politics and sociology", *Quality and Quantity* 10(3), sep 76 : 189-206.

380   NISBETT, Richard E.; BELLOWS, Nancy. "Verbal reports about causal influences on social judgments: private access versus public theories", *J. Person. soc. Psychol.* 35(9), sep 77 : 613-624.

381   REEDER, Glenn D.; MESSICK, David M.; VAN AVERMAET, Eddy. "Dimensional asymmetry in attributional inference", *J. exp. soc. Psychol.* 13(1), jan 77 : 46-57.

382   TAKEMURA, Takahiko; FUNAHASHI, Kazuo. "Inga suiteiho no kentô - 4-hensû moderu o chushin to shite" (A study of the method for making causal inferences - the case of four-variable causal models), *Shigakenritsu-tankidaigaku Gakujutsu-zasshi.* 18, 1977 : 108-112.

383   WELLS, G. L. *et al.* "Anticipated discussion of interpretation eliminates actor-observer differences in the attribution of causality", *Sociometry* 40(3), 1977 : 247-253.

11127.

384   HELLWIG, Zdzisław. "On the testing of hypothesis that an *n*-dimension random variable is normal", in: SZANIAWSKI, Klemens (ed.). *Problems of formalization in the social sciences.* Wrocław-Warszawa-Kraków-Gdańsk, Zakład Narodowy Imienia Ossolińskich Wydawnictwo, 1977 : 203-215.

385   KOLARSKA, Lena. "Formalization, standardization and centralization. A critical analysis of selected research", *Polish sociol. B.* 1977 : 63-74.

386   NAGASAWA, Richard H.; BRETZEL, Philip VON. "The utility of formalization in constructing theories in sociology: an illustration", *Pacific sociol. R.* 20(2), apr 77 : 221-240.

387   SOZAŃSKI, Tadeusz. "Measures of association for nominal variables", in: SZANIAWSKI, Klemens (ed.). *Problems of formalization in the social sciences.* Wrocław-Warszawa-Kraków-Gdańsk, Zakład Narodowy Imienia Ossolińskich Wydawnictwo, 1977 : 247-255.

388   SZANIAWSKI, Klemens (ed.). *Problems of formalization in the social sciences.* Wrocław-Warszawa-Kraków-Gdańsk, Zakład Narodowy Imienia Ossolińskich Wydawnictwo, 77, 255 p.

11130. Research method. Sociological analysis
      Méthode de recherche. Analyse sociologique

11131.

[See also / Voir aussi: 131, 231, 250, 578, 3852, 5260, 5263, 5264, 5267]

389   ABGARJAN, É. "Metodika i tehnika izmerenija social'nyh javlenij" (Methods and techniques of social events measurement), *Vestn. obšč. Nauk Akad. Nauk Arm. SSR* (10), 1976 : 42-53.

390   ATOJI, Yoshio. "Simmel shakaigaku hohoron ni tsuite" (On the sociological methodology of Georg Simmel), *Soshiorojika* 2(1), 1977 : 1-25.

391   Bibl.XXVI-371. BOGDAN, Robert; TAYLOR, Steven J. *Introduction of
       qualitative research methods: a phenomenological approach to
       the social sciences.* CR: Kathy CALKINS CHARMAZ, *Contemp. Sociol.
       (Washington)* 6(1), jan 77 : 114-115.

392   CHERNS, Albert; SINCLAIR, Ruth (eds.). *Sociotechnics.* London,
       Malaby Press, 76, x-310 p.

393   ECKHARDT, Kenneth W.; ERMANN, M. David. *Social research methods:
       perspective, theory, and analysis.* New York, Random House, 77,
       xx-410 p.

394   FINSTERBUSCH, Kurt; WOLF, Charles Parker (eds.). *Methodology of
       social impact assessment.* Stroudsburg, Pa., Dowden, Hutchinston
       and Ross, 77, xii-387 p.

395   GOLDEN, M. Patricia (ed.). *The research experience.* Itasca, Ill.,
       F. E. Peacock Publishers, 76, 528 p. CR: Norman K. DENZIN,
       Contemp. Sociol. (Washington) 6(3), mai 77 : 321-322.

396   IOVČUK, M. T. "Teoretiko-metodologičeskie problemy sociologii"
       (Theoretical and methodological problems of sociology), *Sociol.
       Issled. (Moskva)* (3), 1976 : 3-11.

397   KARPIŃSKI, Jakub. "Schematy metodologiczne" (Methodological schemes),
       Stud. socjol. 60(1), 1976 : 57-60.

398   KÖPECZI, B. "A társadalomtudományi kutatás néhány kérdéséről"
       (Some questions of research in the social sciences), *Szociológia*
       5(3-4), 1976 : 389-397.

399   MALAHOV, V. A. "Vybor ob'ektov v sociologičeskom issledovanii"
       (Choice of objects in sociological research), in: *Social'nye
       problemy migracii.* Moskva, 1976 : 47-60.

400   MANHEIM, Henry L.; SIMON, Bradley A. *Sociological research: phi-
       losophy and methods.* Homewood, Ill., Dorsey Press, 77, xvii-
       391 p.

401   MARČENKO, G. I. "O ponjatii 'sociologičeskoe issledovanie'" (On
       the concept "sociological research"), in: *Voprosy teorii i
       metodov sociologičeskih issledovanij. II.* Moskva, 1976 : 12-23.

402   McTAVISH, Donald G. *et al.* "Assessing research methodology: the
       structure of professional assessments of methodology", *Sociol.
       Meth. Res.* 6(1), aug 77 : 3-44.

403   NACHMIAS, David; NACHMIAS, Chava. *Research methods in social
       sciences.* New York, St. Martin's Press, 76, 335 p. CR: S. PAD-
       mini RAVINDHRAN, *Contemp. Sociol. (Washington)* 6(3), mai 77 :
       323.

404   OPP, Karl-Dieter. *Methodologie der Sozialwissenschaften: Einfüh-
       rung in Probleme ihrer Theorienbildung* (Methodology of the
       social sciences: introduction to problems of their theory for-
       mation). Rev. enl. ed. Reinbek-bei-Hamburg, Rowohlt, 76, 429 p.

405   REX, John. "Value-relevance, scientific laws, and ideal types:
       the sociological methodology", *Canad. J. Sociol.* 2(2), 1977 :
       151-166.

406   ŠEREGI, F. È. "Metodičeskie problemy vyborki i reprezentivnosti
       sociologičeskoj praktike" (Methodological problems of choice
       and representativity in sociological practice), *Sociol. Issled.
       (Moskva)* (1), 1977 : 112-122.

407   ŠLJAPENTOH, V. È. "Mnogostupenčataja vyborka v sociologičeskih
       issledovanijah" (Multi-degree choice in sociological research),
       Sociol. Issled. (Moskva) (4), 1976 : 98-108.

408   SUSLOV, V. Ja. "Nekotorye metodologičeskie voprosy sistemnogo pod-
       hoda v sociologii" (Some methodological approach in sociology),
       in: *Materialisticeskaja dialektika i častnye nauki.* Leningrad,
       1976 : 135-145.

409   SUZUKI, Masahito. "Weber shakai-kagaku no bunseki ronri" (On Max
       Weber's methodology of social science), *Shakaigaku Hyōron* 27(4),
       1977 : 2-21.

410   WASILEWSKI, Rainer; STOSBERG, Manfred. *Aspekte soziologischer
       Forschung: Karl Gustav Specht zum 60. Geburtstag* (Aspects of

sociological research: Karl Gustav Specht on the 60th anniversary). Nürnberg, Selbstverlag, 76; 212 p.

411   WILLIAMSON, John B. *et al. The research craft: an introduction to social science methods.* Boston, Little, Brown, 77, xii-468 p.

11132.
[See also / Voir aussi: 374, 391, 1202, 2457]

412   BALFET, H. *et al. Pratiques et représentations de l'espace dans les communautés méditerranéennes.* Paris, Editions du Centre national de la recherche scientifique, 76, 155 p.

413   HAMM, Bernd. "Zur Revision der Sozialraumanalyse" (Towards a revision of social area analysis), *Z. Soziol.* 6(2), apr 77 : 174-188.

414   JULKUNEN, Raija. "A contribution to the categories of social time and the economy of time", *Acta sociol.* 20(1), 1977 : 5-24.

415   Bibl.XXVI-389. SHILS, Edward A. *Center and periphery: essays in macrosociology.* CR: Ellen R. ROBERT, *Contemp. Sociol. (Washington)* 6(2), mar 77 : 257-258.

416   ZERUBAVEL, Eviatar. "The French Republican calendar: a case study in the sociology of time", *Amer. sociol. R.* 42(6), dec 77 : 868-877.

11133.
[See also / Voir aussi: 627, 1098, 1107, 1370, 1481, 1542, 1576, 2537, 2945, 2946, 2953, 3107, 3280, 3315, 3339, 3500, 3735, 4691, 4960, 5316, 5369]

417   ANTAL, L. *A tartalomelemzés alapjai* (The foundations of content analysis). Budapest, Magvető, 76, 151 p.

418   BARDIN, Laurence. *L'analyse de contenu.* Paris, Presses universitaires de France, 77, 240 p.

419   BÉTEILLE, André. *Six essays in comparative sociology.* New York, Oxford University Press, 76, 113 p. CR: Joseph R. GUSFIELD, *Contemp. Sociol. (Washington)* 6(3), mai 77 : 357-358.

420   CHAI, Tron- R. "A content analysis of the obituary notices on Mao Tse-Tung", *Publ. Opin. Quart.* 41(4), 1977 : 475-487.

421   DeWEESE, L. Carroll III. "Computer content analysis of 'day-old' newspapers: a feasibility study", *Publ. Opin. Quart.* 41(1), 1977 : 91-94.

422   ESCOTET, M. A. "Metodología de la investigación transcultural: un esquema" (Methodology of cross-cultural research: a scheme), *R. latinoamer. Psicol.* 9(2), 1977 : 159-176.

423   FÜSTÖS, L. *Szociológiai kutatások sokváltozós matematikai statisztikai módszerei* (Methods of multivariate mathematical statistics applied in sociological research). Budapest, Sociological Research Institute of the Hungarian Academy of Sciences, 77, 220 p.

424   GENDRE, Francis. *L'analyse statistique multivariée.* Genève, Droz, 76, 294-101 p.

425   GREEN, Paul E.; CARROLL, J. Douglas. *Mathematical tools for applied multivariate analysis.* New York, Academic Press, 76, xiii-376 p.

426   HUGHES, John A. *Sociological analysis: methods of discovery.* London, Nelson, 76, xi-291 p.

427   JENNINGS, M. Kent; FARAH, Barbara G. "Continuities in comparative research strategies. The Mannheim Data Confrontation Seminar", *Sociol. Sci. Inform.* 16(2), 1977 : 231-249.

428   JOBERT, Bruno. "L'essentiel est le résidu (bis). Pour une critique de l'analyse systémique stratégique", *R. franç. Sociol.* 17(4), oct-dec 76 : 633-642. Suivi d'une réponse par Jean-Paul THOENIG: 641-642.

429   KATO, Sadao. "Shakaigakuteki kinōshugi ni okeru inga-bunseki no mondai ni tsuite" (The problem of causal analysis in sociologic-

al functionalism), *Shakaigaku Hyoron* 27(3), 1977 : 35-49.

430 LUCHSINGER, Vincent P.; DOCK, V. Thomas. *The system approach: a primer.* Dubuque, Kendall/Hunt Publishing Co., 76, vii-145 p.

431 LUTYŃSKA, Krystyna. "Kilka refleksji w zwiazku z publikacją 'Standaryzacja zmiennych socjologicznych'" (Some reflections on "The standardization of sociological variables"), *Przegl. socjol.* 29, 1977 : 307-325.

432 NIGSCH, Otto. "Theoretische und praktische Bedeutung der Mehreben- analyse" (Theoretical and practical meaning of the multivariate level analysis), *Kölner Z. Soziol. u. soz.-Psychol.* 29(3), sep 77 : 561-576.

433 REYNOLDS, H. T. "Some comments on the causal analysis of surveys with log-linear models", *Amer. J. Sociol.* 83(1), jul 77 : 127- 143.

434 RIZ, Liliana DE. "Algunos problemas teórico-metodológicos en el análisis sociológico y político de América Latina" (Some theo- retical and methodological problems in the sociological and political analysis of Latin America), *R. mexic. Sociol.* 39(1), jan-mar 77 : 157-171.

435 RONDANINI, Piero. "Riflessioni su alcuni aspetti metodologici dell'analisi per sistemi" (Considerations on some methodologi- cal aspects of systems analysis), *Studi Sociol.* 15(1), 1977 : 71-80.

436 TASSEIT, Siegfried. "Einige Bemerkungen zu Niklas Luhmanns Begriff der funktionalen Äquivalenz als Ausgangspunkt einer vergleichen- den Methode für die Sozialwissenschaften" (Some remarks on N. Luhmann's concept of functional equivalence as an introduction to a comparative method for social sciences), *Sociol. int. (Berlin)* 12(1-2), 1974 : 69-91.

11200. DATA COLLECTION. EXPERIMENT
RASSEMBLEMENT DES DONNÉES. EXPÉRIENCE

11210. Experimentation. Observation
Expérimentation. Observation

11211.

[See also / Voir aussi: 1467, 1821, 5233, 5274, 5590]

437 DOUGLAS, Jack D. *Investigative social research: individual and team field research.* Beverly Hills, Calif., Sage Publications, 76, 229 p. CR: Sherri CAVAN, *Amer. J. Sociol.* 83(3), nov 77 : 009-011.

438 FAIRBROTHER, Peter. "Experience and trust in sociological work", *Sociology (London)* 11(2), mai 77 : 359-368.

439 ter HAVE, Paul. *Sociologisch veldonderzoek* (Sociological field- work). Meppel, Boom, 77, 121 p.

440 VASIL'EV, G. G. "Specifika konkretnyh sociologičeskih issledova- nij kak sredstva sbora i pererabotki informacii v social'nom upravlenii" (The specificity of concrete sociological research as means of information choice and treatment in social planning), in: *Voprosy teorii i metodov sociologičeskih issledovanij. II.* Moskva, 1976 : 73-80.

441 ZICH, František. "K problematice charakteru empirických dat v sociologickém výzkumu" (On problems relating to the character of empirical data in sociological research), *Sociol. Čas.* 13(2), 1977 : 187-197.

11212.

[See also / Voir aussi: 2586, 3183, 3225]

442 LEVINE, John M.; RANELLI, Candice J. "Observer visibility and comfort in a surveillance situation", *Sociometry* 40(4), dec 77 : 343-350.

443   MONSON, Thomas C.; SNYDER, Mark. "Actors, observers, and the
        attribution process: toward a reconceptualization", *J. exp.
        soc. Psychol.* 13(1), jan 77 : 89-111.
444   WOLFSON, Michael R.; SALANCIK, Gerald R. "Observer orientation and
        actor-observer differences in attributions for failure", *J. exp.
        soc. Psychol.* 13(5), sep 77 : 441-451.

11213.

445   KLEINKE, Chris L. "Compliance to requests made by gazing and touch-
        ing experimenters in field settings", *J. exp. soc. Psychol.* 13(3),
        mai 77 : 218-223.
446   KUZNECOV, V. P. "Obščestvennaja praktika i èksperiment" (Social
        practice and experiment), in: *Voprosy teorii i metodov sociolo-
        gičeskih issledovanij. II.* Moskva, 1976 : 151-159.
447   ŽELEZKO, S. N. *et al.* "Metodologičeskie voprosy realizacii social'-
        no-èkonomičeskogo èksperimenta" (Methodological questions on the
        realization of a socio-economic experiment), in: *Voprosy teorii
        i metodov sociologičeskih issledovanij. II.* Moskva, 1976 : 159-
        166.

11215.

448   BERNSTEIN, Ilene N. (ed.). *Validity issues in evaluation.* Beverly
        Hills, Sage Publications, 76, 134 p. CR: Lynne G. ZUCKER, *Con-
        temp. Sociol. (Washington)* 6(3), mai 77 : 317-317.
449   FALTER, Jürgen W. "Zur Validierung theoretischer Konstrukte" (On
        the validation of theoretical constructs), *Z. Soziol.* 6(4), oct
        77 : 370-385.
450   GREENE, Vernon L. "A note on theta reliability and metric invari-
        ance", *Sociol. Meth. Res.* 6(1), aug 77 : 123-128.

11220. Sampling. Survey
       Échantillonnage. Enquête

11221.

[See also / Voir aussi: 4375, 4662]
451   ALCOBENDAS, Pilar. "El panel, técnica para la medida del cambio"
        (Panel survey: a technique for the measurement of change), *R.
        esp. Opin. públ.* 50, 1977 : 75-94.
452   GARDNER, Godfrey James. *Social surveys for social planners.* Sydney-
        New York, Holt, Rinehart and Winston, 76, 165 p.
453   GOSTKOWSKI, Zygmut. "Toward qualitative improvement of survey res-
        earch", *Polish sociol. B.* 1976 : 113-136.
454   NEGROTTI, Massimo. "Indagine pilota su alcune tendenze di riadatta-
        mento culturale in relazione all'ambiente tecnico" (Pilot res-
        earch on some tendencies of cultural re-adjustment in relation
        with technical environment), *Sociologia (Roma)* 11(1), jan-apr
        77 : 9-30.
455   POWERS, Edward A. *et al.* "Serial order preference in survey res-
        earch", *Publ. Opin. Quart.* 41(1), 1977 : 80-85.
456   SMITH, Gilbert. "The place of 'professional ideology' in the analy-
        sis of "social policy': some theoretical conclusions from a pi-
        lot study of the children's panels", *Sociol. R.* 25(4), nov 77 :
        843-865.
457   STINSON, J. G. "Nonprinted data from census and surveys", *Demogra-
        phy* 14(1), feb 77 : 121-145.
458   WEISBERG, Herbert F.; BOWEN, Bruce D. *An introduction to survey
        research and data analysis.* San Francisco, W. H. Freeman, 77,
        x-243 p.

11222.

[See also / Voir aussi: 1264]

459 ANTOINE, J. "Le rôle des sondages d'opinion et des indicateurs sociaux subjectifs dans la régulation sociale", *R. franç. Mkting* 64-65, oct-dec 76 : 121-135.

460 BEZOUŠKA, Jiři. "K nové organizaci výběrových šetřeni u obyvatelstva v ČSSR" (The new organization of Gallup polls in Czechoslovakia), *Statistika (Praha)* (3-4), 1977 : 90-98.

461 BOER, Connie DE. "The polls: nuclear energy", *Publ. Opin. Quart.* 41(3), 1977 : 402-411.

462 CONVERSE, Jean M. "Predicting no opinion in the polls", *Publ. Opin. Quart.* 40(4), 1976 : 515-530.

463 HART, Harm 't. "Selection and selfselection of respondents in sample surveys", *Netherlands J. Sociol.* 12(1), jul 76 : 39-45.

464 LADD, E. C. Jr. "The polls: the question of confidence", *Publ. Opin. Quart.* 40(4), 1976-1977 : 544-552.

11230. Interview. Questionnaire
Entretien. Questionnaire

465 BERMAN, John; McCOMS, Harriet; BORUCH, Robert. "Notes on the contamination method: two small experiments in assuring confidentiality of response", *Sociol. Meth. Res.* 6(1), aug 77 : 45-62.

466 BOKSZANSKI, Zbigniew; PIOTROWSKI, Andrzej. "Socjolingwistyczne aspekty stosowania wywiadu kwestionariuszowego" (Sociolinguistic aspects of the use of a questionnaire interview), *Stud. socjol.* 64(1), 1977 : 81-116.

467 BRIDGE, R. Gary *et al.* "Interviewing changes attitudes - sometimes", *Publ. Opin. Quart.* 41(1), 1977 : 56-64.

468 CARPENTER, Edwin H. "Evaluation of mail questionnaires for obtaining data from more than one respondent in a household", *Rur. Sociol.* 42(2), 1977 : 250-259.

469 COLLOMB, Philippe. "Les non réponses aux questions d'opinion sur la politique de population", *Population* 32(4-5), jul-oct 77 : 835-866.

470 CONEY, Kenneth A. "Order-bias: the special case of letter preference", *Publ. Opin. Quart.* 41(3), 1977 : 385-388.

471 CUNNINGHAM, William H.; CUNNINGHAM, Isabella C. M.; GREEN, Robert T. "The ipsative process to reduce response set bias", *Publ. Opin. Quart.* 41(3), 1977 : 379-384.

472 ESSER, Hartmut. "Response set - methodische Problematik und soziologische Interpretation" (Response-set. Methodological problems and sociological interpretation), *Z. Soziol.* 6(3), jul 77 : 253-263.

473 FLAMENT, Claude. *L'analyse booléenne de questionnaire.* Paris-La Haye, Mouton, 76. CR: Alain DEGENNE, *R. franç. Sociol.* 18(3), jul-sep 77 : 511-519.

474 GRAHAM, William K. "Commensurate characterization of persons, groups, and organizations: development of the trait ascription questionnaire", *Hum. Relat.* 29(7), jul 76 : 607-622.

475 HOUSE, James S.; GERBER, Wayne; McMICHAEL, Anthony J. "Increasing mail questionnaire: a controlled replication and extension", *Publ. Opin. Quart.* 41(1), 1977 : 95-99.

476 KUCZYŃSKI, Pawel. "Metoda ankietowa w badaniu zachowań" (The use of questionnaire as a method of behavioural research), *Stud. socjol.* 64(1), 1977 : 117-138.

477 KVIZ, Frederick J. "Toward a standard definition of response rate", *Publ. Opin. Quart.* 41(2), 1977 : 265-267.

478 MEŠČERIN, V. P. "Sravnitel'noe izučenie priemov količestvennoj obrabotki v oprosnyh metodah" (A comparative study on quantitative treatment means in questionnaire methods), in: *Problemy industrial'noj psihologii. II.* Jaroslavl', 1975 : 100-105.

479   MONTGOMERY, Andrew C.; CRITTENDEN, Kathleen C. "Improving coding reliability for open-ended questions", *Publ. Opin. Quart.* 41(2), 1977 : 235-243.

480   STEFANOWSKA, Małgorzata. "Poczucie 'nieadekwatności kulturalnej' a trafnosc odpowiedzi respondentów na pytania o czytelnictwo ksiązek" (The feeling of "cultural inadequacy" and the validity of respondent's answers to questions about book reading), *Stud. socjol.* 65(2), 1977 : 133-143.

481   TULL, Donald S.; ALBAUM, Gerald S. "Bias in random digit dialed surveys", *Publ. Opin. Quart.* 41(3), 1977 : 389-395.

482   WILDMAN, Richard C. "Effects of anonymity and social setting on survey responses", *Publ. Opin. Quart.* 41(1), 1977 : 74-79.

483   ZDEP, S. M.; RHODES, Isabelle N. "Making the randomized response technique work", *Publ. Opin. Quart.* 40(4), 1976 : 531-537.

11240. Personality measurement. Test
Mesure de la personnalité. Test

11241.
[See also / Voir aussi: 360]

484   BOURNE, Edmund. "Can we describe an individual's personality ? Agreement on stereotype versus individual attribute", *J. Person. soc. Psychol.* 35(12), dec 77 : 863-872.

485   BROMLEY, Dennis Basil. *Personality description in ordinary language.* London-New York, Wiley, 77, x-278 p.

486   EYSENCK, Hans Jürgen. *The measurement of personality.* Baltimore, University Park Press; Lancaster, Eng., MTP, 76, xviii-511 p.

487   EYSENCK, S. B. G.; EYSENCK, Hans Jürgen. "The place of impulsiveness in a dimensional system of personality description", *Brit. J. soc. clinic. Psychol.* 16(1), feb 77 : 57-68.

488   VARELA, Julia. "La medida del desarrollo psicosocial" (The measurement of psycho-social development), *RS Cuad. Realidad soc.* 12, jan 1977 : 133-188.

11242.
[See also / Voir aussi: 1158]

489   SMITH, Kent W. "Test-factor standardization and marginal standardization", *Soc. Forces* 56(1), sep 77 : 240-249.

490   ZURFLUH, Jean. *Les tests mentaux. Expériences, chronologie, présentation et critiques des tests mentaux.* Paris, J.-P. Delarge, 76, 498 p.

11250. Sociodrama
Sociodrame

491   KAEPPELIN, Philippe. *Le psychodrame, moyen de formation.* Paris, le Centurion, 77, 189 p.

492   STARR, Adaline. *Rehearsal for living: psychodrama.* Chicago, Nelson-Hall, 77, xiii-379 p.

11300. MATHEMATICAL ANALYSIS. STATISTICAL ANALYSIS
ANALYSE MATHÉMATIQUE. ANALYSE STATISTIQUE

11310. Algebra. Calculus. Logic
Algèbre. Calcul. Logique
[See also / Voir aussi: 377, 382, 1391, 2720, 3804, 5265]

493   COPLAN, Bette S.; GOLDMAN, Harvey. "The utility of a model: an application of the global matrix", *Hum. Relat.* 29(12), dec 76 : 1131-1145.

494   DOREIAN, Patrick. HUMMON, Norman P. *Modeling social processes.* New York, Elsevier, 76, 172 p.

495   FARARO, Thomas J.; KOSAKA, Kenji. "A mathematical analysis of Boudon's IEO model", *Soc. Sci. Inform.* 15(2-3), 1976 : 341-475.

496   FELDMAN, Jacqueline. "Regards sur la sociologie mathématique",
       Archiv. europ. Sociol. 18(1), 1977 : 179-193.
497   LEIK, Robert K.; MEEKER, Barbara F. *Mathematical sociology.* Engle-
       wood Cliffs, N.J., Prentice-Hall, 75, 242 p. CR: Phillip BONACICH,
       Contemp. Sociol. (Washington) 5(2), mar 76 : 159.
498   O'CONNOR, James F. "A logarithmic technique for decomposing change",
       Sociol. Meth. Res. 6(1), aug 77 : 91-102.
499   SCHANZ, Hans-Jørgen. "Einige Probleme des Verhältnisses swischen
       Wesenslogik und Umfangslogik" (Some problems in the relations
       between essential logic and extensional logic), *Acta sociol.*
       20(4), 1977 : 335-348.
500   VIGUIER, Marie-Claire. "Sur l'usage de la mathématique et de l'in-
       formatique en sociologie", *C. int. Sociol.* 23(61), jul-dec 76 :
       329-340.

11320. Statistical analysis
       Analyse statistique

11321.
       [See also / Voir aussi: 473, 535, 2861, 4782]

501   ANDERSON, O. D. *Time series analysis and forecasting. The Box-
       Jenkins approach.* London, Butterworths, 76, viii-182 p.
502   BASU, Asoke; DOCTOROW, Osher; AMES, Richard G. *Elementary statis-
       tical theory in sociology.* Leiden, Brill, 76, 98 p.
503   BIJNEN, E. J. "Bayesiaanse statistiek" (Bayesian statistics), *Soc.
       Wetensch.* 19(4), 1976 : 229-246.
504   COHEN, Jacob. *Statistical power analysis for the behavioral scien-
       ces.* New York, Academic Press, 77, xv-474pp.
505   FLAMENT, Claude. "Boolean analysis of data", in: SZANIAWSKI, Kle-
       mens (ed.). *Problems of formalization in the social sciences.*
       Wrocław-Warszawa-Kraków-Gdańsk, Zakład Narodowy Imienia Ossolin-
       skich Wydawnictwo, 1977 : 163-176.
506   GOLDSTONE, Leo. "Amélioration des statistiques sociales des pays
       en développement", *R. int. Sci. soc.* 29(4), 1977 : 802-818.
507   HANUSHEK, Eric Alan; JACKSON, John E. *Statistical methods for soc-
       cial scientists.* New York, Academic Press, 77, xiii-374 p.
508   JOHNSON, Allan G. *Social statistics without tears.* New York, McGraw-
       Hill, 77, xiv-270 p.
509   JOHNSON, Marcia K.; LIEBERT, Robert M. *Statistics: tool of the be-
       havioral sciences.* Englewood Cliffs, N.J., Prentice-Hall, 77,
       xiv-237 p.
510   KESSLER, Ronald C. "Rethinking the 16-fold table problem", *Soc.
       Sci. Res.* 6(1), mar 77 : 84-107.
511   KJØLBY, Henning. *Statistik og samfund* (Statistics and society).
       København, Erhvervsøkonomisk Forlag; Nyt Nordisk Forlag, 76,
       236 p.
512   KUPRIJAN, A. P. "Statističeskij ěksperiment",(Statistical experi-
       ment), in: *Voprosy teorii i metodov sociologičeskih issledovanij.*
       II. Moskva, 1976 : 141-151.
513   LISSOWSKI, Grzegorz. "Interpretation of statistical measures",
       Polish sociol. B. 1976 : 89-111.
514   LISSOWSKI, Grzegorz. "Statistical association and prediction", in:
       SZANIAWSKI, Klemens (ed.). *Problems of formalization in the so-
       cial sciences.* Wrocław-Warszawa-Kraków-Gdańsk, Zakład Narodowy
       Imienia Ossolińskich Wydawnictwo, 1977 : 217-245.
515   MALEC, Michael A. *Essential statistics for social research.* New
       York, Lippincott, 77, x-235 p.
516   MYCKAN, J. "Metodologiczne problemy statystycznej kwantifikacji
       minimum społecznego" (Methodological problems of statistical
       quantification of the social minimum), *Biul. IGS* 20(3), 1977 :
       43-57.

517   PINE, Vanderlyn R. *Introduction to social statistics.* Englewood
       Cliffs, N.J., Prentice-Hall, 77, xiv-415 p.
518   STOETZEL, Antoine. "L'impossibilité théorique: Arrow", *Soc. Sci.*
       Inform. 15(4-5), 1976 : 757-786.
519   VIGDERHOUS, G. "The level of measurement and 'permissible' statis-
       tical analysis in social research", *Pacific sociol. B.* 20(1),
       jan 77 : 61-72.
520   YASUDA, Saburô; UMINO, Michio. *Shakai-tokeigaku* (Social statistics).
       Rev. ed. Tokyo, Maruzen, 77, 340 p.

       11322.
       [See also / Voir aussi: 4308]
521   ALLISON, Paul D. "Testing for interaction in multiple regression",
       Amer. J. Sociol. 83(1), jul 77 : 144-153.
522   ANDORKA, Rudolf. "A faktoranalizis alkalmazása ökologiai vizsgá-
       latokban" (The application of factor analysis in social ecolo-
       gical investigations), *Szigma* 9(3), 1976 : 159-177.
523   Bibl.XXVI-489. COHEN, Jacob; COHEN, Patricia. *Applied multiple*
       regression-correlation analysis for the behavioral sciences.
       CR: Neil W. HENRY, *Contemp. Sociol. (Washington)* 6(3), mai 77 :
       320-321.
524   DRECKENDORFF, H. Otis. "Towards a theory of n-tuple binds", *So-*
       ciol. Inquiry 47(2), 1977 : 143-147.
525   EDWARDS, Allen L. *An introduction to linear regression and corre-*
       lation. San Francisco, Freeman, 76, xviii-213 p.
526   GILLESPIE, Michael W. "Log-linear techniques and the regression
       analysis of dummy dependent variables: further bases for compa-
       rison", *Sociol. Meth. Res.* 6(1), aug 77 : 103-122.
527   SMITH, Robert B. "Proportional reduction in error interpretations
       for the squared generalized multiple, partial, and multiple-
       partial correlation coefficients and their special class", *Soc.*
       Forces 56(2), dec 77 : 688-702.
528   WEEDE, Erich; JAGODZINSKI, Wolfgang. "Einführung in die konfirma-
       torische Faktorenanalyse" (Introduction to confirmatory factor
       analysis), *Z. Soziol.* 6(3), jul 77 : 315-333.

       11323.
       [See also / Voir aussi: 459, 4200, 4613, 5495]
529   ANDERSON, James G. "A social indicator model of a health service
       system", *Soc. Forces* 56(2), dec 77 : 661-687.
530   ANDORKA, Rudolf. "A társadalmi jelzöszámok és társadalmi mérlegek
       rendszerének felépítésére irányuló vizsgálatok a Központi Sta-
       tisztikai Hivatal Társadalomstatisztikai Föosztályán" (The
       attempt by the Department for Social Statistics of the Central
       Statistical Office to construct a system of social index numbers
       and social scales), *Szociológia* 5(3-4), 1976 : 575-582.
531   BORŠČEVSKIJ, M. V. "K metodologii opredelenija indikatorov social'-
       nogo i ěkonomičeskogo razvitija socialisticeskogo goroda" (Me-
       thodology of elaboration indicators for the economic and social
       development of socialist town), in: *Social'nye aspekty ěkonomi-*
       českogo i kul'turnogo razvitija i vyrabotka asocial'nyh i kul'-
       turnyh indikatorov v modeljah mira. II. Moskva, 1976 : 70-83.
532   CARMONA GUILLEN, J. A. "Los indicadores sociales y la planifica-
       cion" (Social indicators and planning), *De Economia* 29(138),
       jul-sep 76 : 341-351.
533   DIEKMANN, A.; SCHMIDT, P. "Soziale Indikatoren – Modelle und So-
       zialplanung" (Social indicators: models and social planning),
       Neue Gesellsch. 24(2), feb 77 : 124-129.
534   FORET, Miroslav. "K něktrým problémům tvorby sociálních ukazatelů"
       (On some problems of the formation of social indicators), *Sociol.*
       Čas. 13(3), 1977 : 288-302.

535   JOHNSTON, Robert. "Review of new compendia of social statistics and social indicators in five Western countries", *Soc. Sci. Inform.* 15(2-3), 1976 : 349-370.

536   MICLET, Georges. "Indicateurs sociaux, indicateurs d'environnement", *Écon. rur.* 120, jul-aug 77 : 11-17.

537   MIENO, Takashi. "Development of a weighting model for social indicator", *Behaviormetrika* (4), 1977 : 45-64.

538   MIENO, Takashi. "Shakai-shihyô kenkyu ni okeru ichi-shiten" (A viewpoint on the study of social indicator), *Kikan Shakai-hoshô-Kenkyû* 13(2), 1977 : 73-90.

539   MOOTZ, M.; NAUTA, A. "The activities of the Social and Cultural Planning Office in the area of social indicators", *Planning Develop. Netherl.* 9(1), 1977 : 50-66.

540   SIVALINGAM, G. "Problems involved in developing indicators of administrative performance", *Ind. J. publ. Adm.* 22(1), jan-mar 76 : 101-105.

541   "Soziale Indikatoren und Planung" (Social indicators and planning), *Neue Gesellsch.* 23(12), 1976 : 1002-1016.

542   UNESCO. *The use of socio-economic indicators in development planning.* Paris, Unesco, 76, 282 p.

11330. Cybernetics. Information theory
Cybernétique. Théorie de l'information
[See also / Voir aussi: 3848]

543   GEORGE, Frank Honywill. *Cybernetics and the environment.* London, Elek, 77, 69-1 p.

544   HORN, M. "Learning strategies for public learning: a cybernetic approach", *Gen. Systems* 21, 1976 : 125-129.

545   KRAJZMER, L. P. *Kibernetika* (Cybernetics). Moskva, Ékonomika, 77, 279 p.

546   LIMONE, Donato A. *Le scienze dell'uomo e la cibernetica* (The sciences of man and cybernetics). Assisi-Roma, B. Carucci, 76, 128 p.

11340. Graph theory
Théorie des graphes
[See also / Voir aussi: 1097]

547   CARTWRIGHT, Dorwin; HARARY, Frank. "A graph theoretic approach to the investigation of system-environment relationships", *J. math. Sociol.* 5(1), 1977 : 87-112.

548   WASSERMAN, Stanley S. "Random directed graph distributions and the triad census in social networks", *J. math. Sociol.* 5(1), 1977 : 61-86.

11350. Stochastic processes. Statistical decision. Game theory
Processus stochastique. Décision statistique. Théorie des jeux

11351.
[See also / Voir aussi: 2905, 3661]

549   BARTHOLOMEW, David J. "Applications of stochastic processes to social phenomena", in: SZANIAWSKI, Klemens (ed.). *Problems of formalization in the social sciences.* Wrocław-Warszawa-Kraków-Gdańsk, Zakład Narodowy Imienia Ossolińskich Wydawnictwo, 1977 : 177-202.

550   EATON, William; WHITMORE, G. A. "Length of stay as a stochastic process: a general approach and application to hospitalization for schizophrenia", *J. math. Sociol.* 5(2), 1977 : 272-292.

551   ISAACSON, Dean L.; MADSEN, Richard W. *Markov chains theory and applications.* New York, Wiley, 76, 256 p. CR: Robert McGINNIS, *Contemp. Sociol. (Washington)* 6(3), mai 77 : 322-323.

552   MOVAHEDI, Siamak; OGLES, Richard H. "Probability of a hypothesis
       or of a theory: some uses and misuses of the concept of proba-
       bility", *Sociol. soc. Res.* 62(1), oct 77 : 43-62.

11352.
[See also / Voir aussi: 609, 1109, 1218]

553   BECKER, Heinz Alfred. *Simulatie in de sociale wetenschappen* (Simu-
       lation in social sciences). Alphen aan den Rijn, Samson, 76,
       252 p.
554   GORN, Gerald J.; GOLDBERG, Marvin E. "The effects of intrinsic and
       extrinsic rewards in a risk-taking situation", *J. exp. soc.
       Psychol.* 13(4), jul 77 : 333-339.
555   NORLEN, Urban. *Simulation model building: a statistical approach to
       modelling in the social sciences with the simulation method.* New
       York, Halsted Press, 76, 172 p. CR: Theodore L. REED, *Contemp.
       Sociol. (Washington)* 6(3), mai 77 : 323-324.
556   PERARNAU, Germain. *Sur un type de fonction d'utilité.* Toulouse,
       Université des sciences sociales, 76, 60 f. multigr.

11353.

557   ELSTER, Jon. "Boudon, education and the theory of games", *Soc. Sci.
       Inform.* 15(4-5), 1976 : 733-740. [R. Boudon.]
558   GROFMAN, Bernard; POOL, Jonathan. "How to make cooperation the op-
       timizing strategy in a two-person game", *J. math. Sociol.* 5(2),
       1977 : 173-186.

11360. Attitude scale
       Échelle d'attitude

559   ALT, James; SÄRLVIK, Bo; CREWE, Ivor. "Individual differences
       scaling and group attitude structures: British party imagery in
       1974", *Quality and Quantity* 10(4), dec 76 : 297-320.
560   BECHTEL, Gordon G. *Multidimensional preference scaling.* The Hague,
       Mouton, 76, xii-170 p.
561   CRESPI, Irving. "Attitude measurement, theory, and prediction",
       Publ. Opin. Quart. 41(3), 1977 : 285-294.
562   CRONKHITE, Gary. "Scales measuring general evaluation with minimal
       distortion", *Publ. Opin. Quart.* 41(1), 1977 : 65-73.
563   FALBO, Toni. "Multidimensional scaling of power strategies", *J.
       Person. soc. Psychol.* 35(8), aug 77 : 537-547.
564   FITZSIMMONS, Stephen J.; FERB, Thomas E. "Developing a community
       attitudes assessment scale", *Publ. Opin. Quart.* 41(3), 1977 :
       356-378.
565   GORDEN, Raymond L. *Unidimensional scaling of social variables:
       concepts and procedures.* New York, Free Press, 77, xii-175 p.
566   HENNING, H. Jörg; SIX, Bernd. "Konstruktion einer Machiavellismus-
       Skala" (Construction of a Machiavellianism scale), *Z. soz.-Psy-
       chol.* 8(3), 1977 : 185-198.
567   JONES, Pauline A. "The validity of traditional-modern attitude
       measures", *J. cross-cult. Psychol.* 8(2), jun 77 : 207-239.
568   KÜHN, Wolfgang. *Einführung in die multidimensionale Skalierung*
       (Introduction to the multidimensional scaling). München, Rein-
       hardt, 76, 186 p.
569   LANTERMANN, Ernst-Dieter; GEHLEN, Hans. "Skalierung von Items und
       Individuen unter Beachtung individueller Urteilsstrukturen"
       (Scaling of items and individuals on the basis of individual
       judgment structures), *Z. soz.-Psychol.* 8(4), 1977 : 242-246.
570   LOUNSBURY, John W.; TORNATZKY, Louis G. "A scale for assessing atti-
       tudes toward environmental quality", *J. soc. Psychol.* 101(2),
       apr 77 : 299-305.

571   SCHUMAN, Howard; PRESSER, Stanley. "Attitude measurement and the
        gun control parados", *Publ. Opin. Quart.* 41(4), 1977 : 427-438.
572   THOMES, Charles W.; WILLIAMS, J. Sherwood. "The construction of
        Likert-type attitude scales", *Int. J. contemp. Sociol.* 14(1-2),
        jan-apr 77 : 45-60.

12100. PSYCHOLOGY. SOCIAL PSYCHOLOGY. SOCIOMETRY
PSYCHOLOGIE. PSYCHOLOGIE SOCIALE. SOCIOMÉTRIE

12110. Psychoanalysis. Social psychology
Psychanalyse. Psychologie sociale

[See also / Voir aussi: 885, 894, 896, 1808, 2275, 3237]

573 BACK, Kurt W. (ed.). *Social psychology*. New York, Wiley, 77, xi-498 p.

574 BERGIUS, Rudolf. *Sozialpsychologie* (Social psychology). Hamburg, Hoffmann und Campe, 76, 262 p.

575 BINTIG, Arnfried et al. *Kritische Einführung in die Sozialpsychologie* (Critical introduction to social psychology). Weinheim-Basel, Beltz, 76, 164 p.

576 BOCOCK, R. J. "Freud and the centrality of instincts in psychoanalytic sociology", *Brit. J. Sociol.* 28(4), dec 77 : 467-480.

577 BORNEWASSER, Manfred et al. *Einführung in die Sozialpsychologie* (Introduction to social psychology). Heidelberg, Quelle und Meyer, 76, 242 p.

578 CARLSMITH, J. Merrill; ELLSWORTH, Phoebe C.; ARONSON, Elliot. *Methods of research in social psychology*. Reading, Mass., Addison-Wesley, 76, 326 p. CR: Royce SINGLETON, Jr. *Contemp. Sociol. (Washington)* 6(3), mai 77 : 319-320.

579 CHESSICK, Richard D. *Great ideas in psychotherapy*. New York, J. Aronson, 77, 462 p.

580 DOISE, Willem. "Structural homologies, sociology and experimental social psychology", *Soc. Sci. Inform.* 15(6), 1976 : 929-942.

581 FERNANDEZ, Ronald. *The I, the me, and you: an introduction to social psychology*. New York, Praeger, 77, xi-430 p.

582 GERGEN, Kenneth J. *The positivist image in social psychological theory*. Paris, LPS, 76, 29 p. Ronéo.

583 GERHARDT, Walter. *Psychoanalyse und Sozialisationstheorie: Probleme einer kritischen Theorie des Subjekts* (Psychoanalysis and socialization theory: the problem of a critical theory of the subjects). Frankfurt-am-Main-New York, Campus-Verlag, 77, 112 p.

584 HARVEY, John H.; SMITH, William P. *Social psychology: an attributional approach*. Saint Louis-Mosby-London, Henry Kimpton, 77, xvi-426 p.

585 HORWITZ, Allan. "Social networks and pathways to psychiatric treatment", *Soc. Forces* 56(1), sep 77 : 86-105.

586 HOUSE, James S. "The three faces of social psychology", *Sociometry* 40(2), jun 77 : 161-177.

587 "Interventions psychosociales et recherche action", *Connexions* 21, 1977 : 3-134.

588 JIMENEZ BURILLO, Florencio. "Algunas cuestiones actuales en la psicología social" (Some present problems of social psychology), *R. esp. Opin. públ.* 47, 1977 : 139-146.

589 LAUER, Robert H.; HANDEL, Warren H. *Social psychology: the theory and application of symbolic interactionism*. Boston, Houghton Mifflin, 77, xviii-467 p.

590 LEVINE, Ned. "On the metaphysics of social psychology", *Hum. Relat.* 29(4), apr 76 : 385-400.

591   LISKA, Allen E. *et al.* "The dissipation of sociological social
        psychology", *Amer. Sociologist* 12(1), feb 77 : 2-23.
592   PALMONARI, Augusto. *Problemi attuali della psicologia sociale*
        (Present problems of social psychology). Bologna, Mulino, 76,
        113 p.
593   MANAHI, Badi. "Die psychoanalytische Soziologie von Talcott Par-
        sons" (Talcott Parsons' psychological sociology), *Sociol. int.*
        (Berlin) 12(1-2), 1974 : 25-67.
594   PATAKI, F. *Társadalomlélektan és társadalmi valóság* (Social psy-
        chology and social reality). Budapest, Kossuth, 77, 362-5 p.
595   ROUDINESCO, Elisabeth. *Pour une politique de la psychanalyse.* Pa-
        ris, F. Mespéro, 77, 179 p.
596   SEIDENBERG, Bernard; SHANOWSKY, Alvin (eds.). *Social psychology:*
        an introduction. New York, Free Press, 76, 561 p. CR: Mary Ann
        GROVES, *Contemp. Sociol. (Washington)* 6(2), mar 77 : 248-249.
597   SEVERY, Lawrence J.; VRIGHAM, John C.; SCHLENKER, Barry R. *A con-*
        temporary introduction to social pscyhology. New York, McGraw-
        Hill, 76, 462 p. CR: Mary Ann GROVES, *Contemp. Sociol. (Washing-*
        ton) 6(2), mar 77 : 248-249.
598   SÉVIGNY, Robert; MORISSETTE, Luc (éds.). "Psychologie - sociologie
        - intervention", *Sociol. et Soc.* 9(2), oct 77 : 3-193.
599   SHAVER, Kelly G. *Principles of social psychology.* Cambridge, Mass.,
        Winthrop Publishers, 77, xix-636 p.
600   SHERIF, Carolyn Wood. *Orientation in social pscyhology.* New York,
        Harper and Row, 76, 441 p. CR: Sylvia CLAVAN, *Contemp. Sociol.*
        (Washington) 6(2), mar 77 : 247-248.
601   STREAN, Herbert S. *Crucial issues in psychotherapy.* Metuchen, N.J.,
        Scarecrow Press, 76, vii-312 p.
602   STRICKLAND, Lloyd H.; ABOUD, Frances E.; GERGEN, Kenneth J. *Social*
        psychology in transition. New York, Plenum Press, 76, ix-361 p.
603   STRYKER, Sheldon. "Developments in 'two social psychologies': to-
        ward an appreciation of mutual relevance", *Sociometry* 40(2),
        jun 77 : 145-160.
604   TAKI, Hirotsugu. "G. H. Mead to konnichi no shakai-shinrigaku"
        (G. H. Mead and social psychology today), *Ningen-kagaku* (10),
        1977 : 31-54.
605   TEDESCHI, James T.; LINDSKOLD, Svenn. *Social psychology: interde-*
        pendence, interaction, and influence. New York, Wiley, 76, 705 p.
        CR: Mary Ann GROVES, *Contemp. Sociol. (Washington)* 6(2), mar
        77 : 248-249.
606   VANDER ZANDEN, James Wilfrid. *Social psychology.* New York, Random
        House, 77, xiv-464 p.

12200. INDIVIDUAL. PERSONALITY
INDIVIDU. PERSONNALITÉ

12210. Ego. Identity
Ego. Identité
[See also / Voir aussi: 842, 1326]

607   BIAGI, Adriano. "L'individuo tra movimento e istituzione" (The in-
        dividual between movement and institution), *Rass. ital. Sociol.*
        18(3), jul-sep 77 : 363-392.
608   CARVETH, Donald L. "The Hobbesian microcosm: on the dialectics of
        the self in social theory", *Sociol. Inquiry* 47(1), 1977 : 3-12.
609   DOWNEY, H. Kirk; HELLRIEGEL, Don; SLOCUM, John W. Jr. "Individual
        characteristics as sources of perceived uncertainty variability",
        Hum. Relat. 30(2), feb 77 : 161-174.
610   FUNATSU, Mamoru. "Jiga to Ningen shtuaisei" (Self and human subjec-
        tivity), *Gendai Shakaigaku* 4(7), 1977 : 3-19.
611   FUNATSU, Mamoru. "Jigaron to Busshôkaron" (Self theory and reifi-
        cation theory), *Shakaigaku Kenkyû* 35, 1977 : 56-75.

612   GRINIŠIN, D. M.; NEFEDOV, M. V. "Aktual'nye problemy ličnosti v
        uslovijah razvitogo socializma" (Topical problems on individual
        under conditions of developed socialism), *Ličnost' i Obščestvo*
        (2), 1976 : 3-15.

613   INKELES, Alex. "Understanding and misunderstanding individual",
        J. cross-cult. Psychol. 8(2), jun 77 : 135-176.

614   KALOCSAI, D. "Egyén és közösség - a polgári társadalomban" (The
        individual and the community in bourgeois society), *Társadtud.*
        Közl. (2), 1977 : 64-85.

615   KUSATSU, Osamu. "Ego development and sociocultural process in Ja-
        pan", *Keizaigaku Kiyo* 3(1), 1977 : 41-109.

616   LADENSON, Robert F. "Mill's conception of individuality", *Soc.*
        Theory Practice 4(2), 1977 : 167-182.

617   LOEVINGER, Jane; BLASI, Augusto. *Ego development: conceptions and*
        theories. San Francisco, Jossey-Bass Publishers, 76, xx-504 p.

618   MAGNÉR, Björn; MAGNÉR, Helena. *Medveten människa: en metod att ut-*
        forska förhållandet mellan individ och samhälle (The conscious
        human being: a method of studying the relationship between in-
        dividual and society). Stockholm, Wahlström och Widstrand, 76,
        204-1 p.

619   NIKONOV, K. M. (ed.). *Social'naja aktivnost' ličnosti* (Social acti-
        vity of an individual). Volgograd, 76, 176 p.

620   PEDROSA IZARRA, Ciriaco. *La psicología evolutiva: desarrollo del*
        individuo normal por etapas (Developmental psychology: develop-
        ment of normal individual by stages). Madrid, Ediciones Marova,
        76, 458 p.

621   SKUJA, Eric; SHEEHAN, Peter W. "The human subject: a study of in-
        dividual experimental participation", *Hum. Relat.* 30(2), feb
        77 : 143-154.

622   VATIN, I. V.; TIŠČENKO, Ju. R. "Istoričeskij process kak stanovle-
        nie čelovečeskoj individual'nosti" (Historical process as the
        future of human individuality), in: *Problema čeloveka v "Ēkono-*
        mičeskih rukopisjah 1857-1859 godov" K. Marksa. Rostov, 1977 :
        1977 : 84-115.

623   VRONSKIJ, G. T. "Individual'nost' i aktivnost' ličnosti. Nekotorye
        aspekty teorii i metodologii" (Individuality and personality ac-
        tivity. Some theoretical and methodological aspects), in: *Vop-*
        rosy razvitija duhovnoj žizni v socialističeskom obščestve. V.
        Tula, 1976 : 3-15.

        12220. Egocentrism. Self concept
               Egocentrisme. Conception de soi
        [See also / Voir aussi: 916, 1112, 1148, 1380, 1711, 3468, 3558,
        3577, 3580, 3593, 3636]

624   BACHMAN, Jerald G.; O'MALLEY, Patric M. "Self-esteem in young men:
        a longitudinal analysis of the impact of educational and occupa-
        tional attainment", *J. Person. soc. Psychol.* 35(6), jun 77 :
        365-380.

625   BALSWICK, Jack O.; BALKWELL, James W. "Self-disclosure to same-
        and opposite-sex parents: an empirical test of insights from
        role theory", *Sociometry* 40(3), 1977 : 282-286.

626   BANKS, W. Curtis *et al.* "Perceived objectivity and the effects of
        evaluative reinforcement upon compliance and self-evaluation in
        Blacks", *J. exp. soc. Psychol.* 13(5), sep 77 : 452-463.

627   BUEHLER, Charles J.; WEIGERT, Andrew J.; THOMAS, Darwin. "Antece-
        dents of adolescent self evaluation: a cross-national applica-
        tion of a model", *J. comp. Family Stud.* 8(1), 1977 : 29-45.

628   CAÏN, Jacques. *Le double jeu: essai psychanalytique sur l'identi-*
        té. Paris, Payot, 77, 200 p.

629   DRIEDGER, Leo; PETERS, Jacob. "Identity and social distance: to-
        wards understanding Simmel's *The stranger*", *Canad. R. Sociol.*
        Anthropol. 14(2), mai 77 : 158-173.

630   FALK, Dennis R.; JOHNSON, David W. "The effects of perspective-
       taking and egocentrism on problem solving in heterogenous and
       homogeneous groups", *J. soc. Psychol.* 102(1), jun 77 : 63-72.

631   FLUDE, R. A. "The development of an occupational self-concept and
       commitment to an occupation in a group of skilled manual workers",
       Sociol. R. 25(1), feb 77 : 41-49.

632   FORSITH, Donelson R.; SCHLENKER, Barry R. "Attributional egocen-
       trism following performance of a competitive task", *J. soc.
       Psychol.* 102(2), aug 77 : 215-222.

633   GAEV, Dorothy Meyer. *The psychology of loneliness.* Philadelphia,
       author, 76, 160 p. CR: Robert A. STEBBINS, *Contemp. Sociol. (Wa-
       shington)* 6(4), jul 77 : 490.

634   GUIOT, Jean M. "Attribution and identity construction: some com-
       ments", *Amer. sociol. R.* 42(5), oct 77 : 692-704.

635   HAAN, Norma *et al. Coping and defending: processes of self-envi-
       ronment organization.* New York, Academic Press, 77, xiv-346 p.

636   HARRIS, Anthony; TESSLER, Richard; POTTER, Joanne. "The induction
       of self-reliance: an experimental study of independence in the
       face of failure", *J. appl. soc. Psychol.* 7(4), oct-dec 77 : 313-
       331.

637   HEWITT, John P. *Self and society: a symbolic interactionist social
       psychology.* Boston, Allyn and Bacon, 76, 248 p. CR: Sylvia CLA-
       VAN, *Contemp. Sociol. (Washington)* 6(2), mar 77 : 247-248.

638   JACQUES, Jeffrey M.; CHASON, Karen J. "Self-esteem and low status
       groups: a changing scene ?", *Sociol. Quart.* 18(3), 1977 : 399-
       412.

639   KREILKAMP, Thomas. *The corrosion of the self: society's effects
       on people.* New York, New York University Press, 76, 235 p. CR:
       Sylvia CLAVAN, *Contemp. Sociol. (Washington)* 6(2), mar 77 : 247-
       248.

640   KOSATSU, Osamu. "Identity to Shakai" (Identity and society), *Gen-
       dai Shakaigaku* 4(7), 1977 : 32-53.

641   LÉVI-STRAUSS, Claude (ed.). *L'identité: séminaire interdiscipli-
       naire.* Paris, B. Grasset, 77, 344 p.

642   MOMBERG, A. P.; PAGE, H. W. "Self-esteem of colored and white
       scholars and students in South Africa", *J. soc. Psychol.* 102(2),
       aug 77 : 179-182.

643   "Obedience under conditions demanding self-immolation", *Hum. Relat.*
       29(4), apr 76 : 345-356.

644   RECIO ADRADOS, J. L. "Evolución de la identidad en la sociedad tec-
       nocrática" (Evolution of the identity in technocratic society),
       R. Fomento soc. 30(120), oct-dec 75 : 377-390; 31(123), jul-sep
       76 : 285-297; 31(124), oct-dec 76 : 417-428.

645   ROSS, Lee; GREENE, David; HOUSE, Pamela. "The 'false consensus ef-
       fect': an egocentric bias in social perception and attribution
       processes", *J. exp. soc. Psychol.* 13(3), mai 77 : 279-301.

646   RUBINSTEIN, Ruth P. "Changes in self-esteem and anxiety in compe-
       titive and noncompetitive camps", *J. soc. Psychol.* 102(1), jun
       77 : 55-57.

647   SAINSAULIEU, Renaud. *L'identité au travail: les effets culturels
de   de l'organisation.* Paris, Presses de la Fondation nationale des
       sciences politiques, 77, 486 p.

648   SCHLENKER, Barry R.; MILLER, Rowland S. "Egocentrism in groups:
       self-serving biases or logical information processing ?", *J.
       Person. soc. Psychol.* 35(10), oct 77 : 755-764.

649   SCHLENKER, Barry R.; SORACI, Salvatore; McCARTHY, Bernhard. "Self-
       esteem and group performance as determinants of egocentric per-
       ceptions in cooperative groups", *Hum. Relat.* 29(12), dec 76 :
       1163-1176.

650   SENNETT, Richard. "Il narcisimo e la cultura moderna" (Narci-
       cism and modern culture), *Rass. ital. Sociol.* 18(2), apr-jun
       77 : 307-315.

651   SIGALL, Harodl; GOULD, Robert. "The effects of self-esteem and
       evaluator demandingness on effort expenditure", *J. Person. soc.*
       Psychol. 35(1), jan 77 : 12-20.

652   STARK, Alan E. "Diagnostic d'identité de deux jumeaux", *Soc. Sci.*
       Inform. 15(4-5), 1976 : 787-792.

653   UDRY, J. Rochard. "The importance of being beautiful: a reexamina-
       tion and racial comparison", *Amer. J. Sociol.* 83(1), jul 77 :
       154)160.

654   WEIGERT, Andrew J.; HASTINGS, Ross. "Identity loss, family, and
       social change", *Amer. J. Sociol.* 82(6), mai 77 : 1171-1185.

       12230. Personality
              Personnalité
       [See also / Voir aussi: 1142, 1308, 1404, 1980, 2776, 2872, 2926,
       3392, 4364, 4385, 4571, 4846, 4847, 4849, 5250]

655   BIERHOFF, Hans Werner; BIERHOFF-ALFERMANN, Dorothee. "Attribution
       impliziter Persönlichkeitstheorien in einer Interaktionssitua-
       tion durch Beurteiler" (Implicit attribution personality theo-
       ries in a situation of interaction between judges), *Z. soz.-*
       Psychol. 8(1), 1977 : 50-66.

656   BLASS, Thomas (ed.). *Personality variables in social behavior.*
       Hillsdale, N.J., L. Erlbaum; New York, Halsted Press Division,
       Wiley, 77, x-405 p.

657   BOLOTNIKOV, I. M. "Socialističeskoe upravlenie i stanovlenie lič-
       nosti" (Socialist management and future of personality), *Učen.*
       Zap. Kaf. obšč. Nauk Vuzov Leningrada Probl. nauč. Kommunizma
       (9), 1976 : 76-83.

658   CORSINI, Raymond J. (ed.). *Current personality theories.* Itasca,
       Ill., F. E. Peacock Publishers, 77, xiv-465 p.

659   DEMIN, M. V. *Problemy teorii ličnosti (social'no-filosofskij as-*
       pect) (Problems of the personality theory; socio-philosophical
       aspect). Moskva, Izdatel'stvo Moskovskogo Universiteta, 77,
       240 p.

660   EYSENCK, S. B. C.; EYSENCK, H. J, "A comparative study of perso-
       nality in Nigerian and English subjects", *J. soc. Psychol.*
       102(2), aug 77 : 171-178.

661   FIL'ČIKOV, G. S. "Soderzanie truda i razvitie ličnosti" (Labour
       content and personality development), in: *Voprosy sociologii*
       ličnosti. Rjazan', 1976 : 42-56.

662   GOLOVKOV, S. I. "Vzaimo-svjaz' potrebnostej i dejatel'nosti v
       formirovanie ličnosti. (Metodologičeskie aspekty)" (Interaction
       of needs and activity in the personality formation. Methodolo-
       gical aspects), in: *Metodologičeskie aspekty upravlnija processom*
       som vospitanija i formirovanija ličnosti novogo tipa. Smolensk,
       1976 : 57-65.

663   HESKIN, K. J. *et al.* "Prisoners' personality: a factory analytical-
       ly derived structure", *Brit. J. soc. clinic. Psychol.* 16(3),
       sep 77 : 203-206.

664   IWAWAKI, S.; EYSENCK, S. B, G.; EYSENCK, H. J. "Differences in
       personality between Japanese and English", *J. soc. Psychol.*
       102(1), jun 77 : 27-33.

665   KIČATINOV, L. P. "Problema suščnosti obščestvennoj aktivnosti kak
       kačestva ličnosti" (Problem of the social activity as a deter-
       minant quality of the personality), *Obšč.-polit. Vospitanie*
       učašč. (1), 1975 : 16-29.

666   KONSTANTINOV, F. V. "Zaknomernosti formirovanija vsestoronne raz-
       vitej ličnosti" (Laws of formation of an entirely developed
       personality), in: *Filosofija i sovremennost'.* Moskva, 1976 :
       15-26.

667   KREML, William P. *The anti-authoritarian personality.* Oxford,
       Pergamon Press, 77, xi-118 p.

668   LIPPOLD, Gerhard. "Personality formation and time budget in the

GDR between 1965 and 1972", *Soc. and Leisure* 8(3), 1976 : 181-197.

669 MAGNUSSON, David; ENDLER, Norman S. (eds.). *Personality at the crossroads: current issues in interactional psychology*. Hillsdale, N.J., Lawrence Erlbaum Associates; New York, Halsted Press Division of Wiley, 77, x-454 p.

670 MAL'CEV, V. A. "Sorevnovanie i razvitie ličnosti rabotnika" (Competition and development of the worker's personality), *Sorevnov. Ličnost' Social.* (1), 1976 : 48-55.

671 MANZ, Günter. "Personality formation and time use - fundamental problems of their correlation", *Soc. and Leisure* 8(3), 1976 : 199-208.

672 MIHOVILOVIC, Miro A. "The factors influencing the use of time and the development of the personality of women", *Soc. and Leisure* 8(3), 1976 : 209-221.

673 MONTE, Christopher F. *Beneath the mask: an introduction to theories of personality*. New York, Praeger, 77, xxii-693 p.

674 NAKAMURA, Masao; SUZUKI, Hiroshi (eds.). *Ningen sonzai no shakai-gaku-teki kôzô* (Sociological structure of human being). Kyoto, Akademia Shuppankai, 77, 260 p.

675 NAKANISHI, Shigeyuki. "Fromm no shakaiteki seikaku-riron ni okeru 'Seisan-sei' gainen" (The concept of "productiveness" in E. Fromm's theory of social character), *Shakaigaku Ronsô* 69, 1977 : 44-55.

676 PAMFIL, Eduard; OGODESCU, Dorn. *Persoană și devenire;eseu de antropologie* (Personality development; essays on anthropology). București, Editura Știinţifică și Enciclopedică, 76, 269 p.

677 ŠAJHUTDINOV, L. G. "O sootnošenii social'nogo tipa i haraktera ličnosti" (On the correlation of social type and personality characteristics), *Učen. Zap. Kazan. pedag. Inst.* 155, 1976 : 106-120.

678 SCHULTZ, Duane P. *Growth psychology: models of the healthy personality*. New York, Van Nostrand Reinhold Co., 77, vii-151 p.

679 TAMBOVCEV, I. V. "Formirovanie social'no-odnorodnoj ličnosti" (Formation of a social homogeneous personality), in: *Voprosy sociologii ličnosti*. Rjazan', 1976 : 57-67.

680 URJUPIN, A. I. "Problemy ličnosti v trudah klasskov marksizma-leninizma" (Problems of the personality in the marxism-leninism classics' works), in: *Voprosy sociologii ličnosti*. Rjazan', 1976 : 11-28.

681 ZENKIN, S. N. "Nekotorye metodologičeskie problemy formirovanija socialističeskogo tipa ličnosti" (Some methodological problems of the socialist type of personality formation), in: *Problemy social'no-političeskogo razvitija obščestva*. Moskva, 1975 : 160-180.

682 ZIEGLER, Robert G.; MUSLINER, Peter J. "Persistent themes: a naturalistic study of personality development in the family", *Family Process* 16(3), sep 77 : 293-305.

683 ZOTOVA, O. I.; SOROHOVA, Ê. V. "Formirovanie ličnosti v proizvodstvennom kollektive" (Personality formation in a production collectivity), in: *Psihologija upravlenija. II*. Moskva, 1976 : 3-17.

12240. Cognition. Emotion. Motivation
Cognition. Émotion. Motivation

12241.

[See also / Voir aussi: 215, 3717]

684 BERTRAM, Hans. "Sozialstruktur und Intelligenz. Ein altes Thema - eine neue Antwort ?" (Social structure and intelligence: an old subjet - a new answer ?), *Kölner Z. Soziol. u. soz.-Psychol.* 29(3), sep 77 : 461-486.

685 BOWER, Gordon H. (ed.). *The psychology of learning and motivation*.

Advances in research and theory. X. New York-London, Academic Press, 76, xiii-247 p.

686   CARROLL, John S.; PAYNE, John W. (eds.). *Cognition and social behavior.* Hillsdale, N.J., Erlbaum Associates; New York, Halsted Press Division of Wiley, 76, xiii-290 p.

687   FLAVELL, John H. *Cognitive development.* Englewood Cliffs, N.J., Prentice-Hall, 77, x-286 p.

688   HAMILTON, Vernon; VERNON, Magdalen D. (eds). *The development of cognitive processes.* London-New York, Academic Press, 76, 772 p.

689   HIGGINS, E. Tory; RHOLES, William S.; JONES, Carl R. "Category accessibility and impression formation", *J. exp. soc. Psychol.* 13(2), mar 77 : 141-154.

690   KÖRNER, Wolfgang. *Kognitive Strukturen und soziales Verhalten. Psychologische und soziologische Implikationen der Balancetheorie* (Cognitive structures and social behaviour. Psychological and sociological implications of the balance theory). s.l., s.e., 76, viii-204 p.

691   KREITLER, Hans; KREITLER, Shulamith. *Cognitive orientation and behavior.* New York, Springer Publishing Co., 76, xv-447 p.

692   LEWIS, Michael (ed.). *Origins of intelligence; infancy and early childhood.* New York, Plenum Press, 76, 413 p. CR: Barbara G. CASHION, *Contemp. Sociol. (Washington)* 6(2), mar 77 : 242-243.

693   LINSKIE, Rosella. *The learning process: theory and practice.* New York, D. Van Nostrand Co., 77, x-310 p.

694   MARX, Melvin H.; BUNCH, Marion E. (eds.). *Fundamentals and applications of learning.* New York, Macmillan, 77, vii-550 p.

695   MAYER, Richard E. *Thinking and problem solving; an introduction to human cognition and learning.* Glenview, Ill., Scott, Foresman, 77, 214 p.

696   MEDINA, C. A. DE; ALMEIDA, M. L. Rodriguez DE. "Hábitos de leitura: uma abordagem sociológica" (Reading habits: a sociological approach), *Amer. lat. (Rio de Janeiro)* 17, 1976 : 70-129.

697   MEICHENBAUM, Donald. *Cognitive-behavior modification: an integrative approach.* New York, Plenum Press, 77, 305 p.

698   MILNE, Robert A.; MEIER, Kenneth J. "A graphic approach to Rosenberg's affective-cognitive consistency theory", *Hum. Relat.* 29(3), mar 76 : 273-285.

699   NACHSON, Israel; SHEFLER, Gabriel E.; SAMOCHA, Dalia. "Directional scanning as a function of stimulus characteristics, reading habits, and directional set", *J. cross-cult. Psychol.* 8(1), mar 77 : 83-100.

700   OSTROM, Thomas M. "Between-theory and within-theory conflict in explaining context effects in impression formation", *J. exp. soc. Psychol.* 13(5), sep 77 : 492-503.

701   PRICE-WILLIAMS, Douglas R.; RAMIREZ, Manuel III. "Divergent thinking, cultural differences, and bilingualism", *J. soc. Psychol.* 103(1), oct 77 : 3-11.

702   RA, John Oh; BOURDEAUX, Robert M. "Intelligence, creativity, and political socialization. A theoretical model", *Youth and Soc.* 9(1), sep 77 : 3-28.

703   RICATEAU, Michel. *Mémoire sémantique et mémoire à long terme.* Paris, Éditions du CNRS, 76, 119 p.

704   TESSER, Abraham; LEONE, Christopher. "Cognitive schemas and thought as determinants of attitude change", *J. exp. soc. Psychol.* 13(4), jul 77 : 340-356.

705   WEST, Charles K.; FOSTER, Stephen F. *The psychology of human learning and instruction in education.* Belmont, Calif., Wadsworth Publishing Co., 76, xiii-278 p.

706   WICKELGREN, Wayne A. *Learning and memory.* Englewood Cliffs, N.J., Prentice-Hall, 77, xiv-448 p.

707   ZANNA, Mark P.; HAMILTON, D. L. "Further evidence for meaning change in impression formation", *J. exp. soc. Psychol.* 13(3).

mai 77 : 224-238.

12242.
[See also / Voir aussi: 646, 698, 5369]
708   CHAPMAN, Anthony J.; FOOT, Hugh C. *Humour and laughter: theory,
      research and applications*. London-New York, John Wiley, 76, x-
      348 p.
709   CLYNES, Manfred. *Sentics: the touch of emotions*. Garden City, N.
      Y., Anchor Press, 77, xxxii-249 p.-8 1.
710   ČOKUŠEV, K. "O smysle social'nyh čvostv" (On the sense of social
      feelings), in: *Semantika i social'naja psihologija*. Frunze,
      1976 : 129-135.
711   GEERKEN, Michael; GOVE, Walter R. "Deterrence, overload, and inca-
      pacitation: an empirical evaluation", *Soc. Forces* 56(2), dec 77
      : 424-447.
712   HAAS, Jack. "Learning real feelings: a study of high steel iron-
      workers' reactions to fear and danger", *Sociol. Wk Occupat.* 4(3),
      mai 77 : 147-170.
713   SCOTT, J. P.; DEGHETT, V.; STEWART, J. M. "El desarrollo del afec-
      to social: efectos de las experiencias contemporáneas sobre la an-
      gustia de separación" (The development of social affect: effects
      of contemporary experience on separation anxiety), *R. latinoamer.
      Psicol.* 9(2), 1977 : 247-257.
714   SKILBECK, Clive; TULIPS, James; LEY, Philip. "The effects of fear
      arousal, fear position, fear exposure, and sidedness on complian-
      ce with dietary instructions", *Europ. J. soc. Psychol.* 7(2),
      1977 : 221-239.
715   ZILLMANN, Dofl; CANTOR, Joanne R. "Affective responses to the emo-
      tions of a protagonist", *J. exp. soc. Psychol.* 13(2), mar 77 :
      155-165.

12243.
[See also / Voir aussi: 444, 685, 843, 4445, 5193]
716   ARIYOSHI, Hiroyuki. "Sôtaiteki kachi hakudatsu to shakai-hendō"
      (Relative deprivation and social change), *Dokkyô-daigaku Kyôyô-
      shogaku* (11), 1977 : 9-30.
717   ARKES, Hal R.; GARSKE, J. P. *Psychological theories of motivation*.
      Monterey, Calif. Brooks/Cole Publishing Co., 77, xi-339 p.
718   BESTUŽEV-LADA, I. V. (ed.). *Prognozirovanie social'nyh potrebnostej*
      (Forecast of social needs). Moskva, 76, 208 p.
719   BOUDON, Raymond. "La logique de la frustration relative", *Archiv.
      europ. Sociol.* 18(1), 1977 : 3-26.
720   CHUNG, Kae H. *Motivational theories and practices*. Columbus, Ohio,
      Grid, 77, xii-324 p.
721   DELLA FAVE, L. R. "Aspirations through four years of high school:
      an inquiry into the value sketching process", *Pacific sociol. R.*
      20(3), jul 77 : 371-388.
722   GALLUP, George H. "Human needs and satisfactions: a global survey",
      Publ. Opin. Quart. 40(4), 1976 : 468-481.
723   HAMBY, Russell R. "The effects of motivational orientation on dein-
      dividuation", *Hum. Relat.* 29(7), jul 76 : 687-697.
724   "Human needs and satisfactions: a global survey of mankind", *Mthly
      publ. Opin. Surv.* 21(9-10), jul-jul 76 : 3-54.
725   ISRAEL, Joachim. "From level of aspiration to cognitive dissonance,
      or, what the middle class worries about", *Acta sociol.* 20(2),
      1977 : 125-143.
726   ISRAEL, Joachim. "From level of aspiration to dissonance, or, what
      the petty-bourgeoisie worries about", *Insurgent Sociologist* 7(1),
      1977 : 31-39.
727   KIDDER, Louise H.; BELLETTIRIE, Gerlad; COHN, Ellen S. "Secret ambi-
      tions and public performances. The effects of anonymyty on reward

allocations made by men and women", *J. exp. soc. Psychol.* 13(1), jan 77 : 70-80.

728   LEVAŠKO, N. N. "Voprosy klassifikacii potrebnostej" (Question on needs classification), in: *Mehanizm, funkcionirovanija i razvitija proizvodstvennyh otnošenij socializma.* Moskva, 1975 : 51-75.

729   McCLELLAND, David Clarence *et al. The achievement motive.* New York, Halsted Press, 76, xxii-386 p.

730   MOROZOV, V. S. *Social'nyj interes i povedenie ličnosti* (Social interest and individual behavior). Moskva, Žnanie, 77, 64 p.

731   NEL'GA, A. V. "Motivacionnyj aspekt problemy potrebnosti" (Motivational aspect of the needs problem), *Probl. Filos.* 40, 1977 : 60-65.

732   PRIHOD'KO, D. N.; SYSOEVA, L. S. "Sistemnyj podhod v analize kategorii 'potrebnost'" (A systemic approach in the analysis of "needs" category), in: *Voprosy teorii vospitanija i obrazovanija.* Tomsk, 1976 : 164-177.

733   SOKOLOVIĆ, Džemal. "Ljudske patrebe izmettu rasta i razvoja" (Human needs between growth and development), *Sociologija* 19(2-3), 1977 : 265-284.

734   TURNER, Charles F.; MARTINEZ, Daniel C. "Socio-economic achievement and the Machiavellian personality", *Sociometry* 40(4), dec 77 : 325-336.

735   VARGA, KÁROLY. "N-achievement, n-affiliation and exposure to media according to the sexes", *Soc. and Leisure* 8(3), 1976 : 223-240.

736   VARGA, Károly. "Teljesítménymotivácio a magyar ifjúsági sajtóban" (Achievement motivation in Hungarian youth press), *Pedag. Szle* 27(5), 1977 : 396-407.

737   WANKEL, Leonard M.; THOMPSON, Carol. "Motivating people to be physically active: self-persuasion vs. balanced decision making", *J. appl. soc. Psychol.* 7(4), oct-dec 77 : 332-340.

738   ZVIRBULIS, Ju. Ja. "Vazaimosvjaz' material'nyh i duhovnyh potrebnostej ličnosti" (Interrelation between material and intellectual needs of man), in: *Problemy formirovanija celostnoj ličnosti.* Riga, 1976 : 109-121.

       112244.
       [See also / Voir aussi: 244, 630, 702, 887, 970, 1015, 1030, 1214, 1530, 3811]

739   ARASTEH, A. Reza; ARASTEH, Josephine D. *Creativity in human development: an interpretive and annotated bibliography.* Cambridge, Mass., Schenkman Publishing Co., New York, Halsted Press, 76, 154 p.

740   ARIETI, Silvano. *Creativity: the magic synthesis.* New York, Basic Books, 76, 448 p. CR: William A. SADLER, Jr. *Contemp. Sociol. (Washington)* 6(2), mar 77 : 156-159.

741   ARROW, Kenneth J. "Current developments in the theory of social choice", *Soc. Res.* 44(4), 1977 : 607-622.

742   ASCHINGER, G. A. "Das 'dynamic social choice' Modell. Ein dynamisches Modell der Gruppenentscheidung" (The 'dynamic social choice' model. A dynamic model of group decision), *Z. ges. Staatswiss.* 132(4), oct 76 : 571-581.

743   AXELROD, Robert (ed.). *Structure of decision: the cognitive maps of political elites.* Princeton, N.Y., Princeton University Press, 76, xvi-404 p.

744   BORGIDA, Eugene; NISBETT, Richard E. "The differential impact of abstract vs. concrete information on decisions", *J. appl. soc. Psychol.* 7(3), jul-sep 77 : 258-271.

745   BUEVA, L. P. "Nekotorye metodologičeskie problemy izučenija dejatel'nosti v sociologii i social'noj psihologii" (Some methodological problems of the activity study in sociology and social psychology), in: *Problemy social'noj psihologii.* Tbilisi, 1976 : 47-54.

746   CONNER, Thomas L. "Performance expectations and the initiation of
        problem-solving attempts", *J. math. Sociol.* 5(2), 1977 : 187-198.
747   CORNELIS, Arnold. *Creativity in society as a learning process: the
        epistemological relation between norms and value.* Amsterdam, So-
        ciologisch Instituut, 76, 18 p.
748   ELSTER, Jon. "Ulysses and the sirens: a theory of imperfect ratio-
        nality", *Soc. Sci. Inform.* 16(5), 1977 : 469-526.
749   FRANKE, Heinz. *Problemlösen als soziale Interaktion* (Problem solv-
        ing as social interaction). Berlin, Duncker und Humblot, 76,
        150 p.
750   HELD, Virginia. "Rationality and reasonable cooperation", *Soc. Res.*
        44(4), 1977 : 708-744.
751   HELLER, Frank A. *et al.* "A longitudinal study in participative de-
        cision-making", *Hum. Relat.* 30(7), jul 77 : 567-587.
752   JANIS, Irving Lester; MANN, Leon. *Decision making: a psychological
        analysis of conflict, choice, and commitment.* New York, Free
        Press, 77, xx-488 p.
753   KROSS, P. A. "Ispol'zovanie metoda situacii pri issledovanii prin-
        jatija rešenija" (Utilization of the situation method for deci-
        sion research), *Trudy Tallinsk. politehn. Inst.* 24, 1977 : 3-16.
754   KUTEPOV, V. P. "Struktura čelovečeskojndejatel'nosti; metodologi-
        českij analiz" (Structure of human activity; a methodological
        analysis), *Trudy Kirgiz. Univ. Ser. obšč. Nauk* (6), 1976 : 28-47.
755   MOUSTAKAS, Clark E. *Creative life.* New York, Van Nostrand Reinhold
        Co., 77, ix-114 p.
756   OTTOMEYER, Klaus. *Anthropologieproblem und marxistische Handlungs-
        theorie* (Anthropological problem and marxist action theory).
        Giessen, Focus-Verlag, 76. CR: Arto NORO, *Acta sociol.* 20(4),
        1977 : 396-400.
757   OVCINNIKOV, V. F.; MOKSALENKO, V. A. "Suščnost' tvorčeskoj aktivnos-
        nosti ličnosti" (Nature of the man's creative activity), *Ličnost'
        i Obščestvo* (2), 1976 : 16-24.
758   RADFORD, K. J. *Complex decision-problems: an integrated strategy
        for resolution.* Reston, Va., Reston Publishing Co., 77, xv-208 p.
759   RAJECKI, D. W. *et al.* "Social facilitation of human performance:
        mere presence effects", *J. soc. Psychol.* 102(2), aug 77 : 297-
        310.
760   ROŽKO, K. G. "Filosofska sociologičeskoe ponjatie čelovečeskoj de-
        jatel'nosti'" (Philosophical and sociological concept of human
        activity), in: *Metodologičeskie problemy istoričeskogo materia-
        lizma.* Barnaul, 1976 : 158-165.
761   SEGUIER, Michel. *Critique institutionnelle et créativite collec-
        tive.* Paris, L'Harmattan, 76, 159 p.
762   SHIRLEY, Robert C.; PETERS, Michael H.; EL-ANSARY, Adel I. *Strate-
        gy and policy formation: a multifunctional orientation.* Santa
        Barbara, Calif., Wiley, 76, xiv-261 p.
763   SIMONTON, Dean Keith. "Creative productivity, age, and stress: a
        biographical time-series analysis of 10 classical composers",
        J. Person. soc. Psychol. 35(11), nov 77 : 791-804.
764   SZANIAWSKI, Klemens. "Information and decision making. Some logical
        aspects", in: SZANIAWSKI, Klemens (ed.), *Problems of formaliza-
        tion in the social sciences.* Wrocław-Warszawa-Kraków-Gdańsk,
        Zaklad Narodowy Imienia Ossolińskich Wydawnictwo, 1977 : 77-90.
765   SZEGÖ, A. "A célracionális cselekvés történetfilozofiai problémái
        Max Weber szociologiájában" (Historical philosophical problems
        of goal-rational action in Max Weber's sociology), *Magyar filoz.
        Szle* 21(6), 1977 : 635-664.
766   TOURAINE, Alain. "Huit manières de se débarrasser de la sociologie
        de l'action", *Inform. Sci. soc.* 15(6), 1976 : 879-903.
767   ULLMANN-MARGALIT, Edna; MORGENBESSER, Sidney. "Picking and choos-
        ing", *Soc. Res.* 44(4), 1977 : 757-785.
768   VICKREY, William. "Economic rationality and social choice", *Soc.
        Res.* 44(4), 1977 : 691-707.

769 WHITE, Douglas John. *Fundamentals of decision theory*. New York,
North-Holland, 76, xiii-387 p.

770 WOLFF, Stephan; CONFURIUS, Gerritt; HELLER, Hartmut. "Entscheidun-
gen als praktische Herstellungen" (Decisions as a practical making), *Soz. Welt* 28(3), 1977 : 271-305.

12300. INTERPERSONAL RELATIONS
RELATIONS INTERPERSONNELLES

12310. Human relations. Sociability
Relations humaines. Sociabilité

[See also / Voir aussi: 655, 1211]

771 ARNOLD, Judith W.; SCHWAB, William A.; SCHWIRIAN, Kent P. "Spatial
and temporal aspects of the density-distance relationship", *Soziol. Focus* 10(2), apr 77 : 117-132.

772 BARTELL, Ted. "The human relations ideology. An analysis of the social origins of a belief system", *Hum. Relat.* 29(8), aug 78 :
737-749.

773 CONDON, John C. Jr. *Interpersonal communication*. New York, Macmillan, 77, xiii-210 p.

774 DUNCAN, Starkey Jr.; FISKE, Donald W. *Face-to-face interaction:
research, methods, and theory*. Hillsdale, N.J., L. Erlbaum Associates; New York, Halsted Press, 77, xiii-361 p.

775 EADIE, William F.; KLINE, John A. *Orientations to interpersonal
communication*. Palo Alto, Calif., Science Research Associates,
76, 45 p.

776 FORD, J. Gurhrie; KNIGHT, Martha; CRAMER, Robert. "The phenomenological experience of interpersonal spacing", *Sociometry* 40(4),
dec 77 : 387-390.

777 IWASAKI, Nobuhiko. "'Shakai-kankei'-ron eno shiten" (Points of view
on the concept of social relations), *Atarashii Shakaigaku no ta-
meni* 4(2), 1977 : 4-13.

778 KENDON, Adam; HARRIS, Richard M.; KEY, Mary Ritchie (eds.). *Organization of behavior in face-to-face interaction*. The Hague,
Mouton; Chicago, Aldine, 76, xiii-509 p.-5 l.

779 LOFLAND, John. *Doing social life: the qualitative study of human
interaction in natural settings*. New York, Wiley, 76, xix-328 p.

780 MILLER, Gerlad R. (ed.). *Explorations in interpersonal communication*. Beverly Hills, Calif., Sage Publications, 76, 278 p.

781 MOULTON, Eugene R.; HELD, McDonald Watkins. *Communication: a creative process*. Minneapolis, Burgess Publishing Co., 76, xi-388 p.

782 OTTOMEYER, Klaus. *Ökonomische Zwänge und menschliche Beziehungen.
Soziales Verhalten im Kapitalismus* (Economic compulsions and
human relations. Social behaviour in capitalism). Hamburg, Rowohlt, 77. CR: Arto NORO, *Acta sociol.* 20(4), 1977 : 396-400.

783 PESENKO, V. N. "Sistemno-istoričeskij podhod v analize social'nyh
svjazej i otnošenij" (A systemic and historical basis for analyzing social ties and relations), in: *Problema čeloveka v "Ėkonomi-
českih rukopisjah 1857-1859 godov" K. Marksa*. Rostov, 1977 : 116-
127.

784 PETROVSKIJ, A. V. "O nekotoryh fenomenah mežličnostnyh vzaimo-
otnošenij v kollektive" (On some phenomena of interpersonal relations in a collectivity), *Vopr. Psihol.* (3), 1976 : 16-25.

785 PRESNJAKOV, P. V. *et al. Razvitie socialističeskih obščestvennyh
otnošenij* (Development of socialist social relations). Alma-Ata,
Kazahstan, 76, 216 p.

786 TARDOS, R. "Társas kapcsolatok, kommunikáció fiatalok körében"
(Interpersonal relations and communication among youth), *Rádió
és TV Szle* 9(1), 1977 : 66-75; 9(2), 1977 : 57-64.

787 VERDERBER, Kathleen S.; VERDERBER, Rudolph F. *Inter-act: using
interpersonal communication skills*. Belmont, Calif., Wadsworth
Publishing Co., 77, x-292 p.

788   WISH, Myron; KAPLAN, Susan J. "Toward an implicit theory of inter-
         personal communication", *Sociometry* 40(3), 1977 : 234-246.

12320. Social perception
Perception sociale
[See also / Voir aussi: 830, 948, 967, 1095, 1103, 1391, 5184]

789   BATESON, Gregory. "Les usages sociaux du corps à Bali", *Actes Rech.
         Sci. soc.* 14, apr 77 : 3-33.
790   BLYTH, Dale A. "Adolescent perception of sex-roles in 1968 and
         1975", *Publ. Opin. Quart.* 41(4), 1977 : 459-474.
791   BOURDIEU, Pierre. "Remarques provisoires sur la perception sociale
         du corps", *Actes Rech. Sci. soc.* 14, apr 77 : 51-54.
792   GOITEIN, Bernard; ROTENBERG, Mordechai. "Protestantism and retro-
         spective labeling: a cross-cultural study in person perception",
         Hum. Relat. 30(6), jun 77 : 487-497.
793   MAISONNEUVE, Jean. "Le corps et le corporéisme aujourd'hui", *R.
         franç. Sociol.* 17(4), oct-dec 76 : 551-571.
794   McARTHUR, Leslie Zabrowitz; POST, David L. "Figural emphasis and
         person perception", *J. exp. soc. Psychol.* 13(6), nov 77 : 520-
         535.
795   SNYDER, Mark; TANKE, Elizabeth Decker; BERSCHEID, Ellen. "Social
         perception and interpersonal behavior: on the self-fulfilling
         nature of social stereotypes", *J. Person. soc. Psychol.* 35(9),
         sep 77 : 656-666.

12330. Interpersonal attraction
Attraction interpersonnelle
*[See also / Voir aussi: 715, 750, 929, 938, 1142, 1308, 1404,
2039, 3305, 4586]*

796   ALLAN, Graham. "Class variation in friendship patterns", *Brit. J.
         Sociol.* 28(3), sep 77 : 389-393.
797   AVENI, Adrian F. "The not-so-lonely crowd: friendship groups in
         collective behavior", *Sociometry* 40(1), 1977 : 96-99.
798   BARDIS, Panos D. "Erotometer: a technique for the measurement of
         heterosexual love", *Sociol. int. (Berlin)* 12(1-2), 1974 : 189-
         202.
799   BRAIN, Robert. *Friends and lovers.* New York, Basic Books, 76. CR:
         Craig CALHOUN, *Contemp. Sociol. (Washington)* 6(4), jul 77 : 447-
         448.
800   BRINK, John H. "Effect of interpersonal communication on attraction",
         tion", *J. Person. soc. Psychol.* 35(11), nov 77 : 783-790.
801   DERLEGA, Valerian J.; STEPIEN, Ewa Gurnik. "Norms regulating self-
         disclosure among Polish University students", *J. cross-cult.
         Psychol.* 8(3), sep 77 : 369-376.
802   DOLLASE, Rainer. *Soziometrische Techniken: Techniken der Erfassung
         und Analyse zwischenmenschliche Beziehungen in Gruppen* (Socio-
         metric technics: of the registration and analysis of human rela-
         tions in groups). Weinheim-Basel, Beltz, 76, 417 p.
803   DUCK, Steve; CRAIG, Gordon. "The relative attractiveness of diffe-
         rent types of information about another person", *Brit. J. soc.
         clinic. Psychol.* 16(3), sep 77 : 229-233.
804   FOLKES, Valerie S.; SEARS, David O. "Does everybody like a liker ?",
         J. exp. soc. Psychol. 13(6), nov 77 : 505-519.
805   FOOT, Hugh C.; CHAPMAN, Antony J.; SMITH, Jean R. "Friendship and
         social responsiveness in boys and girls", *J. Person. soc. Psy-
         chol.* 35(6), jun 77 : 401-411.
006   FREEMAN, Harvey R. "Reward vs. reciprocity as related to attrac-
         tion", *J. appl. soc. Psychol.* 7(1), jan-mar 77 : 57-66.
807   FREEMAN, Linton C. "A set of measures of centrality based on bet-
         weenness", *Sociometry* 40(1), 1977 : 35-41.
808   GOLDMAN, William; LEWIS, Philip. "Beautiful is good: evidence that

the physically attractive are more socially skillful", *J. exp. soc. Psychol.* 13(2), mar 77 : 125-130.

809   GOULD, Robert; SIGALL, Harold. "The effects of empathy and outcome on attribution: an examination of the divergent-perspectives hypothesis", *J. exp. soc. Psychol.* 13(5), sep 77 : 480-491.

810   GRAIG, Gordon; Duck, Steven W. "Similarity, interpersonal attitudes and attraction: the evaluative-descriptive distinction", *Brit. J. soc. clinic. Psychol.* 16(1), feb 77 : 15-21.

811   HALLINAN, Maureen T. "Friendship patterns in open and traditional classrooms", *Sociol. Educ.* 49(4), oct 76 : 254-265.

812   HANSSON, Robert O.; SLADE, Kenneth M. "Altruism toward a deviant in city and small town", *J. appl. soc. Psychol.* 7(3), jul-sep 77 : 272-279.

813   HARRIS, Mary B. "Effects of altruism on mood", *J. soc. Psychol.* 102(2), aug 77 : 197-208.

814   INSKO, Chester A.; WILSON, Midge. "Interpersonal attraction as a function of social interaction", *J. Person. soc. Psychol.* 35(12), dec 77 : 903-911.

815   KAHN, Arnold; McGAUGHEY, Timothy A. "Distance and liking: when moving close produces increased liking", *Sociometry* 40(2), jun 77 : 138-144.

816   KRAIN, Mark. "Effects of love and liking in premarital dyads", *Sociol. Focus* 10(3), aug 77 : 249-262.

817   LANGEHEINE, Rolf. "Measures of social proximity and their use in sociometric research", *Z. Soziol.* 6(2), apr 77 : 189-202.

818   LILLI, Waldemar; KROLAGE, Josef. "Zur Stereotypisierung sozialer Reize" (On social attraction stereotyping), *Z. soz.-Psychol.* 8(3), 1977 : 156-166.

819   MILLER, Dale T. "Altruism and threat to a belief in a just world", *J. exp. soc. Psychol.* 13(2), mar 77 : 113-124.

820   MORSE, Stanley J. *et al.* "Reactions to receiving expected and unexpected help from a person who violates or does not violate a norm", *J. exp. soc. Psychol.* 13(4), jul 77 : 397-402.

821   NOESJIRWAN, Jennifer. "Contrasting cultural patterns of interpersonal closeness in doctors' waiting rooms in Sydney and Jakarta", *J. cross-cult. Psychol.* 8(3), sep 77 : 357-368.

822   OLSON, James M.; PARTINGTON, John T. "An integrative analysis of two cognitive models of interpersonal effectiveness", *Brit. J. soc. clinic. Psychol.* 16(1), feb 77 : 13-14.

823   OTTO, Luther B. "Girl friends as significant-others: their influence on young men's career aspirations and achievements", *Sociometry* 40(3), 1977 : 287-293.

824   PERETTI, Peter O. "Closest friendships of black college students; structural characteristics", *Hum. Relat.* 30(1), 1977 : 43-51.

825   SANDERS, Glenn S.; BARON, Robert S. "Is social comparison irrelevant for producing choice shifts ?", *J. exp. soc. Psychol.* 13(4), jul 77 : 304-314.

826   STEPHAN, Cookie; KENNEDY, James C.; ARONSON, Elliot. "The effects of friendship and outcome on task attribution", *Sociometry* 40(2), 1977 : 107-112.

827   SUBOČEV, N. S. "O teoretičeskih osnovanijah sociometričeskogo oprosa" (On theoretical bases of sociometric questionaires), in: *Voprosy teorii i metodov sociologičeskih issledovanij. II.* Moskva, 1976 : 126-134.

828   TEICHMAN, Meir. "Affiliative behaviours among soldiers during wartime", *Brit. J. soc. clinic. Psychol.* 16(1), feb 77 : 3-7.

829   VERBRUGGE, Lois M. "The structure of adult friendship choices", *Soc. Forces* 56(2), dec 77 : 576-597.

830   WALSH, Nancy A.; MEISTER, Lynn A.; KLEINKE, Chris L. "Interpersonal attraction and visual behavior as a function of perceived arousal and evaluation by an opposite sex person", *J. soc. Psychol.* 103(1), oct 77 : 65-74.

831   WEBSTER, Murray Jr. "Equating characteristics and social inter-
       action: two experiments", *Sociometry* 40(1), 1977 : 41-50.
832   WESTACOTT, George H.; WILLIAMS, Lawrence K. "Interpersonal trust
       and modern attitudes in Peru: work orientations, self-efficacy,
       and future orientation", *Int. J. contemp. Sociol.* 13(1-2), jan-
       apr 76 : 117-137.

12340. Interpersonal influence
Influence interpersonnelle

833   BAR-TAL, Daniel *et al.* "Reciprocity behavior in the relationship
       between donor and recipient and between harmdoer and victim",
       Sociometry 40(3), 1977 : 293-298.
834   BUTLER, Suellen R.; SNIZEK, William E. "The waitress-diner rela-
       tionship: a multimethod approach to the study of subordinate
       influence", *Sociol. Wk Occupat.* 3(2), mai 76 : 209-222.
835   PATTERSON, Miles L. "Interpersonal distance, affect, and equilib-
       rium theory", *J. soc. Psychol.* 101(2), apr 77 : 205-214.
836   SCHWARTZ, Shalom H.; AMES, Ruth E. "Positive and negative referent
       others as sources of influence: a case of helping", *Sociometry*
       40(1), 1977 : 12-21.
837   SHAW, John. "Some 'real-life' accounts of influential relation-
       ships", *Hum. Relat.* 30(4), apr 77 : 363-372.
838   SHERROD, Drury R. *et al.* "Environmental attention, affect, and
       altruism", *J. appl. soc. Psychol.* 7(4), oct-dec 77 : 359-371.
839   WALLER, Manfred; PREIS, Herbert. "Kompetenz und Interessantheit
       des Modellverhaltens als Anregungsbedingungen der Imitations-
       bereitschaft" (Validity and interest of model conducts as con-
       ditions of reinforcement of imitation dispositions), *Z. soz.-
       Psychol.* 8(4), 1977 : 256-264.

12350. Interpersonal conflict
Conflit interpersonnel
[See also / Voir aussi: 632, 1222, 2016]

840   BALLE, Catherine. *La menace: un langage de violence.* Paris, Édi-
       tions du CNRS, 76, 169 p.
841   DA GLORIA, Jorge; RIDDER, Richard DE. "Aggression in dyadic inter-
       action", *Europ. J. soc. Psychol.* 7(2), 1977 : 189-219.
842   DANZIGER, Kurt. "Hostility management and ego involvement in dis-
       cussion groups", *J. soc. Psychol.* 102(1), jun 77 : 143-148.
843   DENGERINK, H. A.; MYERS, J. D. "The effects of failure and depres-
       sion on subsequent aggression", *J. Person. soc. Psychol.* 35(2),
       feb 77 : 88-96.
844   DUA, J. K. "Effect of audience on the acquisiton and extinction
       of avoidance", *Brit. J. soc. clinic. Psychol.* 16(3), sep 77 :
       207-212.
845   FROMKIN, Howard L.; GOLDSTEIN, Jeffrey H.; BROCK, Timothy C. "The
       role of 'irrelevant' derogation in vicarious aggression cathar-
       sis: a field experiment", *J. exp. soc. Psychol.* 13(3), mai 77 :
       239-252.
846   GABLER, Hartmut. *Aggressive Handlungen im Sport: ein Beitrag zur
       theoretische und empirische Aggressionsforschung* (Aggressive
       actions in sport: a contribution to the research on aggressive-
       ness). Schorndord, Hofmann, 76, 144 p.
847   JOSEPH, Joanne M. *et al.* "Perceived aggression: a re-evaluation of
       the Bandura modeling paradigm", *J. soc. Psychol.* 103(2), dec 77 :
       277-289.
848   KANE, Thomas R.; JOSEPH, Joanne M.; TEDESCHI, James T. "Perceived
       freedom, aggression, and responsibility, and the assignment of
       punishment", *J. soc. Psychol.* 103(2), dec 77 : 257-263.

849 KIMBLE, Charles E.; FITZ, Don; ONORAD, James R. "Effectiveness of counteraggression strategies in reducing interactive aggression by males", *J. Person. soc. Psychol.* 35(4), apr 77 : 272-278.

850 LARSEN, Knud S. *Aggression: myths and models.* Chicago, Nelson, 76, xiv-317 p.

851 LEFKOWITZ, Monroe M. *et al. Growing up to be violent: a longitudinal study of the development of aggression.* New York, Pergamon Press, 77, ix-236 p.

852 LINNÉ, Olga. "The viewer's aggression as a function of a variously edited TV-Film", *Communications (Köln)* 2(1), 1976 : 101-111.

853 MONTAGU, Ashley. *The nature of human aggression.* New York, Oxford University Press, 76, 381 p. CR: J. P. SCOTT, *Amer. J. Sociol.* 82(6), mai 77 : 1385-1386; Richard McCLINTOCK, *Contemp. Sociol. (Washington)* 6(3), mai 77 : 384-385.

854 SELG, Herbert (ed.). *The making of human aggression: a psychological approach.* New York, St. Martin's Press, 76, 202 p. CR: Karl SCHONBORN, *Contemp. Sociol. (Washington)* 6(1), jan 77 : 123-124.

855 SHERROD, Drury R. *et al.* "Effects of personal causation and perceived control on responses to an aversive environment: the more control, the better", *J. exp. soc. Psychol.* 13(1), jan 77 : 14-27.

856 SMITH, Peter K.; CONNOLLY, Kevin J. "Social and aggressive behaviour in preschool children as a function of crowding", *Soc. Sci. Inform.* 16(5), 1977 : 601-620.

857 SUMMERS, David A.; ASHWORTH, Clar D.; FELDMAN-SUMMERS, Shirley. "Judgment processes and interpersonal conflict related to societal problem solutions", *J. appl. soc. Psychol.* 7(2), apr-jun 77 : 163-174.

858 SUDMAN, Seymour *et al.* "Estimates of threatening behavior based on reports of friends", *Publ. Opin. Quart.* 41(2), 1977 : 261-264.

12360. Intergroup relations
Relations intergroupes
[See also / Voir aussi: 1160, 1167]

859 BILLIG, Michael. *Social psychology and intergroup relations.* London-New York, Academic Press, 76, x-428 p.

860 DOISE, Willem. *L'articulation psychosociologique et les relations entre groupes.* Bruxelles, A. de Boeck, 76, 215 p.

861 GOLDMAN, Morton; STOCKBAUER, Joseph W.; McAULIFFE, Timothy G. "Intergroup and intragroup competition and cooperation", *J. exp. soc. Psychol.* 17(1), jan 77 : 81-88.

862 WORCHEL, Stephen; ANDREOLI, Virginia A.; FOLGER, Robert. "Intergroup cooperation and intergroup attraction: the effect of previous interaction and outcome of combined effort", *J. exp. soc. Psychol.* 13(2), mar 77 : 131-140.

12361.
[See also / Voir aussi: 1100]

863 CHERTKOFF, J. M.; ESSER, J. K. "A test of three theories of coalition formation when agreements can be short-term or long-term", *J. Person. soc. Psychol.* 35(4), apr 77 : 237-249.

864 FOLKES, Valerie S.; WEINER, Bernard. "Motivational determinants of coalition formation", *J. exp. soc. Psychol.* 13(6), nov 77 : 536-542.

865 KOMORITA, Samuel S.; BRINBERG, David. "The effects of equity norms in coalition formation", *Sociometry* 40(4), dec 77 : 351-361.

866 MURNIGHAN, J. Keith; KOMORITA, S. S.; SZWAJKOWSKI, Eugene. "Theories of coalition formation and the effects of reference groups", *J. exp. soc. Psychol.* 13(2), mar 77 : 166-181.

867 SCHNEIDER, Hans-Dieter. "Koalitionstendenzen in der Tetrade" (Coalition tendencies in the tetrad), *Z. Soziol.* 6(1), jan 77 : 77-90.

12362.

[See also / Voir aussi: 1005, 1454, 1475, 1666]

868   BOZEMAN, Adda Bruemmer. *Conflict in Africa, concepts and realities.*
Princeton, N.J., Princeton University Press, 76, xiv-430 p. CR:
David D. LAITIN, *Contemp. Sociol. (Washington)* 6(3), mai 77 :
359-360.

869   BÜHL, Walter Ludwig. *Theorien sozialer Konflikte* (Social conflict
theories). Darmstadt, Wissenschaftliche Buchgesellschaft, 76,
vi-178 p.

870   GENTILE, Roberto. *Contraddizione, conflitto e mutamento* (Contradiction, conflict and change). Napoli, Guida, 76, 131 p.

871   KOMORITA, S. S. "Negotiating from strength and the concept of bargaining strength", *J. Theory soc. Behav.* 7(1), apr 77 : 49-79.

872   KUTY, Olgierd. "Le paradigme de négociation" (The negotiation paradigm), *Sociol. Trav.* 19(2), apr-jun 77 : 157-175.

873   LEVI, A. M.; BENJAMIN, A. "Jews and Arabs rehearse Geneva: a model
of conflict resolution", *Hum. Relat.* 29(11), nov 77 : 1035-1044.

874   LOUIS, Meryl Reis. "How individuals conceptualize conflict: identification of steps in the process and the role of personal/develop-
mental factors", *Hum. Relat.* 30(5), mai 77 : 451-467.

875   McCORD, Arline; McCORD, William. *Urban social conflict.* Saint Louis,
C. V. Mosby Co., 77, xiii-201 p.

876   MELL, Wolf-Dieter. *Ein Beitrag zur Analyse vom Konflikstrategien:
Untersucht an einer dynamischen Konfliktmodell* (A contribution to
to the analysis of conflict strategy: study of a dynamic conflict
model). Meisenheim am Glan, Hain, 76, x-346 p.

877   PETROVSKAJA, L. A. "O ponjatijnoj sheme social'no-psichologičeskogo
analiza konflikta" (On the concept scheme of a socio-psychological analysis of conflict), in: *Teoretičeskie i metodologičeskie
problemy social'noj psihologii.* Moskva, 1977 : 126-143.

878   PFEIFFER, Wolfgang M. "Konflikte, psychoreaktive und psychosomati-
sche Störungen auf Nias (Indonesia)" (Conflicts, psycho-reactive
and psycho-somatic disturbances in Nias, Indonesia), *Sociologus*
27(1), 1977 : 1-35.

879   RIVIÈRE, Claude. "Pour une sociologie des conflits", *C. int. Sociol.*
24(62), jan-jun 77 : 5-26.

880   "Social conflict", *J. soc. Issues* 33(1), 1977 : 1-229.

881   STUMPF, Stephen A. "Using integrators to manage conflict in a
research organization", *J. appl. behav. Sci.* 13(4), oct-dec 77 :
507-517.

882   TJOSVOLD, Dean. "Commitment to justice in conflict between unequal
status persons", *J. appl. soc. Psychol.* 7(2), apr-jun 77 : 149-
162.

883   YANOV, A. "Social contradictions and the social struggle in the
post-stalinist USSR", *Int. J. Sociol.* 6(2-3), 1976 : 219 p.

12363.

884   BURNS, Tom R. "Unequal exchange and uneven development in social
life: continuities in a structural theory of social exchange",
Acta sociol. 20(3), 1977:: 217-245.

885   CHADWICK-JONES, John K. *Social exchange theory: its structure and
influence in social psychology.* London-New York, Academic Press,
76, vi-431 p.

886   COOK, Karen S. "Exchange and power in networks of interorganizational relations", *Sociol. Quart.* 18(1), 1977 : 62-82.

887   Bibl.XXVI-809. HEATH, A. *Rational choice and social exchange: a
critique of exchange theory.* CR: Richard M. EMERSON, *Amer. J.
Sociol.* 82(6), mai 77 : 1364-1366; Mary FARMER, *Brit. J. Sociol.*
28(2), jun 77 : 254-255.

888   KUJI, Toshitake. "Shakai-kôkan riron kara no shakai-kateiron" (Toward an exchange theory of social processes), *Mie-daigaku Kyôiku-*

gakubu Kenkyu Kiyô 28(3), 1977 : 19-33,

889   MICHENER, H. Andrew; COHEN, Eugene D.; SØRENSEN, Aage B. "Social exchange: predicting transactional outcomes in five-event, four-person systems", *Amer. sociol. R.* 42(3), jun 77 : 522-535.

890   VATUK, Sylvia. "Gifts and affines in North India", *Contrib. Ind. Sociol.* 9(2), jul-dec 75 : 155-196.

12400. GROUP
GROUPE

12410. Group dynamics
Dynamique de groupe

[See also / Voir aussi: 638, 939, 1466, 2542, 5306]

891   BABAD, Elisha Y. *et al.* "An all-purpose model for group work", *Hum. Relat.* 30(4), apr 77 : 389-401.

892   BAR-LEVAV, Reuven. "The treatment of preverbal hunger and rage in a group", *Int. J. Group Psychother.* 27(4), oct 77 : 457-469.

893   BARDILL, Ronald R. "A behavior-contracting program of group treatment for early adolescents in a residential treatment setting", *Int. J. Group Psychother.* 27(3), jul 77 : 389-400.

894   BERTRAM, H. Raven; RUBIN, Jeffrey Z. *Social psychology: people in groups.* New York, John Wiley and Sons, 76, 591 p. CR: Morris J. DANIELS, *Contemp. Sociol. (Washington)* 6(2), mar 77 : 241-242.

895   BLUMBERG, Arthur; GOLEMBIEWSKI, Robert T. *Learning and change in groups.* Harmondsworth, Eng.-Baltimore, Penguin Books, 76, 208 p.

896   CALHOUN, Donald W. *Persons-in-groups: a humanistic social psychology.* New York, Harper and Row, 76, 484 p. CR: Morris J. DANIELS, *Contemp. Sociol. (Washington)* 6(2), mar 77 : 241-242.

897   COTINAUD, Olivier. *Groupe et analyse institutionnelle, l'intervention psychosociologique et ses dérivés.* Paris, Centurion, 76, 234 p.

898   FISHER, Harriet S. "Adolescent group psychotherapy: collaborative opportunity for patients, parents, and therapist", *Int. J. Group Psychother.* 27(2), 1977 : 233-239.

899   GANZARAIN, Ramon. "General systems and object-relations theories: their usefulness in group psychotherapy", *Int. J. Group Psychother.* 27(4), oct 77 : 441-456.

900   "Group psychotherapy research: an open forum", *Int. J. Group Psychother.* 27(2), apr 77 : 135-200; 27(3), jul 77 : 281-341.

901   HANSEN, James C.; WARNER, Richard W.; SMITH, Elsie M. *Group counseling: theory and process.* Chicago, Rand McNally College Publishing Co., 76, 460 p.

902   HERSEN, Michael; LUBER, Raymond F. "Use of group psychotherapy in a partial hospitalization service: the remediation of basic skill deficits", *Int. J. Group Psychother.* 27(3), jul 77 : 361-376.

903   HORWITZ, Leonard. "A group-centered approach to group psychotherapy py", *Int. J. Group Psychother.* 27(4), oct 77 : 423-440.

904   HOULIHAN, John P. "Contribution of an intake group to psychiatric impatient milieu therapy", *Int. J. Group Psychother.* 27(2), apr 77 : 215-223.

905   KAËS, René. *L'appareil psychique groupal: constructions du groupe.* Paris, Dunod; New York, SMPF Corporation, 76, xii-273 p.

906   LIEBERMAN, Morton A. "Problems in integrating traditional group therapies with new group forms", *Int. J. Group Psychother.* 27(1), jan 77 : 19-32.

907   LION, John R.; CHRISTOPHER, Russell L.; MADDEN, Denis J. "A group approach with violent outpatients", *Int. J. Group Psychother.* 27(1), jan 77 : 67-74.

908   MacLENNAN, Beryce W. "Modifications of activity group therapy for children", *Int. J. Group Psychother.* 27(1), jan 77 : 85-96.

909   MARTINEZ, Cervando. "Group process and the Chicano: clinical issues" *Int. J. Group Psychother.* 27(2), apr 77 : 225-231.

910   PETERS, Carol B. "It could be worse: effective group psychotherapy
        with the help-rejecting complainer", *Int. J. Group Psychother.*
        27(4), oct 77 : 471-480.
911   PRAGŁOWSKI, Janusz. "Teoria grupy w systemie socjologicznym Ludwika
        Gumplowicza" (Theory of groups in the sociological system of L.
        Gumplowicz), *Stud. socjol.* 63(4), 1976 : 85-105.
912   SBANDI, Pio. *Psicología de grupos* (Group psychology). Barcelona,
        Editorial Herder, 77, 278 p.
913   SCHIFFER, Mortimer. "Activity-interview group psychotherapy: theory,
        principles, and practice", *Int. J. Group Psychother.* 27(3), jul
        77 : 377-388.
914   "Self-help groups", *J. appl. behav. Sci.* 12(3), jul-sep 76 : 261-463.
915   SELIGMAN, Milton (ed.). *Group counseling and group psychotherapy
        with rehabilitation clients.* Springfield, Ill., Thomas, 77, xiv-
        335 p.
916   STONE, Walter N.; WHITMAN, Roy M. "Contributions of the psychology
        of the self to group process and group therapy", *Int. J. Group
        Psychother.* 27(3), jul 77 : 343-359.
917   VAN DEN BERGHE, Pierre L. "Territorial behavior in a natural human
        group", *Soc. Sci. Inform.* 16(3-4), 1977 : 419-430.
918   VASSILIOU, George; VASSILIOU, Vasso G. "On the alternation of group
        transaction patterns and its therapeutic actualization", *Int. J.
        Group Psychother.* 27(1), jan 77 : 75-84.
919   WAXER, Peter H. "Short-term group psychotherapy: some principles and
        techniques", *Int. J. Group Psychother.* 27(1), jan 77 : 33-42.

12420. Primary group. Training group
Groupe primaire. Groupe de formation

[See also / Voir aussi: 842, 946]

920   BRODY, Celeste M. *The peer group.* Morristown, N.J., General Learning
        Press, 76, xiii-47 p.
921   DANILIN, K. È. "Analiz refleksivnyh struktur pri issledovanii malyh
        grupp" (Analysis of reflexive structures research in small groups),
        in: *Teoretičeskie i metodologičeskie problemy social'noj psiholo-
        gii.* Moskva, 1977 : 109-126.
922   GORDON, Michael. "Primary group differentiation in urban Ireland",
        Soc. Forces 55(3), mar 77 : 743-752.
923   GUSTAFSON, James P. "The passive small group: working concepts",
        Hum. Relat. 29(8), aug 76 : 793-803.
924   GUSTAFSON, James P. "The pseudomutual small group or institution",
        Hum. Relat. 29(10), oct 76 : 989-997.
925   HAUSER, Stuart T.; SHAPIRO, Roger L. "An approach to the analysis
        of faculty-student interactions in small groups", *Hum. Relat.*
        29(9), sep 76 : 819-832.
926   KATANO, Takashi. "T-gurupu no yogokaka ni kansuru kenkyu - A-kigyo
        kanri kantokusha no baai" (Study on prognostic effects of T-group
        on managerial staff of a company), *Nara-daigaku Kiyô* (6), 1977 :
        115-126.
927   KOLOMINSKIJ, Ja. L. *Psihologija vzaimo-otnošenij v malyh gruppah
        (Obščie i vozrastnye osobennost)* (Psychology of interrelations in
        small groups. General characteristics and by age), Minsk, Izda-
        tel'stvo BGU imeni V. I. Lenina, 76, 350 p.
928   LUNDGREN, David C.; SCHAEFFER, Catherine. "Feedback processes in
        sensitivity training groups", *Hum. Relat.* 29(8), aug 76 : 763-
        782.
929   PANIOTTO, V. I. "Sociometričeskie metody izucenija malyh social'nyh
        grupp" (Sociometric methods for the study of small social groups),
        Sociol. Issled. (Moskva) (3), 1976 : 141-152.
930   SZMATKA, Jacek. "Grupy pierwotne w strukturze społecznej" (Primary
        groups in the social structure), *Stud. socjol.* 65(2), 1977 : 145-
        166.

930   SZMATKA, Jacek. "Grupy pierwotne w strukturze społecznej" (Primary
       groups in the social structure), *Stud. socjol.* 65(2), 1977 : 145-
       166.
931   VAJSMAN, R. S. "K voprosu ob ěffektivnosti malyh grupp" (Question
       on the small groups efficiency), in: *Teoretičeskie i metodologičes-
       kie problemy social'noj psihologii.* Moskva, 1977 : 74-92.
932   WOODMAN, William F.; GRANT, Marc R. "The persistence and salience of
       small group structures within a successful athletic team: a case
       study over time", *Int. R. Sport Sociol.* 12(2), 1977 : 73-87.
933   WOOTTON, A. J. "Sharing: some notes on the organization of talk in
       a therapeutic community", *Sociology (London)* 11(2), mai 77 : 333-
       350.
934   ZIFFO, P. M. "Communication sequence in small groups: persuasion as
       a two-step process", *J. soc. Psychol.* 102(2), aug 77 : 291-296.

12430. Group size
Dimension du groupe
[See also / Voir aussi: 548, 816, 841, 867, 962, 2878, 3310]

935   ARABIE, Phipps. "Clustering representations of group overlap", *J.
       math. Sociol.* 5(1), 1977 : 113-128.
936   BOORMAN, Scott A. "Informational optima in a formal hierarchy: cal-
       culations using the semigroup", *J. math. Sociol.* 5(1), 1977 : 129-
       147.
937   DAVIS, James A. "Sociometric triads as multivariate systems", *J.
       math. Sociol.* 5(1), 1977 : 41-60.
938   DAVIS, John D. "Effects of communication about interpersonal process
       on the evolution of self-disclosure in dyads", *J. Person. soc. Psy-
       chol.* 35(1), jan 76 : 31-37.
939   LINDSAY, John S. B. "On the number and size of subgroups", *Hum. Re-
       lat.* 29(12), dec 76 : 1103-1114.
940   MULLINS, Nicholas C. *et al.* "The group structure of cocitation clus-
       ters: a comparative study", *Amer. sociol. R.* 42(4), aug 77 : 552-
       562.
941   SEGAL, Mady Wechsler. "A reconformation of the logarithmic effect
       of group size", *Sociometry* 40(2), jun 77 : 187-190.
942   SKOTKO, Vincent P.; LANGMEYER, Daniel. "The effects of interaction
       distance and gender on self-disclosure in the dyad", *Sociometry*
       40(2), jun 77 : 178-182.
943   STAVIG, Gordon R.; BARNETT, Larry D. "Group size and societal con-
       flict", *Hum. Relat.* 30(8), aug 77 : 761-765.

12440. Group integration
Intégration du groupe
[See also / Voir aussi: 559, 630, 861]

944   BIRD, Anne Marie. "Team structure and success as related to cohe-
       siveness and leadership", *J. soc. Psychol.* 103(2), dec 77 : 217-
       223.
945   CALLOWAY, Carolyn R. "Group cohesiveness in the Black Panther Party",
       J. Black Stud. 8(1), sep 77 : 55-74. [USA.]
946   COHEN, Jere M. "Sources of peer group homogeneity", *Sociol. Educ.*
       50(4), oct 77 : 227-241.
947   DONCOV, A. I. "Principy social'no-psihologičeskogo analiza gruppovoj
       spločennosti" (Principles of socio-psychological analysis of group
       cohesiveness), in: *Teoretičeskie i metodologičeskie problemy so-
       cial'noj psihologii.* Moskva, 1977 : 50-74.
948   FORGAS, Joseph P. "Polarization and moderation of person perception
       judgments as a function of group interaction style", *Europ. J.
       soc. Psychol.* 7(2), 1977 : 175-187.
949   KOKURINA, I. G. "K vožmoznosti ižucenija ieharhii gruppovyh cennos-
       tej pri pomošci sociometričeskoj metodiki" (On the possibilities
       of studying group values hierarchy with the help of sociometrical

method), in: *Novoe v psihologii. II.* Moskva, 1977 : 134-139.

950   LEVINE, John M.; SROKA, Karolyn R.; SNYDER, Howard N. "Group support
       and reaction to stable and shifting agreement/disagreement", *Socio-
       metry* 40(3), 1977 : 214-224.

951   ŁOŚ, Maria. "Grupy odniesienia - propozycja modyfikacji zakresu po-
       jęcia" (Preference groups - a proposal to modify the range of the
       concept), *Stud. socjol.* 63(4), 1976 : 107-115.

952   MEEKER, Barbara F. "Interaction in a cooperative game: status, sex
       roles, and task behavior", *Pacific sociol. B.* 20(4), oct 77 : 476-
       491.

953   SCHOFIELD, Janet W.; SAGAR, H. Andrew. "Peer interaction patterns
       in an integrated middle school", *Sociometry* 40(2), jun 77 : 130-
       138.

954   UEMURA, Katsuhiko. "Fessler-Kaneda no 'Chiiki rentaisei shakudo' no
       sai-hensei" (Revision of Fessler-Kaneda's community solidarity
       scale), *Nenpo Shakai-shinrigaku* 18, 1977 : 149-169.

955   UMINO, Michio. "Bunketsu-shisū no kentô -hôhôronteki kôsatsu" (Some
       examinations on the nature of a segregation index), *Kaisei-gakuin-
       daigaku Shakaigakubu Kiyo* 35, 1977 : 49-60.

956   WARD, Russell A. "Aging group consciousness. Implications in an ol-
       der sample", *Sociol. soc. Res.* 61(4), jul 77 : 496-519.

12450. Group membership
Appartenance au groupe

[See also / Voir aussi: 934, 948, 950, 1091, 3585]

957   CARLSTON, Donal E. "Effects of polling order on social influence in
       decision-making groups", *Sociometry* 40(2), jun 77 : 115-123.

958   CHELL, Elizabeth. "A study of situational (cooperative/competitive)
       and personality ('high' and 'low' participation) factors on the
       role enactment of human relations problems", *Hum. Relat.* 29(11),
       nov 76 : 1061-1081.

959   GOLOGOR, Ethan. "Group polarization in a non-risk-taking culture",
       J. cross-cult. Psychol. 8(3), sep 77 : 331-346.

960   KAPLAN, Martin F.; MILLER, Charles E. "Judgments and group discus-
       sion: effect of presentation and memory factors on polarization",
       Sociometry 40(4), dec 77 : 337-343.

961   KENNEDY, James; STEPHAN, Walter G. "The effects of cooperation and
       competition on ingroup-outgroup bias", *J. appl. soc. Psychol.*
       7(2), apr-jun 77 : 115-130.

962   KOOMEN, Willem; SAGEL, Piet K. "The prediction of participation in
       two-person groups", *Sociometry* 40(4), dec 77 : 369-373.

963   KOULACK, David. "Effect of outgroup responses on perceptions of lea-
       der effectiveness", *Soc. Forces* 55(4), jun 77 : 959-965.

964   LIBO, Lester M. *Is there life after group ?* Garden City, N.Y., An-
       chor Press Doubleday, 77, x-148 p.

965   RIDGEWAY, Cecilia L.; JACOBSON, Cardell K. "Sources of status and
       influence in all female and mixed sex groups", *Sociol. Quart.*
       18(3), 1977 : 413-425.

966   ROWAN, John. *The power of the group.* London, Davis-Poynter, 76,
       212 p.

967   WILDER, David A. "Perception of groups, size of opposition, and so-
       cial influence", *J. exp. soc. Psychol.* 13(3), mai 77 : 253-268.

968   WYER, Robert S. Jr. "The role of logical and non-logical factors in
       making inferences about category membership", *J. exp. soc. Psychol.*
       13(6), nov 77 : 577-595.

969   ZANDER, Alvin. "The psychology of removing group members and recruit-
       ing new ones", *Hum. Relat.* 29(10), oct 76 : 969-987.

12460. Group performance
Performance du groupe

[See also / Voir aussi: 632, 649, 749, 826, 952, 2882]

970   BRANDSTÄTTER, Hermann; SCHULER, Heinz (eds.). *Entscheidungsprozesse in Gruppen* (Decion-making processes in groups). Bern, H. Huber, 76, 192 p.

971   KRUGLANSKI, Arie W.; STEIN, Chana; RITER, Aviah. "Contingencies of exogenous reward and task performance: on the 'minimax' strategy in instrumental behavior", *J. appl. soc. Psychol.* 7(2), apr-jun 77 : 141-148.

972   McGUIRE, Mary V.; BERMANT, Gordon. "Individual and group decisions in response to a mock trial: a methodological note", *J. appl. soc. Psychol.* 7(3), jul-sep 77 : 220-226.

12500. BUREAUCRACY. ORGANIZATION
BUREAUCRATIE. ORGANISATION

12510. Sociology of organization
Sociologie des organisations

[See also / Voir aussi: 1399]

973   ANDICS, J.; ROZGONYI, T. "Néhany gondolat a szervezet fogalmának marxista értelmezéséröl" (Some thoughts on the Marxist interpretation of the concept of organization), *Szociológia* 6(1), 1977 : 42-56.

974   BENSON, J. Kenneth. "Innovation and crisis in organizational analysis", *Sociol. Quart.* 18(1), 1977 : 3-16.

975   BOWEY, Angela M. *The sociology of organisations.* London, Hodder and Stoughton, 76, 5-228 p.

976   BÜSCHGES, Günter (ed.). *Organisation und Herrschaft: Klassifikation und moderne Studientexte zur sozialwissenschaftliche Organisationstheorie* (Organization and control: classification and modern study texts of social science organization theories). Reinbek-bei-Hamburg, Rowohlt, 76, 346 p.

977   CLEGG, Stewart; DUNKERLEY, David (eds.). *Critical issues in organizations.* London, Routledge and Kegan Paul, 77, vii-109 p.

978   DRIGGERS, Preston F. "Theoretical blockage: a strategy for the development of organizational theory", *Sociol. Quart.* 18(1), 1977 : 143-159.

979   EVAN, William M. *Organization theory: structures, systems, and environments.* New York, Wiley, 76, xiii-312 p.

980   FUNABASHI, Harutoshi. "Soshiki no sonritsu kozo-ron" (Genetic objectivation theory of organization), *Shiso* (8), aug 77 : 37-63.

981   HANDY, Charles B. *Understanding organizations.* Harmondsworth-Baltimore, Penguin Books, 76, 447 p.

982   HEYDEBRAND, Wolf. "Organizational contradictions in public bureaucracies: toward a Marxian theory of organizations", *Sociol. Quart.* 18(1), 1977 : 83-107.

983   IMERSHEIN, Allen W. "Organizational change is a paradigm shift", *Sociol. Quart.* 18(1), 1977 : 33-43.

984   KOCHAN, Thomas A.; CUMMINGS, L. I.; HUBER, George P. "Operationalizing the concepts of goals and goal incompatibilities in organizational behavior research", *Hum. Relat.* 29(6), jun 76 : 527-544.

985   McMAHON, J. Timothy. "Participative and power-equalized organizational systems. An empirical investigation and theoretical integration", *Hum. Relat.* 29(3), mar 76 : 203-214.

986   MEYER, Marshall W. *Theory of organizational structure.* Indianapolis, Bobbs-Merrill, 77, 82 p.

987   MOUZELIS, Nicos P. *Organisation and bureaucracy. An analysis of modern theories.* Rev. ed. London, Routledge and Kegan Paul, 76, xxxiv-234 p.

988   PFEIFFER, Dietmar K. *Organisationssoziologie: eine Einführung* (Organizational sociology: an introduction). Stuttgart-Berlin-Köln,

Mainz, Kohlhammer, 76, 147 p.

989   SAITŌ, Yoshio. "Kanryôsei riron to keieigaku no kôsaku" (The study of business administration and the theory of bureaucracy), *Soshiki-kagaku* 11(3), 1977 : 34-43.

990   SAITŌ, Yoshio. "Kôeki-kigyôron to kanryôsei riron no kôsaku" (Public utility economics and the theory of bureaucracy), *Kôeki-jigyô Kenkyû* 29(1), 1977 : 97-125.

991   SHERIFF, P. "Sociology of public bureaucracies, 1965-1975", *Curr. Sociol.* 24(2), 1976 : 175 p.

992   SHORTELL, Stephen M. "The role of environment in a configurational theory of organizations", *Hum. Relat.* 30(3), mar 77 : 275-302.

993   TÓTH, I. Ż. *Szervezés- és vezetéselmélet. A szociális rendszerek irányításelmélete* (Organization and management theory. Organizational theory of social systems). Budapest, International Computer Education Center, 76, 432 p.

994   TREUHEIT, Leo J. "Der wissenschaftssystematische und -historische Ort der Organisationspsychologie" (The scientific systematical and historical place of the psychology of organizations), *Z. soz.- Psychol.* 8(4), 1977 : 218-233.

995   ZÜNDORF, Lutz. "Forschungsartefakte bei der Messung der Organisationsstruktur" (Research artifacts in surveying organizational structure), *Soz. Welt* 27(4), 1976 : 468-487.

12520. Complex organization
Organisation complexe
[See also / Voir aussi: 1081]

996   "Associations dans la vie locale (Les)", *Rech. soc. (Paris)* 60, oct-dec 76 : 5-83.

997   KNOKE, David; THOMSON, Randall. "Voluntary association membership trends and the family life cycle", *Soc. Forces* 56(1), sep 77 : 48-65.

998   KRONUS, C. L. "Mobilizing voluntary associations into a social movement: the case of environmental quality", *Sociol. Quart.* 18(2), 1977 : 267-283.

999   LANE, John Hart Jr. *Voluntary associations among Mexican Americans in San Antonio, Texas: organizational and leadership characteristics.* New York, Arno Press, 76, viii-220 p.

1000   MATEJKO, Alexander J. "The sociological nature of complex organizations", *Sociol. int. (Berlin)* 12(1-2), 1974 : 105-146.

1001   MILES, Robert H. "Role-set configuration as a predictor of role conflict and ambiguity in complex organizations", *Sociometry* 40(1), 1977 : 21-34.

1002   MILETI, Dennis S.; GILLESPIE. David F.; HAAS, J. Eugene. "Size and structure in complex organizations", *Soc. Forces* 56(1), sep 77 : 208-217.

1003   RADECKI, Henry. "Ethnic voluntary organizational dynamics in Canada: a report", *Int. J. comp. Sociol.* 17(3-4), sep-dec 76 : 275-284.

1004   YEO, Stephen. *Religion and voluntary organisations in crisis.* London, Croom Helm, 76, 426 p.

12530. Bureaucracy
Bureaucratie
[See also / Voir aussi: 134, 385, 984, 2496, 4375, 4537, 5632]

1005   Bibl.XXVI-917. ABELL, Peter (ed.). *Organisations as bargaining and influence systems.* CR: David SILVERMAN, *Brit. J. Sociol.* 28(1), mar 77 : 113.

1006   AL-SALMAN, F. J. "Some observations on developmental change and bureaucracy in developing countries", *Res publ.* 18(2), 1976 : 237-250.

1007   ARMENAKIS, Achilles A.; FEILD, Hubert S.; HOLLEY, William H. "Guidelines for overcoming empirically identified evaluation problems of organizational development change agents", *Hum. Relat.* 29(12), dec 76 : 1147-1161.

1008   BEKKE, A. J. G. *Organisatieontwikkeling: confrontatie van individu,
        organisatie en maatschappij: een sociologische plaatsbepaling* (De-
        velopment of organizations: confrontation between the individual,
        organizations and society; a sociological field). Rotterdam, Uni-
        versitaire Pers Rotterdam, 76, viii-230 p.

1009   BERK, B. B. "Staff stability and organizational effectiveness", *Pa-
        cific sociol. R.* 20(3), jul 77 : 349-370.

1010   BOWERS, David G.; FANKLIN, Jerome L. *Survey-guided development:
        data based organizational change.* Ann Arbor. Institute for Social
        Research. University of Michigan. 76. v-166 p.

1011   BOZEMAN, Barry; McALPINE, William E. "Goals and bureaucratic deci-
        sion-making: an experiment", *Hum. Relat.* 30(5), mai 77 : 417-429.

1012   BURKE, W. Warner (ed.). *Current issues and strategies in organiza-
        tion development.* New York, Human Sciences Press, 77, 448 p.

1013   CAPLOW, Theodore. *How to run any organization.* New York, Holt, Rine-
        hart and Winston, 76, 222 p.

1014   CARROLL, Stephen J.; TOSI, Henry L. *Organizational behavior.* Chi-
        cago, St. Clair Press, 77, xix-570 p.

1015   CLIFFORD, Jim. *Decision making in organisations.* London, Longman,
        76, xi-273 p.

1016   DAVIS, Louis E. "Evolving alternative organization designs: their
        sociotechnical bases", *Hum. Relat.* 30(3), mar 77 : 261-273.

1017   DEITCHMAN, Seymour J. *The best laid schemes: a tale of social res-
        earch and bureaucracy.* Cambridge, Mass., MIT Press, 76, 483 p.
        CR: David R. SEGAL, *Contemp. Sociol. (Washington)* 6(4), jul 77 :
        502-503.

1018   ÊLENURM, T. A. "K probleme ocenki vlijanija organizacionnyh izmene-
        nij na razvitie organizacii" (To the problem of the evaluation of
        the organizational changes influences on the organization deve-
        lopment), *Trudy Tallinsk. politehn. Inst.* 24, 1977 : 17-24.

1019   ELIZUR, Dov; GUTTMAN, Louis. "The structure of attitudes toward work
        and technological change within an organization", *Adm. Sci. Quart.*
        21(4), dec 76 : 611-622.

1020   FARACE, Richard V.; MONGE, Peter R.; RUSSELL, Hamish M. *Communicat-
        ing and organizing.* Reading, Mass., Addison-Wesley Publishing Co.,
        77, xvii-281 p.

1021   FUJIYAMA, Masahide. "Kanryosei soshiki ni kansuru bunken kadai"
        (Review article: literature on bureaucratic organizations),
        Soshiki-kagaku 11(3), 1977 : 44-53.

1022   GIBSON, James L.; IVANCEVICH, John M.; DONNELLY, James H. Jr. *Or-
        ganizations: behavior, structure, processes.* Rev. ed. Dallas,
        Tex., Business Publications, 76, xiv-506 p.

1023   GOLDMAN, Paul; VAN HOUTEN, Donald R. "Managerial strategies and the
        worker: a Marxist analysis of bureaucracy", *Sociol. Quart.* 18(1),
        1977 : 108-125.

1024   GOLDNER, Fred H.; RITTI, R. Richard; FERENCE, Thomas P. "The produc-
        tion of cyclical knowledge in organizations", *Amer. sociol. R.*
        42(4), aug 77 : 539-551.

1025   GRAY, Jerry L.; STARKE, Frederick A. *Organizational behavior: con-
        cepts and applications.* Columbus, Ohio, Merrill, 77, ix-302 p.

1026   GUEST, Robert H.; HERSEY, Paul; BLANCHARD, Kenneth H. *Organizational
        change through effective leadership.* Englewood Cliffs, N.J., Pren-
        tice-Hall, 77, viii-184 p.

1027   HANNAN, Michael T.; FREEMAN, John. "The population ecology of orga-
        nizations", *Amer. J. Sociol.* 82(5), mar 77 : 929-964.

1028   HANNIGAN, John A.; KUENEMAN, Rodney M. "Legitimacy and public orga-
        nizations: a case study", *Canad. J. Sociol.* 2(1), 1977 : 125-135.

1029   HEGEDÜS, Andras. *Socialism and bureaucracy.* London, Allison and Bus-
        by, 76, 195 p.

1030   HEIRS, Ben J.; PEHRSON, Gordon O. *The mind of the organization: on
        the relevance of the decision-thinking processes of the human mind
        to the decision-thinking processes of organizations.* New York,

Harper and Row, 77, xv-138 p.

1031   JOHNSON, Bonnie McDaniel. *Communication: the process of organizing.*
        Boston, Allyn and Bacon, 77, xi-404 p.

1032   KHANDWALLA, Pradip N. *The design of organizations.* New York, Har-
        court Brace Jovanovich, 77, xvii-713 p.

1033   KIMBERLY, John R. "Organizational size and the structuralist pers-
        pective: a review, critique, and proposal", *Adm. Sci. Quart.*
        21(4), dec 76 : 571-597.

1034   KING, Ambrose Yeo-chi. "A voluntarist model of organization: the
        Maoist version and its critique", *Brit. J. Sociol.* 28(3), sep
        77 : 363-374.

1035   KIRSCHENBAUM, Alan B.; GOLDBERG, Albert I. "Organizational behavior,
        career orientations, and the propensity to move among profession-
        als", *Sociol. Wk Occupat.* 3(3), aug 76 : 357-372.

1036   KOLARSKA, Lena. "Centralizacija i formalizacja" (Centralization and
        formalization), *Stud. socjol.* 64(1), 1977 : 225-240.

1037   KVALE, Steinas. "Examinations: from ritual through bureaucracy to
        technology", *Soc. Praxis* 3(3-4), 1975 : 187-206.

1038   LAKY, T. "A szervezetfogalom vitatott elemei" (Disputed features of
        the concept of "organization"), *Szociológia* 6(1), 1977 : 79-96.

1039   MAAS, P. J. M. *De organisatie als sociall systeem* (The organization
        as a social system). Delft, Delftse Universitaire Pers, 76, vi-
        51 p.

1040   MARCH, James G. *et al. Ambiguity and choice in organizations.* Ber-
        gen, Universitetsforlaget, 76, 408 p.

1041   METCALFE, J. L. "Organizational strategies and interorganizational
        networks", *Hum. Relat.* 29(4), apr 76 : 327-343.

1042   MEYER, John W.; ROWAN, Brian. "Institutionalized organizations: for-
        mal structure as myth and ceremony", *Amer. J. Sociol.* 83(2), sep
        77 : 340-363.

1043   MEYER, Marshall W.; BROWN, M. Craig. "The process of bureaucratiza-
        tion", *Amer. J. Sociol.* 83(2), sep 77 : 364-385.

1044   MREŁA, Krzysztof; STANISZKIS, Jadwiga. "Degree of coherence and me-
        chanisms of transformation of organizational structures", *Polish
        sociol. B.* 38(3), 1977 : 49-62.

1045   NAMIHIRA, Isao. "Keiei-soshiki no kanryôka to sono keieisha-hojû
        no oyobosu eikyô" (Bureaucratization of business organizations
        and its effects on the sources of recruitment of business leaders),
        Shakaigaku Hyôron 27(3), 1977 : 50-69.

1046   NJAIM, Humberto. "La tecnologia organizativa como condicionamiento
        y producto de la sociedad organizacional" (Organizational techno-
        logy as conditioning and product of organizational society), *R.
        Fac. Der. (Caracas)* 54, apr 75 : 22-46. *[Venezuela.]*

1047   OBRADOVIČ, Josip. "Utjecaj veličine organizacija na strukturu od-
        lučivanja i ponašanja pojedinaca u procesu donošenja odluka"
        (The size of an organization and its impact on the decision-
        making structure and the attitude of the individual in decision),
        Sociologija 19(4), 1977 : 559-596.

1048   PARRA LUNA, Francisco. "Las organizaciones y sus sistemas de valores"
        (Organizations and their value systems), *Bol. Docum. Fondo Invest.
        econ. soc.* 9(3), jul-sep 77 : 584-594.

1049   PETERS, J. P. M. *Individu en organisatie: een organisatie-psychologi-
        sche benadering* (Individual and organization: an approach in or-
        ganizational psychology). Deventer, Kluwer, 76, x-116 p.

1050   PFEFFER, Jeffrey; SALANCIK, Gerald R. "Administrator effectiveness:
        the effects of advocacy and information on achieving outcomes in
        an organizational context", *Hum. Relat.* 30(7), jul 77 : 641-656.

1051   PRESTHUS, Robert; MONOPOLI, William. "Bureaucracy in the USA and Ca-
        nada: social, attitudinal and behavioral variables", *Int. J. comp.
        Sociol.* 18(1-2), mar-jun 77 : 176-190.

1052   Bibl.XXVI-933. PRICE, Robert M. *Society and bureaucracy in contempo-
        rary Ghana.* CR: Heidi Schuhr ERLICH, *Amer. J. Sociol.* 83(2), sep
        77 : 530-532.

1053   REITZ, H. Joseph. *Behavior in organizations*. Homewood, Ill., R. D. Irwin, 77, xv-575 p.

1054   RITTI, R. Richard; FUNKHOUSER, G. Ray. *The ropes to skip and the ropes to know: studies in organizational behavior*. Columbus, Ohio, Grid, 77, xx-252 p.

1055   ROCKEY, Edward H. *Communicating in organizations*. Cambridge, Mass., Winthrop Publishers, 77, xix-156 p.

1056   ROMÁN DE SILGADO, Manuel. *Burocracia y cambio social: ensayo sobre las relaciones entre las formas organizacionales y la presión de cambio* (Bureaucracy and social change: essay on the relationships between organizational patterns and the pressure for change). Madrid, Ediciones J. Porrúa Turanzas, 76, xi-338 p.

1057   RYCHARD, Andrzej. "Organizational stereotypes of the economic reform", *Polish sociol. B.* 38(3), 1977 : 75-83.

1058   SOMLAI, P. *Hivatalnoki szervezet és intenziv iparosítás. Max Weber bürokráciaelmélete, a gazdaság és a politika viszonya a századfordulo Németországban* (Bureaucratic system and intensive industrialization. Max Weber's theory of bureaucracy, relations between economy and politics in Germany at the turn of the century). Budapest, Akadémiai Kiadó, 77, 151 p.

1059   STÖCKLI, Alfred. *Allgemeine Organisationsmethodologie* (General organizational methodology). Bern, Herbert Lang; Frankfurt-am-Main, Peter Lang, 76, 370 p.

1060   TAGUCHI, Masahiro. "Gendai soshiki ni okeru ningensei to kanri no chôwa" (The equilibrium of humanity and management in modern organization), *Shakaigaku Ronsô* 68, 1977 : 1-13.

1061   THOMPSON, Victor A. *Bureaucracy and the modern world*. Morristown, N.J., General Learning Press, 76, 141 p. CR: Robert N. STERN, *Contemp. Sociol. (Washington)* 6(3), mai 77 : 391-392.

1062   TNGALLS, John D. *Human energy: the critical factor for individuals and organizations*. Reading, Mass., Addison-Wesley Publishing Co., 76, xviii-285 p.

1063   TÜRK, Klaus. *Grundlagen einer Pathologie der Organisation* (Bases of a pathology of organizations). Stuttgart, Enke, 76, 186 p. CR: Dietmar K. PFEIFFER, *Kölner Z. Soziol. u. soz.-Psychol.* 29(3), sep 76 : 607-608.

1064   UMEZAWA, Tadashi. *Nihon-gata soshiki kaihatsu ~ sono tenkai to jirei* (Organization development in Japan; case and strategy). Tokyo, Daiyamondo-sha, 77, 384 p.

1065   WHITLEY, Richard. "Organisational control and the problem of order", *Soc. Sci. Inform.* 16(2), 1977 : 169-189.

1066   WIGAND, Rolf T. "Some recent developments in organizational communication: network analysis ~ a systemic representation of communication relationships", *Communications (Köln)* 3(2), 1977 : 181-200.

1067   WOFFORD, Jerry C.; GERLOFF, Edwin A.; CUMMINS, Robert C. *Organizational communication:the keystone to managerial effectiveness*. New York, McGraw-Hill, 77, xiv-477 p.

1068   WOOLEYBIGGART, Nicole. "The creative-destructive process of organizational change: the case of the Post Office", *Adm. Sci. Quart.* 22(3), sep 77 : 410-426.

1069   WRIGHT, Robert Granford. *The nature of organizations*. Encino, Calif., Dickenson Publishing Co., 77, viii-232 p.

12600. LEADERSHIP. ROLE
COMMANDEMENT. RÔLE

12610. Authority
Autorité

[See also / Voir aussi: 302]

1070   BAUM, Rainer C. "Authority codes: the invariance hypothesis", *Z. Soziol.* 6(1), jan 77 : 5-28; 6(4), oct 77 : 349-369.

1071 FOX, William S. *et al.* "Authority position, legitimacy of authority
structure, and acquiescence to authority", *Soc. Forces* 55(4),
jun 77 : 966-973.

1072 HARRIS, R. Baine (ed.). *Authority, a philosophical analysis.* University, Ala., University of Alabama Press, 76, vi-173 p.

1073 NASTAVŠEV, I. V. "O prirode avtoriteta ličnosti" (On the nature of
a man's authority), *Ličnost' i Obščestvo* (2), 1976 : 67-74.

1074 SAHAY, Arun. "Virtù, fortuna and charisma: an essay on Machiavelli
and Weber", *Sociol. Anal. Theory* 7(3), oct 77 : 165-183.

1075 SALAMAN, Graeme. "An historical discontinuity: from charisma to
routinization", *Hum. Relat.* 30(4), apr 77 : 373-388.

1076 WALASZEK, Zdzisława. "Power of authority ?", *Polish sociol. B.*
36(4), 1976 : 31-45.

1077 WATERSON, Karolyn. *Molière et l'autorité: structures sociales,
structures comiques.* Lexington, Ky., French Forum, 76, 150 p.

12620. Leadership
Commandement
[See also / Voir aussi: 944, 963, 999, 1026, 1045, 2691]

1078 ARGYRIS, Chris. *Increasing leadership effectiveness.* New York,
Wiley, 76, xvi-286 p.

1079 CLARK, Peter. "Leadership succession among the Hutterites", *Canad.
R. Sociol. Anthropol.* 14(3), aug 77 : 294-302.

1080 CLARK, R. D. III; SECHREST, L. B. "The mandate phenomenon", *J. Person. soc. Psychol.* 34(6), dec 76 : 1057-1061. *[Groups consisting
of six male persons were asked to elect a leader.]*

1081 COMISH, Newel W. *Effective leadership of voluntary organizations.*
Winter Park, Fla., Anna Publishers, 76, xviii-205 p.

1082 ECHOHAWK, Marlene; PARSONS, Oscar A. "Leadership vs. behavioral problems and belief in personal control among American Indian youth",
J. soc. Psychol. 102(1), jun 77 : 47-54.

1083 FRANK, Harold H.; KATSCHER, Aaron H. "The qualities of leadership:
how male medical students evaluate their female peers", *Hum. Relat.* 30(5), mai 77 : 403-416.

1084 GREENLEAF, Robert K. *Servant leadership: a journey into the nature
of legitimate power and greatness.* New York, Paulist Press, 77,
x-335 p.

1085 HELLER, Frank A.; WILPERT, Bernhard. "Limits to participative leadership: task, structure and skill as contingencies - a German-
British comparison", *Europ. J. soc. Psychol.* 7(1), 1977 : 61-84.

1086 LOYE, David. *The leadership passion.* San Francisco, Jossey-Bass
Publishers, 77, xix-249 p.

1087 NELSON, Charles W.; SMITH, Eugene. "A frame of reference for the
measurement of institutional leadership concepts and the analysis
of system states", *Hum. Relat.* 29(6), jun 76 : 589-606.

1088 NIX, Harodl L.; DRESSEL, Paula L.; BATES, Frederick L. "Changing
leaders and leadership structure: a longitudinal study", *Rur.
Sociol.* 42(1), 1977 : 22-41.

1089 RANGASWAMY, Govindarajula; HELMICH, Donald. "A comparative study
of Indian and American executives' leadership styles", *Ind. J.
soc. Res.* 17(2-3), aug-dec 76 : 71-81.

1090 RAY, J. J. "Do authoritarians hold authoritarian attitudes ?", *Hum.
Relat.* 29(4), apr 76 : 307-325.

1091 WEHMAN, Paul *et al.* "Effects of different leadership styles on individual risk-taking in groups", *Hum. Relat.* 30(3), mar 77 : 249-
259.

12630. Role
Rôle

[See also / Voir aussi: 625, 1001, 3276, 3432, 5103]

1092   BERSANI, Carl; GILLHAM, James; NAPADY, Darlene. "Perceived expec-
       tations and role behavior of socialization agents: the case of
       the school counselor and SES areas", *Sociol. Quart.* 18(3), 1977 :
       384-398.

1093   BLASS, Jerome H. "Role preferences among Jewish seminarians",
       Sociol. Anal. (San Antonio) 38(1), 1977 : 59-64.

1094   BURKE, Peter J.; TULLY, Judy C. "The measurement of role identity",
       Soc. Forces 55(4), jun 77 : 881-897.

1095   CALHOUN, Lawrence G.; SELBY, James W.; WARRING, Louise J. "Social
       perception of the victim's causal role in rape: an exploratory
       examination of four factors", *Hum. Relat.* 29(6), jun 76 : 517-
       526.

1096   DOW, Ruth McNABB. *Changing societal roles and teaching.* Washington,
       Home Economics Education association, 76, 44 p.

1097   JAGODZINSKI, Wolfgang; ZÄNGLE, Michael. "Über einige Probleme der
       Anwendung der Pfadanalyse - Bemerkungen zu einer Studie über so-
       ziokulturelle Determinanten der Fähigkeit zum Role-Taking" (On
       some problems in applying path analysis - comments on a study of
       sociocultural determinants of role-taking), *Z. Soziol.* 6(1), jan
       77 : 49-61.

1098   MacKINNON, Neil J.; SUMMERS, Gene F. "Homogeneity and role consen-
       sus: a multivariate exploration in role analysis", *Canad. J. So-
       ciol.* 1(4), 1976 : 439-462.

1099   MARKS, Stephen R. "Multiple roles and role strain: some notes on
       human energy, time and commitment", *Amer. sociol. R.* 42(6), dec
       77 : 921-936.

1100   NELSON, L. D. "Continuity in helping roles: a comparison of every-
       day and emergency role performance", *Pacific sociol. R.* 20(2),
       apr 77 : 263-278.

1101   NYE, F. Ivan; WHITE, Lynn; FRIDERES, James S. "Role competence,
       profit and marital dissolution", *Int. J. contemp. Sociol.* 14(1-
       2), jan-apr 77 : 74-86.

1102   PINKERTON, Todd. *Breaking communication barriers with roleplay.*
       Atlanta, John Knox Press, 76, 132 p.

1103   ROSS, Lee D.; AMABILE, Teresa M.; STEINMETZ, Julia L. "Social roles,
       social control, and biases in social-perception processes", *J.
       Person. soc. Psychol.* 35(7), jul 77 : 485-494.

1104   RUGGIERO, Josephie A.; WESTON, Louise C. "Sex-role characterization
       of women in 'modern gothic' novels", *Pacific sociol. R.* 20(2),
       apr 77 : 279-300.

1105   SAS, J. H. "A nöi és a férfi szerepek bibliai képe a köztudatban"
       (Female and male roles biblical picture in public consciousness),
       Világosság (12), 1977 : 770-777.

1106   SPINNER, Barry; ADAIR, John G.; BARNES, Gordon E. "A reexamination
       of the faithful subject role", *J. exp. soc. Psychol.* 13(6), nov
       77 : 543-551.

1107   STRONG, P. M.; DAVIS, A. G. "Roles, role formats and medical en-
       counters: a cross-cultural analysis of staff-client relationships
       in children's clinics", *Sociol. R.* 25(4), nov 77 : 775-800.

1108   WYER, Robert S.; HENNINGER, Marilyn; HINKLE, Ronald. "An informa-
       tional analysis of actors' and observers' belief attribution in
       a role-playing situation", *J. exp. soc. Psychol.* 13(3), mai 77 :
       199-217.

12700. ATTITUDE. OPINION

12710. Behaviour
Comportement

[See also / Voir aussi: 704, 1145, 1175, 1180, 1305, 1396, 1512, 2037, 2955, 3811, 4501]

1109   ALFIOROV, V.; BORODKIN, Friedrich. "A study of attitudinal differences of rural and urban youth by simulation game", *Polish sociol. B.* 38(3), 1977 : 13-26.

1110   ALVIRA MARTIN, Francisco. "La relación entre actitudes y conducta" (The relation between attitudes and behaviour), *R. esp. Opin. publ.* 49, 1977 : 33-52.

1111   ARTS, W.; LINDENBERG, Siegwart; WIPPLER, R. *Gedrag en struktuur: de relevantie van microtheorieën voor de verklaring van microverschijnselen* (Behaviour and structure: the relevance of microtheories to highlight macrophenomena). Rotterdam, Universitaire Pers Rotterdam, 76, xv-237 p.

1112   BARKOW, Jerome H. "Human ethology and intraindividual systems", *Soc. Sci. Inform.* 16(2), 1977 : 133-145.

1113   BECKER, Gary Stanley. *The economic approach to human behavior.* Chicago, University of Chicago Press, 76, 314 p.

1114   BELLACK, Alan S.; HERSEN, Michael. *Behavior modification: an introductory textbook.* Baltimore, Williams and Wilkins, 77, xi-374 p.

1115   BRAVER, Sanford L. *et al.* "Some conditions that affect admission of attitude change", *J. exp. soc. Psychol.* 13(6), nov 77 : 565-576.

1116   BURNSTEIN, Eugene; VINOKUR, Amiram. "Persuasive argumentation and social comparison as determinants of attitude polarization", *J. exp. soc. Psychol.* 13(4), jul 77 : 315-332.

1117   COZBY, Paul C. *Methods in behavioral research.* Palo Alto, Calif., Mayfield Publishing Co., 77, x-291 p.

1118   DAWES, Robyn M.; McTAVISH, Jeanne; SHAKLEE, Harriet. "Behavior, communication, and assumptions about other people's behavior in a commons dilemma situation", *J. Person. soc. Psychol.* 35(1), jan 77 : 1-11.

1119   EYSENCK, Hans Jürgen. (ed.). *Case studies in behaviour therapy.* London, Routledge and Kegan Paul, 76, xii-355 p.

1120   GILLINGHAM, P. R.; GRIFFITHS, R. D. P.; CARE, D. "Direct assessment of social behaviour from videotape recordings", *Brit. J. soc. clinic. Psychol.* 16(2), jun 77 : 181-187.

1121   GREENSPOON, Joel. *The sources of behavior: abnormal and normal.* Monterey, Calif., Brooks/Cole Publishing Co., 76, xii-224 p.

1122   HAHN, Martin E.; SIMMEL, Edward C. *Communicative behavior and evolution.* New York-London, Academic Press, 76, xvi-176 p.

1123   HARTMANN, Paul. "A perspective on the study of social attitudes", *Europ. J. soc. Psychol.* 7(1), 1977 : 85-96.

1124   MASH, Eric J.; TERDAL, Leif G. (eds.). *Behavior-therapy assessment: diagnosis, design, and evaluation.* New York, Springer, 76, xviii-382 p.

1125   MASTERS, R. D. "Exit, voice, and loyalty in animal and human social behavior", *Soc. Sci. Inform.* 15(6), 1976 : 855-878.

1126   McAULEY, Clark M.; STITT, Christopher L. (eds.). *Frontiers of behavior: perspective and practice.* New York, Praeger, 76, vii-231 p.

1127   MYERS, David G.; WOJCICKI, Sandra Brown; AARDEMA, Bobette S. "Attitude comparison: is there ever a bandwagon effect ?", *J. appl. soc. Psychol.* 7(4), oct-dec 77 : 341-347.

1128   NEWSTON, Darren; ENGQUIST, Gretchen; BOIS, Joyce. "The objective basis of behavior units", *J. Person. soc. Psychol.* 35(12), dec 77 : 847-862.

1129   OSKAMP, Stuart. *et al. Attitudes and opinions.* Englewood Cliffs,

N.J., Prentice-Hall, 77, xiii-466 p.

1130   PAICHELER, Geneviève. "Norms and attitude change. The phenomenon of bipolarization", *Europ. J. soc. Psychol.* 7(1), 1977 : 5-14. *[See for the first part Bibl.XXVI-1002.]*

1131   PEAY, Marilyn Y. "The effects of social power and preexisting attitudes on public and private responses to an induced attitude", *Hum. Relat.* 29(12), dec 76 : 1115-1129.

1132   PIAGET, Jean. *Le comportement, moteur de l'évolution.* Paris, Gallimard, 76, 190 p.

1133   RADEN, David. "Situational thresholds and attitude-behavior consistency", *Sociometry* 40(2), jun 77 : 123-129.

1134   RASSEM, M. H. "Über alte und neue Ethologie" (On old and new ethology), *Z. Polit.* 23(2), jun 76 : 101-113.

1135   REGAN, Dennis T.; FAZIO, Russell. "On the consistency between attitudes and behavior: look to the method of attitude formation", *J. exp. soc. Psychol.* 13(1), jan 77 : 28-45.

1136   RIESS, Marc; SCHLENKER, Barry R. "Attitude change and responsibility avoidance as modes of dilemma resolution in force-compliance situations", *J. Person. soc. Psychol.* 35(1), jan 77 : 21-30.

1137   ROCHE DE COPPENS, Peter. "Orgiastic behavior", *R. int. Sociol. (Madrid)* 35(24), 1977 : 495-522.

1138   ROGERS-WARREN, Ann; WARREN, Steven F. (eds.). *Ecological perspectives in behavior analysis.* Baltimore, University Prek Press, 77, xi-249 p.

1139   ROSENBLATT, Jay S. *et al.* (eds.). *Advances in the study of behavior. VI.* New York-London, Academic Press, 76, xv-284 p.

1140   TYSON, Herbert L. Jr.; KAPLOWITZ, Stan A. "Attitudinal conformity and anonymity", *Publ. Opin. Quart.* 41(2), 1977 : 226-234.

1141   YANDELL, Ben; INSKO, Chester A. "Attribution of attitudes to speakers and listeners under assigned-behavior conditions: does behavior engulf the field ?", *J. exp. soc. Psychol.* 13(3), mai 77 : 26 269-278.

12720. Cognitive dissonance. Prejudice
Dissonance cognitive. Préjugé
[See also / Voir aussi: 484, 725, 726, 795, 818, 2352]

1142   ALBRECHT, Stan L.; BAHR, Howar M.; CHADWICK, Bruce A. "Public stereotyping of sex roles, personality characteristics, and occupations", *Sociol. soc. Res.* 61(2), jan 77 : 223-240.

1143   ATHANASSIADES, John C. "The internationalization of the female stereotype by college women", *Hum. Relat.* 30(2), feb 77 : 187-199.

1144   BAKARE, C. G. M. "Metaperceptual congruence as a measure of the 'kernel of truth' in Nigerian interethnic stereotypes", *J. soc. Psychol.* 102(1), jun 77 : 13-25.

1145   BANDURA, Albert; ADAMS, Nancy E.; BEYER, Janice. "Cognitive processes mediating behavioral change", *J. Person. soc. Psychol.* 35(3), mar 77 : 125-139.

1146   BREWER, Marilyn B. "An information-processing approach to attribution of responsibility", *J. exp. soc. Psychol.* 13(1), jan 77 : 58-69.

1147   ETZEL, Gerhard. "Stereotype Wahrnehmung: eine alternative Interpretation klassifikatorischer Urteile" (Stereotype perception: an alternative interpretation of classificatory judgment), *Z. soz.- Psychol.* 8(4), 1977 : 234-241.

1148   FAZIO, Russell H.; ZANNA, Mark P.; COOPER, Joel. "Dissonance and self-perception: an integrative view of each theory's proper domain of application", *J. exp. soc. Psychol.* 13(5), sep 77 : 464-479.

1149   GOUDY, Willis J.; BAIN, Robert K.; SPIKER, Kathryn S. "Stereotyping as a form of attempted social control", *Sociol. soc. Res.* 61(3), apr 77 : 350-362.

1150   GOULD, Robert; BROUNSTEIN, Paul J.; SIGALL, Harold. "Attributing ability to an opponent: public aggrandizement and private denigration", *Sociometry* 40(3), 1977 : 254-261.

1151   GURWITZ, Sharon B.; DODGE, Kenneth A. "Effects of confirmation and disconfirmations on stereotype-based attributions", *J. Person. soc. Psychol.* 35(7), jul 77 : 495-500.

1152   HAMPEL, Rainer; KRUPP, Burkhard. "The cultural and the political framework of prejudice in South Africa and Great Britain", *J. soc. Psychol.* 103(2), dec 77 : 193-202.

1153   NICHOLS, Michael P.; DUKE, Marshall P. "Cognitive dissonance and locus of control: interface of two paradigms", *J. soc. Psychol.* 101(2), apr 77 : 291-297.

1154   ORNAUER, H. *et al.* (eds.). *Images of the world in the year 2000. A comparative ten nation study.* Atlantic Highlands, N.J., Humanities Press; The Hague, Mouton, 76, xvi-729 p.

1155   PALUBA, Gary V.; NEULINGER, John. "Stereotypes based on free time activities", *Soc. and Leisure* 8(3), 1976 : 89-95.

1156   PETRIE, Brian M. "Examination of a stereotype: athletes as conservatives", *Int. R. Sport Sociol.* 12(3), 1977 : 51-62.

1157   POSKOCIL, Art. "Encounters between Blacks and White liberals: the collision of stereotypes", *Soc. Forces* 55(3), mar 77 : 715-727.

1158   SALAZAR, J. M.; MARIN, G. "National stereotypes as a function of conflict and territorial proximity, a test of the mirror image hypothesis", *J. soc. Psychol.* 101(1), feb 77 : 13-19.

1159   STEADMAN, Henry J.; COCOZZA, Joseph J. "Selective reporting and the public's misconceptions of the criminally insane", *Publ. Opin. Quart.* 41(4), 1977 : 523-533.

1160   STEPHAN, Walter G. "Cognitive differentiation in intergroup perception", *Sociometry* 40(1), 1977 : 50-58.

1161   STEPHAN, Walter G. "Stereotyping: the role of ingroup-outgroup differences in causal attribution for behavior", *J. soc. Psychol.* 101(2), apr 77 : 255-266.

1162   TROPE, Yaacov; BURNSTEIN, Eugene. "A disposition-behavior congruity model of perceived freedom", *J. exp. soc. Psychol.* 13(4), jul 77 : 357-368.

1163   UMINO, Michio; KAGAMI, Yutaka. "Henken no inga kozo" (The causal structure of prejudice), *Kansei-gakuin-daigaku Shakaigakubu Kiyo* 34, 1977 : 51-65.

1164   WILLIAMS, John E. *et al.* "Sex-trait stereotypes in England, Ireland and the United States", *Brit. J. soc. clinic. Psychol.* 16(4), nov 77 : 303-309.

1165   ZUCKERMAN, Miron; SIEGELBAUM, Heidi; WILLIAMS, Restee. "Predicting helping behavior willingness and ascription of responsibility", *J. appl. soc. Psychol.* 7(4), oct-dec 77 : 295-299.

12730. Dogmatism. F scale
Dogmatisme. Échelle F

1166   BAUER, A. Thomas. "Dogmatismus als Strukturbasis ideologischer Aussagen" (Dogmatism as a structural basis for ideological statements), *Communications (Köln)* 2(2), 1976 : 207-232.

1167   BREWER, Marilyn B.; CAMPBELL, Donald T. *Ethnocentrism and intergroup attitudes: East African evidence.* New York, Halsted Press, 76, 218 p. CR: Stanley J. MORSE, *Contemp. Sociol. (Washington)* 6(4), jul 77 : 465.

1168   KARIKÓ, Sandor. "Cselekedj úgy, mint a többiek ? Adalékok a konformizmus fogalmának értelmezéséhez" (Do as the others ? Data about the understanding of the conformism concept), *Világosság* (12), 1976 : 749-756.

1169   NAGELSCHMIDT, Anna M.; JAKOB, Roberto. "Dimensionality of Rotter's I-E scale in a society in the process of modernization", *J. cross-cult. Psychol.* 8(1), mar 77 : 101-112.

1170   STANKOV, Lazar. "Some experience with the F scale in Yugoslavia",

Brit. J. soc. clinic. Psychol. 16(2), jun 77 : 111-121.

12740. Opinion
[See also / Voir aussi: 645, 772, 1218, 1454. 1877, 3648]

1171   BARTON, Allen A.; PARSONS, R. Wayne. "Measuring belief system structure", *Publ. Opin. Quart.* 41(2), 1977 : 159-160.

1172   BOURDIEU, Pierre. "La production de la croyance: contribution à une économie des biens symboliques", *Actes Rech. Sci. soc.* 13, feb 77 : 4-43.

1173   BRUNNER, Ronald D. "An 'international' alternative in public opinion research", *Amer. J. polit. Sci.* 21(3), aug 77 : 435-465.

1174   BUCHHOLZ, Rogene A. "Measurement of beliefs", *Hum. Relat.* 29(12), dec 76 : 1177-1188.

1175   CHISMAN, Forrest P. *Attitude psychology and the study of public opinion.* University Park, Pennsylvania State University Press, 76, xvi-253 p.

1176   DEHLER, Karl-Heinz. *Langfristiger Wandel der Theorien zur öffentlichen Meinung* (Long-term change of public opinion theories). Lollar-am-Lahn, Achenbach, 76, ix-52 p.

1177   FIELDS, James M.; SCHUMAN, Howard. "Public beliefs about the beliefs of the public", *Publ. Opin. Quart.* 40(4), 1976-1977 : 427-448.

1178   GROVES, David L.; KAHALAS, Harvey. "Public opinion sampling as an element in resource allocation decisions: a case study of a technique for reconciling scientific data and citizens desires", *Amer. J. Econ. Sociol.* 36(4), oct 77 : 367-380.

1179   HAJNAL, A.; HOPPÁL, M. "Az egyéni és közösségi hiedelmekről. Interdiszciplináris vázlatok" (About individual and public belief. Interdisciplinary sketches), *Szociológia* 5(3-4), 1976 : 475-493.

1180   HANSEN, Ronald D.; DONOGUE, James M. "The power of consensus: information derived from one's own and others' behavior", *J. Person. soc. Psychol.* 35(5), mai 77 : 294-302.

1181   KEPPLINGER, Hans Mathias. "Probleme der Begriffsbildung in den Sozialwissenschaften: Begriff und Gegenstand öffentliche Meinung" (Problems of concept formation in social sciences: concept and object of public opinion), *Kölner Z. Soziol. u. soc.-Psychol.* 29(2), jun 77 : 233-260.

1182   KOJIMA, Kazuto. "Public opinion trends in Japan", *Publ. Opin. Quart* 41(2), 1977 : 206-216.

1183   KOROBEJNIKOV, V. S. *Sociologičeskie problemy obščestvennogo mnenija i dejatel'nosti sredstv massovoj informacii* (Sociological problems of public opinion and activities of mass informations means). Mosva, 76, 190 p.

1184   MÉREI, F. "A hamistudati hiedelmek egyik forrása: a gyermeki elméletképzés" (One of the sources of various types of the false conscience beliefs: theory construction in childhood), *Szociológia* 5(3-4), 1976 : 502-507.

1185   MURÁNYI, M. "Hamistudat és hiedelemrendszer" (False consciousness and the belief system), *Szoiológia* 5(3-4), 1976 : 469-474.

1186   NOELLE-NEUMANN, Elisabeth. "Turbulences in the climate of opinion: methodological applications of the spiral of silence theory", *Publ. Opin. Quart.* 41(2), 1977 : 143-158.

1187   VOIGT, V. "Miért hiszünk a hiedelmekben ? A hiedelem paradigmatikus és szintagmatikus tengelye" (Why do we believe in beliefs ? The paradigmatic and syntagmatic axis of belief), *Ethnographia* (4), 1977 : 559-569.

1188   WHEELER, Michael. *Lies, damm lies, and statistics: the manipulation of public opinion in America.* New York, Liveright, 76, 300 p. CR: David V. McQUEEN, *Contemp. Sociol. (Washington)* 6(2), mar 77 : 215-216.

12750. Ideology
Idéologie

[See also / Voir aussi: 772, 1260, 1271, 1278, 1306, 1585, 1790,
1819, 1824, 2015, 2065, 2551, 2687, 2693, 2737, 4264, 5486, 5503,
5521]

1189   BISHOP, G. F. "The effect of education on ideological consistency",
Publ. Opin. Quart. 40(3), 1976 : 337-348.

1190   CARLTON, Eric. *Ideology and social order.* London, Boston, Routledge
and K. Paul, 77, 320 p.

1191   DUMONT, Louis. *Homo aequalis: genèse et épanouissement de l'idéologie économique.* Paris, Gallimard, 76, 270 p.

1192   FRIEDMAN, Yona. *Utopies réalisables.* Paris, Union Générale d'éditions, 76, 310 p.

1193   GAZIZULLIN, F. G . "Idejnaja bor'ba v oblasti tatarskoj social'no-
ěkonomičeskoj mysli v načale XX veka" (The ideological struggle
in the Tatar socio-economic thought at the beginning of the twentieth century), *Učen. Zap. Kazan. pedag. Inst.* 152, 1976 : 32-132.

1194   GEDÖ, András. "Vissza az utopiához ?" (Back to utopianism ?), *Polit.
Föisk. Közlem.* (2), 1977 : 3-13.

1195   GOULDNER, Alvin W. *The dialectic of ideology and technology. The
origins, grammar and future of ideology.* London, Macmillan, 76,
xvi-304 p.

1196   GREFFRATH, Mathias. "Das endgültige Ende der Ideologie ? Helmut
Schelsky's Weg von der Technokratie 'zum Klassenkampf'" (The de-
finitive end of ideology ? Helmut Schelsky's way from technocracy
to class struggle), *Argument* 18(100), nov-dec 76 : 949-965.

1197   JAMESON, Frederic R. "Ideology, narrative analysis, and popular culture: review article", *Theory and Soc.* 4(4), 1977 : 543-559.

1198   KAPITONOV, Ê. A. "Nekotorye metodologičeskie aspekty issledovanija
ideologičeskogo processa" (Some methodological aspects of research
on the ideological process), *Metodol. Probl. Nauki* (4), 1976 : 101-
107.

1199   KULCSÁR, K. "Az ideologiai változások hatása a jogi strukturára.
Kisérlet a szocialista tapasztalatok elemzésére" (The impact of
ideological changes on legal structure. An attempt to analyze
experiences in socialist countries), *Szociológia* 6(2), 1977 : 145-
164.

1200   LUDZ, Peter Christian. *Ideologiebegriff und marxistische Theorie.*
(The concept of ideology and Marxist theory). Opladen, Westdeutscher Verlag, 76, 337 p. CR: Dieter VOIGT, *Kölner Z. Soziol. u.
soz.-Psychol.* 29(2), jun 77 : 374-376.

1201   LUDZ, Peter Christian. "Ideologieforschung. Eine Rückbesinnung und
ein Neubeginn" (Ideology research. A retrospective thought and a
new start), *Kölner Z. Soziol. u. soz.-Psychol.* 29(1), mar 77 :
1-31.

1202   MOULIN, L. "Le temps dans les utopies et les idéologies de progrès
R. gén. (12), dec 76 : 21-32.

1203   NELSON, John S. "The ideological connection: or, smuggling in the
goods", *Theory and Soc.* 4(3), 1977 : 421-448; 4(4), 1977 : 573-
590.

1204   PALMADE, Guy. *Interdisciplinarité et idéologies.* Paris, Éditions
Anthropos, 77, 291 p.

1205   POPOVICI, Elena. *Societate, ideologie, cunoaştere* (Society, ideology,
knowledge). Bucureşti, Editura Ştiinţifică şi Enciclopedica, 76,
247 p.

1206   QUINTANILLA, Miguel A. *Ideología y ciencia* (Ideology and science).
Valencia, F. Torres, 76, 155 p.

1207   RAMA, Carlos M. *Ideología, regiones y clases sociales en la España
contemporánea* (Ideology, regions and social classes in contemporary Spain). Madrid, Ediciones Júcar, 77, 165 p.

1208   SANDHU, S. S. "Ideology and social science: a quasi-theory of political change", *Int. J. contemp. Sociol.* 13(1-2), jan-apr 76 : 107-
116.

1209   SKLAIR, Leslie. "Ideology and the sociological utopias", *Sociol. R.*
        25(1), feb 77 : 51-72.

1210   ŽURAVLEV, G. J. "Rol konkretnyh sociologičeskih issledovanij v izu-
        čenii ěffektivnosti ideologičeskoj raboty" (Role of concrete so-
        ciological research in the study of ideological activity effi-
        cience), in: *Problemy povyšenija ěffektivnosti kommunističeskoj
        propagandy. III*. Tomsk, 1976 : 32-43.

        12760. Collective behaviour
               Comportement collectif
               [See also / Voir aussi: 797, 2719]

1211   AIELLO, John R. *et al*. "Crowding and the role of interpersonal dis-
        tance preference", *Sociometry* 40(3), 1977 : 271-282.

1212   BOOTH, Alan. *Urban crowding and its consequences*. New York, Praeger,
        76, xi-139 p.

1213   EDWARDS, John N.; BOOTH, Alan. "Crowding and human sexual behavior"
        Soc. Forces 55(3), mar 77 : 791-808.

1214   FELD, Scott L. "A reconceptualization of the problem of collective
        decisions", *J. math. Sociol.* 5(2), 1977 : 256-271.

1215   GREENBERG, Carl I.; FIRESTONE, Ira J. "Compensatory responses to
        crowding: effects of personal space intrusion and privacy re-
        duction", *J. Person. soc. Psychol.* 35(9), sep 77 : 637-644.

1216   HELLER, Jack F.; GROFF, Bradford D.; SOLOMON, Sheldon H. "Toward
        an understanding of crowding: the role of physical interaction",
        J. Person. soc. Psychol. 35(3), mar 77 : 183-190.

1217   HUNYADI, Zs. *Kollektivitás az iskolai osztályokban. A közösségi be-
        állítodás strukturális meghatározói* (Collective behaviour in
        school classes. Structural determinants of collective attitudes).
        Budapest, Akadémiai Kiado, 77, 203 p.

1218   JOHNSON, Norris R.; FEINBERG, William E. "A computer simulation of
        the emergence of consensus in crowds", *Amer. sociol. R.* 42(3),
        jun 77 : 505-521.

1219   JOHNSON, Norris R.; STEMLER, James G.; HUNTER, Deborah. "Crowd beha-
        vior as 'risky shift': a laboratory experiment", *Sociometry*
        40(2), jun 77 : 183-187.

1220   LANGER, Ellen J.; SAEGERT, Susan. "Crowding and cognitive control",
        J. Person. soc. Psychol. 35(3), mar 77 : 175-182.

1221   MUCCHI, Angelica. "Irrazionalismo e positivismo nella teoria psi-
        cologica della folla di Gustave Le Bon" (Irrationalism and po-
        sitivism in Gustave Le Bon's psychological theory of crowds),
        Riv. Sociol. 14(1-2), jan-dec 76 : 5-30.

1222   RUSSELL, Gordon W.; DREWRY, Bruce R. "Crowd size and competitive
        aspects of aggression in ice hockey: an archival study", *Hum.
        Relat.* 29(8), aug 76 : 723-735.

1223   ZUCKERMAN, Miron; SCHMITZ, Marie; YOSHA, Andrew. "Effects of crowd-
        ing in a student environment", *J. appl. soc. Psychol.* 7(1), jan-
        mar 77 : 67-72.

13. CULTURE. SOCIALIZATION. SOCIAL LIFE
CULTURE. SOCIALISATION. VIE SOCIALE

13100. CULTURE. SOCIAL ENVIRONMENT. VALUE
       CULTURE. MILIEU SOCIAL. VALEUR

13110. Social and cultural anthropology
       Ethnologie
       [See also / Voir aussi: 1534, 3549]

1224   CHUA, Beng-Huat. "Delineating a marxist interest in ethnomethodo-
        logy", Amer. Sociologist 12(1), feb 77 : 24-32.
1225   COLAJANNI, Antonino. "Un classico dell'antropologia sociale trent'-
        anni dopo: I Nuer di E. E. Evans-Pritchard e la teoria delle so-
        cietà segmentarie" (A classics of social anthropology after thir-
        ty years: The Nuer by E. E. Evans-Pritchard and the theory of
        segmentary society), Rass. ital. Sociol. 17(4), oct-dec 76 : 541-
        592.
1226   Bibl.XXVI-1083. CRESSWELL, Robert. Éléments d'ethnologie. CR: Clau-
        de RIVIÈRE, C. int. Sociol. 61, 1976 : 369-372.
1227   "Cultural anthropology", Amer. behav. Scientist 20(5), jun 77 : 619-
        792.
1228   FRIEDL, John. Cultural anthropology. New York, Harper's College
        Press, 76, 486 p.
1229   GODELIER, Maurice. Perspectives in Marxist anthropology. Cambridge,
        Cambridge University Press, 77, vi-243 p.
1230   GROTTANELLI, Vinigi. "Ethnology and/or cultural anthropology in Ita-
        ly: traditions and developments", Curr. Anthropol. 18(4), dec 77 :
        593-614.
1231   HUNTER, David E.; WHITTEN, Phillip. The study of cultural anthropo-
        logy. New York, Harper and Row, 77, xv-477 p.
1232   KEESING, Roger M. Cultural anthropology: a contemporary perspective.
        New York, Holt, Rinehart and Winston, 76, xiii-637 p.
1233   KRZEMINSKI, Ireneusz. "Antropologia a socjologia. W poszukiwaniu
        modelu integracji nauk społecznych" (Anthropology and sociology.
        In quest of a model of integration of the social sciences), Stud.
        socjol. 60(1), 1976 : 33-56.
1236   LEWIS, I. M. Social anthropology in perspective: the relevance of
        social anthropology. Harmondsworth-New York, Penguin, 76, 386 p.
1235   LYNCH, Frederick R. "Field research and future history: problems
        posed for ethnographic sociologists by the 'Doomsday cult' making
        good", Amer. Sociologist 12(2), mai 77 : 80-88.
1236   OBRADOVIĆ, Gradimir. "Etnološka istraživanja Tihimira Đorđevića i
        njihov značaj za sociologiju" (Ethnographical studies by Tihomir
        Đorđević and their significance for sociology), Sociologija 18(3-
        4), 1976 : 379-393.
1237   PLOG, Fred; BATES, Daniel G. Cultural anthropology. New York, Knopf,
        76, vii-449 p.
1238   SCAGLIOSO, Cosimo. Questioni di antropologia culturale (Questions
        of cultural anthropology). Roma, Bulzoni, 76, viii-105 p.

13120. Civilization. Culture. Society
Civilisation. Culture. Société

13121.

[See also / Voir aussi: 454, 701, 1809, 1949, 1969, 2029, 2348, 2635, 2639, 2783, 2951, 3247, 3919, 4421, 4687, 4835, 5503]

1239 ARNOL'DOV, A. I. *Socialističeskij obraz žizni ⊥ kul'tura* (Socialist way of life and culture). Moskva, Mysl', 76, 156 p.

1240 BAKALDIN, S. S. "Vysokaja obščestvenno-političeskaja aktivnost' i otvetstvennost' ličnosti-čerta sovetskogo obraza žizni" (A high socio-political activity and individual responsibility are characteristics of the Soviet way of life), *Nauč. Trudy Kursk. pedag. Inst.* 74, 1976 : 95-109.

1241 BARNETT, Marguerite Ross. *The politics of cultural nationalism in south India.* Princeton, Princeton University Press, 76, xii-368 p.

1242 BEN-DAVID, Joseph; CLARK, Terry, Nichols (eds.). *Culture and its creators: essays in honor of Edward Shils.* Chicago, University of Chicago Press, 77, x-325 p.

1243 BEZRUKOV, A. V. "O nekotoryh problemah socialističeskogo obraza žizni" (On some problems of the socialist way of life), *Nauč. Dokl. vyss. Školy nauč. Kommunizma* (2), 1977 : 56-61.

1244 BORISOV, G. M. "Dialektika ob'ektivnogo i sub'ektivnogo v socialističeskom obraze žizni" (Dialectics of objective and subjective in the socialist way of life), *Učen. Zap. (Vyss. part. Školy CK KPSS)* (5), 1976 : 17-24.

1245 BUTENKO, A. P. (ed.). *Socialističeskij obraz žizni, êgo suščnost' i problemy* (Socialist way of life, its nature and problems). Moskva, 76, 200 p.

1246 CAMPBELL, Angus; CONVERSE, Philip E.; RODGERS, Willard L. *The quality of American life: perceptions, evaluations, and satisfactions.* New York, Russell Sage, 76, 583 p. CR: Richard M. COHN, *Contemp. Sociol. (Washington)* 6(4), jul 77 : 489-490.

1247 CIPKO, A. S. "K aktualizacii problem socialističeskogo obraza žizni v sovremennyh uslovijah" (On actualization of the socialist way of life problems in contemporary conditions), *Probl. nauč. Uprav. social. Obšč.* (3), 1976 : 91-104.

1248 CLANCIER, Georges-Emmanuel; CLANCIER, Pierre Sylvestre. *La vie quotidienne en Limousin au XIXe siècle.* Paris, Hachette, 76, 319 p.

1249 CLARK, S. D. *Canadian society in historical perspective.* Toronto, McGraw-Hill, 76, 144 p. CR: Jean Leonard ELLIOTT, *Contemp. Sociol. (Washington)* 6(2), mar 77 : 174-175.

1250 COTTERELL, Yap Yong; COTTRELL, Arthur. *Chinese civilization from the Ming revival to Chairman Mao.* London, Weidenfeld and Nicolson, 77, 256 p.

1251 CULLEN, Ian G. "An hierarchical interpretation of every day life", *Soc. and Leisure* 8(3), 1976 : 127-144.

1252 DICKSTEIN, Morris. *Gates of Eden: American culture in the sixties.* New York, Basic Books, 77, xi-300 p.-3 1.

1253 DIVINE, Donna Robinson. "Approaching the study of Egyptian society: an analysis of the language of the social sciences", *Sociol. Anal Theory* 7(3), jun 77 : 135-163.

1254 DIXON, Keith. "Is cultural relativism self-refuting ?", *Brit. J. Sociol.* 28(1), mar 77 : 75-88.

1255 DOBRYNINA, V. I. (ed.). *Sovetskij obraz žizni: segodnja i zavtra* (Soviet way of life: today and tomorrow). Moskva, Molodaja Gvardija, 76, 255 p.

1256 DRAGEL', V. "K voprosu o roli soznanija v obraze žizni ljudej" (On the role of consciousness in men's way of life), in: *Obščestvennoe soznanie.* Barnaul, 1975 : 58-66.

1257   FUKÁSZ, Gy. "Az életmód fogalmáról - filozófiai aspektusban" (On
        the concept of way of life - in a philosophical aspect), *Magyar
        filoz. Szle* 21(5), 1977 : 508-529.

1258   GAŁĘSKI, Boguslaw. "Styl zycia i jakość zycia - próba systematyzacji
        pojęć" (Life style and quality of life - an attempt to concept
        systematization), *Stud. socjol.* 64(1), 1977 : 31-50.

1259   GERVAI, Pál; LAJTAI, György. "Vélemények a szocialista életmód kérdé-
        seiröl" (Opinions regarding the socialist way of life), *Társadtud.
        Közl.* (4), 1976 : 81-95.

1260   GLEZERMAN, G. E. et al. *Socialisticeskij obraz zizni i sovremennaja
        ideologiceskaja bor'ba* (The socialist way of life and contempo-
        rary ideological struggle). Moskva, Politizdat, 76, 350 p.

1261   GLUMIN, V. I. *Dve sistemy - dva obraza zizni* (Two systems, two ways
        of life). Alma Ata, Kazahstan, 77, 72 p.

1262   GORDON, L. A.; KLOPOV, E. V.; ONIKOV, L. A. *Certy socialisticeskogo
        obraza zizni: byt gorodskih rabocih vcera, segodnja, zavtra* (Cha-
        racteristics of the socialist way of life: customs of urban wor-
        kers, yesterday, today, tomorrow). Moskva, Znanie, 77, 159 p.

1263   GRAFSKIJ, Ju. A. "Socialisticeskij obraz zizni" (Socialist way of li-
        fe), *Sociol. Issled. (Moskva)* (3), 1976 : 22-32.

1264   GOCU, V. G.; ŠEREGI, F. E. "Metod kvotnoj vyborki v issledovanii
        voprosov obraza zizni" (Method of quota choice in research on
        way of life questions), *Izv. Akad. Nauk Moldav. SSR Ser. obsc.
        Nauk* (3), 1976 : 73-78.

1265   GYÖRI, György. (ed.). *Ember és müveltség* (Man and culture). Budapest,
        Gondolat, 76, 444-3 p.

1266   HERMANN, István. "A kultúra, a müvészet és a szabadidö egysége"
        (The unity of culture, art and leisure), *Társad. Szle* (10), 1976 :
        57-65.

1267   HILLER, Harry H. *Canadian society: a sociological analysis*. Scar-
        borough, Ont., Prentice-Hall of Canada, 76, xvi-200 p.

1268   HOOVER, Thomas. *Zen culture*. New York, Random House, 77, xx-262 p.

1269   HUET, A. et al. *La marchandise culturelle*. Paris, Éditions du CNRS,
        77, 95 p.

1270   HUSZAR, T. "Culture, community and society", *New Hungar. Quart.*
        17(64), 1976 : 42-51; 18(65), 1977 : 72-83.

1271   KABIEV, B. N. "Protivo-poloznost' socialisticeskogo i burzuaznogo
        obraza zizni i sovremennaja ideologiceskaja bor'ba" (Opposition
        between the socialist and bourgeois ways of life and contemporary
        ideological struggle), *Vopr. Teorii Metod. ideol. Raboty* (7),
        1977 : 232-246.

1272   KAPUSTIN, E. I. *Socialisticeskij obraz zizni: ekonomiceskij aspekt*
        (The socialist way of life: economic aspect). Moskva, Mysl',
        76, 301 p.

1273   KARPIŃSKI, Jakub. "Culture and social structure. Troublesome con-
        cepts", *Polish sociol. B.* 38(3), 1977 : 27-35.

1274   KASUMOV, T. K. "Osnovnye faktory formirovanija socialisticeskogo
        obraza zizni" (Essential factors of the socialist way of life
        formation), *Izv. Akad. Nauk Azerb. SSR Ser. Ist. Filos. Prava*
        (1), 1976 : 103-108.

1275   KLASTORNYJ, N. D. "K voprosy o metodologiceskih osnovah opredeleni-
        ja ponjatija 'obraz zizni'" (On methodological bases of determi-
        nation of the "way of life" concept), *Vopr. nauc. Kommunizma
        (Kiev)* 35, 1977 : 58-64.

1276   KÖPECZI, B. *A magyar kultura harminc éve 1945-1975* (Thirty years
        of Hungarian culture, 1945-1975). Budapest, Kossuth Kiado, 77,
        243-4 p.

1277   KOPYRIN, V. A. "Socialisticeskij obraz zizni kak projavlenie koren-
        nyh preimuscestv socializma pered kapitalizmom" (The socialist
        way of life as a demonstration of essential advantages of so-
        cialism in front of capitalism), *Nauc. Trudy Sverdlovsk pedag.
        Inst. Probl. izucen. social. Obraza zizni* 276(1), 1976 : 46-68.

1278   KUZNECOV, V. I.; PLAKSIJ, S. I. "Socialističeskij obraz žizni, molodež' i ideologičeskaja bor'ba" (Socialist way of life, youth
and ideological struggle), in: *Sovremennaja ideologičeskaja bor'ba
i molodež'*. *II*.Moskva, 1976 : 216-229.

1279   LAKTIONOV, I. D.; SOKOLOVA, A. D. "Suščnost' i osnovnye čerty socialističeskogo obraza žizni" (Nature and essential characteristics of the socialist way of life), *Nauč. Trudy Kursk. pedag.
Inst.* 74, 1976 : 3-21.

1280   LEACH, Edmund Donald. *Culture and communication. The logic by which
symbols are connected. An introduction to the use of structuralist
analysis in social anthropology.* Cambridge, Cambridge University
Press, 76, x-105 p. CR: Robert D. LEIGHNINGER, Jr. *Contemp. Sociol.
(Washington)* 6(4), jul 77 : 496-497.

1281   LENT, John A. *et al.* (eds.). *Cultural pluralism in Malaysia: polity,
military, mass media, education, religion, and social class.* De
Kalb, Center for Southeast Asian Studies, Northern Illinois University; Detroit, Cellar Books Shop, 77, x-114 p.

1282   LICHTVELD, L. "Cultuur en arbeid" (Culture and labour), *Social. en
Democr.* 33(12), dec 76 : 560-572.

1283   LOSONCZI, Á. *Az életmód az időben, a tárgyakban és az értékekben*
(The way of life as reflected in the use of time, in objects and
values). Budapest, Gondolat, 77, 795 p.

1284   LOVOLL, Odd S. (ed.). *Cultural pluralism versus assimilation: the
views of Waldemar Ager.* Northfield, Minn., Norwegian-American
Historical Association, 77, 136 p.

1285   MALAŠTOVÁ-DRAGNĚVOVÁ, Raisa. "O mechanismech ovlivňujících osvojení
kultury" (On mechanisms affecting the appropriation of culture),
Sociol. Čas. 13(3), 1977 : 270-279.

1286   MARUYAMA, Tetsuo. *Bunka to Kachi -Bunka taikei-ron noto* (Culture
and value; notes on the theory of culture system). Nagoya, Kinjo-
gakuin-daigaku Jonmon-kagaku Kenkyu-kai, 77, 191 p.

1287   MAYERS, Marvin Keene. *A look at Latin American lifestyles.* Dallas,
SIL Museum of Anthropology, 76, v-119 p.

1288   MERAND, Patrick. *La vie quotidienne en Afrique noire: à travers la
littérature africaine d'expression française.* Paris, L'Harmattan,
77, 239 p.

1289   MONTMOLLIN, E. DE. "Le pluralisme culturel en Suisse", *Cultures*
3(3), 1976 : 161-178.

1290   NAGY, E. "Adalékok a klasszikusaink életmódfelfogásához" (Glosses
on our classics' concept of way of life), *Magyar. filoz. Szle*
21(5), 1977 : 555-574.

1291   PAVAN, Adalberto. *Alle sorgenti della cultura africana* (At the sources of the African culture). Milano, Centro studi Terzo mondo;
Padova, Edizioni laurenzione, 77, 175 p.

1292   PELLIZZI, Camillo. "Una civiltà mummificata ?" (A mummified civilization ?), *Rass. ital. Sociol.* 18(2), apr-jun 77 : 165-169.

1293   PETERSON, Richard A. (ed.). |*The production of culture.* Beverly
Hills, Calif., Sage Publications, 76, 144 p.

1294   POPOV, S. I. "Buržuaznaja sociologija v poiskah novogo 'kačestva
žizni'" (Bourgeois sociology in quest of a new "quality of life"),
Sociol. Issled. (Moskva) (1), 1977 : 149-159.

1295   RAMU, G. N.; JOHNSON, Stuart D. (eds.). *Introduction to Canadian
society: sociological analysis.* Toronto, Macmillan of Canada,
76, vi-530 p.

1296   RAUTY, Raffaele. *Cultura popolare e marxismo* (Folk culture and
Marxism). Roma Editori riuniti, 76, 267 p.

1297   RIBEILL, Georges. "Éléments pour une approche gramscienne du cadre
de vie", *Éspaces et Soc.* 19, dec 76 : 99-116.

1298   RIBEIRO, Darcy. "La cultura latinoamericana" (Latin American culture), *Latino Amér.* (9), 1976 : 9-89.

1299   RODI, Frithjof. "Les traits allusifs culturels et leur rôle dans les propositions interprétatives", *Soc. Sci. Inform.* 15(2-3), 1976 : 269-286.

1300   ROY, Girish Chandra. *Indian culture: the tradition of non-violence and social change in India.* Delhi, Ajanta Publications, Ajanta Books International, 76, ix-198 p.

1301   RUTKEVIČ, M. N. *et al. Problemy socialisticeskogo obraza žizni* (Problems of the socialist way of life). Moskva, Nauka, 77, 288 p.

1302   RUTKEVIČ, M. V. "Obraz žizni i 'kacestvo žizni'" ("Way of life" and "quality of life"), *Sociol. Issled. (Moskva)* (4), 1976 : 13-23.

1303   SAHLINS, Marshall David. *Culture and practical reason.* Chicago, University of Chicago Press, 76, xi-252 p.

1304   SATŌ, Takeshi. "Gendai to bunkateki mujun to bunka kakushin" (Cultural contradiction of modern society), *Gendai to Shiso* 28, 1977 : 2-21.

1305   SERPELL, Robert. *Culture's influence on behaviour.* London, Methuen, 76, 144 p.

1306   SMOLJANSKIJ, V. G. "Socialisticeskij obraz žizni i ideologiceskaja bor'ba" (The socialist way of life and ideological struggle), in: *Filosofija i sovremennost'.* Moskva, 1976 : 63-71.

1307   SPINDLER, George; SPINDLER, Louise (eds.). *Native North American cultures: four cases.* New York, Holt, Rinehart and Winston, 77, 508 p.

1308   SRYL'NIK, A. "Sovetskij obraz žizni i razvitie ličnosti" (Soviet way of life and the development of personality), *Kommunist vooruž. Sil* (14), 1976 : 9-16.

1309   STRAUTIN', A. I. (ed.). *Problemy soversenstvovanija obraza žizni socialisticeskogo obscestva* (Problems of improvement of the socialist way of life). Riga, Zinatne, 76, 161 p.

1310   STRUKOV, E. V. *Socialisticeskij obraz žizni. Teoreticeskie i idejno-vospitatel'nye problemy* (The socialist way of life. Theoretical and educational problems). Moskva, Mysl', 77, 263 p.

1311   SZÁNTÓ, M. "Gondolatok a szocialista életmódról" (Reflections on the socialist way of life), *Magyar. filoz. Szle* 21(5), 1977 : 530-577.

1312   TAYLOR, Arnold H. *Travail and triumph: Black life and culture in the South since the Civil War.* Westport, Conn., Greenwood Press, 76, viii-325 p.

1313   VACCARINI, Italo. "Il modello culturale della società americana" (The cultural pattern of American society), *Aggiorn. soc.* 28(3), mar 77 : 195-214.

1314   VEČERNÍK, Jiří; VÍTEČKOVÁ, Jana. "Changes in some conditions and features of the way of life of working women in Czechoslovakia", *Soc. and Leisure* 8(3), 1976 : 21-41.

1315   VICKERS, Geoffrey. "The weakness of Western culture", *Futures* 9(6), dec 77 : 457-473.

1316   VRONSKIJ, G. T. "Individual'naja specifika obraza žizni i nekotorye voprosy stanovlenija ličnosti i molodežnom kollektive" (Individual specificity of way of life and some questions on the future of individual in a young collectivity), in: *Voprosy razvitija duhovnoj žizni sovetskogo obscestva. VI.* Tula, 1976 : 83-91.

1317   WELLS, Alan. (ed.). *American society; problems and dilemmas.* Pacific Palisades, Calif., Goodyear Publishing Co., 76, viii-391 p. CR: Henry M. BARLOW, *Contemp. Sociol. (Washington)* 6(2), mar 77 : 240.

1318   WOJCIECHOWSKA, Anita *et al.* "Styl zycia - problematyka teoretyczna i badawcza" (Life style - theoretical and research problems), *Stud. socjol.* 64(1), 1977 : 51-80.

1319   Bibl.XXVI-1174. YOUNG, Crawford. *The politics of cultural pluralism.* CR: Richard L. SKLAR, *Amer. J. Sociol.* 83(2), sep 77 : 516-520.

1320   ZBOROVSKIJ, G. E. "Metodologiceskie voprosy izucenija socialisticeskogo obraza žizni" (Methodological questions of the socialist way of life study), *Nauc. Trudy Sverdlovsk. pedag. Inst. Probl.*

izučen. social. Obraza žizni 276(1), 1976 : 5-45.

1321   ZIÓŁKOWSKI, Marek. "Claude Lévi-Straussa koncepcja kultury - próba rekonstrukcji" (Claude Lévi-Strauss's concept of culture - an attempt at reconstruction), *Stud. socjol.* 63(4), 1976 : 47-66.

1322   ZUCKER, Lynne G. "The role of institutionalization in cultural per-sistence", *Amer. sociol. R.* 42(5), oct 77 : 726-743.

1323   ZUKIN, Sharon. "Mimesis in the origins of bourgeois culture", *Theory and Soc.* 4(3), 1977 : 333-358.

13122.
[See also / Voir aussi: 1694]

1324   BANDYOPADHYAYA, Jayantanuja. "National character and international relations", *Int. Stud. (New Delhi)* 15(4), oct-dec 76 : 531-555.

1325   CHAŁASIŃSKI, Josef. "Irlandia - Europa - Ameryka. Problem narodu o związków ponadnarodowych" (Ireland-Europe-America. The problem of the nation and of supranational associations), *Przegl. socjol.* 29, 1977 : 7-31.

1326   DAŠDAMIROV, A. F. *Nacija i ličnost'* (Nation and the individual). Baku, Ėlm, 76, 226 p.

1327   DŽUNUSOV, N. S. "Sbliženie nacij v uslovijah razvitogo socializma (Nekotorye metodologičeskie i metodičeskie problemy)" (The bringing together of nations in conditions of developed socialism. Some methodological problems), *Sociol. Issled. (Moskva)* (4), 1976 : 42-51.

1328   INGLIS, Fred. "Nation and community: a landscape and its morality", *Sociol. R.* 25(3), aug 77 : 489-514.

1329   IWAND, Wolf Michael. "Nationenbilder als Gegenstand der Massenkommunikationsforschung" (The image of the nation as a subject for mass communication research), *Communications (Köln)* 2(2), 1976 : 167-186.

1330   RAŠIDOV, Š. "Socialističeskij obraz žizni i nacional'noe samosozna-nie" (Socialist way of life and national consciousness), in: *Problemy teorii i praktiki razvitogo socializma.* Praga, 1977 : 217-236.

1331   REX, John. "Nations, nationalism, and the social scientist", *Canad. J. Sociol.* 1(4), 1976 : 501-514.

1332   SZABOLCS, O. "A magyar értelmiség nemzeti tudatának kérdéséhez" (The problem of the national consciousness among Hungarian intellectuals), *Tört. Szle* (3), 1976 : 509-518.

13123.
[See also / Voir aussi: 2507, 4537]

1333   DESROCHE, Henri. "Notes sur quelques fragments d'Utopies. Crises de la société: société sans crises ?", *Communications (Paris)* 25, 1976 : 128-137.

1334   GINER, Salvador. *Mass society.* London, Martin Robertson; New York, Academic Press, 76, xvi-288 p.

1335   GRØNBJERG, Kirsten A. *Mass society and the extension of welfare, 1960-1970.* Chicago, University of Chicago Press, 77, xiii-266 p. *[USA.]*

1336   MOSCOVICI, Serge. *Society against nature: the emergence of human societies.* Atlantic Highlands, N.J., Humanities Press, 76, 158 p. CR: Richard McCLINTOCK, *Contemp. Sociol. (Washington)* 6(3), mai 77 : 384-385.

1337   NAKA, Hisao. "Shakaigaku ni okeru shakai-gainen no kôsei" (A conceptual construct of society in sociology), *Kyôto-daigaku Bungakubu Kenkyûkiyô* 17, 1977 : 55-204.

1338   PODGÓRECKI, Adam. "The global analysis of Polish society. A sociological point of view", *Polish sociol. B.* 36(4), 1976 : 17-30.

1339   "Problèmes de la société socialiste développée", *Nouv. Ét. hongr.* (11), 1976 : 3-103.

1340   SANTOS, Milton. "Société et espace: la formation sociale comme
        théorie et comme méthode", *C. int. Sociol.* 24(63), jul-dec 77 :
        261-276.
1341   SLAVIN, B. F.; ČESNOKOV, V. S. "Obščestvo kak ulevaja samoupravlja-
        maja sistema" (Society as a self-managed system), *Nauč. upravl.*
        Obsč. (10), 1976 : 17-58.
1342   STARK, Werner. *Antecedents of the social bond: the phylogeny of*
        sociality. New York, Fordham University Press, 76, ix-229 p.
        CR: Justin STAGL, *Kölner Z. Soziol. u. soz.-Psychol.* 29(2), jun
        77 : 376-378.
1343   TOURAINE, Alain. *La société invisible: regards 1974-1976.* Paris,
        Seuil, 77, 284 p.
1344   WILLMUTH, Sidney. *Mass society, social organization, and democracy.*
        New York, Philosophical Library, 76, 104 p.

        13130. Cultural dynamics. Cultural relations
               Dynamique culturelle. Relations culturelles

        13131.

1345   BENGU, Sibusiso Mandlenkosi Emmanuel. *African cultural identity*
        and international relations: analysis of Ghanaian and Nigerian
        sources, 1958-1974. Pietermaritzburg, Shuter et Shooter, 76,
        xxv-170 p.
1346   "Identité culturelle négro-africaine", *Présence afr.* 98, 2 trim
        76 : 1-241; 3-4 trim 76 : 3-239.
1347   SĘKOWSKI, Stanislaw. "Problematyka uwarunkowań uczestnictwa w kul-
        turze w badaniach Polskich" (The problems of determinants of cul-
        tural participation in the Polish field research), *Stud. socjol.*
        63(4), 1976 : 5-43.
1348   SNYDER, Émile; VALDMAN, Albert (eds.). *Identité culturelle et fran-*
        cophonie dans les Amériques. Québec, Presses de l'Université La-
        val, 76, 290 p.
1349   SZELI, István. "Adalék a nemzetiségi mikrokultúra vizsgálatának el-
        méleti és módszertani kérdéseihez" (Data on the theoretical exa-
        mination and methodological problems of the minorities microcul-
        ture), *Híd* (3), 1977 : 364-377.

        13132.

        [See also / Voir aussi: 1379, 2828, 4382]

1350   AITHNARD, K. M. *Some aspects of cultural policy in Togo.* Paris,
        Unesco Press, 76, 101 p.
1351   BARABAS, Ju. "Nekotorye aspekty razvitija hudozestvennoj kul'tury
        v uslovijah zrelogo socializma" (Some aspects of development of
        culture in the developed socialist society), *Kommunist (Moskva)*
        54(6), apr 77 : 45-56.
1352   BERRY, John W. (ed.). "Psychological perspectives on culture chan-
        ge", *J. cross-cult. Psychol.* 8(2), jun 77 : 131-156.
1353   CAMILLERI, Joseph A. *Civilisation in crisis. Human prospects in a*
        changing world. Cambridge, Cambridge University Press, 76, vii-
        303 p.
1354   CHOMBART DE LAUWE, Paul-Henry. "La culture-action et les transfor-
        mations sociales", *Sociol. contemp.* 22(1-3), 1974 : 35-48.
1355   DIENES, G. (ed.). *Youth, agent and subject of cultural change.* Bu-
        dapest, Népmüvelési Intézet, 76, 104 p.
1356   KIM, Yersu. *Cultural policy in the Republic of Korea.* Paris, Unesco,
        76, 59 p.-2 l.
1357   KOSSOU, B. "Politique culturelle, politique de développement",
        Ethiopiques (8), oct 76 : 14-25.
1358   MACKLIN, Barbara June. *Structural stability and culture change in*
        a Mexican-American community. New York, Arno Press, 76, x-xxxii
        279 p.

1359   MARSAL, Juan F. "La sociología de las instituciones culturales",
        (Sociology of the cultural institutions), *R. esp. Opin. publ.*
        49, 1977 : 77-92.

1360   OSCHLIES, Wolf. *Bulgariens Kulturentwicklung 1944-1975* (Cultural
        development in Bulgaria, 1944-1975). Köln, Bundesinstitut für
        Ostwissenscahftliche und Internationale Studien, 76, 2 vols.

1361   RICARD, A. "Politique culturelle et accès à l'information: sur
        quelques outils récents", *Année afr.* 1975 : 239-246.

1362   ROSSADE, Werner. "Kulturpolitik als Herschaftsinstrument" (Cultural
        policy as an instrument of domination), *Deutschland Archiv* 10(3),
        mar 77 : 288-304.

1363   SPINDLER, Louise S. *Culture change and modernization: mini-models
        and case studies*. New York, Holt, Rinehart and Winston, 77, xiii-
        177 p.

1364   VALADE, Bernard. "L'idée de décadence", *C. int. Sociol.* 24(62),
        jan-jun 77 : 75-88.

        13133.

        [See also / Voir aussi: 4881]

1365   BALDAUF, Richard B. Jr.; AYABE, Harold I. "Acculturation and edu-
        cational achievement in American Samoan adolescents", *J. cross-
        cult. Psychol.* 8(2), jun 77 : 241-256.

1366   DAMMANN, Ernst. "Das Miteinander von Weiss und Schwarz. Probleme
        der Akkulturation in Schwarzafrica" (Cohabitation of Black and
        White. Problem of acculturation in Black Africa), *Hamburg. Jb.
        Wirtsch.- u. Ges.-Polit.* 22, 1977 : 205-219.

1367   DODD, Carley H. *Perspectives on cross-cultural communication*. Du-
        buque, Iowa, Kendall/Hunt Publishing Co., 77, vi-109 p.

1368   GARAUDY, Roger. *Pour un dialogue des civilisations: l'Occident est
        un accident*. Paris, Denoël, 77, 233 p.

1369   GIUSTI, Sonia. "A proposito di acculturazione" (About acculturation),
        Rass. ital. Sociol. 18(3), jul-sep 77 : 465-472.

1370   GROVE, D. John. "A cross-national examination of cross-cutting and
        reinforcing cultural cleavages", *Int. J. comp. Sociol.* 18(3-4),
        sep-dec 77 : 217-227.

1371   HAMZAOUI, S. "L'arabisation: problème idéologique", *R. tunis. Sci.
        soc.* 13(44), 1976 : 173-211.

1372   KNIGHT, George P.; KAGAN, Spencer. "Acculturation of prosocial and
        competitive behaviors among second and third generation Mexican-
        American children", *J. cross-cult. Psychol.* 8(3), sep 77 : 273-
        284.

1373   LENNON, John J. *A comparative study of the patterns of accultura-
        tion of selected Puerto Rican Protestant and Roman Catholic fa-
        milies in an urban metropolitan area*. San Francisco, R and E
        Research Associates, 76, xii-148 p.

1374   PETRICĂ, Ion. *Confluenţe culturale româno-polone* (Romanian-Polish
        cultural confluent). Bucureşti, Minerva, 76, 364 p.

1375   PHILLIPS, Ray Edmund. *The Bantu in the city: a study of cultural
        adjustment on the Witwatersrand*. New York, AMS Press, 77, xxix-
        452 p.

1377   STEGER, Hanns-Albert. "Emancipacion y acculturacion como instrumen-
        tos de dominación de la región latino-americana y del Caribe"
        (Emancipation and acculturation as instruments of domination in
        Latin America and the Caribbean), *Latino Amér.* (8), 1975 : 99-
        117.

1378   TUGANOVA, O. É. "O meždunarodnom kul'turnom sotrudničestve v sovre-
        mennyh uslovijah" (The international cultural co-operation under
        present conditions), *Rabočij Klass sovrem. Mir* 5(5), sep-oct 76 :
        45-56.

13140. Norm. Social control. Value
Norme. Régulation sociale. Valeur

[See also / Voir aussi: 721, 949, 1048, 1103, 1149, 1286, 1413, 1441, 1485, 1507, 1531, 2240, 2486, 3940, 4371]

1379 ACQUAVIVA, Sabino S. "Crise des valeurs et des significations de l'existence dans la société italienne contemporaine", *C. int. Sociol.* 24(63), jul-dec 77 : 197-222.

1380 ALEXANDER, C. Norman Jr.; LAUDERDALE, Pat. "Situated identities and social influence", *Sociometry* 40(3), 1977 : 225-233.

1381 BÉJIN, André. "Crises des valeurs, crises des mesures", *Communications (Paris)* 25, 1976 : 39-72.

1382 COLLETT, Peter (ed.). *Social rules and social behaviour.* Totowa, N.J., Rowman and Littlefield, 77, 185 p.

1383 "Érték a társadalomtudományokban" (Value in social sciences), *Magyar filoz. Szle* 20(4), 1976 : 473-661.

1384 FRITZ, Éva. "Társadalmi értékrend és a társadalmi termelés hatékonyságának összefüggése" (Relations between the efficiency of the social system of value and social productivity), *Acta Fac. polit.-iur. Univ. Sci. budapest.* 19, 1977 : 245-254.

1385 GIBBS, Jack P. "Social control, deterrence, and perspectives on social order", *Soc. Forces* 56(2), dec 77 : 408-423.

1386 HALL, Brian P.; SMITH, Patrick; CANTIN, Eileen. *The development of consciousness: a confluent theory of values.* New York, Paulist Press, 76, xiv-268 p.

1387 HANKISS, Elemér. *Érték és társadalom. Tanulmányok az értékszociológia köréböl* (Value and society. Studies in the field of the sociology of values). Budapest, Magvető, 77, 392 p.

1388 HANKISS, Elemér. *Értékszociológiai kisérlet. (Az ipari dolgozók néhány rétegének értékrendjéröl)* (Experiments in sociology of values. The range of values among some categories of industrial workers). Budapest, NPI, 76, 142 -1 p.

1389 HUGHES, J. R. T. *Social control in the colonial economy.* Charlottesville, University Press of Virginia, 76, vi-178 p. CR: Stanley L. ENGERMAN, *J. econ. Liter.* 15(1), mar 77 : 99-101.

1390 KIRSCHENBAUM, Howard. *Advanced value clarification.* La Jolla, Calif., University Associates, 77, 187 p.

1391 KRIS, Mitchel; KINCHLA, R. A.; DARLEY, John M. "A mathematical model for social influences on perceptual judgments", *J. exp. soc. Psychol.* 13(5), sep 77 : 403-420.

1392 LERNER, Max. *Values in education: notes toward a values philosophy.* Bloomington, Ind., Phi Delta Kappa, 76, x-138 p.

1393 MEIER, Robert F.; JOHNSON, Weldon T. "Deterrence as social control: the legal and extra-legal production of conformity", *Amer. sociol. R.* 42(2), apr 77 : 292-304.

1394 MICKLIN, Michael. "Anticipated reactions to deviance in a South American city: a study of social control", *Pacific sociol. R.* 20(4), oct 77 : 515-535.

1395 PADUČIH, V. V. "Trudovaja disciplina kak élement sistemy cennostnyh orientacij ličnosti" (Labour discipline as an element of the system of the personality value orientations), in: *Proizvodstvennyj kollektiv i disciplina truda.* Omsk, 1976 : 47-54.

1396 PELKMAN, G. H. G. "Wensen, willen, handelen. Waarden als determinanten van gedrag" (To wish, to will, to act. Values as determinants of behaviour), *Sociol. Gids* 24(6), nov-dec 77 : 82-395.

1397 PRENNER, Louis A.; ANH, Tran. "A comparison of American and Vietnamese value systems", *J. soc. Psychol.* 101(2), apr 77 : 187-204.

1398 SANTEE, R. T.; JACKSON, J. "Cultural values as a source of normative sanctions", *Pacific sociol. R.* 20(3), 1977 : 439-454.

1399 SEKULIĆ, Dusko. "Vrijednosne orijentacija kao faktori organizacionog ponašanja" (Value orientations as factors of organized behaviour), *Sociologija* 18(3-4), 1976 : 283-296.

1400 SIMON, Sidney B.; O'ROURKE, Robert D. *Developing values with exceptional children.* Englewood Cliffs, N.J., Prentice-Hall, 77, xii-140 p.

1401 THOMPSON, K. W. "Values and education: a worldwide review", *Yb. Wld Aff.* 31, 1977 : 327-341.

1402 TITTLE, Charles T. (ed.). "Social control and deviance", *Soc. Forces* 56(2), dec 77 : 315-502.

1403 VACCARINI, Italo. "Un'interpretazione sociologica dei valori della società americana",(A sociological interpretation of the values of the American society), *Studi Sociol.* 14(4), oct-dec 76 : 299-337.

13150. Alienation. Socialization. Social conformity
Aliénation. Socialisation. Conformité sociale

13151.

[See also / Voir aussi: 583, 629, 749, 866, 1393, 1440, 1463, 1935, 2136, 2140, 2158, 2265, 2279, 2671, 2838, 2892, 2937, 2969, 2990, 3366, 4433, 4898, 5313, 5329, 5469]

1404 ANDRUŠČENKO, V. P. "Osnovnye metodologičeskie principy issledovanija socializacii ličnosti" (Essential methodological principles of research on personality socialization), *Vop. nauč. Kommunizma (Kiev)* 35, 1977 : 90-99.

1405 BAER, Robert; GOLDMAN, Morton; JUHNKE, Ralph. "Factors affecting prosocial behavior", *J. soc. Psychol.* 103(2), dec 77 : 209-216.

1406 BANDURA, Albert. *Social learning theory.* Englewood Cliffs, N.J., Prentice Hall, 77, viii-247 p.

1407 DABELKO, D. D. "Reference group theory, social comparison theory, and the study of politics", *J. soc. Psychol.* 99(2), aug 76 : 283-287.

1408 ENGELMANN, Hugo O. "Interaction analysis and community typology", *Int. J. contemp. Sociol.* 14(1-2), jan-apr 77 : 1-10.

1409 FEND, Helmut *et al. Sozialisationseffekte der Schule* (Effects of socialization in school). Weinheim-Basel, Beltz, 76, xi-502 p.

1410 FLYNN, Charles P. *Insult and society: patterns of comparative interaction.* Port Washington, N.Y., Kennikat Press, 77, 131 p.

1411 GASC, Jean-Pierre. "A propos du concept d'adaptation", *Soc. Sci. Inform.* 16(5), 1977 : 567-580. Précédé d'une note d'introduction par Jacques BARRAU: 566.

1412 GOTTSCHALCH, Wilfried; NEUMANN-SCHÖNWETTER, Marina; SOUKUP, Gunther. *Sozialisationsforschung: Materialien, Probleme, Kritik* (Socialization research: documents, problems, criticism). Frankfurt-am-Main, Fischer Taschenbuch Verlag, 76, 201-1 p.

1413 HAGAN, John; SIMPSON, J. H. "Ties that bind: conformity and the social control of student discontent", *Sociol. soc. Res.* 61(4), jul 77 : 520-538.

1414 HUNT, Janet G. "Assimilation or marginality ? Some school integration effects reconsidered", *Soc. Forces* 56(2), dec 77 : 604-610.

1415 KANDO, Thomas M. *Social interaction.* Saint Louis, C. V. Mosby Co., 77, xiii-349 p.

1416 KÖHLER, Bernd. "Prosoziales Verhalten: Forschungsschwerpunkte und Forschungsthemen" (Pro-social behaviour: research centre of gravity and research themes), *Z. soz.-Psychol.* 8(1), 1977 : 23-49.

1417 KOMOROWSKI, Z. "Formation de la conscience sociale supratribale en partant des conditions ethniques du Sahara occidental", *Africana B.* 23, 1975 : 95-123.

1418 KRONUS, Carol L. "Occupational versus organizational influences on reference group identification: the case of pharmacy", *Sociol. Wk Occupat.* 3(3), aug 76 : 303-330.

1419 MAILLOUX, Noël. "Quelques observations empiriques sur le processus de socialisation", *A. int. Criminol.* 13(1-2), 1974 : 165-174.

1420   McPHERSON, J. M. "Correlates of social participation: a comparison of the ethnic community and compensatory theories", *Sociol. Quart.* 18(2), 1977 : 197-208.

1421   ORCUTT, James D.; ANDERSON, Ronald E. "Social interaction, dehumanization and the 'computerized other'", *Sociol. soc. Res.* 61(3), apr 77 : 380-397.

1422   PIONTKOWSKI, Ursula. *Psychologie der Interaktion* (The psychology of interaction). München, Juventa-Verlag, 76, 256 p.

1423   PLAKE, Klaus. "Sozialer Identitätsanspruch und die Legitimation der Betreuung: zur Kustodialfunktion der Sozialisationsorganisationen" (Social identity claims and the legitimacy of custory: towards the custodial function of socializing institutions), *Z. Soziol.* 6(3), jul 77 : 264-278.

1424   ROSCH, Ekkehard. "Auf Angemessenheit von Integrationsmodellen in der sozialen Eindrucksbildung" (On the relevance of integration models in social impression formation), *Z. soz.-Psychol.* 8(4), 1977 : 247-255.

1426   SHIBANO, Shozan. "Shakaikaron no sai-kentô - shutaisei keisei-katei no kosatsu" (Reexamination of recent socialization theories - a consideration to the process of subjecthood formation), *Shakai-gaku Hyôron* 27(3), 1977 : 19-34.

1427   SLAVINA, M. A. "O ponjatii 'social'naja adaptacija' v marksistskoj sociologii" (On the concept of social adaptation in marxist sociology), in: *Voprosy marksizma i ideologičeskoj bor'by.* Petrozavodsk, 1976 : 124-133.

1428   TKAČENKO, N. B. "O pravomernosti ispol'zovanija kategorii 'socializacija'" (On the legality of the utilization of the "socialization" category), in: *Voprosy filosofii i sociologii.* Tomsk, 1976 : 101-107.

1429   VAN AKEN, Teun. *Sociologie van de medezeggenschap. Een fenomenologische oriëntatie* (Sociology of participation. A phenomenological orientation). 's-Gravenhage, VUGA, 77, 173 p.

1430   VOGEL, Ulrike. "'Soziales Lernen' als Element soziologischer Sozialisationstheorie" (Social learning as an element of the sociological theory of socialization), *Kölner Z. Soziol. u. soz.-Psychol.* 29(1), mar 77 : 32-44.

1431   WISWEDE, Günter. *Soziologie konformen Verhaltens* (Sociology of conformity behaviour). Stuttgart, W. Kohlhammer, 76, 176 p.

1432   ZAHAROV, V. I. "Značenie optimal'nogo sočetanija različnyh vidov interesov pri socializme dlja social'nogo poznanija" (Meaning of optimal combination of different interests under socialism for social consciousness), in: *Nekotory voprosy marksistsko-leninskoj filosofii i sociologii.* Kišinev, 1976 : 28-50.

13152.

[See also / Voir aussi: 782, 812, 840, 1394, 1402, 1414, 2016, 2496, 2555, 3393, 4123, 4128, 4181, 4824, 5016, 5092, 5151]

1433   ALEXANDER, Yonah (ed.). *International terrorism. National, regional, and global perspectives.* New York, AMS Press, 76, xx-390 p.

1434   ALONSO TORRENS, F. J. "Marginación social de la tercera edad en España" (Social marginality of third age in Spain), *R. Fomento soc.* 31(123), jul-sep 76 : 271-284; 31(124), oct-dec 76 : 427-434.

1435   ARIEL DEL VAL, Fernando. "Escuela, violencia simbólica y dinámica política" (School, symbolic violence and political dynamics), *RS Cuad. Realidad soc.* 12, jan 77 : 77-88.

1436   BASLER, Heinz-Dieter. "Untersuchungen zur Validität der Anomiaskala von Srole" (Studies of the validity of Srole's anomia-scale), *Kölner Z. Soziol. u. soz.-Psychol.* 29(2), jun 77 : 335-342.

1437   BLUMENTHAL, Monica D. *et al. More about justifying violence; me-
        thodological studies of attitudes and behavior.* Ann Arbor, Mich.,
        Institute of Social Research, 76, 411 p. CR: Daniel B. McGILLIS,
        Contemp. Sociol. (Washington) 6(2), mar 77 : 194.

1438   BONANATE, Luigi. "Dimensioni del terrorismo politico" (Dimensions
        of political terrorism), *Comunità* 31(177), feb 77 : 76-122.

1439   BOUDON, Raymond. "Anomie, contradictions et philosophie publique
        dans les sociétés industrielles", *Contrepoint* 22-23, 1976 : 39-
        69.

1440   BRAUN, D. Duane. "Alienation and participation: a replication com-
        paring leaders and the 'mass'", *J. polit. milit. Sociol.* 4(2),
        1976 : 245-259.

1441   BRITT, David W.; CAMPBELL, Ernest Q. "Assessing the linkage of
        norms, environments, and deviance", *Soc. Forces* 56(2), dec 77 :
        532-550.

1442   BRYCE-LAPORTE, Roy S.; THOMAS, Claudewell S. (eds.). *Alienation in
        contemporary society: a multidisciplinary examination.* New York,
        Praeger, 76, xxxv-394 p.

1443   CIPOLLA, Costantino. "Marginalità sociale e pluralismo politico"
        (Social marginality and political pluralism), *Studi Sociol.*
        15(1), jan-mar 77 : 30-56.

1444   "Comunicación y marginalidad" (Communication and marginality),
        Comunicación 12, *[1977]* : 2-117. *[Venezuela.]*

1445   CULLEN, Francis T. Jr.; CULLEN, John B. "The Soviet model of Soviet
        deviance", *Pacific sociol. R.* 20(3), jul 77 : 389-410.

1446   Bibl.XXVI-1309. CURTIS, Lynn A. *Violence, race, and culture.* CR:
        Robert H. HILL, *Amer. J. Sociol.* 82(4), jan 77 : 920-923.

1447   DAVIS, Murray S.; SCHMIDT, Catherine J. "The obnoxious and the nice:
        some sociological consequences of two psychological types", *So-
        ciometry* 40(3), sep 77 : 201-213.

1448   FINE, Bob. "Labelling theory: an investigation into the sociology
        of deviance", *Econ. and Soc.* 6(2), mai 77 : 166-193.

1449   FRAZIER, Charles E. *Theoretical approaches to deviance: an evalua-
        tion.* Columbus, Ohio, Charles E. Merrill, 76, 256 p. CR: Lee
        ELLIS, *Contemp. Sociol. (Washington)* 6(3), mai 77 : 307-308.

1450   GEYER, R. Felix; SCHWEITZER, David R. (eds.). *Theories of aliena-
        tion: critical perspectives in philosophy and the social scien-
        ces.* Leiden, Nijhoff, Stenfert Kroese, 76, xxv-305 p.

1451   GINGERICH, Wallace J.; FELDMAN, Ronald A.; WODARSKI, John S. "A
        behavioral approach toward the labelling of antisocial behavior",
        Sociol. soc. Res. 6(12), jan 77 : 204-222.

1452   GROSS, Harriet Engel. "Micro and macro level implications for a
        sociology of virtue: the case of draft protesters to the Viet-
        nam War", *Sociol. Quart.* 18(3), 1977 : 319-339.

1453   HACKER, Frederick J. *Crusaders, criminals, crazies: terror and
        terrorism in our time.* New Yo-k, Norton, 76, xvi-355 p.

1454   HAGAN, John; SILVA, Edward T.; SIMPSON, John H. "Conflict and con-
        sensus in the designation of deviance", *Soc. Forces* 56(2), dec
        77 : 320-340.

1455   HALPERIN, Ernst. *Terrorism in Latin America.* Beverly Hills, Calif.,
        Sage Publications, 76, 90 p.

1456   HARRIS, Anthony R. "Sex and theories of deviance: toward a func-
        tional theory of deviant type-scripts", *Amer. sociol. R.* 42(1),
        feb 77 : 3-16.

1457   HEUNKS, F. J. "Vervreemding onderzocht" (Alienation research), *Mens
        en Mij* 52(2), 1977 : 172-205.

1458   HEWITT, Christopher. "Majorities and minorities: a comparative sur-
        vey of ethnic violence", *A. Amer. Acad. polit. soc. Sci.* 433, sep
        77 : 150-160.

1459   HØIVIK, Ford. "The demography of structural violence", *J. Peace
        Res.* 14(1), 1977 : 59-73.

1460   HONG, Lawrence K. "Becoming a taxi-dancer: the significance of
       neutralization in a semi-deviant occupation", *Sociol. Wk Occupat.*
       4(3), aug 77 : 327-342.
1461   JOHN, Puthenpeedikail Mathew. *Marx on alienation: elements of ca-*
       pitalism and communism. Calcutta, Minerva Associates Publica-
       tions, 76, xv-267 p.
1462   JOHNSON, Paul. *Enemies of society.* London, Weidenfeld and Nicolson,
       77, viii-278 p.
1463   JUROVSKI, A. "Položenie otdel'nyh lic v processe socializacii v
       molodeži" (Situation of isolated persons in the process of youth
       socialization), in: *Problemy social'noj psihologii.* Tbilisi,
       1976 : 203-211.
1464   KAPLAN, Morton A. *Alienation and identification.* New York, Free
       Press, 76, xiii-206 p.
1465   KEPHART, William M. *Extraordinary groups: the sociology of uncon-*
       ventional lifestyles. New York, St. Martin's Press, 76, vii-311 p.
1466   KÖGLER, Alfred. *Die Entwicklung von Randgruppen in der BRD: Lite-*
       raturstudie zur Entwicklung randständiger Bevölkerungsgruppen
       (The development of marginal groups in the GFR: a review of li-
       terature on the development of marginal population groups). Göt-
       tingen, Schwartz, 76, xxx-511 p.
1467   KÖHLER, Gernot; ALCOCK, Norman. "An empirical table of structural
       violence", *J. Peace Res.* 13(4), 1976 : 343-356.
1468   KWAŚNIEWSKI, Jerzy. "Positive social deviancy", *Polish sociol. B.*
       35(3), 1976 : 31-39.
1469   LASSERRE, René; MUZET, Denis. "La violence, moyen d'information",
       Communications (Köln) 2(2), 1976 : 249-260.
1470   LÉVY-STRINGER, Jacques. *Les marginaux: une nouvelle force politique*
       en France. Paris, Fayolle, 77, 229 p.
1471   MARTINI, Alceo. "La marginalità sociale nella città di Roma" (So-
       cial marginality in the city of Rome), *Riv. Sociol.* 14(1-3),
       jan-dec 76 : 269-294.
1472   MARX, Emmanuel. *The social context of violent behaviour. A social*
       anthropological study in an Israeli immigrant town. London,
       Routledge and Kegan Paul, 76, xv-130 p.
1473   MATSUURA, Kôsaku. *Ningen no shakaiteki kôzô to sogai* (Social struc-
       ture of personality and alienation). Tokyo, Yachiyo Shuppan, 77,
       207 p.
1474   MAUGER, Gérard; FOSSE, Claude. *La vie buissonnière: marginalité*
       petite bourgeoise et marginalité populaire. Paris, F. Maspéro,
       77, 262 p.
1475   McCAGHY, Charles H. *Deviant behavior. Crime, conflict and interest*
       groups. New York, Macmillan, 76, xiv-400 p.
1476   MELUK, Alfonso. *Los marginados: radiografía social de la clase baja*
       en Colombia (Marginals: social radiography of lower class in Co-
       lombia). Bogotá, Ediciones Tercer Mundo, 76, 113 p.
1477   MORENO, Francisco José. "Legitimacy and violence", *Sociol. int.*
       (Berlin) 12(1-2), 1974 : 93-103.
1478   MOSCATI, Roberto. "Violenza politica e giovani" (Political violence
       and youth), *Rass. ital. Sociol.* 18(3), jul-sep 77 : 335-362.
1479   NEAL, Arthur G.; GROAT, H. Theodore. "Alienation and fertility in
       the marital dyad", *Soc. Forces* 56(1), sep 77 : 77-85.
1480   NEWMAN, Graeme R. *Comparative deviance: perception and law in six*
       cultures. New York, Elsevier Scientific Publishing Co., 76, xii-
       332 p.
1481   NEWMAN, Graeme R. "Social institutions and the control of deviance:
       a cross-national opinion survey", *Europ. J. soc. Psychol.* 7(1),
       1977 : 39-59.
1482   NIGAM, Krishna. "Parsonian alienation model", *Ind. J. soc. Res.*
       17(2-3-, aug-dec 76 : 140-145.
1483   ÔMURA, Eisho. "Kon'ichi no Anomî" (Anomie in our time), *Soshioroji*
       22(2), 1977 : 1-32.

1484   PARKER, James H. "Subjective marginality and alienation", *Int. J. contemp. Sociol.* 14(1-2), jan-apr 77 : 39-44.

1485   PAWEŁCZYŃSKA, Anna. "Values and violence, sociology of Auschwitz", *Polish sociol. B.* 35(3), 1976 : 5-17.

1486   PERLMAN, Janice E. *The myth of marginality: urban poverty and politics in Rio de Janeiro.* Berkeley, University of California Press, 76, xxi-341 p.

1487   PHILIBER, William W. "Patterns of alienation in inner city ghettos", *Hum. Relat.* 30(4), apr 77 : 303-310.

1488   PRICE, H. Edward Jr. "The strategy and tactics of revolutionary terrorism", *Comp. Stud. Soc. Hist.* 19(1), jan 77 : 52-66.

1489   REED, Myer S. Jr. et al. "Wayward cops: the functions of deviance in groups reconsidered", *Soc. Probl.* 24(5), jun 77 : 565-575.

1490   ROBINS, Lee N.; WISH, Eric. "Childhood deviance as a developmental process: a study of 223 urban black men from birth to 18", *Soc. Forces* 56(2), dec 77 : 448-473.

1491   ROONEY, James F. "Employment and social integration among the skid row population", *Sociol. Inquiry* 47(2), 1977 : 109-117. [USA.]

1492   RUSHING, William A.; ESCO, Jack. "Status resources and behavioral deviance as contingencies of societal reaction", *Soc. Forces* 56(1), sep 77 : 132-147.

1493   SCHELLENBERG, James A. "Area variations of violence in Northern Ireland", *Sociol. Focus* 10(1), jan 77 : 69-78.

1494   SCHEUCH, Erwin. "Gewalt als politisches Kampfmittel in heutigen Industriegesellschaften" (Violence as mean of political struggle in contemporaneous industrial societies), *Hamburg. Jb. Wirtsch.-u. Ges.-Polit.* 22, 1977 : 281-315.

1495   SCHWENDINGER, H.; SCHWENDINGER, J. R. "Marginal youth and social policy". *Soc. Probl.* 24(2), dec 76 : 184-191.

1496   SENNETT, Richard. *The fall of public man.* New York, Knopf, 77, xii-373-xvi p.

1497   SHOHAM, S. Giora. *Social deviance.* New York, Gardner Press, 76, 162 p. CR: Nanette J. DAVIS, *Contemp. Sociol. (Washington)* 6(3), mai 77 : 312-313.

1498   STOHL, Michael. *War and domestic political violence: the American capacity for repression and reaction.* Beverly Hills, Calif., Sage Publications, 76, 153 p.

1499   SWANSON, Charles H. "The social marketability of self: toward a new theory of social deviance", *Sociol. Focus* 10(3), apr 77 : 263-274.

1500   THÉVENIN, Nicole-Edith. *Révisionnisme et philosophie de l'aliénation.* Paris, C. Bourgois, 77, 248 p.

1501   TOURAINE, Alain. "La marginalité urbaine", *Bol. Estud. latinoamer.* 22, jun 77 : 3-33.

1502   VAN DIJK, J. J. M. *Dominatiegedrag en geweld. Een multidisciplinaire visie op de veroorzaking van geweldmisdrijven* (Dominant behavior and violence. A multidisciplinary view on criminal violence). Nijmegen, Dekker en van de Vegt, 77, 165 p.

1503   VAZ, Edmund W. *Aspects of deviance.* Scarborough, Ont., Prentice-Hall, of Canada, 76, x-188 p.

1504   VEKEMANS, Roger; SILVA FUENZALIDA, Ismael. *Marginalidad, promoción popular y neo-marxismo: críticas y contracríticas* (Marginality, popular promotion and neo-marxism: criticism and contre-criticism) Bogotá, CEDIAL, 76, 327 p.

1505   VINK, N. "Marginalidad: teoria y práctica" (Marginality: theory and practice), *Bol. Estud. latinoamer.* 21, dec 76 : 57-75.

1506   WILLKE, Helmut. "Societal reactions and engendered deviation: the case of offensive groups", *Z. Soziol.* 6(4), oct 77 : 425-433.

1507   WILSON, John. "Social protest and social control", *Soc. Probl.* 24(4), apr 77 : 469-481.

1508   YOUNG, Ann; COCHRANE, Raymond. "Social isolation and reinforcer effectiveness: a test of three theories", *J. soc. Psychol.* 101(2), apr 77 : 281-289.

1509   ZIMMERMANN, Ekkart. *Soziologie der politischen Gewalt. Darstellung und Kritik vergleichender Aggregatdatenanalysen aus den USA* (Sociology of the political violence. Presentation and criticism of comparative aggregate data analysis of the USA). Stuttgart, F. Enke, 77, viii-226 p.

1510   ZORRILLA CASTRESANA, Restituto. *Sociología de las manifestaciones* (Demonstrations sociology). Bilbao, Editorial Vizcaína, 76, 206 p.

13200. CUSTOM. TRADITION
COUTUME. TRADITION

[See also / Voir aussi: 1541, 3266, 3277, 3439]

1511   CHANG, Kuang Chih et al. (eds.). *Food in Chinese culture: anthropological and historical perspectives.* New Haven, Yale University Press, 77, 429 p.

1512   DOBROWOLSKA, Monika. "Stosunek do tradycji w świetle badań socjologicznych" (Attitudes to tradition in the light of sociological research), *Przegl. socjol.* 29, 1977 : 203-217.

1513   DÓZSA, Katalin. "Öltözködési szabályok a századfordulo idején" (Clothing habits at the beginning of the 20th century), *Folia hist.* (4), 1976 : 131-144.

1514   MOSCHETTI, Gregory J. "Individual maintenance and perpetuation of a means/ends arbitrary tradition", *Sociometry* 40(1), 1977 : 78-85.

1515   TRÁSER, László. "Orvosegyetemi hallgatók müvelödési szokásainak elemzése" (Analysis of cultural habits among medicine students), *Tájékoztató* (4), 1976 : 140-170.

13300. ETHICS. MORALS
ÉTHIQUE. MORALE

[See also / Voir aussi: 1136, 1146, 1165, 1398, 1547, 1972, 2964, 3913, 4310, 5545]

1516   ARHANGEL'SKIJ, L. M.; KVASOV, G. G. "Sociologičeskie aspekty ětike: issledovanija i perspektivy" (Sociological aspects of ethics: researches and prospects), *Sociol. Issled. (Moskva)* (4), 1976 : 3-12.

1517   AUDRY, Colette. *Les militants et leurs morales.* Paris, Flammarion, 76, 184 p.

1518   BÁBOSIK, István. "Az erkölcsi irányultság és a magatartás összefüggéseinek vizsgálata" (Examination of relationships between moral principles and behaviour), *Magyar Pedag.* 16(4), 1976 : 358-370.

1519   BAYLES, Michael D. (ed.). *Ethics and population.* Cambridge, Mass., Schenkman, 76, xxviii-190 p.

1520   BENJAMIN, Martin. "Can moral responsibility be collective and non-distributive ?", *Soc. Theory Practice* 4(1), 1976 : 93-106.

1521   BONDY, O. "Das Reich des Sollens" (The realm of duty), *Österr. Z. öff. Recht* 27(1-2), 1976 : 85-90.

1522   ELDER, Carl A. *Values and moral development in children.* Nashville, Broadman Press, 76, 151 p.

1523   ETZIONI-HALEVY, Eva; HALEVY, Zvi. "The 'Jewish ethic' and the 'spirit of achievement'", *J. Sociol.* 19(1), jun 77 : 49-66.

1524   HAJDÚ, Péter. (ed.). *Szocializmus és erkölcs* (Socialism and ethics). Budapest, NIM IGÜSZI, 76, 289 p.

1525   HARSANYI, John C. *Essays on ethics, social behavior, and scientific explanation.* Dordrecht-Boston, D. Reidel Publishing Co., 76, xvi-262 p.

1526   HARSANYI, John C. "Morality and the theory of rational behavior", *Soc. Res.* 44(4), 1977 : 623-656.

1527   KANEKAR, Suresh; KOLSAWALLA, Maharukh B. "Responsibility in rela-
        tion to respectability ?", *J. soc. Psychol.* 102(2), aug 77 :
        183-188.
1528   KAVOLIS, Vytautas. "Moral cultures and moral logics", *Sociol. Anal.*
        (San Antonio) 38(4), 1977 : 331-344.
1529   MAPPES, Thomas A.; ZEMBATY, Jane S. *Social ethics: morality and*
        social policy. New York, McGraw-Hill, 77, viii-375 p.
1530   MORGENBESSER, Sidney (ed.). "Rationality, choice and morality",
        Soc. Res. 44(4), 1977 : 601-606.
1531   NELSON, Jack L. *Values, rights, and the new morality, do they con-*
        flict ? Englewood Cliffs, N.J., Prentice-Hall, 77, vii-120 p.
1532   PODMORE, David; YEOMANS, Keity. "Honesty and size and type of vic-
        tim organization: a British study, including comparisons with
        the United States", *Int. J. comp. Sociol.* 18(3-4), sep-dec 77 :
        293-298.
1533   ROUCEK, Joseph S. "The impact of the American frontier and 'wild
        West' on the American ethos", *Communications (Köln)* 3(1), 1977 :
        81-94.
1534   RYNKIEWICH, Michael A.; SPRADLEY, James P. *Ethics and anthropology:*
        dilemmas in field work. New York, Wiley, 76, 186 p. CR: Elvi
        WHITTAKER, *Contemp. Sociol. (Washington)* 6(4), jul 77 : 508.
1535   SCHLENKER, Barry R.; FORSYTH, Donelson R. "On the ethics of psy-
        chological research", *J. exp. soc. Psychol.* 13(4), jul 77 : 369-
        396.
1536   SHAPIRO, Sheldon. "Morality in religious reformations", *Comp. Stud.*
        Soc. Hist. 18(4), oct 76 : 438-457.
1537   TÄNNSJÖ, Torbjörn. *The relevance of metaethics to ethics.* Stock-
        holm, Almqvist och Wiksell International, 76, 226 p.
1538   THIROUX, Jacques P. *Ethics: theory and practice.* Encino, Calif.,
        Glencoe Press, 77, ix-194 p.
1539   VITÁNYI, Iván. "Az etikai világkép és az etikai magatartás szocioló-
        giája" (The sociology of the image of moral world and the moral
        behaviour), *Valóság* (7), 1976 : 1-16.

        13400. LAW. REGULATION
               LOI. RÉGLEMENTATION

        [See also / Voir aussi: 1199, 4998, 5381]

1540   ALKER, Hayward R. Jr. et al. "Jury selection as a biased social
        process", *Law Soc. R.* 11(1), 1976 : 9-41.
1541   ALLOTT, A. N. "The people as law-makers: customs, practice and
        public opinion as sources of law in Africa and England", *J. Afr.*
        Law 21(1), 1977 : 1-24.
1542   ARAL, Sevgi O.; SUNAR, Diane G. "Interaction and justice norms: a
        cross-national comparison", *J. soc. Psychol.* 101(2), apr 77 : 175-
        186.
1543   "Aspects significatifs de la politique criminelle des pays de l'Af-
        rique noire francophone", *Archiv. Polit. crim.* (1), 1975 : 91-260.
1544   BARKAN, Steven E. "Political trials and the pro se defendant in the
        adversary system", *Soc. Probl.* 24(3), feb 77 : 324-336.
1545   BLACK, Donald J. *The behavior of law.* New York, Academic Press, 76,
        xi-175 p.
1546   BLANKENBURG, E. "Über die Unwirksamkeit von Gesetzen" (On the inef-
        ficacy of laws), *Archiv Rechts- u. soz.-Philos.* 63(4), 1977 : 31-
        58.
1547   BLOM-COOPER, Louis; DREWRY, Gavin (eds.). *Law and morality.* London,
        Duckworth, 76, xvi-265 p.
1548   BOBBIO, Norberto. *Dalla struttura alla funzione: nuovi studi di*
        teoria del diritto (From the structure to the function: recent
        studies on the theory of law). Milano, Edizioni di Comunità, 76,
        278 p.

1549   BRYDE, Brun-Otto. *The politics and sociology of African legal de-*
        velopment. Frankfurt-am-Main, Metzner, 76, viii-290 p.
1550   CAMPBELL, C. M.; WILES, P. "The study of law on society in Britain",
        Law Soc. R. 10(4), 1976 : 547-578.
1551   CHIBA, Masaji. "Hô to Bunka" (Law and culture), *Horitsu Jihô* 49(6),
        1977 : 58-65; 49(8), 1977 : 111-119; 49(9), 1977 : 52-59; 49(11),
        1977 : 98-105; 49(12), 1977 : 148-155; 49(13), 1977 : 90-97.
1552   CLAUSS, Jan Ulrich. *Sozialwissenschaften und Rechtswissenschaft:*
        moderne Administration zwischen Juristendominanz und Verwaltungs-
        reformern (Social sciences and the science of law: modern adminis-
        tration between dominating jurists and governmental reformers).
        Konstanz, Neser, 76, 102 p.
1553   COOK, Karen S.; PARCEL, Toby L. "Equity theory: directions for fu-
        ture research", *Sociol. Inquiry* 47(2), 1977 : 75-88.
1554   DAMM, Richard. *Systemtheorie und Recht. Zur Normentheorie Talcott*
        Parsons (Systems theory and law. On Talcott Parsons theory of
        norms). Berlin, Dunker und Humblot, 76, 189 p. CR: Helmut WILLKE,
        Kölner Z. Soziol. u. soz.-Psychol. 29(3), sep 77 : 581-582.
1555   DÍAZ, Elías. *Sociología y filosofía del derecho* (Sociology and phi-
        losophy of law). Madrid, Taurus, 76, 451 p.
1556   DWORKIN, R. M. (ed.). *The philosophy of law.* London-New York, Ox-
        ford University Press, 77, 176 p.
1557   ECKHOFF, Torstein Einang. *Retten og samfunnet* (Law and society).
        Oslo, Tanum-Norli, 76, 352 p.
1558   FAUGERON, Claude; ROBERT, Philippe. "Les représentations sociales
        de la justice pénale", *C. int. Sociol.* 23(61), jul-dec 76 : 341-
        366.
1559   FRIEDMAN, Lawrence M.; REHBINDER, Manfred (eds.). *Zur Soziologie*
        des Gerichtsverfahrens / Sociology of the judicial process.
        Opladen, Westdeutscher Verlag, 76, 426 p.
1560   GORECKI, Jan (ed.). *Sociology of jurisprudence of Leon Petrazycki.*
        Urbana, University of Illinois Press, 76, 144 p. CR: J. G. HUND,
        Contemp. Sociol. (Washington) 6(2), mar 77 : 176-177.
1561   HAGAN, John. "Criminal justice in rural and urban communities: a
        study of the bureaucratization of justice", *Soc. Forces* 55(3),
        mar 77 : 597-612.
1562   HARTZLER, H. Richard. *Justice, legal systems, and social structure.*
        Port Washington, N.Y., Kennikat Press, 76, x-134 p. CR: A. J.
        BERGESEN, *Contemp. Sociol. (Washington)* 6(3), mai 77 : 310.
1563   HOPPANIA, Olavi. "Oikeussosiologian pääkysymyksesta" (On the so-
        called major question of sociology of law), *Sosiologia* 15(3-4),
        1977 : 123-133.
1564   HURST, James Willard. *Law and social order in the United States.*
        Ithaca, Cornell University Press, 77, 318 p.
1565   KAPLAN, Morton A. *Justice, human nature, and political obligation.*
        New York, Free Press, 76, xviii-283 p.
1566   KOTLJAREVSKIJ, G. S. "Pravnoe regulirovanie-istoričeskaja neobhodi-
        most' klassovogo obščestva" (Legal regulation is an historical
        necessity of a class society), *Trudy Vsesojuz. jur. zaoč. Inst.*
        39, 1975 : 103-134.
1567   KOUDRIAVTSEV, Vladimir. "L'humanisme du droit soviétique", *Sci.*
        soc. (Moscou) (4), 1976 : 53-64.
1568   KULCSÁR, K. "A jog hatékonysága a társadalomban" (The efficiency
        of law in society), *Jogtud. Közl.* 32(8), aug 77 : 448-453.
1569   KULCSÁR, K. "A jog hatékonyságának társadalmi tényezöi" (Social
        factors of the efficiency of law), *Jogtud. Közl.* 32(6), jun 77 :
        301-308.
1570   KULCSÁR, K. "A konzisztencia problémája a jogi rendszerben" (The
        problem of consistency in legal system), *Valóság* (5), 1977 : 19-
        21.
1571   LANG, W.; MORAWSKI, L.; GAWRYSIAK, T. "Koçepcja 'prawodawcy dosko-
        nal'nego' i jej zastosowanie prawodawstwie" (The concept of

"ideal legislator" and its application in jurisprudence), *Pań. i Prawo* 31(1-2), jan-feb 76 : 127-140.

1572   MAL'CEV, G. V. *Social'naja spravedlivost' i pravo* (Social justice and law). Moskva, Mysl', 77, 255 p.

1573   Bibl.XXVI-1400. McDONALD, Lynn. *The sociology of law and order.* CR: John HAGAN, *Contemp. Sociol. (Washington)* 6(2), mar 77 : 161-163.

1574   MICKEVIČ, A. V. "Issledovanie sostojanija pravovogo vospitanija trudjaščihsja" (Research on the content of workers legal education), *Sociol. Issled. (Moskva)* (3), 1976 : 107-112.

1575   MILLER, Dale T. "Personal deserving versus justice for others: an exploration of the justice motive", *J. exp. soc. Psychol.* 13(1), jan 77 : 1-13.

1576   MONOPOLI, William V. "'Equality before the law' and 'equal protection of the law': a comparative view", *Int. J. comp. Sociol.* 18(1-2), mar-jun 77 : 102-126.

1577   OTANI, Tomohiro. "Gurvitch no hô-shakaigaku-teki shiko" (Legal-sociological thought of Gurvitch), *Seikei Ronso* 26(2), 1977 : 271-288.

1578   ROBERT, Philippe; FAUGERON, Claude; KELLENS, George. "Le juge pénal et le justiciable. Représentations et attitudes", *Connexions* 20, 1976 : 39-62.

1579   TURK, Austin T. "The problem of legal order in the United States and South Africa: substantive and analytical considerations", *Sociol. Focus* 10(1), jan 77 : 31-41.

1580   UNGER, Roberto Mangabeira. *Law in modern society: toward a criticism of social theory.* New York, Free Press, 76, 309 p. CR: Allan HORWITZ, *Contemp. Sociol. (Washington)* 6(3), mai 77 : 308-310.

1581   UNITED NATIONS. Social Defence Research Institute. *Juvenile justice: an international survey: country reports, related materials, and suggestions for future research.* Rome, SDRI, 76, 251-xxviii-p.

1582   VEČEŘA, Miloš. "Význam marxistické sociologie práva" (Significance of the Marxist sociology of law), *Sociol. Čas.* 13(4), 1977 : 383-389.

1583   WOLFF, Robert Paul. *Understanding Rawls: a reconstruction and critique of "A theory of justice".* Princeton, N.J., Princeton University Press, 77, x-224 p.

13500. MAGIC. MYTHOLOGY. RELIGION
MAGIE. MYTHOLOGIE. RELIGION

13510. Religion. Sociology of religion
Religion. Sociologie religieuse

[See also / Voir aussi: 1004]

1584   "Ayer, hoy y mañana de la sociología de la religión en España" (Past, present and future of the Spanish sociology of religion), *Mundo soc.* 22(245), jul-aug 76 : 43-49.

1585   BERMUDO, M. "Es la religión una ideología ?" (Is religion an ideology ?), *Razón y Fe* 947, dec 76 : 401-415.

1586   BOURG, Carroll J. "Theory and the study of religion", *Sociol. Anal. (San Antonio)* 38(4), 1977 : 279-280.

1587   ČERNJAK, V. A. *Naučnyj progress i religija* (Scientific progress and religion). Alma Ata, Nauka, 76, 215 p.

1588   "Dimensions sociales de la religion", *R. int. Sci. soc.* 29(2), 1977 : 233-349.

1589   DION, Michel. "Le Groupe de sociologie des religions", *Pensée* 192, apr 77 : 117-127. *[France.]*

1590   el GUINDI, Fadwa. *Religion in culture.* Dubuque, Iowa, W. C. Brown Co., 77, viii-71 p.

1591   FITZPATRICK, Joseph P. *et al.* "Symposium on Thomas F. O'Dea",
Sociol. Anal. (San Antonio) 38(2), 1977 : 131-166. *[On sociology
of religion.]*

1592   HARRISON, Paul M. "Toward a dramaturgical interpretation of religion", *Sociol. Anal. (San Antonio)* 38(4), 1977 : 389-396.

1593   HILHORST, Hendrikus Wilhelmus Antonius. *Religie in verandering.
Een kritische analyse en evalutie van de sociologische optiek
van Peter L. Berger en Thomas Luckmann* (Religion in change. A
critical analysis and evaluation of the sociological points of
view of Peter L. Berger and Thomas Luckmann). Utrecht, s.e.,
76, viii-136 p.

1594   HOUTART, H. "Religion et modes de production précapitalistes",
Rech. sociol. 8(2), 1977 : 137-164.

1595   JOHNSON, Benton. "Sociological theory and religious truth", *Sociol.
Anal. (San Antonio)* 38(4), 1977 : 368-388.

1596   MADURO, Otto. "New Marxist approaches to the relative autonomy of
religion", *Sociol. Anal. (San Antonio)* 38(4), 1977 : 359-367.

1597   PHILLIPS, Dewi Zephaniah. *Religion without explanation.* Oxford,
Blackwell, 76, xi-200 p.

1598   Bibl.XXVI-1438. PICKERING, W. S. F. (ed.). *Durkheim on religion:
a selection of readings with bibliographies and introductory
remarks.* CR: Rendzin N. TAKLA, *Contemp. Sociol. (Washington)*
6(2), mar 77 : 163-165.

1599   POBEE, J. S. (ed.). *Religion in a pluralistic society.* Leiden,
E. J. Brill, 76, viii-236 p.-l 1.

1600   RASCHKE, Carl A.; KIRK, James A.; TAYLOR, Mark C. *Religion and the
human image.* Englewood Cliffs, N.J., Prentice-Hall, 77, xi-274 p.

1601   ROBERTSON, Roland. "Individualism, societalism, worldliness, uni-
versalism: thematizing theoretical sociology of religion", *Sociol. Anal. (San Antonio)* 38(4), 1977 : 281-308.

1602   ROCHE DE COPPENS, Peter. "The rediscovery of Bergson's work: its
implications for sociology in general and the sociology of religion in particular", *R. int. Sociol. (Madrid)* 34(17), jan-mar
76 : 133-160.

1603   SHINN, Larry D. *Two sacred worlds: experience and structure in
the world's religions.* Nashville, Abingdon, 77, 205 p.

1604   SKORUPSKI, John. *Symbol and theory: a philosophical study of theories of religion in social anthropology.* Cambridge-New York,
Cambridge University Press, 76, xv-265 p.

1605   SWATOS, William H. "The comparative method and the special vocation
of the sociology of religion", *Sociol. Anal. (San Antonio)* 38(2),
1977 : 106-114.

1606   WINTER, Jerry Alan. *Continuities in the sociology of religion:
creed, congregation, and community.* New York, Harper and Row,
77, x-307 p.

1607   WÖSSNER, Jakobus. "Die Möglichkeit von Religion. Von der Kirchen-
soziologie zur Religionssoziologie" (The possibility of religion.
From the sociology of church to sociology of religion), *Sociol.
int. (Berlin)* 12(1-2), 1974 : 147-167.

13520. Magic. Primitive religion
Magie. Religion primitive

13521.

[See also / Voir aussi: 1604]

1608   CAVENDISH, Richard. *A history of magic.* New York, Taplinger Publishing Co., 77, 180pp.-9 1.

1609   LORINT, Florica Elena; BERNABE, Jean. *La sorcellerie paysanne:
approche anthropologique de l'Homo magus, avec une étude sur la
Roumanie.* Bruxelles, A. De Boeck; Paris, A. Colin, 77, 207 p.

1610   MAPLE, Eric. *Deadly magic: the power of darkness.* Wellinborough,
        Eng., Thorsons, 76, 96 p.

1611   PEDRAZZANI, Jean Michel. *Geheime Zeichen, magische Kräfte* (Secret
        signs, magic powers). Kastellaun, Henn, 76, 184 p.

1612   TURNER, Harold W. *Bibliography of new religious movements in primal
        societies.* Boston, G. K. Hall, 77.

        13522.

1613   BOOTH, Newell S. (ed.). *African religions: a symposium.* New York,
        NOK Publishers, 77, 390 p.-5 1.

1614   CUCHE, Denys. "La mort des dieux africains et les religions noires
        au Pérou", *Archiv. Sci. soc. Relig.* 43(1), jan-mar 77 : 77-91.

1615   DENIEL, R. "Religions traditionnelles et religions révélées", *R.
        franç. Ét. polit. afr.* 131, nov 76 : 75-84. [Côte d'Ivoire.]

1616   PIERRE, Roland. "Caribbean religion: the Voodoo case", *Sociol.
        Anal. (San Antonio)* 38(1), 1977 : 25-36.

1617   POBEE, John S.; MENDS, Emmanuel H. "Social change and African tra-
        ditional religion", *Sociol. Anal. (San Antonio)* 38(1), 1977 :
        1-12.

        13524.

        [See also / Voir aussi: 792, 1373, 1523, 1718, 1736, 2949, 3306]

1618   DESMANGLES, Leslie Gerald. "African interpretations of the Chris-
        tian cross in Vodun", *Sociol. Anal. (San Antonio)* 38(1), 1977 :
        13-24.

        13530. Buddhism. Christianity
               Bouddhisme. Christianisme

1619   BAUBEROT, Jean. "La place des protestants", *Esprit* 45(4-5), apr-mai
        77 : 28-39. [France.]

1620   BELL, Geoffrey. *The Protestants of Ulster.* London, Pluto Press;
        New York, E. P. Dutton, 76, 159 p.

1621   DARIAN, Jean C. "Social and economic factors in the rise of Buddh-
        ism", *Sociol. Anal. (San Antonio)* 38(3), 1977 : 226-238.

1622   DAWIDOWICZ, Lucy S. *The Jewish presence: essays on identity and
        history.* New York, Holt, Rinehart and Winston, 77, xiii-308 p.

1623   DELLA PERGOLA, Sergio. *Anatomia dell'ebraismo italiano: caratteris-
        tiche demografiche, economiche, sociali, religiose e politiche di
        una minoranza* (Anatomy of the Italian judaism: demographic, eco-
        nomic, social, religious and political characteristics of a mi-
        nority). Assisi-Roma, B. Carucci, 76, xvi-358 p.

1624   DEM'IANOV, A. I. "A contribution to the question of the present
        status of the 'truly orthodox christians'", *Sov. Sociol.* 15(2),
        1976 : 17-37.

1625   DENIEL, Raymond. "Musulmans et chrétiens en Afrique de l'Ouest",
        Études (Paris) oct 77 : 377-386.

1626   ERNST, Eldon G. *Without help or hindrance: religious identity in
        American culture.* Philadelphia, Westminster Press, 77, 240 p.

1627   GOULEY, Bernard. *Les Catholiques français aujourd'hui: suivi d'un
        peuple.* Paris, A. Fayard, 77, 404 p.

1628   GREELEY, Andrew M. *The American Catholic: a social portrait.* New
        York, Basic Books, 77, vi-280 p.

1629   GUPTA, Raghuraja. *Hindu-Muslim relations.* Lucknow, Ethnographic
        and Folk Culture Society, University Press, 76, xvi-208 p.

1630   IRVING, T. B. "Islamic education in Spain and Latin America", *Islam
        mod. Age* 8(4), nov 77 : 65-77.

1631   KIM, Young Oon. *Living religions of the Middle East.* New York,
        Golden Gate Publishing Co., 76, x-275 p. [Judaism, Zoroastrian-
        ism, Islam.]

1632   LEWIS, Bernard (ed.). *Islam and the Arab world: faith, people, culture*. New York, Knopf, Random House, 76, 360 p.

1633   LEWIS, Bernard (ed.). *Le monde de l'Islam*. Paris-Bruxelles, Elsevier, 76, 367 p.

1634   MESSELKEN, Karlheinz. "Zur Durchsetzung des Christentums in der Spätantike. Strukturell-funktionale Analyse eines historischen Gegenstandes" (The infiltration of Christianity in the late classical period. Structural and functional analysis of a historical subject), *Kölner Z. Soziol. u. soz.-Psychol.* 29(2), jun 77 : 261-294.

1635   MOORE, Kenneth. *Those of the street: the Catholic-Jews of Mallorca: a study in urban cultural change*. Notre Dame, Ind., University of Notre Dame Press, 76, viii-218 p.-2 l.

1636   MOSES, Larry. "Mongol Buddhism in the 20th century", *Asian Pacific Quart. cult. soc. Aff.* 8(3), 1976 : 1-30.

1637   OFORI, Patrick E. *Christianity in tropical Africa: a selective annotated bibliography*. Nendeln, Kto Press, 77, 461 p.

1638   STANG, Hakon. *Westernness and Islam*. Oslo, Chair in Conflict and Peace Research, University of Oslo, 76, 96 p.

1639   TRANVOUEZ, Yvon. "La fondation et les débuts de 'La vie intellectuelle' (1928-1929). Contribution à l'histoire du catholicisme intransigeant", *Archiv. Sci. soc. Relig.* 42(2), jul-dec 76 : 57-96.

1640   WILLAIME, Jean-Paul. "La sociologie du protestantisme en France. Des premières recherches aux travaux actuels", *Archiv. Sci. soc. Relig.* 44(1), jul-sep 77 : 103-118.

13540. Church. Religious community. Sect
Église. Communauté religieuse. Secte

13541.

1641   DUBB, Allie A. *Community of the saved: an African revivalist church in the East Cape*. Johannesburg, Witwatersrand University Press for African Studies Institute, 76, xvii-175 p.-10 p.

1642   FIELD, Clive D. "The social structure of English Methodism: eighteenth-twentieth centuries", *Brit. J. Sociol.* 28(2), jun 77 : 199-225.

1643   FLORA, Cornelia Butler. *Pentecostalism in Colombia: baptism by fire and spirit*. Rutherford, N.J., Fairleigh Dickinson University Press, 76, 288 p.

1644   FORD, Josephine Massyngberde. *Which way for Catholic pentecostals ?* New York, Harper and Row, 76, x-143 p.

1645   GARELLI, Franco. "Istituzione ecclesiale e mutamento sociale" (Church institution and social change), *Quad. Sociol.* 27(2), apr-jun 77 : 150-173. [Italy.]

1646   HESSLER, Hans-Wolfgang (ed.). *Protestanten und ihre Kirche in der Bundesrepublik Deutschland* (The protestants and their churches in the German Federal Republic). München, G. Olzog, 76, 373 p.

1647   MANOR, Yohanan; SHEFFER, Gabriel. "L''United Jewish Appeal' ou la métamorphose du don", *R. franç. Sociol.* 18(1), jan-mar 77 : 3-24.

1648   SANTINI, Alceste. "La Chiesa Cattolica di fronte alla crisi del mondo contemporaneo" (The Catholic Church facing the crisis in the contemporary world), *Crit. marx.* 14(5-6), sep-dec 76 : 87-112.

1649   SHAROT, Stephen. "Instrumental and expressive elites in a religious organization. The United Synagogue in London", *Archiv. Sci. soc. Relig.* 43(1), jan-mar 77 : 141-155.

1650   WESTHUES, Kenneth. "Religious organization in Canada and the United States", *Int. J. comp. Sociol.* 17(3-4), sep-dec 76 : 206-225.

13542.

[See also / Voir aussi: 1736]

1651 O'BRIEN, Donal B. Cruise. "A versatile charisma. The Mouride Brotherhood, 1967-1975", *Archiv. europ. Sociol.* 18(1), 1977 : 84-106.

1652 PICKERING, W. S. F. "Hutterites and problems of persistence and social control in religious communities", *Archiv. Sci. soc. Relig.* 4(1), jul-sep 77 : 75-92.

1653 SAMARDZIC, Radovan M. "Religious communities", *Yugosl. Surv.* 18(3), aug 77 : 59-70. *[Yugoslavia.]*

1654 VOISIN, Michel. "Communautés utopiques et structure sociale: le cas de la Belgique francophone", *R. franç. Sociol.* 18(2), apr-jun 77 : 271-300.

13543.

[See also / Voir aussi: 1268, 3380]

1655 Bibl.XXVI-1481. BECKFORD, James A. *The trumpet of prophecy: a sociological study of Jehovah's witnesses.* CR: Philippe, HAMMOND, *Amer. J. Sociol.* 82(4), jan 77 : 896-898.

1656 CERBU, Marcel. *Le combat des francs-maçons: contribution à l'histoire du rite écossais ancien et accepté de 1940 à nos jours.* Marseille, Centre de documentation traditionnelle, 76, 236 p.

1657 COSTON, Henry. *Un État dans l'État: la franc-maçonnerie.* Paris, Librairie française, 76.

1658 COVAR, Prospero R. "General characterization of contemporary religious movements in the Philippires", *Asian Stud.* 13(2), aug 75 : 79-92.

1659 CRAEMER, Willy DE; VANSINA, Jan; FOX, Renée C. "Religious movements in Central Africa: a theoretical study", *Comp. Stud. Soc. Hist.* 18(4), oct 76 : 458-475.

1660 DAVIS, Thomas Brabson. *Aspects of Freemasonry in modern Mexico: an example of social cleavage.* New York, Vantage Press, 76, xxiv-421 p.

1661 LIGOU, Daniel (éd.). *La franc-maçonnerie.* Paris, Presses universitaires de France, 77, 200 p.

1662 MOLA, Aldo Alessandro. *Storia della massoneria italiana dall'unità alla repubblica* (History of the Italian freemasonry from the unity to the Republic). Milano, Bompiani, 76, xvi-822 p.

1663 "Témoins de Jéhovah (Les)", *Soc. Compass* 24(1), 1977 : 5-134.

1664 WALKER, Scheila S. "Religion and modernization in African context: the Harrist Church of the Ivory Coast", *J. Afr. Stud.* 4(1), 1977 : 77-85.

13545.

1665 "Futuro del ecumenismo en América latina (El)" (The future of ecumenism in Latin America), *Crist. y Soc.* 15(2-3), 1977 : 3-54.

1666 KELLY, James R. "Ecumenism and social conflict: the case of Kawaida towars", *J. ecumen. Stud.* 14(2), 1977 : 288-303.

1667 NEWBIGIN, L. "What is 'a local church truly united' ?", *Ecumen. R.* 29(2), apr 77 : 115-128.

1668 POGGI, Vicenzo. "Nuove dimensioni dell'ecumenismo" (New dimensions of oecumenism), *Aggiorn. soc.* 28(11), nov 77 : 635-648.

1669 SANTA ANA, Julio DE. "Notas sobre el futuro del ecumenismo" (Notes on the future of oecumenism), *Crist y Soc.* 15(1), 1 trim 77 : 29-43.

13550. Clergy. Religious authority
       Clergé. Autorité religieuse

13551.

1670   GARCÍA DE CORTÁZAR RUIZ DE AGUIRRE, Fernando. "Análisis sociológi-
        co del Episcopado español de la Restauración" (Sociological ana-
        lysis of the Spanish episcopacy during the Restoration), *R. int.
        Sociol. (Madrid)* 34(18-19-20), apr-dec 76 : 63-90.
1671   POTEL, Julien. *Les prêtres séculiers en France: évolution de 1965
        à 1975.* Paris, Centurion, 77, 143 p.
1672   VIGNERON, Paul. *Histoire des crises du clergé français contemporain.*
        Paris, P. Téqui, 76, 494 p.

13552.

        [See also / Voir aussi: 1093, 5346]

1673   ALTHEIDE, D. L.; JOHNSON, J. M. "Counting souls: a study of coun-
        seling at Evangelical crusades", *Pacific sociol. R.* 20(3), jul
        77 : 323-348. [The perspective and activities of religious coun-
        selors at a Billy Graham Evangelical Crusade are examined.]
1674   ELIFSON, Kirk M.; IRWIN, Joseph. "Black ministers' attitudes to-
        ward population size and birth control", *Sociol. Anal. (San An-
        tonio)* 38(3), 1977 : 252-257.
1675   FRANKEL , E. A. "The maronite Patriarch: an historical view of a
        religious Za'im in the 1958 Lebanese crisis", *Muslim Wld* 66(3),
        jul 76 : 213-225; 66(4), oct 76 : 245-258.
1676   LUNEAU, René. "Monde rural et christianisation. Prêtres et paysans
        français du siècle dernier", *Archiv. Sci. soc. Relig.* 43(1),
        jan-mar 77 : 39-52.
1677   REIDY, M. T. V.; WHITE, L. C. "The measurement of traditionalism
        among Roman Catholics priests: an exploratory study", *Brit. J.
        Sociol.* 28(2), jun 77 : 226-241. [UK.]
1678   VENTIMIGLIA, Joseph C. "Career commitment among continuing and
        exiting seminary students", *Sociol. Anal. (San Antonio)* 38(1),
        1977 : 49-58.

13560. Cult. Rite
       Culte. Rite

        [See also / Voir aussi: 1042, 1692]

1678   BIRKS, J. S. "The Mecca pilgrimage by West African pastoral no-
        mads", *J. mod. Afr. Stud.* 15(1), mar 77 : 47-58.
1680   CAMPBELL, Colin. "Clarifying the cult", *Brit. J. Sociol.* 28(3),
        sep 77 : 375-388.
1681   CHAMPAGNE, Patrick. "La fête au village", *Actes Rech. Sci. soc.*
        17-18, nov 77 : 73-84.
1682   COBOS RUIZ DE ADANA, José; LUQUE-ROMERO ALBORNOZ, F. "La romería
        de San Benito en Obejo. Una aproximación antropológica" (The
        pilgrimage of San Benito in Obejo. An anthropological approach),
        R. int. Sociol. (Madrid) 36(21), 1977 : 77-92.
1683   DUVIGNAUD, Jean. *Le don du rien: essai d'anthropologie de la fête.*
        Paris, Stock, 77, 314 p.
1684   FUJII, Masao. *Bukkyô girei jiten* (Dictionary of Buddhist rituals).
        Tokyo, Tokyo-dô, 77, 373 p.
1685   HALL, Angus. *Strange cults.* Garden City, N.Y., Doubleday, 76,
        144 p.
1686   ISAMBERT, François-A. "Religion populaire, sociologie, histoire et
        folklore", *Archiv. Sci. soc. Relig.* 43(2), apr-jun 77 : 161-184.
1687   MORIOKA, Kiyomi. "The appearance of 'Ancestor Religion' in modern
        Japan", *Japan. J. relig. Stud.* 4(2-3), 1977 : 183-212.

1688   OLIVEIRA, Nei Roberto da Silva; OLIVEIRA, Isabel Montezuma DE.
"Estudo de festivais e seu impacto na comunidade" (Survey of fes-
tivals and its impact on the community), *Amér. lat. (Rio de Janeiro)* 17, 1976 : 130-177. [Brazil.]

1689   PLONGERON, Bernard *et al. La religion populaire dans l'Occident
chrétien: approches historiques.* Paris, Beauchesne, 76, 237 p.

1690   RAPHAEL, Freddy. "Esquisse d'une sociologie de la fête", *Contrepoint* 24, 1977 : 109-131.

1691   RIBEYROL, Monette; SCHNAPPER, Dominique. "Cérémonies funéraires
dans la Yougoslavie orthodoxe", *Archiv. europ. Sociol.* 17(2),
1976 : 220-246.

1692   ROSENBLATT, Paul C.; WALSH, R. Patricia; JACKSON, Douglas A. *Grief
and mourning in cross-cultural perspective.* New Haven, Conn.,
HRAF Press, 76, vii-231 p. [Funeral rites and ceremonies.]

1693   SANCHIS, Pierre. "Les Romarias portugaises", *Archiv. Sci. soc.
Relig.* 43(1), jan-mar 77 : 53-76.

1694   SANSON, Rosemonde. *Les 14 juillet, 1789-1975, fête et conscience
nationale.* Paris, Flammarion, 76, 220 p.

1695   WORKS, John A. Jr. *Pilgrims in a strange land: Hausa communities
in Chad.* New York, Columbia University Press, 76, xiv-280 p.

13570. Myth. Religious doctrine
Mythe. Doctrine religieuse

13571.

1696   BECKER, Lee B. "Predictors of change in religious beliefs and behaviors during college", *Sociol. Anal. (San Antonio)* 58(1), 1977
: 65-74.

1697   FLERE, Sergej. "Dekompozicija religiozne svesti kao oblik procesa
ateizacije" (The desintegration of religious consciousness as a
form of the atheizing process), *Sociologija* 19(4), 1977 : 597-
619.

1698   GONZÁLEZ MONTES, Adolfo. *Razón política de la fe cristiana: un estudio histórico-teológico de la hermeneútica política de la fe*
(Political reason of the Christian faith: an historico-theologic-
al study of the political hermeneutics of faith). Salamanca,
Universidad Pontificia, 76, 244 p.

1699   MURÁNYI, Mihaly; DÖMÖK, Zsuzsa. "Vallásosság, hitközöny, ateizmus ?
Budapesti fiatalok világnézeti orientációinak néhány jellemzöjé-
röl" (Piety, indifference to religion, atheism? Some characteristics about the orientation of the conception of the world among
young people of Budapest), *Világosság* (8-9), 1976 : 590-600.

1700   RUFFAT, Andrée. *La superstition à travers les âges.* Paris, Payot,
76, 292 p.

13572.

1701   DECONCHY, J.-P.; COSNEFROY, L. "Dogmatisme et religion. Études empiriques utilisant la conceptualisation de Milton Rokeach", *Archiv. Sci. soc. Relig.* 44(1), jul-sep 77 : 139-145.

1702   "Sincretismo religioso" (Religious syncretism), *Vozes* 71(7), sep
77 : 5-68. [Brazil.]

1703   SZÁSZ, Thomas Stephen. *Heresies.* New York, Anchor Press, 76, 183 p.
CR: Robert S. BROADHEAD, *Contemp. Sociol. (Washington)* 6(3), mai
77 : 391.

13573.

[See also / Voir aussi: 2042, 2046]

1704   BELL, Daniel. "The return of the sacred ? The argument on the future
of religion", *Brit. J. Sociol.* 28(4), dec 77 : 419-449.

1705   COURTAS, R.; ISAMBERT, François-A. "La notion de 'sacré'. Biblio-
        graphie thématique", *Archiv. Sci. soc. Relig.* 44(1), jul-sep 77
        : 119-138.
1706   GOODICH, Michael. "A profile of thirteenth-century sainthood",
        Comp. Stud. Soc. Hist. 18(4), oct 76 : 429-437.
1707   ISAMBERT, François-A. "L'élaboration de la notion de sacré dans
        l'école durkheimienne", *Archiv. Sci. soc. Relig.* 42(2), jul-dec
        76 : 35-56.
1708   ISAMBERT, François-A. "Symbolisme religieux, séculier, et classes
        sociales. 14e Conférence internationale de sociologie religieuse,
        Strasbourg, 28 août-1 septembre 1977", *Archiv. Sci. soc. Relig.*
        44(1), jul-sep 77 : 147-148.
1709   LEROI-GOURHAN, André. "Interprétation esthétique et religieuse des
        figures et symboles dans la préhistoire", *Archiv. Sci. soc. Relig.*
        42(2), jul-dec 76 : 5-15.
1710   MARTIN, Hervé; MARTIN, Louis. "Croix rurales et sacralisation de
        l'espace. Le cas de la Bretagne au Moyen Âge", *Archiv. Sci. soc.
        Relig.* 22(43), jan-mar 77 : 23-38.
1711   MOL, Hans. *Identity and the sacred: a sketch for a new social-
        scientific theory of religion.* New York, Free Press, 77, xvi-
        326 p.
1712   SEGUY, Jean. "Images et 'religion populaire'", *Archiv. Sci. soc.
        Relig.* 44(1), jul-sep 77 : 25-43.

        13575.

        [See also / Voir aussi: 1042]

1713   CLARKE, Simon. "Lévi-Strauss's structural analysis of myth", *So-
        ciol. R.* 25(4), nov 77 : 743-774.
1714   O'FLAHERTY, Wendy Doniger. *The origins of evil in Hindu mythology.*
        Berkeley, University of California Press, 76, xi-411 p.
1715   PERRY, John Weir. *Roots of renewal in myth and madness.* San Fran-
        cisco, 76, xii-256 p.
1716   RUTHVEN, K. K. *Myth.* London, Methuen; New York, Harper and Row,
        Barnes and Noble, 76, 8-104 p.
1717   TESTART, Alain. "Milieu naturel, mythologie et organisation soci-
        ale: le principe de la classification dualiste chez les Tlingit
        de la Côte nord-ouest de l'Amérique du Nord", *Soc. Sci. Inform.*
        15(2-3), 1976 : 415-426.

        13580. Religious behaviour
        Comportement religieux

        [See also / Voir aussi: 372, 1674, 3144]

1718   BETTEN, Neil. *Catholic activism and the industrial worker.* Gaines-
        ville, University Presses of Florida, 76, x-191 p.
1719   CHAMIE, Joseph. *Religion and population dynamics in Lebanon.* Ann
        Arbor, Population Studies Center, University of Michigan, 77,
        xv-141-13 p.
1720   DAVIDSON, James D. "Socio-economic status and ten dimensions of
        religious commitment", *Sociol. soc. Res.* 61(4), jul 77 : 462-
        485.
1721   DAVIDSON, James D.; KNUDSEN, Dean D. "A new approach to religious
        commitment", *Sociol. Focus* 10(2), apr 77 : 151-173.
1722   EL-GARM, M. S. "The Islamic attitude towards women", *Orita* 10(1),
        jun 76 : 24-45.
1723   GLENN, Morval D.; GOTARD, Erin. "The religion of Blacks in the
        United States: some recent trends and current characteristics",
        Amer. J. Sociol. 83(2), sep 77 : 443-451.
1724   Bibl.XXVI-1540. CLOCK, Charles Y.; BELLAH, Robert N. (eds.). *The
        new religious consciousness.* CR: Roy WALLIS, *Contemp. Sociol.*
        (Washington) 6(4), jul 77 : 472-474.

1725   HEIRICH, Max. "Change of heart: a test of some widely held theories about religious conversion", *Amer. J. Sociol.* 83(3), nov 77 : 653-680.

1726   HUNT, Larry L.; HUNT, Janet G. "Black religion as both opiate and inspiration of civil rights militance: putting Marx's data to the test", *Soc. Forces* 56(1), sep 77 : 1-14.

1727   KRAFT, Virgil A. *The freedom story: a survey of the origin and meaning of the American experiment with civilization's basic freedom, freedom of religion.* Tujunga, Calif., Parthenon Books, 77, x-152 p.

1728   LERNOUX, P. "Popular religiosity: new wind in Latin America", *Nation* 224(7), feb 19, 77 : 199-205.

1729   LLANOS, José Maria DE. "Notas de piedad en una barriada madrileña" (Devotion symptoms in a suburb of Madrid), *Razon y Fe* 956-957, sep-oct 77 : 892-895.

1730   LOUX, Françoise. "Pratiques médicales préventives et recours religieux. Les soins aux enfants en Haute-Normandie", *Archiv. Sci. soc. Relig.* 44(1), jul-sep 77 : 45-58.

1731   PACE, Enzo. "Il dibattito sulla religiosità popolare" (The debate on popular religiosity), *Sociologia (Roma)* 11(1), jan-apr 77 : 95-102.

1732   RANTALA, Lea. "Murrosikäisten uskonnollinen ajattelu tutkimustulosten valossa" (Religious thinking among teenagers in the light of research results), *Kasvatus* 78(5), 1976 : 248-251.

1733   RAZZELL, Peter. "The *Protestant ethics and the spirit of capitalism*: a natural scientific critique", *Brit. J. Sociol.* 28(1), mar 77 : 17-37.

1734   RICHARDSON, James T. (ed.). "Conversion and commitment in contemporary religion", *Amer. behav. Scientist* 20(6), jul-aug 77 : 799-956.

1735   RUSSELL, Margo. "Religion as a social possession. Afrikaner reaction to the conversion of Bushmen to their Church", *Archiv. Sci. soc. Relig.* 44(1), jul-sep 77 : 59-73.

1736   TAPIA, Claude. "Propositions méthodologiques pour l'étude des comportements religieux. Communautés et pratiques religieuses dans le judaïsme français", *Archiv. Sci. soc. Relig.* 4(1), jul-sep 77 : 93-101.

1737   TOMKA, Miklós. "A változó vallásosság mérésének problémái" (Problems of measuring changing religiosity), *Magyar pszichol. Szle* 34(4), 1977 : 363-376.

13590. Church and State. Religious practice
        Église et État. Pratique religieuse

[See also / Voir aussi: 1536, 1675, 1676, 5123]

1738   AHMED, M. D. "Religion and society in Pakistan", *Orient (Opladen)* 17(4), dec 76 : 123-151.

1739   ARROYO, G. "L'Eglise face au néo-fascisme", *Etudes (Paris)* jan 77 : 25-44. [Amérique latine.]

1740   BARKAT, A. M. "Church-State relationships in an ideological Islamic State", *Ecumen. R.* 29(1), jan 77 : 39-51.

1741   BEACH, Stephen W. "Religion and political change in Northern Ireland", *Sociol. Anal. (San Antonio)* 38(1), 1977 : 37-48.

1742   Bibl.XXVI-1555. BELLAH, Robert N. *The broken covenant: American civil religion in time of trial.* CR: Benton JOHNSON, *Contemp. Sociol. (Washington)* 6(1), jan 77 : 82-83.

1743   BOYLE, J. F. "Educational attainment, occupational achievement and religion in Northern Ireland", *Econ. soc. R.* 8(2), jan 77 : 79-100.

1744   DAVIES, John Gordon. *Christians, politics and violent revolution.* London, SCM Press; Maryknoll, N.Y., Orbis Books, 76, 216 p.

1745   DOMENACH, J. M. "Société et Église en Pologne", *Esprit* 44(10),
        oct 76 : 339-352.
1746   "Eurocomunismo y cristianismo" (Eurocommunism and christianity),
        R. Fomento soc. 32(125), jan-mar 77 : 7-101.
1747   GLASNER, Peter E. *The sociology of secularisation. A critique of
        concept.* London, Routledge and Kegan Paul, 77, viii-137 p.
1748   GREIL, Arthur L. "Previous dispositions and conversion to pers-
        pectives of social and religious movements", *Sociol. Anal. (San
        Antonio)* 38(2), 1977 : 115-125.
1749   GRIGNON, Claude. "Sur les relations entre les transformations du
        champ religieux et les transformations de l'espace politique",
        Actes Rech. Sci. soc. 16, sep 77 : 3-34.
1750   GUIZZARDI, Gustavo. "New religious phenomena in Italy: towards a
        post-Catholic era ?", *Archiv. Sci. soc. Relig.* 42(2), jul-dec
        76 : 97-116.
1751   HÄBERLE, P. "'Staatskirchenrecht' als Religionsrecht der verfass-
        ten Gesellschaft" ("State Church law" as a law of religion in
        organized society), *Öff. Verw.* 29(3), feb 76 : 73-80.
1752   HARTMANN, K. "Stagnation in den Beziehungen zwischen Kirche und
        Staat in Polen" (Stagnation in the relations between State and
        Church in Poland), *Osteuropa* 27(1), jan 77 : 20-30.
1753   HEUBEL, E. "Church and State in Spain: transition toward indepen-
        dence and liberty", *West. polit. Quart.* 30(1), mar 77 : 125-139.
1754   HUNT, Larry L.; HUNT, Janet G. "Religious affiliation and militan-
        cy among urban blacks: some catholic-protestant comparisons",
        Soc. Sci. Quart. 57(4), mar 77 : 821-833.
1755   IKADO, Fujio. "Kyôdan-kaikaku no shakaigaku" (A sociological sur-
        vey on religious reforms and revolts in Japan), *Kokusai Shukyo
        News* 16(2), 1977 : 9-27.
1756   IKADO, Fujio. "Sezoku shakai no dendôgijutsu" (Mission in secular
        society - its technique and organization), *Kyoka to Kyogaku* 1(1),
        1977 : 163-223.
1757   ISAMBERT, François-André. "La sécularisation interne du christia-
        nisme", *R. franç. Sociol.* 17(4), oct-dec 76 : 571-590.
1758   KANGE, Ewane. *La politique dans le système religieux catholique
        romain en Afrique de 1815 à 1960.* Lille, Université Lille III;
        Paris, H. Champion, 76, 513 p.
1759   LA HERA, A. DE. "Las relaciones entre la Iglesia y el Estado en
        España, 1953-1974" (Church and State relationships in Spain,
        1953-1974), *R. Estud. polít.* 211, jan-feb 77 : 5-37.
1760   LANGTON, K. P.; RAPOPORT, R. "Religion and leftist mobilization
        in Chile", *Comp. polit. Stud.* 9(3), oct 76 : 277-308.
1761   LE BOT, Yvon. "Le pouvoir de l'Église en pays Quiché", *C. Monde
        hisp. luso-brésil.* 28, 1977 : 225-243. [Guatemala.]
1762   LE BRAS, Gabriel *et al.* "Pratique religieuse et religion populaire",
        Archiv. Sci. soc. Relig. 43(1), jan-mar 77 : 7-22.
1763   LEVINE, Daniel H.; WILDE, Alexander W. "The Catholic Church, 'pol-
        itics' and violence: the Colombian case", *R. Polit.* 39(2), apr
        77 : 220-249.
1764   LEYLAND KAUFFERT, P. "Christianity, education and politics in a
        Ghanaian community", *West Afr. J. Sociol. polit. Sci.* 1(2),
        jan 76 : 134-146.
1765   MEHL, Roger. *Le catholicisme français dans la société actuelle.*
        Paris, Le Centurion, 77, 222 p.
1766   MICHELAT, Guy; SIMON, Michel. "Religion, class and politics",
        Comp. Polit. 10(1), oct 77 : 159-186.
1767   Bibl.XXVI-1571. MORIOKA, Kiyomi. *Religion in a changing Japanese
        society.* CR: David W. PLATH, *Contemp. Sociol. (Washington)* 6(2),
        mar 77 : 227-228.
1768   POWLES, C. "Yasukuni Jinja Hoan: religion and politics in contem-
        porary Japan", *Pacific Aff.* 49(3), 1976 . 491-505.

1769   PRANDI, Carlo. "Religion et classes subalternes en Italie. Trente années de recherches italiennes", *Archiv. Sci. soc. Relig.* 43(1), jan-mar 77 : 93-139.

1770   REGAN, D. "Islam, intellectuals and civil religion in Malaysia", *Sociol. Anal. (San Antonio)* 37(2), 1976 : 95-110.

1771   "Religione, secolarizzazione e politica in Italia" (Religion, secularization and politics in Italy), *IDOC int.* 7(11), dec 76 : 45-64.

1772   "Religious innovations in modern African society", *Afr. Perspect.* (2), 1976 : 7-147.

1773   Bibl.XXVI-1575. RÉMOND, René. *L'anticléricalisme en France, de 1815 à nos jours.* CR: Jean-Marie DONEGANI, *R. franç. Sci. polit.* 27(3), jun 77 : 462-467.

1774   "Russie et chrétienté: la situation religieuse en URSS", *Istina* 22(1), jan-mar 77 : 26-108.

1775   SCHNEIDER, Karlheinz. *Religion in Israel. Eine Studie zum Verhältnis Person, Religion, Gesellschaft* (Religion in Israel. A study of the relations between individual, religion, society). Meisenheim-am-Glan, A. Hain, 76, 267 p.

1776   SHUPE, Anson D. Jr. "Conventional religious and political participation in postwar rural Japan", *Soc. Forces* 55(3), mar 77 : 613-629.

1777   SUHRKE, Astri. "Loyalists and separatists: the Muslims in Southern Thailand", *Asian Surv.* 17(3), mar 77 : 237-250.

1778   "Szocializmus és vallás" (Socialism and religion), *Világosság* (1), 1977 : 2-48. [Conference held on 25-27th October 1976 in Pécs.]

1779   THORBJØRNSEN, Lis. *Kristendom og socialisme* (Christianity and socialism). Århus, Aros, 76, 136 p.

1780   TOMKA, Miklós. "A vallási kultúra maradványai a vidéki fiatalok körében" (The remnants of religious culture among country youth), *Pedag. Szle* 27(1), 1977 : 10-21. [Hungary.]

1781   TOMKA, Miklós. *A mai fiatalok és a vallás vidéken* (Youth and religion in the country today). Budapest, Ifjúsági Lapkiadó, 76, 51 p. [Hungary.]

1782   WILSON, Bryan R. *Contemporary transformations of religion.* London, Oxford University Press, 76, xii-116 p.

1783   WITTMAYER BARON, Salo. "Nationalism and religion in the contemporary world", *J. ecumen. Stud.* 13(4), 1976 : 117-135.

1784   YOUNG, L. C.; FORD, S. R. "God is society: the religious dimension of maoism", *Sociol. Inquiry* 47(2), 1977 : 89-97.

13600. SCIENCE. SOCIOLOGY OF KNOWLEDGE
SCIENCE. SOCIOLOGIE DE LA CONNAISSANCE

[See also / Voir aussi: 83, 262, 747, 1205, 1206, 2061, 2403, 2731]

1785   APEL, Karl Otto. "Types of social science in the light of human interests of knowledge", *Soc. Res.* 44(3), 1977 : 425-470.

1786   AXELROD, Charles D. "Freud and science", *Theory and Soc.* 4(2), 1977 : 273-293.

1787   Bibl.XXVI-1587. BLOOR, David. *Knowledge and social imagery.* CR: James G. CARRIER, *Brit. J. Sociol.* 18(3), sep 77 : 407.

1788   BLUM, Alan. "Criticalness and 'traditional prejudice': science as the perfect art for our times", *Canad. J. Sociol.* 2(1), 1977 : 97-124.

1789   BÖHME, Gernot; VAN DEN DAELE, Wolfgang; KROHN, Wolfgang. "Finalization in science", *Soc. Sci. Inform.* 15(2-3), 1976 : 307-330.

1790   BOUCHIER, David. "Radical ideologies and the sociology of knowledge a model for comparative analysis", *Sociology (London)* 11(1), jan 77 : 25-46.

1791   BROWN, Harold I. *Perception, theory, and commitment: the new phi-
        losophy of science.* Chicago, Precedent Publishers, 77, 203 p.
1792   BRUNNER, August. *Erkenntnis und Überlieferung* (Knowledge and tra-
        dition). München, J. Berchman, 76, 118 p.
1793   CORDÓN, Gaustino. *La función de la ciencia en la sociedad* (The role
        of science in society). Madrid, Editorial Cuadernos para el
        Dialogo, 76, 165 p.
1794   DEAN, Colin. "Are serendipitous discoveries a part of normal scien-
        ce ? The case of the pulsars", *Sociol. R.* 25(1), feb 77 : 73-86.
1795   "Discoveries and interpretations studies in contemporary scholar-
        ship", *Daedalus* 105(2), 1977 : 1-156; 106(3), 1977 : 1-172.
1796   DUHALIN, V. N. "Ob'ekty znanija v strukture sociologičeskoj terrii"
        (Knowledge objects in the structure of sociological theory), in:
        Metodologičeskie problemy razvitija nauki i kul'tury. Kujbišev,
        1976 : 42-57.
1797   EBERLEIN, Gerald. "Wissenschaftstheorie oder Wissenschaftsforschung ?
        Wider eine Dogmatisierung wissenschaftlichen Handelns" (Scientific
        theory or scientific research ? Against a dogmatizing of scienti-
        fic activity), *Soz. Welt* 27(4), 1976 : 488-503.
1798   Bibl.XXVI-1591. FEYERABEND, Paul. *Against method: outline of an
        anarchistic theory of knowledge.* CR: Ernest NAGEL, *Amer. polit.
        Sci. R.* 71(3), sep 77 : 1132-1132.
1799   FORD, Thomas R. "The production of social knowledge for public use",
        Soc. Forces 56(2), dec 77 : 504-518.
1800   GIZYCKI, Rainald VON. *Prozesse wissenschaftlicher Differenzierung.
        Eine organisations- und wissenssoziologische Fallstudie* (Processes
        of scientific differentiation. A case study in sociology of or-
        ganizations and sociology of knowledge). Berlin, Duncker und
        Humblot, 76, 151 p. CR: Heine von ALEMANN, *Kölner Z. Soziol. u.
        soz.-Psychol.* 29(4), dec 77 : 815-817.
1801   HILL, Lewis E.; ROUSE, Robert L. "The sociology of knowledge and
        the history of economic thought", *Amer. J. Econ. Sociol.* 36(3),
        jul 77 : 299-310.
1802   HOLZNER, Burkart; FISHER, Evelyn M.; MARX, John H. "Paul Lazarsfeld
        and the study of knowledge applications", *Sociol. Focus* 10(2),
        apr 77 : 97-116.
1803   HOUSE, J. Douglas. "In defence of Karl Mannheim: the sociology of
        knowledge, epistemology, and methodology", *Sociol. Anal. Theory*
        7(3), oct 77 : 207-225.
1804   JOHNSTON, Ron; ROBBINS, Dave. "The development of specialities in
        industrialised science", *Sociol. R.* 25(1), feb 77 · 87-108.
1805   KEMP, Ray. "Controversy in scientific research and tactics of com-
        munication", *Sociol. R.* 25(3), aug 77 : 515-534.
1806   KEVE, V. Ž. *Social'noe znanie i social'noe upravlenie* (Social know-
        ledge and social management). Moskva, Znanie, 76, 64 p.
1807   KONEV, V. A.; KONEVA, L. A. "Sistema i sistemnost' social'nogo zna-
        nija" (System and systems analysis of social knowledge), in:
        Metodologičeskie problemy razvitija nauki i kul'tury. Kujbišev,
        1976 : 102-108.
1808   KVAČAHIJA, V. M. "K voprosu o vzaimosvjazi sociologii soznanija i
        sosial'noj psihologii" (On the interaction between sociology of
        knowledge and social psychology), in: *Problemy social'noj psiho-
        logii.* Tbilisi, 1976 : 55-61.
1809   LADRIÈRE, Jean. *Les enjeux de la rationalité: le défi de la science
        et de la technologie aux cultures.* Paris, Aubier-Montaigne, Unes-
        co, 77, 219 p.
1810   LATOUR, Bruno; FABBRI, Paolo. "La rhétorique du discours scienti-
        fique", *Actes Rech. Sci. soc.* 13, feb 77 : 81-95.
1811   LEVI, Isaac. "Four types of ignorance", *Soc. Res.* 44(4), 1977 : 745-
        756.
1812   MENDELSOHN, Everett; WEINGART, Peter; WHITLEY, Richard (eds.). *The*

social production of scientific knowledge. Dordrecht, Holland; Boston, D. Reidel Publishing Co., 77, vi-294 p.

1813   MERELMAN, R. M. "On interventionist behavioralism: an essay in the sociology of knowledge", *Polit. and Soc.* 6(1), 1976 : 57-78.

1814   MITROFF, Ian I.; FITZGERALD, Iraz. "On the psychology of the Apollo Moon scientists: a chapter in the psychology of science", *Hum. Relat.* 30(8), aug 77 : 657-674.

1815   MITROFF, Ian I.; KILMANN, Ralph H. "Systemic knowledge: toward an integrated theory of science", *Theory and Soc.* 4(1), 1977 : 103-129.

1816   MOREAU DE BELLAING, Louis. "Catégories politiques et sociologie de la connaissance", *C. int. Sociol.* 24(63), jul-dec 77 : 277-288.

1817   MORRIS, Monica B. *An excursion into creative sociology*. New York, Columbia University Press, 77, x-212 p.

1818   MOTWANI, Kewal (ed.). *Sociology of knowledge*. Bombay, Somaiya Publications, 76, xxiv-407 p.

1819   MULKAY, Michael J. "Norms and ideology in science", *Soc. Sci. Inform.* 15(4-5), 1976 : 637-656.

1820   NAMER, Gérard. "La sociologie de la connaissance et les mass-media", *Communications (Köln)* 2(1), 1976 : 112-126.

1821   OESER, Erhard. *Wissenschaftstheorie und empirische Wissenschaftsforschung* (Science theory and empirical science research). Wien-München, Oldenburg, 76, 158 p.

1822   O'GORMAN, Hubert; GARRY, Stephen L. "Pluralistic ignorance - a replication and extension", *Publ. Opin. Quart.* 40(4), 1976 : 427-448.

1823   ONO, Hiroshi. "K. Mannheim ni okeru chishiki-shakaigaku to kyoiku-shakaigaku - Kyoikuteki chishiki no shakaigaku" (Sociology of knowledge and education in K. Mannheim's sociological thought: toward a sociology of educational knowledge), *Yamanashi-daigaku Kyôikugakubu Kenkyû Hokoku* 27, 1977 : 89-97.

1824   PAPP, Zs. "Látszat és légitimació: ideologia-értelmezések a tudásszociologiában és a kritikai elméletben" (Appearance and legitimation: interpretations of ideology in the sociology of knowledge and critical theory), *Világosság* (10), 1977 : 592-599; (11) 1977 : 699-704.

1825   RESKIN, Barbara F. "Scientific productivity and the reward structure of science", *Amer. sociol. R.* 42(3), jun 77 : 491-504.

1826   SCHÄUBLE, Ingegerd. *Zur Rolle der Wissenschaftspolitik in der Gesellschaft* (The role of science policy in society). Erlangen, Institut für Gesellschaft und Wissenschaft, 76, 43 p.

1827   SHMUELI, Efraim. "Objectivity and presuppositions. A re-evaluation of Karl Mannheim's sociology of knowledge", *Sociol. soc. Res.* 62(1), oct 77 : 99-112.

1828   ŠLTAHTIČ, G. P. "Logiko-gnoseologičeskij analiz special'nyh teorij kak sistem sociologičeskogo znanija" (A logico-gnoseological analysis of the special theories as a system of sociological knowledge), *Probl. Filos.* 40, 1977 : 45-52.

1829   ŠUŠNJIĆ, Duro. "Integrativna funkcija ideja" (The integrative function of ideas), *Sociologija* 19(4), 1977 : 621-639.

1830   ULTEE, Wouter Cornelis. *Groei van kennis en stagnatie in de sociologie* (Growth of knowledge and stagnation in sociology). Utrecht, Rijksuniversiteit Utrecht, 77, 468 p.

1831   VAN DOORN, J. A. A. "Conservatieve gedachten over wetenschap en maatschappij" (Conservative reflections on science and society), *Mens en Mij* 52(1), 1977 : 2-17.

1832   VAN ERP, H. "Maatschappelijke relevantie van de wetenschap. Een betekenisanalyse" (Social relevance of science. A concept analysis), *Soc. Wetensch.* 19(4), 1976 : 279-296.

1833   VITÁNYI, Iván. "Az ismeretek igazságértékének rendszere" (Genuine values' system of knowledge), *Kult. és Köz.* (3), 1976 : 5-17.

1834   WALD, Henri. *Orientări contemporane în teoria cunoașterii* (Contemporary trends in theory of knowledge). București, Editura Academiei Republicii Socialiste România, 76, 206 p.

1835   WEINGART, Peter. *Wissenschaftsplanung und Wissenschaftsbegriff* (Science planning and science concept). Erlangen, Institut für Gesellschaft und Wissenschaft an der Universität Erlangen-Nürnberg, 76, 40 p.

1836   WILSON, H. T. "Attitudes toward science: Canadian and American scientists", *Int. J. comp. Sociol.* 18(1-2), mar-jun 77 : 154-175.

1837   YASUDA, Takashi. "Chishiki shakaigaku to Busshoka-ron" (The sociology of knowledge and the theory of "Versachlichung"), *Shakaigaku Kenkyû* 35, 1977 : 76-96.

13700. COMMUNICATION. LANGUAGE
COMMUNICATION. LANGAGE

13710. Linguistics. Semiotics
Linguistique. Sémiotique

[See also / Voir aussi: 341, 466, 1859, 2014, 2055, 3378, 4854]

1838   AITCHISON, Jean. *The articulate mammal: an introduction to psycholinguistics.* New York, Universe Books, London, Hutchinson, 76, 3-256 p.1839

1839   ANDRÁSSY, Mária. *A társadalmi kommunikáció és a kultura elméletének ujabb szemiotikai problémái* (The new semiotic problems of social communication and culture theory). Budapest, Népmüvelési Intézet, 76, 62 1.

1840   APPEL, René; HUBERS, Gerard; MEIJER, Guns. *Sociolinguistiek* (Sociolinguistics). Utrecht, Het Spectrum, 76, 256 p.

1841   BELL, Roger T. *Sociolinguistics: goals, approaches, and problems.* London, B. T. Batsford, 76, 251 p.

1842   BOUAZIS, Charles. *Essais de la sémiotique du sujet.* Bruxelles, Éditions complexe; Paris, Presses universitaires de France, 77, 95 p.

1843   BOYSSON-BARDIES, Bénédicte DE. *Négation et performance linguistique.* Paris-La Haye, Mouton, 76, 134 p.

1844   BUREAU Conrad. *Linguistique fonctionnelle et stylistique objective.* Paris, Presses universitaires de France, 76, 264 p.

1845   CALAME-GRIAULE, Geneviève (éd.). *Langage et cultures africaines: essais d'ethnolinguistique.* Paris, F. Maspéro, 77, 364 p.

1846   CAPRETTINI, Gian Paolo. *La semiologia: elementi per un'introduzione* (Semiology: elements for an introduction). Torino, G. Giappichelli, 76, vi-147 p.

1847   CARDONA, Giorgio Raimondo. *Introduzione all'etnolinguistica* (Introduction to ethnolinguistics). Bologna, Il Mulino, 76, 327 p.

1848   CORNEILLE, Jean Pierre. *La linguistique structurale: sa portée, ses limites.* Paris, Larousse, 76, 255-1 p.

1849   COULARDEAU, Jacques. *Pour une linguistique formelle: notes de recherche.* Paris, Centre d'études et de recherches marxistes, 76, 53 p.

1850   COURTES, Joseph. *Introduction à la sémiotique narrative et discursive: méthodologie et application.* Paris, Hachette, 76, 143 p.

1851   CRICK, Malcolm. *Explorations in language and meaning: towards a semantic anthropology.* New York, Wiley, 76, vii-212 p.

1852   DASSETTO, F.; HIERNAUX, J. P.; SERVAIS, E. "Recherche sociologique et instrumentation 'linguistique'", *Rech. sociol.* 8(2), 1977 : 165-188.

1853   DILLON, George L. *Introduction to contemporary linguistic semantics.* Englewood Cliffs, N.J., Prentice-Hall, 77, xvii-150 p.

1854   FODOR, Janet Dean. *Semantics: theories of meaning in generative grammar.* Hassocks, Eng., Harvester Press; New York, Crowell, 77, xi-225 p.

1855   HYMES, Dell. "Towards linguistic competence", *Sociol. Gids* 23(4),
        jul-aug 76 : 217-239.
1856   MORTON, John *et al.* (eds.). *Psycholinguistics: developmental and
        pathological.* Ithaca, N.Y., Cornell University Press, 77, vii-
        160 p.
1857   PEARSON, Bruce L.; FISCHER, John L. *Introduction to linguistic
        concepts.* New York, Knopf, 77, vi-376 p.
1858   PÉCSVÁRADY, J. *et al.* "Nyelvtanulmány-vita" (Debate on linguistics),
        Állam és Jogtud. 19(1), 1976 : 133-144.
1859   PIERCE, Joe E. *Languages and linguistics: an introduction.* The Ha-
        gue, Mouton, 76, 188 p.
1860   PILCH, Herbert. *Empirical linguistics.* München, Francke, 76, 246 p.
1861   RENZETTI, Emanuela. "Considerazioni metodologiche sulla teoria
        glossematica di L. Hjelmslev" (Methodological considerations on
        L. Hjelmslev's glossematic theory), *Sociologia (Roma)* 11(1),
        jan-mar 77 : 81-94.
1862   SCHAFF, Adam. (ed.). *Soziolinguistik* (Sociolinguistics). Wien,
        Europaverlag, 76, 250 p.
1863   SHUY, Roger W. (ed.). *Linguistic theory: what can it way about
        reading ?* Newark, Del., International Reading Association, 77,
        x-185 p.
1864   STEWART, Ann Harleman. *Graphic representation of models in linguis-
        tic theory.* Bloomington, Indiana University Press, 76, vii-195 p.
1865   VOIGT, Vilmos. *Bevezetés a szemiotikába* (Introduction to semiotics).
        Budapest, Gondolat, 77, 216-1 p.
1866   WÖLCK, Wolfgang. "Sociolinguistics. Revolution or interdiscipline ?"
        Amer. behav. Scientist 20(5), mar-jun 77 : 733-756.

13720. Communication. Sign
Communication. Signe

[See also / Voir aussi: 773, 775, 780, 781, 787, 788, 886, 1020,
1031, 1055, 1066, 1067, 1172, 1280, 5379]

1867   ALLEAU, René. *La science des symboles: contribution à l'étude des
        principes et des méthodes de la symbolique générale.* Paris, Payot,
        76, 292 p.
1868   BENSON, Thomas W.; FRANDSEN, Kenneth D. *An orientation to nonverbal
        communication.* Palo Alto, Calif., Science Research Associates,
        76, 38 p.
1869   BOFILL, Juan A. *et al. Epistemología de la comunicación* (Epistemo-
        logy of communication). Valencia, F. Torres, 76, 238 p.
1870   BRETSCHER, Georges. "Die Analyse von kommunikativen Erwartungen"
        (Analysis of communicative expectations), *Communications (Köln)*
        2(1), 1976 : 9-24.
1871   BROWN, Richard H. "Métaphore et méthode: de la logique et de la
        découverte en sociologie", *C. int. Sociol.* 24(62), jan-jun 77 :
        61-73.
1872   COMBS, James F.; MANSFIELD, Michael W. (ed.). *Drama in life: the
        uses of communication in society.* New York, HastingsHHouse, 76,
        xxx-444 p.
1873   CYMBAL, V. P. *Teorija informacii i kodirovanie* (Theory of informa-
        tion and code elaboration). Kiev, Višča Škola, 77, 288 p.
1874   DRUŽEROVIĆ, Borisov. "Komuniciravje kao sociološki fenomen" (Commu-
        nication as a sociological phenomenon), *Gledišta* 18(3), mar 77 :
        166-176.
1875   ESCARPIT, Robert. *Théorie générale de l'information et de la com-
        munication.* Paris, Hachette, 76, 218 p.
1876   GAUTHIER, Alain; JEUDY, Henri Pierre. "L'échange à blanc: un essai
        sur les sigles", *C. int. Sociol.* 23(61), jul-dec 76 : 297-308.
1877   GRANBERG, Donald; CAMPBELL, Keith E. "Effect of communication dis-
        crepancy and ambiguity on placement and opinion shift", *Europ.
        J. soc. Psychol.* 7(2), 1977 : 137-150.

1878   HENLEY, Nancy M. *Body politics: power, sex, and nonverbal communication.* Englewood Cliffs, N.J., Prentice-Hall, 77, ix-214 p.

1879   HILBERT, Richard A. "Approaching reason's edge: 'nonsense' as the final solution to the problem of meaning", *Sociol. Inquiry* 47(1), 1977 : 25-31.

1880   HSIA, H. J. "On supranational communication research: a plea for a worldwide communications centre", *Communications (Köln)* 2(3), 1976 : 275-291.

1881   HUND, Wulf D. *Nachricht und Informationsfetisch. Zur Theorie der gesellschaftlichen Kommunikation* (News and information fetish. Theory of the social communication). Darmstadt-Neuwied, Luchterhand, 76, 336 p. CR: Alphons SILBERMANN, *Kölner Z. Soziol. u. soz.-Psychol.* 29(3), sep 76 : 599-600.

1882   KAISER, Heinz Jürgen; WERBIK, Hans. "Der 'Telefonzellenversuch' - ein erstes Experiment zur Überprüfung einer Theorie sozialen Handels" (The "telephone cabin test": a first experimental verification of the theory of social exchange), *Z. soz.-Psychol.* 8(2), 1977 : 115-129.

1883   LA IGLESIA GOMEZ, Angel DE. "La comunicación social" (Social communication), *R. esp. Opin. públ.* 49, 1977 : 107-124.

1884   LA RUSSO, Dominic A. *The shadows of communication: nonverbal dimensions.* Dubuque, Iowa, Kendall-Hunt Publishing Co., 77, x-252 p.

1885   LOHISSE, Jean. "Communication et développement", *Communications (Köln)* 3(1), 1977 : 47-54.

1886   MEDINA, Carlos Alberto DE; MELO, José Marques DE. *Comunicação/incomunicação no Brasil* (Communication/non-communication in Brazil). São Paulo, Edições Loyola, 76, 207 p.

1887   MILLER, George R.; NICHOLSON, Henry E. *Communication inquiry. A perspective on a process.* Reading, Mass., Addison-Wesley, 76, xii-260 p.

1888   MILLER, Robert E.; GIANNINI, A. James; LEVINE, John M. "Nonverbal communication in man with a cooperative conditioning task", *J. soc. Psychol.* 103(1), oct 77 : 101-113.

1889   MOLES, Abraham A. "Image et communication visuelle: vers une méthodologie", *Communications (Köln)* 2(3), 1976 : 330-348.

1890   NOELLE-NEUMANN, Elisabeth. *Öffentlichkeit als Bedrohung, Beiträge zur empirischen Kommunikationsforschung* (The public as a threat: contributions to the empirical communication research). Ed. by Jüngen WILKE. Freiburg-im-Breisgau, K. Alber, 77, 260 p.

1891   PIOTROWSKI, Andrzej. "Sign functions of utilitarian objects", *Polish social R.* 37(1), 1977 : 19-30.

1892   POYATOS, Fernando. *Man beyond words: theory and methodology of nonverbal communication.* Oswego, New York State English Council, 76, xii-207 p.

1893   RAMIREZ, Albert. "Social influence and ethnicity of the communicator", *J. soc. Psychol.* 102(2), aug 77 : 209-213.

1894   ROSENFIELD, Lawrence William; HAYES, Laurie Schultz; FRENTZ, Thomas S. *The communicative experience.* Boston, Allyn and Bacon, 76, vii-452 p.

1895   SARAF, M. J. "Semiotic signs in sports activity", *Int. R. Sport Sociol.* 12(2), 1977 : 89-101.

1896   SAUGSTAD, Per. *A theory of communication and use of language: foundations for the study of psychology.* Oslo, Universitetsforlaget, 77, 263 p.

1897   SERRAN PAGAN, Ginès. "Notas de antropología simbólica en Africa. Poder y estructura de los símbolos" (Notes of symbolic anthropolocy in Africa. Power and structure of symbols), *R. int. Sociol. (Madrid)* 34(18-19-20), apr-dec 76 : 109-121.

1898   SILBERMANN, Alphons. "L'avenir des systèmes de communication et du comportement social", *R. int. Sci. soc.* 29(2), 1977 : 363-367.

1899   SPEIER, Hans. "The communication of hidden meaning", *Soc. Res.* 44(3), 1977 : 471-501.

1900   STEINBUCH, Karl. *Kommunikationstechnik* (Communication technique).
Heidelberg-New York-Berlin,   , 77, 273 p. CR: Alphons
SILBERMANN, *Kölner Z. Soziol. u. soz.-Psychol.* 29(4), dec 77 :
812-813.

1901   VALBUENA, Felicísimo. *Receptores y audiencias en el proceso de la
comunicación* (Receivers and audience in the communication process). Madrid, P. del Río, 76, 198 p.

1902   WATZLAWICK, Paul. *How real is real ? Confusion, disinformation,
communication.* New York, Vintage Books, 77, xiv-266 p.

1903   YATANI, Yoshikuni. "Alfred Schutz no tagen-tekina imi-sekairon to
shôcho no mondai ni tsuite" (On Alfred Schutz' theory of reality
and symbol), *Soshioroji* 22(2), 1977 : 33-54.

13730. Language
Langage

[See also / Voir aussi: 701, 933, 1896, 2241, 2666]

1904   ALLEN, Donald E.; GUY, Rebecca F. "Ocular breaks and verbal output",
Sociometry 40(1), 1977 : 90-96.

1905   BARNETT, George A. "Bilingual semantic organization: a multidimensional analysis", *J. cross-cult. Psychol.* 8(3), sep 77 : 315-330.

1906   BENKÖ, Loránd. "Anyanyelv és társadalom" (Mother tongue and society)
Magyar Nyelv (4), 1976 : 385-394.

1907   BOCK, Michael. "Sprachpsychologische Aspekte der Mediengestaltung.
I. Organisation und Gedächtnis. II. Verstehen und Behalten" (Aspects relating to the psychology of language in the organization
of media. I. Organization and memory. II. Understanding and re-
taining), *Communication (Köln)* 2(1), 1976 : 62-77; 3(1), 1977 :
95-112.

1908   BOLLACK, Jean. "Réflexions sur la politique philologique", *Soc.
Sci. Inform.* 16(3-4), 1977 : 375-384.

1909   BRIGHT, William. *Variation and change in language: essays.* Stanford, Calif., Stanford University Press, 76, xiv-283 p.

1910   CARLSON, Karen; MEYERS, Alan. *Speaking with confidence: a small-
group approach to speech communication.* Glenview, Ill., Scott,
Foresman, 77, xi-308 p.

1911   CASTONGUAY, Charles. "Les transferts linguistiques au foyer", *Rech.
sociogr.* 17(3), sep-dec 76 : 341-351.

1912   DUBARLE, Dominique. *Logos et formalisation du langage.* Paris,
Klincksieck, 77, 301 p.

1913   EDWARDS, Anthony Davies. *Language in culture and class: the sociology of language and education.* London, Heinemann Educational,
76, viii-206 p.

1914   ENGLEFIELD, F. R. H. *Language: its origin and its relation to
thought.* Ed. by G. A. WELLS; D. R. OPPENHEIMER. London, Elek
for Pemberton Publishing, 77, xvi-192 p.

1915   FISHMAN, Joshua A.; LEWIS, E. Glyn. *Bilingual education: an international sociological perspective.* Rowley, Mass., Newbury House,
76, xiii-208 p.

1916   GRABER, Doris A. *Verbal behaviour and politics.* Urbana, University
of Illinois Press, 76, 377 p. CR: M. Glenn NEWKIRK, *Contemp. Sociol. (Washington)* 6(3), mai 77 : 332-333.

1917   GREGERSEN, Edgar A. *Language in Africa; an introductory survey.*
New York, Gordon and Breach, 77, xvii-237 p.

1918   HEAP, J. L. "Verstehen, language and warrants", *Sociol. Quart.*
18(2), 1977 : 177-184.

1919   JACOB, André. *Introduction à la philosophie du langage.* Paris,
Gallimard, 76, 447 p.

1920   JEFFERSON, Gail; SCHENKEIN, Jim. "Some sequential negotiations in
conversation: unexpanded and expanded versions of projected action sequences", *Sociology (London)* 11(1), jan 77 : 87-103.

1921   KATZER, Jeffrey. *Free association behaviour and human language processing: a theoretical model*. The Hague, Mouton, 76, 120 p.

1922   LABOV, William. "La langue des paumés", *Actes Rech. Sci. soc.* 17-18, nov 77 : 113-125.

1923   "Langue et identité nationale: le maintien des communautés linguistiques", *Rech. sociol.* 7(1), 1977 : 3-133.

1924   LANIGEN, Richard L. *Speech act phenomenology*. The Hague, Nijhoff, 77, viii-137 p.

1925   MACKEY, William Francis. *Bilinguisme et contact des langues*. Paris, Klincksieck, 76, 534 p.

1926   MALMBERG, Bertil. *Signes et symboles: les bases du langage humain*. Paris, A. et J. Picard, 77, 454 p.

1927   MILLER, George Armiatage; JOHNSON-LAIRD, Philip N. *Language and perception*. Cambridge, Mass., Belknap Press, 76, viii-760 p.

1928   MOERK, Ernst L. *Pragmatic and semantic aspects of early language development*. Baltimore, University Park Press, 77, x-330 p.

1929   O'BARR, William O.; O'BARR, Jean F. (eds.). *Language and politics*. The Hague, Mouton, 76, xvi-506 p.

1930   O'NEILL, John. "Language and the legitimation problem", *Sociology (London)* 11(2), mai 77 : 351-358.

1931   ROSENTSVEIG, Viktor Julevich. *Linguistic interference and convergent change*. The Hague, Mouton, 76, 58 p.

1932   RUTTER, D. R.; STEPHENSON, G. M. "The role of visual communication in synchronising conversation", *Europ. J. soc. Psychol.* 7(1), 1977 : 29-37.

1933   SKIK, H. "Aspects du bilinguisme à l'école primaire tunisienne", *R. tunis. Sci. soc.* 13(44), 1976 : 73-116.

1934   SKIK, H. "Le passage d'une langue à l'autre chez les tunisiens bilingues. Étude socio-linguistique", *R. tunis. Sci. soc.* 13(45), 1976 : 140-165.

1935   SODEUR, Wolfgang. "Sprachkonsistenz von Jugendlichen als Folge ähnlicher Sozialisationsprozess" (Speech consistency among young people as a consequence of similar socialization processes), *Kölner Z. Soziol. u. soz.-Psychol.* 29(1), mar 77 : 71-94.

1936   VELTMAN, Calvin J. "Les incidences du revenu sur les transferts linguistiques dans la région métropolitaine de Montréal", *Rech. sociogr.* 17(3), sep-dec 76 : 323-339. [Canada.]

1937   VRIES, John DE. "Explorations in the demography of language: estimation of net language shift in Finland", *Acta sociol.* 20(2), 1977 : 145-153.

1938   ZIMMERMAN, Cordon I.; OWEN, James L.; SEIBERT, David R. *Speech communication: a contemporary introduction*. St. Paul, West Publishing Co., 77, xvi-384 p.

13740. Audience

[See also / Voir aussi: 2027, 2051, 2060]

1939   OYABU, Juichi. *Shichôsha sanka bangumi no genjô to shôraizô ni kansuru shakai-shinrigakuteki kenkyû* (A social psychological study on present situations and future images of audience-participant-TV-programs). Osaka, Osaka-shiritsu-daigaku Communication Kenkyûkai, 77, 220 p.

1940   STEBBINS, Robert A. "The amateur: two sociological definitions", *Pacific sociol. R.* 20(4), oct 77 : 582-606.

1941   TAKEUCHI, Ikuo *et al.* "Terebi shichosha-sanka bangumi ni okeru 'Riyo to Manzoku' no jittai" ("Uses and gratifications" in audience participation programs), *Tokyo-daigaku Shinbun Kenkyujo Kiyo* 25, 1977 : 92-201.

13750. Advertising. Propaganda
Publicité. Propagande

[See also / Voir aussi: 2030]

1942   ALBOU, Paul. *Psychologie de la vente et de la publicité*. Paris, Presses universitaires de France, 77, 254 p.

1943   CATHELAT, Bernard; CADET, André. *Publicité et société: de l'instrument économique à l'instrument social* . Paris, Payot, 76, 251 p.

1944   FODOR, G. *Nyilvánosság, közvélemény, tömegkommunikáció* (Publicity, public opinion, mass communication). Budapest, MSZMP KB Társadalomtudományos Intézet, 76, 122 p.

1945   FONTANEL, Jacques. *L'anti-publicité*. Grenoble, Université des sciences sociales, 77, 127 p.

1946   JEUDY, Henri-Pierre. *La publicité et son enjeu social*. Paris, Presses universitaires de France, 77, 206 p.

1947   KLECKIN, A. Ja. "Propaganda v sisteme social'nogo upravlenija" (Propaganda in the social management system), in: *Problemy istorii, teorii i praktiki žurnalistiki*. Voronež, 1977 : 26-42.

1948   LAGNEAU, Gérard. *La sociologie de la publicité*. Paris, Presses universitaires de France, 77, 128 p. CR: David VICTOROFF, *R. franç. Sociol*. 18(3), jul-sep 77 : 519-520.

1949   MADRIÈRES, Frédérique; GAUMONT, Daniel. "Styles de vie et publicité", *R. franç. Mkting* 66, jan-feb 77 : 9-19.

1950   NKPA, Nwokocha K. U. "Rumors of mass poisoning in Biafra", *Publ. Opin. Quart*. 41(3), 1977 : 332-346.

1951   PORCHER, Louis. *Introduction à une sémiotique des images: sur quelques exemples d'images publicitaires*. Paris, Didier, 76, 259 p.- 4 l.

1952   RONIS, David L. *et al*. "In search of reliable persuasion effects. I. A computer-controlled procedure for studying persuasion", *J. Person. soc. Psychol*. 35(8), aug 77 : 548-569.

1953   ROSNOW, Ralph L.; FINE, Gary A. *Rumor and gossip: the social psychology of hearsay*. New York, Elsevier, 76, viii-166 p.

1954   TAMURA, Norio. *Komyuniti kyanpên* (Community communication campaign). Tokyo, Saimura shuppankai, 77, 232 p.

1955   ULANOFF, Stanley M. *Advertising in America: an introduction to persuasive communication*. New York, Hastings House, 77, xvi-492 p.

1956   ZUKIN, Cliff. "A reconsideration of the effects of information on partisan stability", *Publ. Opin. Quart*. 41(2), 1977 : 244-254.

13760. Mass communication
Communication de masse

[See also / Voir aussi: 735, 1183, 1321, 1444, 1820, 1907, 1944, 2276, 4890]

1957   BALDWIN, Elizabeth. "The mass media and the corporate elite: a reanalysis of the overlap between the media and economic elites", *Canad. J. Sociol*. 2(1), 1977 : 1-27.

1958   BISKY, Lothar *et al*. *Massenmedien und ideologische Erziehung der Jugend* (Mass media and ideological education of the youth). Berlin VEB, Deutscher Verlag der Wissenschaften, 76, 177 p. CR: Alphons SILBERMANN, *Kölner Z. Soziol. u. soz.-Psychol*. 29(4), dec 76 : 811-812.

1959   BISKY, Lothar. *Zur Kritik der bürgerlichen Massenkommunikationsforschung* (Criticism of the bourgeois mass communication research) Berlin, VEB, Deutscher Verlag der Wissenschaften, 76, 190 p. CR: Alphons SILBERMANN, *Kölner Z. Soziol. u. soz.-Psychol*. 29(4), dec 76 : 811-812.

1960   BITTNER, John R. *Mass communication, an introduction: theory and practice of mass media in society*. Englewood Cliffs, N.J., Prentice-Hall, 77, xvi-512 p.

1961   BÖCKELMANN, Frank. *Theorie der Massenkommunikation* (Mass communication theory). Frankfurt-am-Main, Suhrkamp, 75, 311 p.

1962   BOEFF, C. "De ontwikkeling van het effectonderzoek in de massa-communicatie" (The development of research on the effects of mass communication), *Sociol. Gids* 24(4), jul-aug 77 : 258-269.

1963   BUDANCEV, Ju. P. "O vzaimodejstvii sistem sredstv massovoj kommunikacii" (On interaction of mass communication media system), in: *Teorija i praktika sovremennoj meždunarodnoj žurnalistiki.* Moskva, 1976 : 3-34.

1964   CAZENEUVE, Jean (éd.). *Les communications de masse: guide alphabétique.* Paris, Denoël-Gonthier, 76, 498 p.

1965   CHRISTIANS, Clifford G. "Jacques Ellul's concern with the amorality of contemporary communications", *Communications (Köln)* 3(1), 1977 : 62-80.

1966   CLEMENT, Wallace. "Overlap of the media and economic elites", *Canad. J. Sociol.* 2(2), 1977 : 205-214. With a discussion by Elizabeth G. BLADWIN: 215-222.

1967   DAVISON, Walter Phillips; BOYLAN, James R.; YU, Frederic T. C. *Mass media: systems and effects.* New York, Praeger, 76, ix-246 p. CR: Moti K. GOKULSING, *Brit. J. Sociol.* 18(3), sep 77 : 413.

1968   FELSENTHAL, Norman. *Orientations to mass communication.* Palo Alto, Calif., Science Research Associates, 76, 54 p.

1969   HANÁK, K. "A tömegkommunikáció életmódalakitó szerepe" (The role of mass communication in moulding the way of living), *Rádió és TV Szle* 9(4), 1977 : 84-93.

1970   KOSCHWITZ, Hansjürgen. "Zwischen Tradition und Reform. Aktuelle Entwicklungstendenzen der Kommunikationspolitik in den Staaten des Sozialismus" (Between tradition and reform. Present development trends of communication in the socialist States), *Communications (Köln)* 2(1), 1976 : 78-100.

1971   MAJOR, Gersh (ed.). *Mass media in Australia.* Sydney, Hodder and Stoughton, 76, 264 p.

1972   McHUGH, Joseph M. *Mass media and public morality: a problem-law-percept analysis with recommendations for self-regulation in the mass media.* New York, Vantage Press, 76, 168 p.

1973   McPHAIL, Thomas L. "An interactive model of mass communication systems", *Communications (Köln)* 2(1), 1976 : 55-61.

1974   MURPHY, Robert D. *Mass communication and human interaction.* Boston, Houghton Mifflin, 77, xvii-430 p.

1975   "Objektivitet i massmedier" (Objectivity in mass media), *Statsvet. Ts.* (3), 1977 : 169-217. [Sweden.]

1976   OHLGREN, Thomas H.; BERK, Lynn M. (eds.). *The new languages: a rhetorical approach to the mass media and popular culture.* Englewood Cliffs, N.J., Prentice-Hall, 77, xvii-395 p.

1977   PIETILÄ, Veikko. "People's conceptions of the mass media", *Communications (Köln)* 2(2), 1976 : 151-166.

1978   REAL, Michael R. *Mass-mediated culture.* Englewood Cliffs, N.J., Prentice-Hall, 77, xii-289 p.

1979   RESCIGNO DI NALLO, Egeria. *Per una teoria della comunicazione di massa* (For a theory of mass communication). Milano, F. Angeli, 77, 296 p.

1980   ROMAŠKINA, P. M. "Sredstva massovoj informacii i formirovanie ličnosti" (Mass communication media and formation of personality), in: *Problemy istorii, teorii i praktiki žurnalistiki.* Voronže, 1977 : 99-108.

1981   ROSENGREN, Karl Erik; WINDAHL, Swen. "Mass media use: causes and effects", *Communications (Köln)* 3(3), 1977 : 336-352.

1982   SCHILLER, Herbert I. *Communication and cultural domination.* White Plains, N.Y., International Arts and Sciences Press, 76, 127 p.

1983   SCHULTZ, Winfried. *Die Konstruktion von Realität in der Nachrichtenmedien. Analyse der aktuellen Berichterstattung* (The construction of reality in the information media. Analysis of the report-

ing today). Freiburg-München, Karl Alber Verlag, 76, 140 p.
CR: Hansjürgen KOSCHWITZ, *Kölner Z. Soziol. u. soz.-Psychol.*
29(3), sep 77 : 598-599.

1984 ŠERKOVIN, Ju. A. "O nekotoryh vozmožnostjah sistemnogo podhoda k social'no-psihologičeskomu issledovaniju massovoj kommunikacii" (On some possibilities of the systemic approach towards socio-psychological research on mass communication), in: *Problemy social'noj psihologii.* Tbilisi, 1976 : 125-134.

1985 SUŁKOWSKI, Boguslaw. "Humor przekasów masowych a integracja społeczna" (Humour in the mass media and social integration), *Stud. socjol.* 60(1), 1976 : 101-114.

1986 TIMORSIN, M. Ž. "Sredstva massovoj kommunikacii kak social'noj institut" (Mass communication media as a social institution), *Žurnalistika* (6), 1976 : 163-173.

1987 TUNSTALL, Jeremy. *The media are American, Anglo-American media in the world.* London, Constable, 77, 352 p.

1988 WATANABE, Yoshimoto. "Soviet ni okeru mass-communication shakaigaku" (Some sociological studies of mass communications in the Soviet Union), *Tokyo-daigaku Shinbun-kenkyujo Kiyô* 25, 1977 : 69-91.

13761.

[See also / Voir aussi: 421, 480, 736, 3523, 3651]

1989 ALBERT, Pierre; FEYEL, Gilles; PICARD, Jean-François. *Documents pour l'histoire de la presse nationale aux XIXe et XXe siècles.* Paris, Éditions du CNRS, 77, 339 p. [France.]

1990 ALTHEIDE, David L.; RASMUSSEN, Paul K. "Becoming news: a study of two newsrooms", *Sociol. Wk Occupat.* 3(2), mai 76 : 223-246.

1991 ARCHAMBAULT, François; LEMOINE, Jean-François. *Quatre milliards de journaux: la presse de province.* Paris, A. Moreau, 77, 482 p. [France.]

1992 BALLE, Francis. "L'avenir des grands quotidiens", *Communications (Köln)* 3(1), 1977 : 55-61.

1993 BOLLINGER, Ernst. *La presse suisse: structure et diversité.* Berne, H. Lang; Francfort-sur-le Main, P. Lang, 76, 327 p.

1994 BROWN, Ronald G.; LEE, Jung-Bock. "The Japanese press and the 'people's right to know'", *J-ism Quart.* 54(3), 1977 : 477-481.

1995 IGOSIN, S. I. "Social'nye vzaimosvjazi gazet" (Newspapers social interaction), *Žurnal. Pressa Audit.* (1), 1975 : 15-23.

1996 JOHNSTONE, John Wallace Claire; SLAWSKI, Edward J.; BOWMAN, William W. *The news people: a sociological portrait of American journalist and their work.* Urbana, University of Illinois Press, 76, ix-257 p.

1997 LENT, J. "Foreign news content of United States and Asian print media: literature review and problem analysis", *Gazette (Amsterdam)* 22(3), 1976 : 169-182.

1998 MASSICOTTE, Guy. "Les éditorialistes canadiens-français et les origines de la seconde guerre mondiale", *Rech. sociogr.* 17(2), mai-aug 76 : 139-165.

1999 McQUAIL, Denis. *Review of sociological writing on the press.* London, HMSO, 76, 86 p.

2000 Bibl.XXVI-1701. ROSHCO, Bernard. *Newsmaking.* CR: Donald M. GILLMOR, *Amer. J. Sociol.* 82(6), mai 77 : 1398-1400.

2001 ROUCEK, Joseph S. "The Soviet press", *Communications (Köln)* 3(2), 1977 : 150-180.

2002 SCHLESINGER, Philip. "Newsmen and their time-machine", *Brit. J. Sociol.* 28(3), sep 77 : 336-350.

2003 SCHWOEBEL, Jean. *Newsroom democracy: the case for independence of the press.* Iowa City, Iowa Center for Communication Study, School of Journalism, University of Iowa, 76, 67 p.

2004 STREUFERT, Siegfried; SUEDFELD, Peter. "Editorial-simulation as a research method: a problem in communication", *J. appl. soc. Psychol.* 7(4), oct-dec 77 : 281-285.

2005   SVITIČ, L. G. "Žurnalist kak ob'ekt sociologičeskogo issledovanija" (The journalist as an object of sociological research), in: *Filologičeskie ètjudy žurnalistika.* Rostov n/D., 1975 : 39-45.

2006   TAMURA, Norio (ed.). *Jânarizumu no shakaigaku* (Sociology of journalism). Tokyo, Burên shuppan, 77, 200 p.

2007   TOPP, H. D. "Die Presse der Volksrepublik Albanien" (The press in the People's Republic of Albania), *Publizistik* 21(4), oct-dec 76 : 445-459.

2008   WAXMAN, Jerry J. "News flow decision-making during consensual community crises", *Communications (Köln)* 2(3), 1976 : 367-376.

13762.

2009   AGEL, Henri. *Métaphysique du cinéma.* Paris, Payot, 76, 207 p.
2010   DÉSI, Ábel. "A film és a mindennapi élet" (The film and the everyday life), *Üzenet* (9), 1976 : 490-496.
2011   FERRO, Marc. *Cinéma et histoire.* Paris, Denoël-Gonthier, 77, 168 p.
2012   FORD, Charles. *Histoire du cinéma français contemporain: 1945-1977.* Paris, Franco-Empire, 77, 349 p.
2013   KRIZSÁN, Zoltán. "Film: kultúra, nyelv, esztétika" (Film: culture, language, aesthetics), *Korunk* (10), 1976 : 749-752.
2014   METZ, Christian. "L'étude sémiologique du langage cinématographique: à quelle distance sommes-nous d'une possibilité réelle de formalisation ?", *Communications (Köln)* 2(2), 1976 : 187-200.
2015   MURA'EV, A. L. "Nekobarye voprosy ideologičeskoj bor'by v sovremennom kinoiskuntve" (Questions concerning the ideological struggle in contemporary cinema), *Vestn. Leningr. Univ. Ser. Ist. Jaz. Lit.* 31(1), jan-mar 77 : 46-53.

13763.

[See also / Voir aussi: 852, 2432, 4446, 5005]

2016   ANDISON, F. Scott, "TV violence and viewer aggression: a cumulation of study results, 1956-1976", *Publ. Opin. Quart.* 41(3), 1977 : 314-331.
2017   ADLER, Richard; CATER, Douglas (eds.). *Television as a cultural force.* New York, Praeger, 76, 191 p.
2018   AUDIGIER, Pierre; LATAPIE, Francis. *Télévision et télécommunications aux États-Unis.* Paris, Presses universitaires de France, 76, 206 p.
2019   BIRESCH, Peter. "Jugendliche produzieren Radiosendungen, Erfahrung und Reflexionen" (Radio programmes for young people. Experiences and reflections), *Dtsche Jugend* 25(4), apr 77 : 174-180.
2020   BLAUKOPF, Kurt. "Senderfärbung und kulturelle Entwicklung" (Television in colours and cultural development), *Communications (Köln)* 3(3), 1977 : 315-335.
2021   BON, Frédéric. "Comment est faite 'La demoiselle d'Avignon'", *R. franç. Sci. polit.* 27(4-5), aug-oct 77 : 643-667. [Feuilleton télévisé.]
2022   BUNCE, Richard. *Television in the corporate interest.* New York, Praeger, 76, 141 p. CR: Robert G. DUNN, *Contemp. Sociol. (Washington)* 6(1), jan 77 : 113-114.
2023   CATER, Douglas; NYHAN, Michael J. (eds.). *The future of public broadcasting.* New York-London, Praeger, 76, ix-372 p.
2024   CAVALLI-SFORZA, Francesco; DONATI, Agnese; EVANS, Huw, "Réseaux indépendants de télévision en Italie. De la transmission par câble à la transmission par ondes", *Communications (Köln)* 3(3), 1977 : 277-288.
2025   COHEN, Akiba A.; WIGAND, Folr T.; HARRISON, Randall P. "The effects of type of event, proximity and repetition on school-children's attention to and learning from television news", *Communications*

(*Köln*) 3(1), 1977 : 30-46.

2026   DUBOIS-DUMÉE, Jean-Pierre. "La télévision par câble en France", *Communications (Köln)* 2(3), 1976 : 315-329.

2027   EGOROV, V. V. *Televidenie i zritel'* (Television and spectator). Moskva, Mysl', 77, 196 p.

2028   FERNANDEZ DE MENEZES, Antonio Carlos *et al.* "Um modelo para o estudo da difusão de emissoras de televisão nas cidades brasileiras. Uma versão preliminar" (A model for the study of television broadcasts dissemination in Brazilian cities. A preliminary version), *R. geogr. (Rio de Janeiro)* 82, jun 75 : 143-165.

2029   HERMANN, Istvan. *Televizio, esztétika, kultúra* (Television, aesthetics, culture). Budapest, Kossuth Kiadó, 76, 322-6 p.

2030   HOFSTETTER, C. Richard. *Bias in the news: network television coverage of the 1972 election campaign.* Columbus, Ohio, State University Press, 76, xv-213 p. CR: Doris A. GRABER, *Amer. J. Sociol.* 83(2), sep 77 : 503-505.

2031   HOWE, Michael J. *Television and children.* Hamden, Conn., Linnet Books, 77, 157 p.

2032   KOSCO, Jan "Der Platz des Fernsehens im System der Massenkommunikationsmittel" (The place of television in the mass media system), *Communications (Köln)* 3(3), 1977 : 304-314.

2033   LIEBERMAN, Leslie; LIEBERMAN, Leonard. "The family in the tube: potential uses of television", *Family Coordinator* 26(3), jul 77 : 235-242.

2034   PALETZ, David L.; VINEGAR, Richard J. "Presidents on television: the effects of instant analysis", *Publ. Opin. Quart.* 41(4), 1977 : 488-497.

2035   PIEPER, Ansgar. *Jugendmagazine zwischen Manipulation und Information* (Television programmes for children between manipulation and information). Köln, Deutscher Instituts-Verlag, 76, 180 p.

2036   SHORT, John; WILLIAMS, Ederyn; CHRISTIE, Bruce. *The social psychology of telecommunications.* London-New York, Wiley, 76, ix-195 p.

2037   "Television and social behavior", *J. soc. Issues* 32(4), 1976 : 1-178.

2038   TOMKA, M. *TV-watching and listening-in of workers.* Budapest, MRT TK, 77, 21 p.

2039   VEITCH, Russell; DE WOOD, Robert; BOSKO, Kathy. "Radio news broadcasts: their effects on interpersonal helping", *Sociometry* 40(4), dec 77 : 383-386.

13800. ART

13810. Aesthetics. Artist. Museum
Esthétique. Artiste. Musée

[See also / Voir aussi: 1266, 2029, 2077, 2704, 5522]

2040   BLUM, Paul VON. *The art of social conscience.* New York, Universe Books, 76, xii-243 p.

2041   BOIXADÓS, Alberto. *El mundo del arte y su proyección en el orden político* (The world of art and its projection into the political order). Buenos Aires, Areté, Huemul, 76, 2 p.

2042   BURCKHARDT, Titus. *Principes et méthodes de l'art sacré.* Paris, Dervy, 76, 230 p.-16 p.

2043   CASTELLANO, Vittorio. "Pour une nouvelle conception de la sociologie de l'art", *R. int. Sociol. (Rome)* 12(1-2); 1976 : 3-15.

2044   CHIARI, Joseph. *Art and knowledge.* London, Elek, 77, ix-132 p.

2045   ETZKORN, K. Peter. "On the sociological potential of the sociology of the arts: introductory comments", *R. int. Sociol. (Rome)* 12(1-2), 1976 : 16-18.

2046   FOUILLOUX, Étienne. "Du spirituel dans l'art. Réflexions sur une exposition", *Archiv. Sci. soc. Relig.* 42(2), jul-dec 76 : 163-172. ["Le symbolisme en Europe", Paris, mai-juin 1976.]

2047   GRIGSBY, J. Eugene Jr. *Art and ethnics: background for teaching youth in a pluralistic society*. Dubuque, Iowa, W.C. Brown Co., 77, xii-147 p.

2048   HARITOS-FATOUROS, M.; CHILD, Irvin L. "Transcultural similarity in personal significance of esthetic interests", *J. cross-cult. Psychol.* 8(3), sep 77 : 285-298.

2049   JÓZSA, Péter. "Az esztétikai értékek társadalmi kommunikációjának mechanizmusai" (Mechanisms of social communication of aesthetic values), *Kult. és Köz.* (4), 1976 : 5-19; [Also published in French, *Soc. Sci. Inform.* 16(2), 1976 : 5-19.]

2050   JÓZSA, Péter. *Esztétikai alkotások társadalmi hatása. Tanulmányok és kutatási beszámolók* (Social impact of works of art. Studies and survey reports). Budapest, Népművelési Propaganda Iroda, 77, 184 p.

2051   LAJDMJAĔ, V. I. Ĕ. *Izobrasitel'noe iskusstvo i ego zritel'. Opyt sociologičeskogo issledovanija* (Plastic arts and their spectator. An essay of sociological research). Tallin, Ĕesti Raamat, 76, 265 p.

2052   LUKŠIN, I. "Sociologičeskie issledovanija iskusstva. Sostojanie i problemy" (Sociological research on art: content and problems), *Iskusstvo* (4), 1977 : 44-47.

2053   MELIÀ, Josep. *Art i capitalisme: una análisi económica del significat social de l'obra d'art* (Art and capitalism: economic anaysis of the social meaning of work of art). Barcelona, Edicions 62, 76, 235 p.

2054   PRONIN, V. A. "Metodika provedenija sociologičeskogo oprosa v muzee" (Methods of holding a sociological inquiry in a museum), *Trudy nauč. issled. Inst. Kul't.* 43(2), 1976 : 152-173.

2055   RAFFA, Piero. *Semiologia delle arti visive* (Semiology of visual arts). Bologna, Pàtron, 76, 225 p.

2056   RECH, Peter. "Überlegungen zur sozialisatorischen Funktion der Kunst. Ein Beitrag zur Zusammenarbeit von Psychoanalyse und Soziologie" (Considerations on the socializing role of art. An essay on the co-operation between psychoanalysis and sociology), *Kölner Z. Soziol. u. soz.-Psychol.* 29(1), mar 77 : 57-70.

2057   SACCA, Antonio. "Considerazioni sulle tesi socio-estetiche marxiste" (Considerations on marxist socio-aesthetic points of view), *R. int. Sociol. (Rome)* 12(1-2), 1976 : 131-149.

2058   SILBERMANN, Alphons (ed.). *Theoretische Ansätze der Kunstsoziologie* (Theoretical introduction to the sociology of art). Stuttgart, Enke, 76, 183 p.

2059   THURN, Hans Peter. "Probleme der ästhetischen Erziehung aus soziologischer Sicht" (Problems of aesthetical education from a sociological point of view), *Kölner Z. Soziol. u. soz.-Psychol.* 29(1), mar 77 : 45-56.

2060   VALKMAN, Otto. *Queuen voor de Nachtwacht. Het Rijksmuseum en zijn bezoekers* (Queu for the Watch Patrol. The Rijksmuseum and its visitors). Amsterdam, E. Boekmanstichting, 76, xviii-151 p.

2061   Bibl.XXVI-1747. WOLFF, Janet. *Hermeneutic philosophy and the sociology of art: an approach to some of the epistemological problems of the sociology of knowledge and the sociology of art and literature*. CR: Barbara ROSENBLUM, *Amer. J. Sociol.* 83(2), sep 77 : 495-499; Batia SHARON. *Contemp. Sociol. (Washington)* 6(3), mai 77 : 304.

13820. Literature
Littérature

[See also / Voir aussi: 1077, 1104, 3930]

2062   BARTHELEMY KNOWLTON, Simone. "The French nouveau roman: a socio-logical inquiry", *R. int. Sociol. (Rome)* 12(1-2), 1976 : 91-99:

2063   BERGER, Morroe. *Real and imagined worlds: the novel and social science*. Cambridge, Mass., Harvard University Press, 77, viii-303 p.

2064   CARRERO ERAS, Pedro. "Notas para sociología de la cultura litera-ria en España desde 1939" (Notes for a sociology of literary culture in Spain since 1939), *R. esp. Opin. publ.* 47, 1977 : 91-122.

2065   CASTELLET, José Maria. *Literatura, ideología y política* (Literature, ideology and politics). Barcelona, Editorial Anagrama, 76, 169 p.

2066   CHAMBOREDON, Jean-Claude; FABIANI, Jean-Louis. "Les albums pour enfants. I. Le champ de l'édition et les définitions sociales de l'enfance", *Actes Rech. Sci. soc.* 13, feb 77 : 60-79; 14, apr 77 : 55-74.

2067   CHARLE, Christophe. "Situation sociale et position spatiale, essai de géographie sociale du champ littéraire à la fin du dix-neuviè-me siècle", *Actes Rech. Sci. soc.* 13, feb 77 : 45-59.

2068   CLARK, Priscilla P. "Polemics and poetics: Peguy and the writer's dilemma", *R. int. Sociol. (Rome)* 12(1-2), 1976 : 100-109.

2069   COUSINS, Albert N. "Creative literature and social change", *Int. J. contemp. Sociol.* 13(3-4), jul-oct 76 : 239-248.

2070   FERNANDES, A. "Literatura e quadrinhos" (Literature and comics), *Vozes* 70(6), aug 76 : 29-48.

2071   FREYRE, G. "Tipos socioantropológicos no romance brasileiro" (Socio-anthropological types in the Brazilian novel), *Ciênc. e Trop.* 2(1), jan-jun 74 : 7-26.

2072   JAMESON, Frederic. "Imaginary and symbolic in *La rabouilleuse*", *Soc. Sci. Inform.* 16(1), 1977 : 59-81.

2073   KIRÁLY, István. *Irodalom és társadalom* (Literature and society). Budapest, Szépirodalmi Könyvtár, 76.

2074   KOVAČEVIĆ, Ivanka. "Sociologija književnosti i tokovi razvoja so-ciologija romana" (A theoretical approach to the sociology of novel), *Sociologija* 18(3-4), 1976 : 269-282.

2075   LABBE, Dominique; MONTES, Arturo. "Introduction thématique à la littérature latino-américaine", *Canad. R. Sociol. Anthropol.* 14(1), feb 77 : 15-33.

2076   "Modern Black literature", *J. Black Stud.* 7(2), dec 76 : 131-240.

2077   PICKOWICZ, Paul G. "Ch'ü Ch'iu-pai and the Chinese Marxist concep-tion of revolutionary popular literature and art", *China Quart.* 70, jun 77 : 269-314.

2078   "Tradition orale (La)", *Cah. ORSTOM Sér. Sci. hum.* 13(2), 1976 : 101-221.

2079   TUNG, Constantine. "The development of the leftist literary con-sciousness in modern China", *Issues and Stud.* 13(1), jan 77 : 55-76.

13830. Fine arts
Beaux-arts

[See also / Voir aussi: 3894]

2080   BLAU, Judith R. "Beautiful buildings and breaching the laws: a study of architectural firms", *R. int. Sociol. (Rome)* 12(1-2), 1976 : 110-128.

2081   BOUDON, Philippe *et al. Intégration et architecture*. Paris, AREA, 76, vii-197 p.

2082   CHEATWOOD, Derral; LINQUIST, Therold (eds.). *The human image: so-ciology and photography*. New York, State University College, 76,

60 p. CR: Philip H. ENNIS, *Contemp. Sociol. (Washington)* 6(3), mai 77 : 302-303.

2083   OLEDZKI, J. "The contemporary African art. Some remarks on new trends in the development of sculpture", *Africana B.* 21, 1974 : 9-36.

2084   SHAPIRO, Theda. *Painters and politics: the European avant-garde and society, 1900-1925.* New York, Elsevier, 76, 341 p. CR: Priscilla P. CLARK, *Amer. J. Sociol.* 83(2), sep 77 : 499-501; Barbara ROSENBLUM, *Contemp. Sociol. (Washington)* 6(4), jul 77 : 509-511.

13840. Music
Musique

2085   ATTALI, Jacques. *Bruits: essai sur l'économie politique de la musique.* Paris, Presses universitaires de France, 77, 301 p.

2086   COSTER, Michel DE. "Le monde des éditeurs phonographiques. Résultats et réflexion critique à propos d'une démarche", *Communications (Köln)* 3(2), 1977 : 201-211.

2087   DASILVA, Fabio B.; DEES, David R. "The social realms of music", *R. int. Sociol. (Rome)* 12(1-2), 1976 : 35-51.

2088   DELTGEN, Florian. "Der Neger im deutschen Kinder- und Jugendlied" (The Negro in German children's songs), *Kölner Z. Soziol. u. soz.-Psychol.* 29(1), mar 77 : 118-136.

2089   JOST. Ekkehard. *Sozialpsychologische Faktoren der Popmusik-Rezeption* (Socio-psychological factors in the reception of pop music). Mainz, Schott, 76, 99 p.

2090   KIER, Herfrid. "Thesen zum Thema des Verhältnisses von Jugend und Schallplatte" (Theses regarding the relations between young people and records), *Communications (Köln)* 3(1), 1977 : 113-120.

2091   MARTORELLA, Rosanne. "The structure of the market and the social organisation of Opera: some inquiries", *R. int. Sociol. (Rome)* 12(1-2), 1976 : 74-90.

2092   MENDOZA DE ARCE, Daniel. "The concept of musical meaning in some modern sociological theories", *R. int. Sociol. (Rome)* 12(1-2), 1976 : 19-34.

2093   RODNITZKY, Jerome L. *Minstrels of the dawn: the folk-protest singer as a cultural hero.* Chicago, Nelson-Hall, 76, 192 p. CR: R. Serge DENISOFF, *Contemp. Sociol. (Washington)* 6(2), mar 77 : 269-270.

2094   STEBBINS, Robert A. "Music among friends: the social networks of amateur musiciens", *R. int. Sociol. (Rome)* 12(1-2), 1976 : 52-73.

2095   VAN ELDEREN, P. L. "Popsociologie" (Pop sociology), *Soc. Wetensch.* 20(2), 1977 : 138-163. [Sociology of the pop music.]

13850. Dramatic art
Art dramatique

2096   BERK, Bernard. "Face-saving at the single dance", *Soc. Probl.* 24(5), jun 77 : 530-544.

2097   DIEZ BORQUE, José María. *Sociología de la comedia española del siglo XVII* (Sociology of the Spanish comedy of the XVIIth century). Madrid, Ediciones Cátedra, 76, 369 p.

2098   LISTOV, V. "El teatro colombiano hoy" (Colombian theatre today), *Amér. lat. (Moscú)* (4), 1976 : 167-182.

2099   MARTORELLA, Rosanne. "The relationship between box office and repertoire: a case study of Opera", *Sociol. Quart.* 18(3), 1977 : 354-366.

2100   MAYER, Rudolf A. M. "Zur Bedeutung des symbolischen Interaktionismus für die Theorie des Theater- und Rollenspiels" (The meaning of symbolic interactionism for the theory of theatre and play performances), *Communications (Köln)* 3(2), 1977 : 223-241.

2101   RICARD, A.; WESTON, J. "Théâtre et communication de masse: l'exemple du concert party au Togo", *Communications (Köln)* 3(3), 1977 : 289-303.

2102   WEINER, Eugene C.; MEINHARD, Agnes C. "The theatre as a strategic research site: an untapped potential", *Communications (Köln)* 3(3), 1977 : 353-374.

13860. Folk art
Art populaire

[See also / Voir aussi: 1686]

2103   AUZIN, Imant. "Foklor i sovremennyj literaturnyj process - rassirenie gorizonta" (Folklore and contemporary literary process for the enlargement of the horizon), *Vopr. Lit.* 21(6), jun 77 : 83-96.

2104   CARPITELLA, Diego. *Folklore e analisi differenziale di cultura* (Folklore and differential analysis of culture). Roma, Bulzoni, 76, xxi-388 p.

2105   CLEMENTE, Pietro; MEONI, Maria Luisa; SQUILLACCIOTTI, Massimo. *Il dibattito sul folklore in Italia* (The debate on folklore in Italy). Milano, Edizioni di cultura popolare, 76, 417 p.

2106   LEVINE, Lawrence W. *Black culture and black consciousness: Afro-American folk thought from slavery to freedom.* New York, Oxford University Press, 77, xx-522 p.

2107   Bibl.XXV-1782. WILSON, William A. *Folklore and nationalism in modern Finland.* CR: Olli ALHO, *Acta sociol.* 20(3), 1977 : 293-299.

13900. EDUCATION

13910. Educational sociology
Sociologie de l'éducation

[See also / Voir aussi: 56, 1189, 1401, 1913, 2417, 2648]

2108   ÁGH, A. "Marxista emberfogalom és müvelödés" (Marxist conception of man and education), *Kult. és Köz.*(2), 1977 : 77-89.

2109   ÁGH, A. *Tudományos-technikai forradalom és müvelödés. Filozofiai tanulmányok* (Scientific-technical revolution and education. Philosophical essays). Budapest, Magvetö, 77, 400 p.

2110   BELKIN, Gary S.; GRAY, Jerry L. *Educational psychology: an introduction.* Dubuque, Iowa; W. C. Brown Co., 77, xvi-697 p.

2111   BERNBAUM, Gerald. *Knowledge and ideology in the sociology of education.* London, Macmillan, 77, 77 p.

2112   BRICKMAN, William W. *Bibliographical essays on educational psychology and sociology of education.* Folcroft, Pa., Folcroft Library Editions, 76, 148 p.

2113   BROWNE, Ronald Kentish; MAGIN, Douglas J. (eds.). *Sociology of education: a source book of Australian studies.* Melbourne, Macmillan, 76, xiv-490 p.

2114   CALHOUN, Craig J.; IANNI, Francis A. J. (eds.). *The anthropological study of education.* The Hague,Mouton; Chicago, Aldine, 76, xii-360 p.

2115   CALLAHAN, Joseph F.; CLARK, Leonard H. (eds.). *Foundations of education.* New York, Macmillan, 77, x-283 p.

2116   CALVIN, Allen D. (ed.). *Perspectives on education.* Reading, Mass., Addison-Wesley Publishing Co., 77, v-265 p.

2117   CHARLOT, Bernard. *La mystification pédagogique: réalités sociales et processus idéologiques dans la théorie de l'éducation.* Paris, Payot, 76, 285 p.

2118   COLEMAN, James S. "Policy decisions, social science information, and education", *Sociol. Educ.* 49(4), oct 76 : 304-312.

2119   DACEY, John S. *New ways to learn: the psychology of education.* Stanford, Conn., Greylock Publishers, 76, xv-207 p.

2120   DAVIES, Brian. *Social control and education.* London, Methuen, 76, 191 p.

2121   DEMAINE, J. "On the new sociology of education: a critique of M.F.D. Young and the radical attack on the politics of educational knowledge", *Econ. and Soc.* 6(2), mai 77 : 111-144.

2122   DUBE, S. C. "Théories et objectifs de l'éducation: perspectives du Tiers Monde", *Perspectives (Unesco)* 6(3), 1976 : 370-385.

2123   DUROJAIYE, M. O. A. *A new introduction to educational psychology*. London, Evans Bros, 76, ix-265 p.

2124   *Explosion de l'éducation (L')*. Paris, R. Laffont; Lausanne, Grammont, 76, 143 p.

2125   FILIPPOV, F. R. *et al*. *Obrazovanie i social'naja struktura* (Education and social structure). Moskva, 76, 199 p.

2126   GLIDEWELL, John (ed.). *The social context of learning and development*. New York, Gardner Press, Halsted Press, 77, x-239 p.

2127   GOODLAD, John I. *Facing the future: issues in education and schooling*. New York, McGraw-Hill, 76, 274 p.

2128   HASSENFORDER, Jean. *Introduction à la recherche bibliographique en sciences de l'éducation*. 2 éd. rév. Paris, Institut national de recherche et de documentation pédagogiques, 76, 32 p.

2129   JOHNSON, M. Clemens. *A review of research methods in education*. Chicago, Rand McNally College Publishing Co., 77, xvii-471 p.

2130   KOZMA, T. *A nevelésszociologia alapjai* (The foundations of educational sociology). Budapest, Tankönyvkiadó, 77, 300 p.

2131   LAPASSADE, Georges; SCHÉRER, René. *Le corps interdit: essais sur l'éducation négative*. Paris, Éditions ESF, 76, 141 p.

2132   MATSUBARA, Haruo (ed.). *Community to kyoiku* (Community and education). Tokyo, Gakuyô Shobô, 77, 219 p.

2133   MEYER, John W. "The effects of education as an institution", *Amer. J. Sociol.* 83(1), jul 77 : 55-77.

2134   NEUFELD, Evelyn M. *The philosophy of Jean Piaget and its educational implications*. Morristown, N. J., General Learning Press, 76, xiv-52 p.

2135   NEZEL, Ivo. *Strukturanalistische Erziehungswissenschaft* (Structuralistic educational science). Weinheim-Basel, Beltz, 76, 157 p.

2136   PIATON, Georges. *Éducation et socialisation: éléments de psychologie de l'éducation*. Toulouse, E. Privat, 77, 205 p.

2137   RICHES, Colin R. *Education and social change: some sociological perspectives*. Hatfield, Hatfield Polytechnic, 76, 26 p.

2138   SATO, Nobuo (ed.). *Kyôiku Shakaigaku* (Sociology of education). Tokyo, Kôbundô shuppansha, 77, 206 p.

2139   SBISÀ, Antonio. *La creatività: il processo educativo tra ideologia ed emancipazione* (Creativity: educational process between ideology and emancipation). Firenze, Le Monnier, 76, 147 p.

2140   SCHORB, Bernd. *Leistung und Sozialisation: Einführung in die Theorien der Leistungsmotivation* (Education and socialization: introduction to the theories of motivation in education). München, Kösel, 76, 206 p.

2141   SEGRÉ, Monique. *École, formation, contradictions*. Paris, Éditions sociales, 76, 254 p. CR: Michel DION, *R. franç. Sociol.* 18(1), jan-mar 77 : 170-173.

2142   SØRENSEN, Aage B.; HALLINAN, Maureen T. "A reconceptualization of school effects", *Sociol. Educ.* 50(4), oct 77 : 273-289.

2143   STONE, Lawrence (ed.). *Schooling and society: studies in the history of education*. Baltimore, Johns Hopkins University Press, 76, xvii-263 p.

2144   TIMAEUS, Ernst; LÜCK, Helmut E. *Sozialpsychologie der Erziehung* (Social psychology of education). Neuwied-Darmstadt, Luchterhand, 76, 109 p.

2145   TYLER, Ralph W. (ed.). *Prospects for research and development in education*. Berkeley, Calif., McCutchan Publishing Corp., 76, ix-183 p.

2146   VARMA, Ved P.; WILLIAM, Phillip (eds.). *Piaget, psychology and education*. London, Hodder and Stoughton, 76, xiv-233 p.

2147   WOODS, Peter; HAMMERSLEY, Martyn (eds.). *School experience: explorations in the sociology of education*. London, Croom Helm; New York, St Martin's Press, 77, 297 p.

13920. Educational system. Educational policy
       Système d'enseignement. Politique de l'enseigne-
       ment

13921.

[See also / Voir aussi: 1574, 2360, 2453, 2860, 3025, 3519, 3640]

2148   "Aspects de l'administration de l'éducation", *Perspectives (Unesco)*
       7(1), 1977 : 62-136.
2149   BACH, Uwe. *Bildungspolitik in Jugoslawien: 1945-1974* (Educational
       policy in Yugoslavia, 1945-1974). Berlin, Osteuropa-Institut;
       Wiesbaden, Harrassowitz, 77, xvi-471 p.
2150   BERGER, Michael; DARILEK, Richards (eds.). *The public education
       system.* New York, F. Watts, 77, vi-108 p. [USA.]
2151   BIZOT, Judith . *La réforme de l'éducation au Pérou.* Paris, Presses
       de l'UNESCO, 76, 67 p.
2152   BOOCOCK, Sarane Spence. *Students, schools, and educational policy:
       a sociological view.* New York, Aspen Institute for Humanistic
       Studies, Program on Education for a Changing Society, 76, 28 p.
2153   Bibl.XXVI-1859. BOWLES, Samuel; GINTIS, Herbert. *Schooling in ca-
       pitalist America: educational reform and the contradictions of
       economic life.* CR: Michael USEEM, *Contemp. Sociol. (Washington)*
       6(1), jan 77 : 19-22.
2154   BROWN, Godfrey N.; HISKETT, Mervyn (eds.). *Conflict and harmony in
       education in tropical Africa.* 1st American ed. Rutherford, N.J.,
       Fairleigh Dickinson University Press, 76, 496 p.
2155   BRUNO, James Edward. *Educational policy analysis: a quantitative
       approach.* New York, Crane, Russak, 76, xii-295 p.
2156   CASE, Harry Lawrence; NIEHOFF, Richard. *Educational alternatives
       in national development: suggestions for policy makers.* East Lan-
       sing, Institute for International Studies in Education, Michigan
       State University, 76, 64 p. [USA.]
2157   CHEN, T. H. E. "The Maoist model of education. I. Origins and
       ideology. II. Theory and practice", *Asian Aff. (New York)* 3(6),
       jul-aug 76 : 384-400; 4(1), sep-oct 76 : 41-61.
2158   CIBOROWSKI, Tom. "The influence of formal education on rule lear-
       ning and attribute identification in a West African society",
       J. cross-cult. Psychol. 8(1), mar 77 : 17-32.
2159   COURT, D. "The education system as a response to inequality in
       Tanzania and Kenya", *J. mod. Afr. Stud.* 14(4), dec 76 : 661-690.
2160   DERMOTT, John E. M. (ed.). *Indeterminacy in education: social scien-
       ce educational policy and the search for standards.* Berkeley,
       Calif., McCutchan Publishing Corp., 76, xx-336 p. [USA.]
2161   "Educación en Colombia, 1975 (La)" (Education in Colombia, 1975),
       Bol. mens. Estadíst. 26(306), jan 77 : 7-48.
2162   "Educación no estatal entre el presente y el futuro (La)" (Private
       education between present and future), *Razon y Fe* 944-945, sep-
       oct 76 : 115-272. [Spain.]
2163   "Enseignement en Tunisie vingt ans après la réforme de 1958 (L')",
       Maghreb-Machrek 78, oct-dec 77 : 43-69.
2164   FERRARO, Oscar Humberto. *Datos y estudios sobre educación en el
       Paraguay* (Data and studies on education in Paraguay). Asunción,
       Centro Paraguayo de Estudios Sociológicos, 76, 71 p.
2165   FILPPULA, Heli-Hanna. "Eiren yleissivistävän koulujarjestelmän
       piirteitä" (Features in the Irish system of general education),
       Kasvatus (3), 1977 : 187-190.
2166   GEORGE, Betty Grace Stein. *Education in Ghana.* Washington, United
       States Government Printing Office, 76, ix-288 p.-1 l.
2167   HALLS, W. D. *Education, culture and politics in modern France.*
       Oxford, Pergamon Press, 76, x-276 p.
2168   HETTWER, Hubert. *Das Bildungswesen in der DDR: strukturelle und in-
       haltliche Entwicklung seit 1945* (The educational system in the

GDR: development of structure and contents since 1975). Köln, Kiepenheuer und Witsch, 76, 138 p.

2169 HSUEH-WEN, Wang. "The Chinese communist educational policy and the leadership struggle", *Issues and Stud.* 13(7), jul 77 : 64-75.

2170 JANSEN, Karel. *Educational planning: the Asian experience.* The Hague, Institute of Social Studies, 76, 31 p.

2171 JOST, Leonhard. *Perspektiven und Horizonte: Gedanken zu Erziehung, Bildung und zum Schulwesen in der Schweiz* (Perspectives and horizons: concepts about training, education and school institutions in Switzerland). Bern-Stuttgart, Paul Haupt, 76, 148 p.

2172 KAMENS, David H. "Legitimating myths and educational organization: the relationship between organizational ideology and formal structure", *Amer. sociol. R.* 42(2), apr 77 : 208-219.

2173 KERR, Donna H. *Educational policy: analysis, structure, and justification.* New York, McKay, 76, x-214 p.

2174 KONDAKOV, Mikhail I. "Perspectives du développement de l'éducation en URSS", *Perspectives (Unesco)* 7(1), 1977 : 137-144.

2175 KOSCHNITZKE, Rudolf (ed.). *Bildung unterm Rotstift, zur Politik nach den Bundestagswahlen 1976* (Education under the red crayon. Politics after the Bundestag elections 1976). Köln, Europäische Verlagsanstalt, 77, 196 p.

2176 LEGRAND, Louis. *Pour une politique démocratique de l'éducation.* Paris, Presses universitaires de France, 77, 293 p. [France.]

2177 LERENA ALESÓN, Carlos. *Escuela, ideología y clases sociales en España: crítica de la sociología empirista de la educación* (School, ideology and social class in Spain: criticism of the empirical sociology of education). Barcelona, Ariel, 76, x-465 p.

2178 LESCHINSKY, Achim; ROEDER, Peter Martin. *Schule im historischen Prozess: zum Wechselverhältnis von institutioneller Erziehung und gesellschaftliche Entwicklung* (The school in the historical process: the interaction of institutional education and social development). Stuttgart, Klett, 76, 545 p. [Germany.]

2179 LOMBARDO-RADICE, Lucio. *Educazione e rivoluzione* (Education and revolution). Roma, Editori riuniti, 76, 278 p.

2180 LUDWIGS, Manfred. "Zur Organisation des Erziehung in der DDR" (Educational organization in the GDR), *Dtsche Stud.* 15(58), jun 77 : 125-138.

2181 MARTINEZ, Eduardo; SILVA, Germán. "La educación en Cuba socialista" (The education in socialist Cuba), *Doc. polít.* 124, mar-apr 77 : 40-54.

2182 MARTINS, Waldemar Valle. *Liberdado do ensino· reflexões a partir de uma situação no Brasil* (Freedom of teaching: reflexions from a situation in Brazil). São Paulo, Edições Loyola, 76, 205 p.

2183 MEYER, John W. *et al.* "The world educational revolution, 1950-1970", *Sociol. Educ.* 50(4), oct 77 : 242-258.

2184 MONTGOMERY, John Dickey. *Alternatives and decisions in educational planning.* Paris, International Institute for Educational Planning, 76, 66 p.

2185 MORRISON, David R. *Education and politics in Africa: the Tanzanian case.* London, C. Hurst; Montreal, McGill-Queen's University Press, 76, 352 p.

2186 MORRISON, Peter A. *The demographic context of educational policy planning.* New York, Aspen Institute for Humanistic Studies, Program on Education for a Changing Society, 76, 32 p.

2187 NIELSEN, François; HANNAN, Michael T. "The expansion of national educational systems: tests of a population ecology model", *Amer. Sociol. R.* 42(3), jun 77 : 479-490.

2188 OLĘDZKI, Michał. "Niektóre przesłanki historyczne programowania modernizacji systemu oświaty i wychowania w Polsce Ludowej" (Some premises of programming the modernization of the system of education in People's Poland), *Biul. IGS* 20(4), 1977 : 54-67.

2189   OLIVER, Donald W. *Education and community: a radical critique of innovative schooling*. Berkeley, Calif., McCutchan Publishing Co., 76, xii-415 p.

2190   PAULSTON, Rolland G. *Conflicting theories of social and educational change: a typological review*. Pittsburgh, University Center for International Studies, 76, vii-62 p. *[USA.]*

2191   PETERSON, Paul E. *School politics, Chicago style*. Chicago, Ill., University of Chicago Press, 76, xiv-304 p.

2192   PETTY, Miguel. *Problemática de la insuficiencia de los sistemas educativos en América Latina* (Problems of educational systems deficiency in Latin America). Buenos Aires, Centro de Investigación y Acción Social, 76, 38 p.

2193   POSTON, Susan L. *Nonformal education in Latin America: an annotated bibliography*. Los Angeles, UCLA Latin American Center Publications, University of California, 76, x-268 p.

2194   ROBLES, M. "Ajustes educativos en la sociedad actual" (Educational reforms in the contemporary society), *Estud. polít.* 2(8), oct-dec 76 : 33-47. *[Mexico.]*

2195   ROTH, Hans-Georg. *Demokratisierung der Schule: Forderung oder Herausforderung der Demokratie ?* (School democratization: demand or challenge of the democracy ?). Mainz, Landeszentrale für Politische Bildung Rheinland-Pfalz, 76, 160 p. *[Germany FR.]*

2196   SACCO, Piero. *L'organizzazione amministrativa della pubblica istruzione* (The administrative organization of the public instruction). Milano, Giuffrè, 76, 230 p. *[Italy.]*

2197   SANCHEZ, Ramon. *Schooling American society: a democratic ideology*. Syracuse, N.Y., Syracuse University Press, 76, xv-175 p. *[USA.]*

2198   SCHIEFELBEIN, Ernesto. *Diagnóstico del sistema educacional chileno en 1970* (Diagnostic of the Chilean educational system in 1970). Santiago de Chile, Universidad de Chile, Facultad de ciencias económicas y administrativas, Departamento de economía, 76, viii-285 p.

2199   SCRIBNER, Jay D. (ed.). *The politics of education*. Chicago, University of Chicago Press, 77, xviii-367 p.

2200   SHUKLA, P. D. *Towards the new pattern of education in India*. New Delhi, Sterling Publishers, 76, 215 p.

2201   SOARES, Orlando. "A problematica do ensino no Brasil" (Educational problems in Brazil), *Vozes* 71(2), mar 77 : 29-40.

2202   SOLJAN, Niksa Nikola. "Problèmes de théorie et de politique de l'éducation en Yougoslavie", *Perspectives (Unesco)* 7(2), 1977 : 200-209.

2203   SUAREZ C., Carlos. "Balance global de la educación en Colombia" (Overall evaluation of education in Colombia), *R. javer.* 90(435), jun 77 : 43-45.

2204   TELMON, Vittorio *et al. Il sistema scolastico italiano* (The Italian educational system). Firenze, Le Monnier, 76, 141 p.

2205   THOMAS, Thomas C.; LARSON, Meredith A. *Educational indicators and educational policy*. New York, Aspen Institute, 76, 23 p. *[USA.]*

2206   WATANABE, Shin'ichi. *A select list of books on the history of education in Japan, and a select list of periodicals on education*. Ann Arbor, Asia Library, Universitynof Michigan, 76, ix-153 p.

2207   ZALTMAN, Gerald; FLORIO, David H.; SIKORSKI, Linda A. *Dynamic educational change: models, strategies, tactics, and management*. New York, Free Press, 77, xvi-364 p. *[USA.]*

         13922.

         [See also / Voir aussi: 557, 2258, 2259, 2312, 2321]

2208   BERTHELOT, Jean-Michel. "Modes de scolarisation et origine sociale", *C. int. Sociol.* 24(63), jul-dec 77 : 299-314.

2209   CAREY, Philip *et al.* "Selection without discrimination: an analy-
        sis of the ASA minority fellowship program", *Sociol. Educ.*
        50(2), apr 77 : 144-150. *[USA.]*

2210   COLLINS, R. "Some comparative principles of educational stratifica-
        tion", *Harvard educ. R.* 47(1), feb 77 : 1-27.

2211   "Education: strait jacket on opportunity", *Soc. Probl.* 24(2), dec
        76 : 143-307.

2212   FILIPPOV, F. R.; BYKOVA, S. N. "Problema 'ravenstva vozmožnostej'
        v sovremennoj buržuaznoj sociologii obrazovanija" (Problem of
        "equal opportunity" in contemporary bourgeois sociology of edu-
        cation), *Sociol. Issled. (Moskva)* (1), 1977 : 160-167.

2213   FLEW, Anthony Garrard Newton. *Sociology, equality, and education:
        philosophical essays in defense of a variety of differences.*
        London, Macmillan; New York, Barnes and Noble Books, 76, 143 p.

2214   GARNIER, M.; HOUT, M. "Inequality of educational opportunity in
        France and the United States", *Soc. Sci. Res.* 5(3), sep 76 : 225-
        246.

2215   KERCKHOFF, Alan C.; CAMPBELL, Richard T. "Black-white differences
        in the educational attainment process", *Sociol. Educ.* 50(1), jan
        77 : 15-27.

2216   MARJORIBANKS, Kevin. "Educational deprivation thesis: a further
        analysis", *Austral. New Zealand J. Sociol.* 13(1), feb 77 : 12-17.

2217   MOENS, Gabriël. *Equality for freedom: a critical study of unresol-
        ved problems of school desegregation cases in the United States.*
        Wien, W. Braumüller, 76, v-73 p.

2218   MORGAN, Edward P. *Inequality in classroom learning: schooling and
        democratic citizenship.* New York, Praeger, 77, xii-224 p.

2219   MÜLLER, Walter. "Further education, division of labour and equality
        of opportunity", *Soc. Sci. Inform.* 16(5), 1977 : 527-556.

2220   NEUWIRTH, G. (ed.). *A fizikai dolgozók gyermekeinek továbbtanulási
        szándékai a magyar középiskolákban* (Aspirations of workers' chil-
        dren after higher education in Hungarian secondary schools). Bu-
        dapest, Felsöoktatási Pedagogiai Kutató Központ, 76, 167 p.

2221   ROBINSON, Philip E. D. *Education and poverty.* London, Methuen, 76,
        126 p.

2222   RYAN, Charlotte. *The open partnership: equality in running the
        schools.* New York, McGraw-Hill, 76, xi-202 p.

2223   SCHÄFER, Hans-Peter. "Chancengleichheit und Begabtenförderung in
        der DDR" (Equal opportunity and encouragement of gifted students
        in the GDR), *Deutschland Archiv* 10(8), aug 77 : 818-828.

2224   SIKULA, P. "Black attitude toward education and schooling: a case
        for American school reform", *R. int. Sociol. (Madrid)* 34(18-19-
        20), apr-dec 76 : 135-143.

2225   SNYDERS, Georges. *École, classe et lutte des classes: une relec-
        ture critique de Baudelot-Establet, Bourdieu-Passeron et Illich.*
        Paris, Presses universitaires de France, 76, 377 p.

2226   WEBER, Silke. *Modèle dominant et aspirations à l'éducation: un
        exemple au Nord-Est du Brésil.* Paris, Éditions du CNRS, 76, 228
        p. *[Également publié en portugais. Petrópolis, Vozes, 76, 141 p.]*

2227   WOLLENBERG, Charles. *All deliberate speed: segregation and exclu-
        sion in California schools, 1855-1975.* Berkeley, University of
        California Press, 76, vi-201 p.

2228   WUTHNOW, Robert. "Is there an academic melting pot ?", *Sociol.
        Educ.* 50(1), jan 77 : 7-15.

13923.

[See also / Voir aussi: 2208, 3926, 4298, 4633*]*

2229   "Analyse des besoins éducatifs (L')", *Éduc. perm.* 34, mai-jun 76 :
        3-106; 35, sep-oct 76 : 1-168. *[France.]*

2230   ASO, Makoto (ed.). *Gakureki kôyôron* (Social functions of schooling).
        Tokyo, Yuhikaku, 77, 256 p.

2231   BÉNÉTON, Philippe. "Niveau d'instruction et comportement politique.
       Quelques éléments d'analyse", *Soc. Sci. Inform.* 16(5), 1977 :
       557-565.
2232   DeBORD, Larry W.; GRIFFIN, Larry; CLARK, Melissa. "Race and sex
       influence in the schooling processes of rural and small town
       youth", *Sociol. Educ.* (2), apr 77 : 85-102.
2233   FAUCHEUX, François. "Rôle de l'école dans la structuration so-
       ciale du Mali", *C. int. Sociol.* 24(63), jul-dec 77 : 315-340.
2234   HIMMELFARB, Harold S. "The impact of schooling comparing different
       types and amounts of Jewish education", *Sociol. Educ.* 50(2),
       apr 77 : 114-132.
2235   IRVINE, D. G. *The reading ability of school-leavers: a study of
       the extent of reading difficulties among school-leavers in
       Liverpool.* Liverpool, University of Liverpool, Institute of
       Extension Studies, 76, 4-31 p.
2236   PINELL, Patrice. "L'école obligatoire et les recherches en psy-
       chopédagogie au début du XXe siècle", *C. int. Sociol.* 24(67),
       jul-dec 77 : 341-362.
2237   "Problèmes de la culture des masses", *Nouv. Ét. hong.* (10), 1975 :
       5-83.
2238   REGNIER, C. "Les disparités régionales de la scolarisation en
       France: situation de l'Alsace", *R. Sci. soc. France Est* (6),
       1977 : 120-146.
2239   ROKICKA, Ewa. "Problematyka badań nad młodzeżą nie kończącą studiów"
       (Topics for research on student drop-outs), *Przegl. socjol.* 29,
       1977 : 241-248.
2240   SACHS, Wolfgang. *Schulzwang und soziale Kontrolle: Argumente für
       eine Entschulung des Lernens* (Compulsory education and social
       control: arguments for a deschooling of the learning). Frankfurt-
       am-Main-Berlin-München, Diesterweg, 76, 174 p.
2241   "Scolarisation en langue maternelle en milieu multilingue", *Pers-
       pectives (Unesco)* 6(3), 1976 : 406-477.

13930. Primary education. Secondary education
Enseignement primaire. Enseignement secondaire

[See also / Voir aussi: 721]

2242   AGUERRONDO, Inés. *El centralismo en la educación primaria argen-
       tina* (The centralism in the Argentine primary education). Buenos
       Aires, Centro de Investigaciones Educativas, 76, 64 p.
2243   AUSTIN, Gilbert R. *Early childhood education: an international
       perspective.* New York, Academic Press, 76, xiii-369 p.
2244   CHOQUET, M.; PHILIPPE, A. "Besoins différentiels de mode de garde
       des jeunes enfants dans une population urbaine", *C. Sociol. Dé-
       mogr. médic.* 17(3), jul-sep 77 : 97-109.
2245   CODD, Joan A.; HERMANSSON, Gary L. (eds.). *Directions in New Zea-
       land secondary education.* Auckland, Hodder and Stoughton, 76,
       372 p.
2246   HOM, Harry L. Jr.; ROBINSON, Paul A. (eds.). *Psychological process-
       es in early education.* New York, Academic Press, 77, xviii-334 p.
2247   JUDGE, Harry George. *The future of secondary education.* Swansea,
       University College of Swansea, 76, 16 p.
2248   LALLEZ, Raymond. *L'innovation en Haute-Volta: éducation rurale et
       enseignement primaire.* Paris, Presses de l'Unesco, 76, 4-107 p.
2249   LANCASTER, Janet; GAUNT, Joan. *Developments in early childhood
       education.* London, Open Books, 76, ix-145 p.
2250   MAYEUR, Françoise. *L'enseignement secondaire des jeunes filles
       sous la Troisième République.* Paris, Presses de la Fondation na-
       tionale des sciences politiques, 77, 488 p.
2251   McCREESH, John; MAHER, Austen. *Preschool education: objectives and
       techniques.* London, Ward Lock, 76, 140 p.

2252   ORGANIZATION FOR ECONOMIC COOPERATION AND DEVELOPMENT. *Beyond compulsory schooling: options and changes in upper secondary education.* Paris-Washington, D.C., OECD Publications Center, 76, 77 p. *[Issued also in French with title: Les options après la scolarité obligatoire.]*

2253   PASSOW, A. Harry. *Secondary education reform: retrospect and prospect.* New York, Teachers College, Columbia University, 76, 61 p. *[USA.]*

2254   ROSS, Elizabeth Dale. *The kindergarten crusade: the establishment of preschool education in the United States.* Athens, Ohio University Press, 76, ix-120 p.

2255   SATO, Mamoru. "Toshika no yoji-kyoiku ni oyobosu eikyo ni jissho-teki kenkyu" (Regional studies on the effects of urbanization on the infant care and young child education), *Akita-daigaku Kenkyu Kiyo* 27, 1977 : 1-128.

2256   SEKIGUCHI, Reiko. "Daigaku ni itaru gakushu katei deno senbatsu yoshiki - Nihon tono hikaku ni okeru Nishi-Doitsu no tokushu to kaikaku no hoko" (Characteristics of the West German secondary education system in comparison with the Japanese system), *Shō-toku-gakuen Gifokyoiku-daigaku Kiyô* (4), 1977 : 131-148.

2257   STUKAT, Karl Gustaf. *Current trends in European pre-school research: with particular regard to compensatory education.* Windsor, NFER; Atlantic Highlands, N.J., Humanities Press, 76, 74 p.

13931.

2258   ACHINGER, Gertrud; FELDMANN, Klaus; MEINTKER, Jürgen. *Grund- und Hauptschule, reformbedürftig ? Empirische Untersuchung zur Selektion und Sozialisation in der Schule* (Primary and secondary school: do they need reforms ? An empirical study about selection and socialization in school). Hannover-Dortmund-Darmstadt-Berlin, Schroedel, 76, 338 p. *[Germany FR.]*

2259   ALEXANDER, Karl L.; ECKLAND, Bruce K. "High school context and college selectivity: institutional constraints in educational stratification", *Soc. Forces* 56(1), sep 77 : 166-188.

2260   BURBY, Raymond J.; DONNELLY, Thomas G. *Schools in new communities.* Cambridge, Mass., Ballinger Publishing Co., 77, xxvii-229 p.

2261   COLUCCI, Celestino. "L'istruzione come consumo di status" (Education as status consumption), *Rass. ital. Sociol.* 17(4), oct-dec 76 : 593-619. *[Secondary education in Italy.]*

2262   "Crèche, l'école maternelle et les parents (La)", *Inform. soc. (Paris)* 31(1-2), jan-feb 77 : 1 118.

2263   FRUNZIO, Ettore. *Vita e funzione della scuola materna* (Life and function of the nursery school). Manduria, Laciata, 76, 279 p.

2264   GOMEZ ORFANEL, German. "Sociedad, educación y escuela: notas para un análisis de sus interrelaciones" (Society, education and school: notes for an analysis of their interrelations), *R. esp. Opin. públ.* 50, 1977 : 143-171.

2265   KÖPECZI, B. "Az iskola szerepe a társadalmi tudat formálásában" (The role of the school in the formation of social consciousness), *Magyar Pedag.* 17(3-4), 1977 : 335-343.

2266   LAMB, Gene. *The school as a social/cultural system.* Morristown, N.J., General Learning Press, 76, xiii-49 p.

2267   McPHERSON, Andrew; NEAVE, Guy. *The Scottish sixth: a sociological evaluation of sixth year studies and the changing relationship between school and university in Scotland.* Windsor, NFER; Atlantic Highlands, N.J., Humanities Press, 76, 3-170 p.

2268   ORATA, Pedro T. "Écoles secondaires de barrio et collèges communautaires aux Philippines", *Perspectives (Unesco)* 7(3), 1977 : 434-447.

2261   PUNCH, M. "A propotype anti-school", *Sociol. Gids* 23(5), sep-oct 76 : 274-284.

2270   REMOTTI, Francesco. "La riforma della scuola secondaria superiore e le scienze sociali" (The reform of high secondary school and the social sciences), *Rass. ital. Sociol.* 17(4), oct–dec 76 : 491–497.

2271   ROSENBAUM, James E. *Making inequality: the hidden curriculum of high school tracking.* New York, Wiley, 76, xviii–238 p.

2272   YARDLEY, Alice. *The organisation of the infant school.* London, Evans Bros, 76, 95 p. *[UK.]*

13932.

[See also / Voir aussi: 856]

2273   BUJAK, Kazimierz. "Postway młodziezy szkolnej wobec pracy jako wartości społecznej" (The attitudes of school youth towards work as social value), *Stud. socjol.* 65(2), 1977 : 107–132.

2274   HARGREAVES, Andy. "Progressivism and pupil autonomy", *Sociol. R.* 25(3), aug 77 : 585–621.

2275   KRÜGER, Hans-Peter. *Soziometrie in der Schule: Verfahren und Ergebnisse zu sozialen Determinanten der Schülerpersönlichkeit* (Sociometry in school: methods and results of social determinants of the personality of school-children). Weinheim-Basel, Beltz, 76, 236 p.

2276   TAP, Pierre; BRAS, André; FERRA, Roger. *Les lycéens, les mass media et le monde contemporain.* Paris, INRDP, 76, 197 p.

13940. School environment
      Milieu scolaire

13941.

2277   ALONSO, Myrtes. *O papel do diretor na administração escolar* (The role of director in school administration). São Paulo, Difel, 76, 197 p.

2278   BRAUN, Carl. *Strategies for instruction and organization.* Calgary, Alta., Detselig Enterprises, 76, 267 p.

2279   CANTA, Carmelina. "Partecipazione sociale e gestione della scuola secondaria" (Social participation and the management of the secondary school), *Sociologia (Roma)* 10(3), sep–dec 76 : 175–212.

2280   GALLOWAY, Charles M. (ed.). *Administration and supervision: leadership in education.* Columbus, College of Education, Ohio State University, 76, 241–313 p.

2281   GALLOWAY, David M. *Case studies in classroom management.* London-New York, Longman, 76, 127 p.

2282   GROSS, Neal; TRASK, Anne E. *The sex factor and the management of schools.* New York, John Wiley, 76, vii–279 p. CR: Charlene HARRINGTON, *Amer. J. Sociol.* 83(3), nov 77 : 818–819; Patricia Yancey MARTIN, *Contemp. Sociol. (Washington)* 6(2), mar 77 : 231–232.

2283   JUNIPER, Dean Francis. *Decision-making for schools and colleges.* Oxford-New York, Pergamon Press, 76, x–302 p.

2284   LANDERS, Thomas J.; MYERS, Judith G. *Essentials of school management.* Philadelphia, Saunders, 77, x–445 p.

2285   MANN, Dale. *Politics of administrative representation. School administrators and local democracy.* Lexington, Mass., Lexington Books, 76, xiii–185 p.

2286   POSTER, Cyril D. *School decision-making: educational management in secondary schools.* London, Heinemann Educational, 76, 180 p.

2287   SMITH, Donald E. P. *The adaptive classroom.* New York, Academic Press, 77, x–320 p.

13942.

[See also / Voir aussi: 1414]

2288   ALWIN, Duane F.; OTTO, Luther B. "High school context effects on aspirations", *Sociol. Educ.* 50(4), oct 77 : 259–273.

2289   ANDREANI SCOPESI, A. M. "Indagine sui problemi psicologici dell'a-
dattamento alla scuola materna" (Survey on psychological problems of adaptation to the nursery school), *Boll. Psicol.* 136-137-
138, aug-dec 76 : 23-37. *[Italy.]*

2290   DELAMONT, Sara. *Interaction in the classroom.* London, Methuen, 76,
124 p.

2291   EIRMBTER, Willy H. *Ökologische und strukturelle Aspekte der Bil-
dungsbeteiligung* (Ecological and structural aspects of the educational participation). Weinheim-Basel, Beltz, 77, 364 p.

2292   GLASER, Robert. *Adaptive education: individual diversity and learning.* New York, Holt, Rinehart and Winston, 77, vii-181 p.

2293   MOTOMURA, Hiroshi. "Gakkô kyôfusho-ji no yogo -shu toshite kazoku
yôin tono kakawari ai ni oite" (Prognostic study of the children
with school phobia: a relation to family factors as intervening),
Ôsaka-shiritsu-daigaku Seikatsu-kagakubu Kiyô 24, 1977 : 171-179.

2294   PINELL, P.; ZAFIROPOULOS, M. "Sociologie différentielle des inadap-
tations scolaires traitées dans les centres médico-psycho-pédago-
giques", *C. Sociol. Démogr. médic.* 17(3), jul-sep 77 : 110-126.

13950. Higher education
Enseignement supérieur

*[See also / Voir aussi: 1413, 2220, 2267, 2421, 2894, 3462, 3601,
3635, 3648, 4647, 5136, 5322]*

2295   ARAI, Katsuhiro; TSUKAHARA, Shûichi; YAMADA, Keiichi. "Kagaku-
gijutsusha no kôtô-kyôiku ni kansuru kenkyû" (Research on higher
education of scientists and engineers), *Daigaku Ronshû* (5),
1977 : 23-44.

2296   BARTOL, Gerda. *Ideologie und studentischer Protest: Untersuchung
zur Entstehung deutscher Studentenbewegungen im 19. und 20. Jh.*
(Ideology and student protest: study of the origin of the German
student movements in the 19th and 20th century). München, Verlag
Dokumentation, 77, viii-272 p.

2297   BASSIS, Michael S. "The campus as a frog pond: a theoretical and
empirical reassessment", *Amer. J. Sociol.* 82(6), mai 77 : 1318-
1326.

2298   BAYER, Hermann; LAWRENCE, Peter. "Effizienz und Traditionalismus:
die Attraktivität akademischer Ausbildungsgänge in Grossbrita-
nien und der Bundesrepublik Deutschland" (Efficiency and traditionalism: the attractiveness of academic education in Great
Britain and in the German Federal Republic), *Soz. Welt* 28(1-2),
1977 : 200-220.

2299   BECHELLONI, Giovanni. "L'università introvabile" (Undiscoverable
university), *Rass. ital. Sociol.* 18(1), jan-mar 77 : 9-18.

2300   BEN-DAVID, Joseph. *Centers of learning: Britain, France, Germany,
United States: an essay.* New York, McGraw-Hill, 77, xiv-208 p.

2301   BLEDSTEIN, Burton J. *The culture of professionalism: the middle
class and the development of higher education in America.* New
York, Norton, 76, xii-354 p.

2302   BOUDON, Raymond. "The French university since 1968", *Comp. Polit.*
10(1), oct 77 : 89-119.

2303   BROWN, Frank; STENT, Madelon D. *Minorities in US institutions of
higher education.* New York, Praeger, 77, xv-178 p.

2304   BRUBACHER, John Seiler. *On the philosophy of higher education.*
San Francisco, Jossey-Bass Publishers, 77, xii-143 p.

2305   BURN, Barbara B. *Higher education in a changing world: reflections
on an international seminar.* New York, International Council for
Educational Development, 76, vi-47 p.

2306   CANGEMI, Joseph P. *Higher education and the development of self-
actualizing personalities.* New York, Philosophical Library, 77,
xxvi-96 p.

2307   CARTON, Michel. *Le Centre universitaire de Roskilde: une interprétation socio-économique d'une innovation au Danemark.* Paris,

Unesco, 76, 113 p.

2308   CHERMESH, Ran. "Students' rating of their faculty – primary impression or a dynamic process", *Sociol. Educ.* 50(4), oct 77 : 290-299.

2309   COURT, D. "East African higher education from the community standpoint", *Higher Educ.* 6(1), feb 77 : 45-66.

2310   CUELLO DE LIZARAZO, Ketty M. *et al.* "El problema universitario en Colombia" (The university problem in Colombia), *R. javer.* 90 (433), mai 77 : 69-79.

2311   DAVIS, Alan G.; STRONG, Philip M. "Working without a net: the bachelor as a social problem", *Sociol. R.* 25(1), feb 77 : 109-129.

2312   EHARA, Takemichi. "Taishūka katei ni okeru kōtōkyōiku kikai no kōzō" (Educational opportunity in Japanese mass higher education), *Daigaku Ronshū* (5), 1977 : 177-199.

2313   ENTWISTLE, Noel James (ed.). *Strategies for research and development in higher education.* Amsterdam, Swets and Zeitlinger, 76, viii-279 p.

2314   GOLDENBERG, Sheldon. "Canadian encouragement of higher educational participation: an empirical assessment", *Int. J. comp. Sociol.* 17(3-4), sep-oct 76 : 284-299.

2315   GUIDUCCI, Roberto; GUIDUCCI, Giuliano; MINOLI, Lorenza. *La scuola superiore in Italia* (Higher education in Italy). Milano, ISEDI, 76, 66 p.-4 l.

2316   HAAR, Jerry. *The politics of higher education in Brazil.* New York, Praeger, 77, xiv-222 p.

2317   HARRISON, B. *et al.* "The decision to enter higher education: the case of polytechnic sociology students", *Higher Educ.* 6(4), nov 77 : 453-476. [UK.]

2318   HILLS, Philip James. *The self-teaching process in higher education.* London, Croom Helm, 76, 144 p.

2319   HOYO A., J. L. "La universidad y la insurgencia estudiantil" (University and student revolt), *Estud. polít.* 1(2), jul-sep 75 : 85-97.

2320   HSUEH-WEN, Wang. "Peking and Tsinghua universities: 1966-1976", *Issues and Stud.* 13(6), jun 77 : 75-90.

2321   HUSEN, T. "Problems of securing equal access to higher education: the dilemma between equality and excellence", *Higher Educ.* 5(4), nov 76 : 407-422.

2322   JABBRA, J. G. "Sectarian affiliation and political orientation of Lebanese students", *Muslim Wld* 66(3), jul 76 : 189-212.

2323   JENCKS, Christopher; RIESMAN, David. *The academic revolution.* Chicago, University of Chicago Press, 77, xxvi-580 p. [USA.]

2324   KAMENS, David H. "Institutional definitions and collective action. The concept of student as a source of school authority and student culture", *Youth and Soc.* 9(1), sep 77 : 55-78.

2325   KELLER, Robert J. "The role of higher education in national development in Southeast Asia", *Higher Educ.* 6(4), nov 77 : 489-498.

2326   KOMYZA, M. A. "V. I. Lenin ob otnošenii marksistskoj partii k studenčeskomu dviženiju" (V. I. Lenin and the relations of the Marxist party with student movement), in: *Studenčestvo v revoljucionnom dviženii i bor'be za socializm v SSSR.* Moskva, 1976 : 6-34.

2327   KONDONASSIS, A. J.; TSENG, S. C. "The demand for higher education in Taiwan: a case study 1950-1969", *Int. J. soc. Econ.* 3(3), 1976 : 146-166.

2328   KÖRCSÖG, A. *et al.* "Experiments of two-level training in Hungarian higher education", *Higher Educ.* 6(1), feb 77 : 1-43.

2329   KULPINSKA, Jolanda. "Les problèmes sociologiques de l'enseignement supérieur en Pologne", *De* (2), 1976 : 9-17.

2330   KUMAGAI, Fumie. "The effects of cross-cultural education on attitudes and personality of Japanese students", *Sociol. Educ.* 50(1), jan 77 : 40-47.

2331   KUO, Hwang Kwang; MARSELLA, Anthony J. "The meaning and measure-
        ment of Machiavellianism in Chinese and American college stu-
        dents", *J. soc. Psychol.* 101(2), apr 77 : 165-173.
2332   LEMENNICIER, Bertrand. "Les tentatives d'explication du comporte-
        ment des étudiants par les économistes et la confrontation des
        hypothèses aux faits", *R. franç. Sociol.* 18(3), jul-sep 77 : 499-
        509.
2333   LIGHT, Donald Jr.; SPIEGEL, John (eds.). *The dynamics of univer-
        sity protest.* Chicago, Nelson-Hall, 77, viii-198 p.
2334   LOMNITZ, Larissa. "Conflict and mediation in a Latin American uni-
        versity", *J. inter-Amer. Stud. Wld Aff.* 19(3), aug 77 : 315-338.
        [Mexico.]
2335   LONG, Samuel. "Student types and the evaluation of the university",
        Higher Educ. 6(4), nov 77 : 417-436. *[USA.]*
2336   MAJALI, Abdel Salam. *The development of higher education in the
        Arab world.* London, Longman, 76, 3-20-16 p.
2337   MARTSINKOVSKI, I. B. "L'enseignement universitaire dans le monde
        capitaliste: les tendances de développement et les problèmes",
        De (1), 1976 : 10-19.
2338   MEHMET, Ozay. "Economic returns on undergraduate fields of study
        in Canadian universities: 1961 to 1972", *Relat. industr.* 32(3),
        1977 : 321-337.
2339   MILLAN PUELLES, Antonio. *Universidad y sociedad* (University and
        society). Madrid, Ediciones Rialp, 76, 154 p.
2340   MØGLESTUE, Idar; JEBER, Arild. *Utdanning og yrke til laererkandida-
        tene fra 1965* (Education and occupation of graduates from teach-
        ers' training colleges in 1965). Oslo, Statistisk sentralbyrå,
        76, 55 p. *[Norway.]*
2341   NAGY-SZEGVÁRI, K.; LADÁNYI, A. *Nök az egyetemeken* (Women in the
        universities). Budapest, s.e., 76, 129-2 p. multigr.
2342   OSBORN, Thomas Noel II. *Higher education in Mexico: history,growth,
        and problems in a dichotomized industry.* El Paso, Tex., Center
        for Inter-American Studies, 76, xv-150 p.
2343   PLOURDE, Paul J. *Experience with analytical models in higher edu-
        cation management.* Amherst, University of Massachusetts at Am-
        herst, 76, 86 p.
2344   RAHMATULLINA, L. K. "Dialektika vospitanija i upravlenija v stu-
        denčeskom kollektive" (Dialectics of education and management
        in a student collectivity), *Filos. Nauki* 19(8), 1976 : 199-208.
2345   RAMSEIER, Erich. "Der Studienerfolg des schweizerischen Immatriku-
        lationsjahrganges 1965" (The result of the studies of the Swiss
        matriculated student group of 1965), *Kölner Z. Soziol. u. soz.-
        Psychol.* 29(3), sep 77 : 511-529.
2346   REYNOLDS, Philip A. "The university in the 1960s: an anachronism",
        Higher Educ. 6(4), nov 77 : 403-415.
2347   RINGER, Fritz K. "Problems in the history of higher education: a
        review article", *Comp. Stud. Soc. Hist.* 19(2), apr 77 : 239-255.
2348   RUBINA, L. Ja. "Obščestvennaja aktivnost' kak pokazatel' obraza
        žizni studenčeskoj molodeži" (Social activity as an index of
        young students way of life), *Nauč. Trudy Sverdlovsk. pedag. Inst.
        Probl. izučen. social. Obraza žizni* 276(1), 1976 : 69-84.
2349   SAHNER, Heinz. "Studentischer Radikalismus" (Student radicalism),
        Z. Soziol. 6(3), jul 77 : 279-296.
2350   SATO, Nobuo. "Komyuniti to kôtô-kyôiku - Beikoku no baai" (Commu-
        nity and higher education - a development of relationship in the
        United States), *Utsunomiya-daigaku Kyôyôbu Kenkyûhôkoku* (10),
        1977 : 15-33.
2351   SAWICKA, Maria. "Szkolnictwo wyższe i ruchu studenckie w Argenty-
        nie" (Universities and student movements in Argentina), *Przegl.
        socjol.* 29, 1977 : 121-140.
2352   SOUZA, Thomas A. DE. "Regional and communal stereotypes of Bombay
        university students", *Ind. J. soc. Wk* 38(1), apr 77 : 37-44.

2353   TAFT, John. *Mayday at Yale: a case study in student radicalism*.
        Boulder, Colo., Westview Press, 76, 224 p. CR: Richard G.
        BRAUNGART, *Contemp. Sociol. (Washington)* 6(4), jul 77 : 461-463.
2354   TENA ARTIGAS, Joaquín et al. *La universidad española: datos para
        un problema* (Spanish university: data for a problem). Madrid,
        Confederación Española de Cajas de Ahorros, D.L., 76, 204 p.-
        7 1.
2355   TROW, M. "Elite higher education: an endanger species ?", *Minerva*
        14(3), 1976 : 355-376.
2356   "Università: ancora tra rivolta e riforma (L')" (The University:
        always between revolt and reform), *Mulino* 26(250), mar-apr 77 :
        153-302. *[Italy.]*
2357   "Università" (University), *Crit. sociol. (Roma)* 39-40, 1976-1977 :
        348 p. *[Italy.]*
2358   VAN WIERINGEN, A. M. L. *De identiteit van het hoger beroepsonder-
        wijs* (The identity of the higher vocational education). Gronin-
        gen, H. D. Tjeenk Willink, 76, 250 p. *[Netherlands.]*
2359   VINOKUR, Annie. "L'économie de l'éducation néoclassique et la
        'crise de l'Université'. Remarques méthodologiques sur l'article
        de Louis Lévy-Garboua", *R. franç. Sociol.* 18(3), jul-sep 77 :
        485-498. *[See Bibl.XXVI-1932.]*
2360   WEISZ, George. "Le corps professoral de l'enseignement supérieur
        et l'idéologie de la réforme universitaire en France, 1860-
        1875", *R. franç. Sociol.* 18(2), apr-jun 77 : 201-232.
2361   WESTBY, David L. *The clouded vision: the student movement in the
        United States in the 1960s*. Cranbury, N.J., Bucknell University
        Press, 76, 291 p. CR: Peter K. MANNING, *Contemp. Sociol. (Wa-
        shington)* 6(3), mai 77 : 348-350.

13960. Adult education
Éducation des adultes

[See also / Voir aussi: 2219, 2402, 5522]

2362   ALBINSON, F. "Adapting curricula and materials to meet new needs
        of adult education in Sweden", *Convergence* 9(3), 1976 : 81-88.
2363   ANDRADE, T. G. DE. "Microplanificação e educação permanente" (Mic-
        ro-planning and continuing education), *Vozes* 70(9), nov 76 : 45-
        56. *[Brazil.]*
2364   BALDISSERA, Eros. "Note sull' analfabetismo in Siria" (Notes on
        illiteracy in Syria), *Oriente mod.* 57(1-2), jan-feb 77 : 16-24.
2365   BEDER, Harold W.; SMITH, Franceska. *Developing and adult education
        program through community linkages: an approach to recruiting
        and retaining students, securing supportive services, and in-
        creasing program visibility, prestige and revenues*. Washington,
        Adult Education Association of the USA, 77, 79-2 p.
2366   BELANGER, Paul. "L'éducation des adultes au Québec ou le projet
        difficile d'une éducation permanente", *Éduc. perm.* 38, mar-apr
        77 : 43-66.
2367   BELORGEY, Jean Michel. *Recurrent education: policy and develop-
        ment in OECD member countries: France*. Paris-Washington, OECD,
        76, 30 p.
2368   BLAUG, Mark; MACE, John. "Recurrent education - the new Jerusalem",
        Higher Educ. 6(3), aug 77 : 277-299.
2369   BOTTANI, N. *et al. Recurrent education: policy and development in
        OECD member countries: Switzerland*. Paris-Washington, D.C.,
        OECD, 76, 114 p.
2370   BOWERS, C. A. "L'alphabétisation culturelle dans les pays déve-
        loppés", *Perspectives (Unesco)* 7(3), 1977 : 349-363.
2371   CAIRNS, John C. "Adult functional illiteracy in Canada", *Conver-
        gence* 10(1), 1977 : 43-52.
2372   CENTRE NATIONAL DE LA RECHERCHE SCIENTIFIQUE. Action thématique
        programmée. *Conception et contrôle d'un programme de formation*

pour adulte: mise au point d'un enseignement scientifique dans
le cadre d'un programme de formation. Paris, CNRS, 77, 142 p.

2373   CHURCHILL, Stacy. The Peruvian model of innovation: the reform of
basic education. Paris, Unesco, 76, 55 p.

2374   CLAMMER, J. R. Literacy and social change: a case study of Fiji.
Leiden, Brill, 76, xiv-218 p.

2375   "Compte-rendu de la journée d'étude sur la formation permanente,
Lyon, 12 juin 1976", B. Soc. franç. Sociol. 3(8), dec 76 : 8-43.

2376   COOK, Wanda Dauksza. Adult literacy education in the United States.
Newark, Del., International Reading Association, 77, x-139 p.

2377   DAVE, R. H. et al. (eds.). Foundations of lifelong education.
Oxford-New York, Pergamon Press, 76, vi-382 p.

2378   DÁVID, J.; KOVÁCS, F.; KASSAI VÉGH, M. A salgotarjáni munkások müveltsége és müvelödése (Workers' culture and education in the
industrial town of Salgotarjan). 3 vols. Budapest, MSZMP KB
Társadalomtudományos Intézet, 76-77, 303 p.; 340 p.; 167 p.

2379   DYMOND, William R. "Répercussion de l'élargissement des possibilités d'éducation sur les marchés de l'emploi. L'éducation permanente", Trav. et Soc. 2(3), jul 77 : 339-349.

2380   "Éducation permanente et cadre de vie", Habitat Vie soc. 20, sep-
oct 77 : 1-69.

2381   "Fins et moyens d'une éducation continue", Perspectives (Unesco)
7(2), 1977 : 246-322.

2382   GROOTHOFF, Hans-Hermann. Erwachsenenbildung und Industriegesell-
schaft: eine Einführung in Geschichte, Theorie und Praxis der
Erwachsenenbildung in der Bundesrepublik (Adult education and
industrial society: an introduction to history, theory and application of the adult education in the Federal Republic). Pader-
born, Schöningh, 76, 352 p.

2383   GROSSENBACHER, J.-P. "Alphabétisation fonctionnelle des membres
des groupements villageois du Bourgou", Dritte Welt 4(3-4), 4
trim 76 : 391-404. [Bénin.]

2384   HANSEN, Berrit. Recurrent education: policy and development in
OECD member countries: Denmark. Paris-Washington, D.C., OECD,
76, 33 p.

2385   HEIN, Roland. Gewerkschaften und Weiterbildung am Beispiel Frankreich (Trade unions and continuing education by the example of
France). Meisenheim-am-Glan, Hain, 77, 266 p.

2386   HERRERA V., J. "Educación de adultos en Guatemala" (Adult education
in Guatemala), Guatemala indíg. 8(1), jan-mar 73 : 23-32.

2387   KANDA, Michiko. "Shôgai Kyôiku no gendankai - fujin kyoiku no shi-
kaku" (The present state of life-long integrated education - from
the viewpoint of women's education), Nihon Shakai-kyoiku gakukai
Kiyô 13, 1977 : 15-20.

2388   KIYOHARA, Keiko. "Toshi no shufu no hôsô riyo gakushu ni kansuru
ichi-kosatsu" (A study of the education of housewives through
television), Shinbun Kenkyûjo Nenpô (9), 1977 : 73-93.

2389   LESNE, Marcel. Travail pédagogique et formation d'adultes: éléments
d'analyse. Paris, Presses universitaires de France, 77, 185 p.

2390   LOWE, John. L'éducation des adultes: perspectives mondiales. Paris, Presses de l'Unesco, 76, 251 p.

2391   MAINDIVE, Jean-Pierre. Le droit des travailleurs à la formation
permanente. Paris, Économie et humanisme; Éditions ouvrières,
76, 296 p.

2392   MAZERES, Jean-Arnaud; CABANIS, André (eds.). La formation continue
enjeu de société. Toulouse, Privat, 76, 498 p.

2393   MONTLIBERT, Christian DE. "L'éducation permanente et la promotion
des classes moyennes", Sociol. Trav. 19(3), jul-sep 77 : 243-
265.

2394   PORCHER, Louis; MARIET, François. Media et formation d'adultes.
Paris, Éditions ESF, 76, 129 p.

2395   SIEBERT, Horst (ed.). *Praxis und Forschung in der Erwachsenen-*
bildung (Practice and research in adult education). Opladen,
Westdeutscher Verlag, 77, 232 p.

2396   ROGERS, Alan (ed.). *The spirit and the form: essays in adult edu-*
cation by and in honour of Professor Harold Wiltshire. Nottingham, Department of Adult Education, University of Nottingham,
76, 7-159 p.

2397   SINKINS, T. "Recurrent education: some economic issues", *Higher*
Educ. 5(4), nov 76 : 363-376.

2398   VAN VOORDEN, W. "Werk en wederkerend onderwijs" (Work and recurrent education), *Beleid en Mij* 3(11), nov 76 : 294-299.

13970. Civic education. Technical education
Instruction civique. Enseignement technique

2399   ASTER, H. "A philosophical commentary on the Canadianization of
political education", *Canad. J. polit. soc. Theory* 1(1), 1977 :
119-126.

2400   DEXTER, Beverly Liebherr. *Special education and the classroom*
teacher: concepts, perspectives, and strategies. Springfield,
Ill., Thomas, 77, xiv-256 p.

2401   GRAPIN, Pierre. "Insertion professionnelle et système d'enseignement: le cas de l'enseignement technologique", *Orientat. scol.*
profes. 6(2), apr-jun 77 : 161-187.

2402   LÉON, Antoine; CHASSIGNAT, Annie. *Enseignement technique et forma-*
tion permanente. Paris, Éditions ESF, 76, 148 p.

2403   NALLETAMBY, Philippe. "Comparative issues and data concerning
science and technical education in some African countries",
Afr. Develop. 1(3), 1976 : 54-63.

2404   TAPPER, Ted. *Political education and stability. Elite responses to*
political conflict. London, J. Wiley, 76, x-265 p.

13980. Academic achievement. School failure
Réussite des études. Échec scolaire

[See also / Voir aussi: 2288]

2405   CAMPIOLI, G. "Enfants migrants et réussite scolaire. Les exceptions"
Rech. sociol. 8(2), 1977 : 245-273.

2406   DeBORD, Larry W. "The achievement syndrome in lower-class boys",
Sociometry 40(2), jun 77 : 190-196.

2407   DRENTH, Pieter J. D. "Prediction of school performance in developing countries: school grades or psychological tests ?", *J.*
cross-cult. Psychol. 8(1), mar 77 : 49-70.

2408   GILBERT, Sid; McROBERTS, Hugh A. "Academic stratification and education plans: a reassessement", *Canad. R. Sociol. Anthropol.*
14(1), feb 77 : 34-47.

2409   HENDERSON, Vernon; MIESZKOWSKI, Peter; SAUVAGEAU, Yvon. *Peer group*
effects and educational production functions. Ottawa, Publications Supply and Services Canada, 76, vii-78 p.

2410   HITCHCOCK, Dale C.; OLIVER, Lincoln I. *Intellectual development*
and school achievement of youths 12-17 years: demographic and
socioeconomic factors. Rockville, Md., United States Government
Printing Office, 76, vii-65 p.

2411   KERCKHOFF, Alan C. "The realism of educational ambitions in England
and the United States", *Amer. sociol. R.* 42(4), aug 77 : 563-
571.

2412   LURÇAT, Liliane. *L'échec et le désintérêt scolaire à l'école pri-*
maire. Paris, Éditions du Cerf, 76, 152 p.

2413   MADDOCK, John. "Academic stratification and the sustaining of
identity types", *Sociol. R.* 25(3), aug 77 : 575-584.

2414   McPARTLAND, James M.; EPSTEIN, Joyce L. "Open schools and achievement: extended tests of a finding of no relationship", *Sociol.*
Educ. 50(2), apr 77 : 133-144.

13990. Pedagogy. Teaching. Teacher
Pédagogie. Enseignement. Enseignant

13991.

[See also / Voir aussi: 1096, 2271, 2362]

2415   BHOLA, H. S. *Diffusion of educational innovation.* Morristown,
N.J., General Learning Press, 77, xvi-29 p.

2416   BORICH, Gary D.; FENTON, Kathleen S. *The appraisal of teaching:
concepts and process.* Reading, Mass., Addison-Wesley Publishing
Co., 77, xvi-396 p.

2417   CAMBI, Franco. *La ricerca in pedagogia: fondamenti e strutture
delle scienze dell'educazione* (Educational research: bases and
structures of educational sciences). Firenze, Le Monnier, 76,
115 p.

2418   DAVIS, Robert Harlan; ABEDOR, Allan J.; WITT, Paul W. F. *Commitment to excellence: a case study of educational innovation.* East
Lansing, Educational Development Program, Michigan State University, 76, x-189 p.

2419   GIRARD, Victor. "L'équipe pluridisciplinaire en institution socio-
éducative. Réflexion sur un exemple de fonctionnement en inter-
nat d'adolescents", *Connexions* 22, 1977 : 81-95.

2420   GOSTKOWSKI, Zygmut. "'Czas smarnowany' w toku studiów na wybranych
kierunkach Uniwersytetu Łodzkiego" (Time wasted in the course of
studies at selected specializations of the University of Łodz),
Przegl. socjol. 29, 1977 : 219-240.

2421   HORAN, Patrick M.; SMAPSON, Gregory B. "The structure of university teaching: some evidence from sociology", *Amer. Sociologist*
12(1), feb 77 : 33-41.

2422   JOHNSON, Mauritz. *Intentionality in education: a conceptual model
of curricular and instructional planning and evaluation.* Albany,
Center for Curriculum Research and Services, 77, vii-264 p.

2423   LAMM, Zvi. *Conflicting theories of instruction: conceptual dimensions.* Berkeley, Calif., McCutchan Publishing Corp., 76, xii-
278 p.

2424   McNEIL, John D. *Curriculum: a comprehensive introduction.* Boston,
Little, Brown, 77, xii-333 p.

2425   McNEIL, John D. *Designing curriculum: self-instructional modules.*
Boston, Little, Brown, 76, 138 p.

2426   "Pédagogie par objectifs", *C. pédag.* 148-149, nov 76 : 9-62.

2427   RUDDUCK, Jean; KELLY, Peter. *The dissemination of curriculum development: current trends.* Ed. by Jack WRIGLEY and Freddio SPARROW.
Windsor, NFER; Atlantic Highlands, N.J., Humanities Press, 76,
111 p.

2428   VIOTTO, Piero. *Pedagogia della scuola di base* (Pedagogy of the
elementary school). Milano, Vita e pensiero, 76, 220 p.

2429   WALTON, Jack; WELTON, John (eds.). *Rational curriculum planning:
four case studies.* London, Ward Lock, 76, 172 p.

13992.

[See also / Voir aussi: 2394]

2430   ASHBY, E. "Technologie et enseignement", *Dialogue (Washington)*
7(2), 1976 : 96-106.

2431   CONTRERAS, Eduardo *et al.* *L'information audio-visuelle transculturelle.* Paris, Unesco, 76, 51 p.

2432   MAYO, John K.; HORNIK, Robert C.; McANANY, Emile G. *Educational
reform with television: the El Salvador experience.* Stanford,
Calif., Stanford University Press, 76, xi-216 p.

13993.

[See alson/ Voir aussi: 2360, 5167]

2433   "Academic profession in comparative perspective (The)", *Higher Educ.* 6(2), mai 77 : 275 p.

2434   BEILLEROT, Jacky. *Un stage d'enseignement ou la régression instituée: sociopsychanalyse et formation continue des enseignants.* Paris, Payot, 77, 278 p.

2435   BERRIDGE, Robert I.; WEST, Philip T.; STARK, Stephen L. *Training the community educator: a case-study approach.* Midland, Mich., Pendell Publishing Co., 77, ix-150 p.

2436   BISHOP, James M. "Organizational influence on the work orientations of elementary teachers", *Sociol. Wk Occupat.* 4(2), mai 77 : 171-208.

2437   BREDO, Eric. "Collaborative relations among elementary school teachers", *Sociol. Educ.* 50(4), oct 77 : 300-309.

2438   CHMIELEWSKA, Bożenna. "Społeczne i dydaktyczne aspekty dokształcania i nauczycieli" (Social and didactic aspects of the further training of teachers), *Przegl. socjol.* 29, 1977 : 275-294.

2439   CHYLIŃSKA, Helena. "Cele wychowania jako składnik samowiedzy nauczycieli" (Educational objectives as an element of teacher's self-knowledge), *Stud. socjol.* 64(1), 1977 : 139-159.

2440   FAIA, Michael. A. "Discrimination and exchange: the double burden of the female academic", *Pacific sociol. R.* 20(1), jan 77 : 3-20.

2441   JAWANDA, J. S. *In-service teacher education in Punjab.* Patiala, J. R. Publications, 76, 130 p.

2442   KERN, Horst J. *Lehrer- und Schulerverhalten: Forschungsergebnisse und Ausleitung zur Verhaltensmodifikation* (Teacher-student relationships: research results and instructions to the modification of behavior). Stuttgart-Berlin-Köln-Mainz, Kohlhammer, 76, 178 p.

2443   KOENIGS, Sharon S.; FIEDLER, Martha L.; DeCHARMS, Richard. "Teacher beliefs, classroom interaction and personal causation", *J. appl. soc. Psychol.* 7(2), apr-jun 77 : 95-114.

2444   Bibl.XXVI-1999. LORTIE, Dan C. *School-teacher: a sociological study.* CR: Blanche GEER, *Contemp. Sociol. (Washington)* 5(2), mar 76 : 169-171.

2445   MURPHY, Raymond. "Societal values and the reactions of teachers to student's backgrounds", *Canad. R. Sociol. Anthropol.* 14(1), feb 77 : 48-56. [Canada.]

2446   POSTIC, Marcel. *Observation et formation des enseignants.* Paris, Presses universitaires de France, 77, 336 p.

2447   RAGGETT, Michael; CLARKSON, Malcolm (eds.). *Changing patterns of teacher education.* London, Falmer Press; Ward Lock, 76, 2-177 p.

2448   RIDGWAY, Lorna. *Task of the teacher in the primary school.* London, Ward Lock, 76, 7-223 p.

2449   TANAKA, Yoshiaki. "Kyôshi no shakaiteki-idô - Fukuokaken kôritsu shogakkô jokyôshi no baai" (Teacher's social mobility - the case of school mistress of public elementary school in Fukuoka), *Tohôdaigaku Kyôyô Kiyô* (8), 1977 : 27-34.

2450   THIELENS, Wagner Jr. "Undergraduate definitions of learning from teachers", *Sociol. Educ.* 50(3), jul 77 : 159-181.

2451   Bibl.XXVI-2001. WILSON, Robert C. *et al. College professors and their impact on students.* CR: Richard T. CAMPBELL, *Amer. J. Sociol.* 82(4), jan 77 : 903-905.

13994.

2452   CROAKE, J. W.; GLOVER, K. E. "A history and evaluation of parent education", *Family Coordinator* 26(2), apr 77 : 151-156.

2453   VINCIGUERRA, Maria Enrica. "Appunti sul rapporto scuola-famiglia in Italia" (Notes on school-family relationships in Italy), *Sociologia (Roma)* 11(1), jan-apr 77 : 179-194.

14100. SOCIAL SYSTEM
SYSTÈME SOCIAL

[See also / Voir aussi: 684, 1190, 1273, 1341, 1385, 2125, 2568, 5187]

2454 ACHARD, Pierre et al. Discours biologique et ordre social. Paris, Seuil, 77, 283 p.

2455 ALEKSEEVA, V. M. "Metodologičeskoe značenia kategorii 'social'naja struktura'" (A methodological meaning of the "social structure" category), in: Rol' i ponjatij v social'nom issledovanii. Leningrad, 1976 : 51-60.

2456 BLAU, Peter M. (ed.). Approaches to the study of social structure. London, Open Books, 76, x-294 p. CR: Jiri KOLAJA, Brit. J. Sociol. 28(2), jun 77 : 255-257.

2457 BLAU, Peter M. "A macrosociological theory of social structure", Amer. J. Sociol. 83(1), jul 77 : 26-54.

2458 BOUDON, Raymond. Effets pervers et ordre social. Paris, Presses universitaires de France, 77, 286 p.

2459 BURNS, Tom R.; BUCKLEY, Walter (eds.). Power and control: social structures and their transformation. London, SAGE, 76, 290 p.

2460 Bibl.XXVI-2010. COSER, Louis A. (ed.). The idea of social structure: papers in honor of Robert K. Merton. CR: Raymond BOUDON, Amer. J. Sociol. 82(6), mai 77 : 1356-1361; David CAPLOVITZ, Randall COLLINS, Maurice R. STEIN, Contemp. Sociol. (Washington) 6(2), mar 77 : 142-156.

2461 DAY, Robert A.; DAY, Joanne V. "A review of the current state of negotiated order theory: an appreciation and a critique", Sociol. Quart. 18(1), 1977 : 126-142.

2462 Bibl.XXVI-2011. FABER, Bernard Lewis (ed.). The social structure of Eastern Europe: transition and process in Czechoslovakia, Hungary, Poland, Romania, and Yugoslavia. CR: Zoltán TAR, Contemp. Sociol. (Washington) 6(3), mai 77 : 381.

2463 HANIFI, M. J. "An ideal model for the analysis of socio-political processes in 'purposive' social systems", East. Anthropologist 29(4), oct-dec 76 : 353-360.

2464 HARCSA, I. "A társadalmi struktura változásainak néhány vonása, 1869-1910" (Some characteristics of the changes of social structure, 1869-1910), Statiszt. Szle 55(3), 1977 : 299-314. [Hungary.]

2465 HAYASE, Toshio. "Taiseiron ni okeru keizai to shakai" (Economy and society in the theory of social systems), Keizaigaku Kenkyu 10(1), 1977 : 95-130.

2466 HOLLAND, Paul W.; LEINHARDT, Samuel. "A dynamic model for social networks", J. math. Sociol. 5(1), 1977 : 5-20.

2467 HOLLAND, Paul W.; LEINHARDT, Samuel. "Social structure as a network process", Z. Soziol. 6(4), oct 77 : 386-402.

2468 KALINOVÁ, Lenka. "Změny sociálnínstruktury české a slovenské společnosti v letech 1945-1948" (Modifications in the social structure of the Czech and Slovak society from 1945 to 1948), Demografie 19(2), apr-jun 77 : 97-105.

2469   KILMANN, Ralph H. *Social systems design: normative theory and the MAPS design technology*. New York, North-Holland, 77, xv-327 p.

2470   KISLOV, S. A. "V. I. Lenin o social'nyh otnošenijah i social'noj strukture obščestva" (V. I. Lenin on social relations and social structure of society), in: *Voprosy marksizma i ideologičeskoj bor'by*. Petrozavodsk, 1976 : 47-58.

2471   KNOLL, R.; PELINKA, A. "L'évolution de la structure sociale en Autriche depuis 1945", *Austriaca* (3), 1976 : 45-65.

2472   LEMIEUX, Vincent. "L'articulation des réseaux sociaux", *Rech. sociogr.* 17(2), mai-aug 76 : 247-260.

2473   LINDENBERG, Siegwart. "The direction of ordering and its relation to social phenomena", *Z. Soziol.* 6(2), apr 77 : 203-221.

2474   LOOMIS, Charles Price *et al.* *Social systems: the study of sociology*. Cambridge, Mass., Schenkman Publishing Co., 76, 458 p.

2475   Bibl.XXVI-2017. LORRAIN, François. *Réseaux sociaux et classifications sociales*. CR: Claude FLAMENT, *R. franç. Sociol.* 18(2), apr-jun 77 : 331-339.

2476   LUHMANN, Niklas. "Interpretation - zum Verhältnis personaler und sozialer Systeme" (Interpretation - on the relation between personal and social systems), *Z. Soziol.* 6(1), jan 77 : 62-76.

2477   MOCULTA, S. "Vers l'homogénéisation des structures sociales en Roumanie", *Nouv. R. int.* 19(12), dec 76 : 49-63.

2476   MÜNCH, Richard. *Theorie sozialer Systeme. Eine Einführung in Grundbegriffe, Grundannahmen und logische Struktur* (Theory of social systems. An introduction to basic concepts, basic hypotheses and logical structure). Opladen, Westdeutscher Verlag, 76, 187 p. CR: Helmut WILLKE, *Kölner Z. Soziol. u. soz.-Psychol.* 29(4), dec 77 : 792-796.

2479   NOGUCHI, Takashi. "Shakai kôzô no gainen to shakaigaku no shiza" (Points of view concerning the concept of social structure), *Shakaigaku Hyôron* 27(4), 1977 : 56-62.

2480   PERNICA, Vladimír. "Systémový přístup a řízení sociálních procesů" (Systems approach and management of social processes), *Sociol. Čas.* 13(2), 1977 : 160-167.

2481   PLEHOV, A. "Razvitie social'noj struktury zrelogo socialistíčeskogo obščestva" (Development of social structure of the mature socialist society), *Kommunist vooruž. Sil* (22), 1976 : 20-30.

2482   SCHÄFERS, Bernhard. *Sozialstruktur und Wandel der Bundesrepublik Deutschland* (Social structure and change in the German Federal Republic). Stuttgart, Enke, 76, xvi-337 p.

2483   SOCKIN, S. N. "Zakonomernosti razvitija social'noj struktury socialistíčeskogo obščestva" (Laws of development of the socialist society social structure), *Filos. Nauki* 19(8), 1976 : 38-49.

2484   STARR, Paul D. "Social patterns and norms in Lebanon and the United States", *Hum. Relat.* 29(4), apr 76 : 357-366.

2485   SUSATO, Shigeru. *Gendai no shakai - kôzô to hendo* (Modern society - structure and change). Tokyo, Nihon Hyôronsha, 77, 264 p.

2486   TITTLE, Charles R. "Sanction fear and the maintenance of social order", *Soc. Forces* 55(3), mar 77 : 579-596.

2487   WHYTE, Marting King *et al.* "Social structure of world regions: Mainland China", *Ann. R. Sociol.* (3), 1977 : 179-207. *[China.]*

2488   ZAVTUR, A. A. *Social'naja struktura Moldavii. Stanovlenie social'no-politíčeskogo ědinstva* (The Moldavian social structure. The future of the socio-political unity). Kišinev, Kartja Moldovenjaskě, 77, 374 p.

14200. SOCIAL STRATIFICATION
STRATIFICATION SOCIALE

14210. Social differentiation
Différenciation sociale

[See also / Voir aussi: 2210, 2219, 2544, 2061, 2663, 2988, 3254, 3638, 3843, 4960, 4964]

2489   BORNSCHIER, Volker. "Arbeitsteilung und soziale Ungleichheit" (Division of labour and social inequality), *Kölner Z. Soziol. u. soz.-Psychol.* 29(3), sep 77 : 438-460.

2490   BRICKMAN, Philip. "Preference for inequality", *Sociometry* 40(4), dec 77 : 303-310.

2491   BROOM, Leonhard; CUSHING, Robert G. "A modest test of an immodest theory: the functional theory of stratification", *Amer. sociol. R.* 42(1), feb 77 : 157-169.

2492   BROOM, Leonhard; JONES, F. Lancaster. "Problematics in stratum consistency and stratum formation: an Australian example", *Amer. J. Sociol.* 82(4), jan 77 : 808-825.

2493   CEPEDE, Michel. "Influence des stratifications sociales sur le développement agricole et l'environnement", *Sociol. rur.* 17(1-2), 1977 : 75-86.

2494   CESSIEUX, R. *et al. Recherches sur les processus de la division du travail.* Grenoble, IREP; Paris, CORDES, 76, 175 p.

2495   CHARVÁT, František. "O jednom možném přístupu k analýze sociálních rozdílů (diferenciaci)" (Analysis of the structure of social differences - one of the possible approaches), *Sociol. Čas.* 13(4), 1977 : 403-415.

2495bis CURTIS, Richard Farnsworth; JACKSON, Elton F. *Inequality in American communities.* New York, Academic Press, 77, xii-254 p.

2496   EVAN, William M. "Hierarchy, alienation, commitment, and organizational effectiveness", *Hum. Relat.* 30(1), jan 77 : 77-94.

2497   GOLDTHORPE, John H.; BEVAN, Philippe. "The study of social stratification in Great Britain: 1946-1976", *Soc. Sci. Inform.* 16(3-4), 1977 : 279-334.

2498   GORZ, André (ed.). *The division of labour: the labour process and class-struggle in modern capitalism.* Atlantic Highlands, N.J., Humanities Press; London, Harvester Press, 76, xiv-189 p. CR: Bryn JONES, *Brit. J. Sociol.* 28(2), jun 77 : 265-267.

2499   HAUSER, Robert Mason; FEATHERMAN, David L. *The process of stratification: trends and analysis.* New York, Academic Press, 77, xxxviii-372 p.

2500   HOLZBERG, Carol S. "Social stratification, cultural nationalism, and political economy in Jamaica: the myths of development and the anti-white bias", *Canad. R. Sociol. Anthropol.* 14(4), nov 77 : 368-380.

2501   HÖRNING, Karl H. (ed.). *Soziale Ungleichheit: Strukturen und Prozesse sozialer Schichtung* (Social inequality: structures and processes of social stratification). Darmstadt, H. Luchterhand, 76, 260 p.

2502   "Inégalités, travail et changement social", *Rech. et Débats* 87, jun 77 : 258 p.

2503   KASPAROV, S. G. "Izmenenie haraktera razdelenija truda pri socializme" (Change of the division of labour character under socialism), in: *Voprosy političeskoj ěkonomii.* Dušanbe, 1976 : 117-132.

2504   KAWAI, Takao. "Kindai Nihon ni okeru shakai seiso kenkyu no seisei" (The creative studies of social stratification in modern Japan), *Hogaku Kenkyu (Tokyo)* 50(5), 1977 : 1-42.

2505   KELLEY, Jonathan; KLEIN, Herbert S. "Revolution and the rebirth of inequality: a theory of stratification in postrevolutionary society", *Amer. J. Sociol.* 83(1), jul 77 : 78-99.

2506   Bibl.XXVI-2043. KIRCHBERGER, Stefan. *Kritik der Schichtungs- und Mobilitätsforschung. Zum Verhältnis von soziologischer Theoriebildung und empirischer Sozialforschung* (Critique of stratification and mobility research. About the relationship between sociological theory formation and empirical sociological research). CR: Thomas HERZ, *Kölner Z. Soziol. u. soz.-Psychol.* 29(3), sep 77 : 595-598.

2507   KRECKEL, R. "Dimensions of social inequality - conceptual analysis and theory of society", *Sociol. Gids* 23(6), nov-dec 76 : 338-362.

2508   KUIPER, G. "Enkele opmerkingen over de relatie tussen stratificatie en mobiliteitsonderzoek" (Some remarks on the relations between stratification and mobility research), *Beleid en Mij* 30(5), mai 76 : 114-117.

2509   LAGNEAU-MARKIEWICZ, J. "La différenciation des groupes sociaux en URSS", *Docum. europ.* (6), dec 75 : 29-42.

2510   LINDENBERG, Siegwart. "Differentiation among people: Blau's revised view of sociology", *Mens en Mij* 52(3), 1977 : 301-323.

2511   LUHMANN, Niklas. "Differentiation of society", *Canad. J. Sociol.* 2(1), 1977 : 29-53.

2512   MARTINUSSEN, Willy. *The distant democracy. Social inequality. Political resources and political influence in Norway.* London, John Wiley, 77. CR: Hannu UUSITALO, *Acta sociol.* 20(3), 1977 : 317-319.

2513   OMORUYI, Omo. "Exploring pattern of alignment in a plural society: Guyana case", *Sociologus* 27(1), 1977 : 35-63.

2514   OPPENHEIM, Felix E. "Equality, groups and quotas", *Amer. J. polit. Sci.* 21(1), feb 77 : 65-59.

2515   PHILLIPS, Derek L. "The equality debate: what does justice require ?", *Theory and Soc.* 4(2), 1977 : 247-272.

2516   POGÁNY, György. "A munkamegosztás hosszu távu fejlödési tendenciájának hatása társadalmunk szerkezetére" (Effect of long-range development trend of labour division on the structure of the Hungarian society), *Társadtud. Közl.* (3), 1977 : 83-95.

2517   POGÁNY, György. "A munkamegosztás rendszere és fogalma" (The system of the division of labour and its concept), *Társadtud. Közl.* (3), 1976 : 35-61.

2518   RESTA, Patrizia. "Stratificazione sociale, potere politico e potere economico nelle Isole Trobriand" (Social stratification, political power and economic power in the Trobriand islands), *Rass. ital. Sociol.* 18(2), apr-jun 77 : 171-219.

2519   ROSENGREN, Bernt. *Jämlikhet är frihet; dribblingar och passningar* (Equality is freedom: dribblings and passes). Stockholm, Rabén och Sjögren, 76, 196 p. [Sweden.]

2520   RUESCHEMEYER, Dietrich. "Structural differentiation, efficiency, and power", *Amer. J. Sociol.* 83(1), jul 77 : 1-25.

2521   SENJAVSKIJ, S. L. *Processy sbliženija klassov i social'nyh sloev sovetskogo obščestva v uslovijah razvitogo socializma* (Processes of bringing together of classes and social strata of the Soviet society under conditions of developed socialism). Moskva, Znanie, 77, 63 p.

2522   SINGH, Jasbir Sarjit. "Social stratification in Petaling Jaya, Malaysia", *Southeast Asian J. soc. Sci.* 2(1-2), 1974 : 75-92.

2523   SØRENSEN, Aage B. "The structure of inequality and the process of attainment", *Amer. sociol. R.* 42(6), dec 77 : 965-978.

2524   SQUIRES, Gregory M. "Education, jobs and inequality: functional and conflict models of social stratification in the United States", *Soc. Probl.* 24(4), apr 77 : 436-450.-

2525   STAFFORD, Rebecca *et al.* "The division of labor among cohabiting and married couples", *J. Marriage Family* 39(1), feb 77 : 43-57.

2526   TURNER, Stephen P. "Blau's theory of differentiation is it explanatory ?", *Sociol. Quart.* 18(1), 1977 : 17-32.

2527   VAN DEN BERGHE, Pierre L. *et al. Inequality in the Peruvian Andes: class and ethnicity in Cuzco.* Columbia, University of Missouri Press, 77, viii-324 p.-5 l.

2528   VILMOS, J. *Munkamegosztás, csere, tulajdon* (Division of labour, exchange, property). Budapest, Közgazdasági és Jogi Kiadó, 77, 214-2 p.

14220. Caste. Slavery
Caste. Esclavage

[See also / Voir aussi: 2106, 2566]

2529   BAIN, Mildred; LEWIS, Erwin (eds.). *From freedom to freedom: African roots in American soil.* New York, Random House, 77, xxi-386 p.

2530   BANGOU, Henri. *La période révolutionnaire à la Guadeloupe: l'abolition et le rétablissement de l'esclavage.* Pointe-à-Pitre, Office municipal de la culture, 76, 102 p.

2531   CARROLL, Patrick J. "Mandinga: the evolution of a Mexican runaway slave community, 1735-1827", *Comp. Stud. Soc. Hist.* 19(4), oct 77 : 488-505.

2532   CEPERO BONILLA, Raul. *Azucar y abolición* (Sugar and abolishment). Barcelona, Editorial Crítica, 76, 218 p. *[Slavery in Cuba.]*

2533   CHAUSSINAND-NOGARET, Guy. *La noblesse au XVIIIe siècle: de la féodalité aux lumières.* Paris, Hachette, 76, 239 p.

2534   CLISSOLD, Stephen. *The Barbary slaves.* London, P. Elek, 77, vii-181 p.-4 l. *[North Africa.]*

2535   COOPER, Frederick. *Plantation slavery on the east coast of Africa.* New Haven, Conn., Yale University Press, 77, xviii-314 p.

2536   CRATON, Michael; MALVIN, James; WRIGHT, David. *Slavery, abolition, and emancipation: Black slaves and the British Empire: a thematic documentary.* London-New York, Longman, 76, xiii-347 p.

2537   DAS,MMan Singh. "A cross-national study of intercaste conflict in India and the United States", *Int. J. contemp. Sociol.* 13(3-4), jul-oct 76 : 261-277.

2538   GOLDIN, Claudia Dale. *Urban slavery in the American South, 1820-1960: a quantitative history.* Chicago-London, University of Chicago Press, 76, xv-168 p.

2539   HALLIBURTON, R. Jr. *Red over Black: Black slavery among the Cherokee Indians.* Westport, Conn., Greenwood Press, 77, x-218 p.-5 l. *[USA.]*

2540   KOLSON, Martin L.; ROTBERG, Robert I. (eds.). *The African diaspora: interpretive essays.* Cambridge, Mass., Harvard University Press, 76, xiii-510 p.

2541   MIERS, Suzanne; KOPYTOFF, Igor (eds.). *Slavery in Africa: historical and anthropological perspectives.* Madison, University of Wisconsin Press, 77, xvii-474 p.

2542   MISHRA, S. N. "Caste structure and group dynamics in an Indian village", *Ind. J. Polit.* 11(1), apr 77 : 31-41. *[India.]*

2543   MORRE, Brian L. "The retention of caste notions among the Indian immigrants in British Guiana during the nineteenth century", *Comp. Stud. Soc. Hist.* 19(1), jan 77 : 96-107.

2544   Bibl.XXVI-2077. SINGH, Vijai P. *Caste, class and democracy: changes in a stratification system.* CR: Baidya Nath VARMA, *Contemp. Sociol. (Washington)* 6(4), jul 77 : 487-489.

2545   STEWART, James Brewer. *Holy warriors: the abolitionists and American slavery.* Ed. by Eric FONER. New York, Hill and Wang, 76, 226 p.

2546   SUZUKI, Jirō; YAJIMA, Tsuneyuki. "Kitakantochiho ni okeru buraku no henbo" (Changing situation of Japan's "untouchables" in Northern Kanto District), *Buraku-mondai Kenkyū* 54, 1977 : 85-110.

14230. Social class
       Classe sociale

*[See also / Voir aussi: 257, 725, 726, 796, 1196, 1207, 1474,
1566, 1708, 1766, 1769, 2225, 2301, 2393, 2406, 2498, 2521,
2544, 2752, 2794, 2947, 3042, 3156, 3311, 3506, 3533, 3540,
3573, 3624, 3803, 3890, 3896, 4099, 4245, 4250, 4307, 4437,
4615, 4701, 4764, 4775, 4783, 4898, 4955, 5062, 5159, 5424,
5425]*

2547 ACCATTATIS, Vincenzo. *Istituzioni e lotte di classe: dalla crisi
dello Stato di diritto al sorgere dello Stato assistenziale*
(Institutions and class struggle: from the crisis of State of
law to the emergence of the welfare State). Milano, Feltrinelli,
76, 147 p.

2548 ALEKSAŠENKO, A. P.; OSINSKIJ, I. I. "XXV s'ezd o vozrastanii veduš-
čej roli rabočego klassa v uslovijah razvitogo-socialističeskogo
obščestva" (The XXVth Congress on the elevation of the working
class leading role under conditions of the developed socialist
society), *Vestn. Moskov. Univ. Teorija nauč. Kommunizma* (5),
1976 : 3-14.

2549 AZAD RANA, Kipkorir Aly. "Class formation and social conflict: a
case study of Kenya", *Ufahamu* 7(3), 1977 : 17-72.

2550 BARBANO, Filippo. *Classi e struttura sociale in Italia: studi e
ricerche, 1955-1975* (Classes and social structure in Italy: studies and researches, 1955-1975). Torino, Valentino, 76, 397 p.

2551 BARTELS, Dennis. "Class conflict and racist ideology in the formation of modern Guyanese society", *Canad. R. Sociol. Anthropol.*
14(4), nov 77 : 396-405.

2552 BENEDEK, S. "Változások a magyar munkásosztály belső strukturájában" (Changes in the internal structure of the Hungarian working
class), *Társadtud. Közl.* (4), 1977 : 28-43.

2553 BEREZINA, Ju. I.; VASZILCOV, Sz. I. "A munkásosztály az olasz társadalom szociális strukturájában" (The working class in the
Italian social structure), *Elmélet és Polit.* (3), 1976 : 19-28.

2554 BERTAUX, Daniel. *Destins personnels et structures de classe. Pour
une critique de l'anthroponomie politique*. Paris, Presses universitaires de France, 77, 322 p.

2555 BLANCO MUÑOZ, Agustín. *Clases sociales y violencia en Venezuela*
(Social class and violence in Venezuela). Caracas, Universidad
central de Venezuela, Facultad de ciencias económicas y sociales,
División de publicaciones, 76, 253 p.

2556 BRANCIARD, Michel. *Société française et luttes de classes. III.
1967-1977*. Lyon, Chronique sociale de France, 77, 246 p.

2557 CERASE, Francesco Paolo; MIGNELLA CALVOSA, Fiammetta. *La nuova
piccola borghesia* (The new small bourgeoisie). Venezia, Marsilio,
76, 231 p. *[Italy.]*

2558 CHARVÁT, František. "Dělnická třida - rozhodujíci síla historické
jednoty komunismu a vědeckotechnické revoluce" (The working
class - a decisive force of the historical unity of communism a
and the scientific-technical revolution), *Sociol. Čas.* 13(3),
1977 : 241-251.

2559 CHARVAT, František; ZICH, František. "Les changements dans la
structure sociale de classe en Tchécoslovaquie", *Aperçus Écon.
tchécosl.* (2), mar 77 : 77-100.

2560 CHERKAOUI, Mohamed; LINDSEY, James. "Problèmes de mesure des classes
sociales: des indices du status aux modèles d'analyse des rapports
de classe", *R. franç. Sociol.* 18(2), apr-jun 77 : 233-270.

2561 CROSSICK, Geoffrey (ed.). *The lower middle class in Britain, 1970-
1914*. London, Croom Helm; New York, St. Martin's Press, 77, 213
p.

2562   CROUCH, Colin. *Class conflict and the industrial relations crisis. Compromise and corporatism in the policies of the British state.* London, Heinemann, 77, xviii-302 p.

2563   DASGUPTA, Satadal. "Rural class structure in India: a comparative study of prestige classes in six Punjab villages", *East. Anthropologist* 29(4), oct-dec 76 : 373-397.

2563   DE BENEDETTI, Augusto. *La classe operaia a Napoli nel primo dopoguerra* (The working class in Naples during the period following the First World War). Napoli, Guida, 76, xi-196 p.

2565   DUBAR, Claude; NASR, Salim. *Les classes sociales au Liban.* Paris, Presses de la Fondation nationale des sciences politiques, 76, xiv-364 p.

2566   DUBEMAN, Lucile. *Social inequality: class and caste in America.* Philadelphia, J. B. Lippincott, 76, 314 p. CR: Joan HUBER, *Contemp. Sociol. (Washington)* 6(2), mar 77 : 250.

2567   EISLER, Ernest; SEIFERT, Michael. "Definitions of the working class", *Marxism today* 21(11), nov 77 : 338-352.

2368   FIGUROVSKAJA, N. K. "O klassah insocial'noj strukture sovetskogo obščestva v ěkonomičeskoj literature 30-X godov" (On classes and social structure of the Soviet society in the economic literature of the thirties). in: *Soversenstvovanie social'noj struktury v razvitom sovetskom obščestve.* Moskva, 1976 : 177-226.

2569   Bibl.XXVI-2104. FORM, William H. *Blue collar stratification: autoworkers in four countries.* CR: William H. FRIEDLAND, *Contemp. Sociol. (Washington)* 6(2), mar 77 : 159-160.

2570   "Formación del proletariado industrial en México (La)" (Formation of the industrial proletariate in Mexico), *R. mexic. Cienc. polít. soc.* 21(83), jan-mar 76 : 3-326.

2571   FOUGEYROLLAS, Pierre. *La révolution prolétarienne et les impasses petites-bourgeoises.* Paris, Anthropos, 76, 294 p.

2572   FRANZ, Hans-Werner. *Klassenkampfe in Spanien heute* (Class struggle in Spain today). Frankfurt-am-Main, Verlag Marxistische Blätter, 76, 235 p.

2573   FREYSSENET, Michel; IMBERT, Françoise. *Capital sidérurgique et classe ouvrière en Lorraine: données statistiques.* Paris, Centre de sociologie urbaine, 76, 350 p.

2574   GARRO, Yakoub. "Le développement de la classe ouvrière en Syrie", *Nouv. R. int.* 20(10), oct 77 : 172-184.

2575   GILLY, A. "Ideologia nazionalista e organizzazione di classe in Argentina" (Nationalist ideology and class organization in Argentina), *Polit. int. (Milano)* (2), feb 77 : 27-36.

2576   GLEZERMAN, G. E. *Klassy i nacii* (Classes and nations). Moskva, Politizdat, 77, 174 p.

2577   GRANOU, André. *La bourgeoisie financière au pouvoir et la lutte de classes en France.* Paris, F. Maspéro, 77, 306 p.

2578   GRUNDMANN, Siegfried; LÖTSCH, Manfred; WEIDIG, Rudi. *Zur Entwicklung der Arbeiterklasse und ihrer Struktur in der DDR* (Development of the working class and its structure in the GDR). Berlin, Dietz, 76, 295 p.

2579   GUTMAN, Herbert George. *Work, culture, and society in industrializing America: essays in American working class and social history.* New York, Vintage Books, 77, xiv-343-xvi p.

2580   HAUG, Wolfgang Fritz Haug. "Zwei Kapitel über ideologischen Klassenkampf" (Two chapters on ideological class struggle), *Argument* 18(100), nov-dec 76 : 905-935.

2581   HEILBRONER, R. "Middle class myths-middle class realities", *Atlantic* 238(4), oct 76 : 37-42. [USA.]

2582   HELMICH, Ursula. *Arbeitskämpfe in Frankreich. Ein Beitrag zur Sozial- und Rechtsgeschichte, 1789-1939* (Class struggles in France: a contribution to the social and juridical history, 1789-1939). Meisenheim-am-Glan, A. Hain, 77, x-351 p.

2583 HOPKINS, Nicholas S. "The emergence of class in a Tunisian town", *Int. J. Mid. East Stud.* 8(4), oct 77 : 453-491. *[Testow.]*

2584 HUTBER, Patrick. *The decline and the fall of the middle class, and how it can fight back.* London, Associated Business Programmes, 76, 184 p. *[UK.]*

2585 IANNI, Octavio. *A classe operaria vai ao campo* (The working class goes to the country). São Paulo, Editora brasiliense, 76, 63 p.

2586 ICKENSAFA, H. "Class consciousness among working class women in Latin America. A case study in Puerto Rico", *Polit. and Soc.* 5(3), 1975 : 377-394.

2587 ISHIKAWA, Akihiro. "'Atarashii rôdôsha kaikyu' (What is the "new working class" ?), *Gendai to Shiso* 27, 1977 : 192-198.

2588 IVANOV, G. I. "Ot otricanija revoljucionnosti rabočego klassa k 'revoljucii institutov'" (From the negation of the working class revolutionary character to the revolution of instincts), in: *Social'naja filosofija Frankfurtskoj Školy (kritičeskie očerki).* Moskva-Praga, 1975 : 161-171.

2589 JAGUIN, Aureliano. *Il geroglifico sociale: forze produttive e strutture di classe in Marx* (The social hieroglyph: productive forces and class structures in Marx). Bari, Dedalo libri, 76, 461 p.

2590 JOHNSON, Terry. "What is to be known ? The structural determination of social class", *Econ. and Soc.* mai 77 : 194-233.

2591 JOHNSTONE, Frederick A. *Class, race, and gold: a study of class relations and racial discrimination in South Africa.* London-Boston, Routledge and K. Paul, 76, xiv-298 p.

2592 KASYMOV, N. "Rabočij klass - veduščaja sila v izmenenii social'noj struktury sovetskogo obščestva" (The working class is the leading force for changing the social structure of the Soviet society), *Nauč. Trudy Taškent. Inst. nar. obšč.* 111, 1975 : 162-170.

2593 KLUEGEL, James R.; SINGLETON, Royce Jr.; STARNES, Charles E. "Subjective class identification: multiple indicator approach", *Amer. sociol. R.* 42(4), aug 77 : 599-611.

2594 KOLBE, Hellmuth *et al. Arbeiterklasse im Kapitalismus: Klassenkampf und Klassenstruktur* (The working class in capitalism: class struggle and class structure). Berlin, Staatsverlag der Deutschen Demokratischen Republik, 76, 255 p.

2595 KOLOSI, T. *A tőkés osztályviszonyok fejlödéstendenciái a Német Szövetségi Köztársaságban. Társadalmi struktura, munkástudat és szakszervezeti érdekképviselet* (Development trends of capitalist class relations in the Federal Republic of Germany. Social structure, workers' consciousness and safeguarding of interests by the trade unions). Budapest, MSZMP KB Társadalomtudományi Intézete, 77, 171 p.

2596 KONDORAKI, V. M. "Vozrastanie social'no-politiceskoj aktivnosti rabočego klassa v uslovijah razvitogo socializma" (Elevation of the working class socio-political activity under the conditions of developed socialism), in: *Nekotorye voprosy marksistsko-leninskoj filosofii i sociologii.* Kišinev, 1976 : 96-111.

2597 KOVÁCS, Ferenc. "A mai magyar munkásosztály kialakulása és jellemzöi" (Formation and characteristics of the Hungarian working class today), *Társadtud. Közl.* (1), 1977 : 47-55.

2598 KOVÁCS, Ferenc. *A munkásosztály politikai-ideológiai müveltségéröl és aktivitásáról. Az 1960-1970-es évtized tapasztalataiból* (On the political and ideological education and activity of the working class. From the experiences of the 60's). Budapest, Kossuth Kiadó, 76, 387 p. *[Hungary.]*

2599 KRAUS, Richard C. "Class conflict and the vocabulary of social analysis in China", *China Quart.* 69, mar 77 : 54-74.

2600 KRUYT, Dirk; VELLINGA, Menno. "Klasse en klassenbewustzijn. Concepten en paradigma's bij klassieke marxisten" (Class and class consciousness. Concepts and paradigms among classical marxists), *Sociol. Gids* 24(3), mai-jun 77 : 167-180.

2601   KUBIK, István. "Társadalmi szerkezet és osztályfejlödés a mai
        Egyiptomban" (Social mechanism and class development in today's
        Egypt), *Valóság* (9), 1976 : 47-57.

2602   KYNASTON, David. *King Labour: the British working class 1850-1914*.
        London, Allen and Unwin, 76, 184 p.2603

2603   LACALLE, Daniel. *Técnicos, científicos y clases sociales* (Techni-
        cians, scientists and social classes). Barcelona, Ediciones
        Guadarrama, 76, 160 p.

2604   LASO, P. "Perspectivas de las clases sociales en España" (Pros-
        pects of social classes in Spain), *Razón y Fe* 950, mar 77 : 242-
        251.

2605   LAZREG, Marnia. *The emergence of classes in Algeria: a study of co-
        lonialism and socio-political change*. Boulder, Colo., Westview
        Press, 76, xv-252 p.

2606   LINHART, Sepp. *Arbeit, Freizeit und Familia in Japan: eine Unter-
        suchunq der Lebensweise von Arbeitern und Anqestellten in Gross-
        betrieben* (Work, leisure and family in Japan: a study of life
        style among workers and employees in big enterprises). Wiesbaden,
        Harrassowitz, 76, 418 p.

2607   LOGAN, John R. "Affluence, class structure, and working-class
        consciousness in modern Spain", *Amer. J. Sociol.* 83(2), sep 77 :
        386-402.

2608   LOREN, Charles. *Classes in the United States: workers against ca-
        pitalists*. Davis, Calif., Cardinal Publishers, 77, 296 p.

2609   MANGHEZI, Alpheus. *Class, elite, and community in African deve-
        lopment*. Uppsala, Scandinavian Institute of African Studies;
        Stockholm, Almqvist och Wiksell, 76, 118 p.

2610   MATSUMURA, Naoko. "Gendai no kaikyû-kaiso to sono seikatsu mondai"
        (Class composition and life problems in contemporary society),
        Ôtani Gakuhô 57(2), 1977 : 36-53.

2611   McDANIEL, Tim. "Class and dependency in Latin America", *Berkeley
        J. Sociol.* 21, 1976-77 : 51-88.

2612   MIKUL'SKIJ, K. I. *Klassovaja struktura obščestva v stranah socia-
        lizma* (The class structure of society in socialist countries).
        Moskva, Nauka, 76, 279 p.

2613   MITCHELL, David F.; PRATTO, David J. "Social class, familism, in-
        terest in children, and childbearing: a preliminary test of a
        'commitment' model of fertility", *Soc. Biology* 24(1), 1977 : 17-
        30.

2614   MOČALOV, A. M. (ed.). *Rabocij klass - veduščaja social'naja sila
        sovetskogo obščestva* (Working class, the leading social force of
        Soviet society). Moskva, 76, 219 p.

2615   MONICH, Z. I. "The industrial component of the rural working class",
        Sov. Sociol. 15(2), 1976 : 3-16.

2616   MORELLI, Ugo. *Classi e movimenti migratori* (Classes and migratory
        movements). Roma, Coines, 76, 100 p. *[Italy.]*

2617   MOURIAUX, René. "Évolutions de la classe ouvrière", *Projet* 120,
        dec 77 : 1213-1222. *[France.]*

2618   Bibl.XXVI-1486. MURASKIN, William Alan. *Middle class blacks in a
        white society*. CR: Ira KATZNELSON, *Amer. J. Sociol.* 82(5), mar
        77 : 1123-1125.

2619   NASH, Irene; SAFA, Helen Icken (eds.). *Sex and class in Latin Amer-
        ica*. New York, Praeger, 76, xiv-330 p.

2620   NEUMANN, Michael. *Methode der Klassenanalyse. Untersuchungen zu
        einem Problem der marxistischen Soziologie* (Method of class
        analysis. Studies on a problem of Marxist sociology). Frankfurt-
        am-Main, Europäische Verlagsanstalt, 76, 209 p.

2621   NÖRLUND, I. "La démocratie et la lutte des classes au Danemark",
        Nouv. R. int. 19(21), dec 76 : 149-160.

2622   PARANHOS, A. "Consciência de classe e consciência possível: refle-
        xões para o estudo da consciência operária" (Class consciousness

and possible consciousness: thought for a study of workers' consciousness), *Vozes* 70(8), oct 76 : 5-28. *[About the concept of class consciousness in G. Lukács' and L. Goldmann's works.]*

2623   "Peru: bourgeois revolution and class struggle", *Latin Amer. Perspect.* 4(3), 1977 : 2-159.

2624   PESTKOVSKAJA, Ê. S. "Êvolucija klassovoj struktury v period 'stabil'nogo' razvitija" (Evolution of the class structure in period of stable development), *Latinsk. Amer.* 8(2), mar-apr 77 : 46-61. *[Mexico.]*

2625   PETRAS, J. F. "Class and politics in the periphery and the transition to socialism", *R. radic. polit. Econ.* 8(2), 1976 : 20-35.

2626   "Puerto Rico: class struggle and national liberation", *Latin Amer. Perspect.* 3(3), 1976 : 3-152.

2627   PULLMAN, D. R.; LOREE, D. J. "Conceptions of class and the Canadian setting", *Int. J. comp. Sociol.* 17(3-4), sep-dec 76 : 164-182.

2628   QUIJANO, Anibal. *Clase obrera en América Latina* (Working classes in Latin America). San José, Ciudad Universitaria Rodrigo Facio, Editorial Universitaria Centroamericana, 76, 101 p.

2629   RAZUVAEVA, N. N. "Novye popolnenija rabočego klassa SSSR v period razvitogo socialisticeskogo obščestva" (The renewal of working class in the USSR at the time of the developed socialist society), *Vestn. Moskov. Univ. Ser. Ist.* 32(5), sep-oct 77 : 61-75.

2630   RECLIFT, M. R. "Agrarian class structure and the State: the case of coastal Ecuador", *Bol. Estud. latino-amer.* 21, dec 76 : 16-31.

2631   REID, Ivan. *Social class differences in Britain.* London, Open Books, 76, xvi-266 p.

2632   RÓZSA, Klára. "A szovjet munkásosztály képzettségének fejlődése" (Development of the formation of the Soviet working class), *Tájékoztató* (4), 1976 : 127-139.

2633   RUBIN, Lillian Breslow. *World of pain: life in the working-class family.* New York, Basic Books, 76, xii-268 p. CR: Kathleen McCOURT, *Amer. J. Sociol.* 83(3), nov 77 : 813-816.

2634   SELINSKAJA, V. M.; SEMENOV, V. S. "Nekotorye voprosy metodologii istoriceskogo issledovanija izmenenij klassovoj struktury sovetskogo obščestva" (Some questions of historical research methodology on the changes of the Soviet society class structure), in: *Voprosy metodologii i istorii istoriceskoj nauki.* Moskva, 1977 : 60-79.

2635   ŠILOBOD, M. I.; PETRUHIN, A. S. "Stiranie klassovyh razlicij v obraze zizni sovetskih ljudej v uslovijah razvitogo socializma" (The retirement of class differences in the Soviet men's way of life under conditions of developed socialism), *Nauč. Trudy Kursk. pedag. Inst.* (7), 1976 : 31-49.

2636   ŠLAJEŠTAJN, Jozef. "O razvitii klassovoj struktury buržuaznogo obščestva" (About the development of class structure of bourgeois society), *Kommunist (Moskva)* 54(5), mar 77 : 96-114. *[Germany, FR.]*

2637   STEPANJAN, Ê. H. "O sootnošenii klassovogo i nacional'nogo v revoljucionnom procese" (On the correlation of class and national aspects in the revolutionary process), *Nauč. Dokl. vysš. Školy nauč. Kommunizma* (6), 1976 : 76-83.

2638   STEVENSON, Paul. "Class and left-wing radicalism", *Canad. R. Sociol. Anthropol.* 14(3), aug 77 : 269-284.

2639   STRAUTIN', A. I. "O formirovanii i razvitii socialisticeskogo obraza zizni rabočego klassa" (On formation and development of the working class socialist way of life), *Probl. nauč. Uprav. social. Obšč.* (3), 1976 : 105-123.

2640   TAYLOR, K. W.; WISEMAN, Nelson. "Class and ethnic voting in Winnipeg; the case of 1941", *Canad. R. Sociol. Anthropol.* 14(2), mai 77 : 174-187.

2641   TEZANOS, José Félix. "Aproximación al estudio de las clases sociales en el campo español" (Approach to the study of social classes in the Spanish countryside), *Sistema* 19, jul 77 : 83-102.

2642   THIAM, H. "De la classe bourgeoise au Sénégal: implications internes et externes", *Ethiopiques* (8), oct 76 : 4-12.

2643   TIMOFEJEV, T. T. "Dělicka trída - těžiště epochy zahájené Velkým říjnem" (Working class - core of the epoch initiated by the Great October Revolution), *Sociol. Čas.* 13(5), 1977 : 455-466.

2644   TRIMIÑO VERGARA, Eddy. "La clase obrera cubana en vísperas de la revolución" (Cuban working class just before the revolution), *Islas* 54, mai-aug 76 : 27-53.

2645   TURNER, Bryan S. "Class solidarity and system integration", *Sociol. Anal. (San Antonio)* 38(4), 1977 : 345-358.

2646   VANNEMAN, Reeve. "The occupational composition of American classes: results from cluster analysis", *Amer. J. Sociol.* 82(4), jan 77 : 783-807.

2647   VANNEMAN, Reeve; PAMPEL, Fred C. "The American perception of class and status", *Amer. sociol. R.* 42(3), jun 77 : 422-437.

2648   VASCONI, Tomás Amadeo. "Educación y lucha de clases: la experiencia chilena" (Education and class struggle: Chilean experience), *R. Univ. industr. Santander* 8(8), jul 77 : 59-70.

2649   VENŽER, V. G. "Problema polnogo izživanija klassovyh različij" (Problem of complete elimination of class differences), in: *Metodologičeskie problemy issledovanija ěkonomiki razvitogo socializma.* Moskva, 1976 : 210-219.

2650   VOROŽEJKIN, I. F.; SENJAVSKIJ, S. L. *Rabočij klass - veduščaja sila sovetskogo obščestva (voprosy metodologii i istoriografii)* (The working class is the leading force of Soviet society. Methodological and historiographical questions). Moskva, Mysl', 77, 374 p.

2651   Bibl.XXVI-2165. WESTERGAARD, John; RESLER, Henrietta. *Class in a capitalist society: a study of contemporary Britain.* CR: Colin CROUCH, *Amer. J. Sociol.* 83(3), nov 77 : 785-787; Frank PARKIN, *Brit. J. Sociol.* 28(1), mar 77 : 102-103; Rochelle FELDMAN, *Contemp. Sociol. (Washington)* 6(2), mar 77 : 251; Leo KRAMER, *J. econ. Liter.* 15(2), jun 77 : 509-510.

2652   WHITE, Gordon. *The politics of class and class origin: the case of the Cultural Revolution.* Canberra, Contemporary China Center, Australian National University, 76, viii-97 p. [China.]

2653   WOLTERS, W. G. *Klasseverhoudingen en politieke processen in Centraal Luzon, Filippijnen* (Class relations and political processes in Central Luzon, Philippines). Amsterdam, Universiteit van Amsterdam, 76, x-386 p.

2654   WRIGHT, Erik Olin; PÉRRONE, Luca. "Marxist class categories and income inequality", *Amer. sociol. R.* 42(1), feb 77 : 32-55.

2655   YOUNG, Philip A.; COCHRANE, Raymond. "Success values and social class: a test of the value stretch hypothesis in Britain", *Int. J. comp. Sociol.* 18(3-4), sep-dec 77 : 280-293.

2656   ŽIVANOV, S. "Sovjetska radnička klasa" (The Soviet working class), *Socijalizam* 20(1), jan 77 : 105-124.

14240. Status

[See also / Voir aussi: 1492, 1720, 2647, 3563, 3899, 4640, 4704, 4707, 5159]

2657   BAKER, Paul Morgan. "On the use of psycho-physical methods in the study of social status: a replication, and some theoretical problems", *Soc. Forces* 55(4), jun 77 : 898-920.

2658   BERGER, Joseph *et al. Status characteristics and social interaction: an expectation-states approach.* New York, Elsevier, 77, xi-196 p.

2659   BIELBY, William T.; HAUSER, Robert M.; FEATHERMAN, David L. "Response errors of black and nonblack males in models of the intergenerational transmission of socioeconomic status", *Amer. J. Sociol.* 82(6), mai 77 : 1242-1288.

2660   BORGSTRÖM, Bengt-Erik. "On rank and hierarchy: status in India and elsewhere", *Archiv. eruop. Sociol.* 18(2), 1977 : 325-334.

2661   BORNSCHIER, Volker; HEINTZ, Peter. "Statusinkonsistenz und Shichtung: eine Erweiterung der Statusinkonsistenztheorie" (Status inconsistency and stratification - an extension of status in consistency theory), *Z. Soziol.* 6(1), jan 77 : 29-48.

2662   BURAWOY, Michael. "Social structure, homogenization, and 'the process of status attainment in the United States and Great Britain'", *Amer. J. Sociol.* 82(5), mar 77 : 1031-1056.

2663   BURT, Ronald S. "Positions in multiple network systems. I. A general conception of stratification and prestige in a system of actors cast as a social topology. II. Stratification and prestige among elite decision-makers in the community of Altneustadt", *Soc. Forces* 56(1), sep 77 : 106-131; 56(2), dec 77 : 551-575.

2664   COBAS, José A. "Status consciousness and leftism: a study of Mexican-American adolescents", *Soc. Forces* 55(4), jun 77 : 1028-1042.

2665   COSBY, Arthur G.; THOMAS, John K.; FALK, William W. "Patterns of early adult status attainment and attitudes in the nonmetropolitan South", *Sociol. Wk Occupat.* 3(4), nov 76 : 411-428.

2666   ENGELS, Hans-Joachim. *Status und nonverbales Verhalten* (Social status and nonverbal behaviour). Köln, Hanstein, 76, 256 p.

2667   FLEISHMAN, John; MARWELL, Gerald. "Status congruence and associativeness: a test of Galtung's theory", *Sociometry* 40(1), 1977 : 1-11.

2668   HORNUNG, Carlton A. "Social status, status inconsistency and psychological stress", *Amer. sociol. R.* 42(4), aug 77 : 623-638.

2669   JOHNES, Frank E. "Social origins in four professions: a comparative study", *Int. J. comp. Sociol.* 17(3-4), sep-dec 76 : 143-163. *[Canada, Sweden, Australia.]*

2670   KEATING, Caroline F.; MAZUR, Allan; SEGALL, Marshall H. "Facial gestures which influence the perception of status", *Sociometry* 40(4), dec 77 : 374-378.

2671   MURPHY, Richard W. *Status and conformity.* New York, Time-Life Books, 76, 176 p.

2672   NIJHOF, Gerhard. "Opvattingen over de persoonlijke maatschappelijke positie van arbeiders" (Considerations on the personal social position of workers), *Sociol. Gids* 24(5), sep-oct 77 : 352-356.

2673   PARCEL, Toby Lee; COOK, Karen S. "Status characteristics, reward allocation, and equity", *Sociometry* 40(4), dec 77 : 311-324.

2674   SHAPIRO, E. Gary. "The estimation of task performance and reward recommendations as a function of status ranks", *Sociol. Focus* 10(2), apr 77 : 189-198.

2675   STARNES, C. E.; SINGLETON, R. Jr. "Objective and subjective status inconsistency: a search for empirical correspondence", *Sociol. Quart.* 18(2), 1977 : 253-266.

2676   TROW, Donald B. "Status equilibration; fueled by uncertainty, frustration, or anxiety ?", *Hum. Relat.* 30(8), aug 77 : 721-736.

2677   WILKINSON, Doris Yvonne; TAYLOR, Roland Lewis. *The Black male in America: perspectives on his status in contemporary society.* Chicago, Nelson-Hall, 77, viii-375 p.

14250. Elite. Intellectual
       Élite. Intellectuel

[See also / Voir aussi: 58, 1332, 1770, 1957, 1966, 2609, 3909, 3927, 4969]

2678   ALATAS, Syed Hussein. *Intellectuals in developing societies*. London, F. Cass, 77, xvi-130 p.

2679   BARRIS, Alexandre DE S.C. "A formaçâo das elites e a continuaçâo da construçâo do Estado nacional brasileiro" (The training of elites and the continuation of Brazilian national state building), *Dados* 15, 1977 : 101-122.

2680   Bibl.XXVI-2192. CLEMENT, Wallace. *The Canadian corporate elite: analysis of economic power.* CR: John L. McMULLAN, *Brit. J. Sociol.* 28(1), mar 77 : 116-117.

2681   CONNELL, R. W. *Ruling class, ruling culture: studies of conflict, power, and hegemony in Australian life.* Cambridge, Eng.-New York, Cambridge University Press, 77, xii-250 p.

2682   CORDOVA, Abraham. "The romantic cénacle: an intellectual coterie in search of status", *Archiv. europ. Sociol.* 18(2), 1977 : 335-355.

2683   "Crise dans la tête (La)", *Arc* 70, 1977 : 103 p. [Place de l'intellectuel dans la société française.]

2684   GELLA, Aleksander (ed.). *The intelligentsia, and the intellectuals.* London, Sage, 76, 235 p.

2685   GERTH, Hans H. *Bürgerliche Intelligenz um 1800. Zur Soziologie des deutschen Frühliberalismus* (Bourgeois intelligentsia about 1800, Sociology of the early liberalism in Germany). Ed. by Ulrich HERRMANN. Göttingen, Vandenhoeck und Ruprecht, 76, 155 p.

2686   HAMAGUCHI, Haruhiko. *Nihon no chishikijin to shakai-undo* (Japanese intellectuals and social movements). Tokyo, Jichosha, 77, 244 p.

2687   HIGLEY, John; FIELD, G. Lowell; GRØHOLT, Knut. *Elite structure and ideology: a theory with applications to Norway.* New York, Columbia University Press, 76, 367 p. CR: Inger J. SAGATUN, *Contemp. Sociol. (Washington)* 6(2), mar 77 : 210-211.

2688   HUSZÁR, T. *Fejezetek az értelmiseg történetéböl* (Chapters from the history of the intellectual class), Budapest, Gondolat, 77, 565 p.

2689   HUSZÁR, T. "Szellemi munkások, értelmiségiek, diplomások" (Brain-workers, intellectuals, professional men), *Társad. Szle* (1), 1977 : 36-49.

2690   IOSOFOVA, M. M. "O roli intelligencii v demokratičeskoj i socialističeskoj revoljucii" (On the intelligentsia role in democratic and socialist revolution), *Iz Ist. sov. Kul't. kul't.-prosvet. Raboty* (2), 1975 : 3-19.

2691   LAUMANN, Edward O.; MARSDEN, Peter V.; GALASKIEWICZ, Joseph. "Community-elite influence structures: extension of a network approach", *Amer. J. Sociol.* 83(3), nov 77 : 594-631.

2692   LÖWENTHAL, Richard. "Die Intellektuellen zwischen Gesellschaftswandel und Kulturkrise" (The intellectuals between social change and cultural crisis), *Schweiz. Mh.* 57(2), mai 77 : 123-136.

2693   LUDZ, Peter C. "Ideology, intellectuals, and organization: the question of their interrelation in early 19th century society", *Soc. Res.* 44(2), 1977 : 260-307.

2694   MALIK, Yogendra K. "North Indian intellectuals: perceptions and images of modernization", *Asian Stud.* 13(2), aug 75 : 55-78.

2695   MALIK, Yogendra K. "North Indian intellectuals: perceptions of their role and status", *Asian Surv.* 17(6), jun 77 : 565-580.

2696   MARKIEWICZ-LAGNEAU, J. "La fin de l'intelligentsia ? Formation et transformation de l'intelligentsia soviétique", *R. Et. comp. Est-Ouest* 7(4), dec 76 : 7-71.

2697   MISTRORIGO, L. "Gli intelettuali e la società italiana oggi" (The intellectuals and the present Italian society), *Civitas (Roma)* 27(11-12), nov-dec 76 : 5-22.

2698   MÓDRA, L. *Az értelmiség falun* (Intellectuals living in villages). Budapest, MSZMP KB Társadalomtudományi Intézet, 77, 149 p. [Hungary.]

2699   NÉMETH, J. *A müszaki értelmiség társadalmunkban* (The technical intelligentsia in our society). Budapest, Kossuth Kiadó, 77, 159-6 p. [Hungary.]

2700   RICCAMBONI, Gianni. "Regioni: una nuova classe politica ?" (Regions: a new political class), *Riv. Sociol.* 14(1-3), jan-dec 76 : 107-178. [Italy.]

2701   ROZENBERG, C. R. "Integracija nauki i proizvodstvom i izmenenija v struktura naučno-tehničeskoj intelligencii" (Integration of science with production and changes in the structure of the scientific and technical intelligentsia), *Filos. Nauki* 19(8), 1976 : 25-38.

2702   TEPPERMAN, Lorne. "Effects of the demographic transition upon access to the Toronto elite", *Canad. R. Sociol. Anthropol.* 14(3), aug 77 : 285-293.

2703   TÓTH-SIKORA, G. *A müszaki értelmiség helyzete, müveltsége, müvelödése* (The situation, culture and education of the technical intelligentsia). Budapest, SZEKI, 76, 109 p. [Hungary.]

2704   WALTER, Just. *Drie generaties museumbeheer, 1890-1930-1970. Een sociologisch onderzoek naar een wulturele elite* (Three generations in museum administration, 1890-1930-1970. A sociological research on a cultural elite). Amsterdam, Boekmanstichting, 76, 97 p.

2705   WEINGROD, Alex; GUREVITCH, Michael. "Who are the Israeli elites ?", *Jew. J. Sociol.* 19(1), jun 77 : 67-77.

14260. Social mobility
Mobilité sociale

[See also / Voir aussi: 2261, 2449, 2506, 2508, 5670]

2706   ANDORKA, Rudolf; ILLÉS, J. "A nemzedékek közötti társadalmi mobilitás változásai" (Changes in social mobility between generations), *Statiszt. Szle* 54(10), oct 76 : 933-950; 54(11), nov 76 : 1045-1055.

2707   BERNARD, Paul; GARON-AUDY, Muriel; RENAUD, Jean (éds.). "La mobilité sociale: pour qui ? pour quoi ?", *Sociol. et Soc.* 8(2), oct 76 : 1-156.

2708   BOGNÁR, László; SIMÓ, Tibor. *Termelöszövetkezeti vezetök társadalmi mobilitása* (Social mobility of the managers of production cooperatives). Budapest, SZÖVORG, 75, 249 p.

2709   BOUCHARD, Gérard. "L'histoire de la population et l'étude de la mobilité sociale au Saguenay, XIXe et XXe siècles", *Rech. sociogr.* 17(3), sep-dec 76 : 353-372. [Canada.]

2710   BROOM, Leonard; McDONNEL, Patrick. "Current research on social mobility: an inventory", *Sociol. contemp.* 22(1-3), 1974 : 354-391.

2711   CHARVÁT, Frantisek; LINHART, Jiri; VEČERNIK, Jiri. "W sprawie badań nad ruchliwością społeczna w społeczenstwie socjalistycznym" (Research on social mobility in socialist society), *Stud. socjol.* 60(1), 1976 : 115-133.

2712   DOBSON, Richard B. "Mobility and stratification in the Soviet Union", *Ann. R. Sociol.* (3), 1977 : 297-329.

2713   GIROD, Roger. *Inégalité - inégalités: analyse de la mobilité sociale.* Paris, Presses universitaires de France, 77, 184 p.

2714   GOLDTHORPE, John H.; LLEWELLYN, Catriona. "Class mobility: intergenerational and worklife patterns", *Brit. J. Sociol.* 28(3), sep 77 : 269-302.

2715   GOLDTHORPE, John H.; LLEWELLYN, Catriona. "Class mobility in modern

Britain: three theses examined", *Sociology (London)* 11(2), mai 77 : 257-288.

2716 McCANN, James C. "A theoretical model for the interpretation of tables of social mobility", *Amer. sociol. R.* 42(1), feb 77 : 74-90.

2717 McCLENDON, McKee J. "Structural and exchange components of vertical mobility", *Amer. sociol. R.* 42(1), feb 77 : 56-74.

2718 MIURA, Noriko. "Chiiki-kan idô no koka o meguru kosatsu" (Some considerations on the effects of intercommunity mobility), *Shakaigaku Kenkyu Nenpô* (7-8), 1977 : 42-49.

2719 MORRIS, Earl W. "Mobility, fertility and residential crowding", *Sociol. soc. Res.* 61(3), apr 77 : 363-379.

2720 NOWOTNY, Sławomir. "Mathematical description of social mobility. An attempt at generalization", *Polish sociol. B.* 38(2), 1977 : 5-11.

2721 PAYNE, G.; FORD, G.; ROBERTSON, C. "A reappraisal of social mobility in Britain", *Sociology (London)* 11(2), mai 77 : 289-310.

2722 RICHARDSON, C. James. *Contemporary social mobility.* London, F. Pinter; New York, Nichols Publishing Co., 77, v-340 p.

2723 RICHARDSON, C. James. "The problem of downward mobility", *Brit. J. Sociol.* 28(3), sep 77 : 303-320.

2724 SCHILDT, Gerhardt. "Wachstum und Stagnation der sozialen Mobilität im 19. und 20. Jahrhundert. Überlegungen zu mobilitätsfordernden und -hemmenden Faktoren" (Growth and stagnation of social mobility in the 19th and 20th centuries. Thoughts about the promoting and stunting factors of mobility), *Kölner Z. Soziol. u. soz.-Psychol.* 28(4), dec 77 : 702-730.

2725 SEEMAN, Melvin. "Some real and imaginary consequences of social mobility: a French-American comparison", *Amer. J. Sociol.* 82(4), jan 77 : 757-782.

2726 STRMISKA, Z.; VAVKOVA, B. "La mobilité sociale dans une société socialiste: l'expérience tchécoslovaque", *R. Ét. comp. Est-Ouest* 7(1), mar 76 : 129-184.

2727 TÓTH, D. J. "Parasztságunk mobilitásának néhány jellemzöje" (Some features of mobility of the peasantry), *Társadtud. Közl.* (4), 1977 : 76-83. *[Hungary.]*

2728 TURGONYI, J. "A kereskedelmi dolgozók társadalmi mobilitása" (The social mobility of commercial employees), *Társadtud. Közl.* (4), 1977 : 44-62. *[Hungary.]*

14300. SOCIAL CHANGE
CHANGEMENT SOCIAL

14310. History
Histoire

[See also / Voir aussi: 313, 1709, 2482]

2729 LACOMBA, Juan Antonio *et al. Historia social de España siglo XX* (Social history of Spain during the XXth century). Madrid, Guadiana de Publicaciones, 76, 372 p.

2730 LUMMIS, Charles Douglas" "On the uses of history: the case of modernization theory", *Berkeley J. Sociol.* 21, 1976-77 : 105-115.

2731 NAMER, Gérard. "La sociologie de la connaissance historique", *C. int. Sociol.* 24(63), jul-dec 77 : 289-297.

2732 SZACKA, Barbara. "Historical consciousness. Conclusions drawn from empirical studies", *Polish sociol. B.* 35(3), 1976 : 19-30.

2733 TOURAINE, Alain. *Un désir d'histoire.* Paris; Stock, 77, 275 p.

2734 VÖRÖS, Károly; ORBÁN, Sándor. "Az új- és legújabbkori társadalomtörténeti kutatásokhoz" (The recent and more recent researches in social history), *Tört. Szle* (4), 1976 : 731-760.

14320. Future
Futur

2735   BESTUŽEV-LADA, I. V. "Ēvoljucija amerikanskoj futurologii" (The evolution of American futurology), *SŠA* 7(3), mar 77 : 37-49.

2736   FERNANDEZ, Ronald (ed.). *The future as a social problem.* Santa Monica, Calif., Goodyear Publishing Co., 77, xvi-348 p.

2737   VERGUN, V. A. "Ēkologičeskie problemy futurologii kak otraženie uglubljajuščego krizisa buržuaznoj ideologii" (Ecological problems of futurology as a reflection of the deepening crisis of bourgeois ideology), *Vopr. polit. Ēkon.* 132, 1977 : 99-106.

14330. Social change
Changement social

[See also / Voir aussi: 654, 716, 870, 1056, 1300, 1354, 1617, 1645, 2069, 2137, 2502, 2694, 2730, 2867, 2944, 3134, 3338, 3485, 3534, 4247, 5217]

2738   AUGUSTINS, Georges. "Reproduction sociale et changement social: l'exemple des baronnies", *R. franç. Sociol.* 18(3), jul-sep 77 : 465-484.

2739   Bibl.XXVI-2254. BLACK, Cyril E. (ed.). *Comparative modernization: a reader.* CR: Randall G. STOKES, *Contemp. Sociol. (Washington)* 6(4), jul 77 : 432-433.

2740   BLACKEY, Robert; PAYNTON, Clifford. *Revolution and the revolutionary ideal.* Cambridge, Mass., Schenkman Publishing Co., 76, 295 p. CR: Ronland Y. L. CHENG, *Contemp. Sociol. (Washington)* 6(3), mai 77 : 329-330.

2741   BLJUM, R. N. "Ponjatija političeskoj i social'noj revoljucii v domarksistskoj i marksistskoj obščestvennoj mysli" (Concept of political and social revolution in pre-marxist and marxist social thought), in: *Problemy teorii social'noj revoljucii.* Moskva, 1976 : 8-29.

2742   BOGGS, Carl Jr. "Revolutionary process, political process, and the dilemma of power", *Theory and Soc.* 4(3), 1977 : 355-393.

2743   CENTRE D'ETHNOLOGIE SOCIALE ET DE PSYCHOSOCIOLOGIE. *Transformations sociales et rapports de pouvoir.* Paris, École des Hautes Études en Sciences sociales, CNRS, 77, 154 p.

2744   CHIROT, D. *Social change in the twentieth century.* Ed. by Robert K. MERTON. New York, Harcourt Brace Jovanovich, 77, xii-273 p.- 2 l.

2745   ELIAS, Norbert. "Zur Grundlegung einer Theorie sozialer Prozesse" (Towards a theory of social processes), *Z. Soziol.* 6(2), apr 77 : 127-149.

2746   FARIÁ, Alvaro DE. *Tempos de mutação* (Mutation time). Rio de Janeiro, Livraria Editora Catedra, 76, 178 p.

2747   Bibl.XXVI-2265. FLORA, Peter. *Indikatoren der Modernisierung: ein historisches Datenhandbuch* (Indicators of modernization: a historical data reference book). CR: Aldo LEGNARO, *Kölner Z. Soziol. u. soz.-Psychol.* 29(2), jun 77 ; 391-392.

2748   GALT, Anthony H.; SMITH, Larry T. *Models and the study of social change.* Cambridge, Mass., Schenkman Publishing Co.; New York, Halsted Press, 76, ix-180 p. CR: Salvador GINER, *Brit. J. Sociol.* 18(3), sep 77 : 405-407.

2749   GARNER, Roberta. *Social change.* Chicago, Rand McNally College Publishing Co., 77, x-430 p.

2750   HILL, Ellen B. "Some notes on innovative processes in social change", *Sociol. contemp.* 22(1-3), 1974 : 123-126.

2751   HIRST, Paul Q. *Social evolution and sociological categories.* New York, Homes and Meier Publishers, 76, 135 p.

2752   HÖRNING, Karl H. *Gesellschaftliche Entwicklung und soziale Schichtung: vergleichende Analyse gesellschaftlichen Strukturwandels*

(Social development and social classes: comparative analysis of social structure change). München, Verlag Dokumentation, 76, 208 p.

2753 HOUŠKA, Jiří. "Poznámky ke kritice některých levičáckých koncepci revoluce" (Comments on the criticism of some leftist conceptions of revolution), *Sociol. Čas.* 13(4), 1977 : 352-363.

2754 KANTOROVIČ, B. Ja. "K voprosu o protivorečivom haraktere sub'ektivnogo faktora social'noj revoljucii" (On the contradictory characteristics of subjective factor in social revolution), *Filos. nauč. Kommunizm* (3), 1976 : 49-54.

2755 KERIMOV, D. A. *et al. Planirovanie social'nogo razvitija* (Planning of social development). Moskva, Mysl', 76, 164 p.

2756 LAUER, Robert H. (ed.). *Social movements and social change.* Carbondale, Southern Illinois University Press, 76, xxviii-292 p.

2757 LAUER, Robert H.; THOMAS, Rance. "A comparative analysis of the psychological consequences of change", *Hum. Relat.* 29(3), mar 76 : 239-248.

2758 LEWANDOWSKI, Edmund. "Rewolucja socjalistyczna a dyktatura proletariatu" (The socialist revolution and the dictatorship of the proletariat), *Przegl. socjol.* 29, 1977 : 141-167.

2759 LIPSKY, W. E. "Comparative approaches to the study of revolution; a historiographic essay", *R. Polit.* 38(4), oct 76 : 494-509.

2760 LOURENÇA, Susan V. "Conflict and failure in planned change", *Hum. Relat.* 29(12), dec 76 : 1189-1203.

2761 LOWENTHAL, R. "Social transformation and democratic legitimacy", *Soc. Res.* 43(2), 1976 : 246-275.

2762 NAFFESOLI, Michel. "Réflexions sur une forme de l'utopie sociale: le mythe du progrès", *Contrepoint* 24, 1977 : 133-141.

2763 MAL'CEV, V. A.; FADEEV, A. N. "Sorevnovanie i social'nyj progress obščestva" (Competition and social progress), *Sorevnov. Ličnost'. Social.* (1), 1976 : 5-14.

2764 McCAUGHRIN, Craig. "An ahistoric view of revolution", *Amer. J. polit. Sci.* 20(4), nov 76 : 637-651.

2765 MAMMEN, M. P. "Theory of sociolysis: a theory of social change and political development", *Ind. polit. Sci. R.* 10(2), jul 76 : 180-189.

2766 MILLER, William L. "Herbert Spencer's factors in social evolution", *Sociol. Anal. Theory* 7(2), jun 77 : 99-115.

2767 MOLNÁR, T. "Was ist Dekadenz ?" (What is decadence ?), *Z. Polit.* 23(4), dec 76 : 313-327.

2768 MOREL, Gyula. "A forradalom szociológiai perspektívában" (Revolution in a sociological perspective), *Katol. Szle* (2), 1976 : 108-117.

2769 MUÑOZ, Luis Joaquin. "El paradigma americano de la modernización" (The American paradigm of modernization), *R. esp. Opin. públ.* 47, jan-mar 77 : 77-90.

2770 NASH, June; DANDLER, Jorge; HOPKINS, Nicholas (eds.). *Popular participation in social change: cooperatives, collectives, and nationalized industry.* The Hague, Mouton; Chicago, Aldine, 76, xviii-621 p.

2771 OLEH, L. G. "Problema psihologičeskogo elementa v sub'ektivnom faktore revoljucii" (Problem of the psychological element in the subjective factor of revolution), in: *Problemy soznanija v uslovijah razvitogo socializma.* Ivanovo, 1976 : 43-52.

2772 PANKOKE, Eckart. "Gesellschaftliche Dynamik und soziokulturelles Lernen" (Social dynamics and socio-cultural learning), *Sociol. int. (Berlin)* 12(1-2), 1974 : 169-188.

2773 PARSONS, Talcott. *The evolution of societies.* Ed. by Jackson TOBY. Englewood Cliffs, N.J., Prentice-Hall, 77, xii-269 p. [Combined and edited version of the author's *Societies* (1966) and *The system of modern societies* (1971).]

2775 ROSE, Richard. "Models of change", *Sociol. Contemp.* 22(1-3), 1974 :

201-221.

2776 ROTTER, Frank. *Sozialer und personaler Wandel. Zur Theorie recht-
licher und therapeutischer Verfahren* (Social and personal change. Theory of legal and therapeutical methods). Stuttgart, F.
Enke, 76. CR: Gerd ABEL, *Kölner Z. Soziol. u. soz.-Psychol.*
29(4), dec 77 : 817-818.

2777 SALERT, Barbara. *Revolutions and revolutionaries: four theories.*
New York, Elsevier, 76, ix-161 p.

2778 SCHUR, Edwin. *The awareness trap: self-absorption instead of social change.* New York, Quadrangle, 76, 213 p. CR: Louis ROWITZ,
Contemp. Sociol. (Washington) 6(2), mar 77 : 239-240.

2779 SHŌJI, Kōkichi. *Gendaika to Gendai shakai no riron* (Theory of modernization and modern society). Tokyo, Tokyo-daigaku Shuppankai,
77, 348 p.

2780 SMITH, Anthony Douglas. *Social change: social theory and historical
processes.* London-New York, Longman, 76, viii-184 p. CR: Salvador
GINER, *Brit. J. Sociol.* 18(3), sep 77 : 405-407.

2781 SOLÉ, Carlota. *Modernización: un análisis sociológico* (Modernization: a sociological analysis). Barcelona, Ediciones Península,
76, 251 p.

2782 STOLJAROV, V. V. *et al. Filosofskie problemy obščestvennogo razvitija* (Philosophical problems of social development). Moskva,
Mysl', 76, 263 p.

2783 SZABÓ, Imre. "Társadalmi átalakulás és az életmód változása" (Social change and way of life transformation), *Társad. Szle* (8-9),
1976 : 35-46.

2784 TOURAINE, Alain (éd.). *Au-delà de la crise.* Paris, Éditions du
Seuil, 76, 252 p.

2785 VASUDEVA, Promila. *Social change: an analysis of attitudes and
personality.* New Delhi, Sterling Publishers, 76, x-224 p.

2786 VROMEN, Suzanne Donner. "Pareto on the inevitability of revolution", *Amer. behav. Scientist* 20(4), apr 77 : 521-528.

2787 WATANABE, Motoki. "Smelser no henkō-riron ni tsuite" (On Smelser's
theory of social change), *Komazawa Shakaigaku Kenkyu* (9), 1977 :
61-80.

2788 WINWOOD, M. G. "Social change and community work: where new ?",
Community Develop. J. 12(1), jan 77 : 4-14.

2789 ZALTMAN, Gerald; DUNCAN, Robert. *Strategies for planned change.*
New York, Wiely, 77, ix-404 p.

14340. Changing society
Société en transformation

[See also / Voir aussi: 506, 2374, 2505, 2579, 2679, 3973, 4080,
4114, 5155]

2790 ABDEL-MALEK, A. "Le 'Tiers-Monde' et l'Orient", *Civilisations*
26(3-4), 1976 : 273-280.

2791 AMIN, Samir. "Social characteristics of peripheral formation: an
outline for an historical sociology", *Berkeley J. Sociol.* 21,
1976-77 : 27-50. [Developing countries.]

2792 ANDERLE, Á. "Változások Peru társadalmában a 20. század első felé-
ben" (Changes in the society of Peru in the first half of the
20th century), *Századok* (2), 1977 : 230-269.

2793 BAKS, Chris; BREMAN, Jan; HOMMES, Enno. *Modernization, stagnation
and steady decline. Sociological contributions on social change
in South Gujarat, India.* Utrecht, Centre for comparative social-
economic studies, University of Utrecht, 76, vi-313 p.

2794 BERTOLA, Giuliana. "Sottosviluppo e classi sociali in Venezuela,
secoli XVI-XIX" (Underdevelopment and social classes in Venezuela, XVIth-XIXth centuries), *Quad. Sociol.* 29(3-4), 1977 :
174-207.

2795   BOLČIĆ, Silvano. "Sociologija i problemi nedovoljno razvijenih
       područja u Jugoslaviji" (Sociology and the problem of less de-
       veloped regions of Yugoslavia), *Sociologija* 19(4), 1977 : 537-
       558.

2796   BRAUN, Oscar. "El nuevo orden internacional desde el punto de vis-
       ta de la dependencia",(The new international order from the point
       of view of dependency), *R. mexic. Sociol.* 38(3), oct-dec 77 :
       853-878.

2797   CALDWELL, Gary; CZARNOCKI, B. Dan. "Un rattrapage raté. Le change-
       ment social dans le Québec d'après-guerre, 1950-1974: une com-
       paraison Québec-Ontario", *Rech. sociogr.* 18(1), jan-apr 77 : 9-
       58.

2798   CARRIER, Fred J. *The third world revolution.* Amsterdam, Grüner,
       76, vii-355 p.

2799   CHALONER, William Henry; RICHARDSON, R. C. *British economic and
       social history: a bibliographical guide.* Manchester, Manchester
       University Press; Totowa, N. J., Rowman and Littlefield, 76,
       xiv-129 p.

2800   CHIROT, Daniel. *Social change in a peripheral society: the crea-
       tion of a Balkan colony.* New York, Academic Press, 76, xvii-179
       p. [Wallachia.]

2801   CLAESSEN, Henri Johannes; KAAYK, J.; LAMBREGTS, R. J. A. *Dekolo-
       nisatie en vrijheid. Een sociaal-wetenschappelijke discussie
       over emancipatieprocessen in de Derde Wereld* (Decolonization
       and freedom. A sociological discussion on emancipation pro-
       cesses in the Third World). Assen, Van Gorcum, 76, xii-286 p.

2802   COHEN, Robin; SHANIN, Teodor; SORJ, Bernardo. "The sociology of
       'developing societies' problems of teaching and definition",
       Sociol. R. 25(2), mai 77 : 351-375.

2803   DAVYDOV, V. M. "Modernizacija otstalostitendencija zavisimogo
       kapitalizma" (Modernization of underdevelopment, trends of de-
       pendent capitalism), *Latinsk. Amer.* 8(1),,jan-feb 77 : 17-37.

2804   DHAR, D. P. *Planning and social change.* New Delhi, Arnold-Heine-
       mann Publishers, 76, xv-210 p.-1 l. [India.]

2805   DIAS, Gentil Martins. "Os novos padrões de controle e dominaçâo
       no campo: mudança e continuidade no Nordeste" (The new control
       and domination patterns in the countryside: change and conti-
       nuity in the Northeast), *Dados* 15, 1977 ; 123-137. [Brazil.]

2806   DURAN S., R.; LOBOS M., F. "Algunas consideraciones sociales sobre
       la estrategía subregional de desarrollo" (Some social reflexions
       on the subregional strategy of development), *Integr. latinoamer.*
       1(5), aug 76 : 20-28.

2807   FITTER, Jörn Carsten. *Entwicklungspolitik, Möglichkeiten und Gren-
       zen des Fortschritts in der Dritten Welt* (Development policy,
       possibilites and limits of the progress in the third world).
       Köln, Deutscher Instituts-Verlag, 76, 56 p.

2808   GOETZE, Dieter. *Entwicklungssoziologie* (Sociology of development).
       München, Goldmann, 76, 220 p. [Underdeveloped areas.]

2809   GUTHRIE, George M. "A social-psychological analysis of moderniza-
       tion in the Philippines", *J. cross-cult. Psychol.* 8(2), jun 77 :
       177-206.

2810   HILOWITZ, Jane. *Economic development and social change in Sicily.*
       Cambridge, Mass., Schenkman Publishing Co., 76, xviii-204 p.

2811   HIMMELSTRAND, U. "Socialism and social liberalism in the context
       of Swedish societal change", *Int. R. Community Develop.* 37-38,
       1977 : 37-67.

2812   HO, Wing Meng. *Asian values and modernisation: a critical inter-
       pretation.* Singapore, Chopmen Enterprises, 76, 16 p.

2813   HURSH-CÉSAR, Gerald; ROY, Prodipto (eds.). *Third world surveys;
       survey research in developing nations.* Delhi, Macmillan Co. of
       India, 76, x-468 p.

2814   "Innovative processes in social change of highly industrialized
        societies", *Int. R. Community Develop.* 37-38, 1977 : 291 p.

2815   JUVILER, Peter H. *Revolutionary law and order: politics and social
        change in the USSR.* New York, Free Press, 76, xii-274 p.

2816   KAHL, Joseph A. *Modernization, exploitation and dependency in La-
        tin America.* New Brunswick, N.J., Transaction Books, 76, 215 p.
        CR: Ira STUDIN, *Contemp. Sociol. (Washington)* 6(4), jul 77 : 442-
        444.

2817   KLINGMAN, David. *Social change, political change, and public pol-
        icy: Norway and Sweden, 1875-1965.* London-Beverly Hills, Sage
        Publications, 76, 54 p.

2818   LA BELLE, Thomas J. *Nonformal education and social change in Latin
        America.* Los Angeles, UCLA Latin American Center Publications,
        University of California, 76, xvii-219 p.

2819   LAMB, David. "Preserving primitive society: reflections on post-
        Wittgensteinian social philosophy", *Sociol. R.* 25(4), nov 77 :
        689-719.

2820   LANDER, Patricia Slade. *In the shadow of the factory: social chan-
        ges in a Finnish community.* Cambridge, Mass., Schenkman Publish-
        ing Co.; New York, Halsted Press, 76, xii-191 p. CR: Kirsti
        SUOLINNA, *Acta sociol.* 20(1), 1977 : 113-115.

2821   LEDER, Arnold. *Catalysts of change: Marxist versus Muslim in a Tur-
        kish community.* Austin, Center for Middle Eastern Studies, Uni-
        versity of Texas at Austin, 76, xii-56 p.-1 l.

2822   LEWIS, Robert A. *et al.* "Modernization, population change and na-
        tionality in Soviet Central Asia and Kazakhstan", *Canad. Slavonic
        Pap.* 17(2-3), jun-sep 75 : 286-301.

2823   MARIEN, Michael. "The two visions of post-industrial society",
        Futures 9(5), oct 77 : 415-431. Also published in French in
        Futuribles (12), 1977 : 429-452.

2824   MATTHEWS, David Ralph. *There's no better place than here: social
        change in three Newfoundland communities.* Toronto, P. Martin
        Associates, 76, xi-164 p.

2825   McHENRY, D. E. Jr. "The under-development theory: a case-study
        from Tanzania", *J. mod. Afr. Stud.* 14(4), dec 76 : 621-636.

2826   MILLER, Rory; SMITH, Clifford Thrope; FISHER, John Robert (eds.).
        Social and economic change in modern Peru. Liverpool, Centre for
        Latin-American Studies, University of Liverpool, 76, 5-198 p.

2827   PAPP, Zsuzsa. "Elméleti nézöpontok a 'kései' tökés allam müködésé-
        hez" (Theoretical points of view on the functioning of the 'be-
        lated' capitalist states), *Szociológia* 5(3-4), 1976 : 398-419.

2828   PEREZ DIAZ, Victor M. "Cambios sociales y transformaciones cultu-
        rales" (Social change and cultural transformations), *Agric. y
        Soc.* (2), 1977 : 97-130. *[Spain, Castilla.]*

2829   PITT, David C. "Social change in Australia and New-Zealand", *Int.
        R. Community Develop.* 37-38, 1977 : 67-111.

2830   PITT, David C. *The social dynamics of development.* Oxford, Pergamon,
        76, viii-162 p.

2831   RAO, V. K. R. V. "Science and social change: emergence of a dual
        society in India", *Sociol. B. (Bombay)* 25(1), mar 76 : 33-44.

2832   SCHMITTER, P. C. "Modalità di mediazione degli interessi e mutamen-
        to sociale in Europa occidentale" (Varieties of interest media-
        tion and social change in Western Europe), *Mulino* 25(248), nov-
        dec 76 : 889-916.

2833   STILLMAN, Peter G.; VROMEN, Suzanne Donner.(eds.). "Revolution in
        advanced industrial society", *Amer. behav. Scientist* 20(4), apr
        77 : 453-616.

2834   TOLNAY, Gy. "A fejlödö országok mai válságai. Válságok vagy a fej-
        lödés ösztönzöi ?" (Contemporary crises of the developing count-
        ries. Are they crises or stimulators of development ?), *Közgazd.
        Szle* 24(3), már 77 : 336-340.

2835   WELLY-BANDARA-SAZRA, A. "Pour une sociologie de la décolonisation. Réflexions critiques à propos du 24e Congrès de l'Institut international de sociologie", *R. algér. Sci. jur. écon. polit.* 12(4), dec 75 : 769-789.

2836   WHYTE, William Foote; ALBERTI, Giorgio. *Power, politics, and progress: social change in rural Peru.* New York, Elsevier, 76, xii-307 p.

2837   YAGO, Glenn. "Whatever happened to the promised land ? Capital flows and the Israeli state ?", *Berkely J. Sociol.* 21, 1976-1977 : 117-146. With a reply by Gershon SHAFIR: 147-155.

15100. DEMOGRAPHY. GENETICS
       DÉMOGRAPHIE. GÉNÉTIQUE

15110. Population research
       Recherche démographique

[See also / Voir aussi: 1459]

2838   ANDERSSON, Åke E.; HOLMBERG, Ingvar (eds.). *Demographic, economic,
        and social interaction.* Cambridge, Mass., Ballinger. Publishing
        Co., 77, xvi-350 p.
2839   BARTOŠOVÁ, M. "Demografický výzkum v Československu 1956-1975"
        (Demographic researches in Czechoslovakia from 1956 to 1975),
        Demografie 18(3), jul-sep 76 : 201-214.
2840   CALOT, G.; SAUVY, Alfred. "La mesure des phénomènes démographiques.
        Hommage à Louis Henry", *Population* 32, sep 77 : 5-500.
2841   CASSEN, Robert; DYSON, Tom. "New population projections in India",
        Popul. Develop. R. 2(1), mar 76 : 101-137.
2842   CHANDER, R. *Unjuran penduduk untuk negeri-negeri Semenanjung Ma-
        laysia, 1970-1980 / Population projections for the states of
        Peninsular Malaysia, 1970-1980.* Kuala Lumpur, Jabatan Perangkaan,
        76, xx-161 p.
2843   FAN, S. C. "The population projection of Hong-Kong", *Southeast
        Asian J. soc. Sci.* 2(1-2), 1974 : 105-117.
2844   FÖRSTER, Erhard; GIERSDORF, Peter. *Grundlagen der Demographie* (Fun-
        damentals of demography). Berlin, Verlag Volk und Gesundheit, 76,
        278 p.
2845   HENRY, Louis; GUTIERREZ, Hector. "Qualité des prévisions démogra-
        phiques à court terme. Étude de l'extrapolation de la population
        totale des départements et villes de France, 1821-1975", *Popula-
        tion* 32(3), mai-jun 77 : 625-647.
2846   MACURA, Milos. "The Third World population conference", *Int. Probl.
        (Beograd)* 16, 1975 : 83-93.
2847   MATRAS, Judah. *Introduction to population: a sociological approach.*
        Englewood Cliffs, N.J., Prentice-Hall, 77, x-452 p.
2848   Bibl.XXVI-2338. NAG, Moni (ed.). *Population and social organization.*
        CR: Nathan KEYFITZ, *Amer. J. Sociol.* 82(6), mai 77 : 1402-1403.
2849   OVERBEEK, Johannes (ed.). *The evolution of population theory; a
        documentary sourcebook.* Westport, Conn., Greenwood Press, 77,
        x-277 p.
2850   PAILLAT, Paul M. *Problèmes démographiques d'aujourd'hui.* Paris,
        Hatier, 76, 79 p.
2851   PARSONS, Jack. *Population fallacies.* London, Elek, 77, xv-286 p.
2852   PONGRÁCZ, Tibor Mme; MOLNÁR, Edit; SZABÓ, Kálmán. *Népesedési kér-
        désekkel kapcsolatos közvéleménykutatás* (Public opinion resear-
        ches concerning population problems). Budapest, Statisztikai
        Kiadó, 76, 199-1 p.
2853   REES, P. H.; WILSON, Alan Geoffrey. *Spatial population analysis.*
        London, E. Arnold, 77, x-356 p.
2854   SALAS, Rafael M. *People: an international choice; the multilateral
        approach to population.* Oxford-New York, Pergamon Press, 76, xv-
        154 p.-10 l.

2855   SAUVY, Alfred; BROWN, Elisabeth; LEFEBVRE, Alain. *Éléments de démographie*. Paris, Presses universitaires de France, 76, 381 p.

2856   SOMOZA, Jorge L. *Systems of demographic measurement: data collection systems: the CELADE demographic survey method*. Chapel Hill, Department of Biostatistics, University of North Carolina, 76, 50 p.

2857   TOMITA, Fujio. *Jinkô shakaigaku no kihon-mondai* (Basic problems of demographic sociology). Tokyo, Shin-hyôron, 77, 226 p.

2858   TORRADO, Susana. "Sociología de la población en América latina" (Sociology of population in Latin America), *Notas Pobl.* 4(11), aug 76 : 65-78.

2859   VALENTEJ, D. I. *Sistema znanij o narodonaselenii* (System of knowledge on population). Moskva, Statistika, 76, 367 p.

2860   VANISTENDAEL, S. "Demografie en onderwijsplanning" (Demography and educational planning), *Bevolking en Gezin* (3), 1976 : 283-306.

2861   VENECKIJ, I. G. *Statisticeskie metody v demografii* (Statistical methods in demography). Moskva, Statistika, 77, 208 p.

2862   VILQUIN, Eric. "La naissance de la démographie", *Popul. et Famille* 39(3), 1976 : 145-164.

2863   WYNNYCZUK, V. "Badania ludnosciowe w Czechoslowacji" (Population research in Czechoslovakia), *Biul. IGS* 20(1), 1977 : 100-119.

2864   ZEIDENSTEIN, George; SCHAERER, Bruce. "Twenty questions to guide research", *Populi* 4(3), 1977 : 12-17. *[In demography.]*

15120. Household. Man. Woman
Ménage. Homme. Femme

[See also / Voir aussi: 830, 849, 1104, 1105, 1142, 1164, 1456, 2232, 2282, 2960, 3260, 3268, 3273, 3382, 3414, 3430, 3507, 4038, 4289, 4441, 4442, 4660, 5022, 5359]

2865   AFANAS'EV, V. G. "Čelovek kak sistema i sistema dejatel'nosti čeloveka" (Man as a system and the human activity system), *Sociol. Issled. (Moskva)* (4), 1976 : 24-33. *[Also published in Czech, Sociol. Čas. 13(4), 1977 : 364-371.]*

2866   AFANAS'EV, V. G. *Čelovek v upravlenii obščestvom* (Man in society management). Moskva, Politizdat, 77, 382 p.

2867   BARKER, Diana Leonard; ALLEN, Sheila (eds.). *Sexual divisions and society: process and change*. London, Tavistock, 76, ix-286 p.

2868   BERNHOLM, Bernt. *Manlig, kvinnlig, stressad* (Male, female, stressed). Stockholm, Aldus, 76, 147 p. *[Sex role.]*

2869   BURNS, Robert B. "Male and female perceptions of their own and the other sex", *Brit. J. soc. clinic. Psychol.* 16(3), sep 77 : 213-220.

2870   DAVID, Deborah S.; BRANNON, Robert (eds.). *The fourty-nine percent majority: the male sex role*. Reading, Mass., Addison-Wesley, 76, 338 p. CR: Jane H. SCHEFF; Thomas J. SCHEFF, *Contemp. Sociol. (Washington)* 6(3), mai 77 : 379.

2871   ENGLISH, Jane (ed.). *Sex equality*. Englewood Cliffs, N.J., Prentice-Hall, 77, vi-250 p.

2872   EYSENCK, Hans Jurgen. *Sex and personality*. Austin, University of Texas Press; London, Open Books, 76, 255 p.

2873   GOFFMAN, Erving. "La ritualisation de la féminité", *Actes Rech. Sci. soc.* 14, apr 77 : 34-50.

2874   GOFFMAN, Erving. "The arrangement between the sexes", *Theory and Soc.* 3(4), 1977 : 301-332.

2875   GONZÁLEZ DURO, Enrique. *Represión sexual, dominación social* (Sexual repression, social domination). Madrid, Akal Editor, 76, 272 p.

2876   GOULD, Meredith; KERN-DANIELS, Rochelle. "Toward a sociological theory of gender and sex", *Amer. Sociologist* 12(4), nov 77 : 182-189.

2877   HAWKINS, M. J. "A re-examination of Durkheim's theory of human nature", *Sociol. R.* 25(2), mai 77 : 229-251.

2878 ICKES, William; BARNES, Richard D. "The role of sex and self-monitoring in unstructured dyadic interactions", *J. Person. soc. Psychol.* 35(5), mai 77 : 315-330.

2879 KANTER, Rosabeth Moss. "Some effects of proportions on group life: skewed sex ratios and responses to token women", *Amer. J. Sociol.* 82(5), mar 77 : 965-990.

2880 KUNITZ, Stephen J.; SLOCUMB, John C. "The changing sex ratio of the Navaho tribe", *Soc. Biology* 23(1), 1976 : 33-44.

2881 LASLETT, Peter; WALL, Richard. *Household and family in past time. Comparative studies in the size and structure of the domestic group over the last three centuries in England, France, Serbia, Japan and colonial North America, with further materials from Western Europe.* Cambridge, Cambridge University Press, 77, 623 p.

2882 MEEKER, B. F.; WEITZEL-O'NEILL, P. A. "Sex roles and interpersonal behavior in task-oriented groups", *Amer. sociol. R.* 42(1), feb 77 : 91-105.

2883 MICHEL, André. "Recherches récentes sur les rôles des sexes dans le monde", *Sociol. contemp.* 22(1-3), 1974 : 393-420.

2884 NEVILL, Dorothy D. "Sex roles and personality correlates", *Hum. Relat.* 30(8), aug 77 : 751-759.

2885 ROPER, Brent S.; LABEEF, Emily. "Sex roles and feminism revisited: an intergenerational attitude comparison", *J. Marriage Family* 39(1), feb 77 : 113-117.

2886 SARGENT, Alice G. *Beyond sex roles.* St. Paul, West Publishing Co., 77, xviii-489 p.

2887 "Sex roles: persistence and change", *J. soc. Issues* 32(3), 1976 : 223 p.

2888 STEINER, Shari. *The female factor; a study of women in five Western European societies.* New York, Putnam, 77, 328 p.

2889 STEMBER, Charles Herbert. *Sexual racism: the emotional barrier to an integrated society.* New York, Elsevier, 76, xviii-234 p.

2890 SUREDA, Leoncio. *Magía y sexo* (Magic and sex). Barcelona, Ediciones Petronio, 76, 247 p.

2891 VERBRUGGE, Los M. "Sex differentials in morbidity and mortality in the United States", *Soc. Biology* 23(4), 1976 : 275-296.

2892 WHEELER, Ladd; NEZLEK, John. "Sex differences in social participation", *J. Person. soc. Psychol.* 35(10), oct 77 : 742-754.

2893 WILLIAMSON, Nancy E. *Sons or daughters: a cross-cultural survey of parental preferences.* Beverly Hills, Calif., Sage Publications, 76, 207 p.

2894 YOUNG, Rosalie F. "Current sex-role attitudes of male and female students", *Sociol. Focus* 10(3), aug 77 : 309-323.

2895 ZIMMERMAN, Carle C. "The proper study of mankind", *Int. J. contemp. Sociol.* 13(3-4), jul-oct 76 : 291-322.

15130. Eugenism. Heredity
Eugénisme. Hérédité

2896 BALLONOFF, Paul A. "On Bernshtein's 'Solution of a mathematical problem in the theory of heredity'", *Soc. Sci. Inform.* 15(4-5), 1976 : 793-795.

2897 BARASH, David P. *Sociobiology and behavior.* New York, Elsevier, 77, xv-378 p.

2898 BERNSHTEIN, Sergei N. "Solution of a mathematical problem in the theory of heredity", *Soc. Sci. Inform.* 15(4-5), 1976 : 797-821.

2899 ELSTER, Jon. "Critique des analogies socio-biologiques. Plaidoyer pour l'autonomie des sciences", *R. franç. Sociol.* 18(3), jul-sep 77 : 369-395.

2900 FEDOSEEV, Piotr. "On the problem of the social and the biological in sociology and psychology", *Soc. Sci. Inform.* 15(4-5), 1976 : 557-570.

2901   IWASAKI, Nobuhiko. "'Seikatsu' no ronri kozo to Zochiâru-na mono" (On the logical structure of the concept of life), *Atarashii Shakaigaku no tame ni* 4(1), 1977 : 1-15.

2902   JONES, Hardy. "Genetic endowment and obligations to future generations", *Soc. Theory Practice* 4(1), 1976 : 29-46.

2903   LOMOV, Boris. "Bio- et socio-: une opposition injustifiée", *Sci. soc. (Moscou)* (4), 1977 : 34-50.

2904   VUILLEMIN, Jules. "De la biologie à la culture", *Soc. Sci. Inform.* 16(5), 1977 : 621-633.

2905   WEN-HSIUNG, Li (ed.). *Stochastic models in population genetics.* Stroudsburg, Pa., Dowden, Hutchinson and Ross; New York, Halsted Press, 77, xiii-471 p.

2906   WILTERDINK, N. "Biology and sociology", *Netherlands J. Sociol.* 12(1), jul 76 : 19-37.

15200. AGE GROUP
GROUPE D'ÂGE

15210. Age. Cohort. Generation
Âge. Cohorte. Génération

[See also / Voir aussi: 3902, 4099, 4532, 5249]

2907   AUERBACH, Lewis; GERBER, Andrea. *Répercussions de l'évolution de la pyramide des âges au Canada.* Ottawa, Approvisionnements et services Canada, 76, ix-125 p.

2908   COBBEN, N. P.; HAGENAARS, J. A. P. "Theoretische betekenis van de begrippen kohort en generatie" (Theoretical meaning of the cohort and generation concepts), *Soc. Wetensch.* 20(1), 1977 : 2-101.

2909   JENNINGS, M. K. "The variable nature of generational conflict. Some examples from West Germany", *Comp. polit. Stud.* 9(2), jul 76 : 171-188.

2910   MOMENI, Djamchid A. "Husband-wife age differentials in Shiraz, Iran", *Soc. Biology* 23(4), 1976 : 341-348.

15220. Childhood
Enfance

[See also / Voir aussi: 692, 908, 1184, 1372, 1490, 1522, 1928, 2025, 2031, 2035, 2066, 3388, 5162]

2911   AMADY, Nathé. "La condition de l'enfant au Tchad", *R. jur. polit.* 31(2), apr-jun 77 : 427-441.

2912   APHALE, Champa. *Growing up in an urban complex: a study of upbringing of children in Maharashtrian Hindu families in Poona.* New Delhi, National Publishing House, 76, viii-175 p.

2913   Bibl.XXVI-2386. ARNOLD, Fred. *et al. The value of children: a cross-national study.* CR: Moni NAG, *Contemp. Sociol. (Washington)* 6(3), mai 77 : 339-340.

2914   BANDIARE, Ali. "L'enfant dans la société nigérienne", *R. jur. polit.* 31(2), apr-jun 77 : 371-379.

2915   BEIT-HALLAHMI, Benjamin; RABIN, Albert I. "The kibbutz as a social experiment and as a child-rearing laboratory", *Amer. Psychol.* 32(7), jul 77 : 532-541.

2916   CHOMBART DE LAUWE, Marie-José *et al. Enfant en-jeu: les pratiques des enfants durant leur temps libre en fonction des types d'environnement et des idéologies.* Paris, Éditions du CNRS, 76, xi-346 p.

2917   CONNEN, Bernard. "L'enfant dans la société contemporaine au Burundi", *R. jur. polit.* 31(2), apr-jun 77 : 213-223.

2918   COOK-GUMPERZ, Jenny; CORSARO, William A. "Social-ecological constraints on children's communicative strategies", *Sociology (London)* 11(3), sep 77 : 411-434.

2919   FERRI, Elsa. *Growing up in a one-parent family: a long-term study of child development*. Windsor, Eng., NFER Publishing Co.; Atlantic Highlands, N.J., Humanities Press, 76, 196 p.

2920   GARDNER, William I. *Learning and behavior characteristics of exceptional children and youth: a humanistic behavioral approach*. Boston, Allyn and Bacon, 77, xii-593 p.

2921   GROSS, Beatrice; GROSS, Ronald (eds.). *The children's rights movement: overcoming the oppression of young people*. Garden City, N.Y., Anchor Books, 77, xvi-390 p.

2922   HABIMANA, Bonaventure. "L'enfant dans la société rwandaise", *R. jur. polit*. 31(2), apr-jun 77 : 381-405.

2923   HENDERSON, Ronald W.; BERGAN, John R. *The cultural context of childhood*. Columbus, Ohio, Merrill, 76, xii-506 p.-8 1.

2924   KAUFFMAN, James M. *Characteristics of children's behavior disorders*. Columbus, Ohio, Merrill, 77, viii-311 p.

2925   KONNER, Melvin J. "Relations among infants and juveniles in comparative perspective", *Soc. Sci. Inform*. 15(2-3), 1976 : 371-402.

2926   LEE, Lee C. *Personality development in childhood*. Monterey, Calif., Books/Cole Publishing Co., 76, viii-166 p.

2927   LEVASSEUR, Georges. "L'enfant victime. Les dispositions répressives protectrices de l'enfant en droit français", *R. jur. polit*. 31(2), apr-jun 77 : 733-753.

2928   Bibl.XXVI-2394. LEVITAN, Sar A.; ALDERMAN, Karen Cleary. *Child care and ABC's too*. CR: Keith D. St. M. EDWARDS, *J. econ. Liter*. 15(1), mar 77 : 155-156.

2929   LLOYD, Barbara B.; EASTON, Brian. "The intellectual development of Yoruba children: additional evidence and a serendipitous finding", *J. cross-cult. Psychol*. 8(1), mar 77 : 3-16.

2930   LOUSTAU-LALANNE, Bernard. "L'enfant dans la société seychelloise contemporaine", *R. jur. polit*. 31(2), apr-jun 77 : 419-426.

2931   LYTTON, Hugh; MARTIN, Nicholas G.; EAVES, Lindon. "Environmental and genetical causes of variation in ethological aspects of behavior in two-year-old boys", *Soc. Biology* 24(3), 1977 : 200-211.

2932   N'DIAYE, Amadou. "La condition de l'enfant dans la société contemporaine au Mali", *R. jur. polit*. 31(2), apr-jun 77 : 329-351.

2933   NEUBAUER, Peter B. (ed.). *The process of child development*. New York, New Academic Library, 76, vi-362 p.

2934   NIPHUIS-NELL, M. "Satisfacties en kosten van het hebben van kinderen" (Satisfaction and costs of children), *Bevolking en Gezin* (3), 1976 : 307-331.

2935   PASSET, Marc. "L'enfant dans la société contemporaine dans l'Empire centrafricain", *R. jur. polit*. 31(2), apr-jun 77 : 245-263.

2936   PFOHL, Stephen J. "The 'discovery' of child abuse", *Soc. Probl*. 24(3), feb 77 : 310-323.

2937   ROEDELL, Wendy Conklin; SLABY, Ronald,G.; ROBINSON, Halbert B. *Social development in young children*. Monterey, Calif., Books/Cole Publishing Co., 77, xiii-90 p.

2938   SHANAB, Mitri E.; YAHYA, Khawla A. "A behavioral study of obedience in children", *J. Person. soc. Psychol*. 35(7), jul 77 : 530-536.

2939   STROMMEN, Ellen A.; McKINNEY, John Paul; FITZGERALD, Hiram E. *Development psychology, the school-aged child*. Homewood Ill., Dorsey Press, 77, xv-300 p.

2940   SUTHERLAND, Neil. *Children in English-Canadian society: framing the twentieth-century consensus*. Toronto-Buffalo, University of Toronto Press, 76, viii-336 p.-6 1.

2941   THORNTON, Arland. "Children and marital stability", *J. Marriage Family* 39(3), aug 77 : 531-540.

2942   WASBURN, Philo C. "Children and Watergate: some neglected considerations", *Sociol. Focus* 10(4), oct 77 : 341-351.

2943   Bibl.XXVI-2404. WHITING, Beatrice; WHITING, John. *Children of six cultures. a psycho-cultural analysis*. CR: Christel ADICK, *Kölner Z. Soziol. u. soz.-Psychol*. 29(4), dec 76 : 807-809.

15230. Youth
Jeunesse

[See also / Voir aussi: 624, 627, 736, 786, 893, 898, 1082, 1109, 1278, 1355, 1365, 1463, 1478, 1495, 1780, 1781, 2019, 2090, 3393, 3940, 4831, 5142, 5143, 5154]

2944   ADAMSKI, Władysław. "Młode pokolenie jako narzędzie zmian społecznych" (The young generation as a means of social change), *Stud. socjol.* 63(4), 1976 : 139-169.

2945   BECKER, Tamar. "Self, family, and community. A cross-cultural comparison of American and Israeli youth", *Youth and Soc.* 8(1), sep 76 : 45-66.

2946   BLAUKOPF, Kurt; MARK, Desmond (eds.). *The cultural behaviour of youth: towards a cross-cultural survey in Europe and Asia.* Vienna, Universal Edition, 76, 135 p.

2947   BLOCH, Richard; MILLER, Steven S. "Educational, social and religious behavior of middleclass suburban youth", *R. int. Sociol. (Madrid)* 34(17), jan-mar 76 : 163-177.

2948   CÁCERES, María Leticia. *Valores y disvalores como probables factores determinantes de la conducta del adolescente peruano en Lima metropolitana: prueba experimental* (Values and non-values as probable factors of the Peruvian adolescent's behaviour in the Lima metropolitan area: experimental test). Lima, Cáceres, 76, iv-293 p.

2949   DIRKS, Sabine. *Islam et jeunesse en Turquie d'aujourd'hui.* Lille, Université de Lille III; Paris, H. Champion, 77, 368 p.

2950   DOROŠENKO, M. M.; PETROV, I. I. "K voprosu o roli kategorij simmetrii i asimmetrii deja analiza social'noj struktury i roli molodeži v žizni buržuaznogo obščestva" (On the role of "symmetry" and "assymmetry" categories for analyzing youth social structure and role in bourgeois society life), in: *Sovremennaja ideologičeskaja bor'ba i molodez'. II.* Moskva, 1976 : 37-46.

2951   DRAGEL', V. S.; ČALKOV, A. A. *Obraz žizni molodogo sovetskogo čeloveka* (The young Soviet man's way of life). Barnaul, Altijskoe Knižnoe Izdatel'stvo, 76, 159 p.

2952   DU POUGET, Bruno. *Adolescents de banlieue: recherche éthologique sur les groupes spontanés de jeunes dans la banlieue de Lyon.* Lyon, Fédérop, 76, 319 p.

2953   FUCHS, Estelle (ed.). *Youth in a changing world: cross-cultural perspectives on adolescence.* The Hague, Mouton; Chicago, Aldine, 76, xiii-346p.-3 l.

2954   GIULIANO, Luca. "La ricerca sociale italiana sul comportamento giovanile dopo la 'contestazione'" (Italian social research on youth behaviour after the protest period), *R. Inst. Sociol. (Rome)* 12(3), 1976 : 242-252.

2955   GUROVA, R. G. "Vlijanie socialističeskogo stroja na social'nuju napravlennost' i cennostnye orientacii škol'noj molodezi" (Influence of the socialist system on social tendencies and value orientations of young scholars), in: *Obščestvenno-političeskoe vospitanie učaščihsja.* Irkutsk, 1976 : 3-17.

2956   HALL, Stuart; JEFFERSON, Tony (eds.). *Resistance through rituals: youth subcultures in post-war Britain.* London, Hutchinson, 76, 287 p.

2957   ICHILOV, Orit. "Youth movements in Israel as agents for transition to adulthood", *Jew. J. Sociol.* 19(1), jun 77 : 21-32.

2958   KIRPAL, Prem. *Youth and established culture (dissent and cooperation).* New Delhi, Sterling Publishers, 76, 96 p.

2959   KOJIMA, Kazuto; AKIYAMA, Toyoko. "Seinen no ishiki no henbo to genjo" (Changing attitudes of Japanese youth), *N.H.K. Hôsôbunka Kenkyu Nenpo* 22, 1977 : 1-36.

2960   KOMAROVSKY, Mirra. *Dilemmas of masculinity: a study of college youth.* New York, W. W. Norton, 76, 274 p. CR: Anna Statham MACKE, *Amer. J. Sociol.* 83(2), sep 77 : 512-513.

2961   LISOVSKIJ, V. J. "Analiz nekotoryh problem molodeži v uslovijah naučno-tehničeskoj revoljucii" (Analysis of some youth problems under conditions of the scientific and technical revolution), in: *Aktual'nye problemy social'nogo planirovanija.* Irkutsk, 1975 : 177-209.

2962   LYSKOV, A. P. "Molodež' e eě mesto v social'noj strukture obščestva" (Youth and its place in society social structure), *Ličnost i Obščestvo* (2), 1976 : 54-66.

2963   MANASTER, Guy J. *Adolescent development and the life tasks.* Boston, Allyn and Bacon, 77, xiii-337 p.

2964   MERELMAN, Richard M. "Moral development and potential radicalism in adolescence. A reconnaissance", *Youth and Soc.* 9(1), sep 77 : 29-54.

2965   MEYER, Katherine; SEIDLER, John; MacGILLAVRAY, Lois. "Youth at a leftist and rightist political rally: reasons for participating", *Sociol. Focus* 10(3), aug 77 : 221-235.

2966   MURY, Gilbert; GAULEJAC, Vincent DE. *Les jeunes de la rue: ce qu'ils disent de leur vie quotidienne: famille, travail, violence, sexualité, drogue.* Toulouse, Privat, 77, 233 p.

2967   NAKA, Hisao. *Japanese youth in a changing society.* Tokyo, International Society for Educational Information, 77, 98 p.

2968   OKADA, Makoto. "'Tekiô to shôjun shûdan' no Scheme no ichi-tenkai" (Merton's scheme applied to Japanese youth problems), *Shakaigaku Hyôron* 27(4), 1977 : 42-55.

2969   ONNA, Ben VAN. *Jugend und Vergesellschaftung: eine Auseinandersetzung mit der Jugendsoziologie* (Youth and socialization: close study of the youth sociology). Frankfurt-am-Main, Aspekte, 76, 208 p.

2970   POLONSKIJ, I. S. "Dejatel'nost' obščenija podrostkov i junošej kak socialno-psihologičeskaja problema" (Relations between adolescents and youth as a socio-psychological problems), *Nauč. Trudy Kursk. pedag. Inst.* 71, 1976 : 33-46.

2971   PRIEUR, N. "Les adolescents, en rupture de famille ?", *Projet* 113, mar 77 : 309-320. *[France.]*

2972   RAK, Tanja. "Omladina i omladinska organizacija" (Young people and youth organization), *Pitanja* 9(3), 1977 : 36-44. *[Yugoslavia.]*

2973   RAMAKRISHNA, Bommathanahalli; VELASQUEZ, Hernan. *Investigacion social sobre la problematica de la juventud rural venezolana* (Social research on the problem of Venezuelan rural youth), Barquisimento, Fundacion para el Desarrollo de la Region Centro Occidental de Venezuela, 76, v-154 p.-3 l.

2974   REŠETOV, P. N. "Nekotorye voprosy izučenija social'no-psihologičeskih osobennostej molodeži" (Some questions for studying socio-psychological characteristics of youth), *Vopr. Teorii Metod. ideol. Raboty* (7), 1977 : 103-118.

2975   TAKSÁS, Imre. "Politika és ifjuságpolitika. Nehány szocialista ország tapasztalatai alapján" (Politics and youth policy, based on some socialist countries experience), *Tarsadtud. Közl.* (4), 1976 : 43-59.

2976   WESTPHAL, Heinz. "Was ist Jugendpolitik ? Abgrenzungen und Orientierungspunkte" (What is youth policy ? Limitation and orientation points), *Dtsche Jugend* 24(12), dec 76 : 543-552.

2977   WOODTLI, O. "Vier Jugendgenerationen" (Four youth generations), *Schweiz. Mh.* 57(1), apr 77 : 41-56. *[Germany, FR.]*

15240. Adult
Adulte

[See also / Voir aussi: 2957]

2978 CHEW, Peter. *The inner world of the middle-aged man.* New York, Macmillan, 76, xix-278 p.

2979 DAVIS, J. A. "Background characteristics in the US adult population in 1952-1973: a survey-metric model", *Soc. Sci. Res.* 5(4), dec 76 : 349-383.

2980 ELIAS, Merrill F.; ELIAS, Penelope K.; ELIAS, Jeffrey W. *Basic processes in adult developmental psychology.* Saint Louis, Mosby, 77, xi-336 p.

2981 SHEEHY, Gail. *Passagers: predictable crises of adult life.* New York, E. P. Dutton, 76, 393 p. CR: Michael S. KIMMEL, *Contemp. Sociol. (Washington)* 6(4), jul 77 : 490-493.

15250. Old age
Vieillesse

[See also / Voir aussi: 956, 3259, 3899, 4190, 5382, 5679]

2982 ANDO, Sadao. "Dokukyo rojin no tashutsu shijo kazoku tono kankei ni tsuite" (The relations between the living-alone aged and their family), *Morioka-tankidaigaku Kenkyu-hokoku* 28, 1977 : 13-19.

2983 AOI, Kazuo. "Nihon no 100-sai rôjin" (Japanese centenarians), *Kazoku Kenkyû Nenpô* (3), 1977 : 1-10.

2984 BELL, Bill D. (ed.). *Contemporary social gerontology: significant developments in the field of aging.* Springfield, Ill., Thomas, 76, xxi-454 p.

2985 BELL, Duran; KASSCHAU, Patricia; ZELLMAN, Gail. *Delivering services to elderly members of minority groups: a critical review of the literature.* Santa Monica, CA., Rand, 76, xvii-103 p. *[USA.]*

2986 BÖSZÖRMÉNYI, Zoltán. "Az öregedési folyamat egyes pszichés vonatkozásairól" (Some psychical features of the ageing process), *Új Irás* (12), 1976 : 110-116.

2987 BURGALASSI, Silvano. "La condizione anziana: un approccio globale, a livello antropologico e sociologico" (Old age status: a global approach at the anthropological and sociological level), *Sicur. soc.* 32(2), mar-apr 77 : 145-160.

2988 CESAREO, Vincenzo. "Divisione sociale del lavoro e condizione dell'anziano" (Social division of labour and the condition of the elderly), *Studi Sociol.* 15(4), oct-dec 77 : 353-362.

2989 DILIĆ, Edhem. "Psihološka prilagođenost starenju u selu" (Psychological adjustment to growing old in the village), *Sociol. sela* 15(1-2), 1977 : 48-61.

2990 DOOGHE, G.; VANDERLEYDEN, L.; VAN LOON, F. "Maatschappelijke aanpassing van bejaarden in rusthuizen. Een multivariate analyse" (Social adaptation of older people living in asylum. A multivariate analysis), *Bevolking en Gezin* (1), 1977 : 25-41.

2991 "Enseignement, recherche et documentation en gérontologie sociale", *Gérontologie 76* 24, oct 76 : 5-50.

2992 FISCHER, David Hackett. *Growing old in America.* New York, Oxford University Press, 77, viii-242 p.

2993 FREZZOTTI, Maria Teresa. "Il problema degli anziani. La popolazione geriatrica di Chieti" (The problem of aged people. The geriatric population of Chieti), *Sociologia (Roma)* 10(3), sep-dec 76 : 145-174.

2994 GUBRIUM, Jaber F. (ed.). *Time, roles and self in old age.* New York, Human Sciences Press, 76, 363 p.

2995 HENDRICKS, Jon; HENDRICKS, C. Davis. *Aging in mass society; myths and realities.* Cambridge, Mass., Winthrop Publishers, 77, xvi-426 p.

2996   KASSCHAU, Patricia L. "Age and race discrimination. Reported by
        middle-aged and older persons", *Soc. Forces* 55(3), mar 77 : 728-
        742.

2997   LACOUR, C.; BARATA, M. "Les besoins socio-culturels des personnes
        âgées. À propos d'une enquête en Dordogne et en Gironde, élé-
        ments de réflexion", *R. écon. Sud-Ouest* 25(4), 1976 : 499-535.

2998   LANTOINE, C. "Enquête auprès des retraités du régime général vi-
        vant dans la région parisienne", *R. franç. Aff. soc.* 30(4),
        oct-dec 76 : 77-113?

2999   LATOUR, Chantal. "La révolte des vieux aux États-Unis", *Temps mod.*
        33(373-374), aug-sep 77 : 147-226.

3000   MAEDA, Daisaku. "Research in social gerontology in Japan", *Shakai-
        rônengaku* (5), 1977 : 3-13.

3001   NARR, Hannelore. *Soziale Probleme des Alters: Altenhilfe, Alten-
        heim* (The social problems of old people: old age assistance,
        old age homes). Stuttgart-Berlin-Köln-Mainz, Kohlhammer, 76,
        156 p.

3002   PAILLAT, P. "Le vieillissement de la France rurale: intensité, évo-
        lution, diffusion et typologie", *Population* 31(6), nov-dec 76 :
        1147-1188.

3003   "Réflexions et études sur le 3e âge", *Serv. soc. (Quebec)* 26(2-3),
        jul-dec 77 : 193 p. *[Canada.]*

3004   ROSS, Jennie-Keith. *Old people new lives: community creation in a
        retirement residence.* Chicago, University of Chicago Press, 77,
        xi-227 p. *[France.]*

3005   SIEGEL, Jacob S. *et al. Demographic aspects of aging and the older
        population in the United States.* Washington, United States Govern-
        ment Printing Office, 76, vii-68 p.

3006   SODEI, Takako; MIYAZAKI, Eiko. "Nichijo-sei no naka no rojin-mon-
        dia" (The problem of the aged in everyday life), *Shakai-ronen-
        gaku* (7), 1977 : 3-23.

3007   TOBIN, Sheldon S.; LIEBERMAN, Morton A. *Last home for the aged.*
        San Francisco, Jossey-Bass, 76, xiii-304 p.

15300. POPULATION EVOLUTION. POPULATION POLICY
ÉVOLUTION DE LA POPULATION. POLITIQUE DÉMOGRAPHI- QUE

15310. Population growth
Accroissement de la population

15311.

[See also / Voir aussi: 1/19, 2822, 2841, 2842, 2043, 4004, 5302]

3008   AFIGBO, A. E.; NWABARA, S. N. "Black civilization and the 'popu-
        lation crisis': a cultural approach", *Civilisations* 26(1-2),
        1976 : 15-35.

3009   AHMAD, Saghir. "Population myths and realities", *Race and Class*
        19(1), jul 77 : 19-28. *[Pakistan.]*

3010   ANDERSON, Charles H. *The sociology of survival. Social problems of
        growth.* Homewood, Ill., Dorsey Press, 76, xii-299 p. CR: Allan
        SCHANIBERG, *Contemp. Sociol. (Washington)* 6(2), mar 77 : 235.

3011   BASTIDE, Henri; GIRARD, Alain. "Attitudes des Français sur la con-
        joncture démographique, la natalité et la politique familiale à
        la fin de 1976", *Population* 32(3), mai-jun 77 : 519-554.

3012   BIRDSALL, Nancy. "Analytical approaches to the relationship of po-
        pulation growth and development", *Popul. Develop. R.* 3(1-2),
        mar-jun 77 : 63-102.

3013   BONGAARTS, J. "A dynamic model of the reproductive process", *Popul.
        Stud.* 31(1), mar 77 : 59-74.

3014   BUXTON, Martin; CRAVEN, Edward (eds.). *The uncertain future: demo-
        graphic change and social policy.* London, Centre for Studies in
        Social Policy, 76, 87 p. *[UK.]*

3015   CALDEIRA BRANT, Vinicius. "Dinámica poblacional, estructura agra-
        ria y desarrollo agrícola en Brazil" (Population dynamics, ag-
        rarian structure and agricultural development in Brazil), *Demogr.*
        y Econ. 10(2), 1976 : 119-126.
3016   CALDWELL, John Charles. *The socio-economic explanation of high*
        fertility: papers on the Yoruba Society of Nigeria. Canberra,
        Department of Demography, Australian National University, 76,
        vii-133 p.
3017   CHESNAIS, Jean-Claude. "Fluctuations démographiques et dépenses de
        sécurité sociale", *Population* 32(2), mar-apr 77 : 373-404.
3018   CROZE, Marcel (éd.). *Tableaux démographiques et sociaux: reliefs*
        géographiques et historiques. Paris, INSÉE, INED, 76, xv-216 p.
3019   D'SOUZA, S.; RAHMAN, S. "Intercensal population growth rates of
        Bangladesh", *Soc. Action* 27(2), apr-jun 77 : 101-118.
3020   ESPENSHADE, Thomas J.; CAMPBELL, Gregory. "The stable equivalent
        population, age composition, and Fisher's reproductive value
        function", *Demography* 14(1), feb 77 : 77-86.
3021   FRANCE. Institut national de la statistique et des études écono-
        miques. *Principaux résultats du recensement de 1975.* Paris,
        INSÉE, 77, 210 p.
3022   FRINKING, G. A. B. "Op weg naar een dalende bevolking; oorzaken en
        gevolgen" (Fertility decline; causes and consequences), *Polit.*
        Perspect. 5(5), sep-oct 76 : 23-31.
3023   GENDREAU, Francis. "La démographie des pays d'Afrique. Revue et
        synthèse", *Population* 32(4-5), jul-oct 77 : 901-943.
3024   HOREV, B. S.; MOISEENKO, V. M. *Sdvigi v razmeščenii naselenija SSSR*
        (Change in the distribution of the USSR population). Moskva, Sta-
        tistika, 76, 102 p.
3025   Bibl.XXVI-2481. JONES, Gavin. *Population growth and educational*
        planning in developing nations. CR: William S. GRIFFITH, *Amer.*
        J. Sociol. 82(4), jan 77 : 916-918; Pranab CHATTERJEE, *Contemp.*
        Sociol. (Washington) 6(1), jan 77 : 36-37.
3026   KALAJDŽIJEV, V. "Tendencje rozwoju demograficznego i polityka lud-
        nościowa w Bułgarii" (Trends in the demographic development and
        population policy in Bulgaria), *Biul. IGS* 20(1), 1977 : 40-67.
3027   KLINGER, András. "Magyarország népesedési helyzete, 1971-1975"
        (The demographic situation in Hungary, 1971-1975), *Statiszt.*
        Szle 55(1), jan 77 : 5-24; 55(2), feb 77 : 117-134.
3028   KOSIŃSKI, Lesek (ed.). *Demographic developments in Eastern Europe:*
        the eighth of eight volumes of papers from the first interna-
        tional conference. New York, Praeger, 77, xx-343 p.
3029   LANE, John S. *On optimal population paths.* Berlin-New York, Sprin-
        ger Verlag, 77, iv-123 p.
3030   LATUCH, M. "Stan i perspektywy oraz podstawowe problemy rozwoju
        demograficznego Polski" (Situation and perspectives, and basic
        problems of Poland's demographic development), *Biul. IGS* 20(2),
        1977 : 6-46.
3031   PERRICK, Thomas W. "Population, development and planning in Brazil"
        Popul. Develop. R. 2(2), jun 76 : 181-199.
3032   MUELLER, Eva. "The impact of demographic factors on economic deve-
        lopment in Taiwan", *Popul. Develop. R.* 3(1-2), mar-jun 77 : 1-22.
3033   ORTEGA, Antonio. "Situación demográfica de Costa Rica y perspecti-
        vas futuras" (Demographic situation of Costa Rica and future
        prospects), *Notas Pobl.* 5(14), aug 77 : 25-57.
3034   PAHL, L. "Rozwój ludności i polityka demograficzna w Czechosłowacji"
        (Population development and demographic policy in Czechoslova-
        kia), *Biul. IGS* 20(1), 1977 : 68-99.
3035   PECHT, Waldomiro. "Agricultura y dinámica de poblacion" (Agricul-
        ture and population dynamics), *Notas Pobl.* 4(12), dec 76 : 11-35.
        [Mexico and Brazil.]
3036   PITIE, Jean. "Sur quelques résultats au niveau départemental du
        recensement de 1975", *Norois* 24(94), apr-jun 77 : 235-249.

3037   POTTER, J. E.; ORDONEZ, M. "The completeness of enumeration in the 1973 census of the population of Colombia", *Popul. Index* 42(3), jul 76 : 377-403.

3038   POTTER, R. G.; WOLOWYNA, O.; KULKARNI, P. M. "Population momentum: a wider definition", *Popul. Stud.* 31(3), nov 77 : 555-569.

3039   PRADEL DE LAMAZE, François. "La connaissance récente de la population des trois pays du Maghreb", *Population* 32(4-5), jul-oct 77 : 992-1001.

3040   PRIOUX, F. "La situation démographique des pays nordiques", *Population* 32(1), jan-feb 77 : 139-174.

3041   SAMMAN, M. L. "La situation démographique de la Syrie", *Population* 31(6), nov-dec 76 : 1253-1288.

3042   SHILOH, Ailon. "Egypt: demography, ecology and the Lumpenproletariat", *Mid. East R.* 7(2), 1974-1975 : 32-42.

3043   "Sixième rapport sur la situation démographique de la France", *Population* 32(2), mar-apr 77 : 255-330.

3044   SOMOZA, J. L. "Encuesta demográfica nacional de Bolivia. Informe sobre aspectos demográficos" (National population survey in Bolivia. Information on demographic aspects), *Notas Pobl.* 4(11), aug 76 : 11-41.

3045   SOUTH AFRICA. Department of Statistics. *Bevolking van Suid-Afrika: 1904-1970 / Population of South Africa: 1904-1970*. Pretoria, Staatsdrukker, 76, xviii-436 p.

3046   SRB, Vladimir. "Le développement de la population en Tchécoslovaquie en 1976", *Demosta* 10(1), 1977 : 21-27.

3047   TOGNETTI, Keith. "Some extensions of the Keyfitz momentum relationship", *Demography* 13(4), nov 76 : 307-512.

3048   VAN DER HARST, H. D. H. "Bevolkingsontwikkeling en woningbehoefte" (Population development and demand for housing), *Bevolking en Gezin* (1), 1977 : 5-24.

3049   VAN PRAAG, P. "Het bevolkingvraagstuk in België: standpunten en opvattingen in het begin van de 20e eeuw" (The population problem in Belgium: points of view and concepts of the first quarter of the 20th century), *Bevolking en Gezin* (1), 1977 : 57-80.

3050   VAN PRAAG, P . "Views and concepts relating to population problems in the Netherlands 1918-1939", *Popul. Stud.* 31(2), jul 77 : 251-265.

3051   VENEZUELA. Centro de investigaciones económicas. *La población de Venezuela* (The population of Venezuela). Paris, CICRED, 76, 167 p.

3052   VINOVSKIS, Maris. *Demographic history and the world population crisis*. Worcester, Mass., Clark University Press, 76, xii-94 p.

3053   WINTER, J. M. "Some aspects of the demographic consequences of the first world war in Britain", *Popul. Stud.* 30(3), nov 76 : 539-552.

3054   WORTON, Stanley N. *Population growth in America*. Rochelle Park, N.J., Hayden Book Co., 76, 182 p.

15312.

[See also / Voir aussi: 2947, 4037, 4410, 5125]

3055   ANTIC, Lazo. "Organiziranje suvremene prehrane gradsog stanovnistva" (Organizing of modern nourishment for urban population), *Sociol. sela* 15(1-2), 1977 : 99-108.

3056   BADARI, V. S. "Disaggregation of urban populations into modern and traditional categories: a methodological note and application to Venezuela", *Estadística (Washington)* 30(114), jul 76 : 30-49.

3057   ESAINKO, Peter. *Ethnic and population changes in San Francisco*. San Francisco, Esainko, 76, 112 p.-1 l.

3058   ERREJON, J. A. "Cambio socioeconómico y evolución de la población activa en España, 1950-1970" (Socio-economic change and evolution of the working population in Spain, 1950-1970), *R. Estud. sindic.* 10(38), jul-sep 76 : 127-149.

3059   FAURE-SOULET, F. "Statistiques annuelles de population active
        (l'exemple du VIe Plan 1971-1975)", *R. Écon. Centre-Est* 19(73-
        74), jul-dec 76 : 11-26. *[France.]*
3060   GARCIA BALLESTEROS, A.; GRANDIS, A.; DEL RIO, I. "Los movimientos
        migratorios de la población de Madrid" (Migratory movements of
        the Madrid population), *R. int. Sociol. (Madrid)* 35(22), 1977 :
        193-224.
3061   ISLAMI, Hivzi. "Poljoprivredno stanovništvo Kosova" (Agricultural
        population of Kosovo), *Sociol. sela* 15(1-2), 1977 : 37-47.
        [Yugoslavia.]
3062   KALMYK, V. A. "Izmenenie uslovij i struktury zanjatosti sel'skogo
        naselenija v processe urbanizacii derevni" (Change of employ-
        ment conditions and structure of rural population in the process
        of village urbanization), *Sociol. Issled. (Moskva)* (3), 1976 :
        50-59.
3063   KORZYBSKI, Stanislas. *Une méthode inductive et peuplement urbain.*
        Lille, Université de Lille III; Paris, H. Champion, 76, xxv-
        812 p.
3064   LULOFF, A. E.; STOKES, C. Shannon. "A note on population size and
        community differentiation in nonmetropolitan communities", *So-
        ciol. soc. Res.* 61(4), jul 77 : 486-495.
3065   PEDERSEN, Peter J. "Arbejdsstyrke og beskaeftigelse 1911-1970"
        (Labour force and employment, 1911-1970), *Soc. Tss.* 53(2), 1977
        : 31-56. *[Denmark.]*
3066   PERNIA, Ernesto M. *A method of decomposing urban population growth
        and an application to Philippine data.* Honolulu, East-West Cen-
        ter, 76, v-26 p.
3067   RYVKINA, R. V. "Tradicionnye i urbanisticeskie cennosti sel'skogo
        naselenija i ih zavisimost' ot mesta žitel'stva" (Traditional
        and urban values of rural population and their dependence upon
        the residence), in: *Sibirskaja derevnja v uslovijah urbanizacii.*
        Novosibirsk, 1976 : 116-134.
3068   SAÁD, J. "A lakosság területi szegregálódása a városnövekedés fo-
        lyamatában" (The territorial segregation of the population in
        the course of city-growing), *Valóság* (3), 1977 : 78-87.
3069   SARIN, Mirja. "Helsingin vaeston yhteiskunnallinen rakenne" (So-
        cial structure of the population of Helsinki), *Tilastoll. kuukau-
        sit. Helsingistä* (3), 1977 : 77-126.

15320. Morbidity
   Morbidité

[See also / Voir aussi: 550, 2891, 2924, 5618, 5636]

3070   ALTHEIDE, David L. "Mental illness and the news: the Eagleton
        story", *Sociol. soc. Res.* 61(2), jan 77 : 138-155.
3071   ARCY, Carl D'; BROCKMAN, Joan. "Public rejection of the ex-mental
        patient: are attitudes changing ?", *Canad. R. Sociol. Anthropol.*
        14(1), feb 77 : 68-80.
3072   ASHFORD, Nicholas Askounes. *Crisis in the workplace: occupational
        disease and injury: a report to the Ford Foundation.* Cambridge,
        Mass.-London, MIT Press, 76, xii-589 p. CR: James R. CHELIUS,
        J. econ. Liter. 15(2), jun 77 : 571-572.
3073   BALLÓ, Robert. "A rokkantság szociálpszichológiai vonatkozása"
        (Psycho-social aspects of disease), *Med. univ.* (2), 1976 : 79-
        81.
3074   BARDEAU, Jean-Marc. *Infirmités et inadaptation sociale: pour une
        étude socio-politique de l'intégration des handicapés dans la
        société capitaliste.* Paris, Payot, 77, 234 p.
3075   BLAXTER, Mildred. *The meaning of disability: a sociological study
        of impairment.* London, Heinemann, 76, x-259 p. *[Great Britain.]*
3076   CARSTAIRS, G. Morris; KAPUR, Ravi L. *The great universe of Kota:
        stress, change, and mental disorder in an Indian village.* London,
        Hogarth Press, 76, 176 p.

3077   ERLENMEYER-KIMLING, L. "Schizophrenia: a bag of dilemmas", *Soc.*
         Biology 23(2), 1976 : 123-134.

3078   FALISE, Michel *et al. Handicap de santé et paupérisation: étude*
         effectuée pour le Centre national de la recherche scientifique.
         Paris, CNRS, 76, 112 p.

3079   HAYES, Kent. "Les droits du patient dans la communauté", *Connexions*
         20, 1976 : 77-86.

3080   KROHN, Marvin D.; AKERS, Ronald L. "An alternative view of the
         labelling versus psychiatric perspectives on societal reaction
         to mental illness", *Soc. Forces* 56(2), dec 77 : 341-361.

3081   MAGARO, Peter A. (ed.). *The construction of madness: emerging con-*
         ceptions into the psychotic process. New York, Pergamon Press,
         76, 221 p.

3082   MAGUIN, P. *et al.* "Les malades mentaux en longue durée-invalidité
         dans une agglomération urbaine universitaire", *C. Sociol. Démogr.*
         médic. 17(1), jan-mar 77 : 17-33.

3083   MANNING, Peter K.; ZUCKER, Martine. *The sociology of mental health*
         and illness. Indianapolis, Bobbs-Merrill, 76, 115 p.

3084   MARAIS, Elizabeth; MARAIS, Michael. *Lives worth living: the right*
         of all the handicapped. London, Souvenir Press, 76, 282 p. -4 1.
         [UK.]

3085   MICKLIN, Michael; LEON, Carlos A. "Perceptions of the distribu-
         tion of mental disorder in a South American city: some neglec-
         ted aspects of the sociology of medical occupations", *Sociol.*
         Wk Occupat. 3(3), aug 76 : 273-302.

3086   MOVAHEDI, Siawak. "Methodological schizophrenia: a problem in the
         sociology of science", *Int. J. contemp. Sociol.* 13(1-2), jan-
         apr 76 : 79-92.

3087   ORFORD, Jim. *The social psychology of mental disorder.* Harmonds-
         worth-New York, Penguin Education, 76, 266 p.

3088   SCULL, Andrew T. "Madness and segregative control: the rise of the
         insane asylum", *Soc. Probl.* 24(3), feb 77 ; 337-351.

3089   SCULL, A. T. "The decarceration of the mentally ill: a critical
         view", *Polit. and Soc.* 6(2), 1976 : 173-212.

3090   SEGAL, Steven P. *et al.* "Falling through the cracks: mental dis-
         order and social margin in a young vagrant population", *Soc.*
         Probl. 24(3), feb 77 : 387-400.

3091   SEYWALD, Aiga. *Körperliche Behinderung: Grundfragen eine Soziolo-*
         gie der Benachteiligten (Physical handicap: basic questions of
         a sociology of the handicapped). Frankfurt-am-Main-New York,
         Campus-Verlag, 77, 144 p.

3092   SIERADZKI, Maciej. "Inwalida w środowisku społecznym" (Disabled
         in a social environment), *Stud. socjol.* 64(1), 1977 : 267-289.

3093   VANIER, J. "La place du handicapé dans la société", *Études (Paris)*
         dec 76 : 641-650.

3094   YOKOYAMA, Minoru. "Shakaigaku kara no seishin shôgai no kenkyu"
         (The sociological study of mental disorders), *Shakaigaku Hyôron*
         28(1), 1977 : 2-18.

         15330. Mortality
                  Mortalité

         [See also / Voir aussi: 1691, 2891, 3132, 3166, 3172, 5665]

3095   ARIES, Philippe. *Essais sur l'histoire de la mort en Occident du*
         Moyen Âge à nos jours. Paris, Éditions du Seuil, 75, 226 p.

3096   BLACKER, J. G. C. "The estimation of adult mortality in Africa
         from data on orphanhood", *Popul. Stud.* 31(1), mar 77 : 107-128.

3097   BUI-DANG-HA, Doan. "Note sur la mortalité chez les médecins", *C.*
         Sociol. Démogr. médic. 17(2), apr-jun 77 : 73-76.

3098   CARVALHO, Alceu Vicente W. DE; MOURA RIBEIRO, Edson DE. "Estudo da
         mortalidade proporsional segundo grupos de idade e causas de obi-
         to em algunas capitais brasileiras em 1970" (Study of propor-

tional according to age groups and causes of death in some Brazilian chief towns in 1970), *R. brasil. Estatíst.* 37(148), oct-dec 76 : 457-482.

3099   Bibl.XXVI-2545. CHESNAIS, Jean-Claude. *Les morts violentes en France depuis 1826. Comparaisons internationales.* CR: Philippe BESNARD, *R. franç. Sociol.* 18(2), apr-jun 77 : 342-344.

3100   CHESNAIS, Jean-Claude; VALLIN, Jacques. "Évolution récente de la mortalité et de la morbidité dues aux accidents de la route, 1968-1977", *Population* 32(6), nov-dec 77 : 1239-1265. *[France.]*

3101   COPENHAGEN. Statistiske kontor. *Dødeligheden i København 1951-1970 / Mortality in Copenhagen, 1951-1970.* Copenhagen, Statistiske kontor, 76, 78 p.

3102   D'AMATO, Marina. "La morte come problema sociologico" (Death as a sociological problem), *Crit. sociol. (Roma)* 37, 1976 : 127-132.

3103   DENNIS, Ruth E. "Social stress and mortality among nonwhite males", *Phylon* 38(3), sep 77 : 315-328. *[USA.]*

3104   DINH, Q. C. "Tables de mortalité de la population de la France pour la période 1966-1970", *Coll. INSÉE Sér. D* 49, nov 76 : 3-96.

3105   FORDYCE, E. James. "Early mortality measures as indicators of socio-economic well-being for whites and non-whites: a re-appraisal", *Sociol. soc. Res.* 61(2), jan 77 : 125-137.

3106   GARROS, Bertrand; VALLIN, Jacques. "La mortalité par cause en Algérie, le cas de Tebessa", *Population* 32(4-5), jul-oct 77 : 807-833.

3107   GEE, Susan C.; LEE, Eun S.; FORTHOFER, Ron N. "Ethnic differentials in neonatal and postneonatal mortality: a birth cohort analysis by a binary variable multiple regression method", *Soc. Biology* 23(4), 1976 : 317-325.

3108   HILL, K. "Estimating adult mortality levels from information on widowhood", *Popul. Stud.* 31(1), mar 77 : 75-84.

3109   HILL, K.; TRUSSELL, J. "Further developments in indirect mortality estimation", *Popul. Stud.* 31(2), jul 77 : 313-334.

3110   KABIR, M. "Levels and patterns of infant and child mortality in Bangladesh", *Soc. Biology* 24(2), 1977 : 158-165.

3111   KALISH, Richard A.; REYNOLDS, David K. *Death and ethnicity: a psychocultural study.* Los Angeles, Ethel Percy Andrus Gerontology Center, University of Southern California, 76, ii-224 p.

3112   KASTENBAUM, Robert. *Death, society and human experience.* Saint Louis, Mosby, 77, x-328 p.

3113   LEE, Anne S. "Maternal mortality in the United States", *Phylon* 38(3), sep 77 : 259-266.

3114   LOSCHKY, David J. "Economic change, mortality and Malthusian theory", *Popul. Stud.* 30(3), nov 76 : 439-452.

3115   MADEIRA, J. L.; FRIAS, L. A. DE M. "Un modelo de regressão para aferir os niveis da mortalidade" (A regression model to evaluate death rate), *R. brasil. Estadíst.* 36(143), jul-sep 75 : 367-384. *[Brazil.]*

3116   MANTON, Kenneth G.; TOLLEY, H. Dennis; POSS, Sharon Sandomirsky. "Life table techniques for multiple-cause mortality", *Demography* 13(4), nov 76 : 541-564.

3117   MARKIDES, Kyriakos S.; BARNES, Donna. "A methodological note on the relationship between infant mortality and socioeconomic status with evidence from San Antonio, Texas", *Soc. Biology* 24(1), 1977 : 38-44.

3118   MOTTA, L. C. DA; THEIAS, M. M. "Selecção e análise das principais causas de morte em Portugal" (Selection and analysis of principal causes of death in Portugal), *R. Centro Estud. demogr.* 21, 1973-1974 : 23-69.

3119   POUCHELLE, Marie-Christine. "La prise en charge de la mort: médecine, médecins et chirurgiens devant les problèmes liés à la mort à la fin du Moyen Âge (XIII-XVe siècles)", *Archiv. europ. Sociol.* 17(2), 1976 : 249-278.

3120   PRESTON, Samuel H. "A halandóság és a gazdasági fejlettség szintje
        közötti változó kapcsolat" (The variable link between mortality
        and the level of economic development), *Demográfia* 19(2-3),
        1976 : 228-255.

3121   PRESTON, Samuel H. *Mortality patterns in national populations: with
        special reference to recorded causes of death.* New York, Academ-
        ic Press, 76, xi-201 p.

3122   SAW-SWEE-HOCK. "Occupational mortality variations in Singapore,
        1970", *J. roy. Statist. Soc.* 139(2), 1976 : 218-226.

3123   SCHOEN, Robert. "Measuring mortality trends and differentials",
        Soc. Biology 23(3), 1976 : 235-243.

3124   SWENSON, Ingrid. "Expected reductions in fetal and infant mortali-
        ty by prolonged pregnancy spacing in rural Bangladesh", *Bangladesh
        Develop. Stud.* 5(1), jan 77 : 1-16.

3125   TABUTEAU, B. "Mortalité régionale suivant le milieu social", *Sud.
        Inform. Provence-Côte d'Azur-Corse* (1), jan 77 : 39-45.

3126   TABUTIN, Dominique. "La mortalité en Algérie, selon le sexe, le
        secteur d'habitat et quelques caractéristiques socio-économiques
        (résultats de l'enquête démographique de 1969-1971)", *Popul. et
        Famille* 39(3), 1976 : 109-144.

3127   TABUTIN, Dominique. *Mortalité infantile et juvénile en Algérie.*
        Paris, Presses universitaires de France, 76, xii-275 p. *[Voir
        aussi Population* 31(6), nov-dec 76 : 1189-1193.*]*

3128   TENTLER, Thomas N. "Death and dying in many disciplines: a review
        article", *Comp. Stud. Soc. Hist.* 19(4), oct 77 : 511-522.

3129   VIDAL, Daniel. "L'article de la mort", *Sociol. Trav.* 19(3), jul-sep
        77 : 295-328.

3130   ZBOŘILOVÁ, Jitka. "Les tables de mortalité infantile par cause.
        Application à la Tchécoslovaquie et à la France 1968-1972",
        Population 32(3), mai-jun 77 : 555-578.

3131   ZIÉGLER, Jean. *Les vivants et la mort.* Paris, Éditions du Seuil,
        75, 314 p.

15340. Fertility. Natality
Fecondité. Natalité

[See also / Voir aussi: 1479, 2613, 2719, 3011, 3197, 3208, 3219,
3256, 3290, 3293, 3301, 3410, 3427, 4510, 4532]

3132   ADEGBOLA, O. "New estimates of fertility and child mortality in
        Africa South of the Sahara", *Popul. Stud.* 31(3), nov 77 : 467-
        486.

3133   AJAMI, I. "Differential fertility in peasant communities: a study
        of six Iranian villages", *Popul. Stud.* 30(3), nov 76 : 453-463.

3134   ARNEY, William Ray. "Socioeconomic change and fertility: a time-
        series model for the United States", *Sociol. Meth. Res.* 6(1),
        aug 77 : 63-90.

3135   ARRETX, Carmen. *Análisis de la fecundidad de Bolivia basado en los
        datos de la encuesta demográfica nacional de 1975* (Analysis of
        fertility in Bolivia founded on data from the 1975 national de-
        mographic census). La Paz, Ministerio de Planeamiento y Coordi-
        nación de la Presidencia de la República, Instituto Nacional de
        Estadística, Centro Latinoamericano de Demografía, 76, 40 p.

3136   Bibl.XXVI-2576. ASKHAM, Janet. *Fertility and deprivation: a study
        of differential fertility amongst working-class families in
        Aberdeen.* CR: Kristen LUKER, *Amer. J. Sociol.* 82(4), jan 77 :
        907-909; Hyman RODMAN, *Contemp. Sociol.* (Washington) 6(1), jan
        77 : 44-45.

3137   BEBARTA, Prafulla C. *Family type and fertility in India.* North
        Quincy, Mass., Christopher Publishing House, 77, 147 p.

3138   BHATTACHARYYA, Amit K. "Role of rural-urban income inequality in
        fertility reduction: cases on Turkey, Taiwan and Morocco", *Econ.
        Develop. cult. Change* 26(1), oct 77 : 11/-138.

3139   BLAYO, Yves; VERON, Jacques. "La fécondité dans quelques pays d'Asie orientale", *Population* 32(4-5), jul-oct 77 : 945-975.

3140   BOURGEOIS-PICHAT, J. "Baisse de la fécondité et descendance familiale", *Population* 31(6), nov-dec 76 : 1045-1097.

3141   CALDWELL, Gary. "La baisse de la fécondité au Québec à la lumière de la sociologie québécoise", *Rech. sociogr.* 17(1), jan-apr 76 : 7-22.

3142   CALDWELL, J. C. "The economic nationality of high fertility: an investigation illustrated with Nigerian survey data", *Popul. Stud.* 31(1), mar 77 : 5-27.

3143   CALDWELL, J. C.; CALDWELL, Pat. "The role of marital sexual abstinence in determining fertility: a study of the Yoruba in Nigeria", *Popul. Stud.* 31(2), jul 77 : 193-217.

3144   CHAMIE, J. "Religious differentials in fertility: Lebanon 1971", *Popul. Stud.* 31(2), jul 77 : 365-382.

3145   CHAUDHURY, Rafiqul Huda. "Education and fertility in Bangladesh", *Bangladesh Develop. Stud.* 5(1), jan 77 : 81-110.

3146   CHAUDHURY, Rafiqul Huda. "Relative income and fertility", *Demography* 14(2), mai 77 : 179-195.

3147   CLIGNET, Rémi. "Rôles matrimoniaux et fécondité en Afrique Noire", *R. franç. Sociol.* 18(3), jul-sep 77 : 439-464.

3148   COLLOMB, Philippe. "Aspects culturels et socio-psychologiques de la fécondité française. Une enquête de l'INED", *Population* 32(3), mai-jun 77 : 655-658.

3149   COLLOMB, Philippe. "De quelques facteurs structurels de baisse de la fécondité française", *Population* 31(6), nov-dec 76 : 1099-1117.

3150   DEFRONZO, James. "Testing the economic theory of fertility with cross-sectional and change data", *Soc. Biology* 23(3), 1976 : 226-234.

3151   FREEDMAN, R. *et al.* "Trends in fertility and in the effects of education on fertility in Taiwan, 1961-1974", *Stud. Family Plan.* 8(1), jan 77 : 11-18.

3152   GARCÍA BALLESTEROS, Aurora. "La fecundidad de la población española en 1970. Aplicación de un nuevo método demográfico" (The fertility of Spanish population in 1970. Application of a new demographical method), *R. int. Sociol. (Madrid)* 34(18-20), apr-dec 76 : 49-62.

3153   GLASS, D. V. "Jelenlegi és távlati termékenységi trendek a gazdaságilag fejlett országokban" (Present trends and prospects of fertility in developed countries), *Demográfia* 19(4), 1976 : 391-454.

3154   GOLDSTEIN, Sidney; TIRASAWAT, Penporn. *The fertility of migrants to urban places in Thailand.* Honolulu, East-West Center, 77, v-49 p.

3155   HENLEY, James R. Jr.; GUSTAVUS, Susan O. "An exploratory technique for measuring fertility norms", *Soc. Biology* 24(2), 1977 : 149-157.

3156   HULL, T. H.; HULL, V. J. "The relation of economic class and fertility: an analysis of some Indonesian data", *Popul. Stud.* 31(1), mar 77 : 43-58.

3157   JONES, G. W. "Fertility levels and trends in Indonesia", *Popul. Stud.* 31(1), mar 77 : 29-41.

3158   JONES, Hwo R. "Fertility decline in Barbados: some spatial considerations", *Stud. Family Plan.* 8(6), jun 77 : 157-163.

3159   JONG, G. F. DE; SELL, R. R. "Changes in childlessness in the United States: a demographic path analysis", *Popul. Stud.* 31(1), mar 77 : 129-142.

3160   JULÉMONT, Gislaine. "Une enquête nationale sur la fécondité. La stabilité des attentes , une analyse longitudinale (1966-1970)", *Popul. et Famille* 37(2), 1976 : 1-70. [Voir aussi Bibl.XXVI-2606.]

3161   KAMINSKY, M. "Tasa de natalidad y variables socio-económicas: una nota" (Birth rate and socio-economic variables: a note), *Notas*

Pobl. 4(11), aug 76 : 97-110.

3162   KONG KYUN RO; KYE CHOON AHN. "Migration and fertility in Korea", *J. Family Planning Stud.* (4), nov 77 : 101-143.

3163   LAYNE, Norman R. Jr.; LOWE, Jay. "The effects of the timing of successive births upon the social organization of American families", *Sociol. Focus* 10(1), jan 77 : 89-96.

3164   LEE-HYO-CHAE; CHOH YOUG. "Fertility and women's labor force participation in Korea", *Korea J.* 17(71), jul 77 : 12-35.

3165   MASSEY, Douglas S.; TEDROW, Lucky M. "Economic development and fertility: a methodological re-evaluation", *Popul. Stud.* 30(3), nov 76 : 429-437.

3166   McDONALD, Peter F.; YASIN, Mohammad; JONES, Gavin W. *Levels and trends in fertility and childhood mortality in Indonesia.* Jakarta, Lembaga Demografi, Fakultas Ekonomi, Universitas Indonesia, 76, ix-79 p.

3167   MONNIER, Alain. *La naissance d'un enfant: incidences sur les conditions de vie des familles.* Paris, Presses universitaires de France, 77, viii-231 p.

3168   OESHSLI, F. W.; ADLAKHA, A. "Variação temporal e regional da natalidade no Brasil, 1940-1970" (Birth rate variations according to periods and regions in Brazil, 1940-1970), *R. brasil. Estatíst.* 36(143), jul-sep 76 : 503-529.

3169   ORGANISATION DES NATIONS UNIES. Département des affaires économiques et sociales. *La fécondité et la planification familiale en Europe aux environs de 1970: étude comparative de douze enquêtes nationales.* New York, NU, 77, xii-197 p. *[Également publié en anglais.]*

3170   PAGE, H. J. "Patterns underlying fertility schedules: a decomposition by both age and marriage duration", *Popul. Stud.* 31(1), mar 77 : 85-106.

3171   PENDLETON, Brian F. "A conceptual model for the identification, organization, and measure of influence of fertility policies and programs", *Soc. Biology* 23(4), 1976 : 326-340.

3172   PICK, James B. "Correlates of fertility and mortality in low-migration standard metropolitan statistical areas", *Soc. Biology* 24(1), 1977 : 69-83.

3173   POTTER, J. E. "Problems in using birth-history analysis to estimate trends in fertility", *Popul. Stud.* 31(2), jul 77 : 335-364.

3174   POTTER, Joseph E. *et al.* "The rapid decline in Columbian fertility", *Popul. Develop. R.* 2(3-4), sep-dec 76 : 509-528.

3175   RAM, B. "Regional sub-cultural explanations of Black fertility in the Unites States", *Popul. Stud.* 30(3), nov 76 : 553-559.

3176   REBELLO, Marina Teixeira Barroso. "Condicionamentos socio-econômicos da fecundidade" (Socio-economic factors of fertility), *R. brasil. Estat.* 37(148), oct-dec 76 : 395-444. *[Brazil.]*

3177   RICHARDS, Toni. "Fertility decline in Germany: an econometric appraisal", *Popul. Stud.* 31(3), nov 77 : 537-553.

3178   RIZK, Hanna. "Trends in fertility and family planning in Jordan", *Stud. Family Plan.* 8(4), apr 77 : 91)99.

3179   RODGERS, G. B. "Fertility and desired fertility; longitudinal evidence from Thailand", *Popul. Stud.* 30(3), nov 76 : 511-526.

3180   SAUVY, Alfred. "Le navire", *R. franç. Sociol.* 18(2), apr-jun 77 : 187-200. *[Baisse de la fécondité en France.]*

3181   SRB, V. "Les tendances à long terme de la fécondité en Tchécoslovaquie", *Demosta* 9(4), 1976 : 122-129.

3182   UKAEGBU, Alfred O. "Fertility of women in polygynous unions in rural Eastern Nigeria", *J. Marriage Family* 39(2), mai 77 : 397-404.

3183   UKAEGBU, Alfred O. "Socio-cultural determination of fertility: a case study of rural Eastern Nigeria", *J. comp. Family Stud.* 8(1), 1977 : 99-115.

3184   VOHRA, H. R. "Problems of conducting a fertility survey in rural areas", *Ind. J. soc. Wk* 37(4), jan 77 : 411-420.

3185   WARE, H. "Fertility and work-force participation: the experience of Melbourne", *Popul. Stud.* 30(3), nov 76 : 413-427.

15350. Family planning
Planification de la famille

[See also / Voir aussi: 469, 1519, 1674, 3026, 3034, 3169, 3178, 3309, 3445, 5505]

3186   AMPOFO, D. A. *et al.* "The Danfa family planning program in rural Ghana", *Stud. Family Plan.* 7(10), oct 76 : 266-274.

3187   ANDERSON, John E. "Planning and births: difference between blacks and whites in the United States", *Phylon* 38(3), sep 77 : 282-296.

3188   ARCY, F. D'. "The Malthusian League and the resistance to birth control propaganda in late Victorian Britain", *Popul. Stud.* 31(3), nov 77 : 429-448.

3189   BADOWSKI, I. "Wychowanie seksualne a planowanie rodziny" (Sexual education and family planning), *Biul. IGS* 20(3), 1977 : 154-173.

3190   BARNES, Josephine. *Essentials of family planning.* Oxford, Blackwell Scientific; Philadelphia, J. B. Lippincott, 76, xi-139 p.

3191   BILSBORROW, Richard E. *Population in development planning: background and bibliography.* Chapel Hill, University of North Carolina, 76, xiii-216 p.

3192   BISSON, Antoine F.; PICHE, Victor. "L'accord conjugal en matière de fécondité et de planification familiale: une enquête au Québec" *Population* 32(1), jan-feb 77 : 184-193.

3193   BLAYO, Chantal. "L'enregistrement de l'avortement provoqué en France", *Population* 32(4-5), jul-oct 77 : 977-987.

3194   BLEEK, Wolf. "Family planning or birth control. The Ghanaian contradiction", *Cult. et Dévelop.* 9(1), 1977 : 64-81.

3195   BULGARU, M. "Niektóre aspekty polityki demograficznej Rumunii" (Some aspects of Romania's population policy), *Biul. IGS* 20(1), 1977 : 154-168.

3196   CALDWELL, J. C.; WARE, Helen. "The evolution of family planning in an African city: Ibadan, Nigeria", *Popul. Stud.* 31(3), nov 77 : 487-507.

3197   CUTRIGHT, Phillips; JAFFE, Frederick S. *Impact of family planning programs on fertility: the US experience.* New York, Praeger, 77, xvi-150 p.

3198   DEMERATH, Nicholas Jay. *Birth control and foreign policy: the alternatives to family planning.* New York, Harper and Row, 76, x-228 p.

3199   DEXEUS, Santiago; RIVIÈRE, Margarita. *Anticonceptivos y control de natalidad* (Contraceptives and birth control). Barcelona, La Gaya Ciencia/Bausán, 76, 231 p.

3200   DZIENIO, K. "Wnioski wynnikające z doświadczeń w zakresis realizacji polityki ludnościowej w wybrannych europejskich krajach socjalistycznych" (Conclusions from experience concerning implementation of population policy in selected European socialist countries), *Biul. IGS* 20(2), 1977 : 47-85.

3201   FORD, Kathleen. "Abortion and family-building models: fertility limitation in Hungary", *Demography* 13(4), nov 76 : 495-505.

3202   FUCHS, Roland F.; DEMKO, Georges S. "Spacial population policies in the socialist countries of Eastern Europe", *Soc. Sci. Quart.* 58(1), jun 77 : 60-73.

3203   HAVEMAN, Robert H. "Benefit-cost analysis and family planning programmes", *Popul. Develop. R.* 2(1), mar 76 : 37-64.

3204   HIRABAYASHI, Gordon; SARAM, P. A. "Factors underlying modernity: birth planning preferences in rural Sri Lanka", *Asian Profile* 5(1), feb 77 : 47-62.

3205   HOLLERBACH, Paula. "Bad luck or good judgment ?", *Populi* 4(3), 1977 48-53. *[About LUKER, Kristin. Taking chances; abortion and the de cision not to contracept.]*

3206   HOUT, Michael. "Family planning program activity and patient enrol‑
        ment rates in the United States, 1969 and 1971", *Demography*
        14(2), mai 77 : 213‑222.

3207   KAHLEY, William J.; GILLASPY, Ronald T. "An economic model of con‑
        traceptive choice: analysis of family planning acceptors in Bogo‑
        tā", *Soc. Biology* 24(2), 1977 : 135‑143.

3208   KAP SUK KOH; NICHOLS, D. J. "Measurement of the impact of the na‑
        tional family planning program on fertility in Korea: 1960‑1975",
        J. Family Planning Stud. (4), nov 77 : 153‑184.

3209   KNODEL, John. "Family limitation and the fertility transition: evi‑
        dence from the age patterns of fertility in Europe and Asia",
        Popul. Stud. 31(2), jul 77 : 219‑249.

3210   KVAŠA, A. Ja. *Upravlenie razvitiem narodonaselenija v SSSR (Prob‑
        lemy i perspektivy)* (The population development management in
        the USSR. Problems and forecasts). Moskva, Statistika, 77, 219 p.

3211   LEDENIG, W.; LUNGWITZ, L. "Podstawowe tezy i srodki polityki de‑
        mograficznej oraz tendencje rozwoju ludnosci w NRD" (Basic pre‑
        mises and means of population policy and trends in the develop‑
        ment of the population of the German Democratic Republic), *Biul.
        IGS* 20(1), 1977 : 119‑136.

3212   LERIDON, Henri *et al.* "La diffusion des méthodes modernes de contra‑
        ception: une étude dans une consultation hospitalière", *Population*
        32(4‑5), jul‑oct 77 : 777‑805.

3213   MATTESON, Richard L.; TERRANOVA, Gerald. "Social acceptance of new
        techniques of child conceptions", *J. soc. Psychol.* 101(2), apr
        77 : 225‑229.

3214   McLAREN, A. "Sex and socialism: the opposition of the French Left
        to birth control in the nineteenth century", *J. Hist. Ideas*
        37(3), jul‑sep 76 : 475‑492.

3215   MOREAU, Yannick. "La situation démographique et la politique fami‑
        liale en France", *R. jur. polit.* 31(2), apr‑jun 77 : 771‑784.

3216   MUÑOZ‑PEREZ, Francisco. "L'avortement provoqué légal dans le monde",
        Population 32(1), jan‑feb 77 : 175‑184.

3217   MUÑOZ PEREZ, Francisco. "La contraception des couples aux États‑
        Unis: évolution récente", *Population* 32(3), mai‑jun 77 : 698‑706.

3218   NESS, Gayl. "Politics and population growth", *Populi* 4(3), 1977 :
        18‑26.

3219   OSTERUD, Nancy; FULTON, John. "Family limitation and age at marriage:
        fertility decline in Sturbridge, Massachusetts, 1730‑1850", *Popul.
        Stud.* 30(3), nov 76 : 481‑494.

3220   PRYOR, Robin J. "Preferences versus policies ? The politics of po‑
        pulation distribution in Australia", *Austral. New Zealand J. So‑
        ciol.* 13(1), feb 77 : 23‑28.

3221   RIDKER, Ronald G. (ed.). *Population and development: the search for
        selective interventions.* Baltimore‑London, Johns Hopkins Univer‑
        sity Press, 76, xviii‑467 p.

3222   SOEJATNI. "Rôle et participation des femmes dans la planification
        des naissances", *Archipel* 13, 1977 : 295‑305. *[Indonésie.]*

3223   SOMERS, Ronlld.L. "Repeat abortion in Denmark: an analysis based
        on national record linkage", *Stud. Family Plan.* 8(6), jun 77 :
        142‑147.

3224   SURJIT KAUR. *Family planning in two industrial units: a study.* New
        Delhi, Sterling Publishers, 76, xiii‑256 p. *[India.]*

3225   THOMPSON, B. "Problems of abortion in Britain‑Aberdeen, a case
        study", *Popul. Stud.* 31(1), mar 77 : 143‑154.

3226   TOWNES, Brenda D. *et al.* "Brith planning values and decisions: the
        prediction of fertility", *J. appl. soc. Psychol.* 7(1), jan‑mar
        77 : 73‑88.

3227   UDRY, J. Richard; BAUMAN, Karl E.; MORRIS, Naomi M. "The effect of
        subsidized family planning services on reproductive behavior in

the United States, 1969-1974", *Demography* 13(4), nov 76 : 463-478.

3228   VAN DE KAA, D. J. "Het lange-termijn bevolkingsbeleid in West-Europa" (Long-term population policy in Western Europe), *Bevolking en Gezin* (2), 1977 : 137-155.

3229   VERON, J. "Niveaux nationaux de la natalité et politique de limitation des naissances", *Population* 31(6), nov-dec 76 : 1235-1246.

3230   VINOKUR-KAPLAN, Diane. "Family planning decision-making: a comparison and analysis of parents' considerations", *J. comp. Family Stud.* 8(1), 1977 : 79-98.

3231   WARE, Helen. "Motivations for the use of birth control: evidence from West Africa", *Demography* 13(4), nov 76 : 479-493.

3232   WESTOFF, Charles F.; RYDER, Norman B. *The contraceptive revolution.* Princeton, N.J., Princeton University Press, 77, vii-388 p. [USA.]

15400. MARRIAGE. FAMILY
MARIAGE. FAMILLE

15410. Sexual behavior
Comportement sexuel

[See also / Voir aussi: 1213]

3233   BARKER-BENFIELD, G. J. *The horrors of the half-known life: male attitudes toward women and sexuality in nineteenth-century America.* New York, Harper and Row, 76, 352 p. CR: Michael GORDON, *Contemp. Sociol. (Washington)* 6(1), jan 77 : 89-90.

3234   BARON, Robert A.; BELL, Paul A. "Sexual arousal and aggression by males: effects of type of erotic stimuli and prior provocation", *J. Person. soc. Psychol.* 35(2), feb 77 : 79-87.

3235   BAYER, Alan E. "Sexual permissiveness and correlates as determined through interaction analyses", *J. Marriage Family* 39(1), feb 77 : 29-40.

3236   BÉJIN, André; POLLAK, Michael. "La rationalisation de la sexualité", *C. int. Sociol.* 24(62), jan-jun 77 : 105-125.

3237   BIROUSTE, Jacques P.; MARTINEAU, Jean-Pierre. *Psychologie et sexualité: Colloque international de sexologie, Toulouse, septembre 1975.* Toulouse, Privat, 76, 275 p.

3238   BUDA, B. *Psychologie der Sexualität* (The psychology of sexuality). Budapest-Frankfurt-am-Main, Akademie Verlag, Marxistische Blätter, 77, 284 p.

3239   CHEVERNY, Julien. *Sexologie de l'Occident.* Paris, Hachette, 76, 661 p.

3240   DAVIDSON, J. Kenneth; LESLIE, Gerald R. "Premarital sexual intercourse: an application of axiomatic theory construction", *J. Marriage Family* 39(1), feb 77 : 15-25.

3241   DeLORA, Joann S. *et al. Understanding sexual interaction.* Boston, Houghton Mifflin, 77, xviii-642 p.

3242   DINNERSTEIN, Dorothy. *The mermaid and the minotaur: sexual arrangements and human malaise.* New York, Harper and Row, 76, xv-288 p. CR: Miriam M. JOHNSON, *Contemp. Sociol. (Washington)* 6(4), jul 77 : 476-478.

3243   ESTEP, Rhoda E.; BURT, Martha R.; MILLIGAN, Herman J. "The socialization of sexual identity", *J. Marriage Family* 39(1), feb 77 : 99-112.

3244   FOUCAULT, Michel. *Histoire de la sexualité.* Paris, Gallimard, 76, 211 p.

3245   GUTHEIL, Thomas G.; AVERY, Nicholas C. "Multiple overt incest as family defense against loss", *Family Process* 16(1), mar 77 : 105-116.

3246   HITE, Shere. *The Hite report: a nationwide study on female sexuality.* New York, Macmillan, 76, xi-438 p. [USA.]

3247   HOHMANN, Joachim Stephan. *Homosexualität und Subkultur* (Homosexuality and sub-culture). Lollar-am-Lahn, Achenbach, 76, 207 p.
        [Germany, FR.]

3248   LAGO, Maria; PARAMELLE, France. *La femme homosexuelle*. Tournai,
        Casterman, 76, 203 p.

3249   LIGHT, Ivan. "The ethic vice industry, 1880-1944", *Amer. sociol.
        R.* 42(3), jun 77 : 464-479.

3250   MÜHLFELD, Claus. "Inzesttabu, familiale Sozialisation und Sozialstruktur" (Incest taboo, socialization of the family and social
        structure), *Soz. Welt* 28(2), 1977 : 221-238.

3251   NAKAJIMA, Akinori. "E. Durkheim no sei-kyô-ikuron" (E. Durkheim's
        theory of sex education), *Aikyôdai Kenpô (Kyôiku Kagaku)* 26,
        1977 : 61-74.

3252   PERICO, Giacomo. "Il problema dell'omosessualità" (Homosexuality
        problem), *Aggiorn. soc.* 28(5), mai 77 : 303-318.

3253   RIVERO, Eneida B. "Educación sexual en Puerto Rico" (Sex education in Puerto Rico), *R. Cienc. soc. (Puerto Rico)* 19(2), jun
        75 : 169-191.

3254   SCHARF, Betty R. "Sexual stratification and social stratification",
        Brit. J. Sociol. 28(4), dec 77 : 450-466.

3255   SCHULZ, Barbara *et al.* "Explaining premarital sexual intercourse
        among college students: a causal model", *Soc. Forces* 56(1), sep
        77 : 148-165.

3256   STEWART, Karen Robb (ed.). *Adolescent sexuality and teenage pregnancy: a selected, annotated bibliography with summary forewords*. Chapel Hill, State Services Office, Carolina Population
        Center, University of North Carolina at Chapel Hill, 76, vii-
        43 p.

3257   SPANIER, Graham B. "Use of recall data in survey research on human
        sexual behavior", *Soc. Biology* 23(3), 1976 : 244-253.

3258   STRACER, C. J. "Research on homosexuality in the Netherlands",
        Netherlands J. Sociol. 12(2), dec 76 : 121-137.

3259   TÜMMERS, Hannelore. *Sozialpsychologische Aspekte der Sexualität
        im Alter* (Social and psychological aspects of the sexuality of
        the aged). Köln-Wien, Böhlau, 76, 186 p.

3260   VANFOSSEN, Beth Ensminger. "Sexual stratification and sex-role socialization", *J. Marriage Family* 39(3), aug 77 : 563-574.

3261   VRGA, Djuro J. "Displacement and differential attitudes of two
        groups of revolutionary fighters toward sexual promiscuity",
        Sociol. int. (Berlin) 12(1-2), 1974 : 203-227.

3262   WEINBERG, Martin S. (ed.). *Sex research: studies from the Kinsey
        Institute*. New York, Oxford University Press, 76, 320 p. CR:
        Marjorie K. LITTLE, *Contemp. Sociol. (Washington)* 6(2), mar 77 :
        234-235.

3263   WHITEHEAD, Antonia; MATHEWS, Andrew. "Attitude change during behavioural treatment of sexual inadequacy", *Brit. J. soc. clinic.
        Psychol.* 16(3), sep 77 : 275-281.

3264   ZURCHER, Louis A. Jr.; KIRKPATRICK, R. George. *Citizens for decency: antipornography crusades as status defense*. Austin, University of Texas Press, 76, 412 p. CR: Albert J. BERGESEN, *Amer.
        J. Sociol.* 82(6), mai 77 : 1420-1422.

        ## 15420. Marriage. Nuptiality
        ## Mariage. Nuptialité

        15421.

        [See also / Voir aussi: 1101, 2525, 3192, 3407, 3522]

3265   ADAMSKI, Franciszek. "Model concepts of marriage in Poland", *Polish
        sociol. B.* 35(3), 1976 : 51-60.

3266   BAKER, Margaret. *Marriage customs and folklore*. Newton Abbot, Eng.,
        David and Charles; Totowa, N.J., Rowman and Littlefield, 77, 144 p.

3267   BALLONOFF, Paul A. "Note on a category arising naturally in marriage theory", *Soc. Sci. Inform.* 15(4-5), 1976 : 823-829.

3268   BROWN, Prudence; PERRY, Lorraine; HARBURG, Ernest. "Sex role attitudes and psychological outcomes for Black and White women experiencing marital dissolution", *J. Marriage Family* 39(3), aug 77 : 549-561.

3269   BUMPASS, Larry L.; MBURUGU, Edward K. "Age at marriage and completed family size", *Soc. Biology* 24(1), 1977 : 31-37.

3270   CALL, Vaughn R. A.; OTTO, Luther B. "Age at marriage as a mobility contingency: estimates for the Nye-Berardo model", *J. Marriage Family* 39(1), feb 77 : 67-79.

3271   CARTER, Hugh; GLICK, Paul C. *Marriage and divorce: a social and economic study.* Cambridge, Mass., Harvard University Press, 76, xxxi-508 p.

3272   CRAFTS, N. F. R.; IRELAND, N. J. "A simulation of the impact of changes in age at marriage before and during the advent of industrialization in England", *Popul. Stud.* 30(3), nov 76 : 495-510.

3273   DORROS, Sybilla G. "The theoretical basis of sexual equality and marriage reform in China", *Asian Stud.* 13(2), aug 75 : 13-25.

3274   FRINKING, G. A. B. "De toekomstige ontwikkeling van het aantal echtscheidingen; een vergelijkende analyse" (The future multiplication of divorces; a comparative analysis), *Soc. Wetensch.* 20(2), 1977 : 105-123.

3275   FRINKING, G. A. B.; VAN POPPEL, F. W. A. *Nuptialiteit in Nederland* (Nuptiality in the Netherlands). Amsterdam, Stichting Interuniversitair Instituut voor Sociaal-wetenschappelijk Onderzoek, 76, x-77 p.

3276   GUNTER, B. G. "Notes on divorce filing as role behavior", *J. Marriage Family* 39(1), feb 77 : 95-98.

3277   HUSAIN, Sheikh Abrar. *Marriage customs among Muslims in India: a sociological study of the Shia marriage customs.* New Delhi, Sterling Publishers, 76, x-226 p.

3278   JOSEPH, Roger. "Sexual dialectics and strategy in Berber marriage", *J. comp. Family Stud.* 7(3), 1976 : 471-481.

3279   KOOY, G. A. "Echtscheiding in België en Nederland" (Divorce in Belgium and the Netherlands), *Bevolking en Gezin* (2), 1977 : 175-194.

3280   LEE, Gary R. "Age at marriage and marital satisfaction: a multivariate analysis with implications for marital stability", *J. Marriage Family* 39(3), aug 77 : 493-504.

3281   LŐCSEI, P. "A házasságbomlás problémái Magyarországon" (Problems of marriage breakdown in Hungary), *Szociológia* 6(2), 1977 : 165-189.

3282   MADAN, T. N. "Structural implications of marriage in North India: wife-givers and wife-takers among the Pandits of Kashmir", *Contrib. Ind. Sociol.* 9(2), jul-dec 75 : 217-243.

3283   MARTIN, J. M. "Marriage and economic stress in the Felden of Warwickshire during the eighteenth century", *Popul. Stud.* 31(3), nov 77 : 519-535.

3284   MAZUR-HART, Stanley F.; BERMAN, John J. "Changing from fault to no-fault divorce: an interrupted time series analysis", *J. appl. Psychol.* 7(4), oct-dec 77 : 300-312.

3285   MUELLER, Charles W.; POPE, H. "Marital instability: a study of its transmission between generations", *J. Marriage Family* 39(1), feb 77 : 83-92.

3286   PERRY, P. J. "Mariage et distance dans le canton du Bleymard (Lozère), 1811-1820 et 1891-1900", *Ét. rur.* 67, jul-sep 77 : 61-70.

3287   REYNA, S. P. "The rationality of divorce: marital instability among the Barma of Chad", *J. comp. Family Stud.* 8(2), 1977 : 269-288.

3288   ROUSSEL, L. "Demographie et mode de vie conjugale au Danemark",
        Population 32(2), mar-apr 77 : 339-359.
3289   RUESCHEMEYER, Marilyn. "The demands of work and the human quality
        of marriage: an exploratory study of professionals in two so-
        cialist societies", *J. comp. Family Stud.* 8(2), 1977 : 243-255.
3290   RUZICKA, L. T. "Age at marriage and timing of the first birth",
        Popul. Stud. 30(3), nov 76 : 527-538.
3291   SRB, V. "L'augmentation de la nuptialité en Tchécoslovaquie", *De-
        mosta* 9(2-3), 1976 : 69-73.
3292   THORNTON, Arland. "Decomposing the re-marriage process", *Popul.
        Stud.* 31(2), jul 77 : 383-392.
3293   TRAY, Dennis N. DE. "Age of marriage and fertility: a policy re-
        view", *Pakistan Develop. R.* 16(1), 1977 : 89-100. *[Pakistan.]*
3294   WAKIL, S. P.; WAKIL, F. B. *Marriage and the family in Canada.*
        Calgary, Alta., Journal of Comparative Family Studies, Depart-
        ment of Sociology, University of Calgary, 76, vi-145 p.

        15422.

        [See also / Voir aussi: 3182, 3748]

3295   KONEČNÁ, Alena. "Národnosti homogamie a heterogamie v ČSSR" (Eth-
        nic homogamy and heterogamy in Czechoslovakia), *Demografie*
        19(1), jan-mar 77 : 1-10.
3296   LEPAGE, Yvan. "Zones d'intermariages de 4 communes du sud-Luxem-
        bourg belge entre 1880 et 1969", *Popul. et Famille* 40(1), 1977 :
        21-36.
3297   MacCLUER, Jean Walters; DYKE, Bennett. "On the minimum size of en-
        dogamous populations", *Soc. Biology* 23(1), 1976 : 1-12.
3298   MOCHIZUKI, Takashi. "Haigûsha sentaku no hensen" (Changes of mate
        selection in Japan), *Jurisuto Gendai no kazoku* (6), 1977 : 181-
        186.
3299   PETERS, John F. "A comparison of mate selection and marriage in the
        first and second marriages in a selected sample of the remarried
        divorced", *J. comp. Family Stud.* 7(3), 1976 : 483-490.
3300   RAO, V. V. Prakasa; RAO, V. Nandini. "Arranged marriages: an assess-
        ment of the attitudes of the college students in India", *J. comp.
        Family Stud.* 7(3), 1976 : 433-453.
3301   SMITH, James E.; KUNZ, Philip. R. "Polygyny and fertility in nine-
        teenth-century America", *Popul. Stud.* 30(3), nov 76 : 465-480.
3302   SPARK, G. M. "Marriage is a family affair", *Family Coordinator*
        26(2), apr 77 : 167-174.
3303   VERNIER, Bernard. "Emigration et déroglement du marché matrimo-
        nial", *Actes Rech. Sci. soc.* 15, jun 77 : 31-58.

        15423.

3304   BARLOW, Brent A. "Notes on Mormon interfaith marriages", *Family
        Coordinator* 26(2), apr 77 : 143-150.
3305   COHEN, Steven Martin. "Socioeconomic determinants of intraethnic
        marriage and friendship", *Soc. Forces* 55(4), jun 77 : 997-1010.
3306   DEPREZ, J. "Mariage mixte, Islam et nation", *R. alger. Sci. jur.
        écon. polit.* 12(1), mar 75 : 97-145.
3307   MONAHAN, Thomas P. "Interracial marriage in a southern area: Mary-
        land, Virginia, and the district of Columbia", *J. comp. Family
        Stud.* 8(2), 1977 : 217-241.

        15424.

        *[See also / Voir aussi: 2910, 2941, 3108, 3469, 4523, 5153, 5349,
        5591]*

3308   ARAJI, Sharon K. "Husbands' and wives' attitude-behavior congruen-
        ce on family roles", *J. Marriage Family* 39(2), mai 77 : 309-320.
3309   DOE, Brenda A. "Husband-wife communication and family planning
        knowledge, attitude and practices in Korea", *J. Family Planning*

Stud. (4), nov 77 : 144-152.

3310 DUBERMAN, Lucile. "The married dyad", *Int. J. contemp. Sociol.* 13(1-2), jan-apr 76 : 93-106.

3311 HAWKINS, James L.; WEISBERG, Carol; RAY, Dixie L. "Marital communication style and social class", *J. Marriage Family* 39(3), aug 77 : 479-490.

3312 KEMPER, Theodore D.; REICHLER, Melvin L. "Work integration, marital satisfaction, and conjugal power", *Hum. Relat.* 29(10), oct 76 : 929-944.

3313 LOBODZINSKA, Barbara. "Married women's gainful employment and housework in contemporary Poland", *J. Marriage Family* 39(2), mai 77 : 405-415.

3314 MEYER, John P.; PEPPER, Susan. "Need compatibility and marital adjustment in young married couples", *J. Person. soc. Psychol.* 35(3), mai 77 : 331-342.

3315 MURSTEIN, Bernard I. "Qualities of desired spouse; a cross-cultural comparison between French and American college students", *J. comp. Family Stud.* 7(3), 1976 : 455-469.

3316 PALISI, Bartolomeo J. "Wife's statuses and husband-wife companionship in an Australian metropolitan area", *J. Marriage Family* 39(1), feb 77 : 185-191.

3317 PEARLIN, Leonard I.; JOHNSON, Joyce S. "Marital status, life-strains and depression", *Amer. sociol. R.* 42(5), oct 77 : 704-715.

3318 POSTON, Dudley L. Jr. "Characteristics of voluntary and involuntarily childless wives", *Soc. Biology* 23(3), 1976 : 198-209.

3319 PRICE-BONHAM, Sharon. "Marital decision-making: congruence of spouses' responses", *Sociol. Inquiry* 47(2), 1977 : 119-125.

3320 WINTER, David G.; STEWART, Abigail J.; McCLELLAND, David C. "Husband's motives and wife's career level", *J. Person. soc. Psychol.* 35(3), mar 77 : 159-166.

15430. Family
Famille

15431.

[See also / Voir aussi: 654, 2033, 3137, 3294, 4292, 4308, 5657, 5673]

3321 ARDIGO, Achille; DONATI, Pierpaolo (eds.). *Famiglia e industrializzazione* (Family and industrialization). Milano, F. Angeli, 76, 366 p.

3322 BANDERA, Joaquín. "Comentario al *Estudio sociológico de la familia española*" (Comment on *The sociological study of the Spanish family*)", *RS Cuad. Realidad. soc.* 13, mar 77 : 111-122.

3323 BUONANNO, Milly. "Condizioni d'origine e orientamenti iniziali della sociologia della famiglia in Italia" (Conditions of origin and first orientations of the sociology of family in Italy), *Rass. ital. Sociol.* 18(1), jan-mar 77 : 85-110.

3324 DELHUMEAU, Antonio. "La familia como celula básica del Estado: el caso mexicano" (Family as a basic cell of the State: the Mexican case), *Estud. polít.* 3(9), jan-mar 77 : 149-158.

3325 DE SANDRE, Paolo. "Aspetti e problemi di demografia della famiglia italiana" (Demographic aspects and problems of the Italian family), *Studi Sociol.* 14(2-3), apr-sep 76 : 168-190.

3326 DONATI, Pierpaolo. "Forme familari e nuovo diritto di famiglia in Italia: una riflessione sociologica" (Family forms and new family law in Italy: a sociological consideration), *Studi Sociol.* 14(2-3), apr-sep 76 : 113-167.

3327 "Family (The)", *Daedalus* 106(2), 1977 ; 220 p.
3328 FISHER, Wesley A.; KHOTIN, Leonid. "Soviet family research", *J. Marriage Family* 39(2), mai 77 ; 365-374.

3329   GROTEVANT, Harold D.; SCARR, Sandra; WEINBERG, Richard A. "Patterns of interest similarity in adoptive and biological families", *J. Person. soc. Psychol.* 35(9), sep 77 : 667-676.

3330   GUICHARD, Jean (éd.). *La famille.* Paris, Larousse, 77, 143 p.

3331   HAYS, William. "Theorists and theoretical frameworks identified by family sociologists", *J. Marriage Family* 39(1), feb 77 : 59-65.

3332   HOOG, C. DE. "De Nederlandse gezinssociologische censusmonografie-ën: een tussentijdse balans" (The Netherlands census monographies concerning family sociology: a tentative review), *Bevolking en Gezin* (3), 1976 : 271-282.

3333   INSTITUTO DE SOCIOLOGIA APLICADA DE MADRID. "Estudios empíricos sobre la familia española" (Empirical studies on the Spanish family), *RS Cuad. Realidad soc.* 13, mar 77 : 83-91.

3334   ISHWARAN, Karigoudar (ed.). *The Canadian family.* Rev. ed. Toronto, Holt, Rinehart and Winston of Canada; 76, xiv-705 p.

3335   IUTAKA, Sugiyama *et al.* "Urbanização e a familia extensa no Brasil" (Urbanization and extended family in Brazil), *R. Cienc. soc. (Ceara)* (1-2), 1975 : 29-50.

3336   JANKOVA, Z. A. (ed.). *Problemy sociologičeskogo izučenija sem'i* (Problems of the sociological study on family). Moskva, 76, 192 p.

3337   LANZETTI, Clemente. "Aspetti istituzionali e aspetti di 'communitas' nella famiglia" (Institutional aspects and "community" aspects in the family), *Studi Sociol.* 14(2-3), 1977 : 191-223.

3338   LASLETT, Barbara. "Social change and the family: Los Angeles, California, 1850-1970", *Amer. sociol. R.* 42(2), apr 77 : 268-291.

3339   LENERO-OTERO, Luis (ed.). *Beyond the nuclear family model. Cross-cultural perspectives.* London, Sage, 77, ii-226 p.

3340   MACKOVSKIJ, M. S.; ÊRMAKOVA, O. V. "Tendencii izmenenija tematiki issledovanij po sociologii sem'i" (Changing research trends in the sociology of family), *Sociol. Issled. (Moskva)* 1976 : 88-97.

3341   MANYONI, Joseph R. "Legitimacy and illegitimacy: misplaced polarities in Caribbean family studies", *Canad. R. Sociol. Anthropol.* 14(4), nov 77 : 417-427.

3342   MASSELL, Gregory J. "Family law and social mobilization in Soviet Central Asia: some comparisons with Communist China", *Canad. Slavonic Pap.* 17(2-3), jun-sep 75 : 374-403.

3343   McCUBBIN, Hamilton; DAHL, Barbara B.; HUNTER, Edna J. (eds.). *Families in the military system.* Beverly Hills, Sage Publications, 76, 400 p. CR: Athena THEODORE, *Contemp. Sociol. (Washington)* 6(3), mai 77 : 327-328.

3344   MILDEN, James Wallace *The family in past time; a guide to the literature.* New York, Garland Publishers, 77, xix-200 p.

3345   MÜHLFELD, Claus. *Familiensoziologie. Eine systematische Einführung* (Sociology of the family. A systematic introduction). Hamburg, Hoffmann und Campe Verlag, 76, 204 p. CR: René KÜNIG, *Kölner Z. Soziol. u. soz.-Psychol.* 29(4), dec 77 : 800-803.

3346   NASU, Sôichi. "Kazoku no henshitsu to kazokuho" (Changing family and the family law), *Jurisuto Gendai no kazoku* (6), 1977 : 6-23.

3347   NONOYAMA, Hisaya. *Gendai kazoku no ronri* (The logic of the modern family). Tokyo, Nihon Hyoronsha, 77, 262 p.

3348   ORTEGA, Félix. "Teorías sobre la familia" (Theories on family), *RS Cuad. Realidad soc.* 12, jan 77 : 49-62.

3349   POULTER, Sebastian M. *Family law and litigation in Basotho society.* Oxford, Clarendon Press, 76, xxxiv-361 p. [Lesotho.]

3350   ROBERTSHAW, P.; CURTIN, C. A. "Legal definition of the family: an historical and sociological exploration", *Sociol. R.* 25(2), mai 77 : 289-308.

3351   SCHMIDT-RELENBERG, Norbert; LUETKENS, Christian; RUPP, Klaus Jürgen. *Familiensoziologie. Eine Kritik* (Family sociology. A criticism). Stuttgart, Kohlhammer, 76, 187 p. CR: Hans-Jürgen HILDEBRANDT, *Kölner Z. Soziol. u. soz.-Psychol.* 29(3), sep 76 :

610-614.

3352   SHORTER, Edward. *The making of the modern family*. London, Collins, 76, 369-xiv p. CR: Olive BANKS, *Brit. J. Sociol.* 28(4), dec 77 : 516-517.

3353   SIDDIQUE, Muhammad. "Changing family patterns: a comparative analysis of immigrant Indian and Pakistani families of Saskatoon, Canada", *J. comp. Family Stud.* 8(2), 1977 : 179-200.

3354   SLATER, Mariam K. *The Caribbean family: legitimacy in Martinique*. New York, St Martin's Press, 77, vii-264 p.

3355   STEIN, Peter J.; RICHMAN, Judith; HANNON, Natalie. *The family: functions, conflicts, symbols*. Reading, Mass., Addison-Wesley Publishing Co., 77, x-452 p.

3356   STOFFLE, Richard W. "Industrial impact on family formation in Barbados, West Indies", *Ethnology* 16(3), jul 77 : 253-267.

3357   SWEET, James A. "Demography and the family", *Ann. R. Sociol.* (3), 1977 : 363-405.

3358   TSUBOUCHI, Yoshihiro; MAEDA, Narifumi. *Kaku-kazoku saikô* (Reconsidering nuclear family). Tokyo, Kôbundô, 77, 218 p.

3359   VAN LEEUWEN, Louis Theodore. *Het gezin als sociologisch studie-object. Een historisch overzicht van de ontwikkeling van een sub-discipline, speciaal met het oog op de situatie in Nederland* (Family as a sociological matter of study. An historical overview of the development of a sub-discipline, with special reference to the situation in the Netherlands). Wageningen, Wageningen Landbouwhogesch., 76, x-420 p.

3360   WEBER-KELLERMANN, Ingeborg. *Dee Familie. Geschichte und Bilder* (The family. History and illustrations). Frankfurt-am-Main, Insel, 76, 347 p. CR: René KÖNIG, *Kölner Z. Soziol. u. soz.-Psychol.* 29(4), dec 77 : 796-799.

3361   WIETING, Stephen G. "Structuralism, systems theory, and ethnomethodology in the sociology of the family", *J. comp. Family Stud.* 7(3), 1976 : 375-395.

3362   WILKE, Arthur S. "Family and civilization: thirty years later", *Int. J. contemp. Sociol.* 13(3-4), jul-oct 76 : 224-238.

15432.

3363   ALLAN, Graham. "Sibling solidarity", *J. Marriage Family* 39(1), feb 77 : 177-184.

3364   BROWN, Cecil H.; SOWAYAN, Saad. "Descent and alliance in an endogamous society: a structural analysis of Arab kinship", *Soc. Sci. Inform.* 16(5), 1977 : 581-599.

3365   DEVILLE, J. C. "Analyse harmonique du calendrier de constitution des familles en France. Disparités sociales et évolution de 1920 à 1960", *Population* 32(1), jan-feb 77 : 17-64.

3366   ESSMAN, C. S. "Sibling relations as socialization for parenthood", *Family Coordinator* 26(3), jul 77 : 259-262.

3367   FARBER, Bernard. "Social context, kinship mapping, and family norms", *J. Marriage Family* 39(2), mai 77 : 227-240.

3368   GOLDENBERG, Sheldon. "Kinship and ethnicity viewed as adaptive responses to location in the opportunity structure", *J. comp. Family Stud.* 8(2), 1977 : 149-165.

3369   INDEN, Ronald B.; NICHOLAS, Ralph W. *Kinship in Bengali culture*. Chicago, University of Chicago Press, 77, xvii-139 p.

3370   JOHNSON, Colleen Leahy. "Interdependence, reciprocity and indebtedness: an analysis of Japanese-American kinship relations", *J. Marriage Family* 39(2), mai 77 : 351-363.

3371   KHARE, R. S. "Embedded affinity and consanguineal ethos: two properties of the northern kinship system", *Contrib. Ind. Sociol.* 9(2), jul-dec 75 : 245-261.

3372   LI, Peter S. "Fictive kinship, conjugal tie and kinship chain among Chinese immigrants in the United States", *J. comp. Family Stud.* 8(1), 1977 : 47-63.

3373   MONAHAN, Thomas P. "Interracial parentage as revealed by birth
        records in the United States, 1970", *J. comp. Family Stud.*
        8(1), 1977 : 65-77.
3374   NIZARD, A. "Droit et statistiques de filiation en France. Le droit
        de la filiation depuis 1804", *Population* 32(1), jan-feb 77 : 91-
        122.
3375   PERISTIANY, Jean G. (ed.). *Kinship and modernization in Mediter-*
        ranean society. Rome, Center for Mediterranean Studies, American
        Universities Field Staff, 76, ix-159 p.
3376   SEKI, Takatoshi. "Toshi Kazoku no Shinzoku kino ni kansuru ichi-
        kosatsu" (A study of kin function in urban families), *Hiroshima*
        Shudo-daigaku Ronshu 18(1), 1977 : 233-267.
3377   THOMPSON, Elizabeth A. "Inference of genealogical structure", *Soc.*
        Sci. Inform. 15(2-3), 1976 : 479-526.
3378   TURNER, James. "A formal semantic analysis of Hindi kinship ter-
        minology", *Contrib. Ind. Sociol.* 9(2), jul-dec 75 : 263-292.
3379   TYRELL, Hartmann. "Historische Familienforschung und Kritik eines
        Forschungsprogramms" (Historical genealogical research and cri-
        ticism of a research programme), *Kölner Z. Soziol. u. soz.-*
        Psychol. 29(4), dec 77 : 677-701.
3380   WILSON, Bryan. "Aspects of kinship and the rise of Jehovah's wit-
        nesses in Japan", *Soc. Compass* 24(1), 1977 : 97-120.
3381   WÖHLKE, Manfred. "Soziologisch relevante Fragen und methodische
        Probleme der Zwillingsforschung" (Sociologically relevant ques-
        tions and methodical problems of the gemellogy), *Kölner Z. Soziol.*
        u. soz.-Psychol. 29(2), jun 77 : 319-334.
3382   YU, Elena S. H. "Kinship structure, post-marital residence and sex-
        role equality in China", *Sociol. Focus* 10(2), apr 77 : 175-188.

15433.

[See also / Voir aussi: 3469, 4389]

3383   BOSS, Pauline. "A clarification of the concept of psychological
        father presence in families experiencing ambiguity of boundary",
        J. Marriage Family 39(1), feb 77 : 141-151.
3384   BRODERICK, Carlfred B. "Fathers", *Family Coordinator* 26(3), jul
        77 : 269-275.
3385   FLEISHER, Belton M. "Mother's home time and the production of child
        quality", *Demography* 14(2), mai 77 : 197-212.
3386   HUNT, Larry L.; HUNT, Janet G. "Race, father identification, and
        achievement orientation. The subjective side of the father-son
        connection, a research note", *Youth and Soc.* 9(1), sep 77 · 113-
        120.
3387   KIM, On-jook Lee; KIM, Kyong-Dong. "A causal interpretation of the
        effect of mother's education and employment status on parental
        decision-making role patterns in the Korean family", *J. comp.*
        Family Stud. 8(1), 1977 ; 117-131.
3388   LAMB, Michael (ed.). *The role of father in child development.* New
        York, Wiley, 76, xii-407 p.
3389   LEACOCK, Eleanor. "The changing family and Lévi-Strauss, or what-
        ever happened to fathers ?", *Soc. Res.* 44(2), 1977 : 235-259.
3390   RICH, Adrienne Cecile. *Of woman born: motherhood as experience and*
        institution. New York, Norton, 76, 318 p. CR: Nona GLAZER, *Con-*
        temp. Sociol. (Washington) 6(4), jul 77 : 480-482.
3391   ROBERTSON, Joan F. "Grandmotherhood: a study of role conception",
        J. Marriage Family 39(1), feb 77 : 165-174.

15434.

[See also / Voir aussi: 625, 682, 997, 2262, 2881, 3167, 3245, 3269, 3302, 3308, 3387, 3902, 3910, 4099, 4165, 4453, 4469, 4844, 4898, 5348, 5417, 5465, 5542]

3392   AOI, Kazuo. "Shinsôkatei kara mita oyako-kankei to pâsonaritî" (Parent-child relationship and personality formation viewed from the depth process), *Jurisuto* (6), 1977 : 210-217.

3393   AVANZINI, Bianca Barbero. "Sistema familiare e comportamento giovanile deviante" (Family system and deviant youth behaviour), *Studi Sociol.* 14(2-3), apr-sep 76 : 224-256.

3394   BEAVERS, W. Robert. *Psychotherapy and growth; a family systems perspective.* New York, Brunner/Mazel, 77, xxi-388 p.

3395   BENET, Mary Kathleen. *The politics of adoption.* New York, The Free Press, 76, 235 p. *[USA.]*

3396   BONHAM, Gordon Scott. "Who adopts: the relationship of adoption and social-demographic characteristics of women", *J. Marriage Family* 39(2), mai 77 : 295-306.

3397   BOUCHALOVA, Marie *et al.* "Reprodukce rodin ve vatahu k jejich sociálně ekonomic kému vývoji" (Family reproduction relating to the social and economic evolution), *Demografie* 19(3), jul-sep 77 : 206-214. *[Czechoslovakia.]*

3398   BOULD, Sally. "Female-headed families: personal fate control and the provider role", *J. Marriage Family* 39(2), mai 77 : 339-349.

3399   BRAUN, Hans; LEITNER, Ute. *Problem Familie - Familienprobleme* (Problem family - family problems). Frankfurt-New York, Campus Verlag, 76, 222 p. CR: René KÖNIG, *Kölner Z. Soziol. u. soz.-Psychol.* 29(4), dec 76 : 803-807.

3400   BRONFENBRENNER, V. "The American family in decline", *Current* 189, jan 77 : 39-47.

3401   BYTHEWAY, Bill. "Problems of representation in 'The generation family study'", *J. Marriage Family* 39(2), mai 77 : 243-252.

3402   CAVALLI, Alessandro. "L'immagine del lavoro dei genitori nell' infanzia" (The image of parents' work during childhood), *Rass. ital. Sociol.* 18(1), jan-mar 77 : 19-56.

3403   CONSTANTINE, Larry L. "Designed experience: a multiple, goal-directed training program in family therapy", *Family Process* 15(4), dec 76 : 373-387.

3404   CONSTANTINE, Larry L. "Open family: a lifestyle for kids and other people", *Family Coordinator* 16(2), apr 77 : 113-121.

3405   CRONKITE, Ruth C. "The determinants of spouses' normative preferences for family roles", *J. Marriage Family* 39(3), aug 77 : 575-585.

3406   DAVID, Annoussamy. "L'adoption dans l'Inde", *R. jur. polit.* 31(2), apr-jun 77 : 561-572.

3407   Bibl.XXVI-2870. DUBERMAN, Lucile. *The reconstituted family; a study of remarried couples and their children.* CR: Michael LEWIS, *Amer. J. Sociol.* 82(4), jan 77 : 910-912.

3408   FIL'JUKOVA, L. F. *Sel'skaja sem'ja* (The rural family). Minsk, Nauka i tehnika, 76, 159 p.

3409   GEDDES, Michael; MEDWAY, Joan. "The symbolic drawing of the family life space", *Family Process* 16(2), jun 77 : 219-228.

3410   GIRARD, A. "Dimension idéale de la famille et tendances de la fécondité; comparaisons internationales", *Population* 31(6), nov-dec 76 : 1119-1146.

3411   GLICK, Paul C. "Updating the life cycle of the family", *J. Marriage Family* 39(1), feb 77 : 5-13.

3412   GOLUBOVIĆ, Zagorka. "Promene u strukturi porodice u Srbiji, prosmatrane u kontekstu društveno-kulturne sredine" (Changes in the family structure in Serbia observed in the context of socio-cultural environment), *Sociologija* 18(3-4), 1976 : 297-316.

3413   GRANDKE, A. "Zur Entwicklung der Familienbeziehungen in der DDR" (Development of family relations in the GDR), *Einheit* 32(2), 1977 : 203-210.

3414   HUMPHREY, Michael. "Sex differences in attitude to parenthood", *Hum. Relat.* 30(8), aug 77 : 737-749.

3415   ICHILOV, Orit; RUBINECK, Bracha. "The relationship between girls' attitudes concerning the family and their perception of the patterns existing in the family of origin", *J. Marriage Family* 39(2), mai 77 : 417-422.

3416   ILLY, L. B. "Afrikanische Familienstrukturen zwischen 'Tradition' und 'Modernität'. Fallstudie Kamerun" (African family structure between tradition and modernity. The case of Cameroon), *Dritte Welt* 4(3-4), 4 trim 76 : 368-390.

3417   JAI-SEUK, Choi. "Family system", *Korea J.* 17(5), mai 77 : 4-14. [Korea, South.]

3418   JIOBU, R.; MARSHALL, H. "Minority states and family size: a comparison of explanations", *Popul. Stud.* 31(3), nov 77 : 509-517.

3419   KIESLER, Sara B. "Post hoc justification of family size", *Sociometry* 40(1), 1977 : 59-67.

3420   KNOWLES, Edmond. *Dynamics of the family unit.* Howell, N.J., E and E Enterprises, 76, 125 p.

3421   KRETZER, David I. "La struttura del gruppo familiare contadino in Europa. Ricerca su una comunità italiana del XIX secolo" (The structure of the rural family group in Europe. Research on a XIXth century Italian community), *Rass. ital. Sociol.* 18(1), jan-mar 77 : 57-83.

3422   KUNZ, Phillip R.; PETERSON, Evan T. "Family size, birth order, and academic achievement", *Soc. Biology* 24(2), 1977 : 144-148.

3423   LADNER, Joyce A. "Mixed families: white parents and black children", *Soc. Sci. mod. Soc.* 14(6), sep-oct 77 : 70-78.

3424   LANTZ, Herman; SCHULTZ, Martin; O'HARA, Mary. "The changing American family from the preindustrial to the industrial period: a final report", *Amer. sociol. R.* 43(3), jun 77 : 406-421.

3425   LARKIN, William E.; LOMAN, L. Anthony. "Labelling in the family context: an experimental study", *Sociol. soc. Res.* 61(2), jan 77 : 192-203.

3426   LEE, Gary R. *Family structure and interaction: a comparative analysis.* Philadelphia, Lippincott, 77, xiv-343 p.

3427   LIRA, Luis Felipe. "Estructura familiar, poblacion y fecundidad en América latina" (Family structure, population and fertility in Latin America), *Notas Pobl.* 5(13), apr 77 : 9-50.

3428   LYTTON, Hugh; CONWAY, Dorice; SAUVE, Reginald. "The impact of twinship on parent-child interaction", *J. Person. soc. Psychol.* 35(2), feb 77 : 97-107.

3429   MAIDMENT, Susan. "Access and family adoptions", *Mod. Law R.* 40(3), mai 77 : 293-313. [UK.]

3430   MARKLE, Gerald E.; WAIT, Robert F. *The development of family size and sex composition norms among US children.* Honolulu, East-West Center, 76, vii-23 p.

3431   MARTIN, J.; LEGER, D. "Capitalisme et famille: réflexions en réponse à une analyse sexiste du patriarcat", *Premier Mai* (4), jan-feb 77 : 28-37.

3432   MATHEW, Anna. "Roles, responsibilities and privileges of parents and children in the rural and urban areas of Chittoor district in Andhra Pradesh", *J. comp. Family Stud.* 8(4), 1977 : 133-138.

3433   McDONALD, Gerald. "Family power: reflection and direction", *Pacific sociol. R.* 20(4), oct 77 : 607-621.

3434   MITTERAUER, Michael; SIEDER, Reinhard. *Vom Patriarchat zur Partnerschaft. Zum Strukturwandel der Familie* (From patriarch to partnership. About the structural change of the family). München,

C. H. Beck, 77, 222 p. CR: René KÖNIG, *Kölner Z. Soziol. u. soz.-Psychol.* 29(4), dec 77 : 800-803.

3435 MOLNÁR, E. S. "A családonként ideálisnak tartott gyermekszam interpretálásának néhány problémája" (Problems raised by the interpretation of the ideal number of children for each family), *Demográfia* 19(2-3), 1976 : 212-226. *[Hungary.]*

3436 MOOS, Rudolf H.; MOOS, Bernice S. "A typology of family social environment", *Family Process* 15(4), dec 76 : 357-371.

3437 MORIOKA, Kiyomi (ed.). *Gendai kazoku no raifu-saikuru* (Life cycle of families in contemporary Japan). Tokyo, Baifu-kan, 77, 266 p.

3438 MOXLEY, Robert L. "Differentiation of family structure and family relative centrality in a rural Peruvian community: a diachronic analysis", *J. comp. Family Stud.* 7(3), 1976 : 409-417.

3439 NAITO, Kanji. "Kirishitan kochi no kazoku-kanko" (Family customs of an old Christian village), *Tetsugaku Nenpô* 36, 1977 : 1-46. *[Japan.]*

3440 NEIDHARDT, Friedhelm. *Systemeigenschaften der Familie: Zwischenberichte einer Tübinger Familienuntersuchung* (System characteristics of the family: progress report on a family study in Tübingen). München, Deutsches Jugendinstitut, 76, 75 p. *[Germany, FR.]*

3441 ODITA, F. C.; JANSSENS, M. A. "Family stability in the context of economic deprivation", *Family Coordinator* 26(3), jun 77 : 252-258.

3442 OLIVER, L. W. "The relationship of parental attitudes and parent identification to career and homemaking orientation in college women", *J. vocat. Behav.* 7'1), aug 75 : 1-12.

3443 OPPONG, Christine. "A note from Ghana on chains of change in family systems and family size", *J. Marriage Family* 39(3), aug 77 : 615-621.

3444 PITROU, Agnès. "Le soutien familial dans la société urbaine", *R. franç. Sociol.* 18(1), jan-mar 77 : 47-84. *[France.]*

3445 POFFENBERGER, Thomas; SEBALY, Kim. *The socialization of family size values: youth and family planning in an Indian village.* Ann Arbor, Center for South and Southeast Asian Studies, University of Michigan, 76, xiv-159 p.

3446 RISKIN, Jules. "'Nonabeled' family interaction: preliminary report on a prospective study", *Family Process* 15(4), dec 76 : 433-439.

3447 RITTERMAN, Michele Klevens. "Paradigmatic classification of family therapy theories", *Family Process* 16(1), mar 77 : 29-48.

3448 ROBINSON, W. P.; ARNOLD, Jenifer. "The question-answer exchange between mothers and young children", *Europ. J. soc. Psychol.* 7(2), 1977 : 151-164.

3449 ROUSSEL, Louis. *La famille après le mariage des enfants: étude des relations entre générations.* Paris, Presses universitaires de France, 76, 258 p. *[Voir aussi Population 31(6), nov-dec 76 : 1195-1206.]*

3450 SAKAI, Toshirô. "Kazoku byôri no Sonzairon-teki Genshogakuteki kosatsu" (An ontological and phenomenological study of family patholody), *Shakai-fukushi Hyoron* 44, 1977 : 1-29.

3451 SARACENO, Chiara. *Anatomia della famiglia: strutture sociali e forme familiari* (Anatomy of the family: social structures and family forms). Bari, De Donato, 76, 161 p.

3452 SECHREST, Lee; SUKSTORF, Steve. "Parental visitation of the institutionalized retarded", *J. appl. soc. Psychol.* 7(4), oct-dec 77 : 286-294.

3453 SMITH, Thomas Ewin. "An empirical comparison of potential determinants of parental authority", *J. Marriage Family* 39(1), feb 77 : 153-164.

3454 SMITH, Thomas Ewin. "Push versus Pull. Intra-family versus peer-group variables as possible determinants of adolescent orientations toward parents", *Youth and Soc.* 8(1), sep 76 : 5-26.

3455   STEINMETZ, Suzanne K. "The use of force for resolving family conflict: the training ground for abuse", *Family Coordinator* 26(1),
jan 77 : 19-26.
3456   STERLINCK, A. H. "Multiple family group therapy: a review of the
literature", *Family Process* 16(3), sep 77 : 307-325.
3457   TOTANI, Osamu; HOTTA, Gôkichi; SUDA, Hiroshi. *Katei-Seikatsuron,
jôkan* (A study of family life). Gifu, Taishû shobô, 77, 210 p.
3458   TREADWAY, R. C. "The model family project in Ispahan, Iran", *Stud.
Family Plan.* 7(11), nov 76 : 308-321.
3459   WALLER, Jerome H. "Sex of children and ultimate family size by
time and class", *Soc. Biology* 23(3), 1976 : 210-225.
3460   WEEKES-VAGLIANI, Winifred. *Vie et structure familiales dans le Sud
Cameroun.* Paris, OCDE, 76, 97 p.
3461   WELLER, Robert H. "Wife's employment and cumulative family size in
the United States, 1970 and 1960", *Demography* 14(1), feb 77 :
43-65.
3462   WON, George; YAMAMURA, Douglas; YANG, Choon. "Parental influence
and plans for higher education among Korean youth", *Pacific sociol. R.* 20(2), apr 77 : 301-320.
3463   WOOD, Charles H.; BEAN, Frank D. "Offspring gender and family
size: implications from a comparison of Mexican-Americans and
Anglo-Americans", *J. Marriage Family* 39(1), feb 77 : 129-139.

15440. Woman's status
Condition de la femme

*[See also / Voir aussi: 672, 1143, 1722, 2341, 2586, 2619, 2873,
3233, 4306, 4312, 4526, 4762, 4846, 5172]*

3464   ABADAN-UNAT, Nermih. "Implications of migration on emancipation
and pseudo-emancipation of Turkish women", *Int. Migration R.*
11(1), 1977 : 31-57.
3465   ABADAN-UNAT, Nermih. "Major challenges faced by Turkish women:
legal emancipation, urbanization, industrialization", *Turk. Yb.
int. Relat.* 14, 1974 : 20-44.
3466   ALBISTUR, Maïté; ARMOGATHE, Daniel. *Histoire du féminisme français:
du Moyen Âge à nos jours.* Paris, Des Femmes, 77, 508 p.
3467   AL-QAZZAZ, Ayad. *Women in the Middle East and North Africa: an
annotated bibliography.* Austin, Center for Middle Eastern Studies,
University of Texas at Austin, 77, 178 p.
3468   ARAFAT, Ibtihaj; YORBURG, Betty. *The new women; attitudes, and
self-image.* Columbus, Ohio, Charles E. Merrill, 76, 142 p. CR:
Nona GLAZER, *Contemp. Sociol. (Washington)* 6(1), jan 77 : 89.
3469   Bibl.XXVI-2919. BERNARD, Jessie. *Women, wives, mothers: values and
options.* CR: Mary LINDENSTEIN WALSHOK, *Contemp. Sociol. (Washington)* 5(2), mar 76 : 137-138.
3470   "Bibliografia sobre a situaçâo da mulher no Brasil" (Bibliography
on women's status in Brazil), *R. brasil. Estatist.* 37(147), jul-
sep 76 : 337-359.
3471   BOULDING, Elise. *Women in the twentieth century world.* Beverly
Hills, Sage Publications; New York, Halsted Press, 77, 264 p.
3472   BOURNE, Paula. *Women in Canadian society.* Toronto, Ontario Institute for Studies in Education, 76, x-158 p.
3473   BUTENSCHON, M. "Frauenemanzipation in der UdSSR: Anspruch und Wirk-
lichkeit" (Women's emancipation in the USSR: claim and reality),
Osteuropa 27(2), feb 77 : 91-104; 27(3), mar 77 : 192-209.
3474   CARROLL, Berenice A. (ed.). *Liberating women's history: theoretical and critical essays.* Urbana, University of Illinois Press,
76, 434 p. CR: Marilyn J. BOXER, *Contemp. Sociol. (Washington)*
6(2), mar 77 : 230-231.
3475   CHARLOT, Monica (éd.). *Les femmes dans la société britannique.*
Paris, A. Colin, 77, 253 p.

3476 CHRISTIANSEN-RUFFMAN, Linda. "Women's problems: private troubles or public issues ?", *Canad. J. Sociol.* 2(2), 1977 : 167-178.

3477 CHUNG, Bethy Jamie. "Some thoughts on the status of women in Southeast Asia: 1975, the International Women's Year", *Southeast Asian Aff.* 1976 : 130-148.

3478 "Condition de la femme en 1975 (La)", *Promotions* 98, [1976] : 111 p. [France.]

3479 "Condizione femminile" (The women's status), *Quad. Azione soc.* 27(7), jul 77 : 3-142; 27(8), aug 77 : 3-177. [Italy.]

3480 COOK, Ramsay; MITCHINSON, Wendy (eds.). *The proper sphere: woman's place in Canadian society.* Toronto, Oxford University Press, 76, 7-334 p.

3481 CORDONNIER, Rita. "De la condition socio-économique des femmes africaines", *Cult. et Dévelop.* 9(3), 1977 : 387-411.

3482 CROLL, Elisabeth. "A recent movement to redefine the role and status of women", *China Quart.* 71, sep 77 : 591-597. [China.]

3483 DAVIN, Delia. *Woman-work: women and the Party in revolutionary China.* Oxford, Eng., Clarendon Press, 76, 244 p. CR: May N. DIAZ, *Contemp. Sociol. (Washington)* 6(3), mai 77 : 377.

3484 DIXSON, Miriam. *The real Matilda: woman and identity in Australia, 1788-1975.* Ringwood, Australia, Penguin Books Australia, 76, 280 p.

3485 DURÁN, María Angeles. *Dominación, sexo y cambio social* (Domination, sex and social change). Madrid, Editorial Cuadernos para el Diálogo, 77, 236 p. [Spain.]

3486 EGOROVA, N. A. "Sovremennoe ženskoe dviženie i ideologija neofeminizma" (Women's movement today and the ideology of the neo-feminism), *Rabočij Klass sovrem. Mir* 6(2), mar-apr 77 : 132-143.

3487 ELMENDORF, Mary Lindsay. *Nine Mayan women: a village faces change.* Cambridge, Mass., Schenkman Publishing Co., 76, xxiv-159 p. [Mexico.]

3488 FRANK, Harold H. *Women in the organization.* Philadelphia, University of Pennsylvania Press, 77, xv-309 p. [USA.]

3489 GEISMAR, Ludwig L.; CAUPIN, Benedicte; DeHAAN, Neil. "Feminist egalitarianism, social action orientation and occupational roles: a cross-national study", *J. comp. Family Stud.* 7(3), 1976 : 419-432.

3490 GIELE, Janet Zollinger; SMOCK, Audrey Chapman (eds.). *Women: roles and status in eight countries.* New York, Wiley, 77, xiii-443 p.

3491 GODELIER, Maurice; BONTE, Pierre. *Le problème des femmes et des fondements de la domination masculine: deux exemples, les Baruya de Nouvelle-Guinée, les Bahima d'Ankole.* Paris, Centre d'études et de recherches marxistes, 76, 61 p. multigr.

3492 GROSMAN, C. P. "Situación de la mujer en la familia argentina" (Woman's condition in the Argentine family), *Universitas (Bogotá)* 51, dec 76 : 319-341.

3493 HAFKIN, Nancy J.; BAY, Edna G. (eds.). *Women in Africa: studies in social and economic change.* Stanford, Calif., Stanford University Press, 76, x-306 p.

3494 HEER, D. M.; YOUSSEF, N. "Female status among Soviet central Asian nationalities: the melding of Islam and Marxism and its implications for population increase", *Popul. Stud.* 31(1), mar 77 : 155-173.

3495 HILLESTRØM, Karsteh. "Nogle overvejelser om ligestilling i arbejdet mellem maend og kvinder. Hvordan kan beskaeftigelses- og regionalpolitiske virkemidler medvirke hertil ?" (Some considerations concerning the equality in the work between men and women. How can the means of the employment policy and the regional policy contribute to this ?), *Soc. Tss.* 52(11-12), 1976 : 293-309.

3496 HOFFMAN, Saul. "Marital instability and the economic status of women", *Demography* 14(1), feb 77 : 67-76.

3497   HUSTON, Perdita. "To be born a woman is a sin", *Populi* 4(3),
        1977 : 27-36.
3498   Bibl.XXVI-2947. IGLITZIN, Lynne B.; ROSS, Ruth (eds.). *Women in
        the world: a comparative study*. CR: Janet Zollinger GIELE,
        Contemp. Sociol. (Washington) 6(4), jul 77 : 478-479.
3499   "Indonesian women: some past and current perspectives", *Courr.
        Extr.-Orient* 10(62), dec 76 : 1-163.
3500   KAROUI, Naïma. "La notion d'émancipation de la femme à travers la
        presse: ébauche d'une analyse de contenu", *R. tunis. Sci. soc.*
        13(47), 1976 : 93-124. [Tunisie.]
3501   KESSLER, Evelyn S. *Women: an anthropological view*. New York, Holt,
        Rinehart and Winston, 76, 267 p. CR: Judith CADITZ, *Contemp.
        Sociol. (Washington)* 6(1), jan 77 : 92-93.
3502   LEBRA, Joyce; PAULSON, Joy; POWERS, Elizabeth (eds.). *Women in a
        changing Japan*. Boulder, Colo., Westview Press, 76, 322 p. CR:
        Cornelia Butler FLORA, *Contemp. Sociol. (Washington)* 6(2), mar
        77 : 232-233.
3503   LÉVI, Florence. "L'évolution des femmes portugaises immigrées à
        Paris et dans la banlieue parisienne", *Année sociol.* 26, 1975 :
        153-177.
3504   LEVY, René. *Der Lebenslauf als Statusbiographie. Die weibliche
        Normalbiographie in makrosoziologiescher Perspektive* (The course
        of life as status biography: the female normal biography in a
        macro-sociological perspective). Stuttgart, Enke, 77, viii-123 p.
3505   LIU, William T.; YU, Elena S. H. "Variations in women's roles and
        family life under the socialist regime in China", *J. comp. Fa-
        mily Stud.* 8(2), 1977 : 201-215.
3506   McCOURT, Kathleen. *Working-class women and grass-roots politics*.
        Bloomington, Indiana University Press, 77, v-256 p.
3507   MICHEL, Andrée *et al. Femmes, sexisme et sociétés*. Paris, Presses
        universitaires de France, 77, 208 p.
3508   MILLER, Jean Baker. *Toward a new psychology of women*. Boston,
        Beacon Press, 76, xi-143 p. CR: Nancy CHODOROW, *Contemp. Sociol.
        (Washington)* 6(4), jul 77 : 479-480.
3509   MORENO, Amparo. *Mujeres en lucha. El movimiento feminista en Es-
        paña* (Fighting women. The feminist movement in Spain). Barcelona,
        Editorial Anagrama, 77, 221 p.
3510   "Mujer en los Andes (La)" (Woman in the Andes), *Estud. andin.*
        5(1), 1976 : 1-171.
3511   "Mujer y la política (La)" (Woman and politics), *R. Inst. Cienc.
        soc.* 29, 1977 : 9-384.
3512   NASH, June. "Women in development: dependency and exploitation",
        Develop. and Change 8(2), apr 77 : 161-182.
3513   NORGES ALMENVITENSKAPELIGE FORSKNINSGRÅD. *Forskning om kvinner*
        (Research about women). Oslo, Universitetsforlaget, 76. CR:
        Elina HAAVIO-MANNILA, *Acta sociol.* 20(1), 1977 : 111-113.
3514   PALMER, I. "La place de la femme dans une stratégie de développe-
        ment rural axée sur les besoins essentiels", *R. int. Trav.*
        115(1), jan-feb 77 : 105-116.
3515   PESCATELLO, Ann M. *Power and pawn: the female in Iberian families,
        societies, and cultures*. Westport, Conn., Greenwood Press, 76,
        281 p. CR: Marta TIENDA, *Contemp. Sociol. (Washington)* 6(3),
        mai 77 : 363-364.
3516   "Regards sur les Indonésiennes", *Archipel* 13, 1977 : 320 p.
3517   Bibl.XXVI-2963. REITER, Rayna R. (ed.). *Toward an anthropology of
        women*. CR: Sherry B. ORTNER, *Amer. J. Sociol.* 82(4), jan 77 :
        870-873.
3518   RESZKE, Irena. "Pozycja społeczna kobiet - przegląd probelmatyki"
        (Women's social position - review of the subject matter), *Stud.
        socjol.* 60(1), 1976 : 135-155.
3519   RIBOLZI, Luisa. "La situazione della donna nel sistema scolastico

italiano" (Woman's status in the Italian educational system),
Studi Sociol. 15(1), jan-mar 77 : 57-70.

3520   ROBERTS, Joan I. (ed.). *Beyond intellectual sexism: a new woman,
a new reality.* New York, David McKay Co., 76, 386 p. CR: Athena
THEODORE, *Contemp. Sociol. (Washington)* 6(4), jul 77 : 482-483.

3521   ROSENBERG, Bernard. "Women's place in Israël - where they are,
where they should be", *Dissent* 24(4), 1977 : 408-417.

3522   SALAFF, J. W. "The status of unmarried Hong Kong women and the
social factors contributing to their delated marriage", *Popul.
Stud.* 30(3), nov 76 : 391-412.

3523   SERES, Zs. "A nöi eszménykép változása a sajtó tükrében" (The
changing women's ideal as reflected by the press), *Radió és TV
Szle* 9(4), 1977 : 119-130.

3524   SHAPIRO, Jane P. "The politization of Soviet women: from passivity
to protest", *Canad. Slavonic Pap.* 17(4), dec 75 : 596-616.

3525   SIEGERS, J. J. "De invloed van de factoren leeftijd en burgelijke
staat op de ontwikkeling van de participatie op de arbeidsmarkt
door vrouwen in Nederland, 1960-1971" (Impact of age and marital
status on women's economic activity in the Netherlands), *Bevolking en Gezin* (3), 1976 : 343-361.

3526   SINGLETON, Royce Jr.; CHRISTIANSEN, John B. "The construct valida-
tion of a short-form attitudes toward feminism scale", *Sociol.
soc. Res.* 61(3), apr 77 : 294-303.

3527   SLADETIEN, Joseleyne. "Women's place in the People's Republic of
China: ideology and practice", *Asian Profile* 5(5), oct 77 : 409-
418.

3528   SOKOŁOWSKA, Magdalena. "The woman image in the awareness of contemporary Polish society", *Polish sociol. B.* 35(3), 1976 : 41-
50.

3529   TILLION, Germaine. "Origines préhistoriques de la condition des
femmes en zones 'civilisées'", *R. int. Sci. soc.* 29(4), 1977 :
725-735.

3530   VILLEMEZ, Wayne J. "Male economic gain from female subordination:
a caveat and reanalysis", *Soc. Forces* 56(2), dec 77 : 626-636.

3531   WEINREICH, Helen. "What future for the female subject ? Some implications of the women's movement for psychological research",
Hum. Relat. 30(6), jun 77 : 535-543.

3532   "Women and change in the developing world", *J. int. Aff.* 30(2),
1976-1977 : 151-268.

3533   "Women and class struggle", *Latin Amer. Perspect.* 4(1-2), 1977 :
2-202.

15500. ETHNIC GROUP
GROUPE ETHNIQUE

15510. Ethnicity. Tribe
Ethnicité. Tribu

15511.

[See also / Voir aussi: 1003, 1375, 1420, 1446, 1458, 2047, 2232,
2527, 2618, 2996, 3107, 3111, 3368, 3386, 4307, 4660, 5123,
5324, 5388]

3534   ABRAMSON, H. "On the sociology of ethnicity and social change: a
model of rootedness and rootlessness", *Econ. soc. R.* 8(1), oct
76 : 43-59.

3535   AHMED, Akbar S. *Social and economic change in the Tribal Areas,
1972-1976.* Karachi, Oxford University Press, 77, vi-81 p.-9 l.
[Pakistan.]

3536   ALLARDT, E. "La minorité d'expression suédoise en Finlande", *Rech.
sociol.* 8(1), 1977 : 35-50.

3537   ARATÓ,-Endre. "A nemzetiségi kutatások fö irányai és eredményei
        Csehszlovákiában az utobbi öt esztendöben" (The main tendencies
        in the minority research in Czechoslovakia and the results
        during the last five years), *Párttört. Közlem.* (3), 1976 : 144-
        164.

3538   BABIŃSKI, Grzegorz. "Problematyka grup etnicznych we wspólczesnej
        socjologii amerykanskiej - próba systematyzacji" (The problem
        of ethnic groups in the contemporary American sociology - an
        attempt at systematization), *Stud. socjol.* 64(3), 1976 : 117-137.

3539   BANTON, Michael P. *The idea of race.* London, Tavistock, 77, 190 p.

3540   BASSAND, Michel. "Le séparatisme jurassien: un conflit de classes
        et/ou un conflit ethnique ?", *C. int. Sociol.* 23(61), jul-dec
        76 : 221-246.

3541   CAREY, Iskandar. *Orang Asli: the aboriginal tribes of peninsular
        Malaysia.* Kuala-Lumpur-New York, Oxford University Press, 76,
        x-376 p.-7 1.

3542   CLAYTON, J. "The transnational protection of ethnic minorities: a
        tentative framework for inquiry", *Canad. Yb. int. Law* 13(13),
        1975 : 25-60.

3543   DASHEFSKY, Arnold (ed.). *Ethnic identity in society.* Chicago,
        Rand McNally, 76, xiv-252 p.

3544   Bibl.XXVI-2988. DESPRES, Leo A. (ed.). *Ethnicity and resource com-
        petition in plural societies.* CR: Leo KUPER, *Amer. J. Sociol.*
        82(5), mar 77 : 1146-1148.

3545   DOUGLASS, William A.; LYMAN, Stanford M. "L'ethnie: structure,
        processus et saillance", *C. int. Sociol.* 23(61), jul-dec 76 :
        197-220.

3546   DRIEDGER, Leo. "Toward a perspective on Canadian pluralism : ethnic
        identity in Winnipeg", *Canad. J. Sociol.* 2(1), 1977 : 77-95.

3547   DWORKIN, Anthony Gary; DWORKIN, Anthony (eds.). *The minority re-
        port: an introduction to racial, ethnic, and gender relations.*
        New York, Praeger, 76, 410 p. CR: Joseph S. ROUCEK, *Contemp.
        Sociol. (Washington)* 6(3), mai 77 : 343-344.

3548   ELKLIT, J.; NOACK, J. P.; TONSGAARD, O. "Allemands et Danois dans
        le Schleswig du Nord", *Rech. sociol.* 8(1), 1977 : 5-34.

3549   GELLNER, Ernest. "Ethnicity and anthropology in the Soviet Union",
        Archiv. europ. Sociol. 18(2), 1977 : 201-220.

3550   GILES, Howard; TAYLOR, Donald M.; BOURHIS, Richard Y. "Dimensions
        of Welsh identity", *Europ. J. soc. Psychol.* 7(2), 1977 : 165-
        174.

3551   GLAZER, Nathan. "Ethnicity: a world phenomenon", *South Afr. int.
        Quart.* 7(4), apr 77 : 197-212. [Also published in French, *Dia-
        logue* 7(2), 1976 : 41-55.]

3552   Bibl.XXVI-2996. GLAZER, Nathan; MOYNIHAN, Daniel P. (eds.). *Eth-
        nicity: theory and experience.* CR: Peter I. ROSE, *Contemp. So-
        ciol. (Washington)* 5(2), mar 76 : 189-190.

3553   GUBERT, R. "Pluralismo etnico e migrazioni internazionali" (Ethnic
        pluralism and international migrations), *Studi Emigr.* 13(43),
        sep 76 : 279-317.

3554   HEIBERG, M. "Insiders/outsiders: Basque nationalism", *Archiv.
        europ. Sociol.* 16(2), 1975 : 169-193.

3555   HENRY, Frances (ed.). *Ethnicity in the Americas.* The Hague, Mouton;
        Chicago, Aldine, 76, xi-456 p.

3556   HERAUD, G. "Nouvelles réflexions sur l'ethnisme et le fédéralisme
        ethnique", *A. Fac. Dr. Univ. Jean Moulin* (1), 1975 : 53-65.

3557   HICKS, George L.; LEIS, Philip E. (eds.). *Ethnic encounters: iden-
        tities and contents.* North Scituate, Mass., Duxbury Press, 77,
        x-289 p.

3558   HUSSAIN, A. "Ethnicity, national identity and praetorianism: the
        case of Pakistan", *Asian Surv.* 16(10), oct 76 : 918-930.

3559   JAFFE, Abram J. CULLEN, Ruth M.; BOSWELL, Thomas D. *Spanish*
        Americans in the United States: changing demographic character-
        istics. New York, Research Institute for the Study of Man, 76,
        xiv-431 p.
3560   JASIEWICZ, Krzysztof. "Czynniki asymilacji narodowej" (Factors in
        national assimilation), *Przegl. socjol.* 29, 1977 : 349-391.
3561   KELMENČIČ, V. "Slovenska manjšina v Avstriji" (The Slovene mino-
        rity in Austria), *Teoriaj in Praksa* 13(11), nov 76 : 915-924.
3562   KEMÉNY, I. (ed.). *Beszámoló a magyarországi cigányok helyzetével*
        foglalkozó 1971-ben végzett kutatásról (Report on the 1971 year
        survey of the situation of gypsies in Hungary). Budapest, MTA
        KESZ, 76, 291 p.
3563   KERCKHOFF, Alan C.; CAMPBELL, Richard T. "Race and social status
        differences in the explanation of educational ambition", *Soc.*
        Forces 55(3), mar 77 : 701-714.
3564   KOMAI, Hiroshi. "Ethnic plurality and national development in
        Thailand", *Shakai-gaku Jânaru* 2(1), 1977 : 23-30.
3565   KÖVÁGÓ, László. *Kisebbség - nemzetiség* (Minorities - nationalities).
        Budapest, Kossuth Kiadó, 77, 155 p. *[Hungary.]*
3566   KÖVÁGÓ, László. *Nemzetiségeink jelene* (The present of our minori-
        ties). Budapest, Sasad Tsz., 76, 83 p. *[Hungary.]*
3567   Bibl.XXVI-3007. KUPER, Leo (ed.). *Race, science and society.* CR:
        Hugh H. SMYTHE, *Contemp. Sociol. (Washington)* 6(1), jan 77 : 77-
        78.
3568   LIÉGEOIS, Jean-Pierre. "Utopie et mutation: l'exemple tzigane",
        C. int. Sociol. 23(61), jul-dec 76 : 247-270.
3569   LUZIK, K. S. *SŠA: naučno-tehničeskaja revoljucija i položenie*
        rassovyh men'sinstv. Social'no-ékonomičeskij aspekt (The USA:
        the scientific technical revolution and the situation of ra-
        cial minorities. The socio-economic aspect). Kiev, Izdatel'stvo
        pri kievskom gosudarstvennom Universitete, 76, 207 p.
3570   MAYER, K. B. "Groupes linguistiques en Suisse", *Rech. sociol.*
        8(1), 1977 : 75-94.
3571   McCAFFREY, Lawrence J. *The Irish diaspora in America.* Bloomington,
        Indiana University Press, 76, 214 p. CR: John Murray DUDDIHY,
        Contemp. Sociol. (Washington) 6(3), mai 77 : 344-345.
3572   MINDEL, Charles H.; HABENSTEIN, Robert W. (eds.). *Ethnic families*
        in America: patterns and variations. New York, Elsevier, 76,
        xiii-429 p. CR: Nicholas TAVUCHIS, *Amer. J. Sociol.* 82(6), mai
        77 : 1422-1424.
3573   NAGATA, J. "The status of ethnicity and the ethnicity of status:
        ethnic and class identity in Malaysia and Latin America", *Int.*
        J. comp. Sociol. 17(3-4), sep-dec 76 : 242-260.
3574   NAKHLEH, Khalil. "Anthropological and sociological studies on the
        Arabs in Israel: a critique", *J. Palestine Stud.* 6(4), 1977 :
        41-70.
3575   NEMETH, Charlan; WACHTLER, Joel; ENDICOTT, Jeffrey. "Increasing
        the size of the minority: some gains and some losses", *Europ.*
        J. soc. Psychol. 7(1), 1977 : 15-27.
3576   PATHY, Jaganath *et al.* "Tribal studies in India: an appraisal",
        East. Anthropologist 29(4), oct-dec 76 : 399-417.
3577   PAVLAK, Thomas J. "Ethnic identity and political alienation"; *Int.*
        J. contemp. Sociol. 14(1-2), jan-apr 77 : 87-101.
3578   PINEO, Peter C. "The social standing of ethnic and racial group-
        ings", *Canad. R. Sociol. Anthropol.* 14(2), mai 77 : 147-157.
        [Canada.]
3579   "Polish Americans (The)", *Polish R.* 21(3), 1976 : 3-148.
3580   RAMIREZ, Albert; LASATER, Thomas L. "Ethnicity of communicator,
        self-esteem, and reactions to fear-arousing communications",
        J. soc. Psychol. 102(1), jun 77 : 79-91.
3581   RAPHAEL, Freddy; WEYL, Robert. *Juifs en Alsace: culture, société,*
        histoire. Toulouse, E. Privat, 77, 458 p.

3582   ROSE, Jerry D. *Peoples: the ethnic dimension in human relations.* Chicago, Rand McNally College, 76, 201 p. CR: Douglas S. SNYDER, *Contemp. Sociol. (Washington)* 6(2), mar 77 : 217-218.

3583   SAID, Abdul; SIMMONS, Luiz R. (eds.). *Ethnicity in an international context.* New Brunswick, N.J., Transaction Books, 76, 241 p.

3584   SCHOLZ, Fred. "Die beduinischen Stämme im östlichen Inner-Oman und ihr Regionalmobilitätsverhalten" (The Bedouin tribes of Eastern Central Oman and their regional mobility behavior), *Sociologus* 27(2), 1977 : 97-133.

3585   SIEMIEŃSKA, Renata. "Przynaleznośc do grupy etnicznej jako czynnik róznicujący postawy członków społeczeństwa amerikańskiego" (Ethnic group membership as a differentiation factor in the attitudes of the American society), *Stud. socjol.* 64(1), 1977 : 241-266.

3586   SOEN, D. "Arabs, social change and ethnicity in Israel", *Orient (Opladen)* 17(4), dec 76 : 109-122.

3587   Bibl.XXVI-3026. SOWELL, Thomas. *Race and economics.* CR: Lynn TURGEON, *Amer. J. Sociol.* 82(5), mar 77 : 1126-1127.

3588   SPADY, Dale R.; THOMPSON, Henrick S. "The Finnish-American: an exploration of ethnic identity", *Siirtolaisuus* (3), 1977 : 12-21.

3589   STEINKE, K. "Les minorités hongroise et allemande de Roumanie", *Rech. sociol.* 8(1), 1977 : 51-74.

3590   Bibl.XXVI-3029. SUTHERLAND, Anne. *Gypsies. The hidden Americans.* CR: Martti GRÖNFORS, *Brit. J. Sociol.* 18(1), sep 77 : 413-414.

3591   Bibl.XXVI-3037. WAGENHEIM, Kal. *A survey of Puerto Ricans on the US mainland in the 1970s.* CR: David Jess LEON, *Contemp. Sociol. (Washington)* 6(2), mar 77 : 224-225.

15512.
[See also / Voir aussi: 909, 2677, 4456, 5100, 5112, 5124, 5140, 5143, 5677]

3592   "American Indian and the law (The)", *Law contemp. Probl.* 40(1), 1976 : 225 p.

3593   Bibl.XXVI-3043. BRAROE, Niels Winther. *Indian and White: self-image and interaction in a Canadian plains community.* CR: Philip A. MAY, *Contemp. Sociol. (Washington)* 6(3), mai 77 : 343-344.

3594   "Brasil indigena" (Indigenous Brazil), *Amer. indíg.* 37(1), jan-mar 77 : 3-196.

3595   CARDOSO DE OLIVEIRA, Roberto. *Identidade, etnia e estrutura social* (Identity, ethnicity and social structure). São Paulo, Livraria Pioneira Editora, 76, xxi-118 p. [Indians of Brazil.]

3596   DA MATTA, Roberto. "Quanto custa ser indio no Brasil ? Considera-çoes sobre o problema da identidade etnica" (How much cost to be Indian in Brazil ? Considerations on the problem of ethnic identity), *Dados* 13, 1976 : 33-54.

3597   DAVIS, Lenwood G. *Blacks in the State of Ohio, 1800-1976: a preliminary survey.* Monticello, Ill., Council of Planning Librarians, 77, 87 p.

3598   "Estados Unidos indígena" (Indigenous United States), *Amér. indíg.* 36(4), oct-dec 76 : 677-874. [North American Indians.]

3599   GARCIA, Richard A. (ed.). *The Chicanos in America, 1540-1974: a chronology and fact book.* Dobbs Ferry, N.Y., Oceana Publications, 77, viii-231 p.

3600   GIGIREY PAREDES, Carlos. "Datos para una sociología del negro brasileño" (Data for a sociology of the Brazilean negro), *R. int. Sociol. (Madrid)* 36(21), 1977 : 29-76.

3601   Bibl.XXVI-3048. GURIN, Patricia; EPPS, Edgar. *Black consciousness, identity, and achievement: a study of students in historically black colleges.* CR: Castellano B. TURNER, *Amer. J. Sociol.* 82(5), mar 77 : 1122-1123.

3602   GUTHRIE, Gerard. "Images of aborigines", *Austral. New Zealand J. Sociol.* 13(1), feb 77 : 69-74.

3603   HUNDLEY, Norris Jr. (ed.). *The Asian Americans: the historical experience*. Santa Barbara, Calif., Clio Press, 76, 186 p. CR: Rawlein G. SOBERANO, *Contemp. Sociol. (Washington)* 6(3), mai 77 : 345.

3604   KRICKUS, Richard. *Pursuing the American dream: White ethnics and the new populism*. Garden City, N.Y., Anchor Books, 76, 424 p. CR: Paul D. STARR, *Contemp. Sociol. (Washington)* 6(1), jan 77 : 77.

3605   MARTINEAU, William H. "Informal social ties among urban black Americans. Some new data and a review of the problem", *J. Black Stud.* 8(1), sep 77 : 83-104.

3606   MOSQUERA, José E. "La 'negritud' en Colombia" (The "negritud" in Colombia), *Doc. polít.* 124, mar-apr 77 : 85-94.

3607   "New perspectives on Black America", *Soc. Sci. Quart.* 57(4), mar 77 : 718-863.

3608   PINKNEY, Alphonso. *Red, Black, and Green: Black nationalism in the United States*. New York, Cambridge University Press, 76, 258 p. CR: Paul T. MURRAY, *Contemp. Sociol. (Washington)* 6(3), mai 77 : 347-348.

3609   SIMMONS, James L. "One little, two little, three little Indians", *Hum. Org.* 36(1), 1977 : 76-79.

3610   SIVANANDAN, A. "The liberation of the black intellectual", *Race and Class* 18(4), mar 77 : 329-343.

3611   SOTO-PEREZ, Hector. "Cikanos: genezis i ěvolucija problemy" (The Chicanos: genesis and evolution of the problem), *Latinsk. Amer.* 8(2), mar-apr 77 : 86-98. *[USA.]*

3612   URBANSKI, E. S. "Les Indiens des Amériques dans le monde contemporain", *Cultures* 3(3), 1976 : 59-79.

15520. Interethnic relations. Racism
Relations interethniques. Racisme

15521.

[See also / Voir aussi: 1144]

3613   BIDWELL, Sidney. *Red, white and black: race relations in Britain*. London, Gordon and Cremonesi, 76, vii-213 p.-8 p.

3614   COX, Oliver C. *Race relations: elements and social dynamics*. Detroit, Wayne State University Press, 76, 337 p. CR: Don O. WATKINS, *Contemp. Sociol. (Washington)* 6(4), jul 77 : 466.

3615   FRANCIS, Emerich K. *Interethnic relations: an essay in sociological theory*. New York, Elsevier, 76, 432 p. CR: Richard T. SCHAEFER, *Contemp. Sociol. (Washington)* 6(4), jul 77 : 466-467.

3616   FRANKLIN, John Hope. *Racial equality in America*. Chicago, University of Chicago Press, 76, ix-113 p. CR: William P. NYE, *Contemp. Sociol. (Washington)* 6(4), jul 77 : 467.

3617   FUKUMOTO SATO, Mary Nancy. *Relaciones raciales en un tugurio de Lima: el caso de Huerta Perdida* (Racial relations in slums of Lima: the case of Huerta Perdida). Lima, Pontificia Universidad Católica del Perú, Programa de Perfeccionamiento en Ciencias Sociales, 76, xix-253 1.

3618   GETTY, Harry T. *Interethnic relationships in the community of Tucson*. New York, Arno Press, 76, 312 p. *[USA.]*

3619   GHIDINELLI, A. "Apuntes para una teoría y metodología de la investigación sobre el roce interétnico" (Notes for a theory and a methodology of the research on the interethnic relations), *Guatemala indíg.* 10(1-2), jan-jun 75 : 9-212. *[Guatemala.]*

3620   HEISLER, Martin O. (ed.). "Ethnic conflict in the world to-day", *A. Amer. Acad. polit. soc. Sci.* 433, sep 77 : 1-160.

3621   KAPUTO, Samba. "Phénomène d'ethnicité et conflit ethnopolitique dans les centres urbains de l'Afrique noire. Le cas des Kusu et des Shi dans la ville de Bukavu", *R. Inst. Sociol.* (1-2), 1987 : 149-172. *[Zaïre.]*

3622   KATZENSTEIN, Peter J. "Ethnic political conflict in South Tyrol",
        Österr. Z. Aussenpolit. 16(4), 1976 : 221-230; 16(5), 1976 :
        275-291.
3623   RAYSIDE, D. M. "Les relations entre groupes linguistiques au Ca-
        nada et en Belgique", *Rech. sociol.* 8(1), 1977 : 95-131.
3624   SANDA, A. O. "Ethnic pluralism and intra-class conflicts in four
        West African societies", *Civilisations* 27(1-2), 1977 : 65-80.
3625   SCHMITZ, H. Walter. "Interethnische Beziehungen in Saraguro (Ecua-
        dor) aus der Sicht einer Anthropologie der Kommunikation" (In-
        terethnic relations in Saraguro, Ecuador, from the point of
        view of an anthropology of communication), *Sociologus* 27(1),
        1977 : 64-85.
3626   TERNON, Yves. *Les Arméniens: histoire d'un génocide.* Paris, Édi-
        tions du Seuil, 77, 317 p.
3627   WINZELER, Robert L. "Ethnic complexity and ethnic relations in an
        East Coast Malay town", *Southeast Asian J. soc. Sci.* 2(1-2),
        1974 : 45-61.

15523.

[See also / Voir aussi: 1417, 1723, 1922, 2224, 2513, 2551,
2591, 2650, 3637, 3730, 4141, 4151, 4172, 5386]

3628   FARLEY, Reynolds. "Trends in racial inequalities: have the gains
        of the 1960s disappeared in the 1970s ?", *Amer. sociol. R.*
        42(2), apr 77 : 189-208. [USA.]
3629   FEIT, F.; STOKES, R. G. "Racial prejudice and economic pragmatism:
        A South African case-study", *J. mod. Afr. Stud.* 14(3), sep 76 :
        487-506.
3630   FOLEY, Linda A. "Personality characteristics and interracial con-
        tact as determinants of black prejudice toward whites", *Hum.
        Relat.* 30(8), aug 77 : 709-720.
3631   FRISBIE, W. Parker; NEIDERT, Lisa. "Inequality and the relative
        size of minority populations: a comparative analysis", *Amer. J.
        Sociol.* 82(5), mar 77 : 1007-1030. [USA.]
3632   FUTERNICK, Allan. "Racial preferences and degree of prejudice
        among white southern ROTC cadets", *J. polit. milit. Sociol.*
        5(1), 1977 : 53-62.
3633   GAERTNER, Samuel L.; DOVIDIO, John F.;"The subtlety of white
        racism, arousal, and helping behavior", *J. Person. soc. Psychol.*
        35(10), oct 77 : 691-707.
3634   HOGAN, Dennis P.; FEATHERMAN, David L. "Racial stratification and
        socioeconomic change in the American North and South", *Amer. J.
        Sociol.* 83(1), jul 77 : 100-126.
3635   HUGO, Pierre J. "Academic dissent and apartheid in South Africa",
        J. Black Stud. 7(3), mar 77 : 243-262.
3636   HUNT, Janet G.; HUNT, Larry L. "Racial inequality and self-image:
        identity maintenance as identity diffusion", *Sociol. soc. Res.*
        61(4), jul 77 : 539-559.
3637   JACOBSON, Cardell K. "Separatism, integrationism, and avoidance
        among Black, White and Latin adolescents", *Soc. Forces* 55(4),
        jun 77 : 1011-1027. [USA.]
3638   JAYARAMAN, R. "Racial inequality in industrial society and theo-
        ries of social stratification", *Sociol. B. (Bombay)* 25(1), mar
        76 : 63-72.
3639   KATZ, Phyllis A. (ed.). *Towards the elimination of racism.* New
        York, Pergamon Press, 76, xiv-444 p. [USA.]
3640   KIRP, D. L. "Race, politics, and the courts: school desegration
        in San Francisco", *Harvard educ. R.* 46(4), nov 76 : 572-611.
3641   KLEIN, Paul. *Urteile junger französischer Arbeitnehmer über Deut-
        sche vor, während und nach einem einjahrigen Arbeitsaufenthalt
        in Deutschland* (Young French workers' judgments towards Germans
        before, during and after a one-year working period in Germany).

Frankfurt-am-Main, Peter Lang; Bern, Herbert Lang, 76, 128 p.

3642 KRIEGEL, Annie. *Les juifs et le monde moderne: essai sur les lo-giques d'émancipation*. Paris, Seuil, 77, 252 p.

3643 LANGMUIR, Gavin I. "Prolegomena to any present analysis of hostility against Jews", *Soc. Sci. Inform.* 15(4-5), 1976 : 689-727.

3644 LEVINE, Daniel U.; MEYER, Yeanic Keeny. "Level and rate of disegregation and white enrolment decline in a big city school district", *Soc. Probl.* 24(4), apr 77 : 451-462. *[USA.]*

3645 LIPSKY, M.; OLSON, D. J. "The processing of racial crisis in America", *Polit. and Soc.* 6(1), 1976 ; 79-103.

3646 MAUCO, Georges. *Les étrangers en France et le problème du racisme*. Paris, La Pensée universelle, 77, 253 p.

3647 MITHUN, Jacqueline S. "Black power and community change", *J. Black Stud.* 7(3), mar 77 : 263-280. *[USA.]*

3648 PATCHEN, Martin *et al.* "Determinants of students' interracial behavior and opinion change", *Sociol. Educ.* 50(1), jan 77 : 55-75.

3649 POLIAKOV, Léon; DELACAMPAGNE, Christian; GIRARD, Patrick. *Le racisme*. Paris, Seghers, 76, 155 p.

3650 SHAPIRO, E. Gary. "Racial differences in the value of job rewards", *Soc. Forces* 56(1), sep 77 : 21-30.

3651 SNYDER, D.; KELLY, W. R. "Conflict intensity, media sensitivity and the validity of newspaper data", *Amer. sociol. R.* 42(1), feb 77 : 105-123. *[Racial conflict in the USA.]*

3652 SYLLA, Lanciné. *Tribalisme et parti unique en Afrique noire: esquisse d'une théorie générale de l'intégration nationale*. Abidjan, Université nationale de Côte d'Ivoire; Paris, Presses de la Fondation nationale des sciences politiques, 77, 391 p.

3653 WOLFENSTEIN, Eugene Victor. "Race, racism and racial liberation", *West. polit. Quart.* 30(2), jun 77 : 163-182.

15600. MIGRATION

15610. Migrant. Migration policy
Migrant. Politique migratoire

[See also / Voir aussi: 2405, 3162, 4191]

3654 ADERANTI ADEPOJU. "Migration and development in Tropical Africa", *Afr. Aff.* 76(303), apr 77 : 210-225.

3655 BACH, Robert L.; SMITH, Joel. "Community satisfaction, expectations of moving, and migration", *Demography* 14(2), mai 77 : 147-167.

3656 CHARBIT, Yves. "La sociologie des migrations en Grande-Bretagne, 1960-1975", *Année sociol.* 26, 1975 : 83-105.

3657 DEGOS, Laurent; CHAVENTRÉ, André; JACQUARD, Albert. "Migration, sélection et système d'histo-compatibilité", *Population* 32(1), jan-feb 77 : 123-136.

3658 GIRARD, Alain. "Sociologie des migrations", *Année sociol.* 26, 1975 : 9-19.

3659 GRZYWNOWICZ, Stanisław. "Procesy migracyjne na tle recesji gospodarczej w rozwiniętych krajach kapitalistycznych" (Migration processes and economic recession in developed capitalist countries), *Biul. IGS* 20(4), 1977 : 6-26.

3660 JONG, Gordon F. DE. "Residential preferences and migration", *Demography* 14(2), mai 77 : 169-178.

3661 KASPARIAN, Robert. "Approximation du calendrier des migrations multiples par un modèle stochastique", *Population* 32(4-5), jul-oct 77 : 867-887.

3662 "Migrations et développement", *Tiers-Monde* 18(69), jan-mar 77 : 5-175.

3663 RYBAKOVSKIJ, L. L. *Social'nye problemy migracii* (Social problems of migration). Moskva, 76, 203 p.

3664 SLY, David F.; TAYMAN, Jeff. "Ecological approach to migration reexamined", *Amer. sociol. R.* 42(5), oct 77 : 783-795.

3665   STAMBOULI, F. "Éléménts de réflexion pour une contribution à une
        nouvelle sociologie des migrations. Tolérance ou droit à la
        différence ?", *IBLA* 39(137), 1 sem 76 : 33-40.
3666   TABOADA-LEONETTI, Isabelle. "Le projet de migration. La nature
        du projet de migration et ses liens avec l'adaptation", *Année
        sociol.* 26, 1975 : 107-123.

        15620. External migration
               Migration externe

        15621.

        [See also / Voir aussi: 3553]

3667   ARAGON, Luis E. "Migracion fronteriza: implicaciones espaciales
        en la cultura kwayker, Colombia" (Frontier migration: special
        implications in the Kwayker culture, Colombia), *R. geogr. (Rio
        de Janeiro)* 83, dec 75 : 87-93.
3668   DIESNER, Hans-Joachim. *Die Völkerwanderung* (Migrations of nations).
        Gütersloh, Bertelsmann Lexikon-Verlag, 76, 255 p.
3669   LOHRMANN, R. "European migration: recent developments and future
        prospects", *Migr. int.* 14(3), 1976 : 229-240.
3670   LOHRMANN, R. "Wanderungsbewegungen in Europa. Politische Auswir-
        kungen der internationalen Migration" (Migrations in Europe.
        The political impact of international migrations), *Europa-
        Archiv* 31(9), mai 10, 76 : 303-312.
3671   MARR, W. L. "The United Kingdom's international migration in the
        inter-war period: theoretical considerations and empirical test-
        ing", *Popul. Stud.* 31(3), nov 77 : 571-579.
3672   PICQUET, Michel R. "Effets démographiques des migrations interna-
        tionales de type conjoncturel sur la structure par âge et sexe
        de la population du Venezuela", *Cah. ORSTOM Sér. Sci. hum.*
        13(3), 1976 : 227-244.
3673   ROSENGREN, Annette. "Migrationen mellan Sverige och Finland efter
        andra världskriget" (Migration between Finland and Sweden after
        the second world war), *Siirtolaisuus* (1), 1977 : 27-32.
3674   SMITH, P. C. "The social demography of Filipino migrations abroad",
        Int. Migration R. 10(3), 1976 : 307-353.
3675   TRINDADE, Maria Beatriz Rocha. "Comunidades migrantes en situação
        bipolar: analise de tres casos de emigração especializada para
        os EUA, para o Brasil e para França" (Migrant communities in
        bipolar situation: analysis of three cases of specialized emig-
        ration for the USA, Brazil and France), *Anál. soc.* 12(48),
        1976 : 983-997. [Portugal.]
3676   WILSON, F. "International migration in Southern Africa", *Int.
        Migration R.* 10(4), 1976 : 451-488.

        15622.

        [See also / Voir aussi: 3303, 3869]

3677   ALBA-HERNÁNDEZ, Francisco. "Exodo silencioso: la emigración de
        trabajadores mexicanos a Estados Unidos" (Silent exodus: the
        Mexican workers' emigration to the United States), *Foro int.*
        17(2), oct-dec 76 : 152-179.
3678   ARBELAEZ C., Alfonso "El éxodo de colombianos en el período 1963-
        1973" (Colombian exodus during the 1963-1973 period), *Bol. mens.
        Estadíst.* 26(310), mai 77 : 7-43.
3679   GINSBURGS, G. "Current legal problems of Jewish emigration from
        the USSR", *Sov. Jew. Aff.* 6(2), 1976 : 3-13.
3680   GOETHALS, A. L. J. "Nederland als emigratieland" (The Netherlands
        as an emigration country), *Bevolking en Gezin* (1), 1977 : 43-
        55.
3681   GRUBEL, H. G. "Reflections on the present state of the brain drain
        and a suggested remedy", *Minerva* 14(2), 1976 : 209-224.

3682   GUHA, Amalendu. "Brain drain issue and indicators on brain drain",
        Migr. int. 15(1), 1977 ; 3-20.

3683   HOPE, K. R. "The emigration to high-level manpower from develop-
        ing to developed countries (with reference to Trinidad and
        Tobago)", *Migr. int.* 14(3), 1976 : 209-218.

3684   KELLY, John J. "Alternative estimates of the volume of emigra-
        tion from Canada, 1961-1971", *Canad. R. Sociol. Anthropol.*
        14(1), feb 77 : 55-67.

3685   LIBERSKA, Barbara. "Socjologiczna problematyka międzynarodowej
        migracji wysoko kwalifikowanych kadr (tzw. drenaż mózgów)"
        (Sociological problems of international migration of profession-
        al personnel; so called brain drain), *Stud. socjol.* 63(4),
        1976 : 171-183.

3686   LYNN, Richard. "Selective emigration and the decline of intelli-
        gence in Scotland", *Soc. Biology* 24(3), 1977 : 173-182.

3687   MALDONADO-DENIS, Manuel. "La emigración puertorriqueña: una in-
        terpretación sociohistórica" (The Puerto-Rican emigration: a
        social and historical interpretation), *Latino Amér.* (8), 1975 :
        69-98.

3688   NAMIHIRA, Isao. "Sonraku no kaisôbunka to kaigai ijûsha no keisei
        - Nogoshi Nakaoji - buraku o chûshin to shite" (Social strati-
        fication in an Okinawan village and formation of emigrants to
        Brazil), *Okinawa kokusai-daigaku Bungakubu Kiyô* 5(2), 1977 :
        36-45.

3689   PORTES, A. "Determinants of the brain drain", *Int. Migration R.*
        10(4); 1976 : 489-508.

3690   PRATO, Ledo. *Sviluppo del capitale ed emigrazione in Europa, la
        Francia* (Capital development and emigration in Europe, the case
        of France). Milano, G. Mazzotta, 76, 160 p.

3691   PUCCIO, F. "Aspetti e problemi dell' emigrazione in Sicilia"
        (Aspects and problems of emigration in Sicily), *Nuovi Quad.
        Merid.* 13(49), jan-mar 75 : 63-79.

3692   ROCHA TRINDADE, M. B. "Analyse de trois ans d'émigration portu-
        gaise vers les ÉUA, le Brésil et la France", *Rech. Migr.* (3),
        jul-oct 76 : 13-29.

3693   SAYAD, Abdelmalek. "Les trois âges de l'émigration algérienne en
        France", *Actes Rech. Sci. soc.* 15, jun 77 : 59-79.

3694   TAPINOS, G. *et al. La population française a l'étranger et les
        flux d'émigration française: rapport.* Paris, Fondation natio-
        nale des sciences politiques, 76, 181 p. multigr.

3695   TASILLO, Carmelina. "Lingua e cultura di emigrati molisani"
        (Language and culture of the emigrants from the region of Mo-
        lisa), *Sociologia (Roma)* 10(3), sep-dec 76 : 65-88.

        15623.

        [See also / Voir aussi: 1472, 3372, 3503, 4511, 4520, 4633]

3696   ALLEN, James P. "Recent immigration from the Philippines and Fi-
        lipino communities in the United States", *Geogr. R.* 67(2), apr
        77 : 195-208.

3697   ANGLADE, Jean. *La vie quotidienne des immigrés en France: de
        1919 à nos jours.* Paris, Hachette, 76, 221 p.

3698   ATH-MESSMOUD, Malek; GILLETTE, Alain. *L'immigration algérienne en
        France.* Paris, Éditions Entente, 76, 127 p.

3699   BASKAUSKAS, L. "Planned incorporation of refugees: the Baltic
        clause", *Migr. int.* 14(3), 1976 ; 219-228. [USA.]

3700   BOGINA, Š. A. *Immigrantskoe naselenie SŠA, 1865-1900 gg.* (The USA
        immigrant population, 1865-1900). Leningrad, Nauka, 76, 275 p.

3701   BONNET, Jean Charles. *Les pouvoirs publics français et l'immig-
        ration dans l'entre-deux-guerres.* Lyon, Centre d'histoire éco-
        nomique et sociale de la région lyonnaise. 76, xxx-414 p.

3702   BOURAOUI, A. "Les travailleurs tunisiens en France. Analyse dé-
           mographique", *R. tunis. Sci. soc.* 13(44), 1976 : 19-36.
3703   BRAGG, Melvyn. *Speak for England.* New York, A. A. Knopf, 77, 512 p.
           CR: Joan GILBERT, *Contemp. Sociol. (Washington)* 6(4), jul 77 :
           501-502.
3704   BRETTELL, Caroline B.; CALLIER-BOISVERT, Colette. "Portuguese im-
           migrants in France: familial and social networks and the struc-
           turing of community", *Studi Emigr.* 14(46), jun 77 : 149-202.
3705   CALVARUSO, Claudio. "Migranti e società industriale",(Migrant and
           industrial society), *Sociologia (Roma)* 11(1), jan-apr 77 : 31-50.
           [Migrant workers assimilation in Italy and France.]
3706   CAMPIOLI, Georges. "De la sociologie des immigrés à la sociologie
           de l'immigration. L'évolution des travaux belges", *Année sociol.*
           26, 1975 : 43-56.
3707   COHEN, Erik. "Expatriate communities", *Sociol. contemp.* 24(3),
           1976 : 5-133.
3708   COHEN, M. "Étude psychologique de l'acculturation des juifs ma-
           rocains", *Dispersion et Unité* 16, 1976 : 173-187.
3709   "Culture immigrée", *Autrement* (11), nov 77 : 3-216.
3710   DAVISON, Victoria F.; SHANNON, Lyle W. "Change in the economic ab-
           sorption of a cohort of immigrant Mexican Americans and Negroes
           between 1960 and 1971", *Int. Migr. R.* 11(2), 1977 : 190-214.
           [USA.]
3711   DECHEZELLES, André. "Les travailleurs migrants et leurs familles
           en France", *R. jur. polit.* 31(2), apr-jun 77 : 845-860.
3712   GOLDSMITH-KASINSKY, Renée. *Refugees from militarism: draft-age
           Americans in Canada.* CR: John C. LEGGETT, *Contemp. Sociol. (Wa-
           shington)* 6(2), mar 77 : 211-212.
3713   GRZEŚKOWIAK, Joanna. "Opinie Anglosasów o polskich emigrantach w
           Kanadzie, 1896-1939" (Anglo-Saxon opinions about Polish immig-
           rants to Canada, 1896-1939), *Przegl. socjol.* 29, 1977 : 45-79.
3714   HAWKINS, F. "Canadian immigration", *Round Table* 265, jan 77 : 50-63.
3715   HAWKINS, Freda. "Canadian immigration: a new law and a new app-
           roach to management", *Int. Migration R.* 11(1), 1977 : 77-93.
3716   HUMBLET, Jean-E. "Problématique de l'adaptation des immigrants au
           Québec", *R. Inst. Sociol.* (1-2), 1976 : 119-147.
3717   INBAR, Michael. "Immigration and learning: the vulnerable age",
           Canad. R. Sociol. Anthropol. 14(2), mai 77 : 218-234.
3718   INBAR, Michael. ADLER, Chaim. *Ethnic integration in Israel: a com-
           parative case study of Moroccan brothers who settled in France
           and in Israel.* New Brunswick, N.J., Transaction Books, 77, 144 p.
3719   INSTITUT NATIONAL D'ÉTUDES DÉMOGRAPHIQUES. *Les immigrés du Maghreb:
           études sur l'adaptation en milieu urbain.* Paris, Presses universi-
           taires de France, 77, xiii-411 p. CR: Alain GIRARD, *Population*
           32(2), mar-apr 77 : 405-410.
3720   ISHII, Yoichi. "Caractéristiques de l'immigration japonaise au Bré-
           sil", *Migr. dans le Monde* 26(2), 1977 : 10-15.
3721   KANAANA, Sharif. *Socio-cultural and psychological adjustment of
           the Arab minority in Israel.* San Francisco, R.and E Research
           Associates, 76, vii-220 p.
3722   KUO, Wen H.; LIN, Nan. "Assimilation of Chinese-Americans in Wa-
           shington",D.C.", *Sociol. Quart.* 18(3), 1977 : 340-353.
3723   LAHALLE, Dominique. "L'insertion des immigrés dans la vie politique",
           Année sociol. 26, 1975 : 189-200.
3724   LEE, Trevor. *Race and residence: the concentration and dispersal
           of immigrants in London.* Oxford, Eng., Clarendon Press, 77, 193 p.
3725   MAGNARELLA, P. "The assimilation of Georgia in Turkey: a case
           study", *Muslim Wld* 66(1), jan 76 : 35-43.
3726   MARKIEWICZ, Wladyslaw. "Tendances et conditions des changements
           dans les communautés polonaises à l'étranger", *Pologne Aff.
           occid.* 12(1-2), 1976 : 28-41.

3727   MEADOWS, Paul *et al. Recent immigration to the United States: the literature of the social sciences.* Washington, Smithsonian Institution Press, 76, 112 p.

3728   MELIKIAN, Levon H.; KARAPETIAN, Aghop DE. "Personality change over time: assimilation of an ethnic minority in Lebanon", *J. soc. Psychol.* 103(2), dec 77 : 185-193.

3729   MOREAU-DEFARGES, Philippe. "L'immigration africaine en France", *R. jur. polit.* 31(3), jul-sep 77 : 967-974.

3730   Bibl.XXVI-3142. MURGUIA, Edward. *Assimilation, colonialism and the Mexican American people.* CR: David T. WELLMAN, *Amer. J. Sociol.* 82(6), mai 77 : 1415-1417.

3731   NOGUCHI, Takashi (ed.). *Imin to bunkahenyo* (Emigration and acculturation). Tokyo, Nihon gakujutsu Shinkôkai, 77, 279 p.

3732   PÁEZ OROPEZA, Carmen Mercedes. *Los libanese en México: asimilación de un grupo étnico* (Lebanese in Mexico: assimilation of an ethnic group). México, Escuela Nacional de Antropología e Historia, 76, iii-266 p.

3733   PARKIN, Andrew. "Ethnic politics: a comparative study of two immigrant societies, Australia and the United States", *J. Commonwealth comp. Polit.* 15(1), mar 77 : 22-38.

3734   PIK, David Wingeate. "L'immigration espagnole en France, 1945-1952", *R. Hist. mod. contemp.* 24, apr-jun 77 : 286-300.

3735   RICHMOND, Anthony H.; RAO, Lakshmana G. "Recent development in immigration to Canada and Australia: a comparative analysis", *Int. J. comp. Sociol.* 17(3-4), sep-dec 76 : 183-205.

3736   RUDDER-PAURD, Véronique DE. "Des projets aux aspirations. Les immigrés et leur logement en France", *Année sociol.* 26, 1975 : 125-151.

3737   SAITO, M. "The integration and participation of the Japanese and their descendants in Brazilian society", *Migr. int.* 14(3), 1976 : 183-197.

3738   SCHNAPPER, D. "Quelques réflexions sur l'assimilation comparée des travailleurs émigrés italiens et des Juifs en France", *B. Soc. franç. Sociol.* 3(7), jul 76 : 11-18.

3739   SKULEY, Michael T. "Australia immigration programme: an evaluation of its effectiveness", *Migr. int.* 15(1), 1977 : 21-34.

3740   STUDLAR, Donley T. "Social context and attitudes towards coloured immigrants", *Brit. J. Sociol.* 28(2), jun 77 : 168-184. [UK.]

3741   TRIPIER, Maryse. "'L'attitude des français à l'égard de l'immigration étrangère'. Note critique", *Année sociol.* 26, 1975 : 179-188.

3742   VARGA, I. *A kivándorlás irányváltozása és a magyar kivándorlók beilleszkedése Latin-Amerikában a két világháború között* (Change in emigration direction and integration of the Hungarian emigrate in Latin America between the two world wars). Szeged, Szegedi nyomda, 76, 51-4 p.

3743   WILKIE, Mary E. "Colonials, marginals and immigrants: contributions to a theory of ethnic stratification", *Comp. Stud. Soc. Hist.* 19(1), jan 77 : 67-95.

15630. Internal migration
Migration interne

[See also / Voir aussi: 2616, 3060, 3154, 3744, 5146, 5408]

3744   ABBOTT, Walter F. "Do we need status-specific migration theories ? A comparison of the effectiveness of the Zipf and Stouffer models in accounting for intermetropolitan and student migration", *Sociol. soc. Res.* 62(1), oct 77 : 85-98.

3745   AMSELLE, Jean-Loup (ed.). *Les migrations africaines: réseaux et processus migratoires.* Paris, F. Maspéro, 76, 126 p.

3746   AUFDERLANDWEHR, Werner. *Mobilität in Indien: stadtgerichtete und innerstädtische Wanderungen im südlichen Indien untersucht am*

Beispiel der drei Städte Vijayawada, Guntur und Tenali (Mobility in India: migration between and inside towns in the South of India studied by the example of the three towns Vijayawada, Guntur and Tenali). Tübingen, H. Erdmann, 76, 205 p.

3747   BARNUM, H. N. "The interrelationship among social and political variables, economic structure, and rural-urban migration", *Econ. Develop. cult. Change* 24(4), jul 76 : 759-764.

3748   BERTRAND, Jean-René. "Aires matrimoniales et migrations rurales en Galice, Espagne", *R. géogr. Pyrénées* 48(3), jul 77 : 303-320.

3749   BREDIMAS-ASSIMOPOULOS, Nadia. "Le phénomène migratoire au Canada et au Québec. Contexte et perspectives", *Année sociol.* 26, 1975 : 57-81.

3750   BRYOR, Robin J. "An analysis of the 'streams' of interstate migrants in peninsula Malaysia", *Southeast Asian J. soc. Sci.* 2(1-2), 1974 : 63-73.

3751   BYERLEE, Derek; TOMMY, Joseph L.; FATOO, Habib. *Rural-urban migration in Sierra Leone: determinants and policy implications.* Njala, University of Sierra Leone, Njala University College; East Lansing, Michigan State University, Department of Agricultural Economics, 76, ix-113 p.

3752   CABRAL, Nelson Enrico. "Les migrations en Afrique du Sud portugaise (Angola et Mozambique avant l'indépendance)", *Ethnographie* 72(2), 1976 : 137-145. *[Exode rural.]*

3753   CHAVUNDUKA, G. L. "Rural and urban life", *Zambezia* 4(2), dec 76 : 69-78. *[Rural exodus in Rhodesia.]*

3754   CONAWAY, Mary Ellen. "Circular migration in Venezuelan frontier areas", *Migr. int.* 15(1), 1977 : 35-42.

3755   DAMAS, H.; VAN HOUTE-MINET, M. "Migrations internes en Belgique (1970). Étude par sexe, âge, nationalité, état civil", *Popul. et Famille* 39(3), 1976 : 41-107.

3756   DAVIS, Lenwood G. *Migration to African cities: an introductory survey.* Monticello, Ill., Council of Planning Librarians, 77, 21 p.

3757   DI FILIPPO, Armando; BRAVO, Rosa. "Los centros nacionales de desarrollo y las migraciones internas en América latina: un estudio de casos, Chile" (National centres of development and internal migrations in Latin America: a case study, Chile), *EURE* 14, nov 77 : 67-101.

3758   DUNBAR, Tony; KRAVITZ, Linda. *Hard travelling: migrant farm workers in America.* Cambridge, Mass., Ballinger, 76, 158 p. CR: David HARVEY, *Contemp. Sociol. (Washington)* 6(4), jul 77 · 453-454.

3759   FRANZINA, Emilio. *La grande emigrazione: l'esodo dei rurali dal Veneto durante il secolo XIX* (The great emigration: rural exodus from the Venetian region during the 19th century). Venezia, Marsilio, 76, 314 p.

3760   GRANT, E. Kenneth; VANDERKAMP, John. *The economic causes and effects of migration: Canada.* Ottawa, Economic Council of Canada, 76, vii-124 p. *[Labour migration.]*

3761   HLOPIN, A. D. "Social'nye funkcii sosedkoj obšćiny v adaptacii sel'skih migrantov k gorodskomu obrazu žizni (Po materialam immigrantskih obšćin v gorodah SŠA)" (Social functions of neighbouring communities in the adaptation of rural migrants to urban way of life), *Sociol. Issled. (Moskva)* (4), 1976 : 148-157.

3762   HUMPHREY, Graig R. *et al.* "Net migration turn around in Pennsylvania non metropolitan minor civil divisions, 1960-1970", *Rur. Sociol.* 42(3), 1977 : 332-351. *[USA.]*

3763   KEMPER, Robert V. *Migration and adaptation: Tzintzuntzan peasants in Mexico City.* Beverly Hills, Sage Publications, 77, 223 p.

3764   KERTÉSZOVÁ, Antonia. "Migrácia obyvatelstva do Košíc v rokoch 1964-1970 a jej vplyvna vekoví štruktúru obycatelstva" (Population migration to Kostice from 1961 to 1970 and its influence on the population age structure), *Demografie* 19(3), jul-sep 77 : 237-242.

3765   KOO, Hagen; BARRINGER, Herbert R. "Cityward migration and socio-economic achievement in two Korean cities", *Rur. Sociol.* 42(1), 1977 : 42-56.

3766   KUBAT, Daniel; RICHMOND, Anthony H. (eds.). *Internal migration. The New World and the Third World.* London, Sage, 76, 320 p.

3767   KURODA, Toshio. *The role of migration and population distribution in Japan's demographic transition.* Honolulu, East-West Center, 77, 17 p.

3768   LARIVIÈRE, J. P. "Remarques sur les destinations de l'émigration rurale en France", *Norois* 23(91), jul-sep 76 : 337-355.

3769   LEGUINA, J. *et al.* "Las migraciones interiores en España, 1961-1970" (Internal migrations in Spain, 1961-1970), *De Economia* 29(138), jul-sep 76 : 353-392.

3770   LI, Wen Lang. "A note on migration and employment", *Demography* 13(4), nov 76 : 565-570.

3771   LONG, Larry H.; HANSEN, Kristin A. "Selectivity of black return migration to the South", *Rur. Sociol.* 42(3), 1977 : 317-331. *[USA.]*

3772   MAAMARY, Samir N. *Attitude towards migration among rural residents: stages and factors involved in the decision to migrate.* San Francisco, R and E Research Associates, 76, xi-130 p.

3773   MAGYAR, Sándor. "Az 'ingázok' társadalmi, gazdasági problémái, valamint megoldásuk lehetöségei Borsod megyében" (Economic and social problems of "commuters" and possibility of solving them in the Borsod district), *Vezetéstud.* (12), 1976 : 22-27.

3774   McKAY, J.; WHITELAW, J. S. "The role of large private and government organizations in generating flows of interregional migrants: the case of Australia", *Econ. Geogr. (Worcester)* 53(1), jan 77 : 28-44.

3775   MENEZES, Claudia. *A mudança: análise da ideologia de um grupo de migrantes* (Migration: analysis of a migrant group's ideology). Rio de Janeiro, Imago Editora, 76, 135 p. *[Rural-urban migration in Brazil.]*

3776   MILLER, Ann R. "Interstate migrants in the United States: some social-economic differences by type of move", *Demography* 14(1), feb 77 : 1-17.

3777   MOUNTFORD, Charles Pearcy. *Nomads of the Australian desert.* Adelaide, Rigby, 76, 628 p.,-7 l.

3778   MUSEUR, M.; PIRSON, R. "Une problématique de passage chez les populations du Hoggar-Tassili: du nomadisme à la sédentarité", *Civilisations* 26(1-2), 1976 : 64-82.

3779   OBRAI, A. S. "Les migrations, le chômage et le marché urbain de l'emploi. Le cas du Soudan", *R. int. Trav.* 115(2), mar-apr 77 : 225-238.

3780   PETERSEN, Gene B.; SHARP, Laure M.; DRURY, Thomas F. *Southern newcomers to northern cities: work and social adjustment in Cleveland.* New York, Praeger, 77, xxxiv-269 p. *[USA.]*

3781   PIRSON, R. "Bilan qualitatif du fait migratoire en Tunisie pré-saharienne", *C. Tunisie* (95-96), 3-4 trim 76 : 273-296.

3782   PRYOR, Robin J. "The migrant to the city in South-East Asia. Can and should we generalise ?", *Asian Profile* 5(1), feb 77 : 63-89.

3783   RAKOWSKI, Witold; KUCINSKI, Kazimierz. "Rejonizacja migracji ludności małych miast" (Regionalization of migration of population in small towns), *Biul. IGS* 20(4), 1977 : 97-121.

3784   RÉMY, Gérard. "Migrations et développement. Mobilité géographique et immobilisme social: un exemple voltaïque", *Tiers-Monde* 18(71), jul-sep 77 : 617-653.

3785   RENAUD, Bertrand. "The economic determinants of internal migra-
       tion in Korea", *Appl. Econ.* 9(4), dec 77 : 307-318.

3786   SHARMA, Ursula M. "Migration from an Indian village: an anthropo-
       logical approach", *Sociol. rur.* 17(4), 1977 : 282-304.

3787   SHIMIZU, Shinji; SUGAWARA, Hiroe. "Chiiki-ido to kazoku no shakai-
       kankei - shinzoku yujin network no hendo o chushin ni" (Migra-
       tion and the family social relationship: changes of kinship and
       friendship networks), *Kenkyujô Nenpô* (5-6), 1977 : 101-130.

3788   SINGH, Ram D. "Les migrations de main-d'oeuvre et leurs effets sur
       l'emploi et les revenus dans une économie agricole où prédomine
       la petite exploitation", *R. int. Trav.* 116(3), nov-dec 77 : 367-
       378. *[Inde.]*

3789   SKELDON, Ronald. "The evolution of migration patterns during ur-
       banization in Peru", *Geogr. R.* 67(4), oct 77 : 394-411.

3790   SLATER, P. B. "Internal migration regions of Argentina and Brazil:
       applications of hierarchical clustering to doubly standardized
       lifetime migration tables", *Estadística (Washington)* 30(114),
       jul 76 : 3-12.

3791   SPITTLER, Gerd. "Urban exodus. Urban-rural and rural-urban migra-
       tion in Gobir (Niger)", *Sociol. rur.* 17(3), 1977 : 223-235.

3792   STANDING, Guy; SUKDEO, Fred. "Les migrations de main-d'oeuvre et
       le développement en Guyane", *R. int. Trav.* 116(3), nov-dec 77 :
       327-338.

3793   STRZELECKI, Zbigniew. "O migracjach mieszkancow Warszawy" (Migra-
       tions of inhabitants of Warsaw), *Biul. IGS* 20(4), 1977 : 122-139.

3794   THOMAS, R. N.; MARTIN, W. W. "Patrones de migración pendular coti-
       diana en Tejucigalpa, Honduras: un ejemplo de movilidad intra-
       urbana" (Commuting patterns in Tejucigalpa, Honduras: an example
       of intraurban mobility), *R. interamer. Planif.* 9(33), mar 75 :
       22-40.

3795   TRABELSI, M. "L'exode rural et son impact sur le développement des
       villes régionales: l'exemple de Kairouan", *R. tunis. Sci. soc.*
       13(44), 1976 : 147-171. *[Tunisie.]*

3796   TUCKER, C. Jack. "Changing patterns of migration between metropo-
       litan and nonmetropolitan areas in the United States: recent
       evidence", *Demography* 13(4), nov 76 : 435-443.

3797   USUI, Wayne M.; LEI, Tzuen-jen; BUTLER, Edgar W. "Patterns of so-
       cial participation of rural and urban migrants to an urban area",
       Sociol. soc. Res. 61(3), apr 77 : 337-349.

3798   ZINOV'EVA, R. A. "Vnutrennie migracii i ih pričiny" (Internal
       migrations and their causes), *Latinsk. Amer.* 8(3), mai-juu 77 :
       111-123. *[Latin America.]*

16. ENVIRONMENT. COMMUNITY. RURAL. URBAN
ENVIRONMENT. COMMUNAUTÉ. RURAL. URBAIN

16100. ECOLOGY. GEOGRAPHY. POPULATION SETTLEMENT
ÉCOLOGIE. GÉOGRAPHIE. HABITAT

16110. Human geography
Géographie humaine

[See also / Voir aussi: 522, 543, 570, 1027, 1138, 3980, 5370]

3799   BUTTEL, Frederick H.; FLINN, William L. "The interdependence of rural and urban environmental problems in advanced capitalist societies: models of linkage", *Sociol. rur.* 17(4), 1977 : 255-281.

3800   CAREY, Phillip. "Crisis in the environment: a sociological perspective", *Amer. J. Econ. Sociol.* 36(3), jul 77 : 263-273.

3801   ČERNIKOV, G. "Ékologičeskij krizis - problemy i resenija" (The ecological crisis: problems and decisions), *Meždun. Zizn'* (1), 1977 : 58-66.

3802   CLAVAL, Paul. *Essai sur l'évolution de la géographie humaine.* Paris, Belles Lettres, 76, 201 p.

3803   COMMONER, Barry; BETTINI, Virginio. *Ecologia e lotte sociali* (Ecology and social struggles). Milano, Feltrinelli, 76, 225 p.

3804   DAGET, J. *Les modèles mathématiques en écologie.* Paris-New York, Masson, 76, viii-172 p.

3805   DOW, James. "Systems models of cultural ecology", *Soc. Sci. Inform.* 16(1), 1977 : 953-976.

3806   DURAND, Michelle; HARFF, Yvette. *La qualité de la vie. Mouvement écologique, mouvement ouvrier.* Paris, Mouton, 77, 257 p.

3807   FEDORENKO, Nikolaï. "Prévisions globales et décisions réelles en écologie", *Nouv. R. int.* 20(5), mai 77 : 208-222.

3808   HOLMES, Nicholas (ed.). *Environment and the industrial society.* Boulder, Colo., Westview Press; London, Hodder and Stoughton, 76, 247 p.

3809   JONES, Emrys; EYLES, John. *An introduction to social geography.* Oxford, Eng.-New York, Oxford University Press, 77, xi-273 p.

3810   KATSOURA, Alexandre; MOVIK, Ilya. "L'interaction des sciences: la biosphère et l'écologie de l'homme", *Sci. soc. (Moscou)* (4), 1977 : 185-197.

3811   MECKTROTH, T. "Ecological inference and the disaggregation of individual decisions", *Polit. Sci. Ann.* (5), 1966 : 113-174.

3812   RAPOPORT, Amos (ed.). *The mutual interaction of people and their built environment: a cross-cultural perspective.* The Hague, Mouton; Chicago, Aldine, 76, xv-505 p.-10 l.

3813   RICHARDSON, Jonathan L. *Dimensions of ecology.* Baltimore, Williams and Wilkins, 77, xiii-412 p.

3814   SCHNAIBERG, Allan. "Obstacles to environmental research by scientists and technologists: a social structural analysis", *Soc. Probl.* 24(5), jun 77 : 500-520.

3815   TESTART, Alain. "Les chasseurs-cueilleurs dans la perspective écologique", *Soc. Sci. Inform.* 16(3-4), 1977 : 389-418.

3816   VIDART, Daniel D. *Colombia, ecología y sociedad* (Colombia, ecology and society). Bogotá, Centro de Investigación y Educación Popular 76, 190 p.

16120. Nature. Soil. Water
Nature. Sol. Eau

16122.

3817   "Living with the desert", *Ekistics* 43(258), mai 77 : 242-324.

16123.

[See also / Voir aussi: 287, 4760]

3818   DOCAVO ALBERTI, Ignacio. "La protección de la naturaleza en la
       planificación territorial" (Nature conservation in regional
       planning), *R. Estud. Vida loc.* 36(194), apr-jun 77 : 249-270.
       [Spain.]
3819   HERSHEY, Marjorie Randon; HILL, David B. "Is pollution 'a white
       thing' ? Racial differences in preadults' attitudes", *Publ. Opin.
       Quart.* 41(4), 1977 : 439-458.
3820   MISIUNA, Małgorzata. "Wkład socjologii w kompleksowy rozwoj zaso-
       bów ludzkich i naturalnych. IV Światowy Kongres Socjologii Wsi"
       (Contribution of sociology to the complex development of human
       and natural resources. Fourth World Congress of Rural Sociology,
       September 9-13 1976, in Torun, Poland), *Przegl. socjol.* 29,
       1977 : 393-403.

16130. Citizen. Inhabitant
Citoyen. Habitant

3821   ALATAS, Syed Hussein. *The myth of the lazy native. A study of the
       image of the Malays. Filipinos and Javanese from the 16th to
       the 20th century and its function in the ideology of colonial
       capitalism.* London, F. Cass, 77, vii-267 p.
3822   ANIZON, Alain. *L'habitat, secteur productif dans l'économie des
       pays en voie de développement / Housing, productive sector in
       the economy of developing countries.* Paris, Secrétariat des
       missions d'urbanisme et d'habitat, 76, 88 p.
3823   BACZKO, Malgorzata *et al. Techniques douces, habitat et société.*
       Paris, Éditions Entente, 77, 164 p.
3824   BELL, Gwenn (ed.). *Strategies for human settlements: habitat and
       environment.* Honolulu, University Press of Hawaii, 76, 172 p.
       CR: Howard M. HAMMERMAN, *Contemp. Sociol. (Washington)* 6(4),
       jul 77 : 445.
3825   ERDEI, F. *Településpolitika, közigazgatás, urbanizació* (Settlement
       policy, local government, urbanisation). Budapest, Akadémiai Ki-
       adó, 77, 558 p.
3826   "Établissements humains (Les)", *Impact* 27(2), apr-jun 77 : 163-
       262.
3827   GÁDOROSI, F. "Lakás és környezet funkcionális összefüggései" (Func-
       tional relations of habitat and environment), *Épit. Kut. Fejleszt.*
       (1), 1976 : 12-21.
3828   GUHUR, A. "Les réformes de l'habitat", *Esprit* 44(10), oct 76 : 35
       455-462. *[France.]*
3829   LANSDOWN, Robert. "Issues of national settlement", *Austral. Quart.*
       49(1), mar 77 : 56-62. *[Australia.]*
3830   PILON-LÊ, Lise. "La condition économique de l'habitat québécois,
       1760-1854", *Anthropol. et Soc.* 1(2), 1977 : 23-35.
3831   SHAMKEH, Ahmed A. "Bedouin settlements", *Ekistics* 43(258), mai 77 :
       249-260. *[Saudi Arabia.]*
3832   TANDAR, L. "The evolution of rural settlements in Cameroon", *Ekis-
       tics* 42(249), aug 76 : 106-109.
3833   VIDAL, Vivian. "Evaluación del estado de desarrollo de las inves-
       tigaciones sobre asentamientos humanos" (Evaluation of the de-
       velopment level of researches upon human settlement), *Estud.
       soc. centroamer.* 6(17), mai-aug 77 : 23-27. *[Cuba.]*

16200. COMMUNITY
COMMUNAUTÉ

[See also / Voir aussi: 141, 1408, 2788, 4228, 5340, 5538]

3834   ANDREEV, Ê. M.; FROLOV, S. F. "Planirovanie social'nogo razvitija kollektivov - êffektivnoe sredstvo upravlenija" (Planning of community social development is an efficient management tool), *Nauc. upravl. Obšč.* (10), 1976 : 88-106.

3835   BURBY, Raymond J.; WEISS, Shirley F. *New communities USA.* Lexington, Mass., Lexington Books, 76, 593 p. CR: Sally S. ROGERS, *Contemp. Sociol. (Washington)* 6(2), mar 77 : 259-260.

3836   EDWARDS, Allan D.; JONES, Dorothy G. *Community and community development.* The Hague, Mouton, 76, 326 p.

3837   EKONG, Chong E. "The administration of community development in Nigeria: a critical appraisal and suggested alternative", *Quart. J. Adm.* 11(3), apr 77 : 153-165.

3838   FUJITA, Kunihiko. "Community-kô MacIver shakaigaku ni kansuru ichi-kosatsu" (A study of community theory), *Kagawa-daigaku Kyoikuga-kubu Kenkyu-hokoku* 1(43), 1977 : 1-32.

3839   GROSSER, Charles F. *New directions in community organization: from enabling to advocacy.* Expanded ed. New York, Praeger, 76, xvii-286 p. *[United States.]*

3840   Bibl.XXVI-3221. GUSFIELD, Joseph R. *Community: a critical response.* CR: C. G. PICKVANCE, *Amer. J. Sociol.* 82(6), mai 77 : 1366-1369; David MARSLAND, *Brit. J. Sociol.* 28(4), dec 77 : 517-518.

3841   HAYASHI, Masataka. "'Ningen kagaku' no chiiki shakaigakuteki waku-gumi" (The frame of local community research for human science), *Yamagachi-daigaku Bungakukaishi* 27, 1977 : 59-73.

3842   KAPOOR, S. "Community development in India", *Ind. J. soc. Res.* 17(2-3), aug-dec 76 : 82-93.

3843   KASS, Roy. "Community structure and the metropolitcan division of labour: the impact of key functions on community social characteristics", *Soc. Forces* 56(1), sep 77 : 218-239.

3844   KELLY, Rita Mae. *Community participation in directing economic development.* Cambridge, Mass., Center for Community Economic Development, 76, x-179 p. *[United States.]*

3845   THORNS, David C. *The quest for community: social aspects of residential growth.* London, Allen and Unwin, 76, 3-164 p. CR: Martin BULMER, *Amer. J. Sociol.* 82(6), mai 77 : 1369-1371.

3846   TWELVETREES, Alain C. *Community associations and centres: a comparative study.* Oxford-New York, Pergamon Press, 76, x-152 p. *[UK.]*

3847   UNIVERSITY OF TOKYO. Institute of Journalism. *Community ishiki no kenkyû* (A study on community consciousness). Tokyo, Tokyo-daigaku Shuppankai, 77, 400 p.

16300. RURAL. URBAN
RURAL. URBAIN

16310. Rural sociology
Sociologie rurale
16311.

[See also / Voir aussi: 192, 3138]

3848   MIHAILESCU, Ioan. "Possibilités et limites de la recherche comparative transnationale: remarques en marge d'une recherche sur 'L'avenir des collectivités rurales dans les sociétés industrialisées'", *Soc. Sci. Inform.* 16(2), 1977 : 213-229.

3849   GARCIA FERRANDO, M. "La sociología rural en perspectiva: una evaluación crítica" (Rural sociology: a critical evaluation), *R. Estud. agro-soc.* 25(96), jul-sep 76 : 25-59.

3850   RAMBAUD, Placide. *Sociologie rurale: recueil de textes.* Paris,
        Mouton, 76, 325 p.
3851   STAROVEROV, V. I. "Sovetskaja sociologija derevni i dostiženija
        problemy" (Soviet rural sociology: results and problems), *So-
        ciol. Issled. (Moskva)* (3), 1976 : 33-40.
3852   ZASLAVSKAIA, T. I. "A falu rendszerszemléletü tanulmányozásának
        metodologiája és metodikája" (Methodology and methods of rural
        sociology), *Szociológia* 5(3-4), 1976 : 548-563.

        16312.

        *[See also / Voir aussi: 1681, 2698, 2989, 3002, 3062, 3076, 3133,
        3688, 3786, 4675]*

3853   BATES, Robert H. *Rural responses to industrialization: a study of
        village Zambia.* New Haven-London, Yale University Press, 76, x-
        380 p.
3854   BLAMONT, Denis. "Un village du Deccan (Inde), Kedgaon", *C. O.-Mer*
        30(119), jul-sep 77 : 209-223.
3855   BOND, George C. *The politics of change in a Zambian community.*
        Chicago, University of Chicago Press, 76, xi-178 p. CR: Robert
        H. BATES, *Amer. J. Sociol.* 83(2), sep 77 : 532-534.
3856   BOUKRAA, R. "La problématique de la communauté rurale au Maghreb:
        quelques observations sur le changement social dans la communau-
        té villageoise de Hammamet", *R. tunis. Sci. soc.* 13(45), 1976 :
        11-48. *[Tunisie.]*
3858   CSÁK, Gy. "Püspökladányi sorsfordulók" (Püspökladány, fragments
        from sociographies), *Szociológia* 6(1), 1977 : 97-107. *[Hungary.]*
3859   DAVYDOV, A. D. *Social'no-ěkonomičeskaja struktura derevni Afgha-
        nistana* (Socio-economic structure of Afghanistan villages).
        Moskva, Nauka, 76, 304 p.
3860   ENYEDI, Gy. "A magyar falu átalakulása" (Transformation of the
        Hungarian village), *Földrajzi Közlem.* 23(2), 1975 : 109-123.
3861   FREEMAN, James M. *Scarcity and opportunity in an Indian village.*
        Menlo Park, Calif., Cummings Publishing Co., 77, xiii-177 p.
3862   FUKUTAKE, Tadashi (ed.). *Nôsanson shakai to chiiki kaihatsu - Ka-
        nagawaken Ôimachi Aiwa-chiku* (Rural community and regional de-
        velopment). Tokyo, Chiiki Shakai Kenkyu-jo 77, 403 p. *[Japan.]*
3863   GORJAČENKO, Ě. Ě. *et al.* "Social'no-ěkonomičeskaja tipologija po-
        selenij kak sredstvo izučenija i prognozirovanija razvitija de-
        revni" (Socio-economic typology of settings as a mean for study-
        ing and forecasting village development), in: *Sibirskaja derevnja
        v uslovijah urbanizacii.* Novosibirsk, 1976 . 7-30.
3864   KENNEDY, John G.; FAHIM, Hussain M. *Struggle for change in a Nu-
        bian community: an individual in society and history.* Palo Alto,
        Calif., Mayfield Publishing Co., 77, x-194 p.
3865   KULCSÁR, Viktor (ed.). *A változó falu* (The changing village). Buda-
        pest, Gondolat, 76, 340-3 p. *[Hungary.]*
3866   LACOSTE-DUJARDIN, Camille. *Un village algérien: structures et évo-
        lution récente.* Alger, Société d'édition et de diffusion, 76,
        164 p.
3867   LANDAU, Yehuda H. *et al.* (eds.). *Rural communities: inter-coope-
        ration and development.* New York, Praeger, 76, xxi-166 p.
3868   MEDUNOV, S. F. *Magistral'nyj pyt' razvitija sela. Social'no-ěkono-
        mičeskie problemy specializacii, koncentracii i agropromyšlennye
        integracii i puti ih rešenija* (The important way of villages de-
        velopment. Socio-economic problems of specialization, concentra-
        tions and agro-industrial integrations, and ways of their reali-
        zation). Moskva, Politizdat, 76, 200 p. *[USSR.]*
3869   MIYAJI, Mieko. *L'émigration et le changement socio-culturel d'un
        village kabyle, Algérie.* Tokyo, Institute for the Study of Lan-
        guages and Cultures of Asia and Africa, 76, 87 p.

3870   NAUMOWA, Stefka. "Modernizacja wsi buɬgarskiej a świadomość praw-
        na" (Modernization of Bulgarian village and legal consciousness),
        Stud. socjol. 65(2), 1977 : 185-206.
3871   ÔTSU, Shôichirô; SAKAI, Shunji. "Gyoson no henyo to gyomin no taio
        (Sokatsu-hen)" (Transformation of a fishing village and adjust-
        ment of fishermen), Suisan-keizai Kenkyû 27, 1977 : 1-160.
3872   RAYNAUT, C. "Transformation du système de production et inégalité
        économique: le cas d'un village haoussa (Niger)", Canad. J.
        Afr. Stud. 10(2), 1976 : 279-306.
3873   ROZE, Jorge P. "Las areas rurales en América latina en relación a
        sus roles regionales: Argentina" (Rural areas in Latin America
        according to their regional functions), Estud. soc. centroamer.
        6(17), mai-aug 77 : 203-220.
3874   SÁNCHEZ JIMÉNEZ, José. Vida rural y mundo contemporáneo: análisis
        sociohistórico de un pueblo del sur (Rural life and contemporary
        world: socio-historical analysis of a southern village). Barce-
        lona, Editorial Planeta, 76, 365 p. [Tolox, Spain.]
3875   SOLEYE, O. O. "A village in commotion: an analysis of the impact
        of a cement factory on a Nigerian village community", Int. J.
        contemp. Sociol. 14(1-2), jan-apr 77 : 61-73.
3876   TAILLARD, Christian. "Le village lao de la région de Vientiane. Un
        pouvoir local face au pouvoir étatique", Homme 17(2-3), apr-sep
        77 : 71-100.
3877   TAVČAR, Jože. "Razvoj slovenskog sela" (Development of the Sloveni-
        an village), Sociol. sela 15(1-2), 1977 : 19-36.
3878   TOEPFER, Helmuth. Untersuchungen zur Wirtschafts- und Sozialstruk-
        tur der Dorfbevölkerung der Provinz Baghlan (Afghanistan) (Res-
        earches on the economic and social structure of the village po-
        pulation of the province of Baghlan, Afghanistan). Meisenheim-
        am-Glan, Hain, 76, 156 p.-4 l.
3879   TONOKI, Norio. "Nihon noson shakai ni okeru buraku no mondai" (The
        reorganization of the hamlet in the Japanese rural community),
        Shaken shirizu (10), 1977 : 110-130.
3880   WATLINGTON-LINARES, Francisco. "Nuevas tendencias en la dinámica
        social de la comunidad agro-rural" (New trends in social dynamics
        of the agro-rural community), R. Cienc. soc. (Puerto-Rico) 19(1),
        mar 75 : 27-45. [Puerto Rico.]
3881   WILKE, George; PHILIP, Mathew. "Village system in Kerala", Ind. J.
        soc. Res. 17(2-3), aug-dec 76 : 132-139.
3882   YORIMITSU, Masatoshi. "Gyoson no keizai kôzô ni kansuru ichi-
        kosatsu" (A study on the economic structure of a fishing village),
        Shakaigaku Kenkyû 35, 1977 : 93-181. [Japan.]
3883   ZASLAVSKAJA, T. I.; KALMYK, V. A. Sociologičeskie issledovanija
        sibirskoj derevni (Sociological research on the Siberian village).
        Novosibirsk, 76, 129 p.

        16313.

        [See also / Voir aussi: 1676, 2563, 2615, 2727, 2805, 3015, 3286,
        3408, 3421, 4513, 4767, 5180]

3884   ALBERTI, Giorgio. "Struttura del potere e movimenti contadini in
        Peru" (Power structure and peasant movements in Peru), Ric. soc.
        (1), 1977 : 89-102.
3885   Bibl.XXVI-3310. BAUER, Arnold J. Chilean rural society from the
        Spanish conquest to 1930. CR: Peter SINGELMANN, Contemp. Sociol.
        (Washington) 6(4), jul 77 : 425-428.
3886   BENOIST, Jean. Structure et changement de la société rurale réu-
        nionnaise: départementalisation et développement dans une "île
        à sucre". Fonds St-Jacques, Ste-Marie, Martinique; Centre de
        recherches caraïbes, Université de Montréal, 76, 127 p.
3887   BERGMANN, Theodor. "Agrarian movements and their context", Sociol.
        rur. 17(3), 1977 : 167-185.

3888 BILIŃSKI, Kazimierz. "Edward Abramowski a ideologija polskiego ruchu ludowego" (Edward Abramowski and the ideology of the Polish peasant movement), *Przegl. socjol.* 29, 1977 : 169-179.

3889 Bibl.XXVI-3313. BODIGUEL, Maryvonne. *Les paysans face au progrès.* CR: Jean-René TRÉANTON, *R. franç. Sociol.* 18(1), jan-mar 77 : 144-146.

3890 BOURDIEU, Pierre. "La paysannerie, une classe objet", *Actes Rech. Sci. soc.* 17-18, nov 77 : 2-5.

3891 CARO BAROJA, Julio. "Caracterizaciones del labrador" (Farmer's characteristics), *Agric. y Soc.* (2), 1977 : 131-182.

3892 CASTEX, Patrick. *"Voie chilienne" au socialisme et luttes paysannes: approche théorique et pratique d'une transition capitaliste non révolutionnaire.* Paris, F. Maspéro, 77, 295 p.

3893 CENTRE D'ÉTUDES FORÉZIENNES. *La vie rurale en France: paysans d'hier et d'aujourd'hui.* Saint-Étienne, Centre d'études foréziennes, 76, 197 p.

3894 CHAMBOREDON, Jean-Claude. "Peinture des rapports sociaux et invention de l'éternel paysan: les deux manières de Jean-François Millet", *Actes Rech. Sci. soc.* 17-18, nov 77 : 6-28.

3895 CHAVES, L. G. "Pesca artesanal no Ceará: tecnologia, sistema cognitivo e relações de produção" (Craftsman fishing at Ceara, technology, cognitive system and relations of production), *R. Cienc. soc. (Ceara)* 6(1-2), 1975 : 5-28. [Brazil.]

3896 CLIFFE, Lionel. "Rural class formation in East Africa", *J. Peasant Stud.* 4(2), jan 77 : 195-224.

3897 COHEN, Eugene N. "Nicknames, social boundaries, and community in an Italian village", *Int. J. contemp. Sociol.* 14(1-2), jan-apr 77 : 102-113.

3898 COHOU, Michel. "La population non agricole au village: différenciation et prolétarisation de la société rurale", *Ét. rur.* 67, jul-sep 77 : 47-59. [France.]

3899 DIMKOVIĆ, Borislav J. "Socijalni položaj starih seljaka u Vojvidini" (Social status of old peasants in Vojvodina), *Sociol. sela* 15(1-2), 1977 : 62-69.

3900 ENYEDI, Gy. "A falusi életkörülmények területi tipusai Magyarországon" (Regional types of rural living conditions in Hungary), *Földrajzi Értes.* 26(1), 1977 : 67-85.

3901 EVANS, Robert H. *Life and politics in a Venetian village community.* Notre Dame, Ind., University of Notre Dame Press, 76, xxi-228 p.- 9 l.

3902 FIRST-DILIĆ, Ruža. "Medugeneracijsko ispomaganje u seoskoj porodici" (Helping out between generations in the rural family), *Sociol. sela* 15(1-2), 1977 : 75-85.

3903 FUNAHASHI, Kazuo. "Kosei Noson ni okeru Suiri to Sorei no kyodososhiki" (Cooperation at irrigation and funeral of a village community in Kosei area), *Soshioroji* 22(1), 1977 : 99-110.

3904 GALJART, Benno Franciscus. *Peasant mobilization and solidarity.* Assen, Van Gorcum, 76, vi-132 p.

3905 GIRARD, Jean-Paul *et al.* "Les agriculteurs. Clés pour une comparaison sociale", *Coll. INSÉE Sér.* E 46-47, apr 77 : 437 p.

3906 GOODY, Jack; THIRSK, Joan; THOMPSON, E. P. (eds.). *Family and inheritance. Rural society in Western Europe, 1200-1800.* Cambridge, Cambridge University Press, 76, vi-421 p.

3907 GUILAINE, Jean. *Premiers bergers et paysans de l'Occident méditerranéen.* Paris-La Haye, Mouton, 76, 286-32 p.

3908 HALPERIN, Rhoda; DOW, James (eds.). *Peasant livelihood; studies in economic anthropology and cultural ecology.* New York, St Martin's Press, 77, x-332 p. [Latin America.]

3909 HAVET, J. "Nouvelles élites locales et stabilité sociale dans les zones rurales boliviennes", *Civilisations* 26(3-4), 1976 : 191-203.

3910 HELLER, Peter K.; QUESADA, Gustavo M. "Rural familism: an interregional analysis", *Rur. Sociol.* 42(2), 1977 : 220-240.

3911 "Inovacije u selu" (Innovations in the village), *Sociol. sela* 14(3-4), jul-dec 76 : 37-97. *[Yugoslavia.]*

3912 JEGOUZO, Guenhaël; BRANGEON, Jean-Louis. *Les paysans et l'école.* Paris, Cujas, 76, 287 p.

3913 JORION, Paul. "L'ordre moral dans une petite île de Bretagne", *Ét. rur.* 67, jul-sep 77 : 31-45.

3914 KATONA, I. "Parasztságunk történelemszemlélete" (The historical consciousness of Hungarian peasantry), *Szociológia* 5(3-4), 1976 : 514-522.

3915 KHOSROVI, Khosrov. "Les marchés hebdomadaires paysans en Iran", *Ét. rur.* 67, jul-sep 77 : 85-91.

3916 KNOX, A. J. G. "Opportunities and opposition: the rise of Jamaica's black peasantry and the nature of the planter resistance", *Canad. R. Sociol. Anthropol.* 14(4), nov 77 : 381-395.

3917 KÓSA, L. "A magyar parasztság történeti tudatának típusai" (Types of historical consciousness of the Hungarian peasantry), *Szociológia* 5(3-4), 1976 : 508-513.

3918 LE BOT, Yvon. *Les paysans, la terre, le pouvoir: étude d'une société agraire à dominante indienne dans les hautes terres du Guatémala.* Paris, CNRS, 77, 415 f multigr.

3919 LENGYEL, Zs. "A szövetkezeti parasztság életmódját alakító tényezőkről" (Some factors influencing cooperative peasants' way of life), *Magyar filoz. Szle* 21(5), 1977 : 538-554.

3920 LUMMIS, Trevor. "The occupational community of East Anglian fishermen: an historical dimension through oral evidence", *Brit. J. Sociol.* 28(1), mar 77 : 51-74.

3921 MEDEIROS, Fernando DA. "Capitalisme et précapitalisme dans les campagnes portugaises de l'entre-deux-guerres", *Ét. rur.* 67, jul-sep 77 : 6-29.

3922 MEDVEDEV, N. A. *Razvitie obsčestvennyh otnošenij v sovetskoj derevne na sovremennom ètape* (Development of social relations in the Soviet village at the present stage). Moskva, Mysl', 76, 188 p.

3923 Bibl.XXVI-3343. MENDRAS, Henri. *Sociétés paysannes.* CR: Jean-René TRÉANTON, *R. franç. Sociol.* 18(1), jan-mar 77 : 144-146.

3924 MESSERSCHMIDT, Don. *The Gurungs of Nepal: conflict and change in a village society.* Warminster, Eng., Arisana Phillips; Forest Grove, Ore., ISBS, 76, 151 p.

3925 MOLLARD, Amédée. *Paysans exploités: essai sur la question paysanne.* Grenoble, Presses universitaires de Grenoble, 77, 244 p.

3926 NACHMIAS, Chava; SADAN, Ezra. "Individual modernity, schooling and economic performance of family farm operators in Israel", *Int. J. comp. Sociol.* 18(3-4), sep-dec 77 : 268-279.

3927 NARAIN, Iqbal; PANDE, K. C.; SHARMA, Mohan Lal. *The rural elite in an Indian state: a case study of Rajasthan.* Colombia, Mo., South Asia Books; New Delhi, Manohar Book Service, 76, xii-256 p.

3928 "New rural America (The)", *A. Amer. Acad. polit. soc. Sci.* 429, jan 77 : 1-208.

3929 OBREBSKI, Jozef. *The changing peasantry of Eastern Europe.* Ed. by Barbara HALPERN and Joel HALPERN. Cambridge, Schenkman Publishing Co., 76, 102 p.-10 l.

3930 PONTON, Rémy. "Les images de la paysannerie dans le roman rural à la fin du dix-neuvième siècle", *Actes Rech. Sci. soc.* 17-18, nov 77 : 62-72.

3931 POTTER, Jack M. *Thai peasant social structure.* Chicago, University of Chicago Press, 76, xi-249 p.-4 l.

3932 ROMERO PITTARI, Salvador. "Movimientos campesinos y estructuras agrarias" (Peasant movement and agrarian structures), *Estud. soc. centroamer.* 6(17), mai-aug 77 : 71-84. *[Bolivia.]*

3933 SAGANT, Philippe. *Le paysan limbu: sa maison et ses champs.* La Haye,

Mouton; Paris, École des hautes études en sciences sociales, 76, 404 p.

3934   SAMANIEGO, Carlos; SORJ, Bernardo. *Articulaciones de modos de producción y campesinado en América Latina* (Links between modes of production and peasantry in Latin America). Lima, Centro de Investigaciones Socio-Económicas, Universidad Nacional Agraria La Molina, 76, 28 p.

3935   SANDERS, Irwin Taylor; WHITAKER, Roger; BISSELLE, Walter C. *East European peasantries: social relations: an annotated bibliography of periodical articles*. Boston, G. K. Hall, 76, vi-179 p.

3936   SCOTT, James C. *The moral economy of the peasant: rebellion and subsistence in Southeast Asia*. London-New Haven, Yale University Press, 76, ix-246 p.

3937   SCOTT, James C. "Protest and profanation: agrarian revolt and the little tradition", *Theory and Soc.* 4(1), 1977 : 1-38; 1(2), 1977 : 211-246.

3938   ŠELEST, P. S. *Sel'skaja ulica - sociologičeskij očerk* (A rural street - a sociological study). Moskva, Sovetskaja Rossija, 77, 156 p.

3939   SELIGSON, Mitchell A. "Prestige among peasants: a multidimensional analysis of preference data", *Amer. J. Sociol.* 83(3), nov 77 : 632-652.

3940   SEMOV, M. "Ob odnoj analitičeskoj koncepcii v issledovanii sistemy cennostej sel'skoj molodeži Bolgarii" (On an analytical conception in the research of value system of Bulgarian rural youth), in: *Problemy social'noj psihologii*. Tbilisi, 1976 : 85-92.

3941   SHARMA, K. L. "Power elite and rural India: some questions and clarifications", *Sociol. B. (Bombay)* 25(1), mar 76 : 45-62.

3942   SIMUŠ, P. I. *Social'nyj portret sovetskogo krest'janstva* (Social portrait of Soviet peasantry). Moskva, Politizdat, 76, 319 p.

3943   "Social contradictions of the countryside in the sixties", *Int. J. Sociol.* 6(2), 1976 : 13-74. [USSR.]

3944   SPITTLER, Gerd. "Staat und Klientelstruktur in Entwicklungsländern. Zum Problem der politischen Organisation von Bauern" (State and clientele structure in developing countries. On the problem of the political organization of farmers), *Archiv. europ. Sociol.* 18(1), 1977 : 57-83.

3945   TAPILINA, V. S. "Tipologija dosuga žitelej sela" (Typology of leisure in the villages), in: *Sibirskaja derevnja v uslovijah urbanizacii*. Novosibirsk, 1976 : 101-115. [USSR.]

3946   "Terre et les paysans en Amérique latine (La)", *C. Monde hisp. luso-brésil.* 28, 1977 : 7-274.

3947   THUILLIER, Guy. *Pour une histoire du quotidien au XIXe siècle*. La Haye-Paris, Mouton, 77, xxiv-490 p.

3948   UEMURA, Katsuhiko. "Nôsanson ni okeru kyodo-tai no henyô to chiiki-rentaisei" (Attitudes in rural community and solidarity), *Chiiki-fukushi Kenkyû* (5), 1977 : 97-117.

3949   UGORJI, Rex Uzo; ACHINIVU, Nnennaya. "The significance of bicycles in a Nigerian village", *J. soc. Psychol.* 102(2), aug 77 : 241-246.

3950   VELLANGA, Dorothy D. "Distinction entre les cultivatrices de deux districts ruraux au Ghana", *Trav. et Soc.* 2(2), apr 77 : 218-228.

3951   WATANABE, Sakae; HANEDA, Arata (eds.). *Dekasegi rodo to Noson no seikatsu* (Dekasegi [Working away from home] and rural life in Japan today). Tokyo, Tokyo-daigaku Shuppankai, 77, 402 p.

3952   WEBER, Eugen. *Peasants into Frenchmen. The modernization of rural France, 1870-1914*. Stanford, Calif., Stanford University Press, 76, xv-615 p.

3953   WEISSER, Michael R. *The peasants of the Montes: the roots of rural rebellion in Spain*. Chicago, University of Chicago Press, 76, xi-143 p.

3954   WILLIAMS, Raymond. "Plaisantes perspectives. Invention du paysage
        et abolition du paysan", *Actes Rech. Sci. soc.* 17-18, nov 77 :
        29-36.

        16314.

        [See also / Voir aussi: 5060]

3955   AGUIRRE AVELLANEDA, Jerjes. *La política ejidal en México* (The
        "ejido" policy in Mexico). México, Instituto Mexicano de Socio-
        logía, 76, 200 p.

3956   ALONSO, V. L. DEL. *Crisis agrarias y luchas campesinas, 1970-1976*
        (Agrarian crises and peasant struggles, 1970-1976). Madrid, Edi-
        torial Ayuso, 76, 322 p.

3957   ARCHER, R. W. "The public land and leasehold system in Canberra,
        Australia: the use of the leasehold land tenure base for financing
        the capital's development, 1958-1971", *Amer. J. Econ. Sociol.*
        36(4), oct 77 : 351-366.

3958   BRINKMAN, G. "Issues in micropolitan (greater rural) development",
        Canad. J. agric. Econ. 24(2), jul 76 : 46-61. *[Canada.]*

3959   CHERRY, Gordon E. (ed.). *Rural planning problems.* New York, Barnes
        and Noble Books, 77, ix-286 p.

3960   CUVI, Pablo; PEREZ, Armando; MARTINEZ, Luciano. "El problema agra-
        rio" (The agrarian problem), *Economía (Quito)* 11(67), dec 76 :
        38-88.

3961   DÍAZ BORDENAVE, Juan E. *Communication and rural development.* Paris,
        Unesco, 77, 107-2 p.

3962   DUMETT, Raymond E.; BRAINARD, Lawrence (eds.). *Problems of rural
        development.* Leiden, E. J. Brill, 76, xiii-148 p. CR: Ruth C.
        YOUNG, *Amer. J. Sociol.* 83(3), nov 77 : 769-771.

3963   GINES ORTEGA, J. "Hacía un modelo educacional de promoción campe-
        sina" (Towards an educational model of rural development), *Pensia-
        miento y Acción* 20, jul-sep 76 : 5-27. *[Latin America.]*

3964   GUICHAOUA, André; GUILLERMOU, Yves. "La réforme agraire algérienne:
        portée et limites", *Tiers-Monde* 18(71), jul-sep 77 : 583-616.

3965   IGBOZURIKE, Martin. *Problem-generating structures in Nigeria's rural
        development.* Uppsala-Stockholm, Almqvist och Wiksell, 76, 140 p.

3966   JANSMA, J. Dean; GOODE, Frank M. "Rural development research: con-
        ceptualizing land measuring key concepts", *Amer. J. agric. Econ.*
        58(5), dec 76 : 922-927.

3967   KAY, Cristobal. "Types of agrarian reform and their contradictions:
        the case of Chile", *Sociol. rur.* 17(3), 1977 : 203-219.

3968   LASSEY, William R. *Planning in rural environments.* New York, McGraw-
        Hill, 77, xii-257 p.

3969   LEUPOLT, Manfred. "Integrated rural development: key elements of an
        integrated rural development strategy", *Sociol. rur.* 17(1-2),
        1977 : 7-28.

3970   "Modèle chinois de développement rural (Le)", *CR Séances Acad. Agric.
        France* (3), 1976 : 186-207.

3971   MOSHER, Arthur Theodore. *Thinking about rural development.* New York,
        Agricultural Development Council, 76, xii-350 p.

3972   OSBORNE, Allan. "Rural development in Botswana: a qualitative view",
        J. South. Afr. Stud. 2(2), apr 76 : 198-213.

3973   RONDINELLI, Dennis; RUDDLE, Kenneth. "Local organization for integ-
        rated rural development: implementing equity policy in developing
        countries", *R. int. Sci. adm.* 43(1), 1977 : 20-30.

3974   ROTH, D. F. "Dimensions of policy change: towards an explanation of
        rural change policies in Thailand", *Asian Surv.* 16(11), nov 76 :
        1043-1063.

3975   RUTLEDGE, Ian. "Land reform and the Portuguese revolution", *J.
        Peasant Stud.* 5(1), oct 77 : 79-98.

3976   SCHULZ, Manfred. "Organizing extension services for integrated rural development in West and East African countries - the commodity approach", *Sociol. rur.* 17(1-2), 1977 : 87-106.

3977   SRINIVAS, Mysore Narasimhachar. *The remembered village.* Berkeley, University of California Press, 76, xvi-356 p.-4 1. *[*Râmpura, India.*]*

3978   WARDWELL, John M. "Equilibrium and change in non-metropolitan growth", *Rur. Sociol.* 42(2), 1977 : 156-179.

16320. Urban sociology
Sociologie urbaine

16321.

*[*See also / Voir aussi: 192, 875, 1212*]*

3979   ABRAHAMSON, Mark. *Urban sociology.* Englewood Cliffs, N.J., Prentice Hall, 76, vi-280 p. CR: William MICHELSON, *Amer. J. Sociol.* 83(3), nov 77 : 803-806.

3980   BERRY, Brian Joe Lobley; KASARDA, John D. *Contemporary urban ecology.* New York, Macmillan, 77, xiii-497 p.

3981   BUTLER, Edgar W. *Urban sociology: a systematic approach.* New York, Harper and Row, 76, xviii-526 p.

3982   EAMES, Edwin; GOODE, Judith Granich. *Anthropology of the city: an introduction to urban anthropology.* Englewood Cliffs, N.J., Prentice Hall, 77, viii-344 p.

3983   FISCHER, Claude S. *The urban experience.* New York, Harcourt Brace Jovanovich, 76, v-309 p. CR: William MICHELSON, *Amer. J. Sociol.* 83(3), nov 77 : 803-806.

3984   FRYSZTACKI, Krzysztof. "O niektórych aspektach kształtowania się kierunków badawczych socjologii miasta w Polsce" (Some aspects of research trends in urban sociology in Poland), *Stud. socjol.* 60(1), 1976 : 235-259.

3985   GORHAM, William; GLAZER, Nathan (eds.). *The urban predicament.* Washington, D.C., Urban Institute, 76, 364 p. CR: Joseph M. CONFORTI, *Contemp. Sociol. (Washington)* 6(3), mai 77 : 372-373.

3986   LEDRUT, Raymond. *L'espace en question ou le nouveau monde urbain.* Paris, Anthropos, 77, 361 p.

3987   LOJKINE, Jean. *Le marxisme, l'État et la question urbaine.* Paris, Presses universitaires de France, 77, 362 p.

3988   MEDAM, Alain. *Conscience de la ville.* Paris, Anthropos, 77, 302 p.

3989   MORGAN, Elaine. *Falling apart: the rise and fall of urban civilization.* New York, Stein and Day, 77, 262 p.

3990   "New trends in urban research", *Comp. urb. Res.* 4(2-3), 1977 : 7-60.

3991   PICKVANCE, C. G. (ed.). *Urban sociology: critical essays.* New York, St Martin's Press, 76, 223 p. CR: John WALTON, *Amer. J. Sociol.* 83(3), nov 77 : 799-803; David TRIESMAN, *Brit. J. Sociol.* 28(4), dec 77 : 514-515.

3992   PORTES, Alejandro; BROWNING, Harley L. (eds.). *Current perspectives in Latin American urban research.* Austin, Institute of Latin American Studies, University of Texas, 77, xi-179 p. CR: Irving Louis HOROWITZ, *Amer. J. Sociol.* 83(3), nov 77 : 761-765.

3993   SCHWIRIAN, Kent P. *et al.* *Contemporary topics in urban sociology.* Morristown, N.J., General Learning Press, 77, 660 p.

3994   SUZUKI, Hiroshi. "Toshi shakai kôzôron josetsu" (An introduction to the theory of urban social structure), *Shakaigaku Kenkyu Nenpo* (7-8), 1977 : 70-85.

3995   YAMAGISHI, Takeshi. "Ningen ruikei kara mita toshi-kenkyu" (Urban studies from the viewpoint of human types), *Nihon Toshi-gakukai Nenpô* (11), 1977 : 155-167.

3996   YAMAGISHI, Takeshi. "Senzen no toshi kenkyû" (Urban studies in the prewar period), *Shakaigaku Hyôron* 28(2), 1977 : 66-78.

16322.

[See also / Voir aussi: 3789, 3797, 3845, 4097, 4397, 5293, 5296, 5487, 5588, 5625]

3997   ABELLAN GARCIA, Antonio. "El cinturón humano de Madrid" (The human belt of Madrid), *R. int. Sociol. (Madrid)* 35(22), 1977 : 289-293.

3998   ABRAHAMSON, Mark; DUBICK, Michael A. "Patterns of urban dominance: the US in 1890", *Amer. sociol. R.* 42(5), oct 77 : 756-768.

3999   Bibl.XXVI-3402. BAUER, Gérard; ROUX, Jean-Michel. *La rurbanisation ou la ville éparpillée.* CR: Henri MENDRAS, *R. franç. Sociol.* 18(1), jan-mar 77 : 147-149.

4000   BERRY, Brian J. L. (ed.). *Urbanization and counterurbanization.* Beverly Hills, Calif., Sage Publications, 76, 334 p.

4001   BEUTEL, Jörg. *Konzentrations- und Verstädterungstendenzen in der Bundesrepublik Deutschland* (Concentration and urbanization tendencies in the German Federal Republic). Meisenheim-am-Glan, Hain, 76, i-234 p.

4002   BOSE, Ashish. *Bibliography on urbanization in India, 1947-1976.* New Delhi, Tata McGraw-Hill Publishing Co., 76, xxxi-179 p.

4003   BOURELLE, Bernard. "Essai sur la production de l'espace stéphanois au XIXème siècle", *Éspaces et Soc.* 20-21, mar-jun 77 : 85-102.

4004   COCHRAN, L. T.; O'KANE, J. M. "Urbanization-industrialization and the theory of demographic transition", *Pacific sociol. R.* 20(1), jan 77 : 113-134.

4005   CONGRESSIONAL URBAN GROWTH STUDY GROUP. *Urban growth in Brazil and Colombia.* Washington, United States Government Printing Office, 76, ix-93 p.

4006   COSTELLO, Vincent Francis. *Urbanization in the Middle East.* Cambridge, Eng.-New York, Cambridge University Press, 77, viii-121 p.

4007   CURRIE, Lauchlin Bernard. *Taming the megalopolis: a design for urban growth.* Oxford-New York, Pergamon Press, 76, ix-127 p.

4008   DOLGIJ, V. M.; LEVADA, Ju. A.; LEVINSON, A. G. "K probleme izmenenija social'nogo prostranstva-vremeni v processe urbanizacii" (Problems of the social space-time change in the urbanization process), in: *Urbanizacija i razvitie novyh rajonov.* Moskva, 1976 : 25-37.

4009   DURAND, Guy. "Le tissu urbain québécois, 1941-1961: évolution des structures urbaines de l'industrie et des occupations", *Rech. sociogr.* 18(1), jan-apr 77 : 133-157.

4010   FONSECA, R. "Growth, transition and the urban environment: a planning frame of reference", *Civilisations* 26(3-4), 1976 : 259-271. [Singapore.]

4011   GERUSON, Richard T.; McGRATH, Dennis. *Cities and urbanization.* New York, Praeger, 77, xviii-233 p.

4012   HALLARON, Shirley Anderson. *Urbanization in the developing nations: a bibliography compiled for the 1960's and 1970's.* Monticello, Ill., Council of Planning Librarians, 76, 46 p.

4013   HAMAGUCHI, Harushiko. "Romania ni okeru toshika to shakai-henyô" (Urbanization and social change in Romania), *Shakaigaku tôkyû* 22(3), 1977 : 39-55.

4014   HARRISON, Geoffrey Ainsworth; GIBSON, John B. (eds.). *Man in urban environments.* Oxford, Oxford University Press, 76, ix-367 p.

4015   HIRSCHMAN, Charles. "Recent urbanization trends in peninsular Malaysia", *Demography* 13(4), nov 76 : 445-461.

4016   HUSZÁR, Paul C. "Equity and urban growth: real property value appreciation in San José, California", *Amer. J. Econ. Sociol.* 36(3), jul 77 : 251-261.

4017   Bibl.XXVI-3422. KAIN, John F. *Essays on urban spatial structure.* CR: Thomas M. GUTERBOCK, *Amer. J. Sociol.* 82(6), mai 77 : 1371-1373.

4018   KANSKY, Karel Joseph. *Urbanization under socializm; the case of*

                Czechoslovakia. New York–London, Praeger, 76, xvi–313 p.

4019   KAPUSTIN, Ě. I. (ed.). *Problemy preodolenija social'no-ěkonomičes-kih različij meždu gorodom i derevnej* (Problems of the socio-economic differences elimination between towns and villages). Moskva, Nauka, 76, 280 p.

4020   LÜHNE, Dietrich. *Urbanisation in Malaysia: Analyse eines Prozesses* (Urbanization in Malaysia: analysis of a process). Wiesbaden, O. Harrassowitz, 76, 400 p-3 1.

4021   LIU, P. K. C. "The relationship between urbanization and socio-economic development in Taiwan", *Industry free China* 46(3), sep 76 : 15–28.

4022   MARTÍN GALÁN, Manuel. "Un ejemplo de estructuras semiurbanas en la España del siglo XVIII: el case de Atienza (análisis socioprofe-sional de su población)" (An example of semi-urban structure in XVIIIth century Spain: the case of Atienza, socio-professional analysis of the population), *R. int. Sociol. (Madrid)* 34(17), jan–mar 77 : 39–94.

4023   MICHELSON, William M. *Man and his urban environment: a sociological approach with revisions*. Reading, Mass., Addison-Wesley Publishing Co., 76, xiii–273 p.

4024   NAJIB, Ahmed. "Urbanisation et habitat au Maroc", *C. Afr. Adm. publ.* 17, jul 77 : 95–106.

4025   OESTEREICH, Jürgen. "Political structure of urbanization", *Viertel-jahresberichte* 69, seo 77 : 201–208.

4026   OTTO, Konrad. *Umweltpolitik der Städte: Materialien zur Umweltpo-litik der Gross- und Mittelstädte auf den Basis von Befragungen* (Urban environmental policy: documents to the environmental po-licy of big and middle size cities based on questionnaires). Karlsruhe, Müller, 76, 108 p.

4027   PČELINCEV, O. S. "Urbanizacija i regulirovanie gorodskogo rosta" (Urbanization and regulation of urban growth), in: *Urbanizacija i razvitie novyh rajonov*. Moskva, 1976 : 5–24.

4028   PERNIA, Ernesto M. *Urbanization in the Philippines: historical and comparative perspectives*. Honolulu, East-West Center, 76, v-38 p.

4029   PIVOVAROV, Ju. L. *Sovremennaja urbanizacija. Osnovnye tendencii rasselenija* (Contemporary urbanization: localization essential tendencies). Moskva, Statistika, 76, 191 p.

4030   POBEDA, N. A. *Socialističeskaja urbanizacija i razvitie kul'tury. (Na materialah MSSR)* (Socialist urbanization and development of culture. From materials of the Moldavian SSR). Kišinev, Stiin-ca, 76, 192 p.

4031   POKATAEVA, T. S. *Razvivajusciesja strany: problemy urbanizacii. Osobennosti formiorvanija i struktury gorodskogo naselenija* (The developing countries: urbanization problem. Characteristics of the urban population formation and structure). Moskva, Mysl', 77, 302 p.

4032   PORTES, Alejandro. "Comparative urbanization and national develop-mznt", *Berkeley J. Sociol.* 21, 1976–1977 : 89–103.

4033   ROWLAND, D. T. "Theories of urbanization in Australia", *Geogr. R.* 67(2), apr 77 : 267–276.

4034   SAINT-MOULIN, L. DE. "Perspectives de la croissance urbaine au Zaïre", *Zaïre-Afr.* 17(111), jan 77 : 35–49.

4035   SANTIAGO, Jacques. "Urbanisation et sous-développement: Santiago du Chili", *C. O.-Mer* 30(118), apr–jun 77 : 153–177.

4036   SMOUT, M. A. H. "Urbanisation of the Rhodesian population", *Zambezia* 4(2), dec 76 : 79–91.

4037   STEPHAN, G. E.; TEDROW, L. M. "A theory of time minimization: the relationship between urban area and population", *Pacific sociol. R.* 20(1), jan 77 : 105–112.

4038   STINNER, William F. "Urbanization and household structure in the Philippines", *J. Marriage Family* 39(2), mar 77 : 377–385.

4039   STONE, C. "Urbanization as a source of political disaffection ᵣ
        the Jamaican experience", *Brit. J. Sociol.* 26(4), dec 75 : 448ᵣ
        464.
4040   "Urbanization and counterurbanization", *Urb. Aff. ann. R.* (11),
        1976 : 7-329.
4041   WHEAT, Leonard F. *Urban growth in the nonmetropolitan South.* Lexing-
        ton, Mass., Lexington Books, 76, xvi-171 p.

        16323.

        *[See also / Voir aussi: 531, 812, 922, 1472, 1635, 2260, 2583,
        3609, 3780, 3783, 4099, 4305, 4409, 5430, 5434]*

4042   ADAMS, John S. (ed.). *Contemporary metropolitan America. Vol. I.
        Book 1. Cities of the nation's historic metropolitan core. Book
        2. Nineteenth century ports. Book 3. Nineteenth century inland
        centers and ports. Book 4. Twentieth century cities.* Cambridge,
        Mass., Lippincott, Ballinger, 76, xvi-354 p.; xiii-314 p.; xix-
        507 p.; XVI-350 p.
4043   ALLEN, Irving Lewis (ed.). *New towns and the suburban dream: ideo-
        logy and utopia in planning and development.* Port Washington,
        N.Y., Kennikat Press, 77, 285 p.
4044   ANDREWS, Richard Bruce. *The urban system: an introduction.* Madison,
        Center for Urban Land Economics Research, University of Wiscon-
        sin, 77, 449 p.
4045   ARCHDEACON, Thomas T. *New York City, 1664-1710: conquest and change.*
        Ithaca, N.Y., Cornell University Press, 76, 197 p. CR: Amy BRIDGES
        Amer. J. Sociol. 82(6), mai 77 : 1417-1418.
4046   ARNAUD, Jean. "Profils démographiques des villes de Mauritanie,
        d'après l'enquête urbaine de 1975", *B. Inst. fondam. Afr. noire*
        38(3), jun 76 : 619-636.
4047   "Barcelone et l'équilibre de la Catalogne", *R. géogr. Pyrénées*
        48(2), apr 77 : 145-220.
4048   BERRY, Brian J. L. *et al. Chicago: transformations of an urban
        system.* Cambridge, Mass., Lippincott, Ballinger, 76, xv-101 p.
4049   BIHARI, Otto; SÁNTHA, János. "Pécs és a pécsi agglomerácio fejlödé-
        sének néhány elvi és sajátos vonása" (Some characteristical and
        theoretical features of the development of the agglomeration of
        Pécs), *Területrendezés* (1), 1976 : 34-38. *[Hungary.]*
4050   BRUNEAU, Jean-Claude. "Libourne (Gironde): exemple d'une ville
        moyenne", *R. géogr. Pyrénées* 48(3), jul 77 : 287-302. *[France.]*
4051   BRUYELLE, Pierre. *Lille et sa communauté urbaine.* Paris, Documen-
        tation française, 76, 132 p.
4052   CAMPBELL, Carlos C. *New towns: another way to live.* Reston, Va.,
        Reston Publishing Co., 76, 283 p. CR: Sally S. ROGERS, *Contemp.
        Sociol. (Washington)* 6(2), mar 77 : 269-260.
4053   CARMONA, M. "Les villes nouvelles de la région parisienne", *Acta
        geogr.* 29, jan 77 : 25-52.
4054   CAVIEDES L.; César. "Chimbote. El caso de una ciudad boom" (Chimbo-
        te. The case of a city boom), *R. geogr. (Rio de Janeiro)* 83, dec
        75 : 51-65. *[Peru.]*
4055   CHECKLAND, S. G. *The upas tree: Glasgow 1875-1975: a study in
        growth and contraction.* Glasgow, University of Glasgow Press,
        76, xi-124 p.-8 p.
4056   CHESNAIS, J. C.; LE BRAS, H. "Villes et bidonvilles du Tiers Monde"
        Population 31(6), nov-dec 76 : 1207-1231.
4057   CORTES ALONSO, Vicenta. *Huelva, población y estructura* (Huelva,
        population and structure). Huelva, Instituto de Estudios Onuben-
        ses, 76, 117 p. *[Spain.]*
4058   COTTEN, A. M.; MARGUERAT, Y. "Deux réseaux urbains africains: Ca-
        meroun et Côte d'Ivoire. I. La mise en place des systèmes ur-
        bains", *C. O.-Mer* 29(116), oct-dec 76 : 348-385.

4059   COUNCIL OF STATE GOVERNMENTS. *State community development policy:
the case of new communities.* Lexington, Ky., Council of State
Governments, 76, viii-121 p. *[USA.]*

4060   DE MICHELIS, Marco; PASINI, Ernesto. *La città sovietica 1925-1937*
(The Soviet city 1925-1937). Venezia, Marsilio, 76, 265 p.

4061   ERDEI, F. *Város és vidéke* (The city and its surroundings). Budapest, Akadémiai Kiadó, 77, 444 p. *[Szeged, Hungary.]*;

4062   FIGUEIREDO FERRAZ, José Carlos DE. *São Paulo e seu futuro, antes
que seja tarde demais* (São Paulo and its future, before it
would be too late). Rio de Janeiro, Instituto Brasileiro de Administração Municipal, 76, 90 p. *[Brazil.]*

4063   GAGNIER-VINET, Annick. *Fontenay-le-Comte: essai sur les rapports
ville-campagne dans la plaine vendéenne.* Poitiers, Centre géographique d'études et de recherches rurales, Université de Poitiers, 76, 147 p.

4064   GARCIA BALLESTEROS, Aurora. "Notas sobre el crecimiento natural y
real de los distritos de Madrid" (Notes on the natural and real
growth of Madrid districts), *R. int. Sociol. (Madrid)* 35(23),
1977 : 429-440.

4065   GOUDY, Willis J. "Evaluations of local attributes and community
satisfaction in small towns", *Rur. Sociol.* 42(3), 1977 : 371-382.

4066   GRANDGUILLAUME, Gilbert. *Nédroma. L'évolution d'une médina.* Leiden,
E.-J. Brill, 76, xv-195 p. *[Algérie.]*

4067   GUEST, Avery M. "The functional reorganization of the metropolis",
Pacific sociol. R. 20(4), oct 77 : 553-567.

4068   GUPTA, Khadija Ansari. *Politics of a small town: a sociological
study.* New Delhi, Impex India, 76, 179 p. *[Aligarh district,
India.]*

4069   HALL, John M. *London, metropolis and region.* Oxford, Oxford University Press, 76, 48 p.

4070   Bibl.XXVI-3470. HAWLEY, Amos H.; ROCK, Vincent P. (eds.). *Metropolitan American in contemporary perspective.* CR: Mary Donahue
STEARNS, *Contemp. Sociol. (Washington)* 6(2), mar 77 : 262-263.

4071   HORASANJAN, G. A. *Nekotorye voprosy èkonomičeskogo razvitija goro-
dov Sovetskoj Armenii* (Some questions on the economic development of Soviet Armenian towns). Èrevan, Ajastan, 76, 106 p.

4072   JOSHI, Heather; LUBELL, Harold; MOULY, Jean. *Abidjan: urban development and employment in the Ivory Coast.* Geneva, International
Labour Office, 76, xi-115 p.

4073   KARIVALO, Lassi. "Helsingin kaupunkialueen kasvu vuoteen 1946"
(The urban expansion of Helsinki to the year 1946), *Terra* 88(4),
1976 : 165-175.

4074   KISS, György. "A városiasodó nagyközségek helyzete és fejlesztésé-
nek kérdései" (Situation and development problems of small-
market towns), *Acta Fac. polit.-iur. Univ. Sci. budapest. Rolando
Eotvos* 20, 1977 : 63-84. *[Hungary.]*

4075   LEWIS, Peirce F. *New Orleans - the making of an urban landscape.*
Cambridge, Mass., Lippincott, Ballinger, 76, xiv-115 p.

4076   MÉRAUD, Marie-Agnès; FLEURY, Michel. "Problèmes de développement
de quelques grandes métropoles", *Aspects statist. Ile de France
Suppl. Ét.* jun-jul 77 : 5-52.

4077   MERLIN, P. "Aménagement régional et urbain et villes nouvelles au
Japon", *Cah. IAURP* dec 76 : 5-95.

4078   NANGIA, Sudesh. *Delhi metropolitan region: a study in settlement
geography.* New Delhi, K. B. Publications, 76, xiv-209 p.

4079   OKADA, Makoto. "'Toshi no kokusaisei' no kihonteki seikaku" (International characteristics of cities), *Nihon Toshigakukai Nenpô*
(11), 1977 : 49-58.

4080   ONOKERHORAYE, A. G. "The influence of different cultures on the
patterns of change in traditional African cities", *Cult. and
Develop.* 8(4), 1976 : 623-645.

4081   PINARD, Jacques. "Réflexions sur les villes scandinaves", *Acta geogr.* 31, jun 77 : 50-63.

4082   PORTER, Paul Robert. *The recovery of American cities*. New York, Two Continents Publishing Group, 76, 213 p.

4083   PORTES, Alejandro; WALTON, John. *Urban Latin America: the political condition from above and below*. Texas-London, University of Texas Press, 76, x-217 p. CR: Irving Louis HOROWITZ, *Amer. J. Sociol.* 83(3), nov 77 : 761-765.

4084   PUMAIN, D.; SAINT-JULIEN T. "Fonctions et hiérarchies des villes françaises. Étude du contenu des classifications réalisées en France entre 1960 et 1974", *A. Géogr.* 85(470), jul-aug 76 : 385-440.

4085   QUILICI, Vieri. *Città russa e città sovietica* (Russian cities and Soviet cities). Milano, G. Mazzotta, 76, 367 p.

4086   ROZMAN, Gilbert. *Urban networks in Russia, 1750-1800, and premodern periodization*. Princeton, N.J., Princeton University Press, 76, 337 p. CR: Theda SKOCPOL, *Contemp. Sociol. (Washington)* 6(1), jan 77 : 120-121.

4087   SAITŌ, Masao. "Chihōtoshi no mityoku yōin - daitoshi tono jakkan no hikaku" (Attractive elements of local cities - some comparisons with the large city), *Risshô-daigaku Jinbun-kagaku kenkyujo nenpo* 14, 1977 : 35-43.

4088   "[Sociologicke aspekty rozvoje Prahy]" (Sociological aspects of the development of Prague), *Sociol. Čas.* 13(1), 1977 : 1-128.

4089   Bibl.XXVI-3492. STERNLEIB, George; HUGHES, James W. (eds.). *Post-industrial America: metropolitan decline and inter-regional job shifts*. CR; John MOLLENKOPF, *Amer. J. Sociol.* 83(2), sep 77 : 474-479.

4090   TAUB, Richard P. *et al.* "Urban voluntary associations, locality based and externally induced", *Amer. J. Sociol.* 83(2), sep 77 : 425-442.

4091   "Toulouse aujourd'hui", *R. géogr. Pyrénées* 48(1), jan 77 : 6-140.

4092   TUROWSKI, Jan. "Kształtowania się zbiorowości osiedlowych w wielkich miastach" (The shaping of settlement collectivities in big cities), *Stud. socjol.* 60(1), 1976 : 203-233.

4093   VANCE, James E. Jr. *This scene of man: the role and structure of the city in the geography of Western civilization*. New York, Harper's College Press, 77, xx-437 p.

4094   VENDITELLI, Manlio. "Sul processo di industrializzazione a Roma", (On the industrialization process in Rome), *Crit. sociol. (Roma)* 41, 1977 : 76-97.

4095   "Villes nouvelles: dix ans après (Les)", *Promotions* 99, 1976 : 130 p. [France.]

4096   WADE, Richard C.; BROWN, Gene (eds.). *The cities*. New York, Arno Press, 76, x-386 p. [USA.]

16324.

[See also / Voir aussi: 1262, 1471, 1486, 1501, 3085, 4834]

4097   APPELBAUM, R. P. "City size and urban life. A preliminary inquiry into some consequences of growth in American cities", *Urb. Aff. Quart.* 12(2), dec 76 : 139-170.

4098   BAGIŃSKI, Eugeniusz. "Wzory wypoczynku preferowane przez ludność miast" (The patterns of recreation preferred by town population), *Stud. socjol.* 63(4), 1976 : 67-84.

4099   BARDO, John W. "Social class, age, sex, mother-daughter role relationships, and community satisfaction in a British new town", *J. soc. Psychol.* 103(2), dec 77 : 251-255.

4100   BASSAND, Michel. "La dynamique du système des collectivités territoriales", *Sociol. contemp.* 22(1-3), 1974 : 299-329. [Suisse.]

4101   BENT, Alan E.; ROSSUM, Ralph A. *Urban administration: management, politics, and change*. Port Washington, N.Y., Kennikat Press, 76, 385 p.

4102   BERRIATUA SAN SEBASTIAN, Javier. "Notas conceptuales de las asocia-
            ciones de vecinos como movimientos sociales urbanos" (Conceptual
            notes on neighbourghood associations as urban social movements),
            R. int. Sociol. (Madrid) 36(21), 1977 : 7-28.
4103   BERTELLI, Sergio. "Oligarchies et gouvernement dans la ville de la
            Renaissance", *Soc. Sci. Inform.* 15(4-5), 1976 : 601-623.
4104   BIAŁOBRZESKI,,Henryk. "Struktura społeczna miasta w świadomości
            jego mieszkańców" (Social structure of the city in the conscious-
            ness of its inhabitants), *Stud. socjol.* 65(2), 1977 : 29-55.
4105   BORJA, Jordi. "Les mouvements sociaux urbains en Espagne", *Espaces
            et Soc.* 19, dec 76 : 37-57.
4106   BORJA, Ricard; BORJA, Jordi; CAMPO, M. J. "Mouvements urbains et
            changements démocratiques aujourd'hui", *Espaces et Soc.* 19, dec
            76 : 59-64.
4107   BRYCE, Herrington J. *Urban governance and minorities.* New York,
            Praeger, 76, xv-220 p.
4108   CODACCIONI, Félix-Paul. *De l'inégalité sociale dans une grande
            ville industrielle: le drame de Lille de 1850 à 1914.* Lille,
            Université de Lille III; Paris, Éditions universitaires, 76, vi-
            444 p.
4109   CSOMOR, Tibor (éd.). *Városi közlekedés* (Urban transport). Budapest,
            Fővárosi Szabó Ervin Könyvtár, 76, 98 p.
4110   DOWDALL, George W. "Models of metropolitan socio-economic diffe-
            rentiation: a comparison among black, latino, and anglo patterns
            in 1970", *Sociol. Focus* 10(2), apr 77 : 133-150.
4111   ECKERT, W. A. "The applicability of the ethos theory to specific
            ethnic groups and the prediction of urban political forms", *Urb.
            Aff. Quart.* 11(3), mar 76 : 357-374.
4112   FAGNANI, Jeanne. "Activités féminines et transports urbains", *A.
            Géogr.* 86(477), sep-oct 77 : 542-561. *[France.]*
4113   GREENSTONE, J. David; PETERSON, Paul E. *Race and authority in ur-
            ban politics: community participation and the war on poverty.*
            Chicago, University of Chicago Press, 76, xxiv-364 p. *[USA.]*
4114   HAMNET, C. "Social change and social segregation in Inner London,
            1961-1971", *Urb. Stud.* 13(3), oct 76 : 261-271.
4115   HOLTERMANN, S. "Areas of urban deprivation in Great Britain: an
            analysis of 1971 Census data", *Soc. Trends* (6), 1975 : 33-47.
4116   IRWING, Henry M. "Social networks in the modern city", *Soc. Forces*
            55(4), jun 77 : 867-880.
4117   JOBERT, Bruno. *Villes et reproduction des différences sociales:
            systèmes scientifiques et développement urbain.* Grenoble, FNSP,
            Centre régional de Grenoble, 76, 162-vii t. multigr.
4118   JOBERT, Bruno; SELLIER, Michèle. "Les grandes villes: autonomie lo-
            cale et innovation politique", *R. franç. Sci. polit.* 27(2), apr
            77 : 205-227. *[France.]*
4119   KARP, David Allen; STONE, Gregory P.; YOELS, William C. *Being ur-
            ban: a social psychological view of city life.* Lexington, Mass.,
            Heath, 77, xiii-242 p.
4120   KILMARTIN, L. A.; THORNS, David. "Urban social problems and pros-
            pects: introduction", *Austral. New Zealand J. Sociol.* 13(1), feb
            77 : 18-22.
4121   LIU, Ben-Chieh. "Economic and non-economic quality of life: empi-
            rical indicators and policy implications for large standard metro-
            politan areas", *Amer. J. Econ. Sociol.* 36(3), jul 77 : 225-240.
4122   MAMON, Joyce A.; MARSHALL, Harvey. "The use of public transporta-
            tion in urban areas: toward a causal model", *Demography* 14(1),
            feb 77 : 19-31.
4123   MARAZZITI, Mario. "Per una sociologia dei marginali nella città"
            (For a sociology of urban marginality), *Crit. sociol. (Roma)*
            41, 1977 : 48-63. *[Italy.]*
4124   MAURICE, Marc; DELOMÉNIE, Dominique. *Mode de vie et espaces sociaux:*

processus d'urbanisation et différenciation sociale dans deux zones urbaines de Marseille. Paris, Mouton, 76, 223 p. *[France.]*

4125 MULLINS, Patrick. "The social base, stake and urban effects of a Brisbane urban social movement", *Austral. New Zealand J. Sociol.* 13(1), feb 77 : 29-35.

4126 NAITŌ, Tatsumi; HANEDA, Arata. "Chiho-toshi no jumin-seikatsu" (Life structure of the people in the city of Fujiyoshida), *Meiji-gakuin Ronsō* 260, 1977 : 65-94. *[Japan.]*

4127 OMI, Tetsuo. "Chiiki shakai seikatsu to shimin dantai" (Community life and associations in an urban society), *Shakaigaku Nenshi* 18, 1977 : 205-218.

4128 OMORI, Motoyoshi. "Violence and legal sanction in an East African town", *Kokuritsu Minzokugaku Hakubutsukan Kenkyu-hokoku* 2(2), 1977 : 38-61.

4129 PETERSON, Mary. "Urban social relations during Divali", *Hum. Relat.* 29(9), sep 76 : 805-817. *[Bombay.]*

4130 PLAX, M. "The use and abuse of political ethos for the study of urban politics", *Urb. Aff. Quart.* 11(3), mar 76 : 375-386.

4131 RABINOVITZ, Francine F.; SIEMBIEDA, William J. *Minorities in suburbs: the Los Angeles experience.* Lexington, Mass., Lexington Books, 77, xiii-100 p.

4132 SAITO, Yoshio. "Chihō-toshi ni okeru 'shakaisanka to seikatsu no shitsu'" (Social participation and quality of life in an urban community), *Nihon Bunka Kenkyūjo Keinkyu-hōkoku* 14, 1977 : 1-88.

4133 Bibl.XXVI-3542. SCHWARTZ, Barry. *Queuing and waiting: studies in the social organization of access and delay.* CR: David GLANZ, *Contemp. Sociol. (Washington)* 6(2), mar 77 : 165-167.

4134 STIPAK, Brian. "Attitudes and belief systems concerning urban services", *Publ. Opin. Quart.* 41(1), 1977 : 41-55.

4135 VAN USSEL, Jos. *Leven in communes. Verslag van een empirisch onderzoek naar communes in Nederland* (Life in communes. Report of an empirical research on communes in the Netherlands). Deventer, Van Loghum Slaterus, 77, 168 p.

4136 WILLENBORG, John F. *et al. The consumer-citizen and community satisfaction.* Columbia, Division of Research, Bureau of Business and Economic Research, College of Business Administration, University of South Carolina, 76, vii-101 p.

4137 YAMAGUCHI, Hiromitsu; KANEKO, Isamu. "Toshi seikatsu yōkenron no kiso-mondai" (The basic problem of urban life prerequisites), *Toshi-mondai* 68(4), 1977 : 63-76.

16325.

[See also / Voir aussi: 1487, 3048, 3382, 3617, 3724, 3724, 3736, 4024, 4056, 4092]

4138 ANDREW, Caroline; BLAIS, André; DESROSIERS, Rachel. *Les élites politiques, les bas-salariés et la politique du logement* à Hull. Ottawa, Éditions de l'Université d'Ottawa, 76, 272 p. *[Canada.]*

4139 ANGYAL, L. "Lakóhelyi sajátosságok tükröződése politikai véleményekben" (The impact of dwelling-place characteristics on political views), *Szociológia* 5(3-4), 1976 : 583-592.

4140 ARIELL, Mordecai; KASHTI, Yitzhak. "The socially disadvantages peer group in the Israeli residential setting", *Jew. J. Sociol.* 19(2), dec 77 : 145-155.

4141 BALAKRISHNAN, T. R. "Ethnic residential segregation in the metropolitan areas of Canada", *Canad. J. Sociol.* 1(4), 1976 : 481-498.

4142 BELL, Colin. "On housing classes", *Austral. New Zealand J. Sociol.* 13(1), feb 77 : 36-40.

4143 BLUM, Jacques; SJØRSLEV, Inger. *Fristaden Christiania: slum, alternativ bykultur eller et socialt eksperiment ?* (The free city of Christiania: slum, alternative city culture or a social experiment ?). Copenhagen, National Museum of Denmark, 76, 67 p.

4144   BOUKRAA, R. "Changement socio-économique et changement socio-cul-
        turel: le cas du gourbiville", *C. Tunisie* 24(95-96), 3-4 trim
        76 : 243-271. *[Tunisie.]*

4145   BROOKS, Mary E. *Housing equity and environmental protection: the
        needless conflict*. Washington, American Institute of Planners,
        76, 136 p.

4146   BUTLER, Rémy; NOISETTE, Patrice. *De la cité ouvrière au grand en-
        semble: la politique capitaliste du logement social, 1815-1975*.
        Paris, F. Maspéro, 77, 193 p.

4147   CANFORA-ARGANDOÑA, Elsie; GUERRAND, Roger H. *La répartititon de la
        population, les conditions de logement des classes ouvrières à
        Paris au 19e siècle*. Paris, Centre de sociologie urbaine, 76,
        325 p.

4148   CARPENTER, Edwin H. "The potential for population dispersal: a
        closer look at residential location preferences", *Rur. Sociol.*
        42(3), 1977 : 352-370.

4149   CESARI, Carlo; GRESLERI, Guiliano. *Residenza operaia e citta neo-
        conservatrice: Bologna, caso esemplare* (Working class housing
        and a neo-conservative city: Bologna as a typical case). Roma,
        Officina, 76, 242 p.-26 l.

4150   CUPAL, Wilhelm. *Die gemeinnützige Wohnungswirtschaft Österreichs
        von 1955-1967* (The housing economy of public interest in Austria
        from 1955-1967). Göttingen, Vandenhoeck und Ruprecht, 76, 88 p.

4151   DANIELSON, Michael N. *The politics of exclusion*. New York, Colum-
        bia University Press, 76, ix-443 p. *[USA.]*

4152   DOWNS, Anthony. "The impact of housing policies on family life in
        the United States since World War II", *Daedalus* 106(2), 1977 :
        163-180.

4153   DUNCAN, S. S. "The housing question and the structure of the housing
        market", *J. soc. Pol.* 6(4), oct 77 : 385-412. *[UK.]*

4154   ENGLISH, John; MADIGAN, Ruth; NORMAN, Peter. *Slum clearance: the
        social and administrative context in England and Wales*. London,
        Croom Helm, 76, 223 p.

4155   FRIEDEN, Bernard J. *et al. The nation's housing, 1975 to 1985*.
        Cambridge, Mass., Joint Center for Urban Studies of the Massa-
        chusetts Institute of Technology and Harvard University, 77,
        155 p. *[USA.]*

4156   HENDON, William S. "Miniparks and urban neighborhood redevelopment",
        Amer. J. Econ. Sociol. 36(3), jul 77 : 275-282.

4157   KAISER, Edward John. *Residential mobility in new communities: an
        analysis of recent in-movers and prospective out-movers*. Camb-
        ridge, Mass., Ballinger Publishing Co., 76, xxxiii-188 p.

4158   KEMÉNY, Jim. "A political sociology of home ownership in Australia",
        Austral. New Zealand J. Sociol. 13(1), feb 77 : 47-52.

4159   KERRI, James N. "A social analysis of the human element in housing:
        a Canadian case", *Hum. Org.* 36(2), 1977 : 173-185.

4160   KERST, Erna W.; MACKENZIE, Donald R. *Housing in developing countries:
        an annotated bibliography*. Charlottesville, Va., Kerst, 76, 279 l.

4161   KOMAI, Hiroshi. "Slum and squatter problems in Asia", *Shakaigaku
        Jânaru* 2(1), 1977 : 5-8.

4162   KUSNETZOFF K. F., "Política de vivienda o política y vivienda ?
        Una evaluación de la experiencia chilena" (Housing policy or
        politics and housing ? An evaluation of the Chilean experience),
        R. interamer. Planif. 9(33), mar 75 : 41-60.

4163   LAKATOS, M. "A lakáshelyzet és a lakáshoz jutás módjai négy orszag-
        ban" (Housing conditions and ways of obtaining dwellings in four
        countries), *Statiszt. Szle* 55(12), dec 77 : 1221-1232. *[USSR,
        Hungary, Italy, France.]*

4164   LANNOY, W. DE. "De woonsegregatie van sociaal-economische groepen
        in de Brusselse agglomeratie" (Housing segregation of socio-
        economic groups in Brussels), *Bovolking en Gezin* (2), 1977 : 195-
        211.

4165   LEE, Trevor R. "Choice and constraints in the housing market: the
        case of one-parent families in Tasmania", *Austral. New Zealand
        J. Sociol.* 13(1), feb 77 : 41-46.

4166   LEVEN, Charles L.; MARK, Jonathan H. "Revealed preferences for
        neighbourhood characteristics", *Urb. Stud.* 14(2), jun 77 : 147-
        159.

4167   LEVEN, Charles L. et al. *Neighborhood change: lessons in the dyna-
        mics of urban decay.* New York, Praeger, 76, xvi-205 p.

4168   MAGRI, Susanna. *Logement et reproduction de l'exploitation: les
        politiques étatiques du logement en France, 1947-1972.* Paris,
        Centre de sociologie urbaine, 77, 312 p.

4169   MANN, Mary Sullivan. *The right to housing: constitutional issues
        and remedies in exclusionary zoning.* New York, Praeger, 76, 191 p.

4170   MARTIN, Albert Edward; KALOYANOVA, Fina; MAZIARKA, Stefan. *Housing,
        the housing environment, and health: an annotated bibliography.*
        Geneva, World Health Organization; New York, United Nations Book-
        shop, 76, iv-113 p.

4171   MASON, T. "Intention and implication in housing policy; a study
        of recent developments in urban renewal", *J. soc. Pol.* 6(1), jan
        77 : 17-30. [UK.]

4172   McKAY, David H. *Housing and race in industrial society: civil
        rights and urban policy in Britain and the United States.* London,
        Croom Helm; Totowa, N.J., Rowman and Littlefield, 77, 193 p.

4173   MILGRAM, Morris. *Good neighborhood: the challenge of open housing.*
        New York, Norton, 77, 248 p.

4174   MORIO, Simone. *Le contrôle des loyers en France: 1914-1948, docu-
        ments pour l'étude comparative des politiques du logement.* Pa-
        ris, Centre de sociologie urbaine, 76, 400 p.

4175   NOËL, Fernando. *Les coopératives dans le domaine de l'habitation
        au Québec: la coopérative, formule d'habitation du futur.* Québec,
        Éditeur officiel du Québec, 76, 116 p. in various pagings.

4176   OKAMOTO, Yukio; SUGAKI, Yoshiko. "Chiiki-idô ni yoru daiichiji kan-
        kei no henka to saihensei" (Residential mobility and changing
        primary relations), *Kazoku Kenkyu Nenpô* (3), 1977 : 26-42.

4177   OLIVE, Maria José; RODRIGUEZ, Jaime; VALLS, Xavier. "La question
        du logement en Espagne", *Espaces et Soc.* 19, dec 76 : 23-36.

4178   ONOKERHORAYE, Andrew Godwin. "The spatial pattern of residential
        districts in Benin, Nigeria", *Urb. Stud.* 14(3), oct 77 : 291-
        302.

4179   ORGANISATION DES NATIONS UNIES. Département des affaires économi-
        ques et sociales. *Principes directeurs d'une politique de l'ha-
        bitation pour les pays en développement.* New York, NU, 77, viii-
        138 p.

4180   OYABU, Juichi. "Toshi kyojû komyuniti no chakaiteki kôzô to chiiki
        kôzôteki tokuchô" (The social structure and area structural cha-
        racteristics of urban-residential communities), *Jinbun Kenkyû
        (Osaka)* 28(3), 1977 : 1-38.

4181   PERLMAN, J. E. "Rio's favelas and the myth of marginality", *Polit.
        and Soc.* 5(2), 1975 : 131-160.

4182   PHILIPPI, Bruno; LUENBERGER, David G. "Neighborhood effects and
        maintenance of the urban housing stock", *J. math. Sociol.* 5(2),
        1977 : 151-172.

4183   PINÇON, Michel; PAYA, Farid. *Les HLM (habitation à loyer modéré),
        structure sociale de la population logée: agglomération de Paris,
        1968.* 2 vols. Paris, Centre de sociologie urgaine, 76, 359 p.;
        306 p.

4184   RIETDORF, Werner. *Neue Wohngebiete sozialistischer Länder: Ent-
        wicklungstendenzen, progressive Beispiele, Planungsgrundsätze*
        (New housing areas in socialist countries: development tenden-
        cies, progressive examples, basic planning principles). Berlin,
        Verlag für Bauwesen, 76, 296 p.

4185   ROBERTSON, Charles *et al.* "Professional elitism or community cont-
        rol ? The Manila housing competition", *Austral. New Zealand J.
        Sociol.* 13(1), feb 77 : 75-84. *[Philippines.]*
4186   ROOF, Wade Clark; SPAIN, Daphne. "A research note on city-suburban
        socioeconomic differences among American Blacks", *Soc. Forces*
        56(1), sep 77 : 15-20.
4187   RUIZ PALOMEQUE, Eulalia. "El barrio de Argüelles" (The neighbour-
        hood of Argüelles), *R. int. Sociol. (Madrid)* 35(23), 1977 : 381-
        426. *[Spain.]*
4188   ŚNIEZYŃSKI, Marian. "Kształtowanie więzi społecznych mieszkańców
        nowych osiedli mieszkaniowych" (Formation of social bonds among
        inhabitants of new housing estates), *Stud. socjol.* 65(2), 1977 :
        57-75.
4189   STINNES, Donald N. "Alternative models of neighborhood change",
        Soc. Forces 55(4), jun 77 : 1043-1057.
4190   Bibl.XXVI-3609. STEPHENS, Joyce. *Loners, losers, and lovers: el-
        derly tenants in a slum hotel.* CR: Andrea FONTANA, *Contemp. So-
        ciol. (Washington)* 6(3), mai 76 : 391.
4191   TALLARD, Michèle. "Les conditions de logement des travailleurs
        migrants en France", *Consommation* 24(1), jan-mar 77 : 71-90.
4192   TUROWSKI, Jan. "Personal relations in the new housing estates,
        theories and Polish experience", *Polish sociol. B.* 37(1), 1977 :
        49-63.
4193   ULACK, R. "Migration to the slum and squatter communities of Caga-
        yan de Oro city, the Philippines", *Int. Migration R.* 10(3),
        1976 : 355-376.
4194   UYEKI, Eugene S. "Occupation and residence: Cleveland, 1940-1970",
        Sociol. Focus 10(4), oct 77 : 325-339.
4195   VAN VALEY, Thomas L.; ROOF, Wade Clark; WILCOX, Jerome E. "Trends
        in residential segregation: 1960-1970", *Amer. J. Sociol.* 82(4),
        jan 77 : 826-844.
4196   WALTER, E. V. "Dreadful enclosures: detoxifying an urban myth",
        Archiv. europ. Sociol. 18(1), 1977 : 151-159.
4197   WARD, P. "The squatter settlement as slum or housing solution:
        evidence from Mexico City", *Land Econ.* 52(3), aug 76 : 330-346.
4198   WINGEN, M. "Wohnbedingungen und Funtionstüchtigkeit der Familien.
        Zur Bedeutung von empirischen Ergebnissen für eine familienge-
        rechte Wohnungspolitik" (Housing conditions and good functioning
        of the families. The meaning of empirical results for a housing
        policy suitable for the families), *Soz. Welt* 27(4), 1976 : 440-
        467.

        16326.

        [See also / Voir aussi: 4131, 4172, 4709, 5109, 5501]

4199   ALFELD, Louis Edward; GRAHAM, Alan K. *Introduction to urban dyna-
        mics.* Cambridge, Mass., Wright-Allen Press, 76, xvii-337 p.
4200   ANGRIST, Shirley S.; BELKIN, Jacob; WALLACE, William. "Social in-
        dicators and urban policy analysis", *Soc.-econ. Plan. Sci.* 10(5),
        1976 : 193-198.
4201   APPLEYARD, Donald. *Planning a pluralist city: conflicting reali-
        ties in Ciudad Guayana.* Cambridge, Mass., MIT Press, 76, 312 p.
4202   ARTEMOV, V. A. (ed.). *Primenenie pokazatelej vremeni v social'no-
        ékonomičeskom planirovanii goroda* (The utilization of time in-
        dexes in the socio-economic planning of a town). Novosibirsk,
        77, 147 p.
4203   ASHTON, Patrick J. "Toward a new conceptualization of suburbs: a
        theoretical and empirical exploration", *Sociol. Focus* 10(3),
        aug 77 : 287-307.
4204   BAS, Carlos Alberto; SEPULVEDA, Anibal. "El desarrollo urbano de
        San Juan y la planificación urbana en Puerto Rico" (Urban deve-
        lopment of San Juan and urban planning in Puerto Rico), *R. in-*

teramer. Planif. 11(43), sep 77 : 112-144.

4205   BORŠČEVSKIJ, M. V. "Strategija kompleksnogo planirovanija goroda"
        (Strategy of complex urban planning), in: *Aktual'nye problemy*
        social'nogo planirovanija. Irkutsk, 1975 : 104-127.

4206   BOYCE, C. P.; BOISIER, S. "Centros de tamaño medio en América la-
        tina y la política de planificación urbana: el caso de Venezuela"
        (Medium-sized cities in Latin America and urban planning policy:
        the case of Venezuela), *EURE* 5(13), jun 76 : 47-60.

4207   CAMAGNI, Roberto; MAZZOCCHI, Giancarlo. "Contrasti nello sviluppo
        urbano: Milano-Torino-Taranto" (Contrasts in urban development:
        Milan-Torino-Taranto), *Riv. int. Sci. soc.* 84(4-5), jul-oct 76 :
        401-418.

4208   CARDENAS, C. "Algunas experiencias del proyecto de desarrollo ur-
        bano de Ciudad Lazaro Cardenas, Michoacan" (Some experience of
        the project of urban development of Ciudad Lazaro Cardenas,
        Michoacan), *R. inter-amer. Planif.* 9(36), dec 75 : 100-113.
        [Mexico.]

4209   ĆIRIĆ, Jovan V. "Iz urbane problematike" (Town planning problems),
        Sociologija 18(3-4), 1976 : 317-324. *[Yugoslavia.]*

4210   CURRIE, Laucklin. "Planeación metropolitana: Moscu y Bogotá" (Met-
        ropolitan planning: Moscow and Bogotá), *R. Plan. Desarr. (Bogotá)*
        8(3), sep-dec 76 : 105-112.

4211   CUTLER, Laurence S.; CUTLER, Sherrie Stephens. *Recycling cities*
        for people: the urban design process. Boston, Cahners Books In-
        ternational, 76, 250 p.

4212   DANAN, Yves Maxime. *Les agences d'urbanisme d'agglomération.* Paris,
        Centre de recherche d'urbanisme, 76, 213 p.

4213   DMITRIEV, A. V.; MEŽEVIČ, M. N. "Kompleksnoe planirovanie v gorodah"
        (Complex planning in towns), *Sociol. Issled. (Moskva)* (4), 1976 :
        52-63.

4214   DRAKAKIS-SMITH, D. W. "Urban renewal in an Asian context: a case
        study in Hong Kong", *Urb. Stud.* 13(3), oct 76 : 295-305.

4215   DUCLOS, Denis. *Orthopédies pour monopolville en crise: hypothèse*
        de recherche sur le redéploiement économique, ses effets sur le
        reclassement des structures de reproduction de la force de tra-
        vail et leurs aspects urbains. Paris, Centre de sociologie ur-
        baine, 76, 139 p.

4216   ELLICKSON, Robert C. "Suburban growth controls: an economic and
        legal analysis", *Yale Law J.* 86(3), jan 77 : 388-509. *[USA.]*

4217   FINKLER, Earl; TONER, William J.; POPPER, Frank J. *Urban nongrowth:*
        city planning for people. New York, Praeger, 76, ix-227 p.

4218   GOLANY, Gideon (ed.). *Innovations for future cities.* New York,
        Praeger, 76, xix-264 p.

4219   GOTTDIENER, Mark. *Planned sprawl: private and public interests in*
        suburbia. Beverly Hills, Sage Publications, 77, 189 p.

4220   "Indian city-urban development and human growth (The)", *Soc. Action*
        27(3), jul-sep 77 : 193-352. *[India.]*

4221   LEVIN, Melvin R. *The urban prospect: planning, policy, and strate-*
        gies for change. North Scituate, Mass., Duxbury Press, 77, xi-
        305 p. *[USA.]*

4222   MASOTTI, Louis H.;;LINEBERRY, Robert L. (eds.). *The new urban po-*
        litics. Cambridge, Mass., Ballinger, 76, xv-266 p.

4223   MATZERATH, Horst; THIENEL, Ingrid. "Stadtentwicklung, Stadtplanung,
        Stadtentwicklungsplanung. Probleme im 20. Jahrhundert am Beispiel
        der Stadt Berlin" (Urban development, urban planning and urban
        development planning. Problems in the 20th century by the example
        of Berlin), *Verwaltung* 10(2), 1977 : 173-196.

4224   McKENZIE, Nigel. "Centre and periphery: the marriage of two minds",
        Acta sociol. 20(1), 1977 : 55-74.

4225   MOLLENKOPF, J. "The post-war politics of urban development", *Polit.*
        and Soc. 5(3), 1975 : 247-295.

4226   PERNOLIA, Mario. "Notes pour une histoire de l'urbanisme labyrin-

thique, le concept labyrinthe", *Espaces et Soc.* 20-21, mar-jun
77 : 121-133.

4227   POPENOE, David. *The suburban environment: Sweden and the United
States.* Chicago, University of Chicago Press, 77, xii-275 p.
4228   QUINN, Ruaici. "Urban design and community development in Ireland",
Administration (Dublin) 24(4), 1976 : 519-527.
4229   RAPOPORT, Amos. *Human aspects of urban form: towards a man-envi-
ronment approach to urban form and design.* Oxford-New York, Pergamon Press, 77, viii-438 p.
4230   ROBERTSON, Ian. *Community self-surveys in urban renewal.* Manchester, Department of Adult Education, University of Manchester,
76, iii-140 p.
4231   SANDERCOCK, Leonie. *Cities for sale: property,-politics and urban
planning in Australia.* London, Heinemann, 76, x-260 p.
4232   STANBACK, Thomas M. Jr.; KNIGHT, Richard. *Suburbanization and the
city.* Montclair, N.J., Allanheld, Osmun, Universe books, 76,
xviii-230 p.
4233   TARRAGO, Marçal. "Modèle de développement et politiques urbaines
en Espagne, 1939-1975", *Éspaces et Soc.* 19, dec 76 : 5-22.
4234   VILLANI, A. "L'urbanistica della partecipazione" (City planning
with participation), *Vita e Pensiero* 60(1), jan)feb 77 : 51-71.

ECONOMICS
SCIENCE ÉCONOMIQUE

17100. ECONOMIC SOCIOLOGY
    SOCIOLOGIE ÉCONOMIQUE

[See also / Voir aussi: 1801]

4235   HUPPES, T. (ed.). *Economics and sociology: towards an integration.*
Leiden, Martinus Nijhoff, 76, vii-181 p.

4236   PÉTYCHAKI-HENZE, Maria. "Georges Gurvitch et la sociologie économique", *C. int. Sociol.* 24(62), jan-jun 77 : 147-170.

4237   RANKOVIĆ, Miodrag. "Nekoliko pitanja o Veberovoj ekonomskoj socio-
logiji" (Some questions relevant to Weber's economic sociology),
Sociologija 18(3-4), 1976 : 371-377.

4238   Bibl.XXVI-3657. REISMAN, David A. *Adam Smith's sociological economics.* CR: Louis SCHNEIDER, *Contemp. Sociol. (Washington)* 6(4),
jul 77 : 497-499.

17200. ECONOMIC SYSTEM
    SYSTÈME ÉCONOMIQUE

17210. Economic doctrine
    Doctrine économique

[See also / Voir aussi: 2528]

4239   KAHULITS, László. "A tulajdon fogalma, a tulajdonviszonyok fejlödése a szocializmus épitésében" (Concept of property, development of property relations in the construction of socialism),
Magyar filoz. Szle 20(5), 1976 : 681-706.

4240   MAKAI, M. "A munka társadalmi jellegének egyes kérdései és a marxi
tulajdonfogalom" (Some questions of the social character of work
and the Marxian concept of property), *Magyar filoz. Szle* 21(3-4),
1977 : 301-327.

17220. Capitalism. Collectivism
    Capitalisme. Collectivisme

17221.

[See also / Voir aussi: 310, 2053, 3431, 3921, 4361, 4916, 4929,
4993]

4241   ABOLTIN, V. Ja. "Cikličeskij krizis kapitalizma i pravota marksizma-leninizma" (Cyclical crisis of capitalism and accuracy of
marxism-leninism), in: *Filosofija i sovremennost'.* Moskva, 1976 :
115-124.

4242   AGUILAR MONTEVERDE, Alonso. "Algunos rasgos de la actual crisis
capitalista" (Some characteristics of the present crisis of capitalism), *R. mexic. Sociol.* 38(4), oct-dec 76 : 751-766.

4243   Bibl.XXVI-3667. BELL, Daniel. *Cultural contradictions of capitalism.*
CR: Roger D. ABRAMS, Alain TOURAINE, *Amer. J. Sociol.* 83(2), sep
77 : 463-473; Jonathan RIEDER, Norbert WILEY, *Contemp. Sociol.*
(Washington) 6(4), jul 77 : 411-424.

4244   DIGGINS, John P. "Reification and the cultural hegemony of capitalism: the perspectives of Marx and Veblen", *Soc. Res.* 44(2),
1977 : 354-383.

4245   FIORAVANTI, Eduardo. "Crísis del capitalismo y lucha de clases"
         (Crisis of capitalism and class struggle), *RS Cuad. Realidad
         soc.* 12, jan 77 : 5-25.
4246   GELLNER, Ernest. "Class before State: the Soviet treatment of
         African feudalism", *Archiv. europ. Sociol.* 18(2), 1977 : 299-
         322.
4247   GOUDZWAARD, B. *Kapitalisme en vooruitgang: een eigentijdse maat-
         schappikritiek* (Capitalism and progress: a contemporary social
         criticism). Assen Van Gorcum, 76, 285 p.
4248   MAYES, Sharon S. "The material requisites for capitalism: a cross-
         cultural study", *Brit. J. Sociol.* 28(2), jun 77 : 155-167.
4249   MINGIONE, Enzo. "Territorial division of labour and capitalist
         development", *Sociol. contemp.* 22(1-3), 1974 : 223-278.
4250   NICHOLS, Theo; BEYLON, Huw. *Living with capitalism. Class relations
         and the modern factory*. London, Routledge and Kegan Paul, 77,
         xvi-204 p.
4251   SAVČENKO, P. V. *Obobešcestvlenie kooperativnogo proizvodstva pri
         socializme* (The socialization of cooperative production under
         socialism). Moskva, Izdatel'stvo Moskovskogo Universiteta, 76,
         224 p.
4252   SCHUMPETER, Joseph A. *Capitalism, socialism and democracy*. London,
         Allen and Unwin, 76, 437 p. CR: *Brit. J. Sociol.* 28(4), dec 77 :
         526.
4253   VOBRUBA, Georg. "Legitimation und Güterknappheit. Ein Beitrag zur
         Rekonstruktion des Legitimationsproblems im Spätkapitalismus"
         (Legitimation and scarcity of goods. A contribution to the re-
         construction of the legitimation problem in the late capitalism),
         Kölner Z. Soziol. u. soz.-Psychol. 29(2), jun 77 : 355-363.
4254   WALLERSTEIN, Immanuel. "L'essor et le déclin éventuel du système
         mondial capitaliste", *R. Inst. Sociol. (Roma)* 12(3), 1976 : 171-
         213.

17222.

[See also / Voir aussi: 1311, 2481, 2711, 4373, 4465, 4686]

4255   BUGAENKO, P. T. "Proizvodstvennyj kollektiv kak social'no-politi-
         českaja jacejka socialisticeskogo obščestva" (Production collec-
         tivity as a socio-political cell of the socialist society), *Nauč.
         Kommunizm* (1), 1977 : 40-47.
4256   DENISJUK, N. P. "Vzaimosvjaz' nacional'nogo i internacional'nogo
         v socialisticeskih tradicijah" (Interaction of national and in-
         ternational in socialist traditions), *Fllos. nauč. Kommunizm*
         (3), 1976 : 121-127.
4257   GEL'BUH, F. N.; LOPATA, P. P. *Razvitoe socialisticeskoe obščestvo:
         istoriceskoe mesto i osnovnye certy* (The developed socialist so-
         ciety: historical place and essential characteristics). Moskva,
         Politizdat, 76, 128 p.
4258   HULÁKOVÁ, Marie. "Kulturní odkaz Velkého říja v praxi socialistické
         výstavby Československa" (Cultural heritage of the Great October
         Revolution in the practice of socialist construction in Czecho-
         slovakia), *Sociol. Čas.* 13(5), 1977 : 446-454.
4259   IGNATOVSKIJ, P. "O kriterijah i étapah razvitija socialisticeskogo
         obščestva v SSSR" (Criteria and stages of development of the so-
         cialist society in the USSR), *Vopr. Ėkon.* 32(8), aug 77 : 30-38.
4260   KAVKO, A. K. "Internacionalizacija obščestvennoj žizni v socialis-
         ticeskom sodružestve" (Internationalization of social life in
         socialist community), *Nauc. Kommunizm* (1), 1977 : 60-67.
4261   KNOBLOM, V. I. "K voprosu o sootnošenii nacional'nyh i interna-
         cional'nyh processov v socialisticeskom obščestve" (On the corre-
         lation of national and international processes in the socialist
         society), in: *Nekotorye voprosy istorii kommunisticeskoj partii
         sovetskogo sojuza. II*. Moskva, 1976 : 82-94.

4262   LAKOS, S. "A szocialista demokrácia egyes kérdései" (Some questions of socialist democracy), *Tarsad. Szle* (5), 1977 : 17-29.

4263   LAŠIN, A. G. "O suščnosti i sisteme socialističeskih obščestvennyh otnosenij" (On nature and system of socialist social relations), *Vestn. Moskov. Univ. Teorija nauč. Kommunizma* (3), 1976 :
74-85.

4264   OVČINNIKOV, V. S. *Idejnoe ědinstvo razvitogo socialističeskogo
obščestva (Filosofskij očerk)* (Ideological unity of the developed socialist society. A philosophical study). Leningrad,
Lenizdat, 76, 184 p.

4265   PAŠKOV, A. I. "K voprosu ov ětapah razvitija socialističeskogo
obščestva" (On the socialist society development stages), in:
Stanovlenie i razvitie ěkonomičeskoj nauki v SSSR. Moskva,
1976 : 8-20.

4266   RUML, Vladimír. "K teoreticko-metodologickým otázkám zkoumání socialistické společnosti" (On theoretical and methodological
issues of the research into socialist society), *Sociol. Čas*.
13(2), 1977 : 129-136.

4267   ŠTEFAŇÁK, Michal. "Vliv úspěchů socialistických zemí na revoluční
a pokrokový vývoj ve světě" (The impact of the socialist countries' achievement on the revolutionary and progressive development in the world), *Sociol. Čas*. 13(5), 1977 : 433-445.

4268   STRMISKA, Z. "Programme socialiste et rapports sociaux en URSS et
dans les pays socialistes", *R. Ét. comp. Est-Ouest* 7(3), sep
76 : 107-233.

4269   TARANOV, A. P. *et al. Politiceskaja organizacija razvitogo socialisticeskogo obščestva. (Pravovye problemy)* (Political organization of developed socialist society. Juridical problems). Kiev,
Naukova Dumka, 76, 516 p.

4270   WERBLAN, Andrzej. "Niektóre problemy teorii budowy rozwiniętego
społeczeństwa socjalistycznego w Polsce" (Some problems of the
theory of construction of the developed socialist society in
Poland), *Stud. socjol*. 65(2), 1977 : 5-27.

4271   ZERKIN, D. P. "Ob ob'ektivnosti rassmotrenija v socialističeskom
obščestva" (On the objectivity of social processes examination
in the socialist society), *Probl. Dialektiki* (6), 1976 : 121-128.

17300. ECONOMIC SITUATION. STANDARD OF LIVING
SITUATION ÉCONOMIQUE. NIVEAU DE VIE

17310. Economy. Economic development
Économie. Développement économique

[See also / Voir aussi: 2810, 3012, 3032, 3165]

4272   BASTIDE, Roger. "Ethno-sociologie des développements. Deux leçons
à l'Université internationale de Monaco (avril 1969). I. Le développement au Brésil. II. Pour un pluralisme du développement",
Archiv. int. Sociol. Coop. Dévelop. 40, jul-dec 76 : 5-14.

4273   BERNARD, Philippe J. "Pour une généralisation de l'étude des facteurs sociaux et culturels du développement", *Tiers-Monde* 18(70),
apr-jun 77 : 339-351.

4274   BOURCIER DE CARBON, Philippe. "À propos de quelques modèles démo-
économiques de développement", *Population* 32(3), mai-jun 77 :
579-624.

4275   BUTENKO, A.; PAVLOVA-SIL'VANSKAJA, M. "Socializm kak faza social'no-
ěkonomičeskogo razvitija" (Socialism as a phase of socio-economic
development), *Obšč. Nauki (Moskva)* 1976 : 33-49.

4276   CARDOSO, F. H. "Quels styles de développement ?", *Études (Paris)*
jan 77 : 7-24.

4277   DAMACHI, Ukandi Godwin. *Leadership ideology in Africa: attitudes
toward socioeconomic development*. New York, Praeger, 76, xi-112 p.

4278   FARMANFARMAIAN, Khodadad. (ed.). *The social sciences and problems
        of development*. Princeton, N.J., Princeton University Program in
        Near Eastern Studies, 76, xv-332 p. CR: J. Bernard MURPHY, *Con-
        temp. Sociol. (Washington)* 6(4), jul 77 : 441.

4279   HIRSCH, Fred. *Social limits to growth*. Cambridge, Mass., Harvard
        University Press, 76, x-208 p.

4280   LANE, Frederic C. "Economic growth in Wallerstein's social systems.
        A review article", *Comp. Stud. Soc. Hist.* 18(4), oct 76 : 517-
        532.

4281   LINDHOLM, Richard W. "A tested program for Third World economic
        development", *Amer. J. Econ. Sociol.* 36(2), apr 77 : 165-169.

4282   MAZUR, Allan; ROSA, Eugene. "An empirical test of McClelland's
        'Achieving society' theory", *Soc. Forces* 55(3), mar 77 : 769-774.

4283   PIPER, Annelotte. *Japans Weg von der Feudalgesellschaft zum In-
        dustriestaat: Wandlungsimpulse und wirtschaftliche Entwicklungs-
        prozesse in ihrer politischen, geistigen und gesellschaftlichen
        Verankerung* (Japan's way from a feudal society to an industrial
        state: change impulses and economic development processes in the
        political, intellectual and social deep rooted ideas). Köln,
        Verlag Wissenschaft und Politik, 76, 259 p.

4284   RITTER, Archibald R. M. "The transferability of socioeconomic de-
        velopment models of revolutionary Cuba", *Cuban Stud.* 7(2), jul
        77 : 183-204.

17320. Income. Living conditions
Revenu. Conditions de vie

[See also / Voir aussi: 1325, 2607, 2654]

4285   AITOV, N. A. "K voprosu o kriterijah sopostavlenija uslovij žizni
        v socialističeskih i kapitalističeskih stranah" (On the compar-
        ison of criteria of conditions of life in the socialist and ca-
        pitalist countries), *Nauč. Dokl. vysš. Školy Nauč. Kommunizma*
        (4), 1976 : 41-53.

4286   ANDREWS, Frank M.; WITHEY, Stephen B. *Social indicators of well-
        being: Americans perceptions of life quality*. New York, Plenum
        Press, 76, xxi-455 p.

4287   BAKER, Sally Hillsman; LEVENSON, Bernard. "Earnings prospects of
        Black and White working-class women", *Sociol. Wk Occupat.* 3(2),
        mai 76 : 123-150.

4288   BELLAMY, R. "*A nemzetek gazdagsága* és a burzsoá politikai gaz-
        dagságtan nyomorúsága" (*Wealth of nations* and poverty of the
        bourgeois political economy), *Beke és Szociál.* (7), 1976 : 107-
        115.

4289   BIBB, Robert; FORM, William H. "The effects of industrial, occupa-
        tional and sex stratification on wages in blue-collar markets",
        Soc. Forces 55(4), jun 77 : 974-996.

4290   BORODKIN, F. M. *et al. Social'no-ěkonomičeskie problemy truda i
        urovnja žizni* (Socio-economic problems of labour and standard
        of living). Novosibirsk, 76, 139 p. [USSR.]

4291   DOWDALL, George W. "Intermetropolitan differences in family income
        inequality: an ecological analysis of total white and nonwhite
        patterns in 1960", *Sociol. soc. Res.* 61(2), jan 77 : 176-191.

4292   EASTON, Brian. "The economic life cycle of the modern New-Zealand
        family", *Austral. New Zealand J. Sociol.* 13(1), feb 77 : 85-89.

4293   EMEREK, Ruth; SIIM, Birte. *Kvinders arbejds- og levevikår: belyst
        gennem kvinder i tobaksindustrien* (Women's working and living
        conditions: illustrated by women in the tobacco industry). Århus,
        Modtryk, 76, 144 p. [Denmark.]

4294   FOLEY, John W. "Trends, determinants and policy implications of
        income inequality in US countries", *Sociol. soc. Res.* 61(4),
        jul 77 : 441-461.

4295 GAERTNER, W. "Zum Problem der Existenz von sozialen Wohlfahrts-funktionen im Sinne von Arrow" (The problem of the existing of social welfare functions according to Arrow), *Z. ges. Staats-wiss.* 133(1), jan 77 : 61-74.

4296 GINSBERT-GEBERT, Adam; MARKOWSKA, Anna; SZULC, Eva. "Warunki zycia w Ostrowcu Swiętokrzyskim w swietle opinii jego mieszkańców" (Living conditions in Ostrowiec Swietokrzyski in the opinion of its inhabitants), *Biul. IGS* 20(4), 1977 : 68-96.

4297 HANNAN, Michael T.; TUMA, Nancy Brandon; GROENEVELD, Lyle P. "Income and marital events: evidence from an income-maintenance experiment", *Amer. J. Sociol.* 82(6), mai 77 : 1186-1211.

4298 HAUSER, Robert M.; DAYMONT, Thomas N. "Schooling, ability, and earnings: cross-sectional findings 8 to 14 years after high school graduation", *Sociol. Educ.* 50(3), jul 77 : 182-206.

4299 HEISKANEN, Heikki. "Palkan yhteiskunnalliset funktiot" (Social functions of wages), *Kansantal. Aikakausk.* 73(3), 1977 : 299-308

4300 HUDIS, Paula M. "Commitment to work and wages: earning differences of Black and White women", *Sociol. Wk. Occupat.* 4(2), mai 77 : 123-146.

4301 JASSO, Guillermina; ROSSI, Peter H. "Distributive justice and earned income", *Amer. sociol. R.* 42(4), aug 77 : 639-651.

4302 KASS, Roy. "Recent changes in male income", *Sociol. Quart.* 18(3), 1977 : 367-377.

4303 KONEVA, L. A. "Metodologičeskie problemy issledovanija obraza žizni" (Methodological problems in research on standard of living), in: *Metodologičeskie problemy razvitija nauki i kul'-tury.* Kujbyšev, 1976 : 137-145.

4304 KOOPMANS, Rudy. *Welzijn als probleem. Sociologie, welzijn, welzijn werk* (Welfare as a problem. Sociology, welfare and social work). Alphen aan den Rijn, Samson, 76, 211 p.

4305 LINCOLN, James R.; FRIEDLAND, Roger. "Metropolitan dominance and income levels in nonmetropolitan cities", *Sociol. soc. Res.* 61(3), apr 77 : 304-319.

4306 NIEMI, Albert W. Jr. "Sexist earnings differences: the cost of fe-male sexuality", *Amer. J. Econ. Sociol.* 36(1), jan 77 : 33-40.

4307 PHILLIBER, William W.; FOX, William S. "Race, class, and percep-tions of affluence", *Sociol. Focus* 10(4), oct 77 : 375-381.

4308 PSACHAROPOULAOS, George. "Family background, education and achieve ment: a path model of earnings determinants in the UK and some alternatives", *Brit. J. Sociol.* 28(3), sep 77 : 321-335.

4309 SELL, Ralph R.; JOHNSON, Michael P. "Income and occupational diffe rences between men and women in the United States", *Sociol. soc. Res.* 62(1), oct 77 : 1-20.

4310 SILK, Leonard Solomon; VOGEL, David. *Ethics and profils: the cris of confidence in American business.* New York, Simon and Schuster 76, 251 p.

4311 SYKES, A. J. M. "Overtime, false returns, and restrictive prac-tices: the perception of an industrial pay system", *Hum. Relat.* 29(11), nov 76 : 1083-1101.

4312 SZYMANSKI, Albert. "The effect of earning discrimination against women on the economic position of men", *Soc. Forces* 56(2), dec 77 : 611-625.

4313 TALBERT, Joan; BOSE, Christine E. "Wage-attainment processes: the retail clerk case", *Amer. J. Sociol.* 83(2), sep 77 : 403-424.

4314 TÖRNBLOM, Kjell Y. "Magnitude and source of compensation in two situations of distributive injustice", *Acta sociol.* 20(1), 1977 75-95; *Hum. Relat.* 30(1), 1977 : 1-24.

431. ZIMBALIST, Sidney Eli. *Historic themes and landmarks in social welfare research.* New York, Harper and Row, 77, xii-432 p.

17400. PRODUCTION. ENTREPRISE
PRODUCTION. ENTERPRISE
17410. Business economics. Management
Économie de l'entreprise. Gestion

4316   ANDICS, J.; ROZGONYI, T. "A vállalati gazdasági döntések társadalmi természetéről" (On the social nature of economic decisions in enterprises), *Közgazd. Szle* 24(12), dec 77 : 1403-1418.

4317   ANDICS, J.; ROZGONYI, T. *Konfliktus és harmonia. A gazdasági szervezetek szociologiájának alapkérdései* (Conflict and harmony. Basic aspects of the sociology of economic organizations). Budapest, Közgazdasági és Jogi Kiadó, 77, 405 p.

4318   BILANDŽIĆ, Dušan. "Neki problemi samoupravljanja" (Some problems of the self-management), *Polit. Misao* 14(2), 1977 : 137-158. *[Yugoslavia.]*

4319   ČALIĆ, Dusan. "Motiviranost omladine za socijalističko samoupravljanje" (The motivation of the young people for the socialist self-management), *Socijalizam* 20(7-8), jul-aug 77 : 1380-1391.

4320   CHIESI, Antonio M. "Una ricercha sulla biografie imprenditoriali nell'Italia liberale e fascista. Problemi teorici, analisi empirica e tipologia" (Research on entrepreneurs' biographies in liberal and fascist Italy. Theoretical problems, empirical analysis and typology), *Quad. Sociol.* 27(2), jun 77 : 109-149.

4321   DESROCHE, Henri *et al.* "Économie et sociologie coopératives: textes et recherches pour une anthologie provisoire", *Communauté* 41-42, jan-dec 77 : 3-405.

4322   DRULOVIĆ, Milojko. *L'autogestion à l'épreuve: le modèle yougoslave.* Éd. rev. Paris, A. Fayard, 77, xxxii-273 p.

4323   "Entreprise face aux transformations sociales (L')", *Personnel (Paris)* 195, mar-apr 77 : 23-88. *[France.]*

4324   EPSTEIN, E. M. "The social role of business enterprise in Britain: an American perspective", *J. Manag. Stud.* 13(3), oct 76 : 113-133; 14(3), oct 77 : 281-316.

4325   FOGARTY, Michael. "La responsabilité sociale de l'entreprise en tant qu'organisation de travail", *Trav. et Soc.* 2(3), jul 77 : 291-314.

4326   GELINIER, Octave. *Stratégie sociale de l'entreprise.* Surennes, Éditions hommes et techniques, 76, 261 p.

4327   HARARI, Ehud; ZEIRA, Yoram. "Limitations and prospects of planned change in multinational corporations", *Hum. Relat.* 29(7), jul 76 : 659-676.

4328   HAZAMA, Hiroshi. *Nihon no kigyô to shakai* (Business and society in Japan). Tokyo, Nihon Keizai Shinbunsha, 77, 290 p.

4329   HODGETTS, Richard M. *The business enterprise: social challenge, social response.* Philadelphia, Saunders, 77, vi-232 p.

4330   HUGHES, Michael; SCOTT, John; MACKENZIE, John. "Trends in interlocking directorships: an international comparison", *Acta sociol.* 20(3), 1977 : 287-299.

4331   JONG, J. H. Th DE. *De maatschappelijke waarde van de onderneming: een bijdrage tot de diskussie over social marketing en social accounting* (The social value of the enterprise: a tentative discussion on social marketing and social accounting). Aalten, Interland, De Graafschap, 76, 128 p.

4332   KARDELJ, E. "L'autogestion socialiste en Yougoslavie", *R. int. Sci. adm.* 42(2), 1976 : 103-110.

4333   LAKY, T. "Attachment to the enterprise in Hungary. Societal determination of enterprise interest in development", *Acta oecon.* 17(3-4), 1976 : 269-284.

4334   MARTÍN MOLINA, Rafael. *Socialización a nivel de empresa: teoria del proporcionalismo* (Socialization at the level of enterprise: theory of proportionalism). Bilbao, Mensajero, 76, 134 p.

4335 MONTIS, Jean-Bernard. *Analyse et mesure du climat social de l'entreprise*. Paris, Entreprise moderne d'édition, 76, 138 p.

4336 ORNSTEIN, Michael D. "The boards and executives of the largest Canadian corporations: size, composition, and interlocks", *Canad. J. Sociol.* 1(4), 1976 : 411-437.

4337 SALLON, Michel. *L'autogestion*. Paris, Presses universitaires de France, 76, 183 p.

4338 ŠARIŠSKY, Marián. "K nektorým poznatkom z aplikácie sociálnej analýzy v podnikovej praxi" (On some findings concerning the application of social analysis in enterprise practice), *Sociol. Čas.* 13(2), 1977 : 168-179.

4339 SEIDER, Maynard S. "Corporate ownership, control and ideology: support for behavioral similarity", *Sociol. soc. Res.* 62(1), oct 77 : 113-128.

4340 SWINDLE, Robert E. *Fundamentals of modern business*. Belmont, Calif. Wadsworth Publishing Co., 77, xi-515 p.

4341 THIERAUF, Robert J.; KLEKAMP, Robert, C.; GEEDING, Daniel W. *Management principles and practices' a contingency and questionnaire approach*. Santa Barbara, Wiley, 77, xv-819 p.

4342 VELIČKO, A. N.; PODMARKOV, V. G. *Sociolog na predprijatii* (The sociologist in an enterprise). Moskva, Moskovskij Rabočij, 76, 240 p.

4343 WINTER, Gerd (ed.). *Sozialisierung von Unternehmen: Bedingungen und Begründungen* (Socialization of enterprises: conditions and reasons). Frankfurt-am-Main-Köln, Europäische Verlagsanstalt, 76, 295 p.

4344 ŽURAVLEV, G. F. "Social'no-psihologičeskaja struktura proizvodstvennogo kollektiva" (Socio-psychological structure of a production collectivity), in: *Psihologija upravlenija. I*. Moskva, 1976 : 26-42.

17420. Productivity. Technology
Productivité. Technologie

[See also / Voir aussi: 1019, 1809, 4672]

4345 ABBOTT, Lewis Frederick. *Social aspects of innovation and industrial technology: a survey of research*. London, HMSO, 76, 131 p.

4346 ADLER, L. M. *et al*. *Sociologia i proizvodstvo* (Sociology and production). Kazan', Tatknigoizdat, 76, 232 p.

4347 ANDICS, Jenö. *A technikai haladás társadalmi problémái a gazdasági szervezetekben* (Social problems of technological progress in eco nomic organizations). Budapest, Akadémiai Kiadó, 77, 262-2 p.

4348 BAINBRIDGE, William Sims. *The spaceflight revolution: a sociological study*. New York, Wiley, 76, x-294 p.

4349 BEREANO, Philip L. (ed.). *Technology as a social and political phe nomenon*. New York, Wiley, 76, viii-544 p.

4350 BHATTACHARYA, K. "Technology is a social product; lessons from India", *Instant Res. Peace Violence* 6(3), 1976 : 130-138.

4351 CHERNS, Albert. "The principles of sociotechnical design", *Hum. Relat.* 29(8), aug 76 : 783-792.

4352 COX, Robert W. "Pour une étude prospective des relations de production", *Sociol. Trav.* 19(2), apr-jun 77 : 113-137.

4353 DAHRENDORF, Ralf *et al*. *Scientific-technological revolution, socia aspects*. London, Sage, 77, 181 p.

4354 ĐURIC, Vojislav. "Prilog konstituisanju socioloske teorija o difuziji inovacija" (A contribution to developing a sociological theory of the diffusion of invocations), *Sociol. sela* 14(3-4), 1976 : 12-36.

4355 FEDORENKO, N. "Naučno-tehničeskij progress. Nekotorye voprosy planirovanija i upravlenija" (The scientific and technical progress Some planning and management questions), *Obšč. Nauk (Moskva)* (1), 1977 : 58-72.

4356   GADAMER, Hans-Georg. "Theory, technology, practice: the task of the
        science of man", *Soc. Res.* 44(3), 1977 : 529-561.
4357   GAILLIE, Duncan. "Automatisation et légitimité de l'entreprise
        capitaliste", *Sociol. Trav.* 19(3), jul-sep 77 : 221-242.
4358   GENDRON, Bernard. *Technology and the human condition.* New York, St.
        Martin's Press, 77, viii-263 p.
4359   GILLESPIE, David F.; MILETI, Dennis S. "An integrative approach to
        the study of organizational technology structure and behaviour",
        Sociol. contemp. 22(1-3), 1974 : 189-200.
4360   GOULET, D. "The suppliers and purchasers of technology: a conflict
        of interests", *Int. Develop. R.* 18(3), 1976 : 14-20.
4361   GROMEKA, V. I. *Naučno-tehničeskaja revoljucia i sovremennyj kapi-
        talizm* (The scientific and technical revolution and contemporary
        capitalism). Moskva, Politizdat, 76, 278 p.
4362   HOLT, R. T. "Technology assessment and technology inducement me-
        chanism", *Amer. J. polit. Sci.* 21(2), mai 77 : 283-301.
4363   IVANOVA, R. K. *Naučno-tehničeskaja revoljucija i razvitie obšcest-
        vennogo truda v SSSR* (The scientific and technical revolution
        and social labour development in the USSR). Moskva, Nauka, 76,
        189 p.
4364   KALININ, A. I. "Naučno-tehničeskaja revoljucija i ličnost' v uslo-
        vijah razvitogo socializma" (The scientific and technical revo-
        lution and personality under conditions of developed socialism),
        in: *Naučno-tehničeskij progress i povyšenie kul'turno-tehničes-
        kogo urovnja trudjašcihsja.* Čeboksary, 1976 : 3-43.
4365   KIRN, Andrej. "Neograničeni i ograničeni razvitak proizvodnih sna-
        ga" (Limited and unlimited development of productive forces),
        Sociologija 18(3-4), 1976 : 249-268.
4366   KOZIK, A. K. "Socialističeskie obšcestvennye otnošenija i naučno-
        tehničeskij progress" (Socialist social relations and scientific
        and technical progress), *Vestn. Moskov. Univ. Teorija nauč. Kom-
        munizma* (4), 1976 : 3-13.
4367   LAKI, László. "A tudományos-technikai haladás szociális következ-
        ményei" (Social consequences of technical scientific progress),
        Létunk (3-4), 1976 : 14-36.
4368   LAKY, T. *Számitógépek alkalmazásának szociológiai problémái az üze-
        mekben* (Sociological problems of introducing computers at fac-
        tories). Budapest, SZÁMKI, 77, 114 p.
4369   LICK, J. "A tudományos-technikai haladás és az emberi fejlödés
        távlatai" (The scientific-technical progress and the perspectives
        of the development of mankind), *Szociológia* 5(3-4), 1976 : 441-
        451.
4370   MOCH, Michael K.; MORSE, Edward V. "Size, centralization and organi-
        zational adoption of innovations", *Amer. sociol. R.* 42(5), oct
        77 : 716-725.
4371   NESÁZAL, Karel. "Vědeckotechnická revoluce a společenské řizeni"
        (The scientific-technological revolution and social control),
        Sociol. Čas. 13(5), 1977 : 481-493.
4372   OGIONWO, W. "Einstellungswandel zu Risikobereitschaft und Innova-
        tionsverhalten. Eine Untersuchung in Nigeria" ("Risky shift" and
        innovative behaviour. A Nigerian experience), *Sociologus* 27(2),
        1977 : 174-187.
4373   PLOTNIKOV, A. A. *Naučno-tehničeskaja revoljucija v uslovijah raz-
        vitogo socialističeskogo obšcestva* (The scientific and technical
        revolution under conditions of the developed socialist society).
        Saratov, Izdatel'stvo Saratovskogo Universiteta, 76, 93 p.
4374   "Povyšenie social'noj aktivnosti sovetskogo čeloveka i razvitie
        tehničeskoj sredy" (Elevation of the Soviet man's social activi-
        ty and development of technical environment), in: *Naučno-tehni-
        českaja revoljucija i soversenstvovanie socialističeskih obšcest-
        vennyh otnošenij.* Leningrad, 1976 : 106-118.

4375   REIMANN, Bernard C. "Dimensions of organizational technology and
        structure: an exploratory study", *Hum. Relat.* 30(6), jun 77 :
        545-566.
4376   RUDAS, J. *Technika, munka, szakképzettség. A müszaki fejlödés és
        az ipari munkások* (Technology, work, qualifications. Technolo-
        gical progress and the industrial workers). Budapest, Kossuth
        Kiado, 77, 185 p.
4377   RYAN, Bryce. "Innovation and innovator in a theory of change",
        Int. J. contemp. Sociol. 13(3-4), jul-oct 76 : 249-260.
4378   SALMONA, Michèle. "Théories de la diffusion des innovations. Ana-
        lyse structurale du discours et pronostics des conduites psycho-
        socio-économiques", *Connexions* 20, 1976 : 105-124.
4379   SANUKOV, K. N. "Vlijanie tehničeskogo progressa na social'noe raz-
        vitie nacij i narodnostej" (Influence of technical progress on
        social development of nations and peoples), in: *Social'nye pos-
        ledstvija mehanizacii i avtomatizacii proizvodstva.* Ufa, 1976 :
        95-113.
4380   SCHMIDT, Peter (ed.). *Innovation. Diffusion von Neuerungen im so-
        zialen Bereich* (Innovation. Diffusion of innovations in the so-
        cial sector). Hamburg, Hoffmann und Campe; 76, 394 p.
4381   SEMPER, Edward *et al.* (eds.). *Hidden factors in technological chan-
        ge.* Oxford, Eng.-New York, Pergamon Press, 76, xiii-252 p.
4382   SERRANO, M. Martin. "Le conflit entre innovation technologique et
        changement culturel", *Communications (Köln)* 2(1), 1976 : 25-39.
4383   SPIEGEL-RÖSING, Ina; SOLLA PRICE, Derek DE (eds.). *Science, techno-
        logy and society. A cross-disciplinary perspective.* London, Sage,
        77, xii-607 p.
4384   WILLEMS, J. G. L. M. *Ondernemingen, bedrijfsleven en maatschappij:
        beknopte inleiding tot de theorie van maatschappelijke produk-
        tieorganisatie* (Enterprises, economy and society: introduction
        notes to the theory of social organization of production). Leiden
        Stenfert Kroese, 77, xix-311 p.
4385   ZLOTNIKOV, R. A. "Naučno-tehničeskij progress i potrebnosti lič-
        nosti" (The scientific and technical progress and personality
        needs), in: *Naučno-tehničeskij progress i ego social'nye pos-
        ledstvija.* Ufa, 1976 : 23-26.

        17430. Agriculture. Commerce. Industry
               Agriculture. Commerce. Industrie

        17431.

        [See also / Voir aussi: 2493, 3035]

4386   BLASI, Joseph R. "The Israeli kibbutz: economic efficiency and
        justice", *Community Develop. J.* 12(3), oct 77 : 201-212.
4387   BRZEZINSKI, Jacek. "Les fonctions sociales des coopératives dans
        la formation des microrégions rurales en Pologne", *Sociol. rur.*
        17(1-2), 1977 : 141-150.
4388   CALISE, Mauro. "Le origini agricole della catena del pomodoro. In-
        dagine sulla struttura socio-economica dell' azienda contadina
        nell' agro nocerino-sarnese" (Agricultural origins of the tomato
        chain. A survey on the socio-economic structure of the agricul-
        tural enterprise in Southern Italy), *Rass. ital. Sociol.* 18(2),
        apr-jun 77 : 273-306.
4389   COUGHENOUR, C. Milton; KOWALSKI, Gregory S. "Status and role of
        fathers and sons on partnership farms", *Rur. Sociol.* 42(2),
        1977 : 180-205.
4390   CRIDEN, Yosef; GELB, Saadia. *The kibbutz experience: dialogue in
        Kfar Blum.* New York, Schocken Books, 76, 277 p. CR: Selma Koss
        BRANDOW, *Contemp. Sociol. (Washington)* 6(2), mar 77 : 172-173.
4391   DON, Jehuda. "Industrialization in advanced rural communities: the
        Israeli kibbutz", *Sociol. rur.* 17(1-2), 1977 : 59-74.

4392   ERDEI, F. *Mezögazdaság és szövetkezet* (Agriculture and coopera-
         tives). Budapest, Akadémiai Kiadó, 77, 4-382 p.

4393   FEDER, Ernest. *Strawberry imperialism. An enquiry into the mecha-
         nism of dependency in Mexican agriculture.* Den Haag, Institute
         of Social Studies, 77, iv-199 p.

4394   FREDERICKS, L. J. "Ideology and organization in agricultural de-
         velopment: the case of Malaysia", *Sociol. rur.* 17(3), 1977 :
         191-200.

4395   GAGNOH, Gabriel. *Coopératives ou autogestion: Sénégal, Cuba, Tuni-
         sie.* Montréal, Presses de l'Université de Montréal, 76, 482 p.

4396   GARTRELL, John W. "Status, inequality and innovation: the Green
         Revolution in Andhra Pradesh, India", *Amer. sociol. R.* 42(2),
         apr 77 : 318-337.

4397   GROTH, Philip. "Plantation agriculture and the urbanization of the
         South", *Rur. Sociol.* 42(2), 1977 : 206-219. *[USA.]*

4398   HEDLEY, Marj. "Independent commodity production and the dynamics
         of tradition", *Canad. R. Sociol. Anthropol.* 13(4), nov 76 :
         413-421. *[Canada.]*

4399   IVANICS, András. "Vezetési és döntési folyamat mezögazdasági szö-
         vetkezetekben" (Management process and decision-making in agri-
         cultural co-operatives), *Vezetéstud.* (2), 1977 : 34-41.

4400   LAMARCHE, Hughes. "Les paysans face au marché: l'élevage hors-sol
         en Bretagne", *Sociol. Trav.* 19(2), apr-jun 77 : 138-156.

4401   LEGENDRE, Camille. "L'environnement et les limites de la bureaucra-
         tisation: la grande industrie forestière du Québec", *Rech. so-
         ciogr.* 17(2), mai-aug 76 : 221-245.

4402   LENGYEL, Zsuzsa. "A mezögazdaság szocialista átszervezése és követ-
         kezményei" (The socialist transformation of agriculture and its
         consequences), *Társadtud. Közl.* (1), 1977 : 68-82.

4403   OPARE, K. Dua. "The role of agricultural extension in the adoption
         of innovations by cocoa growers in Ghana", *Rur. Sociol.* 42(1),
         1977 : 72-82.

4404   SAGARA, Dušan; BLAAŞ, Gejza. "Funkcia sociálno-ekonomického plá-
         novania v integračných procesoch československého socialistické-
         ho pol'nohospodárstva a jeho metodické zásady" (Function of so-
         cio-economic planning in the integration process of Czechoslo-
         vak socialist agriculture and its methodological principles),
         Sociol. Čas. 13(4), 1977 : 390-402.

4405   SIMÓ, T. "Az anyagi tényezök szerepe a termelöszövetkezeti elnö-
         kök mobilitásában" (Role of economic factors in the mobility of
         cooperative farm chairmen), *Társadtud. Közl.* (1), 1977 . 83 95.

4406   SIMUŠ, P. I. "Kolhoz kak social'nyj institut" (Collective farm
         as a social institutions), *Sociol. Issled. (Moskva)* (3), 1976 :
         42-49.

4407   STOCKDALE, Jerry D. "Technology and change in United States agri-
         culture: model or warning ?", *Sociol. rur.* 17(1-2), 1977 : 43-
         58.

4408   WEBER, Ouri. "L'autogestion au kibboutz", *Esprit* 45(3), mar 77 :
         399-412. *[Israel.]*

17432.

[See also / Voir aussi: 3272, 3321, 4357, 4779]

4409   ALOUNATE, Adolfo. "Efectos sociales de la rápida industrializacion:
         el caso de São José dos Campos" (Social effects of accelerated
         industrialization: the case of São José dos Campos), *Notas Pobl.*
         5(13), apr 77 : 51-85. *[Brazil.]*

4410   KARUSH, Gerald E. "Industrialisation et changements de la popula-
         tion active en Belgique de 1846 à 1910", *Popul. et Famille*
         40(1), 1977 : 37-76.

4411   ŁACH, Wiktor. "Tendencje rozwoju i przeobrazen społeczno-ekonomicz-
nych rejonów uprzemyslawianych" (Trends of socio-economic development and change of industrializing areas), *Kult. i Społecz.*
20(4), oct-dec 76 : 219-229. *[Poland.]*
4412   MARSH, Robert M.; MANNARI, Hiroshi. *Kindai-ka to Nihon no kojo*
(Modernization and the Japanese factory). Tokyo, Tokyo-daigaku
Shuppankai, 77, 462 p.
4413   NORR, James L.; NORR, Kathleen L. "Societal complexity or production techniques: another look at Udy's data on the structure of
work organizations", *Amer. J. Sociol.* 82(4), jan 77 : 845-853.
4414   OLESNEVIČ, L. A. *Problemy social'nogo upravlenija na promyslennom
predprijatii* (Problems of social management in an industrial
enterprise). Kiev, 76, 149 p.
4415   OSAKO, Masako. "Technology and social structure in a Japanese automobile factory", *Sociol. Wk Occupat.* 4(4), nov 77 : 397-426.
4416   PATRICK, Hugh; MEISSNER, Larry (eds.). *Japanese industrialization
and its social consequences*. London, University of California
Press, 76, x-505 p.
4417   PINEO, Peter C. "Public evaluations of the social standing of in-
dustries and firms", *Int. J. comp. Sociol.* 17(3-4), sep-dec 76 :
226-241.
4418   ROTSTEIN, Abraham (ed.). *Beyond industrial growth.* Buffalo, University of Toronto Press, 76, 131 p. CR: Irene Taviss THOMSON, *Contemp. Sociol. (Washington)* 6(4), jul 77 : 487-488.
4419   VÁNYAI, J. "Empirical examination of factors influencing workers'
performance in the Hungarian machine-building industry", *Acta
oecon.* 16(2), 1976 : 191-211.

17433.

4420   BOTTACCHIARI, Vinicio. "L'artigianato" (Handicraft), *Riv. Sociol.*
14(1-3), jan-dec 76 : 205-238. *[Italy.]*
4421   DÓKA, Klara. "A pest-budai kézmüvesek életmódja a XIX. században
(1810-1872)" (Budapest craftsmen's way of life in the 19th century, 1810-1872), *Ethnographia* (4), 1975 : 552-586.
4422   EDWARDS, Ronald George. *Australian traditional bush crafts.* New
York, Schocken Books, 77, 143 p.
4423   LOWY, P. "L'artisanat dans les médinas de Tunis et de Sfax", *A.
Géogr.* 85(470), jul-aug 76 : 473-493.
4424   RIQUET, P. "Secteur tertiaire et métiers tertiaires. Approche statistique des activités de service en Allemagne fédérale", *A.
Géogr.* 85(467), jan-feb 76 : 1-33.

17434.

4425   KNEIFEL, John L. *A study on the choice of international transpor-
tation, cars, trains, planes: its assessment and synthesis, with
special regard to the sociological aspects.* Berlin/West, Kneifel,
76, 65 p.
4426   STUTZ, Frederick P. *Social aspects of interaction and transporta-
tion.* Washington, Association of American Geographers, 76, vii-
74 p.
4427   WHITE, Peter R. *Planning for public transport.* London, Hutchinson,
76, 224 p.-4 p. *[UK.]*

17500. CONSUMPTION. MARKET. PRICE
CONSOMMATION. MARCHE. PRIX

17510. Consumer behaviour
Comportement du consommateur

4428   BEARDEN, William O.; WOODSIEDE, Arch G. "The effect of attitudes
and previous behavior on consumer choice", *J. soc. Psychol.* 103(1
oct 77 : 129-137.

4429   BLUM, Milton L. *Psychology and consumer affairs*. New York, Harper and Row, 77, xiii-317 p.

4430   BONIFACE, Jean. *L'homme consommateur: victime ou complice ?* Paris, Société coopérative d'information et d'édition mutualiste, 76, 343 p.

4431   BOSS, Jean-François; BOUDON, Alain. *Comportement du consommateur et prévision des ventes dans la mode: une application au vêtement féminin de dessus*. Jouy-en-Josas, CESA, 76, 61 p. multigr.

4432   "Consommation comparée Est-Ouest (La)", *R. Ét. comp. Est-Ouest* 7(2), jun 76 : 5-258.

4433   HAMILTON, Gary G. "Chinese consumption of foreign commodities: a comparative perspective", *Amer. sociol. R.* 52(6), dec 77 : 877-891.

4434   HENRY, W. A. "Cultural values do correlate with consumer behavior", *J. Mkting Res.* 13(2), mai 76 : 121-127.

4435   KANTECKI, Antoni. "Społeczne aspekty planowania konsumpcji" (Social aspects of consumption planning), *Nowe Drogi* 30(5), mai 77 : 100-109. [Poland.]

4436   KLIMKIEWICZ, Roman; ZALESKI, Janusz. "Zmiany w pozlomie i strukturze spozycia ludnosci" (Change in consumption level and structure), *Nowe Drogi* 30(1), jan 77 : 93-102. [Poland.]

4437   KUZ'MINA, Ê. I. "Social'naja differenciacija potreblenija v SŠA" (The social differentiation of consumption in the USA), *Raboćij Klass sovrem. Mir* 5(6), nov-dec 76 : 49-60.

4438   LEMEL, Y. "Une source d'informations sur les consommations médicales des Français: l'enquête santé 1970-1971", *C. Sociol. Démogr. médic.* 17(3), jul-sep 77 : 81-88.

4439   MARCUS-STEIFF, Joachin. "L'information comme mode d'action des organisations de consommateurs", *R. franç. Sociol.* 18(1), jan-mar 77 : 85-107.

4440   NICOSIA, Francesco; MAYER, Robert. "Verso una sociologia del consumo" (Towards a sociology of consumption), *Impresa* 19(3), 1977 : 257-272.

4441   NORWAY. Statistisk sentralbyrå. *Private husholdningers forbruk, 1973 / Private households' consumption, 1973*. Oslo, H. Aschenhoug, 76, 103 p. [Norway.]

4442   SCOTT, Rosemary. *The female consumer*. London, Associated Business Programmes, 76, xi-352 p. [UK.]

4443   SHIOTA, Shizuo. "Shōhisha kôdô kenkyu to life-style gainen" (Studies of consumer behavior and life-style concept), *Chûkyô-shôgaku Ronsô* 24(2), 1977 ; 41-65.

4444   SOKOLOWSKI, K. "Évolution de la structure de la consommation en Pologne", *R. Et. comp. Est-Ouest* 8(2), jun 76 : 11-29.

4445   VORONOV, V. V. "Osobennosti vzaimodejstvijah material'nogo proizvodstva i potrebnostej v uslovijah naučno-tehničeskoj revoljucii" (Characteristics of material production and needs interaction under conditions of the scientific and technical revolution), in: *Problemy istoričeskogo materializma. IV. Naučno-tehničeskaja revoljucija i material'noe proizvodstva*. Leningrad, 1976 : 30-47.

4446   WARD, Scott; WACKMAN, Daniel B.; WARTELLA, Ellen. *How children learn to buy: the development of consumer information-processing skills*. Beverly Hills, Calif., Sage Publications, 77, 271 p.

4447   WEBER-JOBÉ, Monique. *Mouvements de consommateurs et transformation sociale: la Fédération romande des consommatrices*. Lausanne, Institut de science politique, 76, 220 p. in various pagings.

4448   WELLS, John R. *Underconsumption, market size and expenditure patterns in Brazil*. Cambridge, Eng., Centre of Latin American Studies, University of Cambridge, 76, 57 p.

17520. Demand. Supply
Demande. Offre

4449 DORNSTEIN, Miriam. "Some imperfections in the market exchanges for professional and executive services", *Amer. J. Econ. Sociol.* 36(2), apr 77 : 113-128.

4450 HANSEN, P. "T. H. Green and the moralization of the market", *Canad. J. polit. soc. Theory* 1(1), 1977 : 91-117.

4451 STARK, G. V. *Sociologičeskij analiz poznavatel'nogo processa v "Teorijah pribavočnoj stoimosti" Karla Marksa* (Sociological analysis of perceptive process in the Marx' theories on added value). Rostov n/D., Izdatel'stvo Rostovskogo Universiteta, 76, 148 p.

4452 VORONKOV, I. M.; SIDOROV, A. A.; GULJAEV, V. V. "Sociologičeskie aspekty organizacii socialističeskogo sorevnovanija" (Sociological aspects of the socialist competition organization), *Soc. Probl. nov. proizvodstv. Kollektiv.* (2), 1976 : 13-25.

17600. CREDIT. FINANCING. MONEY
CRÉDIT. FINANCEMENT. MONNAIE

[See also / Voir aussi: 3690]

4453 HERBST, Philip G.; GETZ, Ingri. "Work organization at a banking branch: towards a participative research technique", *Hum. Relat.* 30(2), feb 77 : 129-142.

4454 HOLMES, William. "Goal achievement and budgetary responsiveness of federal agencies", *Sociol. Focus* 10(1), jan 77 : 79-88.

4455 LICK, József. "Az érdek fogalma és társadalmi meghatározottsága" (The concept of interest and its social delimitation), *Társad. Szle* (10), 1976 : 59-73.

4456 LINDLEY, James T.; SELBY, Edward B. Jr. "Differences between Blacks and Whites in the use of selected financial services", *Amer. J. Econ. Sociol.* 36(4), oct 77 : 393-399.

4457 MÜLLER, Rudolf Wolfgang. *Geld und Geist. Zur Entstehungsgeschichte von Identitätsbewusstsein und Rationalität seit der Antike* (Money and spirit. History of the origin of the identity consciousness and rationality since the Antiquity). Frankfurt-am-Main, Campus Verlag, 77, 423 p. CR: Pasi FALK, *Acta sociol.* 20(4), 1977 : 393-396.

4458 PFEFFER, Jeffrey; LEONG, Anthony. "Resource allocations in United Funds: examination of power and dependence", *Soc. Forces* 55(3), mar 77 : 775-790.

4459 PHELPS, Edmund S. "Rational taxation", *Soc. Res.* 44(4), 1977 : 657-667.

4460 SZTUMSKI, Janusz. "Pieniądz w świetle socjologii - społeczne funkcje pieniądza" (Money in the light of sociology - the social functions of money), *Stud. socjol.* 60(1), 1977 : 89-100.

17700. ECONOMIC POLICY. PLANNING
POLITIQUE ÉCONOMIQUE. PLANIFICATION

[See also / Voir aussi: 541, 542, 1057, 4077]

4461 ALKER, Hayward R. Jr.; DEUTSCH, Karl W.; MARKOVITS, Andrei S. "Global opportunities and constraints for regional development: a review of interdisciplinary simulation research toward a world model as a framework of studies of regional development", *Soc. Sci. Inform.* 16(1), 1977 : 83-102.

4462 ATTESLANDER, Peter (ed.). *Soziologie und Raumplanung* (Sociology and regional planning). Berlin-New York, De Gruyter, 76, 272 p.

4463 KRAENZEL, Carl F. "Zimmerman's regional sociology viewed from the standpoint of a regionalist", *Int. J. contemp. Sociol.* 13(3-4), jul-oct 76 : 209-223.

4464 SANDBERG, Åke. *The limits to democratic planning. Power and methods in the struggle for the future.* Stockholm, Liberförlag, 76. CR:

J. P. ROOS, *Acta sociol.* 20(2), 1977 : 205-207.

4465   SUFIN, Zbigniew. "Teoretyczne zagadnienie planowania w społeczeń-
stwie socjalistycznym" (Theoretical problems of planning in the
socialist society), *Stud. socjol.* 64(1), 1977 : 5-29.

18. LABOUR
TRAVAIL

18100. INDUSTRIAL SOCIOLOGY. SOCIOLOGY OF WORK
SOCIOLOGIE INDUSTRIELLE. SOCIOLOGIE DU TRAVAIL

[See also / Voir aussi: 4824]

4466   DUNNETTE, Marvin D. (ed.). *Handbook of industrial and organiza-
        tional psychology.* Chicago, Rand McNally College Publishing Co.,
        76, xxvii-1740 p.
4467   LEPLAT, Jacques; CUNY, Xavier. *Introduction à la psychologie du
        travail.* Paris, Presses universitaires de France, 77, 240 p.
4468   ROZGONYI, T. *Munkaszociológia* (Sociology of work). Budapest, Föva-
        rosi Munkaügyi Nyomda, 76, 47-1 p.

18200. EMPLOYMENT. LABOUR MARKET
EMPLOI. MARCHÉ DU TRAVAIL
18210. Labour. Manpower
Travail. Main-d'oeuvre

[See also / Voir aussi: 647, 670, 1395, 2712, 3820]

4469   EICHARDUS, M. "Arbeidsmarktparticipatie van gehuwde moeders. Gezins-
        grootte en gezinsontwikkeling" (Labour market participation of
        married mothers. Family size and family development), *Bevolking
        en Gezin* (2), 1977 : 221-236.
4470   JACOBS, Frans. *Reflexies over arbeid* (Reflections on labour). Al-
        phen aan den Rijn, Samsom, 76, 115 p.
4471   MONTAGNA, Paul D. *Occupations and society: toward a sociology of
        the labor market.* New York, Wiley, 77, xvii-456 p.
4472   MOURSI, Mahmoud A.; ZUBERI, Habid A. "Experiences with human re-
        source development in some developing countries", *Develop. Pol.
        Adm. R.* 2(2), jul-dec 76 : 131-144.
4473   NAKHLEM, Emil A. "Labor markets and citizenship in Bahrayn and
        Qatar", *Mid. East J.* 31(2), 1977 : 143-156.
4474   O'CONNOR, J. "Productive and unproductive labor", *Polit. and Soc.*
        5(3), 1975 : 297-336.
4475   ORNSTEIN, Michael D. *Entry into the American labor force.* New York,
        Academic Press, 76, 220 p. CR: Jeylan T. MORTIMER, *Contemp. So-
        ciol. (Washington)* 6(1), jan 77 : 57-58.
4476   ŠEVCOV, I. "Trud v socialističeskom obščestve" (Labour in socialist
        society), *Kommunist Tatarii* (10), 1976 : 20-27.
4477   SHIBATA, Shingo. "RŌDO no jiyû to rôdô-undo" (Freedom of labour and
        tasks of labour movement), *Gendai to Shiso* 27, 1977 : 52-71.
4478   SIEGERS, J. J. "Ondersoek van participatie op de arbeidsmarkt door
        middel van regressie-analyse waarbij de afhankelijke variabele
        tweewaardig is" (Research on participation in the labour market
        through regression analysis using two dependent variables), *Be-
        volking en Gezin* (2), 1977 : 213-219.
4479   SPILERMAN, Seymour. "Careers, labor market structure, and socio-
        economic achievement", *Amer. J. Sociol.* 83(3), nov 77 : 551-593.
4480   STREIT, Max. "Experteninformiertheit und ihre Auswirkung auf die
        Bedarfsprognose von hochqualifizierten Arbeitskräften" (Informed

experts and their effects on the prognosis of need of highly qualified manpower), *Kölner Z. Soziol. u. soz.-Psychol.* 29(3), sep 77 : 530-542.

4481 SUSLOV, V. Ja. *Trud v uslovijah razvitogo socializma. (Social'no-filosofskie voprosy)* (Labour under conditions of developed socialism. Socio-philosophical questions). Leningrad, Nauka, 76, 150 p.

4482 VAN HOOF, Jacques J.; MARTENS, Albert (eds.). "Arbeidsmarkt en ongelijkheid" (Labour market and inequality), *Sociol. Gids* 24(1-2), jan-feb/mar-apr 77 : 5-136.

4483 WERNEKE, Diane; BROADFIELD, Robin. "Une politique de main-d'oeuvre orientée vers la satisfaction des besoins dans les pays avancés à économie de marché", *R. int. Trav.* 116(2), sep-oct 77 : 189-201.

4484 ŽELEZKO, S. N. "Opyt sociologičeskogo issledovanija formirovanija rabočej sily na Bajkal-Amurskoj magistrali" (An essay of sociological research on the labour force formation in the Baikal-Amour railway line), in: *Social'nye problemy migracii.* Moskva, 1976 : 84-94.

18220. Employment. Unemployment
Emploi. Chômage

[See also / Voir aussi: 3387, 3495, 3770, 3779, 4072, 4489, 4623, 4638]

4485 "Adéquation emploi-formation: les réflexions et les recherches dans le domaine de l'emploi et de la formation en Lorraine (L')", *Doss. Écon. lorraine* 21-22, jan-feb 77 : 85 p. *[France.]*

4486 ENGELEN-KEFER, Ursula. *Beschäftigungspolitik* (Full employment policy). Köln, Bund-Verlag, 76, 365 p.

4487 FONTANA, Maria Rosaria. "La disoccupazione intellettuale nella provincia di Frosinone" (Intellectual unemployment in the province of Frosinone), *Sociologia (Roma)* 11(1), jan-apr 77 : 141-178. *[Italy.]*

4488 GRUNBERG, K. S. "Le chômage intellectuel en Europe occidentale", *Int. R. Community Develop.* 35-36, 1976 : 253-274.

4489 KRAFELD, Franz Josef. "Auswirkungen der Jugendarbeitslosigkeit als Bedingungskomponenten politischer Bildungsarbeit" (Effects of youth work unemployment as a necessary component of political formation work), *Neue Praxis* 7(4), 1977 : 327-334.

4490 LASHUK, Maureen Wilson; KURIAN, George. "Employment status, feminism, and symptoms of stress: the case of a Canadian prairie city", *Canad. J. Sociol.* 2(2), 1977 : 195-204.

4491 LAUTERBACH, Albert. "Employment, unemployment and underemployment. A conceptual re-examination", *Amer. J. Econ. Sociol.* 36(3), jul 77 : 283-298.

4492 SARTIN, Pierrette. *Jeunes au travail, jeunes sans travail.* Paris, Les Éditions d'organisation, 77, 188 p. *[France.]*

4493 SKOLNIK, M. L.; SIDDIQUI, F. "The paradox of unemployment and job vacancies", *Relat. industr.* 31(1), 1976 : 32-55.

18230. Employment service. Job evaluation
Service d'emploi. Évaluation d'emploi

[See also / Voir aussi: 3650]

4494 LEVITAN, Sar; JOHNSON, Benjamin H. *The job corps: a social experiment that works.* Baltimore, Johns Hopkins Press, 76, viii-118 p. CR: Miriam JOHNSON, *Amer. J. Sociol.* 82(5), mar 77 : 1163-1165.

4495 SCHNEIDER, Benjamin. *Staffing organizations.* Pacific Palisades, Calif., Goodyear Publishing Co., 76, xiii-257 p.

18240. Woman worker. Young worker
Travailleur féminin. Jeune travailleur

[See also / Voir aussi: 182, 1314, 2440, 3164, 3185, 3313, 3320, 3950, 4287, 4293, 4319, 4473, 4666]

4496   AGA, Synnøva. *Kvinnene sin arbeidssituasjon på ein einsidig indus-tristad* (Women's working conditions in a town with one dominating industry). Oslo, Instituttet for sosiologi, Universitetet i Oslo, Norsk Institutt for by- og regionforskning, 76, v-237 p. *[Norway.]*

4497   Bibl.XXVI-3892. ANGRIST, Shirley S.; ALMQUIST, Elizabeth M. *Careers and contingencies: how college women juggle with gender.* CR: Bettina J. HUBER, *Contemp. Sociol. (Washington)* 6(4), jul 77 : 452-453.

4498   BIRCHALL, David; WILD, Ray. "Job characteristics and the attitudes of female manual workers: a research note", *Hum. Relat.* 30(4), apr 77 : 335-342.

4499   Bibl.XXVI-3897. BLAXALL, Martha; REAGAN, Barbara (eds.). *Women and the workplace: the implications of occupational segregation.* CR: Virginia OLESEN, *Contemp. Sociol. (Washington)* 6(3), mai 77 : 376-377.

4500   BRAITO, Rita; POWERS, Edward A. "What the other half thinks: the implications of female perceptions for work demands", *Sociol. Inquiry* 47(1), 1977 : 59-64.

4501   BRUINS, L. "Houdingen van Nederlandse werknemers ten opzichte van buitenlandse werknemers" (Attitudes of Dutch workers towards foreign workers), *Sociol. Gids* 24(5), sep-oct 77 : 332-351.

4502   CHAUDHURY, Rafiqul Huda. "Married women in non-agricultural occupations in a metropolitan urban area of Bangladesh – some issues and problems), *Bangladesh Develop. Stud.* 5(2), apr 77 : 152-200.

4503   CURTIS, Jean. *Working mothers.* New York, Simon and Schuster, 77, 214 p. *[USA.]*

4504   DURAND-DROUHIN, Marianne *et al. Femmes à l'usine et au bureau: enquête sociologique sur la condition des femmes travailleuses, ouvrières et employées.* Paris, CGT, 76, 323 p.

4505   FARKAS, George. "Cohort, age, and period effects upon the employment of white females: evidence for 1957-1968", *Demography* 14(1), feb 77 : 33-42.

4506   FERGE, Zsuzsa. "Nök a munkában" (Working women), *Látóhatár* (8), 1976 : 127-144; *Társad. Szle* (6), 1976 : 39-50.

4507   FIELDS, J. "A comparison of intercity differences in labor force participation rates of married women in 1970 with 1940, 1950 and 1960", *Hum. Resources* 11(4), 1976 : 568-577. *[USA.]*

4508   FINN, M.; JUSENIUS, C. "La posición de la mujer en la fuerza laboral de Ecuador" (Woman position in the labour force of Ecuador), *Estud. andin.* 5(1), 1976 : 99-117.

4509   FIRST-DILIC, Ruža. "Zena u socijalističkom razvoju poljoprivrede" (The woman in the socialist development of the agriculture), *Socijalizam* 20(7-8), jul-aug 77 : 1392-1405. *[Yugoslavia.]*

4510   FONG, Monica S. "Female labor force participation and fertility: some methodological and theoretical considerations", *Soc. Biology* 23(1), 1976 : 45-54.

4511   FOWLER, Bridget; LITTLEWOOD, Barbara; MADIGAN, Ruth. "Immigrant school leavers and the search for work", *Sociology (London)* 11(1), jan 77 : 65-85.

4512   FRITSCHNER, Linda Marie. "Women's work and women's education: the case of home economics, 1870-1920", *Sociol. Wk. Occupat.* 4(2), mai 77 : 209-234.

4513   GARCÍA FERRANDO, Manuel. *Mujer y sociedad rural; un análisis sociológico sobre trabaje i ideología* (Women and rural society: a sociological analysis about work and ideology). Madrid, Editorial Cuadernos para el Diálogo, 77, 263 p. *[Spain.]*

4514   GERMOTSIS, Wassilios. *Die ausländischen Arbeitnehmer in der Gesell-schaft der Bundesrepublik Deutschland: eine empirische-theoreti-sche Untersuchung* (The foreign workers in the West German socie-ty: an empirical-theoretical study). Bochum, Studienverlag Brock-meyer), 77, iv-233 p.

4515   GEURTS, Jan; TESSER, Paul. *Werkende jongeren en hun onderwijs: een studie naar de maatschappelijke situatie en de sociale kenmerken van werkende jongeren* (Young workers in their enterprise: a study on the social situation and social characteristics of young wor-kers). Nijmegen, Postbus 1144, Link, 76, 192 p. *[Netherlands.]*

4516   GIROD, Roger. "Les travailleurs étrangers en Suisse: ouverture et domination", *Année sociol.* 26, 1975 : 21-41.

4517   HARČEV, A. G.; ODINCOV, V. P. *Socialisticeskoe sorevnovanie i vos-pitanie molodyh rabocih* (Socialist competition and young workers' education). Moskva, Znanie, 77, 64 p.

4518   HERMAN, Karel. "Prispevek k stabilizaci mladých pracovniků v pod-niku" (Contribution to the stabilization of young workers in the enterprise), *Sociol. Cas.* 13(3), 1977 : 264-269.

4519   HOWE, Louise Kapp. *Pink collar workers: inside the world of women's work.* New York, Putnam, 77, 301 p.

4520   IPSEN, Detlev. "Aufenthaltsdauer und Integration ausländischer Ar-beiter" (Duration of residence and integration of foreign wor-kers), *Z. Soziol.* 6(4), oct 77 : 403-424.

4521   KOMAROV, Ê. G. *Aktivnost' molodogo pokolenija rabocego klassa* (Ac-tivity of the working class young generations). Krasnojarsk, Kniz-noe Izdatel'stvo, 76, 243 p.

4522   MIHAJLOV, Ê. M. *Inostrannaja rabocaja sila vo Francii. Êkonomices-kie, social'nye i politiceskie aspekty problemy* (Foreign labour force in France. Economic, social and political aspects of the problem). Moskva, Nauka, 77, 151 p.

4523   MUELLER, Charles W.; CAMPBELL, Blair G. "Female occupational achieve-ment and marital status: a research note", *J. Marriage Family* 39(3), aug 77 : 587-593.

4524   MULCAHY, Susan DiGiacomo; FAULKNER, Robert R. "Work individuation among women machine operators", *Sociol. Wk Occupat.* 4(3), aug 77 : 303-326.

4525   OPOLSKI, Krysztof; WŁODARSKI, Włodzimierz. "Niektóre społeczne prob-lemy wykorzystania kwalifikacji zawodowych młodych pracowników przemysłu" (Some social problems involved in young industrial workers acquiring vocational skills), *Stud. socjol.* 60(1), 1976 : 157-169.

4526   OPPENHEIMER, Valerie Kincade. "The sociology of women's economic role in the family", *Amer. sociol. R.* 43(3), jun 77 : 387-406.

4527   PICO DE HERNANDEZ, Isabel. "Estudio sobre el empleo de la mujer en Puerto Rico" (Study on woman employment in Puerto Rico), *R. Cienc. soc. (Puerto Rico)* 19(2), jun 75 : 141-166.

4528   PISELLI, Fortunata. *La donna che lavora: la condizione femminile fra arretratezza e società industriale* (The woman worker: the woman's backward condition and industrial society). Bari, De Do-nato, 76, 396 p.

4529   Bibl.XXVI-3937. SACKS, Michael Paul. *Women's work in Soviet Russia' continuity in the midst of change.* CR: Marilyn Power GOLDBERG, *Contemp. Sociol. (Washington)* 6(3), mai 77 : 378.

4530   SETHI, Raj Mohini. *Modernization of working women in developing so-cieties.* New Delhi, National Publishing House, 76, vi-168 p.

4531   SPENCER, Dunstan S. C. *African women in agricultural development: a case study in Sierra Leone.* East Lansing, Department of Agri-cultural Economics, Michigan State University, 76, 36 p.

4532   STOLZENBERG, Ross M.; WAITE, Linda J. "Age, fertility expectations and plans for employment", *Amer. sociol. R.* 42(5), oct 77 : 769-783.

4533   STRANDELL, Harriet. "Kvalifikationsstruktur och kvinnlig arbets-
kraft i Finlands industri" (Qualification structure and the female labor force in the industry of Finland), *Sociologia* 15(3-4),
1977 : 134-144.

4534   VAJDA, Ágnes. "A nök beilleszkedése a foglalkozási strukturában,
1949-1970" (Insertion of women in the employment structure,
1949-1970), *Statiszt. Szle* 54(7), jul 76 : 672-688.

4535   WADHERA, Kiron. *The new bread winners: a study on the situation of
young working women*. New Delhi, Vishwa Yuvak Kendra, 76, xi-377 p.

18300. PERSONNEL MANAGEMENT. WORKING CONDITIONS
ADMINISTRATION DU PERSONNEL. CONDITIONS DE TRAVAIL

18310. Labour standard. Work study
Norme de travail. Étude du travail

18311.

4536   CUMMINGS, Thomas G.; MOLLOY, Edmond; GLEN, Roy. "A methodological
critique of fifty-eight selected work experiments", *Hum. Relat.*
30(8), aug 77 : 675-708.

4537   DUBIN, Robert (ed.). *Handbook of work, organization and society*.
Chicago, Rand McNally, 76, xi-1068 p. CR: Melvin SEEMAN, *Amer.
J. Sociol.* 82(5), mar 77 : 1127-1130.

4538   "Ergonomía. Una nueva organización de la producción y de la empresa" (Ergonomics. A new organization of production and enterprise),
Bol. Estud. econ. 31(98), aug 76 : 331-516.

4539   GAZDAG, Miklós; SZAKASITS, D. György. "Az ergonómia helyzete Magyarországon" (Ergonomics in Hungary), *Magyar pszichol. Szle*
33(6), 1976 : 585-592.

18312.

[See also / Voir aussi: 1023]

4540   BISANI, Fritz. *Das Personalwesen in der Bundesrepublik Deutschland*
(Personnel management in the German Federal Republic). Köln,
Hanstein, 76, 189 p.

4541   BISANI, Fritz. *Personalwesen: Grundlagen, Organisation, Planung*
(Personnel management: bases, organization, planning). Opladen,
Westdeutscher Verlag, 76, 159 p.

4542   BOTHE, Bernd; SIMON, Harald. *Personalmanagement* (Personnel management). München, Verlag Moderne Industrie, 76, 286 p.

4543   DACHRODT, Heinz-G. *Management und Menschenführung* (Management and
personnel management). Köln, Bund-Verlag, 76, 176 p.

4544   DREYFACK, Raymond. *Sure fail: the art of mismanagement*. New York,
Morrow, 76, 156 p.

4545   HACKMAN, J. Richard; SUTTLE, J. Lloyd (eds.). *Improving life at
work: behavioral science approaches to organizational change*.
Santa Monica, Calif., Goodyear Publishing Co., 77, 494 p.

4546   JANGER, Allen R. *The personnel function: changing objectives and
organization*. New York, Conference Board, 77, ix-133 p. [USA.]

4547   LUZZATTO, Patrizia. "Sul problema dell'organizzazione del lavoro"
(On the problems of labour organization), *R. Inst. Sociol. (Roma)*
12(3), 1976 : 217-241.

4548   PODOROV, G. M. "Opyt sociologičeskih issledovanij trudovoj discipliny na predprijatijah Gor'kovskoj oblasti" (An essay of sociological research on the labour discipline in the Gorki region
enterprises), *Sociol. Issled. (Moskva)* (4), 1976 : 72-78.

4549   "Produktivnost rada" (Labour productivity), *Socijalizam* 20(2), feb
77 : 187-325. [Yugoslavia.]

4550   SUDAKOV, V. N.; LJASNIKOV, N. V. "Social'no-psihologičeskij klimat
kak faktor razvitija socialisticeskoj discipliny truda" (Socio-
psychological climate as a factor of development of the socialist
discipline of labour), in: *Proizvodstvennyj kollektiv i discipli-*

na truda. Omsk, 1976 : 92-111.

4551 TELFORD, Fred. *The principles of public personnel administration*. Newark, University of Delaware, 76, xiv-122 p.

4552 WEXLEY, Kenneth N.; YUKL, Gary A. *Organizational behavior and personnel psychology*. Homewood, Ill., R. D. Irwin, 77, xiv-375 p.

4553 WHATLEY, Arthur A.; KELLEY, Nelson Lane. *Personnel management in action: skill building experiences*. St. Paul, West Publishing Co., 77, xii-305 p.

4554

18320. Working conditions
Conditions de travail

18321.

[See also / Voir aussi: 3062, 4496, 4504, 4524]

4554 BOISVERT, Maurice Philippe. "The quality of working life: an analysis", *Hum. Relat.* 30(2), feb 77 : 155-160.

4555 CARPENTIER, J.; CAZAMIAN, P. *Night work. Its effects on the health and welfare of the worker*. Geneva, ILO, 77, x-82 p.

4556 "Condizioni di lavoro in Cina (Le)" (Working conditions in China), *A. Sociol. (Milano)* 13, 1976 : 16-25.

4557 CORRIGAN, Philip. "Feudal relics or capitalist monuments ? Notes on the sociology of urban labour", *Sociology (London)* 11(3), sep 77 : 435-463.

4558 Bibl.XXVI-3963. DAVIS, Louis E.; CHERNS, Albert B. (eds.). *The quality of working life*. CR: Craig C. LUNDBERG, *Contemp. Sociol. (Washington)* 6(1), jan 77 : 55-57.

4559 FRICKE, Else; FRICKE, Werner. "Industriesoziologie und Humanisierung der Arbeit. Über die Möglichkeiten und Schwiereigkeiten industriesoziologischer Forschung, einen Beitrag zur autonomie-orientierten Gestaltung von Arbeitssystemen zu leisten" (Industrial sociology and humanization of work. Possibilities and difficulties of industrial-sociological research, a contribution to the making o of self-managed working systems), *Soz. Welt* 28(1-2), 1977 : 91-108.

4560 GOTTSCHALCH, Holm. "Humanisierte Arbeit ?" (Humanization of work ?), *Blätt. dtsche int. Polit.* 22(7), jul 77 : 841-854; 22(8), aug 77 : 998-1014.

4561 KAMAGAEV, V. K. "Uslovija truda i social'naja aktivnost' proizvodstvennogo kollektiva" (Labour conditions and social activity of a production collectivity), in: *Social'nye posledstvija mehanizacii i avtomatizacii proizvodstva*. Ufa, 1976 : 129-133.

4562 Bibl.XXVI-3967. KLEIN, Lisl. *New forms of work organization*. CR: Paul GOLDMAN, *Contemp. Sociol. (Washington)* 6(2), mar 77 : 199-200.

4563 LEFEVRE, Claude; ROLLOY, Gerard. *L'amélioration des conditions de travail dans les emplois administratifs*. Paris, Chotard, 76, 260 p.

4564 LØKEN, Bjarne; RAMBERG, Ingrid Greger; ROALDSNES, Jostein. *Vårt arbeidsmiljø* (Work environment). Oslo, NKS forl., 75, 220 p.

4565 PERLAKI, Ivan. "Metodika zlepšovania vzt'ahov medzi pracovnými kolektívmi" (Methodology of improving relations among working teams), *Sociol. Čas.* 13(3), 1977 : 252-263.

4566 RUDAKOV, B. F. "Čelovek kak sub'ekt proizvodstvennyh otnošenij" (Man as a subject of production relations), in: *Voprosy sociologii ličnosti*. Rjazan', 1976 : 29-41.

4567 SUSLOV, V. Ja. "Izmenenie soderžanija i haraktera truda v uslovijah naučno-tehničeskoj revoljucii" (Change of the labour content and characteristics under conditions of the scientific and technical revolution), in: *Naučno-tehničeskaja revoljucija i sovershenstvovanie socialističeskih obščestvennyh otnošenij*. Leningrad, 1976 : 68-88.

18322.

[See also / Voir aussi: 668, 671, 672, 4852]

4568   BEYAERT, A. "La durée du travail et des loisirs en Belgique", *C. écon.* Bruxelles 72, 4 trim 76 : 563-598.

4569   BRESSON, Yoland. *Le capital-temps: pouvoir, répartition et inégalités.* Paris, Calmann-Lévy, 77, 218 p.

4570   BROSSOLLET, Marc; LOUVET, Marc-Noël. *Le statut français du travail temporaire.* Paris, J. Delmas, 77, 271 p.

4571   CSEH-SZOMBATY, László; SURÁNYI, Bálint. "Some comments regarding the interrelation of time budget, the use of time and the personality", *Soc. and Leisure* 8(3), 1976 : 119-126.

4572   ELLIOTT, D. H.; HARVEY, A. S.; PROCOS, D. "An overview of the Halifax time-budget study", *Soc. and Leisure* 8(3), 1976 : 145-159.

4573   FELDHEIM, Pierre. "Essai sur la problématique de la fixation des heures d'ouverture des entreprises commerciales et artisanales et l'étude des budget-temps ou comment utiliser la recherche sociale appliquée pour la prise de décisions politiques", *Soc. and Leisure* 8(3), 1976 : 161-173.

4574   GORDON, L. A.; KLOPOV, È. V. "Racional'nyj bjudžet vremeni: podhod k probleme i opyt nacal'nogo rasceta" (A rational time-budget: approach of the problem and essay of first evaluation), *Sociol. Issled. (Moskva)* (1), 1977 : 19-30.

4575   JAVEAU, Claude. "Note sur une recherche de budgets-temps", *Soc. and Leisure* 8(3), 1976 : 175-180.

4576   ROBINSON, John P. *How Americans use time: a social-psychological analysis of everyday behavior.* New York, Praeger, 77, xii-209 p.

4577   ZBARSKIJ, M. I. *Social'no-èkonomičeskie problemy rabočego dnja pri socializme* (Socio-economic problems of the labour day under socialism). Moskva, Mysl', 76, 222 p.

18323.

[See also / Voir aussi: 1019, 3312, 4605]

4578   ANTHONY, P. D. *The ideology of work.* London, Tavistock, 77, viii-340 p.

4579   BRIEF, Arthur P.; ALDAG, Ramon J. "Work values as moderators of perceived leader behavior-satisfaction relationships", *Sociol. Wk Occupat.* 4(1), feb 77 : 99-112.

4580   DICKSON, John W. "The relation of individual search activity to subjective job characteristics", *Hum. Relat.* 29(10), oct 76 : 911-928.

4581   GARDELL, Bertil. "Reactions at work and their influence on nonwork activities: an analysis of a sociopolitical problem in affluent societies", *Hum. Relat.* 29(9), sep 76 : 885-904.

4582   IVANOV, Ju. K.; PATRUŠEV, V. D. "Vlijanie uslovij truda na udovletvorennost' trudom rabotnikov sel'skogo hozjajstva" (Influence of labour conditions on workers' satisfaction in an agricultural enterprise), *Sociol. Issled. (Moskva)* (3), 1976 : 60-70.

4583   KALLEBERG, Arne L. "Work values and job rewards: a theory of job satisfaction", *Amer. sociol. R.* 42(1), feb 77 : 124-143.

4584   KATZ, Ralph; VAN MAANEN, John. "The loci of work satisfaction: job, interaction, and policy", *Hum. Relat.* 30(5), mai 77 : 469-486.

4585   KERRINKSON, J. H. "Job satisfaction and work improvement: a modern dilemma", *New Zealand J. publ. Adm.* 39(1), mar 77 : 13-19.

4586   MAKREŁOW, Konstantin. "Socjometryczne aspekty atmosfery społecznej w środowisku pracy" (Sociometric aspects of social atmosphere at work), *Stud. socjol.* 65(2), 1977 : 167-184.

4587   MORAWSKI, Bronosław. "Czynniki warunkujące postawy wobec pracy. W świetle wybranych badań" (The factors conditioning attitudes towards work in the light of selected researches), *Stud. socjol.* 64(1), 1977 : 185-206.

4588   OLDHAM, Greg R. "Job characteristics and internal motivation: the moderating effect of interpersonal and individual variables", *Hum. Relat.* 29(6), jun 76 : 559-569.

4589   POPLUCZ, Jan. "Oczekiwania zawodowe pracujących" (Professional expectations of the employed), *Stud. socjol.* 65(2), 1977 : 77-105. [Poland.]

4590   RAINVILLE, Jean-Marie. "Effets comparés de la cadence et de l'enrichissement du travail sur la satisfaction des ouvriers dans leur travail", *Trav. et Soc.* 2(3), jul 77 : 315-326.

4591   ROUSTANG, Guy. "Enquêtes sur la satisfaction au travail ou analyse directe des conditions de travail ?", *R. int. Trav.* 1115(3), mai-jun 77 : 295-310.

4592   SCHAEFER, Susan Davidson. *The motivation process*. Cambridge, Mass., Winthrop Publishers, 77, xvi-189 p.

4593   SPAETH, Joe L. "Differences in the occupational achievement process between male and female college graduates", *Sociol. Educ.* 50(3), jul 77 : 206-217.

4594   WEIR, Mary (ed.). *Job satisfaction: challenge and response in modern Britain*. Glasgow, Fontana/Collins, 76, 288 p.

4595   WNUK-LIPINSKI, E. "La satisfaction au travail et la qualité de la vie professionnelle: l'expérience polonaise", *R. int. Trav.* 115(1), jan-feb 77 : 57-69.

18324.

[See also / Voir aussi: 4667]

4596   JENEI, György. "Az üzemi demokrácia fejlödésének tapasztalataiból" (Experiences from the development of democracy in factories), *Társadtud. Közl.* (3), 1976 : 62-69.

4597   LAKI, L. "A munkahelyi beilleszkedés kutatásáról" (On the research of adjustment at the place of work), *Társadtud. Közl.* (4), 1977 : 63-73.

4598   MAKÓ, Csaba. "Az érdekegyeztetés és a cselekvési egység az üzemben" (Conciliation of interests and the unity of action in the factory), *Társad. Szle* (7-8), 1977 : 58-67.

4599   SIMONYI, Ágnes. "Az üzemi demokrácia a munkások oldaláról nézve. Egy kezdeményezés és tapasztalatai a Budapesti Vegyi Müvekben" (Democracy in the factory from the workers' point of view. A test and its experiences in the Chemical Factory of Budapest), *Társad. Szle* (7), 1976 : 56-65.

18330, Labour turnover
Renouvellement de la main-d'oeuvre

4600   Bibl.XXVI-4000. ATCHLEY, Robert C. *The sociology of retirement*. CR: Sarah MATTHEWS, *Contemp. Sociol. (Washington)* 6(1), jan 77 : 109-110.

4601   BÉRAUD, Jean-Marc. "La mise à pied économique", *A. Univ. Jean Moulin* 13, 1975 : 9-35.

4602   DUBOIS, Pierre. "L'absentéisme ouvrier dans l'industrie", *R. franç. Aff. soc.* 31(2), apr-jun 77 : 15-37. [France.]

4603   FULLER, Robert L.; REDRERING, David L. "Effects of preretirement planning on the retirement adjustment of military personnel", *Sociol. Wk Occupat.* 3(4), nov 76 : 479-488.

4604   HEINTZ, Katherine McMillan. *Retirement communities, for adults only*. New Brunswick, N.J., Center for Urban Policy Research, Rutgers University, 76, xx-239 p. [USA.]

4605   NICHOLSON, Nigel *et al.* "The predictability of absence and propensity to leave from employees: job satisfaction and attitudes toward influence in decision making", *Hum. Relat.* 30(6), jun 77 : 499-514.

4606   SOMOGYI, Miklós. "A fizikai dolgozók munkaidejének kihasználása" (Utilization of manual workers' working time), *Statiszt. Szle*

55(8-9), aug-sep 77 : 864-880. *[Absenteeism in Hungary.]*

18400. OCCUPATION. VOCATIONAL TRAINING
PROFESSION. FORMATION PROFESSIONNELLE

18410. Occupational sociology
Sociologie de la profession

[See also / Voir aussi: 1142, 2340, 2669, 3289, 4194]

4607 BÉLAND, François. "Du paradoxe professionnel: médecins et ingénieurs des années 1800", *Archiv. europ. Sociol.* 17(2), 1976 : 306-330.

4608 COLASANTO, Michele. "Processi di professionalizzazione e condizione di lavoro dipendente. Indicazioni e problemi per un approccio empirico" (Processus of professionalization and dependent labour conditions. Indications and problems for an empirical approach), *Studi Sociol.* 14(4), oct-dec 76 : 338-358.

4609 GALLAGHER, Bernard J.; PALAZZOLO, Charles S. (eds.). *The social world of occupations.* Dubuque, Iowa; Kendall/Hunt Publishing Co., 77, vii-305 p.

4610 GOLDBERG, Albert I. "The relevance of cosmopolitan/local orientations to professional values and behavior", *Sociol. Wk Occupat.* 3(3), aug 76 : 331-356.

4611 HEARN, Jeff. "Toward a concept of non-career", *Sociol. R.* 25(2), mai 77 : 273-288.

4612 MONTIRONI, Marina; MANCINI, Paolo. "Metodologia della ricerca: intervento e analisi della professionalità" (Research methodology: intervention and analysis of the profession), *Riv. Sociol.* 14(1-3), jan-dec 76 : 239-268.

4613 PAMPEL, Fred C.; LAND, Kenneth C.; FELSON, Marucs. "A social indicator model of changes in the occupational structure of the United States: 1947-1974", *Amer. sociol. R.* 42(6), dec 77 : 951-964.

4614 PINEO, Peter C. *et al.* "The 1971 census and the socioeconomic classification of occupations", *Canad. R. Sociol. Anthropol.* 14(1), feb 77 : 91-102. *[Canada.]*

4615 TOUSIJN, Willem. "Verso un analisi di classe delle professioni" (Towards a class-based analysis of occupations), *Rass. ital. Sociol.* 18(3), jul-sep 77 : 393-414. *[Italy.]*

4616 WOESLER, Christine. "Opposition between professionalization and political practice in West German sociology", *Soc. Sci. Inform.* 15(4-5), 1976 : 663-687.

18420. Occupational life. Vocational guidance
Vie professionnelle. Orientation professionnelle

[See also / Voir aussi: 823, 1035, 2358, 2728, 3442, 3646, 3939, 4289, 4309, 4485]

4617 "Általános iskolát végzett fiatalok pályaválasztásának és továbbtanulásának tendenciái néhány megyében (Az)" (The tendencies in the occupational choice and continued training of young graduates of secondary school in some provinces), *Területi Statiszt.* 26(5), 1976 : 565-571. *[Hungary.]*

4618 ANDORKA, Rudolf. *The influence of historical factors in inter- and intragenerational mobility in Hungary, 1939-1973. An attempt to analyze occupational life histories.* Budapest, Statisztikai Kiadó, 77, 21 p.

4619 BIAŁECKI, Ireneusz. "Wyksztatcenie a wybór zawodu" (Vocational training and occupational choice), *Kult. i Społecz.* 20(4), oct-dec 76 : 191-204. *[Poland.]*

4620 BODE, Herbert F. *Arbeit und Qualifikation: Studien zum Verhältnis von Arbeitzplatz- und Qualifikationsstruktur unter besonderer Berücksightigung der aktuellen Entwicklung in den USA* (Work and qualification: studies of the relationship between the structure of working places and that of qualifications considering espe-

cially the actual developments in the USA). Marburg, Marburger
Forschungsstelle für Vergleichende Erziehungswissenschaft, 77,
xi–403 p. multigr.

4621 BRINKERHOFF, Merlin B.; CORRY, David J. "Structural prisons: barriers to occupational and educational goals in a society of
'equal' opportunity", *Int. J. comp. Sociol.* 17(3-4), sep-dec
76 : 261-274.

4622 CALOGERO LA MALFA, Luisa. *La formazione professionale: problemi e
prospettive in Italia* (Vocational training: problems and prospects in Italy). Milano, F. Angeli, 76, 181 p.

4623 CHORDECKI, A. "Zróżnicowanie społeczno-zawodowe a płynność zatrud-
nienie w przedsiębiorstwie przemysłowym" (Socio-professional
differentiation and unstability of employment in an industrial
enterprise), *Biul. IGS* 20(3), 1977 : 126-153.

4624 CRAWFORD, Scott A. G. M. "Occupational prestige rankings and the
New Zealand Olympic athlete", *Int. R. Sport Sociol.* 12(1), 1977 :
5-16.

4625 DUDLEY, Gordon A. *et al. Career development: exploration and commitment.* Muncie, Ind., Accelerated Development, 77, xii-404 p.

4626 FORCESE, Dennis; BRIES, John DE. "Occupational and electoral
success in Canada: the 1974 federal election", *Canad. R. Sociol.
Anthropol.* 14(3), aug 77 : 331-340.

4627 "Formation au travail et travail de formation", *R. Inst. Sociol.*
(3), 1976 : 201-370.

4628 GARELLI, Franco. "Sistema delle garanzie e doppia occupazione"
(System of guarantee and double occupation), *Quad. Sociol.* 25(4),
oct-dec 76 : 392-408. [Italy.]

4629 GILLI, Angelo C. *Modern organizations of vocational education.*
University Park, Pennsylvania State University Press, 76, xiii-
302 p.

4630 GOODALE, J. G.; HALL, D. T. "Inheriting a career: the influence of
sex, values and parents", *J. vocat. Behav.* 8(1), feb 76 : 19-30.
[USA.]

4631 GOYDER, John C.; CURTIS, James E. "Occupational mobility in Canada
over four generations", *Canad. R. Sociol. Anthropol.* 14(3), aug
77 : 303-319.

4632 GUPPY, L. N.; SILTANEN, J. L. "A comparison of the allocation of
male and female occupational prestige", *Canad. R. Sociol. Anthropol.* 14(3), aug 77 : 320-330.

4633 GUPTA, Y. P. "The educational and vocational aspirations of Asian
immigrant and English school leavers: a comparative study", *Brit.
J. Sociol.* 28(2), jun 77 : 185-198.

4634 HONORÉ, Bernard. *Pour une théorie de la formation: dynamique de la
formativité.* Paris, Payot, 77, 252 p.

4635 HORAN, Patrick. "Structure and change in occupational mobility: a
Markov approach", *Quality and Quantity* 10(4), dec 76 : 321-340.

4636 HUNTER, A. A. "A comparative analysis of Anglophone-Francophone
occupational prestige structures in Canada", *Canad. J. Sociol.*
2(2), 1977 : 179-193.

4637 JARDILLIER, Pierre; LUPE, Michel-Claude. *De la qualification du travail à l'évaluation des fonctions.* Paris, Entreprise moderne d'é-
dition, 76, xv-220 p.

4638 JARLOV, Carsten; TOGEBY, Lise. "Arbejdsløshed og uddannelsesløshed
blandt unge. Et socialt problem" (Unemployment and lack of vocational training among young people. A social problem), *Soc.
Tss.* 52(6-7), 1976 : 167-203.

4639 JUSZIG, Renate; WILHELM, Klaus. *Vocational education in the German
Democratic Republic.* Mainz, von Hase und Koehler, 76, 107 p.

4640 LANE, Angela Victoria. "Migration and the processes of occupational
mobility and status attainment", *Sociol. Focus* 10(1), jan 77 :
43-52.

4641   LORBER, Judith; SATOW, Roberta. "Creating a company of unequals: sources of occupational stratification in a ghetto community mental health center", *Sociol. Wk Occupat.* 4(3), aug 77 : 281-302.

4642   MARAFFI, Marco. "La plurioccupazione negli USA. Analisi della letteratura sull'argomento" (Multiple occupation in the USA. A topical analysis of the literature), *Quad. Sociol.* 26(3-4), jul-dec 77 : 232-259.

4643   MARTINEAU, William H.; MacQUEEN, Rhonda Sayres. "Occupational differenciation among the Old Order Amish", *Rur. Sociol.* 42(3), 1977 : 383-397. *[USA.]*

4644   MAYER, Nonna. "Une filière de la mobilité ouvrière: l'accès à la petite entreprise artisanale et commerciale", *R. franç. Sociol.* 18(1), jan-mar 77 : 25-45.

4645   MEDVENE, A.; COLLINS, A. "Occupational prestige and appropriateness: the views of mental health specialists", *J. vocat. Behav.* 9(1), aug 76 : 63-71.

4646   MITCHELL, Eugene F. *Cooperative vocational education: principles, methods, and problems.* Boston, Allyn and Bacon, 77, 398 p.

4647   MORACCO, J. C. "Vocational maturity of Arab and American high school students", *J. vocat. Behav.* 8(3), jun 76 : 367-373.

4648   MORE, Douglas L.; SUCHNER, Robert W. "Occupational situs, prestige, and stereotypes", *Sociol. Wk Occupat.* 3(2), mai 76 : 151-168.

4649   NYSTROM, Dennis C.; BAYNE, G. Keith; McCLELLAN, L. Dean. *Instructional methods in occupational education.* Indianapolis, Bobbs-Merrill, 77, x-267 p.

4650   OLUIGBO NATHAN OSUJI. "Patterns of occupational choice and aspiration in conditions of economic and technological underdevelopment", *J. vocat. Behav.* 8(2), apr 76 : 133-44. *[Nigeria.]*

4651   O'RAND, Angela M. "Professional standing and peer consultation status among biological scientists at a summer research laboratory", *Soc. Forces* 55(4), jun 77 : 921-937.

4652   PAYNE, Geoff. "Occupational transition in advanced industrial societies", *Sociol. R.* 25(1), feb 77 : 5-39.

4653   PERRUCCI, Carolyn Cummings. "University and work organization influences on professional role orientation", *Sociol. Focus* 10(3), aug 77 : 237-247.

4654   PIPPKE, Wolfgang; WOLFMEYER, Peter. *Die berufliche Mobilität von Führungskräften in Wirtschaft und Verwaltung* (The professional mobility of executive officers in economy and administration). Baden-Baden, Nomos Verlagsgesellschaft, 76, 224 p.

4655   POHOSKI, Michał; SŁOMCZYŃSKI, Kazimierz M.; WESOŁOWSKI, Włodzimierz. "Occupational prestige in Poland, 1958-1975", *Polish sociol. B.* 36(4), 1976 : 63-77.

4656   "Probleme der beruflichen Bildung" (Problems of vocational training) *Mater. polit. Bildung* (4), 1976 : 5-37. *[Germany FR.]*

4657   Bibl.XXVI-4019. PULLUM, Thomas W. *Measuring occupational inheritance.* CR: P. H. TRESS, *Contemp. Sociol. (Washington)* 6(1), jan 77 : 42-43.

4658   "Riforma della formazione professionale (La)" (The reform of vocational training), *Quad. Azione soc.* (11-12), nov-dec 76 : 3-218. *[Italy.]*

4659   SAPELLI, Giulio. "Formazione della forza-lavoro e psicotecnica nell'Italia fra la due guerre mondiali" (Vocational training and psychotechnics in Italy after the second world war), *Quad. Sociol* 26(1), jan-mar 77 : 5-27.

4660   STOLZENBERG, Ross M.; D'AMICO, Ronald J. "City differences and non-differences in the effect of race and sex on occupational distribution", *Amer. sociol. R.* 42(6), dec 77 : 937-950.

4661   TECKENBERG, W. "Prestigerangordnungen, berufliche Bewertungen und Präferenzen in der UdSSR im internationalen Vergleich" (Prestige hierarchy, occupational evaluation and preferences in the USSR in international comparison), *Kölner Z. Soziol. u. soz.-Psychol.* 29(4), dec 77 : 731-761.

4662   TINTO, Vincent. "Perceptions of occupational structure and career aspirations among the future Turkish elite", *Int. J. Mid. East Stud.* 8(3), jul 77 : 329-338.

4663   VILLEMEZ, Wayne J.; SILVER, Burton B. "Occupational situs as horizontal social position: a reconsideration", *Sociol. soc. Res.* 61(3), apr 77 : 320-336.

4664   VUILLEMEZ, W. J. "Occupational prestige and the normative hierarchy: a reconsideration", *Pacific sociol. R.* 20(3), 1977 : 455-472.

4665   WILLIAMS, Gregory. "Trends in occupational differentiation by sex", *Sociol. Wk Occupat.* 3(1), feb 76 : 38-62.

4666   YONEZAWA, Kasuhiko. "Jakunen rôdôryoku no ryûshutsu to bunko no secchi" (A study of the young worker's mobility), *Kyûdai Shakaigaku Kenkyû Nenpô* (7-8), 1977 : 50-62.

18500. EMPLOYEE. TECHNICIAN. WORKER
EMPLOYÉ. TECHNICIEN. TRAVAILLEUR

18510. Worker
Travailleur

[See also / Voir aussi: 631, 1388, 2038, 2672, 4376, 5249]

4667   ANDORS, Stephen (ed.). *Workers and workplaces in revolutionary China.* White Plains, N.Y., M. E. Sharpe, 77, xxxiii-403 p.

4668   BONNET, Serge. *L'homme du fer. Mineurs de fer et ouvriers sidérurgiques lorrains, 1889-1930.* Nancy, Centre lorrain d'études sociologiques, 76, 303 p. CR: François-A. ISAMBERT, *R. franç. Sociol.* 17(4), oct-dec 76 : 685-688.

4669   CATTANEO, Angela. "Sul lavoro domestico" (On domestic labour), *Crit. sociol. (Roma)* 37, 1976 : 120-127.

4670   FUJITA, Eishi. "Gendai ni okeru rôdôsha seikatsu no henka" (Changes in the worker's life today), *Soshioroji* 22(1), 1977 : 81-98.

4671   GÁL, R. *Az ipari szakmunkássá válás néhány társadalmi és pedagógiai összefüggése* (Some social and educational relations of the process of transformation into skilled workers). Budapest, MSZMP KB Társadtud. Intézet, 77, 121 p.

4672   HÉTHY, Lajos; MAKÓ, Csaba. "A technikai haladás hatása az ipari munkásokra" (Effect of technical development on industrial workers), *Társadtud. Közl.* (4), 1977 : 3-27.

4673   HOLMSTRÖM, Mark. *South Indian factory workers: their life and their world.* Cambridge, Eng.-New York, Cambridge University Press, 76, x-158 p.

4674   JEAN, Bruno. "Un ouvrier du textile", *Rech. sociogr.* 17(1), jan-apr 76 : 73-114.

4675   LADÁNYI, J. "Községekben élö munkások" (Workers in villages), *Szociológia* 6(1), 1977 : 28-41.

4676   MATEJKO, Alexander J. "The Polish blue collar workers", *Mens en Onderneming* 31(5), sep-oct 77 : 295-313.

4677   MJALKIN, A. V. *Social'nyj portret sovetskogo rabočego. Osnovnye čerty. Process formirovanija* (Social portrait of the Soviet worker. Essential characteristics. Process of formation). Moskva, Profizdat, 77, 135 p.

4678   PAVLENOK, P. D. "Preodolenie suščestvennyh različij meždu rabotnikam umstvennogo i fizičeskogo truda – zakonomernost' razvitija socializma i stroitel'stva kommunizma" (The elimination of existing differences between intellectual and physical workers is a law of the socialism development), *Nauč. Kommunizm* (1), 1977 : 30-39.

4679   REGT, A. J. DE. "Arbeiderssubcultuur in Engeland en Nederland: een vergelijking" (Workers' subculture in England and the Netherlands; a comparison), *Sociol. Gids* 24(5), sep-oct 77 : 310-331.

4680   RIEMER, Jeffrey W. "Becoming a journeyman electrician: some implicit indicators in the apprenticeship process", *Sociol. Wk Occupat.* 4(1), feb 77 : 87-98.

4681   SERFŐZŐ, Simon. "Munkásmüvelődés a nagyüzemekben" (Workers' culture in big factories), *Borsodi Szle* (4), 1976 : 41-46.

4682   SMIRNOV, V. A.; BOJKOV, V. É. "Opyt postroenija tipologii rabočih na osnove sovmeščenija ob'ektivnyh i sub'ektivnyh pokazatelej ih trudovoj aktivnosti" (A tentative typology of workers on the basis of objective and subjective factors of activity), *Sociol. Issled. (Moskva)* (1), 1977 : 31-39.

4683   VAN STIPHOUT, H. A. "Werkers en niet-werkers in de samenleving" (Workers and non-workers in society), *Beleid en Mij* 3(12), dec 76 : 306-318.

4684   YAZAWA, Shujiro. "Rodosha ishiki kenkyu no gendankai" (The present stage of the study of worker's consciousness), *Tsudajuku-daigaku Kiyô* (9), 1977 : 157-171.

4685   ŽELEZKO, S. N. "Stroiteli Bajkalo-Amurskoj magistrale - ob'ekt sociologičeskogo issledovanija" (The builders of the Baikal-Amour road as an object of sociological research), *Sociol. Issled. (Moskva)* (3), 1976 : 99-106.

4686   ŽUKOVA, N. B. "Ličnost' rabočego v uslovijah razvitogo socialističeskogo obščestva" (The personality of the worker in the developed socialist society), *Vopr. Ist.* 51(9), sep 77 : 3-16.

4687   ZUPANČIČ, Beno. *Workers and culture.* Beograd, Komunista, 76, 175 p.

18520. Employee
Employé

[See also / Voir aussi: 2728]

4688   DEYO, F. C. "Ethnicity and work culture in Thailand: a comparison of Thailand and Thai-Chinese white-collar workers", *J. Asian Stud.* 34(4), aug 75 : 995-1015.

4689   DITTON, Jason. "Alibis and aliases: some notes on the 'motives' of fidding bread salesmen", *Sociology (London)* 11(2), mai 77 : 233-255.

4690   ELLIOTT, R. F. "The growth of white-collar employment in Great Britain, 1951 to 1971", *Brit. J. industr. Relat.* 15(1), mar 77 : 39-44.

4691   HARARI, Ehud; ZEIRA, Yoram. "Attitudes of Japanese and non-Japanese employees: a cross-national comparison in uninational and multinational corporations", *Int. J. comp. Sociol.* 18(3-4), sep-dec 77 : 228-241.

4692   Bibl.XXVI-4085. WHEELER, Christopher, *White-collar power: changing patterns of interest group behavior in Sweden.* CR: Nils ELVANDER, *Amer. J. Sociol.* 82(5), mar 77 : 1144-1146.

18530. Manager. Technician
Cadre. Technicien

[See also / Voir aussi: 4607]

4693   ANDRLE, Vladimir. *Managerial power in the Soviet Union,* Farnborough, Hants, Saxon House; Lexington, Mass., Lexington Books, 76, xi-176 p.

4694   CUNEO, Carl J. "The controlled entry of Canadian managers to the United States", *Int. J. comp. Sociol.* 18(1-2), mar-jun 77 : 81-101.

4695   Bibl.XXVI-4068. DUNKERLY, David. *The foreman: aspects of task and structure.* CR: Richard K. BROWN, *Contemp. Sociol. (Washington)* 6(4), jul 77 : 454-455.

4696   GRAU, Gerhard. "Die 'besondere' Verantwortung des Technikers für die Gesellschaft" (The technician's "particular" responsibility for the society), *Communications (Köln)* 2(3), 1976 : 349-366.

4697   HERMAN, Jacques; BRUYNE, Paul DE. "Managers, organisations, idéologies", *A. Sci. écon. appl.* 33(4), 1976-1977 : 33-107.

4698   IZRAELI, D. "'Setting in': an interactionist perspective on the entry of the new manager", *Pacific sociol. R.* 20(1), jan 77 : 135-160.

4699   KOSTECKI, Marian J. "The managerial cadres of the Polish industry: research report", *Polish sociol. B.* 38(3), 1977 : 85-96.

4700   KRASNOGORSKIJ, I. É. "O social'noj roli inženerno-tehničeskoj intelligencii v razvitom socialističeskom obščestve" (On the social role of engineers and technicians in the developed socialist society), *Nauč. Dokl. vyss̆. Školy nauč. Kommunizma* (6), 1976 : 43-49.

4701   LACALLE, Daniel. *Técnicos, científicos y clases sociales* (Technicians, scientists, and social classes). Barcelona, Ediciones Guadarrama, 76, 160 p. *[Spain.]*

4702   MASŁYK, Ewa. "Reforma WOG a zmiany w sytuacji organizacyjnej kadry kierowniczej" (The WOG *[large socialist corporations]* reform and changes in the organizational situation of the executive personnel), *Stud. socjol.* 64(1), 1977 : 207-223.

4703   McKIE, Craig. "American managers in Canada: a comparative profile", *Int. J. comp. Sociol.* 18(1-2), mar-jun 77 : 44-63.

4704   PITROU, A. "Un processus de récupération du statut social: le cas des cadres non diplômés", *Sociol. Trav.* 19(1), jan-mar 77 : 1-22.

4705   ROTONDI, T. Jr. "Identification, personality needs, and managerial position", *Hum. Relat.* 29(6), jun 76 : 507-515.

18540. Liberal profession
Profession libérale

[See also / Voir aussi: 1083]

4706   BRUNOIS, A. "L'avenir des professions libérales", *R. Trav. Acad. Sci. mor. polit.* 128, 1 sem 75 : 5-19. *[France.]*

4707   HUSZÁR, T. (ed.). *A jogászság társadalmi helyzete és szakmai életútja. Kutatási beszámoló* (The social position and professional life of lawyers. A survey report). Budapest, Oktatási Minisztérium, 77, 252 p.

4708   KRONUS, Carol L. "The evolution of occupational power: a historical study of task boundaries between physicians and pharmacists", *Sociol. Wk Occupat.* 3(1), feb 76 : 3-37.

4709   ROSS, Robert J. S. "The impact of social movements on a profession in process: advocacy in urban planning", *Sociol. Wk Occupat.* 3(4), nov 76 : 429-454.

18600. LABOUR MANAGEMENT RELATIONS
RELATIONS DU TRAVAIL

[See also / Voir aussi: 2562]

4710   ALBEDA-WIE. "Changing industrial relations in the Netherlands", *Industr. Relat. (Berkeley)* 16(2), mai 77 : 133-144.

4711   COETZEE, J. A. Grey. *Industrial relations in South Africa: an event-structure of labour.* Cape Town, Juta, 76, xxv-238 p.

4712   COOPER, Bruce M.; BARTLETT, A. F. *Industrial relations: a study in conflict.* London, Heinemann, 76, ix-310 p, *[UK.]*

4713   DAHLSTRÖM, Edmund. "Efficiency, satisfaction and democracy in work: conceptions of industrial relations in post-war Sweden", *Acta sociol.* 20(1), 1977 : 25-53.

4714   DINGWALL, Robert. "'Atrocity stories' and professional relationships", *Sociol. Wk Occupat.* 4(4), nov 77 : 371-396.

4715   HASEGAWA, Tadashi. "Rôshi-kankei no kenryoku kôzo" (Power struc-
        ture in industrial relations), *Shirasagi Ronsô* (10), 1977 : 1-8.
4716   "Industrial democracy in international perspective", *A. Amer. Acad.
        polit. soc. Sci.* 431, mai 77 : 1-193.
4717   KELLER, Berndt. "Zu einer Theorie der Arbeitsbeziehungen im öffent-
        lichen Sektor" (Theory of labour relations in the public sector),
        Hamburg. Jb. Wirtsch.- u. Ges.-Polit. 22, 1977 : 113-129.
4718   SAINT-JOURS, Yves. *Les relations de travail dans le secteur public.*
        Paris, Librairie générale de droit et de jurisprudence, 76, 450 p.
4719   SMURAGLIA, Carlo. "Impresa, sindicati e forze politiche nella pros-
        pettive di un modello italiano di relazioni industriali" (Enter-
        prise, trade unions, and political forces within the framework
        of an Italian model of industrial relations), *Democr. e Dir.*
        17(1), jan-mar 77 : 111-128.
4720   SORGE, A. "The evolution of industrial democracy in the countries
        of the European Community", *Brit. J. industr. Relat.* 14(3), nov
        76 : 274-294.
4721   TREU, Tiziano. "Entwicklungen in den italienischen industriellen
        Beziehungen" (Developments in the Italian industrial relations),
        Gewerkschaftl. Mh. 28(9), sep 77 : 558-568.
4722   WALKER, Kenneth F. "Towards useful theorising about industrial re-
        lations", *Brit. J. industr. Relat.* 15(3), nov 77 : 307-316.
4723   WEDDERBURN, Kenneth William. "Democrazia industriale i recenti svi-
        luppi in Gran Bretagna" (Industrial democracy and recent deve-
        lopments in Great Britain), *Mulino* 26(251), mai-jun 77 : 311-
        338.
4724   WOOD, Stephen; ELLIOTT, Ruth. "A critical evaluation of Fox's ra-
        dicalisation of industrial relations theory", *Sociology (London)*
        11(1), jan 77 : 105-125.

        18610. Labour law
               Droit du travail

4725   EPP, David. *Labor law.* Dobbs Ferry, N.Y., Oceana Publications, 76,
        vii-120 p. *[USA.]*
4726   FRENDL, L. "Kodeks pracy w Polsce" (Labour code in Poland), *Kultura*
        1-2(352-353), jan-feb 77 : 129-136.
4727   IVANOV, S. A. "Funkcii sovetskogo trudovogo prava" (The functions
        of the Soviet labour law), *Sov. Gos. Pravo* 49(12), dec 76 : 48-
        54.
4728   KUNZ, Frijhof; SCHÜSSLER, Gerhard. "Das neue arbeitsgesetzbuchwich-
        tiges Instrument zur Gestaltung der entwickelten sozialistischen
        Gesellschaft" (The new labour law as an important instrument to
        the formation of the developed socialist society), *Staat u. Recht*
        26(3), mar 77 : 229-239. *[Germany DR.]*
4729   MARTIN, Ruperto G. *Reviewer on labor and social legislation.* Rev.
        ed. Manila, Premium Book Store, 76, ix-418 p. *[Philippines.]*
4730   MAZZIOTTI DI CELSO, Fabio. *Diritto del lavoro* (Labour law). Napoli,
        Jovene, 76, xv-598 p. *[Italy.]*
4731   MEYER, Daniel. *Der Gleichbehandlungsgrundsatz im schweizerischen
        Arbeitsrecht* (The principle of equal treatment in the Swiss labour
        law). Bern, Stämpfli, 76, 327 p.
4732   UNIVERSITÉ JEAN MOULIN. *Le droit au travail.* Lyon, Éditions l'Hermès,
        76, 154 p.
4733   WHINCUP, Michael H. *Modern employment law: a guide to job security
        and safety at work.* London, Heinemann, 76, xxxv-266 p. *[UK.]*

        18620. Employer's organization
               Organisation patronale

4734   JACKSON, P.; SISSON, K. "Employers' confederation in Sweden and the
        UK, and the significance of industrial structure", *Brit. J. in-
        dustr. Relat.* 14(3), nov 76 : 306-323.

4735   "Patrons et patronat", *Écon. et Human.* 236, jul-aug 77 : 4-37.
         [France.]

4736   SIMON, Walter. *Macht und Herrschaft der Unternehmerverbände, BDI, BDA und DIHT im ökonomischen und politischen System der BDR* (Power and domination of the employers' associations, BDI, BDA and DIHT in the economic and political system of the Federal Republic of Germany). Köln, Pahl-Rugenstein, 76, 237 p.

18630. Trade union
Syndicat

[See also / Voir aussi: 4477, 5009, 5132, 5221]

4737   ANDERSON, John C. "The union convention. An examination of limitations on democratic decision-making", *Relat. industr.* 32(3), 1977 : 379-396.

4738   ARMSTRONG, K. J. *et al.* "The measurement of trade-union bargaining power", *Brit. J. industr. Relat.* 15(1), mar 77 : 91-100.

4739   BANERJI, S. "The labour movement in India - its dynamics and dimensions", *Ind. Lab. J.* 27(5), mai 76 : 853-880.

4740   COHEN, Robin. "Michael Imoudu and the Nigerian labour movement", *Race and Class* 18(4), mar 77 : 345-362.

4741   COT, Jean-Pierre; MOUNIER, Jean-Pierre. *Les syndicats américains. Conflit ou complicité ?* Paris, Flammarion, 77, 183 p.

4742   CRABBE, Victor. "Administration et syndicats. Cinquante ans de Whitleyisme en Belgique", *R. Inst. Sociol.* (1-2), 1976 : 61-80.

4743   EDELSTEIN, J. David; WARNER, Malcolm. *Comparative union democracy: organisation and opposition in British and American unions.* New York, Halsted Press, 76, 378 p. CR: Edna E. Raphael, *Contemp. Sociol. (Washington)* 6(1), jan 77 : 60-61.

4744   FINK, G. M. (ed.). *Labor unions.* Westport, Conn., Greenwood Press, 77, xiii-520 p.

4745   FRUIT, Elie. *Les syndicats dans les chemins de fer en France, 1890-1910.* Paris, Éditions ouvrières, 76, 216 p.

4746   GEVERS, P. "Du conseil d'entreprise au conseil des travailleurs ? Un dilemme posé au mouvement ouvrier belge", *Rech. sociol.* 8(2), 1977 : 189-210.

4747   "Gewerkschaftsbewegung in Frankreich" (Labour movement in France), *Lendemains* 2(7-8), jun 77 : 5-156.

4748   GROULX, L. H. J. "Syndicalisation locale et action ouvrière", *Relat. industr.* 31(1), 1976 : 84-97. *[Canada.]*

4749   GUERIN, Daniel. *Le mouvement ouvrier aux États-Unis de 1866 à nos jours.* Paris, F. Maspéro, 77, 218 p.

4750   HASKINS, James. *The long struggle: the story of American labor.* Philadelphia, Westminster Press, 76, 160 p.

4751   HOLTON, Bob. *British syndicalism 1900-1914: myths and realities.* London, Pluto Press, 76, 232 p.

4752   JENKINS, J. Craig; PERROW, Charles. "Insurgency of the powerless: farm worker movements, 1946-1972", *Amer. sociol. R.* 42(2), apr 77 : 249-268. *[USA.]*

4753   KAWANISHI, Hirosuke. "Fukusū kumiai heizonka no kumiaikan-kankei no jittai" (Report on the inter-relations of trade unions in the enterprise), *Kenkyū Hōkoku* A(9), 1977 : 169-208.

4754   KAWANISHI, Hirosuke. *Shōsūha rōdōkumiai undoron* (Theory of the minority trade union in the enterprise). Tokyo, Kaien Shobo, 77, 328 p.

4755   KIRKWOOD, F.; MEWES, H. "The limits of trade-union power in capitalist order: the case of West German labour's quest for co-determination", *Brit. J. industr. Relat.* 14(3), nov 76 : 295-305.

4756   KRUIJT, Dirk; VELLINGA, Menno. "Achtergronden van militantie onder arbeiders en syndicaatsleiders: een methodologisch case-study" (Background of combativeness among workers trade union leaders: a methodological case study), *Mens en Mij* 52(1), 1977 : 18-41.

4757   LAMA, Luciano. *Il sindacato nella crisi italiana* (Trade union in
        the Italian crisis). Roma, Editori riuniti, 77, xxvi-301 p.
4758   LOVELL, John Christopher. *British trade unions, 1875-1933*. London,
        Macmillan, 77, 75 p.
4759   MALSCH, T.; STÜCK, H. "Gewerkschaften und 'technische Intelligenz'
        in Frankreich" (Trade unions and "technical intelligentsia" in
        France), *Soz. Welt* 27(4), 1976 : 420-439.
4760   McCARTHY, John D.; ZALD, Mayer N. "Resource mobilization and social
        movements: a partial theory", *Amer. J. Sociol.* 82(6), mai 77 :
        1212-1241.
4761   MONATTE, Pierre. *La lutte syndicale*. Paris, F. Mespéro, 76, 318 p.
4762   NICKELL, S. J. "Trade unions and the position of women in the in-
        dustrial wage structure", *Brit. J. industr. Relat.* 15(2), jul
        77 : 192-210. [UK.]
4763   PALONEN, Kari. "Työväenliikkeen laiminlyödyistä mahdollisuuksista"
        (On neglected possibilities of labour movement), *Politiikka* (3),
        1977 : 253-266.
4764   PARRY, Noel; PARRY, José. "Professionalism and unionism: aspects
        of class conflict in the national health service", *Sociol. R.*
        25(4), nov 77 : 823-841.
4765   PERRY, Ronald W.; GILLESPIE, David F.; PARKER, Howard A. *Social
        movements and the local community*. Beverly Hills, Calif., Sage
        Publications, 76, 66 p.
4766   PHILIPPE, L.; SAINT-JEVIN, P. "Les comités d'entreprise. Étude sta-
        tistique de l'institution et des élections intervenues en 1974",
        R. franç. Aff. soc. 30(4), oct-dec 76 : 3-76.
4767   PREVOST, François. *Mutation dans le syndicalisme agricole. Le cou-
        rant paysans-travailleurs*. Lyon, Chronique sociale de France;
        Paris, Diffusion Gamma, 76, 138 p.
4768   PRICE, R.; BAIN, G. S. "Union growth revisited: 1948-1974 in pers-
        pective", *Brit. J. industr. Relat.* 14(3), nov 76 : 339-355. [UK.]
4769   RAMASWAMY, E. A. "The participatory dimension of trade union democ-
        racy: a comparative sociological view", *Sociology (London)* 11(3),
        sep 77 : 465-480. [India.]
4770   ROJOT, J. "Syndicats français et théorie des relations industriel-
        les", *R. franç. Gestion* (11), sep-oct 77 : 49-58.
4771   ROY, Delwin A. "Labour and trade unionism in Turkey: the Eregli
        coalminers", *Mid. East. Stud.* 12(3), oct 76 : 125-172.
4772   STREECK, Wolfgang. "Strukturdimensionen deutscher Gewerkschaften
        im Jahre 1914: eine Analyse historischer Daten" (Structural di-
        mensions of German trade unions in the year 1914: an analysis of
        historical data), *Soz. Welt* 27(4), 1976 : 399-419.
4773   TALAVERA ALDANA, Luis Fernando. "Organizaciones sindicales obreras
        en la rama textil, 1935-1970" (Trade unions in the textile sector,
        1935-1970), *R. mexic. Cienc. polít. soc.* 21(83), jan-mar 76 :
        227-299. [Mexico.]
4774   TREU, Eckbert. "Gewerkschaftliche Organisation in einer schrumpfen-
        den Branche" (Trade-union organization in a shrinking branch),
        Soz. Welt 28(1-2), 1977 : 167-186. [Germany FR.]
4775   TURONE, Sergio. *Sindacato e classi sociali* (Trade union and social
        classes). Bari, G. Laterza, 76, xi-178 p. [Italy.]
4776   URBANI, Giuliano (ed.). *Sindacati e politica nella società post-
        industriale* (Trade unions and politics in the post-industrial
        society). Bologna, Il Mulino, 76, 232 p.
4777   WIARDA, Howard J. *Corporatism and development: the Portuguese ex-
        perience*. Amherst, University of Massachusetts,Press, 77, xiii-
        447 p.
4778   WITHERS, Glenn A. "Social justice and the unions: a normative app-
        roach to co-operation and conflict under interdependence", *Brit.
        J. industr. Relat.* 15(3), nov 77 : 322-337. [UK.]
4779   YELLOWITZ, Irwin. *Industrialization and the American labor movement,
        1850-1900*. Port Washington, N.Y., Kennikat Press, 77, 183 p.

18640. Labour conflict
Conflit du travail

4780   Bibl.XXVI-4145. BADIE, Bertrand. *Stratégie de la grève, pour une*
        approche fonctionnaliste du Parti communiste français. CR: Jac-
        ques CAPDEVIELLE, *R. franç. Sci. polit.* 27(4-5), aug-oct 77 :
        717-718.

4781   BLASCO SEGURA, Benjamín. "Esquemas de solución de conflictos de
        trabajo en los países de la Comunidad Económica Europea" (Schemes
        of labour conflict resolution in the EEC countries). *R. Polít.*
        soc. 115, 1977 : 5-46.

4782   BUTLER, R. J. "Relative deprivation and power: a switched replica-
        tion design using time series data of strike rates in American
        and British coal mining", *Hum. Relat.* 29(7), jul 76 : 623-641.

4783   COLLONGES, Yann; RANDAL, Pierre Georges. *Les autoréductions: grèves*
        d'usagers et luttes de classes en France et en Italie, 1972-1976.
        Paris, C. Bourgois, 76, 184 p.

4784   DIÉGUEZ CUERVO, Gonzalo. *Orden público y conflictos colectivos*
        (Public order and collective conflicts). Pamplona, Ediciones
        Universidad de Navarra, 76, 144 p.

4785   DURAN LOPEZ, Federico. "La nueva regulación de la huelga y del cier-
        re patronal" (The new regulation of strike and lockout), *R. Polít.*
        soc. 115, 1977 : 47-82.

4786   EDWARDS, P. K. "A critique of the Kerr-Siegel hypothesis of strikes
        and the isolated mass: a study of the falsification of sociolo-
        gical knowledge", *Sociol. R.* 25(3), aub 77 : 551-574.

4787   ERBÈS-SEGUIN, Sabine; CASSASSUS, Cecilia; KOURCHID, Olivier. *Les*
        conditions de développement du conflit industriel. Paris, Groupe
        de sociologie du travail, 77, 240 p.

4788   HIBBS, D. A. Jr. "Industrial conflict in advanced industrial so-
        cieties", *Amer. polit. Sci. R.* 70(4), dec 76 : 1033-1058.

4789   HOPPE, Hans-H.; SCHUMACHER, Jürgen. "Einflussfaktoren auf die Kon-
        fliktbereitschaft von Arbeitern" (Factors of influence in wor-
        kers' readiness to conflicts), *Soz. Welt* 28(1-2), 1977 : 187-207.

4790   KISELEV, I. J. "Kollektivnye trudovye konflikty" (Collective labour
        conflicts), *Rabočij Klass sovrem. Mir* 5(5), sep-oct 76 : 83-96.

4791   KRUIJT, Dir; VELLINGA, Menno. "On strike and strike propensity",
        Netherlands J. Sociol. 12(2), dec 76 : 139-151.

4792   MIRONOV, V. K. "Rassmotrenie trudovyh sporov nå predprijatijah v
        ěvropejskih socialistíceskij stranah" (Analysis of labour con-
        flicts in enterprises of the European socialist countries),
        Vestn. Moskov. Univ. Ser. Pravo 31(6), nov-dec 76 : 32-40.

4793   PICO, J. "La conflictualidad laboral en el país valenciano" (Labour
        conflicts in the Valencian area), *R. esp. Opin. públ.* 46, oct-dec
        76 : 79-102. *[Spain.]*

4794   POSAS AMADOR, M. "El movimiento obrero hondureño: la huelga de
        1954 y sus consecuencias" (Labour movement in Honduras: the 1954
        strike and its consequences), *Estud. soc. centroamer.* 5(15), sep-
        dec 76 : 93-127.

4795   TROCSÁNYI, László. "A munkaügyi viták jogi rendjének fejlödése a
        szocialista országokban" (Evolution and regulation of labour
        conflicts in the socialist countries), *Állam- és Jogtud.* 19(3),
        1976 : 396-417.

4796   TURKINGTON, Don J. *The forms of industrial conflict.* Victoria,
        Victoria University of Wellington, Industrial Relations Centre,
        76, ii-22 p.

4797   VAN DER LINDEN, J. M. *Spelregels bij arbeidsconflicten* (Game rules
        in labour conflicts). Scheveningen, Stichting Maatschappij en
        Onderneming, 76, 168 p.

4798   WIGHAM, Eric L. *Strikes and the government, 1893-1974.* London,
        Macmillan, 76, viii-206 p. *[UK.]*

18650. Arbitration. Mediation
Arbitrage. Médiation

4799   "Action et négociation", *Sociol. Trav.* 19(4), oct-dec 77 : 341-449.
        [France.]

4800   BROOKSHIRE, Michael L.; ROGERS, Michael D. *Collective bargaining
        in public employment: the TVA experience.* Lexington, Mass.,
        Lexington Books, 77, xiv-245 p. *[Tennessee Valley Authority, USA.]*

4801   FENDRICH, James M. "Unions help faculty who help themselves: a par-
        tisan view of a collective bargaining campaign", *Amer. Sociolo-
        gist* 12(4), nov 77 : 162-175.

4802   MORGAN, David R.; KEARNEY, Richard C. "Collective bargaining and
        faculty compensation: a comparative analysis", *Sociol. Educ.*
        50(1), jan 77 : 28-39.

4803   PANKERT, Albert. "La négociation collective", *A. Univ. Jean Moulin*
        14, 1976 : 5-33.

4804   PERRY, J. L.; LEVINE, C. H. "An inter-organizational analysis of
        power, conflict and settlements in public sector collective
        bargaining", *Amer. polit. Sci. R.* 70(4), dec 76 : 1185-1201.
        [USA.]

4805   RICHARDSON, Reed C. *Collective bargaining by objectives: a positive
        approach.* Englewood Cliffs, N.J., Prentice Hall, 77, xii-387 p.
        [USA.]

4806   ROTHMAN, William.A. *A bibliography of collective bargaining in
        hospitals and related facilities, 1972-1974.* Ithaca, New York
        State School of Industrial and Labor Relations, Cornell Univer-
        sity, 76, xxiv-139 p. *[USA.]*

18660. Collective agreement. Joint management
Convention collective. Cogestion

4807   CERI, Paolo. "L'autonomia operaia tra organizzazione del lavoro e
        sistema politico" (Workers' autonomy between labour organization
        and political system), *Quad. Sociol.* 26(1), jan-mar 77 : 28-63.

4808   "Cogestione: esperienze e problemi" (Joint management: experiences
        and problems), *Bibl. Libertà* 13(63), oct-dec 76 : 1-90.

4809   EDLUND, Sten Etson; GUSTAFSSON, Stig. *Medbestämmanderätten: lagar
        med kommentar* (Workers' participation in management: laws with
        comments). Stockholm, Tiden; Solna, Seelig, 76, 280 p. *[Sweden.]*

4810   FERNÁNDEZ VARGAS VARGAS, V.; FRAX ROSALES, E.; CASALS, J. L.
        "Efectos económicos, jurídicos y sociales de los convenios co-
        lectivos" (Economic, legal and social effects of collective
        agreements), *R. int. Sociol. (Madrid)* 34(18-19-20), apr-dec 76 :
        125-127.

4811   GARDELL, Bertil. "Autonomy and participation at work", *Hum. Relat.*
        30(6), jun 77 : 515-533. *[Norway.]*

4812   ISHIKAWA, Akihiro. "Czechoslovakia ni okeru keiei-sanka" (Workers'
        participation in management: the Czechoslovak case), *Nihon Rôdô-
        kyôkai Zasshi* 19(4), 1977 : 2-10.

4813   NYQVIST, Per; SVAHN, Hans. *Styrelserepresentation för anställda*
        (Employees' representation in management). Stockholm, LiberFörlag,
        76, 189 p. *[Sweden.]*

4814   "Participation and industrial democracy", *Hum. Relat.* 29(5), mai
        76 : 401-505.

4815   "Participation (La): quelques expériences étrangères", *R. int. Dr.
        comp.* 28(4), oct-dec 76 : 681-789.

4816   RAMSAY, Harvie. "Cycles of control: worker participation in socio-
        logical and historical perspective", *Sociology (London)* 11(3),
        sep 77 : 481-506.

4817   SMITH, W. Rand. "Attitudes towards workers' control in France: evi-
        dence from a sample of trade union members; research note", *So-
        ciol. R.* 25(4), nov 77 : 877-885.

4818   THOMSON, A. W. J. *et al.* "Bargaining structure and relative earnings in Great Britain", *Brit. J. industr. Relat.* 15(2), jul 77 : 176-191.
4819   TSUDA, Masumi; KISHIDA, Shôyû. *Ôshû no rodô-sha sanka - sono jikken to tenbo* (Workers' participation in Europe). Tokyo, Nihon Seisan sei honbu, 77, 364 p.
4820   WALL, Toby; LISCHERON, Joseph A. *Worker participation: a critique of the literature and some fresh evidence.* New York, McGraw-Hill, 77, 162 p.
4821   WEIR, D. "Radical managerialism: middle managers' perception of collective bargaining", *Brit. J. industr. Relat.* 14(3), nov 76 : 324-338.

18700. LEISURE
       LOISIR

[See also / Voir aussi: 1155, 1266, 3945]

4822   ÁGH, A. "A szabadidö fétise",(The fetish of leisure), *Valóság* (11), 1977 : 18-29.
4823   ARVIDSON, Peter; BUCHT, Rolf. *Fritiden i Sverige: ett sociologiskt perspektiv* (Leisure in Sweden: a sociological perspective). Stockholm, Esselte studium, 76, 109 p.
4824   BAJAGIĆ, Veronika. "A szabadidö és a munka humanizációjának kérdése Marx alienációs elméletenek megvilágításában" (Problem of humanization of leisure and work in the Marxian theory of alienation), *Létünk* (6), 1976 : 14-34.
4825   BURBY, Raymond J. *Recreation and leisure in new communities.* Cambridge, Mass., Ballinger Publishing Co., 76, xxxii-366 p. *[USA.]*
4826   CHEEK, Neil H. Jr.; BURCH, William R. Jr. *The social organization of leisure in human society.* New York, Harper and Row, 76, xx-283 p.
4827   CHRISTIANSEN, G.; LEHMANN, K. D. *Chancenungleichheit in der Freizeit: eine Sekundäranalyse von Umfragedaten* (Unequal chances in leisure: a secondary analysis based on data from sample surveys). Stuttgart, Kohlhammer, 76, 105 p. *[Germany FR.]*
4828   CRANDALL, Rick. "Future directions for the psychology of leisure", *Soc. and Leisure* 8(3), 1976 : 105-109.
4829   FALUSSY, Béla. (ed.). *A szabadidö szociológiája* (Sociology of leisure). Budapest, Gondolat, 76, 400 p.
4830   FRYKLINDH, Pär Urban; JOHANSSON, SvenOve. *En bok om fritiden i sociologiskt perspektiv* (A book about leisure in a sociological perspective). Stockholm, AWE/Geber, 76, 220 p. *[Sweden.]*
4831   GROVES, David L.; DAWSON, Kenneth E. "Toward a theory for the development of a youth leisure program", *Soc. and Leisure* 8(3), 1976 : 43-56.
4832   HARVA, Urpo. "Marxist conception of leisure", *Adult Educ. Finland* (2), 1977 : 3-12.
4833   HIDAKA, Chihiro. "Yoka-shûdan to chiiki-shakai seikatsu" (Leisure groups and community life), *Kokumin seikatsu Kenkyû* 17(3), 1977 : 71-87.
4834   HIDAKA, Chihiro. "Yoka to toshi-seikatsu" (Leisure and urban life), *Shakaigaku Hyôron* 28(1), 1977 : 72-86.
4835   Bibl.XXVI-4174. KATZ, Elihu; GUREVITCH, Michael. *The secularization of leisure: culture and communication in Israel.* CR: Moshe SHOKEID, *Amer. J. Sociol.* 83(2), sep 77 : 485-487.
4836   KELLY, John R. "Leisure as compensation for work constraint", *Soc. and Leisure* 8(3), 1976 : 73-82.
4837   KELLY, John B. "Sociological perspectives and leisure research", *Sociol. contemp.* 22(1-3), 1974 : 127-158.
4838   KÜHL, Werner; TUROWSKI, Gerd. *Systematik der Freizeitinfrastuktur* (The system of leisure infrastructure). Stuttgart-Berlin-Köln-Mainz, Kohlhammer, 76, 128 p. *[Germany FR.]*

4839   KUMASAKA, Kenji. "'Leisure shakai' no ruikeiron. Leisure no konni-
        chi-teki imi" (Typologies of "leisure society". On the meaning
        of leisure in contemporary society), *Tetsugaku* 66, 1977 : 75-97.
4840   LIEBERMAN, J. Nina. "Playfulness, cognitive style, and leisure or
        'do we need to educate for leisure ?'", *Soc. and Leisure* 8(3),
        1976 : 83-88.
4841   MANKIN, Don. "Leisure in the steady-state society", *Soc. and Leisure*
        8(3), 1976 : 97-103.
4842   NEULINGER, John. "Comments on the 1975 American Psychological Asso-
        ciation symposium: directions in the psychology of leisure", *Soc.
        and Leisure* 8(3), 1976 : 57-59.
4843   Bibl.XXVI-4176. PARKER, Stanley. *The sociology of leisure*. CR:
        Worth C. SUMMERS, *Contemp. Sociol. (Washington)* 6(4), jul 77 :
        506-507.
4844   ROBERTS, K. *et al.* "The family life-cycle, domestic roles and the
        meaning of leisure", *Soc. and Leisure* 8(3), 1976 : 7-20. [UK.]
4845   ROEBUCK, Julian B.; FRESE, Wolfgang. *The rendez-vous: a case study
        of an afterhours club*. New York, Free Press, 76, 278 p. CR:
        Edward F. VACHA, *Contemp. Sociol. (Washington)* 6(1), jan 77 : 35.
4846   WNUK-LIPIŃSKI, Edmund. "Patterns of leisure and development of
        women's personality", *Soc. and Leisure* 8(3), 1976 : 241-252.
4847   ZLATE, Camelia. "Le loisir et le développement multilatéral de la
        personnalité", *Soc. and Leisure* 8(3), 1976 : 253-260.

18710. Leisure time
       Temps de loisir

4848   AKKANEN, Riitta; LÖYTTYNIEMI, Leena. "The family mother and leisure
        time", *Adult Educ. Finland* (2), 1977 : 23-33.
4849   METEL'SKIJ, F. M. "Svobodnoe vremja kak odno iz važnejsih uslovij
        Vsestoronnego razvitija čeloveceskoj ličnosti" (Leisure time as
        one of essential conditions of complete development of human per-
        sonality), in: *Socializm i narodnoe blagosostojanie*. Moskva,
        1976 : 352-367.
4850   ŠARAKALIEV, A. Š. "Svobodnoe vremja v razvitom socialisticeskom
        obscestve" (Leisure time in developed socialist society), *Ucen.
        Zap. Azerb. Inst. nar. Hoz. Ser. ekon. Nauk* (2), 1976 : 73-77.
4851   VOLPI, Claudio. *Il tempo libero tra mito e progetto* (Leisure time
        between myth and project). Torino, ERI, 76, 403 p.

18720. Leisure utilization
       Utilisation des loisirs

[See also / Voir aussi: 846, 932, 1156, 1222, 1895, 4098, 4624]

4852   AAS, Dagfinn. "Explorations with alternative methodologies for
        data on time use", *Soc. and Leisure* 8(3), 1976 : 111-117.
4853   Bibl.XXVI-4200. BALL, Donald W.; LOY, John W. *Sport and social or-
        der: contributions to the sociology of sport*. CR: Gregory P.
        STONE, *Contemp. Sociol. (Washington)* 6(1), jan 77 : 110-112.
4854   BOUET, Michel A. "The significance of the Olympic phenomenon. A
        preliminary attempt at systematic and semiotic analysis", *Int.
        R. Sport Sociol.* 12(3), 1977 : 5-22.
4855   BROHM, Jean-Marie. *Sociologie politique du sport*. Paris, Jean
        Pierre Delarge, 76, 360 p. CR: Joffre DUMAZEDIER, *R. franç.
        Sociol.* 18(3), jul-sep 77 : 21-523.
4856   BUHRMANN, Hans G.; BRATTON, Robert D. "Athletic participation and
        status of Alberta High School girls", *Int. R. Sport Sociol.*
        12(1), 1977 : 57-69.
4857   BUTT, Dorcas Susan. *The psychology of sport: the behavior, motiva-
        tion, personality, and performance of athletes*. New York, Van
        Nostrand Reinhold, 76, xii-196 p.
4858   CARRON, Albert V.; BALL, James R. "An analysis of the cause-effect
        characteristics of cohesiveness and participation motivation in

intercollegiate hockey", *Int. R. Sport Sociol.* 12(2), 1977 :
49-60.

4859 DICKINSON, John. *A behavioural analysis of sport.* London, Lepus
Books, 76, x-134 p.

4860 EADINGTON, William R. (ed.). *Gambling and society: interdisciplinary studies on the subject of gambling.* Springfield, Ill., Thomas, 76, xix-466 p.

4861 GEISLER, Charles C.; MARTINSON, Oscar B.; MILKENING, Eugene A.
"Outdoor recreation and environmental concern: a restudy", *Rur.
Sociol.* 42(2), 1977 : 241-249.

4862 GOODGER, B. C.; GOODGER, J. M. "Judo in the light of theory and
sociological research", *Int. R. Sport Sociol.* 12(2), 1977 : 5-34.

4863 GREENDORFER, Susan L. "Intercollegiate football: an approach toward
rationalization", *Int. R. Sport Sociol.* 12(3), 1977 : 23-34.

4864 GRUNEAU, Richard S.; ALBINSON, John G. (eds.). *Canadian sport: sociological perspectives.* Don Mills, Ont., Reading Mass., Addison-
Wesley, 76, xiv-433 p.

4865 HANKS, Michael P.; ECKLAND, Bruce K. "Athletics and social participation in the educational attainment process", *Sociol. Educ.*
49(4), dec 76 : 271-294.

4866 HAYANO, David M. "The professional poker player: career identification and the problem of respectability", *Soc. Probl.* 24(5),
jun 77 : 556-564.

4867 KRAWCZYK, Barbara. "The social origin and ambivalent character of
the ideology of amateur sport", *Int. R. Sport Sociol.* 12(3),
1977 : 35-49.

4868 KRAWCZYK, Zbigniew. "Ke genezi sociologie tělesné výchovy a sportu"
(On the genesis of the sociology of physical culture and sports),
Sociol. Čas. 13(3), 1977 : 280-287.

4869 KRAWCZYK, Zbigniew. "Theory and empiricism in the social sciences
regarding physical culture", *Int. R. Sport Sociol.* 12(1), 1977 :
71-92.

4870 KRÖNER, Sabine. *Sport und Geschlecht: eine soziologische Analyse
sportliches Verhaltens in der Freizeit* (Sports and sexes: a sociological analysis of sport behaviour in leisure). Ahrensburg-
bei-Hamburg, Czwalina, 76, 265 p.

4871 LANDERS, Daniel M. (ed.). *Social problems in athletics: essays in
the sociology of sport.* Urbana, University of Illinois Press, 76,
251 p. CR: Carolyn R. DEXTER, *Contemp. Sociol. (Washington)* 6(2),
mar 77 : 249-250.

4872 LIGHT, Ivan. "Numbers gambling among Blacks: a financial institution", *Amer. sociol. R.* 42(6), dec 77 : 892-904.

4873 LÜSCHEN, Günther; WEIS, Kurt (eds.). *Die Soziologie des Sports*
(Sociology of sport). Darmstadt, Luchterhand, 76, 339 p. CR:
Michael KLEIN, *Kölner Z. Soziol. u. soz.-Psychol.* 29(3), sep
76 : 602-605.

4874 McCANNELL, Dean. *The tourist: a new theory of the leisure class.*
New York, Schocken Books, 76, 214 p. CR: Suzanne WEDOW, *Contemp.
Sociol. (Washington)* 6(2), mar 77 : 200-202.

4875 MEDOFF, Marshal H. "Positional segregation and professional baseball", *Int. R. Sport Sociol.* 12(1), 1977 : 49-56.

4876 MERHAUTOVÁ, J.; JOACHIMSTHALER, F. "Funkce tělesné kultury z hledis-
ka socialistického způsobu života" (Function of physical education
as concerns the formation of the socialist way of life), *Sociol.
Čas.* 13(5), 1977 : 509-521.

4877 MÓDRA, László. "A falusi értelmiség tevékenysége és kulturális szo-
kásai a szabad időben" (The activity of intellectuals from rural
areas and their cultural habits in leisure time), *Társad. Közl.*
(4), 1976 : 60-80.

4878 MORIKAWA, Sadao. "Amateurism - yesterday, today and tomorrow",
Int. R. Sport Sociol. 12(2), 1977 : 61-72.

4879   MURRAY, Louis. "Value categories for Australian sport", *Int. R. Sport Sociol.* 12(3), 1977 : 97-105.

4880   NIETO PIÑEROBA, José Antonio. "Implicaciones socio-económicas, ecológicas y culturales del turismo: su impacto en una pequeña comunidad" (Socio-economic, ecological and cultural implications of tourism: its impact on a small community), *RS Cuad. Realidad soc.* 13, mar 77 : 67-80.

4881   NEITO PIÑEROBA, José Antonio. "Turistas y nativos: el caso de Formentera" (Tourists and indigenens: the case of Formentera), *R. esp. Opin. públ.* 47, jan-mar 77 : 147-165. *[Spain.]*

4882   NIXON, Howard L. *Sport and social organization.* Indianapolis, Ind., Bobbs-Merrill Co., 76, 75 p. CR: Barry D. McPHERSON, *Contemp. Sociol. (Washington)* 6(3), mai 77 : 388-389.

4883   OTTO, Luther B.; ALWIN, Duane F. "Athletics, aspirations, and attainments", *Sociol. Educ.* 50(2), apr 77 : 102-113.

4884   PARKER, Stanley et al. (eds.). *Sport and leisure in contemporary society.* London, School of the Environment, Polytechnic of Central London, 76, 120 p.

4885   PHILLIPS, John C. "Some methodological problems in sport sociology literature", *Int. R. Sport Sociol.* 12(1), 1977 : 93-99.

4886   POLGAR, Sylvia Knopp. "The social context of games: or when play is not play", *Sociol. Educ.* 49(4), oct 76 : 265-271.

4887   RITTNER, Karin. *Sport und Arbeitsteilung: zur sozialen Funktion und Bedeutung des Sports* (Sports and division of labour: the social function and importance of sports). Bad Homburg v.d.H., Limpert, 76, 282 p.

4888   SCHULKE, Hans Jürgen. "Sociology of sport science. Theoretical and methodological aspects of the research situation in the German Federal Republic", *Int. R. Sport Sociol.* 12(3), 1977 : 63-74.

4889   SCHWARTZ, Barry; BARSKY, Stephen F. "The home advantage", *Soc. Forces* 55(3), mar 77 : 641-661. *[Sport.]*

4890   SMIRNOV, S. V. "Svobodnoe vremja i srestva massovoj informacii" (Leisure time and mass media), *Žurnal. Pressa Audit.* (1), 1975 : 31-44.

4891   SNYDER, Eldon E.; SPREITZER, Elmer. "Participation in sport as related to educational expectations among high school girls", *Sociol. Educ.* 50(1), jan 77 : 47-55.

4892   STOLJAROV, V. I. "On a humanistic value of sport", *Int. R. Sport Sociol.* 12(3), 1977 : 75-84.

4893   THUROT, J. M. et al. *Les effets du tourisme sur les valeurs socioculturelles.* Aix-en-Provence, Centre des hautes études touristiques, 76, i-53 f.

4894   VALENTINOVA, N. G. et al. *Obščestvo i sport* (Society and sport). Moskva, 76, 133 p.

4895   VOGT, Dieter; GRÄTZ, Frank. "Probleme der Sportsoziologie in der DDR" (Problems of the sociology of sport in the GDR), *Kölner Z. Soziol. u. soz.-Psychol.* 29(2), jun 77 : 295-318.

4896   VOIGT, David Q. *America through baseball.* Chicago, Nelson-Hall, 76 221 p. CR: Carolyn R. DEXTER, *Contemp. Sociol. (Washington)* 6(2), mar 77 : 249-250.

4897   VOIGT, Dieter; MESSING, Manfred. "Sozialstruktur im deutschen Spor (Social structure of the German sport), *Deutschland Archiv* 10(7) jul 77 : 709-724.

4898   WATSON, Geoffrey G. "Games, socialization and parental values: social class differences in parental evaluation of little league baseball", *Int. R. Sport Sociol.* 12(1), 1977 : 17-48.

4899   WOHL, Andrzej. "Sport and the quality of life", *Int. R. Sport Sociol.* 12(2), 1977 : 35-48.

19. **POLITICS. STATE. INTERNATIONAL RELATIONS
POLITIQUE. ÉTAT. RELATIONS INTERNATIONALES**

19100. POLITICAL SCIENCE. POLITICAL SOCIOLOGY
SCIENCE POLITIQUE. SOCIOLOGIE POLITIQUE

[See also / Voir aussi: 1407]

4900 BRAUNGART, R. G. "A metatheoretical note on Max Weber's political sociology", *Int. J. contemp. Sociol.* 13(1-2), jan-apr 76 : 1-13.
4901 CORES TRASMONTE, Baldomero. *Sociología política de Galicia: orígenes y desarrollo (1846-1936)* (Political sociology of Galicia: origins and development, 1846-1936). La Coruña, Librigal, 76, 349 p.
4902 IWASE, Yôri. "A social function of policy sciences", *Doshisha Amerika Kenkyu* 13, 1977 : 43-49.
4903 KULCSÁR, K. *A politikai szociológia alapjai* (The formulation of political sociology). Budapest, Tanácsakadémia, 77, 189 p.
4904 LEONI, F. "La sociología política como ciencia de actualidad" (Political sociology as a science of actuality), *R. Estud. polit.* 210, nov-dec 76 : 81-96.
4905 LÖRINCZ, Lajos; NAGY, Endre; SZAMEL, Lajos. *A közigazgatás kutatásának tudományos irányzatai* (Scientific orientations of administrative research). Budapest, Közgazdasági és Jogi Kiadó, 76, 471-1 p.
4906 SEGALL, Marshall H. *Human behavior and public policy: a political psychology.* New York, Pergamon Press, 76, xiv-321 p.
4907 WINTER, Herbert R. et al. *People and politics: an introduction to political science.* New York, Wiley, 77, xiv-514 p.

19200. POLITICAL DOCTRINE. POLITICAL THOUGHT
DOCTRINE POLITIQUE. PENSÉE POLITIQUE

19210. Political philosophy
Philosophie politique

[See also / Voir aussi: 314]

4908 BOCKMAN, Sheldon; GAYK, William F. "Political orientations and political ideologies", *Pacific sociol. R.* 20(4), oct 77 : 536-552.
4909 BOWIE, Norman E.; SIMON, Robert L. *The individual and the political order: an introduction to social and political philosophy.* Englewood Cliffs, N.J., Prentice-Hall, 77, viii-280 p.
4910 LARSSON, Reidar. *Politiska ideologier i vår tid* (Political ideologies in our time). Lund, Studentlitt., 76, 71 p.

19220. Power
Pouvoir

[See also / Voir aussi: 563, 966, 1076, 2742, 2743, 3941]

4911 ABELL, Peter. "The many faces of power and liberty: revealed preference, autonomy, and teleological explanation", *Sociology (London)* 11(1), jan 77 : 3-24.
4912 ARCY, Philippe D'. *L'argent et le pouvoir.* Paris, Presses universitaires de France, 76, 161-2 p.
4913 BACHARACH, S. B.; LAWLER, E. J. "The perception of power", *Soc. Forces* 55(1), sep 76 : 123-134.

4914   BURT, Ronald S. "Power in a social topology", *Soc. Sci. Res.* 6(1), mar 77 : 1-83.

4915   Bibl.XXVI-4275. CLEGG, Stewart. *Power, rule and domination.* CR: David Silverman, *Brit. J. Sociol.* 28(1), mar 77 : 113.

4916   GULIEV, V. Ê.; GRAFSKIJ, V. G. *Političeskaja vlast' i demokratija v uslovijah sovremennogo kapitalizma* (Political power and democracy under conditions of contemporary capitalism). Moskva, Znanie, 76, 64 p.

4917   Bibl.XXVI-4279. LAMB, Curt. *Political power in poor neighborhoods.* CR: Richard F. CURTIS, *Amer. J. Sociol.* 82(5), mar 77 : 1112-1113; George W. DOWDALL, *Contemp. Sociol. (Washington)* 6(1), jan 77 : 104-105.

4918   MARTIN, Roderick. *The sociology of power.* London, Routledge and Kegan Paul, 77, ix-203 p.

4919   NAGEL, Jack H. *The descriptive analysis of power.* New Haven, Conn., Yale University Press, 76, xi-200 p. CR: Morton BARATZ, *Amer. J. Sociol.* 82(5), mar 77 : 1165-1168.

4920   ROGERS, Mary F. "Goffman on power", *Amer. Sociologist* 12(2), mai 77 : 88-95.

4921   SWINGLE, Paul G. *The management of power.* Hillsdale, N.J., L. Erlbaum Associates; New York, The Halsted Press Division of Wiley, 76, xi-178 p.

19230. Communism. Nationalism
Communisme. Nationalisme

[See also / Voir aussi: 302, 612, 1327, 1331, 1783, 2107, 2500, 2503, 2575, 3554, 3608, 4252, 4275]

4922   BARTOLI, D. "Der umgestülpte Patriotismus" (Reverse patriotism), *Schweiz. Mh.* 56(12), mar 77 : 1051-1067.

4923   BELYH, A. K. "Suščnost' i kriterii razvitogo socializma" (Nature and criteria of developed socialism), *Učen. Zap. Kaf. obšč. Nauk Vuzov g. Leningr. Probl. nauč. Kommunizma* (9), 1976 : 3-17.

4924   BIARD, Roland. *Histoire du mouvement anarchiste en France, 1945-1975.* Paris, Éditions Galilée, 76, 313 p.

4925   BLOCK, Fred. "Beyond corporate liberalism", *Soc. Probl.* 24(3), feb 77 : 352-361.

4926   BOTZ, Gerhard; BRANDSTETTER, Gerfried; POLLAK, Michael. *Im Schatten der Arbeiterbewegung. Zur Geschichte des Anarchismus in Österreich und Deutschland* (In the shadow of the labour movement: history of the anarchism in Austria and Germany). Wien, Europaverlag, 77, 190 p.

4927   BOUBIL, Alain. *Le socialisme industriel.* Paris, Presses universitaires de France, 77, ix-322 p.

4928   CARRERA DAMAS, German. "El nacionalismo latino-americano en perspectiva histórica" (Latin American nationalism in historical perspective), *R. mexic. Sociol.* 38(4), oct-dec 76 : 783-791.

4929   CUEVA, Agustín. "Crisis del capitalismo y perspectivas del nacionalismo en América latina: análisis del caso ecuatoriano" (Crisis of capitalism and perspectives of nationalism in Latin America: analysis of the case of Ecuador), *R. mexic. Sociol.* 38(4), oct-dec 76 : 825-841.

4930   DÍAZ, Carlos. *Las teorías anarquistas: (utopía y praxis)* (The anarchist theories: utopia and praxis). Bilbao, Zero; Madrid, ZYX, 76, 205 p.

4931   DUDEL', S. P. *Problema protivorečij v uslovijah razvitogo socializma* (Problem of contradictions under conditions of developed socialism). Moskva, Znanie, 76, 63 p.

4932   ÊFENDIEV, S. I. "K voprosu o sootnošenii kategorij patriotizma, nacional'nogo i internacional'nogo" (On the correlation of patriotism, national and international categories), *Učen. Zap. (Azerb. Univ.) Ser. ist. filos. Nauk* (4), 1976 : 52-57.

4933   FEDOSEEV, P. "Teoretičeskie problemy razvitogo socializma: kommu-
        nisticeskogo stroitel'stva" (Theoretical problems of the deve-
        loped socialism and communism edification), Obšč. Nauki (Moskva)
        (2), 1977 : 7-25.
4934   HAMON, Léo. Socialisme et pluralités. Paris, Gallimard, 76, 475 p.
4935   HAUTECOEUR, Jean-Paul. "Nationalisme et développement en Acadie",
        Rech. sociogr. 17(2), mai-apr 76 : 167-188. [Canada.]
4936   HEGEDÜS, András. The structure of socialist society. London, Con-
        stable, 77, viii-230 p.
4937   ISHIKAWA, Akihiro. Kurashi no naka no shakai-shugi. Czechoslovakia
        no shimin seikatsu (Socialism in everyday life. Civic life in
        Czechoslovakia). Tokyo, Aoiki Shoten, 77, 252 p.
4938   ISHIKAWA, Akihiro. "Shakai-shugi-teki chihô-seido ni okeru shūken-
        gata" (Two types of local systems under socialism: centralism
        and decentralism), Chûô-daigaku Bungakubu Kiyô 85, 1977 : 15-39.
4939   JAKUŠIN, S. P. "Diktatura proletariata-obščaja i glavnaja zakono-
        mernost' postroenija socializma" (Dictatorship of the proletariat
        is a general and essential law of the edification of socialism),
        Učen. Zap. Kaf. obšč. nauk Vuzov g. Leningr. Probl. nauč. Kom-
        munizma (9), 1976 : 41-47.
4940   JARVIE, I. C. "Nationalism and the social sciences", Canad. J. So-
        ciol. 1(4), 1976 : 515-528.
4941   KAMENKA, Eugene (ed.). Nationalism: the nature and evolution of an
        idea. London-New York, St. Martin's Press, 76, vi-135 p. CR:
        Ernest GELLNER, Brit. J. Sociol. 28(4), dec 77 : 512-514.
4942   KASJANENKO, V. I. Razvitoj socializm' istoriografija i metodologija
        problemy (The developed socialism: historiography and methodolo-
        gy of the problem). Moskva, Mysl', 76, 270 p.
4943   KHARE, R. S. "Reflections on levels and structures in Indian na-
        tionalism: a case from Northern India", Sociol. B. (Bombay)
        25(1), mar 76 : 1-32.
4944   KOPYLOV, I. Ja.; SALIKOV, R. A. "Internacionalizm, patriotizm i
        obščenacional'naja gordost' grazdan SSSR" (Internationalism,
        patriotism and national pride of the USSR citizens), Nauč. Trudy
        Kursk.-pedag. Inst. 74, 1976 : 70-96.
4945   KOSTIN, L. A. Vysšaja cel' socializma (The highest objective of
        socialism). Moskva, Mysl', 76, 191 p.
4946   LAŠIN, A. G. (ed.). Teorija socialisticeskogo stroitel'stva (Theory
        of socialist edification). Moskva, Izdatel'stvo Moskovskogo Uni-
        versiteta, 76, 318 p.
4947   MALDONADO DENIS, Manuel. "Las perspectivas del nacionalismo lati-
        noamericano: el caso de Puerto Rico" (The perspectives of Latin
        American nationalism: the case of Puerto Rico), R. mexic. So-
        ciol. 38(4), oct-dec 76 : 799-810.
4948   MORAWSKI, Stefan. "The ideology of anarchism. A tentative analysis",
        Polish sociol. B. 37(1), 1977 : 31-47.
4949   PAVLOVA-SIL'VANSKAJA, M. P. "Razvitie socializma na sobstvennoj
        osnove" (Development of socialism on a proper basis), in: Meto-
        dologiceskie problemy issledovanija ekonomiki razvitogo socializ-
        ma. Moskva, 1976 : 94-102.
4950   PRIPUTEN', L. G. "Socialisticeskoe otečestvo-voploščenie dialek-
        ticeskogo edinstva patriotizma i internacionalizma trudjaščihsja"
        (The socialist fatherland is the personification of the dialec-
        tic unity between patriotism and internationalism of workers),
        Vopr. nauč. Kommunizma (Kiev) 35, 1977 : 80-85.
4951   ROSENKO, M. N. Patriotizm i obščesnacional'naja gordost' sovetskogo
        naroda (Patriotism and national pride of the Soviet people). Le-
        ningrad, Lenizdat, 77, 175 p.
4952   SANTOS, Theotonio DOS. "Socialismo y fascismo en América Latina
        hoy" (Socialism and fascism in Latin America today), R. mexic.
        Sociol. 39(1), jan-mar 77 : 173-190.

4953   SMITH, Anthony D. (ed.). *Nationalist movements*. London, Macmillan,
        76, vi-185 p. CR: Ernest GELLNER, *Brit. J. Sociol.* 28(4), dec
        77 : 513-514.

4954   SMITH, N. A. *The new enlightenment: an essay in political and so-
        cial realism*. London, J. Calder, 76, 256 p.

4955   SOLOZÁBAL ECHEVARRIA, J. J. "Nacionalismo y clases sociales: bur-
        guesía, aristocracia y campesinado" (Nationalism and social
        classes: bourgeoisie, aristocracy and peasantry), *R. int. Sociol.
        (Madrid)* 34(18-19-20), apr-dec 76 : 144-149.

4956   STEINER, John M. *Power and social change in National Socialist
        Germany, a process of escalation into mass destruction*. The Ha-
        gue, Mouton, Atlantic Highlands, N.J., Humanities Press, 76, xx-
        466 p.

19240. Democracy. Dictatorship
Démocratie. Dictature

[See also / Voir aussi: 1344, 4252, 4916]

4957   BERDAHL, Robert M. "Prussian aristocracy and conservative ideology:
        a methodological examination", *Soc. Sci. Inform.* 15(4-5), 1976 :
        583-599.

4958   BLOCH, Maurice. "The disconnection between power and rank as a
        process. An outline of the development of kingdoms in Central
        Madagascar", *Archiv. europ. Sociol.* 18(1), 1977 : 107-148.

4959   FORMÁNEK, Miloslav. "Socialistická demokracie" (Socialist democra-
        vy), *Sociol. Čas.* 13(5), 1977 : 467-480.

4960   HEWITT, Christopher. "The effect of political democracy and social
        democracy on equality in industrial societies: a cross-national
        comparison", *Amer. sociol. R.* 42(3), jun 77 : 450-464.

4961   KARLOV, A. A. "Social'noe značenie socialistič eskoj demokratii"
        (Social meaning of socialist democracy), *Probl. Pravovedenija*
        34, 1976 : 132-140.

4962   LEMOS, Ramon M. "A moral argument for democracy", *Soc. Theory
        Practice* 4(1), 1976 : 57-74.

4963   MONGARDINI, Carlo. "Democracy or plutocracy ?", *Sociol. Anal. Theor*
        7(2), jun 77 : 83-97.

4964   RUBINSON, Richard; QUINLAN, Dan. "Democracy and social inequality:
        a reanalysis", *Amer. sociol. R.* 42(4), aug 77 : 611-623.

4965   STRASNICK, Steven. "Ordinality and the spirit of the justified
        dictator", *Soc. Res.* 44(4), 1977 : 668-690.

4966   TAYLOR, Michel. *Anarchy and cooperation*. London, J. Wiley, 76, viii
        151 p.

19300. CONSTITUTION. STATE
CONSTITUTION. ÉTAT

19310. Political system
Système politique

4867   ABBATE, Fred J. *A preface to the philosophy of the state*. Belmont,
        Calif., Wadsworth, 77, 209 p.

4968   ANDREY, G. "La conscience politique romande. Petite contribution
        à l'étude du fédéralisme suisse, 1848-1975", *Annu. suisse Sci.
        polit.* 16, 1976 : 151-161.

4969   BLOCK, Fred. "The ruling class does not rule: notes on the marxist
        theory of the State", *Social. Revol.* 7(3), mai-jun 77 : 6-28.

4970   FREY, Kurt. *Konstruktiver Foderalismus: gesammelte kulturpolitische
        Beitrag, 1948-1975* (Constructive federalism: a collection of cul-
        tural political contributions, 1948-1975). Weinheim-Basel, Beltz,
        76, ix-210 p. [Germany FR.]

4971   GALLINO, Luciano. "Sociologia dello Stato" (The sociology of the
        State), *Quad. Sociol.* 25(4), oct-dec 76 : 351-365.

4972   GEERTZ, Clifford. "The judging of nations: some comments on the

the assessment of regimes in the new states", *Archiv. europ. Sociol.* 18(2), 1977 : 245-261.

4973 GOERTZEL, Ted George. *Political society.* Chicago, Ill., Rand McNally College Publishing Co., 76, xi-272 p.

4974 KAMIŃSKI, Antoni Z. "State bureaucracy and parliamentary democracy in the development of a liberal-democratic state", *Polish sociol. B.* 38(3), 1977 : 37-48.

4975 KANTOROVIČ, B. Ja. "Ideologičeskaja funkcija buržuaznogo gosudarstva" (Ideological function of the bourgeois state), *Nauč. Dokl. vysš. Školy nauč. Kommunizma* (2), 1977 : 86-93.

4976 LECA, Jean. "Pour une analyse comparative des systèmes politiques méditerranéens", *R. franç. Sci. polit.* 27(4-5), aug-oct 77 : 557-581.

4977 LOERTSCHER, C. "Propositions pour une analyse de l'État. Pourquoi et comment étudier l'État ?", *Annu. suisse Sci. polit* 16, 1976 : 43-63.

4978 LUHMANN, Niklas. "Der politische Code. Zur Entwirrung von Verwirrungen" (The political code. The clearing up of confusions), *Kölner Z. Soziol. u. soz.-Psychol.* 29(1), mar 77 : 157-159.

4979 MacPHERSON, C. B. "Do we need a theory of the State", *Archiv. europ. Sociol.* 18(2), 1977 : 223-244.

4980 MANN, Michael. "States, ancient and modern", *Archiv. europ. Sociol.* 18(2), 1977 : 262-298.

4981 MARTINS, Luciano. *Pouvoir et développement économique: formation et évolution des structures politiques au Brésil.* Paris, Éditions Anthropos, 76, 472 p.

4982 MURGA FRASSINETTI, Antonio. "Estado y burguesía industrial en Honduras" (State and industrial bourgeoisie in Honduras), *R. mexic. Sociol.* 39(2), apr-jun 77 : 595-609.

4983 NAGY, E. "Pulszky Ágost társadalom- és államtana" (The theories of Agost Pulszky on state and society), *Szociológia* 6(2), 1977 : 207-213.

4984 O'DONNELL, Guillermo. "Reflexiones sobre las tendencias de cambio del Estado burocrático-autoritario" (Reflections on trends of change of the bureaucratic-authoritarian State), *R. mexic. Sociol.* 39(1), jan-mar 77 : 9-59. *[Latin America.]*

4985 PARK, Richard L. "Political modernization in the developing world: contributions from American experience", *A. Amer. Acad. polit. soc. Sci.* 428, nov 76 : 33-42.

4986 PISIER-KOUCHNER, Evelyne. "Perspective sociologique et théorie de l'État", *R. franç. Sociol.* 18(2), apr-jun 77 : 317-330.

4987 POGGI, Gianfranco. "The constitutional state of the nineteenth century: an elementary conceptual portrait", *Sociology (London)* 11(2), mar 77 : 311-332.

4988 SAMU, M. *A hatalom és az állam* (Power and state). Budapest, Közgazdasági és Jogi Kiadó, 77, 546 p.

4989 SATHYAMURTHY, T. V. "Les nouveaux états: double dynamique et conflits", *C. int. Sociol.* 23(61), jul-dec 76 : 271-296.

4990 SCHMIDT, P. "Szocializmus és államiság" (Socialism and statehood), *Társadtud. Közl.* (1), 1977 : 3-25.

4991 VEYNE, Paul. *Le pain et le cirque: sociologie historique d'un pluralisme politique.* Paris, Éditions du Seuil, 76, 799 p.

4992 ZAJCEVA, Ê. V. "O dialektike ĕdinstva internacional'nogo i nacional'nogo v sovetskoj gosudarstvennosti" (On dialectics of international and national unity in Soviet state structure), *Jur. Nauki* (6), 1976 : 39-59.

4993 ZERMEÑO GARCÍA, Sergio. "Estado y sociedad en el capitalismo tardío" (State and society in the later capitalism), *R. mexic. Sociol.* 39(1), jan-mar 77 : 61-1117.

4994 ZYLBERBERG, Jacques. "État – corporatisme – populisme; contribution à une sociologie politique de l'Amérique latine", *Ét. int.*

7(2), jun 76 : 215-250.

19320. Human rights
Droits de l'homme

[See also / Voir aussi: 4911, 5222]

4995   BOURDIEU, Pierre. "La censure", *Soc. Sci. Inform.* 16(3-4), 1977 : 385-388.

4996   CLAUDE, Richard P. (ed.). *Comparative human rights.* Baltimore, Md., Johns Hopkins University Press, 76, xvi-410 p. CR: Harry M. JOHNSON, *Contemp. Sociol. (Washington)* 6(3), mai 77 : 306-307.

4997   "Droit humanitaire et protection de l'homme", *A. Ét. int.* (8), 1977 : 7-771.

4998   GARCÍA RAMIREZ, Sergio. *Los derechos humanos y el derecho penal* (Human rights and penal law). México, Secretaria de Educación Pública, 76, 205 p.

4999   HILLERY, George A.; DUDLEY, Charles J.; MORROW, Paula C. "Toward a sociology of freedom", *Soc. Forces* 55(3), mar 77 : 685-700.

5000   MHITARJAN, G. Ê. *Svoboda i istoričeskaja neobhodimost'. O strukture social'noj svobody* (Liberty and historical necessity. On the structure of social liberty). Êrevan, Ajastan, 76, 283 p.

5001   O'NEILL, William F.; DEMOS, George D. "Existential freedom", *Int. J. contemp. Sociol.* 13(1-2), jan-apr 76 : 29-42.

5002   SASAKI, Kôken. "Ningen no jiyû to byôdô" (On liberty and equality), *Soshiorojika* 1(2), 1977 : 19-47.

5003   SHIBATA, Shingo (ed.). *Ningen no kenri* (Human rights). Tokyo, Otsuki Shoten, 77, 222 p.

19340. Government
Gouvernement

[See also / Voir aussi: 1489]

5004   ALEX, Nicholas. *New York cops talk back: a study of a beleaguered minority.* New York, John Wiley and Sons, 76, 225 p. CR: Michael WILLIAMS, *Contemp. Sociol. (Washington)* 6(3), mai 77 : 375.

5005   ARCURI, Alan F. "You can't take fingerprints off water: police officers' view toward 'cop' television shows", *Hum. Relat.* 30(3), mar 77 : 237-247.

5006   BROGDEN, M. "A police authority - the denial of conflict", *Sociol. R.* 25(2), mai 77 : 325-349. [UK.]

5007   BUNYAN, Tony. *The political police in Britain.* New York, St. Martin's Press, 76, 320 p.

5008   ENLOE, Cynthia H. "Police and military in the resolution of conflict", *A. Amer. Acad. polit. soc. Sci.* 433, sep 77 : 137-149.

5009   FEUILLE, Peter; JURIS, Hervey A. "Police professionalization and police unions", *Sociol. Wk Occupat.* 3(1), feb 76 : 88-1113.

5010   GOLDSTEIN, Herman. *Policing a free society.* Cambridge, Mass., Ballinger Publishing Co., 77, xi-371 p.

5011   GRIFFETH, Roger W.; GAFFERTY, Thomas P. "Police and citizen value systems: some cross-sectional comparisons", *J. appl. soc. Psychol.* 7(3), jul-sep 77 : 191-204.

5012   HOLDAWAY, Simon. "Changes in urban policing", *Brit. J. Sociol.* 28(2), jun 77 : 119-137.

5013   INN, Andrea; WHEELER, Alan C. "Individual differences, situational constraints, and police shooting incidents", *J. appl. soc. Psychol.* 7(1), jan-mar 77 : 19-26.

5014   INN, Andrea; WHEELER, Alan C.; SPARLING, Cynthia L. "The effects of suspect race and situation hazard on police officer shooting behavior", *J. appl. soc. Psychol.* 7(1), jan-mar 77 : 27-37.

5015   LOTZ, Roy; REGOLI, Robert M. "Police cynism and professionalism", *Hum. Relat.* 30(2), feb 77 : 175-186.

5016   SNYDER, David. "Theoretical and methodological problems in the analysis of governmental coercion and collective violence", *J. polit milit. Sociol.* 4(2), 1976 : 277-293.

5017   TANNAHILL, R. Neal. "The performance of military and civilian go-
        vernments in South America, 1948-1967", *J. polit. milit. Sociol.*
        4(2), 1976 : 233-244.

5018   TOKI, Hiroshi. "Shimin-ishiki to gyôsei shimin kankei" (The rela-
        tion between citizen and municipal government in case of Sendai
        and Hiroshima), *Toshi-mondai* 68(8), 1977 : 53-76.

5019   YINGER, J. Milton. "Presidential address: countercultures and social
        change", *Amer. sociol. R.* 42(6), dec 77 : 833-853.

19350. Parliament
Parlement

[See also / Voir aussi: 5158, 5168]

5020   CAMPBELL, Colin. "Interplay of institutionalization and assignment
        of tasks in parliamentary and congressional systems: House of
        Commons and House of Representatives", *Int. J. comp. Sociol.*
        18(1-2), mar-jun 77 : 127-151.

5021   CLARKE, Harold D.; PRICE, Richard G. "A note on the pre-nomination
        role and socialization of freshmen members of Parliament", *Ca-
        nad. J. polit. Sci.* 10(2), jun 77 : 391-406.

19360. Judiciary power
Pouvoir judiciaire

[See also / Voir aussi: 5470]

5023   HOROWITZ, Donald L. *The courts and social policy.* Washington, Brook-
        ings Institution, 77, 309 p. [USA.]

5024   FEARS, Denise. "Communication in English juvenile courts", *Sociol.
        R.* 25(1), feb 77 : 131-145.

5025   JACOUBOVITCH, M. Daniel *et al.* "Juror responses to direct and me-
        diated presentations of expert testimony", *J. appl. soc. Psychol.*
        7(3), jul-sep 77 : 227-238.

5026   KAPLAN, Martin F. "Discussion polarization effects in a modified
        jury decision paradigm: informational influences", *Sociometry*
        40(3), 1977 : 262-271.

5027   NEMETH, Charlan. "Interactions between jurors as a function of ma-
        jority vs. unanimity decision rules", *J. appl. soc. Psychol.*
        7(1), jan-mar 77 : 38-56.

5028   ROBERT, Philippe; GODEFROY, Thierry. "Le système de justice pénale
        analysé à travers une étude de coûts", *Sociol. Trav.* 19(3),
        jul-sep 77 · 266-294.

5029   WILSON, David W.; DONNERSTEIN, Edward. "Guilty or not guilty ? A
        look at the 'simulated' jury paradigm", *J. appl. soc. Psychol.*
        7(2), apr-jun 77 : 175-190.

5030   WOLF, Sharon; MONTGOMERY, David A. "Effects of inadmissible eviden-
        ce and level of judicial admonishment to disregard on the judg-
        ments of mock jurors", *J. appl. soc. Psychol.* 7(3), jul-sep 77 :
        205-219.

19400. PUBLIC ADMINISTRATION
ADMINISTRATION PUBLIQUE

19410. Civil service. Technocracy
Fonction publique. Technocratie

[See also / Voir aussi: 540]

5031   AKIN, William E. *Technocracy and the American dream: the technocrat
        movement, 1900-1941.* Berkeley, University of California Press,
        77, xv-227 p.

5032   BADILLO NIETO, M. "Hacía un nuevo concepto de control. El control
        interno de la administración: la intervención general del Estado"
        (Towards a new concept of control. The internal control of admi-
        nistration: the general intervention of the State), *Bol. Docum.*

Fondo Invest. econ. soc. 8(1-2), jan-jun 76 : 26-30. *[Spain.]*

5033 BAKKERODE, H. *et al.* "The responsibility of the civil servant
in the Netherlands", *Administration (Dublin)* 23(4), 1975 : 396-
422.

5034 GONZALEZ-HABA GUISADO, Vicente. "La nueva imagen del funcionario
público" (The new image of the civil servant), *Docum. adm.* 174,
apr-jun 77 : 37-67. *[Spain.]*

5035 HÜVELY, I. "A technokrata-fogalom értelmezéséröl és szerepéröl"
(Interpretation and role of the concept of technocrat), *Társadtud. Közl.* 7(1), 1977 : 26-46.

5036 JENSEN, Mogens Braband. *Informationssystemer i den offentlige for-
valtning* (Information systems in public administration). Århus,
Politica, Institut for Statskundskab, Universitetsparken, 76,
200 p. *[Denmark.]*

5037 KÖNIG, Klaus. "Les systèmes européens de formation en matière d'administration publique", *R. franç. Adm. publ.* (2), apr-jun 77 :
105-133.

5038 LETOWSKI, Janusz. "La réforme de la fonction publique en Pologne",
R. franç. Adm. publ. (1), jan-mar 77 : 137-146.

5039 MACRAE, D. "Technical communities and political choice", *Minerva*
14(2), 1976 : 169-190.

5040 MATTERN, Karl-Heinz. "Le perfectionnement des fonctionnaires en
République fédérale d'Allemagne", *R. franç. Adm. publ.* (2),
apr-jun 77 : 133-143.

5041 PATRONO, Marie. "Tecnocrazia e potere politico nei paesi del capitalismo avanzato" (Technocary and political power in the countries of advanced capitalism), *Amministrare* (3), jul-sep 77 : 195-
220.

5042 PRÄTORIUS, Rainer. *Folgen der Planung: Untersuchung zur politische
Verwaltungssoziologie des Interventionsstaates* (Consequences of
planning: study of the political administration sociology of
the intervention states). Lollar-am-Lahn, Achenbach, 77, 262 p.

5043 ROSENTHAL, V. "Communalism and the clientele bureaucracy: research
into the relations between the administration and the adminis-
trated in the Netherlands", *Netherlands J. Sociol.* 12(1), jul
76 : 79-88.

5044 SADRAN, Pierre. "Recrutement et sélection par concours dans l'administration française", *R. franç. Adm. publ.* (1), jan-mar 77 :
53-107.

5045 SHERIFF, P. *Career patterns in the higher civil service.* London,
HMSO, 76, 74 p. CR: Michalina VAUGHAN, *Brit. J. Sociol.* 28(2),
jun 77 : 261-283.

5046 SIMARD, Jean-Jacques. "La longue marche des technocrates", *Rech.
sociogr.* 18(1), jan-apr 77 : 93-132.

5047 SMITH, M. P. "Barriers to organizational democracy in public administration", *Adm. and Soc.* 8(3), nov 76 : 275-317.

5048 SZENTPÉTERI, I. "Az igazgatási struktúra-típusok" (The types of
structure in administration), *Szociológia* 6(1), 1977 : 57-78.

5049 WARWICK, Donald P.; MEADE, Marvin; REED, Theodore. *A theory of
public bureaucracy: politics, personality, and organization in the
State Department.* Cambridge, Mass.-London, Harvard University
Press, 76, xii-252 p.

19420. Central government. Local government
Administration centrale. Administration locale

[See also / Voir aussi: 5135, 5138]

5050 BARTON, Allen *et al. Decentralizing city government: an evaluation
of the New York City district manager experiment.* Lexington,
Mass., Lexington Books, 77, xix-279 p.

5051 BECQUART-LECLERQ, Jeanne. "Légitimité et pouvoir local", *R. franç.
Sci. polit.* 27(2), apr 77 : 228-258.

5053   CALLON, Michel; VIGNOLLE, Jean Pierre. "Breaking down the orga-
        nization: local conflicts and societal systems of action", *Soc.*
        Sci. Inform. 16(2), 1977 : 147-167.
5054   COCKBURN, Cynthia. "The local state management of cities and people",
        Race and Class mar 77 : 363-376.
5055   KOSHI, Heikki. "Developing local planning in Finland", *Planning*
        and Adm. 4(2), 1977 : 39-48.
5056   PAPP, I. "A közigazgatási döntési folyamat vizsgálata megyei ta-
        nácsi szervekben" (Survey on the process of decision-making in
        public administration at the county council bodies), *Állam és*
        Igazg. 27(9), sep 77 : 796-810.
5057   SELLIER, M. "Les groupes d'action municipale", *Sociol. Trav.* 19(1),
        jan-mar 77 : 41-58. *[France.]*
5058   SIEWERT, H.-Jörg. "Verein und Kommunalpolitik" (Associations and
        municipal policy), *Kölner Z. Soziol. u. soz.-Psychol.*29(3), sep
        77 : 487-510.
5059   SZEGÖ, A. "A területi érdekviszonyok, a központosított ujrafelosz-
        tás és a területi igazgatás" (The regional interest relations,
        the centralized redistribution and the regional administration),
        Szociológia 5(3-4), 1976 : 420-440.
5060   ZAWODZIŃSKI, Stefan. "Rola gminy w rozwoju wsi i rolnictwa" (Role
        of commune in rural and agricultural development), *Nowe Drogi*
        30(2), feb 77 : 174-181. *[Poland.]*

        19500. POLITICAL PARTY. PRESSURE GROUP
               PARTI POLITIQUE. GROUPE DE PRESSION

        19510. Party system. Political party
               Système de parti. Parti politique

        [See also / Voir aussi: 559, 2326, 3214, 3652, 4780]

5061   BECK, Nathaniel; PIERCE, John. "Political involvement and party
        allegiances in Canada and the United States", *Int. J. comp. Sociol.*
        18(1-2), mar-jun 77 : 23-44.
5062   CAVAROZZI, Marcelo. "Populismo y 'partidos de clasa media'" (Po-
        pulism and "middle class parties"), *R. mexic. Sociol.* 39(1), jan-
        mar 77 : 119-154. *[Latin America.]*
5063   DOMINGUEZ, J. I.; MITCHELL, C. N. "The roads not taken: institu-
        tionalization and political parties in Cuba and Bolivia", *Comp.*
        Polit. 9(2), jan 77 : 173-195.
5064   ELLEINSTEIN, Jean. *Le PC.* Paris, B. Grasset, 76, 210 p. *[Parti com-*
        muniste, France.]
5065   FABRE, Jean; HINCKER, François; SÈVE, Lucien. *Les Communistes et*
        l'État. Paris, Éditions sociales, 77, 248 p.
5066   FAUVET, Jacques; DUHAMEL, Alain. *Histoire du Parti Communiste Fran-*
        çais: de 1920 à 1976. Paris, A. Fayard, 77, 605 p.
5067   FICKETT, Lewis P. *The major socialist parties of India: a study in*
        leftist fragmentation. Syracuse, N.Y., Syracuse University, 76,
        vii-185 p.
5068   GAXIE, Daniel. "Économie des partis et rétribution du militantisme",
        R. franç. Sci. polit. 27(1), feb 77 : 123-154.
5069   HILLER, Harry H. "Internal problem resolution and third party emer-
        gence", *Canad. J. Sociol.* 2(1), 1977 : 55-75.
5070   JOURNES, Claude. *L'extrême gauche en Grande-Bretagne.* Paris, Lib-
        rairie générale de droit et de jurisprudence, 77, 229 p.
5071   MER, Jacqueline. *Le parti de Maurice Thorez ou le bonheur commu-*
        niste français. Étude anthropologique. Paris, Payot, 77, 241 p.
5072   MONCADA, Alberto. "Notas para une sociología de la extrema derecha"
        (Notes for a sociology of the extreme right), *Sistema* 20, sep
        77 : 111-118.
5073   PADOVANI, Marcelle. *La longue marche: le Parti communiste italien.*
        Paris, Calmann-Lévy, 76, 270 p.

5074   PETERSON, P. E.; KANTOR, P. "Political parties and citizen participation in English city policies", *Comp. Polit.* 9(2), jan 77 :
197-217.

5075   PFISTER, Thierry. *Les socialistes.* Paris, A. Michel, 77, 213 p.

5076   RUDOLPH, Joseph R. Jr. "Ethnonational parties and political change: the Belgian and British experience", *Polity* 9(4), 1977 : 401-
426.

5077   SALLES, René. "Le Parti communiste de Grande Bretagne et les élections", *R. franç. Sci. polit.* 27(3), jun 77 : 407-427.

5078   SARTORI, Giovanni. *Parties and party systems: a framework for
analysis.* Cambridge, Eng.-New York, Cambridge University Press,
76, xiii-370 p.

5079   STEININGER, R. "Pillarization (verzuiling) and political parties",
Sociol. Gids 24(4), jul-aug 77 : 242-257.

5080   TANNAHILL, R. N. "The future of the Communist parties of Western
Europe", *Wld Aff.* 139(2), 1976 : 141-154.

5081   TEMPESTINI, Attilio. "Il problema dei partiti in Ostrogorski"
(The problem of parties in Ostrogorski), *Quad. Sociol.* 25(4),
oct-dec 76 : 366-391.

5082   VAZQUEZ, Verónica. "Selección bibliográfica sobre los principales
partidos políticos mexicanos, 1906-1970" (Selected bibliography
on the main Mexican political parties, 1906-1970), *R. mexic.
Sociol.* 39(2), apr-jun 77 : 677-715.

5083   WOODWARD, C. A. "The emergence of competitive party systems: comparative observations on the custodial party period in the United
States, Sri Lanka and Canada", *Verfassung u. Recht Übersee* 9(3),
1976 : 301-313.

19520. Pressure group. Protest movement
Groupe de pression. Mouvement contestataire

[See also / Voir aussi: 1475, 4692, 5130, 5577]

5084   ADDARIO, Nicolo. "Teoria azionalista e movimenti di rivolta" (Ac-
tionalist theory and protest movements), *Rass. ital. Sociol.*
18(3), jul-sep 77 : 431-438.

5085   ARCHIBALD, Clinton; PALTIEL, Kayyam Z. "Du passage des corps inter-
médiaires aux groupes de pression: la transformation d'une idée
illustrée par le mouvement coopératif Desjardins", *Rech. sociogr.*
18(1), jan-apr 77 : 59-91.

5086   BEACH, Stephen W. "Social movement radicalization: the case of the
People's Democracy in Northern Ireland", *Sociol. Quart.* 18(3),
1977 : 305-318.

5087   BLACKEY, Robert. *Modern revolutions and revolutionists. A bibliography.* Santa Barbara, Calif., American Bibliographical Center-
Clio Press; Oxford, European Bibliographical Center-Clio Press,
76, xxviii-257 p.

5088   BURTON, Michael G. "Elite disunity and collective protest: the
Vietnam case", *J. polit. milit. Sociol.* 5(2), 1977 : 169-183.

5089   DELLI SANTE DE ARROCHA, Angela. "La intervención ideológica de la
empresa transnacional en países dependientes: el caso de México"
(The ideological intervention of transnational corporation in
dependent countries: the case of Mexico), *R. mexic. Sociol.*
39(1), jan-mar 77 : 303-323.

5090   EICHLER, Margrit. "Leadership in social movements", *Sociol. Inquiry*
48(2), 1977 : 99-107.

5091   HARRISON, Michael I. "Dimensions of involvement in social movements",
Sociol. Focus 10(4), oct 77 : 353-366.

5092   KRITZER, Herbert M. "Political protest and political violence: a
nonrecursive causal model", *Soc. Forces* 55(3), mar 77 : 630-640.
[USA.]

5093   KUJI, Toshitake. "Soshiki moderu kara undô moderu e" (From organization model to movement model), *Soshioroji* 22(2), 1977 : 119-
130.

5094   LANZA, Orazio. "Gli enti del settore agricolo nel sistema politico
       italiano" (Agricultural sector agencies in the Italian political
       system), *Rass. ital. Sociol.* 18(2), apr-jun 77 : 247-271.
5095   LEVITAS, R. A. "Some problems of aim-centred models of social
       movements", *Sociology (London)* 11(1), jan 77 : 47-63.
5096   MARX, J. H.; HOLZNER, B. "The social construction of strain and
       ideological models of grievance in contemporary movement", *Pa-
       cific sociol. R.* 20(3), 1977 : 411-438.
5097   OLSEN, Marvin E. "Influence linkages between interest organiza-
       tions and the government in Sweden", *J. polit. milit. Sociol.*
       5(1), 1977 : 35-51.
5098   ORREN, K. "Standing to sue: interest group conflict in the Federal
       Courts", *Amer. polit. Sci. R.* 70(3), sep 76 : 723-741. *[USA.]*

       19530. Political majority. Political opposition
             Majorité politique. Opposition politique

       [See also / Voir aussi: 5112]

5099   HUGLIN, Thomas O. *Tyrannei der Mehrheit* (The tyranny of the majo-
       rity). Bern, P. Haupt, 77, iv-353 p.
5100   SCOTT, Joseph W. "Afro-Americans as a political class: towards
       conceptual clarity", *Sociol. Focus* 10(4), oct 77 : 383-395.

       19600. POLITICAL BEHAVIOUR. ELECTIONS. POLITICS
             COMPORTEMENT POLITIQUE. ÉLECTIONS. POLITIQUE

       19610. Political leader. Political society
             Leader politique. Société politique

       [See also / Voir aussi: 4138, 5088, 5127, 5447]

5102   DE SOUZA, A. "Some social and economic determinants of leadership
       in India", *Soc. Action* 26(4), oct-dec 76 : 329-350.
5103   HALL, J. A. "The role and influence of political intellectuals:
       Tawney vs. Sidney Webb", *Brit. J. Sociol.* 28(3), sep 77 : 351-362.
5104   JOHNSON, Graham E. "Leaders and leadership in an expanding New
       Territories town", *China Quart.* 69, mar 77 : 109-125. *[Hong Kong.]*
5105   KIRKPATRICK, Jeane J. et al. *The new Presidential elite: men and
       women in national politics.* New York, Basic Books, 76, xix-605
       p. *[USA.]*
5106   MAZRUI, Ali A. "Boxer Muhammed Ali and soldier Idi Amin as interna-
       tional political symbols: the bioeconomics of sport and war",
       Comp. Stud. Soc. Hist. 19(2), apr 77 : 189-215.
5107   NAKANO, Hideichirô. "Gendai Malaysia ni okeru seiji-teki Leader-
       ship no shiteki tokusei bunseki" (Malaysia's political leadership),
       Tônan Ajia Kenkyû 15(2), 1977 : 153-177.
5108   ROCKMAN, Bert A. *Studying elite political culture: problems in
       design and interpretation.* Pittsburg, University Center for
       International Studies, University of Pittsburgh, 76, 17 p.
5109   SLOAN, J. W.; WEST, J. P. "Community integration and policies among
       elites in two border-cities: los dos Laredo", *J. inter-Amer.
       Stud. Wld Aff.* 18(4), nov 76 : 451-474. *[Mexico.]*
5110   SPADARO, Robert N. "Political constraints on public policy. The
       folkways of politicians", *Hum. Relat.* 29(3), mar 76 : 287-305.
5111   TUCKER, Robert C. "Personality and political leadership", *Polit.
       Sci. Quart.* 92(3), 1977 : 383-393.

       19620. Political attitude. Political participation
             Attitude politique. Participation politique

       [See also / Voir aussi: 702, 1776, 2231, 2349, 2638, 2664, 2942,
       2965, 3577, 4139, 5074, 5188]

5112   ABRAMSON, Paul R. *The political socialization of Black Americans.*
       New York, Free Press, 77, xi-195 p.

5113   ALFORD, R. R.; FRIEDLAND, R. "Political participation and public policy", *Ann. R. Sociol.* (1), 1975 : 429-479.

5114   AMELANG, Manfred; WENDT, Wolfgang. "Stabilität und Veränderungen von Einstellungen gegenüber Fragen der aktuellen Politik – ein Längsschnittvergleich der Jahre 1972 und 1975" (Stability and change of attitudes towards problems of contemporary politics; a longitudinal comparison between 1972 and 1975 years), *Z. soz.-Psychol.* 8(3), 1977 : 167-184.

5115   BÄCKER, Ferdinand Fred; HARNEY, Klaus. *Politische Sozialisation und politische Bildung* (Political socialization and political education). Opladen, Leske Verlag, 76, 87 p.

5116   BECK, Paul Allen. "Partisan dealignment in the postwar South", *Amer. polit. Sci. R.* 71(2), jun 77 : 477-496. [USA.]

5117   BERGESEN, Albert James. "Political witch hunts: the sacred and the subversive in cross-national perspective", *Amer. sociol. R.* 42(2), apr 77 : 220-233.

5118   BETTINI, Romano. *Istituzionalizzazione e prassi della partecipazione del cittadino: un'indagine a Messina* (Institutionalization and practice of citizen's participation: an investigation in Messina). Roma, B. Carucci, 76, 361 p.

5119   BUDGE, Ian; CREWE, Ivor; FARLIE, Dennis (eds.). *Party identification and beyond: representatives of voting and party competition.* New York, Wiley, 76, x-393 p. CR: David KNOKE, *Amer. J. Sociol.* 83(3), nov 77 : 793-795.

5120   CASSEL, Carol A. "Cohort analysis of party identification among Southern Whites", 1952-1972", *Publ. Opin. Quart.* 41(1), 1977 : 28-33. [USA.]

5121   CHIBNALL, Steven; SAUNDERS, Peter. "Worlds apart: notes on the social reality of corruption", *Brit. J. Sociol.* 28(2), jun 77 : 138-154.

5122   CLAUSSEN, Bernhard (ed.). *Materialien zur politischen Sozialisation* (Materials on political socialization). München-Basel, E. Reinhardt, 76, 231 p.

5123   COHEN, Steven Martin; KAPSIS, Robert E. "Religion, ethnicity, and party affiliation in the US: evidence from pooled electoral surveys, 1968-1972", *Soc. Forces* 56(2), dec 77 : 637-653.

5124   DANIGELIS, Nicholas L. "A theory of Black political participation in the United States", *Soc. Forces* 56(1), sep 77 : 31-47.

5125   DIETZ, H. A. "Political participation by the urban poor in an authoritarian context: the case of Lima, Peru", *J. polit. milit. Sociol.* 5(1), 1977 : 63-77.

5126   DOUGLAS, Jack D.; JOHNSON, John M. *Official deviance: readings in malfeasance, misfeasance, and other forms of corruption.* New York, Lippincott, 77, 426 p. [Corruption in politics in the USA.]

5127   EAGLY, A. H.; CHAIKEN, S. "Why would anyone say that ? Causal attribution of statements about the Watergate scandal", *Sociometry* 39(3), sep 76 : 236-243.

5128   ETZIONI-HALEVY, Eva; SHAPIRA, Rina. *Political culture in Israel: cleavage and integration among Israeli Jews.* New York, Praeger, 77, xxiv-249 p.

5129   FENDRICH, James M. "Black and white activists ten years later. Political socialization and adult left-wing politics", *Youth and Soc.* 8(1), sep 76 : 81-104.

5130   FENDRICH, James M. "Keeping the faith or pursuing the good life: a study of the consequences of participation in the civil rights movement", *Amer. sociol. R.* 42(1), feb 77 : 144-157.

5131   FERGUSON, Le ROY C.; FERGUSON, Lucy R.; BOUTOURLINE-YOUNG, Harben. "An attempt to relate age at puberal maturity to political orientations", *Soc. Sci. Inform.* 15(6), 1976 : 943-952.

5132   GAUDETTE, Gabriel. "La culture politique de la CSD", *Rech. sociogr.* 17(1), jan-apr 76 : 35-72. [Centrale des syndicats démocratiques au Canada.]

5133   GUZMAN, Ralph C. *The political socialization of the Mexican Ameri-can people.* Rev. ed. New York, Arno Press, 76, xiv-266 p.

5134   HUNTINGTON, Samuel P.; NELSON, Joan M. *No easy choice: political participation in developing countries.* Cambridge, Mass., Harvard University Press, 76, x-202 p.

5135   HUTCHESON, John D. Jr.; SHEVIN, Jann. *Citizen groups in local politics: a bibliographic review.* Santa Barbara, Calif., Clio Books, 76, xi-275 p.

5136   IWASE, Yôri. "Seitô shijitaido no keisei to kazoku no yakuwari" (The role of family in party identification process among high school students), *Hyrônsha Shakai-kagaku* (12), 1977 : 28-43.

5137   JABBRA, J. G.; LANDES, R. G. "Political orientations among adolescents in Nova Scotia", *Ind. J. polit. Sci.* 27(4), oct-dec 76 : 75-96. *[Canada.]*

5138   KANEKO, Isamu. "Shimin sanka to toshi-seiji-shakaigaku" (Citizen participation and urban political sociology), *Shakaigaku Kenkyu Nenpo* (7-8), 1977 : 12-19.

5139   KOPPMAN-IWEMA, Agnes M.; THOERRY, Henk. "Participatie, motivatie en machtsafstand" (Participation, motivation and power distance), *Mens en Onderneming* 31(5), sep-oct 77 : 263-284.

5140   KUO, Wen H. "Black political participation; a reconsideration", *J. polit. milit. Sociol.* 5(1), 1977 : 1-16. *[USA.]*

5141   KWILECKI, Andrzej. "Przemiany w świadomości społeczno-politicznej ludności Wielkopolski" (Changes in the social and political consciousness of the population of the region "Great Poland"), *Stud. socjol.* 63(4), 1976 : 185-195.

5142   LANDES, Ronald G. "Political socialization among youth: a comparative study of English-Canadian and American school children", *Int. J. comp. Sociol.* 18(1-2), mar-jun 77 : 63-81.

5143   LONG, S. "Perceived relative deprivation and political orientation: a study of white and black adolescents", *J. polit. milit. Sociol.* 5(1), 1977 : 99-115.

5144   LÜCK, Volker. *Basiskonzepte der politischen Sozialisationsfor-schung: eine Kritik* (Basic concepts of the political socialization research: a criticism). Frankfurt-am-Main, Peter Lang, 76, 222 p.

5146   MANNHEIMER, Renato; MICHELI, Giuseppe. "Luttes à l'usine, luttes à la ville: la participation politique des immigrés méridionaux en Italie du Nord", *Éspaces et Soc.* 19, dec 76 : 65-82.

5147   MARTIN, Colin; MARTIN, Dick. "The decline of Labour Party membership", *Polit. Quart.* 48(4), oct-dec 77 : 459-471. *[UK.]*

5148   MEDDING, Peter Y. "Towards a general theory of Jewish political interests and behaviour", *Jew. J. Sociol.* 19(2), dec 77 : 115-144. *[USA.]*

5149   MORGAN, David R.; REGENS, James L. "Political participation among federal employees: the Hatch Act and political equality", *Midwest R. publ. Adm.* 10(4), dec 76 : 193-200. *[USA.]*

5150   NAKANO, Hideichirô. "Seiji jôhô to seiji-teki shiko" (Information and orientation in political behaviour), *Kansei-gakuin daigaku Shakaigakubu Kiyo* 35, 1977 : 33-47.

5151   NASR, Nafhat; PALMER, Monte. "Alienation and political participation in Lebanon", *Int. J. Mid. East Stud.* 8(4), oct 77 : 493-516.

5152   NATHAN, J. A.; REMY, R. C. "Political structure and political attitudes: a cross-national comparison", *Amer. Polit. Quart.* 4(4), oct 76 : 423-440.

5153   NIEMI, Richard G. *et al.* "The similarity of husband's and wives political views", *Amer. polit. Quart.* 5(2), apr 77 : 133-148. *[USA.]*

5154   O'KANE, James M. *et al.* "Anticipatory socialization and male Catholic adolescent socio-political attitudes", *Sociometry* 40(1), mar 77 : 67-77.

5155   ÖZBUDUN, Ergun. *Social change and political participation in Turkey.*
        Princeton, N.J., Princeton University Press, 76, xiii-254 p.
5156   PARSON, Jack. "Political culture in rural Botswana: a survey re-
        sult", *J. mod. Afr. Stud.* 15(4), dec 77 : 639-650.
5157   PEN, J. "Political behaviour, the rules of the game: fiction and
        reality", *Netherlands J. Sociol.* 12(1), jul 76 : 89-93.
5158   PRESTHUS, Robert. "Aspects of political culture and legislative
        behavior: United States and Canada", *Int. J. comp. Sociol.* 18(1-
        2), mar-jun 77 : 7-23.
5159   RAGIN, Charles. "Class, status, and 'reactive ethnic cleavages':
        the social bases of political regionalism", *Amer. sociol. R.*
        42(3), jun 77 : 438-450.
5160   RICH, Harvey E. "The effect of college on politiwal awareness and
        knowledge", *Youth and Soc.* 8(1), sep 76 : 67-80.
5161   RODGERS, Harrel R. Jr.; TEDIN, Kent L. "Political socialization:
        an assessment of theoretical approaches, methods and findings",
        Youth and Soc. 8(2), dec 76 : 107-207; 8(3), mar 77 : 212-320.
5162   SEGATORI, Roberto. "Socializzazione infantile ed emancipazione po-
        litica" (The socialization of children and political emancipa-
        tion), *Riv. Sociol.* 14(1-3), jan-dec 76 : 179-204.
5163   SELIGSON, M. H.; BOOTH, J. A. "Political participation in Latin
        America: an agenda for research", *Latin Amer. Res. R.* 11(3),
        1976 : 95-119.
5164   VERBA, Sidney; NIE, Norman H. *Political participation in America,
        March-July, 1967.* Ann Arbor, Mich., Inter-university Consortium
        for Political and Social Research, 76, xi-372 p.
5165   WEEDE, Erich. "Politische Kultur, Institutionalisierung und Prä-
        torianismus: Überlegungen zur Theorie und empirischen Forschungs-
        praxis" (Political culture, institutionalization and praetorian-
        ism: thoughts about the theory and empirical research practice),
        Kölner Z. Soziol. u. soz.-Psychol. 29(3), sep 77 : 411-437;
        29(4), dec 77 : 657-676.

        19630. Elections
               Élections

        [See also / Voir aussi: 2030, 2640, 5145]

5166   ALDRICH, John H. "Electoral choice in 1972: a test of some theorems
        of the spatial model of electoral competition", *J. maht. Sociol.*
        5(2), 1977 : 215-238.
5167   BACOT, Paul. "Le comportement électoral des instituteurs: mitteran-
        distes et giscardiens", *R. franç. Sci. polit.* 27(6), dec 77 : 884-
        914. [France.]
5168   BURSTEIN, Paul; FREUDENBURG, William. "Ending the Vietnam War: com-
        ponents of change in Senate voting on Vietnam War bills", *Amer.
        J. Sociol.* 82(5), mar 77 : 991-1006.
5169   DARCY, R.; SCHRAMM, Sarah Slavin. "When women run against men",
        Publ. Opin. Quart. 41(1), 1977 : 1-12. [Voting behaviour in the
        USA.]
5170   GRANBERG, Donald; JENKS, Richard. "Assimilation and contrast effects
        in the 1972 election", *Hum. Relat.* 30(7), jul 77 : 623-640.
5171   GRANBERG, D.; SEIDEL, J. "Social judgments of the urban Vietnam
        issues in 1968 and 1972", *Soc. Forces* 55(1), sep 76 : 1-15.
5172   GRECO, Giacchino. "Il voto femminile a Salerno. Un'indagine prelimi-
        nare" (Female voting in Salerno. A preliminary survey), *Quad. So-
        ciol.* 26(1), jan-mar 77 : 64-86. [Italy.]
5173   HAMMOND, John L. "Race and electoral mobilization white Southerners,
        1952-1968", *Publ. Opin. Quart.* 41(1), 1977 : 13-27. [USA.]
5174   HEDLUND, Ronald D. "Cross-over voting in a 1976 open presidential
        primary", *Publ. Opin. Quart.* 41(4), 1977 : 498-514. [USA.]
5175   HUDON, Raymond. "Les études électorales au Québec: principales
        orientations et quelques débats", *Rech. sociogr.* 17(3), sep-dec

76 : 283-322.

5176 KUKLINSKI, James H. "District competitiveness and legislative roll-call behavior: a reassessment of the marginality hypothesis", *Amer. J. polit. Sci.* 21(3), aug 77 : 627-639. *[USA.]*

5177 KUSHNER, Harvey W.; DE MAIO, Gerald. "Using digraphs to determine the crucial actos in a voting body", *Sociometry* 40(4), dec 77 : 361-369.

5178 LOTZ, Roy; HEWITT, John D. "The influence of legally irrelevant factors on felony sentencing", *Sociol. Inquiry* 47(1), 1977 : 39-48.

5179 MANNHEIMER, Renato; MICHELI, Giuseppe. "Il comportamento elettorale a Milano" (Voting behaviour in Milan), *Rass. ital. Sociol.* 17(4), oct-dec 76 : 619-639. *[Italy.]*

5180 MARTINEZ-ALIER, Verena; BOITO, Armando Jr. "The hoe and the vote rural labourers and the national election in Brazil in 1974", *J. Peasant Stud.* 4(3), apr 77 : 148-170.

5181 McALLISTER, I. "Social influences on voters and non-voters: a note on two Northern Ireland election", *Polit. Stud. (Oxford)* 24(4), dec 76 : 462-468.

5182 MONROE, Alan D. "Urbanism and voter turnout: a note on some unexpected findings", *Amer. J. polit. Sci.* 21(1), feb 77 : 71-78. *[USA, Illinois.]*

5183 NISHIHIRA, Shigeki. "An anatomy of the 1976 election", *Japan Echo* 4(2), 1977 : 67-76. *[Japan.]*

5184 NYGREN, Thomas E.; JONES, Lawrence E. "Individual differences in perceptions and preferences for political candidates", *J. exp. soc. Psychol.* 13(2), mar 77 : 182-197.

5185 POMPER, Gérald M. "Profil de l'électeur américain", *Dialogue (Washington)* 8(1), 1977 : 82-91.

5186 "Sociología electoral" (Electoral sociology), *R. esp. Opin. publ.* 48, apr-jun 77 : 7-343. *[Spain.]*

5187 TROITZSCH, Klaus G. *Sozialstruktur und Wählerverhalten* (Social structure and voting behaviour). Meisenheim-am-Glan, A. Hain, 76, 142 p. *[Germany FR.]*

5188 VALENZUELA, Arturo. "Political participation, agriculture and literacy: communal versus provincial voting patterns in Chile", *Latin Amer. Res. R.* 12(1), 1977 : 105-114.

5189 "Wahlsoziologie heute. Analysen aus Anlass der Bundestagswahl 1976" (Electoral sociology today. Analyses regarding the parliamentary election of 1976), *Polit. Vjschr.* 18(2-3), 1977 : 139-704. *[Germany FR.]*

5190 WIATR, Jerzy J. "Głos za zmianą: amerykanskie wybory prezydenckie 1976" (A voice for change: American presidential elections, 1976), *Stud. socjol.* 65(2), 1977 : 207-229.

5191 WRIGHT, Gerald Jr. "Contextual models of electoral behavior: the Southern Wallace vote", *Amer. polit. Sci. R.* 71(2), jun 77 : 497-508. *[USA.]*

5192 ZUKERMAN, Alan S.; LICHBACH, Mark Irving. "Stability and change in European electorates", *Wld Polit.* 29(4), jul 77 : 523-551.

19640. Politics
Politique

[See also / Voir aussi: 1741, 1744, 1749, 1758, 1763, 1764, 1766, 1768, 1771, 2041, 2065, 2404]

5193 BOWEN, Don R. "Guerilla war in Western Missouri, 1862-1865: historical extensions of the relative deprivation hypothesis", *Comp. Stud. Soc. Hist.* 19(1), jan 77 : 30-51.

5194 HALEBSKY, Sandor. *Mass society and political conflict: toward a reconstruction of theory.* Cambridge-New York, Cambridge University Press, 76, ix-309 p.

5195   LABASTIDA MARTÍN DEL CAMPO, Julio. "Proceso político y dependencia en México, 1970-1976" (Political process and dependency in Mexico, 1970-1976), *R. mexic. Sociol.* 39(1), jan-mar 77 : 193-227.

5196   LAQUEUR, Walter Ze'ev. *Guerrilla: a historical and critical study.* Boston, Little Brown; London, Weidenfeld and Nicolson, 77, x-462 p.

5197   MEWES, H. "On the concept of politics in the early work of Karl Marx", *Soc. Res.* 43(2), 1976 : 276-294.

5198   MORRISON, D. G.; STEVENSON, H. M. "The practice and explanation of coups d'État: measurement or artifact ?", *Amer. J. Sociol.* 82(3), nov 76 : 674-683.

5199   LE ROY LADURIE, Emmanuel. "La crise et l'historien", *Communications (Paris)* 25, 1976 : 19-33.

5200   PIRAGES, Dennis. *Managing political conflict.* New York, Praeger; Sunbury-on-Thames, Nelson, 76, ix-149 p.

5201   ROSENBAUM, H. Jon; SEDERBERG, Peter C. (eds.). *Vigilente politics.* Philadelphia, University of Pennsylvania Press, 76, x-292 p. CR: Glendon SCHUBERT, *Amer. J. Sociol.* 82(6), mai 77 : 1389-1393.

5202   ROUCEK, Joseph S. "Guerrilla warfare: marginal aspects of modern wars", *Int. behav. Scientist* 8(2), dec 76 : 23-35.

5203   STARN, Randolph. "Métamorphoses d'une notion. Les historiens et la 'crise'", *Communications (Paris)* 25, 1976 : 4-18.

5204   WATANUKI, Joji. *Politics in postwar Japanese society.* Tokyo, Tokyo-daigaku Shuppankai, 77, 171 p.

19700. ARMY. MILITARY SOCIOLOGY
ARMÉE. SOCIOLOGIE MILITAIRE

[See also / Voir aussi: 828, 3343, 3632, 5008, 5017]

5205   BONDARENKO, V. M. *Sovremennaja nauka i razvitie voennogo dela. Voenno-sociologičeskie aspekty problemy* (Contemporary science and development of military affairs. Military and sociological aspects of this problem). Moskva, Voenizdat, 76, 192 p.

5206   CORTESE, Charles F. *Modernization, threat, and the power of the military.* Beverly Hills, Calif., Sage Publications, 76, 64 p.

5207   DEATON, John E. *et al.* "Coping activities in solitary confinement of US Navy POWs in Vietnam", *J. appl. soc. Psychol.* 7(3), jul-sep 77 : 239-257.

5208   FELD, Maury D. *The structure of violence; armed forces as social systems.* Beverly Hills, Calif., Sage Publications, 77, 203 p.

5209   GARNIER, M. A.; HAZELRIGG, L. E. "Military organization and distributional inequality: an examination of Andreski's thesis", *J. polit. milit. Sociol.* 5(1), 1977 : 17-33.

5210   GOLDMAN, Nancy L.; SEGAL, David R. (eds.). *The social psychology of military service.* Beverly Hills, Sage Publications, 76, 288 p. CR: Scott G. McNALL, *Contemp. Sociol. (Washington)* 6(3), mai 77 : 325-326.

5211   HARRIES-JENKINS, Gwyn; VAN DOORN, Jacques. *The military and the problem of legitimacy.* Beverly Hills, Sage Publications, 76, 217 p. CR: Richard MACHALEK, *Contemp. Sociol. (Washington)* 6(3), mai 77 : 326-327.

5212   HERNU, Charles. "Ce n'est plus la discipline mais la conviction qui fait la force principale des armées", *A. Univ. Sci. soc. Toulouse* 25, 1977 : 39-46.

5213   HERRY, Joseph-Louis. *La fonction militaire; évolution statutaire.* Paris, Berger-Levrault, 76, 285 p.

5214   HOROWITZ, Irving Louis. "From dependency to determinism: the new structure of Latin American militarism", *J. polit. milit. Sociol.* 5(2), 1977 : 217-238.

5215   HRABE, Josef. "Kritika jedné buržoazní vojenskosociologické konstrukce" (Critique of one bourgeois military-sociological construction), *Sociol. Čas.* 13(5), 1977 : 494-508.

5216   HUNTER, Edna *et al.* "Resistance posture and the Vietnam prisoner of war", *J. polit. milit. Sociol.* 4(2), 1976 : 295-308.

5217   JACKMAN, R. W. "Politicians in uniform: military governments and social change in the Third World", *Amer. polit. Sci. R.* 70(4), dec 76 : 1078-1097.

5218   JANOWITZ, Morris. *Military institutions and coercion in the developing nations.* Chicago, University of Chicago Press, 77, xiii-211 p.

5219   KOURVETARIS, George A.; DOBRATZ, Betty A. (eds.). *World perspectives in the sociology of the military.* New Brunswick, N.J., Transaction Books, 77, xi-294 p.

5220   LEMARCHAND, René. "African armies in historical and contemporary perspectives: the search for connections", *J. polit. milit. Sociol.* 4(2), 1976 : 261-275.

5221   MANDEVILLE, Lucien. "Le système militaire français et le syndicalimse: répression, tentation et solutions de substitution", *A. Univ. Sci. soc. Toulouse* 25, 1977 : 85-102. Également publié en Italien, *Mulino* 25(244), jul-aug 76 : 554-571.

5222   MARICHY, Jean-Pierre. "La liberté d'expression des militaires de carrière en France", *A. Univ. Sci. soc. Toulouse* 25, 1977 : 67-83.

5223   MARTEL, André. "Permanences et pesanteur du système militaire français: l'avenir et la doctrine", *A. Univ. Sci. soc. Toulouse* 25, 1977 : 13-27.

5224   MARTIN, Michel L. "Un cas d'endorecrutement: le corps des officiers français, 1945)1975", *Archiv. europ. Sociol.* 18(1), 1977 : 27-54.

5225   MINELLO, Nelson. "Uruguay: la consolidación del Estado militar" (Uruguay: the consolidation of the military State), *R. mexic. Sociol.* 39(2), apr-jun 77 : 575-594.

5226   MOSKOS, Charles C. Jr. *Peace soldiers: the sociology of a United Nations military force.* Chicago, University of Chicago Press, 76, 171 p. CR: Ruth Harriet JACOBS, *Amer. J. Sociol.* 83(2), sep 77 : 484-485; Phillip BUTLER, *Contemp. Sociol. (Washington)* 6(2), mar 77 : 214.

5227   RADINE, Lawrence B. *The taming of the troops: social control in the United States Army.* Westport, Conn., Greenwood Press, 77, xii-276 p.

5228   REGENS, James L. "Attitudinal dimensions of military professionalism: perceptions among naval personnel", *J. polit. milit. Sociol.* 5(2), 1977 : 239-257.

5229   SCHIFFRIN, Harold Z. (ed.). *Military and State in modern Asia.* Jerusalem, Jerusalem Academic Press, 76, 309 p. CR: Stephen P. COHEN, *Contemp. Sociol. (Washington)* 6(3), mai 77 : 324-325.

5230   SIERRA, Gerómino DE. "Introducción al estudio de las condiciones de ascenso de las dictaduras militares: el caso uruguayo" (Introduction to the study of the conditions of development of military dictatorship: the case of Uruguay), *R. mexic. Sociol.* 39(2), apr-jun 77 : 567-574.

5231   VIEILLESCAZES, F. "Problématique de la sociologie militaire. Quelques exemples tirés de l'expérience américaine", *Déf. nat.* 32(12), dec 76 : 21-40.

5232   VÖLGYES, Iván. "The political and professional perspectives of the Hungarian armed forces", *J. polit. milit. Sociol.* 5(2), 1977 : 279-294.

5233   ZURCHER, Louis A. Jr. "The naval reservist: an empirical assessment of ephemeral role enactment", *Soc. Forces* 55(3), mar 77 : 753-768.

19800. INTERNATIONAL RELATIONS
RELATIONS INTERNATIONALES

19810. International law. International organization
Droit international. Organisation internationale

[See also / Voir aussi: 1345, 4932]

5234   AKEHURST, Michael. "Custom as a source of international law", *Brit. Yb. int. Law* 47, 1974-1975 : 1-53.

5235   "Approches de l'étude des organisations internationales", *R. int. Sci. soc.* 29(1), 1977 : 7-228.

5236   HAMELINK, Cees. "Internationale orde en internationale communicatie" (International order and international communication), *Massacommunicatie* 5(3), 1977 : 99-104.

5237   HOFFMANN, Stanley. "An American social science: international relations", *Daedalus* 106(3), 1977 : 41-60.

5238   SOJAK, Vladimir. "Reconstruction of the system of international relations", *Int. Relat. (Prague)* 1977 : 19-36.

5239   TUCKER, Robert W. *The inequality of nations.* New York, Basic Books, 77 : X-214 p.

5240   WENDZEL, Robert L. *International relations: a policymaker focus.* New York, Wiley, 77, xii-286 p.

19820. Foreign policy. Sovereignty
Politique étrangère. Souveraineté

[See also / Voir aussi: 3198]

5241   FREYMOND, J. "Diplomatie secrète, diplomatie ouverte. Réflexions sur un thème connu", *Relat. int. (Geneve)* (5), 1976 : 3-10.

5242   INFANTINO, Lorenzo. "Schumpeter e la teoria dell'imperialismo" (Schumpeter and the theory of imperialism), *Riv. Sociol.* 14(1-3), jan-dec 76 : 31-60.

5243   KORTUNOV, V. V. "Obostrenie protivorečij imperializma i sovrmennoja ideologičeskaja bor'ba" (Emphasis on the contradictions of imperialism and ideological struggle today), *Vopr. Ist. KPSS* 20(5), mai 77 : 58-70.

5244   PEARSON, Frederic S.; BAUMANN, Robert. "Foreign military intervention and changes in United States business activity", *J. polit. milit. Sociol.* 5(1), 1977 : 79-97.

5245   WATANUKI, Joni; HOSOYA, Hihiro (eds.). *Taigai seisaku takutekikatei no Nichi-Bei hikaku* (Studies in foreign policy making - Japan and US). Tokyo, Tokyo-daigaku Shuppankai, 77, 484 p.

19830. International cooperation. War
Coopération internationale. Guerre

5246   ALTHERR, Marco. "Les origines de la guerre froide: un essai d'historiographie", *Relat. int. (Genève)* (9), 1977 : 69-81.

5247   ANSART, Pierre. "Idéologie stratégique et stratégie politique", *C. int. Sociol.* 63, jul-dec 77 : 223-242.

5248   BRESSLER, Marion A.; BRESSLER, Leo A. *Peace or war: can humanity make the choice ?* Englewood Cliffs, N.J., Prentice-Hall, 77, vii-120 p.

5249   DANKÁNICS, M. "Különböző korú munkások tudati képe a II. világháborúról" (The image of workers of different ages about World War II), *Szociológia* 5(3-4), 1976 : 494-501.

5250   KUSATSU, Osamu. "Personality and international politics", *Kokusai-kankeigaku Kenkyu* (3), 1977 : 89-95.

5251   LEAVITT, Gregory C. "The frequency of warfare: an evolutionary perspective", *Sociol. Inquiry* 47(1), 1977 : 49-58.

5252   MARIÑO, Primitivo. "La guerra en el pensamiento de Origenes y su entorno cristiano" (The war in Origene's thought and its Christian context), *R. int. Sociol. (Madrid)* 34(17), jan-mar 76 : 7-37.

5253   VAYDA, Andrew P. *War in ecological perspective*. New York, Plenum
        Publications, 76, 129 p. CR: Richard MACHALEK, *Contemp. Sociol.*
        (Washington) 6(3), mai 77 : 326-327.
5254   YAZAWA, Shujiro. "Vietnem senso to America shakai" (The Vietnam
        war and American society), *Gendai to Shiso* 30, 1977 : 49-70.
5255   ZIMMERMANN, Ekkart. "Factor analysis of conflicts within and bet-
        ween nations: a critical evaluation", *Quality and Quantity* 10(4),
        dec 76 : 267-296.

        19840. Disarmament. Weapon
               Désarmement. Arme

5256   HAMBLIN, Robert L. *et al.* "Arms races: a test of two models",
        Amer. sociol. R. 42(2), apr 77 : 338-354.
5257   RATTINGER, H. "From war to war. Arms races in the Middle East",
        Int. Stud. Quart. 20(4), dec 76 : 501-531.
5258   SHIBATA, Shingo. "Kakuheiki haizetsu to shiso no mondai" (The abo-
        lition of nuclear weapons and problems of thought), *Kagaku to*
        Shiso 26, 1977 : 2-18.
5259   SHIBATA, Shingo. "Kakuheiki haizetsu to tetsugaku shakaikagaku no
        kadai" (The abolition of nuclear weapons and tasks of philosophy
        and social sciences), *Kagaku to Shiso* 27, 1977 : 65-83.

20. SOCIAL PROBLEM. SOCIAL SERVICE. SOCIAL WORK
PROBLÈME SOCIAL. SERVICE SOCIAL. TRAVAIL SOCIAL

20100. SOCIAL PROBLEM
PROBLÈME SOCIAL

20110. Applied sociology
Sociologie appliquée

5260   CHOW, Napoleon (ed.). *Técnicas de investigación social* (Social research techniques). San José, EDUCA, 76, 400 p.

5261   Bibl.XXVI-4471. LAZARSFELD, Paul F.; REITZ, Jeffrey G. *An introduction to applied sociology.* CR: Terry Nichols CLARK, *Amer. J. Sociol.* 82(6), mai 77 : 1373-1374; Michael HENNESSY, *Contemp. Sociol. (Washington)* 6(1), jan 77 : 118-119.

5262   LIN, Nan. *Foundations of social research.* New York, McGraw Hill, 76, 458 p. CR: Roger SPIELMANN, *Contemp. Sociol. (Washington)* 6(4), jul 77 : 449-450.

5263   MANIS, Jerome G. *Analyzing social problems.* New York, Praeger, 76, xiv-194 p.

5264   OLSON, Sheldon. *Ideas and data. The process and practice of social research.* Homewood, Ill., Dorsey Press, 76, xvi-513 p.

5265   OSIPOV, G. V. "Osnovnye napravlenija primenenija matematičeskih metodov v konkretnyh social'nyh issledovanijah" (Basic trends in the use of mathematical methods in applied social research), *Sociol. Issled. (Moskva)* (3), 1976 : 131-140. [Also published in Czech, *Sociol. Čas.* 13(2), 1977 : 180-186.]

5266   ØYEN, Orjar. "Social research and the protection of privacy: a review of the Norwegian development", *Acta sociol.* 19(3), 1976 : 249-262.

5267   PELLICCIARI, Giovanni; TINTI, Giancarlo. *Tecniche di ricerca sociale* (Social research techniques). Milano, F. Angeli, 76, 276 p.

5268   PETRELLA, Riccardo. "La recherche sociale dans la Communauté européenne", *R. int. Sci. soc.* 29(4), 1977 : 821-836.

5269   PLATT, Jennifer. *Realities of social research: an empirical study of British sociologists.* London, Chatto and Windus, 76, 223 p. CR: Michael PHILLIPSON, *Brit. J. Sociol.* 28(2), jun 77 : 257-258; Bob HININGS, *Contemp. Sociol. (Washington)* 6(4), jul 77 : 451-452.

20120. Social pathology
Pathologie sociale

[See also / Voir aussi: 5263]

5270   CLARKE, M. "Social problem ideologies", *Brit. J. Sociol.* 26(4), dec 75 : 406-416.

5272   HARTJEN, Clayton A. *Possible trouble: an introduction to social problems.* New York, Praeger, 77, xiv-351 p.

5273   HENSHEL, Richard L. *Reacting to social problems.* Don Mills, Ont., Longman Canada, 76, 191 p.

5274   KOJDER, Andrzej. "Zjawiska patologii społecznej w Polsce w świetle badań empirycznych" (The phenomenon of social pathology in Poland in the light of empirical research), *Stud. socjol.* 60(1), 1976 : 171-202.

5275   LE GRAND, Julian; ROBINSON, Ray. *The economics of social problems.* London, Macmillan, 76, xix-245 p. [UK.]

5276   McCORD, William Maxwell; McCORD, Arline. *American social problems: challenges to existence.* Saint Louis-Mosby-London, Henry Kimpton, 77, xi-291 p.

5277   PELLIZZI, Camillo. "La patologia sociale" (Social pathology), *Rass. ital. Sociol.* 18(1), jan-mar 77 : 3-7.

5278   SANADA, Naoshi. "Shakai-mondai shakai-jigyô" (Study of social problems before the war in Japan), *Shakaigaku Hyorôn* 28(2), 1977 : 121-134.

5279   SHEPARD, Jon M.; STEWART, Cyrus S. (eds.). *Sociology and social problems: a conceptual approach.* Englewood Cliffs, N.J., Prentice-Hall, 76, xiv-301 p.

5280   TRUZZI, Marcello; SPRINGER, Philip B. (eds.). *Solving social problems: essays in relevant sociology.* Pacific Palisades, Calif., Goodyear Publishing Co., 76, 347 p. CR: Henry M. BARLOW, *Contemp. Sociol. (Washington)* 6(2), mar 77 : 240.

5281   TURNER, Jonathan H. *Social problems in America.* New York, Harper and Row, 77, xix-555 p.

5282   ZIMMERMAN, Donald H.; WIEDER, D. Lawrence; ZIMMERMAN, Siu (eds.). *Understanding social problems.* New York, Praeger, 76, ix-438 p. CR: Malcolm SPECTOR, *Contemp. Sociol. (Washington)* 6(3), mai 77 : 392-393.

20130. Disaster
Catastrophe

5283   CANNING, John (ed.). *Great disasters: catastrophes of the twentieth century.* London, Octopus Books, 76, 5-124 p.

5284   "Learning from disasters", *Ekistics* 44(260), jul 77 : 3-59.

5285   NAKANO, Takashi. "Mizushima kôgyô-chitai to jishin" (Mizushima industrial area and earthquake), *Kankyô to Ningen* 3(1), 1977 : 13-21.

5286   SASABE, Taketoshi. "Community to saigai" (Community and disaster), *Toshi-mondai Kenkyû* 29(6), 1977 : 62-75.

5287   THOM, René. "Crise et catastrophe", *Communications (Paris)* 25, 1976 : 34-38.

20140. Poverty
Pauvreté

[See also / Voir aussi: 1486, 5143]

5288   COMMONER, Barry. *The poverty of power.* New York, Alfred A. Knopf, 76, 314 p. CR: Noman MILLER, *Contemp. Sociol. (Washington)* 6(2), mar 77 : 187-188.

5289   DREWNOWSKI, Jan. "Poverty: its meaning and measurement", *Develop. and Change* 8(2), apr 77 : 183-208.

5290   IWAMA, Tsuyoshi. "Toshi-chiiki ni okeru hinmin: Philippin shakai-chosa no hokoku" (The poor in the urban areas: a report on a sociological study in the Philippines), *Tamagawa-daigaku Bungakubu Ronsô* 17, 1977 : 19-59.

5291   KAIM-CANDLE, P. "Poverty in Australia", *J. soc. Pol.* 5(4), oct 76 : 401-406.

5292   KALIRAJAN, K. "Calorie intakes of food comparisons across states and classes", *Indian J. agric. Econ.* 31(2), apr-jun 76 : 53-62.

5293   LIPTON, Michael. *Why poor people stay poor: a study of urban bias in world development.* London, Temple Smith, 77, 467 p.

5295   NALSON, J. S. "Periodic and permanent poverty in rural areas", *Asian Pacific Quart. cult. soc. Aff.* 8(3), 1976 : 60-66. *[Australia.]*

5296   ONUORA ONAH, J. "La pauvreté urbaine au Nigéria", *Trav. et Soc.* 1(2), apr 76 : 123-130.

5297   OSOCHOWSKA-RUSAK, Marlene R. "The level and structure dynamics of food consumption in Egypt in the years 1959-60/1970-71", *Africana B.* 24, 1976 : 135-149.

5298   REUTLINGER, Shlomo; SELOWSKY, Marcelo. *Malnutrition and poverty: magnitude and policy options*. Baltimore, Johns Hopkins University Press, 76, xii–82 p.
5299   RODMAN, Hyman. "Culture and poverty: the rise and fall of a concept", *Sociol. R.* 25(4), nov 77 : 867–876.
5300   "Scarcity and society", *Soc. Sci. Quart.* 57(2), sep 76 : 260–472.
5301   SEKUŁA, Włodzimierz; SZCZYGIEL, Aleksander. "Problemy Żywienie w Polsce" (Food problems in Poland), *Gosp. plan.* 32(4), apr 77 : 176–181.
5302   SMITH, T. Lynn. *The race between population and food supply in Latin America*. Albuquerque, University of New Mexico Press, 76, 194 p. CR: William E. BERTRAND, *Contemp. Sociol. (Washington)* 6(3), mai 77 : 369–370.
5303   VAN TIL, Sally Bould. *Work and the culture of poverty: the labor force activity of poor men*. San Francisco, R and E Research Associates, 76, xv–190 p.

20150. Alcoholism. Drug
       Alcoolisme. Stupéfiants

[See also / Voir aussi: 5350, 5461]

5304   ALONSO TORRENS, J. "Alcoholismo, auténtica playa nacional" (Alcoholism, an authentic national plague), *Mundo soc.* 22(244), jun 76 : 40–45. [Spain.]
5305   BECKER, Carolyn; KRONUS, Sidney. "Sex and drinking patterns: an old relationship revisited in a new way", *Soc. Probl.* 24(4), apr 77 : 482–497.
5306   BOVILSKY, Deborah M.; SINGER, David L. "Confrontational group treatment of smoking: a report of three comparative studies", *Int. J. Group Psychother.* 27(4), oct 77 : 481–498.
5307   BOWKER, L. H. "Enquête sur l'incidence de l'usage de drogues dans deux petites villes et sur les facteurs qui s'y rattachent", *B. Stupéfiants* 28(4), oct–dec 76 : 17–25.
5308   BURKETT, Steven R. "School ties, peer influence, and adolescent marijuana use", *Pacific sociol. R.* 20(2), apr 77 : 181–202. [USA.]
5309   CAPLOVITZ, David. "The working addict", *Int. J. Sociol.* 6(4), 1976–1977 : 3–134.
5310   CERFEDA, Giuseppe. "Il fenomeno medico e sociale della droga nei riflessi en la nuova legislazione" (The medical and social phenomenon of drug addiction viewed through the new legislation), *Dif. soc.* 55(4), oct–dec 76 : 101–128. [Italy.]
5311   CLOYD, Jerald W. "The processing of misdemeanor drinking divers: the bureaucratization of the arrest, prosecution, and plea bargaining situations", *Soc. Forces* 56(2), dec 77 : 385–407.
5312   COHEN, H. "Drugs, drug-users and drug-scenes", *Netherlands J. Sociol.* 12(1), jul 76 : 3–17.
5313   COOMBS, Robert H.; FRY, Lincoln J.; LEWIS, Patricia G. *Socialization in drug abuse*. Cambridge, Mass., Schenkman Publishing House, 76, xvi–478 p.
5314   D'ARCANGELO, Enzo. *La droga en la scuola: inchiesta tra gli studenti di Roma* (Drug in the school: an investigation among the Roman students). Torino, G. Einaudi, 77, xiv–246 p.
5315   DENZIN, Norman K. "Notes on the criminogenic hypothesis: a case study of the American liquor industry", *Amer. sociol. R.* 42(6), dec 77 : 905–920.
5316   DOBKIN DE RIOS, Marlene; SMITH, David E. "Drug use and abuse in cross-cultural perspective", *Hum. Org.* 36(1), 1977 : 14–21.
5317   EISER, J. Richard; SUTTON, Stephen R.; WOBER, Mallory. "Smoker, non-smokers and the attribution of addiction", *Brit. J. Psychol.* 16(4), nov 77 : 329–336.

5318   FORTUNA, Saverio. "Il problema della droga" (The problem of drug addiction), *Civitas (Roma)* 28(3-4), mar-apr 77 : 19-54; 28(5), mai 77 : 49-102.

5319   FRÉJAVILLE, Jean-Pierre; DAVIDSON, Françoise; CHOQUET, Maria. *Les jeunes et la drogue*. Paris, Presses universitaires de France, 77, 230 p.

5320   GOSSELIN, Normand. "Désintégration sociale et comportement alcooli- que", *Toxicomanies* 10(1), jan-mar 77 : 5-22. [Canada.]

5321   GRINSPOON, Lester; BALAKAR, James B. *Cocaine: a drug and its social evolution*. New York, Basic Books, 76, x-308 p.

5322   HANSON, D. J. "Trends in drinking attitudes and behaviors among college students", *J. Alcohol Drug. Educ.* 22(3), 1977 : 17-22.

5323   Bibl.XXVI-4526. HELMER, John. *Drugs and minority oppression*. CR: Joseph L. ZENTNER, *Amer. J. Sociol.* 82(4), jan 77 : 918-919.

5324   HODGES, H. Eugene; LOWE, George D. "Race and change in rates of treatment and deaths due to alcoholism in a Southern state: 1970- 1974", *Phylon* 38(2), jun 77 : 152-159. [USA.]

5325   HUNT, Leon Gibson. *Assessment of local drug abuse*. Lexington, Mass., Lexington Books, 77, xvii-153 p. [USA.]

5326   HUNT, Leon Gibson; CHAMBERS, Carl D. *The heroin epidemics: a study of heroin use in the United States, 1965-1975*. New York, Spectrum, 76, 145 p. CR: PAUL ATTEWELL, *Contemp. Sociol. (Washington)* 6(1), jan 77 : 31-32.

5327   JOHNSON, Weldon T.; PETERSEN, Robert E.; WELLS, L. Edward. "Arrest probabilities for marijuana users as indicators of selective law enforcement", *Amer. J. Sociol.* 83(3), nov 77 : 681-699. [USA.]

5328   JONES, Hardin Blair; JONES, Helen C. *Sensual drugs: deprivation and rehabilitation of the mind*. Cambridge-New York, Cambridge University Press, 77, ix-373 p.

5329   KILTY, Keith M.; MEENAGHAN, Thomas M. "Drinking status, labeling, and social rejection", *J. soc. Psychol.* 102(1), jan 77 : 93-104.

5330   KOHN, Paul M.; BARNES, Gordon E. "Subject variables and reactance to persuasive communications about drugs", *Europ. J. soc. Psychol.* 7(1), 1977 : 97-109.

5331   LABRIE, Gisèle; TREMBLAY, Marc-André. "Études psychologiques et soico-culturelles de l'alcoolisme: inventaire des travaux dis- ponibles au Québec depuis 1960", *Toxicomanies* 10(2), apr-jun 77 : 85-125.

5332   LANGER, John. "Drug entrepreneurs and dealing culture", *Soc. Probl.* 24(3), feb 77 : 377-386.

5333   LAREZ ALBORNOZ, A. et al. "Contribution à l'étude de la pharmaco- dépendance chez les jeunes à Caracas", *B. Stupéfiants* 28(4), oct dec 76 : 45-54.

5334   MÄKELÄ, Klaus; VIIKARI, Matti. "Notes on alcohol and the State", *Acta sociol.* 20(2), 1977 : 155-179.

5335   MANNING, Peter K. "Rules in organizational context: narcotics law enforcement in two settings", *Sociol. Quart.* 18(1), 1977 : 44-61.

5336   MOORE, James J. *Investigating drug abuse: a multi-national prog- ramme of pilot studies into the non-medical use of drugs*. Rome, United Nations Social Defence Research Institute, 76, 192 p.

5337   OHASHI, Kaoru et al. "Arukoru izonsha kazoku no shakaigaku-teki shakai-byorigaku-teki Kenkyû" (A sociological study of the alco- holic family), *Meiji-gakuin Ronsô* 260, 1977 : 31-64.

5338   PADIOLEAU, Jean G. "La lutte contre le tabagisme: action politique et régulation étatique de la vie quotidienne", *R. franç. Sci. polit.* 27(6), dec 77 : 932-959. [France.]

5339   PARENTEAU, Fernand. "Épidémiologie de la consommation des drogues et politiques gouvernementales intégrées au Québec", *Toxicomanies* 10(1), jan-mar 77 : 53-65.

5340   PEEK, C. W.; LOWE, G. D. "Wirth, whiskey, and WASP's: some consequen- ces of community size for alcohol use", *Sociol. Quart.* 18(2), 1977 : 209-222.

5341   RETTERSTÖL, N. "La toxicomanie en Norvège: usage et abus des drogues engendrant la dépendance; moyens de traitement; contrôle après traitement; mesures prophylactiques", *B. Stupéfiants* 28(4), oct-dec 76 : 27-44.

5342   ROBINSON, David. *From drinking to alcoholism; a sociological commentary.* New York, Wiley, 76, 187 p. CR: Walter DAVIS, *Contemp. Sociol. (Washington)* 6(4), jul 77 : 507-508.

5343   ROCK, Paul E. (ed.). *Drugs and politics.* New Brunswick, N.J., Transaction Books, 77, 331 p. *[USA.]*

5344   SIMPSON, Herbert M. *et al.* "Étude analytique des accidents mortels de la route au Canada, 1974-1975. Étude orientée sur l'influence de l'alcool", *Toxicomanies* 10(3), jul-sep 77 : 199-232.

5345   SIMPURA, Jussi. "Tilastoimaton alkoholin kulutus uuden alkoholilain aikana" (Statistically unrecorded alcohol consumption during the period of the new alcohol legislation of 1969 in Finland), *Alkoholipolitiikka* (3), 1977 : 107-117.

5346   SORENSEN, Andrew A. *Alcoholic priests: a sociological study.* New York, Seabury Press, 76, x-181 p.

5347   STANG, Hans Jakob. *Ungdom på drift: en sosialpsykiatrisk undersøkelse av 100 unge stoffmisbrukere i Oslo sentrum* (Drifting youth: a socio-psychiatric study of 100 young drug addicts in the center of Oslo). Oslo, Universitetsforlaget, 76, 182 p.

5348   STEINGLASS, Peter; POYER, Janet K. "Assessing alcohol use in family life: a necessary but neglected area for clinical research", *Family Coordinator* 26(1), jan 77 : 53-60.

5349   STEINGLASS, Peter; DAVIS, Donald I.; BERENSON, David. "Observations of a conjointly hospitalized 'alcoholic couples' during sobriety and intoxication: implications for theory and therapy", *Family Process* 16(1), mar 77 : 1-16.

5350   WEBB, Stephen D.; COLLETTE, John. "Rural-urban differences in the use of stress-alleviative drugs", *Amer. J. Sociol.* 83(3), nov 77 : 700-707.

5351   WICKS, Robert J.; PLATT, Jerome J. *Drug abuse: a criminal justice primer.* Beverly Hills, Calif., Glencoe Press, 77, ix-148 p.

20160. Crime. Delinquency
Crime. Délinquance

20161.

[See also / Voir aussi: 140]

5352   AUBUSSON DE CAVARLAY, Bruno; ROBERT, Philippe. "La recherche prévisionnelle en criminologie", *A. int. Criminol.* 13(1-2), 1974 : 83-125.

5353   CARRIER, Daniel M. (ed.). *Perspectives in criminology.* Dubuque, Iowa, Kendall/Hunt Publishing Co., 77, viii-240 p.

5354   CHANG, Dae H. (ed.). *Criminology: a cross-cultural perspective.* 2 vols. Durham, Carolina Academic Press, 76, xiv-1039-xiv p.

5355   GALLIHER, John F.; McCARTNEY, James L. *Criminology: power, crime, and criminal law.* Homewood, Ill., Dorsey Press, 77, xii-548 p.

5356   KLOČKOV, V. V. "Aktualnye voprosy sovetskoj kriminologii" (Today's problems of the Soviet criminology), *Sov. Gos. Pravo* 50(5), mai 77 : 39-47.

5357   RADZINOWICZ, Leon; HOOD, Roger. *Criminology and the administration of criminal justice: a bibliography.* Westport, Conn., Greenwood Press, 76, xiii-400 p.

5358   SMART, Carol. "Criminological theory: its ideology and implications concerning women", *Brit. J. Sociol.* 28(1), mar 77 : 89-100.

5359   SMART, Carol. *Women, crime, and criminology: a feminist critique.* London-Boston, Routledge and K. Paul, 77, xv-208 p.

5360   WILES, Paul (ed.). *The sociology of crime and delinquency: the new criminologies.* New York, Barnes and Noble, 77, 237 p.

20162.

[See also / Voir aussi: 1095, 1475, 1581, 5024]

5361   BALLONI, Augusto. "Il comportamento collettivo e le condotte crimi-
        nose" (Collective behaviour and criminal conducts), *Studi Sociol.*
        15(4), oct-dec 77 : 338-352.

5362   BERENTS, Dirk Arend. *Misdaad in de middeleeuwen. Een onderzoek naar
        de criminaliteit in het laat-middeleeuwawse Utrecht* (Crime in the
        Middle Ages. A research on criminality in Utrecht at the end of
        the Middle Ages). Bloemendaal, Stichtse Historische Reeks, 76,
        viii-176 p.

5363   BICKMAN, Leonard; GREEN, Susan K. "Situational cues and crime re-
        porting: do signs make a difference", *J. appl. soc. Psychol.*
        7(1), jan-mar 77 : 1-18.

5364   BLASIUS, Dirk. *Bürgerliche Gesellschaft und Kriminalität: zur So-
        zialgeschichte Preussens in Vormärz* (Bourgeois society and cri-
        minality: social history of Prussia before the March Revolution
        1848). Göttingen, Vandenhoeck und Ruprecht, 76, 203 p.

5365   BORTOLLAS, Clemens; MILLER, Stuart J.; DINITZ, Simon. *Juvenile vic-
        timization: the institutional paradox.* New York, Wiley, 76, 324
        p. CR: Roy L. AUSTIN, *Contemp. Sociol. (Washington)* 6(4), jul
        77 : 430-432.

5366   BÖSZÖRMÉNYI, Ede. "A magyarországi öngyilkosságok történetéhez"
        (On the history of suicides in Hungary), *Demográfia* 19(1), 1976:
        478-488.

5367   CANADA. Statistics Canada. Judicial Division. *L'homicide au Canada:
        un tableau synoptique.* Ottawa, Statistique Canada, 76, 206 p.

5368   CHESNAIS, Jean-Claude; ZBORILOVA, Jirka. "Le suicide en Europe
        centrale, en France et en Suède depuis un siècle", *R. franç.
        Aff. soc.* 31(1), jan-mar 77 : 105-137.

5369   CLEMENTE, Frank; KLEIMAN, Michael B. "Fear of crime in the United
        States: a multivariate analysis", *Soc. Forces* 56(2), dec 77 :
        519-531.

5370   "Criminal behavior and the physical environment", *Amer. behav.
        Scientist* 20(2), nov-dec 76 : 147-288.

5371   DUKES, Richard L.; MATTLEY, Christine L. "Predicting rape victim
        reportage", *Sociol. soc. Res.* 62(1), oct 77 : 63-84.

5373   ELLIOTT, Ian D. "Theft and related problems - England, Australia
        and the USA compared", *Int. comp. Law Quart.* 26(1), jan 77 :
        110-149.

5374   ESER, Albin; BRINGEWAT, Peter (eds.). *Suizid und Euthanasie als
        human- und sozialwissenschaftliches Problem* (Suicide and eutha-
        nasia as a problem of human and social sciences). Stuttgart,
        Enke, 76, vii-432 p.

5375   FELDMAN, Maurice Philip. *Criminal behaviour: a psychological analy-
        sis.* London-New York, Wiley, 77, xvi-330 p.

5376   FERGUSSON, David Murray; FIFIELD, June; SLATER, S. W. *Social back-
        ground, school performance, adjustment and juvenile offending:
        a path analytic model.* Wellington, Research Unit, Joint Committee
        on Young Offenders, 76, 26 p.

5377   GLENNIE, C. "Crime in England and Wales", *Soc. Trends* (7), 1976 :
        32-42.

5378   GÖDÖNY, József. *A társadalmi-gazdasági fejlödés és a bünözés* (Eco-
        nomic and social development and criminality). Budapest, Közgaz-
        dasági és Jogi Kiadó, 76, 471-1 p.

5379   GOMEZ GRILLO, Elio. "El délito y los medios de comunicación social"
        (Delinquency and social communication media), *Anu. Inst. Cienc.
        pen. criminol.* (5), 1973 : 85-98.

5380   GURR, Ted Robert *et al.* The politics of crime and conflict: a com-
        parative history of four cities. Beverly Hills, Calif., Sage
        Publications, 77, xii-792 p,

5381   HAGAN, John; LEON, Jeffrey. "Rediscovering delinquency: social
        history, political ideology and the sociology of law", *Amer.
        sociol. R.* 42(4), aug 77 : 587-598.

5382   HAHN, Paul H. *Crimes against the elderly: a study in victimology.*
        Santa Cruz, Calif., Davis Publishing Co., 76, iv-207 p.

5383   HIGGINS, Paul C.; ALBRECHT, Gary L. "Hellfire and delinquency re-
        visited", *Soc. Forces* 55(4), jun 77 : 952-958.

5384   HILBERMAN, Elaine. *The rape victim.* Washington, D.C., American
        psychiatric Association, 76, 98 p. CR: Lynda Lytle HOMSTROM,
        Contemp. Sociol. (Washington) 6(2), mar 77 : 178.

5385   HIRSCHI, Travis; HINDELANG, Michael J. "Intelligence and delinquen-
        cy: a revisionist review", *Amer. sociol. R.* 42(4), aug 77 : 571-
        587.

5386   HOROWITZ, Irving Louis. *Genocide: state power and mass murder.* New
        Brunswick, N.J., Transaction Books, 76, 80 p.

5387   IANNI, Francis A. J.; REUSS-IANNI, Elizabeth (eds.). *The crime so-
        ciety: organized crime and corruption in America.* New York, New
        American Library, 76, xvii-379 p.

5388   IBRAHIM, I. B. *et al.* "Ethnicity and suicide in Hawaii", *Soc. Biology*
        24(1), 1977 : 10-16.

5389   INCIARDI, James A.; SIEGAL, Harvey A. (eds.). *Crime: emerging
        issues.* New York, Praeger, 77, viii-206 p. *[USA.]*

5390   KUNZ, Harald J. *Die Ökonomik individueller und organisierter Krimi-
        nalität* (The economic aspects of individual and organized crimi-
        nality). Köln, C. Heymann, 76, xi-193 p..

5391   LABOVITZ, Sanford; BRINKERHOFF, Merlin B. "Structural changes and
        suicide in Canada", *Int. J. comp. Sociol.* 18(3-4), sep-dec 77 :
        254-267.

5392   LAHTI, Raimo. "Rikollisuus tutkimuksen ja päätöksenteon kohteena"
        (Criminality as the object for research and decision-making),
        Lakimies 74(7), 1976 : 507-546.

5393   LEEK, Sybil; SUGAR, Bert R. *The assassination chain.* New York,
        Corwin Books, 76, viii-342-4 p.

5394   LEWIS, Dorothy Otnow *et al. Delinquency and psychopathology.* New
        York, Grune and Stratton, 76, xxii-209 p.

5395   MALEWSKA, Hanna; PEYRE, Vincent. *Juvenile delinquency and develop-
        ment: a cross-national study.* Beverly Hills, Calif., Sage Pub-
        lications, 76, 40 p.

5396   MANGIN, G. "La délinquance juvénile en Afrique noire francophone",
        Archiv. Polit. crim. (1), 1975 : 225-240.

5397   MCKINLEY, James. *Assassination in America.* New York, Harper and
        Row, 77, xii-243 p.

5398   MONESTIER, Martin. *Le suicide.* Paris, J.-C. Simoën, 76, 349 p.

5399   NOBLIT, George W. "The adolescent experience and delinquency.
        School versus subcultural effects", *Youth and Soc.* 8(1), sep
        76 : 27-44.

5400   PEARCE, Frank. *Crimes of the powerful: Marxism, crime, and deviance.*
        London, Pluto Press, 76, 172 p. *[USA.]*

5401   PEPINSKY, Harold E. *Crime and conflict: a study of law and society.*
        New York, Academic Press, 76, x-159 p.

5402   PILLAT, V. N. "Crime and criminal justice system in the next decade
        in developing countries", *Ind. J. soc. Wk* 38(2), jul 77 : 99-112.

5403   POPE, Whitney. *Durkheim's Suicide: a classic analyzed.* Chicago,
        University of Chicago Press, 76, ix-229 p.

5404   RADZINOWICZ, Leon; KING, Joan. *The growth of crime: the interna-
        tional experience.* New York, Basic Books, 77, x-342 p.

5405   ROBERTSON, Alex; COCHRANE, Raymond. "Attempted suicide and cultural
        change: an empirical investigation", *Hum. Relat.* 29(4), sep 76 :
        863-883.

5406   ROSHIER, Bob. "The function of crime myth", *Sociol. R.* 25(2), mai
        77 : 309-323.

5407   ROWE, A. R.; TITTLE, C. R. "Life cycle changes and criminal propensity", *Sociol. Quart.* 18(2), 1977 : 223-236.

5408   RUDAS, Nereide. "Migrazioni e criminalità" (Migrations and criminality), *Studi Emigr.* 14(46), jun 77 : 135-147.

5409   SAHAROV, A. B. "O koncepcii pričin prestupnosti v socialističeskom obščestve" (On the conception of the causes of crime in socialist society), *Sov. Gos. Pravo* 49(4), sep 76 : 25-34. *[Also published in English Sov. Law Gvt* 15(4), 1977 : 37-54.]

5410   SAHAROV, A. B. "Opyt izučenija vlijanija social'nyh uslovij na territorial'nye različija prestupnosti" (Essay of study of social conditions influence on territorial differences in criminality), *Sociol. Issled (Moskva)* (1), 1977 : 75-84.

5411   SANDERS, William B. *Juvenile delinquency.* New York, Praeger, 76, 238 p. CR: Roy L. AUSTIN, *Contemp. Sociol. (Washington)* 6(4), jul 77 : 430-432.

5412   SANDHU, Harjit S. *Juvenile delinquency: causes, control, and prevention.* New York, Gregg Division, McGraw-Hill, 77, x-324 p. *[USA.]*

5413   SATHYAVATHI, K. "Suicides among unemployed persons in Bangalore", *Ind. J. soc. Wk* 37(4), jan 77 : 385-392. *[India.]*

5414   Bibl.XXVI-4549. SCHNEIDMAN, Edwin S. (ed.). *Suicidology: contemporary developments.* CR: James F. SHORT Jr. *Contemp. Sociol. (Washington)* 6(4), jul 77 : 511-512.

5415   SERRANO GOMEZ, A. "Robos con violencia o intimidación en las personas" (Thefts with violence or intimidation on persons), *R. esp. Opin. públ.* 46, oct-dec 76 : 103-140. *[Spain.]*

5416   SHORT, James F. Jr. *et al.* (eds.). *Delinquency, crime, and society.* Chicago, University of Chicago Press, 76, ix-325 p.

5417   SHUKLA, K. S. "Adolescent thieves: family structure", *Ind. J. soc. Wk* 37(4), jan 77 : 393-406. *[India.]*

5418   SOMERHAUSEN, Colette. "Mineur 'délinquant' et protection de la jeunesse en Belgique", *R. jur. polit.* 31(2), apr-jun 77 : 653-665.

5419   SORRENTINO, Anthony. *Organizing against crime: redeveloping the neighborhood.* New York, Human Sciences Press, 77, 272 p.

5420   STEVENS, John. *Suicide: an illicit lover.* Denver, Heritage House Publications, 76, 150 p.

5421   SWIGERT, Victoria Lynn; FARRELL, Ronald A. "Normal homicides and the law", *Amer. sociol. R.* 42(1), feb 77 : 16-32.

5422   TASSÉ, R. "The role of social science in crime and delinquency policy", *Canad. publ. Adm.* 19(2), 1976 : 267-278.

5423   THOMAS, Charles W.; KREPS, Gary A.; CAGE, Robin J. "An application of compliance to the study of juvenile delinquency", *Sociol. soc. Res.* 61(2), jan 77 : 156-175.

5424   TITTLE, Charles R.; VILLEMEZ, Wayne J. "Social class and criminality", *Soc. Forces* 56(2), dec 77 : 474-502.

5425   TURK, Austin T. "Class, conflict, and criminalization", *Sociol. Focus* 10(3), aug 77 : 209-220.

5426   VARMA, Paripurnanand. *Suicide in India and abroad.* Agra Sahitya Bhawan, 76, xi-311 p.

5427   VICTOR, Michael I. "Relations between known crime and police spending in large United States cities", *Sociol. Focus* 10(2), apr 77 : 199-207.

5428   WILKINSON, Doris Y. (ed.). *Social structure and assassination behavior: the sociology of political murder.* Cambridge, Mass., Schenkman Publishing Co., 76, vi-226 p.

5429   ZEHR, Howard. *Crime and the development of modern society: patterns of criminality in nineteenth century Germany and France.* London, Croom Helm; Totowa, N. J., Rowman and Littlefield, 76, 188 p.

20163.

[See also / Voir aussi: 1491]

5430 BALDWIN, John; BOTTOMS, A. E.; WALKER, Monica A. *The urban criminal: a study in Sheffield*. London, Tavistock, 76, ix-262 p. [UK.]

5431 BERNSTEIN, Ilene Nagel; KELLY, William R.; DOYLE, Patricia A. "Societal reaction to deviants: the case of criminal defendants", *Amer. sociol. R.* 42(5), oct 77 : 743-755.

5432 BERNSTEIN, Ilene Nagel *et al.* "Charge reduction: an intermediary stage in the process of labelling criminal defendants", *Soc. Forces* 56(2), dec 77 : 362-384.

5433 CARTER, Robert M.; KLEIN, Malcolm W. (eds.). *Back on the street:: the diversion of juvenile offenders*. Englewood Cliffs, N.J., Prentice-Hall, 76, 368 p. CR: Roy L. Austin, *Contemp. Sociol. (Washington)* 6(4), jul 77 : 430-432.

5434 CARTER, Ronald; HILL, Kim Quaile. "The criminal's image of the city and urban crime patterns", *Soc. Sci. Quart.* 57(3), dec 76 : 597-607.

5435 CRITES, Laura (ed.). *The female offender*. Lexington, Mass., Lexington Books, 76, xii-230 p. [USA.]

5436 DEMING, Richard. *Women: the new criminals*. Nashville, T. Nelson, 77, 191 p. [Female offenders in the USA.]

5437 DITTON, Jason. "Learning to 'fiddle' customers: an essay on the organised production of part-time theft", *Sociol. Wk Occupat.* 4(4), nov 77 : 427-450.

5438 FINESTONE, Harold. *Victims of change: juvenile delinquents in American society*. Westport, Conn., Greenwood Press, 76, xvii-235 p.

5439 FOX, Richard G. "Young persons in conflict with the law in Canada", *Int. comp. Law Quart.* 26(2), apr 77 : 445-467.

5440 HEPBURN, J. R. "Official deviance and spoiled identity: delinquents and their significant others", *Pacific sociol. R.* 20(2), apr 77 : 163-179.

5441 SHUKLA, K. S. "Adolescent thieves and differential association", *Sociol. B. (Bombay)* 25(1), mar 76 : 74-94.

20164.

5442 LISOVSKIJ, Ju. P. "Mafija i sovremennyj ital'janskij kapitalizm" (Maffia and the contemporaneous Italian capitalism), *Nov. novejš. Ist.* 20(3), mai-jun 77 : 13-118; 20(4), jul-aug 77 : 117-129.

20165.

[See also / Voir aussi: 663, 5357, 5664]

5443 ABADINSKY, Howard. *Probation and parole; theory and practice*. Englewood Cliffs, N.J., Prentice-Hall, 77, xiii-431 p. [USA.]

5444 AKERS, Ronald L. "Type of leadership in prison: a structural approach to testing the functional and importation models", *Sociol. Quart.* 18(3), 1977 : 378-383.

5445 ALONZO, F. O. "The constitutional rights of incarcerated juveniles", *South. Quart.* 15(2), jan 77 : 179-192. [USA.]

5446 BEDAU, Hugh Adam; PIERCE, Chester M. (eds.). *Capital punishment in the United States*. New York, AMS Press, 76, xxiii-567 p.

5447 BERK, Richard A.; ROSSI, Peter H. *Prison reform and State elites*. Cambridge, Mass., Ballinger Publishing Co., 77, xvi-207 p. [USA.]

5448 BLANKENBURG, Erhard. "The selectivity of legal sanctions: an empirical investigation of shoplifting", *Law Soc. R.* 11(1), 1976 : 109-130. [Germany FR.]

5449 CARNEY, Louis P. *Probation and parole: legal and social dimensions*. New York, McGraw-Hill, 77, vi-346 p. [USA.]

5450 CICOUREL, Aaron Victor. *The social organization of juvenile justice*. London, Heinemann Educational, 76, xxi-345 p.

5451 CLARKE, Stevens H.; KOCH, Gary G. "The influence of income and other factors on whether criminal defendant go to prison", *Law Soc. R.* 11(1), 1976 : 57-92.

5452 ERICKSON, Maynard L.; GOBBS, Jack P.; JENSEN, Gary F. "The deterrence doctrine and the perceived certainty of legal punishments", *Amer. sociol. R.* 42(2), apr 77 : 305-317.

5453 KING, Roy D.; MORGAN, Rodney. *A taste of prison: custodial conditions for trial and remand prisoners.* London-Boston, Routledge and K. Paul, 76, x-100 p.

5454 KLEIN, Malcolm W. (ed.). *The juvenile justice system.* Beverly Hills, Calif., Sage Publications, 76, 287 p. CR: Roy L. AUSTIN, *Contemp. Sociol. (Washington)* 6(4), jul 77 : 430-432.

5455 LEGER, Robert G.; STRATTON, John R. (eds.). *The sociology of corrections: a book of readings.* New York, Wiley, 77, xv-557 p.

5456 ŁOS, Maria; ANDERSON, Palmer. "The 'second life'. A cross-cultural view of peer subcultures in correctional institutions in Poland and the United States", *Polish sociol. B.* 36(4), 1976 : 47-61.

5457 MACKEY, Philip English (ed.). *Voices against death: American opposition to capital punishment, 1787-1975.* New York, B. Franklin, 76, liii-362 p.

5458 McCONVILLE, Sean (ed.). *The use of imprisonment: essays in the changing state of English penal policy.* Boston, Routledge and Kegan Paul, 76, 128 p. CR: Robert SOMMER, *Contemp. Sociol. (Washington)* 6(1), jan 77 : 32-33.

5459 MONTARON, Jean-Pierre. *Les jeunes en prison: "on nous enfonce".* Paris, Seuil, 77, 253 p.

5460 MURTON, Thomas O. *The dilemma of prison reform.* New York, Holt, Rinehart and Winston, 76, 285 p. CR: W. David WATTS, *Contemp. Sociol. (Washington)* 6(1), jan 77 : 34-35.

5461 NEWMAN, Charles L.; PRICE, Barbara R. *Jails and drug treatment.* Beverly Hills, Calif., Sage Publications, 77, 223 p. *[USA.]*

5462 QUINNEY, Richard. *Class, state, and crime: on the theory and practice of criminal justice.* New York, D. McKay Co., 77, ix-179 p.

5463 RIVES, G. "Les problèmes de l'évolution de la politique criminelle du Sénégal depuis l'indépendance", *Archiv. Polit. crim.* (1), 1975 : 179-212.

5464 SCHEDLER, George. "Capital punishment and its deterrent effect", *Soc. Theory Practice* 4(1), 1976 : 47-56.

5465 SCHNELLER, Donald P. *The prisoner's family: a study of the effects of imprisonment on the families of prisoners.* San Francisco, R and E Research Associates, 76, ix-102 p.

5466 SOSA WAGNER, F. "Administración penitenciaria" (Penitentiary administration), *R. Adm. públ. (Madrid)* 80, mai-aug 76 : 83-125. *[Spain.]*

5467 SWIGERT, Victoria Lynn; FARRELL, Ronald A. *Murder, inequality, and the law: differential treatment in the legal process.* Lexington, Mass., Lexington Books, 76, xv-126 p.

5468 THIBAULT, Laurence. *La peine de mort en France et à l'étranger.* Paris, Gallimard, 77, 248 p.

5469 THOMAS, Charles W. "Prisonization and its consequences: an examination of socialization in a coercive setting", *Sociol. Focus* 10(1), jan 77 : 53-68.

5470 THOMAS, Charles W.; CAGE, R. J. "The effect of social characteristics on juvenile court dispositions", *Sociol. Quart.* 18(2), 1977 : 237-252.

5471 Bibl.XXVI-4641. VAN DEN HAAG, Ernest. *Punishing criminals: concerning a very old and painful question.* CR: Vernon FOX, *Amer. J. Sociol.* 83(2), sep 77 : 537-538.

5472 WHISENAND, Paul M. *Crime prevention.* Boston, Holbrook Press, 77, xi-419 p. *[USA.]*

20200. SOCIAL POLICY
POLITIQUE SOCIALE

20210. Social action. Social planning
Action sociale. Planification sociale

[See also / Voir aussi: 141, 440, 456, 533, 1495, 1529, 1572,
4120, 5023, 5615]

5473   BELORGEY, Jean-Michel. *La politique sociale*. Paris, Seghers, 76,
343 p. [France.]

5474   BLUME, Stuart S. "Policy as theory: a framework for understanding
the contribution of social science to welfare policy", *Acta
sociol.* 20(3), 1977 : 247-262.

5475   BOUDARD, F.; AVRIL, A. M.; ROUCHY, J.-C. "Réflexions sur l'évaluation dans la pratique sociale", *Connexions* 20, 1976 : 95-103.

5476   BRÜCK, Gerhard Wilhelm. *Allgemeine Sozialpolitik: Grundlagen, Zu-
sammenhänge, Leistungen* (General social policy: bases, connections, performance). Köln, Bund-Verlag, 76, 343 p.

5477   GRUGIDOU, Jean-Paul; DELAROCHE, Patrick. "Problème des structures
de l'action sanitaire et sociale à travers le travail pluridisciplinaire", *Connexions* 22, 1977 : 7-23.

5478   COLEMAN, James S. "Social action systems", in: SZANIAWSKI, Klemens
(ed.). *Problems of formalization in the social sciences*. Wrocław-
Warszawa-Kraków-Gdańsk, Zakład Narodowy Imienia Ossolińskich Wydawnictwo, 1977 : 11-50.

5479   DAHL, Robert Alan; LINDBLOM, Charles E. *Politics, economics, and
welfare: planning and politico-economic systems resolved into
basic social processes*. Chicago, University of Chicago Press, 76,
1-557 p.

5480   DAUDT, H. "De politieke toekomst van de versorgingsstaat" (The political future of the welfare state), *Beleid en Mij* 3(7-8), jul-
aug 76 : 175-189.

5481   DAVIDJUK, G. P. et al. *Metodologičeskie osnovy social'nogo upravlenija* (Methodological bases of social planning). Minsk, Izdatel'stvo BGU imeni V. I. Lenina, 77, 239 p.

5482   ERLANGER, Howard S. "Social reform organizations and subsequent
careers of participants: a follow-up study of early participants
in the OEO legal services program", *Amer. sociol. R.* 42(2), apr
77 : 233-248.

5483   FRITLINSKIJ, V. S. "K voprosu o celjah i urovnjah social'nogo
planirovanija" (On objectives and levels of social planning),
in: *Voprosy teorii i metodov sociologičeskih issledovanij. II.*
Moskva, 1976 : 91-98.

5484   FURNISS, Norman; TILTON, Timothy. *The case for the welfare State.
From social security to social equality*. Bloomington, Ind.,
Indiana University Press, 77, xii-249 p.

5485   GÁBOR, Éva. "Válság és tervezés. Korunk polgári társadalomtervezés-
elméletének előfutára: Karl Mannheim" (Crisis and planning. Karl
Mannheim as the forerunner of the theory of bourgeois social
planning in our time), *Bpesti Müsz. Egy. Marx.-Lenin. Közlem.*
(2), 1976 : 226-240.

5486   GEORGE, Victor N.; WILDING, Paul. *Ideology and social welfare*.
London, Routledge and Kegan Paul, 76, x-162 p.

5487   GERMAN, I. M.; MAL'CEV, V. I. *Social'noe planirovanie v gorodskom
rajone* (Social planning in an urban region). Saratov, Privolžskoe
knižnoe izdatel'stvo, 76, 126 p.

5488   GILBERT, Neil; SPECHT, Harry (eds.). *Planning for social welfare:
issues, and tasks*. Englewood Cliffs, N.J., Prentice-Hall, 77,
xiii-398 p.

5489   GORDEEV, I. I.; MALINOVSKIJ, P. A. (eds.). *Problemy social'nogo planirovanija* (Problems of social planning). Kubyšev, 76, 127 p.

5490   Bibl.XXVI-4649. GREFFE, Xavier. *La politique sociale. Étude cri-tique.* CR: Philippe BESNARD, *R. franç. Sociol.* 18(3), jul-sep 77 : 533.

5491   GRIGOROV, V. M. "Opyt v rešenii problem social'nogo upravlenija" (An attempt to resolve social management problems), *Nauč. upravl. Obšč.* (10), 1976 : 107-130.

5492   GULDIMANN, Tim. *Die Grenzen des Wohlfahrtsstaates: am Beispiel Schwedens und der Bundesrepublik* (The limits of the welfare state: the examples of Sweden and the Federal Republic). München, C. H. Beck, 76, 181 p. CR: Risto ERÄSAARI, *Acta sociol.* 20(2), 1977 : 202-205.

5493   Bibl.XXVI-4652. HALL, P. *et al. Change, choice and conflict in social policy.* CR: John CARRIER, *Brit. J. Sociol.* 28(4), dec 77 : 520-522.

5494   HAVEK, Friedrich August VON. *The mirage of social justice.* Chicago, University of Chicago Press, 76, xiv-195 p.

5495   HAYDEN, F. Gregory. "Toward a social welfare construct for social indicators", *Amer. J. Econ. Sociol.* 36(2), apr 77 : 129-146.

5496   JANOWITZ, Morris. *Social control of the Welfare State.* New York, Elsevier, 76, xxii-170 p.

5497   JOBERT, Bruno; RÉVÉSZ, Bruno. "Politiques résiduelles et planification sociale", *C. int. Sociol.* 24(6), jul-dec 77 : 243-260.

5498   JORDAN, Bill. *Freedom and the welfare state.* London-Boston, Routledge and K. Paul, 76, 224 p.

5499   KAĆANSKI UDOVIČIĆ, Gordana. "O planiranju socijalne zastite" (On social welfare planning), *Sociologija* 18(3-4), 1976 : 325-340.

5500   KLEIN, Rudolf. "Democracy, the Welfare State and social policy", *Polit. Quart.* 48(4), oct-dec 77 : 448-458. *[UK.]*

5501   KREFETZ, Sharon Perlman. *Welfare policy making and city politics.* New York, Praeger, 76, xiii-218 p. *[USA: Baltimore, San Francisco.]*

5502   KULCSÁR, K. "A társadalmi tervezés és a jogi szabályozás" (Social planning and legal regulation), *Gazdaság és Jogtud.* 10(1-2), 1976 : 19-34.

5503   KURCZEWSKA, Joanna. "Social engineering, ideology, society and culture", *Polish sociol. B.* 1976 : 22-32.

5504   LAPINE, N. "Théorie et pratique de la planification sociale", *Sci. soc. (Moscou)* (3), 1976 : 120-133. *[URSS.]*

5505   LATUCH, M. "Założenia generalne i cele populacijne polityki społ-ecnej w Polsce" (General assumption and populationist aims of social policy in Poland), *Biul. TGS* 20(1), 1977 : 27-39.

5506   LEHTONEN, Heikki. "Sosiaalipolitiikan käsitteen ja sen teoreettioon perustan kehityksestä Suomessa" (On the changes of concept of social policy and its theoretical base in Finland), *Sosiologia* 15(3-4), 1977 : 114-122.

5507   LITTRELL, W. Boyd; SJOBERG, Gideon (eds.). *Current issues in social policy.* Beverly Hills, Sage Publications, 76, 248 p. *[USA.]*

5508   LÖRCHER, Siegfried. *Zur Quantifizierung der "Sozialen Wohlfahrt" in Japan* (Quantifying of "social welfare" in Japan). Hamburg, Institut für Asienkunde, 76, 205 p.

5509   MILLER, David L. *Social justice.* Oxford, Eng., Clarendon Press, 76, viii-367 p.

5510   MILOSAVLJEVIC, Milosaw. "Sociološki prilog odredivanju pojma socijalna politika" (Sociological contribution to the definition of social policy), *Sociologija* 18(3-4), 1976 : 341-358.

5511   MURSWIECK, Axel (ed.). *Staatliche Politik im Sozialsektor* (State policy in the social sector). München, R. Piper, 76, 214 p.

5512   OKADA, Makoto. "Fukushi, kyoiku ni taisuru zaisei-shishutsu no shakaiteki koka" (Welfare policies under stagflation), *Komazawa Shakaigaku Kenkyū* (9), 1977 : 81-110.

5513   PAŠKOV, A. S.; MEŽEVIC, M. N. "Teoreticeskie voprosy social'nogo
        planirovanija" (Theoretical problems of social planning), in:
        Aktual'nye problemy social'nogo planirovanija. Irkutsk, 1975 :
        21-37.

5514   PIERIS, Ralph. *Social development and planning in Asia*. New Delhi,
        Abhinav Publications, 76, xi-438 p.

5515   "Politique sociale en Belgique", *R. belge Sécur. soc.* 19(3), mar
        77 : 232-325.

5516   POSTRIGAN', G. F. "O metodologiceskom aspekte svjazi interesov i
        social'nogo upravlenija" (On the methodological aspect of the
        connection between interests and social management), *Probl.
        Filos.* 40, 1977 : 52-59.

5517   SANADA, Naoshi (ed.). *Gendai no fukushi* (Welfare today). Tokyo,
        Yûhikaku, 77, 272 p.

5518   SCHUYT, C. "De sociale toekomst van de voerzorgingsstaat" (The
        social future of the welfare state), *Beleid en Mij* 3(7-8), jul-
        aug 76 : 190-201.

5519   SELLERBERG, Ann-Mari. "Social policy and social psychology. 'Social
        welfare interaction' analysed from three theoretical perspectives'
        Acta sociol. 19(3), 1976 : 263-272.

5520   SOKOŁOWSKA, Magdalena. "Polytika społeczna a zdruwie" (Social po-
        licy and health), *Stud. socjol.* 63(4), 1976 : 227-252.

5521   ŠUBNJAKOV, B. P. (ed.). *Sociologiceskie issledovanija i social'noe
        planirovanie - sostavnye casti upravlenija ideologiceskim pro-
        cessom (iz opyta sociologiceskoj razrabotki problemy "svoboda,
        otvetstvennost', upravlenie")* (Sociological researches and social
        planning are component parts of the ideological process manage-
        ment. From an essay of sociological elaboration of the problem:
        freedom, responsibility, management). Jaroslavl', 76, 160 p.

5522   VIŠNEVSKIJ, I. B.; MOSOLOV, Ju. P.; GALOBANOV, V. V. "Esteticeskoe
        razvitie trudjascihsja kak ob'ekt social'nogo planirovanija" (Aes-
        thetic development of workers as an object of social planning),
        in: *Aktual'nye problemy social'nogo planirovanija*. Irkutsk,
        1975 : 210-223.

5523   WILLIAMSON, John B.; FLEMING, Jeanne J. "Convergence theory and the
        social welfare sector", *Int. J. comp. Sociol.* 18(3-4), sep-dec
        77 : 242-253.

5524   YAMASHITA, Kesao; MITONO, Masao (eds.). *Shakai-fukushi-ron' sono
        kadai to tenbô* (Introduction to social welfare). Tokyo, Kawa-
        shima shoten, 77, 222 p.

20220. Social security
Sécurité sociale

[See also / Voir aussi: 3017, 5639]

5525   ABAD GOMEZ, H. "Seguridad social integral en Colombia" (Integral
        social security in Colombia), *Univ. Antioquía* 50(196), jan-mar
        76 : 113-121.

5526   DUE, Johannes. "De familie politiske kontantydelser, 1903-1976"
        (Family allowances policy from 1903 to 1976), *Soc. Tss.* 53(5),
        1977 : 119-139. [Denmark.]

5527   FUHRKE, Monika. *Staatliche Sozialpolitik: eine Untersuchung zur
        Entwicklung des Systems der sozialen Sicherheit im Kapitalismus*
        (State social policy: a study on the development of social secu-
        rity systems in capitalism). Offenbach, Verlag 2000, 76, 134-2 p.

5528   LEMAN, Christopher. "Patterns of policy development: social secu-
        rity in the United States and Canada", *Publ. Pol.* 25(2), 1977 :
        261-291.

5529   MUNNELL, Alicia Haydock. *The future of social security*. Washington,
        Brookings Institution, 77, xiii-190 p. [USA.]

5530   PORCIN, Nadine. *Bibliographie de l'histoire de la Sécurite sociale
        en France de 1789 à nos jours*. Paris, Fondation nationale des

sciences politiques, 76, xx-815 p.

5531 SANADA, Naoshi; OGURA, Jôji (eds.). *Rôdôsha no kurashi to shakai-hoshô* (Workers' life and social security). Kyôto, Horitsu Bunka-sha, 77, 277 p.

5532 SHARMA, Krishna Murti. *Social assistance in India.* NEW Delhi, Macmillan Co. of India, 76, xiii-119 p.

5533 TOMITA, Yoshiro. *Shakai-hoshô yôhen* (Social security). Kyoto, Mine-ruva Shobo, 77, 183 p.

5534 URBANI, R. "Aspetti della sicurezza sociale nei paesi in via di sviluppo" (Aspects of social security in the developing countries), *Previd. soc.* 32(3), mai-jun 76 : 755-772.

5535 VERGÉS, Joaquim. *La seguridad social española y sus cuentas* (Spanish social security and its accounts). Barcelona, Editorial Ariel, 76, 217 p.

20300. SOCIAL WORK
TRAVAIL SOCIAL

[See also / Voir aussi: 2985, 4304, 5630]

5536 ARKAVA, Morton, L.; BRENNEN, E. Clifford (eds.). *Competency-based education for social work: evaluation and curriculum issues.* New York, Council on Social Work Education, 76, XVii-204 p.

5537 BAILEY, Roy; BRAKE, Mike (eds.). *Radical social work.* London, Edward Arnold, 75, 6-170 p. *[UK.]*

5538 CHATTERJEE, P. K. "Social work and community development in India", *Int. R. Community Develop.* 35-36, 1976 : 167-188. *[India.]*

5539 DI CARLO, Enrique. *El trabajo social: teoría, metodología, inves-tigación* (Social work: theory, methodology, research). Buenos Aires, Editorial-Libreria ECRO, 76, 30 p.

5540 FISCHER, Joel. *The effectiveness of social casework.* Springfield, Ill., Thomas, 76, xvi-342 p.

5541 GOTTESFELD, Mary L.; PHARIS, Mary E. *Profiles in social work.* New York, Human Sciences Press, 77, 238 p.

5542 JENNENS, Roger. *Casework with a family at risk.* London, Family Service Units, 76, 1-29 p.

5543 LARBES, Germaine (éd.). *Distances et présences: tâches de la trans-mission en travail social.* Toulouse, E. Privat, 77, 182 p.

5544 LASCOUMES, Pierre. *Prévention et contrôle social: les contradic-tions du travail social.* Genève, Médecine et hygiène; Paris, Masson, 77, 262 p.

5545 LEVY, Charles S. *Social work ethics.* New York, Human Science Press, 76, 266 p.

5546 LIÉGEOIS, Jean-Pierre (éd.). *Idéologie et pratique du travail so-cial de prévention.* Toulouse, Privat, 77, 265 p.

5547 LOEWENBERG, Frank M. *Fundamentals of social intervention: core con-cepts and skills for social work practice.* New York, Columbia University Press, 77, xiv-374 p.

5548 MATSUMOTO, Takeko. "Waga-kuni ni okeru shakai-fukushi kyoiku no genjo to kadai" (The present conditions and issues of social work education in Japan), *Sosharu Wâku Kenkyû* 3(1), 1977 : 2-11.

5549 MORALES, Armando; SHEAFOR, Bradford W. *Social work: a profession of many faces.* Boston, Allyn and Bacon, 77, xiv-286 p.

5550 NAKAMURA, Toshimasa. "Amerika shakai-fukushi ni okeru gijutsuron no nagare" (Current developments of professional social work in America), *Shakaigaku Ronsô* 67, 1977 : 53-65.

5551 OKADA, Tôtarô. *Shakai-fukushi to social work. Social work no tankyu* (Social welfare and social work. Search for social work). Kyoto, Rugâru-sha, 77, 448 p.

5552 RAGG, Nicholas M. *People not cases: a philosophical approach to social work.* London-Boston, Routledge and K. Paul, 77, viii-159 p.

5553 ROBERTS, Robert W.; NORTHEN, Helen (eds.). *Theories of social work with groups.* New York, Columbia University Press, 76, xviii-401 p.

5554   SALOMON, Georges-Michel. "L'homme morcelé ou de quelques handicaps institutionnels au travail social concerté", *Connexions* 22, 1977 : 115-128.
5555   "Travail social. Travailleurs sociaux", *Contradictions* 14, dec 77 : 1-140.
5556   WECHSLER, Henry; REINHERZ, Helen Z.; DOBBIN, Donald D. *Social work research in the human services*. New York, Human Sciences Press, 76, xii-360 p.

20400. SOCIAL SERVICE
SERVICE SOCIAL

20410. Medical sociology. Medicine
Sociologie médicale. Médecine

[See also / Voir aussi: 3085]

5557   ALVAREZ-URIA, Fernando. "Poder médico y orden burgués. Análisis socio-histórico de las condiciones de aparición de la medicina moderna" (Medical power and bourgeois order. Socio-historical analysis of emerging conditions of modern medicine), *RS Cuad. Realidad soc.* 13, mar 77 : 5-26.
5558   ATKINSON, Paul; REID, Margaret; SHELDRAKE, Peter. "Medical mystique" *Sociol. Wk Occupat.* 4(3), aug 77 : 243-280.
5559   Bibl.XXVI-4723. BERLANT, Jeffrey L. *Profession and monopoly. a study of medicine in the United States and Great Britain*. CR: Terence C. HOLLIDAY, *Amer. J. Sociol.* 82(6), mai 77 : 1403-1407; Mike SAKS, *Brit. J. Sociol.* 18(3), sep 77 : 416.
5560   CABANEL, Guy-PIERRE. *Médecine libérale ou nationalisée ? sept politiques à travers le monde*. Paris, Dunod, 77, x-237 p.
5561   CARTWRIGHT, Frederick Fox. *A social history of medicine*. London-New York, Longman, 77, 209 p.
5562   DINGWALL, Robert *et al.* (eds.). *Health care and health knowledge*. London, Croom Helm; New York, Prodist, 77, 209 p.
5563   GORDON, Douglas. *Health, sickness, and society: theoretical concepts in social and preventive medicine*. St. Lucia, University of Queensland Press, 76, xvi-954 p.
5564   HARMAT, P. "Az orvostudomány funkcióváltozása. A társadalmi tényezök növekvö szerepe korunk orvostudományában" (Medical science changes function. The developing role of social factors in contemporary medical science), *Szociológia* 5(3-4), 1976 : 452-465.
5565   JONES, R. Kenneth; JONES, Patricia A. *Sociology in medicine*. New York, Halsted Press, 76, 222 p. CR: Thomas J. SULLIVAN, *Contemp. Sociol. (Washington)* 6(3), mai 77 : 383-384.
5566   KITAHARA, Ryûji. "Iryôshi no shomondai" (Some problems on the history of medicine), *Shakai-jigyôshi Kenkyû* (5), 1977 : 34-48.
5567   KLINKERT, J. J. *Inleiding in de medische sociologie* (Introduction to medical sociology). Assen, Van Gorcum, 77, viii-163 p.
5568   ROBIN, François; ROBIN, Nicole. *Le pouvoir médical*. Paris, Stock, 76, 252 p.
5569   SCULL, Andrew T. "Mad-doctors and magistrates: English psychiatry's struggle for professional autonomy in the nineteenth century", *Archiv. europ. Sociol.* 17(2), 1976 : 279-305.
5570   SMITHURST, Barry Anthony. *Fundamentals of social and preventive medicine*. St. Lucia, University of Queensland Press, 76, 170 p.
5571   *Sociología y medicina* (Sociology and medicine). Barcelona, Universidad Autónoma de Barcelona, 76, 275 p.
5572   STEUDLER, François. "Médecine libérale et conventionnement", *Sociol Trav.* 19(2), apr-jun 77 : 176-198. *[France.]*
5573   THOMAS, Lewis. "Biomedical science and human health: the long-range prospect", *Daedalus* 106(3), 1977 : 163-171.
5574   Bibl.XXVI-4737. TUCKETT, David (ed.). *An introduction to medical sociology*. CR: Agnes MILES, *Brit. J. Sociol.* 18(3), sep 77 : 414-415.

5575   VAN DORMAEL, M.; LACROSSE, J.-M. "La médecine du travail en Bel-
        gique", *Reflets Perspect. Vie écon.* 15(6), dec 76 : 443-452.

20420. Public health
Santé publique

[See also / Voir aussi: 1730, 4170, 4438, 5477, 5520]

5576   ALBRECHT, Gary L. (ed.). *The sociology of physical disability and
        rehabilitation.* Pittsburgh, University of Pittsburgh Press, 76,
        xiv-303 p.
5577   Bibl.XXVI-4742. ALFORD, Robert R. *Health care politics: ideological
        and interest group barriers to reform.* CR: Robert L. CRAIN, *Amer.
        polit. Sci. R.* 71(4), dec 77 : 1659-1660.
5578   BERG, Robert L.; BROOKS, M. Roy Jr.; SAVIČEVIĆ, Miomir. *Health
        care in Yugoslavia and the United States.* Bethesda, Md., United
        States Government Printing Office, 76, vii-251 p.
5579   BONSI, Stephen K. "Persistence and change in traditional medical
        practice in Ghana", *Int. J. contemp. Sociol.* 14(1-2), jan-apr
        77 : 27-38.
5580   CAMPAGNE, Pierre. "L'environnement de la planification sanitaire:
        plan santé et plan développement", *C. Sociol. Démogr. médic.*
        17(2), apr-jun 77 : 45-55.
5581   CARMICHAEL, Lynn P. "Consumerism in health care services", *Phylon*
        38(3), sep 77 : 249-257.
5582   CHEN, Pi-chao. *Population and health policy in the People's Repub-
        lic of China.* Washington, Interdisciplinary Communications Prog-
        ram, Smithsonian Institution, 76, xi-157 p.
5583   CUPERTINO, Fausto. *População e saude pública no Brazil: povo pobre
        e povo doente* (Population and public health in Brazil: poor
        people and ill people). Rio de Janeiro, Civilização Brasileira,
        76, 110 p.
5584   DEAN, Alfred; KRAFT, Alan M.; PEPPER, Bert (eds.). *The social
        setting of mental health.* New York, Basic Books, 76, x-405 p.
5585   "Doing better and feeling worse: health in the United States",
        Daedalus 106(1), 1977 : 278 p.
5586   ESTRYN-BEHAR, Madeleine; BEHAR, Abraham. *Santé publique et méde-
        cine préventive en République populaire d'Albanie.* Paris, Nouveau
        bureau d'édition, 76, 189 p.
5587   FOLEY, John W. "Community structure and the determinants of local
        health care differentiation: a research report", *Soc. Forces*
        56(2), dec 77 : 654-660.
5588   FORD, Amasa B. *Urban health in America.* New York, Oxford University
        Press, 76, 294 p. CR: Jennie J. KRONENFELD, *Contemp. Sociol. (Wa-
        shington)* 6(2), mar 77 : 261.
5589   FRIEDMAN, Kenneth; RAKOFF, Stuart H. (eds.). *Toward a national
        health policy: public policy and the control of health-care costs.*
        Lexington, Mass., Lexington Books, 77, xiii-257 p. [USA.]
5590   GOVE, Walter R.; GEERKEN, Michael R. "Response bias in surveys of
        mental health: an empirical investigation", *Amer. J. Sociol.*
        82(6), mai 77 : 1289-1317.
5591   GOVE, Walter R.; GEERKEN, Michael R. "The effect of children and
        employment on the mental health of married men and women", *Soc.
        Forces* 56(1), sep 77 : 66-76.
5592   "Health and society", *Milbank Memor. Fund Quart.* 55(2), 1977 : 161-
        340. [USA.]
5593   "Health care and the community", *New Univ. Quart.* 31(2), 1977 : 131-
        230. [UK.]
5594   "Health care in America: an overview", *Curr. Hist.* 72(427), mai-jun
        77 : 193-230.
5595   HOUTAUD, Alphonse D'. *Recherches en Lorraine sur les facteurs psy-
        chosociaux de la santé.* 3 vols. Paris, H. Champion, 77, 371 p.;
        232 p.; pagination multiple.

5596   "Improving health care in America", *Curr. Hist.* 73(428), jul-aug
        77 : 1-38.

5597   JONAS, Steven *et al. Health care delivery in the United States.*
        New York, Springer Publishing Co., 77, xviii-492 p.

5598   JONES, Maxwell. *Maturation of the therapeutic community: an organic
        approach to health and mental health.* New York, Human Sciences
        Press, 76, xxviii-169 p.

5599   KASER, Michael Charles. *Health care in the Soviet Union and Eastern
        Europe.* Boulder Colo., Westview Press, 76, 278 p.

5600   KRAUSE, Elliott A. *Power and illness: the political sociology of
        health and medical care.* New York, Elsevier, 77, xiv-383 p.

5601   LAPRÉ, R. M. "Policy objectives of health care planning in the
        Netherlands", *Planning Develop. Netherl.* 9(1), 1977 : 67-91.

5602   LETOURNY, Alain. "Intérêt et limites des indicateurs de santé en
        matière de planification", *C. Sociol. Démogr. médic.* 17(2), apr-
        jun 77 : 66-72.

5603   Bibl.XXVI-4760. MECHANIC, Daniel. *The growth of bureaucratic medici-
        ne: an inquiry into the dynamics of patient behavior and the orga-
        nization of medical care.* CR: Stephen M. SHORTELL, *Amer. J. So-
        ciol.* 82(5), mar 77 : 1134-1139.

5604   MERCKX, Virginie. "Perspectives de la planification sanitaire en
        Tunisie rurale", *C. Sociol. Démogr. médic.*17(2), apr-jun 77 :
        56-65.

5605   NELISSEN, N. J. M. "Sociale oorzaken van milieu-onhygiëne; een on-
        derzoeksnotitie" (Social causes of environment without hygiene;
        a research note), *Sociol. Gids* 24(6), nov-dec 77 : 396-406.

5606   OWEN, David. *In sickness and in health: the politics of medicine.*
        London, Quartet Books, 76, 11-178 p. [UK.]

5607   PATROV, B. D. (ed.). *Social'naja gigiena v SSSR (Očerk istorii)*
        (Social hygiene in the USSR. Historical characteristics). Moskva,
        Medicina, 76, 215 p.

5608   READ, Donald A.; SIMON, Sidney B.; GOODMAN, Joel B. *Health educa-
        tion: the search for values.* Englewood Cliffs, N.J., Prentice-
        Hall, 77, xi-186 p.

5609   RÉGNIER, F. "De la réparation à la maintenance: vers une intégra-
        tion du système de santé", *C. Sociol. Démogr. médic.* 17(1), jan-
        mar 77 : 34-36.

5610   RENAUD, Marc (éd.). "La gestion de la santé", *Sociol. et Soc.* 9(1),
        apr 77 : 3-159.

5611   ROSEN, Marvin; CLARK, Gerald R.; KIVITZ, Marvin S. *Habilitation of
        the handicapped: new dimensions in programs for the developmen-
        tally disabled.* Baltimore, University Park Press, 77, xv-371 p.

5612   ROSSER, James M.; MOSSBERG, Howard E. *An analysis of health care
        delivery.* New York, Wiley, 77, x-176 p. [USA.]

5613   "Santé des nations (La)", *R. int. Sci. soc.* 29(3), 1977 : 393-569.

5614   "Salud mental in Venezuela: problemas y organización" (Mental
        health in Venezuela: problems and organization), *R. venezol.
        Sanid. Asist. soc.* 41(1-2), mar-jun 76 : 15-180.

5615   SARAN, Parmatma. "Medical care and patient perception: a critique",
        Int. J. contemp. Sociol. 14(1-2), jan-apr 77 : 11-26.

5616   SOKOLOWSKA, Magdalena; BEJNAROWICZ, J. "Szociálpolitika és az egész-
        ségi állapot fogalma" (Social policy and the concept of health
        condition), *Szociológia* 5(3-4), 1976 : 564-574.

5617   SOKOLOWSKA, Magdalena *et al.* "The sociology of health of Polish
        society: trends and current state of research", *Sociol. contemp.*
        22(1-3), 1974 : 159-176.

5618   TARISKA, István. "Az elmeegészségügyről, az elmebetegségről és a
        társadalmi felelősségről" (Mental health, mental disease and
        social responsibility), *Valóság* (7), 1976 : 81-91.

5619   THEBAUD, A. "Besoins de santé et réponse de l'institution sanitaire
        en Algérie: réflexe théorique à partir d'un cas concret", *C. So-
        ciol. Démogr. médic.* 17(4), oct-dec 77 : 170-183.

5620   TWADDLE, Andrew C.; HESSLER, Richard M. *A sociology of health*.
        Saint Louis, Mosby, 77, xvi-349 p.
5621   VAN ETTEN, G. M. *Rural health development in Tanzania: a case-
        study of medical sociology in a developing country*. Assen, Van
        Gorcum, 76, 191 p.; CR: Margot JEFFETYS, *Brit. J. Sociol.* 18(3),
        sep 77 : 415.

20430. Hospital
Hôpital

[See also / Voir aussi: 529, 902, 1107, 2990, 4641, 4764]

5622   ANDERSEN, Ronald; LION, Joanna; ANDERSON, Odin W. *Two decades of
        health services: social survey trends in use and expenditure*.
        Cambridge, Mass., Ballinger Publishing Co., 76, xxii-387 p. *[USA.]*
5623   AXELSEN, Thorbjørn. *Det tause sykehuset: en sosialpsykologisk un-
        dersøkelse av kontaktforholdene på en sykehusavdeling* (The silent
        hospital: a socio-psychological study of the contact situation
        in a hospital ward). Oslo, Universitetsforlaget, 76, 151-1 p.
5624   BARNARD, Keith; LEE, Kenneth (eds.). *Conflicts in the National
        Health Service*. London, Croom Helm; New York, Prodist, 77, 252 p.
        [UK.]
5625   BARNETT, J. Ross; NEWTON, Peter. "Intra-urban disparities in the
        provision of primary health care: an examination of three New
        Zealand urban areas", *New Zealand J. Sociol.* 13(1), feb 77 : 60-
        68.
5626   BLOOM, Bernard L. *Community mental health: a general introduction*.
        Monterey, Calif., Brooks/Cole Publishing Co., 77, xi-331 p. *[Com-
        munity mental health services in the USA.]*
5627   CRICHTON, A. "The shift from entrepreneurial to political power in
        the Canadian health system", *Soc. Sci. Medic.* 10(1), jan 76 : 59-
        66.
5628   DEEGAN, Arthur X. *Management by objectives for hospitals*. German-
        town, Md., Aspen Systems Corporation, 77, vii-229 p.
5629   DUMONT, Jacques; LATOUCHE, Jean. *L'hospitalisation malade du pro-
        fit*. Paris, Éditions sociales, 77, 221 p.
5630   DUTRENIT, Jean-Marc. "Fonction médicale et travail social à l'hôpi-
        tal psychiatrique", *R. franç. Sociol.* 18(2), apr-jun 77 : 301-
        315.
5631   GHERMANI, I. "Das rumänische Gesundheitswesen. Bisherige Entwick-
        lung und Ausbauziele" (The health service in Rumania. The deve-
        lopment up to now and expansion aims), *Wiss. Dienst Südosteuropa*
        25(11), nov 76 : 196-200.
5632   GUSTIN, P. "Technocratie, bureaucratie et humanisation à l'hôpital",
        R. hospital. France 41(299), mar 77 : 195-269.
5633   HALL, David J. "Problems of innovation in a hospital setting: the
        example of playleaders", *Sociol. Wk Occupat.* 4(1), feb 77 : 63-86.
5634   KLEIN, Rudolf; LEWIS, Janet. *The politics of consumer representa-
        tion: a study of community health councils*. London, Centre for
        Studies in Social Policy, 76, 3-205 p. *[UK.]*
5635   LEVIN, Arthur (ed.). "Health services: the local perspective",
        Proc. Acad. polit. Sci. 32(3), 1977 : 1-262. *[USA.]*
5636   MIGUEL, Jesus M. "Tendencias mundiales en los servicios sanitarios
        para enfermos mentales" (World-wide trends of health services
        for mental handicaped), *R. int. Sociol. (Madrid)* 34(17), jan-mar
        76 : 95-131.
5637   RUEL, Michel. *Le pouvoir à l'hôpital... le malade*. Paris, Savelli,
        77, 182 p.
5638   STACEY, Margaret (ed.). *The sociology of the National Health Ser-
        vice*. Keele, University of Keele, 76, 6-200 p. *[UK.]*
5639   WEINSTEIN, R. M.; MORAVEC, J. G. "A comparative analysis of health
        and welfare organizations", *Pacific sociol. R.* 20(1), jan 77 :
        79-104.

20440. Social worker
Travailleur social

[See also / Voir aussi: 3097, 4607, 4708, 5555, 5569]

5641 "Aspects de la responsabilité médicale en France, en Italie et en Suisse", *R. int. Dr. comp.* 28(3), jul-sep 76 : 487-577.

5642 BADURA, Bernhard; GROSS, Peter. *Sozialpolitische Perspektiven. Eine Einführung in Grundlagen und Probleme sozialer Dienstleistungen* (Socio-political perspectives. An introduction to basic principles and problems of social services). München, R. Piper, 76, 360 p. CR: Hansjürgen DAHEIM, *Kölner Z. Soziol. u. soz.-Psychol.* 29(3), sep 77 : 590-593.

5643 BELLABY, Paul; ORIBABOR, Patrick. "The growth of trade union consciousness among general hospital nurses viewed as a response to 'proletarianisation'", *Sociol. R.* 25(4), nov 77 : 801-822.

5644 BEYSSAGUET, Anne-Marie; CHAUVIERE, Michel; OHAYON, Annick. *Les socio-clercs: bienfaisance ou travail social.* Paris, F. Maspéro, 76, 248 p.

5645 BIERTER, Willy. "Dangers d'une conception trop scientifique du service social", *R. int. Sci. soc.* 29(4), 1977 : 837-841.

5646 BLINKERT, Baldo *et al. Berufskrisen in der Sozialarbeit: eine empirische Untersuchung uber Verunsicherung, Anpassung und Professionalisierung von Sozialarbeitern* (Professional crisis in the social work: an empirical study of the unsecurity, adaptation and professionalization of social workers). Weinheim-Basel, Beltz, 76, 183 p. [Germany FR.]

5647 "Centres de services sociaux au Québec (Les)", *Serv. soc. (Québec)* 25(2-3), jul-dec 76 : 194 p.

5648 COLE, Jonathan R.; LIPTON, James A. "The reputations of American medical schools", *Soc. Forces* 55(3), mar 77 : 662-684.

5649 Bibl.XXVI-4807. CRANE, Diana. *The sanctity of social life: physicians' treatment of critically ill patients.* CR: Bradford H. GRAY, *Amer. J. Sociol.* 82(4), jan 77 : 885-887.

5650 "Développement des personnels de santé", *Chron. OMS* 30(11), nov 76 : 482-526; 30(12), dec 76 : 553-557.

5651 DUTRÉNIT, Jean-Marc. "Ethos du service social et enfance en danger", *R. franç. Sociol.* 17(4), oct-dec 76 : 615-632.

5652 ERIKSEN, Karin. *Human services today.* Reston, Va., Reston Publishing Co., 77, x-198 p.

5653 FREDERICKS, Marcel A.; MUNDY, Paul. *The making of a physician: a ten-year longitudinal study of social class, academic achievement, and changing professional attitudes of a medical school class.* Chicago, Loyola University Press, 76, 206 p. CR: Robert H. COOMBS, *Contemp. Sociol. (Washington)* 6(2), mar 77 : 191-192.

5654 FROGER-GUALON, Jacqueline. "Le médecin, le psychanalyste et l'enseignant: un exemple de fonctionnement pluridisciplinaire dans un CMPP", *Connexions* 22, 1977 : 47-63.

5655 GILBERT, Neil; SPECHT, Harry. *Coordinating social services: an analysis of community, organizational, and staff characteristics.* New York, Praeger, 77, xv-84 p.

5656 GOLDSTEIN, Harold M.; HOROWITZ, M. A. *Entry-level health occupations: development and future.* Baltimore, Johns Hopkins University Press, 77, ix-100 p. [USA.]

5657 HARRELL-BOND, Barbara. "The influence of the family caseworker on the structure of the family: the Sierra Leone case", *Soc. Res.* 44(2), 1977 : 193-215.

5658 HESSELBART, Susan. "Women doctors win and male nurses lose: a study of sex role and occupational stereotypes", *Sociol. Wk. Occupat.* 4(1), feb 77 : 49-62.

5659 HOERNI, B. *et al.* "Relations entre omnipraticiens et cancérologues", *C. Sociol. Démogr. médic.* 17(1), jan-mar 77 : 11-16.

5660   JEAN, P. "Les personnels sanitaires", *B. trim. École nat. Santé*
        publ. 8(3-4), jul-dec 75 : 355-420. *[France.]*
5661   JEANNET, Maurice. "L'évaluation des interventions du psychologue
        praticien. Une expérience suisse", *Connexions* 20, 1976 : 7-17.
5662   JOUFFROY, C. *et al.* "Déroulement des études médicales du lycée à
        la thèse", *C. Sociol. Démogr. médic.* 17(1), jan-mar 77 : 3-10.
        [France.]
5663   KRAMER, Ralph M. *The voluntary service agency in Israel.* Berkeley,
        Institute of International Studies, University of California,
        76, x-94 p.
5664   LAZARUS, Antoine. "Le médecin pénitentiaire entre deux demandes",
        Connexions 20, 1976 : 63-75.
5665   LEFEBVRE, Alain. "Nombre de médecins et espérance de vie", *Popu-*
        lation 31(6), nov-dec 76 : 1289-1297.
5666   LEPORRIER, Herbert. *Le médecin aujourd'hui.* Paris, Payot, 76, 183 p.
5667   LEVY, D. "Aperçu sur la démographie médicale de la Région pari-
        sienne", *C. Sociol. Démogr. médic.* 17(4), oct-dec 77 : 152-164.
5668   MARSDEN, Lorna R. "Power within a profession: medicine in Ontario",
        Sociol. Wk Occupat. 4(1), feb 77 : 3-26.
5669   OMARK, R. "Practices of psychotherapists: cultural mutuality,
        ideologies, and work settings", *Canad. R. Sociol. Anthropol.*
        14(2), mai 77 : 188-199.
5670   PARRY, Noel; PARRY, José. *The rise of the medical profession: a*
        study of collective social mobility. London, Croom Helm; New
        York, International Publications Service, 76, 282 p. *[UK.]*
5671   REYMÃO, Maria Eunice Garcia. *As atribuições profissionais do assis-*
        tente social (The professional attribution of social worker).
        São Paulo, Edições Loyola, Cortez y Moraes, 76, 174 p. *[Brazil.]*
5672   SCHNELLER, Eugene Stewart. "The design and evolution of the phy-
        sician's assistant", *Sociol. Wk Occupat.* 3(4), nov 76 : 455-478.
5673   "Service social et famille: réalité nouvelle, nouveaux impératifs",
        Serv. soc. (Québec) 26(1), jan-jun 77 : 3-109. *[Canada.]*
5674   SMITH, James P. *Sociology and nursing.* Edinburgh-New York, Chur-
        chill Livingstone, 76, 179 p.
5675   SOLYMOSI, Zs. "Orvosok és települések. Az orvosok területi elhe-
        lyezkedéséről és demográfiai-társadalmi összetételéről" (Phy-
        sicians and settlements. On territorial distribution and de-
        mographic-social stratification of physicians), *Valóság* (10),
        1977 : 73-86. *[Hungary.]*
5676   SOUBEYROL, J. "Les médecins dans la CEE", *R. trim. Dr. europ.*
        12(4), oct-dec 76 : 601-623.
5677   SULLIVAN, Louis W. "The education of Black health professionals",
        Phylon 38(2), jun 77 : 181-193. *[USA.]*
5678   SUSSMAN, George D. "The glut of doctors in mid-nineteenth-century
        France", *Comp. Stud. Soc. Hist.* 19(3), jul 77 : 287-304.
5679   TOBIN, Sheldon S.; DAVIDSON, Stephen M.; SACK, Ann. *Effective so-*
        cial services for older Americans. Ann Arbor, Institute of Ge-
        rontology, University of Michigan, Wayne State University, 76,
        xii-221 p.
5680   TOSQUELLES, François. "Dialogue intérieur sur l'équipe en psycho-
        thérapie institutionnelle", *Connexions* 22, 1977 : 25-46.
5681   TOURNIER, P. "Évolution des disparités de la répartition géogra-
        phique des médecins libéraux en France entre 1962 et 1975", *C.*
        Sociol. Démogr. médic. 17(4), oct-dec 77 : 131-151.

AUTHOR INDEX
INDEX DES AUTEURS

Aardema, Labette S., 1127
Aas, Dagfinn, 4852
Abadan-Unat, Nermih, 3464, 3465
Abad Gomez, H., 5525
Abadinsky, Howard, 5443
Abbate, Fred J., 4967
Abbott, Lewis F., 4345
Abbott, Walter F., 3744
Abdel-Malek, A., 2790
Abe, Minoru, 159
Abedor, Allan J., 2418
Abel, Gerd, 2776
Abell, Peter, 1005, 4911
Abellan Garcia, Antonio, 3997
Abgarjan, Ê., 389
Aboltin, V. Ja., 4241
Aboud, Frances E., 602
Abrahams, Roger D., 4243
Abrahamson, Mark, 3979, 3998
Abramson, H., 3534
Abramson, Paul R., 5112
Accattatis, Vincenzo, 2547
Achard, Pierre, 2454
Achinger, Gertrud, 2258
Achinivu, Nnennaya, 3949
Acquaviva, Sabino S., 1379
Adair, John G., 1106
Adams, J. Mack, 120
Adams, John S., 4042
Adams, Nancy E., 1145
Adamski, Franciszek, 3244
Adamski, Władysław, 2944
Addario, Xicolo, 5084
Adegbola, O., 3132
Aderanti Adepoju, 3654
Adick, Christel, 2943
Adlakha, A., 3168
Adler, Chaim, 3718
Adler, L. M., 4346
Adler, Richard, 2017
Adriaansens, H. P. M., 198
Afanas'ev, V. G., 2865, 2866
Afigbo, A.E., 3008
Aga, Synnova, 4496
Agel, Henri, 2009
Ágh, A., 1, 2108, 2109, 4822
Aguerrondo, Inès, 2242
Aguilar Monteverde, Alonso, 4242
Aguirre Avellaneda, Jerjes, 3955
Ahmad, Saghir, 3009
Ahmed, Akbar S., 3535

Ahmed, M. D., 1738
Aiello, John R., 1211
Aitchison, Jean, 1838
Aithnard, K. M., 1350
Aitov, N.A., 4285
Ajami, I., 3133
Akehurst, Michael, 5234
Akers, Ronald L., 3080, 5444
Akin, William E., 5031
Akiyama, Toyoko, 2959
Akkanen, Riitta, 4848
Alatas, Syed H., 2678, 3821
Alba-Hernández, Francisco, 3677
Albaum,Gerald S., 481
Albeda-Wie, 4710
Albert, Pierre, 1989
Alberti, Giorgio, 2836, 3884
Albinson, F., 2362
Albinson, John G., 4864
Albistur, Maïté, 3466
Albou, Paul, 1942
Albrecht, Gary L., 5383, 5576
Albrecht, Stan L., 1142
Alcobendas, Pilar, 451
Alcock, Norman, 1467
Aldag, Ramon J., 4579
Alderman, Karen C., 2928
Aldrich, John H., 5166
Aleksasenko, A. P., 2548
Alekseeva, V. M., 2455
Alemann, Heine von, 22, 1800
Alex, Nicholas, 5004
Alexander, C. Norman, 1380
Alexander, Karl L., 2259
Alexander, Yonah, 1433
Alfeld, Louis E., 4199
Alfiorov, V., 1109
Alford, Robert R., 5113, 5577
Alho, Olli, 2107
Alker, Hayward R. Jr., 1540, 4461
Allan, Graham, 796, 3363
Allardt, E., 3536
Alleau, René, 1867
Allen, Donald E., 1904
Allen, I. L., 4043
Allen, James P., 3696
Allen, Patricia R. B., 137
Allen, Sheila, 2867
Allison, Paul D., 521
Allott, A. N., 1541
Almeida, M. L., 696

Almquist, Elizabeth M., 4497
Alonso, Myrtes, 2277
Alonso, V. L., 3956
Alonso Torrens, F. J., 1434
Alonso Torrens, J., 5304
Alonzo, F. O., 5445
Alounate, Adolfo, 4409
Al-Qazzaz, Ayad, 3467
Al-Salman, F. J., 1006
Alt, James, 559
Altheide, David L., 1673, 1990, 3070
Altherr, Marco, 5246
Alvarez-Uria, Fernando, 5557
Alvira Martin Francisco, 1110
Alwin, Duane F., 2288, 4883
Amabile, Teresa M., 1103
Amady, Nathé, 2911
Amelang, Manfred, 5114
Ames, Richard G., 502
Ames, Ruth, 836
Amin, Samir, 2791
Ampofo, D. A., 3186
Amselle, Jean-Loup, 3745
Anderle, Á., 2792
Andersen, Ronald, 5622
Anderson, Charles H., 3010
Anderson, James G., 529
Anderson, John C., 4737
Anderson, John E., 3187
Anderson, O. D., 501
Anderson, Odin W., 5622
Anderson, Palmer, 5456
Anderson, Ronald E., 121, 1421
Andersson, A. E., 2838
Andics, Jeno, 973, 4316, 4317, 4347
Andison, F. Scott, 2016
Andō, Sadao, 2982
Andorka, Rudolf, 522, 530, 2706, 4618
Andors, S., 4667
Andrade, T. G. de, 2363
Andrássy, Maria, 1839
Andreani Scopesi, A. M., 2289
Andreev, Ê. M., 3834
Andreoli, Virginia A., 862
Andrew, Caroline, 4138
Andrews, Frank M., 4286
Andrews, Richard B., 4044
Andrey, G., 4968
Andrle, Vladimir, 4693
Andruscenko, V. P., 1404
Anglade, Jean, 3697
Angrist, Shirley S., 4200, 4497
Angyal, V., 4139
Anh, Tran, 1397
Anizon, Alain, 3822
Ansart, Pierre, 5247
Antal, L., 417
Anthony, P. D., 4578
Antic, Lazo, 3055
Antoine, J., 459
Aoi, Kazuo, 2983, 3392

Apel, Karl O., 1785
Aphale, Champa, 2912
Appel, René, 1840
Appelbaum, R. P., 4097
Appleyard, Donald, 4201
Arabie, Phipps, 935
Arafat, Ibtihaj, 3468
Aragon, Luis E., 3667
Arai, Katsuhiro, 2295
Araji, Sharon K., 3308
Aral, Sevgi O., 1542
Arasteh, A. Reza, 739
Arasteh, Josephine D., 739
Arató, Endre, 3537
Arbelaez C., Alfonso, 3678
Archambault, François, 1991
Archideacon, Thomas T., 4045
Archer, R. W., 3957
Archibald, Clinton, 5085
Arcuri, Alan F., 5005
Arcy, Carl d', 3071
Arcy, F. d', 3188
Arcy, Philippe d', 4912
Ardigo, Achille, 3321
Argyris, Chris, 1078
Arhangel'skij, L. M., 1516
Ariel del Val, Fernando, 1435
Arieli, Mordecai, 4140
Aries, Philippe, 3095
Arieti, Silvano, 740
Ariyoshi, Hiroyuki, 716
Arkava, Morton L., 5536
Arkes, Hal R., 717
Armand, Monique, 139
Armenakis, Achilles A., 1007
Armogathe, Daniel, 3466
Armstrong, K. J., 4738
Arnaud, Jean, 4046
Arney, William R., 3134
Arnold, Fred, 2913
Arnold, Jenifer, 3448
Arnold Judith W., 771
Arnol'dov, A. I., 1239
Aronson, Elliot, 578, 826
Arrtex, Carmen, 3135
Arrow, Kenneth J., 741
Arroyo, G., 1739
Artemov, V. A., 4202
Arts, W., 1111
Arvidson, Peter, 4823
Aschinger, G. A., 742
Ashby, E., 2430
Ashford, Nicholas A., 3072
Ashton, Patrick J., 4203
Ashworth, Clark D., 857
Ashworth, C. E., 202
Askham, Janet, 3136
Asō, Makoto, 2230
Aster, H., 2399
Atal, Yogesh, 64
Atchley, Robert C., 4600
Athanassiades, John C., 1143

Ath-Messaoud, Malek, 3698
Atkinson, Paul, 5558
Atoji, Yoshio, 199, 390
Attali, Jacques, 2085
Atteslander, Peter, 4462
Attewell, Paul, 5326
Aubusson de Cavarlay, Bruno, 5352
Audigier, Pierre, 2018
Audry, Colette, 1517
Auerbach, Lewis, 2907
Aufderlandwehr, Werner, 3746
Augustins, Georges, 2738
Austin, Gilbert R., 2243
Austin, Roy L., 5365, 5411, 5433, 5454
Auzin, Imant, 2103
Avanzini, Bianca B., 3393
Aveni, Adrian F., 797
Avery, Nicholas C., 3245
Avril, A. M., 5475
Avvakumov, Ju. G., 200
Axelrod, Charles D., 201, 1786
Axelrod, Robert, 743
Axelsen, Thorbjørn, 5623
Ayala, Francisco J., 160
Aymard, Marguerite, 139
Azad Rana, Kipkorir Aly, 2549

Babad, Alisha Y., 891
Babiński, Grzegorz, 3538
Bábosik, István, 1518
Bach, Robert L., 3655
Bach, Uwe, 2149
Bacharach, S. B., 4913
Bachman, Jerald G., 624
Back, Kurt W., 573
Bäcker, Ferdinand F., 5115
Bacon, Phil, 316
Bacot, Paul, 5167
Baczko, Malgorzata, 3823
Badari, V. S., 3056
Badcock, C. R., 202
Bader, Veit-Michael, 203
Badie, Bertrand, 4780
Badillo Nieto, M., 5032
Badowski, I., 3189
Badura, Bernhard, 5642
Baer, Robert, 1405
Baginski, Eugeniusz, 4098
Bahr, Howard M., 1142
Bailey, F. G., 3857
Bailey, Roy, 5537
Bain, G. S., 4768
Bain, M., 2529
Bain, Robert K., 1149
Bainbridge, William S., 4348
Bajagic, Veronika, 4824
Bakaldin, S. S., 1240
Bakare, C. G. M., 1144
Baker, Margaret, 3268
Baker, Paul M., 2657
Baker, Sally Hillsman, 4287

Bakkerode, H., 5033
Baks, Chris, 2793
Balakar, James B., 5321
Balakrishnan, T. R., 4141
Baldamus, Wilhelm, 376
Baldauf, Richard B. Jr., 1365
Baldissera, Eros, 2364
Baldwin, E$izabeth G., 1957, 1966
Baldwin, John, 5430
Balfet, H., 412
Balkwell, James W., 625
Ball, Donald W., 4853
Ball, James R., 4858
Ball, Richard A., 347
Balle, Catherine, 840
Balle, Francis, 1992
Ballo, Robert, 3073
Balloni, Augusto, 5361
Ballonoff, Paul A., 2896, 3267
Balswick, Jack O., 625
Bandera, Joaquín, 3322
Bandiare, Ali, 2914
Bandura, Albert, 1145, 1406
Bandyopadhyaya, Jayantanuja, 1324
Banerji, S., 4739
Bangou, Henri, 2530
Banks, Olive, 3352
Banks, W. Curtis, 626
Banton, Michael P., 3539
Barabas, Ju., 1351
Barash, David P., 2897
Baratra, M., 2997
Baratz, Morton, 4919
Barbano, Filippo, 2550
Bardeau, Jean-Marc, 3074
Bardill, Ronald, 893
Bardin, Laurence, 418
Bardis, Panos D., 798
Bardo, John W., 4099
Barkan, Steven E., 1544
Barkat, A. M., 1740
Barker, Diana Leonard, 2867
Barker-Benfield, G. J., 3233
Barkow, Jerome H., 1112
Bar-Levav, Reuven, 892
Barlow, Brent A., 3304
Barlow, Henry M., 1317, 5280
Barnard, Keith, 5624
Barnes, Donna, 3117
Barnes, Gordon E., 1106, 5330
Barnes, Josephine, 3190
Barnes, Richard D., 2878
Barnett, George A., 1905
Barnett, J. Ross, 5625
Barnett, Lawry D., 943
Barnett, Marguerite Ross, 1241
Barnum, H. N., 3747
Baron, Robert A., 3234
Baron, Robert S., 825
Barrau, Jacques, 1411

Barringer, Herbert R., 3765
Barritt, Adrian, 111
Barros, Alexandre de S.C., 2679
Barsky, Stephen, F., 4889
Bar-Tal, Daniel, 833
Bartell, Ted, 772
Bartels, Dennis, 2551
Baryhelemy Knowlton, Simone, 2062
Bartholomew, David J., 549
Bartol, Gerda, 2296
Bartoli, D., 4922
Barton, Allen H., 1171, 5050
Bartošová, M., 2839
Bas, Carlos A., 4204
Baskauskas, L., 3699
Basler, Heinz-Dieter, 1436
Bassand, Michel, 3540, 4100
Bassis, Michael S., 2297
Bastide, Henri, 3011
Bastide, Roger, 4272
Basu, Asoke, 502
Bates, Daniel G., 1237
Bates, Frederick, 1088
Bates, Robert H., 3853, 3855
Bateson, Gregory, 789
Batscha, Robert, 131
Bauberot, Jean, 1619
Bauer, Arnold J., 3885
Bauer, A. Thomas, 1166
Bauer, Gérard, 3999
Baum, Rainer C., 1070
Bauman, Karl E., 3227
Baumann, Robert, 5244
Bay, Edna G., 3493
Bayer, Alan E., 3235
Bayer, Hermann, 2298
Bayles, Michael D., 1519
Bayne, G. Keith, 4649
Beach, Stephen W., 1741, 5086
Bean, Frank D., 3463
Bearden, William O., 4428
Beavers, W. Robert, 3394
Bebarta, Prafulla C., 3137
Bechelloni, Giovanni, 2299
Bechtel, Gordon G., 560
Beck, Nathanieĕ, 5061
Beck, Paul A., 5116
Becker, Carolyn, 5305
Becker, Gary S., 1113
Becker, Heinz A., 553
Becker, Lee B., 1696
Becker, Tamar, 2945
Beckford, James A., 1655
Becquart-Leclercq, Jeanne, 5051, 5052
Bedau, Hugh Adam, 5446
Beder, Harold W., 2365
Behar, Abraham, 5586
Beillerot, Jacky, 2434
Beit-Hallahmi, Benjamin, 2915
Béjin, André, 1381, 3236
Bejnarowicz, J., 5616

Bekke, A.J.G.M., 1008
Béland, François, 4607
Belanger, Paul, 2366
Belkin, Gary S., 2110
Belkin, Jacob, 4200
Bell, Bill D., 2984
Bell, Colèn, 4142
Bell, Daniel, 1704, 4243
Bell, Duran, 2985
Bell, Geoffrey, 1620
Bell,Gwenn, 3824
Bell, Paul A., 3234
Bell, Roger T., 1841
Bellaby, Paul, 5643
Bellack, Alan S., 1114
Bellah, Robert N., 1724, 1742
Bellamy, R., 4288
Bellettirie, Gerlad, 727
Bellows, Nancy, 380
Belorgey, Jean-Michel, 2367, 5473
Belyh, A. K., 4923
Ben-David, Joseph, 1242, 2300
Benedek, S., 2552
Benet, Mary K., 3395
Bénéton, Philippe, 2231
Bengu, Sibusio M. E., 1345
Benjamin, A., 873
Benjamin, Martin, 1520
Benkó, Lóránd, 1906
Benn, S. I., 3
Benoist, Jean, 3886
Bensman, Joseph, 186
Benson, J. Kenneth, 974
Benson, Thomas W., 1868
Bent, Alan E., 4101
Benton, Ted, 4
Béraud, Jean-Marc, 4601
Bereano, Philip L., 4349
Berenson, David, 5349
Berezina, Ju. I., 2553
Berdahl, Robert M., 4957
Berents, Dirk A., 5362
Berg, Lars-Erik, 204
Berg, Robert L., 5578
Bergan, John R., 2923
Berger, Joseph, 2658
Berger, Michael, 2150
Berger, Morroe, 2063
Bergesen, Albert James, 1562, 3264
    5117
Bergius, Rudolf, 574
Bergmann, Theodor, 3887
Bergner, Dieter, 205
Berk, Bernard, 2096
Berk, B.B., 1009
Berk, Lynn M., 1976
Berk, Richard A., 5447
Berlant, Jeffrey L., 5559
Berman, John J., 465, 3284
Bermant, Gordon, 972
Bermudo, M., 1585

Bernabé, Jean, 1609
Bernard, Jessie, 3469
Bernard, Paul, 2707
Bernard, Philippe J., 4273
Bernbaum, Gerald, 2111
Bernholm, Bernt, 2868
Bernstein, Sergei N., 2898
Bernstein, Ilene N., 108, 448, 5431, 5432
Bernstein, Richard J., 206
Berriatua San Sebastian, Javier, 4102
Berridge, Robert I., 2435
Berry, Brian J. L., 3980, 4048
Berry, John W., 1352
Bersani, Carl, 1092
Berscheid, Ellen, 795
Bertaux, Daniel, 2554
Bertelli, Sergio, 4103
Berthelot, Jean-Michel, 2209
Bertola, Giuliana, 2794
Bertram, Hans, 684, 894
Bertrand, Jean-René, 3748
Bertrand, William E., 5302
Besnard, Philippe, 3099, 5490
Bestuzev-Lada, I. V., 348, 349, 718, 2735
Béteille, André, 419
Betten, Neil, 1718
Bettini, R., 5118
Beutel, Jörg, 4001
Bevan, Philippe, 2497
Beyaert, A., 4568
Beyer, Janice, 1145
Beylon, Huw, 4250
Beyssaguet, Anne-Marie, 5644
Bezerra, Felte, 207
Bezouska, Jiří, 450
Bezrukov, A. V., 1243
Bhattacharyya, Amit K., 3138
Bhattacharya, K., 4350
Bhola, H. S., 2415
Biagi, Adriano, 607
Biadecki, Ireneusz, 4619
Bialobrzeski, Henryk, 4104
Biard, Roland, 4924
Bibb, Robert, 4289
Bickman, Leonard, 5363
Bidwell, Sidney, 3613
Bielby, William T., 2659
Bierhoff, Hans W., 655
Bierhoff-Alfermann, Dorothée, 655
Bierter, Willy, 5645
Bihari, Ottó, 4049
Bijnen, E. J., 503
Bilandžić, Dušan, 4318
Biliński, Kazimierz, 3888
Billeter, Jean-François, 47
Billig, Michael, 859
Bislborrow, Richard E., 3191
Bintig, Arnfried B., 575
Birchall, David, 4498
Bird, Anne-Marie, 944
Birdsall, Nancy, 3012
Biresch, Peter, 2019
Birks, J. S., 1679
Birouste, Jacques P., 3237
Bisani, Fritz, 4540, 4541
Bishop, G. F., 1189
Bishop, James M., 2436
Bisky, Lothar, 1958, 1959
Bisselle, Walter C., 3935
Bisson, Antoine F., 3192
Bittner, John R., 1960
Bizot, Judithe, 2151
Blaas, Gejza, 4404
Black, Cyril E., 2739
Black, Donald J., 1545
Blacker, J. G. C., 3096
Blackey, Robert, 2740, 5087
Blais, André, 4138
Blamont, Denis, 3854
Blanchard, Kenneth H., 1026
Blanco Muñoz, Agustin, 2555
Blankenburg, Erhard, 1546, 5448
Blasco Segura, Benjamin, 4781
Blasi, Augusto, 617
Blasi, Joseph R., 4386
Blasius, Dirk, 5364
Blass, Jerome H., 1093
Blass, Thomas, 656
Blau, Judith R., 2080
Blau, Peter M., 2456, 2457
Blaug, Mark, 2368
Blaukopf, Kurt, 2020, 2946
Blaxall, Martha, 4499
Blaxter, Mildred, 3075
Blayo, Chantal, 3193
Blayo, Yves, 3139
Blazko, N.I., 109
Bledstein, Burton J., 2301
Bleek, Wolf, 3194
Blinkort, Baldo, 5646
Bljum, R. N., 2741
Bloch, Maurice, 4958
Bloch, Richard, 2947
Block, Fred, 4925, 4969
Blom-Cooper, Louis, 1547
Bloom, Bernard L., 5626
Bloor, David, 1787
Blum, Alan, 1788
Blum, Jacques, 4143
Blum, Milton L., 4429
Blum, Paul von, 2040
Blumberg, Arthur, 895
Blume, Stuart S., 5474
Blumenthal, Monica D., 1437
Blyth, Dale A., 790
Bobbio, Norberto, 1548
Bock, Michael, 1907
Böckelmann, Frank, 1961
Bockman, Sheldon, 4908
Bocock, R. J., 576
Bode, Herbert F., 4620

Bodiguel, Maryvonne, 3889
Boef, C., 1962
Boer, Connie de, 461
Bofill, Juan A., 1869
Bogart, Robert W., 208, 209
Bogdan, Robert, 391
Bogdanovic, Marija, 48, 161
Boggs, Carl, Jr., 2742
Bogina, S. A., 3700
Bognar, Laszlo, 2708
Bogue, Allan G., 5
Böhme, Gernot, 1789
Bois, Joyce, 1128
Boisier, S., 4206
Boisvert, Maurice P., 4554
Boito, Armando Jr., 5180
Boixadós, Alberto, 2041
Bojkov, V. Ê., 4682
Bokszanski, Zbigniew, 466
Bolčić, Silvano, 2795
Bollack, Jean, 1908
Bollinger, Ernst, 1993
Bolotnikov, I. M., 657
Bon, Frédéric, 2024
Bonacich, Phillip, 497
Bonarate, Luigi, 1438
Bond, George C., 3855
Bondarenko, V. M., 5205
Bondy, O., 1521
Bon Espasandin, Mario, 65
Bongaarts, J., 3013
Bonham, Gordon Scott, 3396
Boniface, Jean, 4430
Bonjean, Charles M., 66
Bonnet, Jean-Charles, 3701
Bonnet, Serge, 4668
Bonsi, Stephen K., 5578
Bonte, Pierre, 3491
Boocock, Sarane S., 2152
Boolsen, Merete W., 103
Boorman, Scott A., 936
Booth, Alan, 1212, 1213
Booth, J. A., 5163
Booth, Newell S., 1613
Borgida, Eugene, 744
Borgström, Bengt-Erik, 2660
Borich, Gary D., 2416
Borisov, G. M., 1244
Borja, Jordi, 4105, 4106
Borja, Ricard, 4106
Bornewasser, Manfred, 577
Bornschier, Volker, 2489, 2661
Borodkin, Friedrich, 1109, 4290
Boronev, A. O., 6
Borščevskij, M. V., 531, 4205
Bortollas, Clemens, 5365
Boruch, Robert, 465
Bose, Ashish, 4002
Bose, Christine F., 4313
Bosko, Kathy, 2039
Boss, Jean-François, 4431

Boss, Pauline, 3383
Boswell, Thomas D., 3559
Böszörményi, Ede, 5366
Böszörményi, Zoltan, 2986
Bothe, Bernd, 4542
Bottacchiari, Vinicio, 4420
Bottani, N., 2369
Bottomore, Tom, 210
Bottoms, A. E., 5430
Botz, Gerhard, 4926
Bouazis, Charles, 1842
Boublil, Alain, 4927
Bouchalova, Marie, 3397
Bouchard, Gérard, 2709
Boucbier, David, 1790
Boudard, F., 5475
Boudon, Alain, 4431
Boudon, Philippe, 2081
Boudon, Raymond, 719, 1439, 2302,
    2458, 2460
Bouet, Michel A., 4854
Boukraa, R., 3856, 4144
Bould, Sally, 3398
Boulding, Elise, 3471
Bouraoui, A., 3702
Bourcier de Carbon, Philippe, 4274
Bourdeaux, Robert M., 702
Bourdieu, Pierre, 791, 1172, 3890,
    4995
Bourelle, Bernard, 4003
Bourg, Carroll J., 1586
Bourgeois-Pichat, J., 3140
Bourhis, Richard Y., 3550
Bourne, Edmund, 484
Bourne, Paula, 3472
Bourricaud, François, 211
Boutourline-Young, Harsen, 5131
Bouveresse, Jacques, 212
Bovilsky, Deborah M., 5306
Bovkalov, A. F., 6
Bowen, Bruce D., 458
Bowen, Don R., 5193
Bower, Gordon H., 685
Bowers, C. A., 2370
Bowers, David G., 1010
Bowey, Angela M., 975
Bowie, Norman E., 4909
Bowker, L.H., 5307
Bowles, Samuel, 2153
Bowman, William W., 1996
Boxer, Marilyn J., 3474
Boyce, C. P., 4206
Boylan, James R., 1967
Boyle, J. F., 1743
Boysson-Bardies, Bénédicte de, 1843
Bozeman, Adda B., 868
Bozeman, Barry, 1011
Bragg, Melvyn, 3703
Brain, Robert, 799
Brainard, Lawrence, 3962
Braito, Rita, 4500

Brake, Mike, 5537
Branciard, Michel, 2556
Brand, Arie, 333, 334
Brandis, A., 3060
Brandow, Selma Koss, 4390
Brandstätter, Hermann, 970
Brandstetter, Gerfried, 4926
Brangeon, Jean-Louis, 3912
Brannon, Robert, 2870
Braroe, Niels W., 3593
Bras, André, 2276
Bratton, Robert D., 4856
Braun, Carl, 2278
Braun, D.D., 1440
Braun, Hans, 3399
Braun, Oscar, 2796
Braungart, Richard G., 2353, 4900
Braver, Sanford L., 1115
Bravo, Rosa, 3757
Bradimas-Assimopoulos, Nadia, 3749
Bredo, Eric, 2437
Breman, Jan, 2793
Brennen, E. Clifford, 5536
Bressler, Leo A., 5248
Bressler, Maria A., 5248
Bresson, Yoland, 4569
Bretscher, Georges, 1870
Brettell, Caroline B., 3704
Bretzel, Philip von, 386
Brewer, Marilynn B., 1146, 1167
Brickman, Philip, 2490
Brickman, William W., 2112
Bridge, R. Gary, 467
Bridges, Amy, 4045
Brief, Arthur P., 4579
Bright, William, 1909
Brindberg, David, 865
Bringewat, Peter, 5374
Brink, John H., 800
Brinkerhoff, Merlin B., 4621, 5391
Brinkman, G., 3958
Britt, David W., 1441
Broadhead, Robert S., 1702
Brock, Timothy C., 845
Brockman, Joan, 3071
Broderick, Carlfred B., 3384
Brody, Celeste M., 920
Brogden, M., 5006
Brohm, Jean-Marie, 4855
Bromley, Dennis B., 485
Bronfenbrenner, V., 3400
Brooks, Mary E., 4145
Brooks, M. Roy Jr., 5578
Brookshire, Michael L., 4800
Broom, Leonard, 2491, 2492, 2710
Brossollet, Marc, 4570
Brounstein, Paul J., 1150
Brown, Cecil H., 3364
Brown, Craig M., 1043
Brown, Elisabeth, 2855
Brown, Frank, 2303

Brown, Gene, 4096
Brown, Godfrey, 2154
Brown, Harold I., 1791
Brown, Prudence, 3268
Brown, Richard H., 1871
Brown, Richard K., 4695
Brown, Ronald G., 1994
Browne, Ronald K., 2113
Browning, Harley L., 3992
Brubacher, John S., 2304
Brück, Gerhard Wilhelm, 5476
Brugidou, Jean-Paul, 5477
Bruins, L., 4501
Bruneau, Jean-Claude, 4050
Brunner, August, 1792
Brunner, Ronald D., 1173
Bruno, James Edward, 2155
Brunois, A., 4706
Bruyelle, Pierre, 4051
Bruyne, Paul de, 4697
Bryant, Christopher G. A., 49
Bryce, Herrington J., 4107
Bryce-Laporte, Roy S., 1442
Bryde, Brun-Otto, 1549
Bryor, Robin J., 3750
Brzezinski, Jacek, 4387
Büchholz, Rogene A., 1174
Buchignani, Norman L., 213
Bucht, Rolf, 4823
Buck, Günther, 214
Bücker-Gärtner, Heinz, 50
Buckley, Walter, 2459
Buda, B., 3238
Budančev, Ju. P., 1963
Budge, Ian, 5119
Buehler, Charles J., 627
Bueva, L. P., 745
Bugaenko, P. T., 4255
Bühl, Walter L., 869
Buhrmann, Hans G., 4856
Bui-Dang-Ha, Doan, 3097
Bujak, Kazimierz, 2273
Bulgaru, M., 3195
Bulmer, Martin, 3845
Bumpass, Larry L., 3269
Bunce, Richard, 2022
Bunch, Marion E., 694
Bunyan, Tony, 5007
Buonanno, Milly, 3323
Burawoy, Michael, 210, 2662
Burby, Raymond J., 2260, 3835, 4825
Burch, William R. Jr., 4826
Burckhardt, Titus, 2042
Bureau, Conrad, 1844
Burgalassi, Silvano, 2987
Burger, Thomas, 215, 216, 350, 351
Burke, Peter J., 1094
Burke, W. Warner, 1012
Burkett, Steven R., 5308
Burn, Barbara B., 2305
Burns, Robert B., 2869

Burns, Tom R., 884, 2459
Burnstein, Eugene, 1116, 1162
Burstein, Paul, 5168
Burt, Marta R., 3243
Burt, Ronald S., 2663, 4914
Burton, Michael G., 5088
Büschges, Günter, 976
Buslov, K. P., 67
Butenko, A. P., 1245, 4275
Butenschon, M., 3473
Butler, Edgar W., 3797, 3981
Butler, Phillip, 5226
Butler, Rémy, 4146
Butler, R. J., 4782
Butler, Suellen R., 834
Butt, Dorcas Susan, 4857
Buttel, Frederick H., 3799
Butts, Stewart, 217
Buxton, Martin, 3014
Byerlee, Derek, 3751
Bykova, S. N., 2212
Bytheway, Bill, 3401

Cabanel, Guy-Pierre, 5560
Cabanis, André, 2392
Cabral, Nelson E., 3752
Caccamo de Luca, Rita, 68
Caceres, María L., 2948
Cadet, André, 1943
Caditz, Judith, 3501
Cafferty, Thomas P., 5011
Cage, Robin J., 5423, 5470
Cahnman, Werner J., 218
Caïn, Jacques, 628
Cairns, John C., 2371
Calame-Griaule, Geneviève, 1845
Caldeira Brant, Vinicius, 3015
Caldwell, Gary, 2797, 3141
Caldwell, John Charles, 3016, 3142, 3143, 3196
Caldwell, Pap, 3143
Calhoun, Craig J., 799, 2114
Calhoun, Donald W., 896
Calhoun, Lawrence G., 1095
Calic, Dusan, 4319
Calise, Mauro, 4388
Calkins Charmaz, Kathy, 391
Calkov, A.A., 2951
Call, Vaughn R. A., 3270
Callahan, Joseph F., 2115
Callier-Boisvert, Colette, 3704
Callinicos, Alex, 219
Callon, Michel, 5053
Calloway, Carolyn R., 945
Calobanov, V.V., 5522
Calogero La Malfa, Luisa, 4622
Calot, G., 2840
Calvaruso, Claudio, 3705
Calvin, Allen D., 2116
Camagni, Roberto, 4207
Cambi, Franco, 2417

Camilleri, Joseph A., 1353, 5580
Campbell, Angus, 1246
Campbell, Blair G., 4523
Campbell, Carlos C., 4052
Campbell, Colin, 1680, 5020
Campbell, C.M., 1550
Campbell, Donald T., 1167
Campbell, Ernest Q., 1411
Campbell, Gregory, 3020
Campbell, Keith E., 1877
Campbell, Richard T., 2215, 2451, 3563
Campioli, Georges, 2405, 3706
Campo, M. J., 4106
Canfora-Argandoña, Elsie, 4147
Cangemi, Joseph P., 2306
Canning, John, 5283
Canta, Carmelina, 2279
Cantin, Eileen, 1386
Cantor, Joanne R., 715
Capdevielle, Jacques, 4780
Caplow, Theodore, 1013
Caplowitz, David, 2460, 5309
Caprettini, Gian Paolo, 1846
Caracciolo, Alberto, 220
Cardenas, C., 4208
Cardona, Giorgio R., 1847
Cardoso, F. H., 4276
Cardoso de Oliveira, 3595
Care, D., 1120
Carey, Iskandar, 3541
Carey, Philip, 2209, 3800
Carlsmith, J. Merrill, 578
Carlson, Karen, 1910
Carlston, Donal E., 957
Carlton, Eric, 1190
Carmichael, Lynn, P., 5581
Carmona, M., 4053
Carmona Guillen, J.A., 532
Carney, Louis P., 5449
Caro Baroja, Julio, 3891
Carpenter, Edwin H., 468, 4148
Carpentier, J., 4555
Carpitella, D., 2104
Carrera Damas, German, 4928
Carrero Eras, Pedro, 2064
Carrier, Daniel M., 5353
Carrier, Fred J., 2798
Carrier, James G., 1787
Carrier, John, 5493
Carroll, Berenice A., 3474
Carroll, J. Douglas, 425
Carroll, John S., 686
Carroll, Patrick J., 2531
Carroll, Stephen J., 1014
Carron, Albert V., 4858
Carstairs, G. Morris, 3076
Carter, Hugh, 3271
Carter, Robert M., 5433
Carter, Ronald, 5434
Carton, Michel, 2307

Cartwright, Dorwin, 547
Cartwright, Frederick F., 5561
Carvalho, Alcev V. W. de Moura, 3098
Carveth, Donald L., 221, 608
Casals, J.L., 4810
Casassus, Cecilia, 4787
Case, Harry L., 2156
Cassel, Carol A., 5120
Cassen, Robert, 2841
Castallano, Vittorio, 2043
Castellet, José M., 2065
Castex, Patrick, 3892
Castonguay, Charles, 1911
Cater, Douglas, 2017
Cater, Douglass, 2023
Cathelat, Bernard, 1943
Cattaneo, Angela, 4669
Caupin, Benedicte, 3489
Cavalli, Alessandro, 3402
Cavalli-Sforza, Francesco, 2024
Cavan, Sherri, 437
Cavarozzi, Marcelo, 5062
Cavazutti, Tommaso, 222, 223
Cavendish, Richard, 1608
Caviedes L., César, 4054
Cazamian, P., 4555
Cazeneuve, Jean, 1964
Cepede, Michel, 2493
Cepero Bonilla, Raul, 2532
Cerase, Francesco P., 2557
Cerbu, Marcel, 1656
Cerfeda, Giuseppe, 5310
Ceri, Paolo, 4807
Černikov, G., 3801
Černjak, V. A., 1587
Cerroni, Umberto, 187
Cesareo, Vincenzo, 2988
Cesari, Carlo, 4149
Černokov, V.S., 1341
Cessieux, R., 2494
Chadwick, Bruce A., 1142
Chadwick-Jones, John K., 885
Chai, Trong R., 420
Chaiken, S., 5127
Chałasiński, Josef, 1325
Chaloner, William H., 2799
Chambers, Carl D., 5326
Chamboredon, Jean-Claude, 2066, 3894
Chamie, Jose ph, 1719, 3144
Champagne, Patrick, 1681
Chander, R., 2842
Chang, Dae H., 5354
Chang, Kwang Chih, 1511
Chapman, Anthony J., 708, 805
Charbit, Yves, 3656
Charle, Christophe, 2067
Charlot, Bernard, 2117
Charlot, Monica, 3475
Charval, Frantisek, 2495, 2558, 2559, 2711
Chason, Karen J., 638

Chassignat, Annie, 2402
Chatterjee, Pranab, 3025, 5538
Chaudhury, Rafiqul Hudu, 3145, 3146, 4502
Chaussinand-Nogaret, Guy, 2533
Chauvière, Michel, 5644
Chaventré, André, 3657
Chaves, L.G. Mendes, 3895
Chavunduka, G. L., 3753
Cheatwood, Derral, 2082
Checkland, S. G., 4055
Cheek, Neil H. Jr., 4826
Chelius, James R., 3072
Chell, Elizabeth, 958
Chen, Pi-chao, 5582
Chen, T. H.E., 2157
Cheng, Roland Y. L., 2740
Cherkaoui, Mohamed, 378, 2560
Chermesh, Ran, 2308
Cherns, Albert B., 374, 392, 4351, 4558
Cherry, Gordon E., 3959
Chertkoff, J.M., 863
Chesnais, Jean-Claude, 3017, 3099, 3100, 4056, 5368
Chessick, Richard D., 579
Cheverny, Julien, 3239
Chew, Peter, 2978
Chiari, Joseph, 2044
Chiba, Masaji, 1551
Chibnall, Steven, 5121
Chiesi, Antonio M., 4320
Child, Irvin, L., 2048
Chirot, Daniel, 2744, 2800
Chisman, Forrest P., 1175
Chmielewska, Bożenna, 2438
Chodorow, Nancy, 3508
Choh, Youg, 3164
Chombart de Lauwe, Marie-José, 2916
Chombart de Lauwe, Paul-Henry, 1354
Choquet, Maria, 2244, 5319
Chordecki, A., 4623
Chow, Napoleon, 5260
Christains, Clifford G., 1965
Christiansen, G., 4827
Christainsen, John B., 3526
Christiansen-Ruffman, Linda, 3476
Christie, Bruce, 2036
Christopher, Russel L., 907
Chua, Beng-Huat, 1224
Chung, Bethy J., 3477
Chung, Kae H., 720
Churchill, Stacy, 2373
Chylinska, Helena, 2439
Ciborowski, Tom, 2158
Cicourel, Aaron V., 5450
Ciechocinska, Maria, 69
Cipko, A. S., 1247
Cipolla, Costantino, 1443
Ćirić, Jovan V., 4209
Claassen, Henri Joannes, 2801
Clammer, J.R., 2374

Clancier, Georges-Emmanuel, 1248
Clancier, Pierre-Sylvestre, 1248
Clark, Alfred W., 99
Clark, Gerald R., 5611
Clark, Leonard H., 2115
Clark, Melissa, 2232
Clark, Peter, 1079
Clark, Priscilla P., 2068, 2084
Clark, R.D. III, 1080
Clark, S. D.ù 1249
Clark, Terry N., 1242, 5261
Clarke, Harold D., 5021
Clarke, M., 5270
Clarke, Simon, 1713
Clarke, Stevens H., 5451
Claude, Richard P., 4996
Clauss, Jan U., 1552
Claussen, Bernhard, 5122
Claval, Paul, 3802
Clavan, Sylvia, 637, 639
Claydon, J., 3542
Clegg, Stewart, 977, 4915
Clement, Wallace, 1966, 2680
Clemente, Frank, 5369
Clemente, P., 2105
Cliffe, Lionel, 3896
Clifford, Jim, 1015
Clignet, Rémi, 3147
Clissold, Stephen, 2534
Clowers, Myles L., 7
Cloyd, Jerald W., 5311
Clubb, Jerome M., 5
Clynes, Manfred, 709
Cobas, José A., 2664
Cobben, N. P., 2908
Cobos Ruíz de Adana, José, 1682
Cochran, L. T., 4004
Cochrane, Raymond, 1508, 2655, 5405
Cockburn, Cynthia, 5054
Coco, Nicola, 140
Cocozza, Joseph J., 1159
Codaccioni, Félix-Paul, 4108
Codd, John A., 2245
Coetzee, J. A. Grey, 4711
Cohen, Akiba A., 2025
Cohen, Erik, 3707
Cohen, Eugene, D., 889
Cohen, Eugene N., 3897
Cohen, H., 5312
Cohen, Jacob, 504, 523
Cohen, Jere M., 946
Cohen, M., 3708
Cohen, Patricia, 523
Cohen, Robin, 2802, 4740
Cohen, Stephen P., 5229
Cohen, Steven M., 3305, 5123
Cohn, Richard M., 1246
Cohou, Michel, 3898
Čokušev, K., 710
Colajanni, Antonino, 1225
Colasanto, Michele, 4608
Cole, Jonathan R., 5648

Coleman, James S., 2118, 5478
Collett, Peter, 1382
Collette, John, 5350
Collins, A., 4645
Collins, Randall, 2210, 2460
Collomb, Philippe, 469, 3148, 3149
Collonges, Yann, 4783
Colucci, Celestino, 2261
Combs, James, 1872
Comish, Newel W., 1081
Commoner, Barry, 3803, 5288
Conaway, Mary Ellen, 3754
Condon, John C. Jr., 773
Coney, Kenneth A., 470
Conforti, Joseph M., 3985
Confurius, Gerrit, 770
Congalton, Athol A., 188
Connell, R. W.ù 2681
Conne, Bernard, 2917
Conner, Thomas L., 746
Connolly, Kervin, 856
Constantine, Larry L., 3403, 3404
Constantinescu, Virgil, 224
Contraras, Eduardo, 2431
Converse, Jean M., 462
Converse, Philip E., 1246
Conway, Dorice, 3428
Cook, Karenn S., 886, 1553, 2673
Cook, Ramsay, 3480
Cook, Thomas D., 108
Cook, Wanda Dauksza, 2376
Cook-Gumperz, Jenny, 2918
Coombs, Robert H., 5313, 5653
Cooper, Bruce M., 4712
Cooper, Frederick, 2535
Cooper, Joel, 1148
Coover, Edwin R., 121
Coplan, Bette S., 493
Coppens, Peter R. de, 225
Cordón, Faustino, 1793
Cordonniere, Rita, 3481
Cordova, Abraham, 2682
Cores Trasmonte, Baldomero, 4901
Corneille, Jean-Pierre, 1848
Cornelis, Arnold, 747
Corrigan, Philip, 4557
Corry, David J., 4621
Corsaro, William A., 2918
Corsini, Raymond, 658
Cortes Alonso, Vicenta, 4057
Cortese, Charles F., 5206
Cosby, Arthur G., 2665
Coser, Lewis A., 8, 2460
Cosnefroy, L., 1701
Costello, Vincent F., 4006
Coster, Michel de, 2086
Coston, Henry, 1657
Cot, Jean-Pierre, 4741
Cotinaud, Olivier, 897
Cotten, A. M., 4058
Cotterell, Yap Yong, 1250
Cottrell, Arthur, 1250

Coughenour, C. Milton, 4389
Coulardeau, Jacques, 1849
Court, D., 2159, 2309
Courtas, R., 1705
Courtes, Joseph, 1850
Cousins, Albert N., 2069
Covar, Prospero R., 1658
Cox, Oliver C., 3614
Cox, Robert W., 4352
Cozby, Paul C., 1117
Crabbe, Victor, 4742
Craemer, Willy de, 1659
Crafts, N. F. R., 3272
Craib, Ian, 226
Craig, Gordon, 803
Crain, Robert L., 5577
Cramer, Robert, 776
Crandall, Rick, 4828
Crane, Diana, 5649
Craton, Michael, 2536
Craven, Edward, 3014
Crawford, Elizabeth, 9, 110
Crawford, Scott A. G. M., 4624
Crespi, Irving, 561
Cresswell, Robert, 1226
Crewe, Ivor, 559, 5119
Crichton, A., 5627
Crick, Malcolm, 1851
Criden, Yosef, 4390
Crites, Laura, 5435
Crittenden, Kathleen C., 479
Croake, J. W., 2452
Croll, Elisabeth, 3482
Cronkhite, Gary, 562
Cronkite, Ruth C., 3405
Crossick, Geoffrey, 2561
Crouch, Colin, 2562, 2651
Crowther, John F., 126
Croze, Marcel, 3018
Csák, Gy., 3858
Cseh-Szombaty, László, 4571
Csomor, Tibor, 4109
Cuche, Denys, 1614
Cuello de Lizarazo, Ketty Ma., 2310
Cueva, Agustín, 4929
Culea, Haralambie , 335
Cullen, Francis T. Jr., 1445
Cullen, Ian G., 1251
Cullen, John B., 1445
Cullen, Ruth M., 3559
Cummings, L. I., 984
Cummings, Thomas G., 4536
Cummins, Robert C., 1067
Cuneo, Carl J., 4694
Cunningham, Bart, 100
Cunningham, Isabella C.M., 471
Cunningham, William H., 471
Cuny, Xavier, 4467
Cupal, Wilhelm, 4150
Cupertino, Fausto, 5583
Curelaru, M., 11
Curran, Joseph Jr., 189

Currie, Lauchlin B., 4007, 4210
Curtin, C.A., 3350
Curtis, James E., 4631
Curtis, Jean, 4503
Curtis, Lynn A., 1446
Curtis, Richard F., 2495bis, 4917
Cushing, Robert G., 2491
Cutler, Laurence S., 4211
Cutler, Sherrie S., 4211
Cutright, Phillips, 3197
Cuvi, Pablo, 3960
Cymbal, V. P., 1873
Czarnocki, B. Dan, 2797

Dabelko, D.D., 1407
Dacey, John S., 2119
Dachrodt, Heinz-G., 4543
Daget, J., 3804
Da Gloria, Jorge, 841
Dahiem, Hans, 5642
Dahl, Barbara B., 3343
Dahl, Robert A., 5479
Dahlström, 4713
Dahrendorf, Ralf, 4353
Dallmayr, Fred R., 352
Damachi, Ukandi G., 4277
Damas, H., 3755
D'Amato, Marina, 3102
Da Matta, Roberto, 3596
D'Amico, Ronald J., 4660
Damm, Richard, 1554
Dammann, Ernst, 1366
Danan, Yves M., 4212
Dandler, Jorge, 2770
Daniel, Ann E., 188
Danieljan, M.S., 227
Daniels, Morris J., 894, 896
Danielson, Michael N., 4161
Danigelis, Nicholas L., 5124
Danilin, K. E., 921
Dankanics, M., 5249
Danziger, Kurt, 842
D'Arcangelo, Enzo, 5314
Darcy, R., 5169
Darian, Jean C., 1621
Darilek, Richard, 2150
Darley, John M., 1391
Das, Man Singh, 2537
Dasdamirov, A. F., 1326
Dasgupta, Satadal, 2563
Dashefsky, Arnold, 3545
Dasilva, Fabio B., 2087
Dassetto, F., 1852
Daudt, H., 5480
Dave, R. H., 2377
David, Annoussamy, 3406
David, Deborah S., 2870
David, J., 2378
Davidjuk, G. P., 5481
Davidson, Françoise, 5319
Davidson, James D., 1720, 1721
Davidson, J. Kenneth, 3240

303

Davidson, Stephen M., 5679
Davies, Brian, 2120
Davies, John G., 1744
Davin, Delia, 3483
Davis, Alan G., 1107, 2311
Davis, Ann E., 127
Davis, Donald, I., 5349
Davis, James A., 937, 2979
Davis, John D., 938
Davis, Lenwood G., 3597, 3756
Davis, Louis E., 1016, 4558
Davis, Murray S., 1447
Davis, Nanette J., 1497
Davis, Robert H., 2418
Davis, Thomas B., 1660
Davis, Walter, 5342
Davison, Victoria F., 3710
Davison, Walter P., 1967
Davydov, A. D., 3859
Davydov, V. M., 2803
Dawes, Robyn M., 1118
Dawidowicz, Lucy S., 1622
Dawson, Kenneth E., 4831
Day, Joanne V., 2461
Day, Robert A., 2461
Daymont, Thomas N., 4298
Dean, Alfred, 5584
Dean, Colin, 1794
Deaton, John E., 5207
De Benedetti, Augusto, 2563
DeBord, Larry W., 2232, 2406
DeCharms, Richard, 2443
Decrezelles, André, 3711
Deconchy, J.-P., 1701
Decoufle, André-Clément, 353
Deegan, Arthur X., 5628
Dees, David R., 2087
Defronzo, James, 3150
Degenne, Alain, 473
Deghett, V., 713
Degos, Laurent, 3657
De Haan, Neil, 3489
Dehler, Karl-Heinz, 1176
Deitchman, Seymour J., 1017
Delacampagne, Christian, 3549
Delamont, Sara, 2290
Delaroche, Patrick, 5477
Delhumeau, Antonio, 3324
Della Fave, L.R., 721
Della Pergola, S., 1623
Delli Sante de Arrocha, Angela, 5089
Deloménie, Dominique, 4124
DeLora, Joann S., 3241
Del Rio, I., 3060
Deltgen, Florian, 2088
Demaine, J., 2121
De Maio, Gerald, 5177
Demarchi, Franco, 150
Demerath, Nicholas J., 3198
Dem'Ianov, A. I., 1624
De Michelis, Marco, 4060
Demin, M. V., 659

Deming, Richard, 5436
Demko, Georges S., 3202
Dengerink, H. A., 843
Deniel, Raymond, 1615, 1625
Denisjuk, N.P., 4256
Denisoff, R. Serge, 2093
Dennis, Ruth E., 3103
Denzin, Norman K., 395, 5315
Deprez, J., 3306
Derlega, Valerian J., 801
Dermott, John M., 2160
De Sandre, Paolo, 3325
Desanti, Jean-Toussaint, 228
Dési, Ábel, 2010
Desmangles, Leslie G., 1618
De Souza, A., 5102
Despres, Leo A., 3544
Desroche, Henri, 1333, 4321
Desrosiers, Rachel, 4138
Deutsch, Karl W., 4461
Deutsch, Steven, 70
Deville, J. C., 3365
DeWeese, L. Carroll III, 421
De Wood, Robert, 2039
Dexeus, S., 3199
Dexter, Beverly L., 2400
Dexter, Carolyn R., 4871, 4896
Deyo, F. C., 4688
Dhar, D. P., 2804
Dias, Gentil M., 2805
Díaz, Carlos, 4930
Díaz, Elías, 1555
Díaz, May N., 3483
Díaz Bordenave, Juan E., 3961
Di Carlo, Enrique, 5539
Dickinson, John, 4859
Dickson, John W., 4580
Dickstein, Morris, 1252
Diéguez Cuervo, Gonzalo, 4784
Diekmann, A., 533
Dienes, G., 1355
Diesner, Jans-Joachim, 3668
Dietz, H. A., 5125
Diez Borque, José María, 2097
Di Filippo, Armando, 3757
Diggins, John P., 4244
Dilic, Edhem, 2989
Dillon, George L., 1853
Dimkovic, Borislav J., 3899
Dingwall, Robert, 4714, 5562
Dinh, Q. C., 3104
Dinitz, Simon, 5365
Dinnerstein, Dorothy, 3242
Dion, Mwchel, 1589, 2141
Dires, Sabine, 2949
Ditton, Jason, 4689, 5437
Divine, Donna R., 1253
Dixon, Keith, 1254
Dixson, Miriam, 3484
Dmitriev, A. V., 51, 4213
Dobbin, Donald D., 5556
Dobkin de Rios, Marlene, 5316

Dobratz, Betty A., 5219
Dobrovol'skaja, N. P., 104
Dobrowolska, Monika, 1512
Dobrynina, V. I., 1255
Dobson, Richard B., 2712
Docavo Alberti, Ignacio, 3818
Dock, V. Thomas, 430
Doctorow, Osher, 502
Dodd, Carley H., 1367
Dodge, Kenneth A., 1151
Dodge, Peter, 229
Doe, Brenda A., 3309
Doise, Willem, 580, 860
Doka, Klára, 4421
Dolgij, V. M., 4008
Dollase, Rainer, 802
Domenach, J.M., 1745
Dominguez, J. I., 5063
Dömök, Zsuzsa, 1699
Don, Jehuda, 4391
Donati, Agnese, 2024
Donati, Pier Paolo, 3321, 3326
Doncov, A. I., 947
Donegani, Jean-Marie, 1773
Donnelly, James H. Jr., 1022
Donnelly, Thomas G., 2260
Donnertsien, Edward, 5029
Donoghe, James M., 1180
Dooghe, G., 2990
Doreian, Patrick, 494
Dornstein, Miriam, 4449
Dorošenko, M.M., 2950
Dorros, Sybilla G., 3273
Douglas, Jack D., 437, 5126
Douglass, William A., 3545
Dovidio, John F., 3633
Dow, James, 3805, 3908
Dow, Ruth McN., 1096
Dowdall, George W., 4110, 4291, 4917
Downey, H. Kirk, 609
Downs, Anthony, 4152
Doyle, Patricia A., 5431
Dózsa, Katalin, 1513
Dragel', V. S., 2951
Drakakis-Smith, D. W., 4214
Dreckendorff, H. Otis, 524
Drenth, Pieter J. D., 2407
Dressel, Paula L., 1088
Drewnowski, Jan, 5289
Drewry, Bruce R., 1222
Drewry, Gavin, 1547
Dreyfack, Raymond, 4544
Driedger, Leo, 629, 3546
Driggers, Preston F., 978
Drulovic, Milojko, 4322
Drury, Thomas F., 3780
Druzerović, Borisov, 1874
D'Souza, S., 3019
Dua, J. K., 844
Dubar, Claude, 2565
Dubarle, Dominique, 1912
Dubb, Allie A., 1641

Dube, S. C., 2122
Duberman, Lucile, 2566, 3310, 3407
Dubick, Michael A., 3998
Dubiel, Helmut, 230
Dubin, Robert, 4537
Dubois, Pierre, 4602
Dubois-Dumée, Jean-Pierre, 2026
Duck, Steven, 803, 810
Ducloe, Denis, 4215
Duddihy, John M., 3571
Dudel', S. P., 4931
Dudley, Charles J., 4999
Dudley, Gordon A., 4625
Due, Johannes, 5526
Duhalin, V. N., 1796
Duhamel, Alain, 5066
Duke, Marshall, P., 1153
Dukes, Richard L., 5371
Dulczewski, Zygmut, 162
Dumazedier, Joffre, 4855
Dumett, Raymond E., 3962
Dumont, Jacques, 5629
Dumont, Louis, 151, 1191
Dunbar, Tony, 3758
Duncan, Robert, 2789
Duncan, Starkey Jr., 774
Duncan, S. S., 4153
Dunkerly, David, 977, 4695
Dunnette, Marvin D., 4466
Du Pouget, Bruno, 2952
Durán, María Angeles, 3485
Durán Lopez, Federico, 4785
Durán, S., 2806
Durand, Guy, 4009
Durand, Michelle, 3806
Durand-Drouhin, M., 4504
Đuric, Vojislav, 4354
Durojaive, M. O. A., 2123
Dutrénit, Jean-Marc, 5630, 5651
Duvignaud, Jean, 1683
Dworkin, Anthony Gary, 3547
Dworkin, Anthony, 3547
Dworkin, R. M., 1556
Dyke, Bennett, 3297
Dymond, William R., 2379
Dyzon, Tom, 2841
Dzienio, K., 3200
Džunusov, N. S.y 1327

Eadie, William F., 775
Eadington, William R., 4860
Eagly, A. H., 5127
Eames, Edwin, 3982
Easton, Brian, 2929, 4292
Eaton, William W., 377, 550
Eberlein, Gerald, 1797
Echohawk, Marlene, 1082
Eckert, W. A.ü 4111
Eckhardt, Kenneth W., 393
Eckhoff, Torstein E., 1557
Eckland, Bruce K., 2259, 4865
Edelstein, J. David, 4743

Edlund, Sten E., 4809
Edwards, Allan D., 3896
Edwards, Allen L., 525
Edwards, Anthony D., 1915
Edwards, John N., 1213
Edwards, Keith D. St. M., 2928
Edwards, P. K., 4786
Edwards, Ronald G., 4422
Efendiev, S. I., 4932
Egorov, V. V., 2027
Egorova, N. A., 3486
Ehara, Takemichi, 2312
Eichardus, M., 4469
Eichler, Margrit, 5090
Eirmbter, Willy H., 2291
Eisenstadt, Shmuel Noah, 10, 11
Eiser, J. Richard, 5317
Eisler, Ernest, 2567
Ekong, Chong E., 3837
El-Ansary, Adel I., 762
Elder, Carl A., 1522
Elenurm, T. A., 1018
El-Garm, M. S., 1722
el Guindi, Fadwa, 1590
Eliæson, Sven, 231
Elias, Jeffrey W., 2980
Elias, Merrill F., 2980
Elias, Norbert, 2745
Elias, Penelope K., 2980
Elifson, Kirk W., 1674
Elizur, Dov, 1019
Elklit, J., 3548
Elleinstein, Jean, 5064
Ellemrers, J. E., 163
Ellena, Aldo, 150
Ellickson, Robert C., 4216
Elliott, D. H., 4572
Elliott, Ian D., 5373
Elliott, Jean Leonhard, 1249
Elliott, Ruth, 4724
Elliott, R. F., 4690
Ellis, Lee, 12, 1449
Ellsworth, Phoebe C., 578
Elmendorf, Mary L., 3487
Elster, Jon, 557, 748, 2899
Elvander, Nils, 4692
Emerek, Ruth, 4293
Endicott, Jeffrey, 3575
Endler, Norman S., 669
Engelen-Kefer, Ursula, 4486
Engelmann, Hugo O., 1408
Engle,s Hans-Joachim, 2666
Engerman, Stanley, L., 1389
Englefield, F.R. H., 1914
English, Jane, 2871
English, John B. A., 4154
Engquist, Gretchen, 1128
Enloe, Cynthia H., 5008
Ennis, Philip H., 2082
Entwistle, Noel James, 2313
Enyedi, Gy., 3860, 3900
Epp, David, 4725

Epps, Edgard, 3601
Epstein, E. M., 4324
Epstein, Joyce L., 2414
Eräsaari, Risto, 5492
Erbès-Seguin, Sabine, 4787
Erdei, F., 3825, 4061, 4392
Erickson, Maynard L., 5452
Eriksen, Karin, 5652
Erlanger, Howard S., 5482
Erlenmeyer-Kimling, L., 3077
Erlich, Heidi Schuhr, 1052
Ermakoua, O. V., 3340
Ermann, N. David, 393
Ernst, Eldon G., 1626
Errejon, J. A., 3058
Esainko, Peter, 3057
Escarpit, Robert, 1875
Esco, Jack, 1492
Escotet, M. A., 422
Eser, Albin, 5374
Espenshade, Thomas J., 3020
Esser, Hartmut, 472
Esser, S. K., 863
Essman, C. S., 3366
Estep, Rhoda E., 3243
Estryn-Behar, Madeleine, 5586
Etzel, Gerhard, 1147
Etzioni-Halevy, Eva, 1523, 5128
Etzkorn, K. Peter, 2045
Evan, William M., 979, 2496
Evans, Huw, 2024
Evans, Robert H., 3901
Eversley, David E. C., 111
Eyles, John, 3809
Eysenck, Hans J., 486, 487, 660, 664,
  1119, 2872
Eysenck, S. B. G., 487, 660, 664

Fabbri, Paolo, 1810
Faber, Bernard L., 2462
Fabiani, Jean-Louis, 2066
Fabre, Jean, 5065
Factor, Regis A., 233
Fadeev, A. N., 2763
Fagnani, Jeanne, 4112
Fahim, Hussain M., 3864
Faia, Michael, 2440
Fairbrother, Peter, 438
Falbo, Toni, 563
Falise, Michel, 3078
Falk, Dennis R., 630
Falk, Pasi, 4457
Falk, William W., 2665
Falter, Jürgen W., 449
Falussy, Béla, 4829
Fan, S. C., 2843
Farace, Richard V., 1020
Farah, Barbara G., 427
Fararo, Thomas J., 495
Farber, Bernard, 3367
Faria, Álvaro de, 2746
Farkas, George, 4505

Farley, Reynolds, 3628
Farlie, Dennis, 5119
Farmanfarmaian, Khodadad, 4278
Farmer, Mary, 887
Farrell, Ronald A., 5421, 5467
Fatoo, Habib, 3751
Faucheux, François, 2233
Faygeron, Claude, 1558, 1578
Faulkner, Robert R., 4524
Faure-Soulet, F., 3059
Fauvet, Jacques, 5066
Fazio, Russell, 1135, 1148
Fears, Denise, 5024
Featherman, David L., 2499, 2659, 3634
Feder, Ernest, 4393
Fedorenko, Nikolaï, 3807, 4355
Fedoseev, Piotr, 2900, 4933
Fedoseev, P. N., 112
Feild, Hubert S., 1007
Feit, F., 3629
Feld, Maury D., 5208
Feld, Scott, L., 1214
Feldheim, Pierre, 4573
Feldman, Jacqueline, 496
Feldman, Maurice P., 5375
Feldman, Rochelle, 2651
Feldman, Ronald A., 1451
Feldman-Summers, Shirley, 857
Feldman, Klaus, 2258
Felsenthal, Norman, 1968
Felson, Marcus, 4613
Fend, Helmut, 1409
Fendrich, James M., 4801
Fendrich, James M., 5129,, 5130
Fenner Vargas, R., 71
Fenton, Kathleen S., 2416
Ferb, Thomas E., 564
Ference, Thomas P., 1024
Ferge, Zsuzsa, 4506
Ferguson, Le Roy C., 5131
Ferguson, Lucy R., 5131
Fergusson, David M., 5376
Fernandes, A., 2070
Fernandes, Florestan, 72
Fernandez, Ronald, 581, 2736
Fernandez de Menezes, Antonio C., 2028
Fernández Vargas Vargas, V., 4810
Ferra, Roger, 2276
Ferraro, Oscar H., 2164
Ferri, Elsa, 2919
Ferro, Marc, 2011
Feuille, Peter, 5009
Feyel, Gilles, 1989
Feyerabend, Paul, 1798
Fickett, Lewis P., 5067
Fiedler, Martha L., 2443
Field, Clive D., 1642
Field, G. Lowell, 2687
Fields, J., 4507
Fields, James M., 1177

Fifield, June, 5376
Ferraz, José Carlos de, 4062
Figurovskaja, N. K., 2568
Fil'čikov, G. S., 661
Filippov, F. R., 2125, 2212
Fil'jukova, L. F., 3408
Filppula, Heli-Hanna, 2165
Fine, Bob, 1448
Fine, Gary A., 1953
Finestone, Harold, 5438
Fink, G. M., 4744
Finkler, Earl, 4217
Finley, M. I., 234
Finn, M., 4508
Finsterbusch, Kurt, 394
Fioravanti, Eduardo, 4245
Firestone, Ira J., 1215
First-Dilic, Ruža, 3902, 4509
Fisch, Rudolf, 52
Fischer, Claude S., 3983
Fischer, David H., 2992
Fischer, Joel, 5540
Fischer, John L., 1857
Fisher, Evelyn M., 1802
Fisher, Harriet S., 898
Fisher, John Robert, 2826
Fisher, Wesley A., 3328
Fishman, Joshua A., 1915
Fiske, Donald W., 774
Fitter, Jörn C., 2807
Fitz, Don, 849
Fitzgerald, Hiram F., 2939
Fitzgerald, Inez, 1814
Fitzpatrick, Joseph P., 1591
Fitzsimmons, Stephen J., 564
Flament, Claude, 473, 505, 2475
Flavell, John H., 687
Fleisher, Belton M., 3385
Fleishman, John, 2667
Fleming, Jeanne J., 5523
Flere, Sergej, 1697
Fleury, Michel, 4076
Flew, Anthony G. N., 2213
Flinn, William L., 3799
Flora, Cornelia B., 1643, 3502
Flora, Peter, 2747
Florio, David H., 2207
Flude, R. A., 631
Flynn, Charles P., 1410
Fodor, G., 1944
Fodor, Janet D., 1854
Fogarty, Michael, 4325
Foley, John W., 4294, 5587
Foley, Linda A., 3630
Folger, Robert, 862
Folkes, Valerie S., 804, 864
Foner, Eric, 2545
Fong, Monica S., 4510
Fonseca, R., 4010
Fontana, Andrea, 4190
Fontana, Maria Rosaria, 4487
Fontanel, Jacques, 1945

Foot, Hugh C., 708, 805
Forcese, Dennis, 4626
Ford, Amasa B., 5588
Ford, Charles, 2012
Ford, G., 2721
Ford, Josephine M., 1644
Ford, J. Guthrie, 776
Ford, Kathleen, 3201
Ford, S. R., 1784
Ford, Thomas R., 1799
Fordyce, E. James, 3105
Foret, Miroslav, 534
Forgas, Joseph P., 948
Form, William H., 2569, 4289
Formánek, Miloslav, 235, 4959
FPorster, Erhard, 2844
Forsyth, Donelson R., 632, 1535
Forthofer, Ron N., 3107
Fortuna, Saverio, 5318
Fosse, Claude, 1474
Foster, Stephen F., 705
Foucault, Michel, 3244
Fougeyrollas, Pierre, 2571
Fouilloux, Étienne, 2046
Fowler, Bridget, 4511
Fox, Renée C., 1659
Fox, Richard G., 5439
Fox, Vernon, 5471
Fox, William S., 1071, 4307
Francis, Emerich K., 3615
Frandsen, Kenneth D., 1868
Frank, Harold H., 1083, 3488
Franke, Heinz, 749
Frankel, Charles, 13
Frankel, E. A., 1675
Franklin, Jerome L., 1010
Franklin, John H., 3616
Franz, Hans-Werner, 2572
Franzina, Emilio, 3750
Frax Rosales, E., 4810
Frazier, Charles E., 1449
Fredericks, L. J., 4394
Fredericks, Marcel A., 5653
Freedman, R., 3151
Freeman, Harvey R., 806
Freeman, Howard E., 108
Freeman, James M., 3861
Freeman, John, 1027
Freeman, Linton C., 807
Freidheim, Elizabeth A., 14
Fréjaville, Jean-Pierre, 5319
Frendl, L., 4726
Frese, Wolfgang, 4845
Freudenburg, William, 5168
Frey, Kurt, 4970
Freymond, J., 5241
Freyre, G., 2071
Freyssenet, Michel, 2573
Frezzotti, Maria Teresa, 2993
Frias, L. A. de M., 3115
Fricke, Else, 4559
Fricke, Werner, 4559

Frideres, James S., 1101
Frieden, Bernard J., 4155
Friedl, John, 1228
Friedland, Roger, 4305, 5113
Friedland, William H., 2569
Friedman, Kenneth M., 5589
Friedman, L. M., 1559
Friedman, Yona, 1192
Frinking, G. A. B., 3022, 3274, 3275
Frisbie, W. Parker, 3631
Friss, István, 15
Fritlinskij, V.S., 5483
Fritschner, Linda Marie, 4512
Fritz, Éva, 1384
Froger-Gaulon, Jacqueline, 5654
Frolov, S. F., 3834
Fromkin, Howard L., 845
Fruit, Élie, 4745
Frunzio, Ettore, 2263
Fry, Lincoln. J., 5313
Fryklindh, Pär Urban, 4830
Frysztacki, Krzysztof, 3984
Fuchs, Estelle, 2953
Fuchs, Roland, 3202
Fuhrke, Monika, 5527
Fujii, Masao, 1684
Fujino, Ryuichi, 16
Fujita, Eishi, 4670
Fujita, Kunihiko, 3838
Fujiyama, Masahide, 1021
Fukász, Gy., 1257
Fukumoto Sato, Mary N., 3617
Fukutake, Tadashi, 73, 3862
Fuller, Robert L., 4603
Fulton, John, 3219
Funabashi, Harutoshi, 980
Funahashi, Kazuo, 382, 3903
Funatzu, Mamoru, 610, 611
Funkhouser, G. Ray, 1054
Furniss, Norman, 5484
Futer, Pierre, 236
Füstös, L., 423
Futernick, Allan, 3632

Gabler, Hartmut, 846
Gábor, Éva, 5485
Gadamer, Hans-Georg, 4356
Gádorosi, F., 3827
Gaertner, Samuel L., 3633
Gaertner, W., 4295
Gaev, Dorothy M., 633
Gaeier-Vinet, Annick, 4063
Gagnon, Gabriel, 4395
Gain, Nicole, 113
Gál, R., 4671
Galaskiewicz, Joseph, 2691
Gałęski, Boguslaw, 1258
Galjart, Benno F., 3904
Gallagher, Bernard J. III, 4609
Gallie, Duncan, 4357
Galliher, John F., 5355
Gallino, Luciano, 4971

Galloway, Charles M., 2280
Galloway, David M., 2281
Gallup, George H., 722
Galt, Anthony H., 2748
Ganzarain, Ramon, 899
Garaudy, Roger, 1368
Garcia, Richard A., 3599
García Ballesteros, Aurora, 3060, 3152, 4064
García de Cortázar Ruiz de Aguirre, 1670
García Ferrando, Manuel, 3849, 4513
García Ramírez, Sergio, 4998
Gardell, Bertil, 4581, 4811
Gardner, Godfrey J., 452
Gardner, William, 2920
Garelli, Franco, 1645, 4628
Garner, Roberta, 2749
Garnier, M., 2214
Garnier, M. A., 5209
Garon-Audy, Muriel, 2707
Garro, Yakoub, 2574
Garros, Bertrand, 3106
Garry, Stephen L., 1822
Garske, J. P., 717
Gartrell, John W., 4396
Gasc, Jean-Pierre, 1411
Gaudette, Gabriel, 5132
Gaulejac, Vincent de, 2966
Gaumont, Daniel, 1949
Gaunt, Joan, 2249
Gauthier, Alain, 1876
Gawrysiak, T., 1571
Gaxie, Daniel, 5068
Gayk, William F., 4908
Gazdag, Miklós, 4539
Gazizullin, F. G., 1193
Geddes, Michael, 3409
Gedó, András, 1194
Gee, Susan C., 3107
Geeding, Daniel W., 4344
Geer, Blanche, 2444
Geerken, Michael R., 711, 5590, 5591
Geertz, Clifford, 4972
Gehlen, Hans, 569
Geisler, Charles C., 4861
Geismar, Ludwig L., 3489
Gelb, Saadia, 4390
Gel'buh, F. N., 4257
Gelinier, Octave, 4326
Gella, Aleksander, 2684
Gellner, Ernest, 3549, 4246, 4941, 4953
Gendre, Francis, 424
Gendreau, Francis, 3023
Gendron, Bernard, 4358
Gentile, Roberto, 870
George, Betty G. S., 2166
George, Frank H., 543
George, Victor N., 5486
Gerber, Andrea, 2907

Gerber, Wayne, 475
Gergen, Kenneth J., 582, 502
Gerhardt, Walter, 583
Gerloff, Edwain A., 1067
German, I. M., 5487
Germotsis, Wassilios, 4514
Gerth, Hans H., 2685
Geruson, Richard T., 4011
Gervai, Pál, 1259
Geser, Hans, 105
Getty, Harry T., 3618
Getz, Ingri, 4453
Geurts, Jan, 4515
Gevers, P., 4746
Geyer, R. Félix, 1450
Ghermani, I., 5631
Ghidinelli, A., 3619
Giannini, A. James, 1888
Gibbs, Jack P., 1385, 5452
Gibson, James L., 1022
Gibson, John B., 4014
Giddens, Anthony, 354
Giele, Janet Zollinger, 3490, 3498
Giersdorf, Peter, 2844
Giesen, Bernard, 53, 190
Gigirey Paredes, Carlos, 3600
Gilbert, Joan, 3703
Gilbert, Neil, 5488, 5655
Gilbert, Sid, 2408
Giles, Howard, 3550
Gillaspy, Ronald T., 3207
Gillespie, David F., 1002, 4359, 4765
Gillespie, Michael, W., 526
Gillette, Alain, 3698
Gillham, James, 1092
Gilli, Angelo C., 4629
Gillingham, P. R., 1120
Gillmor, Donald M., 2000
Gilly, A., 2575
Giner, Salvador, 237, 1334, 2748, 2780
Cinco Ortega, J., 3963
Gingerich, Wallace J., 1451
Ginsbert-Gebert, Adam, 4296
Ginsburgs, G., 3679
Gintis, Herbert, 2153
Girard, Alain, 3011, 3410, 3658
Girard, Jean-Paul, 3905
Girard, Patrick, 3649
Girard, Thierry, 122
Girard, Victor, 2419
Girod, Roger, 2713, 4516
Giuliano, Luca, 2954
Giusti, Sonia, 1369
Gizycki, Rainald von, 1800
Glanz, David, 4133
Glaser, Barney G., 238
Glaser, Robert, 2292
Glasner, Peter E., 1747
Glass, D. V., 3163
Glazer, Myron, 31
Glazer, Nathan, 3551, 3552, 3985

Glazer, Nona, 3468
Glazer, Penina Migdal, 31
Glen, Roy, 4536
Glenn, Morval D., 1723
Glenne, C., 5377
Glezerman, G. E., 1260, 2576
Glick, Paul C., 3271,3411
Glidewell,John, 2126
Glock, Charles Y., 1724
Glover, K. E., 2452
Glumin, V. I., 1261
Godefroy, Thierry, 5028
Godelier, Maurice, 1229, 3491
Gödöny, József, 5378
Goertzel, Ted G., 4973
Goethals, A. L. J., 3680
Goetze, Dieter, 2808
Goffman, Erving, 2873, 2874
Goitein, Bernard, 792
Gokulsing, Moti K., 1967
Golany, Gideon, 4218
Goldberg, Albert I., 1035, 4610
Goldberg, Marilyn P., 4529
Goldberg, Marvin E., 554
Golden, M. Patricia, 395
Goldenberg, Sheldon, 2314, 3368
Goldin, Claudia D., 2538
Goldman, Harvey, 493
Goldman, Morton, 861, 1405
Goldman, Nancy L., 5210
Goldman, Paul, 1023, 4562
Goldman, William, 808
Goldner, Fred H., 1024
Goldsmith Kasinsky, Renée, 3712
Goldstein, Harold M., 5655
Goldstein, Herman, 5010
Goldstein, Jeffrey H., 845
Goldstein, Sidney, 3154
Goldstone, Leo, 506
Goldthorpe, John H., 2497, 2714, 2715
Golembiewski, Robert T., 895
Gologor, Ethan, 959
Golovkov, S. I., 662
Golubović, Zagorka, 3412
Gomez Grillo, Elio, 5379
Gomez Orfanel, German, 2264
Gonos, George, 239
González Duro, Enrique, 2875
Gonzalez-Haba Guisado, Vicente, 5034
González Montes, Adolfo, 1698
Goodale, J. G., 4630
Goode, Frank M., 3966
Goode, Judith G., 3982
Goode, William J., 191
Goodger, B. C., 4862
Goodger, J. M., 4862
Goodich, Michael, 1706
Goodlad, John I., 2127
Goodman, Joel B., 5608
Goody, Jack, 3906
Gordeev, I. I., 5489
Gorden, Raymond L., 565

Gordon, Douglas, 5563
Gordon, L. A., 1262, 4574
Gordon, Michael, 922,3233
Gorecki, Jan, 1560
Gorham, William, 3985
Gorjačenko, Ê. Ê., 3863
Gorman, Robert A., 240
Gorn, Gerald J., 554
Gorz, André, 2498
Gosselin, Normand, 5320
Gostkowski, Zygmut, 453, 2420
Gotard, Erin, 1723
Gottdiener, Mark, 4219
Gottesfeld, Mary L., 5541
Gottschalch, Holm. 4560
Gottschalch, Wilfried, 1412
Goudy, Willis J., 1149, 4065
Goudzwaard, B., 4247
Gould, Meredith, 2876
Gould, Robert, 651, 809, 1150
Gouldner, Alvin W., 1195
Goulet, D., 4360
Gouley, Bernard, 1627
Gove, Walter R., 711,5590, 5591
Goyder, John C., 4631
Graber,Doris A., 1916, 2030
Grafskij, Ju. A., 1263
Grafskij, W. G., 4916
Graham, Alan K., 4199
Graham, William K., 474
Graig, Gordon, 810
Granberg, Donald, 1877, 5170, 5171
Grandguillaume, Gilbert, 4066
Grandke, A., 3413
Granou, André, 2577
Grant, E. Kenneth, 3760
Grant, Marc R., 932
Grapin, Pierre, 2401
Grätz, Frank, 4895
Grau, Gerhard, 4696
Gray, Bradford H., 5649
Gray, Jerry, L., 1025
Gray, Jerry L., 2110
Greco, Gioacchino, 5172
Greeley, Andrew M., 1628
Green, Paul E., 425
Green, Robert T., 471
Green, Susan K., 5363
Greenberg, Carl I., 1215
Greendorfer, Susan L., 4863
Greene, David, 645
Greene, Vernon L., 450
Greenleaf, Robert K., 1084
Greenspoon, Joel, 1121
Greenstone, J. David, 4113
Greffe, Xavier, 63, 5490
Greffrath, Mathias, 1196
Gregersen, Edgar A., 1917
Greil, Arthur L., 1748
Greisman, H. C., 241
Gresleri, Guiliano, 4149
Griffith, Roger W., 5011

Griffin, Larry, 2232
Griffith, William S., 3025
Griffiths, R. D. P., 1120
Grignon, Claude, 1749
Grigorov, V. M., 5491
Grigby, J. Euge Jr., 2047
Grinisin, D. M., 612
Grinspoon, Lester, 5321
Groat, H.Theodore, 1479
Groeneveld, Lyle P., 4297
Groff, Bradford, D., 1216
Grofman, Bernard, 558
Grøholt, Kurt, 2687
Gromeka, V. I., 4361
Grønbjerg, Kirsten A., 1335
Grönfors, Martti, 3590
Groothoff, Hans-Hermann, 2382
Grosman, C. P., 3492
Gross, Beatrice, 2921
Gross, Harriet Engel, 1452
Gross, Neal, 2282
Gross, Peter, 5642
Gaoss, Ronald, 2921
Grossenbacher, J.-P., 2383
Grosser, Charles F., 3839
Grotevant, Harold D., 3329
Groth, Philip, 4397
Grottanelli, Vinigi, 1230
Groulx, L. H. J., 4748
Grove, D. John, 1370
Groves, David L., 1178, 4831
Groves, Mary Ann, 596, 597, 605
Grubel, H. G., 3681
Grunberg, K. S., 488
Grundmann, Siegfried, 2578
Gruneau, Richard S., 4864
Gruper, Michael, 310
Grzeskowiak, Joanna, 3713
Grzywnowicz, Stanisław, 3659
Gubert, R., 3553
Gubrium, Jaber F., 2994
Gucu, V. G., 1264
Guerin, Daniel, 4749
Guerrand, Roger H., 4147
Guest, Avery M., 4067
Guest, Robert H., 1026
Guha, Amalendu, 3682
Guhur, A., 3828
Guichaoua, André, 3964
Guichard, Jean, 3330
Guidicini, Paolo, 192
Guiducci, Giuliano, 2315
Guiducci, Roberto, 2315
Guilaine, Joan, 3907
Guillermou, Yves, 3964
Guiot, Jean M., 634
Guizzardi, Gustavo, 1750
Guldimann, Tim, 5492
Gulian, C. I., 242
Guliev, V. E., 4916
Guljaev, V. V., 4452
Gunter, B. G., 3376

Guppy, L. N., 4632
Gupta, Khadija A., 4068
Gupta, Raghuraja, 1629
Gupta, Y. P., 4633
Gurevitch, Michael, 2705, 4835
Gurin, Patricia, 3601
Gurova, R. G., 2955
Gurr, Ted R., 5380
Gurwitz, Sharon B., 1151
Gusfield, Joseph R., 419, 3840
Gustafson, James P., 923, 924
Gustafsson, Stig, 4809
Gustavus, Susan O., 3155
Gustin, P., 5632
Guterbock, Thomas M., 4017
Gutheil, Thomas G., 3245
Guthrie, George M., 2809
Guthrie, Gerard, 3602
Gutierrez, Hector, 2845
Gutman, Herbert G., 2579
Guttman, Louis, 1019
Guy, Rebecca, 1904
Guzman, Ralph C., 5133
Györi, György, 1265

Haan, Norma, 635
Haar, Jerry, 2316
Haas, Eugene J., 1002
Haas, J. Eugene, 291
Haas, Jack, 712
Haavio-Mannila, Elina, 3513
Habenstein, Robert W., 3572
Häberle, P., 1751
Habermas, Jürgen, 243
Habimana, Bonaventure, 2922
Hacker, Frederick J., 1453
Hackman, J. Richard, 4545
Haden, Douglas H., 120
Haferkamp, Hans, 244
Hafkin, Nancy J., 3493
Hagan, John, 1413, 1454, 1561, 1573, 5381
Hagennaars, J. A.P., 2908
Hahn, Martin E., 1122
Hahn, Paul H., 5382
Hajdu, Péter, 1524
Hajnal, A., 1179
Halebsky, Sandor, 5194
Halevy, Zvi, 1523
Hall, Angus, 1685
Hall, Brian P., 1386
Hall, David J., 5633
Hall, D. T., 4630
Hall, John M., 4069
Hall, J. A., 245, 5103
Hall, P., 5493
Hall, Stuart, 2956
Hallaron, Shirley A., 4012
Halliburton R. Jr., 2539
Halliday, Terence C., 5559
Hallinan, Maureen T., 811, 2142
Halls, W. D., 2167

Halperin, Ernst, 1455
Halpern, Barbara, 3929
Halperin, Rhoda, 3908
Halpern, Joel, 3929
Hamaguchi, Haruhiko, 2686, 4013
Hamashima, Akira, 152
Hamashima, Hikaru, 246
Hamblin, Robert L., 5256
Hamelink, Cees, 5236
Hamilton, David L., 707
Hamilton, Gary C., 4433
Hamilton, Vernon, 688
Hamm, Bernd, 413
Hammerman, Howard M., 3824
Hammersley, Martyn, 2147
Hammond, John L., 5173
Hammond, Philippe, 1655
Hamnet, C., 4114
Hamon, Léo, 4934
Hampel, Rainer, 1152
Hamzaoui, S., 1371
Hanák, K., 1969
Hanák, Tibor, 74
Handel, Warren H., 589
Handy, Charles B., 981
Haneda, Arata, 3951, 4126
Hanifi, M. J., 2463
Hankiss, Elemér, 1387, 1388
Hanks, Micahel P., 4865
Hannan, Michael T., 1027, 2187, 4297
Hannigan, John A., 1028
Hannon, Natalie, 3355
Hansen, Berrit, 2384
Hansen, Donald A., 17
Hansen, James C., 901
Hansen, Kristin A., 3771
Hansen, P., 4450
Hansen, Ronald D., 1180
Hanson, D. J., 5322
Hansson, Robert O., 812
Hanushek, Eric A., 507
Harari, Ehud, 4327, 4691
Harary, Franck, 547
Harburg, Ernest, 3268
Harčev, A. G., 4517
Harcsa, I., 2464
Harding, Neil, 248
Harff, Yvette, 3806
Hargreaves, Andy, 2274
Haritos-Fatouros, M., 2048
Harmat, P., 5564
Harney, Klaus, 5115
Harrell-Bond, Barbara, 5657
Harries-Jenkins, 5211
Harrington, Charlene, 2282
Harris, Anthony R., 636, 1456
Harris, Mary B., 813
Harris, Richard M., 778
Harris, R. Baine, 1072
Harrison, B., 2317
Harrison, Geoffrey A., 4014
Harrison, Michael I., 5091

Harrison, Paul M., 1592
Harrison, Randall P., 2025
Harsanyi, John C., 1525, 1526
Hart, Harm't, 463
Hartfiel, Günter, 153
Hartmann, K., 1752
Hartmann, Paul, 1123
Hartzler, H. Richard, 1562
Harva, Urpo, 4832
Harvey, A. S., 4572
Harvey, David, 3758
Harvey, John H., 584
Hasegawa, Tadashi, 4715
Haskins, James, 4750
Hassenforder, Jean, 2128
Hastings, Ross, 654
Haug, Wolfgang F. H., 2580
Hauser, Robert M., 2499, 2659, 4298
Hauser, Stuart T., 925
Hautecoeur. Jean-Paul, 4935
Have, Paul ten, 439
Havek, Friedrich August von, 5494
Haveman, Robert H., 3205
Havet, J., 3909
Hawkins, Freda, 3714, 3715
Hawkins, James L., 3311
Hawkins, M. J., 2877
Hawley, Amos H., 4070
Hawthorn, Geoffrey, 18
Hayano, David M., 4866
Hayase, Toshio, 75, 2465
Hayashi, Masataka, 3841
Hayden, F. Gregory, 5495
Hayes, Kent, 3079
Hayes, Laurie S., 1894
Hays, William, 3331
Hazama, Hiroshi, 4328
Hazelrigg, L. E., 5209
Heap, J. L., 1918
Hearn, Jeff, 4611
Heath, A., 887
Hedley, Marj, 4398
Hedley, R. Alain, 184
Hedlund, Ronald D., 5174
Heer, D. M., 3494
Hegedüs, András, 1029, 4936
Heiberg, M., 3554
Heilbroner, R., 2581
Hein, Roland, 2385
Heintz, Katherine McM., 4604
Heintz, Peter, 2661
Heirich, Max, 1725
Heirs, Ben J., 1030
Heiskanen, Heikki, 4299
Heisler, Martin O., 3620
Held, McDonald Watkins, 781
Held, Virginia, 750
Heller, Frank A., 751, 1085
Heller, Hartmut, 770
Heller, Jack F., 1216
Heller, Peter K., 3910
Hellriegel, Don, 609

Hellwig, Zdzisław, 384
Helmer, John, 5323
Helmich, Donald, 1089
Helmich, Ursula, 2582
Henderson, Ronald W., 2923
Henderson, Vernon, 2409
Hendon, William S., 4156
Hendricks, C. Davis, 2995
Hendricks, Jon, 2995
Henley, James R. Jr., 3155
Henley, Nancy M., 1878
Hennessy, Michael, 5261
Henning, H. Jörg, 566
Henninger, Marilyn, 1108
Henry, F., 3555
Henry, Louis, 2845
Henry, W. A., 4434
Henshel, Richard L., 5273
Hepburn, J. R., 5440
Héraud, G., 3556
Herbst, Philip G., 4453
Herman, Jacques, 4697
Herman, Karel, 4518
Hermann, István, 1266, 2029
Hermansson, Gary L., 2245
Hernu, Charles, 5212
Herrera V., J., 2386
Herrmann, Ulrich, 2685
Herry, Joseph-Louis, 5213
Hersen, Michael, 902, 1114
Hersey, Paul, 1026
Hershey, Marjorie R., 3819
Herz, Thomas, 2506
Heskin, K. J., 663
Hesselbart, Susan, 5658
Hessler, Hans W., 1646
Hessler, Richard M., 5620
Héthy, Lajos, 4672
Hetrick, Barbara, 128
Hettwer, Hubert, 2168
Heubel, E., 1753
Heunks, F. J., 1457
Hewitt, Christopher, 1458, 4960
Hewitt, John D., 5178
Hewitt, John P., 637
Heydebrand, Wolf, 982
Hibberd, Dominic, 249
Hibbs, D. A. Jr., 4788
Hickox, M. S., 38
Hicks, George L., 3557
Hidaka, Chihiro, 4833, 4834
Hiernaux, J. P., 1852
Higgins, E. Tory, 689
Higgins, Paul C., 5383
Higley, John, 2687
Hilberman, Elaine, 5384
Hilbert, Richard A., 1879
Hildebrandt, Hans-Jürgen, 3351
Hilhorst, Hendrikus W. A., 1593
Hill, David B., 3819
Hill, Ellen B., 2750
Hill, Kim Quaile, 5434

Hill, K., 3108, 3109
Hill, Lewis E., 1801
Hill, Robert H., 1446
Hiller, Harry H., 1267, 5069
Hillery, George A., 4999
Hilleström, Karstén, 3495
Hills, Philip J., 2318
Hilowitz, Jane, 2810
Himmelfarb, Harold S., 2234
Himmelstrand, U., 2811
Hincker, François, 5065
Hindelang, Michael J., 5385
Hindess, Barry, 250, 354, 376
Hinings, Bob, 5269
Hinkle, Ronald, 1108
Hirabayashi, Gordon, 3204
Hirsch, Fred, 4279
Hirschi, Travis, 5385
Hirschman, Charles, 4015
Hirst, Paul Q., 251, 2751
Hiskett, Mervyn, 2154
Hitchcock, Dale C., 2410
Hite, Shere, 3246
Hlopin, A. D., 3761
Ho, Wing Meng, 2812
Hodges, H. Eugene, 5324
Hodgetts, Richard M., 4329
Hoeben-Kruisinga, Renée, 252
Hoerni, B., 5659
Hoffman, Saul, 3496
Hoffmann, Stanley, 5237
Hofstetter, C. Richard, 2039
Hogan, Dennis P., 3634
Hogeweg-de-Haart, H., 76
Hohmann, Joachim S., 3247
Høivik, Ford, 1459
Holdaway, Simon, 5012
Holland, Paul W., 2466, 2467
Hollerbach, Paula, 3205
Holley, William H., 1007
Holmberg, Ingvar, 2838
Holmes, David S., 5022
Homes, N., 3808
Holmes, William, 4454
Holmström, Lynda Lytte, 5384
Holmström, Mark, 4673
Holt, R. T., 4362
Holtermann, S., 4115
Holton, Bob, 4751
Holzberg, Carol S., 2500
Holzner, Burkaert, 1802, 5096
Hom, Harry L. Jr., 2246
Hommes, Enno, 2793
Hong, Lawrence K., 1460
Hong, Sung Chick, 77
Honore, Bernard, 4634
Hood, Roger, 5357
Hoog, C. de, 3332
Hoover, Thomas, 1268
Hope, K. R., 3683
Hopkins, Nicholas S., 2583, 2770
Hoppa'l, M., 1179

Hoppania, Olavi, 1563
Hoppe, Hans-H., 4789
Horan, Patrick M., 2421, 4635
Horasanjan, G. A., 4071
Horev, B. S., 3024
Horn, M., 544
Hornik, Robert C., 2432
Hörning, Karl H., 2501, 2752
Hornung, Carlton A., 2668
Horowitz, Donald L., 5023
Horowitz, Irving Louis, 3992, 4083, 5214, 5386
Horowitz, Morris A., 5656
Arowitz, Allan, 585, 1580
Horwitz, Leonard, 903
Hosoya, Chihiro, 5245
Hosoya, Takashi, 19
Hotta, Gôkichi, 3457
Houghton, John, 253
Houlihan, John P., 904
House, James S., 475, 586
House, J. Douglas, 1803
House, Pamela, 645
Houška, Jiří, 2753
Hout, Michael, 2214, 3206
Houtart, H., 1594
Houtaud, Alphonse d', 5595
Howe, Louise K., 4519
Howe, Michel, 2031
Hoyo A., J. L., 2319
Hrabě, Josef, 5215
Hsia, H. J., 1880
Hsueh-Wen, Wang, 2169, 2320
Huber, Bettina J., 4497
Huber, George P., 984
Huber, Joan, 2566
Hubers, Gérard, 1840
Hudis, Paula M., 4300
Hudon, Raymond, 5175
Huet, A., 1269
Hughes, James W., 4089
Hughes, John A., 254, 426
Hughes, J. R. T., 1389
Hughes, Michael, 4330
Huglin, Thomas O., 5099
Hugo, Pierre J., 3635
Hula, Erich, 166
Hulaková, Marie, 4258
Hull, T. H., 3156
Hull, V. J., 3156
Hülvely, I., 5035
Humblet, Jean-E., 3716
Hummel, Hans J., 378
Hummon, Norman P., 494
Humphrey, Graig R., 3762
Humphrey, Michael, 3414
Hund, J. G., 1560
Hund, Wulf D., 1881
Hundley, Norris Jr., 3603
Hunt, Janet G., 1414, 1726, 1754, 3386, 3636
Hunt, Larry L., 1726, 1754, 3386, 3636

Hunt, Leon G., 5325, 5326
Hunter, A. A., 4636
Hunter, David E., 1231
Hunter, Edna J., 3343, 5216
Huntington, Samuel P., 5134
Hunyady, Zs., 1217
Huppes, T., 4235
Hursh-César, Gerald, 2813
Hurst, James W., 1564
Hurtubise, Rolland, 132
Husain, Sheikh A., 3277
Husen, T., 2321
Hussain, A., 3558
Huston, Perdita, 3497
Huszár, Paul C., 4016
Huszár, T., 1270, 2688, 2689, 4707
Hutber, Patrick, 2584
Hutcheson, John D. Jr., 5135
Hy, Ronn J., 123
Hymes, Dell, 1855

Ianni, Francis A. J., 2114, 5387
Ianni, Octavio, 2585
Ibrahim, I. B., 5388
Ichikawa, Akihiro, 152
Ichilov, Orit, 2957, 3415
Ickensafa, H., 2586
Ickes, William, 2878
Igbozurike, Martin, 3965
Iglitzin, Lynne B., 3498
Ignatovskij, P., 4259
Igosin, S. I., 1995
Ikado, Fujio, 1755, 1756
Ikeda, Giyū, 20
Illés, J., 2706
Illy, L. B., 3416
Imbert, Françoise, 2573
Imershein, Allen W., 983
Inbar, Michael, 3717, 3718
Inciardi, James A., 5389
Inden, Ronald B., 3369
Infantino, Lorenzo, 5242
Ingalls, John D., 1062
Inglis, Fred, 1328
Inkeles, Alex, 613
Inn, Andres, 5013, 5014
Inoshita, Osamu, 21
Insko, Chester A., 814, 1141
Iosifova, M. M., 2690
Iovčuk, M. T., 396
Ipsen, Detlev, 4520
Ireland, N. J., 3272
Irvine, D. G., 2235
Irving, T. B., 1630
Irwin, Joseph, 1674
Irwing, Henry W., 4116
Isaacson, Dean L., 551
Isambert, François-André, 1686, 1705, 1707, 1708, 1757, 4668
Ishii, Yoichi, 3729
Ishikawa, Akihiro, 2587, 4812, 4937, 4938

Ishwaran, Karigoudar,3334
Islami, Hivzi, 3061
Israel, Joachim, 725, 726
Iutaka, Sugiuama, 3335
Ivancevich, John M., 1022
Ivanics, András, 4399
Ivanov, G. I., 2588
Ivanov, Ju. K., 4582
Ivanov, S. A., 4727
Ivanova, R. K., 4363
Iwama, Tsuyoshi, 5290
Iwand, Wolf Michael, 1329
Iwasaki, Nobuhiko, 777, 2901
Iwase, Yōri, 5136
Iwawaki, S., 664
Izraeli, D., 4698

Jabbra, J. G., 2322, 5137
Jackman, R. W., 5217
Jackson, Douglas A., 1692
Jackson, Elton F., 2495
Jackson, John E., 507
Jackson, J., 1398
Jackson, P., 4734
Jacob, André, 1919
Jacobs, Frans, 4470
Jacobs, Ruth Harriet, 5226
Jacobson, Cardell K., 965, 3637
Jacoubovitch, M.-Daniel, 5025
Jacquard, Albert, 3657
Jacques, Jeffrey M., 638
Jadov, V. A., 355
Jaffe, Abram J., 3559
Jaffe, Frederick S., 3197
Jagodzinski, Wolfgang, 528, 1097
Jaguin, Aureliano, 2589
Jai-Seuk, Choi, 3417
Jakob, Roberto, 1169
Jakušin, S. P., 4939
Jameson, Frederic R., 1197, 2072
Janger, Allen R., 4546
Janicijević, M., 256
Janis, Irving L., 752
Jankova, Z. A., 3336
Janowitz, Morris, 5218, 5496
Jansen, Karel, 2170
Jansha, J. Dean, 3966
Janssens, M. A., 3441
Jardillier, Pierre, 4637
Jarlov, Carsten, 4638
Jarvie, I. C., 4940
Jasiewicz, Krzysztof, 3560
Jasso, Guillermina, 4301
Jáveau, Claude, 4575
Jawanda, J. S., 2441
Jayaraman, R., 3638
Jean, Bruno, 4674
Jean, P., 5660
Jeannet, Maurice, 5661
Jeber, A., 2340
Jefferson, Gail, 1920
Jefferson, Tony, 2956

Jefferys, Margot, 5621
Jegouzo, Guenhaël, 3912
Jencks, Christopher, 2323
Jenei, György, 4596
Jenkins, J. Craig, 4752
Jenks, Craig, 257
Jenks, Richard, 5170
Jennens, Roger, 5542
Jennings, M. Kent, 427, 2909
Jensen, Gary F., 5452
Jensen, Mogens B., 5036
Jeudy, Henri-Pierre, 1876, 1946
Jimenez Burillo, Florencio, 588
Jiobu, R., 3418
Joachmsthaler, F., 4876
Jobert, Bruno, 428, 4117, 4118, 5497
Johansson, Sven Ove, 4830
John, Puthenpeedikail M., 1461
Johnes, Frank E., 2669
Johnson, Allan G., 508
Johnson, Benjamin H., 4494
Johnson, Benton, 1595, 1742
Johnson, Bonnie McD., 1031
Johnson, Colleen L., 3370
Johnson, David W., 630
Johnson, Graham E., 5104
Johnson, Harry M., 4996
Johnson, John M., 1673, 5126
Johnson, Joyce S., 3317
Johnson, Marcia K., 509
Johnson, Mauritz, 2422
Johnson, Michael P., 4309
Johnson, Miriam M., 3242, 4494
Johnson, M. Clemens, 2129
Johnson, Norris R., 1218, 1219
Johnson, Paul, 1462
Johnson, Stuart D., 1295
Johnson, Terry, 251, 2590
Johnson, Weldon T., 1393, 5327
Johnson-Laird, Philip N., 1927
Johnston, Robert, 535
Johnston, Ron, 114, 1804
Johnstone, Frederick A., 2591
Johnstone, John W. C., 1996
Jonas, Steven, 5597
Jones, Bryn, 2498
Jones, Carl R., 689
Jones, Dorothy G., 3836
Jones, Emrys, 3809
Jones, F. Lancaster, 2492
Jones, Gavin W., 3025, 3157, 3166
Jones, Hardin B., 5328
Jones, Hardy, 2902
Jones, Helen C., 5328
Jones, Hwo R., 3158
Jones, Kenneth, 336
Jones, Lawrence E., 5184
Jones, Maxwell, 5598
Jones, Patricia A., 5565
Jones, Pauline A., 567
Jones, Robert Alun, 258
Jones, R. Kenneth, 5565

Jong, Gordon F. de, 3159, 3669
Jong, J. H. Th. de, 4331
Joravsky, David, 259
Jordan, Bill, 5498
Jorion, Paul, 3915
Joseph, Joanne M., 847, 848
Joseph, Roger, 3278
Joshi, Heather, 4072
Jost, Ekkehard, 2089
Jost, Leonhard, 2171
Jouffroy, C., 5662
Journes, Claude, 5070
Jozsa, Péter, 2049, 2050
Judge, Harry G., 2247
Juanke, Ralph, 1405
Julémont, Gislaine, 3160
Julkunen, Raija, 414
Juniper, Dean F., 2283
Juris, Hervey A., 5009
Jurovski, A., 1463
Jusenius, C., 4508
Juszig, Renate, 4639
Juviler, Peter H., 2815

Kaayk, J., 2801
Kabiev, B. N., 1271
Kabir, M., 3110
Kacanski Udovicic, Gordana, 5499
Kaeppelin, Philippe, 491
Kaës, René, 905
Kagami, Yutaka, 1163
Kagan, Spencer, 1372
Kahalas, Harvey, 1178
Kahl, Joachim, 260
Kahl, Joseph A., 2816
Kahley, William J., 3207
Kahn, Arnold, 815
Kahulits, László, 4239
Kaim-Candle, P., 5291
Kain, John F., 4017
Kaiser, Edward J., 4157
Kaiser, Heinz J., 1882
Kalajdzijev, V., 3026
Kalinin, A. I., 4364
Kalinova, Lenka, 2468
Kalirajan, K., 5292
Kalish, Richard A., 3111
Kalleberg, Arne L., 4583
Kalmyk, V. A., 3062, 3883
Kalocsai, D., 614
Kaloyanova, Fina, 4170
Kamagaev, V. K., 4561
Kamenka, Eugene, 4941
Kamens, David H., 2172, 2324
Kaminski, Antoni Z., 4974
Kaminsky, M., 3161
Kanaana, Sharif, 3721
Kanda, Michiko, 2387
Kando, Thomas M., 1415
Kane, Thomas R., 848
Kanekar, Suresh, 1527
Kaneko, Isamu, 4137, 5138

Kange, Ewane, 1758
Kansky, Karel J., 4018
Kantecki, Antoni, 4435
Kanter, Rosabeth M., 2879
Kantor, P., 5074
Kantorovic, B. Ja, 2754, 4975
Kapitonov, E. A., 1198
Kaplan, Martin F., 960, 5026
Kaplan, Morton A., 1464, 1565
Kaplan, Susan J., 788
Kaplowitz, Stan A., 1140
Kapoor, S., 3842
Kapsis, Robert E., 5123
Kap Sur Koh, 3208
Kapur, Ravi L., 3076
Kapustin, E. I., 1272, 4019
Kaputo, Samba, 3621
Karady, Victor, 261
Karapetian, Aghop de, 3728
Kardelj, E., 4332
Kariko, Sandor, 1168
Karivalo, Lassi, 4073
Karlov, A. A., 4961
Karoui, Naima, 3500
Karp, David A., 4119
Karpinski, Jakub, 397, 1273
Karush, Gerald E., 4410
Kasarda, John D., 3980
Kaser, Michael C., 5599
Kashti, Yitzhak, 4140
Kasjanenko, V. I., 4942
Kasparian, Robert, 3661
Kasparov, S. G., 2503
Kass, Roy, 3843, 4302
Kassai Végh, M., 2378
Kasschau, Patricia L., 2996
Kastenbaum, Robert, 3112
Kasumov, T. K., 1274
Kasymov, N., 2592
Katano, Takashi, 926
Kato, Sadao, 429
Katona, I., 3914
Katscher, Aaron H., 1083
Katsoura, Alexandre, 3810
Katz, Elihu, 4835
Katz, Fred E., 262
Katz, Phyllis A., 3639
Katz, Ralph, 4584
Katzenstein, Peter J., 3622
Katzer, Jeffrey, 1921
Katznelson, Ira, 2618
Kauffman, James M., 2924
Kavko, A. K., 4260
Kavolis, Vytautas, 1528
Kawai, Takao, 2504
Kawanishi, Hirosuke, 4753, 4754
Kay, Cristobal, 3967
Keane, John, 263
Kearney, Richard C., 4803
Keating, Caroline F., 2670
Keesing, Roger M., 1232
Kellens, George, 1578

Keller, Berndt, 4717
Keller, Robert J., 2325
Kelley, Jonathan, 2505
Kelley, Nelson L., 4553
Kelly, James R., 1666
Kelly, John B., 4837
Kelly, John J., 3684
Kelly, John R., 4836
Kelly, Peter, 2427
Kelly, Rita Mae, 3844
Kelly, William R., 3651, 5431
Kelmenčič, V., 3561
Kemény, I., 3562
Kemény, Jim, 4158
Kemp, Ray, 1805
Kemper, Robert V., 3763
Kemper, Theodore D., 3312
Kendon, Adam, 778
Kennedy, James C., 826, 961
Kennedy, John G., 3864
Kephart, William M., 1465
Kepplinger, Hans M., 1181
Kerckhoff, Alan C., 2215, 2411, 3563
Kerimov, D. A., 2755
Kern, Horst J., 2442
Kern-Daniels, Rochelle, 2876
Kerr, Donna H.) 2173
Kerri, James N., 4159
Kerrinkson, J. H., 4585
Kerst, Erna W., 4160
Kertészová, Antonia, 3764
Kervin, John B., 367
Kessler, Evelyn S., 3501
Kessler, Ronald C., 510
Keve, V. Ž., 1806
Key, Mary Riteline, 778
Keyfitz, Nathan, 2848
Khandwalla, Pradip N., 1032
Khare, R. S., 3371, 4943
Khosrovi, Khosrov, 3915
Khotin, Leonid, 3320
Khozine, Grigori, 264
Kičatinov, L. P., 665
Kicinski, Krzysztof, 337
Kidder, Louise H., 727
Kier, Herfrid, 2090
Kiesler, Sara B., 3419
Kilmann, Ralph H., 1815, 2469
Kilmartin, L. A., 4120
Kilty, Keith M., 5329
Kim, Kyong-Dong, 3387
Kim, On-Jook Lee, 3387
Kim, Yersu, 1356
Kim, Young Oon, 1631
Kimberly, John R., 1033
Kimble, Chales E., 849
Kimmel, Michael S., 2981
Kinchla, R. A., 1391
King, Ambrose Yeo-chi, 1034
King, Joan, 5404
King, Roy D., 5453
Kinloch, Graham C., 265

Kira'ly, Istvan, 2073
Kirchberger, Stefan, 2506
Kirk, James A., 1600
Kirkpatrick, James J., 5105
Kirpatrick, R. George, 3264
Kirkwood, F., 4755
Kirn, Andrej, 4365
Kirn, M., 266
Kirp, D. L., 3640
Kirpal, Prem, 2958
Kirschenbaum, Alan B., 1035
Kirschenbaum, Howard, 1390
Kiselev, I. J., 4790
Kishida, Shôyû, 4819
Kislov, S. A., 2470
Kiss, Cyörgy, 4074
Kiss, Gabor, 193
Kitahara, Ryūji, 5566
Kivitz, Marvin S., 5611
Kiyohara, Keiko, 2388
Kjølby, Henning, 511
Kleckin, A. Ja, 1947
Kleiman, Michael B., 5369
Klein, Herbert S., 2505
Klein, Lisl, 4562
Klein, Malcolm W., 5433, 5454
Klein, Michael, 4873
Klein, Paul, 3641
Klein, Rudolf, 5500, 5634
Kleinke, Chris L., 445, 830
Klekamp, Robert C., 4341
Klinkiewicz, Roman, 4436
Kline, John A., 775
Klinger, Andras, 3027
Klingman, David, 2817
Klinkert, J. J., 5567
Kljastornyj, N. D., 1275
Kločkov, V. V., 5356
Klopov, Ê. V., 1262, 4574
Kluegel, James R., 2593
Kneifel, John L., 4425
Knight, George F., 1372
Knight, Martha, 776
Knight, Richard, 4232
Knoblom, L. V., 4261
Knodel, John, 3209
Knoke, David, 997, 5119
Knoll, R., 2471
Knowles, Edmond, 3420
Knox, A. J. G., 3916
Knudsen, Dean D., 1721
Koch, Gary G., 5451
Koch, Ursula, 78
Kochan, Thomas Z., 984
Koenigs, Sharon S., 2443
Kögler, Alfred, 1466
Köhl, Werner, 4838
Köhler, Bernd, 1416
Köhler, Gernot, 1467
Kohn, Paul M., 5330
Kojder, Andrzej, 5274
Kojima, Kazuto, 1182, 2959

Kokurina, I. G., 949
Kolaja, Jiri, 2456
Kolarska, Lena, 385, 1036
Kolbe, H., 2594
Kolominskij, Ja. L., 927
Kolosi, T., 2595
Kolsawalla, Maharukh B., 1527
Kolson, Martin L., 2540
Komai, Hiroshi, 3564, 4161
Komarov, Ê. G., 4521
Komarovsky, Mirra, 2960
Komorita, Samuel S., 865, 866, 871
Komorowski, Z., 1417
Komyza, M. A., 2326
Kondakov, Mikhail I., 2174
Kondonassis, A. J., 2327
Kondoraki, V. M., 2596
Konečná, Alena, 3295
Konev, V. A., 1807
Koneva, L. A.p 1807, 4308
Kong Kyun Ro, 3162
König, Klaus, 5037
König, René, 3345, 3360, 3399, 3434
Konner, Melvin J., 2925
Konstantinov, F. V., 666
Koo, Hagen, 3765
Koomen, Willem, 962
Koopmans, Rudy, 4304
Kooy, G. A., 3279
Köpeczi, B., 398, 1276, 2265
Koppman-Iwema, Agnes M., 5139
Kopylov, I. Ja., 4944
Kopyrin, V. A., 1277
Kopytoff, Igor, 2541
Körcsög, A., 2328
Körner, Wolfgang, 690
Körobejnikov, V. S., 1183
Kortunov, V. V., 5243
Korzybski, Stanislas, 3063
Kosa, L., 3917
Kosaka, Kenji, 495
Koschnitzke, Rudolf, 2175
Koschwitz, Hansjürgen, 1970, 1983
Kosco, Jan, 2032
Koshi, Heikki, 5055
Kosinski, Leszek A., 3028
Kossou, B., 1357
Kostecki, Marian J., 4699
Kostin, L. A., 4945
Kotljarevskij, G. S., 1566
Kōtō, Yosuke, 267, 356
Koudriavtsev, Vladimir, 1567
Koulack, David, 963
Kourchid, Olivier, 4787
Kourvetaris, George A., 5219
Kovačedić, Ivanka, 2074
Kovács, Ferenc, 2378, 2597, 2598
Kóvágó, László, 3565, 3566
Kowalski, Gregory S., 4389
Koyano, S., 79
Kozik, A. K., 4366
Kozma, T., 2130

Kraenzel, Carl F., 4463
Krafeld, Franz Josef, 4489
Kraft, Virgil A., 1727
Krain, Mark, 816
Krajzmer, L. P., 545
Kramer, Leo, 2651
Kramer, Ralph M., 5663
Kramm, L., 338
Krasnogorskij, I. Ê., 4700
Kraus, Richard C., 2599
Krause, Elliott A., 5609
Kravitz, Linda, 3758
Krawczyk, Barbara, 4867
Krawczyk, Zbigniew, 4868, 4869
Kreckel, R., 2507
Krefetz, Sharon P., 5501
Kreilkamp, Thomas, 639
Kreitler, Hans, 691
Kreitler, Shulamith, 691
Kreml, William P., 667
Kreps, Gary A., 5423
Kretzer, David I., 3421
Krickus, Richard, 3604
Kriegel, Annie, 3642
Kris, Michel, 1391
Krizsán, Zoltán, 2013
Kritzer, Herbert M., 5092
Krohn, Marvin D., 3080
Krohn, Wolfgang, 1789
Krolage, Joseph, 818
Kronenfeld, Jennie J., 5588
Kröner, Sabine, 4870
Kronus, Carol L., 998, 1418, 4708
Kronus, Sidney, 5305
Kross, P. A., 753
Krüger, Hans-Peter, 2275
Kruglanski, Arie W., 971
Kruijt, Dirk, 2600, 4756, 4791
Krupp, Burkhard, 1152
Krzemiński, Ireneusz, 1233
Kubat, Daniel, 3766
Kubik, István, 2601
Kubik, Włodzimierz, 268
Kucinski, Kazimierz, 3783
Kuczyński, Pawel, 476
Kueneman, Redney M., 1028
Kühn, Wolfgang, 568
Kühne, Dietrich, 4020
Kuiper, G., 2508
Kuji, Toshitake, 888, 5093
Kuklinski, James H., 5176
Kulcsár, Kálmán, 80, 116, 1199, 1568, 1569, 1570, 4903, 5502
Kulcsár, Viktor, 3865
Kulkarni, P. M., 3038
Kulminska, Jolanda, 2329
Kumagai, Fumie, 2330
Kumasaka, Kenji, 4839
Kunitz, Stephen J., 2880
Kunz, Frithjof, 4728
Kunz, Harald J., 5390
Kunz, Philip R., 3301, 3422

Kuo, Hwang Kwang, 2331
Kuo, Wen H., 3722, 5140
Kuper, Leo, 3544, 3567
Kuprijan, A. P., 512
Kurczewska, Joanna, 5503
Kurian, George Thomas, 154, 4490
Kuroda, Toshio, 3767
Kurzweil, Edith, 269
Kusatsu, Osamu, 615, 640, 5250
Kushner, Harvey W., 5177
Kusnetzoff K., F., 4162
Kutepov, V. P., 754
Kuty, Olgierd, 872
Kuz'mina, Ê. I., 4437
Kuznecov, V. I., 1278
Kuznecov, V. P., 446
Kvacahija, V. M., 1808
Kvale, Steinas, 1037
Kvasa, A. Ja, 3210
Kvason, G. G., 1516
Kviz, Frederick J., 477
Kwasniewski, Jerzy, 1468
Kwilecki, Andrzej, 5141
Kye Choon Ahn, 3162
Kynaston, David, 2602

Labastida Martin del Campo, Julio,
   5195
Labbe, Dominique, 2075
Labeff, Emily, 2885
La Belle, Thomas J., 2818
Labov, William, 1922
Labovitz, Sanford, 155, 5391
Labrie, Gisèle, 5331
Lacalle, Daniel, 2603
Łach, Wiktor, 4411
Lacomba, Juan Antonio, 2729
Lacoste-Dujardin, Camille, 3866
Lacour, C., 2997
Lacroix, Bernard, 270
Lacrosse, J.-M., 5575
La Da'nyi, A., 2041
Ladanyi, J., 4675
Ladd, E. C. Jr., 464
Ladenson, Robert F., 616
Ladner, Joyce A., 3423
Ladrière, Jean, 1809
Lagneau, Gérard, 1948
Lagneau-Markiewicz, J., 2509
Lago, Maria, 3248
Lahalle, Dominique, 3723
La Hera, A. de, 1759
Lahti, Raimo, 5392
La Iglesia Gomez, Angel de, 1883
Lajdmjaê, V. I. Ê., 2051
Lajtai, György, 1259
Lakatos, M., 4163
Laki, László, 4597, 4867
Lakos, S., 4262
Laktionov, I. D., 1279
Laky, T., 4333, 4368
Lallez, Raymond, 2248

Lama, Luciano, 4757
Lamarche, Hugues, 4409
Lamb, Curt, 4917
Lamb, David, 2819
Lamb, Gene, 2266
Lamb, Michael E., 3388
Lambregts, R. J. A., 2801
Lamm, Zvi, 2423
Lancaster, Janet, 2249
Land, Kenneth C., 4613
Landau, Yehuda H., 3867
Lander, Patricia S., 2820
Landers, Daniel M., 4871
Landers, Thomas J., 2284
Landes, R. G., 5137, 5142
Lane, Angela V., 4640
Lane, Frederic C., 4280
Lane, John Hart Jr., 999
Lane, John S., 3029
Lang, W., 1571
Langeheine, Rolf, 817
Langer, Ellen J., 1220
Langer, John, 5332
Langmeyer, Daniel, 942
Langmuir, Gavin I., 3643
Langton, K. P., 1760
Lanigen, Richard L., 1924
Lannoy, W. de, 4164
Lansdown, Robert, 3829
Lantermann, Ernst-Dieter, 569
Lantoine, C., 2998
Lantz, Herman, 3424
Lanza, Orazio, 5094
Lanzetti, Clemente, 3337
Lapassade, Georges, 2131
Lapine, N., 5504
Lapointe, Claire C., 271
Lapointe, François, 271
Lapré, R. M., 5601
Laqueur, Walter Se'ev, 5196
Larbes, Germaine de, 5543
Larez Alhornoz, A., 5333
Larivière, J. P., 3768
Larkin, William E., 3425
Larsen, Knud S., 850
Larsen, Otto, N., 8
Larson, Meredith A., 2205
Larsson, Reidar, 4910
LaRusso, Dominic A., 1884
Lasater, Thomas L., 3580
Lascoumes, Pierre, 5544
Lashuk, Maureen W., 4490
Lasin, A. G., 4268, 4946
Laslett, Barbara, 3338
Laslett, Peter, 2881
Laso, P., 2604
Lasserre, René, 1469
Lassey, William R., 3968
Latapie, Francis, 2018
Latouche, Jean, 5629
Latour, Bruno, 1810
Latour, Chantal, 2999

Latuch, M., 3030, 5505
Lauderdale, Pat, 1380
Lauer, Robert H., 2756, 2757,
Laumann, Edward O., 2691
Lauterbach, Albert, 4491
Lawler, E. J., 4913
Lawrence, Peter A., 272, 2298
Layne, Norman R. Jr., 3163
Lazarsfeld, Paul F., 5261
Lazarus, Antoine, 5664
Lazreg, Marnia, 2605
Leach, Edmund D., 1280
Leacock, Eleanor, 3389
Leavitt, Gregory C., 5251
Lebel, M., 145
Leblebici, Husejin, 134
Le Bot, Yvon, 1761, 3918
Lebra, Joyce, 3502
Le Bras, Gabriel, 1762
Le Bras, H., 4056
Leca, Jean, 4976
Ledenig, W., 3211
Leder, Arnold, 2821
Lederman, Bobbie, 342
Ledrut, Raymond, 3986
Lee, Anne S., 3113
Lee, Eun Sul, 3107
Lee, Gary R., 3280, 3426
Lee, Jung-Bock, 1994
Lee, Kenneth, 5624
Lee, Lee C., 2926
Lee, Trevor R., 3724, 4165
Lee-Hyo-Chae, 3164
Leek, Sybil, 5393
Lefebure, Alain, 2855
Lefebvre, Alin, 5665
Lefevre, Claude, 4563
Lefkowitz, Monroe M., 851
Legendre, Camille, 4401
Leger, D., 3431
Leger, Robert G., 5455
Leggett, John C., 3712
Legnaro, Aldo, 2747
Le Grand, Julian, 5275
Legrand, Louis, 2176
Leguina, J., 3769
Lehmann, K. D., 4827
Lehtonen, Heikki, 5506
Lei, Tzuen-jen, 3797
Leighninger, Robert D. Jr., 1280
Leik, Robert K., 497
Leimu, Heikki, 81
Leinhardt, Samuel, 2466, 2467
Leis, Philip E., 3557
Leitner, Ute, 3399
Leman, Christopher, 5528
Lemarchand, René, 5220
Lemel, Y., 4438
Lemennicier, Bertrand, 2332
Lemieux, Vincent, 2472
Lemoine, Jean-François, 1991
Lemos, Ramon R., 4962

Lenero-Otero, L., 3339
Lengyel, Zsuzsa, 3919, 4402
Lennon, John J., 1373
Lent,J.A., 1281, 1997
Léon, Antoine, 2402
Leon, Carlos A., 3085
Leon, David Jess, 3591
Leon, Jeffrey, 5381
Leone, Christopher, 704
Leong, Anthony, 4458
Leoni, F., 4904
Lepage, Yvan, 3296
Leplat, Jacques, 4467
Leporrier, Herbert, 5666
Lepsius, 22
Lerena Aleson, Carlos, 2177
Leridon, Henri, 3212
Lerner, Max, 1392
Lernoux, P., 1728
Leroi-Gourhan, André, 1709
Le Roy Ladurie, Emmanuel, 5199
Leschinsky, Achim, 2178
Leschiutta, Pier Paolo, 1425
Leslie, Gerald R., 3240
Lesne, Marcel, 2389
Letourny, Alain, 5602
Letowski, Janusz, 5038
Leupolt, Manfred, 3969
Levada, Ju. A., 4008
Levasko, N. N., 728
Levasseur, Georges, 2927
Leven, Charles L., 4166, 4167
Levenson, Bernard, 4287
Levi, A. M., 873
Lévi, Florence, 3503
Levi, Isaac, 1811
Levin, Arthur, 5635
Levin, Melvin R., 4221
Levine, C. H., 4804
Levine, Daniel H., 1763
Levine, Daniel U., 3644
Levine, Donald N., 273
Levine, Herbert M., 117
Levine, John M., 442, 950, 1888
Levine, Lawrence W., 2106
Levine, Ned, 590
Levinson, A. G., 4008
Levi-Strauss, Claude,641
Levitan, Sar A., 2928, 4494
Levitas, R. A., 5095
Levy, Charles S., 5545
Levy, D., 5667
Levy, René, 3504
Lévy-Stringer, Jacques, 1470
Lewandowski, Edmund, 2758
Lewis, Bernard, 1632, 1633
Lewis, Dorothy Otnow, 5394
Lewis, Erwin, 2529
Lewis E., Glyn, 1915
Lewis, I. M., 1234
Lewis, Janet, 5634
Lewis, J. David, 3

Lewis, Michael, 692, 3407
Lewis, Patricia G., 5313
Lewis, Peirce F., 4075
Lewis, Philip, 308
Lewis, Robert A., 2822
Ley, Philip, 714
Leyland Kauffert, P., 1764
Li, Peter S., 3372
Li, Wen Lang, 3770
Liberska, Barbara, 3685
Libo, Lester M., 964
Lichbach, Mark Irving, 5192
Lichtveld, L., 1282
Lick, József, 4369, 4455
Lieberman, J. Nina, 4840
Lieberman, Leonard, 2033
Lieberman, Leslie, 2033
Lieberman, Morton A., 906, 3007
Liebert, Robert M., 509
Liégeois, Jean-Pierre, 3568, 5546
Light, Donald, 2333
Light, Ivan, 3249, 4872
Ligou, Daniel, 1661
Lilli, Waldemar, 818
Limone, Donato A., 546
Lin, Nan, 3722, 5262
Lincoln, James R., 4305
Lindblom, Charles E., 5479
Lindenberg, Siegwart, 2473, 2510
Lindenberg, S., 1111
Lindenstein, Mary, 3469
Lindholm, Richard W., 4281
Lindley, James T., 4456
Lindsay, John S. B., 939
Lindsey, James, 2560
Lindskold, Svenn, 605
Lineberry, Robert L., 66, 4222
Linhart, Jiri, 2711
Linhart, Sepp, 2606
Linné, Olga, 852
Linquist, Therold, 2082
Linskie, Rosella, 693
Lion, Joanna, 5622
Lion, John R., 907
Lippold, Gerhard, 668
Lipset, S. M., 82
Lipsky, M., 3645
Lipsky, W. E., 2759
Lipton, James A., 5648
Lipton, Michel, 5293
Lira, Luis F., 3427
Lischeron, Joseph A., 4820
Liska, Allen E., 591
Lisovskij, Ju. P., 5442
Lisovskij, V. J., 2961
Lissner, Will, 170, 171, 172
Lissowski, Grzegorz, 513, 514
Listov, V., 2098
Little, Marjorie K., 3262
Littlewood, Barbara, 4511
Littrell, W. Boyd, 5507
Liu, Ben-Chieh, 4121

Liu, P. K. C., 4021
Liu, William T., 3505
Ljasnikov, N. V., 4550
Llanos, José Maria, 1729
Llewellyn, Catriona, 2715
Lloyd, Barbara B., 2929
Lobodzinska, Barbara, 3313
Lobos M., F., 2806
Lócsei, P., 3281
Loertscher, C., 4977
Loevinger, Jane, 617
Loewenberg, Frank M., 5547
Lofland, John, 779
Logan, John R., 2607
Lohisse, Jean, 1885
Lohrmann, R., 3669, 3670
Lojkine, Jean, 3987
Løken, Bjarne, 4564
Loman, L. Anthony, 3425
Lombardo-Radice, Lucio, 2179
Lomnitz, Larissa, 2334
Lomov, Boris, 2903
Long, Larry H., 3771
Long, Samuel, 2335
Long, S., 5143
Loomis, Charles P., 2474
Lopata, P. P., 4257
López Tejeiro, L., 173
Lorber, Judith, 4641
Lörcher, Siegfried, 5508
Loree, D. J., 2627
Loren, Charles, 2608
Lórincz, Lajos, 4905
Lorint, Florica E., 1609
Lorrain, François, 2475
Lortie, Dan C., 2444
Łoś, Maria, 951, 5456
Loschky, David J., 3114
Losonczi, A., 1283
Lötsch, Manfred, 2578
Lotz, Roy, 5015, 5178
Loubser, Jan C., 274
Louis, Meryl Reis, 874
Lounsbury, John W., 570
Lourau, René, 23, 54
Lourença, Susan V., 2760
Loustau-Lalanne, Bernard, 2930
Louvet, Marc Noël, 4570
Loux, Françoise, 1730
Lovell, John C., 4758
Lovoll, Odd S., 1284
Lowe, George D., 5324, 5340
Lowe, Jay, 3163
Lowe, John, 2390
Löwenthal, Richard, 2692, 2761
Lowy, P., 4423
Loy, John W., 4853
Loye, David, 1086
Löyttyniemi, Leena, 4848
Lubell, Harold, 4072
Luber, Raymond F., 902
Luchsinger, Vincent P., 430

Lück, Helmut E., 2144
Lück, Volker, 5144
Ludwigs, Manfred, 2180
Ludz, Peter C., 1200, 1201, 2693
Luenberger, David G., 4182
Luetkens, Christian, 3351
Luhmann, Niklas, 275, 2476, 2511, 4978
Luker, Kristen, 3136
Luksin, I., 2052
Luloff, A. E., 3064
Lummis, Charles D., 2730
Lummis, Trevor, 3920
Ludnberg, Craig C., 4558
Ludgren, David C., 928
Ludnström, Karl J., 5294
Luneau, René, 1676
Lungwitz, L., 3211
Lupe, Michel-Claude, 4637
Luque-Romero Albornoz, F., 1682
Lurçat, Liliane, 2412
Lüschen, Günther, 4873
Lutyńska, Krystyna, 431
Luzik, K. S., 3569
Luzzatto, Patrizia, 4547
Lyman, Stanford M., 3545
Lynch, 276, 1235
Lynn, Richard, 3686
Lyskov, A. P., 2962
Lytton, Hugh, 2931, 3428

Maamary, Samir N., 3772
Maas, P. J. M., 1039
MacCluer, Jean W., 3297
Mac Donald, K. I., 379
Mace, John, 2368
Mac Gillivray, Lois, 2965
Machalek, Richard, 5211, 5253
Macke, Anna S., 2960
Mac Kenzie, Donald R., 4160
Mackenzie, John, 4330
Mackey, Philip E., 5457
Mackey, William Francis, 1925
Mackie, Marlene, 182
MacKinnon, Neil J., 1098
Macklin, Barbara J., 1358
Mackovskij, M. S., 3340
MacLennan, Beryce W., 908
MacPherson, C.B., 4979
MacQueen, Rhonda S., 4643
MacRae, Duncan Jr., 24, 5039
Macura, Milos, 2846
Madan, T. N., 3282
Madden, Denis J., 907
Maddock, John, 2413
Madeira, J. L., 3115
Madigan, Ruth, 4154, 4511
Madrières, Frédérique, 1949
Madsen, Allan, 277
Madsen, Richard W., 551
Maduro, Otto, 1596
Maeda, Daisaku, 3000

Maeda, Nari Lumi, 3358
Maffesoli, Michel, 2762
Magaro, Peter A., 3081
Maggioni, Guido, 278
Maghami, Farhat Ghaem, 279
Magin, Douglas J., 2113
Magnarella, P., 3725
Magnér, Björn, 618
Magnér, Helena, 618
Magnusson, David, 669
Magri, Susanna, 4168
Maguin, P., 3082
Magyar, Sándor, 3773
Maher, Austen, 2251
Maidment, Susan, 3429
Mailloux, Noël, 1419
Maindive, Jean-Pierre, 2391
Maisonneuve, Jean, 793
Majali, Andel S., 2336
Major, Gersh, 1971
Makai, M., 4240
Mäkelä, Klaus, 5334
Makó, Csaba, 4598, 4672
Makrełow, Konstantin, 4586
Malahov, V. A., 399
Malastová-Dragnevová, Raisa, 1285
Mal'cev, G. V., 1572
Mal'cev, V. A., 670, 2763
Mal'cev, V. I., 5487
Maldonado-Denis, Manuel, 3687, 4947
Malec, Michael A., 515
Malewska, Hanna, 5395
Malik, Yogendra K., 2694, 2695
Malinovskij, P. A., 5489
Malmberg, Bertil, 1926
Malsch, T., 4759
Mammen, M. P., 2765
Mamon, Joyce A., 4122
Manaster, Guy J., 2963
Mancini, Paolo, 4612
Mandeville, Lucien, 5221
Manghezi, Alpheus, 2609
Mangin, G., 5396
Manheim, Henry L., 400
Manis, Jerome G., 5263
Mankin, Don, 4841
Mann, Dale, 2285
Mann, Leon, 752
Mann, Mary S., 4169
Mann, Michael, 4980
Mannari, Hiroshi, 4412
Mannheimer, Renato, 5146, 5179
Manning, Peter K., 2261, 3083, 5335
Manor, Yohanan, 1647
Mansfield, Michael W., 1872
Mansilla, H. C. F., 280
Manton, Kenneth G., 3116
Manyoni, Joseph R., 3341
Manz, Günther, 671
Maple, Eric, 1610
Mappes, Thomas A., 1529
Maraffi, Marco, 4642

Marais, Elizabeth, 3084
Marais, Michael, 3084
Marazziti, Mario, 4123
Marčenko, G. I., 401
March, James G., 1040
Marchello, Giusepp, 174
Marcus-Steiff, Joachin, 4439
Marguerat, Y., 4058
Marichy, Jean-Pierre, 5222
Marien, Michael, 2823
Mariet, Frabçois, 2394
Marin, G., 1158
Mariño, Primitivo, 5252
Marjoribanks, Kevin, 2216
Mark, Desmond, 2946
Mark, J;nathan H., 4166
Markides, Kyriakos S., 3117
Markiewicz, Wladyslaw, 3726
Markiewicz-Lagneau, Janina, 175,2696
Markle, Gerald E., 3430
Markowska, Anna, 4296
Marks, Stephen R., 1099
Marr, W. L., 3671
Marsal, Juan F., 1359
Marsden, Lorna R., 5668
Marsden, Peter V., 2691
Marsella, Anthony J., 2331
Marsh, Robert M., 4412
Marshall, Harvey, 3418, 4122
Marsland, David, 3840
Martel, André, 5223
Martens, Albert, 4482
Martidale, Don, 55
Martin, Albert E., 4170
Martin, Colin, 5147
Martin, Dick, 5147
Martin, Hervé, 1710
Martin, J., 3431
Martin, J. M., 3283
Martin, Louis, 1710
Martin, Michel L., 5224
Martin, Nicholas G., 2931
Martin, Patricia Y., 2282
Martin, Roderick, 4918
Martin, Ruperto G., 4729
Martin, W. W., 3794
Martineau, Jean-Pierre, 3237
Martineau, William H., 3605, 4643
Martinez, Cervando, 909
Martinez, Daniel C., 834
Martinez, Eduardo, 2181
Martinez, Luciano, 3960
Martinez-Alier, Verena, 5189
Martín Galán, Manuel, 4022
Martini, Alcoo, 1471
Martín Molina, Rafael, 4334
Martins, Luciano, 4981
Martins, Waldemar V., 2182
Martín Serrano, Manuel, 281, 339
Martinson, Oscar B., 4861
Martinussen, Willy, 2512
Martorella, Rosanne, 2091, 2099

Martsinkovski, I. B., 2337
Matsumoto, Takeko, 5548
Maruyama, Sadami, 16
Maruyama, Tetsuo, 1286
Marwell, Gerald, 2667
Marx, Emmanuel, 1472
Marx, John H., 1802, 5096
Marx, Melvin H., 694
Mash, Eric J., 1124
Masłyk, Ewa, 4702
Mason, T., 4171
Masotti, Louis J., 4222
Massell, Gregory J., 3342
Massey, Douglas S., 3165
Massicotte, Guy, 1998
Masters, R. D., 1125
Matejko, Alexander J., 1000, 4676
Mathew, Anna, 3432
Mathews, Andrew, 3263
Matras, Judah, 2847
Matsubara, Haruo, 2132
Matsumara, Naoko, 2610
Matsuura, Kôsaku, 1473
Mattern, Karl-Heinz, 5040
Matteson, Richard L., 3213
Matthews, David R., 2824
Matthews, Sarah, 4600
Mattley, Christine, 5371
Matzerath, Horst, 4225
Mauco, Georges, 3646
Mauger, Gérard, 1474
Maurice, Marc, 4124
May, Philip A., 3593
Mayer, K. B., 3570
Mayer, Nonna, 4644
Mayer, Richard E., 695
Mayer, Robert, 4440
Mayer, Rudolf A. M., 2100
Mayers, Marvin K., 1287
Mayes, Sharon S., 4248
Mayeur, Françoise, 2250
Mayo, John K., 2432
Mazeres, Jean-Arnaud, 2392
Maziarka, Stefan, 4170
Mazrui, Ali A., 5106
Mazur, Allan, 2670, 4282
Mazur-Hart, Stanley F., 3284
Mazziotti Di Celso, Fabio, 4730
Mazzocchi, Giancarlo, 4207
Mburugu, Edward K., 3269
McAllister, I., 5181
McAlpine, William E., 1011
McAnany, Emile G., 2432
McArthur, Leslie Z., 794
McAuliffe, Timothy G., 861
McCaffrey, Lawrence J., 3571
McCaghy, Charles H., 1475
McCann, James C., 2716
McCannell, Dean,226, 4874
McCarthy, Bernhard, 649
McCarthy, John D., 4760
McCarthy, Thomas A., 352

McCartney, James L., 5355
McCaughrin, Craig, 2764
McCauley, Clark R., 1126
McClellan, L. Dean, 4649
McClelland, David C., 729
McClelland, Robyn, 141
McClendon, McKee G., 2717
McClintock, Richard, 1336
McClung Lee, Alfred,282
McCons, Harriet, 465
McConville, Sean, 5458
McCord, Arline, 875, 5276
McCord, William, 875
McCord, William M., 5276
McCourt, Kathleen, 2633, 3506
McCreesh, John, 2251
McCubbin, Hamilton, 3343
McDaniel, Tim, 2611
McDonald, Gerald,3433
McDonald, Lynn, 1573
McDonald, Peter F., 3166
McDonnel, Patrick, 2710
McGaughey, Timothy A., 815
McGee, Reece, 184, 194
McGillis, Daniel B., 1437
McGinnis, Robert, 551
McGrath, Dennis, 4011
McGuire, Mary V., 972
McHale, John, 133
McHenry, D. E. Jr., 2825
McHugh, Joseph M., 1972
McIntosh, Donald, 283
McKay, David H., 4172
McKay, J., 3774
McKenzie, Nigel, 4224
McKie, Craig, 4703
McKinley, James, 5397
McKinney, John P., 2939
McKnight, S. A., 284
McLaren, A., 3214
McMahon, J. Timothy, 985
McMichael, Anthony J., 475
McMullan, John L., 2680
McNall, Scott G., 5210
McNeil, John D., 2424, 2425
McPartland, James M., 2414
McPhail, Thomas L., 1973
McPherson, Andrew, 2267
McPherson, Barry D., 4882
McPherson, J. M., 1420
McQuail, Denis, 1990
McQuuen, David V., 1188
McRoberts, Hugh A., 2408
McTavish, Donald G., 402
McTaush, Jeanne, 1118
Meade, Marvin, 5049
Meadows, Paul, 3727
Mechanic, Daniel, 5603
Mecktroth, T., 3811
Medan, Alain, 3988
Medding, Peter Y., 5148
Medeiros, Fernando Da, 3921

Medina, Carlos, 696, 1886
Medoff, Marshal H., 4875
Medunov, S. F., 3868
Medvedev, N. A., 3922
Medvene, A., 4645
Medway, Joan, 3409
Meeker, Barbara F., 497, 952, 2882
Meenaghan, Thomas M., 5329
Mehl, Roger, 1765
Mehmet, Ozay, 2338
Meichenbaum, Donald, 697
Meier, Kenneth J., 698
Meier, Robert F., 1393
Meinhard, Agnes C., 2102
Meintker, Jürgen, 2258
Meissner, L., 4416
Meister, Lynn A., 830
Meilà, Josep, 2053
Melikian, Levon H., 3728
Mell, Wolf-Dieter, 876
Melo, José Marquès de,
Meluk, Alfonso, 1476
Mendelsohn, Everett, 1812
Mendoza de Arce, Daniel, 2092
Mendras, Henri, 3923, 3999
Mends, Emmanuel H., 1617
Menezes, Claudia, 3775
Mennell, Stephen, 49
Meoni, Maria Louisa, 2105
Mer, Jacqueline, 5071
Merand,Patrick, 1288
Meraud, Marie-Agnès, 4076
Merckx, Virginie, 5604
Mérei, F., 1184
Merelman, Richard M., 1813, 2964
Merhautová, J., 4876
Merlin, P., 4077
Mérrick, Thomas W., 3031
Merton, Robert K., 25, 2744
Mescerin, V. P., 478
Messelken, Karlheinz, 1634
Messerschmidt, Don, 3924
Messick, David M., 381
Messing, Manfred, 4897
Metcalfe, J. L., 1041
Metel'skij, F. M., 4849
Metz, Christian, 2014
Mewes, H., 4755, 5197
Meyer, A. G., 285
Meyer, Daniel, 4731
Meyer, John P., 3314
Meyer, John W., 1042, 2133,2183
Meyer, Katherine, 2965
Meyer, Marshall W., 986, 1043
Meyer, Yeanic Keeny, 3644
Meyers, Alan, 1910
Meževic, M. N., 4213, 5513
Mhitarjan, G. E., 5000
Michel, Andrée, 2883, 3507
Michelat, Guy, 1766
Micheli, Giuseppe, 5146, 5179
Michelson, William M., 3979, 3983,4023

Michener, H. Andrew, 889
Mickevic̆, A. V., 1574
Micklin, MIchael, 1394, 3085
Miclet, Georges, 530
Mieno, Takashi, 537, 538
Miers, Suzanne, 2541
Mieszkowski, Peter, 2409
Mignella Calvosa, Fiammetta, 2557
Micguel, Jésus M., 5636
Mihailescu, Ioan, 3848
Mihajlov, Ê. M., 4522
Mihovilovic̆, MIro A., 672
Mikul'skij, K. I., 2612
Milden, James W., 3344
Miles, Agnes, 5574
Miles, Robert H., 1001
Mileti, Dennis S., 1002, 4359
Milgram, Morris, 4173
Milkening, Eugene A., 4861
Millan Puelles, Antonio, 2339
Miller, Ann R., 3776
Miller, Charles E., 960
Miller, Dale T., 819, 1575
Miller, David L., 550
Miller, George A., 1927
Miller, George R., 1887
Miller, Gerald R., 780
Miller, Jean B., 3508
Miller, J. S., 56
Miller, Norman, 5288
Miller, Robert E., 1888
Miller, Rory, 2826
Miller, Rowland S., 648
Miller, Steven S., 2947
Miller, Stuart J., 5365
Miller, William L., 2766
Milligan, Herman J., 3243
Milne, Robert A., 698
Milosavljevic, Milosaw, 5510
Mindel, Charles H., 3572
Minello, Nelson, 5225
Mingione, Enzo, 4249
Minoli, Lorenza, 2315
Mirkin, Boris G., 368
Mironov, V. K., 4792
Mishra, S. N., 2542
Misiuna, Ma₹gorzata, 3820
Mistrorigo, L., 2697
Misuraca, Pasquale, 369
Mitchell, C. N., 5063
Mitchell, David F., 2613
Mitchell, Eugene F., 4646
Mitchell, G. Duncan, 26
Mitchell, Mark, 18
Mitchinson, Wendy, 3480
Mithun, Jacqueline, 3647
Mitono, Masao, 5524
Mitroff, Ian I., 1814, 1815
Mitterauer, Michael, 3434
Miura, Noriko, 2718
Miyaji, Nieko, 3869
Miyazaki, Eiko, 3006

Mjalkin, A. V., 4677
Moc̆alov, A. M., 2614
Mocek, Reinhard, 205
Moch, Michael K., 4370
Mochizuki, Takashi, 3298
Moculta, S., 2477
Módra, László, 2698, 4877
Moens, Gabriel, 2217
Moerk, Ernst L., 1928
Moglestue, Idar, 2340
Mohan, Raj P., 286
Moiseenko, V. M., 3024
Mokrzycki, Edmund, 287
Moksalenko, V. A., 757
Mol, Hans, 1711
Mola, Aldo A., 1662
Moles, Abraham A., 1889
Mollard, Amédée, 3925
Mollenkopf, John, 4089, 4225
Molloy, Edmond S., 4536
Molnár, Edith S., 2852, 3435
Molnár, T., 2767
Momberg, A. P., 642
Momeni, Djamchid A., 2910
Monahan, Thomas P., 3307, 3373
Monatte, Pierre, 4761
Moncada, Alberto, 5072
Monestier, Martin, 5398
Mongardini, Carlo, 4963
Monge, Peter R., 1020
Monich, Z. I., 2615
Monnier, Alain, 3167
Monod-Herzen, Gabriel E., 340
Monopoli, William V., 1051, 1576
Monroe, Alan D., 5182
Monson, Thomas C., 443
Montagna, Paul D., 4471
Montagu, Ashley, 853
Montaron, Jean-Pierre, 5459
Monte, Christopher F., 673
Montes, Arturo, 2075
Montgomery, Andrew C., 479
Montgomery, David A., 5030
Montgomery, John D., 2184
Montironi, Marina, 4612
Montis, Jean-Bernard, 4335
Montlibert, Christian de, 2393
Montmollin, E. de, 1289
Moody, Mary, 111
Moore, Brian L., 2543
Moore, Kenneth, 1635
Moos, Bernice S., 3436
Moos, Rudolf H., 3436
Mootz, M., 539
Moracco, J. C., 4647
Morales, Armando, 5549
Moravec, J. G., 5639
Morawski, Bronos₹aw, 4587
Morawski, L., 1571
Morawski, Stefan, 4948
More, Douglas M., 4648
Moreau, Yannick, 3215

Moreau de Bellaing, Louis, 1816
Moreau-Defarges, Philippe, 3729
Morel, Giyla, 2768
Morel, Julius, 27
Morelli, Ugo, 2616
Moreno, Amparo, 3509
Moreno, Francisco J., 1477
Morgan, David R., 4802, 5149
Morgan, Edward P., 2218
Morgan, Elaine, 3988
Morgan, Rodney, 5453
Morgenbesser, Sidney, 1530
Mori, Steven H., 7
Morikawa, Sadao, 4878
Morio, Simone, 4174
Morioka, Kiyomi, 1687, 1767, 3437
Morissette, Luc, 598
Morozov, V. S., 730
Morris, Earl W., 2719
Morris, Monica B., 1817
Morris, Naomi M., 3227
Morrison, David R., 2185
Morrison, D. G., 5198
Morrison, Peter A., 2186
Morrissey, Joseph P., 57
Morrissey, M., 83
Morrow, Paula C., 4999
Morse, Edward S., 4370
Morse, Stanley J., 820, 1167
Mortimer, Jeylan T., 4475
Mortimore, G. W., 3
Morton, John, 1856

Moscati, Roberto, 1478
Moschetti, Gregory J., 1514
Moscovici, Serge, 1336
Moskos, Charles C. Jr., 5226
Moses, Larry, 1636
Mosher, Arthur T., 3971
Mosolov, Ju. P., 5522
Mosquera, José E., 3606
Mossberg, Howard E., 5612
Motomura, Hiroshi, 2293
Motta, L. C. da, 3118
Motwani, Kewal, 1818
Moulin, L., 1202
Mouloud, Noël, 341
Moulton, Eugene R., 781
Mouly, Jean, 4072
Mounier, Jean-Pierre, 4741
Mountford, Charles Pearcy, 3777
Moura Ribeiro, Edson de, 3098
Mouriaux, René, 2617
Moursi, Mahmoud A., 4472
Moustakas, Clark E., 755
Mouzelis, Nicos P., 987
Movahedi, Siamak, 552, 3086
Movik, Jeya, 3810
Moxley, Robert L., 3438
Moyer, Janet K., 5348
Moynihan, Daniel P., 3552
Mreła, Krzysztof, 1044
Mrksic, Danilo, 288

Mucchi, Angelica, 1221
Mueller, Charles W., 3285, 4523
Mueller, Eva, 3032
Mühlfeld, Claus, 3250, 3345
Mulcahy, Susan DiGiacomo, 4524
Mulkay, Michael J., 1819
Müller, Rudolf W., 4457
Müller, Walter, 2219
Mulligan, Glenn, 342
Mullins, Nicholas C., 940
Mullins, Patrick, 4125
Münch, Richard, 2478
Mundy, Paul, 5653
Munnel, Alicia H., 5529
Muñoz, Luis J., 2769
Muñoz-Perez, Francisco, 3216, 3217
Mura'ev, A. L., 2015
Murányi, Mihály, 1185, 1699
Muraskin, William A., 2618
Murga Frassinetti, Antonio, 4982
Murguia, Edward, 3730
Murnighan, J. Keith, 866
Murphy, Raymond, 2445
Murphy, Robert D., 1974
Murray, Louis, 4879
Murray, Paul T., 3608
Murstein, Bernard L., 3315
Murswieck, Axel, 5511
Murton, Thomas O., 5460
Mury, Gilbert, 2966
Museur, M., 3778
Muzet, Denis, 1469
Myckan, J., 516
Myers, David G., 1127
Myers, J. D., 843
Myers, Judith G., 2284

Nachmias, Chava, 3926,
Nachmias, David, 403
Nachshon, Israel, 699
Nag, Moni, 2848, 2913
Nagasawa, Richard, 386
Nagata, J., 3573
Nagel, Ernest, 1798
Nagel, Jack H., 4919
Nagelschmidt, Anna M., 1169
Nagy, Endre, 1290, 4905, 4983
Nagy-Szegvari, K., 2341
Naitô, Kanji, 3439
Naitô, Tatsumi, 4126
Najib, Ahmed, 4024
Naka, Hisao, 1337, 2967
Nakajima, Akinori, 3251
Nakamura, Masao, 674
Nakamura, Toshimasa, 5550
Nakanishi, Shigeyuki, 675
Nakano, Hideichirô, 5107, 5150
Nakano, Takashi, 176, 5285
Nakhleh, Khalil, 3574
Nakhlem, Emile A., 4473
Nalletamby, Philippe, 2403
Nalson, J. S., 5295

Namer, Gérard, 1820, 2731
Namihira, Isao, 1045, 3688
Nangia, Sudesh, 4078
Napady, Darlene, 1092
Narain, Iqbal, 3927
Narr, Hannelore, 3001
Nash, Jene, 2619
Nash, June, 2770, 3512
Nasr, Nafhat, 5151
Nasr, Salim, 2565
Nastavšev, I. V., 1073
Nasu, Sôichi, 3346
Nathan, J. A., 5152
Natsukari, Yasuo, 289
Naumona, Stefka, 3870
Nauta,A.P.N., 539
N'diaye, Amadou, 2932
Neal, Arthur G., 1479
Neave, Guy, 2267
Nefedou, M. V., 612
Negrotti, Massimo, 106, 454
Neidert, Lisa, 3631
Neidhardt, Friedhelm, 3440
Nel'ga, A. V., 731
Nelissen, N. J. M., 5605
Nelson, Charles W., 1087
Nelson, Jack L., 1531
Nelson, Joan M., 5134
Nelson, John S., 1203
Nelson, L. D., 1100
Nemeth, Charlan, 3575, 5027
Németh, J., 2699
Nesázal, Karel, 4371
Ness, Gayl, 3218
Neubauer, Peter B., 2933
Neufeld, Evelyn M., 2134
Neulinger, John, 1155, 4842
Neumann, Michael, 2620
Neumann-Schönwetter, Marina, 1412
Neuwirth, G., 2220
Nevill, Dorothy D., 2884
Newbigin, L., 1667
Newkirk, Glenn, 1916
Newman, Charles L., 5461
Newman, Graeme R., 1480, 1481
Newton, Peter, 5625
Newtson, Darren, 1128
Nezel, Ivo, 2135
Nezlek, John, 2892
Niang, Mamadou, 28
Nicholas, Ralph W., 3369
Nichols, D. J., 3208
Nichols, Michael P., 1153
Nichols, Theo, 4250
Nicholson, Henry E., 1887
Nicholson, Nigel, 4605
Nickell, S. J., 4762
Nicosia, Francesco, 4440
Nie, Norman H., 5164
Niehoff, Richard O., 2156
Nielsen, François, 2187
Nielsen, Joyce McC., 291

Niemi, Albert W. Jr., 4306
Niemi, Richard G., 5153
Nieto Piñeorba, José Antonio, 4880, 4881
Nigam, Krishna, 1482
Nigsch, Otto, 432
Nijhof, Gerhard, 2672
Nikonov, K. M., 619
Niphuis-Nell, M., 2924
Nisbet, Robert, 29
Nisbett, Richard E., 380, 744
Nishihira, Shigeki, 5183
Nix, Harold L., 1088
Nixon, Howard L., 4882
Nizard, A., 3374
Njaim, Humberto, 1046
Nkpa, Nwokocha K. U., 1950
Noack,J. P., 3548
Noblit, George W., 5399
Noël, Fernando, 4175
Noëlle-Neumann, Elisabeth, 1186, 1890
Noesjirwan, Jennifer, 821
Noguchi,Takashi, 2479, 3731
Noisette, Patrice, 4146
Nonoyama, Hisaya, 3347
Norlen, Urban, 555
Nörlund, I., 2621
Norman, Peter, 4154
Noro, Arto, 38
Norr, James L., 4413
Norr, Kathleen L., 4413
Northen, Helen, 5553
Nowak, Stefan, 357
Nowotny, Sławomir, 2720
Nuñez Encabo, Manuel, 84
Núñez Velásquez, Hernán, 2973
Nwabara, S. N., 3008
Nye, F. Ivan, 1101
Nye, William P., 292, 3616
Nygren, Thomas E., 5184
Nyhan, Michael J., 2023
Nyqcist, Pel, 4813
Nystrom, Dennis C., 4649

O'Barr, Jean F., 1929
O'Barr, William O., 1929
Oberai, A. S., 3779
Obradović, Gradimir, 1236
Obradović, Josip, 1047
Obrębski, Józef, 3929
O'Brien, Donal B. Cruise, 1651
O'Connor, James F., 498
O'Connor, J., 4474
Odincov, V. P., 4517
Odita, F. C., 3441
O'Donnell, Guillermo, 4984
Oeser, Erhard, 1821
Oeshsli, F. W., 3168
Oestereich, Jürgen, 4025
O'Flaherty, Wendy D., 1714
Ofori, Patrick E., 1637
Ogionwo, W., 4372

Ogles, Richard H., 552
Ogodescu, Doru, 676
O'Gorman, Hubert, 1822
Ogura, Jôgi, 5531
O'Hara, Mary, 3424
Ôhashi, Kaoru, 5337
Ohayon, Annick, 5644
Ohlgren, Thomas H., 1976
Okada, Makoto, 2968, 4079, 5512
Okada, Tôtarô, 5551
Okamoto, Yukio, 4176
O'Kane, James M., 4004, 5154
O'Keefe, Eileen, 3
Oldham, Greg R., 4588
Oledzki, J., 2083
Olędzki, Michał, 2188
Oleh, L. G., 2771
Olesen, Virginia, 4499
Olesnevič, L. A., 4414
Olive, Maria José, 4177
Oliveira, Isabel Montezuma de, 1688
Oliveira, Nei Roberto da Silva, 1688
Oliver, Donald W., 2189
Oliver, Lincoln I., 2410
Oliver, L. W., 3442
Olsen, Marvin E., 5097
Olson, D. J., 3645
Olson, James M., 822
Olson, Sheldon, 5264
Oluigbo Nathan Osuji, 4650
O'Malley, Patrick M., 624
Omark, R., 5669
Ômi, Tetsuo, 4127
Omori, Motoyoshi, 4128
Omoruyi, Omo, 2513
Ômura, Eisho, 1483
O'Neill, John, 1930
O'Neill, William F., 5001
Onikov, L. A., 1262
Ono, Hiroshi, 1823
Onokerhoraye, Andrew G., 4080, 4178
Onorad, James R., 849
Onuora Onah, J., 5296
Opare, K. Dua, 4403
Opolski, Krysztof, 4525
Opp, Karl-Dieter, 404
Oppenheim, Felix E., 2514
Oppenheimer, D. R., 1914
Oppenheimer, Valerie K., 4526
Oppong, Christine, 3443
O'Rand, Angela M., 4651
Orata, Pedro T., 2268
Orbán, Sándor, 2734
Orcutt, James D., 1421
Ordonez, M., 3037
Orford, Jim, 3087
Oribador, Patrick, 5643
Orlik, Jacek, 185
Ornauer, H., 1154
Ornstein, Michael D., 4336, 4475
O'Rourke, Robert D., 1400
Orren, K., 5098

Ortega, Antonio, 3033
Ortner, Sherry B., 3517
Osako, Masako, 4415
Osborn, Thomas Noel.II, 2342
Osborne, Allan, 3972
Oschlies, Wolf, 1360
Osinskij, I. I., 2548
Osipov, G. V., 195, 5265
Oskamp, Stuart, 1129
Osochowska-Rusak, Marlene B., 5297
Osterud, Nancy, 3219
Ostrom, Thomas M., 700
Otani, Tomohiro, 1577
Oteiza, Enrique, 85
Ôtsu, Shôichirô, 3871
Otto, KOnrad, 4026
Otto, Luther B., 823, 2288, 3270, 4883
Ottomeyer, Klaus, 756, 782
Ovčinnikov, V. F., 757
Ovčinnikov, V. S., 4264
Overbeek, Johannes, 2849
Overington, Michael A., 293, 294
Owen, David, 5606
Owen, Dolores B., 117
Owen, James L., 1938
Oyabu, Juichi, 1939, 4180
Øyen, Ørjar, 5266
Ozbudun, Ergun, 5155

Pace, Enzo, 1731
Pach, Zsigmond Pál, 30
Padioleau, Jean G., 5338
Padovani, Giuseppe, 106
Padovani, Marcelle, 5073
Paducih, V. V., 1395
Paez Oropeza, Carmen M., 3732
Page, H. J., 3170
Page, H. W., 642
Pahl, L., 3034
Paicheler, Geneviève, 1130
Paillat, Paul M., 2850, 3002
Palazzolo, Charles J., 4609
Paletz, David L., 2034
Palisi, Bartolomeo J., 3316
Palmade, Guy, 1204
Palmer, I., 3514
Palmer, Monte, 5151
Palmonari, Augusto, 592
Palonen, Kari, 4763
Paltiel, Kayyam Z., 5085
Paluba, Gary V., 1155
Pamfil, Eduard, 676
Pampel, Fred C., 2647, 4613
Panahi, Badi, 593
Pande, K. C., 3927
Paniotto, V. I., 929
Pankert, Albert, 4803
Pankoke, Eckart, 2772
Papp, I., 5056
Papp, Zs., 1824, 2827

Paramelle, France, 3248
Paranhos, A., 2622
Parcel, Toby Lee, 1553, 2673
Parenteau, Fernand, 5339
Park, Richard L., 4985
Parker, Howard A., 4765
Parker, James H., 1484
Parker, Stanley, 4843, 4884
Parkin, Andrew, 3733
Parkin, Frank, 2651
Parra Luna, Francisco, 1048
Parry, José, 4764, 5670
Party, Noel, 4764, 5670
Parson, Jack, 5156
Parsons, Jack, 2851
Parsons, Oscar A., 1082
Parsons, R. Wayne, 1171
Parsons, Talcott, 216, 2773
Partington, John T., 822
Parys, Jan, 295
Pasini, Ernesto, 4060
Paškov, A. I., 4265
Paškov, A. S., 5513
Passet, Marc, 2935
Passow, A. Harry, 2253
Pataki, F., 594
Patchen, Martin, 3648
Pathy, Jaganath, 3576
Patrick, Hugh, 4416
Patrono, Mario, 5041
Patrov, B. D., 5607
Patrušev, V. D., 4582
Patterson, Miles L., 835
Paulson, Joy, 3502
Paulston, Rolland G., 2190
Pavan, Adalberto, 1291
Pavlak, Thomas J., 3577
Pavlenok, P. D., 4678
Pavlova-Sil'vanskaja, M. P., 4275, 4949
Pawełczyńska, Anna, 1485
Pawłowski, Zbigniew, 358
Paya, Farid, 4183
Payne, Geoff, 2721, 4652
Payne, John W., 686
Paynton, Clifford, 2740
Pčelincev, O. S., 4027
Pearce, Frank, 5400
Pearlin, Leonard I., 3317
Pearson, Bruce L., 1857
Pearson, Frederic S., 5244
Pease, John, 128
Peay, Edmund R., 370
Peay, Marilyn Y., 1131
Pecht, Waldomiro, 3035
Péczvárady, J., 1858
Pedersen, Peter J., 3065
Pedrazzani, Jean Michel, 1611
Pedrosa Izarra, Ciriaco, 620
Peek, C. W., 5340
Pehrson, Gordon O., 1030
Pelinka, A., 2471

Pelkman, G. H. G., 1396
Pallicani, LUciano, 296, 2774
Pellicciari, Giovanni, 5267
Pellizzi, Camillo, 1292, 5277
Pen, J., 5157
Pendleton, Brian F., 3171
Pepinsky, Harold E., 5401
Pepper, Bert, 5584
Pepper, Susan, 3314
Perarnau, Germain, 556
Peretti, Peter O., 824
Perez, Armando, 3960
Perez Alvarez-Osorio, J. R., 146
Perez Diaz, Victor M., 2828
Perico, Giacomo, 3252
Peristiany, Jean G., 3375
Perlaki, Ivan, 4565
Perlman, Janice E., 1486, 4181
Pernia, Ernesto M., 3066, 4028
Pernica, V., 2480
Pernolla, Mario, 4226
Perrone, Luca, 2654
Perrucci, Carolyn C., 4653
Perry, John Weir, 1715
Perry, J. L., 4804
Perry, Lorraine, 3268
Perry, P. J., 3286
Perry, Ronald W., 4765
Pescatello, Ann M., 3515
Pesenko, V. N., 783
Pestkovskaja, Ê. S., 2624
Peters, Carol B.ù 910
Peters, Jacob, 629
Peters, John F., 3299
Peters, J. P. M., 1049
Peters, Michael n., 762
Petersen, Gene B., 3780
Petersen, Robert E., 5327
Peterson, Evan T., 3422
Peterson, Mary, 4129
Peterson, Paul E., 2191, 4113, 5074
Peterson, Richard A., 1293
Petras, J. F., 2625
Petrella, Riccardo, 5268
Petrică, Ion, 1374
Petrie, Brian M., 1156
Petrov, I. I., 2950
Petrovskaja, L. A., 877
Petrovskij, A. V., 784
Petrumin, A. S., 2635
Petty, Miguel, 2192
Petychaki-Henze, Maria, 4236
Peyre, Vincent, 5395
Pfaff, M., 297
Pfeffer, Jeffrey, 134, 1050, 4458
Pfeiffer, Dietmar K., 988, 1063
Pfeiffer, Wolfgang M., 878
Pfister, Thierry, 5075
Pfohl, Stephen J., 2936
Pharis, Mary E., 5541
Phelps, Edmund S., 4459
Philiber, William W., 148/

Philip, Mathew, 3881
Philippe, A., 2244
Philippe, L., 4766
Philippi, Bruno, 4182
Philliber, William W., 4307
Phillips, Derek L.,2515
Phillips, Dewi Z., 1597
Phillips, John C., 4885
Phillips, Ray E., 1375
Phillipson, Michael, 5269
Piaget, Jean, 1132
Piaton, Georges, 2136
Picard, Jean-François, 1989
Pick, James B., 3172
Pckering, W. S. F., 1598, 1652
Pickowicz, Paul G., 2077
Pickvance, C. G., 3840, 3991
Pico, J., 4793
Pico de Hernandez, Isabel, 4527
Picquet, Michel R., 3672
Pieper, Ansgar, 2035
Pierce, Chester M., 5446
Pierce, Joe E., 1859
Pierce, John, 5061
Pieris, Ralph, 5514
Pierre, Roland, 1616
Pietilä, Veikko, 1977
Pik, David W., 3734
Pilch, Herbert, 1860
Pillat, V. N., 5402
Pilon-Lê, Lise, 3830
Pinard, Jacques, 4081
Pinçon, Michel, 4183
Pine, Vanderlyn R., 517
Pinell, Patrice, 2236, 2294
Pineo, Peter C., 3578, 4417, 4614
Pinkerton, Todd, 1102
Pinkney, Alphonso, 3608
Piontkowski, Ursula, 1422
Piotrowski, Andrzej, 466, 1891
Piper, Antoinette, 4283
Pippke, Wolfgang, 4654
Pirages, Dennis, 5200
Pirson, R., 3778, 3781
Piselli, Fortunata, 4528
Pisier-Kouchner, Evelyne, 4986
Pitié, Jean, 3036
Pitrou, Agnès, 3444, 4704
Pitt, Daniel, 2829, 2830
Pivovarov, Ju. L., 4029
Plake, Klaus, 1423
Plaksij, S. I., 1278
Plath, David W., 1767
Platt, Jennifer, 5269
Platt, Jerome J., 5351
Plax, M., 4130
Plehov, A., 2481
Plog, Fred, 1237
Plongeron, Bernard, 1689
Plotnikov, A. A., 4373
Plourde, Paul J., 2343
Pobeda, N. A., 4030

Pobee, John S., 1599, 1617
Podgórecki, Adam, 86, 298, 1338
Podmarkov, V. G., 4342
Podmore, David, 1532
Pdorov, G. M., 4548
Poffenberger, Thomas, 3445
Pogány,György, 2516, 2517
Poggi, Gianfranco, 4987
Poggi, Vincenzo, 1668
Pohoski, Mihaľ, 4655
Pokataeva, T. S., 4031
Polgar, Sylvia Knopp,4886
Poliakov, Léon, 3649
Pollak, Michael, 3236, 4926
Pollini, Gabriele, 299
Polonskij, I. S., 2970
Pomper, Gérald M., 5185
Pongrácz, Tibor, 2852
Ponton, Rémy, 3930
Pool, Jonathan, 558
Pope, H., 3285
Pope, Whitney, 5403
Popenoe, David, 4227
Poplucz, Jan, 4589
Popov, S. I., 1294
Popovici, Elna, 1205
Poppen, Paul J., 331
Popper, Frank J., 4217
Porcher,Louis, 1951, 2394
Porcin, Nadine, 5530
Porter, Paul R., 4082
Portes, Alejandro, 3689, 3992, 4032,
    4083
Portis, Edward B., 300
Posas Amador, M., 4794
Poskocil, Art, 1157
Poss, Sharon Sandomirsky, 3116
Post, David L., 794
Poster, C. D., 2286
Poster, Mark, 226, 301
Mostic, Marcel, 2446
Poston, Dudley L. Jr.,3318
Poston, Susan L., 2193
Postrigan', G. F., 5516
Potel, Julien, 1671
Potter, Jack M., 3931
Potter, Joanne, 636
Potter, Joseph E., 3037, 3173, 3174
Potter, R. G., 3038
Pouchelle, Marie-Christine, 3119
Poulter, Sebastian M., 3349
Poviña, Alfredo, 156
Powers, Edward A., 455, 4500
Powers, Elizabeth, 3502
Powles, C., 1768
Poyatos, Fernando, 1892
Pradel de Lamaze, François, 3039
Praglowski, Janusz, 911
Prandi, Carlo, 1769
Prato, Ledo, 3690
Prätorius, Rainer, 5042
Pratto, David J., 2613

Preibisha, 147
Preis, Herbert, 839
Prenner, Louis A., 1397
Presnjakov, P. V., 785
Presser, Stanley, 571
Presthus, Robert, 1051, 5158
Preston, Samuel H., 3120,3121
Prevost, François, 4767
Price, Barbara R., 5461
Price, H. Edward, 1488
Price, Richard G., 5021
Price, Robert M., 1052
Price, R., 4768
Price-Bonham, Sharon, 3319
Price-Williams, Douglass R., 701
Prieur, N., 2971
Prihod'ko, D. N., 732
Prioux, F., 3040
Priputen', L. G., 4950
Procos, D., 4572
Pronin, V. A., 2054
Prout, Timothy, 160
Pryor, Robin J., 3220, 3782
Psacharopoulaos, George, 4308
Puccio, F., 3691
Pullman, D. R., 2627
Pullum, Thomas W., 4657
Pumain, D., 4084
Punch, M., 2269

Quasada, Gustavo M., 3910
Quijano, Aníbal, 2628
Quilici, Vieri, 4085
Quinlan, Dan, 4964
Quinn, Ruaici, 4228
Quinney, Richard, 5462
Quintanilla, Miguel A., 1206

Ra, John Oh, 702
Rabier, Jean-Claude, 87
Rabin, Albert I., 2915
Rabinovitz, Francine F., 4131
Radecki, Henry, 1003
Raden, David, 1133
Radford, K. J., 758
Radine, Lawrence B., 5227
Radzinowicz, Leon, 5357, 5409
Raffa, Piero, 2055
Ragg, Nicholas M., 5552
Raggett, Michael, 2447
Ragin, Charles, 5159
Rahman, S., 3019
Rahmatullina, L. K., 2344
Rainville, Jean-Marie, 4590
Rajecki, D. W., 759
Rak, Tanja, 2972
Rakoff, Stuart H., 5589
Rakowski, Witold, 3783
Ram, B., 3175
Rama, Carlos M., 1207
Ramakrishna, Bommathanahalli, 2973
Ramaswamy, E. A., 4769

Rambaud, Placide, 3850
Rambers, Ingrid Gregor, 4564
Ramirez, Albert, 1893, 3580
Ramirez, Manuel III, 701
Ramsay, Harvie, 4816
Ramseier, Erich, 2345
Ramu, G. N., 1295
Randal, Pierre G., 4783
Ranelli, Candice J., 442
Rangaswamy, Govindarajula, 1089
Ranković, Miodrag, 4237
Rantala, Lea, 1732
Rao, G. Lakshmana, 3735
Rao, V. K. R. V., 2831
Rao, V. Nandini, 3300
Rao, V.V. Prakasa, 3300
Rapaport, Elizabeth, 302
Raphael, Edna E., 4743
Raphael, Freddy, 1690, 3581, 3812,
Rapoport, Amos, 3812, 4229
Rapoport, R., 1760
Raschke, Carl A., 1600
Rasidov, S., 1330
Rasmussen, Paul K., 1990
Rassem, M. H., 1134
Rattinger, H., 5257
Rauty, R., 1296
Ravindhran, S. Padmini, 403
Ray, Dixie L., 3311
Ray, J. J., 1090
Raynaut, C., 3872
Rayside, D. M., 3623
Razuvaeva, N. N., 2629
Razzell, Peter, 1733
Read, Donald A., 5608
Reading, Hugo F., 157
Reagan, Barbara, 4499
Real, Michael R., 1977
Rebello, Marina Teixeira B., 3176
Rech, Peter, 2056
Recio Adrados, J. L., 644
Redcliff, M. R., 2630
Redfering, David L., 4603
Reed, Myer S. Jr., 1489
Reed,Theodore, 5049
Reeder, Glenn D., 381
Rees, P. H., 2853
Regan, Dennis T., 1135
Regan D., 1770
Regens,James L., 5149, 5228
Regnier, C., 2238
Regnier, F., 5609
Regoli, Robert M., 5015
Regt, A. J. de, 4679
Rehbinder, Manfred, 1559
Reichler, Melvin L., 3312
Reid, Ivan, 2631
Reid,Margaret, 5558
Reidy, M. T. V., 1677
Reimann, Bernard C., 4375
Reinarth, Leon, 371
Reinherz, Helen Z., 5556

Reisman, David A., 4238
Reiter, Rayna R., 3517
Reitz, H. Joseph, 1053
Reitz, Jeffrey G., 5261
Rémond, René, 1773
Remotti, Francesco, 2270
Remy, Gérard, 3784
Remy, R. C., 5152
Renaud, Bertrand, 3785
Renaud, Jean, 2707
Renaud, Marc, 5610
Renzetti, Emanuela, 1861
Renzina, I. M., 303
Rescigno Di Nallo, Egeria, 1979
Rešetov, P. N., 2974
Reskin, Barbara F., 1825
Resler, Henrietta, 2651
Resta, Patrizia, 2518
Reszke, Irena, 3518
Retterstöl, N., 5341
Reuss-Ianni, Elizabeth, 5387
Reutlinger, Shlomo, 5298
Révész, Bruno, 5497
Rex, John, 405, 1331
Reyes, Román, 343
Reymão, Maria E., 5671
Reyna, S. P., 3287
Reynolds, David K., 3111
Reynolds, H. T., 433
Reynolds, Philip A., 2346
Rhodes, William S., 689
Ribeill, Georges, 1297
Ribeiro, Darcy, 1298
Ribeyrol, Monette, 1691
Ribolzi, Luisa, 3519
Ricard, A., 1361, 2101
Ricateau, Michel, 703
Riccamboni, Gianni, 2700
Rich, Adrienne C., 3390
Rich, Harvey E., 5160
Richards, Toni, 3177
Richardson, C. James, 2722, 2723
Richardson, James T., 1734
Richardson, Jonathan L., 3813
Richardson, Reed C., 2799, 4805
Riches, Colin, R., 2137
Richman, Judith, 3355
Richmond, Anthony H., 3735, 3766
Ricks, David F., 331
Ridder, Richard de, 841
Ridgeway, Cecilia L., 965
Ridgway, Lorna, 2448
Ridker, Ronald G., 3221
Rieder, Jonathan, 4243
Riemer, Jeffrey W., 4680
Riesman, David, 2323
Riess, Marc, 1136
Rietdorf, Werner, 4184
Ringer, Fritz K., 2347
Riquet, P., 4424
Riskin, Jules, 3446
Rist, R. C., 118

Riter, Anah, 971
Ritter, Archibald R. M., 4284
Ritterman, Michele K., 3447
Ritti, Richard R., 1024
Ritti, R., Richard, 1054
Rittner, Karin, 4887
Rivero, Eneida B., 3253
Rives, G., 5463
Rivière, Claude, 879, 1226
Riz, Liliana de, 434
Rizk, Hanna, 3178
Roaldsnes, Jostein, 4564
Robbins, Dave, 1804
Robert, Ellen R., 415
Robert, Philippe, 1558, 1578, 5028, 5352
Roberts, Joan I., 3520
Roberts, K., 4844
Roberts, Robert W., 5553
Robertshaw, P., 3350
Robertson, Alex, 5405
Robertson, Charles, 4185
Robertson, C., 2721
Robertson, Ian, 4230
Robertson, Joan F., 3391
Robertson, Roland, 1601
Robin, François, 5568
Robin, Nicole, 5568
Robins, Lee N., 1490
Robinson, David, 5342
Robinson, Halbert B., 2937
Robinson, John P., 4576
Robinson, Paul A., 2246
Robinson, Philip E. D., 2221
Robinson, Ray, 5275
Robinson, W. P., 3448
Robles, M., 2194
Rocha Trindade, 3692
Roche de Coppens, Peter, 1137, 1602
Rock, Paul E., 5343
Rock, Vincent P., 4070
Rockey, Edward H., 1055
Rockman, Bert A., 5108
Rodgers, G. B., 3179
Rodgers, Harrel R. Jr., 5161
Rodgers, Willard L., 1246
Rodi, Frithjof, 1299
Rodman, Hyman, 3136, 5299
Rodnitzky, Jerome L., 2093
Rodriquez, Jaime, 4177
Roebuck, Julian B., 4845
Roedell, Wendy C., 2937
Roeder, Peter M., 2178
Rogers, Alan, 2396
Rogers, Mary F., 4920
Rogers, Michael D., 4800
Rogers, Sally S., 3835, 4052
Rogers, Tommy W., 359
Rogers-Warren, A., 1138
Rojot, Jacques, 4770
Rokicka, Ewa, 2239
Rokkan, Stein, 9

Rolloy, Gerard, 4563
Román de Silgado, Manuel, 1056
Romaškina, P. M., 1980
Romero Pittari, Salvador, 3932
Ronayne, J., 58
Rondanini, PAero, 435
Rondinelli, Dennis, 3973
Ronis, David L., 1952
Roof, Wade C., 4186
Rooney, James F., 1491
Roos, J. P., 4464
Roper, Brent S., 2885
Rosa, Eugene, 4282
Rosch, Ekkehard, 1424
Rose, Jerry D., 3582
Rose, Peter I., 31, 3552
Rose, Richard, 2775
Rosen, Marvin, 5611
Rosenbaum, H. Jon, 5201
Rosenbaum, James E., 2271
Rosenberg, Bernard, 186, 3521
Rosenblatt, Jay S., 1139
Rosenblatt, Paul C., 1692
Rosenblum, Barbara, 2061, 2084
Rosenfield, Lawrence W., 1894
Rosengren, Annette, 3673
Rosengren, Bernt, 2519
Rosengren, Karl E., 1981
Rosenko, M. N., 4951
Rosenthal, V., 5043
Roshco, Bernard, 2000
Roshier, Bob, 5406
Rosnow, Ralph L., 1953
Ross, Elizabeth D., 2254
Ross, Jennie-Keith, 3004
Ross, Lee, 360, 645
Ross, Lee D., 1103
Ross, Robert J. S., 4709
Ross, Ruth, 3498
Rossade, Werner, 1362
Rosser, James M., 5612
Rossi, Ino, 262
Rossi, Peter H., 4301, 5447
Rossun, Ralph A., 4101
Rotberg, Robert I., 2540
Rotenberg, Mordechai, 792
Roth, D. F., 3974
Roth, Guenther, 143, 215
Roth, Hans-Georg, 2195
Rothman, William A., 4806
Rotondi, Th. Jr., 4705
Rotstein, Abraham, 4418
Rotter, Frank, 2776
Roucek, Joseph S., 1533, 2004, 3547, 5202
Rouchy, J.-C., 5475
Roudinesco, Elisabeth, 595
Rouse, Robert L., 1801
Roussel, Louis, 3288, 3449
Roustang, Guy, 4591
Roux, Jean-Michel, 3999
Roux, Yvonne, 88

Rowan, Brian, 1042
Rowan, John, 966
Rowe, A. R., 5407
Rowitz, Louis, 2778
Rowland, D. T., 4033
Roy, Delwin A., 4771
Roy, Girish C., 1300
Roy, Prodipto, 2813
Roze, Jorge P., 3873
Rozenberg, C. R., 2701
Rozentsveig, Viktor IUI'evich, 1931
Rozgony, T., 973, 4316, 4317, 4468
Rozko, K. G., 760
Rozman, Gilbert, 4086
Rózsa, Klára, 2632
Rubin, Jeffrey Z., 894
Rubin, Lillian B., 2633
Rubina, L. Ja, 2348
Rubineck, Bracha, 3415
Rubinson, Richard, 4964
Rubinstein, Ruth P., 646
Rubio Carracedo, José, 304
Rudakov, B. F., 4566
Rudas, J., 4376
Rudas, Nereide, 5408
Rudder-Payrd, Véronique de, 3736
Ruddle, Kenneth, 3973
Rudduck, Jean, 2427
Rudolph, Joseph R. Jr., 5076
Ruel, Michel, 5637
Rueschemeyer, Dietrich, 2520
Rueschemeyer, Marilyn, 3289
Ruffat, Andrée, 1700
Ruggiero, Joséphine, 1104
Ruhly, Sharon, 1376
Ruiz Palomeque, Eulalia, 4187
Ruml, Vladimir, 4266
Rupp, Klaus J., 3351
Rushing, William A., 1492
Russell, Gordon W., 1222
Russell, Hamish M., 1020
Russell, Margo, 1735
Russo, F., 135
Rust, Holger, 305
Ruthven, K. K., 1716
Rutkevič, M. N., 1301
Rutkevič, M. V., 1302
Rutledge, Albert J., 137
Rutledge, Ian, 3975
Rutter, D. R., 1932
Ruzicka, L. T., 3290
Ryan, Bryce, 4377
Ryan, Charlotte, 2222
Rybakovskij, L. L., 3663
Rybicki, Pawel, 32
Rychard, Andrzej, 1057
Rychtarik, Karel, 361
Ryder, Norman B., 3232
Rynkiewich, Michael A., 1534
Ryvkina, R. V., 3067

Saād, J., 3068
Saal, C. D., 177
Sacca, Antonio, 2057
Sacco, Piero, 2196
Sachs, Wolfgang, 2240
Sack, Ann, 5679
Sacks, Michael P., 4529
Sadan, Ezra, 3926
Sadran, Pierre, 5044
Saegert, Susan, 1220
Safa, Helen Icken, 2619
Sagant, Philippe, 3933
Sagar, Andrew H., 953
Sagara, D., 4404
Sagatun, Inger J., 2687
Sagel, Piet K., 962
Saharov, A. B., 5409, 5410
Sahay, Arun, 372, 1074
Sahlins, Marshall D., 1303
Sahner, Heinz, 2349
Said, Abdul, 3583
Sainsaulieu, Renaud, 647
Saint-Jevin, P., 4766
Saint-Jours, Yves, 4718
Saint-Julien, T., 4084
Saint-Moulin, L. de, 4034
Saitō, Masao, 4087
Saito, M., 3737
Saitō, Shōji, 33, 196, 197
Saitō, Yoshio, 989, 990, 4132
Šajhutdinov, L. G., 677
Sakai, Shunji, 3871
Sakai, Toshirō, 3450
Saks, Mike, 5559
Salaff, J. W., 3522
Salaman, Graeme, 1075
Salancik, Gerald R., 444, 1050
Salas, Rafael M., 2854
Salazar, J. M., 1158
Salcedo, Juan, 237
Salert, Barbara, 2777
Salikov, R. A., 4944
Salles, René, 5077
Sallon, Michel, 4337
Salmona, Michèle, 4378
Salomon, Georges-Michel, 5554
Samaniego, Carlos, 3934
Samardzič, Radovan M., 1653
Samman, M. L., 3041
Samocha, Dalia, 699
Sampson, Gregory B., 2421
Samu, M., 4988
Sanada, Naoshi, 5278, 5517, 5531
Sanchez, Ramon, 2197
Sanchez Jiménez, José, 3874
Sanchis, Pierre, 1693
Sanda, A. O., 3624
Sandberg, Åke, 4464
Sandercock, Leonie, 4231
Sanders, Glenn S., 825
Sanders, Irwin T., 3935
Sanders, William B., 5411

Sandhu, Harjit S., 5412
Sandhu, S.S., 1208
Sandor, Pal, 2734
Sano, Makoto, 89
Sanson, Rosemonde, 1694
Santa Ana, Julio de, 1669
Santee, R. T., 1398
Sántha, János, 4049
Santiago, Jacques, 4035
Santini, Alceste, 1648
Santos, Milton, 1340
Santos, Theotonio Dos, 4952
Sanukov, K. N., 4379
Sapelli, Giulio, 4659
Saporiti, Angelo, 1425
Saraceno, Chiara, 3451
Saraf, M. J., 1895
Šarakaliev, A. Š., 4850
Saram, P. A., 3204
Saran, Parmatma, 5615
Sargent, Alice G., 2886
Sarin, Mirja, 3069
Šarisský, Marián, 4338
Särlvik, Bo, 559
Sartin, PIerrette, 4492
Sartori, Giovanni, 5078
Sas, J. H., 1105
Sasabe, Taketoshi, 5286
Sasaki, Kōken, 5002
Sathyamurthy, T. V., 4989
Sathyavathi, K., 5413
Satō, Mamoru, 2255
Satō, Nobuo, 2138, 2350
Satō, Takeshi, 1304
Satow, Roberta, 4641
Saugstad, Per, 1896
Saunders, Peter, 5121
Sauvageau, Yvon, 2409
Sauve, Reginald, 3428
Sauvy, Alfred, 2840, 2855, 3180
Savčenko, P. V., 4251
Savićevič, Miomir, 5578
Sawicka, Maria, 2351
Saw-Swee-Hock, 3122
Sayad, Abdelmalek, 3693
Sbandi, Pio, 912
Sbisà, Antonio, 2139
Scaglioso, Cosimo, 1238
Scalia, Gianni, 220
Scaramucci, Fabio, 140
Scarr, Sandra, 3329
Schaeffer, Richard T., 3615
Schaefer, Susan D., 4592
Schaeffer, Catherine, 928
Schäfer, Hans-Peter, 2223
Schäfers, Bernhard, 2482
Schaff, Adam, 1862
Schanz, Hans-Jørgen, 499
Scharf, Betty R., 3254
Schäuble, Ingegerd, 1826
Shaw, John, 837
Schearer, Bruce, 2864

Schedler, George, 5464
Scheff, Jane H., 2870
Scheff, Thomas J., 2870
Schellenberg, James A., 1493
Schenkein, Jim, 1920
Schérer, René, 2131
Scheuch, Erwin, 1494
Schiefelbein, Ernesto, 2198
Schiffer, Mortimer, 913
Schiffrin, Harold Z., 5229
Schildt, Gerhardt, 2724
Schiller, Herbert I., 1982
Schlenker, Barry R., 597, 632, 648, 649, 1535
Schlesinger, Philip, 2002
Schmid, Michael, 190
Schmidt, Catherine J., 1447
Schmidt, Peter, 533, 4380, 4990
Schmidt-Relenberg, Norbert, 3351
Schmitter, P. C., 2832
Schmitz, H. Walter, 3625
Schmitz, Marie, 1223
Schnaiberg, Allan, 3010, 3814
Schnapper, D., 3738
Schneider, Benjamin, 4495
Schnieder, Hans-Dieter, 867
Schneider, Karlheinz, 1775
Schneider, Louis, 66, 4238
Schneidman, Edwin S., 5414
Schneller, Donald P., 5465
Schneller, Eugene St., 5672
Schoen, Robert, 3123
Schofield, Janet W., 953
Scholz, Fred, 3584
Schorb, Bernd, 2140
Schramm, Sarah S., 5169
Schubert, Glendon, 5201
Schuler, Heinz, 970
Schulke, Hans J., 4888
Schultz, Duane P., 678
Schultz, Martin, 3424
Schultz, Winfried, 1983
Schulz, Barbara, 3255
Schulz, Manfred, 3976
Schumacher, Jürgen, 4789
Schumna, Howard, 571, 1177
Schumpeter, Joseph A., 4252
Schur, Edwin, 2778
Schüsser, Gerhard, 4728
Schuyt, C., 5518
Schwab, William A., 771
Schwartz, Barry, 4133, 4889
Schwartz, Shalom H., 836
Schweitzer, David R., 1450
Schwendinger, H., 1495
Schwendinger, J. R., 1495
Schwirian, Kent P., 771, 3993
Schwoebel, Jean, 2003
Scimecca, Joseph A., 307
Scivoletto, Angelo, 344
Scott, James C., 3936, 3937
Scott, John, 4330

Scott, Joseph W., 5100
Scott, J. P., 713
Scott, Rosemary, 4442
Scribner, Jay D., 2199
Scull, Andrew T., 3088, 3089, 5569
Sears, David, 804
Sebaly, Kim, 3445
Sechrest, Lee B., 1080, 3452
Sederberg, Peter C., 5201
Seeman, Melvin, 2725, 4537
Segal, David R., 1017, 5210
Segal, Mady W., 941
Segal, Steven P., 3090
Segall, Marshall H., 2670, 4906
Segatori, Roberto, 5162
Segatti, Paolo, 308
Segré, Monique, 2141
Segre, Sandra, 309
Seguier, Michel, 761
Seguy, Jean, 1712
Seidel, J., 5171
Seidenberg, Bernard, 596
Seider, Maynard S., 4339
Seidler, John, 2965
Seidman, Steven, 310
Seifert, Michael, 2567
Seki, Takatoshi, 3376
Sekuguchi, Reiko, 2256
Sękowski, Stanislaw, 1347
Sekuła, Włodzimierz, 5301
Sekulić, Dusko, 1399
Selby, Edward B. Jr., 4456
Selby, James W., 1095
Šelest, P. S., 3938
Selg, Herbert, 854
Seligman, Milton, 915
Seligson, Mitchell A., 3939
Seligson, M. H., 5163
Selinskaja, V. M., 2634
Sell, Ralph R., 3159, 4309
Sellerberg, Ann-Mari, 5519
Sellier, Michèle, 4118, 5057
Selowsky, Marcelo, 5298
Semenov, V. S., 2634
Semov, M., 3940
Semper, E., 4381
'Senguko, Joshiro, 16
Senjavskij, S. L., 2521, 2650
Sennett, Richard, 650, 1496
Sepulveda, Anibal, 4204
Šeregi, F. É., 406, 1264
Seres, Zs., 3523
Serfözö, Simon, 4681
Šerkovin, Ju. A., 1984
Serpell, Robert, 1305
Serrano, M. Martin, 4382
Serrán Pagan, Ginès, 1897
Serrano Gomez, 5415
Serravezza Antonio, 311
Sethi, Raj Mohini, 4530
Ševcov, I., 4476
Sève, Lucien, 5065

Severy, Lawrence J., 597
Sévigny, Robert, 598
Seywald, Aiga, 3091
Sgritta, Giovanni B., 1425
Shafir, Gershon, 2837
Shaklee, Harriet, 1118
Shalin, Dmitri N., 91
Shamkeh, Ahmed A., 3831
Shanab, Mitri E., 2938
Shanin, Teodor, 2802
Shannon, Lyle W., 3710
Shanowsky, Alvin, 596
Shapira, Rina, 5128
Shapiro, E. Gary, 2674, 3650
Shapiro, Jane P., 3524
Shapiro, Roger L., 925
Shapiro, Sheldon, 1536
Shapiro, Theda, 2084
Sharma, K. L., 3941
Sharma, Krishna Murti, 5532
Sharma, Mohan Lal, 3927
Sharma, Ursula M., 3786
Sharon, Bahia, 2061
Sharot, Stephen, 1649
Sharp, Laure M., 3780
Shaver, Kelly G., 599
Shclenker, Barry R., 1136
Sheafor, Bradford W., 5549
Sheeman, Peter W., 621
Sheehy, Gail, 2981
Sheffer, Gabriel E., 699, 1647
Shelby, Bo, 291
Sheldrake, Peter, 5558
Shepard, Jan M., 5279
Sherif, Carolyn W., 600
Sheriff, P., 991, 5045
Sherrod, Drury R., 838, 855
Sherwood, F. P., 102
Shevin, Jann, 5135
Shibano, Shozan, 1426
Shibata, Shingo, 4477, 5003, 5258, 5259
Shiloh, Ailon, 3042
Shils, Edward A., 415
Shimizu, Shinji, 3787
Shimoda, Naoharu, 362, 363
Shinn, Larry D., 1603
Shiota, Shizuo, 4443
Shirley, Robert C., 762
Shmuelli, Efraim, 1827
Shoham, S. Giora, 1497
Shôji, Kôkichi, 2779
Shokeid, Moshe, 4835
Short, James F. Jr., 5414, 5416
Short, John, 2036
Shortell, Stephen M., 992, 5603
Shorter, Edward, 3352
Shukla, K. S., 5417, 5441
Shukla, P. D., 2200
Shupe, Anson D., 1776
Shuy, Roger W., 1863
Sicard, Gerald L., 34

Siddique, Muhammad, 3353
Siddiqui, F., 4493
Sidorov, A. A., 4452
Siebert, Horst, 2395
Sieder, Reinhard, 3434
Siegal, Harvey A., 5389
Siegel, Jacobs, 3005
Siegelbaum, Heidi, 1165
Siegers, J. J., 3525, 4478
Siembieda, William J., 4131
Siemienska, Renata, 3585
Sieradzki, Maciej, 3092
Sierra, G. de, 5230
Siewert, H.-Jörg, 5058
Sigall, Harold, 651, 809, 1150
Siim, Birte, 4293
Sikorski, Linde A., 2207
Sikula, P., 2224
Silbermann, Alphons, 1881, 1898, 1900, 1958, 1959, 2058
Silk, Leonard S., 4310
Šilobod, M. I., 2635
Siltanen, J. L., 4632
Silva, Edward T., 1454
Silva, Germain, 2181
Silva de Mejía, Luz M., 124
Silva Fuenzalida, Ismael, 1504
Silver, Burton B., 4663
Silverman, David, 1005, 4915
Simard, Jean-Jacques, 5046
Simmel, Edward C., 1122
Simmons, James L., 3609
Simmons, Luiz R., 3583
Simo, Tibor, 2708, 4405
Simon, Bradley A., 400
Simon, Harald, 4542
Simon, Michel, 1766
Simon, Robert L., 4909
Simon, Sidney B., 1400, 5608
Simon, Walter, 4736
Simonen, Leila, 59
Simonton, Dean K., 763
Simonyi, Agnes, 4599
Simpson, Herbert M., 5344
Simpson, John H., 1413, 1454
Simpura, Jussi, 5345
Simuš, P. I., 3942, 4406
Sinclair, Ruth, 392
Singelmann, Peter, 3885
Singer, David L., 5306
Singh, Jasbir S., 2522
Singh, Ram D., 3788
Singh, Vijai P., 2544
Singleton, Royce Jr., 578, 2593, 2675, 3526
Sinkins, T., 2397
Sisson, K., 4734
Sivalingam, G., 540
Sivanandan, A., 3610
Six, Bernd, 566
Sjoberg, Gideon, 5507
Sjørslev, Inger, 4143

Skeldon, Ronald, 3789
Skik, H., 1933, 1934
Skilbeck, Clive, 714
Sklair, Leslie, 1209
Sklar, Richard L., 1319
Skocpol, Theda, 4086
Skolnik, M. L., 4493
Skorupski, John, 1604
Skotko, Vincent P., 942
Skuja, Eric, 621
Skulley, Michael T., 3739
Slaby, Ronald G., 2937
Slade, Kenneth M., 812
Sladetien, Joseleyne, 3527
Ślajfśtajn, Jozef, 2636
Slater, Mariam, 3354
Slater, P. B., 3790
Slater, S. W., 5376
Slavin, B. F., 1341
Slavina, M. A., 1427
Slawski, Edward J., 1996
Śljapentoh, V. Ê., 407
Sloan, J. W., 5109
Slocum, John W., 609
Slocumb, John C., 2880
Słomczyński, Kazimierz M., 4655
Śltahtič, G. P., 1828
Sly, David F., 3664
Smart, Barry, 301
Smart, Carol, 5358, 5359
Smelser, Neil J., 312
Smirnov, S. V., 4890
Smirnov, V. A., 4682
Smith, Anthony D., 2780, 4953
Smith, Clifford T., 2826
Smith, David E., 5316
Smith, Donald E. P., 2287
Smith, Elsie M., 901
Smith, Eugene V., 1087
Smith, Franceska, 2365
Smith, Gilvert, 456
Smith, James E., 3301
Smith, James P., 5674
Smith, Jean R., 805
Smith, Joel, 3655
Smith, Kent W.,489
Smith, Larry J., 2748
Smith, M. P., 5047
Smith, N. A., 4954
Smith, Patrick, 1386
Smith, Peter K., 856
Smith, P. C., 3674
Smith, Robert B., 527
Smith, Thomas E., 3453, 3454
Smith, T. Lynn, 5302
Smith, William P., 584
Smith, W. Rand, 4817
Smithurst, Barry A., 5570
Smock, Andrey Chapman, 3490
Smoljanskij, V. G., 1306
Smout, M. A. H., 4036
Smuraglia, Carlo, 4719

Smythe, Hugh H., 3567
Śniezyński, Marian, 4188
Snizek, William E., 834
Snyder, David, 5016
Snyder, Douglas S., 3582
Snyder, D., 3651
Snyder, Eldon E., 4891
Snyder, Emile, 1348
Snyder, Howard N., 950
Snyder, Mark, 443, 795
Snyders, Georges, 2225
Soares, Orlando, 2201
Soberano, Rawlein G., 3603
Sodei, Takako, 3006
Sodeur, Wolfgang, 1935
Soejatni, 3222
Soen, D., 3586
Sojak, Vladimir, 5238
Sokolova, A. D., 1279
Sokolovic, D., 733
Sokołowska, Magdalena, 3528, 5520,
    5616, 5617
Sokolowski, K., 4444
Solé, Carlota, 2781
Soleye, O. O., 3875
Soljan, Niksa Nikola, 2202
Solla Price, Derek de , 4383
Solomon, Sheldon H., 1216
Solozábal Echevarria, J. J., 4955
Solymosi, Zs., 5675
Somerhausen, Colette, 5418
Somers, Ronald L., 3223
Somlai, P., 1058
Sommer, Robert, 5458
Somogyi, M., 4606
Somoza, Jorge L., 2856, 3044
Soraci, Salvatore, 649
Sørensen, Aage B., 889, 2142, 2523,
Sorensen, Andrew A., 5346
Sørensen, Ole A., 103
Sorge, A., 4720
Sorj, Bernardo, 2802, 3934
sorohova, Ê. V., 683
Sorrentino, Anthony,5419
Sosa Wagner, F., 5466
Soskin, S. N., 2483
Soto-Perez, Hector, 3611
Soubeyrol, J., 5676
Soukup, Gunther, 1412
Souza, Thomas A., 2352
Sowayan, Saad, 3364
Sowell, Thomas, 3587
Sozański, Tadeusz, 387
Spadaro, Robert N., 5110
Spady, Dale R., 3588
Spaeth, Joe L., 4593
Spain, Daphne, 4186
Spanier, Graham B., 3257
Spark, G. M., 3302
Sparling, Cynthia L., 5014
Sparrow, Freddie, 2427
Specht, Harry, 5488, 5655

Spector, Malcolm, 5282
Speier, Hans, 1899
Spencer, Dunstan S. C., 4531
Spencer, Martin E., 313
Spiegel, John, 2333
Spiegel-Rösing, Ina, 4383
Spielmann, Roger, 5262
Spiker, Kathryn S., 1149
Spilerman, Seymour, 4479
Spindler, George, 1307
Spindler, Louise S., 1307, 1363
Spinner, Barry, 1106
Spittler, Gerd, 3791, 3944
Spradley, James P., 1534
Spreitzer, Elmer, 4891
Springer, Philip B., 5280
Squillacciotti, Massimo, 2105
Squires, Gregory M., 2524
Srb, Vladimír, 3046, 3181, 3291
Srinivas, Mysore N.,3977
Sroka, Karolyn R., 950
Sryl'nik, A., 1308
Srzednicki, Jan T.J., 314
Stacey, Margaret, 5638
Stafford, Rebecca, 2525
Stagl, Justin, 1342
Stambouli, F., 3665
Stanback, Thomas M. Jr., 4232
Standing, Guy, 3792
Stang, Hakon, 1638
Stang, Hans J., 5347
Staniszkis, Jadwiga, 1044
Stankov, Lazar, 1170
Stark, Alan E., 652
Stark, G. V., 4451
Stark, Stephen L., 2435
Stark, Werner, 1342
Starke, Frederick A., 1025
Starn, Randolph, 5203
Starnes, Charles E., 2593, 2675
Staroverov, V. I., 3851
Starr, Adaline, 492
Starr, Paul D., 2484, 3604
Stavig, Gordon R., 943
Steadman, Henry J., 57, 1159
Stearns, Mary D., 4070
Stebbins, Robert A., 633, 1940, 2094
Štefaňak, Michal, 4267
Stefanowska, Maɫgorzata, 480
Steger, Hanns-Albert, 1377
Stein, Chana, 971
Stein, Maurice R., 2460
Stein, Peter J., 3355
Steinbuch, Karl, 1900
Steiner, John M., 4956
Steiner, Shari, 2888
Steinglass, Peter, 5348, 5349
Steininger, R., 5079
Steinke, K., 3589
Steinmetz, Julia L., 1103
Steinmetz, Suzanne K., 3455
Steinnes, Donald N., 4189

Steinvorth, Ulrich, 315
Stember, Charles Herbert, 2889
Stent, Madelon D., 2303
Stepanjan, Ė. H., 2637
Stephan, Cookie, 826
Stephan, G. E., 4037
Stephan, Walter G., 961, 1160, 1161
Stephens, Joyce, 4190
Stephenson, G. M., 1932
Stepien, Ewa Gurwik, 801
Sternberg, David J., 93
Sternleib, George, 4089
Steudler, François, 5572
Stevens, John, 5420
Stevenson, H. M., 5198
Stevenson, Paul, 2638
Stewart, Ann H., 1864
Stewart, Cyrus S., 5279
Stewart, James B., 2545
Stewart, J. M., 713
Stewart, Karen R., 3256
Stillman, Peter G., 2833
Stinner, William F., 4038
Stinson, J. G., 457
Stipak, Brian, 4134
Stitt, Christopher L., 1126
Stockbauer, Joseph W., 861
Stockdale, Jerry D., 4407
Stöckli, Alfred,1059
Stoetzel, Antoine, 518
Stoffle, Richard W., 3356
Stohl, Michael, 1498
Stokes, C. Shannon, 3064
Stokes, Randall G., 2739, 3629
Stoljarov, V. I., 4892
Stoljarov, V. V., 2782
Stolzenberg, Ross M., 4532, 4660
Stone, C., 4039
Stonz, Gregory P., 4119, 4853
Stone, Lawrence, 2143
Stone, Walter N., 916
Stosberg, Manfred,410
Stracer, C. J., 3258
Strandell, Harriet, 4533
Strasnick, Steven, 4965
Strasser, Hermann, 316
Stratton, John R., 5455
Strauss, Anselm I, 238
Strautin', A. I., 1309, 2639
Strean, Herbert S., 601
Streeck, Wolfgang, 4772
Streit, Max, 4480
Strelnick, A. H., 3456
Streufert, Siegfried, 2004
Strickland, Lloyd H., 602
Strmiska, Z., 2726, 4268
Strommen, Ellen A., 2939
Strong, Philip, 1107, 2311
Strukov, Ė. V., 1310
Stryker, 603
Strzelecki, Zbigniew, 3793
Stück. H., 4759

Studin, Ira, 2816
Studlar, Donley T., 3740
Stukat, Karl G., 2257
Stumpf, Stephen A., 881
Stutz, Frederick P., 4426
Sryczeń, Marek
Suarez C., Carlos, 2203
Subnjakov, B. P., 5521
Subočev, N. S., 827
Suchner, Robert W., 4648
Suda, Hiroshi, 3457
Sudakov, V. N., 4550
Sudman, Seymour, 858
Suefeld, Peter, 2004
Sufin, Zbigniew, 4465
Sugaki, Yoshito, 4176
Sugar, Bert R., 5393
Sugawara, Hiroe, 3787
Suhonen, Pertti, 59
Suhrke, Astri, 1777
Sukdeo, Fred, 3792
Sukstorf, Steve, 3452
Sułek, Antoni, 144
Sułowski, Boguslaw, 1985
Sullivan, Louis W., 5677
Sullivan,Thomas J., 5565
Summers, David A., 857
Summers, Gene F., 1098
Summers, Worth C., 4843
Sunar, Diane G., 1542
Suolinna, Kirsti, 2820
Suranyi, B., 4571
Surdda, Leoncio, 2890
Surjit Kaur, 3224
Susato, Shigeru, 2485
Suslov, V. Ja, 408, 4481, 4567
Sušnjić, Duro, 1829
Sussman, George D., 5678
Sutherland, Anne, 3590
Sutherland, Neil, 2940
Suttle, J. Lloyd, 4545
Sutton, Stephen, R., 5317
Suzuki, Hiroshi, 674, 3994
Suzuki, Jirô, 2546
Suzuki, Masahito, 409
Svahn, Hans, 4813
Svitič, L. G., 2005
Swanson, Charles H., 1499
Swatos, William H., 1605
Sweet, James A., 3357
Swenson, Ingrid, 3124
Swigert, Victoria L., 5421, 5467
Swindle, Robert E., 4340
Swingle, Paul G., 4921
Sykes, A. J. M., 4311
Sylla, Lanciné, 3652
Symes, John M. D., 119
Sysoeva, L. S., 732
Szabó, Imre, 2783
Szabó, Kálmán, 2852
Szabolcz, U., 1332
Szacka, Barbara, 2732

Szacki, Jerzy, 317
Szakasits, D. György, 4539
Szalai, S., 178
Szamel, Lajos, 4905
Szaniawski, Klemens, 388, 764
Szántó, M., 1311
Szász, Thomas, 1704
Szczepański, Jan, 35
Szczygiel, Aleksander, 5301
Szegö, A., 765, 5059
Szeli, István, 1349
Szentpéteri, I., 5048
Szmatka, Jacek, 930
Sztompka, Piotr, 37, 318
Sztumski, Janusz, 4460
Szulc, Eva, 4296
Szwajkowski, Eugene, 866
Szymanski, Albert, 4312

Taboada-Leonetti, Isabelle, 3666
Tabuteau, B., 3125
Tabutin, Dominique, 3126, 3127
Taft, John, 2353
Taguchi, Masahiro, 1060
Taillard, Christian, 3876
Takahashi, Yoshinori, 319
Takemura, Takahiko, 382
Takeuchi, Ikuo, 152, 1941
Taki, Hirotsugu, 604
Takla, Tendzin N., 1598
Taksás, Imre, 2975
Takuba, Ê. A., 320
Talavera Aldana, Luis Fernando, 4773
Talbert, Joan, 4313
Tallard, Michèle, 4191
Tambovcev,679
Tamura, Norio, 1954, 2006
Tanaka, Yoshiaki, 2449
Tandar, L., 3832
Tange, Ryûichi, 321
Tanke, Elizabeth D., 795
Tannahill, R. Neal, 5017, 5080
Tännsjö, Torbjörn, 1537
Tap, Pierre, 2276
Tapia, Claude, 1736
Tapilina, V. S., 3945
Tapinos, G., 3694
Tapper, Ted, 2404
Tar, Zoltán, 2462
Taranov, A. P., 4269
Tardos, R., 786
Tariska, István, 5618
Tarrago, Mraçal, 4233
Tasillo, Carmelina, 3695
Tassé, R., 5422
Tasseit, Siegfried, 436
Taub, Richard, 4090
Tavčar, Jože, 3877
Taveggia, Thomas C., 184
Tavuchis, Nicholas, 3572
Taylor, Arnold H., 1312
Taylor, Donald M., 3550

Taylor, K. W., 2640
Taylor, Mark C., 1600
Taylor, Michel, 4966
Taylor, Roland L., 2677
Taylor, Steven J., 391
Tayman, Jeft, 3664
Teckenberg, W., 4661
Tedeschi, James T., 605, 848
Tedin, Kent L., 5161
Tedrow, Lucky M., 3165, 4037
Teichman, Meir, 828
Telford, Fred, 4551
Telmon, V., 2204
Tempestini, Attilio, 5081
Tena Artigas, J., 2354
Tentler, Thomas N., 3128
Tepperman, Lorne, 2702
Terdal, Leif G., 1124
Ternon,Yves, 3626
Terranova, Gerald, 3213
Terwindt, Jan G. F., 148
Tesser, Abraham, 704
Tesser, Paul, 4515
Tessler, Richard, 636
Testart, Alain, 1717, 3815
Tezanos, José Félix, 2641
Thebaud, A., 5619
Theias, M. M., 3118
Theodore, Athena, 3343, 3520
Therborn, Göran, 38
Thévenin, Nicole-Edith, 1500
Thiam, H., 2642
Thibault, Laurence, 5468
Thielens, Wagner, Jr., 2450
Thienel, Ingrid, 4223
Thierauf, Robert J., 4341
Thiroux, Jacques P., 1538
Thirsk, Joan, 3906
Thoenig, Jean-Paul, 428
Thoerry, Henk, 5139
Thom, René, 5287
Thomas, Charles W., 5423, 5469, 5470
Thomas, Claudewell S., 1442
Thomas, Darwin, 627
Thomas, John K., 2665
Thomas, Lewis, 5573
Thomas, Rance, 2757
Thomas, R. N., 3794
Thomas, Thomas C., 2205
Thomes, Charles W., 572
Thompson, B., 3225
Thompson, Carel, 737
Thompson, Elizabeth A., 3377
Thompson, E. P., 3906
Thompson, Henrick S., 3588
Thompson, K. W., 1401
Thompson, Victor A., 1061
Thomsen, Hand J., 345
Thomson, A. W. J., 4818
Thomson, Irene Y., 4418
Thomson, Randall, 997
Thorbjørnsen, Lis, 1779

Thorns, David C., 3845, 4120
Thornton, Arland, 2941, 3292
Thuillier, Guy, 3947
Thurlings, J. M. G., 39
Thurn, Hans Peter, 2059
Thurot, J. M., 4893
Tienda, Marta, 3515
Tillion,Germaine, 3529
Tilton, Timothy, 5484
Timaeus, Ernst, 2144
Timofejev, T. T., 2643
Timorsin, M. Z., 1986
Tinti, Giancarlo, 5267
Tinto, Vincent, 4662
Tirasawat, Penporn, 3154
Tiryakian, Edward A., 261
Tiscenko, Ju. R., 622
Tittle, Charles T., 1402, 2486
Tittle, Charles R., 5424
Tjosvold, Dean, 882
Tkacenko, N. B., 1428
Tobin, Sheldon S., 3007, 5679
Toby, Jackson, 2773
Toepfer, Helmuth, 3878
Togeby, Lise, 4638
Tognetti, Keith, 3047
Toiviainen, Seppo, 40
Toki, Hiroshi, 5018
Tolley, H. Dennis, 3116
Tolnai, Gy, 2834
Tomita, Fujio, 2857
Tomita, Yoshiro, 5533
Tomka, Miklós, 1737, 1780, 1781, 2038
Tommy, Joseph L., 3751
Toner, William J., 4217
Tonoki, Norio, 3879
Tonsgaard, O., 3548
Topp, H.D., 2007
Tornatzky, Louis G., 570
Törnblom, Kjell Y., 4314
Torrado, Susana, 2858
Torrance, John, 94
Tosi, Henry L., 1014
Tosquelles, François, 5680
Totani, Osamu, 3457
Toth, D. J., 2727
Toth, I. Z., 993
Toth-Sikora, G., 2703
Touraine, Alain, 766, 1343, 1501, 2733, 2784, 4243
Tournier, P., 5681
Tousijn, Willem, 4615
Townes, Brenda D., 3226
Trabelsi, M., 3795
Tranvouez, Yvon, 1639
Traser, Laszlo, 1515
Trask, Anne E., 2282
Tray, Dennis N. de,3293
Treadway, R. C., 3458
Tréanton, Jean-René, 3889, 3923
Tremblay, Marc-André, 5331
Tress, P. H., 4657

Treu, Eckbert, 4774
Treu, Tiziano, 4721
Treuheit, Leo J., 994
Triesman, David, 3991
Trimiño Vergara, Eddy, 2644
Trindade, Maria Beatriz R., 3675
Tripier, Maryse, 3741
Trocsanyi, László, 4795
Troitzsch, Klaus G., 5187
Trope, Yaacov, 1162
Troskina, V. P., 322
Trow, Donald B., 2676
Trow, M., 2355
Trussell, J., 3109
Truzzi, Marcello, 5280
Trystram, Jean-Paul, 122
Tseng, S. C., 2327
Tsubouchi, Yoshihiro, 3358
Tsuda, Masumi, 4819
Tsukahara, Shûichi, 2295
Tsutsui, Kiyotada, 346
Tucker, C. Jack, 3796
Tucker, Robert C., 5111
Tucker, Robert W., 5239
Tuckett, David, 5574
Tuganova, O. É., 1378
Tulips, James, 714
Tull, Donald, S., 481
Tully, Judy P., 1094
Tuma, Nancy Brandon, 4297
Tümmers, Hannelore, 3259
Tung, Constantine, 2079
Tunstall, Jeremy, 1987
Turgeon, Lynn, 3587
Turgonyi, J., 2728
Turk, Austin T., 1579, 5425
Türk, 1063
Turkington,Don J., 4796
Turner, Bryan S., 323, 2645
Turner, Castellano B., 3601
Turner, Charles F., 734
Turner, Harold W., 1612
Turner,James, 3378
Turner, Jonathan, 324, 5281
Turner, Stephen P., 233, 2526
Turone, Sergio, 4775
Turowski, Gerd, 4838
Turowski, Jan, 4092, 4192
Turuk, G. P., 364
Twaddle, Andrew C., 5620
Twelvetrees, Alan C., 3846
Tyler, Ralph W., 2145
Tyrell, Hartmann, 3379
Tyson, Herbert L. Jr., 1140

Udry, J. Richard, 653, 3227
Uemura, Katsuhiko, 954, 3948
Ugorji, Rex U., 3949
Ukaegbu, Alfred O., 3182, 3183
Ulack, R., 4193
Ulanoff, Stanley M, 1955
Ullmann-Margalit, Edna, 767

Ultee, Wouter C., 1830
Umezawa, Tadashi, 1064
Umino, Michio, 520, 955, 1163
Unger, Roberto M., 1580
Urbani, G., 4776
Urbani, R., 5534
Urbanski, E. S., 3612
Urdanoz, T., 325
Urjupin, A. I., 680
Useem, Michael, 2153
Usui, Wayne M., 3797
Unsitalo, Hannu, 2512
Uyeki, Eugene S., 4194

Vaccarini, Italo, 326, 1313, 1403
Vacha, Edward F., 4845
Vajda, Agnes, 4534
Vajsman, R. S., 931
Valade, Bernard, 1364
Valbuena, Felicisimo, 1901
Valdman, Albert, 1348
Valentej, D. I., 2859
Valentinova, N. G., 4894
Valenzuela, Arturo, 5188
Valk, J. M. M. de, 158
Valkman, Otto, 2060
Vallin, Jacques, 3100, 3106
Valls, Xavier, 4177
Vamos, Vera, 327
Van Aken, Teun, 1429
Van Avermaet, Eddy, 381
Vance, James E. Jr., 4093
Van de Kaa, D.J., 3228
Van den Berghe, Pierre, 917, 2527
Van den Daele, Wolfgang, 1789
Van den Haag, Ernest, 5471
Van der Harst, H. D. H., 3048
Vanderkamp, John, 3760
Vanderleyden, L., 2990
Van der Linden, J. M., 4797
Vander Zanden, James W., 606
Van de Ven, Andrew H., 99
Van Dijk, J.J.M., 1502
Van Doorn, Jacques, 5211
Van Doorn, J.A.A., 1831
Van Dormael, M., 5575
Van Elderen, P.L., 2095
Van Erp, H., 1832
Van Etten, G. M., 5621
Vanfossen, Beth E., 3260
Van Hoof, Jacques J., 4482
Van Houte-Minet, M., 3755
Van Houten, B.C., 179
Van Houten, Donald R., 1023
Vanier, J., 3093
Vanistendael, S., 2860
Van Leeuwen, Louis Theodore, 3359
Van Loon, F., 2990
Van Maanen, John, 4584
Vanneman, Reeve, 2646, 2647
Van Onna, Ben, 2969
Van Parys, P., 365

Van Poppel, F.W.A., 3275
Van Praag, P., 3049, 3050
Vansina, Jan, 1659
Van Stiphout, H.A., 4683
Van Til, Sally B., 5303
Van Ussel, Jos, 4135
Van Valey, Thomas L., 4195
Van Voorden, W., 2398
Van Wieringen, A. M. L., 2358
Vanyai, J., 4419
Varela, Julia, 488
Varga, I., 3742
Varga, Károly, 61, 735, 736
Varma, Baidya Nath, 41,2544
Varma, Paripurnanand, 5426
Varma, Ved P., 2146
Vasconi, Tomas Amadeo, 2648
Vasil'ev, G.G., 440
Vassiliou, George, 918
Vassiliou, Vasso G., 918
Vasudeva, Promila, 2785
Vaszilcov, Sz. I., 2553
Vatin, I.V., 622
Vatuk, Sylvia, 890
Vaughan, Michalina, 5045
Vavakova, B., 2726
Vayda, Andrew P., 5253
Vaz, Edmund W., 1503
Vazquez, V., 5082
Večeřa, Milos, 1582
Večerník, Jiri, 1314
Večerník, Jiri, 2711
Veitch, Russell, 2031
Vekemans, Roger, 1504
Veličko, A.N., 4342
Vellanga, Dorothy D., 3950
Vellinga, Menno, 2600, 4756, 4791
Veltman, Calvin J., 1936
Venditelli, Manlio, 4094
Veneckij, I. G., 2861
Ventimiglia, Joseph C., 1678
Venžer, V. G., 2649
Verba, Sidney, 5164
Verbrugge, Lois M., 829, 2891
Verderber, Kathleen S., 787
Verderber, Rudolph F., 787
Vergati, Stefania, 328
Vergés, Joaquim, 5535
Vergun, V.A., 2737
Verhargen, B., 62
Verigat, José, 329
Vernier, Bernard, 3303
Vernon, Magdalen D., 688
Veron, Jacques, 3139, 3229
Veyne, Paul, 4991
Vickers, Geoffrey, 1315
Vickrey, William, 768
Victor, Michael I., 5427
Victoroff, David, 1948
Vidal, Daniel, 3129
Vidal, Vivian, 3833
Vidart, Daniel D., 3816

Vieillescazes, F., 5231
Vigderhous, G., 519
Vigneron, Paul, 1672
Vignolle, Jean-Pierre, 5053
Viguier, Marie-Claire, 500
Viikari, Matti, 5334
Villani, A., 4234
Villemez, Wayne J.ù 3530, 4663, 5424
Vilmos, J., 2528
Vilquin, Eric, 2862
Vinciguerra, Maria Enrica, 2453
Vinegar, Richard J., 2034
Vink, N., 1505
Vinokur, Amiram, 1116
Vinokur, Annie, 2359
Vinokur-Kaplan, 3230
Vinovkis, Maris, 3052
Viotto, Piero, 2428
Višnevskij, I.B., 5522
Vitányi, Ivána, 1539; 1833
Vítečkova, Jana, 1314
Vobruba, Georg, 4253
Vogel, David, 4310
Vogel, Ulrike, 330, 1430
Vohra, H. R., 3184
Voigt, David Q., 4896
Voigt, Dieter, 1200, 4895, 4897
Voigt, Vilmas, 1187, 1865
Voisin, Michel, 1654
Völgyes, Ivan, 5232
Volpi, Claudio, 4851
Voronkov, I.M., 4452
Voronov, V.V., 4445
Vörös, K., 2734
Vorožejkin, I. F., 2650
Vrga, Djuro J., 3261
Vries, John de, 1937, 4626
Vrigham, John C., 597
Vromen, Suzamme Donner, 2786, 2833
Vronskij, G. T., 623, 1316
Vuillemez, W. J., 4664
Vuillemin, Jules, 2904

Wachtler, Joel, 3575
Wackman, Daniel B., 4440
Wade, Richard C., 4096
Wadhera, Kiron, 4535
Wagenheim, Kal, 3594
Wahba, Mahmoud A., 371
Wait, Robert F., 3430
Waite, Linda J., 4532
Wakil, F. P., 3294
Wakil, S. P., 3294
Walaszek, Zdzisława, 1076
Wald, Henri, 1834
Walker, Kenneth F., 4722
Walker, Monica A., 5430
Walker, Scheila S., 1664
Wall, Richard, 2881
Wall, Toby, 4820
Wallace, William A., 4200
Waller, Jerome H., 3459

Waller, Manfred, 839
Wallerstein, Immanuel, 4254
Wallis, Roy, 1724
Walsh, Nancy A., 830
Walsh, R. Patricia, 1692
Walter, E. V., 4196
Walter, Just, 2704
Walton, Jack, 2429
Walton, John, 3991, 4083
Walvin, James, 2536
Wandersman, A., 331
Wankel, Leonard M., 737
Ward, P., 4197
Ward, Russell A., 956
Ward, Scott, 4446
Wardwell, John M., 3978
Ware, Helen, 3185, 3196, 3231
Warner, Malcolm, 4743
Warner, R. Stephen, 312
Warner, Richard W., 901
Warren, Carol A. B., 42
Warren, Steven, F., 1138
Warring, Louise J., 1095
Wartella, Ellen, 4446
Warwick, Donald , 5049
Wasburn, Philo C., 2942
Wasilewski, Rainer, 410
Wasserman, Stanley S., 548
Watanabe, Motoki, 2787
Watanabe, Sakae, 3951
Watanabe, Shin'ichi, 2206
Watanabe, Yoshitomo, 1988
Watanuki, Joji, 5204, 5245
Waterson, Karolyn, 1077
Watkins, Don O., 3614
Watlington-Linares, Francisco, 3880
Watson, Geoffrey G., 4898
Watson, Roy E.L., 180
Watts, W. David, 5460
Watzlawick, Paul, 1902
Waxer, Peter H., 919
Waxman, Jerry L., 2008
Webb, Stephen D., 5350
Weber, Eugen, 3952
Weber, Ouri, 4408
Weber, Silke, 2226
Weber-Jobé, Monique, 4447
Weber-Kellermann, Ingeborg, 3360
Webstr, Murray, Jr., 831
Wechsler, Henry, 5556
Wedderburn, Kenneth W., 4723
Wedow, Suzanne, 4874
Weede, Erich, 528, 5165
Weekes-Vagliani, Winifred, 3460
Wehman, Paul, 1091
Weidig, Rudi, 2578
Weigert, Andrew J., 627, 654
Weinberg, Martin S., 3262
Weinberg, Richard A., 3329
Weinberger, Philip, 34
Weiner, Bernard, 864
Weiner, Eugene, 2102

Weingart, Peter, 1812, 1835
Weingrod, Alex, 2705
Weinrich, Helen, 3531
Weinstein, Deena, 43
Weinstein, Michael A., 43
Weinstein, R. M., 5639
Weir, D., 4821
Weir, Mary, 4594
Weis, Kurt, 4873
Wiesberg, Carole, 334
Weisberg, Herbert F., 458
Weiss, Johannes, 215
Weiss, Shirley F., 3835
Weisser, Michael R., 3953
Weisz, George, 2360
Weitzel-O'Neill, P.A., 2882
Weizenbaum, Joseph, 126
Weller, Robert H., 3461
Wellman, David T., 3730
Wells, Alan, 1317
Wells, G.A., 1914
Wells, G. L., 383
Wells, JohnR., 4448
Wells, L. Edward, 5327
Welly-Bandara-Sazra, A., 2835
Welton, John, 2429
Wendt, Wolfgang, 5114
Wendzel, Robert L., 5240
Wen-Hsiung, Li, 2905
Werbik, Hans, 1882
Werblan, Andrzej, 4270
Werneke, Diane, 4483
Werner, Jana C., 5022
Wesołowski, Włodzimierz, 4655
Wessel, Andrew E., 136
West, Charles K., 705
West, J.P., 5109
West, Philip T., 2435
Westacott, George H., 832
Westby, David L., 2361
Westergaard, John, 2651
Westhues, Kenneth, 1650
Westoff, Charles ü., 3232
Weston, J., 2101
Weston, Louise C., 1104
Westphal, Heinz, 2976
Wexley, Kenneth N., 4552
Weyl, Robert, 3581
Whatley, Arthur A., 4553
Wheat, Leonard F., 4041
Wheeler, Alan C., 5013, 5014
Wheeler, Christopher, 4692
Wheeler, Ladd, 2892
Wheeler, Michael, 1188
Whincup, Michael H., 4733
Whisenand, Paul M., 5472
Whitaker, Roger, 3935
White, Douglas J., 769
White, Gordon, 2652
White, L.C., 1677
White, Lynn, 1101
White, Peter R., 4427

Whitehead Antonia, 3263
Whitelaw, J.S., 3774
Whiting, Beatrice, 2943
Whiting, John, 2943
Whitley, Ricgard, 1065, 1812
Whitman,Roy M., 916
Whitmore, G.A., 550
Whittaker, Elvi, 1534
Whitten, Phillip, 1231
Whyte, Marting K., 2487
Whyte, William F., 2836
Wiarda, Howard J., 4777
Wiatr, Jerzy J., 5190
Wickelgren, Wayne A., 706
Wicks, Robert J., 5351
Wieder, D. Lawrence, 5282
Wieting, Stephen G., 3361
Wigand, Rolf T., 1066, 2025
Wigham, Eric L., 4798
Wild, Ray, 4498
Wilde, Alexander W., 1763
Wilder, David A., 967
Wilding, Paul, 5486
Wildman,Richard C., 482
Wiles, Paul, 1550, 5360
Wiley, Norbert, 4243
Wilhelm, Klaus, 4639
Wilke, Arthur S., 3362
Wilke, George, 3881
Wilkie, Mary E., 3743
Wilkinson, Doris Y., 2677, 5428
Willaime, Jean-Paul, 373, 1640
Willems, J. G. L. M., 4384
Willenborg, John F., 4136
Williams, Ederyn, 2036
Williams, Gregory, 4665
Williams, John E., 1164
Williams, J., 572
Williams, Lawrence K., 832
Williams, Michael, 5004
Williams, Phillip, 2146
Williams, Raymond, 3954
Williams, Restee, 1165
Williamson, John B., 411, 5523
Williamson, Nancy E., 2893
Willke, Helmut, 1506, 1554, 2478
Willmot, Peter, 44
Willmuth, Sidney, 1344
Wilpert, Bernhard, 1085
Wilson, Alan Geoffrey, 2853
Wilson, Bryan R., 1782, 3380
Wilson, David W., 5029
Wilson, F., 3676
Wilson, H. T., 1836
Wilson, John, 1507
Wilson, Midge, 814
Wilson, Pauline, 149
Wilson, Robert C., 2451
Wilson, William A., 2107
Wilterdink, N., 2906
Windahl, Swen, 1981
Wingen, M., 4198

Winter, David G., 3320
Winter, G., 4343
Winter, Herbert R., 4907
Winter, Jerry A., 1606
Winter, J.M., 3053
Winwood, M. G., 2788
Winzeler,Robert L., 3627
Wippler, R., 1111
Wisan, Gail, 95
Wiseman,Nelson, 2640
Wish, Eric, 1490
Wish, Myron, 788
Wiswede, Günter, 1431
Withers, Glenn A., 4778
Withey, Stephen B., 4286
Witjes, Claus W., 293
Witt, Paul W. F., 2418
Wittmayer Baron, Salo, 1783
Włodarski, Wledzimierz, 4525
Wnuk-Lipinski, Edmund,4595, 4846
Wober, Mallory, 5317
Wodarski, John S., 1451
Woesler,Christine, 4616
Wofford, Jerry C., 1067
Wohl, Andrzej, 4899
Wöhlcke, Manfred, 3381
Wojcicki, Sandra B., 1127
Wojciechowska, Anita, 1318
Wölck, Wolfgang, 1866
Wolf, Charles P., 394
Wolf, Sharon, 5030
Wolfelsperger, Alain,63
Wolfenstein, Eugene V., 3653
Wolff, Janet, 2061
Wolff, Robert P., 1583
Wolff, Stephan, 770
Wolfmeyer, Peter, 4654
Wolfson, Pichael R., 444
Wollenberg, Charles, 2227
Wolowyna, O., 3038
Wolters, W. G., 2653
Won, George, 3462
Wood, Charles H., 3463
Wood, Stephen, 4724
Woodman, William F., 932
Woods, Peter, 2147
Woodsiede, Arch G., 4428
Woodtli, O., 2977
Woodward, C. A., 5083
Wooleybiggart, Nicole, 1068
Wootton, A. J., 933
Worchel, Stephen, 862
Works, John A.Jr., 1695
Worton, Stanley N., 3054
Wössner, Jakobus, 1607
Wright, David, 2536
Wright, Erik Olin, 2654
Wright, Gerald, Jr., 5191
Wright, Robert G., 1069
Wrigley, Jack, 2427
Wrong, Dennis H., 45
Wuthnow, Robert, 2228

Wyer, Robert S. Jr., 968, 1108
Wynnyczuk, V., 2863

Yagi, Tadashi, 19
Yago, Glenn, 2837
Yahya, Khawla A., 2938
Yajima, Tsuneuiki, 2546
Yamada, Keiichi, 2295
Yamagishi, Takeshi, 3995, 3996
Yamaguchi, Hiromitsu, 4137
Yamamoto, Shizuo, 96
Yamamura, Douglas, 3462
Yamashita, Kesao, 5524
Yandell, Ben, 1141
Yang, Choon, 3462
Yanov, A., 883
Yardley, Alice, 2272
Yasin, Mohammad, 3166
Yasuda, Saburô, 520
Yasuda, Takashi, 1837
Yatani, Yoshikuni, 1903
Yazawa, Shujiro, 4684, 5254
Yellowitz, Irwin, 4779
Yeo, Stephen, 1004
Yeomans, Keith, 1532
Yinger, J. Milton, 5019
Yoels, William C., 4119
Yokoyama, Minoru, 3094
Yonezawa, Kasuhiko, 129, 4686
Yorburg, Betty, 3468
Yorimitsu, Masatoshi, 3882
Yosha, Andrew, 1223
Yoshida, Hiroshi, 366
Young, Ann, 1508
Young, Crawford, 1319
Young, L. C., 1784
Young, Philip A., 2655
Young, Rosalie F., 2894
Young, Ruth C., 3962
Young, T. R., 97
Youssef, N., 3494
Yu, Elena S.H., 3382, 3505
Yu, Frederick T. C., 1967
Yukl, Gary A., 4552

Zafiropoulos, M., 2294
Zaharov, V. I., 1432
Zajceva, Ê. V., 4992
Zald, Mayer N., 4760
Zaleski, Janusz, 4436
Zaltman, Gerald, 2207, 2789
Zander, Alvin, 969
Zängle, MIchael, 1097
Zanna, Mark P., 707, 1148
Zaslavskaia, T.I., 3852, 3883
Zaslavsky, V., 98

Zavtur, A. A., 2488
Zawodzinski, Stefan, 5060
Zbarskij, M. I., 4577
Zborilova, Jitka, 3130, 5368
Zborovskij, G. E.G 1320
Zdep, S. M., 483
Zdravomyslov, A. G., 332
Zehr, Howard, 5429
Zeidenstein, George, 2864
Zeira, Yoram, 4327, 4691
Zelezko, S. N., 447, 4484, 4685
Zembaty, Jane S., 1529
Zenkin, S. N., 681
Zentner, Joseph L., 5323
Zerkin, D. P., 4271
Zermeño Garcia, Sergio, 4993
Zerubavel, Ebiatar, 416
Zich, Frantisek, 441, 2559
Ziégler, Jean, 3131
Ziegler, Robert G., 682
Ziegler, Rolf, 378
Ziffo, P. M., 934
Zillmann, Dofl, 715
Zimbalist, Sidney E., 4315
Zimmerman, Carle C., 2895
Zimmerman, Donald H., 5282
Zimmerman, Ekkart, 1509, 5255
Zimmerman, Gordon I., 1938
Zimmerman, Siu, 5282
Zinov'eva, R. A., 3798
Ziolkowski, Marek, 1321
Zivanov, S., 2656
Zlate, Camelia, 4847
Zlotnikov, R. A., 4385
Zorrilla Castresana, Restituto, 1510
Zotova, O. I., 683
Zuberi, Habib A., 4472
Zucker, Lynne G., 448, 1322
Zucker, Martine, 3083
Zuckerman, MIron, 1165, 1223
Zukerman, Alan S., 5192
Zukin, Clift, 1956
Zukin, Sharon, 1323
Zukova, N. B., 4686
Zulke, Frank, 46
Zündorf, Lutz, 995
Zupancic, Beno, 4687
Zuralev, G. F., 4344
Zuravlev, G. J., 1210
Zurcher, Louis A. Jr., 3264, 5233
Zurfluh, Jean, 490
Zvirbulis, Ju, Ja., 738
Zylberberg, Jacques, 4994

SUBJECT INDEX

Abortion, 3193, 3201, 3205, 3216, 3223, 3225
Abramowski, Edward, 3888
Absenteeism, 4602, 4605, 4606
Academic achievement, *use* Academic success
Academic administration, 2148, 2178, 2189, 2201, 2206, 2453
Academic aptitude, 2411, 2413
Academic freedom, 2182
Academic profession, 2433, 2440
Academic success, 2288, 2405, 2406, 2409, 2414
Access to education, 2208, 2216, 2221, 2224-2226
Acculturation, 1365, 1366, 1369, 1372, 1373, 1377
Achievement, 734
Achievement motivation, 735, 736
Action, 244, 745, 754, 756, 760, 761, 763, 765, 766, 887
Action research, 99, 100, 102, 587
Actionalism, 766, 5084
Administrative science, 4905
Adolescence, 2953, 2964
Adolescent, 624, 627, 893, 898, 1365, 2948, 2951, 2952, 2963, 2966, 2970, 2971, 3637, 5143, 5154
Adorno, Th. W., 311
Adult, 2957, 2980, 2981
Adult age, 2979
Adult education, 2219, 2362, 2365, 2366, 2372, 2375-2377, 2382, 2387-2390, 2394-2396
Advertising, 1942-1946, 1948, 1949, 1951, 1955, 1956
Aesthetics, 2029, 2048, 2049, 2057, 2059, 5522
Affectivity, 843
Affiliation motive, 828
Affinity, 715, 1142
Affluent society, 2607, 4307

Afghanistan, village, 3859, 3878
Africa
  acculturation, 1366
  army, 5220
  bibliography, 3468
  child, 2935
  Church : 1641; and State, 1758
  conflict, 868

cultural identification, 1345
divorce, 3287
educational system, 2150, 2158
elite, 2609
ethnocentrism, 1167
family planning, 3196
fertility, 3147
fertility rate, 3132
higher education, 2309
infant mortality, 3132
interethnic relations, 3624
internal migration, 3745, 3784
international relations, 1345
juvenile delinquency, 5396
law, 1541
migration, 3654
monarchy, 4958
mortality, 3096
Moslem, 1625
one party system, 3652
politics, 1758
population evolution, 3023, 3039
primitive religion, 1613, 1617
racial discrimination, 2591
religious revival, 1772
rural development, 3976
rural migration, 3756
rural society, 3896
science, 2403
sculpture, 2083
sect, 1659
slavery, 2530, 2534, 2535, 2540, 2541
social change, 1617
social class, 2591
symbol, 1897
technical education, 2403
tribalism, 1417, 3652
urban life, 4128
violence, 4128
way od life, 1288
woman's status, 3467, 3481, 3493
Age, 4532, 5249
Age difference, 2910
Aged, 2982, 2985, 2988, 2990, 2993, 2997-2999, 3004, 3006, 3007, 3259, 5382, 5679
Ageing, 956, 2986, 2989, 2995, 3002, 3005
Ager, Waldemar, 1384
Aggression, 841, 843, 845, 847-854, 1222, 2016

Aggressiveness, 846, 856
Agrarian reform, 3955, 3956, 3967, 3975
Agricultural cooperative, 4387, 4392,
    4395, 4399, 4405
Agricultural development, 2493, 4394,
    4402, 4403
Agricultural economics, 4389, 4396,
    4397, 4401
Agricultural enterprise, 4388
Agricultural population, 3061
Agricultural production, 4398
Agricultural worker, 3937, 4767
Agriculture, 3035, 4393, 4400, 4404,
    4407
Albania, press, 2007
Alcoholism, 5304, 5315, 5320, 5322,
    5324, 5329, 5331, 5334, 5337, 5340,
    5344, 5345, 5348
Algeria
  agrarian reform, 3964
  emigration, 3693, 3869
  health, 5619
  infant mortality, 3127
  mortality, 3106, 3126
  nomadism , 3778
  social class, 2605
  town, 4066
  village, 3866, 3869
Algorithm, 498
Alienation, 1440, 1442, 1450, 1457,
    1461, 1464, 1473, 1479, 1482, 1487,
    1500, 2496, 4824, 5151
Althusser, Louis, 219, 222, 301
Ambition, 727
Anarchism, 302, 4924, 4926, 4930, 4948
Anarchy, 4966
Anomia, 1436, 1447
Anomie, 1439, 1483
Antisemitism, 3642, 3643
Antisocial behaviour, 1451, 1462
Anxiety, 646, 713
Apartheid, 3635
Applied sociology, 5261, 5263
Apprentice, 4680
Architecture, 2080, 2081
Argentina
  internal migration, 3790
  nationalism, 2575
  social class, 2575
  student movement, 2351
  woman's status, 3492
Aristocracy, 4957
Arms race, 5256, 5257
Army, 3632, 5207, 5208, 5212, 5213,
    5220, 5227
Arrow, 4295
Art, 2042, 2044, 2046, 2047, 2050, 2051,
    2053, 2055, 2077
Asia
  cross cultural analysis, 2946
  educational planning, 2170
  family planning, 3209

farmer, 3936
fertility, 3139
higher education, 2325
military, 5229
rural migration, 3782
slum, 4161
social planning, 5514
traditional society, 2812
woman's status, 3477
youth, 2946
Aspiration, 721, 725, 726
Assassination, *see* Homicide
Assistance, 1100
Asylum, 2990
Atheism, 1697, 1699
Attitude, 1109, 1110, 1123, 1127,
    1129, 1131, 1140, 1141, 1175,
    1512, 4501
Attitude change, 704, 1115, 1116,
    1130, 1136, 1145
Attitude scale, 561, 562, 564, 566,
    567, 570-572
Attitude to work, 1019, 3312, 4578,
    4579, 4581, 4586, 4587, 4593
Audience, 1941, 2060
Audience analysis, 1939
Audio visual material, 2394, 2431,
    2432
Australia
  coloured person, 3602
  female labour, 3185
  fertility, 3185
  handicraft, 4422
  housing, 4158
  immigrant, 3733
  immigration, 3739
  internal migration, 3774
  mass communication, 1971
  nomadism, 3777
  occupation, 2669
  population policy, 3220
  population settlement, 3829
  poverty, 5291, 5295
  ruling class, 2680
  social origina, 2669
  sociology of development, 2829
  sport, 4879
  theft, 5373
  town planning, 4231
  urbanization, 4033
  wife, 3316
  woman's rights, 3484
Austria
  anarchism, 4926
  housing, 4150
  national minority, 3561
  research, 94
  social structure, 2471
Authoritarian leadership, 1090
Authority, 302, 1070-1073, 1076,
    1077
Automation, 4357

Automobile, 4425
Avoidance, 844

Bahrain
  foreign worker, 4473
  labour market, 4473
Ball, Donald W., 180
Bangladesh
  fertility, 3145
  infant mortality, 3110, 3124
  kinship, 3369
  woman worker, 4502
Bank, 4453
Barbados
  family, 3356
  fertility, 3158
Bargaining, 871, 872, 874, 879, 881,
  1005
Basic education, 2373
Battaglia, Felice, 174
Baudelot, 2225
Becker, Ernest, 282
Behaviour, 1111, 1112-1114, 1117-1122,
  1124-1126, 1128, 1132, 1133, 1134,
  1135, 1137-1139, 1180, 1305, 1396,
  2037
Behaviour in group, 958, 960, 1091
Behavioural sciences, 21
Behaviourism, 249, 266, 331
Belgium
  divorce, 3279
  housing policy, 4164
  industrialization, 4410
  interethnic relations, 3623
  internal migration, 3755
  juvenile delinquency, 5418
  manager, 4697
  political party, 5076
  population equilibrium, 3049
  religious community, 1654
  social medicine, 5575
  social policy, 5515
  vocational training, 4627
  workers' committee, 4746
  working population, 4410
  working time, 4568
Belief, 1696, 1698
Benin, illiteracy, 2383
Berger, Peter L., 1593
Bernard, Claude, 261
Bibliography, 89, 137, 138, 140, 141,
  143, 144, 271, 739, 1612, 1637,
  2112, 2128, 2193, 2206, 3191, 3344,
  3468, 3470, 3727, 4002, 4012, 4160,
  4170, 4806, 5082, 5087, 5135, 5357,
  5530
Bilingualism, 701, 1915, 1925, 1933,
  1934
Biography, 159, 161, 162, 164-166, 172,
  176, 178, 180
Biological family, *see* Nuclear family

Birth control, 1674, 3187, 3194,
  3198, 3210, 3214, 3222, 3226,
  3229
Birth interval, 3163
Birth rate, 3161, 3168
Birth spacing, 3204, 3213
Bloch, Ernst, 236
Bloch, Herman D., 167
Bolivia
  elite, 3909
  farmer, 3932
  fertility, 3135
  political party, 5063
  population density, 3044
  rural environment, 3909
Bonengant, Jean-Charles, 168
Book, 480
Booth, Charles, 159
Botswana
  developing country, 3973
  political culture, 5156
  rural development, 3972
Boudon, R., 557
Boulding, Kenneth, E., 297
Bouman, P.J., 177, 179
Bourdieu, Pierre, 2225
Bourgeois sociology, 205, 322, 2636
Bourgeoisie, 726, 1474, 2557, 2642,
  4982
Boy, 2960
Brain drain, 3681, 3682, 3685, 3689
Brazil
  academic administration, 2201
  academic freedom, 2182
  agriculture, 3035
  bibliography, 3470
  birth rate, 3168
  changing society, 2805
  coloured person, 3594
  communication, 1886
  consumption, 4448
  continuing education, 2363
  death rate, 3115
  economic development, 4272
  elections, 5180
  elite, 2679
  emigrant, 3688
  extended family, 3335
  family planning, 3169
  farmer, 5180
  fertility, 3176
  higher education, 2316
  immigrant assimilation, 3737
  immigration, 3720
  indian, 3595, 3596
  industrialization, 4409
  internal migration, 3790
  marginality, 1486, 4181
  mortality, 3098
  national development, 2679
  negro, 3600
  novel, 2071

Brazil *[contd]*
  political modernization, 4981
  population evolution, 3031, 3035
  public health, 5583
  religious syncretism, 1702
  rural life, 3895
  rural migration, 3775
  rural society, 2805
  slum, 4181
  social worker, 5671
  television, 2028
  town, 4062, 4409
  urban growth, 4005
  urban society, 1486
  woman's status, 3470
Brecht, Arnold, 166
British Guinea, caste, 2543
Broadcast, 2019, 2039
Broadcasting, *see* Radio
Brotherhood, 1651
Buddhism, 1621
Budget, 4454
Bulgaria
  cultural dynamics, 1360
  population growth, 3026
  population policy, 3026
  rural society, 3940
  value system, 3940
  village, 3870
  youth, 3940
Bureaucracy, 1006, 1017, 1023, 1029,
    1036, 1037, 1051, 1052, 1056, 1058,
    1061
Bureaucratic control, 1009, 1011, 1020,
    1021, 1025, 1031, 1035, 1041, 1046,
    1050, 1057, 1059, 1066, 1067
Bureaucratic organization, *see* Bureau-
    cracy
Bureaucratization, 1043, 1045, 5632
Burke, Kenneth, 294
Burundi, child, 2917
Business community, 4328
Business economics, 4317
Business management, 4327

Cameroon
  family group, 3416
  family life, 3460
  population settlement, 3832
  town, 4058
Canada
  academic success, 2409
  adult education, 2366
  agricultural production, 4398
  alcoholism, 5320, 5344
  child, 2940
  culture pattern, 1249
  delinquent, 5439
  electoral sociology, 5175
  elite, 2680, 2702
  emigration, 3684
  employment, 4490

  ethnic group, 1003, 3578
  ethnicity, 3546
  family, 3294, 3334, 5673
  family planning, 3192
  fertility, 3141
  health service, 5627
  higher education, 2314
  homicide, 5367
  housing, 4159
  housing policy, 4138
  illiteracy, 2371
  immigrant, 3713
  immigrant assimilation, 3716
  immigration, 3714, 3715, 3735
  indian, 3593
  intellectual development, 2408
  interethnic relations, 3623
  internal migration, 3749
  labour migration, 3760
  legislative behaviour, 5158
  library, 145
  manager, 4694, 4703
  marriage, 3192, 3294
  middle class, 5062
  nationalism, 4935
  occupation, 2669, 4614
  occupational mobility, 4631
  occupational prestige, 4626, 4632
    4636
  old age, 3003
  party system, 5061
  political culture, 5132, 5158
  political education, 2399
  political party, 5083
  political socialization, 5142
  politicization, 5137
  population pyramid, 2907
  population settlement, 3830
  racial segregation, 4141
  refugee, 3712
  religious institution, 1650
  residential segregation, 4141
  rural development, 3958
  social class, 2627
  social mobility, 2709
  social origin, 2669
  social security, 5528
  social service, 5673
  social worker, 5647
  sociology of development, 2797,
    2824
  sport, 4864
  suicide, 5391
  teacher, 2445
  trade union, 5132
  trade unionism, 4748
  university, 2338
  urban structure, 4009
  verbal behaviour, 1936
  white, 3593
  woman's status, 3472, 3480
  youth, 5142

Capital city, 4045, 4064, 4088
Capital market, *see* Stock market
Capital punishment, 5446, 5457, 5464, 5468
Capitalism, 310, 2053, 3431, 3921, 4241-4245, 4247-4250, 4252-4254, 4361, 4916, 4929, 4993
Career, *see* Occupation
Case study, 2586, 3183, 3225
Casework, 5542
Caste, 2537, 2542-2544, 2546, 2566
Catholic, 1627, 1628
Catholicism, 1639
Causal analysis, 429, 433
Causal explanation, 377, 379, 380, 429, 3255
Causal inference, 376, 381, 382
Causality, 378, 383
Censorship, 4995
Central government, 5050
Centralization, 385
Ceremonial, *see* Rite
Ceremony, 1042, 1691, 1693
Chad, child, 2911
Changing society, 2374, 2505, 2801, 2805, 2811, 2821, 4114
Character, 675
Charisma, 1074, 1075
Child, 2927, 2928, 2930, 2932, 2934, 2935, 2936, 2938, 2940-2943, 5162
Child adoption, 3395, 3396, 3406, 3429
Child development, 2912, 2916, 2918, 2919, 2926, 2929, 2933, 2937, 2939, 3388
Childhood, 1184, 1490, 2923
Child rearing, 2915
Chile
  agrarian reform, 3967
  Church and State, 1760
  civilization, 1267, 1295
  class struggle, 2648
  education, 2648
  educational system, 2198
  elections, 5188
  housing policy, 4162
  political participation, 5188
  rural environment, 3892
  rural society, 3885
  urbanization, 4035
China
  civilization, 1250
  class conflict, 2599
  consumption, 4433
  educational policy, 2169
  family, 3342
  food habits, 1511
  health, 5582
  housing, 3382
  immigrant, 3372
  kinship, 3372, 3382
  literacy criticism, 2077
  marriage, 3273

  rural development, 3970
  sex, 3382
  sex differentiation, 3273
  social class, 2652
  social structure, 2488
  sociology of literature, 2079
  university, 2320
  woman's rights, 3483, 3505
  woman's status, 3482, 3527
  worker, 4667
  working conditions, 4556
  working place, 4667
Ch'iu-pai, Ch'ü, 2077
Christianity, 1637
Christianization, 1676
Church, 1641-1644, 1648
Church and State, 1675, 1738-1746, 1749, 1751-1753, 1758, 1761, 1763, 1764, 1766-1769, 1773, 1775, 1777-1779, 1783
Church attendance, *see* Religious practice
Church hierarchy, 1670
Cinema, 2009, 2011, 2012, 2014, 2015
City, *see* Town
Civic education, 2400
Civil law, 1544
Civil liberties, *see* Human rights
Civil servant, 5034, 5040
Civil service, 5033, 5038, 5045
Civilization, 1250, 1267, 1292, 1295, 1315
Civism, 2942
Clan, 3363, 3366
Class, *see* Social class
Class conflict, 2549, 2551, 2562, 2599, 4764, 5425
Class consciousness, 2586, 2595, 2600, 2607, 2622
Class differentiation, 2635, 2649, 4437, 4898
Class structure, 2554, 2559, 2563, 2578, 2589, 2594, 2607, 2610, 2612, 2624, 2630, 2634, 2636
Class struggle, 1196, 2225, 2498, 2547, 2556, 2572, 2577, 2580, 2582, 2594, 2621, 2623, 2626, 2648, 3540, 3803, 4245, 4783
Class value, 2593, 2645
Classification, 368
Classroom, 2287
Clergy, 1671, 1672
Clinical psychology, 585
Clothing, 1513
Coalition, 863-867
Cognition, 686-688, 690, 691, 697, 698, 704
Cognitive dissonance, 725, 726, 1145, 1146, 1148, 1153, 1160
Cohort, 2908
Collective agreement, 4810, 4818, 4821

Collective bargaining, 4799-4806
Collective behaviour, 797, 1217
Collective consciousness, 1214
Collective farm, 4386, 4390, 4391,
    4406, 4408
Colombia
  Church and State, 1763
  contraception, 3207
  ecology, 3816
  educational planning, 2203
  educational system, 2161
  exodus, 3678
  external migration, 3667
  fertility, 3174
  higher education, 2310
  marginal man, 1476
  negro, 3606
  politics, 1763
  population density, 3037
  protestant Church, 1643
  social security, 5525
  theatre, 2098
  town planning, 4210
  urban growth, 4005
Coloured person, 3594, 3602, 3603,5100
Commercial worker, 2728, 4689
Communication, 773, 775, 780, 781,787,
    788, 1020, 1031, 1055, 1066, 1067,
    1172, 1280, 1868-1870, 1872, 1874,
    1876, 1878, 1880-1890, 1892-1894,
    1896, 1900-1902
Communication code, 1873
Communication network, 886, 1898
Communication theory, *see* Information
    theory
Communism, 4933
Community, 141, 1408, 2788, 3835,3838-
    3841, 3843, 3845, 3847, 5340
Community development, 3834, 3836,3837,
    3842, 3846, 5538
Community participation, 3844
Commuting, 3773, 3794
Comparative analysis, 419, 427, 3848
Competition, 4452
Complex organization, 996-999, 1003,
    1004
Compulsory education, 2236
Computer, 120-126
Comte, Auguste, 225, 281, 322
Concept, 215
Conference, 1708, 2846
Conflict, 868, 869, 870, 875, 877, 878,
    880, 882, 883, 1454, 1475, 1666
Conflict resolution, 873, 876
Conformism, 1168
Congruity model, 1162
Consensus, 772, 1180, 1218, 1454
Consumer, 4429, 4430, 4439, 4442, 4446,
    4447
Consumer behaviour, 4428, 4431, 4434,
    4438, 4441, 4443

Consumption, 4432, 4433, 4435-4437,
    4444, 4448
Content analysis, 417, 418, 420, 421
Contextual analysis, 3500
Continuing education, 2363, 2367-
    2369, 2379-2381, 2392, 2393,
    2397, 2398, 2402
Contraception, 3199, 3207, 3217,
    3232
Contraceptive method, 3212
Cooperative, 4321, 4344
Cooperative system, 4251
Corporatism, 4777
Correlation, 523, 525-527
Costa Rica, population evolution,
    3033
Coup d'Etat, 5198
Court, 5023, 5024, 5029, 5470
Creativity, 702, 739,740, 747,
    755, 757, 2139
Crime, 1475, 5362, 5363, 5369,
    5370, 5375, 5377, 5380, 5382,
    5387, 5389, 5400, 5401, 5404,
    5406, 5409, 5419, 5427
Criminal, *see* Delinquent
Criminal law, *see* Penal law
Criminal sociology, 5360
Criminality, *see* Delinquency
Criminology, 140, 5352-5359
Cross-cultural analysis, 422, 1107,
    2945, 2946, 2953, 3315, 5316,
    5354
Cross-national analysis, 627, 1370,
    1481, 1542, 2537, 3339, 3848,
    4960, 5152, 5395
Crowd, 1211-1213, 1215, 1216, 1218-
    1223, 2719
Cuba
  agricultural cooperative, 4395
  economic development, 4284
  educational system, 2181
  political party, 5063
  population settlement, 3833
  slavery, 2532
  working class, 2644
Cult, 1680, 1685, 1689, 1692
Cultural anthropology, *see* Social
    and cultural anthropology
Cultural conflict, 1370
Cultural crisis, 1353, 1364, 1379
Cultural differentiation, 701,1304,
    1322
Cultural diffusion, 1351, 1354
Cultural dynamics, 1350, 1356,1360-
    1362
Cultural environment, 1299
Cultural heritage, 557
Cultural history, 1359
Cultural identification, 1345,1346,
    1348
Cultural integration, 1347
Cultural minority, 1349

Cultural nationalism, 1241
Cultural pluralism, 1281, 1284, 1289, 1319
Cultural property, 1280, 1291, 1300, 1307
Cultural relations, 1367, 1375, 4881
Culture, 454, 1242, 1252, 1253, 1265, 1266, 1268-1270, 1273, 1276, 1282, 1285, 1286, 1293, 1298, 1303,1312, 1321, 1323, 1809, 2029, 3247,4687, 4835, 5503
Culture and personality, 1296
Culture area, 1254, 1305
Culture change, 1352, 1355, 1358,1363, 2828, 4382
Culture contact, 1368, 1374, 1378
Culture pattern, 1249, 1313
Cumulative scale, *see* Unidimensional scale
Current research, 64, 65, 67, 69, 70, 72-74, 77-79, 81, 84-86, 89, 92, 95, 97, 98, 1230, 1584, 3332, 3549, 3992
Curriculum, 2271, 2362, 2422, 2424, 2425, 2427, 2429
Custom, 1541
Cybernetic model, 544
Cybernetics, 543, 545, 546
Czechoslovakia
  agriculture, 4404
  class structure, 2559
  ethnic group, 3215
  fertility, 3181
  heterogamy, 3295
  homogamy, 3295
  internal migration, 3764
  life table, 3130
  national minority, 3537
  nuptiality, 3291
  poll, 460
  population evolution, 3034, 3046
  population policy, 3034
  population research, 2839, 2863
  social mobility, 2726
  social structure, 2462, 2468
  socialism, 4937
  socialist country, 4258
  urbanization, 4018
  way of life, 1314
  workers'participation, 4812
  young worker, 4518

Dance, 2096
Data archives, *see* Data bank
Data bank, 132
Davy, George, 164
Death, 1691, 3095, 3099, 3102, 3111, 3112, 3118, 3119, 3128, 3129, 3131
Death rate, 3115
Decision, 741, 743, 744, 753, 758, 768, 769, 1030, 1214, 1530

Decision making, 742, 751, 752,764, 767, 770, 970, 1015
Decolonization, 2835
Delinquency, 5361, 5364, 5378, 5379, 5381, 5383, 5385, 5390, 5392, 5394, 5402, 5407, 5408, 5410, 5416, 5422, 5424, 5425, 5429
Delinquent, 1491, 5402, 5430-5432, 5434, 5436, 5438, 5440
Democracy, 1344, 4252, 4916, 4959, 4960-4964
Demography, 1459, 2838, 2840, 2844, 2850, 2855, 2856, 2857, 2860-2862
Denmark
  abortion, 3223
  class struggle, 2621
  continuing education, 2384
  employment, 3495
  family allowances, 5526
  living onditions, 4293
  marriage, 3288
  mortality, 3101
  public administration, 5036
  research institution, 103
  slum, 4143
  university college, 2307
  vocational training, 4638
  woman worker, 4293
  women's rights, 3495
Dependency relationship, 833, 838
Deprivation, 5143
Descent, 3365, 3374
Desert, 3817
Developing country, 506, 2790, 2791, 2809, 2810, 2813, 2834, 3973
Deviance, 812, 1394, 1402, 1441, 1445, 1448, 1449, 1454, 1456, 1460, 1468, 1475, 1480, 1481, 1489, 1490, 1491, 1497, 1499, 1503, 1506, 3393
Dialectical materialism, *see* Marxism
Dialectics, 200, 221, 248, 259, 305, 308, 339, 361, 608
Diary, *see* Biography
Dictatorship, 4965
Dictionary, 150, 152-154, 156, 157
Di Leonardis, C., 308
Diploma, 2311
Diplomacy, 5241
Directive interview, 470, 471
Directory, 90, 991
Disability, 3079, 3092
Disaster, 5283-5287
Discussion group, 842
Disease, 3072, 3074, 3078
Dismissal, 4601
Dispute, *see* Conflict
Division of labour, 2494, 2498, 2503, 2516, 2517, 2525, 2528, 2988

Divorce, 1101, 3268, 3271, 3274, 3276,
   3279, 3284, 3287
Dobzhansky, Theodosius, 160
Document analysis, 139
Documentation, 135
Documentation centre, 146
Dogma, 1701
Dogmatism, 1166
Downward mobility, 2723
Dragicescu, Dimitrie, 224
Dramatic art, 2099
Dream, 730
Drinker, 5305, 5311, 5342
Drug, 5309, 5310, 5312, 5314,5319,
   5321, 5323, 5326-5328, 5330, 5332,
   5335, 5339, 5347, 5461
Drug addition, 5307, 5308, 5313, 5316,
   5318, 5325, 5333, 5336, 5341,5343,
   5350, 5351
Duricu, Vojislavu, 169
Durkheim, Emile, 218, 225, 261, 270,
   289, 300, 321, 344, 1598, 2877,
   3251, 5403
Duty, 1521
Dwelling, 3826
Dyad, 816, 841, 938, 942, 2878, 3310

E Scale, 1169
Early childhood, 692, 856, 1928,2925,
   2931
Eastern Europe
   health care, 5599
   population equilibrium, 3028
   population policy, 3202
Ecological analysis, 522
Ecology, 1027, 1138, 3799, 3801,3803-
   3807, 3810, 3811) 3813, 3815,3816
Economic behaviour, 4440, 4445
Economic change, *see* Economic development
Economic development, 2810, 3012,3032,
   3165, 4272-4278, 4281, 4283, 4284
Economic growth, 4279, 4280
Economic life, 4282
Economic sociology, 1801, 4236, 4237
Economics, 4235, 4238
Economics of education, 2128, 2137,2142
Economist, 63
Ecuador
   agrarian reform, 3960
   class structure, 2630
   female labour, 4508
   interethnic relations, 3625
   nationalism, 4929
Education, 1189, 1401, 2108, 2109,2114-
   2116, 2118, 2122, 2124, 2125, 2127,
   2129, 2131, 2132-2134, 2139-2141,
   2145, 2648
Educational guidance, 2220
Educational history, 2143
Educational institution, 2171
Educational level, 2231

Educational material, 2430
Educational needs, 2229
Educationa planning, 2156, 2170,
   2172, 2180, 2184,2186, 2203,
   2207, 3025
Educational policy, 1574, 2149,
   2152, 2155, 2160, 2169, 2173,
   2174, 2176, 2179, 2185, 2191,
   2195, 2199, 2202, 2205, 3640
Educational psychology, 2110, 2112,
   2119, 2123, 2136, 2144, 2146
Educational reform, 2151, 2153,
   2175, 2183, 2190, 2194, 2360
Educational sociology, 56, 1913,
   2111, 2113, 2117, 2120, 2121,
   2126, 2130, 2135, 2138, 2147,
   2417
Educational system, 2150, 2154,
   2157, 2158, 2159, 2161, 2163-
   2168, 2177, 2181, 2187, 2188,
   2192, 2193, 2197, 2200, 2204
Effect, 1962
Ego, 608, 610, 611? 615, 617,842
Egocentrism, 630, 632, 645, 648,
   650
Egypt
   culture, 1253
   food, 5297
   population growth, 3042
   proletariat, 3042
   social class, 2601
Elections, 5173, 5180, 5183,5188,
   5190
Electoral abstentionism, 5145
Electoral campaigning, 2030, 5176
Electoral sociology, 5166, 5170,
   5171, 5175, 5177, 5178, 5186,
   5189
Elementary family, *see* Nuclear
   family
Elite, 58, 1957, 1966, 2609, 2679,
   2680, 2687, 2691, 2702, 2704,
   2705, 3909
Emigrant, 3688, 3695
Emigration, 3303, 3679, 3680,3683,
   3684, 3686, 3690-3694, 3869
Emotion, 708-710, 715
Empathy, 809
Empirical research, 440, 441, 1467,
   1821, 5274, 5590
Employee, 4688, 4690
Employers' organization, 4734-4736
Employment, 3387, 3495-3770, 4485,
   4490-4492, 4623
Enculturation, 1371
Encyclopedia, 158
Endogamy, 3297
Engineer, 4607
Enterprise, 4316, 4323-4326, 4329,
   4331, 4333, 4335, 4338, 4342,
   4343
Entertainment, 4877

Entrepreneur, 4320
Entrepreneurship, 4330, 4336, 4339
Environment, 543, 570, 3800, 3808,3812,
    3814, 5370
Epistemology, 222, 333, 335, 336, 339-
    341, 344, 345, 1803, 1869
Equal opportunity, 2209-2215, 2217
    2221-2223, 2227, 2228, 2259, 2312,
    2321
Equality, 2219, 2514, 2515, 2519, 4960
Ergonomics, 4536-4539
Establishment, *see* Ruling class
Esty, Geoffrey W., 170
Ethics, 1136, 1516, 1519, 1523-1525,
    1534, 1535, 1537, 1538, 4310
Ethiopia, hunger, 5294
Ethnic group, 1003, 1420, 3295, 3538,
    3540, 3545, 3548, 3553, 3556, 3564,
    3570, 3572, 3574, 3578, 3585, 3590,
    3591
Ethnic minority, *see* National minority
Ethnicity, 2047, 2527, 3107, 3111,3368,
    3534, 3543, 3544, 3546, 3549-3552,
    3555, 3557, 3558, 3573, 3577, 3580,
    3582, 3583, 3586, 3588, 5123
Ethnocentrism, 1167
Ethnography, 1235, 1236
Ethnolinguistics, 1845, 1847
Ethnology, *see* Social and cultural
    anthropology
Ethos, 1533
Europe
    cross-cultural analysis, 2946
    emigration, 3690
    external migration, 3669, 3670
    family planning, 3209
    fertility, 3169
    housing, 4184
    industrial relations, 4720
    labour conflict, 4781
    peasantry, 3935
    physician, 5676
    public administration, 5037
    social research, 5268
    suicide, 5368
    voter, 5192
    workers' participation, 4819
    youth, 2946
Evaluation, 347, 355, 448
Evolutionism, 218, 251, 261, 270, 289,
    300, 321
Exchange, 884-889
Exchange value, 4451
Existentialism, 208, 226, 245, 301
Exodus, 3677, 3678
Experiment, 446, 447
Experimental group, 926
Experimenter, 445
Explanation, 355, 359, 360, 362-365
Extended family, *see* Joint family
External migration, 3553, 3667-3676

F scale, 1170
Factor analysis, 522, 528
Factory, 4596, 4598, 4599
Factory worker, 4668, 4673
Faith, *see* Belief
Family, 654, 2033, 3137, 3294,
    3321-3328, 3330-3334, 3336,
    3338, 3340-3357, 3359-3361,
    5657, 5673
Family allowances, 5526
Family disorganization, 3450,3455,
Family environment, 3308, 3403,
    3412, 3424, 3436, 3441, 3444,
    5465
Family group, 3302, 3393, 3394,
    3400, 3408, 3416, 3421, 3438,
    3440, 3449, 3456, 5417
Family integration, 682, 3405,
    3417, 3447, 3452, 5542
Familylife,2881, 3167, 3399, 3404,
    3409, 3411? 3420, 3433, 3437,
    3439, 3457, 3460, 3910, 4844,
    5348
Family planning, 3169, 3178, 3186,
    3189-3192, 3194, 3196-3198,
    3203, 3206, 3208, 3209, 3219,
    3221, 3224, 3227, 3230, 3309,
    3445
Family size, 3269, 3397, 3401,
    3407, 3410, 3418, 3419, 3422,
    3426, 3427, 3430, 3435, 3443,
    3445, 3451, 3458, 3459, 3461,
    3463, 4165, 4469
Farm, *see* Agricultural enterprise
Farmer, 3888, 3889, 3891? 3894,
    3904, 3905, 3907, 3908, 3912,
    3920, 3926, 3932, 3933, 3936,
    3939, 3944, 3946, 3952, 3953,
    5180
Farming, *see* Agriculture
Fascism, 4952
Father, 3383, 3384, 3386, 3388,
    3389
Fear, 714, 5369
Federalism , 4968, 4970
Female, 1105, 2873, 2888, 4442
Female labour, 182, 3185, 3313,
    4497, 4498, 4500, 4505, 4507,
    4508, 4510, 4619, 4523, 4527,
    4533
Female worker, *see* Woman worker
Feminism, 672, 1143, 2873, 3466,
    3474, 3486, 3489, 3507, 3509,
    3517, 3520, 3526, 3531
Ferenc, Erdei, 232
Fertility, 2613, 2719, 3016,3133-
    3154, 3156, 3158, 3160, 3164-
    3166, 3169, 3171-3185, 3197,
    3208, 3219, 3293, 3301, 3410,
    3427, 4510, 4532
Fertility rate, 3132, 3155

Fertility table, 3170
Festival, 1681, 1683, 1686, 1688, 1690, 1694
Fiji Islands
  changing society, 2374
  illiteracy, 2374
Field experiment, *see* Field work
Field work, 437-439
Film, 2010, 2013
Financial market, *see* Stock market
Finland
  alcoholism, 5346
  current research, 81
  ethnicity, 3588
  external migration, 3673
  female labour, 4533
  folklore, 2107
  language, 1937
  local government, 5055
  metropolis, 4073
  nationalism, 2107
  research, 87
  social policy, 5506
  sociology of development, 2820
  urban population, 3069
Firm, *see* Enterprise
Folk art, 2106
Folklore, 1686, 2103-2105, 2107
Food, 5292, 5297, 5301, 5302
Food habits, 1511
Forecasting, 348, 349, 353, 358, 501, 2845
Foreign labour, 3646, 4511, 4522, 4531
Foreign policy, 3198, 5244, 5245
Foreign worker, 4473, 4501, 4514, 4516, 4520
Formalization, 384-388
Foucault, Michel, 269
France
  abortion, 3193
  absenteeism, 4602
  adolescent, 2952, 2966, 2971
  aged, 2997, 2998, 3004
  ageing, 3002
  agriculture, 4400
  anarchism, 4924
  automation, 4357
  bibliography, 5530
  birth control, 3214
  capital punishment, 5468
  catholic, 1627
  Church and State, 1773
  class struggle, 2556, 2577, 2582, 4783
  clergy, 1672
  collective bargaining, 4799
  consumer behaviour, 4438
  continuing education, 2367, 2379, 2385, 2393
  contraceptive method, 3212
  death, 3099

  delinquency, 5429
  demography, 2850, 2855
  descent, 3365, 3374
  educational needs, 2229
  educational policy, 2176
  educational system, 2167
  emigration, 3690, 3694
  employment, 4485
  enterprise, 4323
  equal opportunity, 2214
  family environment, 3444
  farmer, 3952
  feminism, 3466
  fertility, 3148, 3149, 3180
  foreign labour, 3646, 4522
  gerontology, 2991
  higher education, 2360
  housing conditions, 4163, 4191
  housing policy, 4168, 4174
  immigrant, 3709, 3711, 3736
  immigrant acculturation, 3708
  immigrant assimilation, 3697, 3705, 3718, 3738
  immigration, 3698, 3701? 3702, 3704, 3729, 3734, 3741
  industrial town, 4094
  industry, 4357
  intellectual, 2683
  labour movement, 4747
  liberal profession, 4706
  life table, 3104, 3130
  local government, 5057
  marriage, 3286
  medicine, 5572
  medical care, 4438
  middle class, 2393
  migrant, 4191
  military, 5221-5224
  mortality, 3100, 3125
  national minority, 3581
  negro, 2677
  new town, 4053, 4095
  nobility, 2533
  physician, 5641, 5662, 5678, 5681
  political attitude, 2664
  political party, 3214, 4780, 5064, 5066, 5071
  population density, 3036
  population equilibrium, 3043
  population policy, 3215
  population settlement, 3828
  power, 2743
  press, 1989, 1991
  priest, 1676
  protestantism, 1640
  public administration, 5044
  racism, 3646
  religious behaviour, 1730
  religious practice, 1765
  research, 88
  rural life, 3893, 3898
  rural migration, 3768

France *[contd]*
  rural society, 3286
  scholarization, 2238
  small town, 4050, 4063
  smoking, 5338
  social change, 2743
  social mobility, 2725
  social policy, 5473
  social security, 5530
  social worker, 5660
  sociology of religion, 1589
  status, 2647, 2662, 2664
  strike, 4783
  suicide, 5368
  teacher, 5167
  television, 2021, 2026
  time budget, 4570
  town, 4052, 4084, 4091
  trade union, 4745, 4759, 4770
  trade unionism, 5221
  university, 2302
  university college, 2300
  urban government, 4118
  urban life, 4124
  urban space, 4003
  urban transport, 4112
  voting bejaviour, 5167
  way of life, 1248
  woman's status, 3478
  workers'committee, 4766
  workers'participation, 4817
  working class, 2573, 2617
  working population, 3059
Freedom, 4911, 4999-5002
Freemasonry, 1656, 1657, 1660-1662
Freud, S., 283, 576
Friedmann, Georges, 165
Friendship, 796, 797,799, 805, 811,
    823, 826, 829, 3305
Frustration, 719
Full employment, 4486
Functional analysis, 436
Fustel de Coulanges, 234
Future, 2736
Futurology, 264, 2735, 2737

Galtung, 2667
Game theory, 557
Ganon, Isaac, 65
General theory, 212, 227, 238, 274,
    282, 284, 286, 287, 294, 296,
    306, 310, 312, 313, 323, 324,
    330, 4237
Generation, 2909
Genetics, 2901, 2902, 2905
Geography, 3800
Gerontology, 2984, 2991, 3000
Germany
  academic administration, 2178
  anarchism, 4926

  fertility, 3177
  intelligentsia, 2685
  meeting, 130
  national minority, 3548
  national socialism, 4956
  sport, 4897
  student movement, 2296
  trade union, 4772
  university college, 2300
  urban development, 4223
Germany (Democratic Republic)
  class structure, 2578
  current research, 78
  educational planning, 2180
  educational system, 2168
  labour law, 4728
  parent child relations, 3413
  personality, 668
  population policy, 3211
  sport, 4895
  vocational training, 4639
  working class, 2578
Germany (Federal Republic)
  adult education
  bourgeois sociology, 2636
  class consciousness, 2595
  class structure, 2636
  culture, 3247
  educational policy, 2195
  educational reform, 2175
  electoral sociology, 5189
  employers' organization, 4736
  family group, 3440
  foreign worker, 4514
  generation, 2909
  higher education, 2298
  homosexuality, 3247
  leisure, 4827, 4838
  marginal man, 1466
  old age, 3001
  personnel management, 4540
  primary school, 2250
  professionalization, 4616
  protestant church, 1646
  punishment, 5448
  research trend, 96
  secondary school, 2258
  social history, 2482
  social structure, 2482, 5187
  social worker, 5646
  tertiary sector, 4424
  trade union, 4755, 4774
  unemployment, 4489
  urban concentration, 4001
  vocational training, 4656
  voting behaviour, 5187
  welfare State, 5492
  young worker, 4489
  youth, 2977
Gestalt psychology, 293

Ghana
  agricultural development, 4403
  birth control, 3194
  Church and State, 1764
  educational system, 2166
  family planning, 3186, 3194
  family size, 3443
  farmer, 3950
  medical care, 5579
  politics, 1764
  woman worker, 3950
Ghetto, 1922, 5386
Gift, 890
Givens, Meredith B., 171
Goffman, 245
Government, 5017
Government policy, 5016
Gramsci, Antonio, 220, 369
Graph theory, 547, 548
Green, T.H., 257
Group, 638, 891-897, 907, 911, 912,
  914, 917, 939
Group affiliation, *see* Group member-
  ship
Group analysis, 901, 909, 1466
Group attraction, 948
Group behaviour, 559
Group cohesiveness, 630, 944-947
Group composition, 935, 940, 962
Group dynamics, 905, 2542
Group effect, 931, 957
Group identification, 964
Group influence, 950, 965, 967
Group interaction, 861, 948, 952,
  953
Group membership, 968, 969
Group participation, 962
Group performance, 971
Group pressure, 959
Group psychotherapy, 898-900, 902-
  904, 906, 908, 910, 913, 915,
  916, 918, 919
Group size, 941, 943
Group task, 970, 972
Group value, 966
Guatemala
  adult education, 2386
  Church and State, 1761
  interethnic relations, 3619
  rural society, 3918
Guerilla, 5193, 5196, 5202
Gurvitch, Georges, 1577, 4236
Guyana
  class conflict, 2551
  ideology, 2551
  labour migration, 3792
  racial discrimination, 2513
  racism, 2551
  social pluralism, 2513

Habermas, Jürgen, 263, 283, 333,
  334

Habit, 1515
Handicapped, 3075, 3084, 3091, 3093
Handicapped rehabilitation, 5576, 5611
Handicraft, 4420, 4421-4423
Hawaii, suicide, 5388
Health, 4170, 5520, 5573, 5577, 5578,
  5580-5582, 5585, 5587, 5588,
  5592, 5595, 5602, 5606, 5608-
  5610, 5616, 5617, 5620
Health service, 529, 4764, 5622, 5624,
  5626, 5627, 5632, 5634-5636, 5638,
  5639
Henry, Luis, 2840
Heredity, 2896, 2898
Heresy, 1703
Hermeneutics, 214
Heterogamy, 3295
High school, *see* Secondary school
Higher education, 2220, 2295, 2298,
  2301, 2303-2306, 2309, 2310, 2312-
  2318, 2321, 2323, 2325, 2327-2329,
  2336, 2342, 2343, 2347, 2350,
  2355, 2358, 2360
Hindu, 1629
Historical science, 2731, 2732
Historicism, 217, 231, 252, 295
History, 313, 2730, 2733
History of ideas, 1829
History of sciences, 1797
Hjelmslev, L., 1861
Hollander, A.N.J. den, 163
Holy object, 1711
Homan, 324
Homicide, 5367, 5386, 5393, 5397,
  5421, 5428
Homogamy, 3295
Homosexuality, 3247, 3248, 3252, 3258
Honduras
  bourgeoisie, 4982
  commuting, 3794
  labour conflict, 4794
  State, 4982
  strike, 4794
Hong Kong
  marriage, 3522
  political leadership, 5104, 5107
  population evolution, 2843
  population projection, 2843
  urban renewal, 4214
  woman's status, 3522
Hospital, 1107, 5623, 5628, 5632,
  5633, 5637
Hospital service, 902, 5625
Hospital treatment, 5629
Hostility, 840, 842, 855, 858
Household, 2881, 4038
Housing, 3382, 3724, 3736, 4024, 4142,
  4146, 4149, 4150, 4153, 4158-4160,
  4169, 4175, 4177, 4184, 4194

Housing conditions, 1487, 4147, 4155,
    4156, 4163, 4165, 4170, 4180, 4183,
    4191, 4198
Housing policy, 3048, 4138, 4145, 4151,
    4152, 4162, 4164, 4168, 4171, 4172,
    4174, 4179, 4196
Human biology, 2897, 2899, 2900, 2903,
    2904, 2906
Human capital, *see* Human resources
Human geography, 3802
Human nature, 2877
Human relations, 772, 782, 783
Human resources, 3820, 4472
Human rights, 4996-4998, 5003
Hungary
    abortion, 3201
    absenteeism, 4606
    army, 5232
    atheism, 1699
    commercial worker, 2728
    commuting, 3773
    culture, 1276
    current research, 74
    division of labour, 2516
    educational guidance, 2220
    enterprise, 4333
    ergonomics, 4539
    family size, 3435
    handicraft, 4421
    higher education, 2220, 2328
    housing conditions, 4163
    immigration assimilation, 3742
    industry, 4419
    intellectual, 1332, 2698
    intelligentsia, 2699, 2703
    marriage, 3281
    mass culture, 2237
    national consciousness, 1332
    national minority, 3562, 3565, 3566
    occupational choice. 4617. 4619
    occupational mobility, 2728, 4618
    peasantry, 2727, 3914, 3917
    physician, 5675
    population evolution, 3027
    press, 736
    religious practice, 1780, 1781
    rural life, 3900
    small town, 4074
    social mobility, 2727
    social structure, 2462
    suicide, 5366
    town, 4049, 4061
    trend report, 80
    village, 2698, 3858, 3860, 3865
    working class, 2552, 2597, 2598
    youth, 736
Hunger, 5294
Husband, 2910, 3309, 3320, 5153

Ideal type, 215, 372, 405
Identity, 628, 629, 634, 640, 641, 644,
    647, 652, 654, 1380, 1711, 3558, 3577

Ideology, 772, 1189-1191, 1193,
    1195-1201, 1203-1210, 1260,
    1271, 1306, 1585, 1790, 1819,
    1824, 2015, 2065, 2139, 2551,
    2687, 2693, 2737, 4264, 5486,
    5503, 5521
Illich, Ivan, 2225
Illiteracy, 2364, 2370, 2371, 2383-
    2385
Illness, *see* Disease
Image, 1154
Imitation, 839
Immigrant, 1472, 3372, 3707, 3709,
    3710, 3711, 3713, 3716, 3719,
    3724, 3726, 3733, 3736, 3740,
    3743, 4511
Immigrant acculturation, 3708, 3731
Immigrant assimilation, 3503, 3697,
    3702, 3705, 3716, 3718, 3721,
    3723, 3725, 3728, 3730, 3732,
    3737, 3738, 3742, 4520
Immigration, 3696, 3698, 3701, 3703,
    3706, 3714, 3715, 3717, 3720,
    3727, 3735, 3739
Imperialism, 5242, 5243
India
    agricultural economics, 4396
    bibliography, 4002
    caste, 2537, 2542
    child adoption, 3406
    child development, 2912
    class structure, 2563
    community development, 3842,
        5538
    cross-national analysis, 2537
    cultural property, 1300
    current research, 64
    dictionary, 154
    educational system, 2200
    factory worker, 4673
    family group, 5417
    family planning, 3224, 3445
    family size, 3445
    fertility, 3137, 3184
    food, 5292
    group dynamics, 2542
    intellectual, 2694, 2695
    internal migration, 3746, 3786
    labour migration, 3788
    labour movement, 4739
    marriage, 3277, 3282
    mate selection, 3300
    mental disease, 3076
    metropolis, 4078
    modernization, 2694
    nationalism, 4943
    political leadership, 5102
    political party, 5067
    population projection, 2841
    population replacement, 2841
    power, 3941
    rural life, 3941

India [contd.]
  rural planning, 3977
  rural society, 2563, 3927
  small town, 4068
  social change, 1300
  social security, 5532
  social work, 5538
  sociology of development, 2831
  status, 2660
  stereotype, 2352
  suicide, 5413, 5426
  survey, 3184
  theft, 5417
  tradition, 3277
  tribe, 3576
  underdevelopment, 2793
  university, 2352
  urban development, 4220
  urban society, 4129
  urbanization, 4002
  village, 3076, 3786, 3854, 3857, 3861
Indonesia
  birth control, 3222
  conflict, 878
  fertility, 3156, 3157
  infant mortality, 3166
  woman's status, 3499, 3516
In group, 961
Incest taboo, 3245, 3250
Income, 4292, 4297, 4301, 4302, 4309
Income distribution, 2654, 4291, 4294,
    4305, 4314
Index, 530
Indian, 909, 3592, 3593, 3595, 3596,
    3598, 3599, 3609, 3611, 3612
Indicator, 459, 529, 531-542, 4200,
    4286, 4613, 5495
Individual, 607, 609, 612-614, 616,
    618-623, 1326
Individualism, 633, 1112
Industrial conflict, see Labour con-
    flict
Industrial development, 4418
Industrial economics, 4411
Industrial enterprise, 4414
Industrial participation, see Workers
    participation
Industrial production, 4413
Industrial psychology, 4466
Industrial relations, 2562, 4710-4716,
    4718-4724
Industrial revolution, 4371, 4373
Industrial society, 2579, 2823, 2833
Industrial town, 4055, 4094
Industrialization, 3272, 3321, 4409,
    4410, 4412, 4416, 4779
Industry, 4357, 4415, 4417, 4419
Inequality, 2489, 2490, 2495, 2501,
    2502, 2505, 2507, 2512, 2523, 2524,
    2527, 4964
Infancy, see Early childhood

Infant mortality, 3110, 3117, 3124,
    3127, 3132, 3166
Infant school, see Nursery school
Infertility, 3159
Information dissemination, 131
Information processing, 132-134, 136
Information service, see Documen-
    tation centre
Information theory, 1875
Innovation, 4354, 4372, 4377, 4378-
    4380, 4382
Intellectual, 1332, 1770, 2678,
    2683, 2684, 2686, 2688, 2689,
    2692-2695, 2697, 2698
Intellectual ability, 2407
Intellectual development, 2408,
    2410
Intelligence, 684, 692, 702
Intelligentsia, 2682, 2685, 2690,
    2696, 2699, 2701, 2703
Interdisciplinary research, 101
Interest, 4455
Interest group, see Pressure group
Interethnic relations, 1144, 3615,
    3618, 3619-3625, 3627
Intergroup relations, 859-862,
    1160, 1167
Interindividual relationships, see
    Interpersonal relations
Internal migration, 3154, 3744-
    3746, 3749, 3754, 3755, 3757,
    3762-3767, 3769, 3774, 3776,
    3783-3787, 3789, 3790, 3793,
    5408
International law, 5234, 5239
International migration, see
    External migration
International organization, 5235
International politics, 5247,
    5250, 5255
International relations, 1345,
    4932, 5236-5238, 5240
Interpersonal attraction, 800, 801,
    803, 806, 808, 810, 814, 818,
    821, 822, 830, 832, 938, 2038
Interpersonal conflict, 632, 857
Interpersonal influence, 834-837
Interpersonal perception, 789, 792-
    794, 830, 948
Interpersonal relations, 655, 771,
    773-780, 784, 786, 788, 1211
Interpretation, 341, 351, 354,
    366, 514
Interval scale, 559, 569
Interview, 465, 467, 472, 477, 482,
    483
Intra group relations, 949-951
Iran
  family size, 3458
  fertility, 3133
  rural life, 3915
  village, 3133

Ireland
  Church and State, 1741, 1743
  educational system, 2165
  Nation, 1325
  political conflict, 1741
  revolutionary movement, 5084
  stereotype, 1164
  town, 922
  urban design, 4228
  violence, 1493
  voter, 5181
Islam, 1630, 1632, 1633, 1638, 2949,
  3306
Islamism, *see* Islam
Isolate, 3296, 3303
Israel
  adult, 2957
  child rearing, 2915
  Church and State, 1775
  collective farm, 4386, 4391, 4408
  cross cultural analysis, 2945
  culture, 4835
  elite, 2705
  ethnic group, 3574
  ethnicity, 3586
  farmer, 3926
  immigrant, 1472
  immigrant assimilation, 3718, 3721
  national development, 2837
  political culture, 5128
  residential segregation, 4140
  social service, 5663
  sociology of leisure, 4835
  town, 1472
  woman's status, 3521
  youth, 2945
  youth movement, 2957
Italy
  aged, 2993
  agricultural enterprise, 4388
  bibliography, 140
  bourgeoisie, 2557
  Church and State, 1769
  class struggle, 4783
  drug, 5310, 5314
  economic development, 2810
  educational system, 2204
  emigrant, 3695
  emigration, 3691
  entrepreneur, 4320
  family, 3323, 3325, 3326
  family group, 3421
  freemasonry, 1662
  handicraft, 4420
  higher education, 2315
  housing, 4149
  housing conditions, 4163
  immigrant assimilation, 3705
  industrial relations, 4719, 4721
  intellectual, 2697
  Jew, 1623
  labour law, 4730

  labour migration, 2616, 5146
  mafia, 5442
  marginality, 1471, 4123
  occupational sociology, 4612, 4615
  occupational stratification, 4628
  old age, 2987
  parent-child relations, 3402
  parent-teacher relations, 2453
  peasantry, 3421
  physician, 5641
  political participation, 5118, 5146
  political party, 5073
  power elite, 2700
  pressure group, 5094
  public education, 2196
  religious movement, 1750
  rural life, 3897, 3901
  rural migration, 3750
  school adjustment, 2289
  secularization, 1771
  social and cultural anthropology,
    1230
  social change, 1645
  social class, 2550, 2616, 4615, 4775
  strike, 4783
  trade union, 4757, 4775
  trend report, 3323
  unemployment, 4487
  university, 2356, 2357
  urban development, 4207
  urban life, 4123
  urban society, 1471
  value, 1379
  vocational training, 4622, 4658,
    4659
  voter, 5172
  voting behaviour, 5179
  women's rights, 5172
  women's status, 3479, 3519
  working class, 2553, 2563
  youth, 2954
Ivory Coast, town, 4058, 4072

Jamaica, urbanization, 4039
Japan
  academic administration, 2206
  business community, 4328
  caste, 2546
  Church and State, 1767, 1768
  cult, 1687
  current research, 73, 79, 89
  economic development, 4283
  elections, 5183
  employee, 4691
  family life, 3437, 3439
  foreign policy, 5245
  gerontology, 3000
  government, 5018
  higher education, 2312
  industrialization, 4412, 4416
  industry, 4415
  intellectual, 2686

Japan *[contd]*
  internal migration, 3767
  kinship, 3370, 3380
  mate selection, 3298
  new town, 4077
  old age, 2983
  organizational change, 1064
  political participation, 1776
  politics, 1768, 1771, 5204
  press, 1994
  regional planning, 4077
  religious practice, 1776
  religious reform, 1755
  research, 75
  rural life, 3951
  sect, 3380
  social problem, 5278
  social stratification, 2504
  social work, 5548
  student, 2330
  tradition, 3439
  urban life, 4126
  village, 3862, 3879, 3882
  woman's status, 3502
  working class, 2606
  youth, 2959, 2967, 2968
Jaspers, Karl, 199
Jew, 1622, 1623
Job classification, 4494
Job satisfaction, 4580, 4582-4585,
  4590, 4591, 4605
Joint family, 3335
Joint management, 4808, 4813
Jordan
  family planning, 3178
  fertility, 3178
Journal, 182, 184
Journalism, 2004, 2006
Journalist, 1996, 1998, 2002, 2005
Journey to work, *see* Labour migration
Judiciary behaviour, 5025, 5026,
  5030
Judiciary power, 5027, 5028
Justice, 1542, 1553, 1562, 1565,
  1575, 1581, 1583
Juvenile delinquency, 1581, 5024,
  5365, 5372, 5376, 5395, 5396,
  5399, 5411, 5412, 5418, 5423

Kenya, conflict class, 2549
Kinship, 3364, 3367-3373, 3375,
  3376, 3378, 3380, 3382
Knowledge, 262, 1205, 1785, 1787,
  1792, 1795, 1796, 1798, 1799,
  1802, 1806-1808, 1811, 1812,
  1822, 1828, 1830, 1833, 1834
Korea (Republic of)
  cultural dynamics, 1356
  current research, 77
  employment, 3387
  family planning, 3208, 3309

  family system, 3417
  fertility, 3162, 3164, 3208
  husband, 3309
  internal migration, 3765, 3785
  migration, 3162
  parent-child relations, 3387, 3462
  wife, 3309
  woman worker, 3164

Labour, 647, 1395, 4470, 4474, 4476,
  4477, 4481
Labour conditions, *see* Working con-
  ditions
Labour conflict, 4781, 4784, 4787-
  4790, 4792-4797
Labour force, *see* Manpower
Labour law, 4725-4733
Labour management relations, 4717
Labour market, 4469, 4471, 4473,
  4478, 4479, 4482
Labour migration, 2616, 3154, 3758,
  3760, 3770, 3792, 5146
Labour mobility, 2712
Labour movement, 4477, 4739, 4740-
  4747, 4749, 4752, 4760, 4763,
  4765, 4768, 4779
Labour standard, 4550
Land reform, *see* Agrarian reform
Land tenure, 3957
Language, 1896, 1906, 1907, 1909,
  1911-1914, 1917-1919, 1922, 1923,
  1926, 1927, 1929, 1930, 1937
Lao PDR,
  village, 3876
Latin America
  acculturation, 1377
  capitalism, 4929
  case study, 2586
  class consciousness, 2586
  culture, 1298
  current research, 3992
  educational system, 2192, 2193
  family size, 3427
  farmer, 3908, 3946
  fascism, 4952
  fertility, 3427
  food, 5302
  immigration assimilation, 3742
  internal migration, 3757, 3798
  Islam, 1630
  literature, 2075
  military sociology, 5214
  nationalism, 4928, 4929, 4947
  oecumenism, 1665
  peasantry, 3934
  political participation, 5163
  political party, 5062
  population growth, 5302
  population research, 2858
  religious behaviour, 1728
  rural area, 3873
  rural development, 3963

Latin America *[contd]*
  social class, 2611, 2619
  sociology of development, 2818
  State, 4984, 4994
  terrorism, 1455
  town, 4083
  underdevelopment, 2816
  urban sociology, 3992
  way of life, 1287
  woman's rights, 2619
  women's status, 2586, 3510
  working class, 2628
Law, 1541, 1545-1548, 1550-1552, 1554, 1557, 1564, 1567-1569, 1572, 1580
Law of nations, *see* International Law
Lawyer, 4707, 4709
Lazarsfeld, Paul, 161, 172, 178, 1802
Leader, 963, 1045, 1080
Leadership, 944, 999; 1026, 1078, 1079, 1081-1089, 1091, 2691, 5444
Learning, 685, 693, 694, 705, 3717,
Lebanon
  alienation, 5151
  fertility, 3144
  immigrant assimilation, 3728, 3732
  political participation, 5151
  population evolution, 1719
  religious behaviour, 1719, 3144
  social class, 2565
  social system, 2484
  student, 2322
Le Bon, Gustave, 1221
Legal protection, 1574, 1576
Legal system, 1199, 1566, 1570, 1579
Legislation, 1571
Legislative behaviour, 5158
Leisure, 1155, 1266, 4822, 4825-4827, 4833, 4834, 4836, 4838, 4840, 4841n 4845-4847
Leisure time, 4848-4851
Leisure utilization, 4852, 4890
Lénine, V.I., 248
Lesotho, family, 3349
Lévi-Strauss, Claude, 202, 207, 271, 304, 1321, 1713, 3389
Lévy-Garboua, Louis, 2359
Lexicology, 1861
Liberal profession, 4706
Liberalism, 4925, 4954
Liberty, *see* Freedom
Library, 145, 147-149
Life expectancy, 5665
Life history, *see* Biography
Life table, 3104, 3116, 3130
Lineage, 3371, 3379, 3381

Linguistics, 1843, 1844, 1848, 1849, 1852, 1855, 1859-1860, 1863, 1864, 3378
Listener, 1940
Literacy criticism, 2067, 2077
Literature, 2062, 2065, 2066, 2069, 2070, 2073, 2076
Living conditions, 4285, 4293, 4296
Local government, 5051-5058, 5135, 5138
Lockout, 4785
Logic, 499
Love, 798, 816
Lower class, 1769, 2406
Luckmann, Thomas, 1593

Macro, 415, 2457
Mafia, 5442
Magic, 1608, 1610, 1611
Mail questionnaire, 468
Mail survey, 481
Malaysia
  cultural pluralism, 1281
  intellectual, 1770
  interethnic relations, 3627
  internal migration, 3750
  population evolution, 2842
  population projection, 2842
  religious practice, 1770
  social stratification, 2522
  tribe, 3541
  urbanization, 4015, 4020
Male, 849, 1105, 2870
Mali
  child, 2932
  scholarization, 2233
Malthus, 278
Malthusianism, 3188
Man, 2865, 2866
Man, Hendrik de, 229
Management, 4340, 4341
Manager, 4693, 4694, 4697-4699, 4703, 4705
Mankind, 2895
Mannheim, Karl, 1803, 1823, 1827
Manpower, 670, 4475, 4480, 4483, 4484
Manual worker, 631, 4669
Marginal man, 1463, 1465, 1466, 1470, 1476, 1495
Marginality, 1434, 1443, 1444, 1471, 1474, 1484, 1486, 1501, 1504, 1505, 4123, 4181
Marital status, 2941, 3311, 3312, 3314, 3317, 3319, 4523
Market, 4449, 4450
Markley Znaniecka, Eileen, 162
Markovian processes, 551
Marriage, 2525, 3192, 3265-3267, 3269-3273, 3277, 3278, 3280-3283, 3285, 3286, 3288-3290, 3292-3294, 3522

Married man, 3308, 3310, 5349
Married woman, 3308, 3310, 3313,
    5349
Marx, Karl, 203, 223, 256, 259, 302,
    315, 1461, 1726, 4451, 5197
Marxism, 80, 199, 203, 210, 219,
    223, 235, 253, 256, 285, 302,
    315, 320, 326, 327, 329, 332,
    756, 2326, 4244
Mass communication, 735, 1183, 1321,
    1444, 1820, 1907, 1944, 1957-
    1988, 2276, 4890, 5379
Mass culture, 2237
Mass media, *see* Mass communication
Mass society, 1334, 1335, 1342,
    1344
Mate selection, 3298, 3299, 3300,
    3302
Materialism, 143, 237, 243
Mathematical analysis, 495, 2720
Mathematical model, 377, 382, 494,
    1391, 3804
Mathematics, 496, 497, 500, 5265
Matriarchy, 3398
Matrix calculus, 493
Maturity, 2978
Mauritania, town, 4046
Mc Clelland, 4282
Mead, George Herbert, 204, 292
Meaning, 1879, 1890
Mechanization, 4368
Medical care, 1730, 4438, 5579,
    5593, 5594, 5596, 5597, 5599,
    5600, 5601, 5603, 5612, 5615
Medical occupation, 1083, 4708
Medical sociology, 3085, 5558, 5561,
    5564, 5565, 5567, 5571, 5574,
    5621
Medicine, 5557, 5559, 5560, 5566,
    5568, 5570, 5572, 5573
Meeting, 130
Membership group, 3585
Memory, 703, 706
Mental disease, 2924, 3070, 3071,
    3076, 3080, 3082,3083, 3085,
    3087-3090, 3094
Mental health, 5584, 5590, 5598,
    5614, 5618
Merton, R. K., 288
Methodology, 231, 250, 390, 394,
    396, 397, 402, 404-406, 408,
    409, 411, 3852, 5263
Metropolis, 4042, 4067, 4069, 4070,
    4073, 4076, 4078, 4087, 4089,
    4092, 4305
Metropolitan area, 3997
Mexico
  agrarian reform, 3955
  agriculture, 3035
  class structure, 2624
  educational reform, 2194
  family, 3324

  freemasonry, 1660
  higher education, 2342
  immigrant assimilation, 3730
  political elite, 5109
  political life, 5195
  political party, 5082
  political socialization, 5133
  population evolution, 3035
  pressure group, 5089
  proletariate, 2570
  slum, 4197
  trade union, 4773
  university, 2334
  urban development, 4208
  women's promotion, 3487
Middle class, 257, 725, 2301, 2393,
    2561, 2581, 2584, 2618, 2947,
    5062
Middle East
  arms race, 5257
  urbanization, 4006
Middle management, 4702, 4704
Migrant, 2405, 4191
Migration, 3162, 3654-3666
Military, 828, 5008, 5017, 5206,
    5211, 5216, 5217, 5218, 5221-
    5225, 5228-5230, 5233, 5244
Military service, 5210
Military sociology, 3343, 4603, 5205,
    5209, 5214, 5215, 5219, 5226,
    5231
Mills, Wright, 307
Minority group, 936, 939
Missionary, 1673
Mixed marriage, 3304-3307
Model, 367, 371, 2466
Modernization,2694, 2730, 2739, 2747,
    2769, 2779, 2781
Mohammedanism, *see* Islam
Monarchy, 4958
Money, 4457, 4460
Morality, 1522, 1526, 1529-1531,
    1536, 1547, 1972
Morals, 1165, 1517, 1518, 1528,
    1532, 1539, 3913
Morbidity, 28911
Morocco
  fertility, 3138
  housing, 4024
  immigrant assimilation, 3718
  rural-urban, 3138
  urbanization, 4024
Mortality, 2891, 3096, 3098, 3100,
    3103, 3105-3109, 3113, 3114,
    3120-3123, 3125, 3126, 3172
Moslem, 1625
Mother, 3385, 3387, 3390, 3391,3469
Motion picture, *see* Film
Motivation, 717, 720, 722, 723, 729,
    737
Motivation to work, 4588, 4589, 4592,
    4594, 4595

Movie, *see* Cinema
Multidimensional scale, 560, 563, 568
Multidisciplinary research, *see*
    Interdisciplinary research
Multivariate analysis, 423-425, 432,
    1098, 3280, 5369
Municipal administration, *see* Local
    government
Murder, *see* Homicide
Museum, 2054, 2060, 2704
Music, 2087, 2094
Musicology, 2086
Myth, 1042, 1713, 1715, 1716
Mythology, 1714, 1717

Natality, 3011, 3167
Nation, 1325-1329, 1331
National character, 1324
National consciousness, 1330, 1332,
    1694
National development, 2679, 2822,
    2837
National minority, 1375, 1458, 2618,
    3536, 3537, 3542, 3547, 3554,
    3559-3562, 3565, 3566, 3568,
    3569, 3571, 3575, 3579, 3581,
    3589
National planning, 4464
National socialism, 4956
Nationalism, 1331, 1783, 2107, 2500,
    2575, 3554, 3608, 4928, 4935,
    4940, 4941, 4943, 4947, 4953,
    4955
Native, 3821
Natural resources, 3820
Nature, 287
Need, 718, 724, 728, 731-733, 738,
    4445
Negro, 2677, 3597, 3600, 3601, 3605-
    3608, 3610, 4456, 5112, 5124,
    5140, 5143
Neighbourhood, 4166, 4167, 4173,
    4182, 4187, 4189
Neocolonialism, 4246
Netherlands
  attitude, 4501
  audience, 2060
  civil service, 5033
  current research, 3332, 3359
  divorce, 3279
  emigration, 3680
  family, 3332, 3359
  foreign worker, 4501
  health care, 5601
  industrial relation, 4710
  museum, 2060
  nuptiality, 3275
  population equilibrium, 3050
  public administration, 5043
  university, 2358
  urban life, 4135

women's promotion, 3525
  young worker, 4515
New town, 2260, 4043, 4053, 4059,
    4077, 4099
New Zealand
  hospital service, 5625
  occupational prestige, 4624
  secondary education, 2245
  sport, 4624
  urban area, 5625
Newspaper, *see* Press
Niger
  rural migration, 3791
  village, 3872
Nigeria
  case study, 3183
  child, 2914
  community development, 3837
  fertility, 3016, 3142, 3143, 3182,
    3183
  innovation, 4372
  interethnic relations, 1144
  labour movement, 4740
  occupational choice, 4650
  polygyny, 3182
  poverty, 5296
  residential segregation, 4178
  rural development, 3965
  rural environment, 3949
  stereotype, 1144
  town, 4080
  traditional society, 4080
  village, 3875
Nobility, 2533
Nomadism, 3777, 3778, 3781
Nonmanual worker, *see* Employee
Norm, 1441
Norway
  consumer behaviour, 4441
  drug addiction, 5341
  elite, 2687
  ideology, 2687
  inequality, 2512
  occupation, 2340
  social research, 5266
  sociology of development, 2817
  university, 2340
  woman worker, 4496
  workers' participation, 4811
  working conditions, 4496
Novel, 1104, 2071, 2072, 2074, 2075,
    3930
Nuclear family, 3329, 3339, 3358
Nuptiality, 3275, 3291
Nurse, 5643, 5658, 5674
Nursery school, 2262, 2263, 2271

Obituary, 160, 163, 167-171, 173,
    174, 177, 179, 420
Objectiveness, 343, 346, 1827
Observer, 442
Occupation, 1142, 2340, 2669, 4194,
    4609, 4611- 4612, 4614

Occupational choice, 823, 3442, 3939, 4617, 4619, 4630, 4642, 4650
Occupational mobility, 2728, 4618, 4635, 4640, 4644, 4654, 4666
Occupational prestige, 4620, 4624, 4626, 4636, 4645, 4648, 4651, 4655, 4661, 4664
Occupational promotion, 4637, 4657, 4663
Occupational sociology, 4607, 4610, 4612, 4613, 4615
Occupational stratification, 4289, 4309, 4621, 4623, 4641, 4643, 4647, 4660, 4665
Oecumenism, 1665-1669
Old age, 2983, 2987, 2992, 2994, 2996, 3001, 3003, 3899
Old people, see Aged
One party system, 3652
Opinion, 645, 1172, 1174, 1184, 1185, 1187, 1877
Opinion change, 3648
Oral literature, 2078
Organization, 964, 1005, 1008, 1012, 1013, 1015, 1016, 1022, 1024, 1027, 1028, 1030, 1032, 1034, 1038-1040, 1042, 1047-1049, 1053, 1055, 1060, 1062, 1063, 1069, 2496, 4537
Organization theory, 973, 976, 979, 980, 982, 986, 990, 992, 993, 1399
Organizational analysis, 974, 978, 984, 987, 989, 995
Organizational change, 1007, 1010, 1014, 1018, 1019, 1026, 1033, 1044, 1054, 1064, 1065, 1068
Organisational control, see Bureaucratic control
Organizational size, 134
Ortega y Gasset, 296
Orthodox christian, 1624
Out group, 963
Overpopulation, 3009, 3052
Owen, Wilfred, 249

Painting, 2084, 3894
Pakistan
  Church and State, 1738
  ethnicity, 3558
  family, 3353
  fertility, 3293
  identity, 3558
  marriage, 3293
  overpopulation, 3009
  teacher, 2441
  tribe, 3535
Panel survey, 451, 456
Panic, 711
Paraguay, educational system, 2164
Parent-child relations, 625, 2262, 3245, 3387, 3392, 3402, 3413,

Parent-child relations [contd.] 3415, 3423, 3428, 3432, 3442, 3446, 3448, 3453, 3454, 3462, 4099, 4898
Parent-teacher relations, 2453
Parents' education, 2452
Pareto, Vilfredo, 225
Parliament, 5020, 5021
Parliamentary system, 4974
Parsons, Talcott, 198, 211, 216, 217, 255, 299, 308, 593, 1482, 1554
Participant observation, 443, 444
Party identification, 5119, 5120, 5136, 5145
Party system, 5061 q 5078
Patriarchy, 3431, 3434
Patriotism, 4922, 4932, 4944, 4950, 4951
Pattern, see Model
Peace, 5248
Peaceful co-existence, 5246
Peasant, see Farmer
Peasantry, 3421, 3884, 3890, 3914, 3916, 3917, 3925, 3929, 3930, 3934, 3942
Pedagogical relationship, 2419
Pedagogical research, 2415, 2417, 2418, 2420
Pedagogy, 2426, 2428
Penal law, 1543, 1558, 1561, 1578, 4998
Penitentiary system, 5445, 5466
People Republic of Albania, public health, 5586
Perception, 689, 700, 707
Perception of others, 967
Performance, 748, 750, 759
Periodical, 181, 183, 185
Personality, 655, 659, 662, 665, 668, 669, 671, 673, 674, 677-681, 683, 1308, 1404, 1980, 2926, 4385, 4571, 5250
Personality assessment, see Personality measurement
Personality change, 656, 2776
Personality development, 657, 661, 666, 670, 672, 682, 3392, 4846, 4847, 4849
Personality inventory, 484, 485, 487
Personality measurement, 486, 488
Personality system, see Personality
Personality trait, 660, 663, 664, 667, 1142
Personnel management, 1023, 4540-4547, 4551-4553
Personnel supervision, see Personnel management
Persuasion, 1952, 2030
Peru
  adolescent, 2948
  basic education, 2373

Peru *[contd]*
  class struggle, 2623, 2626
  educational reform, 2151
  ethnicity, 2527
  family group, 3438
  inequality, 2527
  internal migration, 3789
  peasantry, 3884
  political participation, 5125
  primitive religion, 1614
  race relations, 3617
  slum, 3617
  sociology of development, 2826,
    2836
  town, 4054
  traditional society, 2792
  urban population, 5125
  urbanization, 3789
Petrazycki, Leon, 1560
Phenomenology, 228, 240, 246
Philippines
  developing country, 2809
  household, 4038
  housing policy, 4185
  immigration, 3696
  labour law, 4729
  poor, 5290
  sect, 1658
  secondary school, 2268
  slum, 4193
  social class, 2653
  urban population, 3066
  urban sociology, 5290
  urbanization, 4028, 4038
Philosophy, 198, 201, 216, 229, 236,
    250, 255, 257, 264, 268, 269,
    271, 278, 283, 297, 299, 309,
    311, 314, 319, 325
Photography, 2082
Physician, 3097, 4607, 4708, 5641,
    5648, 5649, 5653, 5654, 5659,
    5662, 5667-5668, 5670, 5672,
    5675, 5676, 5678, 5681
Piaget, Jean, 204, 306, 2134
Pilgrimage, 1678, 1682, 1695
Pilot survey, 454, 4375
Planned parenthood, *see* Family plan-
    ning
Planning, 541, 542,1057, 4465
Play, 4854, 4860, 4866, 4872, 4886
Plural society, *see* Social pluralism
Poland
  agricultural cooperative, 4387
  bibliography, 144
  biography, 175
  Church and State, 1745, 1752
  civil service, 5038
  consumption, 4435, 4436, 4444
  cultural contact, 1374
  cultural integration, 1347
  current research, 69, 86
  educational system, 2188

  farmer, 3888
  female labour, 3313
  food, 5301
  health, 5617
  higher education, 2329
  immigrant, 3713, 3726
  industrial economics, 4411
  internal migration, 3793
  job satisfaction, 4595
  labour law, 4726
  library, 147
  manager, 4699
  marriage, 3265
  married woman, 3313
  motivation to work, 4589
  national minority, 3579
  occupational prestige, 4655
  periodical, 185
  political behaviour, 5141
  population equilibrium, 3030
  population policy, 5505
  punishment, 5456
  regional government, 5060
  research trend, 68, 3984
  rural development, 5060
  social pathology, 5274
  social policy, 5505
  social structure, 2462
  socialist society, 4270
  society, 1338
  town dweller, 4192
  urban sociology, 3984
  vocational training, 4619
  woman's status, 3538
  worker, 4676
Police, 1489, 5004-5015
Political attitude, 2664, 3577, 5114,
    5116, 5127, 5152, 5154
Political behaviour, 2241, 4139,
    5126, 5141, 5148, 5150, 5153,
    5157
Political communication, 5117, 5159
Political conflict, 1741, 2404, 5194,
    5200
Political crisis, 5199, 5203
Political culture, 5128, 5132, 5156,
    5158, 5165
Political development, 4978
Political education, 2399, 2404
Political elite, 5088, 5101, 5105,
    5108, 5109
Political faction, 5100, 5112
Political ideology, 4908, 4910
Political institution, 4973
Political leader, 5127
Political leadership, 5102, 5104,
    5107, 5111
Political life, 1749, 2041, 5195
Political majority, 5099
Political man, 5103, 5106, 5110
Political modernization, 4981, 4985

Political participation, 1776, 2965,
    5074, 5113, 5118, 5124, 5125,
    5130, 5134, 5135, 5138-5140,
    5146, 5149, 5151, 5155, 5163,
    5164, 5188
Political party, 559, 2326, 3214,
    4780, 5062-5083
Political philosophy, 314, 4909
Political psychology, 4906
Political science, 1407, 4902, 4907
Political scientist, 58
Political socialization, 702, 5112,
    5115, 5122, 5129, 5133, 5142,
    5144, 5161, 5162
Political sociology, 4901, 4903,
    4904
Political system, 4972, 4976, 4991
Politicization, 5131, 5137, 5143,
    5160
Politics, 1744, 1758, 1763, 1764,
    1766, 1768, 1771, 2065, 5197,
    5201, 5204
Poll, 459-462, 464
Pollution, 3819
Polygyny, 3182, 3301
Poor, 5290, 5293, 5303
Popper, Karl R., 346
Population, 2846-2848, 2851, 2854,
    2859
Population control, *see* Birth con-
    trol
Population decrease, 3053
Population density, 3036, 3037,
    3044
Population dynamics, *see* Population
    evolution
Population equilibrium, 3008, 3021,
    3024, 3028, 3030, 3032, 3038,
    3043, 3047, 3049
Population evolution, 1719, 2822,
    2842, 2843, 3011, 3014-3018,
    3023, 3027, 3031, 3033-3035,
    3039-3041, 3045, 3046
Population growth, 3010, 3012, 3019,
    3022, 3025, 3026, 3042, 3048,
    3054, 3218, 5302
Population movement, *see* Migration
Population optimum, 3029
Population policy, 469, 1519, 3026,
    3034, 3195, 3200, 3202, 3211,
    3215, 3218, 3220, 3228, 5505
Population projection, 2841, 2842,
    2843, 2845
Population pyramid, 2907
Population replacement, 2841, 3013
Population research, 2838, 2852,
    2853, 2858, 2864
Population settlement, 3822-3825,
    3827-3833
Population theory, 2849
Portugal
  agrarian reform, 3975

capitalism, 3921
corporatism, 4777
death, 3118
emigration, 3692
external migration, 3675
immigrant assimilation, 3503
rural society, 3921
woman's promotion, 3503
Positivism, 209, 225, 233, 260, 279-
    281, 1221
Poulantzas, Nicos, 237
Poverty, 1486, 5288, 5291, 5295,
    5296, 5298, 5299
Power, 563, 966, 1076, 2842, 2743,
    3941, 4911-4921
Power elite, 2700
Pregnancy, 3256
Prehistory, 1709
Prejudice, 1150, 1152, 1163
Preschool child, *see* Childhood
Preschool education, 2243, 2244,
    2246, 2249, 2251, 2254, 2255,
    2257
Presidency, 5019
Press, 421, 736, 1988-1995, 1997,
    1999-2001, 2003, 2007, 2008,
    3523, 3651
Pressure group, 1475, 4692, 5085,
    5089, 5094, 5097, 5098, 5577
Prevention of delinquency, 5357,
    5450, 5454, 5462, 5463, 5467,
    5470, 5472
Priest, 1676, 1677, 5346
Primary education, 2242, 2248
Primary school, 2258, 2412, 2428,
    2448
Primitive religion, 1604, 1612-1618
Primitive society, 2819
Principal components analysis, 524
Prison, 663, 5444, 5447, 5451, 5453,
    5458-5461, 5465, 5469
Private education, 2162
Probability calculus, 552
Probability model *see* Stochastic
    model
Probation system, 5443, 5449
Problem solving, 630, 746, 749
Production, 4346, 4352, 4365, 4384
Profession, *see* Occupation
Professionalization, 4608, 4616
Professor, 2360
Profit, 4310
Proletariate, 2570, 2571, 3042, 4939
Propaganda, 1947, 1954
Property, 2528, 4239, 4240
Protest movement, 5084, 5088, 5091-
    5093, 5095, 5096, 5130
Protestant, 1619, 1620
Protestant church, 1642, 1643, 1646
Protestant ethics, 372, 1733
Protestantism, 1640
Proust, M., 245

Psychiatrist, 5569, 5640, 5661, 5669, 5680
Psychiatry, 5569
Psychoanalysis, 576, 583, 593, 595
Psychodrama, 491, 492
Psycholinguistics, 1838, 1856
Psychosociology, 587, 598
Psychotherapy, 579, 601
Public administration, 5032, 5036, 5037, 5042-5044, 5047-5049
Public education, 2196
Public finance, 4458
Public health, 5477, 5583, 5586, 5589, 5613
Public opinion, 1171, 1173, 1175-1179, 1181-1183, 1186, 1188
Public school, *see* Secondary school
Puerto Rico
  emigration, 3687
  female labour, 4527
  nationalism, 4947
  sexology, 3253
  urban development, 4204
  village, 3880
Pulszky, Agost, 4983
Punishment, 5448, 5452, 5455, 5456, 5471
Pupil, 2274, 2276
Puritanism, *see* Protestant ethics

Questionnaire, 466, 469, 473-476, 478-480
Quota sampling, 1264

Race, 1446, 2996, 3386, 3539, 3563, 3567, 3587, 4307, 4660
Race relations, 3613, 3614, 3616, 3617, 3626
Racial attitude, 2224, 2640, 3637, 3648, 4172
Racial conflict, 3641, 3651
Racial discrimination, 1723, 2513, 2591, 3631, 3636, 3647, 4151
Racial prejudice, 3628-3630, 3632, 3650
Racial segregation, 3634, 3638, 3640, 3644, 4141
Racism, 2551, 3633, 3639, 3645, 3646, 3649, 3653
Radicalism, 2349, 2638
Radio, 2023
Reading, 696, 699
Readings, 197
Recreation, 4098, 4861
Recruitment, 4495
Reference group, 866, 1407, 1418, 4443
Reference work, 142
Refugee, 3699, 3712
Regional government, 5059, 5060
Regional planning, 4077, 4461-4463
Regression analysis, 521

Relative deprivation, 716, 5193
Reliability, 450
Religion, 1004, 1585-1588, 1590, 1594, 1595, 1597, 1599, 1600
Religious assembly, 1647
Religious behaviour, 1718-1726, 1728-1732, 1734-1737, 3144
Religious community, 1652-1654, 1736
Religious freedom, 1727
Religious history, 1598
Religious institution, 1645, 1649, 1650
Religious minister, 1093, 1674, 1675, 1678
Religious mission, 1756
Religious movement, 1748, 1750, 1784
Religious participation, 5123
Religious practice, 1754, 1762, 1765, 1770, 1780
Religious prosecution, 1774
Religious reform, 1536, 1755, 1782
Religious representation, 1712, 2042, 2046
Religious revival, 1772
Religious sciences, 1592, 1596, 1603
Religious symbolism, 1708, 1709
Religious syncretism, 1702
Research, 75, 76, 87, 88, 90, 94, 317, 3328, 3538
Research centre, 104, 106, 1589
Research coordination, 108, 117
Research council, 111
Research foundation, 116
Research institution, 103, 107
Research method, 131, 391, 395, 399, 401, 403, 578, 5264
Research policy, 112-114, 119
Research priority, 109, 110, 118
Research strategy, 398
Research technique, 389, 392, 393, 400, 407, 410, 5260, 5267
Research trend, 68, 82, 83, 91, 96, 3340, 3984
Research unit, 105
Research worker, 61, 62, 1535
Residential mobility, 4148, 4157, 4176
Residential segregation, 4140, 4141, 4178, 4186, 4195
Resistance to change, 2767
Responsibility, 1146, 1520, 1527
Retirement, 4600, 4603, 4604
Reunion Island, rural society, 3886
Review, *see* Journal
Revolt, 1452, 1510
Revolution,2740-2742, 2753, 2754, 2758, 2759, 2764, 2768, 2771, 2774, 2777, 2786
Revolutionary movement, 5086, 5087, 5090
Rhodesia
  rural migration, 3753

Rhodesia *[contd]*
  urbanization, 4036
Rickert, H., 199
Risk, 554
Rite, 1684, 1692
Ritual, *see* Rite
Rokeach, Milton, 1701
Role, 625, 1092, 1094, 1098, 1100, 1103, 1104, 1106, 1107, 3276, 3432, 5103
Role change, 1096
Role chart, 1101, 1105
Role conflict, 1001
Role differentiation, 1093
Role perception, 1095
Role playing, 1102, 1108
Role set, 1099
Role taking, 1097
Romania
  cultural contact, 1374
  health service, 5631
  national minority, 3589
  physician, 5641
  population policy, 3195
  social structure, 2462
  sociology of development, 2800
  urbanization, 4013
  witchcraft, 1609
Rothvoss, Mariano Gonzalez, 173
Round table, *see* Symposium
Rule, *see* Norm
Ruling class, 2681, 4969
Rumour, 1950, 1953
Rural area, 3002, 3873
Rural community, *see* Village
Rural development, 3958, 3961-3963, 3965, 3966, 3969, 3973, 3976, 3978, 5060
Rural environment, 3887, 3892, 3903, 3909, 3938, 3949, 3954
Rural exodus, *see* Rural migration
Rural life, 3893, 3895, 3897-3902, 3910, 3913, 3915, 3919, 3922, 3940, 3943, 3945, 3947, 3951
Rural migration, 3747, 3748, 3751, 3752, 3759, 3771, 3772, 3775, 3779, 3780, 3782, 3786, 3791, 3795, 3797
Rural planning, 3959, 3968, 3974
Rural population, 3062, 3067
Rural society, 1676, 2563, 2615, 2805, 3015, 3286, 3408, 3885, 3886, 3896, 3898, 3906, 3918, 3921, 3923, 3924, 3927, 3928, 3931, 3940, 3948, 4513
Rural sociology, 192, 3848-3852
Rural-urban, 3138, 3989, 5350
Rwanda, child, 2922

Sacred, 1704, 1705, 1707
Saint, 1706
Salesman, *see* Commercial worker

Sample survey, 463
Sanction, 1398
Sartre, Jean-Paul, 226, 301
Saudi Arabia
  higher education, 2336
  kinship, 3364
  occupational stratification, 4647
  sedentarization, 3831
  student, 4647
Scandinavia, town, 4081
Scarcity, 5300
Schelsky, Helmut, 1196
Schizophrenia, 550, 3077, 3081, 3086
Scholarization, 2208, 2233, 2238, 2241
School, 2260, 2264, 2265, 2267, 2269, 3912
School achievement, *see* Academic success
School adjustment, 1414, 2289, 2292, 2294
School administration, 2277-2286
School attendance, 2291
School child, 2273, 2275
School dropout, 2235, 2239
School environment, 2288, 2290, 2293
School failure, 2412
Schooling, 2230, 2232, 2234, 2240, 3927, 4298
Schutz, Alfred, 240, 344, 1903
Science, 747, 1206, 1786, 1788, 1789, 1791, 1793, 1794, 1804, 1805, 1809, 1810, 1814, 1815, 1819, 1821, 1825, 1826, 1831, 1832, 1835, 1836, 2403
Science policy, 115
Sciences of man, *see* Social sciences
Scotland
  emigration, 3686
  school, 2267
  university, 2267
Sculpture, 2083
Secondary education, 721, 2245, 2247, 2250, 2252, 2253, 2256
Secondary school, 2258, 2259, 2261, 2268, 2270, 2271
Secret society, 1268
Sect, 1655, 1658, 1659, 1663, 1664, 3380
Sectarianism, 1674
Secularization, 1747, 1757, 1771
Sedentarization, 3831
Self concept, 631, 635-637, 639, 643, 916
Self-esteem, 624, 638, 642, 646, 649, 651, 3580
Self-evaluation, 626, 627
Self-management, 4318, 4319, 4322, 4332, 4337
Self-perception, 625, 653, 1148, 3468
Semantic differential, 1905, 1928

Semantics, 341, 1851, 1853, 1854
Seminar, 427
Semiology, 1846, 2014, 2055
Semiotics, 1839, 1842, 1850, 1865,
    4854
Semiskilled worker, 4674
Senegal
    agricultural cooperative, 4395
    bourgeoisie, 2642
Sex, 830, 1104, 1142, 1164, 1456,
    2232, 2868, 2869, 2871, 2872,
    2874-2876, 2878-2880, 2882-2887,
    2889, 2890, 2893, 2894, 3260,
    3268, 3382, 3507, 4099
Sex differentiation, 2282, 2867, 2891,
    2892, 3273, 3314, 4660
Sex distribution, 3430, 4289
Sexology, 3237, 3239, 3249, 3251,
    3253, 3264
Sexual behaviour, 1213, 3234, 3235,
    3241, 3242, 3254, 3256, 3257,
    3260, 3261, 3263
Sexual intercourse, 3240, 3255
Sexuality, 3236, 3238, 3243, 3244,
    3246, 3259, 3262
Seychelles, child, 2930
Shils, Edward, 1242
Sierra Leone
    family, 5657
    foreign labour, 4531
    social worker, 5657
Sign, 1891, 1895
Simmel, Georg, 201, 272, 273
Simulation, 553, 555, 1109, 1218
Singapore
    mortality, 3122
    urban environment, 4010
Skilled worker, 4671
Slavery, 2106, 2529, 2532, 2534-2536,
    2538-2541, 2545
Slum, 3617, 4056, 4143, 4144, 4154,
    4161, 4181, 4190, 4193, 4197
Small group, 921-925, 927, 929-932,
    934
Small town, 812, 3783, 4050, 4063,
    4065, 4068, 4074
Smith, Adam, 4238
Smoking, 5306, 5317, 5338
Sociability, 781
Social action, 5475, 5477, 5478, 5503
Social adjustment, 1411, 1427, 2990
Social and cultural anthropology,
    1224-1234, 1237, 1238, 1534
Social anthropology, *see* Social and
    cultural anthropology
Social assimilation, 2158
Social assistant, *see* Social worker
Social casework, *see* Casework
Social change, 654, 716, 870, 1056,
    1300, 1354, 1617, 1645, 2069,
    2137, 2502, 2738, 2743, 2744,
    2746, 2748-2752, 2755-2757, 2760,

2761, 2765, 2766, 2770, 2772,
    2773, 2775, 2776, 2778, 2780,
    2782-2785, 2787-2789, 2944, 3134,
    3338, 3485, 3534, 5217
Social class, 796, 1207, 1566, 1708,
    1766, 2521, 2544, 2550, 2555,
    2560, 2565, 2566, 2568, 2575,
    2576, 2590, 2591, 2601, 2603-
    2605, 2608, 2609, 2611, 2613,
    2616, 2620, 2625, 2627, 2631,
    2637, 2638, 2640, 2641, 2646,
    2647, 2651-2655, 2752, 2794,
    3156, 3311, 3890, 3896, 4099,
    4250, 4308, 4615, 4701, 4775,
    4955, 5159, 5424
Social communication, *see* Communica-
    tion
Social conflict, *see* Conflict
Social conformity, 1493, 1413, 1431,
    2671
Social consciousness, 1405, 1416,
    1417, 1432
Social control, 1103, 1149, 1385,
    1389, 1393, 1394, 1402, 1413,
    1485, 1507, 1531, 2486
Social desirability, 5329
Social development, *see* Social change
Social differentiation, 2495, 2509-
    2511, 2520, 2526
Social distance, 629
Social dynamics, 2466
Social evolution, *see* Social change
Social fact, 342
Social factor, 1337
Social group, *see* Group
Social group work, 2985
Social hierarchy, 2496
Social history, 2482, 2729, 2734
Social hygiene, 5605
Social influence, 1380, 1391
Social insurance, *see* Social security
Social integration, 1414, 1424
Social interaction, 749, 1406, 1408,
    1410, 1415, 1421, 1422, 2838
Social isolation, 1496, 1508
Social justice, 1572, 5494, 5509
Social medicine, 5562, 5563, 5575
Social mobility, 2261, 2449, 2506,
    2508, 2706-2716, 2718-2722, 2724-
    2728, 5670
Social order, 1190, 1385, 2454, 2458,
    2461, 2473, 2486
Social origin, 2663, 2669, 2672
Social participation, 1420, 1429,
    1440, 2279, 2892
Social pathology, 5274, 5277
Social perception, 790, 791, 795,
    1095, 1103, 1391, 5184
Social planning, 141, 440, 533, 4120,
    5481, 5483, 5485, 5487, 5489,
    5491, 5497, 5502, 5504, 5514,
    5516, 5521, 5522

Social pluralism, 2513
Social policy, 456, 1495, 1529, 5023,
    5473, 5476, 5490, 5493, 5505,
    5507, 5510, 5511, 5513, 5515,
    5519, 5520
Social power, *see* Social control
Social pressure, *see* Social control
Social problem, 5263, 5270, 5272,
    5273, 5275, 5276, 5278
Social progress, 2745, 2762, 2763,
    4247
Social protest, 1507
Social psychologist, 52
Social psychology, 573-575, 577,
    578, 580-582, 584, 586, 588-
    592, 594, 596, 597, 599, 600,
    602-606, 885, 894, 896, 1808
Social reform, 5482
Social representation, 1159, 1165
Social research, 5260, 5262, 5264-
    5269
Social role, *see* Role
Social sciences, 1-3, 5, 6, 13, 15,
    24, 28, 30, 31, 35, 37, 41, 44,
    46
Social security, 3017, 5525, 5527,
    5528-5535, 5639
Social service, 5642, 5644, 5645,
    5647, 5651, 5652, 5655, 5663,
    5673, 5679
Social status, *see* Status
Social stratification, 2210, 2491,
    2493, 2497, 2499, 2500, 2501,
    2506, 2508, 2518, 2522, 2544,
    2661, 2663, 3254
Social stratum, 2492, 2521
Social structure, 684, 1273, 2455-
    2457, 2459, 2460, 2462, 2464,
    2467, 2468, 2470, 2471, 2477,
    2479, 2481-2483, 2485, 2487,
    2488, 2568, 5187
Social system, 1341, 2463, 2465,
    2469, 2472, 2474-2476, 2478,
    2480, 2484
Social work, 4304, 5536, 5537-5541,
    5543-5556, 5630
Social worker, 5555, 5646, 5650,
    5656, 5657, 5660, 5671, 5677
Socialism, 612, 1327, 2503, 4252,
    4275, 4923, 4927, 4931, 4934,
    4936-4939, 4942, 4945, 4946,
    4949
Socialist country, 4256, 4258, 4260,
    4267, 4268
Socialist society, 1311, 2481, 2711,
    4255, 4257, 4259, 4261, 4266,
    4269-4271, 4373, 4465, 4686
Socialization, 583, 1404, 1409, 1412,
    1419, 1423, 1426, 1428, 1430,
    1463, 1935, 2136, 2140, 2969,
    3366, 4898, 5313, 5469

Society, 1333, 1336, 1338-1340, 1343,
    2507, 4537
Socioeconomic status, 2659, 4704
Sociolinguistics, 466, 1840, 1841,
    1862, 1866
Sociological analysis, 426, 431, 434
Sociological association, 127-129
Sociological society, *see* Sociolo-
    gical association
Sociologism, 272, 273
Sociologist, 47-51, 53-57, 59, 60,
    4342, 5269
Sociology, 4, 7-12, 14, 16-20, 22,
    23, 25-27, 29, 31, 33, 34, 36,
    38-40, 42, 43, 45
Sociology of art, 2040, 2041, 2043,
    2045, 2052, 2056, 2058, 2061
Sociology of development, 2795-2797,
    2802, 2804, 2806, 2808, 2814,
    2815, 2817, 2818, 2820, 2824,
    2826, 2828-2832, 2836
Sociology of knowledge, 83, 1790,
    1800, 1801, 1803, 1813, 1816-
    1818, 1820, 1823, 1824, 1827,
    1837, 2061, 2731
Sociology of law, 1540, 1549, 1555,
    1556, 1559, 1560, 1563, 1573,
    1577, 1582, 5381
Sociology of leisure, 3945, 4823,
    4824, 4828-4831, 4835, 4837,
    4839, 4842-4844
Sociology of literature, 2063, 2064,
    2079
Sociology of music, 2085, 2089, 2090,
    2092, 2095
Sociology of organizations, 975,
    977, 981, 983, 985, 988, 991,
    994
Sociology of religion, 1584, 1588,
    1591, 1593, 1601, 1602, 1604-
    1606, 1607
Sociology of theatre, 2097
Sociology of work, 4467, 4468, 4824
Sociometric choice, 825, 827
Sociometric relations, 750, 802,
    807, 831, 929, 1404
Sociometric status, 817, 4586
Sociometry, 2275
Soldier, *see* Military
Solidarity, 812, 813, 819, 820
Song, 2088, 2091, 2093
Sorcery, *see* Witchcraft
South Africa (Republic of)
  apartheid, 3635
  external migration, 3676
  government, 5017
  industrial relations, 4711
  military, 5017
  population evolution, 3045
  prejudice, 1152
  racial prejudice, 3629

South Africa *[contd]*
  rural migration, 3752
  university, 3635
South Tirol, interethnic relations,
  3622
Space, 412,413
Spain
  affluent society, 2607
  alcoholism, 5304
  Church and State, 1753, 1759
  civil servant, 5034
  class consciousness, 2607
  class structure, 2607
  class struggle, 2572
  cultural relations, 4881
  culture change, 2828
  current research, 84
  documentation centre, 146
  electoral sociology, 5186
  family, 3322, 3333
  farmer, 3953
  feminism, 3509
  fertility, 3152
  housing, 4177
  ideology, 1207
  internal migration, 3769
  Islam, 1630
  labour conflict, 4793
  marginality, 1434
  metropolitan area, 3997
  neighbourhood, 4187
  penitentiary system, 5466
  political sociology, 4901
  private education, 2162
  religious behaviour, 1729
  rural migration, 3748
  rural society, 4513
  social change, 3485
  social class, 1207, 2604, 2641,
    4701
  social consciousness, 1417
  social history, 2729
  social security, 5535
  sociology of development, 2828
  sociology of literature, 2064
  sociology of religion, 1584
  sociology of theatre, 1385
  technician, 4701
  tourism, 4881
  town, 1635, 4047, 4057, 4064
  university, 2354
  urban population, 3060
  urban society, 4105
  urban structure, 4022
  urbanism, 4233
  village, 3874
  wildlife protection, 3818
  woman worker, 4513
  woman's status, 3485
  working class, 2607
  working population, 3058
Spectator, 1374, 2027

Speech, 933, 1910, 1924, 1932, 1935,
  1938
Spencer, Herbert, 268
Sport, 846, 932, 1156, 1222, 1895,
  4624, 4853, 4855-4859, 4862-4865,
  4867-4871, 4873, 4875, 4876,
  4878, 4879, 4882-4885, 4887-4889,
  4891, 4892, 4894-4899
Sri Lanka
  birth control, 3204
  political party, 5083
Srole's scale, *see* Anomia
Stable population, 3020
Standard of living, 4290, 4303
State, 4967, 4969, 4971, 4975, 4977,
  4979, 4980, 4982-4984, 4986-4990,
  4992-4994
Statistical analysis, 473, 501, 504,
  510, 514, 518, 519
Statistical data, 505
Statistical model, 502, 507, 513,516
Statistics, 503, 506, 508, 509, 511,
  512, 515, 517, 520, 535
Status, 1492, 1720, 2647, 2657, 2658,
  2660-2662, 2664-2666, 2668, 2670,
  2671, 2673-2677, 3563, 3899, 4707,
  5159
Status congruency, 2667
Stereotype, 484, 795, 818, 1142-1144,
  1147, 1149, 1151, 1155-1158, 1161,
  1164, 2352
Stochastic model, 2905
Stochastic processes, 549, 550
Stock market, 4456
Strategy, 762
Strauss, Leo, 223
Strike, 4780, 4782, 4783, 4785, 4786,
  4791, 4794, 4798
Structuralism, 202, 207, 239, 242,
  262, 304, 316, 1280, 1713, 3361
Structure, 368-370, 373
Student, 1413, 2300, 2311, 2322,
  2324, 2330, 2332, 2335, 2344,
  2348, 4647, 5136
Student movement, 2296, 2319, 2326,
  2333, 2351, 2361
Student organization, 2345, 2349,
  2353
Suburb, 4131, 4203, 4216, 4219, 4227,
  4232
Sudan
  rural migration, 3779
  unemployment, 3779
  village, 3853
Suicide, 5366, 5368, 5374, 5388,
  5391, 5398, 5403, 5405, 5413,
  5414, 5420, 5426
Superstition, 1700
Supervisor, 4695
Survey, 452, 453, 455, 3184, 4662
Survey data, 457, 458

Sweden
  adult education, 2362
  changing society, 2811
  curriculum, 2362
  employee, 4692
  employers'organization, 4734
  external migration, 3673
  industrial relations, 4713
  joint management, 4813
  national minority, 3536
  occupation, 2669
  pressure group, 4692, 5097
  social origin, 2669
  sociology of development, 2817
  sociology of leisure, 4823
  suburb, 4227
  suicide, 5368
  welfare State, 5492
  workers'participation, 4809
Switzerland
  consumer, 4447
  cultural pluralism, 2170
  educational institution, 2171
  federalism, 4968
  foreign worker, 4516
  labour law, 4731
  press, 1993
  psychiatrist, 5661
  student organization, 2345
  urban government, 4100
Syllabus, *see* Curriculum
Symbol, 1867, 1876, 1897, 1903
Symbolism, 1871
Sympathy, 804, 815
Symposium, 1613, 3237
Syria
  illiteracy, 2364
  population evolution, 3041
  working class, 2574
Systems analysis, 428, 430, 435

Taiwan
  economic development, 3032
  fertility, 3138, 3151
  higher education, 2327
  population equilibrium, 3032
  rural-urban, 3138
  urbanization, 4021
Tanzania
  educational policy, 2185
  health, 5621
  medical sociology, 5621
  underdevelopment, 2825
Taxation, 4459
Taxonomy, 374, 375
Teacher, 2434, 2436, 2437, 2439,
  2441-2445, 2448-2450, 5167
Teacher training, 2435, 2438, 2446,
  2447
Teaching, 1096, 2416, 2421, 2423
Technical education, 2401-2403

Technical progress, 4347, 4351, 4355,
  4361, 4363, 4364, 4366, 4367,
  4369, 4374, 4379, 4385, 4672
Technician, 4696, 4700, 4701
Technocracy, 5031, 5035, 5039, 5041,
  5046
Technology, 1019, 1809, 4345, 4348-
  4350, 4353, 4356, 4358-4360,
  4362, 4370, 4375, 4376, 4381,
  4383
Telecommunication, 2018, 2036
Television, 1852, 2016, 2017, 2020-
  2022, 2024-2035, 2037, 2038,
  2432, 4446
Terminology, 151
Terror, 712
Terrorism, 1433, 1438, 1453, 1455,
  1488, 1491
Tertiary sector, 4424
Test, 489, 490, 1158
Textbook, 189, 192, 193, 195, 2206
Thailand
  Church and State, 1777
  employee, 4688
  ethnic group, 3564
  fertility, 3154, 3179
  internal migration, 3154
  labour migration, 3154
  rural planning, 3974
  rural society, 3931
Theatre, 2100-2102
Theft, 1095, 5371, 5373, 5384, 5415,
  5417
Theory, 206, 211, 213, 215, 220,222,
  230, 232, 234, 241, 244, 247,
  254, 258, 263, 265, 267, 275-277,
  288, 291, 292, 303, 307, 317,
  318, 328, 1034, 1796, 1802, 4786
Therapeutic group, 933, 946
Thesis, 186-188, 190, 191, 194, 196
Thief, 5437, 5441
Thinking, 695, 701
Time, 414, 416
Time budget, 668, 671, 672, 4569,
  4570-4576, 4852
Toffler, Alvin, 264
Tönnies, F., 218
Topitsch, Ernst, 260
Topological analysis, 1097
Tourism, 4874, 4880, 4881, 4893
Town, 531, 922, 1472, 1635, 2583,
  3609, 4044, 4046-4051, 4054,
  4056-4058, 4060, 4066, 4071,
  4072, 4075, 4079, 4080, 4081-
  4086, 4090, 4091, 4093, 4409,
  5434
Town centre, 4224
Town dweller, 4139, 4188, 4192
Town planning, 4172, 4200-4202, 4205,
  4206,4209, 4210, 4213,4217, 4218,
  4221, 4222, 4234, 4709, 5501

Trade union, 4738, 4741–4745, 4753–
    4759, 4762, 4769, 4770, 4772–
    4776, 4778, 5009, 5132
Trade unionism, 4737, 4748, 4751,
    4761, 4764, 4767, 4771, 5221
Tradition, 1512, 1514, 3266, 3277,
    3439
Traditional society, 2792, 2812,
    2827, 4080
Training group, 928
Tramp, 5433
Transport, 4425–4427
Trend report, 66, 71, 80, 93, 3323,
    3851
Triad, 548, 867, 937
Tribalism, 1417, 3652
Tribe, 3535, 3541, 3576, 3584
Trinidad, emigration, 3683
Trobriand Islands, social strati-
    fication, 2518
Tunisia
    agricultural cooperative, 4395
    educational system, 2163
    handicraft, 4423
    health care, 5604
    immigrant, 3702
    nomadism, 3781
    rural migration, 3795
    slum, 4144
    social class, 2583
    town, 2583
    village, 3856
    women's promotion, 3500
Turkey
    changing society, 2821
    fertility, 3138
    immigrant assimilation, 3725
    Islam, 2949
    political participation, 5155
    rural-urban, 3138
    survey, 4662
    trade unionism, 4771
    vocational guidance, 4662
    women's promotion, 3464
    women's rights, 3465
    youth, 2949
Two person game, 558
Typology, 1408

Uncertainty, 609
Underdevelopment, 2790, 2793, 2798,
    2803, 2807, 2808, 2816, 2825
Underemployment, 4488, 4491
Understanding, 214, 352, 357, 362
Unemployment, 3779, 4487, 4489,
    4491–4493
Unidimensional scale, 565
Union of Soviet Socialist Republics
    adolescent, 2951
    birth control, 3210
    class differentiation, 2635
    class structure, 2634

criminology, 5356
current research, 98, 3549
deviance, 1445
document analysis, 139
educational policy, 2174
emigration, 3679
ethnicity, 3549
family, 3328, 3342
health care, 5599
housing conditions, 4163
intelligentsia, 2696
labour law, 4727
labour mobility, 2712
manager, 4693
mass communication, 1988
national development, 2822
occupational prestige, 4661
patriotism, 4944, 4951
peasantry, 3942
population equilibrium, 3024
population evolution, 2822
press, 2001
reference, 142
religious prosecution, 1774
research trend, 91
rural life, 3922, 3943, 3945
social and cultural anthropology,
    3549
social class, 2568
social hygiene, 5607
social mobility, 2712
social stratum, 2521
social structure, 2568
socialist country, 4268
socialist society, 4259
sociology of development, 2815
sociology of leisure, 3945
standard of living, 4290
State, 4992
technical progress, 4374
town, 4060, 4071, 4085, 4086
town planning, 4210
village, 3868, 3883
way of life, 1256, 2635
woman worker, 4529
women's promotion, 3473
women's rights, 3524
women's status, 3494
worker, 4677
working class, 2614, 2629, 2592,
    2632, 2650, 2656
United Kingdom
    abortion, 3225
    academic aptitude, 2411
    automation, 4357
    case study, 3225
    changing society, 4114
    child adoption, 3429
    class conflict, 2562
    collective agreement, 4818, 4821
    community development, 3846
    consumption, 4442

United Kingdom *[contd]*
  crime, 5377
  delinquent, 5430
  employee, 4690
  employers'organization, 4734
  enterprise, 4324
  family life, 4844
  female, 4442
  health : 5593, 5606 ; service,
    5624, 5634, 5638
  higher education, 2298, 2317
  housing : 4153 ; policy, 4171,
    4172
  immigrant, 3724, 3740
  industrial relations, 2562, 4723
  industrialization, 3272
  industry, 4357
  labour law, 4733
  labour movement, 4768
  law, 1541, 1550
  malthusianism, 3188
  marriage, 3272
  medicine, 5559
  metropolis, 4069
  middle class, 2561, 2584
  migration, 3656
  national development, 2799
  new town, 4099
  parent-child relations, 4099
  party membership, 5147
  physician, 5670
  police, 5006, 5007
  political participation, 5074
  political party, 5070, 5074, 5076,
    5077
  prejudice, 1152
  prison, 5458
  protestant Church, 1642
  psychiatrist, 5569
  psychiatry, 5569
  race relations, 3613
  racial attitude, 4172
  rural planning, 3959
  school dropout, 2235
  sex, 4099
  slavery, 2536
  slum, 4154
  social class, 2631, 2651, 2655,
    4099
  social medecine, 5562
  social mobility, 2721,2722, 5670
  social problem, 5275
  social research, 5269
  social stratification, 2497
  social work, 5537
  sociology of leisure, 4844
  status, 2662
  stereotype, 1164
  strike, 4782, 4798
  theft, 5373
  town planning, 4172

  trade union, 4738, 4743, 4758,
    4762, 4778
  trade unionism, 4751
  university college, 2300
  urban government, 4099
  urban life, 4114
  urban society, 4115
  vocational interest, 4633
  wage, 4308
  welfare State, 5500
  women's rights, 4762
  women's status, 3475
  worker, 4679
  workers'participation, 4816
  working class, 2602
United States of America
  academic aptitude, 2411
  adolescent, 3637
  adult age, 2979
  adult education, 2365, 2376, 2377
  advertising, 1945
  aged, 2985, 2999, 5679
  ageing, 3005
  agricultural economics, 4397
  agriculture, 4407
  alcoholism, 5324
  army, 3632, 5207, 5227
  bibliography, 3727
  birth control, 3187
  birth interval, 3163
  capital city, 4045
  capital punishment, 5446, 5457
  caste, 2537, 2566
  catholic, 1628
  central government, 5050
  child : 2962 ; adoption, 3395
  civism, 2942
  class differentiation, 4437
  collective bargaining, 4800, 4804,
    4806
  coloured person, 3603
  community, 3835, 3840
  community participation, 3844
  consumption, 4437
  contraception, 3217, 3232
  crime, 5369, 5387, 5389, 5400, 5427
  cross cultural analysis, 2945
  cross national analysis, 2537
  delinquent, 5435, 5436
  drug : 5326, 5327, 5461 ; addiction,
    5325, 5343
  educational planning, 2156, 2186,
    2207
  educational policy, 2205, 3640
  educational reform, 2153, 2190
  educational system, 2150, 2197
  elections, 5173, 5190
  electoral campaigning, 5176
  enterprise, 4324
  equal opportunity, 2209, 2214,
    2217, 2227

United States of America *[contd]*
ethnic group, 3538, 3572, 3590, 3591
ethnicity, 3555, 5123
ethos, 1533
exodus, 3677
family : 3338, 3355 ; environment, 3424 ; group, 3400 ; planning, 3197, 3206, 3219, 3227 ; size, 3418, 3430, 3461, 3463
fear, 5369
female labour, 4507
fertility, 3134, 3175, 3197, 3219, 3301
foreign policy, 5244, 5245
futurology, 2735
guerilla, 5193
health, 5578, 5585, 5588, 5592
health service, 5622, 5626, 5635
higher education, 2301, 2303, 2323, 2343, 2350
homicide, 5397
housing conditions, 4155
housing policy, 4151, 4152, 4172
husband, 5153
income distribution, 4294
indian, 3592, 3598, 3599, 3609, 3611, 3612
industrial society, 2579
industrialization, 4779
immigrant : 3700, 3710, 3723 ; assimilation, 3722
immigration, 3727
inequality, 3725
infant mortality, 3117
interethnic relations, 3618
internal migration, 3762, 3776, 3796
international relations, 5237
journalist, 1996
juvenile delinquency, 4512
kinship, 3370, 3372, 3373
labour migration, 3758
labour movement, 4749, 4750, 4779
law, 1564
legal system, 1579
legislative behaviour, 5158
leisure, 4825
manager, 4703
medicine, 5559
medicine, sociology, 3085
medical care, 5589, 5594, 5596, 5597, 5612
mental disease, 3085, 3090
metropolis, 4042, 4070, 4089
middle class, 2581, 5062
military, 5244
military sociology, 5231
mixed marriage, 3307
modernization, 2769
morals, 1532
morbidity, 2891

mortality, 2891, 3103, 3113
multivariate analysis, 5369
mythology, 1717
national minority, 3359, 3571, 3579
nationalism, 3608
negro, 3597, 3605, 3607, 3608, 5112, 5124, 5140
new town, 2260, 4059
occupational choice, 4630, 4642
occupational sociology, 4613
occupational stratification, 4643, 4647
old age, 2992
parent-child relations, 3423
party identification, 5120
party membership, 5123
party system, 5061
penitentiary system, 5445
personnel management, 4546
police, 5004
political attitude, 2127, 5116
political behaviour, 5126, 5148, 5153
political culture, 5158
political elite, 5101, 5105
political faction, 5112
political leader, 5127
political modernization, 4985
political participation, 5124, 5140, 5149, 5164
political party, 5083
political socialization, 5112, 5142
polygyny, 3301
population growth, 3054
press, 3651
pressure group, 5098
prevention of delinquency, 5472
prison, 5447, 5461
probation system, 5443
profit, 4310
protest movement, 5092
punishment, 5456
race relations, 3616
racial attitude, 3637, 4172
racial conflict, 3651
racial discrimination, 3631, 3647, 4151
racial prejudice, 3632
racial segregation, 3634, 3640, 3644
racism, 3645
refugee, 3699
relative deprivation, 5193
religious behaviour, 1723
religious freedom, 1727
religious institution, 1650
religious participation, 5123
research, 3538
residential segregation, 4186, 4195

United States of America [contd]
  retirement, 4604
  rural migration, 3751, 3771, 3772, 3780
  rural society, 3928
  sex differentiation, 2891
  sex distribution, 3430
  sexuality, 3233
  slavery, 2529, 2538, 2539, 2545
  social change, 3134, 3338
  social class, 2566, 2608, 2609, 2646, 2647
  social group work, 2985
  social mobility, 2725
  social policy, 5507
  social problem, 5276, 5281
  social security, 5528
  social service, 5652, 5679
  social system, 2484
  social work, 5550
  social worker, 5656, 5677
  sport, 4896
  stereotype, 1164
  strike, 4782
  student : 2335, 4647 ; movement, 2361; organization, 2361
  suburb, 4216, 4227, 4131
  technocracy, 5031
  theft, 5373
  town, 3609, 4044, 4048, 4082, 4096
  town planning, 4172, 5501
  trade union, 4741, 4743
  urban government, 4113
  urban growth, 3998, 4097
  urban life, 3085, 4097
  urban planning, 4221
  urban population, 3057
  urbanization, 4011, 4016, 4397
  value, 1397, 1403
  violence, 1509, 5092
  voter, 5185
  voting behaviour, 5169, 5191
  voting turnout, 5174
  war, 5254
  way of life, 1317
  welfare : 4286; policy, 5501
  white, 3604
  wife, 5153
  woman worker, 4503
  women's rights, 3488
  working class, 2579
  youth, 2945, 5142
University, 1413, 2267, 2299, 2302, 2320, 2334, 2337-2341, 2346, 2352, 2354, 2356, 2357, 2359, 2421, 3635
University campus, 2297
University college, 2300, 2307, 2331, 5322
Upper class, 2569
Urban, 1212, 3983, 3985, 3988, 3991, 3994, 3996, 5293, 5296

Urban agglomeration, *see* Town
Urban area, 3797, 4019, 4037, 5588, 5625
Urban community, *see* Town
Urban concentration, 4001, 5487
Urban design, 4211, 4228, 4229
Urban development, 4204, 4207, 4208, 4220, 4223, 4225
Urban environment, 4010, 4014, 4023, 4026
Urban geography, 3986, 3995
Urban government, 4099-4101, 4103, 4107, 4111, 5113, 4118, 4130, 4133, 4134 ; *see also* Local Government
Urban growth, 3845, 3998, 4007, 4016, 4027, 4034, 4041, 4097
Urban life, 1262, 3085, 4097, 4098, 4114, 4116, 4119, 4121, 4123, 4124, 4126, 4128, 4131, 4132, 4135, 4137, 4834
Urban planning, *see* Town planning
Urban population, 2947, 3055-3057, 3060, 3063, 3066, 3068, 3069, 4037, 5125
Urban renewal, 4199, 4214, 4215, 4230
Urban-rural, *see* Rural-urban
Urban society, 1471, 1486, 1501, 4102, 4104-4106, 4108, 4110, 4115, 4117, 4120, 4125, 4127, 4129, 4136
Urban sociology, 192, 875, 3979-3982, 3984, 3987, 3990, 3992, 3993, 5290
Urban space, 4003
Urban structure, 4009, 4017, 4022, 4031
Urban transport, 4109, 4112, 4122
Urbanism, 4212, 4226, 4233
Urbanization, 3789, 3999, 4000, 4002, 4004, 4006, 4008, 4011-4013, 4015, 4016, 4018, 4020, 4021, 4024, 4025, 4028-4033, 4035, 4036, 4038-4040, 4397
Uruguay
  current research, 65
  military, 5225, 5230
Utility theory, 556
Utopia, 1192, 1194, 1202,

Validity, 448, 449
Value, 1379, 1383, 1386-1388, 1390, 1392, 1396, 1398-1401, 1403
Value system, 1048, 1286, 1384, 1395, 1397, 3940
Venezuela
  external migration, 3672
  internal migration, 3754
  marginality, 1444
  mental health, 5614
  population evolution, 3051

Venezuela *[contd]*
  social class, 2555, 2794
  town planning, 4206
  underdevelopment, 2794
  urban population, 3056
  violence, 2555
  youth, 2973
Verbal behaviour, 1904, 1908, 1916,
    1920, 1921, 1931, 1936, 2666
Verification, 361
Vertical mobility, 2717
Vietnam
  military, 5216
  political elite, 5088
  protest movement, 5088
  value, 1397
  war, 5254
Village, 1681, 2698, 2989, 3062,
    3076, 3133,3688, 3786, 3853-
    3872, 3873-3883, 4675
Violence, 782, 840, 1435, 1437,
    1458, 1459, 1467, 1469, 1472,
    1477, 1478, 1485, 1493, 1494,
    1498, 1502, 1509, 2016, 2555,
    4128, 5016, 5092
Vocabulary, 155
Vocational guidance, 1035, 4625,
    4629, 4653, 4662
Vocational interest, 4633, 4652
Vocational training, 2358, 4619,
    4622, 4627, 4634, 4639, 4646,
    4649, 4656, 4658, 4659
Voegelin, 284
Voluntary association, 1000-1002,
    1081
Voter, 5172, 5181, 5185, 5192
Voting behaviour, 2640, 5168, 5169,
    5184, 5187, 5191
Voting turnout, 5174, 5182

Wage, 4287, 4289, 4298, 4299, 4300,
    4306, 4311-4313
Wallerstein, 4280
War, 5248, 5251-5254
Way of life, 1239, 1240, 1243-1248,
    1251, 1255-1264, 1271, 1272,
    1274, 1275, 1277-1279, 1283,
    1287, 1288, 1290, 1294, 1297,
    1301, 1302, 1306, 1308-1311,
    1314, 1316-1318, 1320, 1949,
    1969, 2348, 2635, 2639, 2783,
    2951, 3919
Wealth, 4288
Weapon, 5258, 5259
Weber, Max,129, 143, 199, 203, 209,
    213, 215, 217, 218, 225, 231,
    234, 256, 267, 309, 310, 313,
    319, 323, 329, 330, 332, 333,
    346, 350, 351, 356, 366, 409,
    1058, 4237
Welfare, 1335, 4286, 4295, 4304,
    4315

Welfare policy, 5474, 5479, 5486,
    5488, 5495, 5499, 5501, 5508,
    5512, 5517, 5523, 5524
Welfare State, 5480, 5484, 5492,
    5496, 5498, 5500, 5518
Western Europe
  political party, 5080
  population policy, 3228
  underemployment, 4488
White, 3593, 3604, 4456
White collar worker, *see* Employee
Widowhood, 3108
Wife, 2910, 3309, 3315, 3316, 3318,
    3320, 3469, 5153
Wildlife protection, 3818
Wirth, Louis, 328
Witchcraft, 1609
Wittgenstein, L., 212, 254
Woman, 5359
Woman worker, 1314, 2440, 3950, 4287,
    4293, 4496, 4499, 4501-4507,
    4506, 4509, 4512, 4513, 4524,
    4526, 4528-4530, 4532, 4534
Woman's promotion, 2341, 3464,3473,
    3487, 3500, 3503, 3504, 3506,
    3512, 3523, 3525, 3532, 4846
Woman's status, 1722, 2586, 3467-
    3472, 3475-3482, 3490-3494, 3496-
    3499, 3501, 3502, 3510, 3513,
    3515, 3518, 3519, 3521, 3522,
    3527-3529, 4312, 4526
Woman's rights, 2619, 3465, 3483,
    3488, 3495, 3505, 3511, 3514,
    3524, 3530, 3533, 4762, 5172
Work study, *see* Ergonomics
Worker, 1388, 2038, 2672, 4667,4670,
    4672, 4675-4679, 4681-4687,5249
Workers'committee, 4746, 4766
Workers'education, 2378, 2391, 5522
Workers'participation, 4807, 4809,
    4811, 4812, 4814-4817, 4819,4820
Working class,2548, 2552, 2558, 2563,
    2567, 2573, 2574, 2578, 2579,
    2585, 2587, 2588, 2592, 2594,
    2596-2598, 2602, 2606, 2607, 2614,
    2615, 2617, 2628, 2629, 2632,
    2633, 2639, 2643, 2644, 2650,
    2656, 3136, 3506
Working conditions, 3062, 4496, 4504,
    4524, 4554-4567
Working group, 6
Working place, 4597, 4667
Working population, 3058, 3059,3064,
    3065, 4410
Working time, 4568, 4577
World politics, *see* International
    politics
World war, 5249
Worship, *see* Cult
Writer, 1077, 2068

Young worker, 4319, 4489, 4515, 4517, 4518, 4521, 4525, 4535, 4666
Youth, 736, 786, 1082, 1109, 1278, 1355, 1463, 1478, 1495, 1780, 1781, 2019, 2090, 2944-2947, 2949, 2950, 2954-2956, 2958-2962, 2965, 2967-2969, 2973-2977, 3393, 3940, 4831, 5142
Youth movement, 2957, 2972
Yugoslavia
  agricultural population, 3061
  current research, 70
  death, 1691
  educational policy, 2149, 2202
  F scale, 1170
  family environment, 3412
  health, 5578
  labour productivity, 4549
  rural environment, 3911
  self-management, 4318, 4332
  social structure, 2462
  sociology of development, 2795
  town planning, 4209
  woman worker, 4509
  youth movement, 2972

Zaire
  interethnic relations, 3621
  urban growth, 4034
Zambia
  village, 3853, 3855
Zimmerman, Carle C., 286

INDEX DES MATIERES

Abandon d'études, 2235, 2239
Abramowski, Edward, 3888
Absentéisme, 4602, 4605, 4606
Abstentionnisme électoral, 5145
Accès à l'éducation, 2208, 2216,
    2221, 2224-2226
Accomplissement, 734
Accroissement de la population, 3010,
    3012, 3019, 3022, 3025, 3026,
    3042, 3048, 3054, 3218, 5302
Acculturation, 1365, 1366, 1369,
    1372, 1373, 1377
Acculturation des immigrés, 3708,
    3731
Action, 244, 745, 754, 756, 760,
    761, 763, 765, 766, 887
Action sociale, 5475, 5477, 5478,
    5503
Actionnalisme, 766, 5084
Adaptation scolaire, 1414, 2289,
    2292, 2294
Adaptation sociale, 1411, 1427, 2990
Administration centrale, 5050
Administration communale, voir
    Administration locale
Administration de l'enseignement,
    2148, 2178, 2189, 2201, 2206,
    2453
Administration du personnel, 1023,
    4540-4547, 4551-4553
Administration locale, 5051, 5058,
    5135, 5138
Administration publique, 5032, 5036,
    5037, 5042-5044, 5047-5049
Administration régionale, 5059, 5060
Administration scolaire, 2277-2286
Administration urbaine, 4099-4101,
    4103, 4107, 4111, 4113, 4118,
    4130, 4133, 4134 ; voir aussi
    Administration locale
Adolescence, 2953, 2964
Adolescent, 624, 627, 893, 898, 1365,
    2948, 2951, 2952, 2963, 2966,
    2970, 2971, 3637, 5143, 5154
Adoption d'enfant, 3395, 3396, 3406,
    3429
Adorno, Th. W., 311
Adulte, 2957, 2980, 2981

Affectivité, 843
Affiliation au groupe, voir Appar-
    tenance au groupe
Affinité, 715, 1142
Afghanistan, village, 3859, 3878
Afrique
    acculturation, 1366
    armée, 5220
    bibliographie, 3468
    changement social, 1617
    classe sociale, 2591
    condition de la femme, 3467, 3481,
        3493
    conflit, 868
    délinquance juvénile, 5396
    développement rural, 3976
    discrimination raciale, 2591
    divorce, 3287
    droit, 1541
    église, 1641 ; église et état,
        1758
    élite, 2609
    enfant, 2935
    enseignement supérieur, 2309
    enseignement technique, 2403
    esclavage, 2530, 2534, 2535, 2540,
        2541
    ethnocentrisme, 1167
    évolution de la population, 3023,
        3039
    fécondité, 3147
    genre de vie, 1288
    identification culturelle, 1345
    migration : 3654; interne, 3745,
        3784 ; rurale, 3756
    monarchie, 4958
    mortalité : 3096 ; infantile, 3132
    musulman, 1625
    parti unique, 3652
    planification de la famille, 3196
    politique, 1758
    relations interethniques, 3624
    relations internationales, 1345
    religion primitive, 1613, 1617
    renouveau religieux, 1772
    science, 2403
    sculpture, 2083
    secte, 1659
    société rurale, 3896
    symbole, 1897

Afrique [suite]
  système d'éducation, 2150, 2158
  taux de fécondité, 3132
  tribalisme, 1417, 3652
  vie urbaine, 4128
  violence, 4127
Afrique du Sud (République d')
  apartheid, 3635
  évolution de la population, 3045
  gouvernement, 5017
  migration externe, 3676
  migration rurale, 3752
  militaire, 5017
  préjudice, 1152
  préjugé racial, 3629
  relations industrielles, 4711
  université, 3635
  urbanisation, 4036
Age, 4532, 5249
Age adulte, 2979
Ager, Waldemar, 1284
Agglomération urbaine, *voir* Ville
Agression, 841, 843, 845, 847-854,
  1222, 2016
Agressivité, 846, 856
Agriculteur, 3888, 3889, 3891, 3894,
  3904, 3905, 3907, 3908, 3912,
  3920, 3926, 3932, 3933, 3936,
  3939, 3944, 3946, 3952, 3953,
  5180
Agriculture, 3035, 4393, 4400, 4404,
  4407
Aire culturelle, 1254, 1305
Aire métropolitaine, 3997
Albanie, 2007, 5586
Alcoolique, 5305, 5311,5342
Alcoolisme, 5304, 5315,5320, 5322,
  5324, 5329, 5331, 5334, 5337,
  5340, 5344, 5345, 5348
Algérie
  classe sociale, 2605
  émigration, 3693, 3869
  mortalité : 3106, 3126 ; infantile,
    3127
  nomadisme, 3778
  réforme agraire, 3964
  santé, 5619
  village, 3866, 3869
  ville, 4066
Algorithme, 498
Aliénation,1440, 1442, 1450, 1457,
  1461, 1464, 1473, 1479, 1482,
  1487, 1500, 2496, 4824, 5151
Alimentation, 5292, 5297, 5301, 5302
Allemagne
  administration de l'enseignement,
    2178
  anarchisme, 4926
  collège universitaire, 2300
  développement urbain, 4223
  fécondité, 3177
  intelligentsia, 2685

  minorité nationale, 3548
  mouvement étudiant, 2296
  national-socialisme, 4956
  réunion, 130
  sport, 4897
  syndicat, 4772
Allemagne (République démocratique)
  classe ouvrière, 2578
  droit du travail, 4728
  formation professionnelle, 4639
  personnalité, 668
  planification de l'enseignement,
    2180
  politique démographique, 3211
  recherche en cours, 78
  relations parent-enfant, 3413
  sport, 4895
  structure de classe, 2578
  système d'éducation, 2168
Allemagne (République fédérale)
  administration du personnel, 4540
  châtiment, 5448
  chômage, 4489
  comportement électoral, 5187
  concentration urbaine, 4001
  conscience de classe, 2595
  culture, 3247
  école primaire, 2258
  école secondaire, 2258
  éducation des adultes, 2260
  église protestante, 1646
  enseignement supérieur, 2298
  état provisoire, 5492
  formation professionnelle, 4656
  génération, 2909
  groupe familial, 3440
  histoire sociale, 2482
  homme marginal, 1466
  homosexualité, 3247
  jeune travailleur, 4489
  jeunesse, 2977
  loisir, 4827, 4838
  organisation patronale, 4736
  politique d'éducation, 2195
  professionalisation, 4616
  réforme de l'enseignement, 2175
  secteur tertiaire, 4424
  sociologie bourgeoise, 2636
  sociologie électorale, 5189
  structure de classe, 2636
  structure sociale, 2482, 5187
  syndicat, 4755, 4774
  tendance de recherche, 96
  travailleur étranger, 4514
  travailleur social, 5646
  vieillesse, 3001
Allocations familiales, 5526
Althusser, Louis, 219, 222, 301
Ambition, 727
Amérique latine
  accroissement de la population,
    5302

Amérique latine [suite]
  acculturation, 1377
  agriculteur, 3908, 3946
  alimentation, 5302
  assimilation des immigrés, 3742
  capitalisme, 4929
  classe ouvrière, 2628
  classe sociale, 2611, 2619
  comportement religieux, 1728
  condition de la femme, 2586, 3510
  conscience de classe, 2586
  culture, 1298
  développement rural, 3963
  dimension de la famille, 3427
  droits de la femme, 2619
  état, 4984, 4994
  étude de cas, 2586
  fascisme, 4952
  fécondité, 3427
  genre de vie, 1287
  Islam, 1630
  littérature, 2075
  migration interne, 3757, 3798
  nationalisme, 4928, 4929, 4947
  oecuménisme, 1665
  parti politique, 5062
  participation politique, 5163
  paysannerie, 3934
  recherche démographique, 2858
  recherche en cours, 3992
  sociologie du développement, 2818
  sociologie militaire, 5214
  sociologie urbaine, 3992
  sous-développement, 2816
  système d'éducation, 2192, 2193
  terrorisme, 1455
  ville, 4083
  zone rurale, 3873
Amitié, 796,797,799,805,811,823,826,
  829,3305
Amour, 798, 816
Analphabétisme, 2364, 2370, 2371,
  2383, 2385
Analyse causale, 429, 433
Analyse comparative, 419, 427, 3848
Analyse contextuelle, 3500
Analyse d'audience, 1939
Analyse de contenu, 417,418,420,421
Analyse de groupe, 901, 909, 1466
Analyse de régression, 521
Analyse des composantes principales,524
Analyse documentaire, 139
Analyse écologique, 522
Analyse factorielle, 522? 528
Analyse fonctionnelle, 436
Analyse mathématique, 495, 2720
Analyse multivariée, 423-425,432,1098,
  3280,5369
Analyse organisationnelle, 974, 978,
  984, 987, 989, 995
Analyse sociologique, 426, 431, 434
Analyse statistique, 475, 501, 504,
  510, 514, 518, 519

Analyse systémique, 428, 430, 435
Analyse topologique, 1097
Analyse transculturelle, 422, 1107,
  2945, 2946,2953,3315,5316,5354
Analyse transnationale, 627, 1370,
  1481, 1542, 2537, 3339, 3848,
  4960, 5152, 5395
Anarchie, 4966
Anarchisme, 302,4924,4926,4930,4948
Angoisse, 646, 713
Anomia, 1436, 1447
Anomie, 1439, 1483
Anthropologie culturelle, *voir* Eth-
  nologie
Anthropologie sociale, *voir* Ethnolo-
  gie
Antisémitisme, 3642, 3643
Apartheid, 3635
Appartenance au groupe, 968, 969
Apprenti, 4680
Apprentissage, 685, 693,694,705,3717
Aptitude aux études, 2411, 2413
Arabie Saoudite
  enseignement supérieur, 2336
  étudiant, 4647
  parenté, 3364
  sédentarisation, 3831
  stratification professionnelle,4647
Architecture, 2080, 2081
Archives de données, *voir* Banque
  de données
Argentine
  classe sociale, 2575
  condition de la femme, 3492
  migration interne, 3790
  mouvement étudiant, 2351
  nationalisme, 2575
Aristocratie, 4957
Arme, 5258, 5259
Armée, 3632, 5207, 5208, 5212, 5213,
  5220, 5227
Arrow, 4295
Art, 1266, 2042, 2044, 2046, 2047,
  2050, 2051, 2053, 2055, 2077
Art dramatique, 2099
Art populaire, 2106
Artisanat, 4420, 4421-4423
Ascension sociale, *voir* Promotion
  sociale
Asie
  agriculteur, 3936
  analyse transculturelle, 2946
  condition de la femme, 3477
  enseignement supérieur, 2325
  fécondité, 3139
  jeunesse, 2946
  migration rurale, 3782
  militaire, 5229
  planification de l'enseignement,
    2170
  planification de la famille, 3209
  planification sociale, 5514

Asie [suite]
  société traditionnelle, 2812
  taudis, 4161
Asile, 2990
Aspiration, 721, 725, 726
Assassinat, *voir* Homicide
Assemblée religieuse, 1647
Assimilation des immigrés, 3503,
  3697, 3702, 3705, 3716, 3718,
  3721, 3723, 3725, 3728, 3730,
  3732, 3737, 3738, 3742, 4520
Assimilation sociale, 2158
Assistance, 1100
Assistante sociale, *voir* Travailleur
  social
Association de sociologie, 127-129
Association volontaire, 1000-1003,
  1081
Assurances sociales, *voir* Sécurité
  sociale
Athéisme, 1697, 1699
Attitude, 1109, 1110, 1123, 1127,
  1129, 1131, 1140, 1141, 1175,
  1512, 4501
Attitude envers le travail, 1019,
  3312, 4578, 4579, 4581, 4586,
  4587, 4593
Attitude politique, 2664, 3577,
  5114, 5116, 5127, 5152, 5154
Attitude raciale, 2224, 2640, 3637,
  3648, 4172
Attraction du groupe, 948
Attraction interpersonnelle, 800,
  801, 803, 806, 808, 810, 814,
  818, 821, 822, 830, 832, 938,
  2039
Audience, 1941, 2060
Auditeur, 1940
Australie
  artisanat, 4422
  classe dirigeante, 2680
  communication de masse, 1971
  droits de la femme, 3484
  épouse, 3316
  fécondité, 3185
  habitat, 3829
  immigrant, 3733
  immigration, 3739
  logement, 4158
  main d'oeuvre féminine, 3185
  migration interne, 3774
  nomadisme, 3777
  origine sociale, 2669
  pauvreté, 5291, 5295
  personne de couleur, 3602
  planification urbaine, 4231
  politique démographique, 3220
  profession, 2669
  sociologie du développement, 2829
  sport, 4879
  urbanisation, 4033
  vol, 5373

Autogestion, 4318, 4319, 4322, 4332
  4337
Automation, 4357
Automobile, 4425
Autorité, 302, 1070-1073, 1076, 1077
Autriche
  anarchisme, 4926
  logement, 4150
  minorité nationale, 3561
  recherche, 94
  structure sociale, 2471
Avenir *voir* Futur
Avortement, 3193, 3201, 3205, 3216,
  3223, 3225

Bahrein
  marché du travail, 4473
  travailleur étranger, 4473
Ball, Donald W., 180
Bangladesh
  fécondité, 3145
  mortalité infantile, 3110, 3124
  parenté, 3369
  travailleur féminin, 4502
Banlieue, 4131, 4203, 4216, 4219,
  4227, 4232
Banque, 4453
Banque de données, 132
Barbades
  famille, 3356
  fécondité, 3158
Battaglia, Felice, 174
Baudelot, 2225
Becker, Ernest, 282
Behaviourisme, 249, 266, 331
Belgique
  comité d'entreprise, 4746
  communauté religieuse, 1654
  délinquance juvénile, 5418
  divorce, 3279
  équilibre démographique, 3049
  formation professionnelle, 4627
  industrialisation, 4410
  manager, 4697
  médecine sociale, 5575
  migration interne, 3755
  parti politique, 5076
  politique du logement, 4164
  politique sociale, 5515
  population active, 4410
  relations interethniques, 3623
  temps de travail, 4568
Bénin, analphabétisme, 2383
Berger, Peter L., 1593
Bernard, Claude, 261
Besoin, 718, 724, 728, 731-733, 738,
  4445
Besoin d'affiliation, 828
Besoins d'éducation, 2229
Bibliographie, 89, 137, 138, 140,
  141, 143, 144, 271, 739, 1612,
  1637, 2112, 2128, 2193, 2206,

Bibliographie [suite]
    3191, 3344, 3468, 3470, 3727,
    4002, 4012, 4160, 4170, 4806,
    5082, 5087, 5135, 5357, 5530
Bibliothèque, 145, 147-149
Bien-être, 1335, 4286, 4295, 4304,
    4315
Bilinguisme, 701, 1915, 1925, 1933,
    1934
Biographie, 159, 161, 162, 164-166,
    172, 176, 178, 180
Biologie humaine, 2897, 2899, 2900,
    2903, 2904, 2906
Blanc, 3593, 3604, 4456
Bloch, Ernst, 236
Bloch, Herman D., 167
Bolivie
    agriculteur, 3932
    densité de la population, 3044
    élite, 3909
    fécondité, 3135
    milieu rural, 3909
    parti politique, 5063
Bonenfant, Jean-Charles, 168
Booth, Charles, 159
Botswana
    culture politique, 5156
    développement rural, 3972
    pays en développement, 3973
Bouddhisme, 1621
Boudon, R., 557
Boulding, Kenneth E., 297
Bouman, P. J., 177, 179
Bourdieu, Pierre, 2225
Bourgeoisie, 726, 1474, 2557, 2642,
    4982
Brecht, Arnold, 166
Brésil
    administration de l'enseignement,
        2201
    agriculteur, 5180
    agriculture, 3035
    assimilation des immigrés, 3737
    bibliographie, 3470
    communication, 1886
    condition de la femme, 3470
    consommation, 4448
    croissance urbaine, 4005
    développement économique, 4272
    développement national, 2679
    éducation permanente, 2363
    élections, 5180
    élite, 2679
    émigrant, 3688
    enseignement supérieur, 2316
    évolution de la population, 3031,
        3035
    famille étendue, 3335
    fécondité, 3176
    immigration, 3720
    indien, 3595, 3596

industrialisation, 4409
liberté de l'enseignement, 2182
marginalité, 1486, 4181
migration interne, 3790
migration rurale, 3775
modernisation politique, 4981
mortalité, 3098
noir, 3600
personne de couleur, 3594
planification de la famille, 3169
roman, 2071
santé publique, 5583
société en transformation, 2805
société rurale, 2805
société urbaine, 1486
syncrétisme religieux, 1702
taudis, 4181
taux de mortalité, 3115
taux de natalité, 3168
télévision, 2028
travailleur social, 5671
vie rurale, 3895
ville, 4062, 4409
Budget, 4454
Budget temps, 668, 671, 672, 4569,
    4570-4576, 4852
Bulgarie
    accroissement de la population,
        3026
    dynamique culturelle, 1360
    jeunesse, 3940
    politique démographique, 3026
    société rurale, 3940
    système de valeurs, 3940
    village, 3870
Bureaucratie, 1006, 1017, 1023, 1029,
    1036, 1037, 1051, 1052, 1056,
    1058, 1061
Bureaucratisation, 1043, 1045, 5632
Burke, Kenneth, 294
Burundi, enfant, 2917

Cadres moyens, 4702, 4704
Calcul des probabilités, 552
Calcul matriciel, 493
Calculateur électronique, *voir* Ordi-
    nateur
Cameroun
    groupe familial, 3416
    habitat, 3832
    vie familiale, 3460
    ville, 4058
Campagne électorale, 2030, 5176
Campus universitaire, 2297
Canada
    alcoolisme, 5320, 5344
    analphabétisme, 2371
    assimilation des immigrés, 3716
    bibliothèque, 145
    blanc, 3593

Canada *[suite]*
  classe moyenne, 5062
  classe sociale, 2627
  comportement législatif, 5158
  comportement verbal, 1936
  condition de la femme, 3472, 3480
  culture politique, 5132, 5158
  délinquant, 5439
  développement intellectuel, 2408
  développement rural, 3958
  éducation des adultes, 2366
  éducation politique, 2399
  élite, 2680, 2702
  émigration, 3684
  emploi, 4490
  enfant, 2940
  enseignant, 2445
  enseignement supérieur, 2314
  ethnicité, 3546
  famille, 3294, 3334, 5673
  fécondité, 3141
  groupe ethnique, 1003, 3578
  habitat, 3830
  homicide, 5367
  immigrant, 3713
  immigration, 3714, 3715, 3735
  indien, 3593
  institution religieuse, 1650
  jeunesse, 5142
  logement, 4159
  manager, 4694, 4703
  mariage, 3192, 3294
  migration de travail, 3760
  migration interne, 3749
  mobilité professionnelle, 4631
  mobilité sociale, 2709
  modèle culturel, 1249
  nationalisme, 4935
  origine sociale, 2669
  parti politique, 5083
  planification de la famille, 3192
  politique du logement, 4138
  politisation, 5137
  prestige professionnel, 4626, 4632,
    4636
  production agricole, 4398
  profession, 2669, 4614
  pyramide des âges, 2907
  réfugié, 3712
  relations interethniques, 3623
  réussite dans les études, 2409
  sécurité sociale, 5528
  ségrégation raciale, 4141
  ségrégation résidentielle, 4141
  service de santé, 5627
  service social, 5673
  socialisation politique, 5142
  sociologie du développement, 2797,
    2824
  sociologie électorale, 5175
  sport, 4864
  structure urbaine, 4009

  suicide, 5391
  syndicalisme, 4748
  syndicat, 5132
  système de parti, 5061
  travailleur social, 5647
  université, 2338
  vieillesse, 3003
Capacité intellectuelle, 2407
Capital humain, *voir* Ressources humaines
Capitale, 4045, 4064, 4088
Capitalisme, 310, 2053, 3431, 3921,
    4241-4245, 4247-4250, 4252-4254,
    4361, 4916, 4929, 4993
Caractère, 675
Caractère national, 1324
Carrière, *voir* Profession
Carte des rôles, 1101, 1105
Caste, 2537, 2542-2544, 2546, 2566
Catastrophe, 5283-5287
Catholicisme, 1639
Catholique, 1627, 1628
Causalité, 378, 383
Censure, 4995
Centralisation, 385
Centre de documentation, 146
Centre de recherche, 104, 106, 1589
Centre ville, 4224
Cérémonial, *voir* Rite
Cérémonie, 1042, 1691, 1693
Changement culturel, 1352, 1355,
    1358, 1363, 2828, 4382
Changement d'attitude, 704, 1115,
    1116, 1130, 1136, 1145
Changement d'opinion, 3648
Changement d'organisation, 1007, 1010,
    1014, 1018, 1019, 1026, 1033,
    1044, 1054, 1064, 1065, 1068
Changement de personnalité, 656, 2776
Changement de rôle, 1096
Changement économique, *voir* Développement économique
Changement social, 654, 716, 870,
    1056, 1300, 1354, 1617, 1645,
    2069, 2137, 2502, 2738, 2743,
    2744, 2746, 2748-2752, 2755-
    2757, 2760, 2761, 2765, 2766,
    2770, 2772, 2773, 2775, 2776,
    2778, 2780, 2782-2785, 2787-
    2789, 2944, 3134, 3338, 3485,
    3534, 5217
Chant, 2088, 2091, 2093
Charisme, 1074, 1075
Chatiment, 5448, 5452, 5455, 5456,
    5471
Chercheur, 61, 62, 1535
Chili
  civilisation, 1267, 1295
  église et état, 1760
  éducation, 2648
  élection, 5188
  lutte de classes, 2648

Chili *[suite]*
  milieu rural, 3892
  participation politique, 5188
  politique du logement, 4162
  réforme agraire, 3967
  société rurale, 3885
  système d'éducation, 2198
  urbanisation, 4035
Chine
  civilisation, 1250
  classe sociale, 2652
  condition de la femme, 3482, 3527
  conditions de travail, 4556
  conflit de classe, 2599
  consommation, 4433
  critique littéraire, 2077
  développement rural, 3970
  différenciation sexuelle, 3273
  droits de la femme, 3483
  famille, 3342
  immigrant, 3372
  lieu de travail, 4667
  logement, 3382
  manières de table, 1511
  mariage, 3273
  parenté, 3372, 3382
  politique d'éducation, 2169
  santé, 5582
  sexe, 3382
  sociologie de la littérature,
    2079
  structure sociale, 2488
  travailleur, 4667
  université, 2320
Ch'iu-pai, Ch'ü, 2077
Choix d'une profession, 823, 3442,
    3939, 4617, 4619, 4630, 4642,
    4650
Choix du conjoint, 3298, 3299,
    3300, 3302
Choix sociométrique, 825, 827
Chômage, 3779, 4487, 4489, 4491-
    4493
Chômage partiel, 4488, 4491
Chrétien orthodoxe, 1624
Christianisation, 1676
Christianisme, 1637
Cinéma, 2009, 2011, 2012, 2014,
    2015
Citadin, 4139, 4188, 4192
Cité, *voir* Ville
Civilisation, 1250, 1267, 1292, 1295,
    1315
Civisme, 2942
Clan, 3363, 3366
Classe, *voir* Classe sociale
Classe dirigeante, 2681, 4969
Classe inférieure, 1769, 2406
Classe moyenne, 257, 725, 2301,2393,
    2561, 2581, 2584, 2618, 2947,
    5062

Classe ouvrière, 2548, 2552, 2558,
    2563, 2567, 2573, 2574, 2578,
    2579, 2585, 2587, 2588, 2592,
    2594, 2596-2598, 2602, 2606, 2607,
    2614, 2615, 2617, 2628, 2629,
    2632, 2633, 2639, 2643, 2644,
    2650, 2656, 3136, 3506
Classe sociale, 796, 1207, 1566,
    1708, 1766, 2521, 2544, 2550,
    2555, 2560, 2565, 2566, 2568,
    2575, 2576, 2590, 2591, 2601,
    2603-2605, 2608, 2609, 2611, 2613,
    2616, 2620, 2625, 2627, 2631,
    2637, 2638, 2640, 2641, 2646,
    2647, 2651-2655, 2752, 2794, 3156,
    3311, 3890, 3896, 4099, 4250,
    4308, 4615, 4701, 4775, 4955,
    5159, 5424
Classe supérieure, 2569
Classification, 368
Classification des emplois, 4494
Clergé, 1671, 1672
Clochard, 5433
Coalition, 863-867
Code de communication, 1873
Coexistence pacifique, 5246
Cogestion, 4808, 4813
Cognition, 686-688, 690, 691, 697,
    698, 704
Cohésion du groupe, 630, 944-947
Cohorte, 2908
Collectivité urbaine, *voir* Ville
Collège universitaire, 2300, 2307,
    2331, 5322
Colloque, 1613, 3237
Colombie
  contraception, 3207
  croissance urbaine, 4005
  densité de la population, 3037
  écologie, 3816
  église et état, 1763
  église protestante, 1643
  enseignement supérieur, 2310
  exode, 3678
  fécondité, 3174
  homme marginal, 1476
  migration externe, 3667
  noir, 3606
  planification de l'enseignement,
    2203
  planification urbaine, 4210
  politique, 1763
  sécurité sociale, 5525
  système d'éducation, 2161
  théâtre, 2098
Comité d'entreprise, 4746, 4766
Commandement, 944, 999, 1026, 1078,
    1079, 1081-1089, 1091, 2691,
    5444
Commandement autoritaire, 1090
Commandement politique, 5102, 5104,
    5107, 5111

Communauté, 141, 1408, 2788, 3835, 3838-3841, 3843, 3845, 3847, 5340

Communauté religieuse, 1652-1654, 1736

Communauté rurale, *voir* Village

Communication, 773, 775, 780, 781, 787, 788, 1020, 1031, 1055, 1066, 1067, 1172, 1290, 1868-1870, 1872, 1874, 1876, 1878, 1880-1890, 1892-1894, 1896,1900-1901

Communication de masse, 735, 1183, 1321, 1444, 1820, 1907, 1944, 1957-1988, 2276, 4890, 5379

Communication politique, 5117, 5159

Communication sociale, *voir* Communication

Communisme, 4933

Comportement, 1111, 1112-1114, 1117-1122, 1124-1126, 1128, 1132, 1133, 1134, 1135, 1137-1139, 1180, 1305, 1396, 2037

Comportement antisocial, 1451, 1462

Comportement collectif, 797, 1217

Comportement du consommateur, 4428, 4431, 4434, 4438, 4441, 4443

Comportement du groupe, 559

Comportement économique, 4440,4445

Comportement électoral, 2640, 5168, 5169, 5184, 5187, 5191

Comportement en groupe, 958, 960, 1091

Comportement judiciaire, 5025,5026, 5030

Comportement législatif, 5158

Comportement politique, 2241, 4139, 5126, 5141, 5148, 5150, 5153, 5157

Comportement religieux, 1718-1726, 1728-1732, 1734-1737, 3144

Comportement sexuel, 1213, 3234, 3235, 3241, 3242, 3254, 3256, 3257, 3260, 3261, 3263

Comportement verbal, 1904, 1908, 1916, 1920, 1921, 1931, 1936, 2666

Composition du groupe, 935, 940,962

Compréhension, 214, 352, 357, 362

Comte, Auguste, 225, 281, 322

Concentration urbaine, 4001, 5487

Concept, 215

Conception de soi, 631, 635-637, 639, 643, 916

Concurrence, 4452

Condition de la femme,1722, 2586, 3467-3472, 3475-3482, 3490-3494, 3496-3499, 3501, 3502, 3510, 3513, 3515, 3518, 3519, 3521, 3522, 3527-3529, 4312, 4526

Conditions de logement, 1487,4147, 4155, 4156, 4163, 4165, 4170, 4180, 4183, 4191, 4198

Conditions de travail, 3062, 4496, 4504, 4524, 4554-4567

Conditions de vie, 4285, 4293, 4296

Conférence, 1708, 2846

Conflit, 868, 869, 870, 875, 877, 878,880, 882, 883, 1454, 1475, 1666

Conflit culturel, 1370

Conflit de classe, 2549, 2551, 2562, 2599, 4764, 5425

Conflit de rôle, 1001

Conflit du travail, 4781, 4784,4787-4790, 4792-4797

Conflit industriel, *voir* Conflit du travail

Conflit interpersonnel, 632, 857

Conflit politique, 1741, 2404, 5194, 5200

Conflit racial, 3641, 3651

Conflit social, *voir* Conflit

Conformisme, 1168

Conformité sociale, 1393, 1413, 1431, 2671

Confrérie, 1651

Congruence du status, 2667

Connaissance, 262, 1205, 1785, 1787, 1792, 1795, 1796, 1798, 1799, 1802, 1806,1808, 1811, 1812,1822, 1828, 1830, 1833, 1834

Conscience collective, 1214

Conscience de classe, 2586, 2595, 2600, 2607, 2622

Conscience nationale, 1330, 1332, 1694

Conscience sociale, 1405, 1416,1417, 1432

Conseil de recherche, 111

Consensus, 772, 1180, 1218, 1454

Consommateur, 4429, 4430, 4439,4442, 4446, 4447

Consommation, 4432, 4433, 4435-4437, 4444,4448

Contact entre cultures, 1368, 1374, 1378

Contestation sociale, 1507

Contraception, 3199, 3207, 3217,3232

Contrainte sociale, 1103,1149,1385, 1389, 1393, 1394, 1402, 1413, 1485, 1507, 1531, 2486

Contremaître, 4695

Contrôle bureaucratique, 1009, 1011, 1020, 1021,1025, 1031, 1035, 1041, 1046, 1050, 1057, 1059, 1066, 1067

Convention collective, 4810, 4818, 4821

Coopérative, 4321, 4344

Coopérative agricole, 4387, 4392, 4395, 4399, 4405

Coordination des recherches, 108,117

Corée (République de)
  dynamique culturelle, 1356
  emploi, 3387

Corée (République de) *[suite]*
épouse, 3309
fécondité, 3162, 3164, 3208
mari, 3309
migration : 3162; interne, 3765
planification de la famille, 3208, 3309
recherche en cours, 77
relations parent-enfant, 3387, 3462
système familial, 3417
travailleur féminin, 3164
Corporatisme, 4777
Corrélation, 523, 525-527
Costa Rica, évolution de la population, 3033
Côte d'Ivoire, ville, 4058, 4072
Coup d'État, 5198
Course aux armements, 5256, 5257
Coutume, 1541
Créativité, 702, 739, 740, 747,755, 757, 2139
Crime, 1475, 5362, 5363, 5369,5370, 5375, 5377, 5380, 5382, 5387, 5389, 5400, 5401, 5404, 5406, 5409, 5419, 5427
Criminalité, *voir* Délinquance
Criminel, *voir* Délinquant
Criminologie, 140, 5352-5359
Crise culturelle, 1353, 1364,1379
Crise politique, 5199, 5203
Critique littéraire, 2067, 2077
Croissance économique, 4279, 4280
Croissance urbaine, 3845, 3998, 4007, 4016, 4027, 4034, 4041, 4097
Croyance, 1696, 1698
Cuba
classe ouvrière, 2644
coopérative agricole, 4395
développement économique, 4284
esclavage, 2532
habitat, 3833
parti politique, 5063
système d'éducation, 2181
Culte, 1680, 1685, 1689, 1692
Culture, 454, 1242, 1252, 1253, 1265, 1266, 1268-1270, 1273, 1276, 1282, 1285, 1286, 1293, 1298, 1303, 1312, 1321, 1323, 1809, 2029, 3247, 4687, 4835, 5503
Culture de masse, 2237
Culture et personnalité, 1296
Culture politique, 5128, 5132, 5156, 5158, 5165
Cybernétique, 543, 545, 546

Danemark
administration publique, 5036
allocations familiales, 5526
avortement, 3223
collège universitaire, 2307
conditions de vie, 4293
droits de la femme, 3495
éducation permanente, 2384
emploi, 3495
formation professionnelle, 4638
institution de recherche, 103
lutte de classes, 2621
mariage, 3288
mortalité, 3101
taudis, 4143
travailleur féminin, 4293
Danse,2096
Davy, George, 164
Décès, *voir* Mort
Décision, 741, 743, 744, 753, 758, 768, 769, 1030, 1214, 1530
Décolonisation, 2835
Délinquance, 5361, 5364, 5378, 5379, 5381, 5383, 5385, 5390, 5392, 5394, 5402, 5407, 5408, 5410, 5416, 5422, 5424, 5425, 5429
Délinquance juvénile, 1581; 5024, 5365, 5372, 5376, 5395, 5396, 5399, 5411, 5412, 5418, 5423
Délinquant, 1491, 5402, 5430-5432, 5434, 5436, 5438, 5440
Démocratie, 1344, 4252, 4916, 4959, 4960-4964
Démographie, 1459, 2838, 2840,2844, 2850, 2855, 2856, 2857, 2860-2862
Densité de la population, 3036,3037, 3044
Dépeuplement, 3053
Désert, 3817
Désirabilité sociale, 5329
Désorganisation de la famille, 3450, 3455
Développement agricole, 2493, 4394, 4402, 4403
Développement de l'enfant, 2912, 2916, 2918, 2919, 2926, 2929, 2933,2937, 2939, 3388
Développement de la personnalité, 657, 661, 666, 670, 672, 682, 3392, 4846, 4847, 4849
Développement des collectivités, 3834, 3836, 3837, 3842, 3846, 5538
Développement économique, 2810,3012, 3032,3165, 4272-4278, 4281,4283, 4284
Développement industriel, 4418
Développement intellectuel, 2408, 2410
Développement national, 2679, 2822, 2837

Développement politique, 4978
Développement rural, 3958, 3961-3963,
  3965, 3966, 3969, 3973, 3976,
  3978, 5060
Développement social, *voir* Changement
  social
Développement urbain, 4204, 4207,
  4208, 4220, 4223, 4225
Déviance, 812, 1394, 1402, 1441,
  1445, 1448, 1449, 1454, 1456,
  1460, 1468, 1475, 1480, 1481,
  1489, 1490, 1492, 1497, 1499,
  1503, 1506, 3393
Devoir, 1521
Dialectique, 2002? 221, 248, 259,
  305, 308, 339, 361, 608
Dictature, 4965
Dictionnaire, 150, 152-154, 156, 157
Différence d'âge, 2910
Différenciation culturelle, 701, 1304,
  1322
Différenciation de classes, 2635,
  2649, 4437, 4898
Différenciation des rôles, 1093
Différenciation sémantique, 1905,
  1928
Différenciation sexuelle, 2282, 2867,
  2891, 2892, 3273, 3314, 4660
Différenciation sociale, 2495, 2509-
  2511, 2520, 2526
Diffusion culturelle, 1351, 1354
Diffusion de l'information, 131
Di Leonardis, C., 308
Dimension de l'organisation, 134
Dimension de la famille, 3269, 3397,
  3401, 3407, 3410, 3418, 3419,
  3422, 3426, 3427, 3430, 3435,
  3443, 3445, 3451, 3458, 3459,
  3461, 3463, 4165, 4469
Dimension du groupe, 941, 943
Diplomatie, 5241
Diplôme, 2311
Direction de l'entreprise, 4330,
  4336, 4339
Discrimination raciale, 1723, 2513,
  2591, 3631, 3636, 3647, 4151
Dissonance cognitive, 725, 726,1145,
  1146, 1148, 1153, 1160
Distance sociale, 629
Divertissement, 4877
Division du travail, 2494, 2498,
  2503, 2516, 2517, 2525, 2528,
  2988
Divorce, 1101, 3268, 3271, 3274,3276,
  3279, 3284, 3287
Dobzhansky, Theodosius, 160
Documentation, 135
Dogmatisme, 1166
Dogme, 1701
Don, 890
Données d'enquête, 457, 458
Données statistiques, 505

Dragicescu, Dimitrie, 224
Droit civil, 1544
Droit criminel, *voir* Droit pénal
Droit des gens, *voir* Droit inter-
  national
Droit du travail, 4725-4733
Droit international, 5234, 5239
Droit pénal, 1543, 1557, 1561, 1578,
  4998
Droits de l'homme, 4996-4998,5003
Droits de la femme, 2619, 3465,
  3483, 3488, 3495, 3505, 3511,
  3514, 3524, 3530, 3533, 4762,
  5172
Droits du citoyen, *voir* Droits
  de l'homme
Durée du travail, *voir* Temps de
  travail
Duricu, Vojislavu, 169
Durkheim, Emile, 218, 225, 261,
  270, 289, 300, 321, 344, 1598,
  2877; 3251, 5403
Dyade, 816, 841, 938, 942, 2878,
  3310
Dynamique culturelle, 1350, 1356,
  1360-1362
Dynamique de groupe, 904, 2542
Dynamique de la population, *voir*
  Évolution de la population
Dynamique sociale, 2466

Échange, 884-889
Échantillonnage par quotas, 1264
Échec scolaire, 2412
Échelle cumulative, *voir* Échelle
  unidimensionnelle
Échelle d'attitude, 561, 562, 564,
  566, 567, 570-572
Échelle d'intervalle, 559, 569
Échelle de Srole, *voir* Anomia
Échelle E, 1179
Échelle F, 1170
Échelle multidimensionnelle, 560,
  563
Échelle unidimensionnelle, 565
École, 2260, 2264, 2265, 2267,2269,
  3912
École maternelle, 2262, 2263, 2271
École primaire, 2258, 2412, 2428,
  2448
École secondaire, 2258, 2259, 2261,
  2268, 2270, 2271
Écolier, 2273, 2275
Écologie, 1027, 1138, 3791, 3801,
  3803-3807, 3810, 3811, 3813,
  3815, 3816
Économie agricole, 4389, 4396, 4397,
  4401
Économie de l'éducation, 2128,2137,
  2142
Économie de l'entreprise, 4317
Économie industrielle, 4411

Économiste, 63
Écosse
  école, 2267
  émigration, 3686
  université, 2267
Écrivain, 2068, 2077
Éducation, 1189, 1401, 2108, 2109,
  2114-2116, 2118, 2122, 2124, 2125,
  2127, 2129, 2131, 2132-2134,2139,
  2141, 2145, 2648
Éducation de base, 2373
Éducation des adultes, 2219, 2362,
  2365, 2366, 2372, 2375-2377,
  2382, 2387-2390, 2394-2396
Éducation des parents, 2452
Éducation ouvrière, 2378, 2391,
  5522
Éducation permanente, 2363, 2367-
  2369, 2379-2381, 2392, 2393,
  2397, 2398, 2402
Éducation politique, 2399, 2404
Éducation préscolaire, 2243, 2244,
  2246, 2249, 2251, 2254, 2255,
  2257
Effet, 1962
Effet de groupe, 934, 957
Égalité, 2219, 2514, 2515, 2519,4960
Égalité de chances, 2209-2215,2217,
  2221-2223, 2227, 2228, 2259,
  2312, 2321
Église, 1641-1644, 1648,
Église et Etat, 1675, 1738-1746,
  1749, 1751-1753, 1758, 1761,
  1763, 1764, 1766-1769, 1773,
  1775, 1777-1779, 1783
Église protestante, 1642, 1643, 1646
Ego, 608, 610, 611, 615, 617, 842
Egocentrisme, 630, 632, 645, 648,
  650
Égypte
  accroissement de la population,3042
  alimentation, 5297
  culture, 1253
  prolétariat, 3042
Électeur, 5172, 5181,5185, 5192
Élections, 5173, 5180, 5183, 5188,
  5190
Élevage de l'enfant, 2915
Élève, 2274, 2276
Élite, 58, 1957, 1966, 2609, 2679,
  2680, 2687, 2691, 2702, 2704,
  2705, 3909
Élite du pouvoir, 2700
Élite politique, 5088, 5101, 5105,
  5108, 5109
Émigrant, 3688, 3695
Émigration, 3303, 3679, 3680, 3683,
  3684, 3686, 3690-3694, 3869
Émission radiophonique, 2019, 2039
Émotion, 708-710, 715
Empathie, 809
Emploi, 3387, 3495, 3770, 4485, 4490-
  4492, 4623

Employé, 4688, 4690
Employé de commerce, 2728, 4689
Enculturation, 1371
Encyclopédie, 158
Endogamie, 3297
Enfance, 1184, 1490, 2923
Enfant, 908, 1372, 1522,2025,2031,
  2035, 2066, 2913, 2914, 2917,
  2920-2922, 2924,2927,2928,2930,
  2932,2934, 2935, 2936, 2938,
  2940, 2943, 5162
En groupe, 961
Enquête, 452, 453, 455, 3184, 4662
Enquête par correspondance, 481
Enquête par panel, 451, 456
Enquête sociale, *voir* Enquête
Enquête sur échantillon, 463
Enseignant, 2343, 2436, 2437, 2439,
  2441-2445, 2448-2450, 5167
Enseignement, 1096, 2416, 2421,
  2423
Enseignement obligatoire, 2236
Enseignement primaire, 2242, 2248
Enseignement privé, 2162
Enseignement public, 2196
Enseignement secondaire, 721,2245,
  2247, 2250, 2252, 2253, 2256
Enseignement supérieur, 2220, 2295,
  2298, 2301, 2303-2306, 2309,
  2310, 2312-2318, 2321, 2323,
  2325, 2327-2329, 2336, 2342,
  2343, 2347, 2350, 2355, 2358,
  2360
Enseignement technique, 2401-2403
Entrepreneur, 4320
Entreprise, 4316, 4323-4326, 4329,
  4331, 4333, 4335, 4338, 4342,
  4343
Entreprise agricole, 4388
Entreprise industrielle, 4414
Entretien, 465, 467, 472, 477, 482,
  483
Entretien directif, 470, 471
Environnement, 543, 570, 3800, 3808,
  3812, 3814, 5370
Épistémologie, 222, 333, 335, 336,
  339-341, 344, 345, 1803, 1869
Épouse, 2910, 3309, 3315, 3316,
  3318, 3320, 3469, 5143
Équateur
  main d'oeuvre féminine, 4508
  nationalisme, 4929
  réforme agraire, 3960
  relations interethniques, 3625
  structure de classe,2630
Équilibre démographique, 3008, 3021,
  3024, 3028, 3030, 3032, 3038,
  3043, 3047, 3049
Ergonomie, 4536-4539
Esclavage, 2106, 2529-2532, 2534-
  2536, 2538-2541, 2545
Espace, 412, 413

Espace urbain, 4003
Espacement des naissances, 3204, 3213
Espagne
  agriculteur, 3953
  aire métropolitaine, 3997
  alcoolisme, 5304
  centre de documentation, 146
  changement culturel, 2828
  changement social, 3485
  classe ouvrière, 2607
  classe sociale, 1207, 2604, 2641,
    4701
  comportement religieux, 1729
  condition de la femme, 3485
  conflit du travail, 4793
  conscience de classe, 2607
  conscience sociale, 1417
  église et état, 1753, 1759
  enseignement privé, 2162
  famille, 3322, 3333
  fécondité, 3152
  féminisme, 3509
  fonctionnaire public, 5034
  histoire sociale, 2729
  idéologie, 1207
  Islam, 1630
  logement, 4177
  lutte de classes, 2572
  marginalité, 1434
  migration interne, 3769
  migration rurale, 3748
  population active, 3058
  population urbaine, 3060
  protection de la nature, 3818
  recherche en cours, 84
  relations culturelles, 4881
  sécurité sociale, 5535
  société d'abondance, 2607
  société rurale, 4513
  société urbaine, 4105
  sociologie de la littérature, 2064
  sociologie de la religion, 1583
  sociologie du développement, 2828
  sociologie du théâtre, 1385
  sociologie électorale, 5186
  sociologie politique, 4901
  structure de classe, 2607
  structure urbaine, 4022
  système pénitentiaire, 5466
  technicien, 4701
  tourisme, 4881
  travailleur féminin, 4513
  yniversité, 2354
  urbanisme, 4233
  village, 3874
  ville, 1635, 4047, 4057, 4064
  voisinage, 4187
Espérance de vie, 5665
Esthétique, 2029, 2048, 2049, 2057,
  2059, 5522
Esthétique urbaine, 4211, 4228, 4229
Estime de soi, 624, 638, 642, 646, 649,
  651, 3580

Esty, Geoffrey W., 170
Établissement d'enseignement, 2171
État, 4967, 4969, 4971, 4975, 4977,
  4979, 4980, 4982-4984, 4986-
  4990, 4992-4994
État des tendances, 66, 71, 80, 93,
  3323, 3851
État providence, 5480, 5484, 5492,
  5496, 5498, 5500, 5518
États-Unis d'Amérique
  accroissement de la population,
    3054
  administration du personnel, 4546
  administration urbaine, 4113
  adolescent, 3637
  adoption d'enfant, 3395
  âge adulte, 2979
  agriculture, 4407
  alcoolisme, 5324
  analyse multivariée, 5369
  analyse transculturelle, 2945
  analyse transnationale, 2537
  appartenance au parti, 5123
  aptitude aux études, 2411
  armée, 3632, 5207, 5227
  assimilation des immigrés, 3722
  attitude politique, 2127, 5116
  attitude raciale, 3637, 172
  banlieue, 4216, 4227, 4131
  bibliographie, 3727
  bien-être, 4286
  Blanc, 3604
  campagne électorale, 5176
  capitale, 4045
  caste, 2537, 2566
  catholique, 1628
  changement social, 3134, 3338
  châtiment, 5456
  choix d'une profession, 4630,
    4642
  civisme, 2942
  classe moyenne, 2581, 5062
  classe ouvrière, 2579
  classe sociale, 2566, 2608, 2609,
    2646, 2647
  communauté, 3835, 3840
  comportement électoral, 5169,
    5191
  comportement législatif, 5158
  comportement politique, 5126,
    5148, 5153
  comportement religieux, 1723
  conditions de logement, 4155
  conflit racial, 3651
  consommation, 4437
  contraception, 3217, 3232
  contrôle des naissances, 3187
  crime, 5369, 5387, 5389, 5400,
    5427
  croissance urbaine, 3998, 4097
  culture politique, 5158
  délinquance juvénile, 5412

États-Unis *[suite]*
  délinquant, 5435, 5436
  différenciation de classes, 4437
  différenciation sexuelle, 2891
  dimension de la famille, 3418,3430,
    3461, 3463
  discrimination raciale, 3631, 3647,
    4151
  droit, 1564
  droits de la femme, 3488
  économie agricole, 4397
  éducation des adultes, 2365, 2376,
    2377
  égalité des chances, 2209, 2214,
    2217, 2227
  électeur, 5185
  élections, 5173, 5190
  élite politique, 5101, 5105
  enfant, 2942
  enseignement suéprieur, 2301, 2303,
    2323, 2343, 2350
  entreprise, 4324
  esclavage, 2529, 2538, 2539, 2545
  ethnicité, 3555, 5123
  éthos, 1533
  étudiant, 2335, 4647
  exode, 3677
  faction politique, 5112
  famille, 3338, 3355
  fécondité,3134, 3175, 3197, 3219,
    3301
  femme, 5153
  futurologie, 2735
  genre de vie, 1317
  gouvernement central, 5050
  grève, 4782
  groupe de pression, 5098
  groupe ethnique, 3538, 3572, 3590,
    3591
  groupe familial, 3400
  guerilla, 5193
  guerre, 5254
  homicide, 5397
  identification au parti, 5120
  immigrant, 3700, 3710, 3723
  immigration, 3727
  indien, 3592,3598, 3599, 3609,3611,
    3612
  industrialisation, 4779
  inégalité, 3725
  institution religieuse, 1650
  intervalle génésique, 3163
  jeunesse, 2945, 5142
  journaliste, 1996
  leader politique, 5127
  liberté religieuse, 1727
  liberté surveillée, 5443
  loisir, 4825
  main d'oeuvre féminine, 4507
  maladie mentale, 3085, 3090
  manager, 4703
  mari, 5153

mariage mixte, 3307
médecine, 5559
métropole, 4042, 4070, 4089
migration de travail, 3758
migration interne, 3762, 3776,
  3796
migration rurale, 3751, 3771,
  3772, 3780
milieu familial, 3424
militaire, 5244
minorité nationale, 3359, 3571,
  3579
mobilité sociale, 2725
modernisation, 2769
modernisation politique, 4985
morale, 1532
morbidité, 2891
mortalité, 2891, 3103, 3113
mortalité infantile, 3117
mouvement contestataire, 5092
mouvement étudiant, 2361
mouvement ouvrier, 4749, 4750,
  4779
mythologie, 1717
nationalisme, 3608
négociation collective, 4800,
  4804, 4806
Noir, 3597, 3605, 3607, 3608,
  5112, 5124, 5140
organisation d'étudiants, 2361
parenté, 3370, 3372, 3373
parti politique, 5083
participation à la collectivité,
  3844
participation électorale, 5174
participation politique, 5124,
  5140, 5149, 5164
participation religieuse, 5123
peine capitale, 5446, 5457
personne de couleur, 3603
peur, 5369
planification de l'enseignement,
  2156, 2186, 2207
planification de la famille, 3197,
  3206, 3219, 3227
planification urbaine, 4172,
  4221,5501
police, 5004
politique d'éducation, 2205,3640
politique de bien-être, 5501
politique du logement, 4151,4152,
  4172
politique étrangère, 5244, 5245
politique sociale, 5507
population urbaine, 3057
polygynie, 3301
préjudice racial, 3632
presse, 3651
prévention de la délinquance,
  5472
prison, 5447, 5461
privation relative, 5193

États-Unis *[suite]*
  problème social, 5275, 5281
  profit, 4310
  publicité, 1945
  racisme, 3645
  recherche, 3538
  réforme de l'enseignement, 2153,
    2190
  réfugié, 3699
  relations interethniques, 3618
  relations internationales, 5237
  relations parent-enfant, 3423
  relations raciales, 3616
  répartition du revenu, 4294
  répartition par sexe, 3430
  retraite, 4604
  santé, 5578, 5585, 5588, 5592
  sécurité sociale, 5528
  ségrégation raciale, 3634, 3640,
    3644
  ségrégation résidentielle, 4186, 4195
  service de santé, 5622, 5626, 5635
  service social, 5652, 5679
  sexualité, 3233
  socialisation politique, 5112, 5142
  société industrielle, 2579
  société rurale, 3928
  sociologie de la profession, 4613
  sociologie médicale, 3085
  sociologie militaire, 5231
  soins médicaux, 5589, 5594, 5596,
    5597, 5612
  sport, 4896
  stéréotype, 1164
  stratification professionnelle,
    4643, 4647
  stupéfiants, 5326, 5327, 5461
  syndicat, 4741, 4743
  système d'éducation, 2150, 2197
  système de parti, 5061
  système juridique, 1579
  système pénitentiaire, 5445
  système social, 2484
  technocratie, 5031
  travail social : 550; des groupes,
    2985
  travailleur féminin, 4503
  travailleur social, 5656, 5677
  urbanisation, 4011, 4016, 4397
  usage de drogue, 5325, 5343
  valeur, 1397, 1403
  vie urbaine, 3085, 4097
  vieillard, 2985, 2999, 5679
  vieillesse, 2992
  vieillissement, 3005
  ville, 3609, 4044, 4048, 4082,
    4096
  ville nouvelle, 2260, 4059
  violence, 1509, 5092
  vol, 5373

Éthiopie, faim, 5294
Éthique, 1136, 1516, 1519, 1523-
    1525, 1534, 1535, 1537, 1538,
    4310
Éthique protestante, 372, 1733
Ethnicité, 2047, 2527, 3107, 3111,
    3368, 3534, 3543, 3544, 3546,
    3549-3552, 3555n 3557, 3558,
    3573, 3577, 3580, 3582, 3583,
    3586, 3588, 5123
Ethnie, *voir* Groupe ethnique
Ethnocentrisme, 1167
Ethnographie, 1235, 1236
Ethnolinguistique, 1845, 1847
Ethnologie, 1224-1234, 1237, 1238,
    1534
Éthos, 1533
Étude de cas, 2586, 3183, 3225
Étude du travail, *voir* Ergonomie
Étudiants, 1413, 2308, 2311, 2322,
    2324, 2330, 2332, 2335, 2344,
    2348, 4647, 5136
Europe
  administration publique, 5037
  analyse transculturelle, 2946
  conflit du travail, 4781
  électeur, 5192
  émigration, 3690
  fécondité, 3169
  jeunesse, 2946
  logement, 4184
  médecin, 5676
  migration externe, 3669, 3670
  participation des travailleurs,
    4819
  paysannerie, 3935
  planification de la famille, 3209
  recherche sociale, 5268
  relations industrielles, 4720
  suicide, 5368
Europe de l'Est
  équilibre démographique, 3028
  politique démographique, 3202
  soins médicaux, 5599
Europe de l'Ouest
  chômage partiel, 4488
  parti politique, 5080
  politique démographique, 3228
Évaluation, 347, 355, 448
Évaluation de soi, 626, 627
Évitement, 844
Évolution de la population, 1719,
    2822, 2842, 2843, 3011, 3014-
    3018, 3023, 3027, 3031, 3033-
    3035, 3039-3041, 3045, 3046
Évolution sociale, *voir* Changement
    social
Évolutionnisme, 218, 251, 262, 270,
    289, 300, 321
Existentialisme, 208, 226, 245,
    301

Exode, 3677, 3678
Exode des cerveaux, 3681, 3682, 3685, 3689
Exode rural, *voir* Migration rurale
Expérience, 446, 447
Expérience sur le terrain, *voir* Travail sur le terrain
Expérimentateur, 445
Explication, 355, 359, 360, 362-365
Explication causale, 377, 379, 380, 429, 3255
Extrémisme, 2849, 2638

Facteur social, 1337
Faction politique, 5100, 5112
Faim, 5294
Faisceau de rôles, 1099
Fait social, 342
Famille, 654, 2033, 3137, 3294, 3321-3328, 3330-3334, 3336, 3338, 3340-3357, 3359-3361, 5657, 5673
Famille biologique, *voir* Famille conjugale
Famille conjugale, 3329, 3339, 3358
Famille étendue, *voir* Famille indivise
Famille indivise, 3335
Fascisme, 4952
Fécondité, 2613, 2719, 3016, 3133-3154, 3156, 3158, 3160, 3164-3166, 3169, 3171-3185, 3197, 3208, 3219, 3293, 3301, 3410, 3427, 4510, 4532
Fédéralisme, 4968, 4970
Féminisme, 672, 1143, 2872, 3466, 3474, 3486, 3489, 3507, 3509, 3517, 3520, 3526, 3531
Femme, 1105, 2873, 2888, 4442, 5359
Femme mariée, 3308, 3310, 3313, 5349
Ferenc, Erdei, 232
Ferme, *voir* Entreprise agricole
Ferme collective, 4386, 4390, 4391, 4406, 4408
Fête, 1681, 1683, 1686, 1688, 1690, 1694
Fiabilité, 450
Filiation, 3365, 3374
Film, 2010, 2013
Finances publiques, 4458
Finlande
  alcoolisme, 5346
  ethnicité, 3588
  folklore, 2107
  gouvernement local, 5055
  langage, 1937
  main d'oeuvre féminine, 4533
  métropole, 4073
  migration externe, 3673
  nationalisme, 2107
  politique sociale, 5506
  population urbaine, 3069
  recherche, 87 ; en cours, 81

  sociologie du développement, 2820
Firme, *voir* Entreprise
Fiscalité, 4459
Foi, *voir* Croyance
Folklore, 1686, 2103-2105, 2107
Fonction publique, 5033, 5038, 5045
Fonctionnaire, 5034, 5040
Fondation de recherche, 116
Formalisation, 384-388
Formation des enseignants, 2435, 2438, 2446, 2447
Formation professionnelle, 2358, 4619, 4622, 4627, 4634, 4639, 4646, 4649, 4656, 4658, 4659
Foucault, Michel, 269
Foule, 1211-1213, 1215, 1216, 1218-1223, 2719
France
  absentéisme, 4602
  acculturation des immigrés, 3708
  administration publique, 5044
  administration urbaine, 4118
  adolescent, 2952, 2966, 2971
  agriculteur, 3952
  agriculture, 4400
  anarchisme, 4924
  assimilation des immigrés, 3697, 3705, 3718, 3738
  attitude politique, 2664
  automation, 4357
  avortement, 3193
  besoins d'éducation, 2229
  bibliographie, 5530
  budget temps, 4570
  catholique, 1627
  changement social, 2743
  classe moyenne, 2393
  classe ouvrière, 2573, 2617
  clergé, 1672
  collège universitaire, 2300
  comité d'entreprise, 4766
  comportement du consommateur, 4438
  comportement électoral, 5167
  comportement religieux, 1730
  condition de la femme, 3478
  conditions de logement, 4163, 4191
  délinquance, 5429
  démographie, 2850, 2855
  densité de la population, 3036
  éducation permanente, 2367, 2379, 2385, 2393
  égalité des chances, 2214
  église et état, 1773
  émigration, 3690, 3694
  emploi, 4485
  enseignant, 5167
  enseignement supérieur, 2360
  entreprise, 4323

France [suite]
  équilibre démographique, 3043
  espace urbain, 4003
  fécondité, 3148, 3149, 3180
  féminisme, 3466
  filiation, 3365, 3374
  genre de vie, 1248
  gérontologie, 2991
  gouvernement local, 5057
  grève, 4783
  habitat, 3828
  immigrant, 3709, 3711, 3736
  immigration, 3698, 3701, 3702,
    3704, 3729, 3734, 3741
  industrie, 4357
  intellectuel, 2683
  lutte de classes, 2556, 2577,
    2582, 4783
  main d'oeuvre étrangère, 3646, 4522
  mariage, 3286
  médecin, 5641, 5662, 5678, 5681
  médecine, 5572
  méthode contraceptive, 3212
  migrant, 4191
  migration rurale, 3768
  militaire, 5221-5224
  minorité nationale, 3581
  mobilité sociale, 2725
  mort, 3099
  mortalité, 3100, 3125
  mouvement ouvrier, 4747
  négociation collective, 4799
  noblesse, 2533
  noir, 2677
  parti politique, 3214, 4780, 5064,
    5066, 5071
  participation des travailleurs,
    4817
  peine capitale, 5468
  petite ville, 4050, 4063
  politique de l'enseignement, 2176
  politique démographique, 3215
  politique du logement, 4168, 4174
  politique sociale, 5473
  population active, 3059
  pouvoir, 2743
  pratique religieuse, 1765
  presse, 1989, 1991
  prêtre, 1676
  profession libérale, 4706
  protestantisme, 1640
  racisme, 3646
  recherche, 88
  régulation des naissances, 3214
  scolarisation, 2238
  sécurité sociale, 5530
  société rurale, 3286
  sociologie de la religion, 1589
  soins médicaux, 4438
  soutien familial, 3444
  suicide, 5368
  syndicalisme, 5221
  syndicat, 4745, 4759, 4770
  système d'éducation, 2167
  table de mortalité, 3104, 3130
  télévision, 2021, 2026
  transport urbain, 4112
  travailleur social, 5660
  université, 2302
  usage du tabac, 5338
  vie rurale, 3893, 3898
  vie urbaine, 4124
  vieillard, 2997, 2998, 3004
  vieillissement, 3003
  ville, 4052, 4084, 4091
  ville industrielle, 4094
  ville nouvelle, 4053, 4095
Franc maçonnerie, 1656, 1657, 1660-
    1662
Fréquentation de l'école, 2291
Fréquentation de l'église, *voir*
    Pratique religieuse
Freud, S., 283, 576
Friedmann, Georges, 165
Frustration, 719
Fustel de Coulanges, 234
Futur, 2736
Futurologie, 264, 2735, 2737

Galtung, 2667
Ganon, Isaac, 65
Garçon, 2960
Génération, 2909
Génétique, 2901, 2902, 2905
Genre de vie, 1239, 1240, 1243-1248,
    1251, 1255-1264, 1271, 1272,
    1274, 1275, 1277-1279, 1283,
    1287, 1288, 1290, 1294, 1297,
    1301, 1302, 1306, 1308-1311,
    1314, 1316-1318, 1320, 1949,
    1969, 2348, 2635, 2639, 2783,
    2951, 3919
Genre humain, 2895
Géographie, 3800
Géographie humaine, 3802
Géographie urbaine, 3986, 3995
Gérontologie, 2984, 2991, 3000
Gestion, 4340, 4341
Gestion d'entreprise, 4327
Ghana
  agriculteur, 3950
  contrôle des naissances, 3194
  développement agricole, 4403
  dimension de la famille, 3443
  église et état, 1764
  planification de la famille, 3186,
    3194
  politique, 1764
  soins médicaux, 5579
  système d'éducation, 2166
  travailleur féminin, 3950
Ghetto, 1922, 5386
Givens, Meredith, B., 171
Goffman, 245

Gouvernement, 5017
Gramsci, Antonio, 220, 369
Green, T. H., 257
Grève, 4780, 4782, 4783, 4785, 4786, 4791, 4794, 4798
Grossesse, 3256
Groupe, 638, 891-897, 907, 911, 912, 914, 917, 939
Groupe d'appartenance, 3585
Groupe d'intérêt, *voir* Groupe de pression
Groupe de discussion, 842
Groupe de formation, 928
Groupe de pression, 1475, 4692, 5085, 5089, 5094, 5097, 5098, 5577
Groupe de référence, 866, 1407, 1418, 4443
Groupe de travail, 6
Groupe élémentaire, *voir* Groupe restreint
Groupe ethnique, 1003, 1420, 3295, 3538, 3540, 3545, 3548, 3553, 3556, 3564, 3570, 3572, 3574, 3578, 3585, 3590, 3591
Groupe expérimental, 926
Groupe familial, 3302, 3393, 3394, 3400, 3408, 3416, 3421, 3438, 3440, 3440, 3449, 3456, 5417
Groupe minoritaire, 936, 939
Groupe primaire, *voir* Groupe restreint
Groupe restreint, 921-925, 927, 929-932, 934
Groupe social, *voir* Groupe
Groupe thérapeutique, 933, 946
Guatemala
  éducation des adultes, 2386
  église et état, 1761
  relations interethniques, 3619
  société rurale, 3918
Guerilla, 5193, 5196, 5202
Guerre, 5248, 5251-5254
Guerre mondiale, 5249
Guinée britannique, caste, 2543
Gurvitch, Georges, 1577, 4236
Guyane
  conflit de classe, 2551
  discrimination raciale, 2513
  idéologie, 2551
  migration de travail, 3792
  pluralisme social, 2513
  racisme, 2551

Habermas, Jürgen, 263, 283, 333, 334
Habitat, 3822-3825, 3827-3833
Habitation, 3826
Habitude, 1515
Hawaï, suicide, 5388
Henry, Luis, 2840
Hérédité, 2896, 2898
Hérésie, 1703
Héritage culturel, 557

Herméneutique, 214
Hétérogamie, 3295
Hiérarchie ecclésiastique, 1670
Hiérarchie sociale, 2496
Hindou, 1629
Histoire, 313, 2730, 2733
Histoire culturelle, 1359
Histoire de l'éducation, 2143
Histoire de vie, *voir* Biographie
Histoire des idées, 1829
Histoire des sciences, 1797
Histoire religieuse, 1598
Histoire sociale, 2482, 2729, 2734
Historicisme, 217, 231, 252, 295
Hjelmslev, L., 1861
Hollander, A. N. J. den, 163
Homan, 324
Homicide, 5367, 5386, 5393, 5397, 5421, 5428
Homme, 849, 1105, 2865, 2866, 2870
Homme de loi, 4707, 4709
Homme marginal, 1463, 1465, 1466, 1470, 1476, 1495
Homme marié, 3308, 3310, 5349
Homme politique, 5103, 5106, 5110
Homogamie, 3295
Homosexualité, 3247, 3248, 3252, 3258
Honduras
  bourgeoisie, 4982
  conflit du travail, 4794
  état, 4982
  grève, 4794
  migration pendulaire, 3794
Hong Kong
  commandement politique, 5104, 5107
  condition de la femme, 3522
  évolution de la population, 2843
  mariage, 3522
  projection démographique, 2843
  rénovation urbaine, 4214
Hongrie
  absentéisme, 4606
  armée, 5232
  artisanat, 4421
  assimilation des immigrés, 3742
  athéisme, 1699
  avortement, 3201
  choix d'une profession, 4617, 4619
  classe ouvrière, 2552, 2597, 2598
  conditions de logement, 4163
  conscience nationale, 1332
  culture, 1276
  culture de masse, 2237
  dimension de la famille, 3435
  division du travail, 2516
  employé de commerce, 2728
  enseignement supérieur, 2220, 2328
  entreprise, 4333
  ergonomie, 4539
  état des tendances, 80
  évolution de la population, 3027
  industrie, 4419

Hongrie *[suite]*
  intellectuel, 1332, 2698
  intelligentsia, 2699, 2703
  jeunesse, 736
  mariage, 3281
  médecin, 5675
  migration pendulaire, 3773
  minorité nationale, 3562, 3565,
    3566
  mobilité professionnelle, 2728,
    4618
  mobilité sociale, 2727
  orientation scolaire, 2220
  paysannerie, 2727, 3914, 3917
  petite ville, 4074
  pratique religieuse, 1780, 1781
  presse, 736
  recherche en cours, 74
  structure sociale, 2462
  suicide, 5366
  vie rurale, 3900
  village, 2698, 3858, 3860, 3865
  ville, 4049, 4061
Hôpital, 1107, 5623, 5628, 5632,
    5633, 5637
Hors groupe, 963
Hostilité, 840, 842, 855, 858
Hygiène sociale, 5605

Identification au groupe, 964
Identification au parti, 5119, 5120,
    5136, 5145
Identification culturelle, 1345,
    1346, 1348
Identité, 628, 629, 634, 640, 641,
    644, 647, 652, 654, 1380, 1711,
    3558, 3577
Idéologie, 772, 1189-1191, 1193,
    1195-1201, 1203-1210, 1260,
    1271, 1306, 1585, 1790, 1819,
    1824, 2015, 2065, 2139, 2551,
    2687, 2693, 2737, 4265, 5486,
    5503, 5521
Idéologie politique, 4908, 4910
Ile de la Réunion, société rurale,
    3886
Iles Fidji
  analphabétisme, 2374
  société en transformation, 2374
Iles Trobriand, stratification so-
    ciale, 2518
Illich, Ivan, 2225
Image, 1154
Imitation, 839
Immigrant, 1472, 3372, 3707, 3709,
    3710, 3711, 3713, 3716, 3719,
    3724, 3726, 3733, 3736, 3740,
    3743, 4511
Immigration 3696, 3698, 3701, 3703,
    3706, 3714, 3715, 3717, 3720,
    3727, 3735, 3739
Impérialisme, 5242, 5243

Incertitude, 609
Inde
  adoption d'enfant, 3406
  alimentation, 5292
  analyse transnationale, 2537
  bibliographie, 4002
  caste, 2537, 2542
  changement social, 1300
  choix du conjoint, 3300
  commandement politique, 5102
  développement de l'enfant, 2912
  développement des collectivités,
    3842, 5538
  développement urbain, 4220
  dictionnaire, 154
  dimension de la famille, 3445
  dynamique de groupe, 2542
  économie agricole, 4396
  enquête, 3184
  fécondité, 3137, 3184
  groupe familial, 5417
  intellectuel, 2694, 2695
  maladie mentale, 3076
  mariage, 3277, 3282
  métropole, 4078
  migration de travail, 3788
  migration interne, 3746, 3786
  modernisation, 2694
  mouvement ouvrier, 4739
  nationalisme, 4943
  ouvrier, 4673
  parti politique, 5067
  patrimoine culturel, 1300
  petite ville, 4068
  planification de la famille, 3224,
    3445
  planification rurale, 3977
  pouvoir, 3941
  projection démographique, 2841
  recherche en cours, 64
  reproduction de la population,
    2841
  sécurité sociale, 5532
  société rurale, 2563, 3927
  société urbaine, 4129
  sociologie du développement, 2831
  sous-développement, 2793
  status, 2660
  stéréotype, 2352
  structure de classe, 2563
  suicide, 5413, 5426
  système d'éducation, 2200
  tradition, 3277
  travail social, 5538
  tribu, 3576
  université, 2352
  urbanisation, 4002
  vie rurale, 3941
  village, 3076, 3786, 3854, 3857,
    3861
  vol, 5417

Indicateur, 459, 529, 531-542, 4200, 4286, 4613, 5495
Indice, 530
Indien, 909, 3592, 3593, 3595, 3596, 3598, 3599, 3609, 3611,3612
Indigène, 3821
Individu, 607, 609, 612-614, 616, 618-623, 1326
Individualisme, 633, 1112
Indonésie
  condition de la femme, 3499, 3516
  conflit, 878
  · contrôle des naissances, 3222
  fécondité, 3156, 3157
  mortalité infantile, 3166
Industrialisation, 3272, 3321, 4409, 4410, 4412, 4416, 4779
Industrie, 4357, 4415, 4417, 4419
Inégalité, 2489, 2490, 2495, 2501, 2502, 2505, 2507, 2512, 2523, 2524, 2527, 4964
Inférence causale, 376, 381, 382
Infirmière, 5643, 5658, 5674
Influence du groupe, 950, 965, 967
Influence interpersonnelle, 834-837
Influence sociale, 1380, 1391
Ingénieur, 4607
Innovation, 4354, 4372, 4377, 4378, 4380, 4382
Institution de recherche, 103, 107
Institution politique, 4973
Institution religieuse, 1645, 1649, 1650
Instruction civique, 2400
Intégration culturelle, 1347
Intégration familiale, 682, 3405, 3417, 3447, 3452, 5542
Intégration sociale, 1414, 1424
Intellectuel, 1332,1770, 2678, 2683, 2684, 2686, 2688, 2689, 2692-2695, 2697, 2698
Intelligence, 684, 692, 702
Intelligentsia, 2682, 2685, 2690, 2696, 2699, 2701, 2703
Interaction en groupe, 861, 948,952, 953
Interaction sociale, 749, 1406, 1408, 1410, 1415, 1421, 1422, 2838
Intérêt, 4455
Intérêt professionnel, 4633, 4652
Interprétation, 341, 351, 354, 366, 514
Intervalle génésique, 3163
Invalide, 3075, 3084, 3091, 3093
Invalidité, 3079, 3092
Inventaire de personnalité, 484, 485, 487
Iran
  dimension de la famille, 3458
  fécondité, 3133
  vie rurale, 3915
  village, 3133

Irlande
  conflit politique, 1741
  église et état, 1741, 1743
  électeur, 5181
  mouvement révolutionnaire, 5084
  nation, 1325
  rénovation urbaine, 4228
  stéréotype, 1164
  système d'éducation, 2165
  ville, 922
  violence, 1492
Islam, 1630, 1632, 1633, 1638, 2949, 3306
Islamisme, *voir* Islam
Isolat, 3296, 3303
Isolement social, 1496, 1508
Israel
  adulte, 2957
  agriculteur, 3926
  analyse transculturelle, 2945
  assimilation des immigrés, 3718, 3721
  condition de la femme, 3521
  culture, 4835
  culture politique, 5128
  développement national, 2837
  église et état, 1775
  élevage de l'enfant, 2915
  élite, 2705
  ethnicité, 3586
  ferme collective, 4386, 4391, 4408
  groupe ethnique, 3574
  immigrant, 1472
  jeunesse, 2945
  mouvement de jeunesse, 2957
  ségrégation résidentielle, 4140
  service social, 5663
  sociologie du loisir, 4835
  ville, 1472
Italie
  adaptation scolaire, 2289
  artisanat, 4420
  assimilation des immigrés, 3705
  bibliographie, 140
  bourgeoisie, 2557
  changement social, 1645
  chômage, 4487
  classe ouvrière, 2553, 2563
  classe sociale, 2550, 2616, 4615, 4775
  comportement électoral, 5179
  condition de la femme, 3479, 3519
  conditions de logement, 4163
  développement économique, 2810
  développement urbain, 4207
  droit du travail, 4730
  droits de la femme, 5172
  église et état, 1769
  électeur, 5172
  élite du pouvoir, 2700
  émigrant, 3695
  émigration, 3691
  enseignement public, 2196

Italie *[suite]*
enseignement supérieur, 2315
entrepreneur, 4320
entreprise agricole, 4388
état des tendances, 3323
ethnologie, 1230
famille, 3323, 3325, 3326
formation professionnelle, 4622,
  4658, 4659
franc maçonnerie, 1662
grève, 4783
groupe de pression, 5094
groupe familial, 3421
intellectuel, 2697
jeunesse, 2954
juif, 1623
logement, 4149
lutte de classe, 4783
mafia, 5442
marginalité, 1471, 4123
médecin, 5641
migration de travail, 2616, 5146
migration rurale, 3750
mouvement religieux, 1750
parti politique, 5073
participation politique, 5118,
  5156
paysannerie, 3421
relations industrielles, 4719,
  4721
relations parents-enfant, 3402
relations parents enseignants,
  2453
sécularisation, 1771
société urbaine, 1471
sociologie de la profession, 4612,
  4615
stratification professionnelle,
  4628
stupéfiants,5310, 5314
syndicat, 4757, 4775
système d'éducation, 2204
université, 2356, 2357
valeur, 1379
vie rurale, 3897, 3901
vie urbaine, 4123
vieillard, 2993
vieillesse, 2987

Jamaïque, urbanisation, 4039
Japon
administration de l'enseignement,
  2206
caste, 2546
changement d'organisation, 1064
choix du conjoint, 3298
classe ouvrière, 2606
condition de la femme, 3502
culte, 1687
développement économique, 4283
église et état, 1767, 1768
élections, 5183

employé, 4691
enseignemmt supérieur, 2312
étudiant, 2330
gérontologie, 3000
gouvernement, 5018
industrialisation, 4412, 4416
industrie, 4415
intellectuel, 2686
jeunesse, 2959, 2967, 2968
migration interne, 3767
milieu d'affaires, 4328
parenté, 3370, 3380
participation politique, 1776
planification régionale, 4077
politique, 1768, 1771, 5204
politique étrangère, 5245
pratique religieuse, 1776
presse, 1994
problème social, 5278
recherche, 75
recherche en cours, 73, 79, 89
réforme religieuse, 1755
secte, 3380
stratification sociale, 2504
tradition, 3439
travail social, 5548
vie familiale, 3437, 3439
vie rurale, 3951
vie urbaine, 4126
vieillesse, 2983
village, 3862, 3879, 3882
ville nouvelle, 4077
Jaspers, Karl, 199
Jeu, 4854, 4860, 4866, 4872, 4886
Jeu à deux personnes, 558
Jeu de rôle, 1102, 1108
Jeune travailleur, 4319, 4489, 4515,
  4517, 4518, 4521, 4525, 4535,
  4666
Jeunesse, 736, 786, 1082, 1109, 1278,
  1355, 1463, 1478, 1495, 1780,
  1781, 2019, 2090, 2944-2947, 2949,
  2950, 2954-2956, 2958-2962, 2965,
  2967-2969, 2973-2977, 3393, 3940,
  4831, 5142
Jordanie
fécondité, 3178
planification de la famille, 3178
Journal, *voir* Presse
Journal intime, *voir* Biographie
Journalisme, 2004, 2006
Journaliste, 1996, 1998, 2002, 2005
Juif, 1622, 1623
Justice, 1542, 1553, 1562, 1565, 1575,
  1581, 1583
Justice sociale, 1572, 5494, 5509

Kenya, conflit de classe, 2549

Langage, 1896, 1906, 1907, 1909, 1911-
  1914, 1917-1919, 1922, 1923, 1926,
  1927, 1929, 1930, 1937

Langue, *voir* Langage
Lazarsfeld, Paul, 161, 172, 178, 1802
Leader, 963, 1045, 1080
Leader politique, 5127
Le Bon, Gustave, 1221
Lecture, 696, 699
Législation, 1571
Lénine, V. I., 248
Lesotho, famille, 3349
Lévi-Strauss, Claude, 202, 207, 271, 304, 1321, 1713, 3389
Lévy-Garboua, Louis, 2359
Lexicologie, 1861
Liban
  aliénation, 5151
  assimilation des immigrés, 3728, 3732
  classe sociale, 2565
  comportement religieux, 1719, 3144
  étudiant, 2322
  évolution de la population, 1719
  fécondité, 3144
  participation politique, 5151
  système social, 2484
Libéralisme, 4925, 4954
Liberté, 4911, 4999-5002
Liberté de l'enseignement, 2182
Liberté religieuse, 1727
Liberté surveillée, 5443, 5449
Licenciement, 4601
Lieu de travail, 4597, 4667
Lignage, 3371, 3379, 3381
Linguistique, 1843, 1844, 1848, 1849, 1855, 1859-1860, 1863, 1864, 3378
Littérature, 2062, 2065, 2066, 2069, 2070, 2073, 2076
Littérature orale, 2078
Livre, 480
Lockout, 4705
Logement, 3382, 3724, 3736, 4024, 4142, 4146, 4149, 4150, 4153, 4158-4160, 4169, 4175, 4177, 4184, 4194
Logique, 499
Loi, 1541, 1545-1548, 1550-1552, 1554, 1557, 1564, 1567-1569, 1572, 1580
Loisir, 1155, 1266, 4822, 4825-4827, 4833, 4834, 4836, 4838, 4840, 4841, 4845-4847
Luckmann, Thomas, 1593
Lutte de classes, 1196, 2225, 2498, 2547, 2556, 2572, 2577, 2580, 2582, 2594, 2621, 2623, 2626, 2648, 3540, 3803, 4245, 4783
Lycée, *voir* École secondaire

Macro, 415, 2457
Mafia, 5442
Magie, 1608, 1610, 1611

Mahométanisme, *voir* Islam
Main d'oeuvre, 670, 4475, 4480, 4483, 4484
Main d'oeuvre étrangère, 3646, 4511, 4522, 4531
Main d'oeuvre féminine, 182, 3185, 3313, 4497, 4498, 4500, 4505, 4507, 4508, 4510, 4519, 4523, 4527, 4533
Majorité politique, 5099
Maladie, 3072-3074, 3078
Maladie mentale, 2924, 3070, 3071, 3076, 3080, 3082, 3083, 3085, 3087-3090, 3094
Malaisie
  évolution de la population, 2842
  intellectuel, 1770
  migration interne, 3750
  pluralisme culturel, 1281
  pratique religieuse, 1770
  projection démographique, 2842
  relations interethniques, 3627
  stratification sociale, 2522
  tribu, 3541
  urbanisation, 4015, 4020
Mali
  enfant, 2932,
  scolarisation, 2233
Malthus, 278
Malthusianisme, 3188
Man, Hendrik de, 229
Manager, 4693, 4694, 4697-4699, 4703, 4705
Manières de table, 1511
Mannheim, Karl, 1803, 1823, 1827
Manuel, 189, 192, 193, 195, 2206
Marché, 4449, 4450
Marché du travail, 4469, 4471, 4473, 4478, 4479, 4482
Marché financier, 4456
Marginalité, 1434, 1443, 1444, 1471, 1474, 1484, 1486, 1501, 1504, 1505, 4123, 4181
Mari, 2910, 3309, 3320, 5153
Mariage, 2525, 3192, 3265-3267, 3269-3273, 3277, 3278, 3280-3283, 3285, 3286, 3288, 3290, 3292-3294, 3522
Mariage mixte, 3304-3307
Markley Znaniecka, Eileen, 162
Maroc
  assimilation des immigrés, 3718
  fécondité, 3138
  logement, 4024
  rural-urbain, 3138
  urbanisation, 4024
Marx, Karl, 203, 223, 256, 259, 302, 315, 1461, 1726, 4452, 5197
Marxisme, 80, 199, 203, 210, 219, 223, 235, 253, 256, 285, 302, 315, 320, 326, 327, 329, 332, 756, 2326, 4244
Matérialisme, 143, 237, 243
Matérialisme dialectique, *voir* Marxisme
Matériel audio-visuel, 2394, 2431, 2432

Matériel éducatif, 2430
Mathématiques, 496, 497, 500, 5265
Matriarcat, 3398
Maturité, 2978
Mauritanie, ville, 4046
McClelland, 4282
Mead, George Herbert, 204, 292
Mécanisation, 4368
Médecin, 3097, 4607, 4708, 5641,
    5648, 5649, 5653, 5654, 5659,
    5662, 5661-5668, 5670, 5672,
    5675, 5676, 5678, 5681
Médecine, 5557, 5559, 5560, 5566,
    5568, 5570, 5572, 5573
Médecine sociale, 5562, 5563, 5575
Mémoire, 703, 706
Ménage, 2881, 4038
Meneur, *voir* Leader
Mère, 3385, 3387, 3390, 3391, 3469
Merton, R. K., 288
Mesure de la personnalité, 486, 488
Méthode contraceptive, 3212
Méthode de recherche, 131, 391, 395,
    399, 401, 403, 578, 5264
Méthodologie, 231, 250, 390, 394,
    396, 397 , 402,404-406, 408,
    409, 411, 3852, 5263
Métier, *voir* Profession
Métropole, 4042, 4067, 4069, 4070,
    4073, 4076, 4078, 4087, 4089,
    4092, 4305
Meurtre, *voir* Homicide
Mexique
    agriculture, 3035
    assimilation des immigrés, 3730
    développement urbain, 4208
    élite politique, 5109
    enseignement supérieur, 2342
    évolution de la population, 3035
    famille, 3324
    franc maçonnerie, 1660
    groupe de pression, 5089
    parti politique, 5082
    prolétariat, 2570
    promotion de la femme, 3487
    réforme agraire, 3955
    réforme de l'enseignement, 2194
    socialisation politique, 5133
    structure de classe, 2624
    syndicat, 4773
    taudis, 4197
    université, 2334
    vie politique, 5195
Migrant, 2405, 4191
Migration, 3162, 3654-3666
Migration de travail, 2616, 3154,
    3758, 3760, 3770, 3792, 5146
Migration externe, 3553, 3667-3676
Migration internationale, *voir* Mi-
    gration externe

Migration interne, 3154, 3744-3746,
    3749, 3754, 3755, 3757, 3762-3767,
    3769, 3774, 3776, 3783-3787, 3789,
    3790, 3793, 5408
Migration pendulaire, 3773, 3794
Migration rurale, 3747, 3748, 3751,
    3752, 3759, 3771, 3772, 3775,
    3779, 3780, 3782, 3786, 3791,
    3795, 3797
Migrations alternantes, *voir* Migration
    de travail
Milieu culturel, 1299
Milieu d'affaires, 4328
Milieu familial, 3308, 3403, 3412, 3424,
    3436, 3441, 3444, 5465
Milieu rural, 3887, 3892, 3903, 3909,
    3938, 3949, 3954
Milieu scolaire, 2288, 2290, 2293
Milieu urbain, 4010, 4014, 4023, 4026
Militaire, 828, 5008, 5017, 5206,
    5211, 5216, 5217, 5218, 5221-5225,
    5228-5230, 5233, 5244
Mills, Wright, 307
Ministre du culte, 1093, 1674, 1675,
    1678
Minorité culturelle, 1349
Minorité ethnique, *voir* Minorité na-
    tionale
Minorité nationale, 1375, 1458, 2618,
    3536, 3537, 3542, 3547, 3554, 3559-
    3562, 3565, 3566, 3568, 3569, 3571,
    3575, 3579, 3581, 3589
Mission religieuse, 1756
Missionnaire, 1673
Mobilité de la main d'oeuvre, 2712
Mobilité descendante, 2723
Mobilité professionnelle, 2728, 4618,
    4635, 4640, 4644, 4654, 4666
Mobilité résidentielle, 4148, 4157,
    4176
Mobilité sociale, 2261, 2449, 2506,
    2706-2716, 2718-2722, 2724-2728,
    5670
Mobilité verticale, 2717
Modèle, 367, 371, 2466
Modèle culturel, 1249, 1313
Modèle cybernétique, 544
Modèle de congruité, 1162
Modèle mathématique, 377, 382, 494,
    1391, 3804
Modèle probabiliste, *voir* Modèle sto-
    chastique
Modèle statistique, 502, 507, 513, 516
Modèle stochastique, 2905
Modernisation, 2694, 2730, 2739, 2747,
    2769, 2779, 2781
Modernisation politique, 4981, 4985
Monarchie, 4958
Monnaie, 4457, 4460
Morale, 1165, 1517, 1518, 1528, 1532,
    1539, 3913

Moralité, 1522, 1526, 1529-1531, 1536, 1547, 1972
Morbidité, 2891
Mort, 1691, 3095, 3099, 3102, 3111, 3112, 3118, 3119, 3128, 3129, 3131
Mortalité, 2891, 3096, 3098, 3100, 3103, 3105-3109, 3113, 3114, 3120-3123, 3125, 3126, 3172
Mortalité infantile, 3110, 3117, 3124, 3127, 3132, 3166
Motivation, 717, 720, 722, 723, 729, 737
Motivation au travail, 4588, 4589, 4592, 4594, 4595
Motivation d'accomplissement, 735, 736
Mouvement contestataire, 5084, 5088, 5091-5093, 5095, 5096, 5130
Mouvement de jeunesse, 2957, 2972
Mouvement de population, *voir* Migration
Mouvement étudiant, 2296, 2319, 2326, 2333, 2351, 2361
Mouvement ouvrier, 4477, 4739, 4740-4747, 4749, 4752, 4760, 4763, 4765, 4768, 4779
Mouvement religieux, 1748, 1750, 1784
Mouvement révolutionnaire, 5086, 5087, 5090
Moyen Orient
  course aux armements, 5257
  urbanisation, 4006
Moyens de communication de masse, *voir* Communiation de masse
Musée, 3054, 2060, 2704
Musicologie, 2086
Musique, 2087, 2094
Musulman, 1625
Mythe, 1042, 1713, 1715, 1716
Mythologie, 1714, 1717

Natalité, 3011, 3167
Nation, 1325-1329, 1331
National-socialisme, 4956
Nationalisme, 1331, 1783, 2107, 2500, 2575, 3554, 3608, 4928, 4935, 4940, 4941, 4943, 4947, 4953, 4955
Nationalisme culturel, 1241
Nature, 287
Nature humaine, 2877
Négociation, 871, 872, 874, 879, 881, 1005
Négociation collective, 4799-4806
Néocolonialisme, 4246
Niger
  migration rurale, 3791
  village, 3872

Nigeria
  choix professionnel, 4650
  développement des collectivités, 3837
  développement rural, 3965
  enfant, 2914
  étude de cas, 3183
  fécondité, 3016, 3142, 3143, 3182, 3183
  innovation, 4372
  milieu rural, 3949
  mouvement ouvrier, 4740
  pauvreté, 5296
  polygynie, 3182
  relations interethniques, 1144
  ségrégation résidentielle, 4178
  société traditionnelle, 4080
  stéréotype, 1144
  village, 3875
  ville, 4080
Niveau d'éducation, 2231
Niveau de vie, 4290, 4303
Noblesse, 2533
Noir, 2677, 3597, 3600, 3601, 3605-3608, 3610, 4456, 5112, 5124, 5140, 5143
Nomadisme, 3777, 3778, 3781
Norme, 1441
Norme de travail, 4550
Norvège
  comportement du consommateur, 4441
  conditions de travail, 4496
  élite, 2687
  idéologie, 2687
  inégalité, 2512
  participation des travailleurs, 4811
  profession, 2340
  recherche sociale, 5266
  sociologie du développement, 2817
  travailleur féminin, 4496
  université, 2340
  usage de drogue, 5341
Notice nécrologique, 160, 163, 167-171, 173, 174, 177, 179, 420
Nouvelle-Zélande
  enseignement secondaire, 2245
  prestige professionnel, 4624
  service hospitalier, 5625
  sport, 4624
  zone urbaine, 5625
Nuptialité, 3275, 3291

Objectivité, 343, 346, 1827
Objet sacré, 1711
Observateur, 442
Observation participante, 443, 444
Observation sur le terrain, *voir* Travail sur le terrain
Oecuménisme, 1665-1669

Opinion, 645, 1172, 1174, 1184, 1185, 1187, 1877
Opinion publique, 1171, 1173, 1175–1179, 1181–1183, 1186, 1188
Optimum de peuplement, 3029
Ordinateur, 120–126
Ordre social, 1190, 1385, 2454, 2458, 2461, 2473, 2486
Organisation, 984, 1005, 1008, 1012, 1013, 1015, 1016, 1022, 1024, 1027, 1028, 1030, 1032, 1034, 1038–1040, 1042, 1047–1049, 1053, 1055, 1060, 1062, 1063, 1069, 2496, 4537
Organisation bureaucratique, *voir* Bureaucratie
Organisation complexe, 996–999, 1003, 1004
Organisation d'étudiants, 2345, 2349, 2353
Organisation internationale, 5235
Organisation patronale, 4734–4736
Orientation professionnelle, 1035, 4625, 4629, 4653, 4662
Orientation scolaire, 2220
Origine sociale, 2663, 2669, 2672
Ortega y Gasset, 296
Ouvrage de référence, 142
Ouvrier, 4668, 4673
Ouvrier agricole, 3937, 4767
Ouvrier qualifié, 4671
Ouvrier spécialisé, 4674
Owen, Wilfred, 249

Paix, 5248
Pakistan
    église et état, 1738
    enseignant, 2441
    ethnicité, 3558
    famille, 3353
    fécondité, 3293
    identité, 3558
    mariage, 3293
    surpeuplement, 3009
    tribu, 3535
Panique, 711
Paraguay, système d'éducation, 2164
Parenté, 3364, 3367–3373, 3375, 3376, 3378, 3380, 3382
Pareto, Vilfredo, 225
Parlement, 5020, 5021
Parole, 933, 1910, 1924, 1932, 1935, 1938
Parsons, Talcott, 198, 211, 216, 217, 255, 299, 308, 593, 1482, 1554
Parti politique, 559, 2326, 3214, 4780, 5062–5083
Parti unique, 3652
Participation à la collectivité, 3844
Participation au groupe, 962

Participation des travailleurs, 4807, 4809, 4811, 4812, 4814–4817, 4819–4820
Participation électorale, 5174, 5182
Participation politique, 1776, 2965, 5074, 5113, 5118, 5124, 5125, 5130, 5134, 5135, 5138–5140, 5146, 5149, 5151, 5155, 5163, 5164, 5188
Participation religieuse, 5123
Participation sociale, 1420, 1429, 1440, 2279, 2892
Pathologie sociale, 5274, 5277
Patriarcat, 3431, 3434
Patrimoine culturel, 1280, 1291, 1300, 1307
Patriotisme, 4922, 4932, 4944, 4950, 4951
Pauvre, 5290, 5293, 5303
Pauvreté, 1486, 5288, 5291, 5295, 5296, 5298, 5299
Pays-Bas
    administration publique, 5043
    attitude, 4501
    audience, 2060
    divorce, 3279
    émigration, 3680
    équilibre démographique, 3050
    famille, 3332, 3359
    fonction publique, 5033
    jeune travailleur, 4515
    musée, 2060
    nuptialité, 3275
    promotion de la femme, 3525
    recherche en cours, 3332, 3359
    relations industrielles, 4710
    soins médicaux, 5601
    travailleur étranger, 4501
    université, 2358
    vie urbaine, 4135
Pays en développement, 506, 2790, 2791, 2809, 2810, 2813, 2834, 3973
Pays socialiste, 4256, 4258, 4260, 4267, 4268
Paysan, *voir* Agriculteur
Paysannerie, 3421, 3884, 3890, 3914, 3916, 3917, 3925, 3929, 3930, 3934, 3942
Pédagogie, 2426, 2428
Peine capitale, 5446, 5457, 5464, 5468
Peinture, 2084, 3894
Pélerinage, 1678, 1682, 1695
Pensée, 695, 701
Perception, 689, 700, 707
Perception d'autrui; 967
Perception de soi, 625, 653, 1148, 3468
Perception du rôle, 1095
Perception interpersonnelle, 789, 792–794, 830, 948

Perception sociale, 790, 791, 795, 1095, 1103, 1391, 5184
Père, 3383, 3384, 3386, 3388, 3389
Performance, 748, 750, 759
Performance du groupe, 971
Périodique, 181, 183, 185
Pérou
  adolescent, 2948
  éducation de base, 2373
  ethnicité, 2527
  groupe familial, 2438
  inégalité, 2527
  lutte de classes, 2623, 2626
  migration interne, 3789
  participation politique, 5125
  paysannerie, 3884
  population urbaine, 5125
  réforme de l'enseignement, 2151
  relations raciales, 3617
  religion primitive, 1614
  société traditionnelle, 2792
  sociologie du développement, 2826, 2836
  taudis, 3617
  urbanisation, 3789
  ville, 4054
Persécution religieuse, 1774
Personnalité, 655, 658, 659, 662, 665, 668, 669, 671, 673, 674, 677-681, 683, 1308, 1404, 1980, 2926, 4385, 4571, 5250
Personne âgée, *voir* Vieillard
Personne de couleur, 3594, 3602, 3603, 5100
Persuasion, 1952, 2030
Petit groupe, *voir* Groupe restreint
Petite ville, 812, 3783, 4050, 4063, 4065, 4068, 4074
Petrazycki, Leon, 1560
Peur, 714, 5369
Phénoménologie, 228, 240, 246
Philippines
  classe sociale, 2653
  droit du travail, 4729
  école secondaire, 2268
  immigration, 3696
  ménage, 4038
  pauvre, 5290
  pays en développement, 2809
  politique du logement, 4185
  population urbaine, 3066
  secte, 1658
  sociologie urbaine, 5290
  taudis, 4193
  urbanisation, 4028, 4038
Philosophie, 198, 201, 216, 229, 236, 250, 255, 257, 264, 268, 269, 271, 278, 283, 297, 299, 309, 311, 314, 319, 325
Philosophie politique, 314, 4909
Photographie, 2082
Piaget, Jean, 204, 306, 2134

Planification, 541, 542, 1057, 4465
Planification de l'enseignement, 2156, 2170, 2172, 2180, 2184, 2186, 2203, 2207, 3025
Planification de la famille, 3169, 3178, 3186, 3189-3192, 3194, 3196-3198, 3203, 3206, 3208, 209, 3219, 3221, 3224, 3227, 3230, 3309, 3445
Planification nationale, 4465
Planification régionale, 4077, 4461-4463
Planification rurale, 3959, 3968, 3974
Planification sociale, 141, 440, 533, 4120, 5481, 5483, 5485, 5487, 5489, 5491, 5497, 5502, 5504, 5514, 5516, 5521, 5522
Planification urbaine, 4172, 4200-4202, 4205, 4206, 4209, 4210, 4213, 4217, 4218, 4221, 4222, 4234, 4709, 5501
Planning familial, *voir* Planification de la famille
Plein emploi, 4486
Pluralisme culturel, 1281, 1284, 1289, 1319
Pluralisme social, 2513
Police, 1489, 5004-5015
Politique, 1744, 1758, 1763, 1764, 1766, 1768, 1771, 2065, 5197, 5201, 5204
Politique d'éducation, 1574, 2149, 2152, 2155, 2160, 2169, 2173, 2174, 2176, 2179, 2185, 2191, 2195, 2199, 2202, 2205, 3640
Politique de bien-être, 5474, 5479, 5486, 5488, 5495, 5499, 5501, 5508, 5512, 5517, 5523, 5524
Politique de la recherche, 112-114, 119
Politique démographique, 469, 1519, 3026, 3034, 3195, 3200, 3202, 3211, 3215, 3218, 3220, 3228, 5505
Politique du logement, 3048, 4138, 4145, 4151, 4152, 4162, 4164, 4168, 4171, 4172, 4174, 4179, 4196
Politique étrangère, 3198, 5244, 5245
Politique gouvernementale, 5016
Politique internationale, 5247, 5250, 5255
Politique mondiale, *voir* Politique internationale
Politique scientifique, 115
Politique sociale, 456, 1495, 1529, 5023, 5473, 5476, 5490, 5493, 5505, 5507, 5510, 5511, 5513, 5515, 5519, 5520
Politisation, 5131, 5137, 5143, 5160

Politiste, 58
Pollution, 3819
Pologne
  administration régionale, 5060
  agriculteur, 3888
  alimentation, 5301
  bibliographie, 144
  bibliothèque, 147
  biographie, 175
  châtiment, 5456
  citadin, 4192
  comportement politique, 5141
  consommation, 4435, 4436, 4444
  contact entre cultures, 1374
  coopérative agricole, 4387
  développement rural, 5060
  droit du travail, 4726
  économie industrielle, 4411
  église et état, 1745, 1752
  enseignement supérieur, 2329
  équilibre démographique, 4030
  femme mariée, 3313
  fonction publique, 5038
  formation professionnelle, 4619
  immigrant, 3713, 3726
  intégration culturelle, 1347
  main d'oeuvre féminine, 3313
  manager, 4699
  mariage, 3265
  migration interne, 3793
  minorité nationale, 3579
  motivation au travail, 4589
  pathologie sociale, 5274
  périodique, 185
  politique démographique, 5505
  politique sociale, 5505
  prestige professionnel, 4655
  recherche en cours, 69, 86
  santé, 5617
  satisfaction au travail, 4595
  société, 1338
  société socialiste, 4270
  sociologie urbaine, 3984
  status de la femme, 3528
  structure sociale, 2462
  système d'éducation, 2188
  tendance de recherche, 68, 3984
  travailleur, 4676
Polygynie, 3182, 3301
Popper, Karl R., 346
Population, 2846-2848, 2851, 2854,
  2859
Population active, 3058, 3059, 3064,
  3065, 4410
Population agricole, 3061
Population rurale, 3062, 3067
Population stable, 3020
Population urbaine, 2947, 3055-3057,
  3060, 3063, 3066, 3068, 3069,
  4037, 5125
Porto Rico
  développement urbain, 4204

émigration, 3687
main d'oeuvre féminine, 4527
nationalisme, 4947
sexologie, 3253
village, 3880
Portugal
  assimilation des immigrés, 3503
  capitalisme, 3921
  corporatisme, 4777
  émigration, 3692
  migration externe, 3675
  mort, 3118
  promotion de la femme, 3503
  réforme agraire, 3975
  société rurale, 3921
Positivisme, 233, 260, 279-281, 1221
Poulantzas, Nicos, 237
Pouvoir, 563, 966, 1076, 2742, 2743,
  3941, 4911-4921
Pouvoir judiciaire, 5027, 5028
Pouvoir social, *voir* Contrainte sociale
Pratique religieuse, 1754, 1762,
  1765, 1770, 1780
Pré-enquête, 454, 4375
Préhistoire, 1709
Préjugé, 1150, 1152, 1163
Préjugé racial, 3628-3630, 3632,
  3650
Première enfance, 692, 856, 1928,
  2925, 2931
Présidence, 5019
Presse, 421, 736, 1989-1995, 1997,
  1999-2001, 2003, 2007, 2008,
  3523, 3651
Pression du groupe, 959
Pression sociale, *voir* Contrainte
  sociale
Prestige professionnel, 4620, 4624,
  4626, 4636, 4645, 4648, 4651,
  4655, 4661, 4664
Prêtre, 1676, 1677, 5346
Prévention de la délinquance, 5357,
  5450, 5454, 5462, 5463, 5467,
  5470, 5472
Prévision, 348, 349, 353, 358, 501,
  2845
Priorité de recherche, 109, 110, 118
Prise de décision, 742, 751, 752,
  764, 767, 770, 970, 1015
Prise de rôle, 1097
Prison, 663, 5444, 5447, 5451, 5453,
  5458-5461, 5465, 5469
Privation, 5143
Privation relative, 716, 5193
Problème social, 5263, 5270, 5272,
  5273, 5275, 5276, 5278
Processus markoviens, 551
Processus stochastiques, 549, 550
Production, 4346, 4352, 4365, 4384
Production agricole, 4398
Production industrielle, 4413

Professeur, 2360
Profession,1142, 2340, 2669, 4194,
    4609, 4611, 4612, 4614
Profession libérale, 4706
Profession médicale, 1083, 4708
Professionalisation, 4608, 4616
Professorat, 2433, 2440
Profit, 4310
Programme d'enseignement, 2271, 2362,
    2422, 2424, 2425, 2427, 2429
Progrès social, 2745, 2762, 2763,
    4247
Progrès technique, 4347, 4351, 4355,
    4361, 4363, 4364, 4366, 4367,
    4369, 4374, 4379, 4385, 4672
Prohibition de l'inceste, 3245,3250
Projection démographique, 2841, 2842,
    2843, 2845
Prolétariat, 2570, 2571, 3042, 4939
Promotion de la femme, 2341, 3464,
    3473, 3487, 3500, 3503, 3504,
    3506, 3512, 3523, 3525, 3532,
    4846
Promotion professionnelle, 4637, 4657,
    4663
Propagande, 1947, 1954
Propriété, 2528, 4239, 4240
Protection de la nature, 3818
Protection légale, 1574, 1576
Protestant, 1619, 1620
Protestantisme, 1640
Proust, M., 245
Psychanalyse, 576, 583, 593, 595
Psychiatre, 5569, 5640, 5661, 5669,
    5680
Psychiatrie, 5569
Psychodrame, 491, 492
Psycholinguistique, 1838, 1856
Psychologie clinique, 585
Psychologie de l'éducation, 2110,
    2112, 2119, 2123, 2136, 2144,
    2146
Psychologie de la forme, 293
Psychologie industrielle, 4466
Psychologie politique, 4906
Psychologie sociale, 573-575, 577,
    578, 580-582, 584, 586, 588-592,
    594, 596, 597, 599, 600, 602-606,
    885, 894, 896, 1808
Psychosociologie, 587, 598
Psychosociologue, 52
Psychothérapie, 579, 601
Psychothérapie de groupe, 898-900,
    902-904, 906, 908, 910, 913,915,
    916, 918, 919
Publicité, 1942-1946, 1948, 1949,
    1951, 1955, 1956
Pulszky, Agost, 4983
Puritanisme, *voir* Éthique protestante
Pyramide des âges, 2907

Questionnaire, 466, 469, 473-476,
    478-480
Questionnaire par poste, 468

Race, 1446, 2996, 3386, 3539, 3563,
    3567, 3587, 4307, 4660
Racisme, 2551, 3633, 3639, 3645,
    3646, 3649, 3653
Radio, 2023
Rapports sexuels, 3240, 3255
Rareté, 5300
Réadaptation des invalides, 5576,
    5611
Recherche, 75, 76, 87, 88, 90, 94,
    317, 3328, 3538
Recherche action, 99, 100, 102, 587
Recherche démographique, 2838, 2852,
    2853, 2858, 2864
Recherche empirique, 440, 441, 1467,
    1821, 5274, 5590
Recherche en cours, 64,65, 67, 69, 70,
    72-74, 77-79, 81, 84-86, 89, 92,
    95, 97, 98, 1230, 1584, 3332, 3549,
    3992
Recherche interdisciplinaire, 101
Recherche multidisciplinaire, *voir*
    Recherche interdisciplinaire
Recherche pédagogique, 2415, 2417,
    2418, 2420
Recherche sociale, 5260, 5262, 5264-
    5269
Récréation, 4098, 4861
Recrutement, 4495
Recueil de textes, 197
Réforme agraire, 3955, 3956, 3964,
    3967, 3975
Réforme de l'enseignement, 2151,2153,
    2175, 2183, 2190, 2194, 2360
Réforme religieuse, 1536, 1755,
    1782
Réforme sociale, 5482
Réfugié, 3699, 3712
Régime parlementaire, 4974
Règle, *voir* Morale
Régulation des naissances, 1674, 3187,
    3194, 3198, 3210, 3214, 3222,
    3226, 3229
Relation de dépendance, 833, 838
Relation pédagogique, 2419
Relations culturelles, 1367, 1375,
    4881
Relations du travail, 4717
Relations humaines, 772, 782, 783
Relations industrielles, 2562, 4710-
    4716, 4718-4724
Relations interethniques, 1144, 3615,
    3618, 3619-3625, 3627
Relations intergroupes, 859-862,
    1160, 1167

Relations interindividuelles, *voir*
Relations interpersonnelles
Relations internationales, 1345,
4932, 5236-5238, 5240
Relations interpersonnelles, 655,
771, 773-780, 784, 786, 788,
1211
Relations intra-groupe, 949-951
Relations parents-enfants, 625, 2262,
3245, 3387, 3392, 3402, 3413,
3415, 3423; 3428, 3432, 3442,
3446, 3448, 3453, 3454, 3462,
4099, 4898
Relations parents-enseignants, 2453
Relations raciales, 3613, 3614, 3616,
3617, 3626
Relations sociométriques, 750, 802,
807, 831, 929, 1404
Religion, 1004, 1585-1588, 1590,1594,
1595, 1597, 1599, 1600
Religion primitive, 1604, 1612-1618
Renouveau religieux, 1772
Rénovation urbaine, 4199, 4214, 4215,
4230
Répartition du revenu, 2654, 4291,
4294, 4305, 4314
Répartition par sexe, 3430, 4289
Répertoire, 90, 991
Représentation religieuse, 1712, 2042,
2046
Représentation sociale, 1159, 1165
Reproduction de la population, 2841,
3013
Réseau de communication, 886, 1898
Résistance au changement, 2767
Résolution de conflit, 873, 876
Résolution de problème, 630, 746,749
Responsabilité, 1146, 1520, 1527
Ressources humaines, 3820, 4472
Ressources naturelles, 3820
Retraite, 4600, 4603, 4604
Réunion, 130
Réussite dans les études, 2288, 2405,
2406, 2409, 2414
Rêve, 730
Revenu, 4292, 4297, 4301, 4302, 4309
Révolte, 1452, 1510
Révolution, 2740, 2742, 2753, 2754,
2758, 2759, 2764, 2768, 2771,
2774, 2777, 2786
Révolution industrielle, 4371, 4373
Revue, 182, 184
Rhodésie, migration rurale, 3753
Richesse, 4288
Rickert, H., 199
Risque, 554
Rite, 1684, 1692
Rituel, *voir* Rite
Rokeach, Milton, 1701

Rôle, 625, 1092, 1094, 1098, 1100,
1103, 1104, 1106, 1107, 3276,
3432, 5103
Rôle social, *voir* Rôle
Roman, 1104, 2071, 2072, 2074, 2075,
3930
Rothvoss, Mariano Gonzalez,173
Roumanie
contact entre cultures, 1374
médecin, 5641
minorité nationale, 3589
politique démographique, 3195
service de santé, 5631
sociologie du développement, 2800
sorcellerie, 1609
structure sociale, 2462
urbanisation, 4013
Royaume-Uni
abandon d'études, 2235
administration urbaine, 4099
adoption d'enfant, 3429
appartenance au parti, 5147
aptitude aux études, 2411
attitude raciale, 4172
automation, 4357
avortement, 3225
classe moyenne, 2561, 2584
classe ouvrière, 2602
classe sociale, 2631, 2651, 2655,
4099
collège universitaire, 2300
condition de la femme, 3475
conflit de classe, 2562
consommation, 4442
convention collective, 4818, 4821
crime, 5377
délinquant, 5430
développement des collectivités,
3846
développement national, 2799
droit du travail, 4733
droits de la femme, 4762
église protestante, 1642
employé, 4690
enseignement supérieur, 2298, 2317
entreprise, 4324
esclavage, 2546
état providence, 5500
étude de cas, 3225
femme, 4442
grève, 4782, 4798
immigrant, 3724, 3740
industrialisation, 3272
industrie, 4357
intérêt professionnel, 4633
logement, 4153
loi, 1541, 1550
malthusianisme, 3188
mariage, 3272
médecin, 5670
médecine : 5559; sociale, 5562
métropole, 4069

Royaume-Uni *[suite]*
  migration, 3656
  mobilité sociale, 2721, 2722, 5670
  mouvement ouvrier, 4768
  organisation patronale, 4734
  parti politique, 5070, 5074,5076, 5077
  participation des travailleurs, 4816
  participation politique, 5074
  planification rurale, 3959
  planification urbaine, 4172
  police, 5006, 5007
  politique du logement, 4171, 4172
  préjudice, 1152
  prison, 5458
  problème social, 5275
  psychiatre, 5569
  psychiatrie, 5569
  recherche sociale, 5269
  relations industrielles, 2562, 4723
  relations parents-enfant, 4099
  relations raciales, 3613
  salaire, 4308
  santé, 5593, 5606
  sexe, 4099
  service de santé, 5624, 5634,5638
  société en transformation, 4114
  société urbaine, 4115
  sociologie du loisir, 4844
  status, 2662
  stéréotype, 1164
  stratification sociale, 2497
  syndicalisme, 4751
  syndicat, 4738, 4743, 4758, 4762, 4778
  taudis, 4154
  travail social, 5537
  travailleur, 4679
  vie familiale, 4844
  vie urbaine, 4114
  ville nouvelle, 4099
  vol, 5373
RDP Lao (République démocratique populaire), village, 3876
Ruanda, enfant, 2922
Rumeur, 1950, 1953
Rural-urbain, 3138, 3989, 5350

Sacré, 1704, 1705, 1707
Saint, 1706
Salaire, 4287, 4289, 4298, 4299, 4300, 4306, 4311-4313
Salle de classe, 2287
Sanction, 1398
Santé, 4170, 5520, 5573, 5577, 5578, 5580-5582, 5585, 5587, 5588, 5592, 5595, 5602, 5606, 5608-5610, 5616, 5617, 5620
Santé mentale, 5584, 5590, 5598, 5614, 5618

Santé publique, 5477, 5583, 5586, 5589, 5613
Sartre, Jean-Paul, 226, 301
Satisfaction au travail, 4580, 4582-4585, 4590, 4591, 4605
Scalogramme, *voir* Echelle de Guttmann
Scandinavie, ville, 4081
Schelsky, Helmut, 1196
Schizophrénie, 550, 3077, 3081, 3086
Schutz, Alfred, 240, 344, 1903
Science, 747, 1206, 1786, 1788,1789, 1791,1793,1794,1804,1805,1809, 1810,1814,1815,1819,1821,1825, 1826,1831,1832,1835,1836,2403
Science économique, 4235, 4238
Science historique, 2731, 2732
Science politique, 1407, 4902, 4907
Sciences administratives, 4905
Sciences de l'homme, *voir* Sciences sociales
Sciences du comportement, 21
Sciences religieuses, 1592, 1596, 1603
Sciences sociales, 1-3, 5, 6, 13, 15, 24, 28, 30, 32, 35, 37, 41, 44, 46
Scolarisation, 2208, 2233, 2238,2241
Scolarité, 2230, 2232, 2234, 2240, 3927, 4298
Sculpture, 2083
Sectarisme, 1674
Secte, 1655, 1658, 1659, 1663, 1664, 3380
Secteur tertiaire, 4424
Sécularisation, 1747, 1757, 1771
Sécurité sociale, 3017, 5525, 5527, 5528-5535, 5639
Sédentarisation, 3831
Ségrégation raciale, 3634, 3638, 3640, 3644, 4141
Ségrégation résidentielle, 4140, 4141, 4178, 4186, 4195
Sémantique, 341, 1851, 1853, 1854
Séminaire, 427
Sémiologie, 1846, 2014, 2055
Sémiotique, 1839, 1842, 1850, 1865, 4854
Sénégal
  bourgeoisie, 2642
  coopérative agricole, 4395
Service d'information, *voir* Centre de documentation
Service de santé, 529, 4764, 5622, 5624, 5626, 5627, 5632, 5634-5636, 5638, 5639
Service hospitalier, 902, 5625
Service militaire, 5210
Service social, 5642, 5644, 5645, 5647, 5651, 5652, 5655, 5663, 5673, 5679

Sexe, 830, 1104, 1142, 1164, 1456, 2232, 2868, 2869, 2871, 2872, 2874-2876, 2878-2880, 2882-2887, 2889, 2890, 2893, 2894, 3260, 3268, 3382, 3507, 4099

Sexologie, 3237, 3239, 3249, 3251, 3253, 3264

Sexualité, 3236, 3238, 3243, 3244, 3246, 3259, 3262

Seychelles, enfant, 2930

Shils, Edward, 1242

Sierra Léone
  famille, 5657
  main d'oeuvre étrangère, 4531
  travailleur social, 5657

Signe, 1891, 1895

Signification, 1879, 1890

Simmel, Georg, 201, 272, 273

Simulation, 553, 555, 1109, 1218

Singapour
  milieu urbain, 4010
  mortalité, 3122

Situation de famille, 2941, 3311, 3312, 3314, 3317, 3319, 4523

Smith, Adam, 4238

Sociabilité, 781

Socialisation, 583, 1404, 1409, 1412, 1419, 1423, 1426, 1428, 1430, 1463, 1935, 2136, 2140, 2969, 3366, 4898, 5313, 5469

Socialisation politique, 702, 5112, 5115, 5122, 5129, 5133, 5142, 5144, 5161, 5162

Socialisme, 612, 1327, 2503, 4252, 4275, 4923, 4927, 4931, 4934, 4936-4939, 4942, 4945, 4946, 4949

Société, 1333, 1336, 1338-1340, 1343, 2507, 4537

Société d'abondance, 2607, 4307

Société de masse, 1334, 1335, 1342, 1344

Société de sociologie , *voir* Association de sociologie

Société en transformation, 2474, 2505, 2801, 2805, 2811, 2821, 4114

Société industrielle, 2579, 2823, 2833

Société pluraliste, *voir* Pluralisme social

Société primitive, 2819

Société rurale, 1676, 2563, 2615, 2805, 3015, 3286, 3408, 3885, 3886, 3896, 3898, 3906, 3918, 3921, 3923, 3924, 3927, 3928, 3931, 3940, 3948, 4513

Société secrète, 1268

Société socialiste, 1311, 2481, 2711, 4255, 4257, 4259, 4261, 4266, 4269-4271, 4373, 4465, 4686

Société traditionnelle, 2792, 2812, 2827, 4080

Société urbaine, 1471, 1486, 1501, 4102, 4104-4106, 4108, 4110, 4115, 4117, 4120, 4125, 4127, 4129, 4136

Sociolinguistique, 466, 1840, 1841, 1862, 1866

Sociologie, 4, 7-12, 14, 16-20, 22, 23, 25-27, 29, 31, 33, 34, 36, 38-40, 42, 43, 45

Sociologie appliquée, 5261, 5263

Sociologie bourgeoise, 205, 322, 2636

Sociologie criminelle, 5360

Sociologie de l'art, 2040, 2041, 2043, 2045, 2052, 2056, 2058, 2061

Sociologie de l'éducation, 56, 1913, 2111, 2113, 2117, 2120, 2121, 2126, 2130, 2135, 2138, 2147, 2417

Sociologie de la connaissance, 83, 1790, 1800, 1801, 1802, 1813, 1816-1818, 1820, 1823, 1824, 1827, 1837, 2061, 2731

Sociologie de la littérature, 2063, 2064, 2079

Sociologie de la musique, 2085, 2089, 2090, 2092, 2095

Sociologie de la profession, 4607, 4610, 4612, 4613, 4615

Sociologie des organisations, 975, 977, 981, 983, 985, 988, 991, 994

Sociologie du développement, 2795-2797, 2802, 2804, 2806, 2808, 2814, 2815, 2817, 2818, 2820, 2824, 2826, 2828-2832, 2836

Sociologie du droit, 1540, 1549, 1555, 1556, 1559, 1560, 1563, 1573, 1577, 1582, 5381

Sociologie du loisir, 3945, 4823, 4824, 4828-4831, 4835, 4837, 4839, 4842-4844

Sociologie du théâtre, 2097

Sociologie du travail, 4467, 4468, 4824

Sociologie économique, 1801, 4236, 4237

Sociologie électorale, 5166, 5170, 5171, 5175, 5177, 5178, 5186, 5189

Sociologie médicale, 3085, 5558, 5561, 5564, 5565, 5567, 5571, 5574, 5621

Sociologie militaire, 3343, 4603, 5205, 5209, 5214, 5215, 5219-5226, 5231

Sociologie politique, 4901, 4903, 4904

Sociologie religieuse, 1584, 1589, 1591, 1593, 1601, 1602, 1604-1606, 1607

Sociologie rurale, 192, 3848-3852

Sociologie urbaine, 192, 875, 3979, 3982, 3984, 3987, 3990, 3882, 3993, 5290
Sociologisme, 272, 273
Sociologue, 47-51, 53-57, 59, 60, 4342, 5269
Sociométrie, 2275
Soins médicaux, 1730, 4438, 5579, 5593, 5594, 5596, 5597, 5599, 5600, 5601, 5603, 5612, 5615
Soldat, *voir* Militaire
Solidarité, 812, 813, 819, 820
Sondage, 459-462, 464
Sorcellerie, 1609
Soudan
  chômage, 3779
  migration rurale, 3779
  village, 3864
Sous-développement, 2790, 2793, 2798, 2803, 2807, 2808, 2816, 2825
Spectateur, 1374, 2027
Spencer, Herbert, 268
Sport, 846, 932, 1156, 1222, 1895, 4624-4853, 4855-4859, 4862-4865, 4867-4871, 4873, 4875, 4876, 4878, 4879, 4882-4885, 4887-4889, 4891, 4892, 4894-4899
Sri Lanka
  contrôle des naissances, 3204
  parti politique, 5083
Statistique, 503- 506, 508, 509,511, 512, 515, 517, 520, 535
Status, 1492, 1720, 2647, 2657, 2658, 2660-2662, 2664-2666, 2668, 2670, 2671, 2673-2677, 3563, 3899,4707, 5159
Status social, *voir* Status
Status socio-économique, 2659, 4704
Status sociométrique, 817, 4586
Stéréotype, 484, 795, 818, 1142-1144, 1147, 1149, 1151, 1155-1158,1161, 1164, 2352
Stérilité, 3159
Strate sociale, 2492, 2521
Stratégie, 762
Stratégie de recherche, 398
Stratification professionnelle, 4289, 4309, 4621, 4623, 4641, 4643, 4647, 4660, 4665
Stratification sociale, 2210, 2491, 2493, 2497, 2499, 2500, 2501, 2506, 2508, 2518, 2522, 2544, 2661, 2663, 3254
Strauss, Leo, 223
Structuralisme, 202, 207, 239, 242, 262, 304, 316, 1280, 1713, 3361
Structure, 368-370, 373
Structure de classe, 2554, 2559,2563, 2578, 2589, 2594, 2607, 2610, 2612, 2624, 2630, 2634, 2636
Structure sociale, 684, 1273, 2455-2457, 2459, 2460, 2462, 2464,

Structure sociale *[suite]*
  2467, 2468, 2470, 2471, 2477, 2479, 2481-2483, 2485, 2487, 2488, 2568, 5187
Structure urbaine, 4009, 4017, 4022, 4031
Stupéfiants, 5309, 5310, 5312, 5314, 5319, 5321, 5323, 5326-5328,5330-5332, 5335, 5339, 5347, 5461
Succès scolaire, *voir* Réussite dans les études
Sud-Tyrol, relations interethniques, 3622
Suède
  banlieue, 4227
  cogestion, 4813
  éducation des adultes, 2362
  employé, 4692
  état-providence, 5492
  groupe de pression, 4692, 5097
  migration externe, 3673
  minorité ethnique, 3536
  organisation patronale, 4734
  origine sociale, 2669
  participation des travailleurs, 4809
  profession, 2669
  programme d'enseignement, 2362
  relations industrielles, 4713
  société en transformation, 2811
  sociologie du développement, 2817
  sociologie du loisir, 4823
  suicide, 5368
Suicide, 5366, 5368, 5374, 5388, 5391, 5398, 5403, 5405, 5413, 5414, 5420, 5426
Suisse
  administration urbaine, 4100
  consommateur, 4447
  droit du travail, 4731
  établissement d'enseignement, 2171
  fédéralisme, 4968
  organisation d'étudiants, 2345
  pluralisme culturel, 2170
  presse, 1993
  psychiatre, 56611
  travailleur étranger, 4516
Superstition, 1700
Supervision du personnel, *voir* Administration du personnel
Surpeuplement, 3009, 3052
Symbole, 1867, 1876, 1897, 1903
Symbolisme, 1871
Symbolisme religieux, 1708, 1709
Sympathie, 804, 815
Syncrétisme religieux, 1702
Syndicalisme, 4737, 4748, 4751, 4761-4764, 4767, 4771, 5221
Syndicat, 4738, 4741-4745, 4753-4759, 4762, 4769, 4770, 4772-4776, 4778, 5009, 5132

Syrie
  analphabétisme, 2364
  classe ouvrière, 2574
  évolution de la population, 3041
Système coopératif, 4251
Système d'éducation, 2150, 2154,
    2157, 2158, 2159, 2161, 2163-2168,
    2177, 2181, 2187, 2188, 2192,2193,
    2197, 2200, 2204
Système de parti, 5061-5078
Système de valeurs, 1048, 1286, 1384,
    1395, 1397, 3940
Système juridique, 1199, 1566, 1570,
    1579
Système pénitentiaire, 5445, 5466
Système politique, 4972, 4976, 4991
Système social, 1341, 2463, 2465,
    2469, 2472, 2474-2476, 2478,
    2480, 2484

Table de fécondité, 3170
Table de mortalité, 3104, 3116, 3130
Table ronde, *voir* Colloque
Tâche du groupe, 970, 972
Taïwan
  développement économique, 3032
  enseignement supérieur, 2327
  équilibre de la population, 3032
  fécondité, 3138, 3151
  rural-urbain, 3138
  urbanisation, 4021
Tanzanie
  politique d'éducation, 2185
  santé, 5621
  sociologie médicale, 5621
  sous-développement, 2825
Taudis, 3617, 4056, 4143, 4144,4154,
    4161, 4181, 4190, 4193, 4197
Taux de fécondité, 3132, 3155
Taux de mortalité, 3115
Taux de natalité, 3161, 3168
Taxonomie, 374, 375
Tchad, enfant, 2911
Tchécoslovaquie
  agriculture, 4404
  évolution démographique, 3034, 3046
  fécondité, 3181
  genre de vie, 1314
  groupe ethnique, 3295
  hétérogamie, 3295
  homogamie, 3295
  jeune travailleur, 4518
  migration interne, 3764
  minorité nationale, 3537
  mobilité sociale, 2726
  nuptialité, 3291
  participation des travailleurs,4812
  pays socialiste, 4258
  politique démographique, 3034
  recherche démographique, 2839,
    2863
  socialisme, 4937

sondage, 460
structure de classe, 2559
structure sociale, 2462, 2468
table de mortalité, 3130
urbanisation, 4018
Technicien, 4696, 4700, 4701
Technique de recherche 389, 392,
    393, 400, 407, 410, 5260, 5267
Technocratie, 5031, 5035, 5039,
    5041, 5046
Technologie, 1019, 1809, 4345,4348-
    4350, 4353, 4356, 4358-4360,
    4362, 4370, 4375, 4376, 4381,
    4383
Télécommunications, 2018, 2036
Télévision, 852, 2016, 2017, 2020
    2022, 2024-2035, 2037, 2038,
    2432, 4446
Temps, 414, 416
Temps de loisir, 4848-4851
Temps de travail, 4568, 4577
Tendance de recherche, 68, 82,83,
    91, 96, 3340, 3184
Tenure foncière, 3957
Terminologie, 151
Terreur, 712
Terrorisme, 1433, 1438, 1453, 1455,
    1488, 1491
Test, 489, 490, 1158
Thaïlande
  église et état, 1777
  employé, 4688
  fécondité, 3154, 3179
  groupe ethnique, 3564
  migration de travail, 3154
  migration interne, 3154
  planification rurale, 3974
  société rurale, 3931
Théâtre, 2100-2102
Théorie, 206, 211, 213, 215, 220,
    222, 230, 232, 234, 241, 244,
    247, 254,258, 263, 265, 267,
    275-277, 288, 291, 292, 303,
    307, 317, 318, 328, 1034, 1796,
    1802, 4786
Théorie de l'information, 1875
Théorie de l'utilité, 556
Théorie de la communication, *voir*
    Théorie de l'information
Théorie de la population, 2849
Théorie des graphes, 547, 548
Théorie des jeux, 557
Théorie des organisations, 973,
    976, 979, 980, 982, 986, 990,
    992, 993, 1399
Théorie générale, 212, 227, 238,
    274, 282, 284, 286, 287, 294,
    306, 310, 312, 313, 323, 324,
    330, 4237
Thèse, 186-188, 190, 191, 194, 196
Toffler, Alvin, 264
Tönnies, F., 218

Topitsch, Ernst, 260
Tourisme, 4874, 4880, 4881, 4893
Tradition, 1512, 1514, 3266, 3277,
   3439
Trait de personnalité, 660, 663, 664
   667, 1142
Traitement de l'information, 132-134,
   136
Traitement hospitalier, 5629
Transport, 4425-4427
Transport urbain, 4109, 4112, 4122
Travail, 647, 1395, 4470, 4474, 4476,
   4477, 4481
Travail des cas individuels, 5542
Travail social, 4304, 5536, 5537-
   5541, 5543-5556, 5630
Travail social des groupes, 2985
Travail sur le terrain, 437-439
Travailleur, 1388, 2038, 2672, 4667,
   4670, 4672, 4675-4679, 4681-4687,
   5249
Travailleur en col blanc, *voir* Em-
   ployé
Travailleur étranger, 4473, 4501,
   4514, 4516, 4520
Travailleur féminin, 1314, 2440, 3164,
   3950, 4287, 4293, 4496, 4499,
   4502-4504, 4506, 4509, 4512,
   4513, 4524, 4526, 4528-4530,
   4532, 4534
Travailleur manuel, 631, 4669
Travailleur non manuel, *voir* Employé
Travailleur social, 5555, 5646, 5650,
   5656, 5657, 5660, 5671, 5677
Triade, 548, 867, 937
Tribalisme, 1417, 3652
Tribu, 3535, 3541, 3576, 3584
Tribunal, 5023, 5024, 5029, 5470
Trinidad, émigration, 3683
Tunisie
   artisanat, 4423
   classe sociale, 2583
   coopérative agricole, 4395
   immigrant, 3702
   migration rurale, 3795
   nomadisme, 3781
   promotion de la femme, 3500
   soins médicaux, 5604
   système d'éducation, 2163
   taudis, 4144
   village, 3856
   ville, 2583
Turquie
   assimilation des immigrés, 3725
   droits de la femme, 3465
   enquête, 4662
   fécondité, 3138
   Islam, 2949
   jeunesse, 2949
   orientation professionnelle, 4662
   participation politique, 5155
   promotion de la femme, 3464

rural-urbain, 3138
société en transformation, 2821
syndicalisme, 4771
Type idéal, 215, 372, 405
Typologie, 1408

Union des Républiques Socialistes
   Soviétiques
   adolescent, 2951
   analyse documentaire, 139
   classe ouvrière, 2614, 2629,
      2592, 2632, 2650, 2656
   classe sociale, 2568
   communication de masse, 1988
   condition de la femme, 3494
   conditions de logement, 4163
   contrôle des naissances, 3210
   criminologie, 5356
   développement national, 2822
   déviance, 1445
   différenciation de classes, 2635
   droit du travail, 4727
   droits de la femme, 3524
   émigration, 3679
   équilibre démographique, 3024
   état, 4992
   ethnicité, 3549
   ethnologie, 3549
   évolution de la population, 2822
   famille, 3328, 3342
   genre de vie, 1256, 2635
   hygiène sociale, 5607
   intelligentsia, 2696
   manager, 4693
   mobilité de la main-d'oeuvre,
      2712
   mobilité sociale, 2712
   niveau de vie, 4290
   ouvrage de référence, 142
   patriotisme, 4944, 4951
   pays socialiste, 4268
   paysannerie, 3942
   persécution religieuse, 1774
   planification urbaine, 4210
   politique d'éducation, 2174
   presse, 2001
   prestige professionnel, 4661
   progrès technique, 4374
   promotion de la femme, 3473
   recherche en cours, 98, 3549
   société socialiste, 4259
   sociologie du développement,
      2815
   sociologie du loisir, 3945
   soins médicaux, 5599
   strate sociale, 2521
   structure de classe, 2634
   structure sociale, 2568
   tendance de recherche, 91
   travailleur : 4677; féminin,
      4529
   vie rurale, 3922, 3943, 3945

Union des Républiques Socialistes
 Soviétiques *[suite]*
 village, 3868, 3883
 ville, 4060, 4071, 4085, 4086
Unité de recherche, 105
Université, 1413, 2267, 2299, 2302,
 2320, 2334, 2337-2341, 2346,
 2352, 2354, 2356, 2357, 2359,
 2421, 3635
Urbain, 1212, 3983, 3985, 3988,3991,
 3994, 3996, 5293, 5296
Urbain-rural, *voir* Rural-urbain
Urbanisation, 3789, 3999, 4000,4002?
 4004, 4006, 4008, 4011-4013,
 4015, 4016, 4018, 4020, 4021,
 4024, 4025, 4028-4033, 4035,
 4036, 4038-4040, 4397
Urbanisme, 4212, 4226, 4233
Uruguay
 recherche en cours, 65
 militaire, 5225, 5230
Usage de drogue, 5307, 5308, 5313,
 5316, 5318, 5325, 5333, 5336,
 5341, 5343, 5350, 5351
Usage du tabac, 5306, 5317, 5338
Usine, 4596, 4598, 4599
Utilisation des loisirs, 4852, 4890
Utopie, 1192, 1194, 1202

Valeur, 1379, 1383, 1386-1388,1390,
 1392, 1396, 1398-1401, 1403
Valeur d'échange, 4451
Valeur de classe, 2593, 2645
Valeur de groupe, 966
Validité, 448, 449
Vendeur, *voir* Employé de commerce
Venezuela
 classe sociale, 2555, 2794
 évolution de la population, 3051
 jeunesse, 2973
 marginalité, 1444
 migration externe, 3672
 migration interne, 3754
 planification urbaine, 4206
 population urbaine, 3056
 santé mentale, 5614
 sous-développement, 2794
 violence, 2555
Vérification, 361
Vêtement, 1513
Veuvage, 3108
Vie économique, 4282
Vie familiale, 2881, 3167, 3399, 3404,
 3409, 3411, 3420, 3433, 3437,
 3439, 3457, 3460, 3910, 4844,
 5348
Vie politique, 1749, 2041, 5195
Vie rurale, 3893, 3895, 3897-3902,
 3910, 3913, 3915, 3919, 3922,
 3940, 3943, 3945, 3947, 3951
Vie urbaine,1262, 3085, 4097, 4098,
 4114, 4116, 4119, 4121, 4123,

Vie urbaine *[suite]*
 4124,4126,4128,4131,4132
 4135, 4137, 4834
Vieillard, 2982, 2985, 2988,2990,
 2993, 2997-2999, 3004, 3006,
 3007, 3259, 5382, 5679
Vieillesse, 2983, 2987, 2992,2994,
 2996, 3001, 3003, 3899
Vieillissement, 956, 2986, 2989,
 2995, 3002, 3005
Vietnam
 élite politique, 5088
 guerre, 5254
 militaire, 5216
 mouvement contestataire, 5088
 valeur, 1397
Village, 1681, 2698, 2989, 3062,
 3076, 3133, 3688, 3786, 3853-
 3872, 3873-3883, 4675
Ville, 531, 922, 1472, 1635, 2583,
 3609, 4044, 4046-4051, 4054,
 4056-4058, 4060, 4066, 4071,
 4072, 4075, 4079, 4080, 4081-
 4086, 4090, 4091, 4093, 4409,
 5434
Ville industrielle, 4055, 4094
Ville nouvelle, 2260, 4043, 4053,
 4059, 4077, 4099
Violence, 782, 840, 1435, 1437,
 1458, 1459, 1467, 1469, 1472,
 1477, 1478, 1485, 1493, 1494,
 1498, 1502, 1509, 2016, 2555,
 4128, 5016, 5092
Vocabulaire, 155
Voegelin, 284
Voisinage, 4166, 4167, 4173, 4182,
 4187, 4189
Vol, 1095, 5371, 5373, 5384, 5415,
 5417
Voleur, 5437, 5441

Wallerstein, 4280
Weber, Max, 129, 143, 199, 203,209,
 213, 215, 217, 218, 225, 231,
 234, 256, 267, 309, 310, 313,
 319, 323, 329, 330, 332, 333,
 346, 350, 351, 356, 366, 409,
 1058, 4237
Wirth, Louis, 328
Wittgenstein, L., 212, 254

Yougoslavie
 autogestion, 4318, 4332
 échelle F, 1170
 milieu familial, 3412
 milieu rural, 3911
 mort, 1691
 mouvement de jeunesse, 2972
 planification urbaine, 4209
 politique d'éducation, 2149,2202
 population agricole, 3061
 productivité du travail, 4549

Yougoslavie *[suite]*
    recherche en cours, 70
    santé, 5578
    sociologie du développement, 2795
    structure sociale, 2462
    travailleur féminin, 4509

Zaïre
    croissance urbaine, 4034
    relations interethniques, 3621
Zambie, village, 3853, 3855
Zimmerman, Carle C., 286
Zone rurale, 3002, 3873
Zone urbaine, 3797,4019,4037,5588